¯¯K L(

The SAGE
Handbook of
Criminological
Research Methods

The SAGE
Handbook of

Criminological
Research Methods

Edited by
David Gadd, Susanne Karstedt,
Steven F. Messner

Los Angeles | London | New Delhi
Singapore | Washington DC

Editorial Introduction and Arrangement © David Gadd,
  Susanne Karstedt, Steven F. Messner, 2012
Chapter 1 © Neal Shover, 2012
Chapter 2 © Marvin D. Krohn, Terence P. Thornberry,
  Kristin A. Bell, Alan J. Lizotte, Matthew D. Phillips, 2012
Chapter 3 © David Gadd, 2012
Chapter 4 © Jody Miller, 2012
Chapter 5 © Yu Gao, Andrea L. Glenn, Melissa Peskin,
  Anna Rudo-Hutt, Robert A. Schug, Yaling Yang,
  Adrian Raine, 2012
Chapter 6 © Tomislav Kovandzic, Mark E. Schaffer,
  Gary Kleck, 2012
Chapter 7 © Eric P. Baumer, Ashley N. Arnio, 2012
Chapter 8 © Per-Olof H. Wikström, Kyle Treiber,
  Beth Hardie, 2012
Chapter 9 © George E. Tita, Adam Boessen, 2012
Chapter 10 © Robert D. Crutchfield,
  Suzanna R. Ramirez, 2012
Chapter 11 © Barry Godfrey, 2012
Chapter 12 © Laura Dugan, 2012
Chapter 13 © Cécile Van de Voorde, 2012
Chapter 14 © Jeff Ferrell, 2012

Chapter 15 © Elizabeth Stanley, 2012
Chapter 16 © Moira Peelo, Keith Soothill, 2012
Chapter 17 © Pat Mayhew, Jan Van Dijk, 2012
Chapter 18 © Emily Gray, Jonathan Jackson,
  Stephen Farrall, 2012
Chapter 19 © Julian Roberts, Martina Feilzer,
  Mike Hough, 2012
Chapter 20 © Janet Chan, 2012
Chapter 21 © Wesley G. Skogan, 2012
Chapter 22 © Aaron Kupchik, Joseph De Angelis,
  Nicole L. Bracy, 2012
Chapter 23 © Karin Tusinski Miofsky, James M. Byrne, 2012
Chapter 24 © Alison Liebling Susie Hulley, Ben Crewe, 2012
Chapter 25 © Susanne Karstedt, 2012
Chapter 26 © Heather Strang, Lawrence W. Sherman, 2012
Chapter 27 © Manuel Eisner, Tina Malti, Denis Ribeaud, 2012
Chapter 28 © Martin Schmucker, Friedrich Lösel, 2012
Chapter 29 © Ken Pease, 2012
Chapter 30 © Michael Levi, 2012
Chapter 31 © Cyndi Banks, 2012
Chapter 32 © Gail Mason, Julie Stubbs, 2012
Chapter 33 © Mark Israel, Iain Hay, 2012

First published 2012

SAGE Publications Ltd
1 Oliver's Yard
55 City Road
London EC1Y 1SP

SAGE Publications Inc.
2455 Teller Road
Thousand Oaks,
California 91320

SAGE Publications India Pvt Ltd
B 1/I 1 Mohan Cooperative Industrial Area
Mathura Road
New Delhi 110 044

SAGE Publications Asia-Pacific Pte Ltd
33 Pekin Street #02-01 Far East Square
Singapore 048763

Library of Congress Control Number 2011920225

British Library Cataloguing in Publication data
A catalogue record for this book is available from the British Library

ISBN 978-1-84920-175-9

Typeset by Cenveo Publisher Services, Bangalore, India
Printed in Great Britain by MPG Books Group, Bodmin, Cornwall
Printed on paper from sustainable resources

MIX
Paper from
responsible sources
FSC
www.fsc.org   FSC® C018575

Contents

Notes on Contributors

Ashley N. Arnio is a PhD candidate in the College of Criminology and Criminal Justice at Florida State University. Her current research focuses on assessing racial and ethnic disparities in crime and justice within temporal and spatial contexts, specifically addressing the relationship between minority threat and criminal justice outcomes. Her other research interests include exploring community influences on attitudes and behaviour using multi-level methods and assessing geographic variation in crime using spatial analysis techniques.

Cyndi Banks is Professor and Chair of the Department of Criminology and Criminal Justice at Northern Arizona University. She is internationally recognized for her work as a criminologist in the Asia/Pacific region, Bangladesh, Myanmar, Iraq, Sudan, East Timor and Iraqi Kurdistan in international children's rights, juvenile justice reform and community justice. She has published widely on comparative and cultural criminology, international children's rights, indigenous incarceration, and professional women justice workers. She has authored eight books including an upcoming third edition of *Criminal Justice Ethics*, Sage, *Alaska Native Juveniles in Detention*, Mellen Press and a forthcoming book, *Youth, Crime and Justice* for Routledge.

Eric P. Baumer is the Allen E. Liska Professor of Criminology at Florida State University. His research focuses on temporal and spatial dimensions of crime and justice, and especially how structural and cultural features of communities affect crime, social control, and other aspects of human behaviour. He has examined these issues empirically in multi-level studies of the influence of community characteristics on individual attitudes and behaviours, macro-level studies of spatial and temporal patterns in crime and social control, and in case studies of crime and justice in Iceland, Malta, and Ireland. Recent publications have appeared in *Criminology*, *American Sociological Review*, and the *American Journal of Sociology*.

Kristin A. Bell is a doctoral student in the School of Criminology and Criminal Justice at Northeastern University. After receiving her BA in Criminology and BS in Psychology, she completed her Masters degree in Criminology, Law, & Society at the University of Florida. She is currently a project manager at the Center for Criminal Justice Policy Research and the Institute on Race and Justice at Northeastern University. Her interests include victim behavior and help-seeking, human rights violations, and the use of mixed research methods.

Adam Boessen is a doctoral student in the Department of Criminology, Law and Society at the University of California Irvine. His primary research interests include the community context of crime, spatial analysis, social network analysis, and juvenile delinquency. His work uses quantitative methodologies to examine the relationship between residential mobility and crime, the measurement and conceptualization of neighbourhoods, and the impact of incarceration on juvenile offenders.

Nicole L. Bracy is a Research Scientist and Adjunct Professor at San Diego State University. Her research interests include police practices with youth, understandings and negotiations of juveniles' legal rights, and policing and punishment strategies in schools. She has authored and co-authored several book chapters on these issues and has published articles in *Youth and Society* and *Youth Violence and Juvenile Justice*.

James M. Byrne (PhD, Rutgers University, 1983) has more than 30 years of experience conducting research on a wide range of justice topics. He has taught in the Department of Criminal Justice and Criminology at the University of Massachusetts Lowell since 1984. Professor Byrne's books include *The Social Ecology of Crime* (Springer Verlag, 1986, with Robert Sampson), *Smart Sentencing: The Emergence of Intermediate Sanctions* (Sage, 1994, with Arthur Lurigio and Joan Petersilia), *The New Technology of Crime, Law, and Social Control* (Criminal Justice Press, 2007, with Donald Rebovich), and *The Culture of Prison Violence* (Pearson, 2008, with Don Hummer and Faye Taxman). He is also the author of monographs and journal articles on the subjects of offender change, offender re-entry, risk classification, the link between prison culture and community culture, and the community context of crime and crime control. Professor Byrne serves as the editor of the journal *Victims and Offenders: Journal of Evidence-Based Practices* and he is currently the Vice Chair of the Division on Corrections and Sentencing at the American Society of Criminology.

Janet Chan is Associate Dean (Research) and Professor in the School of Law at the University of New South Wales (UNSW) and a Fellow of the Academy of Social Sciences in Australia. Her research interests include: reform and innovation in criminal justice, organizational culture, and the sociology of creativity. She has worked as a consultant for a number of government organizations and has published numerous books and articles on criminal justice and policing issues, including the books *Changing Police Culture* (1997), *Fair Cop: Learning the Art of Policing* (2003), *Reshaping Juvenile Justice* (2005). Her recent research projects have focused on understanding individual and collective creative practice among artists, scientists and art–science collaborations.

Ben Crewe is a Senior Research Associate at the Institute of Criminology, University of Cambridge. He has published on various aspects of prison life, including staff–prisoner relationships, the drugs economy within prison, and the 'inmate code'. His most recent book, *The Prisoner Society: Power, Adaptation and Social Life*, was published in 2009.

Robert D. Crutchfield is Professor and Chair of Sociology at the University of Washington. His research interests include the effects of employment and labour markets on crime, neighbourhoods and social disorganization and race and ethnic stratification.

Joseph De Angelis is a Senior Research Analyst with the Office of the Independent Monitor in Denver, Colorado. His research explores issues relating to legitimacy and criminal justice, police misconduct, and citizen oversight of police. His recent work has been published in the *Journal of Criminal Justice, Criminal Justice Review, Teaching Sociology, Police Quarterly,* and *Policing: An International Journal of Police Strategies and Management.*

Laura Dugan is an Associate Professor in the Department of Criminology and Criminal Justice at the University of Maryland. She is a member of the National Center for the Study of Terrorism and the Response to Terrorism. Her research focuses on violence, its consequences, and the efficacy of violence prevention/intervention policy and practice. She also designs methodological strategies to overcome data limitations inherent in the social sciences.

Manuel Eisner is Professor of Developmental and Comparative Criminology at the Institute of Criminology, University of Cambridge. His research interests include the history of violence, cross-cultural comparison of violence, human development and aggressive behaviour, and experimental research on violence prevention. He is principal investigator of the Zurich Project on the Social Development of

Children, a longitudinal study on a cohort of 1,200 children that is combined with a dissemination trial on the effectiveness of violence prevention at the start of primary school. In 2011 he was recipient of the Sellin-Glueck award of the American Society of Criminology.

Stephen Farrall is Professor of Criminology and Director of the Centre for Criminological Research at Sheffield University. He has held numerous grants from the UK's Economic and Social Research Council, the Leverhulme Trust, the European Commission and UK Government Departments. His most recent publications include "Escape Routes: Contemporary Perspectives on Life After Punishment", (co-edited with Richard Sparks, Mike Hough and Shadd Maruna, and published by Routledge in 2011) and "Serious Criminals: A Historical Study of Habitual Criminals", (co-authored with Barry Godfrey and David Cox, and published by Oxford University Press in 2011). He has recently completed a further round of interviews with a cohort of ex-probationers he has been studying since the late 1990s.

Martina Feilzer is a Lecturer in Criminology and Criminal Justice at Bangor University. She has particular interests in mixed-methods research, the media influence on public perceptions of crime and criminal justice, public opinion of crime and criminal justice, and policing and has published a number of papers in these areas.

Jeff Ferrell is currently Professor of Sociology at Texas Christian University, and Visiting Professor of Criminology at the University of Kent. He is the author of *Crimes of Style* (1993; 1996), *Tearing Down the Streets* (2001/2002), *Empire of Scrounge* (2006), and, with Keith Hayward and Jock Young, *Cultural Criminology: An Invitation* (2008), winner of the 2009 Distinguished Book Award from the Division of International Criminology, American Society of Criminology. He is also the co-editor of the books *Cultural Criminology* (1995), *Ethnography at the Edge* (1998), *Making Trouble* (1999), *Cultural Criminology Unleashed* (2004), and *Cultural Criminology: Theories of Crime* (2011). Jeff Ferrell is the founding and current editor of the New York University Press book series *Alternative Criminology*, and one of the founding editors of the journal *Crime, Media, Culture: An International Journal*, winner of the Association of Learned and Professional Society Publishers' 2006 Charlesworth Award for Best New Journal. In 1998 he received the Critical Criminologist of the Year Award from the Division of Critical Criminology, American Society of Criminology.

David Gadd is Professor of Criminology at Manchester University where he is also Director of the Centre for Criminology and Criminal Justice. He has over a decade of experience of conducting and analyzing in-depth interview research with offenders, and has written extensively on the subjects of domestic abuse, masculinities and crime, racial harassment, offender motivation and desistance from crime. His first book *Psychosocial Criminology* (co-written with Tony Jefferson) was published in 2007 with Sage. His second book, *Losing the Race* (co-written with Bill Dixon), about racial harassment perpetrators and how to respond to them, was published by Karnac in 2011.

Yu Gao is an Assistant Professor in the Department of Psychology at the Brooklyn College of the City University of New York. Her overarching research focus has been the identification of biosocial markers for aggressive, antisocial, psychopathic and criminal behaviour in children, adolescents, and adults. Her approach has been to integrate multiple methodologies within the field of psychology (including developmental, clinical, social, and cognitive neuroscience perspectives) to gain a more comprehensive cross-area perspective on antisocial and criminal behaviour using non-invasive and easily accessible psychophysiological approaches (e.g. event-related potentials) and advanced statistical methods (e.g. latent growth curve and multilevel modelling).

Andrea L. Glenn received her PhD from the University of Pennsylvania is currently a post-doctoral research fellow in the Department of Child and Adolescent Psychiatry at the Institute of Mental Health in Singapore. Her research focuses on the neurobiological bases of psychopathic personality using a variety of methods including structural and function MRI and hormone measurements. Additional interests include moral decision making, neuroethics, and emotional processing. Her current work involves biosocial interventions for youth with conduct disorder.

Barry Godfrey is Professor of Social Justice at Liverpool University. He has twenty years of experience in researching comparative criminology, particularly international crime history; desistence studies; and longitudinal studies of offending. He has published a number of books, most recently Godfrey, Cox, and Farrall (2010) *Serious Offenders: A Historical Study of Habitual Offenders 1850-1950*, Clarendon Series in Criminology, Oxford University Press; Godfrey, Lawrence, and Williams (2007) *History and Crime,* SAGE; and Godfrey, Cox, and Farrall (2007) *Criminal Lives: Family, Employment and Offending*, Clarendon Series in Criminology, Oxford University Press.

Emily Gray is a Researcher in the Institute of Law, Politics and Justice, Keele University. Her research interests focus on public attitudes towards crime, youth justice and persistent offending. Her work in these areas explores how results are shaped by the choice of methodological and interpretive tools.

Beth Hardie is Research Manager of the Peterborough Adolescent and Young Adult Development Study (PADS+) at the University of Cambridge. Her main research interest is the study of temporal and spatial dynamics of people's activities and criminal involvement. She is currently completing a PhD using PADS+ data.

Iain Hay is Professor of Geography at Flinders University, South Australia. He completed his PhD at the University of Washington as a Fulbright Scholar and recently received a LittD from the University of Canterbury for work on geographies of domination and oppression. He is author or editor of ten books including *Money, Medicine and Malpractice in American Society* (Praeger, 1992) and *Qualitative Research Methods in Human Geography* (3rd edn Oxford, 2010). He has had editorial roles with journals that include *Applied Geography; Ethics, Place and Environment;* and *Social and Cultural Geography.* In 2006, Iain received the Prime Minister's award for Australian University Teacher of the Year. He received the 2009 Taylor and Francis Award of the Royal Geographical Society (with the Institute of British Geographers) and the 2010 inaugural Association of American Geographers' E. Willard and Ruby S. Miller Award in 2010 for 'outstanding contributions to the discipline of geography'. Iain is currently President of the Institute of Australian Geographers.

Mike Hough is Professor of Criminal Policy and Co-Director of the Institute for Criminal Policy Research in the School of Law, Birkbeck, University of London. He has published extensively on a range of criminological topics including policing, crime prevention and community safety, anti-social behaviour, probation and drugs, and public attitudes to crime and justice. Current work includes research on sentencing, on drugs, on youth justice and on public trust in justice.

Susie Hulley is a Research Associate at the Institute of Criminology, Cambridge University, working primarily on a study of 'Values, Practices and Outcomes in Public and Private Sector Corrections'. She was awarded a PhD from the University of London in 2008 for her thesis on the perceptions and experiences of anti-social behaviour amongst adults and young people.

Mark Israel is Winthrop Professor of Law and Criminology at the University of Western Australia and Adjunct Professor at Flinders University. He has published over 50 books, book chapters and journal articles in the areas of research ethics, criminology and socio-legal studies, higher education policy and practice. His books include *South African Political Exile in the United Kingdom* (Palgrave Macmillan, 1999), and *Research Ethics for Social Scientists: Between Ethical Conduct and Regulatory Compliance* (Sage, 2006 with Iain Hay). He won the Prime Minister's Award for Australian University Teacher of the Year in 2004; the Radzinowicz Memorial Prize from the *British Journal of Criminology* in 2005; the

Critical Criminologist of the Year Award from the Critical Criminology Division of the American Society of Criminology in 2006; and the American Society of Criminology Teaching Award in 2010. He has undertaken research ethics-related consultancy for, among others, Australian Federal and State government departments and research organisations, and a range of public and private higher education institutions.

Jonathan Jackson is Senior Lecturer in Research Methodology at the London School of Economics. His research focuses on public attitudes towards crime, policing and punishment. He is currently involved in a number of comparative European projects, including a rotating module on trust in justice in Round 5 of the European Social Survey (ESS), and the scaling of new measures of fear of crime introduced in Round 3 of the ESS.

Susanne Karstedt is Professor of Criminology and Criminal Justice at the Centre for Criminal Justice Studies, University of Leeds, UK. Her research focuses on cross-national and cross-cultural studies of violence, white collar and middle class crime, and criminal justice, and especially how democratic values and institutions affect crime and justice. Additional areas of research interest and publications include transitional justice and the prevention of genocide and mass atrocities. Besides publications in professional journals and edited books, she is editor of *Legal Institutions and Collective Memories* (2009); and co-editor of *Emotions, Crime and Justice* (2011), *Democracy, Crime and Justice* (2006) and *Social Dynamics of Crime and Control* (2000) in addition to a number of co-edited special issues of major journals.

Gary Kleck is the David J. Bordua Professor of Criminology and Criminal Justice at Florida State University. He received his doctorate in Sociology from the University of Illinois in 1979, where he received the University of Illinois Foundation Fellowship in Sociology. He has been at Florida State since 1978. His research has focused on the topics of the impact of firearms and gun control on violence, deterrence, crime control, and violence. He is the author of *Point Blank: Guns and Violence in America*, which won the 1993 Michael J. Hindelang Award of the American Society of Criminology, awarded to the book of the previous several years which 'made the most outstanding contribution to criminology'. More recently, he is the author of *Targeting Guns* (1997) and, with Don B. Kates, Jr., *The Great American Gun Debate* (1997) and *Armed* (2001). Kleck has testified before Congress and state legislatures on gun control issues, and worked as a consultant to the National Research Council, National Academy of Sciences Panel on the Understanding and Prevention of Violence and as a member of the US Sentencing Commission's Drugs-Violence Task Force. He is a referee for over a dozen professional journals, and serves as a grants consultant to the National Science Foundation.

Tomislav Kovandzic is an Associate Professor in the School of Economic, Political and Policy Sciences at the University of Texas, Dallas. He holds a PhD in Criminology, Florida State University, 1999. His research interests include the impact of firearms and gun control on violence, deterrence, incapacitation, crime control, and structural correlates of violence. His work has appeared in *Criminology*, *Justice Quarterly*, *Criminology & Public Policy* and other journals

Marvin D. Krohn is a Professor in the Department of Sociology and Criminology & Law at the University of Florida. He is primarily interested in developmental approaches to the explanation of delinquency, drug use and crime and has pursued those interests with his work on the Rochester Youth Development Study. His co-authored book (with Thornberry, Lizotte, Smith and Tobin) *Gangs and Delinquency in Developmental Perspective*, won the 2003 American Society of Criminology's Michael J. Hindelang award for Outstanding Scholarship.

Aaron Kupchik is an Associate Professor in the Department of Sociology and Criminal Justice at the University of Delaware. His work focuses on the punishment and control of youth in a variety of institutions, including schools, courts, and correctional facilities. He is the author of *Judging Juveniles:*

Prosecuting Adolescents in Adult and Juvenile Courts (NYU Press, 2006), and *Homeroom Security: School Discipline in an Age of Fear* (NYU Press, 2010), as well as articles recently published in *Punishment & Society, Youth & Society, British Journal of Sociology of Education, Crime and Delinquency, Youth Violence and Juvenile Justice*, and the *Prison Journal*.

Michael Levi is Professor of Criminology and former ESRC Professorial Fellow at the Cardiff School of Social Sciences, Cardiff University. Professor Levi's research was funded via ESRC RES-051-27-0208. He has been researching and writing about fraud, money laundering and organised crime since 1972. Recent books include the 2nd edition of *The Phantom Capitalists: the Organisation and Control of Long-Firm Fraud*, and *Drugs and Money* (with Petrus van Duyne).

Alison Liebling is Professor of Criminology and Criminal Justice and Director of the Prisons Research Centre at the University of Cambridge. She has carried out research on suicides in prison, staff–prisoner relationships, the work of prison officers, small units for difficult prisoners, incentives and earned privileges, prison privatization and measuring the quality of prison life. She has published several books, including *Suicides in Prison* (1992), *Prisons and their Moral Performance* (2004) and (with Shadd Maruna) (2005) *The Effects of Imprisonment*.

Alan J. Lizotte is Dean and Professor in the School of Criminal Justice, The University at Albany. He is co-principal investigator on the Rochester Youth Development Study, a more than 20-year ongoing longitudinal study of juvenile delinquency and drug use covering three generations of subjects. His substantive interests include illegal firearms ownership and use and developmental criminology. In 2003, he and several co-authors were awarded the American Society of Criminology's Hindelang Award for the book *Gangs and Delinquency in Developmental Perspective*.

Friedrich Lösel is Director of the Institute of Criminology at Cambridge University (UK) and Professor of Psychology at the University of Erlangen-Nuremberg (Germany). He was Professor of Psychology at Bielefeld, Director of the Social Science Research Centre at Nuremberg, Senior Lecturer at Bamberg and worked in two Advanced Research Centres. He has published 18 books and 300 articles/chapters on delinquency, violence, offender treatment, hooliganism, bullying, psychopathy, resilience, and prevention. He was President of the European Association of Psychology and Law and the German Criminological Society. He serves on the Campbell Crime and Justice Collaboration and the Correctional Services Accreditation Panel. He is a Fellow of the Academy of Experimental Criminology and received the Sellin-Glueck Award of the American Society of Criminology, the EAPL Lifetime Award, an honorary Doctorate, the German Psychology Prize and the Stockholm Prize in Criminology.

Tina Malti is Assistant Professor of Developmental Psychology at the Department of Psychology, University of Toronto Mississauga. Trained as a developmental and clinical child psychologist, her research interests include the development of moral emotions, social competence and mental health, and the promotion of resilience and the prevention of aggression and problem behaviours in children and adolescents. She is a research collaborator in the Zurich Project on the Social Development of Children. In 2010, she was named recipient of the Young Investigator Award from the Society for Research on Adolescence.

Gail Mason is Director of the Sydney Institute of Criminology, Faculty of Law, University of Sydney. She is the author of *The Spectacle of Violence: Homophobia, Gender and Knowledge* (Routledge, 2002) and has published widely in *Social and Legal Studies, British Journal of Criminology* and *Hypatia*. Her current research centres on emotion, punitiveness and hate crime law.

Pat Mayhew worked for much of her career as a researcher in the British Home Office. Between 2004 and 2008 she was Director of the Crime and Justice Research Centre at Victoria University of Wellington, New Zealand. Since then, she has worked as a freelance criminologist consultant.

Steven F. Messner is Distinguished Teaching Professor of Sociology, University at Albany, State University of New York. His research focuses on social institutions and crime, understanding spatial distributions and trends in crime, and crime and social control in China. In addition to his publications in professional journals, he is co-author of *Crime and the American Dream*, and *Perspectives on Crime and Deviance*; and co-editor of *Theoretical Integration in the Study of Deviance and Crime*, and *Crime and Social Control in a Changing China*.

Jody Miller is Professor in the School of Criminal Justice at Rutgers University. She is author of *One of the Guys: Girls, Gangs and Gender* (Oxford University Press, 2001) and *Getting Played: African American Girls, Urban Inequality, and Gendered Violence* (New York University Press, 2008), as well as numerous articles and chapters.

Karin Tusinski Miofsky is an Assistant Professor in the Department of Sociology and Criminal Justice at the University of Hartford. Her current work explores patterns of bullying and victimizations within schools, contextualizing teen sexting, and nature of community crime control. Professor Miofsky serves as the associate editor of the journal *Victims and Offenders: Journal of Evidence-Based Practices*.

Ken Pease is Visiting Professor at the Jill Dando Institute, University College London. A Chartered Forensic Psychologist, his published work over forty years has included studies of repeat and near-repeat victimisation, and methods of prioritising police work on the basis of criminal career trajectories.

Moira Peelo is a freelance researcher and consultant. She has researched into aspects of marginality in crime, education and health and has co-written (with Soothill and Taylor) *Making Sense of Criminology* (Polity Press, 2002) and co-edited *Questioning Crime and Criminology* (Willan Press, 2005).

Melissa Peskin is a Ph.D. candidate in the Department of Psychology at the University of Pennsylvania. Her research focuses on the relationship between chronic stress and neurobiological functioning. She is particularly interested in examining how psychosocial factors, such as trauma, maltreatment, and abuse, affect neuroendocrinological functioning.

Matthew D. Phillips is a doctoral candidate at the University at Albany and currently works as a research analyst for the Rochester Youth Development Study. His doctoral dissertation focuses on adolescent drug use and drug selling and their consequences later in the life course. He is primarily interested in drug offending, violence, drug trafficking, causal analysis, and quantitative methods.

Adrian Raine is University Professor and the Richard Perry Professor of Criminology, Psychiatry, and Psychology, as well as Chair of the Department of Criminology at the University of Pennsylvania. His main area of interest is Neurocriminology – an emerging sub-discipline of Criminology which applies neuroscience techniques to probe the causes and cures of crime. Using techniques including structural and functional brain imaging, autonomic and central nervous system psychophysiology, neuroendocrinology, neuropsychology, and x-ray fluorescence, his research focuses on risk and protective factors for childhood conduct disorder, reactive and proactive aggression, adult antisocial personality disorder, homicide, and psychopathy. He has published five books, 257 journal articles and book chapters, and given 228 invited presentations in 25 countries.

Suzanna R. Ramirez is a PhD candidate in the Department of Sociology, University of Washington. Her current work explores the relationships between neighbourhoods collective efficacy and crime for immigrant neighbourhoods and populations. Other areas of work include the juvenile justice system and collective action.

Denis Ribeaud is Scientific Project Coordinator of the Zurich Project on the Social Development of Children. He has an MPhil in Sociology and a PhD in Criminology. His research interests include human development and aggressive behaviour, experimental research on violence prevention, indicators and secular trends of youth violence, and the links between migration and violence.

Julian Roberts is Professor of Criminology at the University of Oxford. He is the Editor of the *European Journal of Criminology* and Associate Editor of the *Canadian Journal of Criminology*. He has been conducting research in the field of public opinion and criminal justice since 1977.

Anna Rudo-Hutt is a PhD candidate in the Department of Psychology at the University of Pennsylvania. Her research interests include the psychophysiology and neuroendocrinology of antisocial behavior, juvenile delinquency, and externalizing disorders in children and adolescents. She is also interested in the interaction between biological, psychological, and social factors in the prediction of antisocial behavior.

Mark E. Schaffer is Professor of Economics at Heriot-Watt University, Edinburgh, UK. His fields of research include applied econometrics, economic reform in transition and emerging economies, industrial organization, labour markets, quantitative criminology and energy economics. Prof. Schaffer is a Fellow of the Royal Society of Edinburgh and a Research Fellow of the Centre for Economic Policy Research, London, and of IZA, the Institute for the Study of Labor, Bonn.

Martin Schmucker is Assistant Professor ("Akademischer Rat") at the Institute of Psychology of the University of Erlangen-Nuremberg, Germany, where he earned his doctorate in 2004. He received the Young Scientist Award for his thesis on sexual offender treatment from the Section on Forensic Psychology of the German Psychological Association. Since 2009 he has been Vice-President of this Section. His research interests include delinquency treatment and prevention, evaluation research, and psychopathy.

Robert A. Schug is Assistant Professor of Criminal Justice and Forensic Psychology in the Department of Criminal Justice at California State University, Long Beach. His area of specialization is the biology and psychology of the criminal mind. His research interests are predominantly focused upon understanding the relationship between extreme forms of psychopathology and antisocial, criminal, and violent behavior from a biopsychosocial perspective—with the application of advanced neuroscience techniques from areas such as neuropsychology, psychophysiology, and brain imaging. He is particularly interested in the etiological mechanisms, risk factors, and developmental progression of antisocial behavior within major mental disorders such as psychopathy and schizophrenia, as well as the ability to predict antisocial behavioral outcomes within mentally ill individuals.

Lawrence W. Sherman is the Wolfson Professor of Criminology and Director of the Jerry Lee Centre for Experimental Criminology at Cambridge University, where he is also a Fellow of Darwin College. He also serves as Distinguished University Professor in the Department of Criminology and Criminal Justice at the University of Maryland. He has conducted field research and experiments in over 30 police agencies in the US, UK and Australia. Publications of the results have appeared in the *American Sociological Review, Law and Society Review, Criminology, Journal of the Royal Statistical Society (Series A), Journal of Experimental Criminology* and the *Journal of the American Medical Association*. His work covers a wide range of issues, from predicting crime locations and serious offences by individual offenders to historical analyses of the control of police corruption.

Neal Shover is Professor Emeritus at the University of Tennessee, Knoxville. A Fellow of the American Society of Criminology, he is author or co-author of numerous papers and books including, most recently (with Andy Hochstetler), *Choosing White-Collar Crime* (Cambridge University Press, 2006). He has been a visiting fellow in the US Department of Justice and a visiting scholar at universities both in the US and overseas. His current work, which explores the significance of social class for crime control and the dynamics of crime-control bureaucracies, is the basis for the book project *Managing Criminal Misfits: Crime Control and Class Control.*

Wesley G. Skogan is a Professor of Political Science and a Faculty Fellow of the Institute for Policy Research at Northwestern University. His research focuses on victimization, fear of crime, the impact of crime on communities, public involvement in crime prevention, and policing. His books on police include *Police and Community in Chicago* (2006), *On the Beat* (1999), and *Community Policing, Chicago Style* (1997). In 2003 he edited *Community Policing: Can It Work?*, a collection of original essays on innovation in policing. In the 2000s, he chaired a committee reviewing research on police policies and practices for the National Academy of Sciences, and was co-editor of the committee's 2004 report, *Fairness and Effectiveness in Policing: The Evidence.*

Keith Soothill is Emeritus Professor of Social Research in the Department of Applied Social Science, Lancaster University and currently is attached to the Centre for Applied Statistics, Lancaster University. He has taught criminology for over 30 years with well over 200 publications. He co-edited (with Moira Peelo) the book, *Questioning Crime and Criminology* (Willan Press, 2005) and co-authored *Understanding Criminal Careers* (Willan Press, 2009).

Elizabeth Stanley is Senior Lecturer in Criminology at Victoria University of Wellington, New Zealand. She teaches and researches on the issues of state crimes, human rights, transitional justice and social justice. Her previous work (undertaken in South Africa, Chile and Timor-Leste) has focused on how victims of state violence have experienced the truth commissions and judicial processes established to 'deal with the past'. Her 2009 book, *Torture, Truth and Justice: The Case of Timor-Leste*, is published by Routledge.

Heather Strang is Director of the Centre for Restorative Justice at the Australian National University and Senior Research Fellow at the Institute of Criminology, University of Cambridge. She has been involved in a series of experimental tests of the effects of restorative justice in Australia and the United Kingdom over the past 15 years and is currently analysing a 10-year follow-up of victims and offenders who participated in the Australian study. She has published extensively in this area, including her victim-focused book, *Repair or Revenge: Victims and Restorative Justice.*

Julie Stubbs is a Professor in the Faculty of Law, University of New South Wales. Her research focuses on violence against women and her publications address domestic violence law reforms, intimate homicide, battered woman syndrome, a critical appraisal of restorative justice, post-separation violence and child contact, sexual assault, and cross-cultural issues in the legal system.

Terence P. Thornberry, Ph.D., is Professor in the Department of Criminology and Criminal Justice at the University of Maryland and the Principal Investigator of the Rochester Youth Development Study, a three-generation panel study begun in 1986 to examine the causes and consequences of delinquency and other forms of antisocial behaviours. In 1995, he was elected a Fellow of the American Society of Criminology, and in 2008, he was the recipient of that society's Edwin H. Sutherland Award. He is the author of a number of books, including *Gangs and Delinquency in Developmental Perspective* which received the American Society of Criminology's Michael J. Hindelang Award in 2004.

George E. Tita is an Associate Professor in the Department of Criminology, Law and Society at the University of California, Irvine. His research is anchored in the community and crime literature with a special focus on the causes and correlates of interpersonal violence. In addition to exploring how youth gangs impact the spatial distribution of crime, he is also interested in examining how racial and ethnic change at the neighbourhood-level impacts levels and patterns of crime. Much of his policy research has been devoted to issues surrounding gun violence including the design and implementation of effective strategies aimed at reducing gun violence as well as study of illegal gun markets in Los Angeles. In addition to spatial analysis, Dr. Tita has employed diverse sets of methodologies in his research including quasi-experimental methods (propensity score matching), hedonic models, agent-based models, and social network analysis. Currently, he is working with an interdisciplinary team of social scientists and mathematicians at UCLA studying the formation and dissipation of crime 'hot spots'. Professor Tita has published in a wide variety of journals in the social sciences (e.g., *Criminology, Social Forces, Journal of Quantitative Criminology, Urban Studies*, and the *Annals of the Association of American Geographers*) as well as the natural sciences (e.g., *Proceedings of the National Academy of Sciences, Physics Review E*, and *Mathematical Models and Methods in the Applied Sciences*).

Kyle Treiber (BS in Psychology, University of North Carolina at Chapel Hill, PhD in Criminology, University of Cambridge), is a Research Associate with of the Peterborough Adolescent and Young Adult Development Study (PADS+) at the University of Cambridge. Her research interests include biosocial aspects of morality, self-control, and the interaction between individuals and environments.

Cécile Van de Voorde, LL.M., Ph.D., is a former Assistant Professor in the Department of Law & Police Science at John Jay College of Criminal Justice (CUNY). She is a cultural criminologist, an international human rights activist, and a social documentary photographer whose ethnographic work focuses primarily on cultural genocide and ethnocide, child soldiers, and the use of sexual violence in armed conflict.

Jan Van Dijk was director of the Research and Documentation Centre of the Dutch Ministry of Justice. Between 1998 and 2005 he worked for the United Nations in Vienna and Turin. He acted as president of the World Society of Victimology between 1997 and 2000. In 2008 he received the Sellin-Glueck Award of the American society of Criminology for his lifelong contribution to international criminology and victimology. He currently holds the Pieter van Vollenhoven chair in victimology and human security at the University of Tilburg (The Netherlands).

Per-Olof H. Wikström (PhD, Docent, Stockholm University) is Professor of Ecological and Developmental Criminology at the Institute of Criminology, University of Cambridge. He is the director of the Peterborough Adolescent and Young Adult Development Study (PADS+), a major ESRC-funded research project which aims to advance knowledge about crime causation and prevention (see www.pads.ac.uk). Professor Wikström's main research interests are developing unified theory of the causes of crime (Situational Action Theory), its empirical testing and its application to devising knowledge-based prevention policies. In 1994, he received the Sellin-Glueck Award for outstanding contributions to international criminology from the American Society of Criminology. In 2002 he was made a Fellow of the Center for Advanced Study in the Behavioral Sciences (Stanford University) and in 2010 he was named a Fellow of the American Society of Criminology.

Yaling Yang is a Postdoctoral Research Fellow in the Department of Neurology at University of California, Los Angeles (UCLA) School of Medical. Her research focuses on applying both traditional and novel image analysis methods to explore the neural mechanisms underlying a broad range of externalizing behavior including psychopathy, antisocial behavior and substance use in developmental and adult populations. She has received an NIH Pathway to Independence Career Award in 2011 to identify brain morphological variations as endophenotypes for psychopathic traits using a longitudinal adolescent twin sample.

Editorial Introduction

David Gadd, Susanne Karstedt,
Steven F. Messner

WHY CRIMINOLOGICAL METHODS?

The subject of methodology is never far from the top of the criminological agenda. In part, this reflects the centrality of 'method' – understood to encompass not only techniques for researching the empirical world, but also the logics that underlie their application – to any systematic field of inquiry. In this respect criminology is little different to any other branch of social science. Criminologists engaged in research attempt to deploy systematic approaches to considering human behaviour which, if not borrowed wholesale, are to a large extent common practice or adapted from the neighbouring disciplines of sociology, psychology, history, law and economics.

At the same time, however, criminology has its own distinctive history as a discipline which at the present time leaves it prone to pressures to establish its methodological credentials which fall rather less forcefully on its social scientific neighbours. This is because criminology's subject matter – crime, criminality, victimization and social control – are currently all so densely political that criminologists who want their research to be taken seriously have always to be ready to explain in the public arena how they know what they claim to know, and why their claims to expertise are to be trusted more than those advanced by journalists, politicians or members of the public. Ian Loader and Richard Sparks (2011: 125) suggest that this politicization induces within criminology three recurring moments:

1   A moment of *discovery* involving the pro-
    duction of knowledge about such matters as
    crime causes, patterns and trends, offender

motivations and behaviour, the social distribution and impact of victimization, and the effects of programmes that aim to reduce crime ... or make societies safer.

2   An *institutional-critical* moment in which criminologists seek to 'explain why criminal justice stubbornly refuses to make much room for criminological reason and research' through, for example, examinations of the processes by which crime is socially and politically constituted in everyday conversation, the media and/or in the organizational cultures of criminal justice professionals (ibid. 126).

3   A *normative* moment that involves 'disciplined reflection' on both the 'nature of justice' and more broadly 'what is at stake in criminological and public debate about crime' including 'the value conflicts and trade-offs that lie therein' (ibid. 126–7). The normative moment entails reflecting upon whether the right questions have been asked by academics and policy makers alike, so that, for example, we do not forget that there is 'more to evaluation than finding out "what works"' (ibid. 127).

Self-evidently the first two of these recurring moments necessitate a level of methodological competency. Both the moment of discovery and the institutional-critical moment require criminologists able to design reliable, generalizable and persuasive studies. But Loader and Sparks' third normative stage also requires a capacity to appreciate the principles behind a range of different approaches to methodology. All criminologists need to be able to understand how and why some of their colleagues approach quite similar research problems in quite different ways. They need also to be able to reflect upon how different approaches to method and data generate competing positions in relation to debates about crime and justice in order to engage with these positions on their own terms.

Put more prosaically, criminological 'reasoning' is constantly 'mediated and contested by a range of vociferous interest groups, activists and a multitude of institutional actors and public opinions' as well as from within its own ranks (McLaughlin and Newburn, 2010: 5). Within these contexts, the expertise of professional criminologists is rarely paramount. Criminologists, perhaps more often than many other kinds of social scientists, have to establish why it is that their expertise should be regarded as any better than commonsensical ways of looking at crime and justice. Whether the debates have to do with fluctuations in crime rates, the effectiveness of particular approaches to policing or punishment, or more basic 'why do some people commit crime?' type questions, methodology ought to be a crucial arbiter of the value of competing criminological expertise. It is therefore important that those undertaking criminological research have a sound grasp of best practice in methodology as it pertains both to their own enquiries and those studies conducted by others.

Criminologists' purchase on public debates, whether these be fuelled by empirically grounded public concerns or the folk devils and moral panics that so litter the history of Western crime policy, rests in no small part on our abilities to develop effective research methodologies: to pose deeper questions about social problems; to suggest ways and means of studying these problems so conceived that they yield evidence that is meaningful, suitably contextualized and accurate; to find strategies of organizing this information in ways that are orderly and logical enough to shed new light on the problems under study; and to make our methods sufficiently transparent so that our analyses and diagnoses make sense to others, even if these others are not fully persuaded by them. Integrity of method is a crucial foundation on which criminological expertise rests. Few criminologists would probably want it to be otherwise.

Of course, good methodology alone cannot guarantee practical answers, since these almost always require a political or theoretical leap from analysis to real-world application. Rather, what good methodology enables is a widening of the remit of enquiry, from the merely anecdotal to a much more thoroughgoing appraisal of relevant cases, samples and sources. As many of the contributors to this volume show, what matters in the service of public debates about crime and punishment is not always whether or not we as criminologists can proffer solutions but, as any good maths teacher knows, that we are always ready to 'show our workings': that we are able to explain to those who have not benefitted from a criminological training why the wider field matters and how we arrived at the perspectives we hold; on what terms our perspectives were formed; and on what empirical grounds these perspectives can be challenged.

At present the importance of attending to these matters of methodology could not be greater. The global financial crises mean that budgets for social science research are likely to suffer in many universities, and the prioritizing of research on crime and punishment in many jurisdictions will almost certainly yield to budgetary cuts. Criminological research is becoming a more precious commodity, especially in those parts of the English speaking world where it was once quite abundant. At the same time, academic social scientists in the UK, US and Australia are under increasing pressure to demonstrate the impact of their research on social policy. This pressure not only affects established criminologists accustomed to having their research sidelined by populist policy making, but it may also redirect many young researchers to areas where the recognition of policy audiences is instantaneous. Unless we clearly articulate what constitutes good methodological practice we could well witness the compromising of the critical distance researchers need to pose big questions, to establish robust research designs, and to contemplate competing interpretations of research data.

AIMS OF THE VOLUME

One of the reasons for having a handbook like this is to help new and established researchers in criminology share experiences so others can learn from them. But what was our vision for this volume? We were asked to produce a state-of-the-art compendium of the scholarly literature on criminological research methods that would fit within the SAGE Handbook series. At first, we were unsure about whether this was desirable. Why should professional criminologists read a general criminology methods book when there are more specialized volumes to choose from? Why shouldn't they simply reach straight for a specific methods textbook on, say, 'survey research', 'participatory enquiry' or 'discourse analysis', or any other book that begins with general methodological principles in social science and moves onto the specialized techniques? The conclusion we came to was that the success of this enterprise would depend upon the nature of the criminological research methods the handbook would encompass and the quality of the explication of these methods. If the chapters worked in the way that criminologists tend to – moving from field of study, to research problematic, to methodological tool – then a handbook of criminological research methods might effectively fill an important gap in the literature. For the *SAGE Handbook of Criminological Research Methods* to be of most use, we thought, it would need to attend very squarely to the logic of research enquiry – the particular problems that criminologists face in conducting research, the specific methodological approaches that have evolved to overcome them, and the range of techniques now at criminologists' disposals for converting information about the world into insightful commentary on crime, victimization and justice issues.

In what follows, therefore, we want to suggest that there are some methodological issues – in terms of the challenges of research design, implementation, data collection, data analysis and dissemination – that take on a fairly unique character when worked through in criminological contexts. We think there are at least four key challenges in criminological research which, as a constellation, have conferred upon the discipline a relatively distinct methodological profile. These four challenges can be summarized as follows.

Challenge 1: The illicit nature of crime

Crime by its very definition is an illicit activity, presenting criminologists across the generations with the problem of how to access information on behaviour that is intended to be covert. To study, for example, the stealthy activities of burglars, the shame-inducing experience of sexual victimization, and the discriminatory workings of criminal justice agents, criminologists confront the challenge of finding ways of asking questions that uncover the nature of the behaviours under investigation without leaving research participants vulnerable to adverse consequences. Question design, the protocols used to pose questions, and the parameters of what counts as sound ethical practice are all elements of this challenge that have generated some distinctly criminological solutions. As some of the chapters in this volume testify, some of these solutions have evolved across different jurisdictions producing what are increasingly globalized methodological arts. At the same time, other contributions in this volume ably demonstrate that some of the most damaging illicit behaviour occurs in those parts of the world where

human and economic insecurities are most acute, and where crime and justice problems are the most urgent. The world's war zones are perhaps the most obvious examples, although we should not lose sight of those countries also facing environmental disasters (Jamieson and McEvoy, 2007; Karstedt, forthcoming). In many such places there is a need for research into the culture, values, and vulnerabilities of populations facing acute problems of crime and insecurity in the absence of policing or effective justice systems. Developing effective methodologies able to gain a purchase on illicit behaviour in these parts of the world remains an ongoing challenge for criminology.

Challenge 2: The diversity of crime

Even within those parts of the world where criminology has long flourished, however, the scope and range of the phenomena that constitute the focus of criminological enquiry can be dazzling. This is primarily because criminological enquiry is directed towards a collection of diverse behaviours, many of which have relatively little in common beyond their relationship to law. For example, criminologists fundamentally disagree over whether conventional crimes such as shoplifting, fraud, prostitution, and interpersonal violence can be explained in terms of the same aetiological factors, or if the only common elements are the modes of control applied to regulate them (Becker, 1953; Gottfredson and Hirschi, 1990; Lemert, 1964). And for some criminologists it is the absence of modes of control that defines what really should be of criminological interest: why, for example, it is that some institutions, nation states, or international corporations, are able to get away with actions that result in loss, injury or death when comparable actions by ordinary citizens do not (Box, 1983)? Definitional issues are frequently a major challenge in criminological research; and not only for those involved in deconstructing representation. As many of the chapters in this volume make clear, the difficulties of finding the right words and phrases to operationalize ideas and concepts is no less a challenge for those involved in designing surveys, self-report studies and programme evaluations. Potential miscommunication and the slipperiness of meaning are constant concerns shared by most criminological researchers whatever their methodological specialism.

Challenge 3: Multi-level phenomena

The problem of multiple levels in criminological research serves only to complicate these definitional issues further. As criminologists we are indebted to many of the classic sociological works on the micro-detail of social interaction: Harold Garfinkel's (1956) ethnomethodological analysis of the administration of successful degradation ceremonies; Erving Goffman's (1961) participant observation study of institutionalization within mental asylums; Howard Becker's (1953) influential essay on how to become a marijuana user – to mention only the most famous. But as criminologists our fascination with processes is derived in large measure from our need to conceptualize the relationships between individuals – whether they be offenders, victims, the general public or criminal justice agents; and the wider environments in which they exist – families, institutions, communities, countries, continents. Many of the major paradigm shifts in twentieth-century criminology can be understood in terms of the complexities, tensions caused, and ideas generated as criminologists have attempted to work between these different levels, to explain for example: changes in rates of victimization, arrest, and/or use of particular criminal justice sanctions; why some of the best-laid plans in criminal corrections fail so spectacularly; or differences within and between communities and countries in terms of how problematic crime is. Garland's (2002) classic essay, 'Of Crime and Criminals', captures the tensions between some of criminology's early psychoanalytic founders and the quest for harder social scientific evidence that enabled the expansion of a governmentally oriented criminology in Britain after the Second World War. Likewise, histories of the Chicago School typically begin with Robert Park's admonition to his students to 'tramp' around crime-prone neighbourhoods (Lilly et al., 2007: 39). This inspired a methodological journey that combined ethnographic observations of city life and the collation of numerous biographies or life histories – of which the story of Stanley the Jackroller is the most famous (Shaw, 1930) – with the spatial modelling of crime rates (Shaw and McKay, 1942). In so doing, the Chicagoans stimulated many a methodological venture in criminology, including the development of alternatives to official statistics for measuring rates of offending and victimization, and the development of more sophisticated observational methods for recording the relationships between crime, disorder, and street life than were hitherto the case (Sampson and Raudenbusch, 1999).

Challenge 4: The messiness of criminological research.

There are probably few research fields where research data come readily packaged in tidy forms. But because the subjects of criminological enquiry include a disproportionate number of those sections of the population deemed dangerous, deprived and disorderly, collecting and making sense of the data we obtain from our research subjects may well be rather harder to handle than in some allied fields. Of course the vulnerable and the powerless are not the only subjects of criminological research. Powerful law avoiders, law enforcers and law makers are also our research subjects; subpopulations that are perhaps no less likely, in certain circumstances, to want to avoid leaving the kinds of evidence trails social scientists find useful.

Paradoxically, the disorderliness of the criminological research field has been a source of disunity within a discipline that often presents itself in terms of the following binaries: quantitative/qualitative, theoretical/empirical; critical/policy-orientated. Often these differences of emphasis are reactions to the volatility of the research field. So, within quantitative, empirical and policy-orientated projects the temptation has sometimes been *to impose order on the field of study in order for research to commence.* Randomized control designs exemplify this methodological pre-ordering approach (Sherman, 2009). Research participants are randomly assigned to control and experimental groups, a carefully managed trial is implemented, with participants' reactions measured pre- and post-test. How effective such experiments can ever be at achieving orderliness is currently the subject of much debate, causing some to argue that in the fields of crime and its control quasi-experimental designs are as good as we are ever likely to get (Carr, 2010; Hough, 2010; Sampson, 2008). Meanwhile, others have expressed the view that 'anarchist understanding' is preferable to all quantification and methodological rigour (Ferrell et al., 2008). Yet ultimately these dissenters share the view of many of the experimentalists whose voices find effect in this volume: in its implementation most criminological research methods turn out to be a little more 'ragged around the edges … not fully conceptualized or completed' than we had hoped they might be (ibid. 160–1).

The contributions to this volume are all in their own unique ways illustrative of the approaches that criminologists have adopted to meet the challenges forced upon us by an inherently messy field of illicit behaviour, fraught with definitional issues across many levels. They reveal how criminologists have positioned themselves within the debates these challenges have given rise to as well as how they have dealt with the more practical day-to-day methodological issues they generate. What these contributions have revealed to us is that making sense of criminological data is as formidable a challenge as it has ever been. Datasets pertaining to crime and victimization continue to proliferate. Official statistics tell us part of the story but never the whole story. But then so do the people we observe and interview, whatever our approach. And perhaps so too do the reports we write about research. Many of the tales from the field recounted in this volume, including some of those most attuned to the tenets of experimental design, reveal that it is only when we have attempted to implement research strategies that we have discovered just where our methods are most under-conceptualized or incomplete. Talking about method is part of the process of discovering methodological limitations and overcoming them as much as possible.

The conclusion we have drawn from this observation is not that criminology is in some state of disarray or that criminologists are deluded about the power of method, but that methodology is very much alive and well in our discipline; constantly evolving to new challenges; fit for purpose in so many respects; and more often than not about learning from experience. Evaluation and action researchers, in-depth interviewer and international survey designers, statistical modellers and ethnomethodologists have at least this much in common. Indeed, the tidy alignments between theoretical perspective, political philosophy, and methodological approach appear to be becoming a part of criminological history that many scholars are less comfortable with than their predecessors. The development of feminist work within criminology is surely the most obvious example of this trend. Within the study of violence against women, for example, a succession of reflexive turns have not only steered the discipline out of its more positivistic preoccupations, but have also fostered a considerable rapprochement between theoretically sophisticated and in-depth qualitative work on victimization and the kinds of statistical, evaluation and econometric methodologies that are needed to persuade policy audiences of the importance of preventative intervention (Gelsthorpe, 2002; Stanko, 2001; Walby, 2004).

ORGANIZATION OF THE VOLUME

Criminological research methodology is therefore nearly always about deciding how to respond in circumstances where the best-laid research designs fall short of expectations. Research on illicit, secretive and stigmatizing phenomena cannot possibly be otherwise. Empirical research in criminology is as much about making difficult decisions

under imperfect conditions as it is about how to do it. What we think needs to be better understood is in what ways our models of what constitutes good research genuinely differ. Would anyone, for example, in the field of survey research now disagree with the argument qualitative researchers often make about the importance of the quality of the relationships between interviewers and interviewees in determining how meaningful the data produced are? How many criminologists would disagree with the observation that quantitative and qualitative methods are not so much rivals, but different tools for different jobs? In order to aid the reader looking to come to their own conclusions about methodological questions we have chosen to organize the volume in a way that aids comparison and is consistent with our commitment to the logic of criminological enquiry. The book's chapters are ordered as far as possible in terms of the intellectual terrain of research problems with which criminologists are routinely confronted. We commissioned chapters to fit into the following five sections around which the volume is now organized:

1 Crime and Criminals
2 Contextualizing Crime in Space and Time: Networks, Communities, and Culture
3 Perceptual Dimensions of Crime
4 Criminal Justice Systems: Organizations and Institutions
5 Preventing Crime and Improving Justice.

To enable readers to move quickly to the contributions of most relevance to them, each of the five sections begins with a short overview of the chapters contained within it. Abstracts summarizing the contents of each chapter are also to be found at the SAGE website. Most of the chapters have been written to a common format of which four key elements are worthy of note.

1 They address the kinds of research approaches and strategies that have become imperative, even orthodox, in relation to very specific fields of criminological enquiry.
2 They explicate what each contributor perceives to have become best practice, methodologically, within that specific field.
3 They provide one or more worked examples of best or innovative methodological practice, typically using textboxes to work through technical detail and practicalities.
4 They provide a conclusion that directs the reader towards new horizons, methodological applications and developments, supported by a short list of further reading and/or web-based resources for the interested reader to follow-up.

As a means of further synthesizing the volume, we have located Mark Israel and Iain Hay's chapter on 'Research Ethics in Criminology' at the very end of the volume. Israel and Hay draw eclectically on examples taken from within some of the other contributions to illustrate how criminologists have attempted to resolve the tensions between ethical conduct and research ethics governance.

A WORD OF THANKS

Throughout the process of collating material for this volume we relied heavily on colleagues to secure the best accounts of methodological innovation in criminology we could find. We are indebted both to our editorial board (Pat Carlen, Frank Cullen, Manuel Eisner, Aaron Kupchik, Eric Baumer, Heather Strang, Mechthild Bereswill, Susan McVie, Tim Newburn, Welsey Skogan) and a number of other colleagues who provided suggestions, recommendations and advice to ourselves and our authors. All chapter contributions were subject to anonymous peer review. We are grateful both to the editorial board and a number of friends and colleagues who assisted with this process. It has vastly enriched the quality of the volume. In addition to those already mentioned, the following people are also deserving of thanks for their assistance along the way: Cyndi Banks, Sarah-Jayne Boyd, Peter Chevins, Clive Emsley, Stephen Farrall, Jeff Ferrell, Mark Israel, Chris Kershaw, Mike Hough, Gary LaFree, Tony Jefferson, Tony Kearon, Caroline Porter, Majid Yar, Shadd Maruna, Robin Robinson, Cécile Van de Voorde, and Anne Worrall.

Finally we want to say a few things about what this handbook is not about. This is a book dedicated to the job of providing a helping hand, a second opinion and a word to the wise. It is not about methodological imperialism. Its contents, we hope, are introductory enough to support those new to particular methodologies, but not so basic that the skilled practitioner of any particular method cannot learn from them. All contributions should be read as pragmatic but not prescriptive. Too keep within length, we asked for reference lists to be kept short, but the chapters themselves should be read as summaries of many complex conversations involving many more individuals, groups and networks. We hope that each contribution will be read as an invitation to join these conversations, and by no means treated as the end of the debate.

REFERENCES

Becker, H.S. (1953) 'Becoming a marijuana user'. *The American Journal of Sociology* 59(3): 235–242.

Box, S. (1983) *Power, Crime and Mystification*. London: Routledge.

Carr, P.J. (2010) 'The problem with experimental criminology: a response to Sherman's 'Evidence and Liberty'. *Criminology and Criminal Justice* 10(1): 3–10.

Garfinkel, H. (1956) 'Conditions of successful degradation ceremonies'. *American Journal of Sociology* 61(5): 420–424.

Garland, D. (2002) 'Of crimes and criminals' in M. Maguire, R. Morgan and R. Reiner (eds), *The Oxford Handbook of Criminology*, 3rd Edition (pp. 7–50). Oxford: Oxford University Press.

Gelsthorpe, L. (2002) 'Feminism and criminology' in M. Maguire, R. Morgan and R. Reiner (eds), *The Oxford Handbook of Criminology*, 3rd Edition (pp. 112–143). Oxford: Oxford University Press.

Goffman, E. (1961) *Asylums: Essays on the Social Situation of Mental Patients and Other Inmates*. New York: Doubleday.

Gottfredson, M. and Hirschi, T. (1990) *A General Theory of Crime*. Stanford: Stanford University Press.

Hough, M. (2010) 'Gold standard or fool's gold? The pursuit of certainty in experimental criminology'. *Criminology and Criminal Justice* 10(1): 11–22.

Jamieson, R. and McEvoy (2007) 'Conflict, suffering and the promise of human rights' in D. Downes, P. Rock C. Chinkin and C. Gearthy (eds), *Crime, Social Control and Human Rights* (pp. 422–441). Collumpton: Willan.

Karstedt, S. (forthcoming) 'Looking back into the future: Migration, Crime and Revolution in Southwest Germany 1840–1850' in S. Farrall (ed.), *The Legal and Criminological Consequences of Climate Change*. Oxford: Hart.

Lemert, E. (1964) 'Social structure, social control and deviation' in M. Clinard (ed.), *Anomie and Deviant Behaviour* (pp. 57–97). New York: Free Press.

Lilly, J.R., Cullen, F.T. and Ball, R.A. (2007) *Criminological Theory: Context and Consequences*, 4th Edition. Thousand Oaks, CA: Sage.

Loader, I. and Sparks, R. (2011) *Public Criminology*. London: Routledge.

McLaughlin, E. and Newburn, T. (2010) 'Introduction' in E. McLaughlin and T. Newburn (eds), *The SAGE Handbook of Criminological Theory* (pp. 1-18) London: Sage.

Sampson, R. (2008) 'Moving to inequality: neighborhood effects and experiments meet social structure'. *American Journal of Sociology* 114(1): 189–231.

Sampson, R.J. and Raudenbush, S.W. (1999) 'Systematic social observation of public spaces: a new look at disorder in urban neighborhoods'. *American Journal of Sociology* 105(3): 603–651.

Shaw, C. (1930) *The Jack-Roller: A Delinquent Boy's Own Story*. Chicago: University of Chicago Press.

Shaw, C. and McKay, H.D. (1942) *Juvenile Delinquency and Urban Areas*. Chicago: University of Chicago Press.

Sherman, L.W. (2009) 'Evidence and liberty: the promise of experimental criminology'. *Criminology and Criminal Justice* 9(1): 5–28.

Stanko, E.A. (2001) 'The day to count: reflections on a methodology to raise awareness about the impact of domestic violence in the UK'. *Criminology and Criminal Justice* 1(1): 215–226.

Walby, S. (2004) *The Cost of Domestic Violence*. London: Women and Equality Unit.

Crime and Criminals

This first section of the handbook includes six chapters that reflect the rich diversity of methodological approaches in the contemporary study of crime and criminals. The contributions encompass both quantitative and quantitative approaches, and highlight the multi-disciplinary character of criminology as a field of inquiry. The chapters review relevant empirical studies, describe principal data sources, explain analytic techniques, and identify the more important challenges associated with the different methodologies.

The initial chapter in the section by Neal Shover focuses on how life histories and autobiographies can be used to address a wide range of important topics in criminology. Although scholars sometimes draw a formal distinction between these two types of materials, Shover chooses to incorporate autobiographies under the broader rubric of life histories, which he defines as 'documents or productions written or in other ways recorded and made available to others that consist largely or entirely of first-person narrative about all or much of the subject's life'. Similar to other forms of ethnographic data, these materials allow the researcher to 'get close' to the subject matter and to understand it from the vantage point of the actors involved. Such an understanding enables researchers to assess key assumptions about human agency that underlie influential criminological theories and criminal justice policies (assumptions that are sometimes implicit). Shover illustrates techniques for the analysis of these qualitative materials and carefully assesses both the strengths and limitations associated with the use of life history materials. In addition, by recounting his own experiences in the discovery and use of life history materials, Shover reveals the interesting intersection of personal biography and the development of professional research

interests that often characterizes the criminological enterprise. The chapter concludes on the optimistic note that vastly improved technological resources to gain access to documents and to manage textual material are likely to enhance the potential of research based on life histories in the years ahead.

The next chapter, by Marvin Krohn, Terence Thornberry, Kirstin Bell, Alan Lizotte, and Matthew Phillips, shifts the focus from qualitative to quantitative criminological analysis. The authors discuss one of the most important tools used by quantitative researchers to measure involvement in delinquent and criminal activity: the self-report survey. In such a survey, respondents are asked to report their personal involvement in specified forms of illegal behaviour with guarantees of either confidentiality or anonymity. The chapter begins with a history of self-report studies, illustrating how the development of this measurement technique raised questions about the widely presumed inverse association between social class and offending that had been reported in research based on official statistics. The somewhat surprising results of the early self-report surveys stimulated further development of the basic methodology. As the authors explain, researchers were sensitized to the importance of considering the 'domains' of behaviour captured by the items included in the surveys (e.g., rather trivial *versus* serious offences) and the types of response sets offered to respondents (e.g., enumeration of the actual counts of illegal acts *versus* the use of truncated categories). The authors also describe some of the continuing challenges associated with the application of the self-report methodology in general and with its application in longitudinal studies in particular. These challenges, along with proposed solutions, are explicated with illustrations from the authors' path-breaking longitudinal research that has employed the self-report methodology, the Rochester Youth Development Survey (RYDS).

David Gadd's chapter explicates the in-depth interviewing technique known as the Free Association Narrative Interview Method, which can be employed in the psychosocial case study. Researchers adopting this methodological approach strive to capture the complexity of human agency by exploring 'how the psychological and social constitute each other, without collapsing one into the other'. In contrast with virtually all other paradigms in contemporary criminology, the Free Association Narrative Interview Method takes seriously the role of unconscious motivation and, in particular, the role of unconscious defences against anxiety. Moreover, as the author explains, this methodology places heavy emotional and intellectual demands on researchers conducting the interviews, who must wrestle with their own defensiveness. Gadd richly illustrates the procedures for such interviews and the associated analytic techniques with excerpts from his own research based on case studies of perpetrators of domestic violence and racially motivated assault. In addition, he lays out some practical guidelines for researchers who would like to implement this distinctive type of in-depth interviewing in conjunction with psychosocial case studies.

Jodie Miller's chapter explains how another qualitative data collection technique – what she refers to as 'qualitative in-depth interviewing' – has been applied productively to advance feminist criminology. Feminist criminology takes as its point of departure the underlying premise that gender is more than an individual-level independent variable. Rather, the relations of sex and gender systematically structure the social world in fundamental ways. Feminist criminologists are accordingly concerned with the ways in which 'gender and gender inequality shape the experiences of those involved in crime'. Miller argues that the qualitative in-depth interview serves the objectives of feminist criminology particularly well by providing 'reflective accounts of social life offered from the points of view of research participants', which can stimulate insights about the cultural frames that participants use to make sense of their lives. Drawing upon grounded theory, Miller illustrates in detail useful techniques for the analysis of the data yielded by qualitative in-depth interviewing, including the development of systematic coding schemes, the formulation of emergent hypotheses, and the assessment of internal validity through comparative methods and deviant case analysis. Miller also calls attention to the importance of paying close attention the dynamics of the interviewer/participant relationship, especially in research on

sexual violence. An overarching theme of the chapter is that realization of the potential of the qualitative in-depth interview requires rigorous inductive analysis.

The chapter by Yu Gao, Andrea Glenn, Melissa Peskin, Anna Rudo-Hutt, Robert Schug, Yaling Yang and Adrian Raine reviews the range of methodologies that are employed in contemporary research on neurobiological factors associated with crime and anti-social behaviour more generally. The authors observe that interest in this field has increased dramatically over recent years due in part to the development of new technologies that have greatly enhanced the capacity of researchers to measure neurobiological structures and functioning with increased precision. The chapter explains key research designs (e.g., behavioural genetic and molecular genetic designs), analytic frameworks (e.g., the decomposition of influences to those attributable to genes, shared environment, and non-shared environment), and sophisticated measurement techniques (e.g., structural and functional imaging, standardized assessments of neuropsychology) that characterize the field today. The emerging body of research summarized in the chapter identifies an array of neurobiological risk factors for anti-social behaviour. At the same time, the research points to important interactions between neurobiological factors and the social environment. The authors conclude the chapter with a call for "an integrative perspective on anti-social and criminal behaviour," a perspective that is on the lookout for biosocial interactions. Greater knowledge about such interactions can enhance our understanding of etiological processes and inform potential intervention and prevention programs.

The final chapter in this section, by Tomislav Kovandzic, Mark Schaffer, and Gary Kleck, addresses a vexing source of erroneous statistical inference: 'endogeneity bias'. As the authors explain, three common sources of such bias are reverse causality (when the outcome variable of interest exerts a causal influence on the theorized predictor variable), omitted variable bias (when the researcher is unable to include in the statistical model variables that are empirically related to both the outcome variable and the predictor variable), and measurement error (when the researcher has no alternative but to use an imperfectly measured proxy for the predictor variable). Drawing on econometric techniques, the authors explicate the Generalized Method of Moments (GMM) framework for dealing with such bias, illustrating its criminological application through the study of the relationships between gun prevalence and homicide rates. Their analyses demonstrate the potentially serious consequences of endogeneity bias in research based on conventional multivariate regression modelling.

Life Histories and Autobiographies as Ethnographic Data

Neal Shover

Underlying the choice and use of ethnographic research methods is belief that regardless of the focus of criminological inquiry, investigators should get close to their subject matter and strive to understand it through the lived experience and perspectives of critical actors. Whether data are collected for what analysis of them reveals about the adequacy of theoretical explanations or because of interest in better-informed policy making, it can be helpful to build on or in other ways take account of first-person understandings and perspectives. Ethnographic investigators employ a variety of techniques for capturing these, including analysis of life histories and autobiographies. Generally a distinction is drawn between these, but they are alike in their essential composition: first-person narratives of all or a significant part of an individual's life. Likewise, both autobiographies and life histories are retrospective descriptions and commentary on persons, situations and events considered significant by their authors.

The potential value of these materials can be appreciated by reflection on how historians use them as windows on past events, times and individuals of scholarly interest. Examining life history narratives enables historical investigators to see how significant events were understood and collectively constructed or responded to by persons who were living at the time. Along with examination of personal diaries, life histories are one of the most revealing ways contemporary readers can gain better understanding of the human dimensions of past cataclysmic events (Smith and Watson, 2001). Some of the most evocative and compelling pictures of the human destruction caused by warfare, for example, is available through the eyes of those affected by it who chanced to record their observations and experiences. Likewise, many feminist scholars count analysis of autobiographies and other life narratives among the most useful of materials (Cotterhill and Letherby, 1993; Smith and Watson, 2001; Swindells, 1995). Thus, investigators intent on understanding and chronicling the twentieth-century women's movement, its origins and its struggles, would not deign to attempt this without consulting the life histories of key and lesser participants. Autobiographical materials are employed by investigators from a range of disciplines, but they are used most typically in the humanities and by criminological investigators with a humanistic theoretical bent.

The value of life histories and autobiographies for criminological research on a range of problems potentially is great. They can inform on topics as diverse as the social psychology of deterrence, criminal organization and crime desistance. Life histories can shine revealing light on criminalization movements and outcomes, the sources and dynamics of crime, and diverse reactions to it. They can educate about the operations of crime-control bureaucracies; those penned by criminal prosecutors, for example, might draw into sharper relief both the demands of their work and also how they are managed day to day in a web of organizational and interpersonal relationships. There may be no more telling or useful perspectives on plea bargaining than the recounted ones of lawyers and court personnel whose work routines and decisions give it life. Likewise, life histories penned by police officers who have worked undercover can inform readers about the practical challenges of these demanding and stressful assignments and how they are managed by officers.

This chapter discusses and discounts a distinction between autobiographies and life histories before retracing briefly my happenstance introduction to and use of them in several criminological investigations. This is followed by noting the limited value of individual life histories and the greatly increased analytic potential from examining multiple ones. The discussion throughout is limited primarily to how life histories can be used to examine criminal offending and criminal careers. Next the essay turns to the logic and mechanics of analyzing multiple documents and some of the strengths and challenges of doing so. An examination of what is known about the validity of information provided in published criminal life histories is then presented before the chapter concludes with comments on technological developments that have reduced the operational difficulties of using them to examine not only criminal offending but also other topics of criminological interest.

FIRST-PERSON LIFE NARRATIVES

Whether a life narrative is classed as autobiography or life history largely hinges on whether the idea and impetus for it originated with others and the extensiveness of their influence. The authors of autobiographies generally decide on their own to write their life story before setting out to do so. Whilst others may provide assistance of one kind or another before the project is completed, the subject provides the initiative and is sole arbiter of what is reported (e.g., Connor, 2009). By contrast, the idea and much of the initiative for compiling and publishing life histories generally originates with someone other than the subject. Academicians who become acquainted with and get to know ex-offenders, perhaps from the latter's visits to classes to talk to students, sometimes will urge them to consider writing their life story (e.g., Edwards, 1972). Other life histories are born from research projects that bring academic investigators into contact with offenders or ex-offenders. Regardless of how the relationship begins, the

typical pattern sees collaborators from the outset providing initiative and direction. In this they differ from the archetypical autobiography. Many life histories include commentary or interpretive materials by the collaborator(s), which can range from a few to many pages. Some draw extensively from contacts with and in many cases tape-recorded interviews with their subjects over a period of years (King, 1972; Singer, 2006; Steffensmeier and Ulmer, 2005).

Maintaining a bright-line, formal distinction between autobiographies and life histories is rendered nearly impossible, however, by the large number of hybrids. The idea for compiling and publishing an autobiography generally rests with the subject, but this is not always the case. Some are launched, adopted belatedly or pursued to completion by collaborators (Behn, 1977; Hapgood, 1903). And whilst the subjects of life histories typically work with direction from others, the same is true of some autobiographers. The latter sometimes are products of ghostwriters, and in these cases it can be nearly impossible to trace their influence or to distinguish first-person narrative from the author's editorial reworking of materials (James and Considine, 1961; Tosches, 1986). Regardless of the label assigned to published memoirs, collaborators may provide guidance or in other ways exercise a formative hand in the project. Where academicians are co-authors or editorial organizers, for example, interest in scholarly issues typically shapes the collection and reporting of narrative (e.g., Steffensmeier and Ulmer, 2005). To the extent that criminal autobiographies are shaped by collaborators' assumptions, priorities and editorial hand they become less autobiography and more life history. The respective contributions of collaborators and subjects can become obscured in the process of compiling and publishing life stories, but the same is true of some autobiographies. Frequently the subject is omitted from the listed authors. Given the difficulty of drawing a sharp line between autobiographies and life histories, this chapter treats both under the latter rubric. As the label is employed here, life histories are documents or productions written or in other ways recorded and made available to others that consist largely or entirely of first-person narrative about all or much of the subject's life.

Collection and analysis of life histories was touted as a research method by sociologists based in Chicago in the early decades of the twentieth century. They saw them as key to understanding the interplay of individual and social factors in development of delinquency and adult crime. In books and essays, Chicago criminologists presented the life histories of individuals with records of criminal participation and highlighted how social factors helped explain this. Shaw's *Jack-Roller* (1930) is perhaps the best known of these studies. First published in 1930 and reissued in 1966, it is the life history of 'Stanley', a 23-year-old man who had compiled by the time of its initial publication an extensive record of delinquency, crime and incarceration. The author, Clifford Shaw, was trained at the University of Chicago where he also acquired an interpretation of crime and other forms of 'social pathology' as products in large part of socially disorganized urban conditions. Like his mentors and colleagues, Shaw believed that life histories could lay bare the criminogenic interaction of these conditions with individual characteristics, family dynamics and the influence of peers.

The passage of time has diminished neither the validity nor the persuasiveness of the justifications for examining life histories offered by Chicago sociologists. Now, as then, the 'boy's story' can show how various risk factors for criminality are understood and responded to by individuals and how they affect its onset, development and sequencing. The influence of criminal acquaintances, long recognized as a contributor to delinquency participation, is obvious in most if not all of the life narratives developed and published by Chicago criminologists (e.g., Landesco, 1933). Likewise it is clear in the great majority of similar narratives published since. Criminal life histories also show that the potential influence of criminal associates does not diminish when offenders move beyond their delinquency years; acquisition of new friends or acquaintances can lead to changes in criminal offending and career trajectories. They can make available new criminal opportunities rooted in the skills and knowledge the new associates bring with them. And the fact that the former have shown few compunctions about breaking the law or paying the price when caught can increase their attractiveness to peers for an array of illicit projects and enterprises. Notwithstanding their considerable research potential, however, analysis of life histories fell into disuse not long after Chicago sociologists championed them, and few investigators now employ them for research purposes (Hunter, 2009).

CRIMINAL LIFE HISTORIES: NUMBERS AND PROPERTIES

The desire to turn their life story into a book is surprisingly common among criminal offenders, particularly street-level thieves and hustlers. Many follow through. A great number of life histories of burglars, robbers and similar offenders are published annually and have been for a century or more. One of the most striking characteristics of this body of materials is how few are authored by women, who generally seem far less inclined than men to own up to and recount publicly a life of transgressions (Clark and Hughes, 1961; Hannington, 2002; Harris, 1986, 1988). Sex offenders generally do not publish their life histories. Convicted white-collar criminals do not match street offenders in their output of life histories, but they are steady contributors nonetheless.

The authors of some life histories use pseudonyms (Clark and Hughes, 1961), but it is a rare author who elects to publish anonymously (Anonymous, 1922). Many works have single authors, but perhaps an equal number do not. Publication by academicians of criminal life histories is a steady though not a large stream of first-person narrative materials on the lives and pursuits of criminal offenders (Clark and Eubank, 1927; Clark and Hughes, 1961; Hills and Santiago, 1992; Jackson, 1969; King, 1972; Rettig et al., 1977; Singer, 2006; Steffensmeier, 1986). As a group they are among the more useful documents for research purposes, but their collective and cumulative significance for criminological theory development and testing has been negligible.

The reasons offenders and ex-offenders write are few, although they are rarely spelled out in detail by authors and not always obvious to readers. Some apparently hope their recounted lives communicate both lessons and an implicit warning not to make the same mistakes. Others see their self-narratives as grist for understanding why their lives took unrewarding and even painful turns; for these authors, the opportunity to examine the past for self-understanding is cause for the venture. As one remarks, the reward for 'shining a light' on the past is the ability to 'see exactly where I went wrong' (Smith, 2005: 478). Few offenders are openly defiant, unrepentant, insist they would 'do it all again' or 'wouldn't change anything' (Kray, 1993: 156). Discernible in some life histories is a sense of unease about the future now that the years of unremunerative crime and incarceration are behind them.

Too late some authors see and regret how they exchanged short-term pleasures and material success for investment in the future. A key participant in one of the most lucrative bank burglaries in U.S. history spent some 32 years of his life in prison and readily acknowledged looking back that for him, as for many, crime pays, but 'just not for long'. In the meantime, lives go on:

> When I get out of prison, I'll be sixty-five. I've broken [my wife's] heart and squandered away the best part of my son's youth. I was never there for the birthdays, the Little League games, and

bedtime stories. I wasn't there when my son got married and had children of his own. I couldn't be there when my father was sick and dying. I pray that God keeps my mother around so I can spend time with her when I'm released ... My plans are to live lawfully and in peace ... I want to ... enjoy watching our grandchildren grow. That sounds good to me (Porrello, 2006: 241–2).

By the time their life story is published, the great majority of subjects have abandoned their criminal careers or turned their criminal efforts to less confrontational, less visible and, therefore, less risky offenses. They have desisted from or significantly changed their criminal ways.

Offenders' narratives range from detailed descriptions and interpretations of their entire life to shorter and more focused accounts of significant parts. Most, however, recount large swaths of the life course, which makes their life histories well suited for examining not only the onset of delinquency but also the later stages of criminal careers and crime desistance. Familiarity with a large number of criminal life histories suggests that some subjects either lack the capacity or apparently see little need to put their finger on the reason(s) for the twists and turns of their lives. If their narratives are read carefully, however, most authors note contingencies of various kinds that appear responsible (Shover, 1996). Readers rarely get to see the end of offenders' lives, but clearly there is variation here. Like Stanley, the one-time street mugger, some eventually die of old age after a circuitous route to a materially adequate legitimate income and a circle of more or less conventional acquaintances (Snodgrass, 1982; Steffensmeier and Ulmer, 2005). Others are not as fortunate as Stanley, and some end their lives by suicide when prospects for anything better in life seem bleak (King, 1972).

Most persons with lengthy records of street-crime involvement know nothing about the publishing industry, the publishing process or how to go about getting their life story into book form. They know only belief it would make a 'good story' and perhaps could be financially rewarding. A substantial majority succeed on the first count, but almost none achieve the second. The reasons for this typically begin with failure to work with a skilled and knowledgeable collaborator or a major publisher. Authors who go it alone make up a sizeable proportion of those who publish with local presses or who self-publish (Gagnon, 2006; Mitchell, 2002; Watson, 1976; Woodroff, 1970). Nearly all subjects are competent writers, but some are more competent than others. Of the latter some developed or honed their writing skills while incarcerated and later put them to use recounting their lives (Baca, 2001; Braly, 1976;

Bunker, 2000; Smith, 2005). Others became proficient writers apart from their criminal justice odyssey (McCall, 1994). Whilst some authors say little or nothing about the crimes they committed (Leopold, 1958), most describe one or more in detail. Most authors write when their crime years are behind them, but some do so while imprisoned or at risk of committing further crime. Not all are successful avoiding return to their criminal ways (e.g., Maas, 1997; Parker, 1981).

DISCOVERING AND USING CRIMINAL LIFE HISTORIES

My discovery and use of life history materials for research purposes was largely fortuitous, but a lifelong interest in biographies combined with an occupational interest in crime perhaps increased the odds that eventually I would find and find value in the self narratives of criminal offenders. As an undergraduate student, *Cell 2455, Death Row* (Chessman, 1954) was one of the first I recall reading, almost certainly while neglecting more important matters. (Its author, Caryl Chessman, was a highly publicized author and inmate on California's death row, the subject of both protracted legal battles and strong support from death penalty opponents. He was executed in 1960.)

Employment later as a prison sociologist at Joliet-Stateville (Illinois) penitentiaries was a catalyst in the process of finding something beyond entertainment in the life histories of criminal offenders. My work duties there in part consisted of collecting information for and writing inmate 'social histories'. These reports were recognizably biographical in format, albeit this was refracted through ideological and bureaucratic prisms. Also, during coffee breaks and other occasions when my work mates and I talked informally, the names of ex-convicts who had published their life stories occasionally came up. In this way I was made aware of and read *The Courage of His Convictions* (Parker and Allerton, 1962), a copy of which was in the staff library. (Its lead author, Tony Parker, would later publish several additional life histories of men who persisted at crime well into adulthood; Parker, 1963, 1967.) While employed at Joliet-Stateville I became aware also of the autobiography of a former Joliet inmate who one of my co-workers had known during his incarceration (Warren, 1953). Near the end of my prison employment, a colleague chanced to comment one day about an unusual inmate he recently had encountered; the inmate was also the author/subject of a just-published autobiography. I read it (Williamson, 1965).

Prison employment made me aware of several criminal autobiographies, but it was only later that their research value became apparent. Near the end of graduate studies, by which time I had begun dissertation research on the lives and pursuits of burglars, I traveled to another university for a job interview. Left unattended during a break in the schedule, I wandered to the library and chanced upon a section of the holdings where offender autobiographies were shelved. Hasty examination of several caused me to see what I had not seen previously, namely that published life history materials are sufficiently numerous and accessible to inform about the worlds of thieves and therefore could be an additional source of ethnographic data for the dissertation. I became a determined searcher for and reader of criminal autobiographies. I read *The Courage of His Convictions* again and photocopied many of its pages, as I did also with several dozen additional criminal life histories. The resulting body of materials were used as part of the data for my doctoral thesis and for subsequent publications.

Over nearly four decades I have returned from time to time to reading and mining life history materials for what they reveal about offenders, why and how they commit crime, how they perceive and experience punishment, and crime desistance. Including life histories of approximately 30 white-collar criminals, I have read an estimated 200 in total. I once compiled and occasionally updated a list of the authors and titles, but more pressing matters eventually led to its neglect. I misplaced it years ago.

ANALYSIS OF LIFE HISTORY MATERIALS

Analysis of life histories can be approached from a host of disciplinary and theoretical vantage points. They are data sources open equally to psychiatrists and economists, and for this reason readers may be interested in and attuned to very different aspects of offenders' self-described lives. Not all disciplines or investigators, however, are inclined by professional training or interest to accept at face value subjects' descriptions and apparent meanings. Instead, the analytic focus for some is on what is thought to lie behind subjects' recollections. They are interested in what is said chiefly for what it reveals about what subjects may not recognize, understand or acknowledge (Gadd and Jefferson, 2007). This can be anything from unvarnished psychopathy to pathological notions of masculinity.

Contrasting with this stance, ethnographers generally assign 'major importance to the interpretations people place on their experience as explanation for behavior' (Becker, 1966: vi). They assume that most offenders are capable of understanding and describing their lives with considerable insight and accuracy. Despite their criminal records, they are competent adults. With this as starting point, the analytic stance when examining life histories is to assume there are common *patterns* and *themes* in authors' recollected and recounted experiences. The investigator's job is to identify these and map their covariates. In this 'thematic analysis', 'the subject is more or less allowed to speak for him or herself … [while the investigator] slowly accumulates a series of themes – partly derived from the subject's account and partly derived from … theory' (Plummer, 1983: 113–14). When they alert to possible themes, investigators shift to assessing how frequently they appear and possible correlates. This may necessitate examining additional but similar narratives and returning perhaps for another look at ones that were read earlier. Likewise, other data may be scrutinized for evidence on the matter one way or the other.

Individual narratives

For ethnographic investigators, individual criminal life histories essentially are case studies and suffer the analytic limitations of this research design. Chief among them is their limited value for developing and refining theoretical propositions. Individual life histories of criminal offenders are useful to investigators whose professional interests lie in offenders' psychological makeup, emotional dynamics or other intra-individual conditions (Maruna and Matravers, 2007). For them and for all investigators, however, individual life histories, if they do nothing else, can make readers better informed about a subject matter and better able, therefore, to comprehend and describe it accurately.

More important, individual life histories, because their descriptions or interpretations sometimes surprise investigators, can cause them to see matters in a different light. Explanations for delinquency, for example, often cast it as the product of material disadvantage, emotional neglect or abuse or psychological dynamics that function as 'push' factors for the onset of crime. Some life histories, however, point unambiguously to attractions and positive aspects of delinquency which operate as 'pull' factors for juveniles. Many times these take the form of older, successful offenders who are looked to as positive role models: 'Johnny D … was about the hippest cat on Eighth Avenue, the slickest nigger in the neighborhood … Johnny did everything. He used to sell all the horse [heroin] in the neighborhood … He was a pimp. He had all kinds of chicks hustling for him" (Brown, 1966: 108–9). Encounters with materials of this kind caused in me renewed awareness of and appreciation for what has come to be known as the 'seductions of crime' (Katz, 1988). By doing so it also caused me to think more systematically about the diverse attractions of what many street offenders know simply as 'doin' wrong'. Life histories make clear that a great deal of youthful transgression stems from a quest for material success, interpersonal respect, or acceptance from others who are similarly engaged in delinquency.

Materials in individual life histories also can cause analytic puzzlement for investigators. Illustrative of this are descriptions of residential burglary penned by offenders whose crime years enwrapped the dawn of the twentieth century. An occasional author from that era dwells on the challenges posed by breaking into occupied dwellings at night:

> [T]he man doesn't breathe who can break into a place in the early hours of the morning without feeling the qualms of fear. He may be shot dead the moment he becomes a burglar. The alarm may be given while he is doing the job. A dog may bark, and of all the horrible sensations any housebreaker can experience let me recommend waiting inside a house, afraid to move one way or the other, with a dog incessantly barking. Then you know what it is to die a thousand deaths (Guerin, 1929: 163).

Those familiar with the target preferences of twenty-first century burglars know that above all they want to avoid their victims and generally try to do so by entering residences during the daylight hours, when occupants are away. Since there is a bountiful supply of these targets, contemporary burglars need not commit residential break-ins at night and risk injury or death in doing so. This may be the reason readers search in vain for descriptions of nighttime residential burglaries in their life histories. Burglars of earlier eras had to contend with residences that more often than not were occupied nearly all hours of the day and night; the larger, extended families of that era and the fact that proportionately few women worked outside the home meant that nearly always someone was there.

In addition to causing analytic puzzlement, perspectives or experiences reported by individual subjects can unsettle the intellect and challenge investigators' interpretive skills. Encounters with the unexpected or poignant, for example, can point them in new directions analytically.

Consider the retrospective reflections of a man who persisted at crime well into adulthood:

> Looking back on my life, I suppose my ambitions were too fast for the normal ways of making money. I took what I thought was the easiest way and it's turned out to be the hardest really. If I'd had an honest job I don't think I'd have earned the money I've earned, but then I wouldn't have had all the aggravation to put with, like prison and all that. I wouldn't be as grey and bald-headed as I am. I've got nothing in the future really (Crookston, 1967: 155).

Shortly after I encountered and made note of this material there was much discussion in academic and literary circles about possible 'seasons of a man's life' and the tendency for men in their later years to look back on, to see and to assess earlier stages of their lives from an emergent vantage point (Levinson, 1978). Taken together these experiences caused me to broaden my interpretive focus from criminal offenders to the larger population of aging males, and the result was a more general interpretation and understanding of the life course (Shover, 1996).

Multiple narratives

The analytic payoffs from using life history materials are strengthened substantially when multiple sources are examined. Just as an interview with one informant is limited in what it can teach, reading a life history generally yields few analytic payoffs. The story is different when multiple life histories are used as data, because this makes possible a wider range of analytic options and benefits.

Analysis of multiple life histories can be useful for developing or casting critical light on theoretical propositions and for arbitrating alternative theoretical explanations. Testing cannot be done with the level of confidence or precision of studies that use large samples and multi-variate statistical methods, but the explanatory merits of theories can be tested using experiential standards and metrics. Implicit in and underlying abstractly conceptualized criminological theories are assumptions about how the day-to-day experiences of individuals and groups constitute their hypothesized causal relationships. Most structural-level explanations – anomie theory is an example – 'either assume something about the way people experience such processes or at least raise a question about the nature of that experience' (Becker, 1966: xii). Analysis of multiple life histories is an opportunity to assess these agency-level underpinnings using the reports of men and women whose lives and experiences make them most appropriate for the exercise. Both the predictive and explanatory merits of theoretical propositions can be assessed. When the relationship between variables reported in life histories appears contrary to the nature and direction predicted by theory, this can be powerful evidence that something is wrong theoretically. It can make obvious the need to modify or in other ways rethink theoretical models. The example of crime-as-choice theory is instructive.

The notion of crime as *choice* has animated policy makers and shaped their approach to crime control in the U.S. for nearly four decades. In keeping with this interpretation, criminal decision making was cast as a process in which offenders carefully weigh the potential costs and benefits of criminal acts. As a result, policy makers embraced the belief that increasing the threatened penalties and punishment for crime would have a demonstrable deterrent effect and would lower crime rates. If there is merit in this assumption, supporting evidence should be available in the life histories of offenders; readers should expect to find descriptions of or materials on the beneficial or career-altering effects on decision making by offenders who were punished. Offender life histories generally are bereft of such testimony. It is remarkable how few pages of criminal life histories are devoted to talking about legal penalties and how they constrain calculation and criminal decision making. This suggests strongly that the process of choosing crime diverges significantly from what is postulated in crime-as-choice theory, and it is a major reason for questioning its explanatory limitations.

At the same time, what is striking in some offender life histories are descriptions of 'hardening effects' of harsh punishment:

> I am glad now … that they lashed me. It did me good. Not in the way it was intended to, of course, but in a better way. I went away from the tripod with fresh confidence … I had taken everything they had in the way of violence and could take it again. Instead of going away in fear, I found my fears removed. The whipping post is a strange place to gather fresh confidence and courage, yet that's what it gave me, and in that dark cell I left behind many fears and misgivings (Black, 1926: 278).

In similar fashion, multiple offenders writing over the span of many decades describe a thirst for revenge with its origins in punishment thought to be unfair or excessively harsh. This from a man who committed crime and experienced imprisonment in the early years of the previous century:

> What was the motive behind [my crimes]? …The answer … is that I wanted to get even with society for the wrong which I felt it had done me … I left prison with a feeling of bitterness and of hatred in my heart, which made me like a wild animal … [T]he spirit of revenge was the chief motive that urged me on in crime (Anonymous, 1922: 149–50).

Nearly a century later, an imprisoned offender reflects similarly on an earlier release from confinement:

> When I stepped off the train [after release from borstal] … I still suffered from bouts of paranoia, and rage and bitterness bubbled just below the surface, ready to be unleashed at a moment's notice. I had changed … I was a bundle of spite and viciousness … a war looking for somewhere to declare itself. I wanted some sort of revenge for the months I had spent in solitary, for the beatings I had suffered at the hands of the prison system, and for the shit I had to swallow in order to be released. Someone was going to suffer (Smith, 2004: 208).

The hardening effects of punishment for other offenders include strengthened determination and confidence in their ability to commit crime successfully. One remarks that after release from prison, 'I was no longer intimidated by anything less than a twelve-gauge shotgun two inches from my head. Surviving five years in San Quentin will do wonders for self-confidence' (Bunker, 2000: 175). Generally evidence of this kind is dismissed as anecdotal, but its appearance in multiple life histories suggests such a dismissive response may be short sighted. In proportional terms, offenders made vengeful and determined by harsh punishment may be few, but the harm they cause may far exceed the damage done by their more numerous peers. Evidence of this kind hardly constitutes a rigorous test of propositions at the core of crime-as-choice theory, but it does suggest need for increased modesty from advocates for gratuitously punitive crime-control measures.

When investigators analyze multiple life histories they are not limited to describing variation in single variables. Bivariate relationships can be identified also. The relationships between offenders' class background and the way they describe themselves and the crimes they committed illustrates how bivariate relationships can be identified and mapped (Shover and Hunter, 2010). Few if any former street-level thieves and hustlers dispute the criminal nature of the acts they commited or their moral status as criminals. Their common response to criminal justice is resignation and accommodation. The memoirs of convicted white-collar criminals are markedly different; typically they write to dispute and correct what they see as misinformation others may believe about them and their crimes. Invariably white-collar offenders discount the latter while hoping to 'set the record straight' on themselves and their misfortune. White-collar criminals generally do not employ the appellations 'crime' or 'criminal' in their stories, preferring instead to characterize their acts as 'mistakes' and to see themselves as victims of treachery, persecution, or official ineptitude.

Clearly, the ways offenders interpret and talk about themselves and their lives varies with social class. The remarks of a former high-level elected public official in the US is emblematic of self-descriptions of offenders from middle-class and upper-class worlds:

> I am writing this book because I am innocent of the [criminal] allegations against me which compelled me to resign from the vice-presidency of the United States … This is not to say I have not made mistakes, or failed to do things I ought to have done, or done things I ought not to have done. I am human, and my conduct has been no better and no worse than that of other officeholders in these United States (Agnew, 1980: 9).

Like this offender, white-collar criminals generally recount with umbrage their treatment by agencies and agents of criminal justice who they charge acted needlessly, improperly or out of malice. Comparable materials and charges are almost entirely absent from the life histories of street offenders, who generally see their crimes as their own fault and criminal justice functionaries as individuals doing a job.

STRENGTHS AND CHALLENGES

One of the greatest strengths of life history materials is the fact that most are compiled without researcher influence. Rarely are academicians or others at their authors' side suggesting this or that when words are put to paper. Nor are authors responding to questions from investigators spontaneously and without time for reflection. During their periods of confinement many offenders devote hours to examining their pasts, the forces that shaped them and significant contingencies in their lives. The descriptions and interpretations contained in their life histories typically reflect this, and readers are the beneficiaries. They can be confident also that subjects generally will highlight and describe what they see as the most important contingencies in their lives. Investigators need not probe for them (Maruna, 1997).

In addition to analytic approaches made possible by numeric variables, code books and multi-variate procedures there are other ways of assessing the merits of propositions and theories. They are grounded in experience rather than statistics. Analysis of life histories presents investigators with opportunities to bring to bear their own experiences and competence as adults. The frequency with which authors describe specific topics and the ways they do so can be assessed on the basis of how squarely they match or give expression to what investigators know to be true from experience. This kind of test is different from but potentially no less important than one presented in the language and logic, for example, of multiple regression analysis. As important, the extent to which descriptions or interpretations square with the investigator's understandings can open up for the investigator understanding of matters removed from and more theoretical than its content. There can be few adults who cannot appreciate the influence of pull factors in causing some delinquency or who would dispute that gratuitously excessive punishment can produce negative if unintended consequences in those subjected to it.

The underlying assumptions and practical challenges of analyzing multiple life histories are thrown into relief when they are contrasted with use of survey methods. When the latter are employed for research purposes, investigators strive to ensure that all respondents are presented with a complete list of relevant questions and pushed to respond to every applicable item. Data are collected on a predetermined list of variables, and missing cases and missing data are proportionately few. This differs substantially from what is available to life history investigators who invariably will not have comparable data on all variables for all subjects. Because subjects have enormous discretion in recounting the events of their past, understandably there is variation in any sample of life histories. The discretion subjects have in what to tell means there will be limited consistency in the topics they highlight and discuss in their life histories. Always there is substantial missing data. Investigators must become accustomed to the fact they may read more than several before anything approaching themes or patterns become apparent. This is one reason criminal life histories are best used in combination with other data collection methods.

The contrast so obvious when analysis of multiple life histories is compared with survey methods is reduced enormously when comparison is made with use of semi-structured interviews. This research technique permits subjects to expound freely in response to general questions. Materials elicited in semi-structured interviews can reinforce or call into question themes identified in life histories. Thus, the unintended hardening effects of punishment are pointed to by an interview subject who was confined as a youth in an austere and harsh institution: 'At a tender age ... you can build up a pretty good well of hate from being mishandled and abused ... And I'll guarantee you, when you came out of there, you would either never steal again or you didn't fear God himself' (Shover, 1985: 47). This suggests that if official policies that emphasize unflinching use of punishment are meant to increase the numbers of those who will 'never steal again' then the price may be a larger number also who do not fear 'God himself'.

Investigators who analyze published life histories for research purposes almost certainly will examine materials produced over the span of a century or more. This is both a challenge and an opportunity. Nearly all aspects of everyday life and routine activities change enormously over such spans of time, and this is no less true of the lives of criminal offenders. Contemporary readers may be unfamiliar with some aspects of the activities of street-level criminals that were commonplace in earlier eras but are no longer part of the lives or experiences of these offenders. One of the most important qualities investigators must develop or sharpen when analyzing large numbers of life histories is the ability to see and appreciate commonalities despite the era they represent. These are harder to ferret out and identify than surface qualities of offenders' chronicles. Some of the commonalities are obvious; the effects of meeting, taking a liking to and being accepted by criminal companions are evident in countless life histories, and probably this will escape the notice of few readers. Likewise visits to 'gin-mills' or 'whiskey houses', retold in the narratives of earlier generations of street thieves and hustlers, parallel in most respects the more contemporary experience of going to 'dope houses' to buy or use heroin by substance-abusing offenders. Surface dissimilarities notwithstanding, these are experientially parallel accounts with similar consequences for those who negotiate markets in disreputable goods and services. Investigators incapable of appreciating that stimulating and useful materials can be found in chronicles produced by offenders of bygone times and generations probably will not reap the full potential of life history analysis. The advantage instead goes to readers less affected by temporal analytic myopia.

DATA VALIDITY

That the authors/subjects of criminal life histories are offenders or ex-offenders doubtless makes many wonder how truthful they are in telling their stories. Can their descriptions be taken at face value, or do they systematically deny, lie or distort? The question cannot be answered with a high level of confidence, because little is known about these matters. But there are reasons to believe that for the most part offenders are forthcoming and truthful in recounting their lives and actions. One reason is because large and morally damaging swaths of their lives repose in the archives of multiple public and social agencies. Over many years authorities have built dossiers on them and perhaps on other family members. The schools they attended as children, the social agencies that investigated and reported on the family for one reason or another during their early years, the juvenile court and certainly the prisons where they were incarcerated all have files. In some cases this glut of material can be used to check the validity of what offenders say about their past. Most authors, for example, include much of their arrest and confinement history in their memoirs. These and other external facts generally are verifiable, and investigators who use officially recorded background information to assess the validity of offenders' reports generally come away from the exercise reassured (e.g., Shover, 1985). Probably few subjects see anything to be gained from falsification of their past, and most assume they would be unsuccessful in any case in trying to hide or distort their past moral and legal failings. The officially archived nature of many key incidents in their lives probably reinforces their assumption there is little reason to deny or distort.

More important, the broad outline and most significant parts of offenders' lives and crimes can be described without need for extensive detail. Individual crimes, particularly any for which the author was never arrested, can be omitted from the narrative or can be described in general terms. The names of crime partners can be changed. In short, the lives of offenders can be chronicled in considerable detail without resorting to detailed descriptions of specific individuals or criminal acts that might make them or the subject culpable.

A final reason for confidence in the validity of what is revealed in criminal life histories is because whatever variation in veracity there may be in the life histories of *individual* offenders, there is little reason to dispute the data *generally*. Simply put, descriptions and patterns that appear repeatedly in them closely match pictures of the lives and careers of offenders developed using other kinds of data. This counts among the most important reason why confidence in their validity is high. Methods as diverse as interviews and analysis of arrest records all yield a picture that deviates in few, if any, significant ways from what is revealed in life histories. The patterns and tendencies revealed in them are remarkably consistent, for example, with what is known about offenders based on ethnographic studies (e.g., Shover, 1996; Wright and Decker, 1994, 1997).

Interviews with street offenders generally leave investigators satisfied with how carefully they try to recall incidents and transitions in their lives. Most give the appearance of good-faith commitment to truthfulness:

> In light of the intimate details of his life and the suffering that he has shared, the consistency of his comments over time, and verification from interviews conducted with many other street drug users, I have grown confident that within reason he tries to tell the truth about his drug use behaviors, his life, and his hopes about somehow, some day turning his life around (Singer, 2006: 5).

What authors openly reveal about themselves and their actions gives little reason to think they are holding back or being untruthful. Some can be unsparing, for example, in acknowledging and recounting harmful or morally reprehensible failings:

> Our apartment opened on a small rear court we shared with a grocery store, and I managed to loosen some boards on the side of the grocery so I could enter anytime I liked ... [O]ne night, looking around, I found the canvas cash bag ... There was six hundred dollars in it. The next day I was in the store and the owner was behind the counter ... and was telling another customer how the money he had been saving for his wife's operation had been stolen, and he didn't know what to do ... [W]hen I say this made me feel awful, you will be able to judge how awful, when I go on to tell you I didn't return the money (Braly, 1976: 210–11).

Many offenders readily admit to a record of criminal participation that is considerably lengthier than arrest records reveal. Others candidly acknowledge intention to continue or resume their criminal pursuits:

> I content myself with the dream – the one that all criminals have – that one day I'll get the really big tickle ... I've no intention of going straight, I'm just being more careful, that's all – and I'm getting cagey, I won't take unnecessary risks ... But sooner or later it'll come, the job will be there. I'll do it, get the big tickle, and then I'll retire ... This is it, this is the dream, the great rock candy mountain that beckons us all (Parker and Allerton, 1962: 188–9).

(This man resumed his criminal pursuits and later served at least one additional term of imprisonment; Parker, 1981.)

Questions about the honesty of ex-offenders can be disposed of with some confidence, but there is also the possibility that some subjects and authors romanticize the former's lives and crimes or exaggerate their criminal success. Remarkably few of the subjects whose lives are recounted in published life histories managed any lasting success from crime, but collaborators may see or choose to tell things differently (e.g., James and Considine, 1961). When contrasted with the worlds of material privilege and respectability from which the latter hail, the lives and exploits of their criminals have an allure that may be difficult to suspend. Exaggerated stories of criminal success or romanticized criminal exploits may be the result. Editors and collaborators may wax about offenders they have gotten to know as 'king of the thieves' (Morton, 1950) or as 'king of the safe-crackers' (Wilson, 1949), or they may tout their 'incredible immunity from criminal prosecution' (King, 1972: 173). Hyperbole like this is rare, but novice investigators may assign to these narratives more analytic importance than they deserve and draw erroneous conclusions about the lives and pursuits of offenders. There are few reported significant problems of truthfulness in accounts and information provided by common criminals, but this in no way denies that one must approach with caution their published life histories. It is clear, however, that most are written by men sincerely motivated to acknowledge their mistakes and to share their belated understandings with a wider audience.

CONCLUSION

Whether used alone or with other data, criminal life histories potentially are a rich source of materials and understandings for developing and assessing theoretical understanding. Anyone intent on using them for research purposes today can employ vastly improved search processes and draw from greatly expanded but easily accessed resources that were not available when I elected to do so. The personal computer, the Internet and readily accessible digital records from hundreds of libraries have made it possible to identify dozens of criminal life histories in a matter of minutes. While preparing this essay, my search on WorldCat (www.worldcat.org/) for English language 'autobiographies of criminals' published after 1999 produced a list of several dozen.

In addition to breakthroughs in the process of identifying life histories, the technical process of managing materials from a large number of them has been made immeasurably less difficult and time consuming by the availability of computer software for analyzing textual materials. This typically begins by denoting sections of text that theory, the investigator's developing understanding, or interpretive hunches suggest may be of value later in the study.

After text segments are denoted they can be pasted into word-processing electronic files for later use along with any conjecturally analytic notes. Coding schemes can be developed easily, but generally these are not complex; the total number of thematically similar text segments identified from reading dozens of life histories may be fewer than a dozen. The availability of e-books has made it possible for investigators to use N-Vivo and similar software programs to organize, search for and analyze text in multiple life histories. Returning to these analytic files from time to time is an opportunity to rethink previous interpretations or to find additional meaning or significance in them. This is the case particularly when analysis of life history materials is used along with other data collection methods. Materials elicited in personal interviews of comparable subjects, for example, can cause investigators to appreciate anew or to see in new ways text segments captured from life history narratives. Recall earlier comments encountered in some life histories about the attractions of crime. They gain added analytic credence alongside comparable materials elicited in interviews with older, ex-offenders. For example:

> The thing was to make it big, to get in the rackets, sell whiskey. (There wasn't no drugs then but whiskey and gambling, see.) And these were the people I looked up to. I can remember very clearly now, there was a man named Mr. Leon in our neighborhood who had two cars and several homes. People looked up to him, because … most people was poor… I wanted to be like Mr. Leon. Yeah, I wanted to be all of that (Shover, 1996: 11).

But it is not only criminal offenders whose lives and pursuits can be examined usefully through analysis of life histories. The narratives of legislators, whose decisions determine what is treated as crime; police officers, who are charged with enforcing it; and prison wardens, who must manage day-to-day the aggregate populations generated by the actions of both legislators and police, can teach investigators important lessons about crime and reactions to it.

ACKNOWLEDGEMENTS

Thanks to Heith Copes for helpful comments on a draft of this paper.

RECOMMENDED READING

In addition to the material cited previously, interested readers may wish to consult Plummer, K. (2001) *Documents of Life2* (London: Sage) and Roberts, B. (2002) *Biographical Research* (Buckingham: Open University Press) for useful introductions to life history research.

The special issue of the journal *Sociology* 27(1) has a series of papers on the rationale for and methodology of using life histories and autobiographies.

Of the sources cited previously, Shover's (1996) *Great Pretenders* (Boulder, CO: Westview) is an example of how multiple life histories and autobiographies can be used in the context of the analysis of criminal lives and careers.

REFERENCES

Agnew, S. (1980) *Go Quietly … Or Else*. New York: Morrow.

Anonymous (1922) *In the Clutch of Circumstance*. New York: D. Appleton.

Baca, J. (2001) *A Place to Stand*. New York: Grove/Atlantic.

Becker, H. (1966) 'Introduction' in C.R. Shaw, *The Jack-Roller* (pp. v–xviii). Chicago: University of Chicago Press.

Behn, N. (1977) *Big Stickup at Brinks*. New York: G.P. Putnam's & Sons.

Black, J. (1926) *You Can't Win*. New York: A.L. Burt.

Braly, M. (1976) *False Starts*. New York: Penguin.

Brown, C. (1966) *Manchild in the Promised Land*. New York: Signet Books.

Bunker, E. (2000) *Education of a Felon*. New York: St. Martin's.

Chessman, C. (1954) *Cell 2455, Death Row*. New York: Prentice-Hall.

Clark, C. and Eubank, E. (1927) *Lockstep and Corridor*. Cincinnati: University of Cincinnati Press.

Clark, J. and Hughes, H. (1961) *The Fantastic Lodge*. Boston: Houghton Mifflin.

Connor, M., Jr. (2009) *The Art of the Heist* (with J. Siler). New York: HarperCollins.

Cotterhill, P. and Letherby, G. (1993) 'Weaving stories: Personal auto/biographies in feminist research'. *Sociology* 27(1): 67–79.

Crookston, P. (1967) *Villain*. London: Jonathan Cape.

Edwards, E. (1972) *Metamorphosis of a Criminal*. New York: Hart.

Gadd, D. and Jefferson, T. (2007) 'On the defensive: A psychoanalytically informed psychosocial reading of *The Jack-Roller'. Theoretical Criminology* 11(4): 443–467.

Gagnon, R. (2006) *053803: Life at Fifteen*. R. J. Gagnon Publishing.

Guerin, E. (1929) *I Was a Bandit*. Garden City, NY: Doubleday.

Hannington, J. (2002) *I Am What I Am*. London: Headline.

Hapgood, H. (1903) *Autobiography of a Thief.* New York: Duffield.

Harris, J. (1986) *Stranger in Two Worlds.* New York: Macmillan.

Harris, J. (1988) *They Always Call Us Ladies.* New York: Scribner's.

Hills, S. and Santiago, R. (1992) *Tragic Magic.* Chicago: Nelson-Hall.

Hunter, B. (2009) 'White-collar offenders after the fall from grace: Stigma, blocked paths and resettlement' in R. Lippens and D. Crewe (eds), *Existentialist Criminology* (pp. 145–168). London: Routledge-Cavendish.

Jackson, B. (1969) *A Thief's Primer.* New York: Macmillan.

James, J. and Considine, B. (1961) *The Men Who Robbed Brinks* (as told by S. O'Keefe). New York: Random House.

Katz, J. (1988) *Seductions of Crime.* New York: Basic Books.

King, H. (1972) *Box Man* (as told to and edited by B. Chambliss). New York: Harper.

Kray, R. (1993) *My Story* (with F. Dineage). London: Sidgwick and Jackson.

Landesco, J. (1933). 'The life history of a member of the 42 gang'. *Journal of Criminal Law and Criminology* 23(6): 964–998.

Levinson, D. (1978) *The Seasons of a Man's Life.* New York: Alfred A. Knopf.

Maas, P. (1997) *Underboss.* New York: HarperCollins.

Martin, J. (1952) *My Life in Crime.* New York: Harper & Brothers.

Maruna, S. (1997) 'Going straight: Desistance from crime and life narratives of reform' in A. Lieblich and R. Josselson (eds.), *The Narrative Study of Lives* (Vol. 5, pp. 59–93). London: Sage.

Maruna, S. and Matravers, A. (2007) 'N = 1: Criminology and the person'. *Theoretical Criminology* 11(4): 427–442.

McCall, N. (1994) *Makes Me Wanna Holler.* New York: Random House.

Mitchell, P. (2002) *This Bank Robber's Life.* Stittsville: P. Mitchell.

Morton, J. (1950) 'I was king of the thieves' (with D. Wittels). *Saturday Evening Post* (August 5, 12 and 19).

Parker, T. (1963) *The Unknown Citizen.* London: Hutchinson.

Parker, T. (1967) *A Man of Good Abilities.* London: Hutchinson.

Parker, T. (1981) Letter to Shover (July 10).

Parker, T. and Allerton, R. (1962) *The Courage of His Convictions.* London: Hutchinson.

Pileggi, N. (1985) *Wiseguy.* New York: Pocket Books.

Plummer, K. (1983) *Documents of Life.* London: George Allen & Unwin.

Porrello, R. (2006) *Superthief.* Cleveland, OH: Next Hat Press.

Rettig, R., Torres, M. and Garrett, G. (1977) *Manny.* Boston: Houghton Mifflin.

Shaw, C. (1930) *The Jack-Roller.* Chicago: University of Chicago Press.

Shover, N. (1985) *Aging Criminals.* Beverly Hills, CA: Sage.

Shover, N. (1996) *Great Pretenders.* Boulder, CO: Westview.

Shover, N. and Hunter, B. (2010) 'Blue-collar, white-collar: Crimes and mistakes.' in W. Bernasco (ed.), *Offenders on Offending* (pp. 205–227). Collompton, UK: Willan.

Singer, M. (2006) *The Face of Social Suffering.* Long Grove, IL: Waveland.

Smith, R. (2005) *A Few Kind Words and a Loaded Gun.* Chicago: Chicago Review Press.

Smith, S. and Watson, J. (2001) *Reading Autobiography.* Minneapolis: University of Minnesota Press.

Snodgrass, J. (ed.) (1982) *The Jack-Roller at Seventy.* Lexington, MA: D.C. Heath.

Steffensmeier, D. (1986) *The Fence.* Rowman and Littlefield.

Steffensmeier, D.J. and Ulmer, J. (2005) *Confessions of a Dying Thief.* Edison, NJ: Transaction.

Swindells, J. (ed.) (1995) *The Uses of Autobiography.* London: Taylor & Francis.

Tosches, N. (1986) *Power on Earth.* New York: Arbor House.

Warren, P. (1953) *Next Time Is for Life.* New York: Dell.

Watson, F. (1976) *Been There and Back.* Winston-Salem, NC: J. F. Blair.

Williamson, H. (1965) *Hustler!* (edited by R. Lincoln Keiser). New York: Avon.

Wilson, H. (1949) 'I was king of the safecrackers' *Colliers* 123 (May 21; and June 4, 11 and 18).

Woodroof, H. (1970) *Stone Wall College.* Nashville, TN: Aurora.

Wright, R. and Decker, S. (1994) *Burglars on the Job.* Boston: Northeastern University Press.

Wright, R. and Decker, S. (1997) *Armed Robbers in Action.* Boston: Northeastern University Press.

2

Self-report Surveys within Longitudinal Panel Designs

Marvin D. Krohn, Terence P. Thornberry,
Kristin A. Bell, Alan J. Lizotte,
Matthew D. Phillips

Abraham Kaplan (1964: 24) has suggested that the most important contribution that methodology makes to science is 'to help unblock the roads of inquiry'. There are numerous examples throughout the development of criminology that illustrate how theory and methods have traversed the roads of inquiry together. Over the past 30 years we have witnessed the emergence and continuing sophistication of life course criminology, exploring the hows and whys of criminal behavior from early childhood (and in some cases birth) to old age (Benson, 2002; Farrington, 2005; Thornberry, 1997). The progress in our understanding of the interplay of crime and other trajectories in the life course would not have been possible without the development of theoretically derived concepts and hypotheses (Elder, 1998) coupled with research designs (such as longitudinal panel studies) and analytical techniques (such as Structural Equation Modeling (SEM), trajectory analysis) that provide for innovative ways to examine those hypotheses and, in turn, point the way to further theoretical development. Equally important, of course, is the development of valid and reliable measures.

Indeed, many years before the use of longitudinal designs and sophisticated statistical techniques with which to analyze the data collected, a much less complex and almost self-evident methodological development in measurement served to open a multitude of avenues for theoretical inquiry. The simple act of asking people to tell us about their criminal and delinquent behavior (and other aspects of their lives) in a manner that would allow for a systematic and quantifiable categorization of their responses fostered what might be seen as a paradigmatic shift in theories of criminal behavior and an empirical basis for questioning the way in which our criminal and juvenile justice systems operate. One could make an argument that the development of the self-report research design was the most significant methodological innovation to date in our pursuit of understanding criminal behavior.

The main focus of this chapter is on the difficulties encountered in implementing self-report research designs and the ways in which researchers have addressed those pitfalls. Our own work on the Rochester Youth Development Study (RYDS), a longitudinal panel study that has followed adolescents from the age of approximately 14 to the age of 31, has made extensive use of the self-report methodology. As we identify issues in the implementation of self-report studies, we will examine not only how other researchers have dealt with them, but also detail what we have done to maximize the quality of the data we have collected. We begin with a brief history of the use of self-report research designs and their importance to the development of criminological thought.

HISTORY OF SELF-REPORT STUDIES

Systematic examination of the crime problem in the US dates back to the beginning of the twentieth century and the ascendency of the Chicago School. The Chicago School focused much of its early efforts on discovering where in that city problems such as crime and delinquency were more likely to be disproportionately represented. To identify patterns of crime within areas of the city, researchers like Park, Burgess and McKenzie (1925) and Shaw and McKay (1942) relied on the use of rate maps, using official data to measure the rate of crime. This, coupled with ethnographic work intended to uncover the sociological dynamics behind the numbers, led those scholars to build on the insights from human ecology and develop social disorganization theory. The areas in which crime was found to be most prevalent, the zones of transition, were also characterized by high poverty rates, high residential mobility, and racial and ethnic heterogeneity. High crime rates came to be associated with disadvantaged neighborhoods and, by implication, the poor.

The assumption, fortified by an examination of official data, that crime was disproportionately committed by the poor and lower classes was evident in other early criminological theories. Although Merton, in presenting his theory that became the basis for strain perspectives, recognized the problems with official data (1968: 198), he nevertheless stated that 'the greatest pressures toward deviation are exerted upon the lower strata'. Even theories more oriented toward the social processes by which individuals come to be delinquent, like Sutherland's (1939) differential association theory, suggested that areas socially organized to foster criminal behavior would be more likely to have residents who were economically disadvantaged. Both Merton and Sutherland recognized that there were other crimes, particularly those committed by the wealthy, that were not included in the official data. Gibbons (1979) credited this insight as the impetus for self-report studies.

The first published paper reporting findings from the use of a self-report survey on delinquency was authored by Austin Porterfield (1943). Porterfield identified 55 offenses from court records of adjudicated delinquents. Using these offenses, he administered a self-report survey to 200 men and 137 women who were enrolled in college, asking them how frequently they had committed any of the 55 offenses. Although all of the students had committed at least one of these offenses, very few had come into contact with the police or the courts. Interpreting these findings as an indication of how legal authorities pay more attention to children who live in disadvantaged

areas, Porterfield questioned whether official data reflected the actual distribution of delinquent behavior.

Wallerstein and Wylie (1947) published another early study based on data collected through a self-report survey. They mailed questionnaires to 1,698 adult men and women asking them whether they had committed any of 49 offenses contained on their checklist. Again, almost all of the respondents reported committing at least one of those acts. Interestingly, a majority of men (64 percent) and about one-third of the women (29 percent) indicated that they had committed one of the felony offenses. By today's standards, these studies are replete with methodological problems. However, they were instrumental in underscoring the limitations of exclusive reliance on official data and in identifying the potential of a new methodology for examining the distribution of crime.

Short and Nye's research

The series of research articles and monographs published by James Short and F. Ivan Nye in the 1950s and early 1960s were both methodologically more sophisticated and substantively more intriguing than the early precursors. Short and Nye surveyed high school students in three Midwestern communities. Included in the three communities were a rural town, a town on the rural–urban fringe and a suburban community. In addition to the high school samples, Short and Nye also collected data from a training school for delinquents. The main findings from these studies confirmed what the earlier self-report studies had discovered. Dividing their sample into four socio-economic groups, they found few differences in the rates of delinquent behavior that were statistically significant (Nye et al., 1958). Even in those instances where there was a significant difference across the groups, it was evident that the differences were much less than what we had come to expect from official data.

A more important aspect of Short and Nye's research, however, was the recognition that the self-report methodology could be used not only to collect data on delinquency and socio-economic status, but it could also be used to acquire information on a host of potential predictors of delinquent behavior. They collected data on family structure and dynamics allowing Nye, in his 1958 monograph, to explore the impact of families on the probability of committing delinquent behavior. Short (1957) focused more on the impact of associating with delinquent peers on delinquent behavior, providing the first systematic examination of hypotheses derived from Sutherland's differential association theory.

The focus on social process issues – like the influence of parents, peers and the school system – was a major shift in emphasis in explanations of crime. Long dominated by a concern with neighborhood-level factors as contained in social disorganization theory and social structural factors such as the centrality of socio-economic status within strain theories, the popularization of the self-report methodology encouraged a movement away from epidemiological issues and toward etiological issues. Research on social disorganization theories was critiqued because of the tenuous match between concepts and measures (Bursik, 1988) while the failure to find significant differences among different socio-economic classes called strain theories into question. Questions contained on self-report instruments could more closely approximate the meaning of social process concepts, and social process theories were not necessarily burdened by the assumption of crime being disproportionately located in the lower class. Thus, a methodological innovation introduced a different way of thinking about crime.

Developing self-report methodology

Once the value of self-report studies was evident, a number of studies sought to use the research design in different types of locations. Porterfield (1943) and Short and Nye's (1958) research had only included smaller communities in rural and suburban areas. A number of studies surveyed more urban areas to determine if the failure to find the presumed inverse relationship between social class and delinquent behavior was due to a sampling bias (Akers, 1964; Dentler and Monroe, 1961; Empey and Erickson, 1966; Erickson and Empey, 1963; Gold, 1966; Slocum and Stone, 1963; Vaz, 1966). For example, Gold (1966) surveyed teenagers in Flint, Michigan, an industrial town with more ethnic and social class diversity than the towns included in the Short and Nye studies. Gold found a statistically significant, albeit relatively moderate, relationship between social class and delinquency, raising the issue of whether the inverse relationship would only be found in urban locations with sufficient variation along social class lines. Clark and Wenninger's (1962) results also seemed to suggest this. Dividing their sample across four different locations ranging from rural to the industrial areas of a city, Clark and Wenninger found a significant inverse relationship only within the latter area.

In addition to administering the self-report surveys to different samples, improvement in the questions used to measure delinquency was evident. Studies began to reflect a concern for the items that were included in the instrument and subscales were developed that included more serious events in order to examine whether the failure to find an inverse relationship between social class and delinquency was due to the trivial nature of the items included (Gold, 1966; Williams and Gold, 1972). Inventive ways were developed to determine if respondents were being truthful, including the use of informants (friends) (Gold, 1966) and the implied threat of lie detector tests (Clark and Tifft, 1966). These studies demonstrated that crime and delinquency data collected with self-report instruments were more valid than not, with estimates indicating that people told the truth 70–80 percent of the time.

By the 1970s, the self-report methodology was being used in nationwide studies. Williams and Gold (1972) did a nationwide survey of a probability sample of 847 13–16-year-old adolescents. The now famous National Youth Survey (NYS) represented a large-scale nation wide effort in administering a self-report instrument to a national probability sample of 1,725 11–17-year-old adolescents (Elliott et al., 1985). The NYS study was noteworthy for two reasons. Elliott and his colleagues were particularly concerned with improving the measure of self-reported delinquent behavior and their measurement strategy has become a standard in the discipline. In addition, the NYS was the first self-report study to be designed as a longitudinal panel design; a trend that was to inform longitudinal criminological research commencing in the 1980s.

A number of longitudinal panel studies employing the self-report methodology were launched around this time period. Among them were projects in Seattle (Hawkins et al., 2003), New Zealand (Moffitt, 2003), Montreal (Tremblay et al., 2003), and Houston (Kaplan, 2003). In addition, the Office of Juvenile Justice and Delinquency Prevention began their Program of Research on the Causes and Correlates of Delinquency, which funded three sister projects in Denver, Pittsburgh and Rochester (Huizinga et al., 1991). Although the three projects differed in their specific theoretical orientations and in aspects of their research designs, their common mission was to focus on those youth who were at high risk for serious delinquent behavior. These prospective longitudinal self-report studies added new challenges to doing self-report surveys.

The remainder of this chapter will explore the problems that one can encounter in performing self-report studies. To illustrate many of these challenges, we will refer to our own work on the RYDS, indicating both the problems we faced and, when appropriate, the resolutions to those problems that we developed. To provide a backdrop to our exploration of research design issues in doing self-report surveys, we briefly describe the overall research design of the RYDS.

DESIGN OF THE ROCHESTER YOUTH DEVELOPMENT STUDY

The RYDS has actually spawned two intertwined longitudinal studies. The original design, which we still refer to as the RYDS, can be divided into three phases. During Phase 1 we interviewed adolescents (generation 2 or G2) and their parent or guardian (G1) every six months for nine waves from the ages of about 14 to the age of 18. After a 2.5-year hiatus, we interviewed them once a year from the ages of approximately 20 to the age of 22. In Phase 3, we interviewed only our target subjects two additional times, when they were about 28 or 29 and when they were about 30 to 31. Thus, we have followed them from the age of about 14 to 31. In addition to the self-report data, we collected information from official agencies such as the police, schools, and department of social services.

In 1999, we began a new initiative, which we call the Rochester Intergenerational Study or RIGS. Recognizing that many of our G2s had children of their own, we began collecting data (both self-report and observational) on the first-born children (G3) if they were two years old or older. In addition, we continued to collect information from G2 and G3's other primary caregiver. We currently have 11 waves of data on these respondents. Thus, the overall study is now a three-generational study that has collected self-report data on respondents ranging in age from 8 (G3 interviews began at age 8) through adolescence to young adulthood (G2) to later adulthood (G1). For G1, we only have self-report data on drug use and not crime or delinquency.

Although we collect data from official sources and from observations of youngsters interacting with their parents, the heart of our data collection efforts are self-report interviews. As such, we have encountered many of the problems that are generic to self-report studies. However, we have also had to deal with issues that are either specific to or enhanced by longitudinal panel designs. As we examine those issues, we will discuss the particular difficulties in dealing with them within a longitudinal panel design and, where applicable, how we addressed those issues.

ANONYMITY AND CONFIDENTIALITY

A key concern that respondents may have about any self-report study is whether their identity can be matched to the responses that they provide. This is particularly problematic the more sensitive the questions become. Researchers have used two procedures to reduce respondents' apprehensions concerning reporting sensitive information. Confidentiality refers to an implicit or explicit agreement that no traceable record of the participant's data will be disclosed; only the researcher knows the response. Anonymity, however, refers to a condition in which the researcher does not know the identity of the respondent (Ong and Weiss, 2000).

In the broader literature on response bias, Ong and Weiss (2000) performed an experiment to examine the impact of level of privacy on students' responses to questions about whether they had ever used unauthorized material on an exam, quiz or any other form of a test. The researchers were able to validate the participants' responses with information from an earlier phase of the experiment. Significant differences between the anonymous and confidential conditions were found; 74 percent of those who had cheated admitted the behavior under the anonymous condition, whereas only 25 percent of those who cheated did so when guaranteed confidentiality.

Studies focusing on crime and drug use, however, generally come to a different conclusion about the impact of confidentiality and anonymity. Hindelang et al. (1981) randomly assigned respondents to four conditions: non-anonymous questionnaire, anonymous questionnaire, non-anonymous interview and anonymous interview. They found that there was little difference among the different modes of presentation. In an earlier study by Krohn et al. (1974) similar results were reported. These findings also are consistent with more recent studies examining drug use. Several researchers have concluded that the differences they have found are not of practical significance (Bjarnason and Adalbjarnardottir, 2000; Latimer et al., 2006; O'Malley et al., 2000).

For example, O'Malley et al. (2000) used data from the Monitoring the Future study to compare the reporting of drug use in national samples of eighth- and tenth-grade students under either an anonymous or confidential administration condition. Results indicated no differences in self-reported drug use between the anonymous and confidential conditions for tenth graders and only a very modest mode of administration effect for eighth graders, who reported higher levels of substance use in the anonymous condition. The pattern of higher reporting was consistent across substances, but was not always significant. Additionally, in several cases, statistically significant differences were rendered non-significant once demographic characteristics were included as controls. The authors conclude that the results show, at most, a very modest mode of administration effect and, quite possibly, no effect at all.

Bjarnason and Adalbjarnardottir (2000) also examine privacy issues by comparing the self-reported drug and alcohol use of a cross-sectional, anonymous survey and a longitudinal, confidential survey. The results show that the differences in non-response are only significant for the most sensitive question, regarding cannabis use, where both males and females were slightly more likely to skip the question in the confidential survey than the anonymous survey. Differences in reporting lifetime use of substances between conditions were minor and did not reach statistical significance for males. Females were just as likely to report lifetime cigarette smoking in both surveys, but those who admitted smoking in the confidential survey admitted to fewer occasions. Fewer females admit to lifetime use of both alcohol and cannabis in the confidential survey. Those who admitted to drinking reported fewer occasions in the confidential condition, but there were no differences in reported frequency of cannabis use. Bjarnason and Adalbjarnardottir (2000) conclude that although the confidential survey yielded slightly more conservative estimates of substance use, the consequences of this minor bias are limited for most research purposes.

It is virtually impossible to assure anonymity in conducting longitudinal panel research designs such as the RYDS study. The researcher needs to be able to match the responses from data collection wave to data collection wave in order to assess change over time. Typically these studies collect other data (e.g., school records, parent reports) that require identifiable interviews.

There has been some exploration of having respondents generate their own number code using numbers that they can regenerate from wave to wave. For example, one might ask respondents to use every other number in their social security number. The assumption would be that they would be able to duplicate this for the next administration of the self-report instrument and the researcher could match the responses from one wave to another. The difficulty with this approach is that many respondents, especially adolescents, are not very good at self-generating a code and duplicating it from administration to administration. Thus, a number of cases are lost because the researcher cannot match the data.

The RYDS, like most longitudinal studies, promised confidentiality. We provided a thorough explanation of the uses of the data (examining aggregate responses to find relationships among variables) coupled with a detailed description of how identifying information was to be handled separately from information gathered with the self-report instrument. As we did not compare responses of an anonymous self-report administration to a confidential one, we cannot say with certainty whether our procedures provided respondents with the necessary confidence to be honest in their responses to sensitive questions. However, some of the results of comparing self-report responses to official responses (see later) seem to suggest that not assuring them anonymity was not problematic.

MODE OF ADMINISTRATION

The second condition that has been explored in the response bias literature is mode of data collection. A large body of research, reviewed by Tourangeau and Smith (1996), supports the conclusion that self-administered questionnaires (SAQs) typically result in higher levels of self-reported drug use than techniques administered by an interviewer. Additionally, the increased use of computerized methods for collecting self-report data has led researchers to assess the strengths and weaknesses of different methods of self-administration. Computer-based methods, for instance, are techniques researchers have employed to deal with issues of confidentiality and anonymity in the investigation of sensitive topics. Recent studies have shown that participants feel as though they have greater levels of privacy when computer-based methods are used (Bates and Cox, 2008; DiLillo et al., 2006). In a true experiment, Bates and Cox (2008) recently employed a 2×3 factorial design, randomly assigning 180 participants to one of six conditions. The independent variables were data collection method (computer-based [CB] *versus* paper-and-pencil [PP]) and administration setting (group setting, alone in a designated office, or being mailed/emailed the survey at home). The questionnaires asked respondents about alcohol, tobacco, drug use, sexual behavior, and eating behavior. Bates and Cox (2008) found that across all three settings, the CB method was seen as more confidential; however, the participants' reports of perceived confidentiality and anonymity did not have a statistically significant difference on responses.

In their own research, Tourangeau and Smith (1996) compare response rate and level of reporting of sensitive behaviors across three modes of CB data collection: computer-assisted personal interviewing (CAPI), computer-assisted self-administered interviewing (CASI), and audio computer-assisted self-administered interviewing (ACASI). CAPI differs from CASI and ACASI in that the interviewer administers the schedule. In CASI, the respondent reads the questions on the computer screen and enters his or her own responses. ACASI allows the respondents to listen to an audio version of the questions, rather than having them read by an interviewer or reading the questions themselves. Although not all results reached statistical significance, Tourangeau and Smith (1996) found that ACASI and CASI elicited higher rates of drug use and sexual behavior than CAPI.

Not unlike the privacy literature, however, the results of comparisons between different data collection techniques may also be described as 'conflicting'. Studies examining a possible mode of administration effect between CB and PP questionnaires have shown differing results, and have also drawn attention to the existence of potential moderators. Research has shown that the sensitivity level of the questions asked may have an impact on response bias (Supple et al., 1999; Richman et al., 1999). In a meta-analysis of the response bias literature, Richman et al. (1999) examined three modes of administration across 61 studies published between 1967 and 1997: CB questionnaires, traditional PP questionnaires and face-to-face interviews. They found a near-zero overall effect size for CB versus PP questionnaires on general, non-sensitive questions, but also found that the impact of modality on internal validity was greater as question sensitivity increased. Supple et al. (1999) found that adolescents were significantly more likely to report substance use in a CASI mode than a PP SAQ. Their results also supported the finding that the size of mode differences increased with sensitivity level of the questions. Some recent research has indicated that mode of administration may not have an effect for questions regarding behavior, but results in less response bias in CB surveys for questions regarding feelings and affective states (DiLillo et al., 2006; Vereecken and Maes, 2006). The results of these studies highlight the issue of varying perceptions of sensitivity both between researchers and their participants and also across respondents.

Additionally, Richman et al. (1999) discuss the fact that studies published more recently may have used CB instruments that more closely match the format of PP questionnaires. One feature that is significant is whether participants have the ability to go back to previous questions, as they would on a paper-based survey. The literature suggests that when CB questionnaires are administered to respondents who are alone and can backtrack among their responses, response bias will be lower (Richman et al., 1999). Overall, Richman et al. conclude that while moderating factors may be present, the evidence suggests that for practical purposes, computer- and paper-based questionnaires can be expected to give similar results.

The RYDS introduced the use of a computer-assisted administration of the delinquency checklist in Year 5 of the RIGS and have continued to use it for both the RYDS and the RIGS study. For the self-reported delinquency (SRD) administration for G2, G3, and the other caregiver (OCG), the respondent wears headphones and the questions are asked via computer audio. Responses are verbal and the interviewer types in the response (no one but interviewer and respondent can hear the questions).

Although we moved to the computer-assisted administration to make respondents more comfortable in answering questions about sensitive issues, our main concern was not with whether respondents were reluctant to verbally admit to interviewers their delinquent behavior. Rather, we encountered a more serious threat to the validity of our data. Our interviewers reported that in many homes in which they conducted their interviews it was impossible to completely isolate the respondent from other members of their family or household. This was especially the case for the younger G3 children. Some reluctance to answer sensitive questions might have stemmed from parents and others being able to hear both the questions and answers. The use of the computer-assisted technique largely solved that problem. Again, we do not have comparative data to demonstrate whether the rate of valid responses or the rate of delinquent behavior rose with this technique, but reports from the field suggested that respondents did feel more comfortable with the computer-assisted presentation of sensitive items.[1]

SELECTION OF DELINQUENCY ITEMS

Any self-report instrument will contain a sample of questions from a potentially much larger population of deviant acts (Christie et al., 1965, as cited in Farrington, 1973). The challenge is to include items that range in the level of seriousness while having a sufficient affirmative response rate to allow for statistical comparisons. This latter concern also raises the issue of sample selection, since some samples are less likely to exhibit serious delinquent behaviors than are other samples.

Early self-report studies tended to focus on less serious forms of delinquency. A prime example of this can be illustrated by the case history of one of the most delinquent adolescents in Gold's (1970) study. Gold used a probe technique to screen out non-chargeable offenses and scored the remaining chargeable offenses by frequency and seriousness.

A respondent in the 10 percent most delinquent category of Gold's sample participated in offenses such as shoplifting chewing gum, lying to a movie theater clerk about his age, drinking beer from a friend's refrigerator, stealing fruit from an orchard and throwing it at various targets, and carrying a hunting knife.

The difficulty with failing to include serious offenses among the items in a self-report instrument (and the related failure to have sufficient numbers of respondents who committed such offenses) can be illustrated by focusing on the controversy concerning the direction and significance of the relationship between social class and delinquency. When the findings from early studies either failed to find a significant inverse relationship between social class and delinquency, or found a smaller association than what official data would reflect (see, for example, Short and Nye, 1958), critics attributed the finding to the relatively minor forms of delinquent behavior that were assessed. Hindelang et al. (1979) identify two vital components relevant to comparing official records versus self-report data. The first component is behavioral content or type of offense. The authors note that Uniform Crime Report (UCR) data most commonly distinguished between violent and property offenses, while self-report data at that time distinguished between offense types such as theft, property damage, drugs, school offenses, and violence. The second factor relates directly to offense seriousness, both within offense types (such as amount of theft) and across offense type (such as a school offense versus a violent offense). Seriousness is often judged based on harm to the victim or potential consequences for the offender. Hindelang et al. (1979) stress that failure to take these considerations into account will lead to an invalid comparison between self-report and official data.

In their review of the literature, Hindelang et al.'s (1979) chief criticism of early self-report measures of crime and delinquency is that they were routinely treated as equivalent to official offenses when comparing correlates of delinquency, despite the fact that it had previously been acknowledged that self-report measures tapped rather trivial offenses. The authors compared a third source of data, victimization surveys, to both official and self-report data. They concluded that both official records and victimization surveys tapped more serious offenses, while self-reports at that time remained focused on less serious offenses. The authors also voiced a criticism of global simple sum scales of delinquency items in the early self-reports of delinquent behavior, as this technique masked the differences between self-report and official statistics, with the global

scales more likely to reflect the correlates of trivial offenses. Hindelang et al. (1979) concluded that both official records and self-report data provide valid indicators of the demographic characteristics of offenders, within the domain of behavior effectively tapped by the respective method.

Some of the most advanced and influential work on the self-report method has been done by Elliott and his colleagues (Elliott and Ageton, 1980; Elliott et al., 1985; Huizinga and Elliott, 1986). Elliott and Ageton (1980) addressed the controversy regarding the relationship between social class and race and self-reported delinquency. They recognized the problem with not including serious offenses and developed a revised measure of self-reported delinquency (SRD) that they used in the National Youth Survey (NYS). The SRD scale included a representative set of offenses, based on categories in the UCR. However, the unique contribution of their study was the recognition of the effect of the response set available to respondents. Elliott and Ageton (1980) argued that a relatively small group of adolescents contributed disproportionately to the overall rate of delinquency. Prior studies had asked respondents to record the frequency of offenses within response sets that were typically capped at a relatively low number of offenses (say, ten or more). This does not capture the true contribution of the very frequent offenders who are more likely to be arrested. They allowed respondents to indicate the actual number of offenses they committed, enabling an examination of whether there was a relationship between social class or race and very frequent offenders. Their findings suggested that among high-rate offenders, class and race differences were observed within some categories of offending. They conclude that earlier measures of SRD, which truncated response sets and did not include high-rate, serious offenders, may not have been sensitive enough to capture the theoretically important differences in delinquent behavior.

The basic RYDS self-report instrument includes 32 items that tap general delinquency and 12 items that measure drug use. These items range in seriousness to include the more serious offenses as well as the common less serious offenses. If respondents reported having committed the offense since the previous interview, they were asked a series of follow-up questions including how often they had committed the act. To make sure that they were reporting 'actionable' offenses, we also asked them to describe the event and evaluated their answers. We have developed several subscales of these behaviors to reflect both type and seriousness of offense.

Longitudinal studies and item selection

As demonstrated earlier, the selection of items to measure delinquent and criminal behavior and the response sets available to the respondents can have important effects on the results and their interpretation. A related issue is the changing meaning of what we might consider delinquent or criminal, or at least anti-social, behavior, for people at different ages in their developmental cycle. A key concern that guides the RYDS and the RIGS is the examination of the development of anti-social behavior across the life course. Thornberry (1987) and later Thornberry and Krohn (2001, 2005) have developed interactional theory to account for anti-social behavior during childhood, adolescence, and adulthood, motivating the dual longitudinal panel designs described previously. To measure the general construct of anti-social behavior in a way that would allow us to examine issues of continuity and change throughout the life course, we needed to develop age-appropriate items.

We have already discussed the measurement of delinquency appropriate for adolescents. However, many of these items may be age-inappropriate for children and adults. In incorporating items that would be age-appropriate for children, we borrowed extensively from prior work by developmental psychologists. For very young children under the age of eight, we did not collect any self-report data. Rather, we collected observational data from which we could code behavioral characteristics such as impulsivity, non-compliance, disobedience and aggression. In addition, as part of our parent, other guardian, and teacher surveys, we incorporated the Child Behavior Checklist (CBCL), designed to assess 'externalizing' problem behaviors (Achenbach, 1992). Both observational measures and the CBCL have been shown to be related to problem behavior among school-age children (Belsky et al., 1996; Campbell, 1987: Richman et al., 1982: Shaw and Bell, 1993).

When the G3 participants reach the age of eight, we begin to interview them and incorporate an anti-social behavior checklist. This checklist is based on the work of Rolf Loeber and colleagues (1989). Some of these items overlap with the delinquency index used in the RYDS (Huizinga et al., 1991), but a number are age-specific for young children. Loeber found that responses to these items were correlated with parental reports (CBCL) about their children's behavior, particularly for those behaviors that are likely to come to the attention of parents. As our subjects moved into adolescence (age 12 and beyond) we used the basic RYDS self-reported inventory.

PANEL OR TESTING EFFECTS

With increased use of self-report methods in longitudinal panel designs, a new threat to the quality of the data has arisen. Testing effects are alterations of the respondent's response to an item that are caused by the prior administration of the same item or scale (Thornberry, 1989: 351). To improve the quality of self-report data regarding anti-social behavior, many studies have incorporated a number of follow-up questions if respondents answer affirmatively to committing a type of behavior. The concern is that having learned that an affirmative response elicits these follow-up questions at time T, respondents will be reluctant to respond affirmatively when administered similar items at $T + 1$. An alternative explanation for unexpected reductions in affirmative responses to delinquency items on self-report surveys is simply generalized fatigue. For example, Lehnen and Reiss (1978) report that there was a reduction in the reporting of victimization data on the National Crime Survey that was not attributable to the number of victimizations reported in prior interviews, but due to the number of prior interviews.

Thornberry (1989) presented the first systematic examination of this potential threat to longitudinal self-report data. Using data from the NYS (Elliott et al., 1985), he found that for most offenses, age-specific prevalence rates across adjacent waves decreased more often than they increased. This was evident for all the waves of data collection, despite the fact that the NYS did not introduce follow-up questions until the fourth wave. Thornberry concluded that it was the panel design, and possibly the general fatigue factor, instead of the design of specific questions, that seemed to cause the unexpected decline in delinquency rates.

Menard and Elliott (1993) and Lauritsen (1998) also looked into this same issue with the NYS data. Menard and Elliott observe the same declining trends, but point out that few of the year-to-year changes are statistically significant. However, in a more sophisticated analysis using hierarchical linear models (HLM), Lauritsen (1998) found that the downward trajectory in the rate of delinquency for the seven different cohorts in the NYS was not consistent with the age–crime curve or what we would theoretically expect. She concurs with Thornberry (1989) that one possible explanation might be generalized panel fatigue. However, she adds that another explanation may be that as youth mature, some of the items may not mean the same for respondents. A behavior that is considered an assault at age 11 might not be so considered at age 15.

Bosick (2009) re-examines the 'panel fatigue' and 'changing content validity' explanations of testing effects in the NYS data, along with an examination of three alternate explanations: issues of scale construction, item-specific age–crime curves, and selective attrition. Bosick (2009) found support for item-specific age–crime curves, implying that the NYS taps offenses that peak at an earlier age than the standard age–crime curve. She also found support for changing content validity of some survey items, including those questions regarding gang involvement. Overall, the author concludes that the declines stem from item-specific issues rather than broader limitations of the panel design as a whole.

The substantive interpretation of this effect is also somewhat ambiguous. Assuming that the frequency of affirmative responses in self-report inventories declines with repeated assessments, absent a 'gold standard', it is not clear whether the earlier or later responses have more validity. The reduction in affirmative responses is typically interpreted as respondents underreporting their involvement in delinquency. The assumption is that the earlier responses are more accurate and later responses less accurate. It is also plausible that the respondents over-report offending in the early assessments in part because they take the wording of the questions literally and report behaviors that technically conform to the question but miss the intent of the question to measure criminal offending; recall Gold's respondent in the high delinquency category. For example, in the Rochester pre-test, one participant responded affirmatively to a question about serious theft and then described an event that was clearly a prank. With repeated assessments, it is possible that respondents learn that the researchers are really interested in delinquent and criminal behavior and censor their responses accordingly. If so, the declining responses may be more accurate than the earlier ones. Of course, it is also possible that both processes are operating.

While we have not systematically examined the RYDS data for testing or panel effects, in some analyses it has been evident that our data are threatened by the same tendency observed in the NYS data. If there are either panel or testing effects in the RYDS data (or any of the other large-scale longitudinal panel studies), we need to determine if those vary by the characteristic of the respondents. For example, if the effect is greater for frequent offenders than it is for less frequent offenders, it has more serious consequences than if the effect was randomly distributed across all respondents. As Thornberry and Krohn (2000: 71) conclude, 'Additional research to identify the extensiveness of testing effects, their sources, and ways of remedying them are certainly a high priority.'

QUALITY OF SELF-REPORT DATA

Overall, the main concern that we have in implementing self-report surveys is acquiring data that are useful in examining the myriad of theoretical and practical issues that are of interest to those who study crime and the criminal justice system. Generally, we use two criteria to assess the quality of our data: reliability and validity.

Reliability is whether there is consistency in the reporting of the information. Stated more precisely, it is the 'extent to which a measuring procedure yields the same result on repeated trials' (Thornberry and Krohn, 2000: 44). For a measure to be useful, we need to be confident that if we ask the question (or a similar question) again we will get the same (or a similar) response. For some measures where we have multiple questions referring to the same concept and where we expect respondents to answer similarly to all the questions (such as attachment to parents), we are concerned with internal consistency of the items. Although many researchers do examine the internal consistency of self-report items, we suggest that there is no necessary expectation that a person who has stolen a CD from a music store would have also assaulted someone. As a result, internal consistency measures are of limited value in assessing the reliability of SRD measures (Huizinga and Elliott, 1986).

Whether the same or similar answers are obtained on a test–retest administration of self-report surveys is of greater interest. In a limited examination of the test–retest approach (the second presentation was administered only 45 minutes after the first), Hindelang et al. (1981) demonstrated that the reliability of the self-reported delinquent behavior was better than many of the attitudinal measures. Huizinga and Elliott (1986) examined the reliability of the NYS data by reinterviewing a subsample of the overall sample four weeks after the initial assessment. They not only found high reliability overall, but also report that the reliability did not vary much across subgroups of the sample.

Validity refers to whether a measure accurately captures the concept of interest. When examining self-report instruments, there are a number of different forms of validity that could be assessed. These have been thoroughly reviewed by Thornberry and Krohn (2000) and we will not repeat that discussion here. Rather, the main concern that most researchers have with responses to self-reported delinquency or crime measures is whether respondents are giving truthful answers. Researchers have employed creative ways to compare self-reported responses to some external criterion that is believed to be an adequate measure of the concept (criterion validity). Group comparisons of those with and without official arrest records have demonstrated that those officially involved are more likely to report a higher number of delinquent acts (Farrington, 1973; Hirschi, 1969; Hindelang et al., 1981; Short and Nye, 1958). For drug use and tobacco use, saliva and urine samples can be obtained to compare with self-reported responses. For example, Akers et al. (1983) collected saliva samples from youth and compared their self-reported tobacco use, estimating that 95 percent of the self-reported responses were accurate. The other common way to assess criterion validity is to compare self-report responses with official data on arrest or self-reported arrests. Group comparisons of those with and without official arrest records have demonstrated that those officially involved are more likely to report a higher number of delinquent acts (Farrington, 1973; Hirschi, 1969; Hindelang et al., 1981; Short and Nye, 1958) and correlations between the two data sources are moderate to strong (Farrington et al., 1996; Hindelang et al., 1981; Huizinga and Elliott, 1986).

While the estimate of the percentage of respondents who tell the truth is certainly important, what is of particular concern is whether there is any systematic bias among those who do not tell the truth. That is, is one type of respondent more likely to not tell the truth than other types of respondents? This is critical in doing correlational research. If we are concerned with the relationship between gender and crime, and if males are more likely than females to lie on self-report instruments, our estimates of the relationship will be seriously flawed. In studies by Hindelang et al. (1981), Huizinga and Elliott (1986), and Kirk (2006), African-American respondents were more likely to under-report their involvement in delinquency. However, the Farrington et al. study (1996) showed that African-Americans are no more or less likely to self-report delinquent behavior. A more recent study using a sample of serious adolescent offenders, as opposed to a general cross-section of the population, similarly did not result in consistent race differences (Piquero and Brame, 2008).

We have begun to systematically examine the criterion validity of self-reported arrest data from the RYDS study, paying particular attention to systematic bias in these data. The analysis is incomplete, but it appears that respondents are as likely to over-report being arrested as they are to under-report being arrested. Moreover, white respondents are more likely than African-American respondents to over-report arrests while African-Americans are more likely to under-report arrests.

CONCLUSION

The use of self-report surveys to acquire data on delinquency, crime, and other variables of interest has presented challenges and held out the promise of significant insights since they were first used. Early research, while methodologically flawed, caused us to question the strength of the relationship between social conditions and crime. This resulted in a rethinking of our theories and a critique of the juvenile and criminal justice systems. The potential of this methodology was realized when it began to be used to research theoretical hypotheses concerning a myriad of potential predictors of crime and delinquency. More sophisticated ways of measuring crime that better accounted for the seriousness of the offense and the frequency with which it was committed, along with strategies to increase the reliability and validity of the data, increased the quality of the data. Longitudinal panel studies brought to bear additional problems with implementing self-report instruments, including creating age-appropriate measures and dealing with testing effects.

In this chapter, we have examined the history of the self-report method and some of the continuing methodological issues in implementing such studies. In discussing the latter, we paid particular attention to how the RYDS study dealt with these issues to illustrate both the difficulties, and in some cases their resolutions, in doing a self-report survey within the context of a longitudinal design.

Although the self-report technique has improved greatly since its introduction to criminology, there are many challenges remaining as we try to perfect this approach to measurement. Four issues will be discussed here.

First, because criminological research increasingly relies upon longitudinal designs to address important theoretical and policy issues, it remains important to investigate further the issue of testing effects or panel bias. The most direct way of doing so would be a longitudinal study in which the sample is randomly divided into groups, with some groups receiving all assessments starting at time T and others entering the panel at later assessments, $T + 1$, $T + 2$, and so on. If there are systematic differences in responses at $T + 1$, or at subsequent assessments, it would provide direct evidence of testing effects. In doing this, it would be important to include behaviors for which there are valid independent measures; for example, substance use, which can be assessed with physiological measures. A study with this type of design would not only assess the direction of the effect, but would also help address the question of whether the temporal change reflects earlier under-reporting versus earlier over-reporting.

Second, it would be desirable to develop one, or a few, standardized self-report instruments. At the present time, there are many self-report instruments used in criminology and many studies develop their own measures that are typically variations of existing instruments. This tendency hampers our ability to make cross-study comparisons, to generate national estimates from the results of individual studies, and also to assess trends over time. Standardized instruments that could be used in many studies would move the field forward. There are many examples of standardized measures in other areas of study; for example, family violence (Straus et al., 1980), child behavior problems (Achenbach, 1992) and so forth. For a standardized instrument to be widely adopted it would be incumbent upon the developers to clearly demonstrate the validity and reliability of the instrument as well as the scope conditions under which it can be properly utilized. There are several good starting points for this effort including the self-reported delinquency measures from the NYS (Huizinga and Elliott, 1986), from the Program of Research on the Causes and Correlates of Delinquency (Huizinga et al., 1991), and from the Second International Self-Report Delinquency Study (Junger-Tas et al., 2010).

Third, it would also be advantageous to develop a 'short form' of the instrument. Many studies need to have a general indicator of involvement in delinquent and criminal behavior, but do not need to have all the items and detail found in the self-report inventories most commonly used in criminological research. The availability of a short form with strong psychometric properties and bearing an identifiable relationship to the long form from which it is developed (see, e.g., Lizotte et al., 1992) would both assist researchers in related areas and disciplines and, by so doing, extend our understanding of the correlates of delinquency and crime.

Fourth, it would also be helpful to future research to develop sub-inventories for various types of offending such as violent, property, and white-collar crimes. These offenses are typically included in the longer inventories but they may not have acceptable psychometric properties as stand-alone indicators. Constructing them so that they can both be used as part of the broader indicator, as well as indicators of separate behavior patterns, would also improve the utility of the self-report method.

Clearly, there are many directions for the future development of this particular approach to measuring involvement in delinquent and criminal behavior. We will never have a perfect indicator since by its very nature crime is secretive and difficult to assess. Nevertheless, the self-report method has improved greatly over the years and there are numerous avenues along which it can be improved by the next generation of researchers.

NOTE

1 These issues did not emerge in the original RYDS data collection since the adolescent interviews were conducted in private settings at school and for the adult interviews it was easier to obtain private settings.

RECOMMENDED READING

In addition to the material cited previously, interested readers may wish to consult Brame, R., Fagan, J. Piquero, A.R., Schubert, C.A. and Steinberg, L. (2004) 'Criminal careers of serious delinquents in two cities'. *Youth Violence and Juvenile Justice* 2: 256–272 for an examination of the relationship between self-reported delinquency and official data that shows similar relationships across demographic subgroups.

Also, Le Blanc, M. (1989) 'Designing a self-report instrument for the study of the development of offending from childhood to adulthood: Issues and problems' in Klein, M. (ed.) *Cross-National Research in Self-Reported Crime and Delinquency* (Kluwer Academic Publishers, Los Angeles) give a thorough discussion of the challenges of creating age appropriate measures of crime and delinquency.

Maxfield, M.G., Weiler, B.L. and Widom, C.S. (2000) 'Comparing Self-Reports and Official Records of Arrests' *Journal of Quantitative Criminology* 16: 87–110 give a comparison of self-reported arrests and official arrests concluding that there is a relatively strong relationship between the two measures.

Raudenbush, S., Johnson, C. and Sampson, R.J. (2003). 'A multivariate, multilevel Raschch model with application to self-reported criminal behavior' *Sociological Methodology* 33: 169–211 give a description and application of an innovative approach to examining the validity of self-report measures.

REFERENCES

Achenbach, T. (1992) *Manual for the Child Behavior Checklist/2-3 and 1992 Profile.* Burlington: University of Vermont.

Akers, R. (1964) 'Socio-economic status and delinquent behavior: A retest'. *Journal of Research in Crime and Delinquency* 1(1): 38–46.

Akers, R., Massey, J., Clarke, W. and Lauer, R. (1983) 'Are self-reports of adolescent deviance valid? Biochemical measures, randomized response, and the bogus pipeline in smoking behavior'. *Social Forces* 62(1): 234–251.

Bates, S. and Cox, J. (2008) 'The impact of computer versus paper-pencil survey, and individual versus group administration, on self-reports of sensitive behaviors'. *Computers in Human Behavior* 24(3): 903–916.

Belsky, J., Woodworth, S. and Crnic, K. (1996) 'Troubled family interaction during toddlerhood'. *Development and Psychopathology* 8(3): 477–495.

Benson, M. (2002) *Crime and the Life Course*. Los Angeles: Roxbury.

Bjarnason, T. and Adalbjarnardottir, S. (2000) 'Anonymity and confidentiality in school surveys on alcohol, tobacco, and cannabis use'. *Journal of Drug Issues* 30(2): 335–344.

Bosick, S. (2009) 'Operationalizing crime over the life course'. *Crime and Delinquency* 55(3): 472–496.

Bursik, R. (1988) 'Social disorganization and theories of crime and delinquency: Problems and prospects'. *Criminology* 26(4): 519–551.

Campbell, S. (1987) 'Parent-referred problem three-year-olds: Developmental changes in symptoms'. *Journal of Child Psychology and Psychiatry* 28(6): 835–845.

Clark, J. and Tifft, L. (1966) 'Polygraph and interview validation of self-reported delinquent behavior'. *American Sociological Review* 31(4): 516–523.

Clark, J. and Wenninger, E. (1962) 'Socioeconomic class and area as correlates of illegal behavior among juveniles'. *American Sociological Review* 27(6): 826–834.

Dentler, R. and Monroe, L. (1961) 'Social correlates of early adolescent theft'. *American Sociological Review* 26(5): 733–743.

Di Lillo, D., DeGue, S., Kras, A., Di Loreto-Colgan, A. and Nash, C. (2006) 'Participant responses to retrospective surveys of child maltreatment: Does mode of assessment matter?' *Violence and Victims* 21(4): 410–424.

Elder, G. (1998) 'The life course as developmental theory'. *Child Development* 69(1): 1–12.

Elliott, D. and Ageton, S. (1980) 'Reconciling race and class differences in self-reported and official estimates of delinquency'. *American Sociological Review* 45(1): 95–110.

Elliott, D., Huizinga, D. and Ageton, S. (1985) *Explaining Delinquency and Drug Use*. Beverly Hills: Sage.

Empey, L. and Erickson, M. (1966) 'Hidden delinquency and social status'. *Social Forces* 44(4): 546–554.

Erickson, M. and Empey, L. (1963) 'Court records, undetected delinquency and decision-making'. *Journal of Criminal Law, Criminology, and Police Science* 54(4): 456–469.

Farrington, D. (1973) 'Self-reports of deviant behavior: Predictive and stable?' *Journal of Criminal Law and Criminology* 64(1): 99–110.

Farrington, D. (ed.) (2005) *Integrated Developmental and Life-Course of Offending*. New Brunswick: Transaction Publishers.

Farrington, D., Loeber, R., Stouthamer-Loeber, M., Van Kammen, W. and Schmidt, L. (1996) 'Self-reported delinquency and a combined delinquency seriousness scale based on boys, mothers, and teachers: Concurrent and predictive validity for African-American and Caucasians'. *Criminology* 34(4): 493–517.

Gibbons, D. (1979) *The Criminological Enterprise: Theories and Perspectives*. New Jersey: Prentice-Hall.

Gold, M. (1966) 'Undetected delinquent behavior'. *Journal of Research in Crime and Delinquency* 3(1): 27–46.

Gold, M. (1970) *Delinquent Behavior in an American City*. Belmont, CA: Brooks/Cole.

Hawkins, D., Smith, B., Hill, K. et al. (2003) 'Understanding and preventing crime and violence: Findings from the Seattle Social Development Project' in T. Thornberry and M. Krohn (eds.), *Taking Stock of Delinquency* (pp. 255–312). New York: Plenum Publishers.

Hindelang, M., Hirschi, T. and Weis, J. (1979) 'Correlates of delinquency: The illusion of discrepancy between self-report and official measures'. *American Sociological Review* 44(6): 995–1014.

Hindelang, M., Hirschi, T. and Weis, J. (1981) *Measuring Delinquency*, Beverly Hills: Sage.

Hirschi, T. (1969). *Causes of Delinquency*, Berkeley: University of California Press.

Huizinga, D. and Elliott, D. (1986) 'Reassessing the reliability and validity of self-report delinquent measures'. *Journal of Quantitative Criminology* 2(4): 293–327.

Huizinga, D., Loeber, R. and Thornberry, T. (1991) *Program of Research on the Causes and Correlates of Delinquency* (Vols 1–3). Washington DC: Office of Juvenile Justice and Delinquency Prevention.

Junger-Tas, J., Marshall, I.H., Enzmann, D., Killias, M., Steketee, M. and Gruszczynska, B. (Eds.) (2010) *Juvenile Delinquency in Europe and Beyond*. New York: Springer.

Kaplan, A. (1964) *The Conduct of Inquiry*. San Francisco: Chandler Publishing.

Kaplan, H. (2003) 'Testing an integrative theory of deviant behavior: Theory-syntonic findings from a long-term multi-generational study' in T. Thornberry and M. Krohn (eds.), *Taking Stock of Delinquency* (pp. 185–204). New York: Plenum.

Kirk, D. (2006) 'Examining the divergence across self-report and official data sources on inferences about the adolescent life-course of crime'. *Journal of Quantitative Criminology* 22(2): 107–129.

Krohn, M., Waldo, G. and Chiricos, T. (1974) 'Self-reported delinquency: A comparison of structured interviews and self-administered checklists'. *Journal of Criminal Law and Criminology* 65(4): 545–553.

Latimer, W., O'Brien, M., Vasquez, M., Medina-Mora, M., Rios-Bedoya, C. and Floyd, L. (2006) 'Adolescent substance abuse in Mexico, Puerto Rico and the United States: Effect of anonymous versus confidential survey formats'. *Journal of Child Adolescent Substance Abuse* 16(1): 69–89.

Lauritsen, J. (1998). 'The age-crime debate: Assessing the limits of longitudinal self-report data'. *Social Forces* 76(4): 1–29.

Lehnen, R. and Reiss, A. (1978) 'Response effects in the National Crime Survey'. *Victimology: An International Journal* 3: 110–124.

Lizotte, A., Chard-Wierschem, D., Loeber, R. and Stern, S.B. (1992) 'A shortened behavior checklist for delinquency studies'. *Journal of Quantitative Criminology* 8: 233–245.

Loeber, R., Stouthamer-Loeber, M., Van Kammen, W. and Farrington, D. (1989) 'Development of a new measure of self-reported antisocial behavior for young children: Prevalence and reliability' in Malcolm W. Klein (ed.), *Cross-National Research in Self-Reported Crime and Delinquency* (pp. 203–225). Los Angeles: Kluwer Academic Publishers.

Menard, S. and Elliott, D. (1993) 'Data set comparability and short-term trends in crime and delinquency'. *Journal of Criminal Justice* 21(5): 433–445.

Merton, R. (1968) 'Social structure and anomie' in R. Merton (ed.), *Social Theory and Social Structure*. New York: Free Press.

Moffitt, T. (2003) 'Life course persistent and adolescence-limited antisocial behavior: A 10-year research review and research agenda' in B. Lahey, T. Moffitt, and A. Caspi (eds.), *Causes of Conduct Disorder and Juvenile Delinquency*. New York: Guilford.

Nye, F. (1958) *Family Relationships and Delinquent Behavior*. New York: John Wiley.

Nye, F., Short, J. and Olson, V. (1958) 'Socio-economic status and delinquent behavior'. *The American Journal of Sociology* 63(4): 381–389.

O'Malley, P., Johnston, L., Bachman, J. and Schulenberg, J. (2000) 'A comparison of confidential versus anonymous survey procedures'. *Journal of Drug Issues* 30(1): 35–54.

Ong, A. and Weiss, D. (2000) 'The impact of anonymity on responses to sensitive questions'. *Journal of Applied Social Psychology* 30(8): 1691–1708.

Park, R., Burgess, E. and McKenzie, R.. (1925) *The City*. Chicago: University of Chicago Press.

Piquero, A. and Brame, R. (2008) 'Assessing the race-crime and ethnicity-crime relationship in a sample of serious adolescent delinquents'. *Crime and Delinquency* 54(3): 390–422.

Porterfield, A. (1943) 'Delinquency and its outcome in court and college'. *American Journal of Sociology* 49(3): 199–208.

Richman, W., Kiesler, S., Weisband, S. and Drasgow, F. (1999) 'A meta-analytic study of social desirability distortion in computer administered questionnaires, traditional questionnaires, and interviews'. *Journal of Applied Psychology* 84(5): 754–775.

Richman, N., Stevenson, J. and Graham, P. (1982) *Preschool to School*. London: Academic Press.

Shaw, D. and Bell, R. (1993) 'Developmental theories of parental contributors to antisocial behavior'. *Journal of Abnormal Child Psychology* 21(5): 493–518.

Shaw, C. and McKay, H. (1942) *Juvenile Delinquency and Urban Areas*. Chicago: University of Chicago Press.

Short, J. (1957) 'Differential association and delinquency'. *Social Problems* 4(3): 233–239.

Short, J. and Nye, F. (1958) 'Extent of unrecorded juvenile delinquency'. *Journal of Criminal Law and Criminology* 49(4): 296–302.

Slocum, W. and Stone, C. (1963) 'Family culture patterns and delinquent-type behavior'. *Marriage and Family Living* 25(2): 202–208.

Straus, M.A., Gelles, R.J. and Steinmetz, S.K. (1980) *Behind Closed Doors: Violence in the American Family*. Beverly Hills: Sage Publications.

Supple, A. Aquilino, W. and Wright, D. (1999) 'Collecting sensitive self-report data with laptop computers'. *Journal of Research on Adolescence* 9(4): 467–488.

Sutherland, E. (1939) *Principles of Criminology*, 3rd Edition. Philadelphia: J.B. Lippincott.

Thornberry, T. (1987) 'Toward an interactional theory of delinquency'. *Criminology* 25(4): 863–891.

Thornberry, T. (1989) 'Panel effects and the use of self-reported measures of delinquency in longitudinal studies' in Malcolm W. Klein (ed.), *Cross-National Research in Self-Reported Crime and Delinquency* (pp. 347–369). Los Angeles: Kluwer.

Thornberry, T. (1997) *Developmental Theories of Crime and Delinquency*. New Brunswick: Transaction.

Thornberry, T. and Krohn, M. (2000) 'The self-report method for measuring delinquency and crime' in D. Duffee, R. Crutchfield, S. Mastrofski, L. Mazerolle and D. McDowall (eds.), *Criminal Justice 2000 (Vol. 4): Measurement and Analysis of Crime and Justice*. Washington DC: National Institute of Justice.

Thornberry, T. and Krohn, M. (2001) 'The development of delinquency: An interactional perspective' in S. White (ed.), *Handbook of Law and Social Science: Youth and Justice* (pp. 289–305). New York: Plenum.

Thornberry, T. and Krohn, M. (2005) 'Applying interactional theory to the explanation of continuity and change in antisocial behavior' in D.P. Farrington (ed.), *Integrated Developmental and Life-Course Theories of Offending* (pp. 183–209). New Brunswick: Transaction.

Tourangeau, R. and Smith, T. (1996) 'Asking sensitive questions'. *Public Opinion Quarterly* 60(2): 275–304.

Tremblay, R., Vitaro, F., Nagin, D. et al. (2003) 'The Montreal Longitudinal Experimental Study' in T.P. Thornberry and M.D. Krohn (eds.), *Taking Stock of Delinquency* (pp. 205–254). New York: Plenum.

Vaz, E. (1966) 'Self-reported juvenile delinquency and social status'. *Canadian Journal of Corrections* 8: 20–27.

Vereecken, C. and Maes, L. (2006) 'Comparison of a computer-administered and paper-and-pencil-administered questionnaire on health and lifestyle behaviors'. *Journal of Adolescent Health* 38(4): 426–432.

Wallerstein, J. and Wylie, C. (1947) 'Our law-abiding law-breakers'. *Probation* 25: 107–112.

Williams, J. and Gold, M. (1972) 'From delinquent behavior to official delinquency'. *Social Problems* 20(2): 209–229.

3

In-depth Interviewing and Psychosocial Case Study Analysis

David Gadd

PSYCHOSOCIAL CRIMINOLOGY: SOMETHING OLD, SOMETHING NEW

Although the psychosocial approach has emerged relatively recently as a specialism within criminology, it is possible to chart a history of delinquency research that addressed the relationships between inner-world psychological and outer-world sociological issues dating back to the 1920s. Often, this work is dismissed for its limited empirical basis and Freudian orthodoxy (Radzinowicz and King, 1977). In some cases this criticism is justified (Hamblin Smith, 1922; Glover, 1960), but it should not cause us to forget the endeavours of a number of early twentieth-century writers to put psychoanalytic concepts to the empirical test. Take, for example, E.W. Burgess' (1930) analysis of the defensiveness of Clifford Shaw's (1930) *Jack-Roller*; John Bowlby's (1946) case notes on 'juvenile thieves', variously traumatised by experiences of war, estrangement, illness, institutional care, abuse or neglect; or Mark Benney's (1936) critical autobiography of working-class life and how it contributed to his life as a thief. The best of this work used empirical evidence to engage with the wider social scientific debates that have always mattered to sociological criminologists – crime, its causes and consequences, and their relation to poverty, politics and social control – while at the same time taking the complexity of criminal subjectivities, their potentially conflicted nature and the possibility of motives that were not always consciously accessible to the individuals concerned, very seriously.

By way of contrast, contemporary criminology is more exclusively sociological in focus, concerned with the cultures, structures and modes of social control to which we are all subject, but not so much with the peculiarities of how these intersect with individual biographies, or the meaning making involved when they impinge upon, or are resisted by, particular individuals. Criminological psychology has done little to rectify this, risk-focused crime prevention merely compounding the problem with a model of the offender that reduces him or her to the aggregate of 'factors' liable to instil a 'propensity' for offending. All of this is rather unfortunate since some of the most interesting developments in social theory over the last 20 years have come from those willing to explore a rapprochement between sociological work attendant to the intersections between power and knowledge and the kind of psycho*dynamic* thinking that the different strands of psychoanalysis are variously concerned with (Du Gay et al., 2000; Henriques et al., 1984). Across the social sciences these theoretical developments have given impetus to a new field of 'psychosocial studies' which seeks to explore how the psychological and social constitute each other, without collapsing one into the other. The website of the UK's fledgling *Psychosocial Network*, for example, defines the focus of psychosocial studies as the 'the tensions between and mutual constitution of the social and the psychic', while the website of the *International Research Group of Psycho-Societal Analysis* draws attention to the 'dialectic between inner experience and the social conditions of people's lives, paying attention to the conflictual and dynamic nature of both psychological and social processes and their mutual effects on social action and change'. This is not the place to chart the debates that gave rise to these formulations (Clarke, 2006; Frosh, 2003; Layton, 2008), but two features of it are worthy of note. First, that in order to posit human subjects with depth and complexity, those working within psychosocial studies have tended to find it necessary to assume unconscious motivations inaccessible to the individual but nevertheless having effects on their behaviour and their relationships with other people. Second, that in the process of addressing the irreducible relationships between the psychic and the social, psychosocial theorists and practitioners have often turned to criminological subject matter for answers. For them, the problems of crime and violence, racism and fundamentalism, abuse and how it is remembered, fear and anxiety, retributive sensibilities, what lies behind them and what it is like to be subject to them, require approaches that engage with issues of social structure, power and discourse, without requiring us – as academics, practitioners, and researchers – to assume that particular people inevitably think or feel in particular ways simply because of the things they have done, the groups they belong to, or because of the times and places in which they have lived. Breaking with these assumptions is particularly difficult for academics schooled in criminology, not least because so much of our discipline is rooted in governmental projects that presume that certain segments of the population, especially the poor, share a common outlook because of their structural positioning; that is, that people offend because they have experienced 'strain', have inherited poor self-control from the 'problem families' in which they were raised, or because they have been labelled as deviant by law enforcers or other agents of social control (Jefferson, 2002). Capturing agency, without resort to rational choice models, is something criminologists have yet to prove very adept at, some notable exceptions notwithstanding (Katz, 1988; Sykes and Matza, 1957).

PRODUCING RICH ENOUGH DATA

At the time of writing, readers looking to begin their enquiries with a new body of psychosocial criminology imbued with a more agentic model of the subject have only a small body of literature to contend with. Until relatively recently the psychosocial criminological literature was largely theoretical (Anderson and Quinney, 1999; Brown, 2003; Hood-Williams, 2001), confined in its more empirical instances to the analysis of case material produced initially, not for academic research, but in the course of criminal justice processes and/or in the course of journalistic enquiry (Evans, 2003; Hollway and Jefferson, 1998; Jefferson, 1997). In this context, Hollway and Jefferson's (2000) account of how they sought to develop an adequately psychosocial approach to researching the fear of crime, *Doing Qualitative Research Differently*, established itself as the pioneering text with respect to methodology, although there are other psychosocial methodology texts worth engaging with beyond the criminological domain (Clarke et al., 2008a; Hollway, 1989; Kvale, 1996; Wengraf, 2001). Within this wider field of psychosocial studies there is a marked preference for material that is richly textual, the advent of portable tape recorders and, subsequently, digital recording devices, making it possible for a new generation of researchers to not only test out hypotheses about subjective inner-world reactions in a way that was near impossible when psychoanalysis was first conceived, but also to evidence their arguments about them through the production of highly detailed interview transcripts. *Doing Qualitative Research Differently* capitalised on this moment. It was the first book in 40 years to make a sustained case for the production of criminological data informed by psychoanalytic hypotheses. It was also a text that resuscitated what had become a long dormant, but nevertheless invaluable, tradition of life-story work within criminology, the methodological tenets of which had never been properly articulated (cf. Carlen, 1980; Shaw, 1930; Soothill, 1999). More than anything else, however, it was a book that underlined the importance of attending as carefully as possible not only to *what people say* about themselves, but also *how they say it, what they struggle to say* and *what they cannot or do not (quite) say*. What mattered most to Hollway and Jefferson was the ability of their approach to produce analyses that did justice to the complexity of the people they were researching: their guardedness and their bold assertions; their principles and their prejudices; the tensions between their values and their desires; the contradictions between what they claim and their actual experiences. Adapting ideas from the psychoanalytic work of Melanie Klein, Hollway and Jefferson adopted a model of subjectivity that has anxiety at its core. Essentially, we are all anxious beings and much of what we say and do is motivated by a desire to defend against the feelings of vulnerability this anxiety arouses in us. For them, incomplete, contradictory or con-fused sentences are just as important as word-perfect responses, since both can read as evidence of the character structure of inherently *defended subjects*. What was most critical was that com-plexities in the data were treated as evidence of the nature and depth of the people under study, and not written out of the analysis as mere idio-syncratic noise of no criminological interest. For Hollway and Jefferson it is only when both the unique and the culturally common features of people's lives are adequately grasped that they become truly recognisable, enabling us to see which aspects of our experiences are akin to our research participants' as well as what it is that makes us different.

In writing their own methodology book, Hollway and Jefferson took inspiration from a then emerging body of German sociological research being conducted on Holocaust survivors and service personnel who had served the Nazis during the Second World War (Bar-On, 2004; Breckner, 1998; Rosenthal, 1993; Rosenthal and Bar-On, 1992). Noting how the methods used in that research elicited rich material from interview-ees who had good reason to deceive both them-selves and the researchers, Hollway and Jefferson (2000) spotted the potential of narrative methods to grapple with the more commonplace phenom-enon of human defensiveness. Troubled by a British policy debate that assumed that people ought to be able to calibrate their fearfulness according to what is known about their risk of victimisation, Hollway and Jefferson elaborated on the dangers of research that failed to take the issue of subjectivity seriously. In the 1980s people who ticked the same boxes in the British Crime Survey were assumed both to be 'telling it like it is' and to have meant the same thing, with no checks being made to test the validity of these unquestioned presumptions. Arguing that the problem was not so much the public per se, but about a failure to anticipate in the design of research instruments how the public experience crime and fear, Hollway and Jefferson began to develop an alternative methodological approach that would encourage individuals to convey the complexity of their experiences and preserve as much of the uniqueness of what was disclosed in the course of the data analysis.

Through the use of a narrative-focused, experi-entially responsive approach to interviewing, Hollway and Jefferson attempted to 'transform' themselves 'from the highly visible asker[s] of … questions to the almost invisible, facilitating cata-lyst' of their interviewees' 'stories' (ibid. 36). The essence of their approach was to encourage people to tell their own stories and then to ask questions that invited participants to elaborate further about their own particular experiences. Rather than asking people to score how safe they felt walking around their neighbourhoods at night, Hollway and Jefferson encouraged their interviewees to recall whatever came to mind – even if seemingly irrelevant to the topic – when invited to talk about how crime had impacted on their lives since they had been living wherever they were. As the fol-lowing extract reveals, participants often rose admirably to this invitation, introducing aspects of their experience that would not have been elicited using closed questions, and narrating those expe-riences with the kind of meaningful disclosures that have to be taken account of if one wants to understand why some people are more fearful than others.

Extract 1: Interview conducted by Tony Jefferson with 'Arthur', October 1995

TJ: Can you tell me about how crime has impacted on your life since you've been living here?

A: Well the only thing that you've got to be wary about really is er, like at the moment I've er, I've got a disability because – on account of this injury at work I had to retire and now I'm having to walk about with a stick. (light laugh) [*TJ:* Yeah.] And I dread – you know, I'm a bit nerv-ous about going out at night. [*TJ:* Um hum.] Er, you never know who's at back of you. Whereas when I were fit it wouldn't have both-ered me. [*TJ:* Mmm.] But there is a lot of er, things happen on this estate that er, you know, last few years it's got really worse. [*TJ:* Um hum.] I don't know whether that answers your ques-tion but, it don't em, it don't bother me really but only thing you worry about is if you go away, you never know when you're gonna come home er, who's been in your house.

TJ: Can I just take those things one at a time that you mentioned?

As the extract reveals, the strength of this approach was in its capacity to generate the nuanced mate-rial needed to make sense of how particular indi-viduals feel about crime and the disjunction between this and what, in certain circumstances, they might be prepared to say about it. Tony Jefferson's invitation to Arthur to tell him how crime had impacted on his life enabled Arthur to explain that he is not so much afraid but 'nervous', and not necessarily on account of having been victimised. On the one hand, Arthur was 'both-ered' about being out at night and leaving his house unattended now, but he had not always been so back in the days before he was injured at work, lost his 'fitness', and retired; changes in his life which he considered to have coincided with when the 'estate … got really worse', whatever that meant. On the other, we learn that Arthur was either not unambiguously bothered or, perhaps more likely if his 'light laughter' is read as 'nervous laughter', that he did not want the interviewer to think he was, hence his retraction, 'it don't bother me really'. Making sure that such ambiguities and tensions are retained as data to be made sense of within the analysis is critical for researchers trying to undertake psychosocial analysis. Hollway and Jefferson, in particular, refer to this as the *Gestalt* principle (an idea they borrow from the German methodologies discussed earlier), meaning that the whole of any one case – including how it is organised, presented and structured – is always greater than the sum of its individual parts.

In terms of how the Free Association Narrative Interview Method works, the dialogue between Tony Jefferson and Arthur illustrates well the nature of the 'free' or spontaneous 'associations' that are being sought. Having *facilitated* Arthur's responses to the opening question through the use of a string of very *minimal cues* – 'Yeah', 'Mmm' 'Um hum', Jefferson's next prompt prepared Arthur to go back through his initial reactions, 'one at a time'. The full version of the transcript (available via the Economic and Social Data Service's website listed at the end of this chapter) reveals that Jefferson achieved this through a combination of techniques that became the principal tenets of the Free Association Narrative Interview Method: presenting elements of what Arthur had disclosed back to him (his 'disability' feeling a 'bit nervous about going out at night' the 'things' that 'happen on the estate') in the order Arthur had revealed them; asking Arthur to say a bit more about these; reflecting back some of Arthur's reactions in order to encourage him to elaborate further; and by posing further narrative-eliciting questions that used Arthur's words and phrases as prompts.

Importantly, for practitioners of the Free Association Narrative Interview Method, these follow-up questions are never 'why?' questions. In this method, 'why?' questions are *explicitly avoided* because in asking participants to explain things they may not be able to explicate, 'why?' questions have a tendency to elicit clichéd rationalisations, further obscuring the uniqueness of the interviewees' biographical experiences from view. Often interviewees do not know very much about the problem under study – at least when expressed in the policy-relevant terms through which research projects are increasingly conceived – and are hence uncertain both as to what caused it and what should be done about it. As Adorno (1950) once perceptively noted, and as a swathe of

psychological research in the social identity tradition now confirms (Branscombe, 1999), when pressured to give an opinion, respondents who are otherwise unsure in their viewpoints can feel inclined to express authoritarian attitudes so as to avoid appearing like naïve outsiders (see also the chapter by Roberts et al., this volume). The same can be true of people's understandings of aspects of their own personal experiences. As Hydén (2008: 125) remarks: 'The significance of the difference between "having been through a lot" and "knowing about" what happened is that of reflection and giving meaning to experience.'

In criminological research it is not uncommon to encounter people who have not benefited from this kind of knowledge-enhancing reflection, who do not know why they did what they did, nor why terrible things have happened to them. In such circumstances, it is rarely productive to pressurise interviewees into providing an explanation. At the same time, it is not always easy to find narrative-eliciting questions to ask such interviewees, especially when the focus of the research is on behaviour that is illicit, attitudes that are taboo, or experiences that are potentially shameful. Not everyone who agrees to participate in this kind of research finds it easy to tell – or construct afresh – their stories. Most need the interviewer to help facilitate and many need to be convinced that they are genuinely allowed to introduce any aspects of their experience they deem relevant. As Hollway and Jefferson explain:

> Interviewees' preparedness to open out intimate material also reflects the building up of an expectation that stories are what the researcher wants – that they are interesting, relevant and valued. This expectation has to be actively built because the normal expectation is otherwise; that is the interviewer will come round with a batch of questions, for which one-word or short replies are required (Hollway and Jefferson 2000: 44).

The beauty of the Free Association Narrative Interview Method is that with skill and practice even short one-word replies can be used to elicit accounts that might otherwise have proved inaccessible to research. Consider, for example, the extract from an interview I conducted with a former far-right activist that follows. The numerical values in square brackets signify the length of paused silences in seconds.

Extract 2: Interview conducted by David Gadd with 'Frank', April 2004

DG: I was wondering if you could start by sort of telling me the story of your life in Stoke-on-Trent, obviously start as far back as you can remember and take as much time as you need. What I'll do is, I'll take some notes so that I can ask you some questions as we go along.

F: Well, I was born in [mining estate], come off a family of seven, five brothers and one sister. [16 second pause] Basically I don't really know what you want like. That's the thing about it. I mean a lot has gone on in me life like. What specific points, like?

DG: Well if you, I mean, perhaps you could tell me the story of growing up in [mining estate] to start with.

F: Growing up, well, we had nothing, never had nothing like, you know coming off a big family (DG: Hm, hm). Me dad wasn't too kind to us.

DG: He wasn't kind?

F: No not really. [3 second pause] Always fighting at school, you know. Cos me dad said so (DG: Hm, hm). [25 second pause]. What basically do you want to know, like?

DG: Well what you've told me so far is that, you told me, you had nothing and your dad wasn't kind and you were into fighting at school, got into fighting at school. So maybe we could start with that. If you could kind of tell me how having nothing kind of impacted upon your upbringing.

Even in this highly reticent retort, littered as it was with painfully long pauses, the interviewee, Frank, provided several leads through which further narration could be pursued. From it, new narrative questions could be formulated about the estate where Frank was born, his family, his siblings, or even about the whole 'lot' that had 'gone on' in his life. I initially responded with a narrative question about life on Frank's estate, then with some reflection ('He wasn't kind?'), some minimal encouragement ('hm, hm'), toleration of long pauses, and then by offering back, as a narrative-evoking question what appeared to be one of the more meaning-laden of Frank's initial disclosures, namely that his family 'never had nothing, like'. My response was not perfect. The reflection might have been more precise had it been phrased: 'Your dad wasn't *too* kind?'; and one of the questions clumsily exposed Frank to my disarray, 'Well if you, I mean, perhaps…'. But in combination the techniques did ultimately elicit many more in-depth disclosures from Frank, a man who was not accustomed to talking about himself in this way, but who nevertheless had a very important story to tell (Gadd, 2006).

Of course practitioners of the Free Association Narrative Interview Method also run the risk of being overwhelmed by the extensiveness of what is revealed when interviewees begin to 'freely associate'. This may be especially likely to happen

in research with participants who have been waiting to tell somebody – perhaps anybody – about things they have done or have happened to them, safe in the knowledge that assurances of confidentiality will be honoured. It is not uncommon for novice researchers to approach this challenge with the view that it does not matter if they do not hear and remember what the interviewee tells them because they can always listen to the recording later. There is an element of truth to this. The Free Association Narrative Interview Method works by *returning to participants for a second follow-up interview*, informed by an analysis of the first interview – a process to which this chapter returns. Nevertheless, it is a mistake to assume that the first interview is not compromised when the interviewer fails to demonstrate to the interviewee – by accurately utilising the their words and phrases to pose further questions – that they have listened attentively to what has been disclosed. Re-expressing what the interviewee has disclosed in words that were not their own can make them feel misconstrued, or, worse still, prejudged for their particular mode of expression; and this, in turn may make them much more guarded than they would ordinarily be in terms of what they are prepared to say and how they are prepared to say it.

Learning to take notes while retaining a level of eye contact with the interviewee is one of the more difficult skills practitioners of the Free Association Narrative Interview Method must develop if they are to gain the interviewee's confidence. Being able to keep eye contact at the same time as taking notes is often crucial in the opening moments of the interview because, if captured accurately, what is revealed when the interviewee does begin to open up can be utilised to structure the rest of the interview. Consider, for example, how many lines of enquiry were opened up by the following response to an invitation to Alan – a 39 year-old man on probation for a racially aggravated assault – to tell his life story.

Extract 3: Interview conducted by David Gadd with 'Alan', May 2004

A: I'm the youngest boy out of ten children. I got a younger sister. And everybody else is older than me. I've got five brothers, four sisters. Em, my mum was from Stoke on Trent, and me dad was from South Wales. So I'm half Welsh, half English. Em. Earliest memories is infant school, which is now closed, em moved on to … Middle School, and then … High School. Em, I got into football at an early age. I went to me first. I'm a big Stoke City fan. Went to me first football match when I was ten. And I, I have been crazy about Stoke City ever since and that has played an integral part of me life. Em … Went off the rails, early teens. From being quite a bright lad I just got no interest in school whatsoever. I was bunking off to work on the markets, em ice cream vans and things like that to earn some cash. [*DG:* Hm, hm] I got into the punk rock movement in me early teens. Em, followed me through until I left school, basically … I left school at 15. I vastly under achieved. Got into drinking again while I was still at school. Going to local pubs and that. Started getting into trouble just after I left school. Em basically, em drink related incidents and football hooliganism. … Eh … Got sentenced, got sent to detention centre, when I was 19, for 3 months … That was for fighting on the pitch at [away game]. 1984. Em, come out of there, drifted from one job to another. … Em lost me driving licence through drink driving. Signed meself up in college and got my City in Guilds in painting and decorating. That was me line of work then for, until like 6 years ago. Em I've suffered mental health problems some very severe. Em, one in 2000 lasted about three to four months and again in 2002 which lasted a similar time. Em I've suffered from depression again since me teens, em I've dabbled with drugs. Er, oh, alcohol has always been a big problem in me life. Em about me two spots of mental illness, em we're not talking just depression there. We're talking severe psychotic bouts. [*DG:* Right.] A: Em probably caused by long term cannabis and alcohol abuse. Not 100% certain on that we're not, but it's the probable cause of it. Em, … I'm sorry mate, I'm blanking here, I'm, I could do with more questioning.

This extensive disclosure is testimony to the richness of human experience that can be captured

with the right methodological approach. In it Alan provided enough material for the interviewer to map out a provisional list of questions that exceeded what was possible within the confines of a ninety-minute interview. Responding to Alan's request for more questioning, while being guided by the ordering of his disclosures, a Free Association Narrative interviewer could respond by asking Alan to 'tell the stories of': growing up in a large family of five brothers and four sisters; his schooling; getting into football; going to his first match aged ten; 'going off the rails' and 'losing interest' in school; working on the markets, ice cream vans and 'things like that'; getting into punk rock; drinking, drug use, and/or football hooliganism; being arrested and detained; drifting from one job to another; getting his 'City and Guilds'; his experiences of psychosis and depression; or more specifically his 'two spots' of mental illness and their possible connection to drink and drug abuse. With a forthcoming interviewee like Alan, the interviewer was almost sure to elicit detailed narrations that could be probed even further, as long as the questions posed invited more stories and accurately utilised his meaning frame.

PREPARING FOLLOW-UP INTERVIEWS

While questions left over from the first interview can be pursued in the second interview, this is not the primary purpose of the follow-up interview. For those using the Free Association Narrative Interview Method the analysis starts when the first interview ends. What is gathered in the first interview is used to formulate provisional hypotheses

---

Box 3.1 Key tenets of the Free Association Narrative Interview Method

- Before the interview commences prepare the interviewee for the kind of research encounter that will follow.
- As the interview commences reassure the interviewee that what they have said has been interesting and that you would like to hear more of their stories.
- Ask narrative-focussed questions wherever possible.
- Avoid 'closed' questions and 'why?' questions.
- Do not interrupt the interviewee when they are talking or fill their pauses and silences when they are thinking.
- Keep notes while remaining attentive.
- Facilitate with minimalist cues. This can mean simply nodding, saying 'Hm, hm', 'right', or encouraging the interviewee to 'go on'.
- Reflect back the interviewee's sentences or phrases in order to facilitate further disclosures while showing that one has listened properly to what has already been divulged.
- Use the interviewee's frames of meaning to pose new narrative questions.
- As far as possible, ask questions in an order that mirrors the way the interviewee has ordered their disclosures.

about the interviewee which are tested in the second; 'to interrogate critically what was said, to pick up on the contradictions, inconsistencies, avoidances and changes of tone' (Hollway and Jefferson 2000: 43); and to think about what more one would like to know and how best to ask about it. Both for reasons of continuity and to minimise the risk of losing contact with the participant, most people using this method tend to arrange follow-up interviews within two weeks of the first interview. The available time between interviews can, therefore, put constraints on how thoroughly one can prepare for the second interviews. It is worth remembering this when scheduling both research encounters. If it is possible to generate a full transcript of the first interview ahead of preparing the questions for the second, this is worth doing. If not, listening to the recording several times may be the best substitute. In order to make sure the dynamics of the interview remain in view, transcripts need to be as full as possible, incorporating half finished words and sentences, noting changes of tone and/or accent, gesturing and other non-verbal and non-linguistic modes of expression.

There are no hard and fast rules for working on the data produced in the first interview, not least because what one picks out will always be partially informed by the focus of the research being undertaken. That said, this is not the kind of research that is best undertaken completely alone. Often, how the interviewee comes across at interview, on tape and through the transcript will vary, and this should be the subject of reflection among the research team during the preparation for the follow-up interview. It is often helpful for the interviewer to develop their own working hypothesis, hunches and queries, informed both by the substance of the interview and any other information they picked up about the interviewee, and then to share this with a supervisor, co-researcher, or interested group of scholars who are willing to either listen to the recording, read the transcript, or both. At this stage it is not necessary to resolve differences of opinion with regard to the interpretation of the first interview, and some of those using this approach have found that such differences can be fruitfully harnessed in print as a means of conveying both the complexity of the people studied and the risks inherent in reducing them to the sum of their attitudes (Clarke, 2008b). What does matter, however, is that the interviewer develops a sense of what might be distinctive, revelatory or perplexing about the interviewee. Sometimes these puzzling qualities are connected to unusual things the interviewee has said or claims they repeatedly make without contextualising or explaining them. But, at a more everyday level, what can also be puzzling is why people tell their story one way and not another. Although not an exhaustive list, I have found the following facets of interviewees' accounts particularly worth exploring in follow-up interviews:

1   *Avoidances.* Does the interviewee avoid answering particular questions, appear reluctant to talk about particular events or periods in their life, or change the subject for no apparent reason? Is there a way of drawing their attention to what appears to have been avoided without causing offence?

2   *Conflations.* Are there points in the interview where several events are inextricably conflated, making their ordering difficult to decipher? For example, is the recollection of something in the recent past being told as if it followed the logic of something that happened much earlier, or vice versa?

3   *Inconsistencies.* Are there inconsistencies or contradictions in the stories told? Are two or more different accounts of the same event offered? Are assertions made that are not supported by the examples given? Does the chronology of events seem plausible, or are there events that are unlikely to have happened when the interviewee claims they did? Is the story consistent with the historical record as well as internally consistent? How does the story told measure up against what other interviewees have said about the same event or phenomenon?

4   *Delivery style.* Are there sudden changes of pace or tone during the interview? Is there a pattern to the pauses or hesitations? Is a third person perspective introduced when a first person account might have been expected? Are some events depicted as things that 'just happened', as a product of good or bad fortune, when other are construed as entirely under the interviewee's control and of their own making? Does the interviewee ask the interviewer to endorse their viewpoint, become inexplicably defensive, or seek some additional recognition or validation beyond the affirmative facilitation provided? Was this recognition forthcoming, and if so – or if not – with what effect?

5   *Unsubstantiated generalisations and projection.* Are there certain descriptive terms that are repeatedly applied to a range of quite different events or relationships? Does the interviewee accuse others of doing things that they have done? Are insinuations made – whether about significant others, the government, or people like the interviewer – that merit further exploration?

Reconciling the need to follow-up issues like these with the need to pose more topic-focused questions that the project or its funders require can be difficult. Anticipating how the second interview may unfold and being able to prioritise is therefore critical, not least because interviewees often wish to introduce new stories or revise their first interview accounts in the second interview. Space needs to be made for this, not only out of courtesy to the interviewee, but also because such revisions can be revelatory in and of themselves.

PEN PORTRAITS AND THE CHALLENGE OF INTERPRETATION

Because of their commitment to the *Gestalt* principle – the idea that the whole of the person being interviewed is greater than the sum of any of their particular attitudes, experiences or other disclosures – those using the Free Association Narrative Interview Method tend to favour modes of analysis that endeavour to preserve as much the data's complexity as possible until an analysis that can be presented to a wider audience has been produced. A case study approach is often used, not only because of the depth of the material garnered about interviewees' experiences, but also because there are almost always

- multiple dimensions to these experiences that are difficult to disentangle from each other;
- a range of hypothesis that ought to be considered in relation to these experiences, and;
- conceptual difficulties to overcome with respect to deciding what is distinctively personal and/or biographical about the person's life and what is a relatively common product of pervasive cultural or social attitudes (Yin, 2009).

Hollway and Jefferson's response to these challenges has been to construct textual 'pen portraits' of their interviewees that bring their case material alive to readers unfamiliar with the original sources. Essentially these pen portraits are descriptive pictures that bring together all the information to hand about a particular individual – including any 'inconsistencies, contradictions and puzzles' evident within the interview transcripts – enabling 'subsequent interpretations' to be 'assessed' against them (Hollway and Johnson, 2000: 70).

Critics of this approach have argued that such pen portraits are more 'constructed' than Hollway and Jefferson concede; constructed with a particular hypothesis – that we are all 'defended subjects', motivated by anxieties of which we were not fully conscious – fully in mind. For some such pen portraits present us with too 'definitive' a story, leading almost 'automatically' to revelations about the 'real character' of the people

under study (Wetherell, 2005: 171). This is indeed a real risk of the method, although one that can be countered if one is both aware of it and upfront about the hypotheses that have informed the data analysis. It certainly helps that today's psychoanalytic interpreters – unlike those of the early twentieth century – can and do make their data available through archives so they can be interrogated by others, and furthermore, that some cases are analysed not only by academic groups (as they are in the approaches advocated by Oevermann et al., 1987 and Wengraf, 2001, discussed later) but in the course of public debate; that is, through special issues of journals and conference sessions specifically devoted to single cases.

Moreover, in the contexts where I have conducted research using the Free Association Narrative Interview Method – in research with domestic violence perpetrators and racially motivated offenders – the converse risk is just as great. Too often the orthodox criminological position relies upon a one-dimensional model of offender motivation – for example, the idea that racially motivated offenders offend simply because of their 'biases' or that domestic abusers are driven exclusively by a will to power – that oversimplifies the complex humanity of the people whose behaviour it purports to understand. Of course, none of us can avoid simplification, but when it comes to writing about offenders, academic work that does not do full justice to the humanity of the people it studies runs the additional risk of compounding the very demonising discourses folk devils and moral panics are made of. Showing that more complex models of criminal motivation can be sustained with the right kind of evidence has been the aim of all my research using the Free Association Narrative Interview Method and the reason why I have pursued modes of analysis that are sensitive to ambiguities of meaning and the interpretive challenges these pose. The following extract, abbreviated from a pen portrait of 'Alan' published in Gadd (2009) illustrates this point, while at the same time revealing more about whom this particular interviewee – introduced earlier – turned out to be.

PSYCHOSOCIAL CASE ANALYSIS

Before one begins to develop an analysis of data like this it is often helpful to refine one's research questions further, focusing the interpretive work required more precisely. For example, it was when I began to wonder why so many people accused of racial aggravated assaults resist becoming labelled as racist more than they resist being known as offenders (Burney and Rose, 2002), that I started

Box 3.2 Abbreviated pen portrait of Alan

Alan was a 39-year-old white English man of muscular build, on probation for the racially aggravated assault of an Asian taxi driver. He claimed not to be able to recall the assault for which he was convicted because he was mentally ill at the time. Alan accepted that he might have spat in the face of the taxi driver in the 'heat' of the moment – 'I'm terrible for it. I think it's like the ultimate insult' – but doubted he was guilty of the racially aggravated element of his conviction. He could not imagine using the words 'Paki bastard' he was alleged to have said.

Alan's disavowal of the racial dimension to the assault appeared to be consistent with his the non-racist beliefs. When, as a schoolboy, he worked on the markets, he 'got on like house on fire' with the 'Indian or Pakistani' traders. As a teenage football hooligan, he remembered two 'coloured' guys in their gang and that 'they never got no racist abuse off us'. He used to wear a 'Rock Against Racism' badge and would take issue with younger hooligans who purported to have connections with militant far-right groups. Nowadays he was appalled by post-9/11 Islamaphobia. This kind of racism had, in his view, done 'a lot of damage to the Muslim community … which they don't deserve'. Alan even claimed to be 'good friends' with the other Asian taxi drivers who worked for the 'same firm' as the man he had assaulted. He had taken one to a local soccer match and 'introduced him' to all of his 'friends down the match'. Three of his niece's children, all of whom he loves 'to bits', have a father who is Pakistani (and also a taxi driver). While there had been some family animosity over this niece's choice of husband, it was, according to Alan, 'nothing racial'. The animosity, Alan said, had more to do with 'how they treat their women' and the strong suspicion that the father, with whom 'everybody gets on', has a second family in Pakistan.

As for the taxi driver who had been assaulted, Alan had hired him on two previous occasions before the alleged assault. On both of those two previous occasions the taxi driver, according to Alan, had made sexually derogatory remarks about women. The taxi driver's offensive remarks on the first occasion were with reference to two young girls walking past. In his first account of this journey, Alan claimed the taxi driver had said: 'I wouldn't mind giving it her up the arse', to which Alan said he replied: 'I'm not like that. I don't enjoy people speaking like that about women.' In the second interview, however, Alan recalled the taxi driver's remarks as 'I bet you like having it up her arse mate' to which Alan said he had replied: 'I'm not like that … I don't enjoy people speaking like that about women … You don't know me'.

Returning from a night out, at the time of the second taxi journey, Alan had 'had a few to drink', when the driver allegedly asked him: 'Where you been mate? You been fucking?' Alan said he replied:

> No offence mate, but this is twice you've made derogatory offence like remarks about women and now you're asking me if I been shagging … You're nothing but a pervert.

For this reason, Alan thought that during the third taxi journey, when he was alleged to have spat at the driver, he would have called him a 'pervert' not a 'Paki': 'because that's what I genuinely thought of him'.

Asked whether he could recall other times when he felt offended by 'sexist or sexually derogatory comments', Alan remembered a boy at school with 'dark-looking skin', now serving a life sentence in prison for rape. Alan knew some of the victims and said he would 'joyfully' act as the rapist's executioner. Another instance when questions of sexuality were touched upon by Alan arose in relation to his explanation of the 'male bonding' dimension of the football hooliganism he had found so 'addictive' since his teens. 'It was' he said,

> always nice if … you was on the coach and you were a bit scared … and some older lad would say, 'stick with us kid… You'll be alright'. It's like a … a male bonding type of thing. I'm not homosexual, or nothing like that.

This male bonding often involved the bloodiest of violence, Alan's fights with rival fans and police officers exposing him to some serious injuries, numerous bans from the club, and a stint in a detention centre in his late teens. It also involved overt sexism: 'It's something different when ten thousand lads are singing to a pretty model parading round the pitch, "Get your tits out for the lads". That's a bit of a laugh.'

The bravado this male-bonding entailed contrasted sharply with the pain Alan felt in relation to his own relationships with women. When his first fiancée discovered that Alan had been unfaithful, she ended the relationship. Alan was so 'devastated' that he took an 'overdose', 'slit his wrist', and became 'really down depressed'. His 'stormy' ten-year marriage to another woman ended when he discovered she was having an affair with a neighbour, whereupon Alan hit his wife hard enough to put 'her arm in a sling' and 'spat in her face'. His father dying the same week, Alan was 'cut up' with grief. He started 'drinking heavily' and began 'trawling' the pubs and clubs 'looking for another partnership'. The assault on the taxi driver occurred around this time, in the midst of mental health problems that were subsequently diagnosed as 'psychotic bouts'.

to revisit the pen portraits of racially motivated offenders, we, as a research team, had constructed several years earlier (Gadd et al., 2005). Remembering that when I had interviewed Alan I had quite liked him and did not experience him as particularly racist or spiteful, I began to wonder how it was possible that his victim might have experienced him otherwise. In hindsight, I suspect I identified closely with Alan and his vicarious accounts of violent hooliganism at the time of the interviews, and only became fully conscious of this when I began to anticipate how his account would be received by people from minority ethnic groups and/or others who might see themselves as potential victims of men like him. I looked again at the transcripts and began to contrast the evidence suggesting that Alan was not racist with those elements of his disclosures which appeared, at least potentially, to have some connection to racialisable hatred. Alan did not have particularly racist attitudes, disliked the racism he witnessed in others, and was not regarded as 'a racist' by his probation officer. Other researchers, working within different traditions, might have concluded on this basis that Alan was most likely not guilty of the racially aggravated element of the assault for which he had been convicted, his own perspective affirmed through triangulation with the researcher's assessment of it and that of a knowledgeable and critical third party. To settle on this interpretation would, however, have meant losing sight of that fact that the police, the courts and the taxi driver had all perceived things rather differently. Was it not equally possible, given his self-confessed propensity for violence, proclivity for spitting, drinking and mental health problems, that there was another side to Alan, a more unpredictable, frightening and abusive side than the one both I and his probation officer had seen? In order to answer this question I returned to the pen portrait armed with theories and hypothesis drawn from the literatures on hate crime and racism. Thereafter, two further contradictions began to stand out in the transcripts:

1   The contradiction in Alan's attitudes towards women. Alan's self-professed 'respect' for women sat uncomfortably with the chauvinism he indulged in with other football hooligans and the disrespectful behaviour his ex-partners had experienced from him.
2   The contradiction in how he recalled what the taxi driver had said on the first journey. The first account of this journey entailed a story about what the taxi driver said he *would not mind doing*; the second entailed a story in which the taxi driver appeared to be making insinuations about what he thought *Alan would have liked to do* to two female strangers.

Could a fuller understanding of the role of these contradictions in Alan's thinking help explain why Alan had wanted to deliver the 'ultimate insult' – spitting – to the taxi driver? Had this act somehow enabled him to temporarily avoid the feelings of loneliness and grief he was trying to satiate with alcohol while 'trawling' for another relationship? Was there a projective dimension to the generalisation Alan made about the way in which Asian men, like the taxi driver and his nieces' husband, 'treat their women'? Was there a connection to be made between Alan's own assertions about his sexuality and what he presumed, probably erroneously, the taxi driver was insinuating about him? Returning to the transcripts with these questions, I was able to produce an analysis that showed how it was possible for someone who was not overtly racist, like Alan, to become susceptible, in the 'heat' of the moment, to a racialised form of hatred of which he was not ordinarily conscious, and hence to make a much wider argument about why racial aggravated crime remains such an elusive phenomenon for those trying to tackle it in, despite a swathe of reform to the law and the institutions of criminal justice in recent years.

Readers interested in the exact substance of this analysis should consult Gadd (2009). What is important to underline here, however, is that psychosocial analysis requires the researcher to commit to an ongoing dialogue with the original data in all its complexity, their own and other's people's queries about it, potential explanations, and a continuous sensitivity to the tensions within and between inner world experiences (like love and hate) and outer-world phenomenon (like racist attacks). Working in this way it becomes possible to achieve more holistic interpretations than are often achieved by other approaches to criminological research studies, including the kinds of qualitative research that construct a common, but often quite meaningless, mindset out of many different people's responses. Often, however, it is only possible to achieve a more nuanced analysis by cultivating, over time, a heightened level of reflexivity in the research process, something which is much harder to do than those sceptical about the worth of positing 'defended subjects' usually realise. This, as Wengraf (2001: 144, emphases in original) surmises, is because

[i]n an interview, there are two anxious defended subjects, not one. In the interview, *the researcher also* must be assumed to be at least potentially 'motivated to not know' certain things that would be upsetting for him or her, and thus subtly or obviously influencing the production of some or all of the text of the interview. In addition, the researcher's anxieties do not vanish after the end of the interview. They may even be exacerbated.

Defence and anxiety are features of the researcher-position right through data-analysis and into the writing up and publication. The operation of such anxiety in the stages of analysis and interpretation cannot be avoided, but its shape and implications need to be detected and combated.

CURRENT CONTROVERSIES AND NEW HORIZONS

Wengraf's own view is that such anxieties are best combated through panel discussions. Advancing the objective hermeneutical approach advocated by Ulrich Oevermann and colleagues (1987), those using the method preferred by Wengraf, bring together groups of people – often colleagues, doctoral students and co-researchers – to examine extracts from the transcript and to hypothesise about what kinds of meanings may lie latent within the spoken words. For Wengraf, bolstering the diversity within the panel is the best protection against the hindrances of the researcher's defensiveness: 'the more intercultural and cross cultural the panel, the more the "sleeping assumptions" of any given researcher are likely to be disturbed and raised to consciousness' (Wengraf, 2001: 145). But it is also the case that whether or not people are able to overcome their defensiveness can depend as much upon *how the issues are presented* to them, *who is doing the presenting*, and, critically, their perception of *whether that person holds them in high esteem*, as the actual substance of challenge being made. In panel discussions many of these moderating prerequisites are often lacking. Consequently, when panel members interrogate the role of the interviewer they run the risk of entrenching the researcher's defensiveness further (Froggett and Wengraf, 2004).

In criminology we are only just starting to come to terms with the ways in which the relationships between interviewers and interviewees have shaped what we think we know about crime and criminals, Loraine Gelsthorpe's (2007) intricate analysis of the relationship between Clifford Shaw and Stanley unearthing an untold story of such dynamics that changed the direction of our discipline for the course of century (ibid. 2007). Rarely are criminologists privileged enough to get to know their subjects as well as Shaw got to know Stanley, even if those of us who do a lot of biographical and narrative work often leave our research encounters with the perception that our research participants are more like us than we had anticipated. How, when and why we identify with some research subjects and not others ought to be reflected upon much more frequently and in much greater depth. As I have documented in my research about domestic violence, it is all too tempting to pass over those research encounters where one has struggled to identify with the interviewee as simply 'bad interviews', rather than ponder what it was about the research relationship that mired the interviewee's participation (Gadd, 2004). Shoshanna Garfield and her colleagues (2010), by contrast, have illustrated, how identification with what research participants say can blind one to the meanings behind the words spoken. Garfield's analysis exposes how her unconscious (over)identification with an interviewee who complained about how little his partner did around the house caused her to overlook what she already knew about him, namely that he had blinded his wife by hitting her in the face with a rolling pin.

What both my own work and that of Garfield et al. reveals therefore is just how emotionally and intellectually demanding engaging with the kind of 'toxic' material the Free Association Narrative Interview Method can elicit from violence perpetrators often is; how acute the desire 'to have company in the hard task of bearing witness' to this material can be (ibid. 166); and how unnerving it is to confront the 'wounded parts' of oneself that often underscore interviewer–interviewee identifications when they come to the fore in data analysis, or even in the course of presenting this kind of research to wider audiences (ibid: 167). The opportunity to bear witness to the toxicity of what some criminological research participants say and the distress, pain and trauma that often lie behind it is, of course, both what attracts some researchers to using the Free Association Narrative Interview Method in research with offenders and also what puts others off it. It is a method that often enlarges one's own emotional repertoire while putting intense demands on it. These demands tend to persist long after the interviews have ended and the writing up has commenced, for they also – as my experiences of revisiting the case of Alan reveals – provide the nagging doubts that inspire intellectually driven analyses. To put the matter starkly, *in research addressed to why violence perpetrators do what they do*, criminologists are often faced with a moral dilemma: to conduct research which avoids eliciting subject matter that is distressing and complicated but, at the same time, has its limits with respect to the extent to which it can realistically hope to challenge preconceptions about populations that are feared, despised or little understood; or to conduct research that is prepared to engage with the distress of its subject population as a matter of course, less sure what it means to secure informed consent from participants whose spontaneous disclosures may lead in any direction, takes longer to digest the meaning of the data it produces, and more cautious in terms of what it promises with respect to the generalisabilty of its findings. To the extent that psychosocial research is offered in the service of rehumanising some of the most demonised sections of our populations, this second approach remains for me, the more promising; but only if those of us engaged in it are prepared to separate our data from the layers of interpretation we subject to it so that both can be interrogated critically by others. I hope, therefore, that this chapter is a contribution to preparing those looking to acquire the skills and foresight needed to embark on these tasks.

RECOMMENDED READING

In addition to the material cited previously, interested readers may wish to consult: Gadd, D. and Jefferson, T. (2007) *Psychosocial Criminology* (London: Sage) for an overview of criminological research conducted using the methods described in this chapter.

Also, *Theoretical Criminology* 11(4) gives an illustration of what different psychosocial approaches can bring to a single case.

In Bereswill, M. (2008) 'Gender and subjectivity in the interview situation'. *Psychoanalysis, Culture and Society* 13(3): 316–324, the author gives an example of how to utilise the transference relationships between interviewers and research participants to enhance criminological analyses.

In Frosh, S. and Saville Young, L. (2008) 'Psychoanalytic approaches to qualitative psychology' in C. Willig and W. Stainton-Rogers, (eds) *The SAGE Handbook of Qualitative Research in Psychology*, pp. 108–125 (London: Sage), the authors give a wider ranging appraisal of psychodynamically informed qualitative methods.

Datasets produced using the Free Association Narrative Interview Method, together with advanced teaching resources for training postgraduate students and researchers in it, can be accessed via the Economic and Social Data Service online at www.esds.ac.uk. The website of the UK based *Psychosocial Network* can be accessed at www.psychosocial-network.org. The website of the *International Research Group of Psycho-Societal Analysis* can be accessed at www. irgfpsa.org.

REFERENCES

Adorno, T.W. (1950) 'Politics and economics in interview material' in T.W. Adorno, T.W., E. Frenkel-Brunswik, D.J. Levinson, and R. Nevitt Sanford (eds), *The Authoritarian Personality* (pp. 654–726). New York: John Harper.

Anderson, K. and Quinney, R. (1999) *Erich Fromm and Critical Criminology*. Illinois: University of Illinois Press.

Bar-On, D. (2004) 'A socially and historically contextualised psychoanalytic perspective: holocaust survival and suffering' in P. Chamberlayne, J. Bornat and U. Apitzsch (eds), *Biographical Methods and Professional Practice* (pp. 101–113). Bristol: Policy Press.

Benney, M. (1936) *Low Company*. London: Peter Davies.

Bowlby, J. (1946) *Forty-four Juvenile Thieves.* London: Balliére, Tindall and Cox.

Branscombe, N., Ellemers, N., Spears, R. and Doosje, B. (1999) 'The context and content of social identity threat' in N. Ellemers, R. Spears, and B. Doosje (eds), *Social Identity* (pp. 35–58). Oxford: Blackwell.

Breckner, R. (1998) 'The Biographical-Interpretive Method – principles and procedures' in *SOSTRIS Working Paper 2* (pp. 91–104). London: UEL.

Brown, A.P. (2003) 'From individual to social defences in psycho-social criminology'. *Theoretical Criminology* 7(4): 421–437.

Burgess, E.W. (1930) 'Discussion' in C. Shaw (ed.)*The Jack* (pp. 184–197). Chicago: University of Chicago Press.

Burney, E. and Rose. G., (2002) *Racist Offences – How is the Law Working?* London: Home Office.

Carlen, P. (1980) (eds) *Criminal Women*. Cambridge: Polity.

Clarke, S. (2006) 'Theory and practice: psychoanalytic sociology as psycho-social studies'. *Sociology* 40(6): 1153–1169.

Clarke, S. Hahn, H. and Hoggett, P. (2008a) (eds) *Object Relations and Social Relations*, London: Karnac.

Clarke, S. (2008b) 'Psycho-social research: relating self, identity and otherness' in S. Clarke, H. Hahn and P. Hoggett (eds), *Object Relations and Social Relations* (pp. 113–136). London: Karnac.

Du Gay, P., Evans, J. and Redman, P. (2000) *Identity: A Reader*. London: Sage.

Evans, J. (2003) 'Victims and vigilantes: thinking psychoanalytically about anti-paedophile action'. *Theoretical Criminology* 7(2): 163–189.

Froggett, L. and Wengraf, T. (2004) 'Interpreting interviews in the light of research team dynamics'. *Critical Psychology* 10(1): 94–122.

Frosh, S. (2003) 'Psychosocial studies and psychology: is a critical approach emerging'? *Human Relations* 56(12): 1545–1567.

Gadd, D (2004) 'Making sense of interviewee-interviewer dynamics in narratives about violence in intimate relationships'. *International Journal of Social Research Methodology* 7(5): 383–401.

Gadd, D. (2006) 'The role of recognition in the desistance process: a case study of a far-right activist'. *Theoretical Criminology* 10(2): 179–202.

Gadd, D. (2009) 'Aggravating racism and elusive motivation'. *British Journal of Criminology* 49(6): 755–771.

Gadd, D. Dixon, B. Jefferson, T. (2005) *Why Do They Do It? Racial Harassment in North Staffordshire,* Keele University: Staffs.

Garfield, S., Reavey, P. and Kotecha, M. (2010) 'Footprints in a toxic landscape: reflexivity and validation in the Free

Association Narrative Analysis method'. *Qualitative Research in Psychology* 7(2): 156–169.

Gelsthorpe, L. (2007) 'The Jack-Roller: telling a story?' *Theoretical Criminology* 11(4): 515–542.

Glover, E. (1960) *The Roots of Crime.* London: Imago.

Hamblin Smith, M. (1922/1933) *The Psychology of the Criminal,* 2nd Edition. London: Metheun.

Henriques, J., Hollway, W., Urwin, C., Venn. C. and Walkerdine, V. (1984) *Changing the Subject.* London: Methuen.

Hood-Williams, J. (2001) 'Gender, masculinities and crime: from structures to psyches'. *Theoretical Criminology* 5(1): 37–60.

Hollway, W. (1989) *Subjectivity and Method in Psychology.* London: Sage.

Hollway, W. and Jefferson, T. (1998) '"A kiss is just a kiss": date rape, gender and subjectivity'. *Sexualities* 1(4): 405–423.

Hollway, W. and Jefferson, T. (2000) *Doing Qualitative Research Differently.* London: Sage.

Hydén, M. (2008) 'Narrating sensitive topics' in C. Squire, M. Andrews, and M. Tamoukou (eds), *Doing Narrative Research* (pp. 121–136). London: Sage.

Jefferson, T. (1997) 'The Tyson rape trial'. *Social and Legal Studies* 6(2): 281–301.

Jefferson, T. (2002) 'For a psychosocial criminology' in K. Carrington and R. Hogg (eds), *Critical Criminology* (pp. 145–167). Collumpton: Willan.

Katz, J. (1988) *Seductions of Crime.* New York: Basic Books.

Kvale, S. (1996) *InterViews,* London: Sage.

Layton, L. (2008) (ed.) 'British Psycho(-)Social Studies'. *Psychoanalysis, Culture and Society* 13(4): 339–40.

Oevermann, U., with Allert, T., Konau, E. and Krambeck, J. (1987) 'Structures of meaning and objective hermeneutics' in V. Meja (ed.), *Modern German Sociology* (pp. 436–448). New York: Columbia Press.

Radzinowicz, L. and King, J. (1977) *The Growth of Crime.* London: Hamish Hamilton.

Rosenthal, G. (1993) 'Reconstruction of life stories' in R. Josselson and A. Lieblich (eds), *The Narrative Study of Lives 1* (pp. 59–91). London: Sage.

Rosenthal, G. and Bar-On. (1992) 'A biographical case study of a victimizer's daughter's strategy'. *Journal of Narrative and Life History* 2(2): 105–127.

Shaw, C. (1930) *The Jack-Roller.* Chicago: University of Chicago Press.

Soothill, K. (1999) (ed.) *Criminal Conversations.* London: Routledge.

Sykes, G. and Matza, D. (1957) 'Techniques of neutralization' *American Sociological Review* 22(6): 664–670.

Wengraf, T. (2001) *Qualitative Research Interviewing.* London: Sage.

Wetherell, M. (2005) 'Unconscious conflict or everyday accountability?' *Social Psychology* 44(2): 169–173.

Yin, R. (2009) *Case Study Research,* 4th Edition. London: Sage.

4

Grounding the Analysis of Gender and Crime: Accomplishing and Interpreting Qualitative Interview Research

Jody Miller

INTRODUCTION

As a feminist scholar and sociological criminologist, a primary question guiding my research concerns the impact of gender stratification, gendered practices, and gender ideologies on criminal offending. I seek to challenge and complicate binary assumptions about women and men, and in doing so carefully attend to the complex ways in which gender – as one of the most basic organizing structures within and across societies – configures individuals' life experiences in ways that lead them to crime, and influences their motivations for offending, strategies for accomplishing it, and the situations and contexts in which this offending takes place. My method of choice for doing this research is the analysis of qualitative in-depth interview data.

In this chapter, I address the following questions: What makes in-depth interviewing a particularly useful methodological approach for feminist criminology? How is research that utilizes interview data put to use for understanding the relationships between gender, inequality, and crime? Finally, how do those of us who analyze in-depth interviews in our research go about doing so – what's the actual process by which we turn our data into meaningful theoretical contributions?

I draw from three of my research projects – on young women's participation in gangs, women's and men's accomplishment of robbery, and young men's sexual violence against young women – to describe why qualitative interviews are my data of choice, and how I use inductive analytic techniques to produce my research findings.

FEMINIST CRIMINOLOGY AND QUALITATIVE INTERVIEW ACCOUNTS

Sociologist Christine Williams (2000: 9) describes academic feminism as 'a general approach to understanding the status of women in society'. Notwithstanding the range of theoretical and methodological approaches brought to bear on the question, she observes that 'all feminist social scientists share the goals of understanding the sources of inequality and advocating changes to empower women' (ibid.). Thus, what differentiates *feminist* criminology from other criminological analyses that consider 'women and crime' is the conceptual understanding of gender that guides our research: a concern with understanding *gender* is as much a starting point in feminist criminological analyses as is the concern with understanding *crime* (Daly, 1998).

Early treatises on feminist methodology, particularly the use of in-depth interview techniques, were situated in women's standpoint theory (Oakley, 1981). These were grounded in feminist goals of 'giving voice' to women and their experiences, which had historically been silenced (see DeVault, 1999; Smith, 1987). This remains an important goal of feminist scholars, though with critical understandings of its challenges. Initially there was a relatively uncritical assumption that when women interviewed women, their shared experiences *as women* would result in identification, rapport, and consequently, the authentic revelation of 'women's experiences'. These rather romanticized assumptions have since been problematized, however. Most scholars now recognize, for example, that no research can provide authentic access to individuals' 'experiences' or unmediated access to 'truth', and this includes the accounts produced in the context of interviews (see Miller and Glassner, 2004; Silverman, 2006). Moreover, feminist scholars now recognize that women don't simply share experiences *as women*. Instead, many facets of difference come into play when we attempt to understand women's and men's lives, including race, ethnicity, cultural identity, nation, class, and age, as well as individual life trajectories and experiences (Presser, 2005; Song and Parker, 1995; Veroff and DiStefano, 2002).

Given this multifaceted understanding of the research process and its goals, many feminist scholars identify unique contributions that qualitative interview approaches can make in theorizing about gender and crime. This results both from how feminist scholars conceptualize gender, and from our insistence that examining the meaning and nature of gender relations and inequalities are a critical component of understanding and theorizing about crime and criminality. To begin with, feminist scholarship challenges the premise that gender is simply an individual-level independent variable. Instead, our research starts with the understanding that the social world is systematically shaped by relations of sex and gender, and these operate at all levels of society, including individual, interactional, organizational and structural (see Connell, 2002; Risman, 2004). As Daly and Chesney-Lind (1988: 504) sum up, '[G]ender and gender relations order social life and social institutions in fundamental ways.'

As a consequence, feminist scholars recognize that gender operates both within the practices and organization of social life, as well as within 'the discursive fields by which women [and men] are constructed or construct themselves' (Daly and Maher, 1998: 4). Taken for granted ideologies about gender are profoundly embedded in social life, and often include common-sense notions of fundamental difference between women and men, coupled with the perception of maleness as the normative standard. These deeply engrained assumptions are regularly found in academic research and theory; the policies, practices and operation of organizations and institutions; and in the interpretive frameworks women and men bring to their daily lives. Moreover, it is through the enactment of these gendered meanings that the most persistent, yet often invisible, facets of gender inequality are reproduced.

Perhaps most pronounced is the tendency to reproduce conventional understandings of gender *difference* (see Miller, 2002). Such interpretive frameworks – particularly cultural emphases on a psychologically based 'character dichotomy' between women and men (Connell, 2002: 40) often guide the understandings of those we investigate, and can also seep into researchers' conceptualizations. Thus, feminist scholars grapple with what Daly and Maher (1998: 1) refer to as an *intellectual double shift*: the dual challenge of examining the impact of gender and gender inequality in 'real' life, while simultaneously deconstructing the intertwined ideologies about gender that guide social practices (see Connell, 2002). Indeed, illuminating the relationship between ideological features of gender and gendered practice is a key facet of feminist scholarship.

In addition, feminist conceptualizations of gender often require us to move beyond what broad, global explanations provide. While our starting point is the recognition that social life is patterned by gender, we also recognize – and empirical evidence demonstrates – that this gender order (Connell, 2002) is complex and shifting. For this reason, a key feature of feminist scholarship is the development of what Daly (1998) refers to as 'middle range' theorizing – developing theoretical understandings that seek primarily to explain how broader structural forces are realized within particular organizational, situational and interactional contexts.

So what does the analysis of qualitative in-depth interviews have to offer in our attempts to attend to these complexities and challenges? From my point of view, the strength of such interviews lies in what they are: reflective accounts of social life offered from the points of view of research participants. As such, they provide two intertwined kinds of data: descriptive evidence of the nature of the phenomena under investigation – including the contexts and situations in which it emerges – as well as insights into the cultural frames that people use to make sense of their experiences (Miller and Glassner, 2004). Both are especially useful for feminist theorizing about gender and crime, particularly in the context of the intellectual double shift I noted previously.

In general, qualitative research is oriented toward the creation of contextual understandings of social worlds, emphasizing complexities in the meanings and social processes that operate within them. Interview data, in which people describe and explain their behaviors and experiences, help us identify and understand social processes and patterns at the interactional and situational levels, as well as the meanings people attribute to their experiences and behaviors (see Charmaz, 2006; Spradley, 1979; but compare Silverman, 2006). In criminology, this includes, for example, examining *in situ* motivations for behaviors such as offending or desistance (Maruna, 2001), social processes associated with crime, criminally involved groups, or the streets (Maher, 1997), situational analyses of crime events (Mullins and Wright, 2004; Wright and Decker, 1997), as well as life history analyses that examine pathways into and out of offending (Giordano, 2010). As such, qualitative in-depth interviews can provide us with ground level understandings of crime and criminal behavior.

In addition, because in-depth interviews are *accounts*, they hold promise for examining the social world from the points of view of research participants, and for exploring how meanings are constructed together, including in the interview itself (see Miller, 2010). When analyzed not just as a source of information about the 'who, what, when, where, and how' of criminal offending, but also as a 'linguistic device employed whenever an action is subjected to valuative inquiry' (Scott and Lyman, 1968: 46), the narrative accounts within in-depth interviews provide insight into 'culturally embedded normative explanations [of events and behaviors, because they] represent ways in which people organize views of themselves, of others, and of their social worlds' (Orbuch, 1997: 455).

Given feminist scholars' concerns with how language and discourse 'reflect and help constitute' gendered meaning systems (Cameron, 1998: 946), the analysis of in-depth interviews thus offers an especially useful tool for feminist scholars in simultaneously examining both social patterns and social meanings associated with gender, inequality and crime. Recognizing interview accounts as evidence of both the nature of the phenomenon under investigation and the cultural frameworks that individuals use to interpret their experiences means that, in one's analysis, juxtaposing these facets of accounts – even or especially when they appear incongruous – can be useful for developing theoretical insight. Qualitative interview data is thus particularly well suited for addressing the goals of feminist

criminologists for understanding how gender and gender inequality shape the experiences of those involved in crime.

ANALYZING QUALITATIVE INTERVIEW DATA

Most qualitative researchers use some version of grounded theory techniques in their data analysis. Charmaz (2006: 2–3) provides the following explanation of what this entails:

> Stated simply, grounded theory methods consist of systematic, yet flexible guidelines for collecting and analyzing qualitative data to construct theories 'grounded' in the data themselves. The guidelines offer a set of general principles and heuristic devices rather than formulaic rules … Thus, data form the foundation of our theory and our analysis of these data generates the concepts we construct.

One of the most important principles of grounded theory analyses is that preliminary data analysis begins at the start of the project. Initial analyses of both what people say and how they say it open up new avenues of inquiry and also generate preliminary hypotheses to be further explored during ongoing data collection and analysis. This is accomplished through close and continuous reading of the data, during which the researcher codes the data and begins documenting preliminary analytic observations and hypotheses, which are then compared with and analyzed in light of additional data collected. Coding, as Charmaz explains, is a process by which 'we attach labels to segments of data that depict what each segment is about. Coding distills data, sorts them, and gives us a handle for making comparisons with other segments of data' (ibid. 3).

The particular analysis strategy a qualitative interview researcher uses may vary for any given project. What they share in common, however, is recognition of the importance of beginning initial data coding by using grounded, open coding strategies. This process helps avoid the application of pre-conceived concepts, assists in generating new ideas, and keeps the researcher thoroughly grounded in the data (Charmaz, 2006). Initial coding can take a variety of forms, including reading the interview text word by word, line by line, and incident by incident. The more closely we read the data, the more readily we can move beyond taken for granted or preconceived ideas we bring to our research, and the more likely we are to discover emergent concepts and patterns in the data.

An important part of the process is paying specific attention to interview participants' unique language and speech patterns (Spradley, 1979). Charmaz (2006: 55) refers to these as *in vivo* codes – terms or phrases that provide telling insights into social worlds or processes. In my recent work, *Getting Played* (2008), for example, the insider term 'play' and its iterations became central to my analysis, and was even the basis of the book's title. While analyzing interviews with urban African-American youth about interactions between young women and young men, and their relation to gendered violence, I was struck by the common and varied ways in which the term 'play' entered into youths' accounts. Treating this as an *in vivo* code, I carefully examined its usage to identify the actions it represented and the implicit meanings 'play' attached to them. This led me to an analysis of the variety of ways that 'play' claims are used to minimize the significance of behavioral patterns that are harmful to girls. To illustrate, Box 4.1 provides a partial excerpt of my analysis of play claims associated with sexual harassment.

In vivo codes can also be phrases that condense and distill significant analytic concepts. During

---

Box 4.1 Contested play claims: humor or disrespect?

[Y]oung men often downplayed the seriousness of sexual harassment by couching it in terms of 'play'. Antwoin said, '[Y]eah, I grabbed a girl bootie a couple of times … we was playing.' Such touching, he said, was best understood as 'like playing around. Sometimes the boys'll be messing with the girls and they'll just grab they bootie or something.' … Similarly, asked why he and his friends touched on girls, Curtis said, 'I don't know, just to have fun. Just playing.'

'Just playing', however, was a characterization young women roundly rejected. Instead, to quote Nicole, girls found boys' sexually harassing behaviors to be 'too much playing'.… Katie complained, '[M]ost of the time boys and girls get into it because boys, they play too much … Like they try to touch you and stuff, or try to talk about you, or put you down in front of they friends to make them feel better … Just talk about you or something like in front of they friends so they can laugh.'

Katie's comments tapped into an important feature of boys' play claims: The primary audience for this 'play' was other young men. As Anishika argued young men's 'humor' was for the benefit of their friends, and at the expense of the young woman:

> They just tryin' to be like this person and that person. They already know, they know what's right. They know right from wrong. But when it's a lot of 'em, they think that stuff is cute, calling girls B's [bitches] and rats and all that stuff. They think that stuff cute, and some of these girls think that stuff cute. But it's not cute.

In fact, [young men's accounts] are indicative of the role male peers played in facilitating young men's behaviors. Thus, Frank [explained], 'some people, when they see [you touch on a girl], they'll laugh or they give you some props. They give you like a little five or something like that. That's what the dudes do.'… Thus, a number of girls said boys simply used play claims as an excuse for their behavior, and described explicitly rejecting these claims. For example, angry after a young man made sexual comments about her, Destiny said he responded to her anger by saying, 'you ain't even gotta get that serious. I was just playin' wit' you.' She replied, 'I don't care. I don't want you playin' with me like that, stop playin' with me like that.' And Nicole explained, 'sometimes boys make it like, act like it's funny. But it's not. 'Cause you touchin' a girl and she don't wanna be touched. So don't touch me, period. Don't even think about touchin' me.'

Indeed, despite young men's routine use of play claims, their own accounts belied the notion that their behaviors were simply intended as harmless fun. For example, several young men said part of the fun in taunting girls was getting an angry response … Moreover, several young men described treating girls in a derogatory way specifically to demarcate their (male) space and make it clear to the girl that she wasn't welcome … [O]ne additional factor belies young men's characterizations of their behavior as 'just play'. Asked when harassing behaviors took place or whether they were directed at particular girls, a number of young men described targeting young women they deemed to be 'stuck up', unwilling to show sexual or romantic interest, or otherwise unimpressed with the boy … Curtis said, '[W]e'll see a girl in like a short skirt or short shorts, and we be kind of talking to her, and she don't, she ain't giving nobody no play. So we just get to playing with her, touching on her butt and all that.'

From Miller 2008: 82–7

her interview for *Getting Played*, one of the young women described offering the following advice to her sister for avoiding sexual violence: 'Protect yourself, respect yourself. 'Cause if you don't, guys won't.' Read in passing, it could easily be seen as simple advice. But my line-by-line coding flagged it as a phrase worth further examination. I made note of it in an analytic memo, and then paid close attention to how youths talked about protection and respect. Ultimately, my analysis revealed that it succinctly crystallized youths' understandings of the causes of sexual violence, and girls' risk-management strategies in the face of limited interpersonal and institutional support (see Miller, 2008: 143–9).

Beyond the importance of open and *in vivo* coding, qualitative researchers employ a variety of specific coding and analysis strategies, depending on the research question at hand. Charmaz (2006) recommends that grounded theory research should code for *action* within the data, using gerund codes to preserve social processes. Lofland and Lofland (1984) encourage scholars to identify *topics* for analysis by combining particular units of analysis (e.g., practices, episodes, encounters or relationships) with their aspects (e.g., cognitive, emotional or hierarchical). Once identified, the researcher rigorously examines the data for instances that are topically relevant. Spradley (1979) utilizes domain analysis, by using semantic relationships to ask structured questions from the data (e.g., X is a kind of Y; X is a way to do Y). Each of these strategies allow us to approach the data in a systematic way, with the goal of moving from initial coding to systematic theoretical analyses.

Good qualitative research emerges from the thoroughness and rigor of the inductive analysis. In the process, *emergent* hypotheses are identified in the course of analysis as patterns begin to emerge. These hypotheses are then tested, refined or rejected using the project data. A variety of strategies have been devised to ensure the rigor of the analytic induction process. Most important is the use of constant comparative methods, which are strengthened through the use of tabulations to identify the strength of patterns (see Silverman, 2006: 296–301, for a concise description of these strategies), and aid in the identification of and analysis of deviant cases. As Charmaz (2006: 54) describes, 'you use "*constant comparative methods*" … to establish analytic distinctions – and thus make comparisons at each level of analytic work … For example, compare interview statements and incidents within the same interview and compare statements and incidents in different interviews.' This allows you to test and refine emergent hypotheses against the data. It is also the case that qualitative researchers tend to

reject the position that any research can tap into 'pure' objective data, regardless of the methodological approach of the researcher. Thus, consideration of the researcher's place in the research process – from formulating research questions, to data collection, to analysis – is necessary. To illustrate these analytic strategies – focusing specifically on the utility of qualitative interview research for studying gender and crime – I now turn to a more detailed description of several of my research projects.

Up it up: Studying gender stratification and the accomplishment of robbery

Early in my career, I was afforded the opportunity to utilize my colleagues' in-depth interview data with armed robbers (Wright and Decker, 1997) to examine the impact of gender on the enactment of robbery (Miller, 1998). My analysis of this data helps illustrate several key features of qualitative analysis techniques. I approached the data with two guiding questions: How do women, as compared to men, account for their motivations to commit robbery? And how do women, as compared to men, describe the process by which they accomplish robbery? The use of comparative samples – in this case female and male robbers – is a particularly useful approach when doing qualitative research, because it allows for some specification of similarities and variations in social processes and meaning systems across groups or settings.

In this particular investigation, I coded the data with these two specific research questions in mind. First, I looked for evidence in the data for how robbers described their motivations to commit robbery, and compared accounts both within and across gender. Next, I coded incident-by-incident, examining how women and men in the sample described accomplishing the robberies they committed. My identification within the data of both similarities and differences across gender led me to theorize about the impact of gender stratification in offender networks on women's participation in crime. This is an example of the type of 'middle range' theorizing described previously – my research findings pointed me in the direction of stratification as the best fit for explaining the patterns I identified, and offered 'an incisive analytic framework' for explaining the structures and processes I uncovered.

Specifically, I found congruence across gender in interview participants' accounts of their *motivations* for committing robberies. For both women and men, the incentives to commit robbery were primarily economic – to get money, jewelry and other status-conferring goods, but also included elements of thrill-seeking, attempting to overcome boredom, and revenge. However, women's and men's accounts of *how* they went about committing robberies were strikingly different. And within gender comparisons of incident accounts were equally illuminating.

Specifically, men's descriptions of their commission of robbery were markedly similar to one another. Their accounts were variations around a single theme: using physical violence and/or a gun placed on or at close proximity to the victim in a confrontational manner. The key, one explained, was to make sure the victim knew 'that we ain't playing'. Another described confronting his victims by placing the gun at the back of their head, where 'they feel it', while saying, 'Give it up, motherfucker, don't move or I'll blow your brains out.' Explaining the positioning of the gun, he noted, 'When you feel that steel against your head … [it] carries a lot of weight.' Closely examining each man's accounts of their strategies for committing robberies, as well as their descriptions of particular incidents, revealed that they accomplished robberies in noticeably uniform ways.

In contrast, women's accounts were notable both for the greater variation in the strategies they described using to accomplish robberies, and for their absence of accounts that paralleled those provided by men, except under very specific circumstances: when they committed robberies in partnership with male accomplices. In short, though men described routinely using firearms to commit robberies, and placing them on or in close proximity to the back of the victim's head, women's strategies for committing robberies varied according to the gender of their victim, and the presence or absence of co-offenders. They described three predominant ways in which they committed robberies: targeting female victims in physically confrontational robberies that did not involve firearms, targeting male victims by appearing sexually available, and participating with male co-offenders during street robberies of men.

Insights about the role of gender stratification in the commission of robbery emerged particularly prominently when I examined women's accounts of robbing men. These incidents nearly always involved firearms, but rarely involved physical contact. Notably, the rationale women provided for this strategy was especially telling. As one explained, '[I]f we waste time touching men there is a possibility that they can get the gun off of us, while we wasting time touching them they could do anything. So we just keep the gun

straight on them. No touching, no moving, just straight gun at you.' The circumstances surrounding the enactment of female-on-male robberies were unique as well. The key, in each case, was that the woman pretended to be sexually interested in her male victim. When his guard dropped, this provided a safe opportunity for the robbery to occur.

Moreover, women specifically described playing on the stereotypes men held about women in order to accomplish these robberies – including the assumptions that women wouldn't be armed, wouldn't attempt to rob them, and could be taken advantage of sexually. For example, one woman explained

> [T]hey don't suspect that a girl gonna try to get 'em. You know what I'm saying? So it's kind of easier 'cause they like, she looks innocent, she ain't gonna do this, but that's how I get 'em. They put they guard down to a woman … Most of the time, when girls get high they think they can take advantage of us so they always, let's go to a hotel or my crib or something.

Another said, '[T]hey easy to get, we know what they after – sex.'

This and other evidence of the role that gender ideologies played in the enactment of robberies pointed explicitly to the importance of gendered organizational features of the street environment as an important explanatory factor. Most notable was the incongruity between the similarities in women's and men's motives for committing robbery and the dramatic differences in their strategies for accomplishing robbery. As such, the research highlighted the gender hierarchy present on the streets: while some women were able to carve out a niche for themselves in this setting, they were participating in a male-dominated environment and their robbery strategies reflected an understanding of this. The differences in the way women, as compared to men, accomplished robberies were not a result of differences in their goals or needs. Instead, they reflected practical choices women made in the context of a gender-stratified environment – one in which, on the whole, men were perceived as strong and women as weak. In this particular project, it was not just the availability of in-depth interview data that resulted in the analysis briefly described here, but also specifically the *comparative* nature of the data. My ability to juxtapose women's and men's accounts facilitated the identification of commonalities and differences across gender, and thus allowed me to build an analytic framework to make sense of them. Moreover, as illustrated in Box 4.2, deviant case analysis further strengthened my analytic framework.

Box 4.2 Deviant case analysis: the 'masculine' woman robber

Once emergent hypotheses are identified in inductive analysis, it is necessary to actively seek out and account for cases in the data that are counter to the emergent hypotheses. In the robbery project, my emergent hypothesis what that women's enactment of robbery differs from men's based on strategic choices they make in recognition of gender stratification on the streets, including men's perceptions of women as weak, and thus ineffectual or non-threatening as robbers.

   Closely examining robbery incident accounts, there was one clear outlier: a lone woman who described committing a 'masculine' style robbery by herself and against a male victim. When using analytic induction techniques, it is necessary for researchers to revise their emergent hypotheses until such deviant cases can be accounted for by their analysis. In this case, the answer was straightforward, and actually buttressed the original hypothesis. The outlier (or deviant case) perfectly fit my explanatory framework:

> Ne-Ne explicitly indicates that this robbery was possible because the victim did not know she was a woman. Describing herself physically, she says, 'I'm big, you know.' In addition, her dress and manner masked her gender. 'I had a baseball cap in my car and I seen him … I just turned around the corner, came back down the street, he was out by hisself and I got out of the car, had the cap pulled down over my face and I just went to the back and upped him. Put the gun up to his head.' Being large, wearing a ballcap and enacting the robbery in a masculine style (e.g. putting a gun to his head), allowed her to disguise the fact that she was a woman and thus decrease the victim's likelihood of resisting. She says, 'he don't know right now to this day if it was a girl or a dude' (Miller, 1998: 60).

While it is rare to have such a seamless answer when analyzing deviant cases, this example illustrates both its utility and import for ensuring rigorous inductive analysis in qualitative research.

One of the guys: Studying gender inequality and gender ideologies in youth gangs

The next example I draw from is especially useful for illustrating the 'intellectual double shift' described earlier – in which feminist researchers seek to analyze both the reality of experiences and the sometimes incongruent cultural frames used to make sense of them – as well as the importance of constant comparative techniques for enhancing qualitative analysis. When analyzing in-depth interviews in a study of young women's experiences in gangs, I was faced with two sets of discrepancies that required address. First, while most young women I interviewed were adamant that they were 'equals' with the boys in their gangs,[1] they simultaneously described systematic gender inequalities within these groups. Second, while much of the extant literature on young women in gangs led me to expect strong bonds of solidarity among young women, instead I found the opposite. Many of the young women I spoke with held openly misogynistic attitudes about other girls. Thus, my analysis required me both to make sense of the disconnect between girls' claims that they were 'one of the guys' and their experiences of inequality, and to account for why my research findings were so disparate from the reports of previous research.

A dominant theme in my interviews with young women was their insistence that their gangs were a space of gender equality, where males and females were treated as equals. As one explained, '[T]hey give every last one of us respect the way they give the males.' Another was visibly frustrated with my line of questions about gender, and repeatedly cut me off in response:

> JM: You said before that the gang was about half girls and half guys? Can you tell me more about that? Like you said you don't think there are any differences in terms of what –
> Interviewee: There isn't!
> JM: Ok, can you tell me more –
> Interviewee: Like what? There isn't, there isn't like, there's nothing – boy, girl, white, black, Mexican, Chinese.

Another explained: 'We just like dudes to them. We just like dudes, they treat us like that 'cause we act so much like dudes they can't do nothing. They respect us as females though, but we just so much like dudes that they just don't trip off of it.'

   Despite this prevailing discursive construction of gender equality, the young women's descriptions of the activities and behaviors of gang members markedly contradicted these statements. Instead, without exception, young women described a distinct gender hierarchy within mixed-gender gangs that included male leadership, a sexual double standard with regard to sexual activity, the sexual exploitation of some young women, perceptions of girls as 'weak' and boys as 'strong', and most girls' exclusion from serious gang crime – specifically, those acts that built status and reputation within their groups (Miller, 2001).

It would be easy to simply discount girls' claims of gender equality as wrong or misguided. But, as I noted earlier, making sense of such contradictions provides an important basis for building theoretical insight. My task, then, was to explain the basis on which girls made claims to gender equality and the functions that such claims served. First, I looked carefully at *how* girls made the case that they were treated as equals. Examining their accounts closely, it became apparent that the means by which this was accomplished was not to make broad claims that all women should be treated as equals, but to differentiate themselves from *other* girls – and in the process, uphold the masculine status norms of their groups. As one explained:

> A lot of girls get scared. Don't wanna break their nails and stuff like that. So, ain't no need for them to try to be in no gang. And the ones that's in it, most of the girls that's in act like boys. That's why they in, 'cause they like to fight and stuff. They know how to fight and they use guns and stuff.

In addition, because the young women I interviewed also described a range of gender inequalities in their gangs, they also had to account for these descriptions of girls' mistreatment, and do so in ways that were consistent with their central belief in the norm of gender equality. Again, this required me to look at not only *what* they said about girls' mistreatment, but also *how* they made sense of it. Closely analyzing their accounts, I discovered that young women drew on two types of frames. First, they individualized acts they recognized as involving the mistreatment of females, describing them as unique or exceptional cases. When this was not possible – for instance, when the mistreatment was recurring or routine – they sought ways to hold young women accountable for their mistreatment. They did so both by justifying particular acts as deserved because of the behaviors of the young women in question, and by characterizing *other* young women as possessing particular negative 'female' traits – having 'big mouths', being 'troublemakers', or being 'ho's' or 'wrecks'.[2]

The other piece of the puzzle that required explanation was *why* young women both insisted on their equality and strongly differentiated themselves from other girls. Answering this question

was key to providing an analytic framework that could link the structures of gender inequality in gangs to the processes by which they were reproduced and maintained. I did so by situating their gang participation in the broader contexts of their environments and life experiences, including evidence that gender hierarchies in girls' gangs were not unique, but embedded within a broader social environment in which gender inequalities were entrenched.

Thus, to the extent that there *was* normative space within gangs for 'gender equality' – however narrowly defined – gang participation actually provided individual young women with a means of empowerment and self-definition not available in other contexts. But this required them to accept a 'patriarchal bargain' (Kandiyoti, 1988) by which *they* could lay claim to being 'one of the guys' only by supporting and justifying the mistreatment of *other* girls. Identifying with dominant beliefs about women, and rejecting such images for themselves, allowed them to construct a space of gender equality *for themselves*, and draw particular advantages from their gangs that were less available in other social spaces in their lives (see Miller, 2001: chapter 8, for a more detailed account of the analysis).

As noted, the other challenge I faced with this research was that my findings were in contrast to previous research on young women in gangs, which tended to uncover bonds of solidarity among young women (see Joe and Chesney-Lind, 1995; Lauderback et al., 1992). This also required an explanation. I began by looking closely at what differences might exist between the gangs previous researchers had studied and those represented in my sample, and what I noticed was that the gender composition of many of the gangs from which my sample was drawn were 'skewed' groups, in which the preponderance of members were male. In contrast, other studies reported findings on gangs that appeared to be either gender-balanced, or were all female. This led me to think about the role of group proportion in shaping gender dynamics in gangs. Sociological research on organizations, for example, has long found that the '*relative* numbers of socially and culturally different people in a group are … critical in shaping interactional dynamics' (Kanter, 1977: 965). Why wouldn't this also apply in youth gangs?

To test this hypothesis, I employed a constant comparative method within my own data, whereby the researcher 'always attempt[s] to find another case through which to test out a provisional hypothesis' (Silverman, 2006: 296). I carefully sought instances in my data in which girls strongly articulated their position as 'one of the guys', as well as instances in which girls were critical of gender inequalities and espoused more close and supportive relationships with other girls. What I discovered supported my hypothesis – the handful of girls in my study who were in gender-balanced or all-female gangs tended not to match the pattern I had previously uncovered. My distinct findings about 'one of the guys' were shaped by the gendered organizational structure of their groups, and this pattern was revealed to me through the use of constant comparative methods in the analytic process.

Running trains: Gaining insight through attention to the interview as a joint accomplishment

Earlier in the chapter, I noted that qualitative researchers tend to reject the position that research can uncover 'pure' objective data. In the context of in-depth interviewing, an important part of this is recognizing that the interview itself is a particular kind of interaction, in which both participants – the interviewer and the interviewee – are constructing narrative versions of the social world. The accounts produced in the context of interviews are, as noted earlier, 'linguistic device[s] employed whenever an action is subjected to valuative inquiry' (Scott and Lyman, 1968: 46). We saw this in gang girls' claims of being 'one of the guys.' It is also the case that our social positioning vis-à-vis those we interview affects the interview exchange. Attention to these interactional dynamics within the interview exchange offers an important site for social inquiry (Grenz, 2005; Miller, 2010; Presser, 2005). This is not about trying to control for interviewer effects per se; instead 'what matters is to understand how and where the stories [we collect] are produced, which sort of stories they are, and how we can put them to honest and intelligent use in theorizing about social life' (Miller and Glassner, 2004: 138).

Earlier, I argued that in-depth interview research utilizing comparative *samples* is particularly useful for theory building. Here, I provide an illustration of how comparative analysis of the data collected by different *interviewers* also provides an important opportunity for theorizing about social life. I draw from one particular set of data from my recent project on violence against young women in urban African-American neighborhoods (Miller, 2008) – young men's accounts of 'running trains' on girls: a sexual encounter that involved two or more young men engaging in penetrative sexual acts with a single young woman. Specifically, this example shows that paying attention to how interviewers' social positioning matters in the interview context can reveal a great deal about how individuals construct particular sorts of accounts of their offending, and about the contexts and meanings of this behavior.

Running trains was an all too common phenomenon in the data, with nearly half of the boys interviewed admitting that they had done so. Though researchers routinely classify such incidents as gang rape, and the young women interviewed described their experiences in this way as well, the young men in the study defined girls' participation in trains as consensual. Thus, it was particularly important in the project to examine how young men understood running trains, and especially how they came to perceive these behaviors as consensual. In this case, interviews conducted by two different research assistants – one a white European man (Dennis), the other an African-American woman who grew up in the same community as the research participants (Toya) – revealed two sets of findings about boys' constructions of running trains. These offered distinct types of accounts of the behavior, each of which revealed different dimensions of the meaning and enactment of running trains. Box 4.3 provides excerpts from several of Dennis' and Toya's interviews with young men.

Comparing these two sets of accounts suggests a variety of ways in which Dennis's and Toya's social positions of similarity and difference with these African-American adolescent boys shaped the ways in which they spoke about their participation in running trains. Moreover, the interviewers themselves took different approaches toward the interview exchanges, tied to their interviewing techniques, the kinds of information they were most interested in obtaining, and their own positionality vis-à-vis the interviewees.

An especially striking feature of the accounts provided in young men's interviews with Dennis was the adamancy with which boys claimed that girls were willing, even eager participants. Moreover, their descriptions were particularly graphic, focusing specific attention on the details of their sexual performances. Dennis was responded to by the young men as a naïve white male academic who knows little about street life (see also Miller, 2008: 232–4). His foreignness, as evidenced by his Dutch accent, further heightened the young men's perceptions of him as different. Thus, they appear to tell their stories in ways that simultaneously play on what they do have in common – maleness (and thus a perceived shared understanding of women as sexual objects) – and position themselves as particularly successful in their sexual prowess, an exaggerated feature of hegemonic masculinity in distressed urban neighborhoods in the US (Anderson, 1999) that marks their difference from Dennis.

Notice that both Lamont's and Frank's accounts emphasized their sexual performance. In fact, research on gang rape suggests that group processes play a central role. The enactment of such

---

Box 4.3 Young men's accounts of running trains

INTERVIEW EXCERPTS WITH DENNIS

Lamont: I mean, one be in front, one be in back. You know sometimes, you know like, say, you getting in her ass and she might be sucking the other dude dick. Then you probably get her, you probably get her to suck your dick while he get her in the ass. Or he probably, either I'll watch, and so she sucking your dick, or while you fuck her in the ass. It, I mean, it's a lot of ways you can do it.

Frank: There's this one girl, she a real, real freak ... She wanted me and my friend to run a train on her.... [Beforehand], we was at the park, hopping and talking about it and everything. I was like, 'man, dawg, I ain't hitting her from the back.' Like, 'she gonna mess up my dick.'... He like, 'oh, I got her from the back dude.' So we went up there ... [and] she like, 'which one you all hitting me from the back?' [I'm] like, 'there he go, right there. I got the front.' She's like, 'okay.' And then he took off her clothes, pulled his pants down. I didn't, just unzipped mine 'cause I was getting head. She got to slurping me. I'm like, my partner back there 'cause we was in the dark so I ain't see nuttin'. He was back, I just heard her [making noises]. I'm like, 'damn girl, what's wrong with you?' [More noises] [I'm like], 'you hitting her from the back?' He's like, 'yeah, I'm hitting it.'

INTERVIEW EXCERPT WITH TOYA

Terence: It was some girl that my friend had knew for a minute, and he, I guess he just came to her and asked her, 'is you gon' do everybody?' or whatever and she said 'yeah.' So he went first and then, I think my other partna went, then I went, then it was like two other dudes behind me ... It was at [my friend's] crib.
Toya: Were you all like there for a get together or party or something?
Terence: It was specifically for that for real, 'cause he had already let us know that she was gon' do that, so.
Toya: So it was five boys and just her?
Terence: Yeah.
....

Toya: And so he asked her first, and then he told you all to come over that day?
Terence: We had already came over. 'Cause I guess he knew she was already gon' say yeah or whatever. We was already there when she got there.
Toya: Did you know the girl?
Terence: Naw, I ain't know her, know her like for real know her. But I knew her name or whatever. I had seen her before. That was it though.
...

Toya: So when you all got there, she was in the room already?
Terence: Naw, when we got there, she hadn't even got there yet. And when she came, she went in the room with my friend, the one she had already knew. And then after they was in there for a minute, he came out and let us know that she was 'gon, you know, run a train or whatever. So after that, we just went one by one.

---

violence increases solidarity and cohesion among groups of young men, and the victim has symbolic status and is treated as an object (Franklin, 2004; Sanday, 1990). Just as performance played a central role in young men's accounts of these incidents, their accounts were themselves a particular sort of masculine performance in the context of their interview exchange with a young white male researcher far removed from their world on the streets (see also Presser, 2005).

In contrast, when young men were interviewed about their participation in 'running trains' by Toya – the African-American female interviewer – two different features emerged. First, they were much less sexually graphic in their accounts. Second, due in part to Toya's interview style and the specific concerns about consent she brought to the interview exchange, her conversations with young men about running trains challenged their attempts to construct the events as consensual. The interview excerpt with Terence in Box 4.3 reveals, for example, that the young woman in this incident arrived at a boy's house that she knew and may have been interested in; waiting on her arrival were four additional young men whom she did not know or know well. And they had come specifically for the purpose of running a train on her. Because Terence's friend said 'she was down for it', he either did not consider or discounted the question of whether the young woman may have felt threatened or had not freely consented. Instead, he took his turn and left.

Similar inconsistencies were revealed in Tyrell's account, again precisely because of Toya's particular style of probing and concern with issues of consent:

> This girl was just like, I ain't even know her, but like I knew her 'cause I had went to work [where she did] last year ... Then my boy, when he started working there, he already had knew her, 'cause he said he had went to a party with her last year. And he was gonna have sex with her then, but ... [her] grandmamma came home or something, so they ain't get to do it. So one day he was just like, we was all sitting watching this movie [at work] and it was real dark or whatever. And she had come in there or whatever, and he was just talking to her, and he was like, 'Let's all go 'head and run a train on you.' She was like, 'What?' And she started like, 'You better go on.' Then, like, [he said], 'For real, let's go over to my house.' And then, you know what I'm saying, she was like, 'Naw.'

Tyrell explained that later that day, he and his friend were leaving work and saw the girl 'walking over there to the bus stop'. His friend invited the girl over to his house, and she agreed to go. Tyrell admitted, 'I think she liked him,' and this was the reason she came over. However, because they had previously introduced the idea of running a train on her, Tyrell and his friend appear to have decided that her consent to go to his house was consent to have a train run on her. The discussion continued:

> *Toya:* Do you think she really wanted to do it?
> *Tyrell:* I can't really say. 'Cause at first she was like laughing and stuff, like, 'Don't!' But we didn't pressure her. I didn't say nothing to her for the rest of the [work] day. I probably talked to her, but I say nothing about like that. And then she just came with us, so I mean, she had to want to.

Thus, in his account, Tyrell maintained his interpretation that the incident was consensual, offering evidence that the fact that he and his friend did not mention running a train on the girl again during the day they spent at work together meant they had not 'pressured' her. He did not appear to consider an alternative interpretation – that their silence on the issue allowed the girl to interpret the earlier comments as innocuous. Instead, he insisted that 'she knew' (see also King, 2003; Willan and Pollard, 2003).

Further, Tyrell's account of the young woman's behavior afterwards – which, again, emerged as a result of Toya's continued questioning, also belied his insistence that she had engaged willingly. He explained that 'she missed like a week of work after that'. And while he believed the girl liked his friend before the incident, he said, 'I know she didn't like him after that ... She don't even talk to him at all. Every time they see each other they'll argue.' In addition, Tyrell said, 'She go to my cousin's school now, and she be talking all stuff like, "I hate your cousin!" But I don't care, I mean I don't even care. She shouldn't have did that.'

Given this evidence, Toya asked whether he thought she felt bad about it, the conversation continued:

> *Tyrell:* I can't even say. I don't even know her like that. I really can't say. She do that kinda stuff all the time.
> *Toya:* She does?
> *Tyrell:* No. I'm just saying. I don't know. If she don't she probably did feel bad, but if she do she probably wouldn't feel bad ... But if she didn't really wanna do it, she shouldn't have did it.

Notice how Tyrell slipped easily into noting that 'she do that kinda stuff all the time', but when pressed, conceded that he had no basis on which to draw such a conclusion.

In part, accounts like Terence's and Tyrell's emerged because they responded to Toya as a young African-American woman who had an understanding of life in their neighborhoods. She was marked by similarities where Dennis was marked by difference, except when it came to gender. Young men thus did not portray running trains as graphic sexual exploits that demonstrated their manhood. And the commonalities Toya shared with them allowed her to probe for factual details without evoking a defensive response that closed down communication within the interview.

These differences could be read as support for the position that social distance between researcher and research participant results in suspicion and lack of trust, which affects the process of disclosure (DeVault, 1995; Taylor et al., 1995). My reading is somewhat different. While the role that social similarities and differences played in producing these disparate accounts of the same phenomenon is notable, both sets of interviews revealed important insights about the nature and meanings of 'running trains'. Dennis' interviews demonstrated their function as masculine performance. In fact, young men's acts of *telling* Dennis about the events were themselves masculine performances, constructed in response to *whom* they were doing the telling. In contrast, Toya's interviews revealed important evidence of the processes by which young men construct their interpretations of girls' consent, and reveal the various ways in which they do so by discounting the points of view of their female victims (see King, 2003).

This example suggests that it is both necessary and useful to pay close attention to how the interview context shapes accounts. Doing so can reveal multifaceted features of behaviors and their meanings, as they emerge in disparate accounts. Moreover, it reveals the benefits for data analysis that can emerge by utilizing diverse research teams, particularly when using this diversity itself as a means of furthering the analysis (see Miller, 2010).

CONCLUSION

A primary concern of feminist scholars in criminology is to examine, understand, and ameliorate the gender inequalities that shape crime, victimization, and justice practices. In this chapter, my goals were to describe why the use of in-depth interviews is an especially valuable methodological approach for conducting research on these issues, and to explain how research that utilizes interview data puts it to use for understanding the relationships between gender, inequality, and crime.

What I find most useful with interview data is the simultaneous access it provides to both social processes – the 'who, what, when, where, and how' of crime – and the cultural frames that individuals use to make sense of these activities and their social worlds. This makes interview accounts particularly useful for addressing the intellectual double shift I noted earlier: the dual challenge of examining the impact of gender and gender inequality in 'real' life, while simultaneously deconstructing the intertwined ideologies about gender that guide social practices, including the strong tendency to view gender through an individualistic and binary lens.

Drawing on my own research, I have shown some of the ways in which the analysis of interview data can illuminate the impact of gender stratification, gendered practices, and gender ideologies on criminal offending. Key to the success of doing so is ensuring the rigor of one's inductive analyses. This includes, for example, working to ensure that initial data coding begins early in the process and remains open; and further into the project, utilizing techniques such as constant comparative methods and deviant case analyses to strengthen the internal validity of one's findings.

Finally, I have illustrated how attention to the social locations of interview participants – researchers and those researched alike – offer important opportunities to advance our understandings.

As a feminist scholar, the relevance of qualitative interview research for studying gender is specific to my particular theoretical goal of 'illuminat[ing] gender as central to our understanding of social life' (Lewis, 2007: 274). Nonetheless, my discussion in this chapter has import for a broader criminological audience. It illustrates the unique contributions that qualitative interview research can provide in theorizing about crime and justice by offering a vital window through which to better understand the life worlds and experiences of those we study, and the social processes and patterns in which they are embedded.

NOTES

1 Thus, again note that the title of the book – *One of the Guys* – made direct use of an *in vivo* code that became central to my analysis.

2 Wreck was a slang term used by young women to refer to girls who were seen as sexually promiscuous.

RECOMMENDED READING

For a contemporary introduction to grounded theory, see Charmaz, K. (2006) *Constructing Grounded Theory: A Practical Guide through Qualitative Analysis* (Thousand Oaks, CA: Sage Publications).

The classic text on grounded theory research is Glaser, B. and A. Strauss. (1967) *The Discovery of Grounded Theory* (Chicago: Aldine).

For further discussion of how social position shapes the interview process and can be put to use in theorizing about crime, see Miller, J. (2010) 'The impact of gender when studying "Offenders on Offending"' in W. Bernasco and M. Tonry (eds), *Offenders on Offending: Learning about Crime from Criminals* (London: Willan Press), pp. 161–183.

A classic feminist account of qualitative interviewing is Oakley, A. (1981) 'Interviewing women: a contradiction in terms' in H. Roberts (ed.), *Doing Feminist Research* (London: Routledge and Kegan Paul) pp. 30–61.

For a discussion of how accounts can be used to gain insight into social worlds, see Orbuch, T.L. (1997) 'People's accounts count: The sociology of accounts'. *Annual Review of Sociology* 23: 455–478.

An excellent discussion of qualitative analysis techniques can be found in Silverman, D. (2006) *Interpreting Qualitative Data: Methods for Analyzing Talk, Text, and Interaction* (Thousand Oaks, CA: Sage Publications).

For a thorough overview of interviewing, including concrete advice on data collection, see Spradley, J. (1979) *The Ethnographic Interview* (New York: Holt).

REFERENCES

Anderson, E. (1999) *Code of the Street.* New York: W.W. Norton & Co.

Cameron, D. (1998) 'Gender, language, and discourse: a review essay'. *Signs* 23: 945–973.

Charmaz, K. (2006) *Constructing Grounded Theory: A Practical Guide through Qualitative Analysis.* Thousand Oaks, CA: Sage Publications.

Connell, R.W. (2002) *Gender.* Cambridge: Polity Press.

Daly, K. (1998) 'Gender, crime and criminology'. in M. Tonry (ed.), *The Handbook of Crime and Justice* (pp. 85–108). Oxford: Oxford University Press.

Daly, K. and Chesney-Lind, M. (1988) 'Feminism and criminology'. *Justice Quarterly* 5: 497–538.

Daly, K. and Maher, L. (1998) 'Crossroads and intersections: building from feminist critique' in K. Daly and L. Maher (eds), *Criminology at the Crossroads: Feminist Readings in Crime and Justice* (pp. 1–17). Oxford: Oxford University Press.

DeVault, M.L. (1999) *Liberating Method: Feminism and Social Research.* Philadelphia, PA: Temple University Press.

Franklin, K. (2004) 'Enacting masculinity: antigay violence and group rape as participatory theater'. *Sexuality Research & Social Policy* 1: 25–40.

Giordano, P. (2010) *Legacies of Crime: A Follow-Up of the Children of Highly Delinquent Girls and Boys.* Cambridge: Cambridge University Press.

Grenz, S. (2005) 'Intersections of sex and power in research on prostitution: a female researcher interviewing male heterosexual clients'. *Signs* 30: 2092–2113.

Joe, K.A. and Chesney-Lind, M. (1995) '"Just every mother's angel": an analysis of gender and ethnic variations in youth gang membership'. *Gender & Society* 9: 408–430.

Kandiyoti, D. (1988) 'Bargaining with patriarchy'. *Gender & Society* 2: 274–290.

Kanter, R.M. (1977) 'Some effects of proportions of group life: skewed sex ratios and responses to token women'. *American Journal of Sociology* 82: 965–990.

King, N. (2003) 'Knowing women: straight men and sexual certainty'. *Gender & Society* 17: 861–877.

Lauderback, D., Hansen, J. and Waldorf, D. (1992) '"Sisters are doin' it for themselves": a black female gang in San Francisco'. *The Gang Journal* 1: 57–70.

Lewis, L. (2007) 'Epistemic authority and the gender lens'. *The Sociological Review* 55: 273–292.

Lofland, J. and Lofland, L.H. (1984) *Analyzing Social Settings: A Guide to Qualitative Observation and Analysis.* Belmont, CA: Wadsworth.

Maher, L. (1997) *Sexed Work: Gender, Race and Resistance in a Brooklyn Drug Market.* Oxford: Clarendon Press.

Maruna, S. (2001) *Making Good.* Washington DC: American Psychological Association.

Miller, J. (1998) 'Up it up: gender and the accomplishment of street robbery'. *Criminology* 36: 37–66.

Miller, J. (2001) *One of the Guys: Girls, Gangs and Gender.* New York: Oxford University Press.

Miller, J. (2002) 'The strengths and limits of "doing gender" for understanding street crime'. *Theoretical Criminology.* 6: 433–460.

Miller, J. (2008) *Getting Played: African American Girls, Urban Inequality, and Gendered Violence.* New York: New York University Press.

Miller, J. (2010) 'The impact of gender when studying "Offenders on Offending"' in W. Bernasco and M. Tonry (eds), *Offenders on Offending: Learning about Crime from Criminals* (pp. 161–183). London, UK: Willan Press.

Miller, J. and Glassner, B. (2004) 'The "inside" and the "outside": finding realities in interviews' in D. Silverman (ed.), *Qualitative Research,* 2nd Edition (pp. 125–139). London: Sage Publications.

Mullins, C.W. and Wright, R. (2003) 'Gender, social networks, and residential burglary'. *Criminology* 41: 813–840.

Oakley, A. (1981) 'Interviewing Women: A Contradiction in Terms' in H. Roberts (ed.) *Doing Feminist Research* (pp. 30–61). London: Routledge and Kegan Paul.

Orbuch, T.L. (1997) 'People's accounts count: The sociology of accounts'. *Annual Review of Sociology* 23: 455–478.

Presser, L. (2005) 'Negotiating power and narrative in research: implications for feminist methodology.' *Signs* 30: 2067–2090.

Risman, B.J. (2004) 'Gender as social structure: theory wrestling with activism'. *Gender & Society* 18: 429–450.

Sanday, P.R. (1990) *Fraternity Gang Rape: Sex, Brotherhood, and Privilege on Campus.* New York: New York University Press.

Scott, M.B. and Lyman, S.M. (1968) 'Accounts'. *American Sociological Review* 33: 46–62.

Silverman, D. (2006) *Interpreting Qualitative Data: Methods for Analyzing Talk, Text, and Interaction.* Thousand Oaks, CA: Sage Publications.

Smith, D.E. (1987) *The Everyday World as Problematic: A Feminist Sociology.* Boston, MA: Northeastern University Press.

Song, M. and Parker, D. (1995) 'Commonality, difference and the dynamics of disclosure in in-depth interviewing'. *Sociology* 29: 241–256.

Spradley, J. (1979) *The Ethnographic Interview.* New York: Holt.

Taylor, J.M., Gilligan, C. and Sullivan, A.M. (1995) *Between Voice and Silence: Women and Girls, Race and Relationship.* Cambridge, MA: Harvard University Press.

Veroff, J. and DiStefano, A. (2002) 'Researching across difference: a reprise'. *American Behavioral Scientist* 45: 1297–1307.

Willan, V.J. and Pollard, P. (2003) 'Likelihood of acquaintance rape as a function of males' sexual expectations, disappointment, and adherence to rape-conducive attitudes'. *Journal of Social and Personal Relationships* 20: 637–661.

Williams, C.L. (2000) 'Preface'. *The Annals of the American Academy of Political and Social Science* 571: 8–13.

Wright, R. and Decker, S.H. (1997) *Armed Robbers in Action: Stick Ups and Street Culture*. Boston: Northeastern University Press.

5

Neurocriminological Approaches

Yu Gao, Andrea L. Glenn, Melissa Peskin,
Anna Rudo-Hutt, Robert A. Schug,
Yaling Yang, Adrian Raine

INTRODUCTION

Although important progress has been made in delineating replicable psychosocial risk factors for antisocial and criminal behavior, interest in the neurobiological correlates of crime and violence has increased in recent years. This may be partly due to the development of new technologies including brain imaging, molecular genetics, as well as the increasingly easier application of psychophysiological approaches alongside the computer revolution. However, the discipline of criminology has largely been reluctant to conduct neurobiological studies. Part of the reason may be lack of the understanding of biological background and approaches. The current chapter attempts to help criminologists by introducing to them contemporary neurobiological methodologies commonly used in criminological research. We take a broad perspective on crime and include antisocial, aggressive and psychopathic behavior. Relevant findings are briefly summarized in the fields of genetics, structural and functional brain imaging, neuropsychology, psychophysiology and hormones.

GENETICS

Genetically informative designs offer a useful method for addressing questions of causality within the criminological domain. Genetic research can be further subdivided into two areas: behavioral genetics and molecular genetics. Behavioral genetic designs help to address questions such as, 'Do genes influence antisocial and criminal behavior?' and 'How much of antisocial behavior is influenced by genes?' One of the strongest features of behavioral genetic designs is to allow researchers to control for and rule out genetic influences on the relationship between a putative environmental risk factor and an antisocial outcome (Moffitt, 2005). For example, researchers have argued that child maltreatment, including abuse and neglect, plays a causal role in the development of aggression (Lahey et al., 2003; Thornberry, 1996). However, without controlling for the possibility that some third variable, namely genes, accounts for the association between child maltreatment and antisocial behavior, researchers cannot conclude that maltreatment *causes* aggression, and thus efforts to eliminate maltreatment may do nothing to reduce antisocial behavior (Moffitt, 2005). Similar problems arise when attempting to interpret the relationship between numerous other risk factors (e.g., parent criminality) and offspring antisocial behavior because, again, environmental causality cannot be assumed (i.e., genes may account for the association between parent criminality and offspring antisocial behavior). In contrast, molecular genetic studies offer the opportunity to investigate a different type of question such as, '*Which* genes predispose to which kinds of antisocial behavior?' (Raine, 2008). Molecular genetic studies thus allow researchers to hone in on specific genes that influence antisocial behavior.

The two types of designs commonly used in behavioral genetic studies are twin and adoption designs. Researchers are interested in determining how much antisocial behavior is accounted for by genes and how much by environmental influences. One way to address this issue is to test whether any of the family members in a study are more similar than can be explained by the proportion of genes they share (Moffitt, 2005). The proportion of variance that is due to genetic influences is termed 'heritability', and is represented by the letter 'A' in genetic models. Monozygotic (MZ), or identical twins share all of their genes. In contrast, dizygotic (DZ), or fraternal twins, share 50 percent of their genes. Therefore, the genetic similarity of MZ twins is twice the genetic similarity of DZ twins. Thus, if genes were the only factor that influenced antisocial behavior, MZ twins' behavior should be at least twice as similar as that of DZ twins. If researchers discover that this is not true, then they can conclude that some environmental factor has influenced the twins and increased their similarity (Moffitt, 2005). Another way to detect genetic and environmental effects on antisocial behavior is to examine whether family members are less alike than predicted from the percentage of genes they share (Moffitt, 2005; Plomin and Daniels, 1987). Because MZ twins share all of their genes, if their antisocial behavior is not equal, experience must have decreased their behavioral resemblance.

In behavioral genetic research, environmental factors are divided into those that are shared by family members (e.g., growing up in an impoverished neighborhood), termed the family wide, common, or shared environment, and represented by the letter 'C', and those that are not shared by family members (e.g., having a head injury, being the victim of bullying), termed unique, person-specific, or non-shared environmental experiences, and represented by the letter 'E'. A meta-analysis on over 100 studies investigating genetic and environmental influences on antisocial behavior has suggested that 40–50 percent of the variance in antisocial behavior is due to genetic influences, 15–20 percent to shared environmental influences, and 30 percent to non-shared environmental influences (Miles and Carey, 1997; Moffitt, 2005; Raine, 2008; Rhee and Waldman, 2002).

One recent paper demonstrates how a genetically informative design can be used to investigate whether there are differential genetic and environmental contributions to proactive and reactive forms of aggression in children (Baker et al., 2008). Prior to this study little was known about differential genetic and environmental influences on proactive (or planned), instrumental and 'cold-blooded' aggression; and reactive (or impulsive), affective, and 'hot-blooded' aggression. Challenges involved in implementing this type of study include recruiting a large, socio-economically and ethnically diverse sample of twins and their families to participate in a longitudinal research study. Another challenge includes ensuring that multiple informants provide reports on antisocial behavior. This is important because parent, teacher and child reports of antisocial behavior are often only weakly correlated, thus the possibility of different etiologies across informants exists.

This study, from the University of Southern California Twin Study of Risk Factors for Antisocial Behavior, represents an ethnically and socio-economically diverse set of 606 families of male and female twins or triplets who were first assessed at age nine years. Caregiver, teacher and child reports were taken on the Reactive-Proactive Aggression Questionnaire (RPQ; Raine et al., 2006) to measure reactive and proactive aggression. An 'ACE model', typically employed by twin studies, was used to estimate the magnitude and significance of additive genetic (A), shared environmental (C), and non-shared environmental (E) influences. Findings revealed that there is significant heritability for, or genetic influences on, proactive and reactive aggression in nine-year olds. However, there were striking differences across gender and informant (caregiver, teacher and child). While there were no sex differences in genetic and environmental influences using caregiver and teacher reports of aggression, child's self-reports of aggression revealed strong genetic influences on proactive (50 percent) and reactive (38 percent) aggression for boys, whereas no genetic influences were found for female self-reports of either proactive or reactive aggression. Instead, shared and non-shared environmental influences almost completely accounted for variance in female self-reports of proactive and reactive aggression. This study illustrates some of the challenges and complexities involved in conducting research that investigates the genetic contribution to aggression, and some of the methodologies that may be used to disentangle genetic from environmental influences on antisocial behavior and crime.

STRUCTURAL IMAGING

The speculations that antisocial, criminal behavior may be linked to neuroanatomical predispositions could be traced back to as early as the eighteenth century. Phrenology, developed by a German physician Franz Joseph Gall, argued that the topography of the cranial bones reflects underlying regional brain sizes, and that mental functions related to different brain regions could be determined by measuring that area of the skull. However, phrenology was largely discarded in the early twentieth century when numerous cases of violent individuals were observed to have well-developed skulls. In the early twentieth century, a new technique called 'pneumoencephalography' allowed for the first time the visualization of the ventricular system of living human beings using an X-ray after injecting air into the subarachnoid space through a lumbar puncture, and draining the cerebrospinal fluid. This technique was not only very invasive, but often painful and dangerous, and therefore was largely abandoned after the rise of computed tomography (CT) in the early 1970s.

In CT, a sequence of X-ray images is taken across the head. These images are then processed to create a three-dimensional representation of the brain. CT images provide details that allow better differentiation between soft tissue with different densities. With increasing availability, CT soon became a gold standard in medical diagnosis and was employed in early brain imaging studies to assess the brain pathology of criminal offenders. For example, by examining the CT scans of a group of violent sadists, Langevin and colleague (1988) showed that about 50 percent of them have brain structural abnormalities, especially in temporal lobe regions. Similarly, Blake et al. (1995) found brain atrophy in 9 of 19 subjects charged with murder. However, CT presents several limitations such as limited spatial resolution (difficulty in differentiating gray and white matter) and the exposure to radioactivity (unsafe for longitudinal research) (Duerk, 1999; Sanders, 1995). In 1973, the first image using magnetic resonance imaging (MRI) was published, and this new technology quickly replaced CT as the most commonly used imaging technique in many research fields including criminology.

MRI is based on the principle that atoms in the human brain are like small bar magnets that possess magnetic charge in random orientations. When immersed in a strong magnetic field (usually 0.5–3.0 Tesla), the nuclei of these atoms tend to align and reach an equilibrium state. A radiofrequency electromagnetic field is then briefly introduced to excite the atoms and induce a transient phase coherence among the nuclei that creates a signal, which can be detected by the MRI scanner receiver. Typically, MRI detects the resonance of ^1H atoms in water, and because this element is abundant in the brain, images with excellent anatomical details (better than CT images) can be produced without the use of radiation. More importantly, MRI has the flexibility of acquiring images with different image contrast that highlight different properties of the nuclei of ^1H atoms. For example, diffusion tensor imaging (DTI) is used to map white matter fiber tracts, and magnetic resonance spectroscopy (MRS) is used to illustrate the concentration of a variety of metabolites. Most MRI studies on criminal offenders utilize three-dimensional T1-weighted images, which provide superb gray and white matter contrast. Earlier MRI studies reported similar findings as observed in CT studies, namely that violent offenders show gross brain atrophy, especially in the fronto-temporal area. For example, Chesterman and colleague (1994) found six out of ten violent psychiatric inpatients to show atrophy in the temporal region. However, the majority of these MRI studies had small and heterogeneous samples, was not quantitative, and could not pinpoint the precise brain regions affected.

Recently, advances in computational imaging analysis methods have permitted researchers to examine the brain structure of criminal offenders in a much more precise manner. Using either manual or automated methods, a sequence of preprocessing steps is first performed to remove the non-brain tissue and brainstem, and to classify the remaining tissue into gray matter, white matter and cerebrospinal fluid. Then the following steps are undertaken: correction of motion (slight head movements during the scan), head alignment (usually put in line with the anterior–posterior commissure), and the placement of the individual brain in a common stereotactic space (e.g. Montreal Neurological Institute 305-template, Talairach coordinate system). Next, trained researchers or technicians who are blind to the group membership follow a previously validated protocol to manually delineate the 'region of interest (ROI)'. The estimated volume for this structure is then obtained from each individual, averaged within each group, and statistically compared between groups. For example, by comparing 21 individuals with antisocial personality disorder (APD) to normal controls and individuals with a history of substance abuse, Raine and colleague (2000) found APD individuals showed an 11 percent reduction in gray matter volume in the prefrontal cortex. Another study found higher psychopathy scores to correlate negatively with smaller volumes in the bilateral posterior hippocampus in a group of violent offenders with APD and type-II alcoholism (Laakso et al., 2001). In a follow-up study by our group, we found reduced prefrontal gray matter volume in unsuccessful psychopaths (psychopaths who had at least one criminal conviction) compared to successful psychopaths (psychopaths without convictions) and normal controls (Yang et al., 2005). Although somewhat subjective due to individual anatomical variations and errors introduced by the scorers, this approach has generated extremely important knowledge for the field of criminology and remains a standard approach to examining hypothesized ROIs, especially those relatively small sub-cortical structures such as the amygdala and hippocampus that are critical to emotional information processing and regulation.

Recently, alternative approaches of using fully automated or semi-automated algorithms to identify morphological changes throughout the whole brain have been increasingly used to examine the brain structure of antisocial, violent individuals. These methods are less labor-intensive and can be designed to identify abnormalities in different aspects of brain structure, such as gray matter concentration (using voxel-based morphometry) or the shape of a certain structure (using tensor-based morphometry). For example, Müller et al. (2008) found reduced gray matter concentrations in frontal and temporal brain regions in criminal psychopaths compared to controls. However, despite several algorithms currently under development, fully automated methods are not yet accurate enough to trace anatomical structures without human intervention, thus studies targeting certain ROIs still largely depend on manual approaches. In summary, preliminary evidence accumulated from structural brain imaging studies in the past decade has provided an important framework for the development of neurobiological models of antisocial and criminal behavior that can be tested in future studies.

FUNCTIONAL IMAGING

Functional MRI (fMRI) is a type of MRI scan that can measure changes in brain activity during a task. The use of fMRI to study antisocial and criminal individuals is still in its infancy, but has great potential for improving our understanding of brain functioning in this population. For a review of brain imaging studies in antisocial individuals to date, see Wahlund and Kristiansson (2009).

Several limitations must be considered when designing an fMRI study. In order to obtain sufficient power to detect a signal, the task must involve events of a similar type that are repeated many times (e.g., looking at a series of familiar objects *versus* looking at a series of unfamiliar objects). Thus, it may be challenging to create tasks that closely resemble real-world events. Generally there need to be two or more types of events that can be contrasted. For example, if the research question is, 'What areas of the brain are active when looking at emotional pictures?', then one would need an 'emotional pictures' condition as well as a 'neutral pictures' condition in order to subtract out the areas that are simply activated by looking at pictures in general.

Another consideration is that the participant must keep their head very still while in the scanner,

thus limiting their range of movements and means for responding; participants cannot speak during the task, and instead must make responses by pressing buttons on a button box. The head movement issue also affects the length of time an individual can be scanned – individuals tend to get restless the longer they are in the scanner, so the shorter the scan the better, particularly when scanning children.

Needless to say, it may take some creativity to develop a task that can account for the limitations of fMRI and still measure a process of interest with real-world applicability. However, there are numerous tasks that have already been developed, particularly in the field of social neuroscience, that are applicable to the study of antisocial behavior (Decety et al., 2009). It is also possible to do interactive tasks – the setup is such that the computer controlling the stimuli presentation is outside the scanner, so the participant may play a game with another person via a computer outside of the scanner, given that the task involves considerable repetition of similar trials (Rilling et al., 2007).

Functional MRI sessions are typically very expensive, so it is important to run a power analysis to determine how many subjects are needed. This will vary depending on the number of repetitions of each event, and the number of contrasts one plans to run. A typical fMRI session for one subject will involve a high-resolution structural scan, and then the functional scan(s). Most imaging centers have technicians or experts who will help with selecting the appropriate scan and will run the scanner. The data is available immediately after the scan.

Data analysis involves preprocessing the data, which includes a series of steps such as correcting for head movement and aligning the scans. Images from each subject's functional scans are aligned so that images from multiple subjects can be averaged. The timing of each event during the scan must be entered. Contrasts are set up to compare brain activity during different events or blocks of events. For example, the contrast Familiar minus Unfamiliar would show which areas are more active when looking at familiar objects than unfamiliar objects, for each subject or for the group on average. *T*-tests can be used to compare this activity in two different groups (e.g., patients and controls) or correlational analyses by entering scores (e.g., psychopathy scores). Co-variates can also be entered (e.g., gender, IQ).

The most commonly used software to analyze fMRI data includes SPM (http://www.fil.ion.ucl.ac.uk/spm/), FSL (http://www.fmrib.ox.ac.uk/fsl/index.html), Brain Voyager (http://www.brainvoyager.com/) and Afni (http://afni.nimh.nih.gov/afni). SPM, FSL and Afni are freely available.

Brain Voyager must be purchased, but is said to have a friendlier user interface and is superior for certain types of analyses. There are a number of additional programs that may be used either alone or in conjunction with those listed. When choosing a software program one should consider several factors, including support available (both from colleagues and online from the software organization), familiarity with Unix, and the types of analyses one wishes to perform. For tips on reporting fMRI data, see Poldrack et al. (2008).

One of the advantages of fMRI is that it provides an objective measure beyond that of self-report. For example, in a recent study from our laboratory, we found that psychopathic individuals made similar moral judgments to controls on a series of moral dilemmas. However, we found that more psychopathic individuals had reduced activity in the amygdala, but more activity in the dorsolateral prefrontal cortex (DLPFC) when making those judgments. The amygdala is thought to respond to the emotional aspect of the moral dilemmas, whereas the DLPFC is involved in cognitive processing. This suggests that more psychopathic individuals may be relying less on emotion and more on purely cognitive processes when making moral judgments, which may partially explain why psychopathic individuals fail to translate their moral judgments into moral behavior (Glenn et al., 2009). Future fMRI studies exploring morality, lying, emotion processing and other social cognitive processes will be beneficial in furthering our understanding of brain functioning in antisocial and criminal behavior.

NEUROPSYCHOLOGY

Neuropsychological assessment provides unique insight into criminality by measuring the indirect behavioral expression of brain dysfunction. Practically speaking, neuropsychological tests offer several advantages. First, they are non-invasive and relatively inexpensive to administer (commonly as paper-and-pencil tests or by computer) – making them desirable for research settings where more-advanced imaging equipment may not be readily available, as for example in facilities housing incarcerated or institutionalized populations. Additionally, although imaging techniques can identify various forms of structural and functional deficits, neuropsychological assessment is needed to identify the nature of behavioral strengths and deficits associated with these deficits – something imaging cannot do. Furthermore, neuropsychological assessment can document mental abilities that are inconsistent with anatomic findings, and can aid in the prediction of

future behavior (Lezak et al., 2004). This makes it particularly valuable in both criminological research and forensic applications (Schug et al., 2010).

Neuropsychological investigations of antisocial and criminal behavior have focused upon intelligence or IQ (Wilson and Herrnstein, 1985), left *versus* right hemispheric functioning (Raine, 1993), and functioning in individual neuropsychological domains. For example, research studies of psychopathy have examined performance deficits in domains of attention, language and executive functioning (Gao et al., 2009). Executive functioning (EF) refers to the cognitive processes that allow for goal-oriented, contextually appropriate behavior and effective self-serving conduct (Lezak et al., 2004). Poor EF is thought to reflect frontal lobe impairment, and is indicated by performance errors on neuropsychological measures of strategy formation, cognitive flexibility, or impulsivity. In a meta-analysis, Morgan and Lilienfeld (2000) specify six reasonably well-validated EF tests in antisocial research.

Recent research has focused upon the differentiation of prefrontal volumes using neuropsychological measures – though caution is suggested against the automatic assumption of regional specificity of function in neuropsychological assessment. Examples of purported tests of functioning in two key subregions (orbitofrontal and dorsolateral prefrontal cortex) that can be examined in criminological research are as follows:

Porteus Maze Test (Porteus, 1959, 1965)

In this test, the participant uses a pencil to trace a series of mazes of increasing difficulty. Three scores are obtained: the test age (the maze with the highest level of difficulty that participants complete); the quantitative score (number of wrong entries or 'blind alleys'); and the qualitative score (Q score; i.e., the number of 'rule-breaking' errors such as crossed lines, pencil lifts and changed directions; Morgan and Lilienfeld, 2000). The Q score has demonstrated a strong effect size in antisocial research (Morgan and Lilienfeld, 2000) and numerous investigations have utilized the Porteus Maze Test Q score as an orbitofrontal/ventromedial measure (Lapierre, 1995).

Iowa Gambling Task (Bechara et al., 1994)

In this computerized test, the participant attempts to win 'money' by picking 'cards' from four decks (labeled A, B, C and D) on the screen.

The selected cards are tracked by the computer, and the amount of money won/lost after each selection, along with the total, are displayed. The final score is the number of selections from 'advantageous' decks (i.e., modest winnings and milder penalties—decks C and D) minus the number of selections from 'disadvantageous' decks (larger winnings but more-severe penalties—decks A and B). Numerous investigations (e.g. Ritter et al., 2004), including studies of psychopathy (see Blair and Frith, 2000), have utilized the Iowa Gambling Task as an orbitofrontal/ventromedial task.

Tower of London (Shallice, 1982)

This test consists of 12 problems of graded difficulty in which the subject must plan the order of moves necessary to rearrange three colored rings or balls from their initial position to match a predetermined goal arrangement on one or more of the sticks (only one piece may be moved at a time, each piece may be moved only from peg to peg, and only a specified number of pieces may be left on each peg at a time). Scoring is based upon the number of problems completed in the minimum number of moves specified (perfect solutions), the average number of excess moves executed at each difficulty level, and planning times at each level. Previous investigations (Dolan and Park, 2002) have utilized this test as a dorsolateral prefrontal task, due to the significant load that it places on spatial working memory (a function which engages the dorsolateral prefrontal cortex; Dolan and Park, 2002).

Wisconsin Card Sorting Test (WCST; Heaton et al., 1993)

The WCST is a reliable and valid EF test (see Lezak et al., 2004) and demonstrated a strong effect size in Morgan and Lilienfeld's (2000) meta-analysis of EF and antisocial behavior. In this test, the participant is required to sort a deck of 64 cards according to a changing rule pattern (color, form or number) that must be deduced from the pattern of the administrator's or computer's responses (right or wrong) to the participant's placement of the cards. Scores for categories achieved (the number of times a participant correctly sorts ten consecutive cards) and perseverative errors (the number of times a participant continues to sort cards according to a previously correct rule or, on the first category, the number of times he/she continues to sort according to an incorrect initial guess) are computed to reflect dorsolateral prefrontal functioning (e.g. Lapierre et al., 1995).

Go/No-Go task (Malloy et al., 1985)

In this test, a series of letters (either 'P' or 'R') are presented individually in variable computer screen locations, and the participant must respond to the appropriate letter by pressing a response button, while inhibiting responses to the non-appropriate letter. Previous investigations (e.g. Dolan and Park, 2002) have utilized the Go/No-Go task as an orbitofrontal/ventromedial measure, and Go/No-Go deficits have been described in an orbitomedial frontal behavioral syndrome (Malloy et al., 1993). Recent imaging studies, however, have indicated the involvement of other cortical regions, including the dorsolateral prefrontal cortex, in Go/No-Go task performance (Ridderinkhof et al., 2004).

More recent neuropsychological investigations of antisocial behavior have incorporated extensive batteries of measures which assess multiple domains of cognitive functioning (rather than merely focusing upon EF) – which may assist in elucidating neuropsychological profiles of antisocial behavioral subtypes. The importance of this multi-domain approach is emphasized in a recent meta-analyses (Schug and Raine, 2009), in which antisocial schizophrenic individuals demonstrated: (1) widespread deficits across multiple domains (full-scale IQ, verbal and performance IQ, attention, broadly defined EF and memory) in comparison to antisocial individuals without schizophrenia, and (2) more-specific full-scale IQ and memory deficits in comparison to non-antisocial individuals with schizophrenia. These divergent neuropsychological profiles suggest biological underpinnings specific to differential forms of antisocial behavior.

PSYCHOPHYSIOLOGY

Psychophysiological research has significantly contributed to our empirical understanding of the neurobiological mechanisms underlying crime. The advantages of psychophysiological measures include relatively easy data collection (especially heart rate) and non-invasive recording features. These measures have proved to be valuable in filling the gap between genetic risk for crime and the brain abnormalities which give rise to antisocial and criminal behavior. The psychophysiological approach on criminality research is summarized in the following two main areas: central nervous system (including electroencephalography [EEG] and event-related potentials [ERPs]) and autonomic nervous system (including skin conductance and heart rate). Extensive introductions to psychophysiological instrumentation, recording techniques, and other methodological issues may be found in Cacioppo et al. (2007). The interested reader is also referred to the review by Patrick (2008) for a more updated summary of research findings on the psychophysiological correlates of antisocial and aggressive behavior.

Central nervous system (CNS)

EEG is a non-invasive measure of brain electrical activity (Hugdahl, 2001). To measure EEG, electrodes are placed in specified locations on the head with reference to certain points on the skull. Standardized placement of electrodes has been made easier by the use of EEG caps, which are spandex caps in which electrodes have been embedded. Electrical activity picked up by the electrodes is then fed through a series of amplifiers and filters and finally to a computer for offline cleaning and analysis. It is critical to remove movement artifacts, including muscle activity and eye blinks, from the data by using algorithms or comparison to a preset maximum signal value.

EEG data is analyzed into different bands based on the frequency components of the EEG wave pattern, ranging from slow-wave frequencies (delta [generally below 3 Hz] and theta [4–7 Hz]), to more moderate (alpha [8–12 Hz]) and high frequency activity (beta [above 15 Hz]). Increasing frequency is associated with increasing arousal: delta and theta waves are predominant during sleep; alpha waves are common during wakeful relaxation; and beta waves are indicative of increased activation and arousal, or rapid eye movement sleep (Hugdahl, 2001).

Most EEG research on criminality has focused on recording EEG when participants are at rest or during sleep. Evidence from past research suggests that EEG abnormalities (e.g., an increase in theta and delta activity) are common in antisocial and criminal individuals. Importantly, this pattern has also been shown to precede criminal behavior. For example, Raine and colleagues (1990a) found that young men who would become criminals by age 24 had more theta power at rest than their non-criminal peers at age 15. Such increases in slow-wave EEG activity may suggest that criminals are physiologically underaroused and thus seek stimulation (Raine et al., 1990a). Alternately, this pattern may indicate that their cortical maturation is delayed, as the dominant EEG frequency tends to increase with age (Dustman et al., 1999).

ERPs (also called evoked potentials) have also been used to study antisocial and criminal behavior. An ERP is a deflection in brain electrical activity that is time-locked to a specific event. The deflection may be positive (P; traditionally depicted downward) or negative (N) and occurs within milliseconds of the onset of the stimulus.

Three commonly studied ERP components, N1, P2 and P3, occur at about 100, 200 and 300 milliseconds (ms), respectively, and therefore are also called N100, P200, and P300. ERPs are thought to be correlates of specific psychological processes (Hugdahl, 2001). As such they may differentiate the brain activity of criminals and non-criminals.

ERPs are recorded using the same equipment as EEG, with the addition of computer software to average the signal of multiple ERP trials. Many trials must be averaged together so that the ERP components can be distinguished from random variation in the brain signal. Perhaps the most simple paradigm is one in which participants passively attend to some stimuli, such as auditory clicks. Passive attending will evoke early ERP components (i.e., within the first 10–12 ms). Later components may be elicited by more active tasks. For example, in the oddball paradigm which is frequently used to study the P3 ERP component, two stimuli (e.g., a low and a high pitch tone) are presented repeatedly, with one more frequent than the other. The participant is asked to respond selectively to the less frequent stimulus, in which case the amplitude of the P3 component will be enhanced.

Studies of criminals using ERPs have focused on whether they have selective attention deficits. This proposal has been supported by studies which show reduced P3 amplitudes in response to target stimuli in aggressive, alcoholic and antisocial participants. For example, early onset of substance use and criminal behavior has been found to be associated with smaller P3 amplitudes (Iacono and McGue, 2006). Other studies, in contrast, have found possible evidence of enhanced attention. For instance, greater N1 amplitude and faster P3 latency at age 15 have been found to predict criminality at age 24 years (Raine et al., 1990b). A recent meta-analysis of P3 studies in antisocial individuals has revealed that in general antisocial individuals are characterized by reduced P3 amplitudes and longer latencies, indicating information-processing deficits in this population (Gao and Raine, 2009).

The precise meaning of specific ERP components is still under study. However, as interest in ERP has increased in recent years, it is likely to become better understood and a good candidate for criminology research. Similarly, EEG provides a direct measure of the electrical activity of the brain, and in the absence of brain imaging it can give rough estimates of where in the brain abnormalities are present.

Autonomic nervous system (ANS)

A large number of studies have been conducted on the autonomic nervous system (ANS) activity in antisocial and criminal individuals. The ANS serves as a link between the CNS and internal organs (e.g., heart, lungs, salivary glands, sweat glands) and is critically involved in mobilizing the body for action when threatened or under stress. The most frequently used measures in criminological research include skin conductance (SC) and heart rate.

SC is a relatively simple but powerful measure of ANS processing. It reflects very small changes in the electrical activity of the skin, with increased sweating leading to an increase in SC. It is recorded by attaching silver–silver chloride electrodes onto the palmer surface of the hands (usually the non-dominant hand) or fingers (distal phalanges of the index and middle fingers), where the concentration of eccrine sweat glands is highest. Electrode jelly is used as the conductive medium between the electrodes and the skin, and adhesive collars are used to control the area of contact between the electrode and the skin. Subject variable such as age, sex, race and stage of menstrual cycle, as well as environmental factors including temperature, humidity, time of day, day of week and season, are found to affect SC (Boucsein, 1992), and therefore need to be considered as potential covariates in SC data analyses.

SC is specifically affected by the sympathetic branch of the ANS and reflects both arousal (measured from SC levels and number of non-specific SC responses) and responsivity (SC reactivity to neutral or emotional stimuli). SC orienting (reflecting degree of information processing) and conditioning (reflecting associative learning and emotional processing) paradigms have been examined extensively in antisocial and criminal individuals. In a typical orienting paradigm, three or more identical stimuli (usually a neutral tone) are presented with several seconds interval between them. In normal individuals the SC response is expected to occur within 1–3 seconds after the onset of each stimulus. Reduced orienting responses, indicating reduced cognitive processing capability, have been linked to antisocial behavior, especially in psychopathic, antisocial and criminal subjects who also exhibit schizotypal features, such as paranoia, reduced emotionality and inability to make close friends. The cognitive deficits indexed by reduced orienting responses in antisocial individuals may contribute to their fear-conditioning deficits (see later) because lack of attentional processing to initially neutral stimuli which warn of impending punishment would be expected to result in poorer conditioning. Similarly, lack of orienting may also partly account for underarousal, since arousal reflects tonic levels of activity, which may in part be a function of moment-to-moment responsivity to events in the environment (Raine, 1996).

The SC fear-conditioning paradigm is often used to examine emotional deficits in antisocial and criminal behavior. In a typical conditioning paradigm, a neutral, non-aversive tone (conditioned stimulus, CS) is presented to the subject, followed a few seconds later by either a loud tone or an electric shock (unconditioned stimulus, UCS). The key measure is the size of the SC response elicited by the CS after a number of CS–UCS pairings. The larger the response to the CS after pairing with the UCS, the better the conditioning is. Reduced SC fear conditioning has been a key concept of aggressive/antisocial behavior and crime. Conscience has been conceptualized as a set of classically conditioned emotional responses. Individuals with good fear conditioning are hypothesized to develop a conscience that deters them from criminal behavior. Empirical studies have generally supported this hypothesis. For example, a longitudinal study conducted by our laboratory has shown that poor SC conditioning at age 3 years predisposes to criminal offending at ages 23 years (Gao et al., 2010), suggesting a neurodevelopmental basis to criminality.

Heart rate measures the number of heart beats per minute and reflects the complex interactions between sympathetic and parasympathetic nervous system activity. To record heart rate, the skin is first cleaned with alcohol on a gauze pad to remove dead skin and skin oils. Silver–silver chloride electrodes are then attached to two body parts that are fairly far apart, for example, one electrode on the distal end of the right collarbone and the other on the lower left rib cage. Similar to SC recording, electrode gel and adhesive collars are used. The most common problems for heart rate recordings are 60 Hz interference and movement artifacts. Careful choices of electrode site and electrodes and preparation are necessary to correct these problems.

Both cross-sectional and longitudinal psychophysiological studies have identified low resting heart rate as the best replicated finding in non-institutionalized antisocial populations (Ortiz and Raine, 2004), particularly in children and adolescents. It has been theorized that criminals generally have lower arousal levels than the non-criminals, and that by engaging in pathological stimulation-seeking behaviors, including aggressive and antisocial behavior, criminals bring their arousal back to an optimal level. Alternatively, it is also argued that ANS under-arousal indicates lack of fear or anxiety in criminals, which may reduce the effectiveness of punishments and socialization processes and in turn predispose them to antisocial behavior (Raine, 1993). In summary, certain psychophysiological measures, including heart rate, can be recorded relatively easily (e.g., using portable equipment or taking a pulse), and as such they are especially valuable to criminologists attempting to explore the biological bases of crime.

HORMONES

Hormones are chemical messengers that travel through the bloodstream and bind to receptors in the brain and body. Hormones are an important aspect of the neurobiological approach to studying crime because they have a direct influence on brain functioning and thus behavior. Examples of theoretically relevant hormones to criminal behavior include, but are not limited to, cortisol, testosterone, alpha-amylase and dehydroepiandrosterone (DHEA). Testosterone is most commonly linked to aggression, though recent meta-analyses suggest it may be related to dominant behavior more generally (Archer, 2006). DHEA is a precursor to testosterone and may be more relevant in studies of youth. Cortisol is a hormone that is released during stress. In relation to aggression, it is hypothesized that the stress response in antisocial individuals is reduced, which may contribute to fearlessness and poor conditioning. Cortisol is released by the hypothalamic–pituitary–adrenal axis and represents a slower-acting stress response. In contrast, recent research suggests that the salivary enzyme alpha-amylase is a promising new marker of a faster-acting stress response system, the sympathetic nervous system. Several studies have examined the role of hormones in antisocial populations (e.g., McBurnett et al., 2005; van Goozen et al., 1998), yet some findings have been mixed, and additional studies in different populations, using different tasks, and in combination with additional factors are needed to clarify the role that hormones may play in the development and maintenance of criminal behavior.

Hormones are typically measured either through saliva or blood samples. Most hormones can be measured from saliva reliably and in a less stressful manner than collecting blood samples, as the process is non-invasive. Hormones can either be measured at baseline, or in response to some type of stressor or event to gain information about the reactivity of the system. According to a recent meta-analysis (Dickerson and Kemeny, 2004), tasks that are most effective at eliciting a stress response involve elements of either uncontrollability, social stress, or both.

Different hormones have different times for optimal measurement, so when measuring multiple hormones it is important to design a study that attempts to maximize the accuracy for each hormone. Cortisol and testosterone, for example, display diurnal rhythms with concentrations highest in the mornings and lowest in the evenings (Yehuda et al., 2003). Saliva sample collection in the morning hours is optimal for detecting individual differences in resting cortisol, while afternoons are optimal for detecting differences in reactivity because levels are more variable (Yehuda et al., 2003). Different hormones may also take different times to reach peak levels in response to a stressor or other event. Cortisol typically peaks 20 minutes post-task and returns to baseline by 40 minutes post-task, whereas alpha-amylase peaks 5 minutes post-task and returns to baseline 20–30 minutes post-task (Granger et al., 2007a).

To improve accuracy of hormone measurement, it is often beneficial to take samples over the course of multiple days. In addition, there are a number of factors that may influence hormone measurement from saliva that should be considered. Gender and age both have significant influences on hormone levels. Phase of the menstrual cycle and current medications should be held constant or controlled for. Participants should abstain from exercise, smoking, eating, and consuming caffeinated beverages or alcohol for at least one hour prior to collection of saliva. Blood and food contamination are also significant confounding factors. For a review, see Granger et al. (2007b).

There are various methods for saliva sample collection. One method is by passive drool, in which participants use a short straw to deposit approximately 6 ml of saliva into a collection vial. There are various methods for stimulating saliva production and for dealing with saliva collection in children. After saliva collection, samples should be immediately frozen at –85° Celsius.

Saliva samples may be analyzed in the laboratory using commercially available enzyme immunoassay kits (e.g., Salimetrics), or by sending them to an external company for analysis. Although the in-house method is likely to be the most cost-effective, it is time and labor-intensive, requires laboratory space (minimum 10 × 7 ft) with water hook-up and adequate counter space, and professional training. The basic components of the in-house assay involve pipetting the saliva into wells coated with antibodies to the respective hormone, adding additional chemicals to facilitate the reaction, and reading the color (i.e., concentration) of the samples using a standard laboratory plate reader. Software is available to translate the output and calculate reliability. The assay procedure takes a minimum of three hours, depending on familiarity with the procedure, and results are available immediately. Thirty-eight samples can be assayed at one time. Samples are usually assayed in duplicate and the average value is used for statistical analyses. Alpha-amylase assays involve creating dilutions of the sample, incubation and reading the color via a plate reader at two time points, two minutes apart.

The methodology for hormone assessments in behavioral research is continually advancing; new research is identifying better methods for study design, sample collection and assaying, so a thorough review of recent literature is recommended before undertaking a study involving hormones. The study of hormones in criminal behavior can help to address a critically important gap in the literature by providing insight into the biological mechanisms underlying antisocial behavior.

OTHER ISSUES

It is critical to mention that psychosocial factors may interact with neurobiological factors in predisposing individuals to antisocial and criminal behavior (Farrington, 1997; Raine et al., 1994). For example, birth complications, including anoxia, interact with negative home environments including early maternal rejection of the child, in predisposing to adult violent behavior (ibid.). Similarly, there is evidence showing that an abnormality in the MAOA gene interacts with early child abuse in predisposing to adult antisocial behavior (Caspi et al., 2002).

Alternatively, neurobiological factors may show stronger relationships to antisocial behavior in those from benign social backgrounds. For example, Raine and Venables (1981) found that antisocial children from higher social class, but not those from lower social class showed poor SC conditioning. In a prospective longitudinal study, Raine et al. (1997) found that low heart rate at age 3 years predicted aggression at age 11 years in children from high but not low social classes. A recent study from our laboratory has found that poor Iowa Gambling Task performance predicted psychopathic tendencies only in adolescents from benign home environments, but not in those from low socio-economic backgrounds (Gao et al., 2009). These findings suggest that biological predispositions including under-arousal, reduced SC conditioning, and decision-making deficits may assume greater importance when social predispositions to crime are minimized. In contrast, social causes may be more important explanations of antisocial behavior in those exposed to adverse early home conditions.

Although most studies conducted to date have examined the neurobiological basis of criminal behavior using cross-sectional data, prospective studies are clearly needed to address questions such as, 'What are the predispositions for criminal behavior?' Prospective longitudinal research is one type of research that follows people repeatedly though their lives. Although it is difficult to execute prospective research, preliminary evidence has suggested that criminal behavior may have a neurodevelopmental basis (Gao et al., 2010). For example, in a nine-year prospective study of crime, Raine and colleagues (1990a) has shown that low resting heart rate, low resting SC activity, and excessive slow-wave theta EEG measured at age 15 years in normal schoolboys predicted criminal behavior at age 24 years. Cavum septum pellucidum, a marker of limbic neural maldevelopment, has been associated with higher levels of antisocial personality, psychopathy, and arrests and convictions in a community sample (Raine et al., 2010). Child and adolescents imaging studies also provide some limited, initial support for the neurodevelopmental perspective in that children and adolescents with conduct disorder show brain structural and functional abnormalities (Gao et al., 2009), which may be possibly caused by child abuse and neglect in infancy. To test the neurodevelopmental hypothesis of crime, prospective studies examining the development of neurobiological measures for antisocial and criminal behavior from an early age are crucial. If criminal offending is partly determined neurodevelopmentally, successful prevention and intervention efforts would be most effective when they start in early childhood or even prenatally.

CONCLUSION

In summary, among the commonly used neurobiological approaches in criminality research, neuropsychological and psychophysiological (especially heart rate) research are relatively easier to operationalize, particularly in children and adolescents. On the other hand, while more expensive, structural and functional imaging techniques may provide more direct information on brain anatomy and activity in relation to criminal behavior. Empirical findings indicate that antisocial and criminal individuals are characterized by structural and functional brain abnormalities (especially in the prefrontal cortex and amygdala), CNS and ANS underarousal, executive functioning deficits and atypical hormone patterns. These biological impairments are hypothesized to give rise to the cognitive, emotional and behavioral risk factors predisposing to antisocial and criminal behavior. In addition, increasing evidence has shown that there is clearly a genetic predisposition to antisocial behavior and crime. One of the possible reasons that have stopped criminologists from conducting neurobiological research on crime may be the assumption that crime may be genetically determined and that genes are fixed and immutable. However, with the technological advances, research has started to show that environmental influences early in development can directly change gene expression, which in turn alters brain functioning and the resulting behavior changes (see Raine, 2008).

To further develop the integrative perspective on antisocial and criminal behavior, longitudinal prospective studies using a biosocial interaction design are necessary. In addition, to addressing the scientific question of the etiology of crime, perhaps the more important reason to understand the biosocial interaction is to potentially inform intervention and prevention programs. One possible way to change/prevent antisocial behavior is to alter biological risk factors by manipulating environmental factors. For example, early environmental enrichment including better nutrition, more physical exercise and cognitive stimulation at ages 3–5 years has been found to improve brain functioning (as indicated by a reduction in slow-wave EEG power) and to enhance attention 8 years later at age 11 years (Raine et al., 2001). Furthermore, early environment enhancement also reduced adult criminal offending by 35 percent (Raine et al., 2003). Such programs applied early in life and combining multi-disciplinary health services from clinical, social and educational domains have the potential to improve brain functioning and make a public health contribution to the reduction of criminal offending throughout the world.

RECOMMENDED READING

Lorber, M.F. (2004) 'Psychophysiology of aggression, psychopathy, and conduct problems: A meta-analysis'. *Psychological Bulletin* 130(4): 531–552. The relationships between three measures of heart rate and SC – resting, task, and reactivity; and three types of antisocial spectrum behavior – aggression, psychopathy, and conduct problems, were examined in this meta-analysis. Results indicated multiple interactive effects and complicated associations which vary with age, stimulus valence and type of antisocial behavior.

Interested readers can consult an atlas of normal and abnormal structure and blood flow of the brain. Specifically, brain structures mentioned in the text can be found at the following website: http://www.med.harvard.edu/AANLIB/cases/caseM/case.html

REFERENCES

Archer, J. (2006) 'Testosterone and human aggression'. *Neuroscience and Biobehavioral Reviews* 30(3): 319–345.

Baker, L.A., Raine, A., Liu, J. and Jacobson, K.C. (2008) 'Differential genetic and environmental influences on reactive and proactive aggression in children'. *Journal of Abnormal Child Psychology* 36(8): 1265–1278.

Bechara, A., Damasio, A.R., Damasio, H. and Anderson, S.W. (1994) 'Insensitivity to future consequences following damage to human prefrontal cortex'. *Cognition* 50(1–3): 7–15.

Blair, J. and Frith, U. (2000) 'Neurocognitive explanations of the antisocial personality disorders'. *Criminal Behaviour and Mental Health* 10: S66–S81.

Blake, P.Y., Pincus, J.H. and Buckner, C. (1995) 'Neurologic abnormalities in murderers'. *Neurology*. 45(9): 1641–1647.

Boucsein, W. (1992) *Electrodermal Activity*. New York: Plenum Press.

Cacioppo, J.T., Tassinary, L.G. and Berntson, G. (Eds) (2007) *Handbook of Psychophysiology*, 3rd Edition. New York: Cambridge University Press.

Caspi, A., McClay, J., Moffitt, T.E., Mill, J., Martin, J., Craig, I.W. et al. (2002) 'Role of genotype in the cycle of violence in maltreated children'. *Science* 297(5582): 851–854.

Chesterman, L., Taylor, P., Cox, T., Hill, M. and Lumsden, J. (1994) 'Multiple measures of cerebral state in dangerous mentally disordered inpatients'. *Criminal Behaviour and Mental Health* 4(3): 228–239.

Decety, J., Michalska, K.J., Akitsuki, Y. and Lahey, B.B. (2009) 'Atypical empathic responses in adolescents with aggressive conduct disorder'. *Biological Psychology* 80(2): 203–211.

Dickerson, S.S. and Kemeny, M.E. (2004) 'Acute stressors and cortisol responses'. *Psychological Bulletin* 130(3): 355–391.

Dolan, M. and Park, I. (2002) 'The neuropsychology of antisocial personality disorder'. *Psychological Medicine* 32(3): 417–427.

Duerk, J.L. (1999) 'Principles of MR image formation and reconstruction'. *Magnetic Resonance Imaging Clinics of North America* 7(4): 629–659.

Dustman, R.E., Shearer, D.E. and Emmerson, R.Y. (1999) 'Life-span changes in EEG spectral amplitude, amplitude variability and mean frequency'. *Clinical Neurophysiology* 110(8): 1399–1409.

Farrington, D.P. (1997) 'The relationship between low resting heart rate and violence'. In A. Raine, P.A. Brennan, D.P. Farrington and S.A. Mednick (Eds.), *Biosocial Bases of Violence* (pp. 89–106). New York: Prenum Press.

Gao, Y., Baker, L.A., Raine, A., Wu, H. and Bezdjian, S. (2009) 'Brief report: Interaction between social class and risky decision-making in children with psychopathic tendencies'. *Journal of Adolescence* 32(2): 409–414.

Gao, Y., Glenn, A.L., Schug, R.A., Yang, Y. and Raine, A. (2009) 'The neurobiology of psychopathy: A neurodevelopmental perspective'. *Canadian Journal of Psychiatry*, 54, 813–823.

Gao, Y. and Raine, A. (2009) 'P3 event-related potential impairments in antisocial and psychopathic individuals'. *Biological Psychology* 82(3): 199–210.

Gao, Y., Raine, A., Venables, P.H., Dawson, M.E. and Mednick, S.A. (2010) 'Association between poor childhood fear conditioning and adult crime'. *American Journal of Psychiatry*, 167, 56–60.

Glenn, A.L., Raine, A. and Schug, R.A. (2009) 'The neural correlates of moral decision-making in psychopathy'. *Molecular Psychiatry* 14(1): 5–6.

Granger, D.A., Kivlighan, K.T., El-Sheikh, M., Gordis, E.B. and Stroud, L. (2007a) 'Salivary alpha-amylase in biobehavioral research'. *Annals of the New York Academy of Sciences* 1098(1): 122–144.

Granger, D.A., Kivlighan, K.T., Fortunato, C., Harmon, A.G., Hibel, L.C., Schwartz, E.B. and Whembolua, G.L. (2007b) 'Integration of salivary biomarkers into developmental and behaviorally-oriented research'. *Physiology and Behavior* 92(4): 583–590.

Heaton, R.K., Chelune, G.J., Talley, J.L., Kay, G.G. and Curtis, G. (1993) *Wisconsin Card Sorting Test manual—revised and expanded*. Odessa, FL: Psychological Assessment Resources.

Hugdahl, K. (2001) *Psychophysiology: The Mind-Body Perspective*. Cambridge, MA: Harvard University Press.

Iacono, W.G. and McGue, M. (2006) 'Association between P3 event-related brain potential amplitude and adolescent problem behavior'. *Psychophysiology* 43(5): 465–469.

Laakso, M.P., Vaurio, O., Koivisto, E., Savolainen, L., Eronen, M., Aronen, H.J., Hakola, P., Repo, E., Soininen, H. and Tiihonen, J. (2001) 'Psychopathy and the posterior hippocampus'. *Behavioural Brain Research* 118(2): 187–193.

Lahey, B., Moffitt, T.E. and Caspi, A. (Eds.) (2003) *Causes of Conduct Disorder and Juvenile Delinquency*. New York: Guilford Press.

Langevin, R., Bain, J., Wortzman, G., Hucker, S., Dickey, R. and Wright, P. (1988) 'Sexual sadism'. *Annals of the New York Academy of Sciences* 528(1): 163–171.

Lapierre, D., Braun, C.M.J. and Hodgins, S. (1995) 'Ventral frontal deficits in psychopathy'. *Neuropsychologia* 33(2): 139–151.

Lezak, M.D., Howieson, D.B., Loring, D.W., Hannay, H.J. and Fischer, J.S. (2004) *Neuropsychological Assessment*, 4th Edition. New York: Oxford University Press.

Malloy, P.F., Bihrle, A., Duffy, J. and Cimino, C. (1993) 'The orbitomedial frontal syndrome'. *Archives of Clinical Neuropsychology* 8(3): 185–201.

Malloy, P.F., Webster, J.S. and Russell, W. (1985) 'Tests of Luria's frontal lobe syndrome'. *International Journal of Clinical Neuropsychology* 7(2): 88–95.

McBurnett, K., Raine, A., Stouthamer-Loeber, M., Loeber, R., Kumar, A.M., Kumar, M. and Lahey, B.B. (2005) 'Mood and hormone responses to psychological challenge in adolescent males with conduct problems'. *Biological Psychiatry* 57(10): 1109–1116.

Miles, D.R. and Carey, G. (1997) 'Genetic and environmental architecture of human aggression'. *Journal of Personality and Social Psychology* 72(1): 207–217.

Moffitt, T.E. (2005) 'The new look of behavioral genetics in developmental psychopathology'. *Psychological Bulletin* 131(4): 533–554.

Morgan, A.B. and Lilienfeld, S.O. (2000) 'A meta-analytic review of the relationship between antisocial behavior and neuropsychological measures of executive function'. *Clinical Psychology Review* 20(1): 113–136.

Müller, J.L., Gänssbauer, S., Sommer, M., Döhnel, K., Weber, T., Schmidt-Wilcke, T. and Hajak, G. (2008) 'Gray matter changes in right superior temporal gyrus in criminal psychopaths'. *Psychiatry Research* 163(3): 213–222.

Ortiz, J. and Raine, A. (2004) 'Heart rate level and antisocial behavior in children and adolescents'. *Journal of American Academy of Child and Adolescent Psychiatry* 43(2): 154–162.

Patrick, C.J. (2008) 'Psychophysiological correlates of aggression and violence'. *Philosophical Transactions of the Royal Society* 363(1503): 2543–2555.

Plomin, R. and Daniels, D. (1987) 'Why are children in the same family so different from each other?' *Behavioral and Brain Sciences* 10(1): 1–16.

Poldrack, R.A., Fletcher, P.C., Henson, R.N., Worsley, K.J., Brett, M. and Nichols, T.E. (2008) 'Guidelines for reporting an fMRI study'. *NeuroImage* 40(2): 409–414.

Porteus, S.D. (1959) *The Maze Test and Clinical Psychology*. Palo Alto, CA: Pacific Books.

Porteus, S.D. (1965) *Porteus Maze Test. Fifty Years' Application*. New York: Psychological Corporation.

Raine, A. (1993) *The Psychopathology of Crime: Criminal Behavior as a Clinical Disorder*. San Diego, California: Academic Press.

Raine, A. (1996) 'Autonomic nervous system activity and violence' in D.M. Stoff and R.B. Cairns (Eds), *Aggression and Violence: Genetic, Neurobiological, and Biosocial Perspective* (pp. 145–168). Mahwah, NJ: Lawrence Erlbaum Associates.

Raine, A. (2008) 'From genes to brain to antisocial behavior'. *Current Directions in Psychological Science* 17(5): 323–328.

Raine, A., Brennan, P. and Mednick, S.A. (1994) 'Birth complications combined with early maternal rejection at age 1 year predispose to violent crime at age 18 years'. *Archives of General Psychiatry*, 51(12): 984–988.

Raine, A., Dodge, K., Loeber, R., Gatzke-Kopp L., Lynam, D., Reynolds, C. et al. (2006) 'The Reactive-Proactive Aggression (RPQ) Questionnaire'. *Aggressive Behavior* 32(2): 159–171.

Raine, A., Lee, L., Yang, Y. and Colletti, P. (2010) 'Neurodevelopmental marker for limbic maldevelopment in antisocial personality disorder and psychopathy'. *British Journal of Psychiatry*, 197, 186–192.

Raine, A., Lencz, T., Bihrle, S., LaCasse, L. and Colletti, P. (2000) 'Reduced prefrontal gray matter volume and reduced autonomic activity in antisocial personality disorder'. *Archives of General Psychiatry* 57(2): 119–127.

Raine, A., Mellingen, K., Liu, J., Venables, P.H. and Mednick, S.A. (2003) 'Effects of environmental enrichment at ages 3–5 years on schizotypal personality and antisocial behavior at ages 17 and 23 years'. *American Journal of Psychiatry* 160(9): 1627–1635.

Raine, A. and Venables, P.H. (1981) 'Classical conditioning and socialization'. *Personality and Individual Differences* 2(4): 273–283.

Raine, A., Venables, P.H., Dalais, C., Mellingen, K., Reynolds, C. and Mendrek, A. (2001) 'Early educational and health enrichment at age 3–5 years is associated with increased autonomic and central nervous system arousal and orienting at age 11 years'. *Psychophysiology* 38(2): 254–266.

Raine, A., Venables, P.H. and Mednick, S.A. (1997) 'Low resting heart rate age 3 years predisposes to aggression at age 11 years'. *Journal of American Academy of Child and Adolescent Psychiatry* 36(10): 1457–1464.

Raine, A., Venables, P.H. and Williams, M. (1990a) 'Relationships between central and autonomic measures of arousal at age 15 years and criminality at age 24 years'. *Archives of General Psychiatry* 47(11): 1003–1007.

Raine, A., Venables, P.H. and Williams, M. (1990b) 'Relationships between N1, P300, and contingent negative variation recorded at age 15 and criminal behavior at age 24'. *Psychophysiology* 27(5): 567–574.

Rhee, S.H. and Waldman, I.D. (2002) 'Genetic and environmental influences on antisocial behavior'. *Psychological Bulletin* 128(3): 490–529.

Ridderinkhof, K.R., Ullsperger, M., Crone, E.A. and Nieuwenhuis, S. (2004) 'The role of medial frontal cortex in cognitive control'. *Science* 306(5695): 443–447.

Rilling, J.K., Glenn, A.L., Jairam, M.R., Pagnoni, G., Goldsmith, D.R., Elfenbein, H.A. and Lilienfeld, S.O. (2007) 'Neural correlates of social cooperation and non-cooperation as a function of psychopathy'. *Biological Psychiatry* 61(11): 1260–1271.

Ritter, L.M., Meador-Woodruff, J.H. and Dalack, G.W. (2004) 'Neurocognitive measures of prefrontal cortical dysfunction in schizophrenia'. *Schizophrenia Research* 68(1): 65–73.

Sanders, J.A. (1995) 'Magnetic resonance imaging' in W.W. Orrison, Jr, J.D. Lewine, J.A. Sanders and M.F. Hartshorne (Eds), *Functional Brain Imaging* (pp 145–186). St. Louise: Mosby.

Schug, R.A., Gao, Y., Glenn, A.L., Peskin, M., Yang, Y. and Raine, A. (2010) 'The developmental bases: Neurobiological research and forensic applications'. In G. J. Towl and D. A. Crighton (Eds.), *Forensic Psychology* (pp. 73–94). UK: Wiley-Blackwell.

Schug, R.A. and Raine, A. (2009) 'Comparative meta-analyses of neuropsychological functioning in antisocial schizophrenic persons'. *Clinical Psychology Review* 29(3): 230–242.

Shallice, T. (1982) 'Specific impairments of planning'. *Philosophical Transactions of the Royal Society of London B* 298(1089): 199–209.

Thornberry, T.P. (Ed.) (1996) *Advances in Criminological Theory: Developmental Theories of Crime and Delinquency.* London: Transactions.

Van Goozen, S.H.M., Matthys, W., Cohen-Kettenis, P.T., Wied, C.G., Wiegant, V.M. and Van Engeland, H. (1998) 'Salivary cortisol and cardiovascular activity during stress in oppositional defiant disorder boys and normal controls'. *Biological Psychiatry* 43(7): 531–539.

Wahlund, K. and Kristiansson, M. (2009) 'Aggression, psychopathy and brain imaging'. *International Journal of Law and Psychiatry* 32(4): 266–271.

Wilson, J.Q. and Herrnstein, R. (1985) *Crime and Human Nature.* New York: Simon & Schuster.

Yang, Y., Raine, A., Lencz, T., Bihrle, S., LaCasse, L. and Colletti, P. (2005) 'Volume reduction in prefrontal gray matter in unsuccessful criminal psychopaths'. *Biological Psychiatry* 57(10): 1103–1108.

Yehuda, R., Halligan, S.L., Yang, R.K., Guo, L.S., Makotkine, I., Singh, B. and Pickholtz, D. (2003) 'Relationship between 24-hour urinary-free cortisol excretion and salivary cortisol levels sampled from awaking to bedtime in healthy subjects'. *Life Sciences* 73(3): 349–358.

6

Gun Prevalence, Homicide Rates and Causality: A GMM Approach to Endogeneity Bias

Tomislav Kovandzic,
Mark E. Schaffer, Gary Kleck

INTRODUCTION

As is well known, guns are heavily involved in violence in America, especially homicide. In 2008, 66.9 percent of homicides were committed by criminals armed with guns (US Federal Bureau of Investigation, 2010). Probably an additional 100,000 to 150,000 individuals were medically treated for non-fatal gunshot wounds (Kleck, 1997: 5). Further, relative to other industrialized nations, the US has higher rates of violent crime, both fatal and non-fatal, a larger private civilian gun stock (about 90 guns of all types for every 100 Americans), and a higher fraction of its violent acts committed with guns (Killias, 1993; Kleck, 1997: 64). These simple facts have led many to the logical conclusion that America's high rate of gun ownership must be at least partially responsible for the nation's high rates of violence, or at least its high homicide rate (e.g., Killias, 1993; Zimring and Hawkins, 1999).

But while gun levels may affect crime rates, higher crime rates may also increase gun levels by stimulating people to acquire guns, especially handguns, for self-protection. At least ten macro-level studies have found effects of crime rates on gun levels (Bordua and Lizotte, 1979; Clotfelter, 1981; Duggan, 2001; Kleck, 1979, 1984; Kleck and Patterson, 1993; Magaddino and Medoff, 1984; McDowall and Loftin, 1983; Rice and Hemley, 2002; Southwick, 1997), and individual-level survey evidence (not afflicted by problems of inferring the direction of causal influences) indicates that people buy guns in response to higher crime rates (Kleck and Kovandzic, 2009).

Thus, causality in the guns–crime relationship may run in either or both directions. If such a simultaneous relationship exists, but analysts fail to take account of it using appropriate methods, their results will be almost meaningless. What is asserted to be the impact of gun levels on crime rates will in fact also include the impact of crime rates on gun levels.

The result is that researchers who want to use macro-level data to estimate the relationship between gun prevalence and crime rates face a classic problem of 'endogeneity bias' resulting from reverse causation. In an econometric estimation in which the dependent variable is a crime measure and the explanatory variable of interest is gun prevalence or a proxy for it, the estimated coefficient on gun prevalence will be biased. Indeed, in such an estimation the crime–guns relationship could quantitatively dominate the guns–crime relationship, in which case the analyst will misinterpret an effect of crime on gun levels as an effect of gun levels on crime. Nor is reverse causality the only reason to expect endogeneity bias in practice; omitted variable bias and measurement error are also likely to be encountered by a researcher seeking to use macro-level data to investigate the gun–crime relationship.

This chapter shows how to address the problem of endogeneity bias by applying the modern estimation and specification testing procedures provided by the generalized method of moments (GMM), using the relationship of gun prevalence to homicide as an illustration. GMM can be thought of as an extension and generalization of the older method of instrumental variables (IV). These extensions are very useful in practice: GMM provides a framework that allows the empirical researcher to address not only endogeneity bias but also other practical problems with standard errors and inference such as heteroskedasticity and correlation of errors across observations (clustering). We apply these procedures in a cross-sectional setting to study the relationship between gun ownership levels and homicide rates using county-level data from the US in 1990. Gun ownership levels were measured using the percent of suicides committed with guns, which recent research indicates is the best measure of gun levels for cross-sectional research (Kleck, 2004). Our application provides a simple and easy-to-follow illustration of how researchers working on empirical problems in criminology can use GMM. Endogeneity problems are widespread in quantitative criminology, especially in aggregate studies of crime rates, as many of the explanatory variables (e.g., adoption of crime-control strategies, police levels, criminal sanctions) are likely to be simultaneously determined with the crime rate. The goal of this chapter is to set out the methodology of GMM in a way that enables an empirical researcher without a specialist training in econometrics to understand and to employ these techniques successfully.

The chapter is organized as follows. The next section discusses the problems of endogeneity bias, unrobustness of standard errors, and a third problem unrelated to GMM, namely the choice and calibration of a proxy when an explanatory variable is not directly available. The method of GMM is then described together with its relationship to other, older estimators such as ordinary least squares (OLS) and instrumental variables (IV), and the various tests of specification that an empirical researcher should employ and report are set out. This is followed by a description of the dataset and variables used. The results are then presented, followed by some conclusions, and finally suggestions for further reading and applications are given.

ENDOGENEITY, ROBUSTNESS AND MISMEASUREMENT

Consider a researcher who wants to estimate the impact of gun availability on the homicide rate.

The researcher has available cross-sectional data on localities (we consider the potential alternative of longitudinal data in the next section). The researcher estimates the following simple linear model using OLS:

$$h_i = \beta g_i + u_i \qquad (6.1)$$

where h_i is the homicide rate in locality i, g_i is the level of gun ownership, u_i is an error term, and for expositional convenience the constant term is suppressed. The parameter of interest to the researcher in equation (6.1) is β, the impact of gun levels on the homicide rate. There are three potential pitfalls facing the researcher that we consider in this section: the variable g_i may be 'endogenous' (correlated with the error u_i), in which case the OLS estimate of β will be biased; the OLS standard errors needed to test the significance of β may not be 'robust'; and a satisfactory direct measure of gun ownership may simply not be available, in which case the researcher needs to work with a proxy measure of gun prevalence. In the next section we outline an estimation strategy built on the GMM that can address the first two pitfalls, as well a practical solution for the proxy problem.

The endogeneity problem

The first property that empirical researchers look for in an estimator is usually that it is unbiased, or at least 'consistent'. ('Consistency' is an 'asymptotic' property of an estimator; i.e., a property that emerges as the sample size increases. Intuitively, an estimator that is consistent is asymptotically unbiased – there might be a bias, but the bias gets small as the sample size gets larger.) The key requirement for the OLS estimator $\hat{\beta}_{OLS}$ to be consistent is that gun levels g_i must be 'exogenous'. This 'exogeneity' requirement can be stated in various ways: g_i is uncorrelated with the error term u_i, g_i and u_i are 'orthogonal' (i.e., independent), or, in statistical terms, $E(g_i u_i) = 0$. This last statistical expression is vsometimes called a 'moment condition' or 'orthogonality condition'. All these are different ways of stating the same requirement.

If the exogeneity condition fails, then we say g_i is 'endogenous'. The consequences for the OLS estimator $\hat{\beta}_{OLS}$ are serious: it is no longer unbiased or even consistent. The bias of $\hat{\beta}_{OLS}$ is upwards if g_i and u_i are positively correlated, and downwards if g_i and u_i are negatively correlated. This bias can arise for various reasons, and the literature sometimes uses different terms for the bias depending on the cause. In this chapter we will use the general term 'endogeneity bias' irrespective of the reason. Unfortunately, there are three good reasons to think that the exogeneity condition will fail and the OLS estimator $\hat{\beta}_{OLS}$ will suffer from endogeneity bias if it is used to estimate the impact of gun prevalence on homicide rates. All three – reverse causality bias, omitted variables bias and measurement error bias – are forms of endogeneity bias.

Reverse (or 'simultaneous') causality arises when there is a second relationship in which gun levels depend on homicide rates:

$$g_i = \delta h_i + e_i \qquad (6.2)$$

As already noted, there is empirical evidence from the US that high crime rates do lead people to acquire guns for self-protection, so this is a serious practical problem for the researcher. The impact of reverse causality on $\hat{\beta}_{OLS}$ depends on δ given that δ and the correlation between g_i and u_i will have the same sign. The evidence cited previously suggests that $\delta > 0$ – high crime levels lead to higher gun levels – and hence g_i and u_i will be positively correlated. The result is that $\hat{\beta}_{OLS}$ will be biased upwards. Indeed, if the reverse causality is strong enough, the researcher could find that $\hat{\beta}_{OLS} > 0$ and conclude that more guns means more crime even if the 'true' β – the true impact of guns on crime, all else being equal – is negligible or negative.

The second reason the exogeneity assumption may fail is because of omitted variable bias. Say that the 'true' relationship between homicide rates and gun prevalence is actually

$$h_i = \hat{a}g_i + \gamma X_i + \varepsilon_i \qquad (6.1b)$$

but the researcher does not include the variable X_i in the estimation, and simply estimates equation (6.1) using OLS. This will result in 'omitted variable bias', depending on whether gun prevalence g_i is correlated with the omitted variable X_i. The reason is straightforward: if equation (6.1b) is the 'true' model, then the error term in the equation actually estimated, equation (6.1), can be written $u_i = \gamma X_i + \varepsilon_i$. It is easy to see that if g_i is correlated with X_i, it will also be correlated with u_i, and the OLS estimate of equation (6.1) will once again suffer from endogeneity bias. The sign of the bias in $\hat{\beta}_{OLS}$ is determined by the sign of γ and the sign of the correlation of g_i and X_i; if both are positive or both are negative, $\hat{\beta}_{OLS}$ will be biased upwards, otherwise it will be biased downwards.

The simplest way to address this problem is to include X_i in the estimation, but often this is impossible because X_i is not available to the researcher, and the guns–homicide application is no exception. For example, we expect that pro-violence sub-cultural norms in a locality will be a positive determinant of homicide, and will also be positively correlated with gun prevalence. The result will be a $\hat{\beta}_{OLS}$ that is biased upwards, because in effect we are mistakenly attributing the pro-violence effect of local norms to gun prevalence. Local laws are another example of a potentially important omitted variable that in practice may not be available to the researcher.

The third reason the exogeneity assumption may fail is because of classical (i.e., random) measurement error: the true relationship between gun and homicide is

$$h_i = \hat{a}g_i^* + u_i \qquad (6.1c)$$

but the observable level of gun prevalence, measured with error η_i, is all we have available:

$$g_i = g_i^* + \eta_i \qquad (6.3)$$

If we estimate (6.1) using g_i instead of the unavailable true g_i^*, the result is again an endogeneity bias in $\hat{\beta}_{OLS}$, because measurement error creates a correlation between g_i and u_i. In this case, the endogeneity bias is a form of attenuation bias, because $\hat{\beta}_{OLS}$ will be biased away from the true β and towards zero.

The standard solution to endogeneity bias is to estimate equation (6.1) using the method of IV or the more modern framework of GMM. These methods require the researcher to have a variable Z_i that is correlated with guns ('instrument relevance') and that is also uncorrelated with the error term u_i in the homicide equation ('instrument exogeneity'). We describe the method of GMM in the next section. First, however, we discuss the issue of robustness of standard errors.

Robustness of standard errors

Exogeneity is all that is required for the OLS estimator to be consistent. But we also need an estimate of the variance of the OLS estimator in order to calculate standard errors, test hypotheses, construct confidence intervals, and so forth.

The classical textbook formula for OLS standard errors can fail for two reasons that are likely to be important in practice. First, u_i, the error term in equation (6.1) may be conditionally heteroskedastic; that is, the variance of the error term u_i may be correlated with the variance of the explanatory variable in (1), g_i. This phenomenon – that when u_i is highly variable, g_i is also highly variable – is very common in cross-sectional and panel data. If, for example, the localities in our dataset – say, US counties – vary a lot in size, we should expect that all our variables will bounce around a lot more in very large counties than in very small ones. The effect on the OLS standard errors is typically to make them 'too small', and hence to lead the researcher to conclude that $\hat{\beta}_{OLS}$ is a more precise estimate than it actually is.

Second, the classical textbook formula for OLS standard errors assumes 'independence'. More precisely, it assumes that $g_i u_i$ is uncorrelated across localities; that is, $g_i u_i$ and $g_j u_j$. This too is likely to be untrue in cross-sectional and panel data. Here omitted variables make an unwelcome reappearance, because they are a prime culprit behind the failure of the independence assumption in cross-sectional data. For example, state-level variables such as laws or economic shocks would affect counties in that state but not in other states; this can be enough to create a correlation between $g_i u_i$ and $g_j u_j$, where i and j refer to two counties in the state. Another example, very common in panel data applications, is serial correlation. If we were using panel data on counties, we should expect that $g_{it} u_{it}$ and $g_{it-1} u_{it-1}$, the observations for county i in periods t and $t-1$, are likely to be correlated. The effect of this 'clustering' or 'within-group correlation' is again typically to make the OLS standard errors 'too small'.

The modern approach to this problem is to use standard errors that are 'robust' to heteroskedasticity and clustering; in other words, to use standard errors that are correct (consistent) whether or not there is heteroskedasticity and/or clustering. These standard errors are known variously as Eicker–Huber–White or 'sandwich' standard errors; for conciseness we will simply call them 'robust'. As we discuss in the next section, this approach to obtaining consistent standard errors is closely linked to the GMM approach to obtaining consistent estimates of β.

The proxy problem

Ideally, researchers investigating the relationship between gun levels and homicide would have well-defined measures of both variables at the level of the locality. Unfortunately, direct measures of gun prevalence have severe drawbacks (which we discuss in the next section), and researchers have to make do with a proxy for gun prevalence. The relationship between the proxy p_i and the (unobserved) level of gun prevalence g_i is

$$p_i = \delta g_i + \eta_i \qquad (6.4)$$

and instead of estimating (6.1), the researcher estimates

$$h_i = b p_i + u_i \qquad (6.1d)$$

The task facing the researcher now is similar to, but more challenging than, the case of classical measurement error discussed previously. In addition to the other problems already discussed, the researcher now has the problem that the parameter δ relating gun prevalence to its proxy is unobservable and can't be directly estimated – if it could, the proxy would of course be unnecessary. This has two practical consequences. First, it is incumbent on the researcher to validate the proxy; that is, to assemble evidence that supports its use. If p_i is uncorrelated with actual gun levels g_i, it is, of course, useless. Second, the researcher should ideally also have available some estimate of the parameter δ (e.g., from a validation exercise). The coefficient b is not the quantitative impact of gun levels on crime rates; this is given by $\beta = b\delta$, and δ is not observed directly. A test of the estimated $\hat{b}$ may enable the researcher to say if there is a statistically significant non-zero impact of guns on crime; but without an estimate of δ, the researcher will be unable to say anything about the actual size of the impact.

INSTRUMENTAL VARIABLES AND GMM

GMM is a modern and increasingly popular approach to the problem of estimation with endogenous regressors. GMM provides a unified framework for estimation and testing that is naturally suited to empirical situations where endogeneity is a central problem. The literature on GMM is now vast and many good expositions are available. All modern graduate-level econometrics textbooks cover it, in varying degrees of detail. Hayashi (2000) is an advanced text that sets out many of the tests and results used and cited in this paper. Baum et al. (2003, 2007) set out the basics of IV and GMM estimation and specification testing, and describe the set of extended estimation and testing routines implemented for the Stata statistical package used here.

In this section we provide a brief non-specialist introduction to GMM. We show how GMM is related to older, standard estimators, how the GMM framework relates to the 'robust' approach to obtaining standard errors, and how GMM can be used in our application to obtain consistent estimates of the impact of gun prevalence on homicide rates. We then provide a checklist of specification tests that a researcher using GMM should employ. Throughout we use our example of the guns–crime relationship, but the recommended procedures and the specification testing checklist are generally applicable.

Box 6.1   A checklist

We have described previously all the tools needed for GMM-based estimation and testing of the guns–homicide relationship. The GMM procedure that we follow is:

1   Estimate equation (6.1) using efficient GMM or inefficient OLS and all the instruments $Z1_i$, $Z2_i$, etc., assuming that the measure of gun prevalence g_i is exogenous. Obtain the J statistic for the efficient GMM estimator. Allow for possible heteroskedasticity or clustering. If the J statistic is large, take this as evidence that one or more of $Z1_i$, $Z2_i$, ..., and g_i is endogenous, and proceed to Step 2. If the J statistic is small, take this as evidence that all the aforementioned variables are exogenous. However, prior research suggests that the assumption that gun prevalence is exogenous is questionable, so we proceed to Step 2 anyway.

2   Estimate equation (6.1) using efficient GMM or inefficient IV, this time treating gun prevalence as endogenous. Obtain the J statistic for the efficient GMM estimator. Allow for possible heteroskedasticity or clustering. If the J statistic is small, take this as evidence that the instruments $Z1_i$, $Z2_i$, ... are exogenous and proceed to Step 3. If the J statistic is large, take this as evidence that one or more of the instruments is endogenous. Unless there are a priori good reasons to suspect one instrument in particular is endogenous (and hence this suspicion can be tested using a C test), stop here – consistent estimation is not possible.

3   Test the relevance of the instruments $Z1_i$, $Z2_i$ in the specification estimated in Step 2. If the first-stage F statistic is large (greater than the Staiger–Stock rule of thumb value of 10 or greater than the Stock–Yogo critical values), proceed to Step 4. If the first-stage F statistic is small, conclude that the instruments are 'weak' and consider using alternative estimation methods (see 'Recommended Reading' section).

4   Test whether gun prevalence is endogenous using a GMM distance test using $J-J2$, where J is the J statistic using all the instruments plus treating gun levels as exogenous (Step 1) and $J2$ is the J statistic that does not assume exogeneity of g_i. If the C statistic is small, take this as evidence that gun prevalence is exogenous, and proceed to Step 5. If the C statistic is large, take this as evidence that gun prevalence is endogenous and go to Step 6.

5   (Where g_i is exogenous): *Consider* using the Step 1 estimates – efficient GMM or OLS – as final estimates. The former is consistent and efficient; the latter is consistent, but inefficient if errors are not homoskedastic and independent. *Alternatively*, because prior evidence and research suggests that gun levels may be subject to endogeneity bias from various sources, treat gun prevalence as endogenous anyway and go to Step 6.

6   (Where g_i is endogenous): Use the Step 2 estimates – efficient GMM or IV – as final estimates. The former is consistent and efficient, but may be more prone to problems in small samples; the latter is consistent, but inefficient if errors are not homoskedastic and independent. In the case IV is used, be sure to use standard errors that are robust to heteroskedasticity and clustering (this is automatic in the case of efficient GMM).

The classical method of moments (MM)

We begin by repeating the equation to be estimated:

$$h_i = \beta g_i + u_i \qquad (6.1)$$

We cannot use the OLS estimator because g_i is endogenous – it is correlated with the error term u_i. If, however, we have available a different variable or 'instrument' Z_i, we can obtain a consistent estimate of β, provided two conditions are met:

Assumption EX: Z_i is exogenous; i.e., uncorrelated with u_i
Assumption R: Z_i is correlated with g_i.

What we have done is replaced the failed requirement that g_i is exogenous with the requirement that the instrument Z_i is exogenous, and added the

requirement that Z_i is 'relevant'; that is, correlated with g_i.

If these two assumptions are satisfied, we can use the classical 'method of moments' (MM) introduced by Karl Pearson in 1894 to obtain a consistent estimate of β. The intuition behind the MM is simple. Formally stated, Assumption EX means that $E(z_i u_i) = 0$. This is an 'orthogonality' or 'moment' condition. It is an assumption, because we cannot observe the true error term u_i. But what we *can* do is calculate the residual, defined in the usual way as $\hat{u}_i \equiv h_i - \hat{\beta} g_i$. The crucial but simple point is that the residual depends on our estimate of β. By choosing a specific estimate $\hat{\beta}$, we are also choosing a set of residuals. But what estimate $\hat{\beta}$ should we choose? Pearson's suggestion was to choose $\hat{\beta}$ so that the residuals $\hat{u}_i$ 'behave like' the true error term u_i. The true error term is uncorrelated with Z_i – it satisfies the 'moment condition' $E(Z_i U_i) = 0$.

Pearson's suggestion is to choose $\hat{\beta}_{MM}$ so that the residuals $\hat{u}_i$ from the sample data we have at hand behave the same way; in other words, so that the sample mean of $(Z_i\hat{u}_i)$ is zero; that is, $\frac{1}{N}\sum Z_i\hat{u}_i = 0$. We refer to this as sample moment condition.

This is just one equation in one unknown, namely $\hat{\beta}_{MM}$. To solve the equation for $\hat{\beta}_{MM}$ we substitute for the residual $\hat{u}_i$ to obtain $\frac{1}{N}\sum Z_i\left(h_i - \hat{\beta}_{MM}g\right) = 0$, and after simplifying and rearranging, we have the MM estimate of the impact of guns on homicide: $\hat{\beta}_{MM} = \sum Z_i h_i / \sum Z_i g_i$. The MM estimator in this simple case is none other than the standard IV estimator. Provided assumptions EX and R are satisfied, $\hat{\beta}_{MM}$ is a consistent estimate of the impact of guns levels on homicide rate.

In fact, OLS is also a special case of a MM estimator. It is a straightforward exercise to replace assumption EX above with our original (but flawed) assumption that g_i is exogenous, and then derive the OLS estimator as the MM estimator.

GMM

A natural question is, what if we have more than one Z_i? Say we want to estimate (6.1), and we have two variables, Z_{1i} and Z_{2i}, that we believe are also exogenous. We now have two exogeneity assumptions; that is, two moment conditions: $E(Z_{1i}U_i) = 0$ (assumption EX1) and $E(Z_{2i}U_i) = 0$ (assumption EX2). We can't use the classical method of moments, for the following reason. MM says to choose $\hat{\beta}_{MM}$ so that vthe sample moment conditions mimic assumptions EX1 and EX2; that is, so that $\frac{1}{N}\sum Z1_i\hat{u}_i = 0$ and $\frac{1}{N}\sum Z2_i\hat{u}_i = 0$. However, we can't, because there is a basic problem: we have two equations but only one unknown, $\hat{\beta}_{MM}$. The parameter β is *overidentified*: there are more exogenous variables than there are parameters to be estimated.

The GMM estimator $\hat{\beta}_{GMM}$ addresses this problem by selecting a $\hat{\beta}_{GMM}$ that gets the two sample moment conditions as 'close' to zero as possible. More precisely, GMM proceeds by defining an objective function $J(.)$ that is a function of the data, the parameters and a set of weights in a weighting matrix **W.** The GMM objective function is a quadratic form in the sample moment conditions; that is, the sample moment conditions are weighted using the weights in **W** and summed to produce a scalar that is minimized: $J(.)$ can be thought of as the 'GMM distance' – the distance from zero, which is the

value the objective function would take if all the sample moment conditions were satisfied – and the definitions of the GMM estimator $\hat{\beta}_{GMM}$ is that it is the value of $\hat{\beta}$ that minimizes J given **W** and the data.

There are as many different GMM estimators as there are different possible **W**s to use in J. Where GMM comes into its own is when an optimal weighting matrix is chosen. Using an optimal weighting matrix guarantees that the GMM estimator is 'efficient' – roughly speaking, it is the most precise estimator possible (it has the smallest possible asymptotic variance) given all the assumptions made by the researcher. Hansen, who introduced GMM in a seminal paper in 1982, showed that the optimal GMM weighting matrix is the inverse of the covariance matrix of moment conditions, which we will denote by Ω. In our example, the elements of Ω are the variances and covariances of $(Z1_iU_i)$ and $(Z2_iU_i)$.

The matrix Ω is unknown, but it can be readily estimated. This is where the link with robust standard errors comes in. The matrix that is used for calculating robust standard errors is none other than an estimate of this same Ω used to calculate the efficient GMM estimator. In GMM estimation, efficiency and robustness go hand-in-hand. Thus:

(a) If we use an $\hat{\Omega}$ that is obtained under the assumption of classical homoskedastic and independent errors as in traditional OLS, the GMM estimator will be efficient under the assumption of homoskedasticity and independence.

(b) If we use an $\hat{\Omega}$ that allows for arbitrary heteroskedasticity, the GMM estimator will be efficient for arbitrary heteroskedasticity, and the GMM standard errors will be robust in the presence of heteroskedasticity.

(c) If we use an $\hat{\Omega}$ that allows for arbitrary heteroskedasticity and within-group correlation ('clustering'), the GMM estimator will be efficient for arbitrary heteroskedasticity and clustering, and the GMM standard errors will be robust in the presence of heteroskedasticity and clustering.

It is helpful to contrast the use of the efficient GMM estimators in (a), (b) and (c) with the use of the IV estimator combined with robust standard errors, a practice commonplace in empirical work. In cases (b) and (c), both the efficient GMM estimator and the IV estimator will be consistent, and the standard errors in both cases will also be consistent. The difference is that the efficient GMM estimator is more precise. In case (a), where we assume that the errors are classical, homoskedastic and independent errors, the efficient GMM estimator *is* the IV estimator – they are one and the same. The IV estimator is simply a special case of a GMM estimator, one that is consistent and efficient under homoskedasticity and independence, but inefficient (although still consistent) if the errors are heteroskedastic or clustered.

We can make a similar contrast between efficient GMM and OLS in (a), (b) and (c) when g_i is considered exogenous. Assumption R about the instruments is no longer needed in this case, but Assumption EX is still useful because it means that efficient GMM can deliver more precise estimates than OLS. The efficient GMM estimator in this special case is known as 'heteroskedastic OLS' or HOLS, and was introduced by Cragg (1983). When g_i is exogenous, OLS is a special case of a GMM estimator, consistent and efficient if errors are classical, and consistent but inefficient if the errors are heteroskedastic or clustered, just like IV.

Specification testing: exogeneity

An attractive feature of GMM for the empirical researcher is that is makes specification testing very straightforward. A 'specification test' is a test of one or more of the assumptions required for the model. In our application, these are tests of the assumptions of exogeneity and relevance. Reporting such tests is now essential in any piece of empirical work using IV or GMM methods.

GMM provides a straightforward framework for testing exogeneity when the equation is overidentified. Under the null hypothesis that the all the exogeneity assumptions are valid – all the variables that were assumed to be exogenous are indeed exogenous – the minimized value of J is distributed as χ^2 with degrees of freedom equal to the degree of overidentification. This 'overidentification test' is known in the literature as the Hansen or Sargan–Hansen J statistic and is, conveniently, an automatic by-product of GMM estimation. The consequence of a failure of exogeneity of instruments is the same as in the case of OLS: the estimated $\hat{\beta}_{GMM}$ will be inconsistent.

The same framework can be used to test the validity of a subset of exogeneity conditions; that is, to test whether or not selected variables are exogenous. For example, say we have doubts about whether $Z1_i$ is actually exogenous. Consider the J statistic resulting from two different efficient GMM estimations: J is the J statistic from an efficient GMM estimation that uses both $Z1_i$ and $Z2_i$ as instruments, and $J2$ is the J statistic from an efficient GMM estimation that uses only $Z2_i$. Under the null hypothesis, both $Z1_i$ and $Z2_i$ are exogenous; under the alternative hypothesis, only $Z2_i$ is exogenous. A 'GMM distance' or 'C' test of the exogeneity of $Z1_i$ is given by the quantity

$C = J - J2$. Under the null hypothesis, C should be distributed as χ^2 with one degree of freedom. A large-test statistic suggests that in fact $Z1_i$ is not a valid instrument, but rather is endogenous.

To take another example that is important for our application: say we want to see if we have evidence that indeed g_i is endogenous. The GMM distance approach suggests that we compare the J statistic from an efficient GMM estimation that uses $Z1_i$ and $Z2_i$ as instruments to a J statistic from an efficient GMM estimation that uses $Z1_i$, $Z2_i$ and g_i. (This means treating g_i as exogenous, which in the GMM framework is either similar to or identical to OLS – but we can still get a J statistic from the estimation.) The difference between these two J statistics will distributed as χ^2 with one degree of freedom if g_i is actually exogenous. For the reasons discussed earlier, a priori we suspect this is unlikely, and the GMM distance statistic will probably be large.

The robustness features of GMM estimation carry over to J and C statistics. If the $\hat{\Omega}$ used in the GMM estimation is robust under arbitrary heteroskedasticity, then not only will the efficient GMM estimator be efficient for arbitrary heteroskedasticity, the J and C statistics will also be consistent for tests of exogeneity. This is one of the most important practical reasons for using the GMM framework. Older specification tests such as Sargan's (1958) NR^2 overidentification statistic and the Durbin–Wu–Hausman endogeneity test are *not* robust – they require the assumptions of homoskedasticity and independence. In fact, these older statistics can be derived as special cases of the more general GMM test statistics. In practice there is rarely any reason for empirical researchers to use these older, un-robust tests given that robust GMM-based statistics can be obtained just as easily.

The intuition behind the J statistic is actually quite straightforward. The power of these tests to detect specification failures – that is, that instruments are endogenous – comes from a 'vector of contrasts'. In our simple one-endogenous-regressor example, we could, if we wanted to, use our two instruments separately, and thereby obtain two different estimates, $\hat{\beta}_{Z1}$ and $\hat{\beta}_{Z2}$. If our two instruments $Z1_i$ and $Z2_i$ are both exogenous, then these two estimates should be fairly similar, since both are consistent estimates of the true β. But what if $\hat{\beta}_{Z1}$ and $\hat{\beta}_{Z2}$ are very *different*? The only way these two estimators can be different is if at least one of them is wrong: either $Z1_i$ is actually endogenous and $\hat{\beta}_{Z1}$ suffers from endogeneity bias; and/or $Z2_i$ is actually endogenous and $\hat{\beta}_{Z2}$ suffers from endogeneity bias. The J statistic in this case is essentially a measure of the difference between $\hat{\beta}_{Z1}$ and $\hat{\beta}_{Z2}$; the bigger the difference, the more likely it is that either $Z1_i$ and/or $Z2_i$ is endogenous. The C statistic has a similar intuitive interpretation for the subset of instruments being tested for endogeneity.

This intuitive interpretation of the J statistic also makes clear when the J test will *not* have the power to detect endogeneity problems. Say that both $Z1_i$ and $Z2_i$ are endogenous, and hence both $\hat{\beta}_{Z1}$ and $\hat{\beta}_{Z2}$ suffer from endogeneity bias. What if the size of the endogeneity bias is similar in both cases? Unfortunately for us, there will be little difference between $\hat{\beta}_{Z1}$ and $\hat{\beta}_{Z2}$, and the J statistic will be small. In other words, the two estimates will be similar – similarly 'wrong', but still similar – and our 'vector of contrasts' test will show a small contrast. One lesson from this discussion is that the J test will have more power to detect problems if the instruments used derive from different sources, since variables from different sources are less likely to share endogeneity biases that are very similar. (For further discussion of this point, see Stock and Watson, 2007, and Wooldridge, 2008, for simple expositions, and Kovandzic et al., 2008, for an application to the guns–homicide model.)

Specification testing: relevance

The second requirement for a GMM estimator is assumption R: an instrument Z_i must be correlated with g_i. This assumption can and should also be subjected to specification testing.

In the case of a single endogenous regressor, as in our application, the standard specification test is straightforward and very easy to implement: the statistic for instrument relevance is the F test of the excluded instruments in the 'first-stage' regression. The 'first-stage' regression is identical to the first stage of 'two-stage least squares' (2SLS), an alternative method of calculating the traditional IV estimator. In the first-stage regression, the endogenous variables are regressed on the instruments plus any exogenous covariates used in the main equation. In our simple example of two instruments and no exogenous covariates, for example, the researcher should estimate

$$g_i = \theta_1 Z1_1 + \theta_2 Z2_1 + v_i \qquad (6.5)$$

and, after examining θ_1 and θ_2, for their consistency with theory and prior evidence, calculate a standard F statistic for their joint significance; a large value indicates that the model is identified. If heteroskedasticity or clustering is suspected, a heteroskedastic- or cluster-robust test statistic can be used. If the main equation (6.1) being estimated includes exogenous covariates, these should also be included in (6.5).

It is not enough for this F statistic to be significant at, say, the 5 percent or 1 percent levels. If the instruments are correlated with the endogenous regressor but only weakly, the F statistic will be significant at conventional levels, but the IV and GMM may still suffer from serious problems. Recent research (e.g., Bound et al., 1995; Staiger and Stock, 1997; Stock et al., 2002, which provides a survey) has shown that when instruments are weak, IV/GMM estimates of parameters will be badly biased (in the same direction as OLS), estimated standard errors will be too small and the null hypothesis will be rejected too often. Staiger and Stock (1997) recommend an F statistic of at least 10 as a rule of thumb for the standard IV estimator Stock and Yogo (2005) provide more detailed advice based on Monte Carlo studies, and show *inter alia* that the Staiger–Stock rule of thumb is a reasonable guideline to follow for the single-endogenous-regressor case when the number of instruments is small.

Caveats

Useful as it is, GMM is not a panacea, and we note here several caveats to its use besides those already mentioned. First, the use of large numbers of instruments can generate bias problems, and the general advice here is to be parsimonious with the number of instruments employed. Second, there is some evidence that the standard errors for some efficient GMM estimators may be biased downwards in small samples. A conservative estimation strategy adopted by some researchers is consequently to use the inefficient IV estimator, rely on robust standard errors for inference, and use the robust GMM J and C statistics for specification testing.

DATA, MODEL AND PROXY VALIDATION

Data and model

To estimate the impact of gun availability on homicide rates, we use cross-sectional data for all US counties from 49 states for which relevant data were available ($N = 3,058$). The missing state is Alaska, which had to be excluded because one of our key variables pertains to election results, and election districts in this state cannot be confidently linked with particular counties (boroughs). The use of 1990 data is dictated by two factors. First, most of the control variables included in the homicide equations to mitigate omitted variable bias are available at the county level only during census years. A second reason for choosing 1990 is the fact that the firearm crime rate (homicide, robbery and assault) had reached its highest level in nearly 30 years by 1990. It is reasonably argued that if gun availability is responsible for higher homicide rates, the high levels of firearm crime in 1990 should provide one of the best opportunities to date for testing the gun availability/homicide relationship.

County-level data were chosen for several reasons. First, the use of counties provides for a diverse sample of ecological units, including urban, suburban and rural areas. Second, counties are more internally homogenous than nations, states or metropolitan areas, thereby reducing potential aggregation bias. Third, counties exhibit great between-unit variability in both gun availability and homicide rates, which is precisely what gun availability and homicide research is trying to explain. Fourth, county data provide a much larger sample than previous gun level studies, which have focused mainly on nations, states, or large cities.

Our estimation equation includes state fixed effects; that is, state dummy variables. This enables us to control for any unobserved county characteristics that vary at the state level and that could be expected to influence both gun levels and homicide rates. Examples of such confounders would be state laws and judicial practice relating directly or indirectly to homicide and gun ownership, state-level resources devoted to law enforcement, and incarceration rates in state prisons. The disadvantage of this approach is that only variables available at the county level can be used in the estimations, because state-level measures would be perfectly collinear with the fixed effects.

Although the used of state fixed effects can address some issues relating to unobservables that vary at the state level, remaining within-state correlation would mean that classical OLS-type standard errors would be inconsistent. Heteroskedasticity is also likely to be present. The standard approach to addressing these problems using disaggregated US locality data is the heteroskedastic and cluster-robust approach, clustering on states. This allows for the county-level errors to be arbitrarily correlated within states, though we still need to assume that they are uncorrelated across states.

We follow the convention for crime policy studies and use a linear model in which most variables are specified in logs. The dependent variable in our model is the log of the gun homicide rate per 100,000 county population (log CRG); if higher gun levels increase the homicide rate at all, they must do so by, at minimum, increasing the *gun* homicide rate. Homicide data for each county were obtained using special Mortality Detail File computer tapes (not the public use tapes) made available by the National

Center for Health Statistics (US National Center for Health Statistics, 1997). The data include all intentional homicides in the county with the exception of those due to legal intervention (e.g., police shootings and executions). Homicide rates are averages for the seven years 1987 to 1993, thus bracketing the census year of 1990 for which data on many of the control variables were available.

The use of logs poses some minor problems, because even though we are using seven-year averages, some variables are zeros prior to logging. The loss of observations because the log of zero is undefined gives us a final sample size of 2,588 counties. Most of the loss of observations is due to counties which had no non-gun murders in 1987–1993. These counties are mostly fairly small (an average population of about 8,000 *versus* 93,000 for the counties in the estimation sample) and together accounted for less than 2 percent of the total population in 1990.

Surveys asking people directly whether they own guns are usually limited to a single large area, such as a nation or state. Instead, we use the best proxy of gun prevalence for cross-sectional research that is available at the county level, the percentage of suicides committed with guns (PSG). Our specification uses the log of the gun suicide percent (log PSG). As was done with homicide rates, PSG was computed for the seven-year period 1987–1993. Similar to homicide, data for the percent of suicides committed with guns were obtained using special Part III Mortality Detail File computer tapes made available by the National Center for Health Statistics. Unlike widely available public-use versions, the tapes permit the aggregation of death counts for even the smallest counties (US National Center for Health Statistics, 1997).

In addition to the gun prevalence measure, we included a set of county-level control variables as regressors. Decisions as to which variables to include in the homicide equations were based on a review of previous macro-level studies linking homicide rates to structural characteristics of ecological units (see Kleck, 1997, chapter 3; Kovandzic et al., 1998; Land et al., 1990; Sampson, 1986; Vieraitis, 2000, and the studies reviewed therein).

We were particularly concerned to control for variables that had opposite-sign associations with gun levels and homicide rates because such variables could suppress evidence of any positive effect of gun levels on homicide rates. Thus, we controlled for the percent of the population that is rural because rural people are more likely to own guns, but less likely to commit homicide. Likewise, we controlled for the poverty rate, the share of the population in the high-homicide ages of 18–24 and 25–34, and the African-American share of the population because people in these groups are less likely to own guns, but more likely to commit homicide, than other people (Cook and Ludwig, 1997; Kleck, 1997; US Federal Bureau of Investigation, 2010). The other controls used were percentage Hispanic, population density, average education level, unemployment rate, transient population (born out-of-state), vacant housing units, female-headed households with children, median household income, households earning less than $15,000, and inequality (ratio of households earning more than $75,000 to households earning less than $15,000).

The sets of controls for rurality and age structure are, exceptionally, used in percentage rather than log form. Because the raw percentages sum to 100, including all categories would generate a perfect collinearity problem, and so one category must be omitted. Using raw percentages has the appealing feature that the results are invariant to whichever percentage is the omitted category. We omit the percentage rural and the percentage aged 65+.

The excluded instrumental variables used are (1) log OMAG, the log of the combined subscription rates of three of the most popular outdoor/sport magazines (*Field and Stream*, *Outdoor Life* and *Sports Afield*) in 1993, per 100,000 county population (Audit Bureau of Circulations, 1993), and (2) log PCTREP88, the log of the percentage of the county population voting for the Republican candidate in the 1988 presidential election.

Both excluded instruments are theoretically important correlates of gun ownership that are plausibly otherwise unrelated to homicide. Log OMAG serves as a measure of interest in outdoor sports such as hunting and fishing, or perhaps as a measure of a firearms-related 'sporting/outdoor culture' (Bordua and Lizotte, 1979). Log PCTREP88 serves as a measure of political conservatism and hence should be positively correlated with gun ownership. The 1988 election results were chosen in preference to the 1992 results because the choice between the two main candidates in 1988 maps more closely to attitudes towards gun ownership. In the 1992 election, unlike the 1988 election, the politically less conservative candidate (negatively correlated with gun ownership) was also a southerner (positively correlated with gun ownership). The 1992 results are also less easily interpreted because of the significant share of the vote that went to the third-party candidate, Ross Perot. Prior research suggests that both variables are important predictors of gun ownership (Cook and Ludwig, 1997: 35; Kleck, 1997: 70–72).

Table 6.1 lists and provides a brief description of each variable used along with their means and standard deviations. Data for the control variables were obtained from the US Bureau of the Census, *County and City Data Book, 1994*, except for log PCTREP88, which is from ICPSR (1995), and rurality, which is from US Census Bureau (1990).

Proxy validation

We need to validate and calibrate our proxy to available survey-based measures of gun levels. Because of its availability in the widely used General Social Surveys (GSS), the most convenient calibration is to the mean percentage of households with guns (HHG). National gun survey prevalence figures have been available since 1959, though not for every year. Using state-level measures from surveys conducted by the Centers for Disease Control (CDC) in 2002 (Okoro et al., 2005) and PSG data for 1995–2002 taken from CDC's WONDER service, a simple OLS regression based on 50 states of log PSG on log HHG is as follows (standard errors are in parentheses):

$$\log \text{PSG} = 2.31 + 0.481 \log \text{HHG} + e$$

$$(0.12)\ (0.035)$$

The coefficient on log HHG can be interpreted as an estimate of the log–log calibration δ of the proxy p_i to the level of gun prevalence g_i in equation (6.4). The figure suggests that in our log–log estimations, the coefficient on our proxy log PSG should be approximately halved $(\delta = 0.481 \approx 0.5)$ in order to be interpreted as elasticity of gun homicide with respect to actual gun levels. This is, however, only an approximation based on limited data and a simple linear calibration, and should be used with caution.

RESULTS

In this section we discuss the estimation results, following the checklist presented earlier. The main estimation results for the estimation of the gun homicide/gun prevalence relationship using efficient GMM, IV and OLS are presented in Table 6.2. Columns 1 and 2 report the efficient GMM and OLS estimations that treat our proxy for gun prevalence, log PSG, as exogenous. Columns 3 and 4 report the efficient GMM estimation and IV estimations in which log PSG is assumed endogenous. The bottom half of Table 6.2 reports the details of the 'first-stage' regression corresponding to the estimations in column 3 and 4. All statistics and standard errors reported are

Table 6.1   Descriptive statistics, estimation sample ($n = 2,588$)

		Mean	Std dev.	Min	Max
Homicide variables, 1987–93 average					
CRGMUR	Gun homicides per 100,000 population	4.62	4.03	0.13	46.08
Log CRGMUR	" logged	1.16	0.91	−2.02	3.83
Gun availability, 1987–93 average					
PSG	% suicides with guns	71.49	15.41	14.29	100.00
Log PSG	" logged	4.24	0.24	2.66	4.61
Instruments					
PCTREP88	% presidential vote Republican, 1988	55.55	10.09	14.83	85.16
Log PCTREP88	" logged	4.00	0.20	2.70	4.44
OMAG	Subscriptions per 100,000 population of 3 top outdoor/sport magazine subscriptions	2558	1099	220	9955
Log OMAG	" logged	7.75	0.45	5.39	9.21
Controls					
DENSITY	Persons per square mile	244	1552	0	53126
Log DENSITY	" logged	3.99	1.47	−1.04	10.88
PCTURBAN	% urban (inside urbanized area)	15.99	30.96	0.00	100.00
PCTSUBURBAN	% suburban (outside urbanized area)	24.40	22.83	0.00	100.00
PCTRURAL	% rural (farm + non-farm)	59.62	29.20	0.00	100.00
PCT0T17	% aged 17 and under	26.74	3.42	11.70	45.10
PCT18T24	% aged 18–24	9.81	3.47	3.70	48.00
PCT25T44	% aged 25–44	29.68	3.29	16.20	50.80
PCT45T64	% aged 45–64	19.42	2.18	3.90	27.60
PCT65PLUS	% aged 65 and over	14.34	4.00	1.40	34.00
PCTBLK	% African-American	10.03	15.03	0.01	86.24
Log PCTBLK	" logged	0.71	2.20	−4.76	4.46
PCTHISP	% Hispanic	4.70	11.53	0.03	97.22
Log PCTHISP	" logged	0.24	1.41	−3.41	4.58
PCTFEM18	% female-headed HHs w/children < 18	57.92	8.11	22.70	85.30
Log PCTFEM18	" logged	4.05	0.15	3.12	4.45
PCTEDUC	% aged 25+ with a BA degree or higher	13.58	6.77	4.10	53.40
Log PCTEDUC	" logged	2.51	0.44	1.41	3.98
PCTTRANS	% born out of state	28.31	15.09	2.76	86.54
Log PCTTRANS	" logged	3.21	0.52	1.02	4.46
Log MEDHHINC	Log median household income, 1989	10.06	0.26	9.06	10.99
PCTINCLT15K	% households with income < $15,000	32.21	10.04	5.00	65.90
Log PCTINCLT15K	" logged	3.42	0.35	1.61	4.19
INEQUALITY	% HHs w/income <$15k / % income >$75k	0.22	0.39	0.01	6.74
Log INEQUALITY	" logged	−2.06	0.92	−5.10	1.91
PCTPOOR	% persons below poverty line, 1989	16.90	8.20	2.20	63.10
Log PCTPOOR	" logged	2.71	0.49	0.79	4.14
PCTUNEMP	% persons unemployed	7.02	2.94	1.20	30.50
Log PCTUNEMP	" logged	1.87	0.40	0.18	3.42
PCTVACANT	% housing units vacant	13.75	9.57	2.70	70.80
Log PCTVACANT	" logged	2.44	0.59	0.99	4.26

Source: US Bureau of the Census, *County and City Data Book* (1994), except for (a) homicide rates and PSG, from US NCHS (1997); (b) PCTREP88, from ICPSR (1995); (c) magazine subscription rates used to construct OMAG, from Audit Bureau of Circulations (1993); (d) rurality measures, from US Bureau of the Census (1990).

Table 6.2   Log gun homicide equation

Dependent variable: Log CRGMUR				
	Log PSG-exogenous		Log PSG-endogenous	
	(1)	(2)	(3)	(4)
	Efficient GMM	OLS	Efficient GMM	IV
Log PSG	0.305**	0.185*	−2.383**	−2.372**
	(0.062)	(0.074)	(0.534)	(0.544)
Log DENSITY	0.086**	0.095**	−0.022	−0.021
	(0.031)	(0.035)	(0.042)	(0.043)
PCTSUBURBAN	−0.003**	−0.003**	−0.003**	−0.004**
	(0.001)	(0.001)	(0.001)	(0.001)
PCTURBAN	0.002*	0.002	0.002	0.001
	(0.001)	(0.001)	(0.001)	(0.001)
PCT0T17	0.035**	0.028**	0.031*	0.030*
	(0.008)	(0.008)	(0.014)	(0.014)
PCT18T24	−0.022**	−0.026**	−0.019*	−0.019
	(0.008)	(0.008)	(0.010)	(0.010)
PCT25T44	0.023**	0.028**	0.028*	0.028*
	(0.008)	(0.008)	(0.012)	(0.012)
PCT45T64	0.035**	0.043**	0.057**	0.057**
	(0.011)	(0.012)	(0.016)	(0.016)
Log PCTBLK	0.084**	0.090**	0.103**	0.102**
	(0.012)	(0.012)	(0.015)	(0.015)
Log PCTHISP	−0.001	0.014	−0.067*	−0.067*
	(0.026)	(0.027)	(0.030)	(0.030)
Log PCTFEM18	−0.281*	−0.274	−0.100	−0.097
	(0.143)	(0.144)	(0.177)	(0.180)
Log PCTEDUC	−0.075	−0.072	−0.185	−0.181
	(0.076)	(0.078)	(0.103)	(0.111)
Log PCTTRANS	−0.017	0.007	0.040	0.037
	(0.036)	(0.040)	(0.045)	(0.051)
Log MEDHHINC	−0.111	−0.116	0.043	0.029
	(0.326)	(0.349)	(0.369)	(0.390)
Log PCTINCLT15K	0.171	0.165	0.538	0.510
	(0.260)	(0.296)	(0.288)	(0.380)
Log INEQUALITY	0.132*	0.100	0.086	0.083
	(0.065)	(0.067)	(0.083)	(0.089)
Log PCTPOOR	0.748**	0.764**	0.498**	0.508**
	(0.151)	(0.161)	(0.150)	(0.176)
Log PCTUNEMP	−0.018	−0.067	0.078	0.081
	(0.053)	(0.058)	(0.088)	(0.092)
Log PCTVACANT	0.170**	0.150**	0.156**	0.154**
	(0.040)	(0.042)	(0.048)	(0.049)
State fixed effects	Yes	Yes	Yes	Yes
J statistic	$\chi^2(2) = 10.98$**, p-value = 0.004		$\chi^2(1) = 0.01$, p-value = 0.913	

(continued)

Table 6.2   Cont'd

Dependent variable: Log CRGMUR				
	Log PSG-exogenous		Log PSG-endogenous	
	(1)	(2)	(3)	(4)
	Efficient GMM	OLS	Efficient GMM	IV
C statistic for exogeneity of Log PGS	$\chi^2(1) = 10.96$**, p-value = 0.001		n.a.	
First-stage regression results				
F statistic			12.9	
Coefficients on IVs	n.a.		Log OMAG: 0.094** (0.022) Log PCTREP88: 0.090** (0.025)	
Observations (counties)	2,588	2,588	2,588	2,588
Clusters (states)	49	49	49	49

Notes: Efficient GMM = two-step efficient GMM, clustering on state.

Excluded instruments are Log OMAG and Log PCTREP88. * $p < 0.05$, ** $p < 0.01$. Standard errors in parentheses. Normal distribution (z-statistics) are used. Standard errors and test statistics in all cases are robust to arbitrary heteroskedasticity and within-state clustering. J statistic, columns (1) and (2) = heteroskedastic and cluster-robust test of the exogeneity of Log PSG, Log OMAG, Log PCTREP88. J statistic, columns (3) and (4) = heteroskedastic and cluster-robust test of the exogeneity of Log PSG, Log OMAG. C statistic, columns (1) and (2) = heteroskedastic and cluster-robust GMM distance test of the exogeneity of Log PSG.

robust to arbitrary heteroskedasticity and within-state correlation (clustering); the efficient GMM estimator is efficient for arbitrary heteroskedasticity and clustering. The efficient GMM estimator used is two-step feasible efficient GMM; see Hayashi (2000) or Baum et al. (2003) for a description.

Step 1 in our checklist is to estimate the equation, treating log PSG as exogenous, and examine the J statistic. The J test in this case is a test of the exogeneity of all the variables assumed to be exogenous: log PSG and all the other regressors, log OMAG and log PCTREP88. There are no endogenous variables in the equation, so the test statistic is distributed as χ^2 with two degrees of freedom, because there are two (excluded) instruments – 0 endogenous regressors = 2. The table reports only the J test statistic for the efficient GMM estimator, because the corresponding test statistic for OLS, the Sargan NR^2 statistic, would not be robust to heteroskedasticity and clustering. The J statistic is 10.98, which is very large for a $\chi^2(2)$ variable ($p = 0.004$). The null hypothesis that all our exogenous variables are actually exogenous is emphatically rejected. We conclude that there is evidence that one or more variables is actually endogenous, or perhaps that the equation is misspecified for other reasons. The immediate implication of this finding is that OLS estimation of the impact of gun prevalence on homicide levels is likely to be biased, resulting in faulty interpretations.

This is not surprising; a priori, we expected that log PSG is endogenous, and the coefficient in the estimation is likely to be biased upwards if log PSG is treated as exogenous. The estimated coefficient on log PSG in columns 1 and 2 is positive and statistically significant: 0.305 and significant at the 1 percent level if estimated using efficient GMM, or 0.185 with a somewhat larger standard error, but still significant at the 5 percent level, if estimated using (inefficient) OLS. Our calibration exercise ($\delta \approx 0.5$) suggests a positive elasticity of gun homicide with respect to gun prevalence of about 10–15 percent: a doubling (100 percent) increase in gun prevalence in a county would raise gun homicide rates by 10–15 percent. We will be able to say something of how much of an upward bias is present in this estimate shortly.

Step 2 in our checklist is to re-estimate the equation, this time treating log PSG as endogenous, and again examine the J statistic. The J test is again a test of the exogeneity of all the variables assumed to be exogenous: the difference is that log PSG is no longer in the list of exogenous variables. There is now one endogenous variable in the equation, log PSG, so the test statistic is distributed as χ^2 with two (excluded) instruments – 1 endogenous regressors = 1 degree of freedom. The table again reports only the J test statistic for the efficient GMM estimator, because the corresponding test statistic for IV, the Sargan NR^2 statistic is again not robust to heteroskedasticity and clustering. The J statistic is now much smaller: 0.012

($p = 0.913$). We cannot now reject the null hypothesis that our exogenous variables are indeed exogenous. So far, the evidence suggests that the estimations in columns 3 and 4 of Table 6.2 are well specified.

The explanation for what is happening is apparent from the estimated coefficient on log PSG in columns 3 and 4: efficient GMM and (inefficient) IV give us almost identical estimates of about –2.4, significant at the 1 percent level. Our calibration exercise ($\delta \approx 0.5$) suggests a *negative* elasticity of gun homicide with respect to gun prevalence of about 1.2: a doubling (100 percent) increase in gun prevalence in a county would *reduce* gun homicide rates by about 120 percent; that is, gun homicide rates would be halved. But before we proceed any further, we have to make sure that we have completed the specification testing of the estimations in columns 3 and 4, namely we have to inspect the instruments log OMAG and log PCTREP88 and confirm that they are 'relevant'. This is Step 3 in our checklist.

The key 'first-stage' regression results are reported at the bottom of Table 6.2 for the IV/GMM estimations in columns 3 and 4. The 'first-stage' regression is a regression of the endogenous variable – here, log PSG – on the two instruments log OMAG and log PCTREP88, plus all the exogenous regressors used in the main equation (including the state fixed effects). The first-stage coefficients on log OMAG and log PCTREP88 are positive and significant at the 1 percent level, as expected: greater local interest in outdoor sports and a politically conservative orientation are both associated with higher levels of gun prevalence as proxied by log PSG. However, the heteroskedastic and cluster-robust first-stage F statistic is 12.9, only slightly higher than the Staiger–Stock rule of thumb that the first-stage F should be >10 if we are to conclude that the instruments are not 'weak'. The Stock–Yogo test critical values (not reported) are similarly marginal. We conclude that our instruments are not so weak that our results likely to be are invalid and that we can proceed to Step 4 in our checklist, but some caution in our conclusions will be warranted on this account. We note here that when we use an alternative (non-GMM-based) estimation method that is robust to weak instruments, our main conclusions continue to be supported. See the 'Recommended Reading' section for details.

Step 4 is to formally test what is already informally apparent, namely that log PSG is endogenous. We do this using a GMM distance test, defined as $C = J$ from Step 1 (gun levels are exogenous, columns 1–2) minus J from Step 2 (gun levels are endogenous, columns 3–4). In fact, the C statistic in Table 6.2, columns 1–2, is very slightly different from this because we report the

exogeneity test statistic provided automatically by the Stata estimation command *xtivreg2*. This GMM test statistic uses a minor adjustment that guarantees it is non-negative, and hence differs slightly from what we would obtain if we calculated C 'by hand' using the two J statistics in columns 1–2 and 3–4. Since we are testing the exogeneity of one variable, the C test is χ^2 with one degree of freedom. The C test statistic is 10.96, which is very large ($p = 0.001$). We therefore reject the null hypothesis that log PSG is exogenous, conclude that gun levels are endogenous, and proceed to Step 6.

Step 6 is to take our Step 2 estimates – using efficient GMM and IV, and treating log PSG as endogenous – our final estimates. We already noted that the estimated coefficient on log PSG, after using our proxy calibration, implies a roughly unitary gun-levels/gun-homicide elasticity; for example, a *ceteris paribus* 10 percent increase in gun prevalence in a locality would lead to a 10 percent decrease in gun homicide. The size of the endogeneity bias if log PSG is treated as exogenous is substantial: the biased estimates from columns 1–2 imply that a 10 percent increase in gun prevalence would be associated with a 1.0–1.5 percent *increase* in gun homicide, rather than the 10 percent *decrease* from the IV/GMM estimations in which log PSG is treated as endogenous. The rest of the estimated coefficients appear reasonable. About half of the 18 control variables are significant, and the significant coefficients have the expected sign. High gun murder rates are associated poverty measures, the percentage of the population that is black and the percentage that is Hispanic. Suburban areas have lower levels of gun homicide compared to urban or rural (the omitted category) areas.

To summarize: our main conclusion is the positive correlation between gun levels and gun homicide rates is driven by endogeneity bias, and when the endogeneity of gun levels is properly addressed in the estimation, any positive correlation vanishes and indeed reverses; our results suggest that greater gun prevalence is, if anything, associated with lower rates of gun homicide. However, because our instruments are marginally weak, and because the calibration exercise is only approximate, our results, and in particular the size of this estimated negative impact, should be treated with some caution.

We offer an additional caveat regarding the interpretation of our results and what our simple model does *not* do. We have argued in other work (Kovandzic et al., 2008) that *heterogeneity in criminality* is a hitherto largely ignored problem in empirical work using ecological data. Heterogeneity in criminality means, in our guns–homicide application, that the impact of an increase in gun prevalence will depend on the composition of the county population: an increase in gun prevalence in a county with a large criminal population should have an impact that is different from an increase in gun prevalence that is the same size but takes place in a county with a small criminal population. More formally, equation (6.1) is replaced with

$$h_i = \beta_i g_i + u_i \qquad (6.1e)$$

and now the impact β_i of gun prevalence on homicide is allowed to vary from county to county, rather than assuming, as we did in this chapter, that β is the same for all counties. It turns out (see Kovandzic et al., 2008, for details) that if equation (6.1e) is an accurate description of 'reality', the estimated $\hat{\beta}$ obtained using IV/GMM methods cannot be interpreted as an estimate of the average impact of gun prevalence; that is, as the impact of gun prevalence in the 'average' county. The correct interpretation depends on the correlations between the instruments used and gun prevalence amongst criminals and non-criminals. This is discussion further in the 'Recommended Reading' section.

CONCLUSION

We have shown in this chapter how an empirical researcher can use the modern framework of GMM to address the problem of endogeneity bias resulting from reverse causality, omitted variable bias, and/or measurement error, and how the GMM framework relates to another modern empirical technique, namely the calculation of 'robust' standard errors. We applied these procedures to US county level data, and found strong evidence of the existence of endogeneity problems. When the problem is ignored, gun levels are associated with higher rates of gun homicide; when the problem is addressed, this association disappears or reverses. Our presentation has been structured in a way that, by following our examples, empirical researchers should be able to employ the same techniques to other problems.

As noted earlier, endogeneity problems stemming from simultaneity bias, omitted variable bias, and measurement error are commonplace in criminology. Take, for example, one of the most often studied topics in criminological research – the link between increases in police levels and crime rates. Simultaneity bias is likely to be present in OLS estimates of the police–crime relationship as increases in crime could encourage policy makers into hiring more police (Levitt,

1997, 2002; Marvell and Moody, 1996; McCrary, 2002). Similarly, studies examining the link between arrest rates and crime rates may also suffer from endogeneity bias if short-term increases in crime reduce the ability of police to affect arrests (Glaser and Sacerdote, 1999; Levitt, 1998). Of course, studies examining individual-level correlates of criminal behaviour are also susceptible to endogeneity bias. A classic example is the plausible two-way relationship between unemployment and criminal behaviour. While the effects of unemployment on crime are obvious, unemployment may be an endogenous regressor if income generated as a result of criminal activities leads to a greater reluctance among criminals to seek out lawful employment (Raphael and Winter-Ebmer, 2001). In all, there are numerous and varied criminological topics where endogeneity bias is a concern. We hope criminologists can use the tools and framework provided in this chapter to overcome endogeneity bias problems.

RECOMMENDED READING

Good discussions of IV/GMM methods can be found in many textbooks. Wooldridge (2008) and Stock and Watson (2007) have good expositions of the simple IV estimator and corresponding specification tests. The statistical package Stata was used for all estimations in this chapter. The main IV/GMM estimation programs, *ivreg2* (Baum et al., 2010) and *xtivreg2* (Schaffer, 2010), were co-authored by one of us (Schaffer), and can be freely downloaded via the RePEc software database (http://repec.org). For further discussion of how the GMM estimators and tests used in this chapter are implemented, see Baum et al. (2003, 2007), and the references therein.

What researchers should do when faced with 'weak instruments' has been the subject of considerable recent research in econometrics. One approach that was first introduced in, remarkably, 1949, by Anderson and Rubin is to eschew obtaining a point estimate of β and instead obtain a confidence interval for it. It turns out that a confidence interval can be constructed that is 'robust to weak instruments' in the intuitive sense that as instruments get weaker, the confidence interval for β – quite naturally – gets wider. See Baum et al. (2007) for a simple discussion and Kovandzic et al. (2005) for an application to the model estimated in this chapter.

Kovandzic et al. (2005, 2008) provide a fuller set of results for the guns–homicide model estimated using US county data, including results using non-gun and total homicide rates. In Kovandzic et al. (2008) we present a framework in which β_i varies according to the criminal/non-criminal composition of the population. Our results suggest that estimation of equation (6.1) using IV/GMM methods provides an estimate primarily reflecting the impact of gun prevalence among non-criminals on homicide rates. This implies a modification of the conclusion in this chapter, namely that the estimated negative impact on homicide rates of an increase in gun prevalence may be largely attributable to the predominantly homicide-reducing effects of gun prevalence among non-criminals.

REFERENCES

Anderson, T.W., and H. Rubin. 1949. 'Estimation of the parameters of a single equation in a complete system of stochastic equations.' *Annals of Mathematical Statistics* 91: 46–63.

Audit Bureau of Circulation. 1993. Supplementary Data Report, covering county paid circulation figures for gun/hunting/outdoor magazines. Chicago: ABC.

Baum, C.F., M. Schaffer, and S. Stillman. 2003. 'Instrumental variables and GMM: Estimation and testing.' *The Stata Journal* 3(1): 1–31.

Baum, C.F., M.E. Schaffer, and S. Stillman. 2007. 'Enhanced routines for instrumental variables/generalized method of moments estimation and testing.' *The Stata Journal* 7(4): 465–506.

Baum, C.F., M.E. Schaffer, and S. Stillman. 2010. 'IVREG2: Stata module for extended instrumental variables/2SLS and GMM estimation'. Available at: http://ideas.repec.org/c/boc/bocode/s425401.html.

Bordua, D.J., and A.J. Lizotte. 1979. 'Patterns of legal firearms ownership: a cultural and situational analysis of Illinois counties.' *Law and Policy Quarterly* 1(2): 147–175.

Bound, J., D.A. Jaeger, and R. Baker. 1995. 'Problems with instrumental variables estimation when the correlation between the instruments and the endogenous explanatory variable is weak.' *Journal of the American Statistical Association* 90(430): 443–450.

Clotfelter, C.T. 1981. 'Crime, disorders, and the demand for handguns.' *Law & Policy Quarterly* 3(4): 425–446.

Cook, P.J., and J. Ludwig. 1997. *Guns in America.* Washington, D.C.: Police Foundation.

Cragg, J. 1983. 'More efficient estimation in the presence of heteroskedasticity of unknown form.' *Econometrica* 51(3): 751–763.

Duggan, M. 2001. 'More guns, more crime.' *Journal of Political Economy* 109(5): 1086–1114.

Glaser, E.L., and B. Sacerdote. 1999. 'Why is there more crime in cities?' *Journal of Political Economy* 107: 225–258.

Hansen, L.P. 1982. 'Large sample properties of generalized method of moments estimators.' *Econometrica* 50(4): 1029–1054.

Hayashi, F. 2000. *Econometrics.* Princeton: Princeton University Press.

ICPSR (Inter-university Consortium for Political and Social Research). 1995. *General Election Data for the United States, 1950-1990.* [Computer file]. Ann Arbor, MI: Inter-university Consortium for Political and Social Research [producer and distributor].

Killias, M. 1993. 'Gun ownership, suicide, and homicide: an international perspective.' in A. del Frate, U. Zvekic, and J. J. M. van Dijk (eds), *Understanding Crime: Experiences of Crime and Crime Control* (pp. 289–303). Rome: UNICRI.

Kleck, G. 1979. 'Capital punishment, gun ownership, and homicide.' *American Journal of Sociology* 84(4): 882–910.

Kleck, G. 1984. 'The relationship between gun ownership levels and rates of violence in the United States.' in Don B. Kates, Jr (ed.) *Firearms and Violence: Issues of Public Policy* (pp. 99–135). Cambridge, MA: Ballinger.

Kleck, G. 1997. *Targeting Guns: Firearms and their Control.* New York: Aldine.

Kleck, G. 2004. 'Measures of gun ownership levels for macro-level crime and violence research.' *Journal of Research in Crime and Delinquency* 41(3): 3–36.

Kleck, G., and T.V. Kovandzic. 2009. 'City-level characteristics and individual handgun ownership: effects of collective security and homicide.' *Journal of Contemporary Criminal Justice* 25(1): 45–66.

Kleck, G., and E.B. Patterson. 1993. 'The impact of gun control and gun ownership levels on violence rates.' *Journal of Quantitative Criminology* 9(3): 249–288.

Kovandzic, T.V., L.M. Vieraitis, and M.R. Yeisley. 1998. 'The structural covariates of urban homicide.' *Criminology* 36(3): 569–600.

Kovandzic, T.V., M.E. Schaffer, and G. Kleck. 2005. 'Gun prevalence, homicide rates and causality: A GMM approach to endogeneity bias.' CEPR Discussion Paper No. 5357. Centre for Economic Policy Research (CEPR), London.

Kovandzic, T.V., M.E. Schaffer, and G. Kleck. 2008. 'Estimating the causal effect of gun prevalence on homicide rates: a local average treatment effect approach.' IZA Discussion Paper No. 3589. Institute for the Study of Labor (IZA), Berlin.

Land, K., P.L. McCall, and L.E. Cohen. 1990. 'Structural covariates of homicide rates.' *American Journal of Sociology* 95(4): 922–963.

Levitt, S.D. 1997. 'Using electoral cycles in police hiring to estimate the effect of police on crime.' *American Economic Review* 87(3): 270–290.

Levitt, S.D. 2002. 'Using electoral cycles in police hiring to estimate the effect of police on crime: Reply.' *American Economic Review* 92(4): 1244–1250.

Magaddino, J.P., and M.H. Medoff. 1984. 'An empirical analysis of federal and state firearm control laws' in Don B. Kates, Jr. (ed.) *Firearms and Violence: Issues of Public Policy* (pp. 225–258). Cambridge, MA: Ballinger.

Marvell, T.B., and C. Moody. 1996. 'Specification problems, police levels, and crime rates.' *Criminology* 34(4): 609–646.

McCrary, J. 2002. 'Using electoral cycles in police hiring to estimate the effect of police on crime: Comment.' *American Economic Review* 92(4): 1236–1243.

McDowall, D., and C. Loftin. 1983. 'Collective security and the demand for handguns.' *American Journal of Sociology* 88(6): 1146–1161.

Okoro, C.A., D.E. Nelson, J.A. Mercy, L.S. Balluz, A.E. Crosby, and A.H. Mokdad. 2005. 'Prevalence of household firearms and firearm-storage practices in the 50 states and the District of Columbia.' *Pediatrics* 116(3): e370–e376.

Raphael, S. and R. Winter-Ebmer. 2001. 'Identifying the effect of unemployment on crime.' *Journal of Law and Economics* 44(1): 259–283.

Rice, D.C. and D.D. Hemley. 2002. 'The market for new handguns.' *Journal of Law and Economics* 45(1): 251–265.

Sampson, R. J. 1986. 'Crime in cities' in Albert J. Reiss Jr. and Michael Tonry (eds.), *Communities and Crime* (pp. 271–311). Chicago: University of Chicago Press.

Sargan, D. 1958. 'The estimation of econometric relationships using instrumental variables.' *Econometrica* 26(3): 393–415.

Schaffer, M.E. 2010. 'XTIVREG2: Stata module to perform extended IV/2SLS, GMM and AC/HAC, LIML and k-class regression for panel data models'. Available at: http://ideas.repec.org/c/boc/bocode/s456501.html.

Southwick, L., Jr. 1997. 'Do guns cause crime? Does crime cause guns?: A Granger test.' *Atlantic Economic Journal* 25(3): 256–273.

Staiger, D., and J.H. Stock. 1997. 'Instrumental variables regression with weak instruments.' *Econometrica* 65: 557–586.

Stock, J.H. and M.W. Watson. 2007. *Introduction to Econometrics*, 2nd edition. Boston: Addison-Wesley and Pearson.

Stock, J.H., J.H. Wright, and M. Yogo, 2002. 'A survey of weak instruments and weak identification in generalized method of moments.' *Journal of Business and Economic Statistics* 20(4): 518–529.

Stock, J.H., and M. Yogo. 2005. 'Testing for weak instruments in linear IV regression' in D.W.K. Andrews and J.H. Stock (eds), *Identification and Inference for Econometric Models: Essays in Honor of Thomas Rothenberg* (pp. 80–108). Cambridge: Cambridge University Press.

US Bureau of the Census. 1994. *County and City Data Book, 1994.* Washington, DC: US Government Printing Office.

US Bureau of the Census. 1990. 'Census 1990 Summary File 3 (SF3) – Sample Data, Table P006 Urban and Rural'. Available at: http://factfinder.census.gov.

US Federal Bureau of Investigation. 2010. *Crime in the United States 2008.* Available at: http://www.fbi.gov/ucr/cius2008/offenses/expanded_information/data/shrtable_07.html.

US National Center for Health Statistics. 1997. Special versions of Mortality Detail Files, 1987–1993, with location detail, supplied to third author.

Vieraitis, L.M. 2000. 'Income inequality, poverty, and violent crime: A review of the empirical evidence.' *Social Pathology* 6(1): 24–45.

Wooldridge, J.M. 2008. *Introductory Econometrics: A Modern Approach*, 4th edition. Mason, Ohio: Thompson and South-Western College Press.

Zimring, F.E., and G. Hawkins. 1997. *Crime is Not the Problem.* New York: Oxford University Press.

Contextualizing Crime in Space and Time: Networks, Communities and Culture

The second section of the handbook contains six chapters that contextualize crime in space and time. The specific topics cover advances in statistical modelling for identifying contextual effects, innovative methods for generating original data of theoretical import and for combining original data with existing data sources, the application of frameworks that have been well developed in other fields for examining collective social processes (i.e., formal network analysis), and data sources and analytic techniques for historical inquiry.

The chapter by Eric Baumer and Ashley Arnio discusses a tool that has become increasingly important in contemporary quantitative criminology: 'multi-level modelling'. As the term implies, the technique is based on the premise that data sets can often be conceptualized as being hierarchically structured in terms of levels, with observations at one level 'nested' within higher levels. The authors explain that with such a hierarchical structure, observations are not independent of one another, which violates assumptions of traditional statistical procedures. Multi-level modelling makes appropriate adjustments for this lack of independence. The authors emphasize, however, the *substantive* contribution of multi-level modelling for understanding spatial and temporal variation in criminological phenomena. This technique has allowed researchers to examine how the larger spatial context, such as the neighbourhood, affects the offending behaviour of individuals, and how the spatial context conditions the effect of individual predictors on offending. Multi-level modelling has also been applied extensively and productively to explain changes in individual involvement in criminal activity over time with the estimation of 'growth curve' models. In these models observations are taken over multiple time points on the same individuals. These observations can thus be conceptualized as being nested within the individuals. The authors provide a brief summary of the historical evolution of multi-level modelling in criminology and explicate the formal statistical properties of the technique. They also illustrate the diverse applications of multi-level modelling with numerous references to the literature. The authors conclude that the 'real value' of the incorporation of multi-level modelling into the toolkit of quantitative criminologists has been to stimulate insights about data and processes that might otherwise have been hidden.

Per-Olof Wikström, Kyle Treiber, and Beth Hardie also address the role of spatial context in understanding crime causation, but they do so from the vantage point of Situational Action Theory (SAT). SAT stipulates that crime is a function of the interaction between an individual's crime propensity and criminogenic features of the environment. From this theoretical perspective, the relevant spatial context for understanding crime is the 'setting', defined as 'the part of the environment a person, at any given moment in time, experienced with his/her senses'. The authors advance the argument that acquiring sound knowledge about the person–environment interaction as conceptualized in SAT requires the development and application of new methodologies. In their view, a key methodological shortcoming of prior criminological work on environmental effects has been the reliance on spatial units that are too large and heterogeneous to capture faithfully the 'settings' that govern social action (e.g. census tracts or neighbourhoods). In addition, standard methodologies typically consider the spatial context of the individual's immediate, home environment (residence), yet people spend much of their time in different locations. To overcome these limitations, the authors propose a methodological approach based on the use of a small-area community survey in combination with a space–time budget. They illustrate these techniques with reference to the Peterborough Adolescent and Young Adult Development Study (PADS). The chapter concludes with an overview of the key steps in designing and combining small community surveys and space–time budgets, including recommendations based on the experiences gained from PADS.

George Tita and Adam Boessen's chapter examines how systematic measurement and analysis of social networks can foster a deeper understanding of the spatial distribution of crime and the nature of the widely studied 'neighbourhood effects' on crime. They begin their discussion by describing the centrality of social networks as the primary mechanism that has linked features of neighbourhoods and communities with crime in influential criminological theories, especially those that follow in the general ecological tradition of the Chicago School. They observe that despite the centrality of social networks to the ecological theorizing about crime, efforts to both measure and analyze social ties explicitly (as opposed to through proxies) are surprisingly rare. To rectify this lacuna, Tita and Boessen explicate some of the principal features of formal network analysis. Their chapter provides numerous illustrations from the literature of the insights about crime that have been yielded by research that has implemented these techniques. Their discussion calls attention in particular to the importance of attending to social networks for understanding both neighbourhood processes of social control that foster safe communities and processes of contagion that facilitate the spread of violence across communities.

The chapter by Robert Crutchfield and Suzanna Ramirez addresses issues of measurement, data sources, and the impact of the larger context of the economy on criminal behaviour, focusing specifically on labour market participation. The authors argue that the focus on unemployment is a major limitation of early research on the relationship between labour market participation and crime. As Crutchfield and Ramirez explain, standard measures of unemployment fail to capture salient features of the operations of the labour market. Moreover, dual labour market theory provides a compelling rationale for expecting that features of the labour market broader than unemployment are likely to be more consequential for criminal behaviour. The authors propose that researchers can gain a much deeper understanding of the link between labour markets and crime by combining census data with survey data. Census data are useful for capturing relevant macro features of the labour market, while survey data often contain information on individual labour market participation and offending. With data from both sources, it is possible to examine the effects of individual characteristics and features of the local economic context through the application of multi-level modelling (as discussed in the chapter by Baumer and Arnio). The authors review exemplary studies based on the use of these multiple data sources that have been conducted in the US. They also illustrate the potential for comparative research in analyses of data for Seattle, Chicago, and Brisbane.

The chapter by Laura Dugan directs attention to the global arena, pointing to a rather glaring gap in the criminological literature – the limited knowledge base on global terrorism. As Dugan explains, criminologists have not contributed much to the understanding of terrorism until very recently. One reason for this rather surprising neglect has been the absence of credible, comprehensive and readily available data. Dugan introduces a data source that should help fill this gap in criminology: the Global Terrorism Database (GTD). She describes the extensive efforts that went into the development of the GTD, along with key technical features of the attributes contained within the database. She also enumerates the strengths and limitations of the GTD. The GTD is the most comprehensive data source on terrorism to date. It includes international and domestic attacks over a 38-year period, and it is based on a broad definition of terrorism to err on the side of inclusiveness. The GTD nevertheless has some inherent weaknesses that reflect its foundations in media accounts. The database is thus best regarded as a comprehensive compilation of those incidents that are likely to be captured in media sources. Dugan illustrates some of the interesting substantive questions that can be addressed with the GTD, such as overall patterns of terrorism over time, life cycles of terrorist organizations, and the level of threat associated with specific terrorist organizations. The chapter highlights how the GTD provides criminologists with a new tool to identify levels of risk associated with terrorism. This tool will enable criminologists to develop better theories about, and policies to deal with, this distinctive form of lethal violence.

Barry Godfrey's chapter provides insight into the methods used by historians 'to contextualize in time' the study of crime and criminals. The chapter begins with an extended review of the development of the sub-discipline of crime history in the period extending from the end of World War II to around 1990. The review describes key topics of inquiry, identifies and assesses a diverse array of documentary sources of historical knowledge, and illustrates the methods applied to analyze these data sources. Godfrey draws upon his own research experience to explain in detail one type of historical methodology in action: 'whole-life' analysis, along with its limitations. The chapter concludes with remarks on new horizons in crime history methodology. These include the explosion of sources for historical research, the redrawing of temporal boundaries such that early criminological studies are becoming historical sources themselves, the wealth of comparative research that has recently appeared, emerging ethical concerns about the use of sources that deal with the lives of deceased persons, and a growing appreciation among many of the common methodological foundations of history and sociology, along with a recognition of the complementary but distinct contributions of each discipline.

7

Multi-level Modeling and Criminological Inquiry

Eric P. Baumer, Ashley N. Arnio

INTRODUCTION

The well-known statement that criminology reflects the study of law-making, law-breaking and law-enforcement still covers most of what we study in the discipline (Sutherland, 1947), but the theoretical and empirical issues of concern within these general categories of inquiry have expanded considerably during the past several decades. Because of this, it is sometimes hard to identify coherence within the vast and continually growing criminological literature. Nonetheless, two themes that, in our judgment, represent cross-cutting hallmarks common in contemporary criminological inquiry are that many of the outcomes on which we focus exhibit considerable variation across space, and they often change notably over time. Indeed, the temporal and spatial dynamics of many aspects of crime and justice have stimulated a large volume of research during the past century. Not unlike other areas of research, there are a variety of methodological considerations to weigh when studying temporal and spatial contexts, and one may find that several potentially relevant or appropriate methods can be rightly applied depending on the specific research issues under investigation and properties of the data being used to do so. Multi-level statistical models in particular have proven quite useful to those who have studied a wide range of issues in which temporal and spatial contexts are thought to play a key role. In this chapter, we outline some of the key parameters of these models as they have been applied in the field.

Spatial and/or temporal variation are common threads in multi-level statistical applications, but these models have been applied to many substantive issues in criminology and have also appeared in a variety of forms in research spanning several nations. They have encompassed the study of individuals or households nested within schools, neighborhoods, and other types of 'communities'. As elaborated in the following, a very common substantive concern in criminology is whether features of community context (e.g., poverty rates, racial composition, and community norms) influence individual attitudes or behaviors, and/or whether they condition the effects of individual/household attributes on such outcomes. Multi-level statistical models are well suited for addressing these types of questions and are advantageous over other methodological approaches that have been used to do so in the literature (e.g., aggregate-level analyses or single-level contextual regression models) because they explicitly adjust for the non-independence of observations from the same community and thereby provide more rigorous statistical assessments of hypothesized relationships. Some of the earliest applications of multi-level modeling in this context appeared in studies of victimization risk (e.g., Rountree et al., 1994), involvement in violent behavior (e.g., Sampson et al., 1997), and attitudes about crime and criminal justice authorities (e.g., Sampson and Bartusch, 1998). More recently, multi-level models of community context have been extended to the study of school context on adolescent deviance (e.g., Payne et al., 2003; Stewart, 2003) and how 'community' context shapes a variety of outcomes, including individual attitudes about punishment policies (e.g., Baumer et al., 2003), citizen reactions to crime (Goudriaan et al., 2006; Tseloni and Zarafonitou, 2008; Zhang et al., 2009), sentencing decisions by judges and juries (e.g., Ulmer and Johnson, 2004), and post-prison outcomes among persons released to different areas (Kubrin and Stewart, 2006).

The other major substantive research problem to which multi-level models have been applied is the analysis of change. Criminologists have long been interested in assessing shifts over time in the prevalence and incidence of individual involvement in crime and deviance, a substantive focus encompassed most visibly within the contemporary era in the 'life-course' perspective (Sampson and Laub, 1993).

A parallel substantive issue studied by scholars who focus on communities and crime concerns temporal variation in rates of crime across samples of neighborhoods, cities and other geographic units (e.g., Bursik and Grasmick, 1992). While other methods (e.g., multivariate repeated measures models [MRM] and structural equation models [SEM]) have been applied to study these issues, several important contributions during the past two decades have illustrated the potential conceptual and empirical utility of approaching them through the lens of multi-level statistical models (e.g., Baumer et al., 1998; Duncan et al., 2006; Johnson et al., 1997; LaFree et al., 2010; Raudenbush and Chan, 1992). As with the examples of research on 'community effects' highlighted previously, studies of individual or community change involve observations that are clustered within the same unit, such as individuals or communities. Thus, one of the motivations for applying multi-level models to study these forms of change is that they account for the clustered nature of repeated observations within subjects and the potential bias that not doing so can have for standard error estimation. Although MRM and SEM also are well equipped to account for this type of data structure and are sometimes the preferred choice, there are a number of conceptual advantages of estimating models of change using multi-level models over MRM and SEM models. As discussed by Bryk and Raudenbush (2002), these advantages include greater flexibility with respect to data requirements (e.g., unbalanced panels are easily handled), explicit modeling of change parameters, and easy extension to more complex hierarchies (e.g., assessing how individual change varies across neighborhoods in a three-level specification).

Multi-level models have been applied in other domains as well. Although space limitations preclude an extensive discussion, three other exciting applications of multi-level models include the analysis of item responses within latent constructs (e.g., Raudenbush et al., 2003; Sampson et al., 1997); meta analyses involving standardized measures of effects across studies and study locations (e.g., Pratt et al., 2006; Rebellon et al., 2008); and repeated observations across years (Baumer, 2009; Diprete and Grusky, 1990a; Quillian, 1996).

Given the advancement of multi-level models in the field during the past few decades, it makes good sense to take stock of how they have evolved, explain how they can yield more suitable answers to important substantive questions, review and illustrate the primary ways they have been applied, and comment on the future prospects of multi-level modeling applications in criminology. We begin by tracing the development of the most basic form in which multi-level models have been applied in criminology: bi-level regression models in which observations are nested within a higher-level grouping of some sort, that more often than not are operationalized as communities (defined in various ways) or schools. We then summarize the evolution of multi-level models into what has amounted to a wide variety of advanced forms, detailing some illustrative applications along the way. Finally, we close with some comments on cutting-edge uses of multi-level models and some thoughts about future applications.

A BRIEF SUMMARY OF THE HISTORICAL EVOLUTION OF MULTI-LEVEL MODELING IN CRIMINOLOGY

The classic example of multi-level modeling in criminology reflects individuals nested within a social or geographic community, such as a school, neighborhood, district, city or metropolitan area. This form of multi-level design reflects a long-standing interest in the social sciences generally, and in criminology specifically, of how exposure to different types of group contexts might generate distinct attitudes and behaviors. This was a major substantive focus of the early Chicago School's research on crime, delinquency, and other forms of deviance, and continues to be a vibrant area of study in the discipline today.

For most of the twentieth century the modal empirical approach to analyzing the role of community conditions in shaping involvement in crime or delinquency was to conduct an aggregate-level analysis using geographic areas as units of analysis (for a review, see Sampson and Lauritsen, 1994). This type of design facilitates an evaluation of the relative rank ordering of, for instance, neighborhood-level crime rates and neighborhood-level poverty rates. Aggregate-level analyses of this type continue to be used and have provided a wealth of valuable information regarding spatial variation in many outcomes of interest to criminologists.

The aggregate-level research design is defensible in contexts where both the relevant explanatory variables and the outcome of interest are 'structural' or 'global' in nature (Liska, 1990). However, it is potentially problematic when the aggregate-level outcome is merely an 'analytical' variable. Lazarsfeld and Menzel (1965) introduce these concepts – structural, global, and analytical – to describe different types of aggregate-level variables. Structural and global attributes refer to group- or aggregate-level conditions that are emergent at only the group level. They do not simply represent (and cannot simply be measured by) the sum of the individual parts within a group context; they are emergent properties that have no individual-level analogue. Analyzing them using an aggregate-level design is thus sensible and usually the only defensible choice. Lazarsfeld and Menzel (1965) distinguish structural and global aggregate variables from 'analytical' variables, which represent group- or aggregate-level properties based on the simple additive combination of individual attributes within a given group or other aggregate unit. Analytical variables often are expressed in terms of a group average (e.g., median income) or rate (e.g., percent unemployed). In research contexts involving analytical outcome variables, the aggregate-level research design can be limiting in some important respects. Two particularly important limitations of aggregate-level designs involving analytical dependent variables is that they ignore variation in the specified outcome within aggregate units, which often is a substantial portion of the overall variation, and they omit individual-level explanatory variables that may be relevant predictors of the outcome under investigation (Liska, 1990). Because of this, aggregate-level analyses can yield misleading conclusions about the role of specified aggregate conditions in shaping behavior, and reliance solely on aggregate-level designs can increase the likelihood of equating to individuals, qualities of group-level characteristics (i.e., the ecological fallacy) (Hauser, 1970; Lincoln and Zeitz, 1980; Blalock, 1984).

In many instances in criminology, the outcomes of interest in studies that focus on the role of aggregate-level explanatory attributes are analytical variables, such as offending or victimization. These can be measured at the aggregate-level in the form of offending or victimization rates, and the aggregate-level design can be applied to describe the association between the resulting crime rates and one or more aggregate-level explanatory variables. Often times, this type of approach is unavoidable because data are expressed only in aggregate-level form. However, it is important to recognize that proceeding in this manner may misrepresent the role of the explanatory variables for reasons outlined previously. As Liska (1990) notes, while this does not render aggregate-level dependent variables or aggregate-level analyses unimportant for assessing the role of group-context on 'analytical' outcomes, it highlights the reality that a multi-level approach in which data on individuals and the community conditions to which they are exposed would be a better fit.

Recognizing the limitations of purely aggregate-level approaches to examining the role of geographically defined social contexts in shaping individual attitudes and behaviors, social science researchers during the past three decades have increasingly used different forms of 'contextual' analyses; in other words, studies that assess the role of indicators of aggregate or group contexts on individual-level attitudes or behaviors. With some notable exceptions (e.g., Johnstone, 1978; Reiss and Rhodes, 1961), the initial studies in this genre focused on substantive issues that were not central to criminology. Some of the initial contextual research simply denoted individual membership in specified aggregate units with dummy variables, often referred to in the literature as 'covariance analysis'. Other studies explicitly paired individual-level data with aggregate-level variables that described social and economic conditions of those units, an approach that paralleled what we typically mean today when we use the phrase 'contextual analysis.' The latter approach proved to be especially popular in criminology during the 1980s and 1990s (see, e.g., Cohen et al., 1981; Gottfredson and Taylor, 1986; Gottfredson et al., 1991; Miethe and McDowall, 1993; Myers and Talarico, 1987; Peeples and Loeber, 1994; Sampson and Wooldredge, 1987; Simcha-Fagan and Schwartz, 1986; Smith and Jarjoura, 1989). Overall, these studies presented empirical evidence consistent with the idea that community context (measured in various ways) plays a significant role in shaping outcomes such as victimization risk, adolescent offending, police behavior towards citizens, and recidivism risk (for a review, see Bursik and Grasmick, 1995). In the vast majority of cases, compared to aggregate-level designs these early contextual multi-level studies revealed a less significant role for factors such as poverty rates and other aggregate conditions emphasized in macro-level theories of crime.

One limitation of the early examples of contextual analysis in criminology and other disciplines was that they did not formally take into account the natural clustering reflected in the multiple levels of data being examined. Instead, studies published during the 1980s and early 1990s essentially treated the contextual indicators, most often features of geographically defined neighborhoods, as an additional attribute of the individuals in their samples, and proceeded to apply conventional 'single-level' regression modeling techniques (ordinary least squares [OLS], logistic etc.). During the decade and a half in which much of this work was being done, several seminal publications appeared that highlighted both methodological and conceptual limitations of the single-level contextual approach (e.g., Bryk and Raudenbush, 1992; Goldstein, 1987; Iversen, 1991; Mason et al., 1983; Wong and Mason, 1985). The key methodological weakness noted was that the typical single-level contextual empirical model assumed independence among observations. This assumption is a precarious one when analyzing data that include observations from the same grouping, such as a neighborhood or school. As Bryk and Raudenbush (1992) elaborate, observations within socially or geographically defined units are likely to have more in common with one another than with observations from other units, and hence the assumption of independent errors made in traditional single-level approaches is often violated when data exhibit significant clustering. From a practical standpoint, ignoring this issue can yield inflated standard errors associated with the estimated coefficients for contextual variables, therefore increasing the likelihood of type II errors (i.e., failing to reject a null hypothesis when it is not true). Additionally, the emerging multi-level methodological literature during the late 1980s and early 1990s made a convincing case that single-level analyses of contextual effects corresponded to a relatively narrow *conceptual* approach for thinking about and estimating the role of social and geographic contexts in shaping individual attitudes and behaviors. As it emerged more widely during the early 1990s in the social sciences, including criminology, a multi-level regression modeling framework offered promise both for providing more robust estimates of standard errors that took into consideration the non-independence of observations, and for broadening the ways in which we hypothesize about and model additive and multiplicative community or contextual effects.

As elaborated in the following, there were a few instances of multi-level modeling being applied in criminology within the area of growth curve estimation during the early 1990s (Bursik and Grasmick, 1992; Raudenbush and Chan, 1992). However, the first study of which we are aware that applied multi-level modeling techniques to the more typical situation in which individuals are clustered in a geographic or social community is the pioneering research examining neighborhood effects on victimization risk by Rountree et al. (1994). This study is especially noteworthy because it explored both additive and multiplicative multi-level models that formally take into account the clustering of observations within neighborhoods, and because it explicitly compared the results from those models with comparable estimations based on the single-level contextual approach that was dominant in earlier eras. In doing so, Rountree et al. (1994) not only introduced multi-level techniques to the discipline in a rigorous way, but also illustrated a key methodological reason as to why such models are more appropriate when analyzing clustered hierarchically structured data.

AN OVERVIEW OF CONTEMPORARY APPLICATIONS OF MULTI-LEVEL MODELS

Multi-level, or hierarchical, regression models have become the norm for analyzing data in which the base units of observations are nested or clustered within one or more higher level units. Some of the more common examples of this type of data structure place emphasis on the potential role of spatial or geographic context, including individuals clustered within neighborhoods, adolescents within schools, criminal defendants within counties, and neighborhoods within cities. Other hierarchical data structures direct our attention to temporal dynamics, including repeated cross-sectional observations across years, and repeated time points within individuals or places. More complex data structures can involve three or more 'levels' including criminal defendants sentenced by judges who represent different counties (e.g., Johnson, 2006) or neighborhoods within cities located in different metropolitan areas (e.g., Krivo et al., 2009), as well as a mixture of temporal and spatial observations, such as repeated observations for persons who live in different neighborhoods or for students who attend different schools (e.g., Raudenbush, 1993). Contemporary applications of multi-level modeling in criminology thus come in a wide variety of forms; they encompass different types of data hierarchies, they are applied to both continuous and discrete outcome measures, and they have been applied in efforts to advance knowledge about both spatial and temporal dynamics.

It is easy to get overwhelmed in the apparent complexity of contemporary applications of multi-level statistical models. However, a solid grasp of the basic two-level hierarchical linear regression model is probably sufficient for most users of the approach and consumers of research in which such models are applied. For this reason, we limit our formal exposition of contemporary models to the basic two-level linear model. More complex multi-level models are, in general, merely elaborations of the basic two-level linear model. To be sure, there are some important distinctions between the two-level linear model and the hierarchical generalized linear models that one increasingly sees in the literature, but with a good foundation in the former, one can easily look elsewhere for technical elaboration of the latter (see Raudenbush and Bryk, 2002; Snijders and Bosker, 1999; Tseloni, 2006). In any event, for balance we illustrate the use of multi-level statistical modeling by referencing some research in this area that engages some of the more complex models (e.g., three-level hierarchical logistic regression models).

A brief primer on the modal bi-level linear regression model: individuals clustered within communities

Bi-level linear regression models are appropriate when the outcome of interest is a continuous variable and the observations for which it is measured exhibit clustering within a set of communities or other groupings based on shared membership. A good example in criminology is the analysis of delinquency among adolescents drawn from different neighborhoods but for which some of the sample members share neighborhoods. Using this example, the basic bi-level linear regression model can be expressed with reference to the following set of three equations, beginning with a level 1 (in this case), individual-level model:

$$Y_{ij} = \beta_{0j}\beta_{1j}X_{ij}r_{ij} \qquad (7.1)$$

where Y_{ij} reflects a delinquency score for person i in neighborhood j, X_{ij} represents one or more individual-level explanatory variables measured for this person, β_{0j} is the estimated intercept, β_{1j} is the estimated slope or effect of a specified X on Y for neighborhood j, and r_{ij} is the level 1 error (i.e., in our example, the unexplained variance in Y varies across individuals, within neighborhoods). A unique feature of this model is that the intercept and slope parameters are estimated separately for each j grouping; in this instance, separate parameters are estimated for each neighborhood. This feature of multi-level models permits exciting possibilities for modeling variation in the regression parameters across neighborhoods. Moreover, by formulating and estimating equation (7.1) separately within each neighborhood, multi-level

models explicitly account for the non-independence of observations within the same neighborhood, which should yield standard errors for neighborhood-level variables that are more precise. This contrasts with the more traditional single-level contextual models discussed previously, in which equation (7.1) – minus the j subscripts – is estimated once for all observations (irrespective of neighborhood membership) and is assumed to yield parameters that are equally applicable across neighborhoods.

In a two-level regression model, the neighborhood-specific parameters β_{0j} and β_{1j} estimated at 'level 1' (i.e., the individual-level model), as expressed in equation (7.1), are modeled through two subsequent equations at 'level 2', which are, in our example, neighborhood-level models of the intercepts (7.2a) and slopes (7.2b):

$$\beta_{0j} = \gamma_{00}\gamma_{01}W_j u_{0j} \qquad (7.2a)$$

$$\beta_{1j} = \gamma_{10}\gamma_{11}W_j u_{1j} \qquad (7.2b)$$

In essence, the neighborhood-specific intercepts (equation 7.2a) and slopes (equation 7.2b) become outcome variables that are then modeled at level 2 as a function of one or more neighborhood-level variables, expressed in the equations as W_j. Equation (7.2a) is often referred to as a random-intercept or means-as-outcomes regression model. The specific interpretation of the γ_{00} in this equation depends on the scaling of W_j. A common strategy is to mean center this variable, and in such a case, γ_{00} reflects the intercept for the average level 2 unit, γ_{01} is the effect of W_j on β_{0j}, and u_{0j} represents the residual variance in β_{0j} after controlling for W_j.

Equation (7.2a) involves the estimated main effect of some aggregate-level explanatory variable (e.g., neighborhood poverty levels) on an individual-level outcome variable (e.g., delinquency). This type of multi-level model permits an assessment of variation in levels of a given outcome variable (Y) across level 2 grouping units, or using our example, variation in delinquency levels across neighborhoods. As noted previously, for much of the history of research in criminology, aggregate-level regression models were applied to examine variation in rates of delinquency across neighborhoods. A key advantage of adopting a multi-level approach to model such variation is that it is possible to control for variation across neighborhoods in the composition of individuals, families, attitudes, and other attributes, something that cannot be done in an aggregate-level design, at least not separately from parallel indicators of neighborhood context.

For example, a classic issue examined in many aggregate-level studies of crime is whether exposure to high rates of poverty increases rates of crime. While aggregate-level studies are suitable for evaluating whether there is a statistical association between rates of poverty and rates of crime across places, they cannot help decipher whether any observed association between these two variables arises because high rates of poverty reflect a unique context that facilitates or motivates crime, or whether it simply reflects the aggregation of an individual relationship between poverty status and criminal involvement. Multi-level data and models can help to adjudicate between these possibilities by assessing the relationship between poverty rates and crime rates after adjusting for the individual-level association between poverty status and criminal involvement.

Equation (7.2b) is typically described in the literature as a random-slope or random-coefficients model (Raudenbush and Bryk, 2002). This is a multiplicative model that involves the estimated effect of some aggregate-level explanatory variable on one or more individual-level slope parameters. In other words, this model assesses a cross-level interaction in which the individual-level, or level 1, variable is the focal variable and the aggregate-level variable is the moderator. (Another form of cross-level interaction – one in which the aggregate-level variable is the focal variable and the individual-level variable is the moderator – arises when a given random-intercept multi-level model is applied to different samples defined by unique values on one of the individual-level variables). This equation assumes that the effect of X_{ij} as expressed in equation (7.1) is specified to vary across level 2 groupings, such as neighborhoods. Under this specification, γ_{10} is the average regression slope of for X_{ij} across the level 2 units after controlling for W_j, γ_{11} represents the effect of W_j (a level 2 attribute) on β_{1j} (i.e., the variation in slopes across level 2 units), and u_{1j} is the residual variance in β_{1j} after accounting for the effect of W_j.

The logic of the three equations presented previously extends in a straightforward way to multi-level analyses of discrete outcome variables, including binary measures, multinomial and ordered categorical measures and counts (Guo and Zhao, 2000; Patterson, 1991; Raudenbush and Byrk, 2002; Tseloni, 2006). In each instance, a key methodological benefit of multi-level statistical approaches, rather than single-level contextual models in which neighborhood or other group-level attributes are treated merely as another individual-level attribute, lies with added precision of the estimated standard errors for γ_{01} (equation 7.2a) and γ_{11} (equation 7.2b), especially if the degree of correlation among observations within

groups (i.e., the intra-class correlation) is relatively large. More directly, if one were to use OLS to estimate the parameters in the basic two-level hierarchical linear regression model outlined previously, the standard errors would tend to be underestimated. Multi-level statistical models minimize this potential bias by estimating the equations using generalized least squares and maximum (or quasi-maximum) likelihood estimators (see also Bursik and Grasmick, 1995). Beyond this, though, and in our view equally important, the multi-level approach has some notable *conceptual* advantages over single-level approaches. Specifically, multi-level statistical models illuminate the importance of full theoretical and empirical specification at each level of the data hierarchy and they explicitly draw attention to the possibility that existing formulations of lower-level models may vary across contexts. As highlighted earlier, during the past two decades these considerations have been instrumental in stimulating a relatively large body of research across several nations as to the role of aggregate-level conditions on a wide range of individual-level outcomes. One example of such a study is an analysis of the role of attitudes about capital punishment by Baumer et al. (2003), described in Box 7.1.

Additional applications of bi-level regression models

The previous description of the two-level regression model is, by design, highly general and simplified. Elucidating more specific interpretations of parameters requires information on how the variables are measured, most notably the metric in which the explanatory variables are expressed. Indeed, a recent example in criminology illustrates this point nicely (cf., Oberwittler, 2004, 2005). Further details on the specifics can be found both in general expositions on multi-level models (Goldstein, 1987; Raudenbush and Bryk, 2002) and in selected overviews of important modeling considerations (see e.g., Enders and Tofighi, 2007; Maas and Hox, 2005; Paccagnella, 2006). As these more selective reviews articulate, features such as sample sizes at different levels and the choice of covariate centering can be consequential for inferences. Nonetheless, this general description outlines the core fundamentals of multi-level statistical approaches and, as noted, more complex versions build off of this foundation in a straightforward way.

Two-level growth-curve models (also referred to as latent growth curve models) represent one natural extension of the traditional bi-level regression framework. Although they are often expressed with different notations in textbook presentations

---

Box 7.1 Exploring geographic variation in support for capital punishment

It is widely known that a majority of Americans support capital punishment, but relatively little attention has been devoted to the possibility of significant variation in levels of support across communities within the United States. Baumer et al. (2003) apply multi-level statistical models to explore this issue.

Baumer et al. (2003) use a version of the American General Social Survey (GSS) that contained identifiers of the sampling units (counties and metropolitan areas) from which respondents were drawn. Using these identifiers permitted the aggregation of responses within sampling units for purposes of estimating area characteristics and also enabled the researchers to merge data on area attributes taken from other sources. In essence, Baumer et al. (2003) were interested in two general issues: (1) do levels of support for capital punishment vary across geographic areas within the US?; and (2) assuming that this is the case, what geographic attributes are related to individual attitudes about capital punishment? They address these two questions by estimating a series of two-level random-intercept regression models.

Their answer to the first question is a clear 'yes', as the data reveal that although approximately 70 percent of respondents sampled indicated support for the death penalty for convicted murderers, levels of support vary from less than 50 percent in some areas to greater than 90 percent in others. Thus, although the US is often described as a nation that exhibits very high levels of support for capital punishment public sentiment about the death penalty is decidedly mixed in many of the geographic areas sampled in the GSS, and in some areas, a majority of persons disapprove of the death penalty for persons convicted of murder.

As outlined previously, the second question considered by Baumer et al. (2003) could be addressed with aggregate-level data on levels of support for capital punishment and other conditions. However, as Baumer et al. (2003) point out, any observed variation across communities in levels of support for capital punishment could simply be a function of the compositional differences across areas, or in other words, it is possible that geographic areas in which levels of support for the death penalty are higher simply contain more individuals with attributes that are associated with support for the death penalty. An aggregate-level analysis could not easily account for such compositional differences, whereas a multi-level regression framework can do so explicitly by modeling the effects of both individual- and aggregate-level attributes. This turns out to be consequential in Baumer et al.'s (2003) analysis; one-quarter of the observed geographic variation in support for capital punishment was due to differences across places in individual attributes. This study also reveals significant effects of 'contextual' geographic factors as well, however. Specifically, controlling for compositional differences, Baumer et al. (2003) find that support for capital punishment is greater in areas characterized by higher homicide rates, a larger concentration of political conservatives, and a greater concentration of African-Americans.

(and there are several nuances to these models that should be given due consideration [see Phillips and Greenberg, 2008]), in their basic form, two-level growth curve models are simply a different expression of equations (7.1), (7.2a), and (7.2b) discussed previously. The key difference is that instead of individuals nested or grouped within neighborhoods (or other shared group settings), the two-level growth curve application for equation (7.1) entails repeated temporal observations grouped within individuals (e.g., Raudenbush and Chan, 1992), neighborhoods (e.g., Bursik and Grasmick, 1992), or cities (e.g., Baumer et al., 1998). Paralleling the description provided previously, in these models an initial task is to estimate a level 1 model for each level 2 unit, which in this instance translates into estimating a panel model of some outcome as a function of one or more variables that represent "time" and other time-varying explanatory variables for each level 2 unit (i.e., persons or places). In a second stage, the resulting intercepts and slopes for these variables

are typically modeled as a function of attributes of level 2 units.

There is a growing volume of multi-level growth curve applications in the literature, some of which focus on repeated observations within individuals (e.g., Duncan et al., 2006; Johnson et al., 1997; Simons et al., 2001; VanderValk et al., 2005) and others that focus on repeated observations within places (Kubrin and Herting, 2003; Ousey and Lee, 2004; Rosenfeld et al., 2007). Two examples we will highlight illustrate the basic foundation of these models as applied to the study of crime trends (Baumer et al., 1998; Rosenfeld et al., 2005). These studies build on the pioneering research of Bursik and Grasmick (1992) on 'community crime trajectories' and explore city-level variation in crime trends across cities in the 1980s and 1990s. Details of both studies are provided in Box 7.2.

In an important contribution, Phillips and Greenberg (2008) outline the advantages and disadvantages of using multi-level growth curve

---

Box 7.2 Multi-level analysis of city crime trends

In the US, there have been two major swings in crime rates since the early 1980s: (1) an abrupt and sharp increase in robbery and youth homicide from the mid-1980s through the early 1990s; and (2) a widespread decline in all major forms of street crime from the early-to-mid-1990s through the first few years or so of the 2000s. Several studies have explored the nature of crime trends during these periods, some of which have applied multi-level growth curve models (for a review, see Baumer, 2008).

Baumer et al. (1998) examine cross-city trends in homicide, robbery, and burglary from 1984 to 1992 using growth curve models. Other methods traditionally had been used to study crime trends involving multiple 'panels' (see, e.g., Bursik and Grasmick, 1992), and such methods are in some cases more appropriate for the task at hand (Phillips and Greenberg, 2008). But, as suggested by Baumer et al. (1998), multi-level growth curve models also provide an appealing alternative for analyzing panel data since they yield some highly intuitive descriptive information about the nature of crime trends, describe how they vary across people or places, and permit an assessment of factors associated with crime trends. Baumer et al. (1998) formulate both random-intercept and random-slope models of city crime trends, showing among other things that between 1984 and 1992 the magnitude of observed increases in robbery and observed decreases in burglary were greater in cities that experienced higher levels of crack cocaine involvement. This pattern is consistent with findings from ethnographic research at the time, which indicated that the proliferation of crack cocaine in many US urban areas during this time was stimulating increases in robbery rates both generally and among many would-be burglars.

Rosenfeld et al. (2005) extend applications of growth curve modeling to city crime trends in two important ways. First, while many of the previous applications of this type included few, if any, time-varying level 1 predictors, the specifications employed by Rosenfeld et al. (2005) contain several relevant attributes in this regard. Second, Rosenfeld et al. (2005) implement 'time' into their analysis in an innovative way by adopting a piecewise approach to estimating cross-city variation in homicide trends before, during, and after notable policy interventions. Substantively, they explore whether crime 'trajectories' during the 1990s were significantly different in New York City, Boston, and Richmond – each of which mounted widely publicized policing interventions during the decade – than other large US cities. Rosenfeld et al. (2005) found that, contrary to expectations, once conditions known to be associated with violent crime rates were controlled, New York City's homicide trend during the 1990s did not differ significantly from those of other large cities. The results for Boston were inconclusive, but this study suggests that Richmond's homicide reduction during the 1990s was significantly greater than the decline in other large cities after the implementation of Project Exile, which is consistent with claims of an intervention effect.

---

models to analyze panel data, including aggregate crime trends. They also situate these models within the larger literature on panel model estimation (see also Raudenbush and Bryk, 2002). While acknowledging that growth curve models provide a flexible means by which to examine panel crime data, they also raise some concerns and highlight some common problems about the implementation of growth curves in practice.

The two issues raised by Phillips and Greenberg that are particularly salient are that (1) many applications of growth curve modeling in criminology do not explicitly account for unmeasured sources of between group heterogeneity, and that (2) growth curve models entail the imposition of a specific functional form for temporal effects that may be unrealistic in some settings. With respect to the first issue, one of the advantages of using panel data to study change is that it better enables researchers to control for unobserved heterogeneity through the inclusion of 'fixed' group-level effects, typically in the form of dummy variables that identify group membership.

Most applications of multi-level growth curve modeling in criminology do not include such fixed effects. This may be in part because some of the popular statistical packages used to estimate multi-level growth curve models (e.g., HLM) do not offer an easily accessible way to do so. However, there are alternative ways of incorporating group-level fixed effects in multi-level models and, in any case, it is vital that researchers be more explicit in acknowledging the strengths and limitations of their analyses. Phillips and Greenberg (2008: 66) go further, strongly encouraging researchers who utilize multi-level growth curve models to 'estimate fixed-effects models where they are appropriate, either by doing the extra work needed in a program like HLM or by using other programs (e.g., Stata, SAS, Eviews) that have built-in capabilities for purging estimates of the influence of stable sources of heterogeneity'.

Another issue that Phillips and Greenberg (2008) mention as a limitation of multi-level growth curve models is that while imposing a particular functional form for time in a panel model (e.g., a linear or quadratic form) may make sense in some instances (e.g., developmental models where change tends to occur in well defined ways), it might not be a reasonable strategy in other settings, including panel analyses of aggregate crime trends where temporal patterns may not be fully captured by linear, quadratic or even more complex functional forms. This is likely a more significant issue for studies that span several decades, but it is an important consideration even for shorter time frames. Piecewise multi-level regression models are one strategy for reducing the potential bias introduced by this concern, as illustrated in the Rosenfeld et al. (2005) study described previously.

A less common application of the basic two-level regression model that has many potentially interesting applications and that involves a different form of data clustering is the multi-level analysis of repeated cross-sectional data (Diprete and Grusky, 1990a). This formulation differs from other applications of multi-level modeling because the data are typically drawn from a single context (e.g., a nation or city) rather than multiple contexts. However, as Diprete and Grusky (1990a) describe, the collection of annual observations in repeated cross-sectional survey designs in a single context or unit can themselves be conceived of as multiple 'contexts.' In multi-level assessments of repeated cross-sectional data, the level 1 observations are individual or household survey responses, and the level 2 units are year 'groupings'. There are some important nuances, however, when a bi-level modeling strategy is adapted to analyze repeated cross-sectional data. Most notably, as Diprete and Grusky (1990a) explain, in a repeated cross-sectional design where different members of a given population are sampled repeatedly over time, there will likely be significant serial correlation across years, or in other words, at level 2 of the multi-level model. To accommodate this error structure, Diprete and Grusky (1990a) derive and illustrate some possible generalized least squares estimators in which the level 2 disturbances are modeled using a first-order autoregressive error structure. To our knowledge, there are only a few applications of multi-level modeling techniques to assess changes over time in repeated cross-sectional data (e.g., Diprete and Grusky, 1990b; Quillian, 1996; Yang and Land, 2008), and no published studies in criminology that have done so. Nonetheless, this form of multi-level modeling has the potential to be useful for studying temporal trends that emerge from repeated cross-sectional data. It has proven useful in some ongoing research on crime reporting trends (Baumer and Stults, 2010) and on sentencing trends (Baumer, 2009). Additional details on the latter study are provided in Box 7.3.

Box 7.3 Temporal variation in the probability of incarceration

Baumer (2009) assesses the nature of changes in racial and gender gaps in the probability of incarceration in the US between 1990 and 2004. Using repeated cross-sectional data from a sample of large urban counties that describes sentencing outcomes for convicted felons, the study aimed to document overall differences in the probability of incarceration by gender and race during this period, and whether such differences have changed over time beyond the fluctuations that would be expected on the basis of shifts in the types of defendants and cases considered for custodial sentences. There are several ways in which these questions could be approached. For instance, one could aggregate the data and describe the resulting trends using uni-variate or multi-variate time-series methods. Alternatively, one could retain the case-level data structure and estimate a single-level model that includes one or more year indicators as a covariate. As Baumer (2009) notes, both approaches are limited in important ways. The first approach does not capture changes over time in the nature of criminal cases and, more generally, ignores all of the within-group (i.e., within year) variation in the outcome. The second approach also has drawbacks because it ignores the dependence of observations from shared groupings (i.e., cases sentenced in the same year), which could yield biased standard errors.

Following Diprete and Grusky (1990a), Baumer (2009) proposes that a two-level hierarchical logistic model would be a preferable approach to assessing these questions. In this model, sentencing outcomes for felony defendants (level 1) are modeled over time (level 2). Note that in the full specification, Baumer (2009) also incorporates geography at level 3, but a key interest in the study is on the two-level model just described, with a particular focus on random-slope specifications of this model that evaluate whether sex and race disparities in the probability of incarceration have differed over time. The results of this model indicated that there was a significant decline in sex differences in the probability of incarceration, but no significant linear change in the magnitude of race or ethnic disparities in the log odds of incarceration.

More complex multi-level models in criminology

There are a variety of more complex multi-level models that can be profitably employed to tackle interesting substantive questions in criminology. Some of these are sophisticated but have not yet been applied extensively in the criminological literature, such as hierarchical item response and measurement models (Molnar et al., 2003; Raudenbush et al., 2003; Sampson et al., 1997), multi-level meta analyses involving standardized measures of effect across studies (Pratt et al., 2006), and cross-classified models (Goldstein, 1987). However, another extension of the bi-level multi-level modeling framework – three-level hierarchical models – have become increasingly common and warrant mention here.

Like their two-level counterparts, three-level regression models come in many different data structures and cover a wide range of different outcomes. Some examples include repeated measurements within individuals nested in different schools or neighborhoods (Raudenbush, 1993), individuals within cities from different nations (Gracia and Herrero, 2006); criminal cases adjudicated by different judges who serve different judicial districts (Johnson, 2006); criminal cases adjudicated in different years within different counties (Baumer, 2009); and survey respondents within metropolitan areas located in different states (Messner et al., 2006). Three-level models are fairly straightforward extensions of the two-level specification outlined earlier (see Raudenbush and Bryk, 2002: chapter 8), but they present a much larger array of modeling possibilities. A good example of creative application of three-level modeling in criminology is Johnson's (2006) study of criminal sentencing outcomes, upon which we elaborate in Box 7.4.

The findings reported by Johnson (2006) are notable and make a significant contribution to the literature, but perhaps equally important, the three-level specification outlined by Johnson (2006) points to some additional questions not addressed explicitly in the study but which become illuminated by the explicit acknowledgment of the complex hierarchy inherent in the criminal justice process. To keep things manageable, Johnson (2006) fixes judge effects across counties. He notes that relaxing this assumption and explicitly modeling judge effects as random might be a fruitful avenue of future inquiry. We agree with this sentiment and think this acknowledgement highlights the conceptual value of thinking in multi-level terms. It would be interesting to examine, for instance, whether the judge-race effect noted previously varied across counties as a function of county racial composition. Alternatively, Johnson (2006) finds no evidence that male judges sentence differently than female judges, a pattern that applies to the data pooled across all Pennsylvania counties; however, it would be interesting to explore whether county gender norms moderate the effect of judge gender on sentencing. In short, three-level hierarchical models add some complexity to estimation but greatly expand the possibilities for analysis by enhancing efforts to address substantively important research questions and opening our eyes to others that we have yet to explore.

CONCLUSION

Multi-level models are an exciting analytical tool, but they are not magical. They are appropriate when the data at hand involve some type of hierarchy or nesting, and when they are suitable to the

---

Box 7.4 The multiple levels of sentencing decisions

Johnson (2006) examines the effect of judge characteristics and county attributes on sentencing outcomes in Pennsylvania. Although some studies had previously examined criminal case outcomes across judges *or* across counties, few had done both simultaneously. Johnson takes an important step in addressing this gap by integrating defendant data from the Pennsylvania Commission on Sentencing (PCS), data on judges from available information on judicial biographies, and a wide array of data on the counties in which these judges presided and their sentencing decisions for the defendants were delivered.

As hypothesized by Johnson (2006), even after controlling for a large number of case attributes, the study indicated significant variation across judges (level 2) and across counties (level 3) in the probability of incarceration among convicted defendants and the sentence length received by sentenced defendants. Additional models revealed several interesting judge and county effects on sentencing outcomes. For example, all else equal, defendants were less likely to receive a prison sentence and, among those who were sentenced to prison, they received a shorter sentence from minority judges as compared to white judges. Johnson (2006) also finds that county attributes, including court size and jail capacity, influence sentencing outcomes in theoretically expected ways.

research question(s) under investigation. As Raudenbush and Bryk (2002) note, many natural data structures involve hierarchies, and thus there may be something to gain by applying multi-level models in these instances. As outlined previously, multi-level models have taken many forms and have been applied across a diverse set of substantive issues in criminology, often on the justification that they provide more accurate estimates of parameters. While often this is an appropriate rationale for applying multi-level models, in our judgment the real value in these models lies beyond merely enhancing the precision with which standard errors are estimated. As we have argued, thinking in a multi-level way can reveal interesting insights about data and substantive issues that might go hidden otherwise. By their very nature, multi-level approaches urge us to consider the possibility that what we know might look different across groups, communities or temporal periods. This, in turn, has potential for generating new knowledge that challenges long-held assumptions, stimulating additional thinking about how we can make sense of our complex and inherently multi-layered world.

There has been much progress in multi-level data analysis over the past few decades. Acquiring the know-how and tools needed to estimate basic two-level linear regression models is relatively straightforward these days; there are good introductions to these models, several existing empirical examples in the literature, and a variety of user-friendly software choices to get the job done. Later, we list some web-based resources that are excellent places to start. Descriptions of the basic models and their purposes have become more accessible and the computer programs capable of estimating these models have grown in number and have become increasingly sophisticated. Additionally, a variety of future directions in multi-level modeling have been spelled out by leading methodologists in this area (e.g., Browne et al., 2001; Raudenbush and Bryk, 2002; Rasbash et al., 2009). Many of the sources typically mentioned are references for extending multi-level modeling to situations in which there is a more complex nesting of data hierarchies (e.g., cross-classified data) or error structures (e.g., auto-regressive errors in models involving repeated observations over time). Other often-voiced hopes for future development in multi-level models center on a desire for better integration of these techniques with high-powered and flexible data management and analysis packages, a demand that has increasingly been met with advancements to multi-level modeling capabilities in SAS, Stata, and MLwin (see Rabe-Hesketh and Skrondal, 2008; Rasbash et al., 2009; SAS, 2010).

The lone addition along these lines we would highlight given our own research interests are to better integrate into multi-level models the capacity to account formally for 'spatial effects' in applications that focus on estimating the role of community conditions on individual outcomes. Spatial regression models have coincidentally been developed during the past few decades with an eye to better enabling researchers to model the spatial clustering of a given phenomenon. Multi-level models, of course, are quite capable of estimating the effect of a given community or spatial attribute on a given outcome; yet, theoretical and empirical work in spatial econometrics and related fields has shown that spatial or community effects can arise through a variety of other mechanisms as well (e.g., through a spatial lag or spatial error process), and that regression models that do not account for these types of spatial effects may yield biased parameters. Although this issue has been given some attention in the multi-level statistical literature (e.g., Browne et al., 2001), additional tools and guidance that would enable researchers to account for spatial correlations in multi-level models of community effects would be useful. The modal contemporary practice in extant research has been to estimate spatial models using a single-level approach either for comparison with a multi-level model or, where evidence of a spatial lag process is found, to simply add a spatially lagged version of the outcome measure to the multi-level model as an explanatory measure. Neither of these approaches is ideal (see Land and Deane, 1992).

Aside from this modest request, in our judgment the most urgent need in the area of multi-level statistical modeling is greater attention to multi-level *theoretical* development. To be sure, there are numerous empirical puzzles for which multi-level models serve as an appropriate and useful tool, and pure data mining is not inherently bad. However, the value of multi-level modeling, in each of its myriad forms, will increase considerably along with the precision and depth of our development of multi-level theoretical models and conceptual frameworks. More than two decades ago, scholars in criminology urged us to begin thinking in ways that might profitably integrate ideas from various theoretical perspectives, including perspectives that outlined explanations of crime and related outcomes across multiple levels of analysis (Messner et al., 1989). There have been some positive developments in accord with those calls, but further consideration of the specific reasons we might expect regression parameters (intercepts and/or slopes) to vary across groups, communities and time would better inform ongoing multi-level investigations and better illuminate the empirical value of multi-level statistical techniques.

RECOMMENDED READING

For those interested in pursuing research questions that require a multi-level framework, the UCLA Academic Technology Services (2010) provide a web-based portal designed to provide a wide range of lessons and applications for many advanced data analysis methods in the social and behavioral sciences. For a more formal, lesson-based approach to learning multi-level modeling, the University of Bristol's Learning Environment for Multilevel Methodology and Applications (LEMMA) provides practical guides for both Stata and MLwiN software packages. Advanced readers might wish to consult Bryk and Raudenbush (1992) for a technical overview of hierarchical linear models and Guo and Zhao (2000) for a discussion on multi-level analysis using binary data.

Bryk, A.S. and Raudenbush, S.W. (1992) *Hierarchical Linear Models: Applications and Data Analysis Methods*. Newbury Park, CA: Sage.
Guo, G., and Zhao, H. (2000) 'Multilevel modeling for binary data'. *Annual Review of Sociology 26*(1): 441–462.
University of Bristol (2010) LEMMA: Multilevel Modelling Online Course. Online course available at http://www.cmm.bristol.ac.uk/learning-training/course.shtml.
UCLA Academic Technology Services (2010) Stat Computing: Text Examples. Available online at http://www.ats.ucla.edu/stat/examples/.

REFERENCES

Baumer, E.P. (2008) 'An Empirical Assessment of the Contemporary Crime Trends Puzzle: A Modest Step Toward a More Comprehensive Research Agenda' in Committee on Law and Justice, National Research Council of the National Academies, *Understanding Crime Trends: Workshop Report* (pp. 127–176). Washington, DC: The National Academies Press.
Baumer, E.P. (2009) 'The probability of imprisonment in the U.S.: Assessing the role of sex and race across time and space'. Unpublished manuscript, Florida State University.
Baumer, E.P., Lauritsen, J.L., Rosenfeld, R. and Wright, R. (1998) 'The influence of crack cocaine on robbery, burglary, and homicide rates: A cross-city, longitudinal analysis'. *Journal of Research in Crime and Delinquency 35*(3): 316–340.
Baumer, E.P., Messner, S.F. and Rosenfeld, R. (2003) 'Explaining spatial variation in support for capital punishment: A multilevel analysis'. *American Journal of Sociology 108*(4), 844–875.
Baumer, E.P. and Stults, B.J. (2010) 'Social change and the mobilization of law: explaining the recent rise in crime reporting in America'. Unpublished manuscript, Florida State University.

Blalock, H.M. (1984) 'Contextual-effects models: Theoretical and methodological issues'. *Annual Review of Sociology 10*(1): 353–372.
Browne, W.J., Goldstein, H. and Rasbash, J. (2001) 'Multiple membership multiple classification (MMMC) models'. *Statistical Modelling 1*(2): 103–124.
Bryk, A.S. and Raudenbush, S.W. (1992) *Hierarchical Linear Models: Applications and Data Analysis Methods*. Newbury Park, CA: Sage.
Bursik, R.J., Jr. and Grasmick, H.G. (1992) 'Longitudinal neighborhood profiles in crime: The decomposition of change'. *Journal of Quantitative Criminology 8*(3): 247–263.
Bursik, R.J., Jr. and Grasmick, H.G. (1995) 'The use of contextual analysis in models of criminal behavior' in J.D. Hawkins (ed.), *Delinquency and Crime: Current Theories*. New York, NY: Cambridge University Press.
Cohen, L.E., Kluegel, J.R. and Land, K.C. (1981) 'Social inequality and predatory criminal victimization: An exposition and test of a formal theory'. *American Sociological Review 46*(5): 505–524.
DiPrete, T.A. and Grusky, D.B. (1990a) 'The multilevel analysis of trends with repeated cross-sectional data'. *Sociological Methodology 20*: 337–368.
DiPrete, T.A. and Grusky, D.B. (1990b) 'Structure and trend in the process of stratification for American men and women'. *The American Journal of Sociology 96*(1): 107–143.
Duncan, S.C., Duncan, T.E. and Strycker, L.A. (2006) 'Alcohol use from ages 9–16: A cohort-sequential latent growth model'. *Drug Alcohol Dependence 81*(1): 71–81.
Enders, C.K. and Tofighi, D. (2007) 'Centering predictor variables in cross-sectional multilevel models: A new look at an old issue'. *Psychological Methods 12*(2): 121–138.
Goldstein, H. (1987) *Multilevel Models in Education and Social Research*. New York, NY: Oxford University Press.
Gottfredson, D.C., McNeil, III, R.J. and Gottfredson, G.D. (1991) 'Social area influences in delinquency: A multilevel analysis'. *Journal of Research in Crime and Delinquency 28*(2): 197–226.
Gottfredson, S.D. and Taylor, R.B. (1986) 'Person-environment interactions in the prediction of recidivism' in J.M. Byrne and R.J. Sampson (eds.), *The Social Ecology of Crime*. New York, NY: Springer-Verlag.
Goudriaan, H., Wittebrood, K. and Nieuwbeerta, P. (2006) 'Neighbourhood characteristics and reporting crime: Effects of social cohesion, confidence in police effectiveness and socioeconomic disadvantage'. *British Journal of Criminology 46*(4): 719–742.
Gracia, E. and Herrero, J. (2006) 'Acceptability of domestic violence against women in the European Union: A multilevel analysis'. *Journal of Epidemiology and Community Health 60*(2): 123–129.
Guo, G. and Zhao, H. (2000) 'Multilevel modeling for binary data'. *Annual Review of Sociology 26*(1): 441–462.
Hauser, R. (1970) 'Context and consex: A cautionary tale'. *American Journal of Sociology 75*(4): 645–664.
Iversen, G.R. (1991) *Contextual Analysis*. Newbury Park, CA: Sage.

Johnson, B.D. (2006) 'The multilevel context of criminal sentencing: Integrating judge- and county-level influences'. *Criminology 44*(2): 259–298.

Johnson, R.A., Hoffmann, J.P., Su, S.S. and Gerstein, D.R. (1997) 'Growth curves of deviant behavior in early adolescence: A multivariate analysis'. *Journal of Quantitative Criminology 13*(4): 429–467.

Johnstone, J.W.C. (1978) 'Social class, social areas and delinquency'. *Sociology and Social Research 63*(1): 49–72.

Krivo, L.J., Peterson, R.D. and Kuhl, D.C. (2009) 'Segregation, racial structure, and neighborhood violent crime'. *American Journal of Sociology, 114*(6): 1765–1802.

Kubrin, C.E. and Herting, J. (2003) 'Neighborhood correlates of homicide trends: An analysis using growth-curve modeling'. *Sociological Quarterly 44*(3): 329–350.

Kubrin, C.E. and Stewart, E.A. (2006) 'Predicting who reoffends: The neglected role of neighborhood context in recidivism studies'. *Criminology 44*(1): 165–197.

LaFree, G., Baumer, E.P. and O'Brien, B. (2010) 'Social context and the racial gap in violence: A city-level analysis of changes in black-white homicide arrest ratios, 1960–2000'. *American Sociological Review 75*(1): 75–100.

Land, K.C. and Deane, G. (1992) 'On the large-sample estimation of regression models with spatial effects terms: A two-stage least squares approach'. *Sociological Methodology 22*: 221–248.

Lazarsfeld, P. and Menzel, H. (1965) 'On the relations between individual and collective properties' in A. Etzioni (ed.), *A Sociological Reader on Complex Organizations* (pp. 422–440). New York, NY: Holt, Rinehart and Winston.

Lincoln, J. and Zeitz, G. (1980) 'Organizational properties from aggregate data: Separating individual and structural effects'. *American Sociological Review 45*(3): 391–408.

Liska, A.E. (1990) 'The significance of aggregate dependent variables and contextual independent variables for linking macro and micro theories'. *Social Psychology Quarterly 53*(4): 292–301.

Maas, C.J. and Hox, J.J. (2005) 'Sufficient sample sizes for multilevel modeling'. *Methodology 1*(3): 86–92.

Mason, W.W., Wong, G.Y. and Entwisle, B. (1983) 'Contextual analysis through the multilevel linear model'. *Sociological Methodology 14*: 72–103.

Messner, S.F., Baumer, E.P. and Rosenfeld, R. (2006) 'Distrust of government, the vigilante tradition, and support for capital punishment'. *Law and Society Review 40*(3): 559–590.

Messner, S.F., Krohn, M.D. and Liska, A.E. (1989) *Theoretical Integration in the Study of Deviance and Crime: Problems and Prospects*. Albany, NY: State University of New York Press.

Miethe, T.D. and McDowall, D. (1993) 'Contextual effects in models of criminal victimization'. *Social Forces 71*(3): 741–759.

Molnar, B.E., Buka, S.L., Brennan, R.T., Holton, J.K. and Earls, F. (2003) 'A multilevel study of neighborhoods and parent-to-child physical aggression: Results from the project on human development in Chicago neighborhoods'. *Child Maltreatment 8*(2): 94–97.

Myers, M.A. and Talarico, S.M. (1987) *The Social Contexts of Criminal Sentencing*. New York, NY: Springer-Verlag.

Oberwittler, D. (2004) 'A multilevel analysis of neighbourhood contextual effects on serious juvenile offending: The role of subcultural values and social disorganization'. *European Journal of Criminology 1*(2): 201–235.

Oberwittler, D. (2005) 'Correction of results: "A multilevel analysis of neighbourhood contextual effects on serious juvenile offending: The role of subcultural values and social disorganization"'. *European Journal of Criminology 2*(1): 93–97.

Ousey, G.C. and Lee, M.R. (2004) 'Investigating the connections between race, illicit drug markets, and lethal violence, 1984–1997'. *Journal of Research in Crime and Delinquency 41*(4): 352–383.

Paccagnella, O. (2006) 'Centering or not centering in multilevel models? The role of the group mean and the assessment of group effects'. *Evaluation Review 30*(1): 66–85.

Patterson, L. (1991) 'Multilevel logistic regression' in R. Prosser, J. Rasbash and H. Goldstein (eds.), *Data Analysis with ML3* (pp. 5–18). London: Institute of Education, University of London.

Payne, A.A., Gottfredson, D.C. and Gottfredson, G. (2003) 'Schools as communities: The relationships among communal school organization, student bonding, and school disorder'. *Criminology 41*(3): 749–777.

Peeples, F. and Loeber, R. (1994) 'Do individual factors and neighborhood context explain ethnic differences in juvenile delinquency?' *Journal of Quantitative Criminology 10*(2): 141–157.

Phillips, J.A. and Greenberg, D.F. (2008) 'A comparison of methods for analyzing criminological panel data'. *Journal of Quantitative Criminology 24*(1): 51–72.

Pratt, T.C., McGloin, J.M. and Fearn, N.E. (2006) 'Maternal cigarette smoking during pregnancy and criminal/deviant behavior: A meta-analysis'. *International Journal of Offender Therapy and Comparative Criminology 50*(6): 672–690.

Quillian, L. (1996) 'Group threat and regional change in attitudes toward African Americans'. *American Journal of Sociology 102*(3): 816–860.

Rabe-Hesketh, S. and Skrondal, A. (2008) *Multilevel and Longitudinal Modeling Using Stata*, 2nd Edition. College Station, TX: Stata Press.

Rasbash, J., Steele, F., Browne, W.J. and Goldstein, H. (2009) *A User's Guide to MLwiN v2.10*. Bristol: Centre for Multilevel Modelling, University of Bristol.

Raudenbush, S.W. (1993) 'Modeling individual and community effects on deviance over time: Multi-level statistical models' in D.P. Farrington, R.J. Sampson and P-O.H. Wikstrom, (eds.), *Intergrating Individual and Ecological Aspects of Crime*. Stockhom: National Crime Council of Sweden.

Raudenbush, S.W. and Bryk, A.S. (2002) *Hierarchical Linear Models: Application and Data Analysis Methods*, 2nd Edition. Thousand Oaks, CA: Sage.

Raudenbush, S.W. and Chan, W. (1992) 'Growth curve analysis in accelerated longitudinal designs'. *Journal of Research in Crime and Delinquency 29*(4): 387–411.

Raudenbush, S.W., Johnson, C. and Sampson, R.J. (2003) 'A multivariate, multilevel Rasch model with application to self-reported criminal behavior'. *Sociological Methodology* 33: 169–211.

Rebellon, C.J., Straus, M.A. and Medeiros, R. (2008) 'Self-control in global perspective: An empirical assessment of Gottfredson and Hirschi's general theory within and across 32 national settings'. *European Journal of Criminology* 5(3): 331–362.

Reiss, A.J. Jr. and Rhodes, A.L. (1961) 'Delinquency and social class structure'. *American Sociological Review* 26(5): 720–732.

Rosenfeld, R., Fornango, R. and Baumer, E.P. (2005) 'Did Ceasefire, Compstat, and Exile reduce homicide?' *Criminology and Public Policy* 4(3): 419–450.

Rosenfeld, R., Fornango, R. and Rengifo, A. (2007) 'The impact of order-maintenance policing on New York City robbery and homicide rates: 1988–2001'. *Criminology* 45(2): 355–383.

Rountree, P.W., Land, K.C. and Miethe, T.D. (1994) 'Macro-micro integration in the study of victimization: A hierarchical logistic model analysis across Seattle neighborhoods'. *Criminology* 32(3): 387–414.

Sampson, R.J. and Bartusch, D.J. (1998) 'Legal cynicism and (subcultural?) tolerance of deviance: The neighborhood context of racial differences'. *Law and Society Review* 32(4): 777–804.

Sampson, R.J. and Laub, J.H. (1993) *Crime in the Making: Pathways and Turning Points Through Life*. Cambridge, MA: Harvard University Press.

Sampson, R.J., Raudenbush, S.W. and Earls, F. (1997) 'Neighborhoods and violent crime: A multilevel study of collective efficacy'. *Science* 277(5328): 918–924.

Sampson, R.J. and Lauritsen, J.L. (1994) 'Violent victimization and offending: Individual-, situational-, and community-level risk factors' in A.J. Reiss Jr. and J. Roth (eds.), *Understanding and Preventing Violence: Social Influences on Violence*. Washington, DC: National Academy Press.

Sampson, R.J. and Wooldredge, J.D. (1987) 'Linking the micro- and macro-level dimensions of lifestyle-routine activity and opportunity models of predatory victimization'. *Journal of Quantitative Criminology* 3(4): 371–393.

SAS Institute Inc (2010) SAS/*STAT® 9.2 User's Guide: The Mixed Procedure*. Cary, NC: SAS Institute Inc.

Simcha-Fagen, O. and Schwartz, J.E. (1986) 'Neighborhood and delinquency: An assessment of contextual effects'. *Criminology* 24(4): 667–703.

Simons, R.L., Chao, W., Conger, R.D. and Elder, G.H. (2001) 'Quality of parenting as mediator of the effect of childhood defiance on adolescent friendship choices and delinquency: A growth curve analysis'. *Journal of Marriage and Family* 63(1): 63–79.

Smith, D.A. and Jarjoura, G.R. (1989) 'Household characteristics, neighborhood composition and victimization risk'. *Social Forces* 68(2): 621–640.

Snijders, T.A.B. and Bosker, R.J. (1999) *Multilevel Analysis: An Introduction to Basic and Advanced Multilevel Modeling*. Thousand Oaks, CA: Sage Publications.

Stewart, E.A. (2003) 'School social bonds, school climate, and school misbehavior: A multilevel analysis'. *Justice Quarterly* 20(3): 575–604.

Sutherland, E.H. (1947) *Principles of Criminology*, 4th Edition. Philadelphia: J.B. Lippincott.

Tseloni, A. (2006) 'Multilevel modeling of the number of property crimes: Household and area effects.' *Journal of the Royal Statistical Society: Series A (Statistics in Society)* 169(2): 205–233.

Tseloni, A. and Zarafonitou, C. (2008) 'Fear of crime and victimization: A multivariate multilevel analysis of competing measurements'. *European Journal of Criminology* 5(4): 387–409.

Ulmer, J.T. and Johnson, B. (2004) 'Sentencing in context: A multilevel analysis'. *Criminology* 42(1): 137–177.

VanderValk, I., Spruijt, E., de Goede, M., Maas, C. and Meeus, W. (2005) 'Family structure and problem behavior of adolescents and young adults: A growth-curve study'. *Journal of Youth and Adolescence* 34(6): 533–546.

Wong, G.Y. and Mason, W.M. (1985) 'Multilevel analysis'. *Journal of the American Statistical Association* 80(391): 513–524.

Yang, Y. and Land, K.C. (2008) 'Age-period-cohort analysis of repeated cross-section surveys: Fixed or random effects?' *Sociological Methods and Research* 36(3): 297–326.

Zhang, L., Messner, S.F., Liu, J. and Zhuo, Y.A. (2009) 'Guanxi and fear of crime in contemporary urban China'. *British Journal of Criminology* 49(4): 472–490.

8

Examining the Role of the Environment in Crime Causation: Small-Area Community Surveys and Space–Time Budgets

Per-Olof H. Wikström,
Kyle Treiber, Beth Hardie

INTRODUCTION

To explain why people commit acts of crime we need to understand the interplay between people's relevant characteristics and experiences and the relevant features of their social lives. One of the major obstacles to advancing knowledge about the causes of crime is the lack of adequate theory to explain, and satisfactory methodologies to test, theoretical propositions about the role of the environment and its interaction with people's personal characteristics and experiences. Criminological theory and research tends to be either person-oriented (focusing on crime propensity) or environment-oriented (focusing on criminogenic exposure) but rarely combines the two approaches effectively within a unified framework (e.g., Wikström, 2004; Wikström and Sampson, 2006).

To get out of the current stalemate, we need to (1) theoretically integrate and develop key criminological insights about crime propensity and criminogenic exposure; and (2) develop new or improved methodologies that can help us better investigate and test resulting hypotheses about the role of the environment and its interaction with people's characteristics and experiences in crime causation.

The Peterborough Adolescent and Young Adult Development Study (PADS+) was specifically set up to help overcome problems of fragmentation and poor integration in the study of crime causation. PADS+ is a large-scale longitudinal research project (see Table 8.1) funded by the ESRC (UK Economic and Social Research Council), which aims to develop (i) new theory amalgamating personal and environmental influences on people's crime involvement within an action theory framework (Situational Action Theory), and (ii) new and improved methodologies (including the *space–time budget* and *small-area community survey*) to explore and test hypotheses about the role of the environment in the person–environment interaction which leads to crime (see www.pads.ac.uk).

The main purpose of this chapter is to introduce advances in methodologies used to explore and test propositions about the role of the environment in crime causation, as developed within PADS+. The chapter (i) gives a brief presentation of Situational Action Theory as the theoretical background against which these methodologies were developed; (ii) provides an overview of the key shortcomings of current approaches to studying environmental influences on crime; (iii) presents the objectives and origins of new methodologies

Table 8.1   The Peterborough Adolescent and Young Adult Development Study (PADS+)

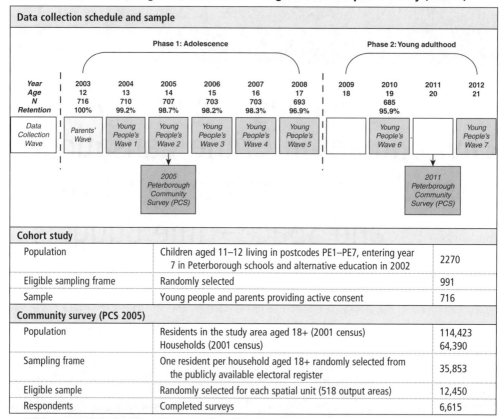

Cohort study		
Population	Children aged 11–12 living in postcodes PE1–PE7, entering year 7 in Peterborough schools and alternative education in 2002	2270
Eligible sampling frame	Randomly selected	991
Sample	Young people and parents providing active consent	716
Community survey (PCS 2005)		
Population	Residents in the study area aged 18+ (2001 census) Households (2001 census)	114,423 64,390
Sampling frame	One resident per household aged 18+ randomly selected from the publicly available electoral register	35,853
Eligible sample	Randomly selected for each spatial unit (518 output areas)	12,450
Respondents	Completed surveys	6,615

For further details see Wikström, Oberwittler, Hardie and Treiber 2011

which address these shortcomings (small-area community surveys and space–time budgets, and their combination) and situates them within the context of a research design aimed at studying the person–environment interaction in crime causation; and (iv) offers an outline of key issues to consider in the implementation of small-area community surveys and space–time budgets, based on experiences from their application in the study of young people and crime within PADS+ (see Wikström et al., 2011).

SITUATIONAL ACTION THEORY

Situational Action Theory (SAT) has been presented in a number of previous publications (e.g., Wikström, 2006, 2010a, 2010b), and here we will only briefly introduce those key propositions which are relevant to the proposed methodological developments.

SAT proposes that acts of crime (C) are ultimately an outcome of a perception–choice process ($\rightarrow$) initiated by the interaction ($\times$) between a person's crime propensity (P) and his/her exposure to a criminogenic setting (E):

$$P \times E \rightarrow C$$

Acts of crime are defined as actions which break moral rules (rules prescribing what it is right or wrong to do, or not do, in a particular circumstance) stated in law (see Wikström, 2006).

SAT suggests that the key personal characteristics relevant to a person's crime propensity are his/her morality (personal moral rules and their related moral emotions) and ability to exercise self-control (see further Wikström and Treiber, 2007). Factors affecting a person's morality (his/her moral education) and ability to exercise self-control (his/her development of relevant cognitive capabilities) are the main causes of crime propensity.

SAT further suggests that the key environmental factor determining whether or not a place is criminogenic is its moral context (its moral rules and their level of enforcement). Social factors affecting a place's moral context are the main causes of its criminogeneity. The extent to which the moral context of a place encourages breaches of moral rules defined in law is the extent to which it is criminogenic.

One of the core assumptions of SAT is that people's development (e.g., of crime propensity) and actions (e.g., acts of crime) are *only* influenced by the settings in which they take part, where a *setting* is defined as the part of the environment a person, at any given moment in time, experiences with his/her senses (including any media present). Moreover, SAT proposes that environmental influences on the development of people's crime propensity (morality and ability to exercise self-control) unfolds as a consequence of their activity field and its changes (their past cumulative exposure to particular factors affecting their moral education and development of relevant cognitive abilities), where an *activity field* is defined as the configuration of settings in which a person takes part during a specific time period. The crucial analytical concept here is that of *exposure*: a particular person's encounter with a particular setting.

To test SAT's hypotheses about the role of the environment in crime causation requires a methodology that can capture, as much as possible, the *exposure* of different *kinds of people* (with different crime propensities) to different *kinds of settings* (with differing criminogeneity). Current methodologies commonly used to study environmental effects on crime (e.g., in the social disorganization/collective efficacy and environmental criminology traditions), we argue, are insufficient.

KEY METHODOLOGICAL SHORTCOMINGS IN THE STUDY OF ENVIRONMENTAL EFFECTS

There has been surprisingly little significant advancement in methods used to study environmental effects in criminology since the works of the early Chicago School (e.g., Shaw and McKay, 1969). The main exceptions are the recent introduction of *large-scale community surveys* and the development of *ecometrics* (a method for assessing the reliability of measures of environments, such as neighbourhoods).

The role of the environment in crime causation has traditionally been studied mostly in terms of the relationship between neighbourhood structural characteristics and neighbourhood levels of crime or offenders. These studies typically use census data on area population characteristics and composition (and occasionally land use data) as predictors of police (or court) recorded data on areas' rates of crime occurrences or resident offenders (e.g., Baldwin and Bottoms, 1976; Schmid, 1960a, 1960b; Shaw and McKay, 1969; Wikström, 1991). Census and land use data provide only limited information on theoretically relevant aspects of the environment.

The introduction of large-scale community surveys (e.g., Kubrin and Weitzer, 2003; Sampson and Wikström, 2008; Sampson et al., 1997; Wikström and Dolmen, 2001) made it possible to measure neighbourhood social conditions more directly, such as levels of social cohesion and informal social control, factors which are often theorized to mediate the influence of structural factors on the occurrence of crime events and the development of residents' crime propensity (see, e.g., Kornhauser, 1978).

The possibility of combining census (and land use) data with data on theoretically relevant area social conditions gathered from community surveys was a big step forward, and the development of ecometrics by Sampson and colleagues (e.g., Raudenbush and Sampson, 1999) further helped to improve the study of environmental factors by providing advanced techniques to assess the reliability of community survey measures of environmental conditions.

However, most of this research suffers from problems with the unit of analysis. Typically, the spatial units are too large and too heterogeneous to qualify as adequate measures of the settings in which people act and develop. While the unit of analysis is rarely a problem where people are concerned, when studying environmental effects it depends on the research question. As previously argued, when studying person–environment interactions the adequate unit is the setting in which a person takes part (and can access with his/her senses). The appropriate spatial unit of analysis is therefore a small area that, as closely as possible, resembles a setting, thereby enabling a better study of the influence of the environments people actually experience.

Most research on environmental effects is conducted at the aggregate level and therefore potentially subject to the problem of the ecological fallacy (meaning it risks drawing the wrong conclusions about individual-level relationships from aggregate data) (see, e.g., Hammond, 1973). While environmental factors (e.g., social climate) are not individual-level factors, action and development always take place at the individual level; therefore we need a methodology that can explore how environments affect a person (not an aggregate of people).

Only a limited number of studies have explored neighbourhood effects at the individual level (e.g., Reiss and Rhodes, 1961; Simcha-Fagan and Schwartz, 1986; Wikström and Loeber, 2000). However, with a few exceptions (Wikström, 2009; Wikström et al., 2010) these studies use large-area units and consider *only* participants' home environments. This is problematic because people spend a substantial portion of their time outside their home environment and hence are subjected to environmental influences from a range of other environments. Even people who live in the same neighbourhood may have very different lifestyles, meaning they may be exposed to very different environments.

To advance the study of environmental effects in crime causation, we need a methodology that allows us (as much as possible) to

1   measure the part of the environment that influences people's acts of crime and development of crime propensity (*the problem of the unit of analysis*);
2   measure relevant aspects of the environment reliably (*the problem of ecometrics*); and
3   account for the fact that people move around in space and encounter a wide range of different environments, not only the environment immediately surrounding their home location (*the problem of exposure*).

PROPOSED METHODOLOGIES

To address the problems discussed previously, PADS+ uses a strategy that combines (matches) data from a small-area community survey (and official data on population composition and land use at the same small-area level) with data from a space–time budget within a research design that allows the investigation of person–environment interactions.

A small-area community survey collects data about the *general social environments* in a study area (such as levels of social cohesion and informal social control). A space–time budget adds to this information about the *circumstances* in which study participants encounter particular social environments (e.g., who they are with and what they are doing in those environments). Combined, these two data sources give us rich information about the settings in which people take part. However, space–time budgets also provide information about the range of settings (the *activity field*) a person takes part in (is exposed to) during the study period. Since it is a new methodology to criminology, the background of the space–time budget will be described here in detail. As far as we are aware, space–time budgets of this kind

were first used in criminology in the cross-sectional Peterborough Youth Study (see Wikström and Butterworth, 2006), and subsequently in PADS+ (Wikström et al., 2010, 2011).

Time diaries measure people's activity patterns over a specified period of time and were first used in the 1920s (for a discussion, see Andorka, 1987). They have been employed in major ongoing time use surveys like the Multinational Time Use Study (MTUS) (see Fisher et al., 2010), the American Time Use Survey (ATUS) (see Phipps and Vernon, 2009), and the Panel Study of Income Dynamics Child Development Supplement (PSID CDS) (see Stafford, 2009) to study differences in time use across different populations. Of all the various methods available for measuring time use (including those mentioned previously), time diaries may be 'the only viable method of obtaining valid and reliable data on activities' (Robinson, 1985: 60).

A *space–time budget* methodology gathers very detailed time diary data linked to a spatial unit and can therefore be used to calculate complex measures of exposure to a range of settings. This method collects information about which individuals interact with which settings (who goes where, under what circumstances, for how long). This provides a more dynamic sense of why particular individuals are in particular places, and the circumstances they encounter.

The term 'space–time budget' can refer to any study which captures activity in space as well as time; such studies are most commonly seen in tourism, urban planning, and transportation research. However, much of this research does not use the same detailed methodology as PADS+. Most studies use less precise geographic data (e.g., larger areas such as regions or cities) and few record as many details about the circumstances of each activity (e.g., who is present). Across all disciplines, only a very small number of studies have collected data which allows for the quantification and examination of activity patterns across time and space, including PADS+ (e.g., Wikström et al., 2010, 2011), the Mobidrive study (Axhausen et al., 2002) and others (Dijst, 1999; Hanson and Hanson, 1980). However, only studies such as these can test theories of human movement and activities (such as that of Hägerstrand, 1970, from the field of geography); hence studies like PADS+ will be the only ones truly capable of testing spatial theories of crime (such as that of Brantingham and Brantingham, 1984). For discussion of the technicalities, wider uses and potential applications of time budgets and space–time budgets see, for example, Anderson (1971), Andorka (1987), Belli et al. (2009); Pentland et al. (1999), and Juster and Stafford (1985). For further reading on the applications and technicalities of space–time budgets within criminology, see Wikström et al. (2011).

An activity field, as previously mentioned, is the configuration of settings an individual is exposed to over a given period of time. Figure 8.1 presents an example of one individual's activity field over one day using space–time budget data. Grey shading indicates areas with poor collective efficacy, a measure of social cohesion and informal social control (Sampson et al., 1997), as measured by the Peterborough Community Survey (PCS), while the activity field represents an example day, as measured by the space–time budget (the coding is shown in Figure 8.3). As the example setting highlighted in Figure 8.1 illustrates, the combination of community survey and space–time budget data can provide information about the kinds of environments and settings to which individuals are exposed. This data can be used to analyse how people spend their time under what conditions, and under which conditions certain activities, such as offending, take place.

STUDYING THE PERSON–ENVIRONMENT INTERACTION: A RESEARCH DESIGN

Measuring settings, and people's exposure to settings, is only part of the challenge of creating a methodology to study the person–environment interaction in crime causation. Measuring people's relevant characteristics and experiences is also required (for further information about collecting relevant data on personal characteristics and experiences, see Wikström et al., 2011). The overall design of PADS+ is illustrated in Figure 8.2. The study focuses on exploring kinds of actions by kinds of people in kinds of settings. It uniquely allows the study of the *convergence in time and space* of people with relevant personal characteristics and experiences (crime propensity), settings with relevant environmental features (criminogenic exposure) and actions (acts of crime). Moreover, since PADS+ uses a longitudinal design, it is also able to study the impact on changes in crime involvement of changes in the interaction between people's crime propensity and criminogenic exposure.

KEY STEPS, AND ISSUES TO CONSIDER, IN THE IMPLEMENTATION OF SMALL-AREA COMMUNITY SURVEYS AND SPACE–TIME BUDGETS TO ASSESS ENVIRONMENTAL EFFECTS IN CRIME CAUSATION

This section provides an overview of the key steps in designing and combining small-area community surveys and space–time budgets (as listed in Table 8.2). We focus on recommendations based on the experiences of PADS+, but also consider alternative methodologies and their comparative strengths and weaknesses.

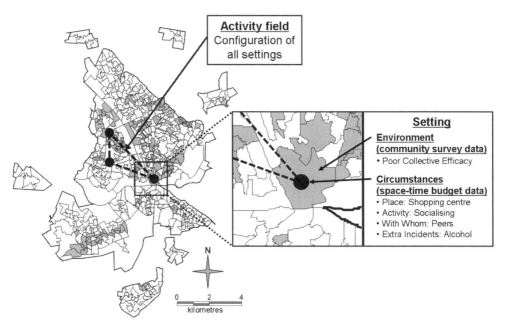

Figure 8.1   Combined small-area community and space-time budget methodology: An illustration from Peterborough (grey shading indicates areas with poor collective efficacy)

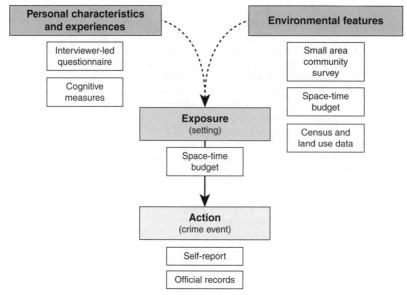

Figure 8.2   Overview of the PADS+ research design (grey boxes) and key methodologies (white boxes)

Table 8.2   Key steps in the design of small-area community surveys and space-time budgets

1. Select the study area	
2. Select the spatial unit of analysis	
Key steps in the design of a small area community survey	*Key steps in the design of a space-time budget*
1. Determine the spatial unit of data collection	1. Select a sample
2. Acquire the study population	2. Select a temporal unit of analysis
3. Select the number of respondents per unit of analysis	3. Select the period for data collection
4. Determine an oversampling strategy for key areas	4. Design the research instrument
5. Decide what kind of data to collect	5. Employ techniques for collecting valid, reliable data
6. Decide what kind of survey to conduct	6. Consider the uses of space-time budget data
7. Employ techniques to improve response rates	
8. Use ecometrics to measure reliability	
9. Validate the resulting environmental measures	
10. Consider the stability of environmental measures	

1 Select the study area

To study the impact of where people spend time on their crime involvement requires inclusive data on the places where they spend time. Consequently, the study area needs to encompass the areas in which they spend time during the period of interest. The most conducive study areas, therefore, will be those which are naturally self-contained, such as a city (or potentially institutions such as prisons). Of course, people are rarely completely confined in their movement patterns and various activities may take them outside of any study area

(e.g., holidays), and this may affect some people more than others (such as those who routinely work outside the study area; e.g., lorry drivers or long-distance commuters). There are reasons to believe that young people's activities tend to be particularly constrained. For example, key locations where they spend much of their time, such as school (except for boarding schools), tend to be situated locally, and they have less personal mobility (Wikström et al., 2010, 2011). Young people may therefore be an especially conducive population for this type of research.

The size of the study area should be taken into account. Study areas need to have adequate variation in social environments to study differential effects, therefore they cannot be too small. As mentioned previously, they also ideally will encompass the general activities of their resident population, which means they need to be able to meet all the fundamental needs of the population (e.g., provide schools, places of work, shopping centres, recreation areas, etc.), all of which demand a particular capacity (depending on the size of the resident population). A very large study area may present its own problems, a significant one being the resources needed to adequately study it (e.g., to collect data on all its social environments). A large study area will also increase the complexity of the space–time budget (see later), already an intensive methodology.

2 Select the spatial unit of analysis

To link data from the community survey, the space–time budget, and official data (such as census and land use data) requires a standard unit of analysis. For our research we have selected the smallest spatial unit available in the UK for official data – the output area (see Oberwittler and Wikström, 2009, on why a smaller unit of analysis is better) – to most closely approximate a behavioural setting. Output areas are geographical units designed to encapsulate approximately 125 'socially homogenous' households, although they are not intended to represent communities (see Martin, 2000). The smallest official geographic unit available for research will of course differ by country; for the American census, for example, census blocks are the smallest unit, which are delineated by natural boundaries (e.g., streets, land formations) and vary considerably in their resident populations from urban to rural areas, but average 100 people. The study area should be comprised of these units, and data must be collected from each unit.

People, however, cannot readily be asked about administrative areas which are unfamiliar to the general public. Similar problems arise from the use of poorly defined areas, such as neighbourhoods, which residents may perceive differently, in part due to their daily activities and/or personal characteristics (Downs and Shea, 1973; Lynch, 1960; Tolman, 1948), meaning that the information residents provide may refer to areas differing in terms of both boundary and size.

In addition, researchers can only assume residents are able to make the required accurate and detailed observations about the area very close to their home (see Brown and Moore, 1970). Studies that employ large spatial units (such as groups of census tracts) and ask survey participants to respond regarding their 'neighbourhood' as a proxy for these units ask for information concerning a large area about which residents can only have limited knowledge. Taking these issues into account, we asked respondents on the Peterborough Community Survey to report on 'the area within a short walking distance (say a couple of minutes) from your home. That is the street you live in and the streets, houses, shops, parks and other areas close to your home.'

We refer to this area as a respondent's *observational space*. Each respondent's observational space was then aggregated to the spatial unit of analysis within which they live (e.g., output area). Although there will be some mismatch between the coverage of the aggregated observational spaces and the boundaries of the spatial unit, this discrepancy will not be problematic as long as the size of the observational space and the spatial unit are of roughly comparable size.

KEY STEPS IN THE DESIGN OF A SMALL SCALE COMMUNITY SURVEY

1 Determine the unit of data collection

The first step in designing a small-scale community survey is to decide on the spatial unit at which one wants to collect data. Arguably, the lower the level of data collection the better, as data can always be aggregated. For spatial data, the most precise data is point data, which for a community survey equates to a single household, or address.

2 Acquire the study population

The population from which to draw one's sample for a small-scale community survey will be all households in the study area. One will need to decide on sampling restrictions (e.g., those in a particular age group) and will ultimately need to randomly select one respondent from each household. Therefore, it is important to acquire a sampling frame of household addresses and occupiers that is accurate and comprehensive for the study area. Different databases on households will be available in different countries and may vary significantly in their accuracy and comprehensiveness. In Sweden, for example, a complete register is available (Swedish Population and Address Register (SPAR); Swedish Tax Agency), whereas in the US there is no such register, and large community studies such as the Project on Human Development in Chicago Neighborhoods (PHDCN) adopt alternative strategies (the PHDCN followed a hierarchical process through which they randomly selected census blocks, then listed households per selected block, randomly selected households, then listed potential respondents per selected household, and finally randomly selected respondents) (see Earls et al., 1997). At the time of the PCS, the most complete and accurate adult population register available for research in the UK was the electoral register (see Wikström et al., 2011, for further details and limitations).

3 Select the number of respondents per spatial unit of analysis

Once one has determined the spatial unit of analysis (e.g., output areas) and has acquired a study population, one needs to develop a sampling strategy which will provide data from all spatial units in the study area. To collect reliable data for each spatial unit, one needs to acquire a minimum number of responses per unit. One should bear in mind that the size of the spatial unit of analysis, and the study area, will determine the number of spatial units for which one requires responses, and must take into account available resources when selecting a sample size per unit. Providentially, to achieve adequate statistical power, even in multi-level models including area-level effects, only a small number of respondents per spatial unit may be necessary; Snijders and Bosker (1999), for example, suggest that just 8–15 respondents per area may be sufficient (see also Murrey et al., 2004, Raudenbush, 1999). However, sufficient statistical power does not ensure reliability. Fewer respondents per area may be sufficiently reliable for the study of area social conditions in which respondents serve as general social observers, as has been shown using ecometric analytical techniques (see Oberwittler and Wikström, 2009; Raudenbush and Sampson, 1999), and as long as respondents are reliable social observers, they need not be fully representative of the general population. However, to reliably study rare individual events, like respondents' own offending and victimization, may require many more observations from a representative sample.

To determine how many residents per spatial unit should be randomly sampled in order to achieve the minimum number of responses, one needs to estimate the response rate. Response rates will vary between countries and study areas; we recommend piloting the survey to measure the expected response rate. Response rates may also vary across units in a study area as a result of certain area characteristics, so one should also consider the need for oversampling in some areas to achieve the minimum number of responses, and ensure pilot surveys address this.

4 Design an oversampling strategy for key areas

Key factors which have been linked to lower response rates include area levels of deprivation and area concentration of ethnic minorities (Goyder, 1987; Groves and Couper, 1998; Stoop, 2005), although other factors may also be relevant depending on the area under study and the focus of the research. Studies should consider the main potential causes of non-response in their sample and take these into account in their sampling strategy (as well as their research design). To effectively oversample from certain kinds of areas requires data on the factor (or factors) of interest, which is often available through official sources. One must then stratify areas by these factors and then oversample to accommodate expected rates of non-response. Piloting the survey in areas which differ along these dimensions may provide a clearer picture of the degree of oversampling required. Such an oversampling strategy can be very effective in counteracting low response rates in particular areas of the sample (e.g., Oberwittler and Wikström, 2009; Wikström et al., 2011).

5 Decide what kind of data to collect

The advantage of community surveys is they are able to collect data which is not readily available from census and land use databases, such as data on social conditions and processes, e.g., cohesion, informal social control, disorder and collective efficacy. A number of instruments have been developed to collect this kind of data (for the measures used in PADS+, see Wikström et al., 2011).

6 Decide what kind of survey to conduct

Various survey techniques are available. We utilized a postal survey for the PCS as they are comparably inexpensive, temporally and financially, to conduct; are suitable for large samples; and, if implemented effectively, can attain good response rates (see de Leeuw and Hox, 2008; Dillman, 2000). Other techniques include phone surveys and personal interviews, and will have their own pros and cons as well as resource demands (for general references on survey methodology and non-response see de Leeuw et al., 2008; Dillman, 2000; Dillman et al., 2008; Edwards et al., 2002; Groves et al., 1992, 2002; Stoop, 2005).

7 Employ techniques to improve response rates

Response rates will vary across different study areas and populations for different reasons.

One reason may be inaccuracies in the sampling frame which mean that the survey fails to reach the intended recipient (such as an addressee who has moved); such cases are often attributed to non-response because they are largely undetectable (see Lynn, 2008; Groves et al., 2004). Other reasons have to do with the research design, the population surveyed and the techniques employed. These techniques need to be tailored to the particular research in order to increase the pros and reduce the cons of participation, both perceived and actual (Dillman, 2000; Dillman et al., 2008; see de Leeuw and Hox, 2008). Common difficulties and solutions include:

- *Accessibility and engagement*: The way a survey is designed (for example, its layout, length, and form of address) can have a substantial impact on participation and item non-response (Dillman et al., 2008; Redline et al., 2005). Personalized surveys and letters, as well as reference to respondents' civic duty and personal interests can increase their response rate (for various aspects of these issues see Dillman, 2000; Edwards et al., 2002; Goyder, 1987; Groves et al., 1992).
- *Legitimacy*: Response rates are generally higher for surveys linked to government agencies or academic institutions (Edwards et al., 2002). Displaying official logos (e.g., a university crest or emblem of local authority) may demonstrate legitimacy and accountability, as can sponsorship by people or groups known to and respected by those in the study area (e.g., the local police constabulary) (see Dillman et al., 2002; Groves et al., 1992; Lynn, 2008). Media releases (such as published articles or radio appearances) may increase public awareness of the survey, further demonstrating legitimacy and encouraging participation.
- *Ethnic minorities*: One of the most significant reasons for non-response amongst ethnic minority groups may be language barriers. Efforts to accommodate respondents; for example, by translating surveys or offering phone interviews into their first language, may help to remove these barriers (see Johnson et al., 2002; Stoop, 2005). Strategies to over-sample in deprived areas may also help to address the typical under representation of minority ethnic respondents, as there is a robust correlation, at least in some countries, between high concentrations of ethnic minority groups (or certain ethnic minority groups) and levels of deprivation. Researchers should take into account conditions in their particular study area (potentially gathering information through a pilot survey).
- *Follow-up letters*: Researchers should be persistent in achieving the minimum number of responses from each spatial unit. The number of reminders has a significant positive effect on response rates in postal surveys (de Leeuw and Hox, 1988; Dillman, 1991). Reminder letters may therefore be particularly important to non-respondents in areas which have not achieved the minimum desired responses. Different approaches can be taken, for example, drawing on the 'social validation heuristic' by emphasizing the number of residents who have already responded, or the 'scarcity principle' by emphasizing how few residents have responded (see Groves et al., 1992). Additional copies of the survey may also be sent. Researchers need to consider their follow-up strategies and schedules carefully, considering their available resources, and ensuring they do not over-burden potential respondents, inadvertently encouraging non-response.

We found these strategies were effective for achieving the minimum number of responses from nearly all spatial units (Oberwittler and Wikström, 2009; Wikström et al., 2011).

8 Use ecometrics to measure reliability

Raudenbush and Sampson (1999) have developed an 'ecometric' technique to test the reliability of ecological measures, in order to ensure that variations in observations reflect area differences in environmental conditions and not differences in respondents' personal characteristics (e.g., socio-demographics). Using this ecometric technique, Oberwittler and Wikström (2009) demonstrated, using PCS data, that respondents' observations of the social characteristics of their area were largely independent of their own socio-demographic characteristics, validating this method of small-area community survey. However, while ecometric analyses can verify the reliability of observational data, the design of the survey and the sampling method are crucial for ensuring the data collected is valid in the first place; that is, it provides accurate information about the spatial unit.

9 Validate the resulting environmental measures

Some environmental measures can be validated by comparison with official data. For example, data on area levels of disorder may be compared with police recorded incidents, and area levels of deprivation may be compared with existing census data (such as the Index of Multiple Deprivation, or IMD, in the UK) if such is available (for these and other methods of cross-validation, see Oberwittler and Wikström, 2009; Wikström et al., 2011). Such comparisons need to take into account differences in the level of measurement (e.g., the IMD is measured at the *super* output area level, in groups of output areas, while PCS data is collected at the output area level) and possible intrinsic changes if measurements are taken at different times. Data on social conditions and processes, such as social cohesion and informal social control, may be more difficult to validate externally, as there may be little comparative data available.

10 Consider the stability of environmental measures

One can generally assume that area social characteristics are reasonably stable over time, although one should take into account any significant changes to the population or physical environment which could impact upon the features of specific areas (e.g., in Peterborough several residential areas have undergone considerable expansion in recent years, which has had an evident impact on their residential stability). To affect overall patterns, however, changes would have to be significant and widespread (e.g., significant urban expansion in nine areas in Peterborough did not significantly impact the general relationships observed between social environmental features and crime). Researchers should, however, bear in mind that these changes will also affect the population's movement and activity patterns, which are recorded by the space–time budget (see Wikström et al., 2011). Levels of change can often be assessed using official data. Because of this general stability, in a longitudinal design it may not be necessary to repeat community surveys frequently; five-year intervals, for example, may be sufficient to account for any significant variation due to gradual changes.

KEY STEPS IN THE DESIGN OF A SPACE–TIME BUDGET

1 Select a sample

The sample for a space–time budget study should be drawn at random from the population of the study area, as the goal is to investigate how the environments in the study area influence those who are regularly exposed to them (develop and act within them). Therefore the sample should aim to represent the general population of the study area. Unlike the sample for the community survey, the sample for the space–time budget does not

need to include residents from all spatial units (e.g., output areas) in the study area; some areas will have more or less residents than others, and residential segregation will affect who lives where, thus sampling by spatial unit would almost inevitably introduce bias into the sample. Utilizing a random sample *across the entire study area* is particularly important for the study of infrequent phenomenon such as crime, as any selectivity in the sample may misrepresent the rate of offenders (and offending) and could exclude people who are of particular interest to criminological research (who are often the most difficult to obtain and retain). The sample also needs to be large enough to satisfy the statistical power requirements for measuring interaction effects for types of people across types of areas (for further discussion on sampling and statistical power, see Cohen, 1988).

2 Select a temporal unit of analysis

One of the key outcomes of the space–time budget is a measure of exposure: how much time a participant has spent in a particular setting during the period of interest. Thus this method requires not only a spatial unit of analysis, but also a temporal unit. Some time budget research uses activity as the core unit of analysis, recording time as a feature of the activity; however, to measure exposure (i.e., time spent), time must be the core unit of analysis. The spatial unit, of course, needs to correspond with that of the community survey if the two methodologies are to be combined.

The temporal unit should be selected to suit the particular research. For criminological research, we recommend an hour as a temporal unit. Hours are a standard unit of time familiar to any participants which can capture the diversity of their core activities throughout the day. Hours are easily quantifiable and interpretable, making them a useful unit of exposure. One can argue that most significant activities in a person's day will take (at least) the larger portion of an hour, therefore recording one's main hourly activities will provide a good representation of one's activity patterns. While smaller units are more detailed (e.g., time use research outside the field of criminology has used units as small as five minutes, such as some diaries administered as part of the Multinational Time Use Study (MTUS) (see Fisher et al., 2010), they also exponentially increase the burden on respondents, the time required for data collection, and may collect a plethora of information which is not of particular interest to criminologists (e.g., time spent brushing teeth). However, many activities of interest, including crime and victimization, take relatively little time and may be omitted in studies relying on larger units of time. Information on these particular activities may be collected in addition to the core space–time budget data, as described later. This is also true of information on secondary activities, such as drug use or weapon possession, which may occur alongside primary activities.

Some research uses temporal duration rather than a standard temporal unit (e.g., they measure the start and end times of an activity and calculate overall duration; for example, see Cullen and Godson, 1975; Phipps and Vernon, 2009). Although this method is temporally precise, it makes it more difficult to tie together multi-modal space–time budget data into complex constructions (e.g., data on what a person is doing, who he/she is with, and where he/she is), as different modalities may vary independently (e.g., three peers may start socializing at time A, move to a new location at time B, and one may leave at time C). This may greatly complicate the analysis of data on exposure. For interpretation and analysis, duration data will have to be transformed into a standard temporal unit; however, it does allow for that unit to be selected after data collection and to vary across analyses if desired.

3 Select the period for data collection

Researchers must decide on the period of time for which they wish to collect space–time budget data. Whether or not this period should be continuous depends on the particular research. Some studies collect data only for random or specified points in time within the study period, such as the beeper or experience sampling method (see Larson and Verma, 1999). However, when measuring people's general activity patterns over time, studies should collect continuous data; most do so covering one day to one week. Data from the Peterborough Youth Study, which served as a pilot for PADS+, collected data over a week, as there is a natural rhythm of activities that people tend to repeat week on week. However, their experiences suggest that collecting data over four days may be just as adequate for capturing the variation in people's general activity patterns (Wikström and Butterworth, 2006). People's activity patterns are reasonably similar across most weekdays, therefore it may be sufficient to collect data for two to three weekdays, rather than all five (see Stewart, 2006). Friday and Saturday evenings are particularly unique, especially for unstructured activities, as they do not precede a weekday, although Sunday evening more closely resembles a weeknight. For these reasons, we determined that measuring two weekdays, Friday and Saturday provides an adequate picture of people's movement and activity patterns during the week.

This does, however, mean that Friday and Saturday hours are over-represented, thus to draw any conclusions at a weekly or yearly level, these data need to be weighted accordingly.

Because of the detail of data desired and the intensity of this methodology, it is best to collect data for the most recent weekdays, Friday and Saturday. This will enable participants to recall their activities and movements more accurately. Recall is always a concern for retrospective space–time budget techniques; some examples of techniques for improving recall are detailed later.

Other considerations include seasonal variations. People's activity patterns may differ throughout the year, therefore it is important that data is collected for all participants at the same time of year, to ensure variation in their activity patterns reflects individual differences and not differences in the season. Researchers should pay attention to the particular variations in, for example, daylight, weather and cultural observances, in the country or region of their study. For longitudinal research it is also important that space–time budget data is collected at the same time of year in all data waves. One also needs to ensure, as much as possible, that the data collected represents a participant's typical activity patterns; hence efforts should be made to avoid collecting data for exceptional events, such as days spent on holiday or in hospital following an accident. The relevance of these considerations depends on the type of research.

4 Design the research instrument

Researchers must decide what kind of data they wish to collect using the space–time budget. The more detailed, arguably, the better. We developed a method for collecting data on a participant's main activity (e.g., socializing, playing football), who he/she was with (e.g., male peers, parents), where he/she was (e.g., home, shopping centre, cinema) and his/her geographical location (the coded spatial unit; e.g., output area), using an extensive hierarchy of hundreds of activity, people and place codes (for the complete list, see Wikström et al., 2011). This data needs to be collected for each temporal unit (e.g., each hour of the day). Due to the complexity of this data, it is important to develop an effective data entry template.

Figure 8.3 illustrates the data entry template used for PADS+, showing data coded for one young person's Friday activity field (the settings and features of those settings he encountered during that day). The boxes in grey highlight the time spent in one particular setting (the city centre). Figure 8.1 illustrates this same activity

Friday							Extra incidents											
							Alcohol / Drugs			Victimisation			Offending			Weapons		
							No ○ Yes ⊙			No ⊙ Yes ○			No ⊙ Yes ○			No ⊙ Yes ○		
Hour	Geocode	Place	Activity	Who	Truancy school	Truancy work	Incident 1	2	3	Incident 1	2	3	Incident 1	2	3	Incident 1	2	3
6	NU19	10	22	23	☐	☐												
7	NU19	10	23	23	☐	☐												
8	NU19	111	59	31	☐	☐												
9	PB17	31	31	71	☐	☐												
10	PB17	31	31	71	☐	☐												
11	PB17	31	31	71	☐	☐												
12	PB17	32	23	35	☐	☐												
13	PB17	31	31	71	☐	☐												
14	PB17	31	31	71	☐	☐												
15	PB17	31	31	71	☐	☐												
16	PB17	111	59	33	☐	☐												
17	NE09	43	571	33	☐	☐												
18	NE09	43	571	33	☐	☐												
19	NE09	43	571	35	☐	☐	35											
20	NE09	43	571	35	☐	☐	35											
21	NE09	111	591	31	☐	☐												
22	NU19	10	23	23	☐	☐												
23	NU19	10	561	23	☐	☐												
24	NU19	10	561	23	☐	☐												
1	NU19	10	22	23	☐	☐												
2	NU19	10	22	23	☐	☐												
3	NU19	10	22	23	☐	☐												
4	NU19	10	22	23	☐	☐												
5	NU19	10	22	23	☐	☐												

Figure 8.3   Example of the space-time budget data entry form

field spatially, in combination with social environmental data from the PCS, drawing particular attention to the highlighted setting and the circumstances under which it was encountered. The young person begins his day at home (waking up at 7:00 and getting ready for school with his parents and siblings), walks to school with a male friend at 8:00, attends school (where he is in classes with classmates and a teacher) until 15:00, and then walks to the city centre with several male peers. Here he socializes at a local shopping centre until 21:00. At 19:00 additional peers (including females) join in and he drinks alcohol between 19:00 and 21:00, when he walks back home with one male peer, watches TV with his family, and then goes to sleep at 01:00.

Researchers also need to consider additional information of relevance to their study, such as specific data on incidents like crime and victimization, drug and alcohol use, weapon possession, and so on, which may not be collected by the core space–time budget. Such data should also be collected by unit of time, so that it can be linked to all other space–time budget (and community survey) data (as shown in Figure 8.3).

5 Employ techniques for collecting valid, reliable data

Although much time-budget and space–time budget research has used self-completion formats, many of the methodological complications and data quality concerns associated with these methods are avoided by using one-to-one interviews (see Phipps and Vernon, 2009, for those specific to time diary methods; and Loosveldt, 2008, for general advantages). We recommend using trained researchers who can help guide participants in recalling and detailing their movements and activities; who can consistently and accurately record only relevant aspects of recollections at the correct level of detail, including matching their locations to the correct spatial unit; and who can control various aspects of the interview. This can be accomplished by eliciting an open verbal description of events from participants, which is then coded hour by hour. This more natural method of relaying events may improve the quality of the data provided. Other examples of the advantages of using a one-to-one interview are:

- *Recall*: Researchers can encourage recollection by leading participants backwards or forwards through a day or a week, or reference participants' regular activities during other days in the interview and also external events, such as extreme weather or much discussed television programmes, to help remind them of their movements and activities. Other similar techniques have also been developed (see Phipps and Vernon, 2009). 'Real time' methods, such as diaries that participants complete at regular intervals throughout the day, are often suggested as a way to reduce recall issues (e.g., Robinson, 1985); however, lack of compliance can reduce the efficacy of this method (see Phipps and Vernon, 2009; Stone and Broderick, 2009). In addition, the nature of real-time methods, unlike retrospective methods, means that participants are constantly aware their activities are being recorded, which may influence their activities and/or responses.
- *Consistency*: The complexity of a detailed space–time budget methodology may make it difficult (or impossible) for untrained participants to effectively and consistently record their activities. A major problem for self-completion studies is participants' differing interpretations of instructions and conceptions of the required level of detail and accuracy. It is also difficult for participants to locate activities in the desired spatial units. Many resources are needed to effectively code such data, including detailed maps of the study area broken into geocoded spatial units (at a geographic level where one can pinpoint

participants' location precisely, if an exact address is not known), comprehensive lists of streets and other relevant features of the study area (the more detailed the better), and familiarity with the study area and the space–time budget codes. We developed many tools to facilitate these interviews, including comprehensive lists of streets in single spatial units (output areas) and local landmarks (specific businesses, recreation venues, etc.) by spatial unit and type. Although geospatial technology, such as GPS tracking and radio telemetry, provides an alternative method for recording participants' geographical locations, it cannot be used to collect information on activities or settings (this, plus other considerations such as validity and the cost of equipping people with expensive technology, make this method currently impractical).

- *Control*: Interviewers can manage distractions and threats to confidentiality; ensure the intended respondent completes the interview; maintain interest to encourage considered and unrushed responses; identify inconsistencies by conversationally double-checking recollections; and request further details about circumstances to ensure they are accurately coded.

To conduct the space–time budget interviews effectively and efficiently and use the required tools and software, researchers need to be intensively trained in house;. For this reason we advocate using qualified researchers employed specifically by the study, rather than temporary staff from private survey companies (see also Lessler et al., 2008). This is particularly important for longitudinal research, for which long-term research staff can ensure consistency in the application of the space–time budget methodology across data waves.

Data also needs to be carefully cleaned and checked following fieldwork. Researchers should check and clean the data from the interviews they themselves have conducted, as soon as possible after the interview, when it is still fresh in their minds. Any data which could not be coded during the interview (e.g., the geographical location of a particular business) should be noted during the interview in as much detail as possible and chased up immediately after. Because the space–time budget involves lots of different kinds of data (e.g., people, places and activities), researchers can and should ensure that related codes make sense (e.g., a participant is not swimming at the movie theatre) and that geocodes are correct (e.g., if there is only one bowling alley in the study area, a participant at the bowling alley should be geographically located in the correct spatial unit). Of particular importance are geocodes referring to places where a participant spends a considerable amount of time, such as his/her home, school or work location. Many of the combinations of codes can be checked using frequencies and cross tables.

6 Using space–time budget data

One of the appeals of space–time budget data is its flexibility. It can be combined in various ways to characterize the circumstances of action. For example, it can be used to measure time spent unsupervised (without an adult guardian) or in unstructured activities (e.g., socializing, hanging around) or unsupervised in unstructured activities, or, by bringing in extra incidents, unsupervised in unstructured activities while drinking alcohol. This means the data can be used for many different kinds of analyses, even before it is combined with other sources of data. By using a standard unit of time, such as an hour, exposure to specific circumstances can be easily quantified and compared.

Although the fundamental unit of analysis is the temporal unit (i.e., each case represents one temporal unit, e.g., an hour), space–time budget data can be aggregated by spatial unit (e.g., hours spent per output area) or by person (e.g., hours spent by a specific participant). This provides many avenues for analysis.

Space–time budget data also has the unique property of being able to place an action in the setting in which it occurred. Other kinds of data may be able to show a correlation between area-level characteristics and activities, such as rates of crime (e.g., that areas where young people spend more time unsupervised have higher rates of crime) but the space–time budget is able to show how those correlations are driven at the situational level (e.g., whether it is those people who spend time unsupervised in the area who commit acts of crime there, and if they commit acts of crime in the area while they are unsupervised).

COMBINING A SMALL-SCALE COMMUNITY SURVEY AND A SPACE–TIME BUDGET

A small-scale community survey provides data on the social characteristics of environments within a study area (which can be supplemented by population statistics and land use data from official sources). A space–time budget provides data on the circumstances of people's activities and their exposure (time spent). In combination, this data can tell us who spends time in what kinds of environments, under what circumstances, and for how long. This unique insight can be used to better understand the role of the social environment in (1) the occurrence of crime events, and (2) (when using longitudinal data) the development of and changes in people's crime propensity. What features of the environment are important for a particular study will depend on whether the study is interested in crime events or crime propensity. For the occurrence of crime events, immediate factors such as the moral context in which someone encounters frictions and opportunities may be more critical, while for the study of development and changes in crime propensity, more long-term factors such as socialization contexts, which influence people's moral education and development of cognitive capabilities, may be more salient.

In combination, small-area community surveys and space–time budgets offer a unique method for exploring differences in social environments, and people's exposure to different social environments, and their relationship to levels of crime. Two aspects make this a particularly powerful instrument:

1 Using a spatial unit of analysis through which community survey, space–time budget, and official census and land use data can be linked, brings together information about environments, circumstances and people's exposure.
2 Where psychometric data is available (e.g., information on key aspects of participants' propensity, such as morality and the ability to exercise self-control), individual characteristics can be linked with exposure, both developmentally (in studying the emergence of propensity) and situationally (in studying the interaction between certain kinds of people and certain kinds of settings).

Such a combination of instruments can be used to answer uniquely specific questions about people's activities, including their crime involvement. Cross-sectional analyses could include the exploration of questions such as: 'In what kinds of social environments, under what circumstances, do certain kinds of people spend time?'; 'Under what circumstances, in what kinds of social environments, are people more likely to offend?'; and 'What kinds of people in what kinds of settings are most likely to offend?' (see, e.g., Wikström et al., 2010, 2011). In addition, data collected longitudinally via these techniques can be used to explore questions that relate to change over time, such as: 'How do changes in exposure influence changes in propensity?'; 'How do changes in exposure and/or changes in propensity relate to changes in crime involvement?' (see, e.g., Wikström, 2009); and 'What are the causal factors influencing change in exposure and/or propensity over time?'

In this chapter we have argued that to advance our knowledge about the role of the environment in crime causation we need theory and methods that can more adequately capture the role of the person–environment interaction. We have outlined a research design aimed at exploring this interaction and, in much more detail, presented how the measurement of people's exposure to criminogenic settings can be improved by combining small-area community surveys and space–time budgets. Initial analyses and findings from PADS+ support the usefulness of this methodology (see Wikström et al., 2011).

RECOMMENDED READING

For the application of this methodology to longitudinal data from a UK study of adolescents, including further details on methodological techniques for both small-area community surveys and space–time budgets, see Wikström, P.-O.H., Oberwittler, D., Treiber, K. and Hardie, B. (2011) *Breaking Rules: The Social and Situational Dynamics of Young People's Urban Crime* (Oxford: Oxford University Press).

For further details of the econometric technique, see Raudenbush, S.W. and Sampson, R.J. (1999) 'Ecometrics: toward a science of assessing ecological settings, with application to the systematic social observation of neighborhoods'. *Sociological Methodology* 29: 1–41.

For arguments why small areas are better for the study of person–environment interaction, see Oberwittler, D. and Wikström, P.-O.H. (2009). 'Why small is better: advancing the study of the role of behavioral contexts in crime causation' in D. Weisburd, W. Bernasco and G.J.N. Bruinsma (eds), *Putting Crime in its Place: Units of Analysis in Geographic Criminology* (Berlin: Springer), pp. 35–59.

A key web resource is the PADS+ website: www.pads.ac.uk.

REFERENCES

Anderson, J. (1971) 'Space–time budgets and activity studies in urban geography and planning'. *Environment and Planning A* 3: 353–368.

Andorka, R. (1987) 'Time budgets and their uses'. *Annual Review of Sociology* 13: 149–164.

Axhausen, K.W., Zimmermann, A., Schönfelder, S., Rindsfüser, G. and Haupt, T. (2002) 'Observing the rhythms of daily life: A six-week travel diary'. *Transportation* 29: 95–124.

Baldwin, J. and Bottoms, A. (1976) *The Urban Criminal*, London: Tavistock Publications.

Belli, R.F., Alwin, D.F. and Stafford, F.P. (2009) 'Introduction: The application of calendar and time diary methods in the collection of life course data' in R.F. Belli, D.F. Alwin and F.P. Stafford (eds) *Calendar and Time Diary Methods in Life Course Research* (pp. 1–10). London: Sage Publications.

Brantingham, P.L. and Brantingham, P.J. (1984) *Patterns in Crime*. New York: Macmillan.

Brown, L.A. and Moore, E.G. (1970) 'The intra-urban migration process: A perspective'. *Geografiska Annaler. Series B, Human Geography* 52: 1–13.

Cohen, J. (1988) *Statistical Power Analysis for the Behavioural Sciences*. Hillsdale, NJ: Lawrence Erlbaum.

Cullen, I.G. and Godson, V. (1975) *Urban Networks: The Structure of Activity Patterns*. Oxford: Pergamon Press.

de Leeuw, E.D. and Hox, J.J. (1988) 'The effects of response-stimulating factors on response rates and data quality in mail surveys'. *Journal of Official Statistics* 4: 241–249.

de Leeuw, E.D. and Hox, J. J. (2008) 'Self-administered questionnaires: Mail surveys and other applications' in E.D. De Leeuw, J.J. Hox and D.A. Dillman (eds) *International Handbook of Survey Methodology* (pp. 239–263). New York: Lawrence Erlbaum.

de Leeuw, E.D., Hox, J.J. and Dillman, D.A. (eds) (2008) *International Handbook of Survey Methodology*. New York: Lawrence Erlbaum.

Dijst, M. (1999) 'Two-earner families and their action spaces: A case study of two dutch communities'. *GeoJournal* 48: 195–206.

Dillman, D.A. (1991) 'The design and administration of mail surveys'. *Annual Review of Sociology* 17: 225–249.

Dillman, D.A. (2000) *Mail and Electronic Surveys: The Tailored Design Method*. New York :Wiley.

Dillman, D.A., Eltinge, J.L., Groves, R.M. and Little, R.J.A. (2002) 'Survey non-response in design, data collection, and analysis' in Groves, R.M., Dillman, D.A., Eltinge, J.L. and Little, R.J.A. (eds) *Survey Nonresponse* (pp. 3–26). New York: Wiley-Interscience.

Dillman, D.A., Smyth, J.D. and Christian, L.M. (2008) *Internet, Mail, and Mixed-mode Surveys: The Tailored Design Method*. New York: Wiley.

Downs, R.M. and Shea, D. (1973) 'Cognitive maps and spatial behaviour: Process and products' in R.M. Downs and D. Shea (eds), *Image and Environment: Cognitive Mapping and Spatial Behaviour* (pp. 8–26). Chicago: Aldine.

Earls, F., Brooks-Gunn, J., Raudenbush, S. and Sampson, R.J. (1997) *Project on Human Development in Chicago Neighborhoods: Community survey 1994–1995* (Individual-level data codebook ICPSR02766). Ann Arbor, MI: Inter-University Consortium for Political and Social Research.

Edwards, P., Roberts, I., Clarke, M., Diguiseppi, C., Pratap, S., Wentz, R. and Kwan, I. (2002) 'Increasing response rates to postal questionnaires: Systematic review'. *British Medical Journal* 324: 1183–1192.

Fisher, K., Gershuny, J. and Gauthier, A. (2010) *Multinational Time Use Study: User's guide and documentation*. Centre for Time Use Research, University of Oxford. See www.timeuse.org.

Goyder, J. (1987) *The Silent Minority: Nonrespondents on Sample Surveys.* Cambridge: Polity Press.

Groves, R.M., Cialdini, R.B. and Couper, M.P. (1992) 'Understanding the decision to participate in a survey'. *The Public Opinion Quarterly* 56: 475–495.

Groves, R.M. and Couper, M. (1998) *Nonresponse in Household Interview Surveys,* New York: Wiley-Interscience.

Groves, R.M., Dillman, D.A., Eltinge, J.L. and Little, R.J.A. (eds) (2002) *Survey Nonresponse.* New York: Wiley-Interscience.

Groves, R.M., Fowler, F.J., Couper, M.P., Lepkowski, J.M., Singer, E. and Tourangeau, R. (2004) *Survey Methodology.* New York: Wiley.

Hägerstrand, T. (1970) 'What about people in regional science?' *Papers in Regional Science* 24: 6–21.

Hammond, J.L. (1973) 'Two sources of error in ecological correlation'. *American Sociological Review* 38: 764–777.

Hanson, S. and Hanson, P. (1980) 'Gender and urban activity patterns in Uppsala, Sweden'. *Geographical Review* 70: 291–299.

Johnson, T.P., O'Rourke, D., Burris, J. and Owens, L. (2002) 'Culture and survey nonresponse' in R.M. Groves, D.A. Dillman, J.L. Eltinge and R.J.A. Little (eds) *Survey Nonresponse* (pp. 55–70). New York: Wiley-Interscience.

Juster, F.T. and Stafford, F.P. (eds) (1985) *Time, Goods, and Well-being.* Ann Arbor, MI: Survey Research Center, University of Michigan.

Kornhauser, R. (1978) *Social Sources of Delinquency.* Chicago: University of Chicago Press.

Kubrin, C.E. and Weitzer, R. (2003) 'New directions in social disorganization theory'. *Journal of Research in Crime and Delinquency* 40: 374–402.

Larson, R.W. and Verma, S. (1999) 'How children and adolescents spend time across the world: Work, play, and developmental opportunities'. *Psychological Bulletin* 125: 701–736.

Lessler, J.T., Eyerman, J. and Wang, K. (2008) 'Interviewer training' in E.D. De Leeuw, J.J. Hox and D.A. Dillman (eds) *International Handbook of Survey Methodology* (pp. 442–460). New York: Lawrence Erlbaum.

Lynn, P. (2008) 'The problem of non-response' in E.D. De Leeuw, J.J. Hox and D.A. Dillman (eds), *International Handbook of Survey Methodology* (pp. 35–55). New York: Lawrence Erlbaum.

Loosveldt, G. (2008) 'Face-to-face interviews' in E.D. De Leeuw, J.J. Hox and D.A. Dillman (eds) *International Handbook of Survey Methodology* (pp. 201–220). New York: Lawrence Erlbaum.

Lynch, K. (1960) *The Image of the City.* Cambridge, MA: MIT Press.

Martin, D. (2000) 'Towards the geographies of the 2001 UK Census of Population'. *Transactions of the Institute of British Geographers* 25: 321–332.

Murrey, D.M., Varnell, S.P. and Blitstein, J.L. (2004) 'Design and analysis of group-randomized trials: A review of recent methodological developments'. *American Journal of Public Health* 94: 423–432.

Oberwittler, D. and Wikström, P.-O.H. (2009) 'Why small is better: Advancing the study of the role of behavioral contexts in crime causation' in D. Weisburd, W. Bernasco and G. Bruinsma (eds), *Putting Crime in its Place: Units of Analysis in Spatial Crime Research* (pp. 35–59). New York: Springer.

Pentland, W.E., Harvey, A.S., Lawton, M.P. and McColl, M.A. (eds) (1999) *Time Use Research in the Social Sciences.* New York: Kluwer Academic/Plenum Publishers.

Phipps, P.A. and Vernon, M.K. (2009) 'Twenty-four hours: An overview of the recall diary method and data quality in the American Time Use Survey' in R.F. Belli, D.F. Alwin and F.P. Stafford (eds) *Calendar and Time Diary Methods in Life Course Research* (pp. 109–120). London: Sage Publications. For more on the ATUS, see http://www.bls.gov/tus/.

Raudenbush, S. (1999) Statistical analysis and optimal design in cluster randomized trials. *Psychological Methods* 2: 173–185.

Raudenbush, S. and Sampson, R.J. (1999) 'Ecometrics: Toward a science of assessing ecological settings, with application to the systematic social observation of neighbourhoods'. *Sociological Methodology* 29: 1–41.

Redline, C.D., Dillman, D.A., Carley–Baxter, L. and Creecy, R.H. (2005) 'Factors that influence reading and comprehension of branching instructions in self–administered questionnaires'. *Advances in Statistical Analysis* 89: 21–38.

Reiss, A.J. and Rhodes, A.L. (1961) 'The distribution of juvenile delinquency in the social class structure'. *American Sociological Review* 26: 720–732.

Robinson, J.P. (1985) 'The validity and reliability of diaries versus alternative time use measures' in F.T. Juster and F.P. Stafford, F.P. (eds), *Time, Goods, and Well-being* (pp. 33–62). Ann Arbor, MI: Survey Research Center, The University of Michigan.

Sampson, R.J., Raudenbush, S.W. and Earls, F. (1997) 'Neighborhoods and violent crime: A multilevel study of collective efficacy'. *Science* 277: 918–924.

Sampson, R.J. and Wikström, P.-O.H. (2008) 'The social order of violence in Chicago and Stockholm neighbourhoods: A comparative inquiry' in S. Kalyvas, I. Shapiro and T. Masoud (eds), *Order, Conflict and Violence* (pp. 97–119). Cambridge: Cambridge University Pres.

Schmid, C.F. (1960a) 'Urban crime areas: Part I'. *American Sociological Review* 25: 527–542.

Schmid, C.F. (1960b) 'Urban crime areas: Part II'. *American Sociological Review* 25: 655–678.

Shaw, C. and McKay, H. (1969) *Juvenile Delinquency and Urban Areas.* Chicago: University of Chicago Press.

Simcha-Fagan, O. and Schwartz, J.E. (1986) 'Neighbourhood and delinquency: An assessment of contextual effects'. *Criminology* 24: 667–703.

Snijders, T. and Bosker, R. (1999) *Multilevel Analysis: An Introduction to Basic and Advanced Multilevel Analysis.* London: Sage.

Stafford, F.P. (2009) 'Timeline data collection and analysis: Time diary and event history calendar methods' in R.F. Belli, D.F. Alwin and F.P. Stafford (eds) *Calendar and Time Diary Methods in Life Course Research* (pp. 13–30).

London: Sage Publications. For more on PSID CDS, see http://psidonline.isr.umich.edu/CDS/.

Stewart, J. (2006) 'Assessing alternative dissimilarity indexes for comparing activity profiles'. *Electronic International Journal of Time Use Research* 3: 49–59.

Stone, A.A. and Broderick, J.E. (2009) 'Protocol compliance in real-time data collection studies' in R.F. Belli, D.F. Alwin and F.P. Stafford (eds) *Calendar and Time Diary Methods in Life Course Research* (pp. 243–256). London: Sage Publications.

Stoop, I.A.L. (2005) *The Hunt for the Last Respondent: Nonresponse in Sample Surveys.* Amsterdam: Aksant Academic.

Tolman, E.C. (1948) 'Cognitive maps in rats and men'. *Psychological Review* 55: 189–208.

Wikström, P.-O.H. (1991) *Urban Crime, Criminals and Victims.* New York: Springer-Verlag.

Wikström, P.-O.H. (2004) 'Crime as alternative: Towards a cross-level situational action theory of crime causation' in J. McCord (ed.), *Beyond Empiricism: Institutions and Intentions in the Study of Crime* (pp. 1–37). *Advances in Criminological Theory.* New Brunswick: Transaction.

Wikström, P.-O.H. (2006) 'Individuals, settings, and acts of crime: Situational mechanisms and the explanation of crime' in P. Wikström and R. Sampson (eds), *The Explanation of Crime: Context, Mechanisms and Development* (pp. 61–107). Cambridge: Cambridge University Press.

Wikström, P.-O.H. (2009) 'Crime propensity, criminogenic exposure and crime involvement in early to mid adolescence'. *Monatsschrift fur Kriminologie und Strafrechtsreform* 92: 253–266.

Wikström, P.-O.H. (2010a) 'Explaining crime as moral action' in S. Hitlin and S. Vaysey, S. (eds), *Handbook of the Sociology of Morality* (pp. 211–239). New York: Springer Verlag.

Wikström, P.-O.H. (2010b) 'Situational Action Theory' in F. Cullen and P. Wilcox (eds), *Encyclopedia of Criminological Theory.* London: Sage Publications.

Wikström, P.-O.H. and Butterworth, D. (2006) *Adolescent Crime: Individual Differences and Lifestyles.* Cullompton: Willan Publishing.

Wikström, P.-O.H., Ceccato, V., Treiber, K. and Hardie, B. (2010) 'Activity fields and the dynamics of crime: Advancing knowledge about the role of the environment in crime causation'. *Journal of Quantitative Criminology. Special edition* 26: 55–87.

Wikström, P.-O.H. and Dolmen, L. (2001) 'Urbanisation, neighbourhood social integration, informal social control, minor social disorder, victimisation and fear of crime'. *International Review of Victimology* 8: 163–182.

Wikström, P.-O.H. and Loeber, R. (2000) 'Do disadvantaged neighbourhoods cause well-adjusted children to become adolescent delinquents?' *Criminology* 38: 1109–1142.

Wikström, P.-O.H., Oberwittler, D., Treiber, K. and Hardie, B. (2011) *Breaking Rules: The Social and Situational Dynamics of Young People's Urban Crime.* Oxford: Oxford University Press.

Wikström, P.-O.H. and Sampson, R. J. (2006) 'Introduction: Toward a unified approach to crime and its explanation' in P.-O.H. Wikström and R.J. Sampson (eds), *The Explanation of crime: Context, Mechanisms and Development* (pp. 1–7). Cambridge: Cambridge University Press.

Wikström, P.-O.H. and Treiber, K. (2007) 'The role of self-control in crime causation: Beyond Gottfredson and Hirschi's general theory of crime'. *European Journal of Criminology* 4: 237–264.

9

Social Networks and the Ecology of Crime: Using Social Network Data to Understand the Spatial Distribution of Crime

George E. Tita, Adam Boessen

INTRODUCTION

The use of social network analysis is becoming widely adopted throughout academia. While once the primary domain of social scientists, social network analysis has recently become a central focus in the natural sciences as well. Physicists, computer scientists and biologists have all begun to realize the power of understanding how entities are linked together within a particular system. As a method for understanding structural relations, social network analysis is utilized to study friendship ties, kinship, protein structures, animal mating habits, and terrorist groups (Borgatti et al., 2009). Formal social network analysis has recently started to appear in the criminology literature with the primary focus being on either peer-effects among individuals (Haynie, 2001, 2002; Haynie and Payne, 2006; McGloin and Shermer, 2009) or gangs and violence (McGloin, 2005, 2007; Papachristos, 2006).

This is not to say that the importance of social networks is new to criminology and the ecology of crime. From the work of the early Chicago School to the more recent work on 'collective efficacy', social networks (especially local social ties) serve as the bedrock upon which all ecological models of crime rest. However, it is true that the formal measurement and analysis of social networks are missing in the advancement of these theories. The magnitude or effect size of, for example, population heterogeneity on the formation of local social ties remains unknown. Nor do we know if a threshold exists at which point the density of local social ties is sufficient to enable adequate levels of informal social control.

Social networks may also provide the key to understanding the spatial distribution of crime. While a consistent set of explanatory variables (e.g., minority population, concentrated poverty, stability of residents, female-headed households) have been shown to be associated with high crime neighborhoods, research has shown that even after controlling for these factors, crime and violence continues to cluster in space (Cohen and Tita, 1999; Morenoff et al., 2001; Sampson et al., 2002). As such, a number of researchers have concluded that crime is contagious and diffuses across space. As Sampson notes, '[N]eighborhoods themselves need to be conceptualized as nodes in a larger network of spatial relations' to suggest that neighborhoods are not independent units of observation and that ecological models of crime need to consider how observable outcomes in one neighborhood are dependent upon the actions and activities occurring in other areas (Sampson, 2004: 163).

We begin this chapter by examining how social networks serve as the primary mechanism by which local residents self-regulate the delinquent and criminal behaviors within a community. We next explore how the spatial dimensions of social networks among individuals and groups might help to better understand the contagious nature of crime. In both instances we highlight not only what has been done with regard to making social networks explicit, but also attempt to demonstrate ways in which the measurement and analysis of social networks can help deepen our understanding of the 'neighborhood effects' that drive crime patterns within local communities. We also provide an example where formal social network data and analysis were used to understand community structures and crime. We argue that it is the careful collection and measurement of local social ties that represents the next frontier within the broad communities and crime literature and conclude by offering our thoughts on how social networks could advance this body of knowledge.

SOCIAL NETWORKS AND THE COMMUNITY CONTEXT OF CRIME

Social networks are often implicated as being important mechanisms in the development and maintenance of safe, low-crime neighborhoods (e.g., Bellair, 2000; Sampson, 1988; Sampson et al., 1997; Taylor et al., 1984; Veysey and Messner, 1999), though some studies question their overall contribution to public safety (Pattillo, 1998; Simcha-Fagan and Schwartz, 1986; Warner and Rountree, 1997). The majority of research on the relative importance of local, as well as nonlocal, social ties among residents is framed within either the systemic model of social disorganization (e.g., Bursik and Grasmick, 1993; Sampson, 1986; Sampson and Groves, 1989), or the more recent conceptual framework of 'collective efficacy' (Sampson, 2004; Sampson et al., 1997). Though both approaches view social networks as facilitating local levels of informal social control within a neighborhood, they take very different views on exactly which types of ties matter.

The systemic model is rooted in the work of Shaw and McKay (1942) and the original Chicago School that focuses on the importance of accruing adequate community levels of 'bonding capital' (Woolcock and Naranyan, 2001). Social disorganization theory posits that the level of community crime is regulated by the amount of self-imposed monitoring and censuring of the local population's activities. Safe communities are expected to result from network ties between residents producing informal social control which is influenced by the amount of poverty, mobility,

heterogeneity, and population density. By attempting to explain why certain types of stable communities exhibit higher levels of crime, the systemic model of social disorganization theory was offered as revision of Shaw and McKay's theory and unpacked three types of social control present in the community (Bursik and Grasmick, 1993; Hunter, 1985). First, the most basic form of control is private, which is defined as the social bonds among family members and close friends. Next, parochial control regulates behaviors through ties that link residents because of co-membership in local community institutions (social clubs, places of worship, neighborhood councils, etc.). Finally, formal social control is dependent upon a community having social networks that extend outward from the neighborhood and is enacted by institutions outside of the community including the police but also other social and political institutions.

Local friendship networks, co-participation in volunteer organizations, and other 'neighboring' activities (Bellair, 2000) increase the frequency of face-to-face interactions, which in turn promote the development of 'strong' ties that bind local residents together. Neighborhoods with dense networks of local ties are more capable of exercising informal social control through the monitoring and censuring of problematic behaviors of residents and visitors alike. The norms and values of the community are expected to informally control the behavior of residents through social networks, and crime results when residents become less knit. In other words, the social networks in the community mediate the relationship between structural neighborhood factors and crime (Bellair, 1997). Although social disorganization theory argues for the importance of social networks for facilitating informal controls in the community, Warner (2007) suggests that social ties *directly* affect whether residents intervene in a community issue (e.g. unruly children). Similarly, local social ties (defined by co-membership within local civic organizations) exhibit both indirect and direct effects on levels of both crime and fear of crime at the block level (Taylor et al., 1984).

The most recent advancement in the ecological explanation of crime is known as collective efficacy. While highlighting the importance of strong community ties as proposed by social disorganization theory and neighborhood characteristics such as poverty, Sampson and colleagues suggest that crime is regulated by residents' perception to collectively organize within the local community (Sampson et al., 1997). Social networks in the community can facilitate collective efficacy and thereby community safety through perceptions of community trust and cohesion (Sampson and Graif, 2009). In contrast to the systemic model's focus on strong ties, collective efficacy focuses on weak ties, or 'bridging capital' (Putnam, 2000), and the existence of latent networks of mutual trust and shared values within the local neighborhood that can be activated in times of need. Collective efficacy questions whether dense local social ties are a necessary, let alone sufficient, condition with regard to the development of safe communities. It has been suggested that strong ties within a community can limit the ability of residents to marshal local municipal goods and services (Wilson, 1978). Strong ties can also inhibit the development of informal social control when networks closely bond law-abiding citizens to local delinquents (Browning et al., 2004; Pattillo-McCoy, 1999).

Recent research has begun to explore the importance of ties outside of the local community. Without access to networks in other neighborhoods, the lack of ties to other neighborhoods has the potential for a neighborhood to become isolated from the geospatial and social infrastructure of the city and nearby communities (Massey and Denton, 1993; Wilson, 1987). By extending social networks to outside the local neighborhood, it is expected that residents will be able to obtain more formal controls (e.g. police) and be more likely to engage in community institutions (e.g. neighborhood councils, places of worship). In fact, drawing from Granovetter's (1973) seminal study, Bellair (1997) argues that connections outside of the local neighborhood rather then just internal ties help communities control crime. Using structural equation modeling, Bellair demonstrates that network ties mediate the direct effect between many structural correlates (e.g. SES, heterogeneity, stability) and crime.

MEASURING LOCAL SOCIAL NETWORKS

To date, most studies measuring social networks within the communities and crime literature use proxies for understanding social structure rather than explicitly measuring the ties in communities or individual networks. Most of the previous approaches to measuring social ties in the community ask respondents about their perceived social ties in the community, but a more explicit analysis of social ties would measure actual ties between residents and incorporate this dependence into the analysis.

The measurement of local social ties can be accomplished using a variety of approaches including surveys, observational studies, or linking together of individuals using archival data such as community meeting minutes, church directories, or other voluntary organizations (for a review, see Marsden, 1990, or Butts, 2008). The majority of neighborhood research, however, substitutes structural measures such as poverty, ethnic/racial heterogeneity, and population instability for implicit measures of local ties. Researchers often argue that increases in these structural characteristics fissure the local community network by making it more difficult for the local community to control the behavior of its residents.

Although few studies have actually measured community ties via observational or survey measures, researchers have explored community cohesion with questions about the number of ties within the local community as well as the frequency of interaction. More explicit measures of social ties in the community beyond community structural characteristics focus on the percent of an individual's family and friends within the local community as an assessment of residents' local social ties. Using the British Crime Survey, Sampson and Groves (1989) and Sampson (1988) used reports of friendship ties to understand residents' networks. Friendship ties were defined using five categories ranging from 'none' to 'all' with respondents being asked: 'How many of your friends live in this area (within about a 15-minute walk of here)?' (Sampson, 1988: 771). Their findings suggest that friendship networks vary across communities and friendship networks are impacted by residential instability. Although the '15-minute walk' is a proxy for how networks are distributed spatially within the local neighborhood and underscores the importance of considering the effects of space on ties, this measure assumes a random spatial distribution where all social ties are equally

---

Box 9.1

For an excellent introduction into the field of social network analysis the reader is referred to Wasserman and Faust, 1994. This text introduces the important topics related to the field including the types of questions one can explore with social network data, how to collect data, and how to analyze and interpret social network data. Methodological detail is presented at both simple and sophisticated levels making it the appropriate 'how to' book for anyone interested in social network analysis.

likely to be connected regardless of the space that they occupy.

Most other measures of local social ties in the communities and crime literature can be referred to as measures of 'neighboring'. Survey questions about neighboring can focus on particular activities, but most often just ask general questions regarding the frequency that socializing occurs among neighbors. For instance, Bellair's (1997) study of crime and local social ties uses data from 60 neighborhoods in St. Louis (Missouri), St. Petersburg/Tampa (Florida), and Rochester (New York) that asked how often residents, or other household members, visit in either person's home. Though this falls short in terms of measuring actual local social ties, Bellair's work suggests that creating ties from outside the local area maximizes social capital within the community. Furthermore, Bellair extends the literature with an assessment of the frequency (or infrequency) of interaction between residents to indicate that informal social controls are more effective for controlling crime when residents interact more than once a year.

Warner (2007) and Sampson and Graif (2009) assess the social ties in communities by asking residents to report how many friends or relatives live in their neighborhood and then residents' responses were aggregated and averaged to get a sense of the social ties within the neighborhood. Using data from the Project on Human Development in Chicago Neighborhoods (PHDCN), Browning et al. (2004) and Sampson and Graif (2009) employed a 'reciprocated exchange scale' to measure residents social networks by asking residents on a scale ranging from 'never', 'rarely', 'sometimes', and 'often': 'How often do you and people in this neighborhood: (1) Have parties or other get-togethers where other people in the neighborhood are invited, (2) Visit in each other's homes or on the street, (3) Ask each other advice about personal things such as child rearing or job openings, and (4) Do favors for each other.' Importantly, this measure recognizes the value of considering the relational nature of social networks and, following Bellair, also

incorporates the frequency of interaction. However, it still does not directly capture dyadic relations between residents.

Most community and crime researchers' measures of social networks are proxies for network structure by asking individuals in the community to report their *perceptions* of social ties as an assessment of their community's social network. In all cases respondents are asked to report their beliefs or perspectives of their ties within the community. Social network researchers have long argued that networks are relational and that to understand social ties, researchers need to move beyond individual perceptions of social ties to examining the actual structure of social ties (e.g., see Entwisle et al., 2007).

One way to assess local social ties is use collect egocentric network data. The egocentric network approach uses traditional random sampling methods to glean information about ties in a respondent's network. Specifically, an ego-centered network captures a respondent's personal network by examining how a focal respondent, or ego, is tied to other individuals (alters). In order to capture one's egocentric network, it is common to ask the ego a series of 'network generating questions' (e.g., with whom do you socialize; who provides material/emotional support). The various alters identified across the different relationships can be collapsed into a single network for each individual. Though it is possible to link individuals across egocentric networks from the sample of egos, this approach is limited because only those individuals known by the focal respondents are included in the 'community' network. Therefore, the representativeness of ties within a community is highly dependent on how the sample of egos was identified and who chose whether or not to participate in the study.

Another approach for gathering network data is to construct a 'complete network'. In this case, the sample becomes community residents and each person is asked if or how they know the other members of the community (for a general review of network data, see Marsden, 1990). Importantly, this type of network data allows for cross-level

Box 9.2

The work of Browning et al. (2004) posits a *negotiated co-existence model* that suggests social ties can be beneficial in facilitating community cohesion and trust but at the same time may have the potential to decrease community controls by integrating residents who commit crimes within the community. Similarly, earlier qualitative work in Chicago by Pattillo (1998) demonstrates that residents who witness a crime may be less likely to cooperate with authorities to avoid disruption within their larger social network since offenders might be friends or share a blood relationship with others in the neighborhood.

analysis of individual actors and the structure of the network itself. This type of network sampling, however, is particularly challenging for community researchers because it is not quite clear on how to bound the network across the city landscape given that ties will likely form across social and physical boundaries. Further, due to data collection challenges, financial considerations, and limitations for mathematically analyzing large-scale networks, datasets with a formal representation of ties among residents in a city is relatively non-existent in the communities and crime literature. With information from residents' social relations and geographic locations, future research could test how community processes (i.e., informal social controls) are structured spatially and socially across the city landscape.

Most studies measuring social networks in the community only examine who an individual interacts with such as family or a friend to suggest the amount of social control in the community. As such, individual conceptualizations of social networks through one respondent's friends or family neglect the interconnections between friends, others in the neighborhood, and friends of friends (Tita and Faust, 2004; Wasserman and Faust, 1994). For example, most studies in the communities and crime literature use individual conceptualizations of social networks that do not capture connections between respondent's friends (X is friends with Y and X is also friends with Z, but it is unclear whether Y and Z are friends). Furthermore, Fischer (1982: 39) notes that social ties among people encompass many types of relations, including co-workers, neighbors, friends, kin, acquaintances, customers, and members of the same organization, but it is unclear how these different types of relations influence social controls. Most network studies in the criminology literature essentially treat all social ties among friends and family as being equally important, but we can all think of friends, relatives and neighbors that we favor more than others.

Network researchers have also argued for the importance of considering the directionality of ties (Grannis, 2009b; Wasserman and Faust, 1994). When measures ask residents to report their friends in the neighborhood, it is unclear whether their friends reciprocate the friendship (i.e. X says he is friends with Y, but Y may not say he is friends with X). Researchers interested in Browning et al.'s (2004) negotiated coexistence model that highlights the paradoxical effect of networks to inhibit as well as facilitate criminal behavior might benefit from exploring the directionality of residents ties. Future research might extend this line of work by analyzing how resident's networks simultaneously foster community cohesion and at the same time inhibit

social controls through potentially the same connections.

Demography plays an important role for forming ties because individuals who are more similar are more likely to be connected (McPherson et al., 2001; Grannis, 2009a). Similarly, age, gender, race, religion and class all shape the social interactions in a community that can result in the formation of social capital needed for fighting crime (Bellair, 1997; Beyerlein and Hipp, 2005; Blau and Blau, 1982; Hipp, 2010; Rountree and Warner, 1999). Controlling for gender, research has demonstrated that ties among females are more effective in controlling local levels of violence than are the density of male neighboring networks (Rountree and Warner, 1999). However, the authors caution that neighboring (as a proxy for local social ties) may not always equate to high levels of local social capital. Though female networks are important, their impact is diminished in communities with greater numbers of female-headed households.

One recent study that tests network relations between residents in micro-neighborhoods suggests that social distance between residents has a curvilinear effect on perceptions of crime in the community. By employing a rich conceptualization of social distance between residents, Hipp (2010) builds on Bellair (1997) by demonstrating that at the lowest levels of social distances (i.e., more dense networks) and the highest levels (more weak ties), residents perceive more crime and disorder in the community. Using a unique sample of residents and their ten spatially proximate neighbors in a micro-neighborhood, Hipp creates a measure of social distance that accounts for the similarity of actors within the networks along such dimensions as education, race, age, income, marital status and presence of children. He argues that including multiple measures of other social characteristics provides a more accurate theoretical representation of social distance within a community. While acknowledging that this measure assumes that all social characteristics are equally weighted for social distance, this study suggests a need to examine how different conceptualizations of social distance impact community collective efficacy. As such, understanding local social networks is critical for understanding how communities respond to crime as well as for developing effective crime fighting strategies.

Most ecological crime studies measure 'neighborhood' by using some type of census aggregation (i.e., tracts, block groups), resident perceptions of their neighborhoods, or a combination of these measures as a way to define the spatial dimension of a place (Hipp, 2007). Capturing the spatial dimension of social networks, however, can also be used to define the geography of a community.

Box 9.3

An important exception is the work of Grannis (2009a), who argues that streets and roads shape social interaction. The probability of a social tie forming among two individuals is determined by whether or not one must cross a major street and thereby networks form among individuals who come into physical contact with one another by walking along, or crossing, only small 'tertiary streets'.

Grannis refers to the areas defined by interconnected tertiary streets as 'T-Communities' and argues that unlike communities defined by boundaries drawn for administrative purposes (e.g., census tracts, zip codes), T-Communities represent a much more realistic definition of a community. By carefully examining local tertiary streets and their effect on the structure of social networks, Grannis suggests that researchers can begin to understand the process by which communities develop social capital for creating and maintaining safe communities (2009a).

In addition to the work by Grannis in which he collected network data on an entire college town (2009a), a study of community in Thailand clearly demonstrates the value of explicitly measuring the social and spatial dimensions of local networks (Entwisle et al., 2007). Over the course of the project, the research team collected complete network data for every member in each household in a sample of villages within the Nang Rong region. In addition to mapping out the residential location of each household, the residential location of offspring/siblings who have moved from the family dwelling, they also noted the location of each household's agricultural field. The richness of both the spatial and social network data (collected on a variety of social relationships) demonstrates the complexity and variability in network structures across the villages in terms of which spatial location or which social tie mattered in explaining a particular outcome. For instance, residential neighborhood networks failed to explain much about the sharing of resources that occurs during the harvest of crops. Instead, the sharing of resources was strongly dependent upon the spatial arrangement of field ownership with farmers of spatially proximate lands being more likely to share resources than were residential neighbors.

USING SOCIAL NETWORKS IN THE SPATIAL ANALYSIS OF CRIME

In addition to using social network analysis to characterize the connectedness of a neighborhood's residents, we can also use social networks to understand the connectedness between neighborhoods. If there is a contagious nature to crime wherein crimes in one neighborhood impact crime in another neighborhood, then defining the linkage or flow of influence from one neighborhood to another is vital. If residents flow between spatially adjacent neighborhoods, then it makes sense that contagion will occur among spatially proximate neighborhoods. However, there are reasons to believe that geographic closeness might not always lead to social interactions. In addition to physical boundaries that might impede social interaction (e.g. waterways, highways, parks) among 'neighbors', there might be 'social boundaries' (i.e., race, ethnicity, social class) that also disrupt the flow of social interactions across space. Thus, the ability of crime in a focal neighborhood to influence crime in another area may also depend upon the social distance between the two areas.

Box 9.4

The combination of spatial analysis and social network analysis is also finding a home within criminal justice circles. Introduced by the architects of the 'Boston Gun Project' (Kennedy et al., 1997), a social network analysis of gang rivalries provide a clear picture of the groups involved in violence. Mapping gang turf as well of the crimes committed by gang members can help local police target their patrols. These methodologies have become standard practice among those using a 'problem solving approach' in the design and implementation of anti-crime strategies.

As documented earlier, crime is not randomly distributed in space. Instead, places that are geographically close to one another tend to have similar levels of crime. From a technical standpoint, we say that crime exhibits patterns of positive spatial autocorrelation.[1] The spatial autocorrelation of crime provides researchers with an important methodological challenge: When levels of crime cluster across our units of observation (neighborhoods, communities, etc.), then we cannot assume that our observations are 'independent'. That is, due to the clustering of similar values, if we know the level of crime in a focal area we likely know something about crime in the neighboring areas. This means that 'ordinary least squares' (OLS) and other regression techniques that 'assume independence among observations' cannot be used. To address this issue, one can rely on spatial regression (or spatial econometric) methods, which take into account the structure of the autocorrelation of crime.

The use of spatial regression grew out of criminologist's desire to understand the unprecedented growth in levels of youth homicide starting in the late 1980s through the early 1990s. Criminologists referring to this era as the 'youth homicide epidemic' adopted epidemiological methods to model the diffusion of violence. Research on the youth crime epidemic finds that urban minority males killed with guns continue to be the subpopulation at greatest risk (Blumstein, 1995). These studies also found evidence that violence diffused at the national level (Blumstein and Rosenfeld, 1998; Cork, 1999; Kellerman, 1996), county level (Baller et al., 2001; Messner and Anselin, 2004; Messner et al., 1999), and local levels (Block and Block, 1993; Cohen and Tita, 1999; Fagan et al., 1998; Kennedy and Braga, 1998; Klein et al., 1991; Morenoff et al., 2001).

These early studies were important in two ways. First, they clearly demonstrated that patterns of violence were consistent with positive spatial autocorrelation. For crime to diffuse through some contagious process, it must first be shown that the crime distribution is not random and exhibits some sort of spatial structure. Thus, positive autocorrelation is a necessary condition of diffusion. Second, many of these studies began to hint at the structures and underpinnings of social processes that might help us understand why violence diffuses across space. The growth of the crack cocaine markets, an increase in the carrying and use of guns, and the diffusion of urban street gangs were proffered as the reason why violence and homicide was growing and spreading throughout the US (Cohen and Tita, 1999; Cork, 1999). It is important to note, however, that all of the early studies of diffusion follow an inductive approach. That is, explanations are posited only after the analysis is complete and the findings are supportive of diffusion.

Only recently have ecological studies of violence begun to take a deductive approach where the specific process driving diffusion (gangs, drugs, adoption of gun carrying) is specified a priori instead of being inferred from the results. For spatial models, this process is all captured in the 'autocorrelation matrix' (**W**). It is this matrix, **W**, that defines which areas (e.g., neighborhoods, census tracts, other geopolitical boundaries) are 'neighbors' of one another. In traditional spatial analysis, **W** is specified using adjacency/contiguity or a distance decay metric. Put another way, the events in one area are either influenced by what happens in the areas immediately adjacent to them, or following Tobler's First Law of Geography (Tobler, 1970), activities nearby matter more than activities farther away. Though this modeling approach has added to the collective understanding of the diffusion of violence, Radil et al. (2010: 2) caution against this sort of 'spatial fetishism' in which the ability to simply map crime patterns takes precedence over attempting to explain the causes of the clusters: 'When spatial analysis is overly dependent on reasoning from spatial form to social process, the risk of reducing people to the spaces they occupy grows while the likelihood of new insights shrinks.' Furthermore, simply relying on a spatial construction of the **W** matrix might ignore more complicated processes driving influence/contagion processes. As Leenders (2002: 22) notes:

> W is supposed to represent the theory a researcher has about the structure of the influence processes in the network. Since any conclusion drawn on the basis of autocorrelation models is conditional upon the specification of **W**, the scarcity of attention and justification researchers pay to the chosen operationalization of **W** is striking and alarming. This is especially so, since different specifications of **W** typically lead to different empirical results.

An emergent body of work is modeling the contagion of violence by considering both geographic neighbors as well as 'social' neighbors. This is being accomplished by combining the social network/social influence framework on the diffusion of innovations/ideas (see Marsden and Friedkin, 1994) with spatial regression models (see Meares and Bhati, 2006; Radil et al., 2010; Tita and Greenbaum, 2009; Tita and Radil, 2010a, 2011). Though a review of the many approaches used in spatial regression models is beyond the scope of this chapter, it is important to know two types of models: spatial error and spatial lag (or spatial dependence) models.

Spatial error models are appropriate for modeling unobservable processes (e.g., norms or beliefs) that are shared among individuals residing in proximate places, or when the boundaries that separate 'places' are arbitrary to the extent that two 'different' places are actually very similar across various social, economic or demographic features. In this case, the research simply creates a spatially lagged version of the error term and includes it as an additional variable in regression model. Failure to account for the non-dependence in the error will still yield unbiased coefficients; however, estimates of the standard errors on those coefficients will be incorrect (Anselin, 2002).

When the level of crime in one neighborhood is directly dependent upon the activities or social processes occurring in a neighboring area, one must apply a spatial lag (spatial dependence) model. Failure to consider spatial dependence in one's model is far more serious than ignoring spatially autocorrelated error terms because the model is mis-specified and the estimates of the coefficients are incorrect. As the name 'spatial lag' suggests, the way to estimate a model with spatial dependence is to include a spatially lagged version of the dependent variable.

In one of the first attempts to geographically 'unbound' the autocorrelation matrix, Mears and Bhati (2006) model the spatial distribution of homicide by considering socio-economic similarity among residents living in different areas (census tracts). That is, census tracts were considered 'neighbors' if the socio-economic and demographic profiles of the residents were similar. Given that homophily (McPherson et al., 2001) is positively related to communication and the adoption of norms, they argue that events in a focal area will be influenced more strongly by events in non-adjacent but socially similar areas than in adjacent, but socially dissimilar areas. The authors find support for this argument and conclude that social distance is important. However, space also matters and the influence of violence in one area has on violence in another is especially powerful when the areas are both spatially and socially proximate.

Tita and Greenbaum (2009) and Tita and Radil (2010a, 2011) provide examples of how the spatial and social dimensions of urban street gangs can be exploited in an inductive approach. Their research argues that gangs are likely to be especially relevant to diffusion because they are organizations that are sustained over time through continuing social interactions within specific geographic locations. Research has also consistently demonstrated that gang 'set space' (Tita et al., 2005a), the area in which gangs hang out, experiences high levels of crime, especially violence (Kennedy et al., 1997; Spergel and Curry, 1990; Tita and Ridgeway, 2007.)

To deductively model the spatial distribution of violence involving gangs one must be able to capture the ties that link gangs to one another

---

Box 9.5

As noted previously, the lack of independence indicative of spatial autocorrelation makes the use of OLS regression techniques inappropriate (see Anselin, 1988, for a more technical treatment of this topic). While there are a variety of methods to address spatially autocorrelated data, simultaneous autoregressive (SAR) models have become the most popular, especially spatial error models and spatial lag (or 'dependence') models.

The spatial error models takes the following form:

$$Y = X\beta + \varepsilon; \ \varepsilon = \lambda \varepsilon + u, \ \text{ with } E[u] = 0, E[uu'] = \sigma^2 I,$$

where $\varepsilon = \mathbf{W} \ \varepsilon$, and $\mathbf{W}$ is the ($N \times N$) autocorrelation weighting matrix that contains information about which spatial units (e.g., census tracts, neighborhoods) are spatially connected and λ measures the spatial correlation of the error term. In the absence of correlation among neighbors' error terms, the λ equals zero, therefore using OLS methods is appropriate.

In the more serious case where particular process is influencing the observed outcome or dependent variable among 'neighboring' unit, then one must estimate a spatial lag model. The spatial lag model takes the form:

$$Y = \rho \mathbf{W} Y + X\beta + \varepsilon, \ \text{ with } E[\varepsilon] = 0, E[\varepsilon\varepsilon'] = \sigma^2 I,$$

where ρ is the spatial coefficient on the spatially lagged dependent variable, and it will be non-zero if outcomes in one location influence outcomes in another location. $\mathbf{W}$ is once again the ($N \times N$) autocorrelation weighting matrix.

(a rivalry network) and then use this network to link the geography of the gangs. This approach is accomplished by taking the $M \times M$ rivalry matrix (R) for all gangs in the area (where M is the number of gangs), the contiguity matrix (C) for the area based upon the N units of observation (such as census block groups or tracts) and the $N \times M$ matrix which locates each of the M gangs within the N geographic units (S). Using matrix algebra we are able to construct a new autocorrelation matrix (W) wherein a non-zero value indicates that a pair of geographic units contains the set space of rival gangs (see Tita and Greenbaum, 2008: 160).

Two studies, one in Pittsburgh (Tita and Greenbaum, 2008) and one in Los Angeles (Tita and Radil, 2011), have employed this modeling approach to the study of gang violence. The results were consistent across sites and demonstrate that the weights matrix that considers the socio-spatial nature of gangs and their rivalries provides a better fit to the data than does the matrix that only considers geographic proximity. It is the hope of the authors that these articles will encourage others to model other types of data in a similar manner. Different types of violence/crime will require different theories and different specifications of the spatial autocorrelation matrix. For instance, one might model the diffusion of youth violence by considering social interactions that occur within schools. In such a case neighborhoods would be linked together if and only if they send students to the same school buildings.

COMMUNITIES, GEOGRAPHY AND EGO-CENTERED NETWORKS: AN EXAMPLE

Motivated by the research in Thailand (Entwisle et al., 2007), a group of researchers demonstrated the efficacy and value of collecting spatial and social network data for understanding community structure. The collection of data on the geographic nature of local social ties took place in the Hollenbeck policing area of Los Angeles. Hollenbeck, and specifically the Boyle Heights neighborhood, is a relatively impoverished area comprised predominately of Latinos of Mexican origin. It also has a long history with gangs and violence (see Tita et al., 2003b). The researchers interviewed subjects and asked questions about their social and economic status. They also asked questions thought to influence the spatial dynamics of social networks. For instance, they ascertain where residents worked (if employed), where they shopped or attended religious services, their tenure both at current and prior places of residence,

and, of particular interest, gang membership. Next, each respondent was asked a series of questions meant to capture one's ego-centered network. The network portion of the survey instrument borrowed heavily from existing surveys such as the General Social Survey (GSS) and the International Social Survey Programme (ISSP) and asked questions regarding friendship, social support, financial support, community participation and job searches. Table 9.1 provides a list of the actual network questions asked.

After the network questions were asked, each respondent was asked about the various alters in their networks. In addition to basic demographic information, the ego was asked questions pertaining to how well and for how long they knew each alter and whether or not any of the alters were gang members. To add the spatial component, the home address was also recorded. For alters that lived within the Hollenbeck area, the specific cross streets nearest their place of residence was recorded. For those that lived outside of Hollenbeck the research team recorded either the neighborhood (for others living within the City of Los Angeles) or the name of the city (state and country) in which they resided. The end result was a rich data set including 97 egos and information on 1,144 alters (mean number of alters per ego = 11.8 with min = 2.0 and max = 27).

As expected, this research found that the participants' social networks were geographically constrained (Tita et al., 2005b). About 70 percent of the 1,144 unique individuals identified in the ego networks resided within the Boyle Heights neighborhood. Another 4 percent lived elsewhere in the City of Los Angeles and 22 percent lived within Los Angeles County leaving less than 50 alters (the remaining 4 percent) to reside in other parts of California ($n = 32$), the US ($n = 13$), or other parts of the globe ($n = 2$).

Important environmental and social factors appear to influence the spatial distribution of ties. Figure 9.1 provides a map of the place of residence for those alters that live within 10 miles of the center of Boyle Heights. Notice that there are no ties to the area immediately to the west of Hollenbeck. This result is not surprising given that the Los Angeles River provides a border between Hollenbeck and the Downtown area of Los Angeles and there are relatively few housing units in the center of the city. In addition to the built environment and land, there are also certain social barriers that limit the geography of local social ties. There appears in Figure 9.1 a particular 'directionality' to the networks as they flow eastward (and to a lesser extent southward) out of Hollenbeck. The participants in the study identify many alters just across the eastern, and to a less extent southern, border of Hollenbeck but notice

Table 9.1 Example of network generating questions

Social support, activities	Financial support	Emotional support/ discussion partners	Neighborhood issues	Other
– Who would care for your home if you went out of town – List the people, who if going out of town, might ask you to look after their home – Who would you ask for a ride to the store, post office or work? – Who have you gone out with socially – to dinner, the movies, or a sports event – in the past six months?	– Suppose you need to borrow a large sum of money. Who would you ask? – Who would turn to you for help if they needed to borrow money? – In you needed help finding a job, whom would you ask about possible jobs?	– With whom do you talk about work-related issues and decisions? – Suppose you needed advice about an important change in your life such as changing jobs or moving to another part of the country. Who would you turn to first for help? – Suppose you are very upset about a problem with your husband, wife or partner. Who would you turn to for help? – Suppose you are just a bit down or depressed, and you wanted to talk about it. Who would you turn to first for help?	– In the past six months have you worked with anyone to help deal with a neighborhood problem – such as public safety issues or traffic problems? – Are there people in your neighborhood that you do not consider friends, but that you are polite to because you do not want to create problems?	– In addition to the people you've identified so far, who else outside your household do you consider important to you that you interact with on a regular basis?

the dearth of ties linking residents of Boyle Heights to the residential neighborhood on the northwestern border. The researchers speculate that the lack of ties is influenced by ethnic differences. While Latinos inhabit both areas, the local residents to the north emigrated from El Salvador. Ethnographic research in Los Angeles has noted the tension between these two ethnic groups noting that Mexicans and El Salvadorians do not frequently mix socially (Vigil, 2002).

The impact of turf-based urban street gangs on the formation of social ties was of particular interest in the Hollenbeck area. By examining the spatial distribution of each ego network and overlaying it on a map of local gang territories[2], it was possible to determine whether the residents living within a gang impacted neighborhood forged ties with individuals residing within a rival gang's turf. In fact, the gang boundaries do appear to limit the ties of local residents. Not surprisingly, the only instances where social ties cross the boundaries of rival gangs is when an alter is a family member (Nakamura and Tita, 2005).

Public housing has long been thought of places that are socially and physically isolated from other areas of urban communities (see Griffiths and Tita, 2009; Massey and Denton, 1993). Social network analysis provides a unique method to fully examine the degree to which this is true. There are several large public housing developments in Boyle Heights and though the number of study participants residing in public housing was small ($n = 8$), one finding emerged that is especially illuminating. All of the egos that resided within public housing identified alters who resided both within the local public housing development as well as outside of the development. However, closer inspection of the spatial distribution of alters who resided outside of public housing finds that none of other 89 egos nominated a single alter residing within any of the local public housing developments. One interpretation of this finding is that residents from the larger community area isolate themselves from public housing residents, rather than public housing residents encapsulating themselves from other communities.

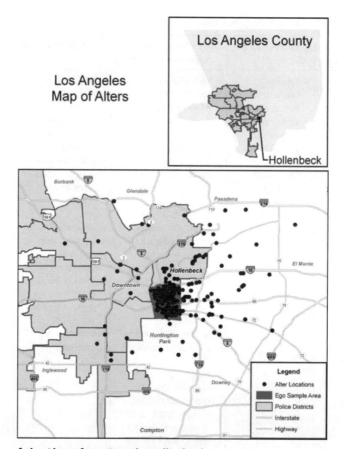

Figure 9.1 Map of the Alters from Egos in Hollenbeck

Box 9.6

Using a 'spatial typology of homicide' that considers the joint distribution of where victims/offenders reside and where the crime occurs, Griffiths and Tita (2009) find evidence that public housing does indeed constrain the geographic scope of its residents' interactions. Victims of homicide who reside within public housing are much more likely to be murdered in their immediate community than are those that do not live in public housing. Similarly, residents who reside in public housing and commit a murder are more likely to commit that murder in their immediate community than are offenders who live in non-public housing neighborhoods.

These examples demonstrate innovative and important ways in which carefully measured local social networks, along with their inherent spatial dimensions, can provide valuable insights into the structure of a community. Though it is well established that geographic distance is inversely related to the probability of individuals interacting (Festinger et al., 1950; Hipp and Perrin, 2009), research has also shown that geographic distance between individuals does not fully explain the

density of ties within the community (Feld, 1981). The network data collected in Hollenbeck demonstrates how both social (gangs) and geographic (distance, public housing) variables impact tie formation and the findings remind us that while distance matters, an individual's social ties are rarely limited to residents of the local community. Although the frequency varied across respondents, nearly everyone identified important alters who resided outside of the ego's neighborhood.

This once again highlights how the networks among individuals may provide important linkages between geographically distant places.

WHERE WE NEED TO GO

In addition to being defined by their social realm (friend, family, co-worker, etc.), social networks clearly have a spatial domain as well. Consequently, a growing number of scholars are beginning to explore both the social and spatial aspects of networks in order to understand neighborhood processes. Though important insights have been gleaned from proxy measures that capture the frequency and density of ties within a community, a more complete picture will emerge by understanding the spatial extent of the ties that link residents both within and across communities.

We believe that the explicit measurement of social networks can aid in our understanding of safe communities and the diffusion of violence. By capturing the social and spatial connections between individual ties, we gain a more precise representation for how communities shape social processes and controls that regulate crime. While it is often suggested that cohesive neighborhoods are essential to successfully fighting crime, this idea suggests that individuals within these cohesive communities all have equal access to the same social resources. Future research might therefore explore the structure of communities by incorporating measures of networks that move beyond the density or perceptions of social ties to actually capturing the extent of how residents are intertwined in space. Additionally, most of the research presented herein only focuses on network relations between residents in a small sample of communities. A challenge for future ecological studies of crime will be to explore how large-scale social networks (e.g. between all communities in a city) transmit into social processes within and between communities. Future research might also capture the dynamic nature of networks with longitudinal studies to explore changes in networks over time and the diffusion of violence across communities.

NOTES

1 In addition to the clustering of like values in space (positive autocorrelation), it is also possible to observe patterns of negative autocorrelation where dissimilar values cluster in space. The pattern observed on a checkerboard is an example of negative autocorrelation.

2 The gang territories and social networks were collected as part of the first author's work on a gun violence reduction program in Hollenbeck (see Tita et al., 2003a)

FURTHER READING

Grannis, R. (2009) *From the Ground Up: Translating Geography into Community Through Neighbor Networks* (Princeton: Princeton University Press). Grannis argues that social interaction (neighboring) patterns should be used to define the geographic extent/boundary of a community. In addition to theory, the book also covers the methods use to collect complete social network data in several different types of neighborhoods.

Entwisle, B. Faust, K. Rindfuss, R. R. and Kaneda, T. (2007), Networks and contexts: variation in the structure of social ties'. *American Journal of Sociology* 112(5): 1495–1533. This paper illustrates the importance of understanding the geographic characteristics of local social ties. The data is collected among local residents in a Thailand village to examine various social processes such as sharing and cooperation. It provides a nice template for the type of study that could be useful for characterizing the nature of social networks within a community.

Marsden, P.V. and Friedkin, N.E. (1994) 'Network studies of social influence' in S. Wasserman and J. Galaskiewicz (eds), *Advances in Social Network Analysis* (Thousand Oaks, CA: Sage), pp. 3–25. This essay outlines the challenges one faces in modeling social processes of influence, adoption and diffusion. Though the focus is solely on social network examples, the work can be applied to the modeling of crime as well (see Tita and Greenbaum, 2008).

Tita, G. and Greenbaum, R. (2009) 'Crime, neighborhoods, and units of analysis: Putting space in its place' in D. Weisburd, W. Bernasco and G. Bruinsma, G. (eds), *Putting Crime in its Place* (New York: Springer), pp. 145–170. Following the principles laid out in Marsden and Friedkin (1994), the authors combine social network analysis with spatial analysis to examine the spatial distribution of violence. They argue that model selection as well as the definition of one's 'spatial autocorrelation matrix' (W) should be driven and supported by one's theory.

For an excellent review of social network methodologies, see Wasserman, S. and Faust, K. (1994) *Social Network Analysis: Methods and Applications*. Cambridge: Cambridge University Press.

REFERENCES

Anselin, L. (1988) *Spatial Econometrics: Methods and Models*. Dordrecht (the Netherlands): Kluwer Academic Publishers.

Anselin, L. (2002) 'Under the hood: issues in the specification and interpretation of spatial regression models'. *Agricultural Economics* 27(3): 247–267.

Baller, R.D. Anselin, L. and Messner, S.F. Deane, G. and Hawkins, D.F. (2001) 'Structural covariates of U.S. county homicide rates: incorporating spatial effects'. *Criminology* 39(3): 561–590.

Bellair, P. (1997) 'Social interaction and community crime: examining the importance of neighborhood networks'. *Criminology* 35(4): 677–703.

Bellair, P. (2000) 'Informal surveillance and street crime: a complex relationship'. *Criminology* 38(1): 137–167.

Beyerlein, K. and Hipp, J.R. (2005) 'Social capital, too much of a good thing? American religious traditions and community crime'. *Social Forces* 84(2): 995–1013.

Blau, J.R. and Blau, P.M. (1982) 'The cost of inequality: metropolitan structure and violent crime'. *American Sociological Review* 47(1): 114–128.

Block, C.B. and Block, R. (1993) *Street Gang Crime in Chicago*. Research in Brief. National Institute of Justice, Washington, DC.

Blumstein, A. (1995) 'Youth violence, guns, and the illicit-drug industry'. *Journal of Criminal Law and Criminology* 86(1): 10–36.

Blumstein, A. and Rosenfeld, R. (1998) 'Explaining recent trends in U.S. homicide rates'. *Journal of Criminal Law and Criminology* 88(4): 1175–1216.

Borgatti, S.P. Mehra, A. Brass, D.J. and Labianca, G. (2009) 'Network analysis in the social sciences'. *Science* 323(5916): 892–895.

Browning, C.R. Feinberg, S.L. and Dietz, R.D. (2004) 'The paradox of social organization: networks, collective efficacy, and violent crime in urban neighborhoods'. *Social Forces* 83(2): 503–534.

Bursik, R. and Grasmick, H. (1993) *Neighborhoods and Crime: the Dimensions of Effective Community Control*. San Francisco: Lexington Books.

Butts, C.T. (2008) 'Social network analysis: A methodological introduction'. *Asian Journal of Social Psychology* 11(1):13–41.

Cohen, J. and Tita, G. (1999) 'Diffusion in homicide: exploring a general method for detecting spatial diffusion processes'. *Journal of Quantitative Criminology* 15(4): 451–493.

Cork, D. (1999) 'Examining space-time interaction in city-level homicide data: crack markets and the diffusion of guns among youth'. *Journal of Quantitative Criminology* 15(4): 379–406.

Entwisle, B. Faust, K. Rindfuss, R.R. and Kaneda, T. (2007) 'Networks and contexts: variation in the structure of social ties'. *American Journal of Sociology* 112(5): 1495–1533.

Fagan, J. Zimring, F.E. and Kim, J. (1998) 'Declining homicide in New York: a tale of two trends'. *Journal of Criminal Law and Criminology* 88(4): 1277–1324.

Feld, S. (1981) 'The focused organization of social ties'. *American Journal of Sociology* 86(5): 1015–1035.

Festinger, L. Schachter, S. and Back, K. (1950) *Social Pressures in Informal Groups*. Stanford, CA: Stanford University Press.

Fischer, C.S. (1982) *To Dwell Among Friends: Personal Networks in Town and City*. Chicago: University of Chicago Press.

Grannis, R. (2009a) *From the Ground Up: Translating Geography Into Community Through Neighbor Networks*. Princeton: Princeton University Press.

Grannis, R. (2009b) 'Paths and semipaths: reconceptualizing structural cohesion in terms of directed relations'. *Sociological Methodology* 39(1): 117–150.

Granovetter, M. (1973) 'The strength of weak ties'. *American Journal of Sociology* 78(6): 1360–1381.

Griffiths, E. and Tita, G.(2009) 'Homicide in and around public housing: is public housing a hotbed, a magnet, or a generator of violence for the surrounding community?' *Social Problems* 56(3): 474–493.

Haynie, D.L. (2001) 'Delinquent peers revisited: does network structure matter?' *American Journal of Sociology* 106(4): 1013–1057.

Haynie, D.L. (2002) 'Friendship networks and adolescent delinquency: the relative nature of peer delinquency'. *Journal of Quantitative Criminology* 18(2): 99–134.

Haynie, D.L. and Payne D.C. (2006) 'Race, friendship networks, and violent delinquency'. *Criminology* 44(4): 775–805.

Hipp, J.R. (2007) 'Block, tract, and levels of aggregation: neighborhood structure and crime and disorder as a case in point'. *American Sociological Review* 72(5): 659–680.

Hipp, J.R. (2010) 'Micro-structure in micro-neighborhoods: a new social distance measure, and its effect on individual and aggregated perceptions of crime and disorder'. *Social Networks* 32(2): 148–159.

Hipp, J.R. and Perrin, A.J. (2009) 'The simultaneous effect of social distance and physical distance on the formation of neighborhood ties'. *City and Community* 8(1): 5–25.

Hunter, A. (1985) 'Private, parochial, and public social orders: the problem of crime and incivility in urban communities' in G.D. Suttles and M.N. Zald (eds), *The Challenge of Social Control: Citizenship and Institution Building in Modern Society* (pp. 230–242). Norwood, NJ: Ablex.

Kellerman, A. (1996) *Understanding and Preventing Violence: a Public Health Perspective*. National Institute of Justice Review. Washington, DC: US Government Printing Office.

Kennedy, D.M. and Braga, A.A. (1998) 'Homicide in Minneapolis: research for problem solving'. *Homicide Studies* 2(3): 263–290.

Kennedy, D.M. Braga, A.A. and Piehl, A.M. (1997) 'The (un) known universe: mapping gangs and gang violence in Boston' in D. Weisburd and T. McEwen (eds), *Crime Mapping and Crime Prevention* (pp. 219–262). Monsey, NY: Criminal Justice Press.

Klein, M. Maxson, C.L. and Cunningham, L.C. (1991) 'Crack, street gangs, and violence'. *Criminology* 29(4): 623–650.

Leenders, R.T.A.J. (2002) 'Modeling social influence through network autocorrelation: constructing the weight matrix'. *Social Networks* 24(1): 21–47.

Marsden, P.V. (1990) 'Network data and measurement'. *Annual Review of Sociology* 16: 435–463.

Marsden, P.V. and Friedkin, N.E. (1994) ,Network studies of social influence' in S. Wasserman and J. Galaskiewicz (eds), *Advances in Social Network Analysis* (pp. 3–25). Thousand Oaks, CA: Sage.

Massey, D.S. and Denton, N.A. (1993) *American Apartheid: Segregation and the Making of the Underclass.* Cambridge, MA: Harvard University Press.

McGloin, J. (2005) 'Policy and intervention considerations of a network analysis of street gangs'. *Criminology and Public Policy* 4(3): 607–636.

McGloin, J. (2007) 'The organizational structure of street gangs in Newark, New Jersey: a network analysis of methodology'. *Journal of Gang Research* 15(1): 1–34.

McGloin, J. and Shermer, L. (2009) 'Self-control and deviant peer network structure'. *Journal of Research in Crime and Delinquency* 46(1): 35–72.

McPherson, M., Smith-Lovin, L. and Cook, J.M. (2001) 'Birds of a feather: homophily in social networks'. *Annual Review of Sociology* 27: 415–444.

Mears, D.P. and Bhati, A.S. (2006) 'No community is an island: The effects of resource deprivation on urban violence in spatially and socially proximate communities'. *Criminology* 44(3): 509–548.

Messner, S.F. and Anselin, L. (2004) 'Spatial analyses of homicide with areal data' in M. Goodchild and D. Janelle (eds), *Spatially Integrated Social Science* (pp. 127–144). New York: Oxford University Press.

Messner, S.F., Anselin, L., Baller, R.D., Hawkins, D.F., Deane, G. and Tolnay, S.E. (1999) 'The spatial patterning county homicide rates: an application of exploratory spatial data.

Morenoff, J.D. (2003) 'Neighborhood mechanisms and the spatial dynamics of birth weight'. *American Journal of Sociology* 108(5): 976–1017.

Morenoff, J.D., Sampson R.J. and Raudenbush, S. (2001) 'Neighborhood inequality, collective efficacy, and the spatial dynamics of urban violence'. *Criminology* 39(3): 517–560.

Nakamura, K. and Tita, G. (2005) 'Gang territory and its impact on community social networks'. Paper presented at the American Society of Criminology, Toronto, Canada.

Papachristos, A.V. (2006) 'Social network analysis and gang research: theory and methods' in J.F. Short and L.A. Hughes (eds), *Studying Youth Gangs* (pp. 99–118). Lanham, MD: Alta Mira.

Pattillo, M. (1998) 'Sweet mothers and gangbangers: Managing crime in a black middle-class neighborhood'. *Social Forces* 76(3): 747–774.

Pattillo-McCoy, M. (1999) *Black Picket Fences: Privilege and Peril Among the Black Middle Class.* Chicago: University of Chicago Press.

Putnam, R.D. (2000) *Bowling Alone: The Collapse and Revival of American Community.* New York: Simon & Schuster.

Radil, S., Flint, C. and Tita, G. (2010) 'Spatializing social networks: Using social network analysis to investigate geographies of gang rivalry, territoriality, and violence in Los Angeles'. *Annals of the Association of American Geographer* 100(2): 307–326.

Rountree, P.W. and Warner, B.D. (1999) 'Social ties and crime: is the relationship gendered?' *Criminology* 37(4): 789–813.

Sampson, R.J. (1986) 'Crime in cities: formal and informal social control' in A.J. Reiss Jr. and T. Michael (eds), *Communities and Crime* (pp. 271–311). Chicago, IL: University of Chicago Press.

Sampson, R.J. (1988) 'Local friendship ties and community attachment in mass society: a multi level systemic model'. *American Sociological Review* 53(5): 766–779.

Sampson, R.J. (2004) 'Networks and neighbourhoods: the implications of connectivity for thinking about crime in the modern city' in H. McCarthy, P. Miller and P. Skidmore (eds), *Network Logic: Who Governs in an Interconnected World?* (pp. 157–166). London: Demos.

Sampson, R.J. and Graif, C. (2009) 'Neighborhood social capital as differential social organization: resident and leadership dimensions'. *American Behavioral Scientist* 52(11): 1579–1605.

Sampson, R.J. and Groves, W.B. (1989) 'Community structure and crime: testing social disorganization theory'. *American Journal of Sociology* 94(4): 774–802.

Sampson, R.J., Morenoff, J.D. and Gannon-Rowley, T. (2002) 'Assessing "neighborhood effects": social processes and new directions in research'. *Annual Review of Sociology* 28: 443–478.

Sampson, R.J., Raudenbush, S.W. and Earls, F. (1997) 'Neighborhoods and violent crime: a multilevel study of collective efficacy'. *Science* 277(5328): 918–924.

Shaw, C.R. and McKay, H.D. (1942) *Juvenile Delinquency and Urban Areas.* Chicago: University of Chicago Press.

Simcha-Fagan, O. and Schwartz, J.E. (1986) 'Neighborhood and delinquency: an assessment of contextual effects'. *Criminology* 24(4): 667–703.

Spergel, I. and Curry, D. (1990) 'Strategies and perceived agency effectiveness in dealing with the youth gang problem' in C.R. Huff (ed.), *Gangs in America: Diffusion, Diversity and Public Policy* (pp. 288–309). Newbury Park, CA: Sage.

Taylor, R.B., Gottfredson, S. and Brower, S. (1984) 'Block crime and fear: Defensible space, local social ties, and territorial functioning'. *Journal of Research on Crime and Delinquency* 21(4): 303–331.

Tita, G., Cohen, J. and Engberg, J. (2005a) 'An ecological study of the location of gang "set space"'. *Social Problems* 52(2): 272–299.

Tita, G. and Faust, K. (2004) The advantages of having 'spaced out' friends: measuring the socio-spatial dimensions of a high crime community. Paper presented at the American Society of Criminology, Nashville, TN.

Tita, G., Faust, K. and Bienenstock, E. (2005b) Spaced out: the spatial dimension of social networks. Paper presented at the Sunbelt Meetings, Redondo Beach, CA.

Tita, G. and Greenbaum, R. (2009) 'Crime, neighborhoods, and units of analysis: Putting space in its place' in D. Weisburd, W. Bernasco and G. Bruinsma (eds), *Putting Crime in its Place* (pp. 145–170). New York: Springer.

Tita, G. and Ridgeway, G. (2007) 'The impact of gang formation on local patterns of crime'. *Journal of Research on Crime and Delinquency* 44(2): 208–237.

Tita, G. and Radil, S. (2010a) 'Spatial regression models in criminology: Modeling social processes in the spatial weights matrix' in A. Piquero and D. Weisburd (eds), *Handbook of Quantitative Criminology* (pp. 101–121). New York: Springer.

Tita, G. and Radil, S. (2011) 'Spatializing the social networks of gangs to explore patterns of violence'. *Journal of Quantitative Criminology* forthcoming.

Tita, G., Riley, K. and Greenwood, P. (2003a) 'From Boston to Boyle Heights: The process and prospects of a 'pulling levers' strategy in a Los Angeles barrio' in S. Decker (ed.) *Policing Gangs and Youth Violence* (pp. 102–130). Belmont, CA: Wadsworth.

Tita, G., Riley, K.J., Ridgeway, G., Grammich, C., Abrahamse, A. and Greenwood, P. (2003b) *Reducing Gun Violence: Results from an Intervention in East Los Angeles.* RAND Press: Santa Monica, CA.

Tobler, W. (1970) 'A computer movie simulating urban growth in the Detroit region'. *Economic Geography* 46(2): 234–240.

Vigil, J.D. (2002) *A Rainbow of Gangs: Street Cultures in the Mega-city.* Austin, TX: University of Texas Press.

Veysey, B.M. and Messner, S.F. (1999) 'Further testing of social disorganization theory: an elaboration of Sampson and Groves "community structure and crime"'. *Journal of Research in Crime and Delinquency* 36(2): 147–156.

Warner, B.D. (2007) 'Directly intervene or call the authorities? A study of forms of neighborhood social control within a social disorganization framework'. *Criminology* 45(1): 99–129.

Warner, B.D. and Rountree, P. (1997) 'Local social ties in a community and crime model: questioning the systemic nature of informal social control'. *Social Problems* 44(4): 520–536.

Wasserman, S. and Faust, K. (1994) *Social Network Analysis: Methods and Applications.* Cambridge: Cambridge University Press.

Wilson, W. (1978) *The Declining Significance of Race.* Chicago: University Chicago Press.

Wilson, W. (1987) *The Truly Disadvantaged: The Inner City, the Underclass and Public Policy.* Chicago: University of Chicago Press.

Woolcock, M. and Narayan, D. (2000) 'Social capital: implications for development theory, research, and policy'. *The World Bank Research Observer* 15(2): 225–249.

10

Using Census Data and Surveys to Study Labor Markets and Crime

Robert D. Crutchfield, Suzanna R. Ramirez

INTRODUCTION

Among the most fundamental questions in sociology are those that ask, 'How do social contexts effect individual and collective behaviors?' Sociological criminologists have long been interested in how the characteristics of neighborhoods, communities, cities, regions and nations affect individual criminality and crime rates. Enduring interests are those focused on how economic characteristics of both populations and individuals effect crime. Employment has been an especially important factor in criminology research, perhaps in large measure because of Merton's treatment of 'legitimate and illegitimate' means of achieving the good life and economic success in his classic paper 'Social Structure and Anomie' (1949).

Employment and aggregate unemployment rates have been frequently included in analyses of individual criminality and aggregate crime rates (see Crutchfield, 1989 for a review). In recent years, criminologists have begun using a wider array of employment and labor market indicators (Krivo and Peterson, 2004; Wadsworth, 2000; and others have used non-employment indicators to measure the influence that the economy has on crime (Rosenfeld and Fornago, 2007; Rosenfeld and Messner, 2009). Here we will be discussing the use of census and survey data to study the relationships between labor market indicators and crime paying special attention to the benefits of using both census data and survey data in combination to measure the macro- and micro-level contributions to crime.

Today, technological advances in statistical analysis and contemporary surveys are allowing researchers to explore the links between macroeconomic forces and individual behavior. The questions we can now answer have moved us beyond simple questions about unemployment and its relationship to crime. Contemporary criminologists are exploring the effect of the quality of jobs and the effect of wages on crime, in addition to how aspects of labor markets differ for particular ethnic groups as well as felons. Research questions such as these are being examined by combining macro-level and micro-level data; census data and survey data, in order to contextualize individual behavior and experiences in neighborhoods, cities, and nations.

Why combine census and survey data in the study of labor markets and crime? As we stated previously, sociological criminology has always been interested in the effects of social contexts on behavior. For instance, the traditional versions of social disorganization theory (Shaw and McKay, 1942), modern versions which emphasize collective efficacy (Sampson et al., 1997), and systemic versions which emphasize neighborhood institutional arrangements (Bursik and Grasmick, 1993), are essentially about how communities influence those who live, work and move through them.

Until recently studying the effect of neighborhoods and contextual influences on individual action has been a challenge. However, increased computing power and software (Kubrin and Weitzer, 2003) have opened new avenues for addressing these questions. Using these technologies with data that measure both aggregate and individual variations, allows us to study multi-level processes more accurately. Censuses of populations provide a wealth of macro or aggregated data and surveys measure individual behavior and attitudes. Some criminologists are especially interested in how variations in labor market participation are an important context effecting collective crime rates and individual criminality.

In the following, we highlight three exemplary studies that use both census data and surveys to study elements of labor markets on crime. In addition, we consider the strengths and weaknesses of census and survey data as sources for criminological research about the labor market and crime relationship, and detail the way in which these sources can be combined to capture the macro and micro variations in the labor market/crime relationship. Finally, we address the nature and collection of census data and some survey data that increasingly allows for a comparing of the labor market/crime relationship across nations. We also suggest further readings in the areas of labor markets and crime, duel labor market theory, and readings on the quantitative approach to analyses we discuss here.

THE LABOR MARKET AND CRIME RELATIONSHIP

The relationship between poverty and crime across neighborhoods, cities and states is well established in the criminological literature. However well established at the macro level, relationships between social class, or unemployment and crime are inconsistent at best at the micro level. For example, research shows that at the macro level, poverty increases crime. The debate here is between those who focus on relative deprivation (Blau and Blau, 1982) and actual poverty rates (Messner, 1983). When individuals are the unit of study it is even less clear. In a classic review, Tittle et al. (1978) report no consistent association between social class and delinquency. The association between unemployment and crime at both the macro and micro levels is even less clear. Chiricos's review (1987) found that unemployment increases crime, Parker and Horwitz (1986) found no significant association, and Cantor and Land (1985) report that it decreases some major crime types. Studies at each level of

analysis have been important in showing that indicators of poverty and labor markets and their relationship to crime are more complex than we once thought.

In addition to these complexities, research has shown that the way in which we measure economic wellbeing and labor market participation, effects the observed association with crime. We believe that to sort out observed anomalies and inconsistencies it is important to take into account social contexts in research on the relationships between economic factors (including both poverty and labor market participation) and crime, as well as different ways to measure both labor market factors and economic climate.

Most often in the criminological literature, unemployment rates or individual employment are used to measure economic climate and labor market participation. As mentioned previously, the research results are not always as most of us would expect. Most of the studies reporting a positive relationship between unemployment and crime interpret this association consistently with variants of strain theory arguments (Baron, 2008). Strain theorists argue that income needs or goals, when blocked, either disrupts the social structure (Merton, 1949) or cause individual stress (Agnew, 1992) which leads to crime. But, the mixed results on the effect of unemployment on crime suggest that singular measures of unemployment do not reveal the whole story about the labor market/crime relationship.

The unemployment rate is misunderstood by many. It is not typically measured by specifying the number of persons out of work, nor those currently receiving unemployment benefits from government-run insurance programs, nor is it usually measured by the decennial census. The unemployment rate is a measure of people who are out of work and are currently seeking employment. Yet there are other aspects of the labor market that the unemployment/employment rate ignores by definition; such as the quality of employment, the types of jobs available, the length of time someone spends looking for work, or the percentage of 'discouraged workers', those who have given up searching for positions, in a population.

In the past two decades criminologists have broadened the methods used to measure labor markets and how they affect criminality (Crutchfield, 1989; Lee and Slack, 2008). To be sure, unemployment rates remain an often-used indicator (Baron, 2008; Worrall, 2008). The primary reason that some have used other measures of work force participation, or labor market activity, is that the unemployment rate is a relatively narrow indicator. After all, all jobs are not created equal (full versus part time, under-employment, etc.) and a growing literature indicates that while some jobs dampen the probability of criminal behavior, others do not (Wadsworth, 2006).

Duel labor market theory and criminology

In recent decades, Steffensmeier and Haynie (1998) and Crutchfield (1989) have argued for a broader conception of employment to study crime rates. Their conceptualizations were drawn from social stratification literature. Crutchfield used dual labor market theory (1989), which dichotomizes jobs into primary-sector (jobs with good pay, benefits, opportunities for advancement, and relative job security; good jobs or family wage jobs) and secondary-sector jobs (positions with low pay, few if any benefits, little or no opportunity for advancement, and very limited job security).

Duel labor market theory states that workers in secondary-sector jobs, due to the job instability, do not form attachments and social ties to co-workers. Their social ties are formed with those in their community rather than in the workplace. This is in contrast to primary-sector workers who are more likely to develop ties to fellow co-workers (Kalleberg and Sorensen, 1979; Piore, 1975). The unstable, low benefits, unlikely promotions, and poor pay of secondary-sector jobs make it less likely that workers will bond to them. Losing such jobs do not have the same costs as losing good, well-paying primary-sector jobs that a person can build a future around. Consequently, employment in each of these sectors not only affects income, but also affects other areas of one's life as well.

For the criminological literature this has implications for multiple theories of crime. Control Theory posits that the lack of attachment to important institutions and units of society, such as work for adults, may weaken an individual's bonds with conventional society, making them more crime prone (cf. Sampson and Laub, 1993). Crutchfield (1989) argued that when a critical mass of such unbonded, unemployed or marginally employed people live in proximity to each other, a lifestyle pattern develops that increases the likelihood of the motivated (to crime) actors, potential victims and absence of guardians, which are central to the routine activities approach (Cohen and Felson, 1979), coming together to form a criminogenic circumstance. Alternatively one can also see how dual labor market theory's conceptions of a segmented labor market, into primary and secondary sectors, might also complement strain or sub-cultural explanations of crime and delinquency.

Duel labor market theory highlights why focusing on unemployment is insufficient to understand the broader impacts of the labor market and the economy on crime. We turn now to illustrating how these notions can be used empirically to build a better understanding of the association between labor markets and crime.

Exemplary studies on the labor market/ crime relationship

Three studies provide good examples of using both census and survey data to study the association between labor markets and crime. Crutchfield and Pitchford (1997) used the National Longitudinal Surveys of Youth (NLSY); Bellair et al.'s (2003) analyses used data from The National Longitudinal Study of Adolescent Health (Add Health); and Crutchfield, Matsueda and Drakulich (2006) used the Seattle Neighborhoods and Crime Survey (SNCS). We will briefly summarize these studies here and then use them later to illustrate the use of individual survey data with census data to do multi-level modeling of relationships between labor markets and crime and delinquency. The NLSY and the Add Health surveys were of national samples, and the SNCS is as an example of a local survey.

Crutchfield and Pitchford (1997), using the initial wave (1979) of the young adult portion (18 and older) in the NLSY sample, in conjunction with their geocoded county of residence data, studied labor force participation, local context, and criminal involvement. Table 10.1, taken from ordinary least squares (OLS) regression analyses, presents standardized regression coefficients from his study. Counties were used for the macro level as a means of measuring social characteristics of the local labor market. The NLSY also includes geo-codes for respondents' census tract of residence, and more is given on those data later.

In the first column of Table 10.1 analyses using just the individual (micro) level variables are included. Column two adds county (macro) level variables and column three includes an interaction term created by multiplying individual time out of the labor force by county level unemployment rates. This was a standard way of examining micro/macro effects before the popularization of superior, contemporary multi-level modeling capacities (discussed later). We would like to highlight three results presented here. First, 'time out of the labor force', a classic dual labor market/ job instability measure, is a significant predictor (but secondary-sector job is not when both are in the model) of violence involvement. Second, of the county level variables, only the percentage of the population that is African-American is a significant predictor. Third, the interaction term for time out of the labor force and unemployment is significant, which means that the former's effect is

Table 10.1   Occupational circumstance and violent crime involvement: standardized regression coefficients*

	Individual level variables only	With aggregate variables added	With interaction terms
Individual variables			
Sex	0.265***	0.264***	0.265***
Race	0.038***	0.027*	0.027*
Age	−0.087***	−0.089***	−0.090***
Marital status	−0.007	−0.008	−0.008
Education	−0.058***	−0.056***	−0.056***
School suspension	0.200***	0.200***	0.200***
In military	0.024*	0.025*	0.026*
Currently student	−0.086***	−0.085***	−0.084***
Secondary sector job	−0.005	0.003	0.002
Time out of lab. force	0.032*	0.033*	−0.133
Job duration	−0.021*	−0.022*	−0.021*
Income	0.001	0.002	0.002
County variables			
Unemployment rate		0.004	0.006
% in labor force		−0.02	0
Poverty rate		0.015	0.009
Population size		−0.011	−0.011
% black		0.046*	0.046*
Interaction term			
Time OLF*% of pop			0.168*
Out of the labor force			
R2	0.169	0.17	0.171

*$p<0.05$ **$p<0.01$ ***$p<0.001$

*From Crutchfield and Pitchford (1997)

'conditioned' by the latter. To explore this further, Crutchfield and Pitchford divided the sample into those living in above-average unemployment rate counties and those living in below-average unemployment rate counties. The analyses (as presented in columns one and two) were repeated for each sub-sample. The time out of the labor market only led to increased violence in those counties that had above-average unemployment. The authors interpreted this to mean that it is in the situation of similarly situated, marginally employed people that being out of work increases criminality. This is a classic contextual effect. The individual-level phenomenon appears in a particular context (here high unemployment rates), but not in another (relatively low unemployment rates).

Bellair et al.'s (2003) article 'Linking Local Labor Market Opportunity to Violent Adolescent Delinquency' is an example of criminological research that investigates the labor market/crime relationship using contemporary multi-level modeling techniques and data sources. They use the National Longitudinal Study of Adolescent Health (Add Health) together with census data to examine the relationship between labor markets and crime, and whether or not this relationship can be explained by mechanisms of family and school attachment, family wellbeing and delinquent peers.

Bellair et al. (2003) use survey data from the first wave of the Add Health study. These survey data are used to measure self-reported delinquency, family and school attachment gathered from both the adolescent as well as a parent of each adolescent. Bellair also uses US census data to measure labor market variables for each county where individual subjects reside. These labor market indicators included low-wage service-sector employment (proportion of county residents that are employed in service, technical, sales and administrative support), unemployment (percentage of county residents who are not working between age 16 and 65), professional-sector employment (employed in managerial and professional occupations), extractive-sector employment (proportion of county residents employed in farming, forestry and fishing), and lastly, county social and economic disadvantage. These county-level indicators are combined in multi-level analysis with individual survey data in order to assess the effect of labor market indicators and family and school attachment on adolescent delinquency.

Bellair et al. (2003) found that delinquency is related to economic and social opportunities for families and adolescents. In particular, low-wage service-sector employment has a positive effect on adolescent delinquency suggesting that in areas where low-wage service-sector jobs are prevalent, adolescents engaging in violence is heightened. Overall, these results suggest support for authors' hypothesis that labor market opportunity influences violent delinquency. The significance of this study is that accounting for the macro and micro context; the authors avoid the pitfalls of only addressing one of these aspects of delinquency; studies that only address micro-level factors overlook the social structural context of behavior, while studies that address only macro factors are often unclear about how structural contexts affect individual behaviors.

Crutchfield et al. (2006) used data from the Seattle Neighborhoods and Crime Survey (SNCS), which were collected in 2002, along with data from the US Bureau of the Census, and the Seattle Police Department. The SNCS is a survey of approximately 5,000 households. This survey, similar to one conducted in Brisbane Australia, which will be briefly discussed later, used a number of items comparable to those collected by Sampson and his colleagues in the Project on Human Development in Chicago Neighborhoods (PHDCN), which will also be briefly discussed shortly. Crutchfield et al.'s purpose was to investigate if the patterns of labor market participation would help us to understand the observed relationship between racial/ethnic composition and neighborhood violence rates.

Like Bellair et al. (2003), Crutchfield et al. used multi-level modeling in their analyses, but while the former focused on individuals and considered their social context, the latter's focus is on the neighborhood. Individual responses to survey items are used to 'inform' about neighborhood characteristics. Crutchfield et al. used census data measures for the census tracts/neighborhoods where respondents live.

Figures 10.1 and 10.2 are taken from Crutchfield et al. (2006). Figure 10.2 displays the distribution of race and ethnic groups in the city (taken from the US census). As is true for all American cities, Seattle is, to a measurable extent, racially residentially segregated, but not nearly as much as some

other places. Figure 10.1 shows the distribution of 2002–2003 average yearly violent crime rates (black dots), which were taken from the Seattle Police Department's Annual Reports, and labor instability as an index across Seattle neighborhoods (also gathered from the census) which combines the unemployment rate and percent in secondary-sector occupations that was described previously. Other variables included in the analyses (e.g. social disorder which was measured by a series of items that asked respondents about how neighbors respond to local problems) were taken from the SNCS. Neighborhoods clustered in the center of the map are higher in both violent crime and labor instability. If readers compare Figures 10.1 and 10.2 one quickly notices these areas of high crime and labor instability are also the same neighborhoods that have great ethnic heterogeneity. Readers might note that dual labor market theory was initially developed to help to explain the long-term disadvantage of racial and ethnic minorities.

Crutchfield et al.'s (2006) major findings were that neighborhood racial composition predicts labor market marginality. Where more African-Americans live, workers are more likely to be unemployed or working in secondary-sector jobs. In turn, this labor market marginality leads to increased disorder, which is related to higher levels of violence. Higher levels of violence in minority communities can thus be attributed to labor market stratification.

These three studies each combine individual (micro) and aggregate (macro) level data to examine aspects of labor market participation and crime. Crutchfield and Pitchford (1997) and Bellair et al. (2003) use counties as the macro level, while Crutchfield et al. (2006) studied individuals nested in neighborhoods (census tracts). Crutchfield and Pitchford use the older methodological approach, combining macro-level data in OLS regressions with individual data and with micro/macro interaction terms. Bellair et al. and Crutchfield et al. both use multi-level modeling techniques, which is the current state of the art (more on this later). Together, these three studies illustrate the kinds of research questions that criminologists are using these types of data and methods to address about the relationships between labor market indicators and crime and delinquency.

MEASURING LABOR MARKET INDICATORS IN CRIME STUDIES

As discussed previously, there are multiple indicators that can be used for studying the labor market/crime relationship. Here we outline some of

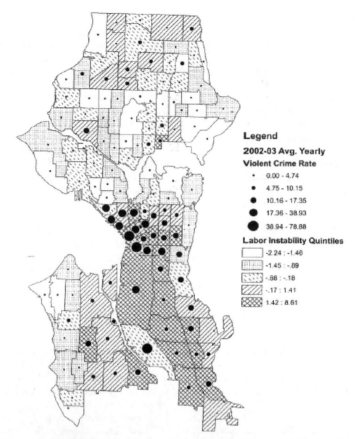

Figure 10.1   2000 Seattle labor market instability by 2002–2003 average yearly violent crime rate. Taken from Crutchfield et al. (2006)

the most common ways that labor market participation can be measured, sources for these measures (from census data and surveys), and examples of criminology that have found these measures useful in studying the labor market/crime relationship. We begin with unemployment as an indicator since, even though we have already discussed it as being an insufficient indicator for understanding economic impacts on crime, it can still be useful in conjunction with other labor market indicators or even a stand-alone measure for some research questions.

Unemployment

The unemployment rate is a measure of people who are out of work and are currently seeking employment. The best measure of unemployment within the US is the Current Population Survey (CPS); a monthly survey of houses which is conducted by the US Bureau of the Census for the

Bureau of Labor Statistics (http://www.census.gov/cps/).[1] Using unemployment as a labor market indicator, Cantor and Land (1985) explore the relationship between unemployment rates and crime rate from 1946 to 1982 and find that, contrary to the expectations of many, unemployment is negatively related to crimes of homicide, burglary, robbery, larceny and auto theft. When unemployment increases, these crimes decrease. They conclude that this is a consequence of reduced public activity when fewer people are working, and because when people spend more time at home, and not going to work, they are guardians against their own and their property's victimization.

Labor force participation/marginal employment

The combination of the unemployment rate and percent of adults working in secondary-sector jobs

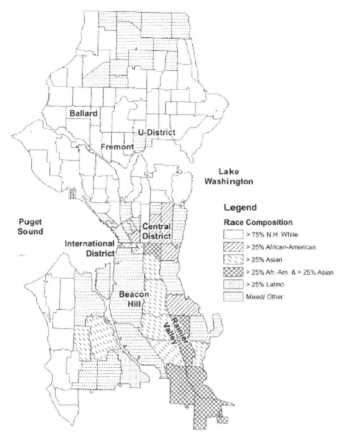

Figure 10.2   2000 Seattle race composition categories and neighborhood names. Taken from Crutchfield et al. (2006)

has been used in several studies to measure neighborhood labor market participation (Crutchfield, 1989; Krivo and Peterson, 2004; Peterson and Krivo, 2005). The division of census tract adults working in the primary and secondary sectors was divided using dual labor market theory conceptualization. Crutchfield (1989: 497) divided US Bureau of the Census categories to define primary- and secondary-sector workers. Placed in the primary sector were managers and professionals, technical, sales and administrative support, precision production, crafts, repair persons, machine operators, assemblers and inspectors, transportation, and material-moving occupations. Placed in the secondary sector were service workers, machine handlers, equipment cleaners, helpers and laborers. The logic for combining the percent unemployed and the percent working in secondary-sector jobs also comes from dual labor market theory. Since secondary-sector employment is unstable, with workers moving in

and out of the active labor force, and the unemployed are people actively searching for jobs, these two indicators are conceptually similar, thus the combination. The new indicator was created by creating Z-scores for both variables and then adding them together. Crutchfield (1989) and Crutchfield et al. (1999) used this combination to measure unstable or marginal employment for the census tract work forces. Unstable employment or 'labor market marginality' has been used to effectively predict violent crime in a number of cities, but not everywhere (see Crutchfield et al., 1999).

The distinction between primary- and secondary-sector occupations is clearly not based simply on income or professionalization, instead it relies on dual labor market logic that groups positions according to job quality characteristics mentioned earlier such as pay level, benefits, job security, and so on. For more on this theory and defining primary- and secondary-sector jobs see Kalleberg and Sorensen (1979) or Piore (1969).

Wages

Gould et al. (2002) use the national average wage in connection with unemployment rates to explain young and unskilled male crime. Gould et al. (2002) find that while both low wages and unemployment are (significantly) associated with increases in crime, low wages plays a larger role in accounting for crime rates over time. Data on wages were collected using the CPS.

STUDYING LABOR MARKETS AND CRIME USING CENSUS DATA

Criminologists have used census data to study states (Sellin, 1967), counties (Cooney and Burt, 2008), metropolitan areas (Stowell et al., 2009), cities (Krivo et al., 2009), and increasingly census tracts (Hipp, 2007) in their efforts to explore the spatial distribution of crimes. Census tracts are usually used as proxies for neighborhoods. Unfortunately while the US Bureau of the Census endeavors to define census tracts to be consistent with neighborhoods as they are understood by residents, they are not the same. Criminologists generally understand this and have elected to accept that using census tracts to represent neighborhoods potentially enters error into their analyses, but they have to decide whether the benefit of what we can learn about the spatial variation in urban crime warrants using them. In some cities, notably Chicago (Sampson et al., 1999) and New York (Fagan et al., 1998) conventions of which census tracts should be combined to make meaningful neighborhoods exists. Unfortunately such conventions do not ordinarily exist in most cities to guide researchers.

Hipp (2007) cautions social scientists about using the appropriate levels of geographical aggregation in studying the effects of structural indicators, such as labor markets, on crime. Ideally, Hipp suggest that block groups (sub-units of tracts) and tracts should be combined to provide more flexible measures of 'the neighborhood' so that each unit provides a better approximation for what residents consider their 'neighborhood'. In Seattle, census tracts have been used effectively to be to approximate Seattle neighborhoods (Crutchfield et al., 2006), and in Brisbane, Australia, suburbs are similarly used (Mazerolle et al., 2010).

Until very recently criminologists have had a difficult time studying these processes at the neighborhood level, unless one were fortunate enough to be interested in studying one of the small number of police departments that aggregated crime statistics for census tracts and were willing to share those data. But now, the National Neighborhood Crime Study (NNCS), which is available through the Inter-university Consortium for Political and Social Research (ICPSR) at the University of Michigan, is a unique assembly of census data and census tract crime statistics for 91 American cities. Included are data for most FBI-Uniform Crime Reports Index crimes (1999–2001), a large number of census variables that have been historically included in criminology studies and an especially rich assemblage of employment and labor market participation variables. Peterson and Krivo (2005) used these data to explore important new research patterns in criminological research, including the importance of labor market participation.

USING SURVEY DATA TO MEASURE INDIVIDUAL BEHAVIOR

Survey data provides individual-level measures needed to complement macro data. What census data and other social aggregate measures cannot provide are the behaviors, perceptions, values and beliefs (micro-level variables) that respondents have about their locations. In this way, survey respondents can be used as informants about their communities. This strategy for studying more localized crime and its relationship to labor markets, is necessary in order to understand how individuals vary within and across places as well as studying how context helps to influence both individual criminality and community crime rates.

The PHDCN is perhaps the most widely known survey of this kind. This survey was deigned to study how neighborhoods, schools and families affect child and adolescent development (Earls et al., 1995). With multiple waves, this survey used individual interviews and survey responses as well as video footage of neighborhoods in order to gather information about neighborhoods and their residents. Not only are these data rich in physical descriptions of neighborhoods, but also a rich source of information about social aspects of families and schools embedded in those neighborhoods. The SNCS (see previous discussion of Crutchfield et al.) is an example of a survey that is designed in part to use residents as informants about their neighborhood. A third such survey, conducted in Brisbane, Australia will be discussed later.

Strengths and weaknesses of census and survey data

Very long lists of references could be made to illustrate how long and how usefully census and survey data have been used separately to address a wide range of criminological questions. And of course, those who are familiar with that literature would make note of both the strengths and the weakness of both. Using them in combination is one way of mitigating the weaknesses and playing to the strengths of each data source, and this is increasingly being done by researchers.

An important strength of census data is that they include data on entire populations with a rich array of indicators of population variations. Their two key weaknesses are that these data are collected for administrative units that do not necessarily correspond to socially important macro units. For example, community influences frequently cross city limits, but the US Bureau of the Census collects data for cities, counties, metropolitan areas and states (some data are also collected for blocks and block groups as well). A second weakness is that the time between complete administration of the census is rather large; every ten years in the US. For many interesting criminology questions this time between data collections is too large.

Of course surveys too have both strengths and weaknesses. Researchers can customize questionnaires and interviews to focus on topics that they are interested in studying. Another strength is that because the research is controlled by a researcher or a team of scientists, rather than an administrative body (the US Bureau of the Census does include many high-quality scientists, but they must be responsive to concerns, questions, and objections from Congress and other political entities), the sampling strategy can be directly tied to the research questions of interest. For contemporary researchers, there are two important weaknesses for collecting data using survey techniques. First, getting a sufficiently large sample, especially for researchers, like criminologists, who are interested in relatively rare events, they are very expensive. That is, they are expensive to do well. Related to the overall cost are response problems with phone surveys, which are more economical than in personal data collection efforts. With increasing numbers of people giving up landlines in favor of cell/mobile phones, they are more difficult to sample. And, now that many screen their calls using caller ID, response rates have fallen for most phone surveys. Some researchers are exploring online survey techniques, but their utility is not yet clear.

COMBINING CENSUS AND SURVEY DATA TO STUDY SOCIAL CONTEXTS

Survey data can also give us macro as well as micro social indicators that can be used in conjunction with census data. For example, survey respondents in Seattle were asked to report their income, size of their monthly house payment, educational experience, how long they have lived in the neighborhood, and who they live with. While aggregate versions of these social indicators can also be gleaned from census data, it is imperative that criminologists account for the individual level variation within and across neighborhoods.

The Add Health (Harris, 2009), which was used in the Bellair et al. (2003) piece described earlier, and the NLSY (OSU, 1997), used by Crutchfield and Pitchford (1997), data sets offer unique opportunities for analyses combining census and survey data. Both have very large nation-wide samples. They are very well designed, ongoing longitudinal data collection efforts. And importantly for our purposes here, the respondents/cases in both data sets are 'geocoded'. That is, individual cases can be linked with US Bureau of the Census data. A note of caution is in order though. Because the administrators and federal funding agencies for both surveys are appropriately concerned about protecting the anonymity of respondents, use of geocoded data is very restricted. In the case of the NLSY surveys (The Center on Human Development Research – CHDR – at Ohio State University has several related data collection efforts, which are funded by the US Bureau of Labor Statistics), researchers can apply for permission to use geocoded data that links respondents to their county of residence, provided they meet certain restrictions and provide institutional assurances. CHDR also has respondents geocoded to census tracts, but these data are far more restricted and are generally used only by at the Center by Center staff. There are two levels of the Add Health data. There is a public-use data set that is easily accessible from ICPSR, but for the kinds of analyses that we are writing about here, a researcher will want to use the restricted version of those data. To use the restricted-use contractual dataset a researcher will have to complete a data use and security agreement with ICPSR. Specific geocoded data are not available for use by researchers who are not at the Carolina Population Center, but the schools data (respondents are nested in schools) can be used at the macro, contextual level, and Bellair et al. were able to use county of residence indicators.

Crutchfield and Pitchford (1997) used interaction terms in OLS regression analyses to link micro- and macro-level data. While this was routinely done in the past, because it was the widely available statistical procedure, it violates an important OLS assumption, namely that the data be independent (because of multiple respondents in each county, appending county data to each of those respondents violates this independence assumption). This might produce inflated standard errors, introducing bias into the results.

In recent years multi-level modeling techniques have become widely available and often used to study contextual effects (Sampson et al., 1997). Hierarchical linear modeling (HLM) (Raudenbush and Bryk, 2002) avoids the problem created by not adhering to the OLS independence assumption. These newer techniques were used by Bellair et al. (2003) and Crutchfield et al. (2006) to study labor markets and crime within community contexts.

POTENTIAL FOR COMPARATIVE WORK IN STUDYING LABOR MARKETS AND CRIME

A virtue of census data is that they are regularly collected in many countries, making census data a useful resource for comparative research. Collected on a regular bases (e.g. every ten years in the US, every five years in Australia), census data provide somewhat consistent information (not totally consistent because aggregate unit boundaries sometimes change and some items come and others go) on the social characteristics of both urban and rural inhabitants. In addition, censuses provide social scientists access to longitudinal measures of social aggregates allowing comparison of these units over time. For example, census data allow criminologists to look at how the racial composition of cities and neighborhoods change over time, and how changes in labor market conditions over time might be related to the distribution of crime within or across cities. These data are increasingly being complemented by criminologists using the surveys that we have been describing. These surveys are not, strictly speaking, co-ordinated, but the researchers conducting them have used similar items and discuss with each other how to make the data comparable. Though other surveys will be mentioned briefly later, most of the forthcoming discussion will center on studies done in Chicago (the PHDCN), Seattle (the SNCS), and Brisbane Australia (the Community Capacity Survey – CCS). In order to illustrate the utility of these data and the censuses for comparative research on labor markets and crime, we will compare the US and Australia.

As is the case when using the US census, labor market variables in the Australian census are also easy to categorize into primary and secondary-sector variables. The Australian Bureau of Statistics publishes counts of persons by occupation. These occupations are grouped easily into primary and secondary categories and are available by sex, age, hours worked in each occupation and average income for each occupation. The Australian census is completed in five-year increments and therefore these population estimates of labor force participation are available over time at regular intervals.

Australian and US census data both collect extensive information on employment and occupation for all census respondents. Census data can not only tell us the status of employment (full time, part time, hourly, etc.), occupation type, wages and income. In addition, the Australian census also contains information on average travel time and mode of transport to work, and how long a respondent has held a job. US census data contain similar information regarding labor market variables. Table 10.2 displays comparative percentages of labor market segmentation for Seattle and Brisbane. Though some categorizations are different, readers can see that occupation categories can be created that are relevant to the labor market context at each site.

Table 10.2 displays frequently used population characteristics for Chicago, Seattle, and Brisbane. Notice that there are no race data for Brisbane (except for indigenous populations). The Australian census does not collect data of the race of inhabitants; rather, region of birth or ancestry are more common measures of ethnic heterogeneity. So, when doing comparative work where important social features may not be collected, researchers should take care to use indicators that are meaningful in the local context. For example, it likely makes more sense if studying Canada to include Aboriginal population or primary language spoken to measure heterogeneity. If comparing nations with important racial divisions with others with different dimensions of diversity, it is more useful to use a measure of population heterogeneity, such as Blau's (1977) heterogeneity statistic, rather than forcing American (or any other nation's) conceptions and categories.

As seen in Table 10.2, though Seattle in comparison to Brisbane has a larger percentage of workers in the primary sector (85.5 percent), both cities have a similar distribution of primary- and secondary-sector workers. However, when these two categories are broken down, more nuanced differences can be seen. While secondary-sector employment is a much smaller part of the labor market in both Seattle and Brisbane, one difference shown here by the percentage of employers in each sector, is that Brisbane has a much higher

Table 10.2   Occupation counts and percentages of total employed for Brisbane (Australia) and Seattle (US)

	Brisbane		Seattle	
	Count	% of Total	Count	% of Total
Primary sector	**533,637**	**72.8**	**367,740**	**85.5**
Managers	80,336	10.9	155,007	36.9
Professionals	143,463	19.5	99,720	23.7
Technicians and trade workers	103,063	14	8,564	2
Administration	126,924	17.3	NA	NA
Sales	79,851	10.9	78,239	18.6
Machine operators	52,888	7.2	26,210	6,2
Secondary sector	**146,617**	**27.2**	**52,269**	**14.48**
Service workers	63,307	8.6	44,326	10.5
Laborers	70,045	9.5	7,034	1.7
Farming, Fishing and Forestry	NA	NA	909	0.2
Inadequate description/not stated	13,265	1.8	NA	NA
Total employed	733,142		420,000	
Total population of working age	1,249,569		482,589	
Total population	1,627,535		560,752	

In the case of Seattle, Administrative jobs included in the category "Sales" as office jobs

Brisbane data taken from Australian Bureau of Statistics

Seattle data taken from US Census Bureau

population of workers in 'laboring' positions (9.5 percent) than does Seattle (1.7 percent). We draw attention to these differences not because of intrinsic value, but because understanding that census data can be separated into detailed segments of the labor market in different settings is important to labor market and crime research for two reasons. First, although there are some minor differences, these data are comparable across labor market sectors and thus have utility for comparative research. Second, understanding the similarities and differences of labor market sector breakdown in two different settings can help lead to important questions for analysis. For example, it may be interesting to explore the relationship of secondary-sector work and its effect on crime in Seattle and Brisbane, knowing that the types of jobs in the secondary-sector labor market are quite different in each city.

Brisbane is a good example of a site which is useful for comparative analyses. Not only are multi waves of neighborhood survey data available, the historical and economic differences in the Australian city make it an interesting comparison to US cities, especially since data are comparable. Census data in the US and Australia are similarly organized. Just as US census data can be organized by tracts, block groups or larger units of analyses, Australian census data can be aggregated for the city/metropolitan area, down to suburbs and statistical local area that approximate census tracts in the US.

The CCS, conducted in Brisbane, was modeled after many aspects of the PHDCN. It includes many of the same measures about perceptions of neighborhood cohesion, trust, collective efficacy, social ties and victimization. This survey includes three waves of data starting in 2006 and includes 82 Brisbane suburbs, and approximately 2,800 survey respondents. These suburbs are used to approximate neighborhoods. Though often larger than US equivalent of census tracts in terms of physical area, information collected in a pilot study showed that residents do perceive their 'neighborhood' as approximate to their suburb of residence (Mazerolle et al., 2010).

Other surveys with comparable measures have been collected in Stockholm, Sweden (Sampson and Wikström, 2007), and Peterborough, UK (Wikström and Treiber, 2009). Consistent measures across these surveys ask about neighborhood problems, victimization, and social networks. Obviously there is a growing capacity for comparative work that can assess the similarities and differences that contribute to neighborhood crime and violence not only in American cities, but cities around the world.

Comparing three cities

The studies described earlier which used the NLSY and ADD Health surveys in conjunction with US Bureau of the Census data demonstrate the utility of combining these rich sources of data to study criminological problems. Here we will focus on the sub-national study of crime with the use of survey data collected in Brisbane, Chicago and Seattle. The three cities which we will focus on are chosen not only because data is available, but also because comparing them is criminologically interesting. Chicago has long been a center for research on neighborhood conditions (Shaw and McKay, 1942; Sampson et al., 1997); however, some believe that it is not a city representative of most, or at least of more medium-sized, American

cities. Chicago has high levels of crime, racial residential segregation, and a larger population of African-Americans than many other US cities. Seattle too has its peculiar differences that distinguish it from many other US cities; for example, a large Asian-American population, small African-American population, and a very educated workforce, it provides an analytical counterpoint to Chicago. Brisbane, which in some respects is more like Seattle than it is like Chicago, is very different from both in quite interesting ways.

Table 10.3 shows the comparative population characteristics, gathered from US census data and the Australian Bureau of Statistics, for Seattle, Brisbane and Chicago. In comparing these three research sites, it is evident that Chicago experiences more extreme levels of poverty and unemployment as well as crime. The percentage of the population living below the poverty line in Seattle (11.8 percent) is approximately half that in Chicago (21.2 percent). The 15.8 percent living under the poverty line in Brisbane most likely

Table 10.3   Demographic profiles of Seattle, Brisbane and Chicago

Demographics	Seattle	Brisbane	Chicago
Population	563,374	1,763,131	2,896,016
% Below Poverty Line	11.8%	15.8%	21.2%
% Unemployed	3.8%	4.4%	6.36%
% Single Parent Families	10.3%	16.1%	23.5%
% Home Ownership	51.9%	65.9%	49.3%
% Renters	48.1%	29.9%	50.7%
% Foreign Born	18.8%	21.7%	21.8%
% Non Native Speakers	9.3%	37.1%	17.8%
Race and Ethnicity			
White	70.0%	NA	36.5%
African-American/Black	8.2%	NA	35.3%
Asian	13.0%	NA	4.4%
Native American	0.9%	NA	0.2%
Latino	5.9%	NA	28.2%
Indigenous	NA	1.7%	NA
Crime			
No. of Homicides	36	1.5*	628
No. of MVT	8386	580*	35570

* Based on national average per 100,000 persons and registered vehicles

2000 census data used for Seattle and Chicago

2001 census data used for Brisbane

reflects Australia's well-established welfare system. While Seattle and Brisbane have similar unemployment rates, Chicago again shows a more extreme experience of unemployment. In Australia, crime rates at the local or city level are not available to the public, therefore only national averages are represented for Brisbane in Table 10.3. However, is it still evident that Chicago experiences more extreme levels of violence and motor vehicle theft than either Seattle or Brisbane. Comparing three cities here is useful for looking at the differences in the structural context for each city in a comparative perspective.

In a recent study, Mazerolle et al. (2010) used multi-level modeling to look at how neighborhood social ties and collective efficacy effects violent victimization in Brisbane. They found that, similar to results in Chicago (Sampson et al., 1999) and Stockholm (Sampson and Wikström, 2007), collective efficacy is important in explaining the spatial distribution of neighborhood violent victimization. These studies are important examples of how census data, crime data and survey data can be effectively used in multi-level regression in order to account for both between and within neighborhood differences.

CONCLUSION

As we stated previously, criminologists have long been asking about both social contextual influences and employment as important forces effecting crime. What has changed for researchers is the technological capability that geographic information systems, and multi-level modeling have given us to effectively address labor market participation rates as a part of the larger context, and to individual employment within those contexts at the same time. When we combine these technological developments with theoretical innovations, the re-emergence of social disorganization theory, the consequent renewed scholarly interests in neighborhood processes, and the growing recognition by social scientists, including criminologists, it has become increasingly clear that we must use measures of labor markets and labor market participation that capture complex social issues and circumstances rather than focusing only on unemployment.

NOTE

1 A wide range of labor market information is available from this source.

RECOMMENDED READING

To develop a better understanding of labor market complexity and duel labor market theory, we recommend readers look to Kalleberg and Sorensen (1979), Doeringer and Piore (1971), and Piore (1969). Though these might be written off by some as too dated, we suggest caution in that premature dismissal since they provide readers a good understanding of segmented labor markets as discussed in this chapter. To be sure, other developments are occurring in the work, employment and stratification literatures, which remain central and important pieces that make the case for more complex considerations of labor markets than just focusing on employment and unemployment.

We also recommend some specific readings from the criminological literature that center on labor market stratification and crime. Crutchfield's (1989) 'Labor Stratification and Violent Crime' article in *Social Forces* is one of the first pieces of research that develops a labor stratification and crime thesis based on duel labor market theory. Crutchfield uses both unemployment and secondary-sector employment as a measure of 'marginal employment', and finds that the distribution of workers in primary- and secondary-sector jobs as well as the unemployment rate mediates the relationship between poverty and the violent crime rate.

We also recommend Wadsworth's (2000) paper on labor markets and delinquency. This paper brings together much of the recent criminology literature on the substantive topics that we have been addressing here. Furthermore, it is a good example of criminological research using labor market indicators other than just employment. Instead, Wadsworth uses other indicators to contextualize a subjects' work sector: whether subject is paid hourly, steady employment, paid by other means, and whether or not subject is unemployed.

The two pieces of research we feature in the earlier discussion (Bellair et al., 2003; Crutchfield et al., 2006) are interesting for bringing together census data and survey data for studying the relationship between labor markets and crime. However, we also recommend reading Sampson et al.'s (1997) work on neighborhoods and violent crime. Although this piece does not focus on the labor market and crime relationship, it is an important work using multi-level regression methods to study macro and micro contexts of violent crime.

The majority of the statistical methods discussed in this chapter involve multi-level modeling or hierarchical linear modeling (HLM). Where survey responses are nested within neighborhoods, neighborhoods within cities, and cities within states, multi-level modeling allows researchers to look at both between and within neighborhood effects. While there are many resources on the mathematics and logic of multi-level modeling, there are two titles that are most frequently referred and used in teaching. These are discussed in the following, along with suggestions for computing resources.

Raudenbush and Bryk's (2002) *Hierarchical Linear Models: Applications and Data Analysis Methods* is an excellent resource for learning multi-level modeling for data analyses. This text is rich in detailed examples, using nested data sets as well as detailed procedures for basic analyses. In particular, the second edition of this book includes two chapters (10 and 11) that provide detailed examples using the PHDCN (1995); data discussed in this chapter. Raudenbush and Bryk's examples primarily rely on analyses performed using HLM, a widely used statistical package (created by the authors) for multi-level modeling. Within this text, the model, algorithm and the software package itself are described in great detail and thus provide a good opportunity for learning HLM as a statistical package for data analyses.

Gelman and Hill's (2007) *Data Analysis Using Regression and Multilevel/Hierarchical Models* is also an excellent resource for multi-level modeling techniques. This text provides a review of basic probability, statistics and regression as well as detailed explanations of the logic, mathematics and execution of multi-level data analyses. Multi-level logistic, linear and generalized linear models as well as likelihood and Bayesian models are also discussed at length, giving any reader the opportunity to learn the tools of multi-level modeling for their specific data needs. The execution of examples in this text relies on the statistical packages R and WinBugs/OpenBugs. Examples are rich in code and computing help for performing data analysis in these packages.

Two other resources are also suggested for further reading for multi-level data analysis. First, Hox's (2002) *Multilevel Analysis: Techniques and Applications* provides an exceptional guide to modeling various multi-level data including dichotomous, longitudinal, and meta-analyses. Rather than providing step-by-step examples in a particular software package, this text is excellent for leaning about the possibilities available with multi-level modeling. Second, Snijders and Bosker's (1999) *Multilevel Analysis: An Introduction to Basic and Advanced Multi-level Modeling* is another excellent guide to multi-level modeling in general; particularly for its discussion of clustered data and discrete

variables. In addition, their chapter 15 includes a detailed discussion of the various statistical packages available for the analysis of multi-level data, including SAS, Stata, R and WinBugs, and HLM.

REFERENCES

Agnew, Robert. 1992. 'Foundation for a general strain theory of crime and delinquency.' *Criminology* 30: 47–87.

Baron, Steven W. 2008. 'Street youth, unemployment, and crime: Is it that simple? Using general strain theory to untangle the relationship.' *The Canadian Journal of Criminology* 50(4): 399–434.

Bellair, Paul E., Vincent J. Roscigno, and Thomas L. McNulty. 2003. 'Linking Local Labor Market Opportunity to Violent Adolescent Delinquency.' *Journal of Research in Crime and Delinquency* 40(1): 6–33.

Blau, Peter M. 1977. *Inequality and Heterogeneity.* New York: The Free Press.

Blau, Judith and Peter Blau. 1982. 'The cost of inequality: metropolitan structure and violent crime.' *American Sociological Review* 47: 114–128.

Bursik, Robert J Jr. and Harold Grasmick. 1993. *Neighborhoods and Crime: The Dimensions of Effective Community Control.* New York: Lexington.

Cantor, David and Kenneth C. Land. 1985. 'The employment and crime rates in the post-World War II United States: A theoretical and empirical analysis.' *American Sociological Review* 50: 317–332.

Chiricos, Theodore G. 1987. 'Rates of crime and unemployment: an analysis of aggregate research evidence.' *Social Problems* 34(2): 187–212.

Cohen, Lawrence and Marcus Felson. 1979. 'Social changes and crime rate trends: a routine activity approach.' *American Sociological Review* 44: 588–608.

Cooney, Mark and Kallie Harbin Burt. 2008. 'Less crime, more punishment.' *American Journal of Sociology* 114(2): 491–527.

Crutchfield, Robert D. 1989. 'Labor stratification and violent crime.' *Social Forces* 62(2): 489–512.

Crutchfield, Robert D., Ann Glusker and George S. Bridges. 1999. 'A tale of three cities: labor markets, and homicide.' *Sociological Focus* 32: 65–83.

Crutchfield, Robert D. and Susan R. Pitchford. 1997. ' Work and crime: The effects of labor stratification.' *Social Forces* 76: 93–118.

Crutchfield, Robert D., Ross Matsueda and Kevin Drakulich. 2006. 'Race, labor markets and neighborhood violence.' In Peterson, Ruth D., Lauren J Krivo and John Hagan (Ed), *The Many Colors of Crime: Inequalities of Race and Ethnicity and Crime in America* (pp. 199–220). New York: NYU Press.

Doeringer, Peter and Michael J. Piore. 1971. *Internal Labor Markets and Manpower Adjustment.* New York: DC Heath and Company.

Earls, Felton, Steven Raudenbush, Albert Reiss and Robert Sampson. 1995. *Project on Human Development for Chicago Neighborhoods (PHDCN): Systematic Social Observation.*

Fagan, Jeffery, Franklin Zimring and June Kim. 1998. 'Declining homicide rates in New York City: A tale of two trends.' *Journal of Criminal Law and Criminology* 88(4): 1277–1324.

Gelman, Andrew and Jennifer Hill. 2007. *Data Analysis Using Regression and Multilevel/Hierarchical Models.* New York: Cambridge University Press.

Gould, Eric d. Bruce A. Weinberg, and David B. Mustard. 2002. 'Crime Rates and Local Labor Market Opportunities in the United States: 1979–1997.' *Review of Economics and statistics* 84 (1): 45–61.

Harris, Kathleen Mullan. 2009. *The National Longitudinal Study of Adolescent Health (Add Health) [machine-readable data file and documentation].* Chapel Hill, NC: Carolina Population Center, University of North Carolina at Chapel Hill.

Hipp, John R. 2007. 'Block, tract, and levels of aggregation: neighborhood structure and crime and disorder as a case in point.' *American Sociological Review* 72(5): 659–680.

Hox, Joop. 2002. *Multilevel Analysis: Techniques and Applications.* Mahwah, NJ: Lawrence Erlbaum.

Kalleberg, Arne L. and Aage B. Sorensen. 1979. 'The sociology of labor markets.' *Annual Review of Sociology* 5: 351–379.

Krivo, Lauren J. and Ruth D. Peterson. 2004. 'Labor market conditions and violent crime among youth and adults.' *Sociological Perspectives* 47(4): 485–505.

Krivo, Lauren, Ruth Peterson and Danielle Kuhl. 2009. 'Segregation, racial structure, and neighborhood violent crime.' *American Journal of Sociology* 114(6): 1765–1802.

Kubrin, Charis and Ronald Weitzer. 2003. 'New directions in disorganization theory.' *Journal of Research in Crime and Delinquency* 40: 374–402.

Lee, Matthew R. and Tim Slack. 2008. 'Labor market conditions and violent crime across the metro-non metro divide.' *Social Science Research* 37(3): 753–768.

Mazerolle, Lorraine, Rebecca Wickes and James McBroom. 2010. 'Community variations in violence: The role of social ties and collective efficacy in comparative context.' *Journal of Research in Crime and Delinquency* 47(1): 3–30.

Merton, Robert K. 1949. *Social Theory and Social Structure:143 Toward the Codification of Theory and Research.* New York: The Free Press.

Messner, Steven F. 1983. 'Regional differences in the economic correlates of the urban homicide rate: some evidence on the importance of cultural context.' *Criminology* 21: 477–488.

Parker, Robert Nash and Allan V. Horwitz. 1986. 'Unemployment, crime, and imprisonment: a panel approach.' *Criminology* 24: 751–73.

Peterson, Ruth and Lauren Krivo. 2005. 'Macrostructural analyses of race, ethnicity, and violent crime: recent lessons and new directions for research.' *Annual Review of Sociology* 31: 331–356.

Piore, Michael J. 1969. 'On-the-job training in a duel labor market.' In Arnold Weber (ed.), *Public and Private Manpower Polices.* Madison: Industrial Relations Research Association.

Piore, Michael J. 1975. 'Notes for a theory of labor market stratification.' In Richard C. Edwards, Michael Reich and David M. Gordon (eds), *Labor Market Segmentation.* New York: Heath.

Raudenbush, Steven W. and Anthony S. Bryk. 2002. *Hierarchical Linear Models: Applications and Data Analysis Methods.* London: Sage.

Rosenfeld, Richard. and R. Fornago. 2007. 'The impact of economic conditions on robbery and property crime: The role of consumer sentiment.' *Criminology* 45(4): 735–769.

Rosenfeld, Richard and Steven F. Messner. 2009. 'The crime drop in comparative perspective: The impact of the economy and imprisonment on American and European burglary rates.' *British Journal of Sociology* 60(3): 445–471.

Sampson, Robert J. and John R. Laub. 1993. *Crime in the Making: Pathways and Turning Points Through Life.* Cambridge, MA: Harvard University Press.

Sampson, Robert J., Jeffery D. Morenoff and Felton Earls. 1999. 'Beyond social capital: spatial dynamics of collective efficacy for children.' *American Sociological Review* 64(3): 633–660.

Sampson, Robert J., Steven Raudenbush and Felton Earls. 1997. 'Neighborhoods and violent crime: A multilevel study of collective efficacy.' *Science* 277: 918–924.

Sampson, Robert and Per-Olof Wikström. 2007. 'The social order of violence in Chicago and Stockholm neighborhoods: A comparative inquiry.' In Kalyvas Shapiro and Masoud (eds), *Order, Conflict and Violence.* New York: Cambridge University Press.

Sellin, Thorsten. 1967. *Capital Punishment.* New York: Harper and Row.

Shaw, Clifford and Henry McKay. 1942. *Juvenile Delinquency in Urban Areas.* Chicago IL: University of Chicago Press.

Snijders, Tom and Roel Boskersl. 1999. *Multilevel Analysis: An Introduction to Basic and Advanced Multilevel Modeling.* London: Sage.

Steffensmeier, Darrell J. and Dana L. Haynie. 1998. 'Gender, structural disadvantage, and urban crime: do macrosocial variables also explain female offending rates?' *Criminology* 38(2): 403–438.

Stowell, Jacob, Messner, Steven, Kelly McGeever and Lawrance Raffalovich. 2009. 'Immigration and the recent violent crime drop in the United States: A pooled, cross-sectional time-series analysis of metropolitan areas.' *Criminology* 47(3): 889–928.

Tittle, Charles R., Wayne J. Villemez and Douglas A. Smith. 1978. 'The myth of social class and criminality: An empirical assessment of the empirical evidence.' *American Sociological Review* 43: 643–656.

Wadsworth, Tim. 2000. 'Labor markets, delinquency, and social control theory: An empirical assessment of mediating processes.' *Social Forces* 78(3): 1041–1066.

Wadsworth, Tim. 2006. 'The meaning of work: Conceptualizing the deterrent effect of employment on crime among young adults.' *Sociological Perspectives* 49(3): 343–368.

Wickström, Per-Olof H., and Kyle H. Treiber. 2009. 'Violence as Situational Action.' *International Journal of Conflict and Violence* 3(1): 75–96.

Worrall, John L. 2008. 'Racial composition, unemployment and crime: Dealing with inconsistencies in panel designs.' *Social Science Research* 37(3): 787–800.

11

Historical and Archival Research Methods

Barry Godfrey

INTRODUCTION

Crime historians tend not to publish books about methodology. Details of research methodology have to be gleaned from the meager descriptions found (usually in footnotes or in a few sentences at the start of the essay) in academic articles. As social science methods become adopted by historians, as seems to be the direction of travel, we may find that historians devote more and more space to describing the methods and frames of analysis they have used in the research. In conversation, if not in print, social scientists often accuse historians of conceptual imprecision in their methods of inquiry, with some justification. The disinclination of historians to reveal the detail of their methods (or their analytical frameworks) seems to imply disinterest at best, and deliberate obfuscation of unsustainable and unjustifiable research methods at worst. The vast majority of crime historians, however, employ such common and well-known approaches to established data sources, and share such similar epistemological frameworks, that a trust has been established between scholars which (at least, to some) obviates the need for lengthy explanations of methodology. Perhaps for that reason most budding historians 'grow up' with a belief that methods are simple, boring, and a thing which may consume social scientists but with which they need not be overly concerned – a view which therefore has tended to prolong the problem.[1] For historians, the sources they exploit (whether archival, oral or visual) *are* the methodology in the sense that the use of particular sources has generally been established over time. Only when new sources that have not been used before are presented, do historians see it as necessary to have a lengthy discussion of the characteristics of the new source, and how they have been used. The problems of interpretation, accuracy and bias, associated with oral history testimony, say, or with the Ordinary of Newgate's Accounts, or published annual statistics, are well known, and have been discussed in many articles and books (Emsley, 2005; Godfrey et al., 2007a; Perks, 1998). Therefore, when one historian acknowledges that they drew upon oral evidence in their studies, another historian nods, implicitly accepting the limitations of the methodology. This can be frustrating to those who are interested in methodology, and also to those who can see the problems with this opaque and at times mystical process of methods/sources sifting and evaluation. But it gets worse, I'm afraid. As will be shown in this chapter, the subjects under historical study, combined with the theoretical/political stance of the researcher, usually dictate the sources consulted (and therefore the methods). For this reason, historical research is often less conservative and more ecumenical in its approaches than social science research. I must confess myself that I find the rich and sometimes unpredictable mix of methods, quantitative and qualitative data, nationally generated and locally focused, unofficial and official data, often all used in just one historical publication, both exciting and illuminating – for example Cox's (2003) *Gender, Justice and Welfare: Bad Girls in Britain 1900–1950*; or Ford's *Settler Sovereignty: Jurisdiction and Indigenous People in America and Australia,*

1788–1836 (2010). This has been especially true for the last decade or so, when experimentation in sources/methods has produced studies that have taken crime history into new waters, such as Davies's *Gangs of Manchester* (2008). As far as crime and its historians are concerned, the past has never looked better. More diverse sources are becoming available and, at last, research methodologies have started to be articulated to a point which allows historians and social scientists together to begin exploring joint enterprises (Brown and Barratt, 2002).

This chapter begins with a discussion of some of the main texts and records that have shaped the sub-discipline of crime history after Second World War; the sources of historical knowledge which dominated research agendas in that period; and the methods adopted by researchers in the mid to late twentieth century; before discussing the position today, and ending by scanning the horizon for future directions in crime history. Discussing the inter-connections between the use of historical sources and the methodologies employed, the chapter also explores some of the ethical and access issues that historians of crime can encounter in their research. So as to embed the theoretical into the practical, these issues will be examined through a case study of the kinds of historical research undertaken by one team of researchers (Godfrey et al., 2007b, 2011) over the last decade.

CRIME HISTORIANS AND THEIR METHODS, 1945–1990

Clive Emsley stated in the preface to his third edition of *Crime and Society in England, 1750–1900* that crime and policing had been a relatively new area for academic historians when the first edition had been published in 1986, but that, since then, 'they seem to be amongst the most popular areas of British social history' (Emsley, 2005). He is undoubtedly right, and the appeal is not just confined to historians, since social scientists are paying as much attention to crime history as they are to any other facet of criminological research, with historical articles regularly being published in the *British Journal of Criminology*, for example, and crime history modules featuring on many undergraduate criminology degree courses. There are now also a number of articles and books reviewing the development of crime history (some of which are listed at the end of this chapter). Notable amongst these are Joanne Innes and John Styles (1986); Jim Sharpe (1999); David Taylor (1998); Philip Rawlings (1999), Clive Emsley (2005), Godfrey and Lawrence (2005), Godfrey et al. (2007a) and Taylor (2009).

These books demonstrate that crime history is a wide-ranging subject. It encompasses the rise of 'scientific criminology', changing conceptions of criminality, gender, and issues around domestic violence, the criminalisation of youths, immigrants and other marginalised groups, and so on.

Although there are very good crime histories of the Middle Ages and Early Modern period (Beattie, 1986; Sharp, 1999; Shoemaker, 1991) and similarly good studies of the twentieth century are now beginning to emerge (D'Cruze, 2012; Jackson, 2006) most crime history is concentrated around the mid eighteenth century to 1914. The First World War has always provided something of a full stop for historians of the nineteenth century since political and social circumstances before and after the First World War are problematic to compare in a straightforward way (Hobsbawm, 1989, 2001). The 1750 to 1914 period has also been identified as the era when the UK was catapulted into social change to an unprecedented degree. That period witnessed a dynamic development of new forms of industrial production, the growth of the great urban towns and cities and unprecedented population growth. Vast social changes created new social conditions and problems that challenged social commentators, politicians, and policy makers to find solutions, and increasingly these solutions involved new laws with coercive agents ready to enforce them. For example, from 1750 up to about 1850, there was an amateur or semi-professional parish or neighborhood watch system organised by local authorities who enforced national legislation and local by-laws. Then, a more consistently professional system of uniformed police force was developed following the setting up of the Metropolitan Police in 1829. The New Police were then extended across the country until police forces in various towns, cities and countryside areas meant that every place in the UK had a publicly funded force that could endeavor to keep the peace, inhibit crime, and re-assure the public. Of course, as is well known, the history of policing is much contested – with scholars demonstrating the resistance shown to middle-class modes of behavior being imposed on the poor and working populations in the mid to late nineteenth century by 'Blue Bottles', 'Blue Locusts', or 'Domestic Missionaries' (Storch, 1975, 1976). The resistance to national forms of regulation that were maintained at local level re-emerged, to an extent, with wartime regulatory breaches ('spivs' and the black market, for example, and the thousands of black-out infringements prosecuted by air-raid wardens) in the First and Second World Wars; in the widespread use of illegal leisure drugs from the 1960s; and in the debates about the legitimacy and purposes of CCTV (Godfrey et al., 2007a) and speed cameras in the last few decades (Emsley, 1993; Wells, 2008).

In addition to significant changes in the forms of policing, the mid to late nineteenth century also witnessed the rise of a system of mass imprisonment which is now culminating in the highest number of people ever imprisoned in this country and the largest prison population in Europe. In the late eighteenth century, execution or transportation (initially to America, and then to Australia) were the norm for offenders (serious and minor). Eighteenth-century castle-like prisons were used sparingly, did not have a reforming mission, and in fact imprisonment was not well used until the mid to late nineteenth century. At that point, local gaols were joined by penitentiary-style national prisons for more serious offenders. Later, the development of community penalties (which have not featured in many historical studies) reduced the prison population, but failed to curb the upward surge in prison numbers in the last half of the twentieth century. The use of capital punishment declined rapidly over this period in England and Wales, though it maintained a fascination for the British public until its final demise (and I suppose it still does). Together with the formation of a system where the police not only arrested suspects but also controlled the prosecution process, replacing victims of crime as active prosecutors (Kearon and Godfrey, 2007) to the introduction of a professional prosecution system (the Crown Prosecution Service) in 1985; the modernisation of the court system, with the introduction of youth courts and female magistrates (both originated in the first decades of the twentieth century; and the introduction of probation services, community-based penalties and supervision, this period was indeed a dynamic period for criminal justice.

However, probably the most significant event that happened in the eighteenth and nineteenth centuries did not happen in the courts, or on the streets, but on paper. During this period the systematic recording of levels of crime was begun by the Home Office (an organisation which itself grew impressively from six clerks in 1817 to a vast bureaucracy in the twentieth century). In order to feed a growing bureaucratic engine that demanded more and more data in order to inform a polity and a system of government that became ever more interested in crime and its control, an information network was created stretching amongst the courts, the police authorities and the prisons. The documents generated by the criminal justice agencies and by governmental enquiries would form the bedrock of research sources for the first generations of crime historians. In the century after criminal statistics were first systematically and annually compiled, however, crime

history had very few adherents (see Garland, 1985; Godfrey et al., 2007a; Rock, 1988). Only after the Second World War did crime history develop as a legitimate area of study, and the criminal statistics become a tool for research.

EARLY DAYS IN CRIME HISTORY

The most significant figure of post-war criminology, Sir Leon Radzinowicz, wrote his works when the Second World War was a recent memory, and the Allies had triumphed over Nazism. It was almost inevitable that he would have a sense that the world was progressing towards a settled future, with British models of democracy and policing brief adopted throughout the world (see Patapan et al., 2005; Reith, 1943). Radzinowicz was himself a Polish refugee who arrived in Britain in the late 1930s, and stayed in the UK until his death in 1999. He was a major figure in the development of criminology, not least because during the Second World War he established the Department of Criminal Science in the Faculty of Law at Cambridge University, and in 1959 became the first Wolfson Professor of Criminology. Undoubtedly his personal experiences and the period in which he was most productive affected his work, and so too did his benign view of official sources. His magnificent study of the development of criminal justice in the UK is drawn principally from published governmental sources – select committee reports, governmental enquiries, and published annual reports of crime, offending, policing, and so on. His research technique is one that would still be recognised by historians today – he read and interpreted the words of the official documents. Although modern criminologists may find this a simplistic approach (see Maguire, 2007, for a review of critiques of official statistics), it was a perfectly reasonable way of proceeding then, and without doubt Sir Leon's account is coherent and manages to maintain an internal consistency. Prevailing social conditions will always affect social commentaries, and one might have anticipated that the more radical times of the 1970s and 1980s would produce a different view of crime history and 'progress' than Sir Leon's work written in the more settled 1950s.

CRIME HISTORY IN THE 1970S AND 1980S: 'ALBION'S PEOPLE'

The publication of Hay et al.'s *Albion's Fatal Tree* in 1975 marked the start of a huge growth in the number of historians exploring the impact of legal changes on the lives of the poor. This group of scholars posited the view that the law and its apparatus was the mechanism for propping up an iniquitous regime. Doug Hay, for example, outlined how the Bloody Code of 200 offences, which could result in the offender hanging from the gallows, was the backdrop to a system where the poor relied on the rich to support them, and to speak for them when they fell foul of the system of laws designed to 'keep them in their place'. This school of history saw the law as being the tool whereby firstly the landed gentry and then the industrial entrepreneurs could control the newly created working class, making them suitable for the new industrial forms of factory-line production. Two of the authors of this seminal book (Thompson and Hay) produced a range of subsequent publications eventually building to a persuasive canon of work.

Edward Thompson's (1963) magnificent survey of the formation of the working class in the early to mid nineteenth century contextualised his and Hay's views on the structural inequalities the law and its agents enforced, although Thompson and Hay differed in their interpretation of how legitimate the ruling classes believed the laws they passed to be. Thompson and other historians then went on to explain how customary entitlements that country dwellers enjoyed were criminalised in a series of parliamentary acts passed towards the end of the eighteenth century (King, 1989; Thompson, 1975). As the creation of a factory system encouraged workers to better wages, and the new urban industrial towns in the Midlands and the north of England, they were subject to new forms of private and public surveillance and control (Godfrey et al., 2007a: 127–49; Styles, 1983). In the factories foremen oversaw their working behaviour, and in the streets the New Police patrolled, assiduously bringing offenders to newly created local courts – the petty sessions or magistrates' courts – that erupted like boils across England in the later nineteenth century. For Hay, Thompson and others, the systems of control – factory discipline, the police, the courts, the creation of oppressive laws – all acted as layers of authority pressing down on the poor and working classes.

Although Thompson and Hay are often described as Marxists, their theoretical leanings were largely submerged by the wealth of documentary and empirical evidence they evaluated. They preferred to let contemporary documents underwrite their arguments without a great engagement with theory, and the documents they chose to evidence their argument were those generated by the courts – Assize trial court records; Quarter Sessions' indictments; pardons and the remarks of judges when pronouncing sentence over the condemned (for a full discussion of these sources, see Gatrell, 1994, and the guides to official crime history records held by the UK's national repository: http://www.nationalarchives.gov.uk/). Although the records created by the courts were just as official in their nature and origin as those used by Radzinowicz, they read them 'against the grain', determined to find an underlying story. These were also the days when simple quantitative analysis was applied to crime history, and this period first saw qualitative and quantitative data presented alongside each other (Beattie, 1986; Davis, 1980, 1984; King, 1984). The annual recording of crime statistics enabled scholars to contextualise the rises and falls in crime with, say, economic conditions, the development of criminal justice agencies, legislative changes and so on. In practice this again meant interpreting data through comparison with existing historical knowledge about class relations in Georgian and Victorian England, and (various forms of) Marxist social theory. Researchers today have far easier access to similar records to those used by Hay and others through the website: http://www.oldbaileyonline.org/. The project which created the website has digitised all surviving editions of the cases dealt with at London's Central Criminal Court or Old Bailey from 1674 to 1913, and the Accounts of the Ordinary of Newgate (the cleric who recorded the life stories of many of the condemned), from 1679 to 1772 (nearly 200 thousand trial details and biographical details of 2,500 men and women sentenced to hang in London). In addition to the text, accessible through both keyword and structured searching, this website provides digital images of all 190,000 original pages of the Proceedings, 4,000 pages of Ordinary's Accounts, advice on methods of searching this resource, information on the historical and legal background to the Old Bailey court and its Proceedings, and a feature whereby simple analysis can be performed. Statistical analysis of the type and number of punishments imposed, for example, can be cross-tabulated against the gender of the accused, or the type of offence. It must be remembered though that any official record, even when rendered electronically in such a tremendous website, is the result of an unknown number of administrative procedures which may limit, expand, exaggerate or otherwise alter the data. Not least, there is the 'dark figure' of crime, which, if anything, has exercised crime historians even more than criminologists, particularly historians of violence. The 'dark figure' of unprosecuted crime (offences never detected, or never proceeded against) remains, as ever, an unknown (Coleman and Moynihan, 1996).

A great number of criminologists and historians have already outlined the severe limitations of both the national and local series of criminal statistics (see Maguire, 2007, for a review of debates) and by historians (Gatrell, 1980; Godfrey and Lawrence, 2005; Godfrey et al., 2007a; Weaver, 1995; Williams, 2001). Difficulties included changes in the ways that crimes were reported, recorded and categorised. Almost exactly a hundred years before these comments, the situation had been simply and concisely summarised thus by a member of the Statistical Society: '[W]e get what we do not want, and do not get what we do want' (MacDonell, 1894: 516).

The police statistical returns, being localised, would at first appear to offer the most reliable official data (Gatrell and Hadden, 1972: 345). However, we still do not know how that those data were secured and classified, or how the classes into which those data were placed had been defined – the method of data collection was not governed by formal or precise national rules, relying instead on the discretionary judgement of the individual forces themselves. The wording on the instructions for compilation of the category 'crimes committed' was that '[t]he officers of police should enter such cases as "in their judgement" from the circumstances attending them, would, "if discovered" be sent for trial' (Hammick, 1867: 393; see Emsley, 2005: 21–55). Hammick's explanation, in part, for what he believed was the increased proportion of crime being detected and prosecuted after the middle of the century was the 'increased vigilance and efficiency of the large body of trained police' (Hammick, 1863: 424). Contemporaries agreed: 'The zeal and activity of the new constabulary added to the number of apprehensions and committals, though there might be no corresponding increases of actual crime' (see Gatrell and Hadden, 1972: 352–5). For these reasons, many researchers have come to treat statistics not as reliable indices of crime, but rather as indicators of some combination of socio-economic conditions, public anxieties, police practice and governmental policy. The bastions of statistical positivism have crumbled away. Recently, even the 'gold standard' of judicial figures – the homicide rates – have also been questioned. Taylor has formulated a theory of 'managerialism' which attempts to account for the apparent decline in murder prosecutions (Taylor, 1998a, 1998b). His theories, that budgetary constraints imposed by national and local government both restricted lengthy (and therefore costly) investigations into suspicious deaths in the mid to late nineteenth century, and also encouraged the police in the twentieth century to further manipulate crime statistics, are unlikely to be the last word on this subject (Archer, 1999; Godfrey, 2003; Morris, 2001; Williams, 2001).

THE CULTURAL TURN IN CRIME HISTORY: 'DISCIPLINE AND PUNISH' AND ITS DISCONTENTS

At the other end of the spectrum from the 'Albion School', and their reliance on official data, a French philosopher, Michel Foucault, constructed strong theoretical models and allowed others to prove or dispute them with historical evidence. Foucault published *Discipline and Punish: The Origin of the Prison*, in 1975. His most influential book, it focuses on the technology of power. Like Thompson, he was interested in factory discipline, though he never studied any particular factory, and was rather more interested in it as an example of panoptic power (similar to the English philosopher Jeremy Bentham's ideal prison – the Panopticon, see Foucault, 1991/1975).

Marxist historians saw the law as being a powerful tool used by particular groups against the poor and dispossessed; Foucault and the scholars following him in the 1980s were more convinced that power was a force that could temporarily be corralled by groups that were then powerful, but that power remained outside of the ownership of those social groups. Power was evident in language of discipline and that was manipulated or resisted by people in society. For the first time, discourse analysis was applied to discussions of criminality, and this was, in essence, the most sophisticated analytical tool that has been applied to crime history up to that point. This is not to say that previous forms of analysis had produced inferior research, but merely to state that crime history researchers now adopted similar methods to those used by social scientists. The results of Foucault's methods and works were much debated and challenged by scholars in the 1990s (Dandeker, 1994; Leps, 1992), and many of those scholars armed themselves with a new range of sources, and ways of using them.

Gender

Foucault remains influential in criminology and crime history. However, alongside his admirers, Foucault has his critics, partly because of his attitudes towards or ignorance of the complications of gender. The rise of the gender paradigm was just one of the challenges made to crime history which particularly came to the fore in the 1990s (following earlier work in the social sciences and influential studies of female criminality;

see Carlen, 1983, 1985; Feeley and Little, 1991; Heidensohn, 1981; Lerner, 1986; Rafter and Stanko, 1982):

> In recent years there has been a spectacular growth in the history of crime and of the agencies and institutions set up from the late eighteenth to the mid nineteenth century to control it. Many historians have suggested that the police and the prisons are best understood as methods of social control, set up to maintain order in a society undergoing rapid urbanization or to impose the social discipline necessary to capitalism ... A number of key questions have to be answered: What determines public perceptions of the social costs of crime? In what ways do attitudes vary according to the type of crime or offender?' (Zedner, 1991: 1)

The type of offender that interested Lucia Zedner most was the female offender, and her book *Women, Crime and Custody in Victorian England* (1991) examined the treatment of women by criminal justice agencies. She showed that, although women were gradually removed from the prosecution process towards the end of the nineteenth century, playing a reduced role as offenders from the 1850s (when statistics were first compiled) and less and less likely to face imprisonment for their crimes, poor women who could not demonstrate their respectability in court were considered doubly deviant – first, for breaking the law; and second, for not living up to dominant conceptions of femininity. Her work was a reaction both to the lack of gendered analysis in crime history, and also to the growing number of criminological studies which showed that women faced barriers to justice in the modern system. Zedner's ideas about double deviancy have been challenged recently (Godfrey et al., 2005) but her work retains importance, and she has influenced the following generation of researchers (D'Cruze, 1998). Crime histories therefore had become part of a larger project of cultural history and feminist criminology. The greater understanding of women's experience in the past offered a new view to women's experiences in the present. D'Cruze's analysis of police occurrence books (which recorded the daily activities of police officers on the beat) and petty sessions' minute books (which recorded cases of domestic violence dealt with in the magistrates' courts) showed that women had suffered violence in the family home that never reached the attention of the courts, and sexual and domestic violence that, when it was brought to courts, was often ignored or downplayed. D'Cruze has taken sources which were once the preserve of cultural or gender historians and used them for crime history research. This trend has continued with historical studies of

masculinity and violence (Wiener, 2004) and the use of cultural material in research:

New historical sources

Ilustrations, broadsides and cartoons

Punch cartoons (http://www.punchcartoons.com), and the lithographs in the *Illustrated London News*, *Police Gazette*, and other contemporary popular journals, show contemporary attitudes towards crime and offending. Good electronic collections of broadsides can now be found at Harvard (http://broadsides.law.harvard.edu/) and the National Library of Scotland collection of 2,000 broadsides with a searchable index, available at: http://www.nls.uk/broadsides/index.html.

Autobiographies, memoirs, and diaries

From the late nineteenth century it became popular for police officers, prison officers and other officials to set down on paper their thoughts on their jobs and crime in general; these can be considered alongside the autobiographies of offenders and prisoners that have been published (mainly in the second half of the twentieth century; see Benney, 1936; Martin, 1952). Some biographies have been constructed jointly by ex-offenders and their academic assistants (Parker and Allerton, 1962; Samuel, 1981).

Institutional records

Alongside the court records that have been described above, there are now available the records of divorce courts (which could reveal details of domestic violence) and coroner's records (for suicides and homicides). There are also business and staff records which can be used to study fraud and workplace appropriation. These are private records, but many businesses have deposited their historical records in the various county records offices. Lastly, there are the quasi-official records of charities such as National Society for the Prevention of Cruelty to Children, and the Prisoners' Aid Societies, which can reveal details of the voluntary sector's involvement in prosecuting crime and helping offenders after imprisonment.

Films, photographs and plans

These can be fictional portrayals of policing, such as 'The Blue Lamp', which introduced Dixon of Dock Green to 1950s audiences; or factual images – for example, newsrooms of the policing of political rallies in the 1930s; or plans of courtrooms, magistrates courts and prisons, which can

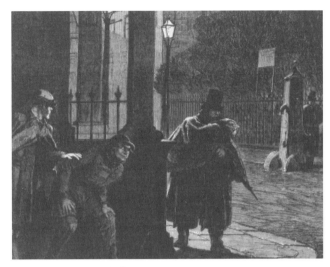

Figure 11.1 Illustration: *Illustrated Times*, 1863

Registered Number
NAME AND PARTICULARS OF PRISONER.
Edward Malia 19
Date of reception
Sessions
3. 1. 14
REMARKS

Registered Number
NAME AND PARTICULARS OF PRISONER.
John Bishop 19
Date of reception
Sessions
3. 1. 14
REMARKS

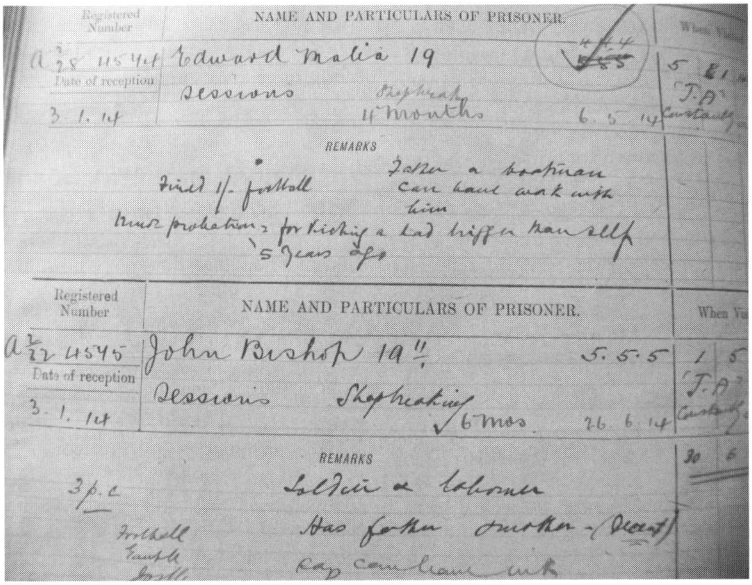

Figure 11.2 Prisoners aid records, 1914

reveal the intentions of the designers. Betham's Panopticon, for example, was never actually built, but his designs show how surveillance had become a dominant aim of penal designers.

New electronic databases

Such databases include the British Academy funded dataset which contains details of prosecutions in the lower courts in Australia, Canada, England, Wales, Scotland, Jersey, New Zealand, and the United States. Approximately 120,000 cases have been recorded. Some contain more details than others (often because of the privacy regulations that operate) and some have had the original details garnered from court records enhanced with data on offenders secured from census data and other sources. The data, which will be available on a dedicated website from 2011, has been entered in both Excel and SPSS

and is designed to be of use to researchers interested in crime rates, prosecution rates, prosecution
practices and sentencing practices, and how they
changed over time. They are aimed at researchers
interested in making comparisons across national
and local jurisdictions for roughly the same period
(broadly 1860–1940) and will complement existing international datasets such as the Criminal
Justice Research Centre at Ohio University
'Historical Violence Database' (http://cjrc.osu.
edu/researchprojects/hvd/) and the Quetelet
Project on Belgian criminal statistics (http://www.
fundp.ac.be/en/research/projects/page_view/
03299003/).

Oral history interviews

These can reveal the attitudes of 'ordinary' people
towards crime and offending, juvenile delinquency, domestic violence, and so on. There are
thousands of hours of interview tapes available to
listen to at The British Library Sound Archive
(http://www.bl.uk/reshelp/bldept/soundarch/
about/soundarchive.html) or at local County
Records Offices. Offering even more possibilities,
many of the hundreds of oral history collections
were formed in the 1980s, and therefore the secondary analysis of transcribed interviews can
extend the reach of historians of crime back to the
1920s. The Oral History Reader (Perks, 1998)
provides a good overview of the problems faced
by researchers using oral evidence. As can be seen
from the two extracts below, both quoted in
Godfrey (2003), oral interviews are not always
straightforward to analyse:

> At the Royal Naval House we got to know the
> police station very well because mother was often
> in there and she used to get escorted home of a
> night time (she was cook at a hotel). She'd call in
> at the police station and always provided with an
> escort home ... She'd been accosted on the street,
> walking the streets. But mother was an attractive
> woman and there was ... she'd be walking home
> at night time, or hurrying home, because she was
> frightened ... and there was steps and alleyways
> and goodness knows what where men could lurk
> (JD, tape 68 Bicentennial Oral History Project, NSW
> State Library).
>
> You could call in at the police station if you
> were frightened, and they would escort you home,
> you see. I remember once I was coming home
> from work when I was grown up and I'd finished
> work at 8 o'clock, and used to walk home because
> it was not that far, and the trams were not that
> frequent. And I was just walking, you know how
> you look in the shops on the way home, and this
> boy must have been following me, and ... every-
> time I'd cross the street or look in a shop window,

> he sort of followed me. And Sergeant Farrell, and
> he knew me cause he knew my dad see, he said
> do you know, called me by name, there's a man
> following you. And I said no. He said I've been
> watching him, so I will escort you home, which he
> did, but you see there was nothing to worry about,
> cause I didn't know about it and I never heard of
> anyone being molested or anything.' (E.G. tape 90
> Bicentennial Oral History Project, NSW State
> Library).

Those two extracts illustrate the contradictory and
counter-factual nature that sometimes presents in
oral evidence ('it was so safe that the police provided escorts'). To suggest that the information
related is complex and relies on the interpretive
skill of the researcher is simply common sense,
and is a point that could be made about all historical sources. However, in oral interviews, there
are numerous references which reveal circumstances mainly hidden from the crime researcher
who relies solely on quantitative or official
sources – situations that were untrustworthy,
places that were to be avoided, suspicious people
not to be approached, crimes never reported to the
authorities, and so on.

HISTORICAL METHODOLOGY IN ACTION: 'WHOLE-LIFE' ANALYSIS

It might be interesting to see how new methodologies are employed by crime historians and criminologists today. For example, in the Leverhulme
Trust funded study of persistent low-level offenders in Crewe, new sources of historical data and
innovative research methods were employed in a
criminological study of persistent offenders. The
small northwest English town of Crewe was
selected because it had an almost complete set of
magistrates court records from 1880 to 1940, and,
because it was a single industry town, we were
able to trace many persistent offenders in the staff
records of the London and North Western Railway
Company. We found that continuity of residence
in one locale, the gaining of 'decent' employment
and the securing of stable familial relationships
were all found to be strongly related to desistance
amongst petty persistent offenders. There were,
however, in our dataset, a group of serious and
persistent offenders who as well as offending in
Crewe, had lengthy offending careers spanning
several decades in various other locations (e.g.
Manchester, London, Stafford, Birmingham,
Leeds, Liverpool) – the highly mobile persistent
serious offenders who appear not to have been so
closely bound in to the processes and structures
which aided desistence from offending for the vast

majority of the petty offenders. The Economic and Social Research Council (ESRC) funded us to examine whether the factors which helped petty criminals to stop offending were absent in the lives of serious offenders, and, by and large, that is what we did in fact find.

Both of these projects used similar records and similar methods to construct the lives of offenders who were operating between 1850 and 1940. For the Leverhulme Trust funded project (written up as Godfrey et al., *Criminal Lives*, 2007b) we first transcribed every court case in Crewe magistrates' courts between 1880 and 1940. When a name appeared five times or more we searched the local newspapers to see if it was the same person being prosecuted in each of those cases (there are a lot of John Smiths in this world!). If we found that it was the same person, we then searched for their names in each census from 1841 to 1911 and, for each census, took details of where they were living, their marital status, occupation, familial status, and so on. Some eluded us and were excluded from the study. To our surprise, however, we found most of the people we were looking for. Even prostitutes and vagrants, who we thought would be impossible to find, were traceable. We then turned to any other record which would provide information on the people – military records, diaries, family papers, or (in the case of the Leverhulme Trust study) employment records. Many of our offenders had worked in the Crewe Railway Works and every detail of their promotions, demotions, wage rates, disciplinary events, and so on, were recorded there. The ESRC study into offenders who were subject to the provisions of habitual offender legislation (written up as *Serious Offenders*, Godfrey et al., 2011) also drew on local and national registers of serious offenders. These documents recorded the antecedent records of previous offences and where they had been committed, the details of punishment, the physical features of the offender (tattoos and scars included) and usually there was a photograph of the offender attached.

Whole-life analysis: constructing life grids

We entered these details into life grids (see Table 11.1) in order to make understandable biographies that could be analysed. We were able to understand the progress of a person's life, how their offending related to life events such as marriage or having children, or was related to periods of punishment and supervision.

There were, of course, some limitations to this methodology. We relied heavily on official records (either generated by the police and the courts, or by other official bodies such as the registers of births, marriages and deaths). We did not have the benefit of self-report studies or interview data – not an unusual state of affairs for researchers of nineteenth century offenders. We were therefore left to make some assumptions – take, for example, the case of a man who had never offended in his life and had reached the age of 50 when his wife died, he then appeared in court for numerous cases of drunkenness and disorderliness. We assumed that the death of his wife caused a life-crisis event which turned him towards alcohol and the attention of the police, rather than any other reason. We also found that details of the lives of some of our offenders were impossible to find for the 1930s and 1940s. This was because our access to court records was sometimes restricted (see essays in Williams, 2004, about the preservation of court records). We were able to follow offenders in magistrates' court records until 1940 – and up to 1970 had we wished. However, the Habitual Offender Registers were closed after 1930. In general the rule which is usually adopted by county records offices (where most lower court records are kept for this period) is a 30-year closure which is designed to protect the identity of people convicted in that period. Some insist on a 75- or even 100-year closure period for reasons which are hard to determine let alone understand – the courts have always been open to the public, and trials are written up by newspapers (which are not restricted in any way). There is more reason for the closure of youth court records because youth courts are not open to the public, and it seems sensible to protect youth from their indiscretions which might damage their chances of gaining employment as an adult. Most archivists take a sensible line and will allow reasonable access to bona fide researchers so long as the names of people named in the records are anonymised, or (occasionally) as long as any images taken by digital camera are transcribed and then destroyed. The time it takes to negotiate access to records should not be under-estimated however (in New Zealand, access requires a letter of permission signed by officials at the Ministry of Justice which can take some time) and occasionally you may find yourself surprised at the restrictions. For example, in Perth's Central Library, I was not allowed to view oral interviews undertaken with prisoners in gaol in 1991 until I had the written permission of each interviewee – the names of which had been anonymised, and who were virtually untraceable, or traceable but dead. Overall, the methodology that we adopted in our study was a robust one which had significant strengths. Not only were we able to layer data, and link together a range of events in a person's

Table 11.1   Life grid of Wilbur B.

Year	Life events	Employment and addresses	Offending and victimization events
1867	Born in Crewe		
1871		Living with his parents (Alice b. 1843 and John b. Middlewich 1842) at 64 Furber Street	
1874–1880	Absent from school	Living at 18 Gladstone Street	
1881	Absent from school	Apprentice slater working for his father	
1884			Assaulted by Chas Poole.
1886	Marries Sally Pryce	Breaks his apprenticeship with his father and tries to establish himself as a contracted slater	Father sues Wilber for £10 unreclaimed wages. His father is described as illiterate and as never having gone to school.
1887	First daughter Elizabeth born		
1888	First son Wilber Jnr born		
1889			Arrested by PC. Booth and convicted for stealing tools from his employer, he was fined £1-00 or twenty-one days in default.
1890	Second son James born		Drunk in Oak Street, no fine but must pay costs of the case
1891		Slater living at 154 Henry Street	
1893	Second daughter Beatrice born		
1896	Third son Donald born	Living in 15 Audley St, and working as a slater	Drunk in charge of horse and cart. In arrears for General District Rates
1897			Education Act × 7, prosecuted by George Plant, School Inspector. Arrears of General District Rates. Arrears of Poor Rates
1898			Drunk in charge of horse and cart. Education Act × 2. Arrears of General District Rates and also arrears of water rates. Education Act × 2 (both charges were withdrawn)
1899		Self-employed master slater living at 19 Audley Street	Drunk and Disorderly in Audley Street. Education Act × 9, prosecuted by School Attendance Officers, William Thompson and Joseph Owen

(continued)

Table 11.1   Cont'd

1900	Wilber Jnr & James sent to Macclesfield County Industrial School for shoplifting. Elizabeth sent to reform school at Stockport for two cases of larceny, and sending fraudulent begging letters to church.		Industrial School Arrears × 3. Ordered to pay 2s. 6d. weekly
1901	Fourth son and third daughter born (Henry and Eleanor).	19 Audley Street, self-employed master slater	
1902		15 Audley Street, slater	
1903	Elizabeth leaves reform school		
1904	Son Henry dies. Sons Wilber jnr and James leave reform school.		
1905			Education Act, prosecuted by William Whitley, fined 6d. Prosecuted under Street Making Expenses Act, for not paying for Audley Street to be paved, × 2. Ordered to pay by the courts.
1906		15 Audley Street, slater	Industrial School Arrears × 4, settled out of court. Malicious Injury against Education Officer, William Whitney. Neglect of 4 Children (with wife). He is bound over for a period of 6 months, but his wife is imprisoned for 21 days. Education Act (withdrawn).
1907	Sally (wife or sister) taken into Upton Asylum Daughter Elizabeth marries Jerry H Coomber, a Nantwich bus driver.		
1908	Daughter Eleanor sent to reform school.		Arrears of General District Rates. Prosecution by Nuisance Inspector, William Urqhuart (nuisance not abated).
1909			Industrial School Arrears
1910		Unemployed slater, 23 Audley St	Arrears for Poor Rates. Education Act. Industrial School arrears of £3-00. Obscene Language. Distress warrant issued and court allowed to seize goods because fines have not been paid.

Table 11.1   Cont'd

Year			
1911		Living at 25 Ludford St	Industrial School Act × 2. Obscene Language, 10s fine. Neglect of 3 Children (with his wife). Both are sentenced to 3 months hard labour. Prosecutes Terrence Olwins for malicious damage to a window – as a result of an attempted burglary when Wilber lives with mother whilst his wife is in gaol.
1912		Living in Cemetery Road	Education Act. Industrial Schools Act
1913	Daughter Eleanor leaves reform school		
1914			Education Act
1915		Living at 10 Grosvenor St	Obscene Language × 3, 10s fine for each. All in Grosvenor Street Education Act. Reported as having 25 previous convictions
1916	Daughter Eleanor in Rescue Home		Conducing by neglect (with his wife) Eleanor to solicit Paid the fine of £2-00 Wilber thought Eleanor was staying with a married sister. He had been working away a great deal, and he could not control Eleanor. 'The parents had drunken habits and at the house there were frequently drunken carousals day and night.' *Crewe Chronicle* 12 July 1916
1917	Daughter Beatrice dies		
1918	Daughter Eleanor leaves Rescue Home		
1922	Son Donald marries Fanny Light Son Donald dies Daughter Eleanor marries Edward Evans		
1937	Death in Crewe		

life with their offending behaviour. We were also able to do this over the whole of their lives, and even follow this through to their children, and in some cases, their children's children. The life-grid analysis and 'whole-life' methodology has now begun to be taken up by a cohort of post-graduate crime history researchers and, in time, a number of publications will follow which will show how they have used and adapted this methodology.

NEW HORIZONS IN CRIME HISTORY METHODOLOGY

It has become clear that there have been recent developments in crime history methodologies which will bring significant changes. The first is the explosion in sources for crime history, which has been well-covered in this chapter. The second is the overlapping of current historical enquiries into the late twentieth century. More and more criminological studies carried out in the 1960s, 1970s and 1980s are themselves becoming historical sources ready for reinterpretation and for placement within their own historical context. The future is getting closer; the past is catching us up. What was once within the ambit of sociology or criminology is now falling within the gaze of historians, and they will continually redraw the temporal boundaries of their subject.

The third factor is the wealth of comparative research across time and across different communities and nations that has characterised recent developments in crime history research. In the 1980s and 1990s regional studies were dominant, but as the twenty-first century dawned, both crime historians and criminologists have grown ambitious and more expansive in their intellectual and geographic horizons. For example, Emsley (2007) has recently published an overview of crime in Europe; a European-wide network of scholars has been established (the International Association for the Study of Crime and Criminal Justice); and comparative meta-studies are becoming influential (Eisner, 2001). In the last few years even wider frameworks for comparative research are being constructed. When these are joined by non-European based initiatives such as the Historical Violence Database (http://cjrc.osu.edu/hvd.html), and the British Academy Prosecution and Sentencing database (discussed earlier) at the very least a statistical basis for international comparison will be available.

The fourth factor is a developing and problematic area for crime historians. The ethical use of sources which uncover details of the lives of dead people is little discussed outside of biographical research (where in the main it is limited only to consideration of the living relatives of recently deceased subjects). Jane Richardson and I have previously discussed the problems when analysing transcribed oral interviews where the subjects (and their children) may well have been dead for a long time. In these cases, it is not the case that an ethical or sensitive approach can simply be put to one side:

> Transcribed archived interviews are a data source which are becoming more widely used across a range of disciplines. Their use raises important ethical issues, particularly in the areas of relationships with research participants; informed consent; and confidentiality. The existing ethical guidelines which are available for social scientists or historians refer to the carrying out of interviews, but not to the secondary use of the transcripts which sometimes result from oral history or qualitative social research projects [We] therefore question whether the ethical relationship between interviewer and interviewee can be adopted and maintained by the reader of a transcripted interview and suggest that the ethical use of transcripted life-narratives cannot be governed by legal or contractual rules of possession, nor solely by the regulations laid down by oral history/archival organisations (Richardson and Godfrey, 2003).

Even when ethical guidelines are observed, they may have been only summarily consulted without any real engagement with what they are trying to achieve (or prevent), and it may be that a more organic approach is desirable:

> We have noted that some historians and researchers have taken a Cassandrian line: that further ethical guidelines are strangling the discipline of oral history. Indeed, some have suggested that an ethical approach inhibits the possibility of the gaining important or necessary information from interviewees, whilst others may have felt constrained by the imposition of 'ethical straightjackets'. Certainly there is a danger that the more prescriptive ethical guidelines become, then the more likelihood there is of them being treated as a 'tickbox' in the research process rather than as intrinsic to good research practice … This blurring of disciplinary boundaries involves a re-thinking of ethical guidelines and points to a need for development of shared guidelines between history and social science. There may be a need for a different kind of ethical practice which considers areas such as how we conceive of participants, whether living or dead and a distinction between codes of ethics and personal morality (Richardson and Godfrey, 2003; see also Godfrey and Richardson, 2004[2]).

The fifth and final factor is the coming together of crime history and criminology into a form where each can be understood by the other and a common methodological foundation can be built between historical and social science research. There is a view that 'we are all sociologists now'; however, the field of crime history research (and researchers!) is much more complicated than that opinion allows for. It is true that the two disciplines of history and sociology have 'come to an understanding' around crime history research methods, and there has been an acceptance that each of those disciplines has a contribution to make. However, there are many literary and cultural historians who focus on crimes committed in our past, historical geographers who focus of the locus of offending, and they can scarcely be lumped in with sociologists, and nor do they employ sociological methods or theory in their work. In fact, many historians would vigorously deny that they had much in common with their sociological or criminological colleagues – even when they share the same source material.

Criminology, of course, has its shortcomings too, with some of its adherents rejecting all but the topical, and denying or ignoring historical legacies or contexts. Nevertheless, the common methodologies employed by historians and social scientists make me optimistic about the future of crime history research. In the diversity of its forms, and the variety of approaches taken by its adherents, lie its strengths.

NOTES

1 Rather perversely, the chapters on methods, sources and analysis that are contained in unpublished doctoral studies of crime history are inexplicably dropped when the thesis is turned into a published book.

2 We tried to maintain a sensitivity when researching the life histories of our offenders for *Criminal Lives* despite, or maybe because of, the fact that they were deceased offenders who had few others to speak up for them. We did, for example, make anonymous the names of all offenders even when this was problematic (e.g., we described the life of a bigamist who had multiple convictions for drunkenness and disorderliness who went on to father two famous war heroes – whose names were, and are, very well known.)

RECOMMENDED READING

Several review books have already been mentioned in this chapter. The guides to available research sources published by the National Archives also provide information on sources and point out their advantages and limitations. Peter King (1999) has provided a guide to navigating the various sources that can be explored (on the web, in bibliographic databases and in journals for example) in the *British Journal of Criminology*. The publications and websites below will provide a good point of reference for further study.

Fowler S. and Paley R. (2005) *Family Skeletons: Exploring the Lives of Our Disreputable Ancestors*. National Archives of England.

Gatrell, V.A.C. and Hadden, T.B. (1972) 'Criminal statistics and their interpretation', in E.A. Wrigley (ed.) *Nineteenth Century Society: Essays in the Use of Quantitative Methods for the Study of Social Data*. Cambridge University Press, Cambridge.

Hawkings, D. (2009) *Criminal Ancestors: A Guide to Historical Criminal Records in England and Wales*. The History Press, London.

Wade, S. (2009) *Tracing Your Criminal Ancestors*. Pen & Sword Books, Barnsley.

http://www.vts.intute.ac.uk/he/tutorial/history. Part of the RDN Virtual Training Suite, this site is an interactive tutorial for historians aiming to provide information skills training and guidance on using the Internet.

http://www.oldbaileyonline.org/. The website contains images and transcriptions of all surviving editions of the Old Bailey Proceedings from 1674 to 1913, and of the Ordinary of Newgate's Accounts, 1679–1772.

http://www.nationalarchives.gov.uk/. The National Archives is the official archive of the UK Government. The archive at Kew in London holds 11 million records, from the Domesday Book to the most recent government papers. The records catalogue can be searched at http://www.nationalarchives.gov.uk/a2a/. Similar archive collections can be found for Scotland (http://www.nas.gov.uk/); for Ireland (http://www.nationalarchives.ie/); and for Wales (http://www.llgc.org.uk/). The catalogue of the US national archives can be found at http://www.archives.gov/. The holdings of county or state archives are detailed on the websites of most individual records offices.

http://www.oralhistory.org.uk/. The Oral History Society promotes the collection, preservation and use of recorded memories of the past. This site holds details of the activities of the society and some guides to accessing and collecting oral histories.

Academic journals which regularly publish articles on crime history include the English/French journal: *Crime, Histoire et Sociétés/Crime, History and Societies* (http://chs.revues.org/index773.html); social history journals such as *Social History* (http://www.tandf.co.uk/journals/routledge/03071022.html), *Cultural and Social History* (http://www.bergpublishers.com/BergJournals/CulturalandSocialHistory/tabid/522/Default.aspx, *Crimes and Misdemeanours: Law in Historical Perspective* (http://www.research.plymouth.ac.uk/solon/journalVol1Issue1.htm); and criminology journals, notably *The British Journal of Criminology* (http://bjc.oxfordjournals.org/).

REFERENCES

Archer, J. (1999) 'The violence we have lost? Body counts, historians and interpersonal violence in England', *Memoria y Civilizacion*, 2, 171–190.

Beattie, J. (1986) *Crime and the Courts in England 1660–1800*, Clarendon, Oxford.

Benney M. (1936) *Low Company, Describing the Evolution of a Burglar*. Peter Davies, London.

Brown, A. and Barratt, D. (2002) *Knowledge of Evil: Child Prostitution and Sexual Abuse in Twentieth-century England*. Willan, Preston.

Carlen, P. (1983) *Women's Imprisonment*. Routledge, London.

Carlen, P. (1985) *Criminal Women*. Polity, Oxford.

Coleman, C. and Moynihan, J. (1996). *Understanding Crime Data: Haunted by the Dark Figure*. Open University Press, Buckingham.

Cox, P. (2003) *Gender, Justice and Welfare*. Palgrave, Basingstoke.

Dandeker, C. (1994) *Surveillance, Power and Modernity*. Polity, London.

Davies, A. (2008) *Gangs of Manchester*, Milo Books. Preston.

Davis, J. (1980) 'The London Garotting Panic of 1862', in V.A.C. Gatrell et al. (eds) *Crime and the Law: The Social History of Crime in Western Europe Since 1500*. Europa, London.

Davis, J. (1984) 'A poor man's system of justice? The London police courts in the second half of the nineteenth century', *The Historical Journal*, 27(2), 309–335.

D'Cruze, S. (1998) *Crimes of Outrage. Sex, Violence and Victorian Working Women*. UCL Press, London.

D'Cruze, S. (2012) *Crime in the Modern Age, 1914–2000*, ABC Clio, Santa Barbara.

Eisner, M. (2001) 'Modernization, self-control and lethal violence – the long-term dynamics of European homicide rates in theoretical perspective', *British Journal of Criminology*, 41, 618–638.

Emsley, C. (1993) '"Mother, what did policemen do when there weren't any motors?" The law, the police and the regulation of motor traffic in England 1900–1939', *Historical Journal*, 37, 357–381.

Emsley, C. (2005) *Crime and Society in England, 1750–1900*, 3rd Edition. Longman, Harlow.

Emsley, C. (2007) *Crime, Police, and Penal Policy. European experiences, 1750–1940*. Oxford University Press, Oxford.

Feeley, M. and Little, D.L. (1991) 'The vanishing female: the decline of women in the criminal process, 1687–1912', *Law and Society Review*, 25(4), 719–759.

Ford, L. (2010) *Settler Sovereignty: Jurisdiction and Indigenous People in America and Australia, 1788–1836*. Harvard University Press, Cambridge.

Foucault, M. (1991) *Discipline and Punish, the Origins of the Prison*. Penguin, London. First published as *Surveiller et Punir: Naissance de la Prison* in 1975.

Garland, D. (1985) 'The criminal and his science: A critical account of the formation of criminology at the end of the nineteenth century', *The British Journal of Criminology*, 25(2), 109–137.

Gatrell, V.A.C. (1994) *The Hanging Tree: Execution and the English People 1770–1868*. Oxford University Press, Oxford.

Gatrell, V.A.C. and Hadden, T.B. (1972) 'Nineteenth-century criminal statistics and their interpretation', in E.A. Wrigley (ed.) *Nineteenth-Century Society: Essays in the Use of Quantitative Methods for the Study of Social Data*. Cambridge University Press, Cambridge, pp.26–99

Gatrell, V.A.C. (1980) 'The decline of theft and violence in Victorian and Edwardian England', in V. Gatrell, B. Lenman and G. Parker (eds), *Crime and the Law: The social history of crime in Western Europe since 1500*, London: Europa. pp.238–337.

Godfrey, B. (2003) 'Counting and accounting for violence', *British Journal of Criminology*, 43, 2.

Godfrey, B., Cox, D. and Farrall, S. (2007b) *Criminal Lives: Family, Employment and Offending*. Clarendon Series in Criminology, Oxford University Press, Oxford.

Godfrey, B., Cox, D. and Farrall, S. (2011) *Serious Offenders*. Clarendon, Oxford.

Godfrey, B. Farrall, S. and Karstedt, S. (2005) 'Explaining gendered sentencing patterns for violent men and women in the late Victorian and Edwardian period', *British Journal of Criminology*, Autumn, 45: 5, 696–720.

Godfrey, B. and Lawrence, P. (2005) *Crime and Justice 1750–1950*. Willan, Cullompton.

Godfrey, B., Lawrence, P. and Williams, C. (2007a) *History and Crime*. Sage, London.

Godfrey, B. and Richardson, J. (2004) 'Loss, collective memory and transcripted oral histories', *International Journal of Social Research Methodology*, 7(2), 143–155. Reprinted in B. Harrison (2008) *Life Story Research*. Sage, London.

Hammick, J.T. (1867) 'On the judicial statistics of England and Wales, with special reference to the recent returns relating to crime', *Transactions of the National Association for the Promotion of Social Sciences*, 30.

Hay, D. (1975) 'Property, authority and the criminal law', in L. Hay et al. (eds) *Albion's Fatal Tree. Crime and Society in Eighteenth-Century England* (pp. 17–63). Allen Lane, London.

Hay, D., Linebaugh, P., Rule, J., Thompson, E.P. and Winslow, C. (1975) *Albion's Fatal Tree: Crime and Society in Eighteenth-Century England*. Penguin, Harmondsworth.

Heidensohn, F. (1981) 'Women and the penal system', in A. Morris and L. Gelsthorpe (eds) *Women and Crime*. Cropwood Conference Series 13, Cambridge.

Hobsbawm, E. (1989) *Age of Empire, 1875–1914*. Vintage, London.

Hobsbawm, E. (2001) *The Age of Extremes: A History of the World, 1914–1991*. Peter Smith, London.

Innes, J. and Styles, J. (1986) 'The crime wave: Recent writing on crime and criminal justice in eighteenth-century England', *Journal of British Studies*, 25(4), 380–435.

Jackson, L. (2006) *Women Police: Gender, Welfare and Surveillance in the Twentieth Century,*. Manchester University Press, Manchester.

Kearon, T. and Godfrey, B. (2007) 'Setting the scene: the history of victims' in S. Walklate (ed.) *The Handbook of Victims and Victimology*. Willan, Cullompton.

King, P.J.R. (1984) 'Decision makers and decision-making in the English criminal law, 1750–1800', *Historical Journal*, 27, 25–58.

King, P. (1989) 'Gleaners, farmers and the failure of legal sanctions in England, 1750–1850' *Past and Present*, 125, 116-50

King, P. (1999) 'Locating histories of crime: a bibliographical study', *British Journal of Criminology*, 39, 161–174.

Leps, M.-C. (1992) *Apprehending the Criminal: The Production of Deviance in Nineteenth-century Discourse*. Duke University Press, Durham, NC.

Lerner, G. (1986) *The Creation of Patriarchy*. Oxford University Press, New York.

MacDonell, J. (1894) 'Statistics of litigation in England and Wales since 1859', *Transactions of the National Association for the Promotion of Social Sciences*, 54.

Maguire, M. (2007) 'Crime data and statistics', in M. Maguire, R. Morgan and R. Reiner (eds) *Oxford Handbook of Criminology*. Oxford University Press, Oxford.

Martin, J. (1952) *My Life in Crime. The Autobiography of a Professional Criminal*. Victor Gollancz, London.

Morris, R.M. (2001) 'Lies, damned lies, and criminal statistics: Reinterpreting criminal statistics in England and Wales'', *Crime, Histoire et Sociétés/Crime, History and Societies*, 5(1), 111–127.

Parker, T. and Allerton, R. (1962) *The Courage of His Convictions*, Hutchinson, London.

Patapan, H., Wanna, J. and Weller, P. (2005) *Westminster Legacies: Democracy and Responsible Government in Asia and the Pacific*. UNSW, Sydney.

Perks, R. (1998) *Oral History Reader*. Routledge, London.

Radzinowicz, L. and Hood, A. (1990) *A History of English Criminal Law and its Administration Since 1750, Vol. V: The Emergence of Penal Policy*. Clarendon, Oxford.

Rafter, N. and Stanko, E. (1982) *Judge, Lawyer, Victim, Thief*. Northeastern University Press, Boston.

Rawlings, P. (1999) *Crime and Power. A History of Criminal Justice 1688–1998*. Longman, London.

Reith, C. (1943) *British Police and the Democratic Ideal*. Oxford University Press, London.

Richardson, J. and Godfrey, B. (2003) 'Towards ethical practice in the use of transcribed oral interviews', *International Journal of Social Research Methodology*, 6(4), 200–214.

Rock, P. (1988) *A History of British Criminology*. Clarendon, Oxford.

Samuel, R. (1981) *Chapters in the Life of Arthur Harding*. Routledge, London.

Sharpe, J.A. (1999) *Crime in Early Modern England, 1550–1750*. Longman, London.

Shoemaker, R. (1991) *Prosecution and Punishment: Petty Crime and the Law in London and Rural Middlesex, 1660–1725*. Cambridge University Press, Cambridge.

Storch, R. (1975) 'The plague of blue locusts: police reform and popular resistance in northern England 1840–57', *International Review of Social History*, 20, 61–90.

Storch, R. (1976) 'The policeman as domestic missionary: urban discipline and popular culture in Northern England, 1850–1880', *Journal of Social History*, IX, 481–511.

Styles, J. (1983), 'Embezzlement, industry and the law in England, 1500–1800', in M. Berg, P. Hudson and M. Sonescher (eds) *Manufacture in Town and Country before the Factory*. Cambridge University Press, Cambridge.

Taylor, D. (1998) *Crime, Policing and Punishment in England, 1750–1914*, Macmillan, Basingstoke.

Taylor, D. (2009) *Hooligans, Harlots, and Hangman: Crime and Punishment in Victorian Britain*. ABC Clio, Santa Barbara.

Taylor, H. (1998a) 'Rationing crime: The political economy of criminal statistics since the 1850s', *Economic History Review*, 49(3), 569–590.

Taylor, H. (1998b) 'The politics of the rising crime statistics of England and Wales', *Crime Histoire and Societies: Crime, History and Societies*, 1(2), 5–28.

Thompson, E.P. (1963) *The Making of the English Working Class*. Penguin, London.

Thompson, E.P. (1975) *Whigs and Hunters: The Origins of the Black Act*. Allen Lane, London.

Weaver, J. (1995) *Crimes, Constables and Courts*. McGill-Queen's University Press, Montreal.

Wells, H. (2008) 'The techno-fix versus the fair cop: procedural (in)justice and automated speed limit enforcement', *British Journal of Criminology*, 48, 798–817.

Wiener, M. (2004) *Men of Blood*. Cambridge University Press, Cambridge.

Williams, C. (2000) 'Counting crimes or counting people: some implications of mid-nineteenth century British police returns', in *Crime, Histoire & Sociétés/Crime, History & Societies*, 4(2), 77–93.

Williams, C. (2004) *Giving the Past a Future: Preserving the Heritage of the UK's Criminal Justice System*. Francis Boutle, London.

Zedner, L. (1991) *Women, Crime and Custody in Victorian England*. Oxford University Press, Oxford.

12

The Making of the Global Terrorism Database and Its Applicability to Studying the Life Cycles of Terrorist Organizations

Laura Dugan

INTRODUCTION

Until the most recent decade, criminologists have contributed very little to the understanding of terrorist violence or the behaviors of those who perpetrate it. Yet, the field of criminology is explicitly purposed to deepen our knowledge about the causes, patterns and consequences of law breaking, including all extralegal violence, which certainly characterizes terrorism. In their essay, LaFree and Dugan (2004) challenge criminologists to expand their expertise by applying criminological ideas and methods to the study of terrorism and those who perpetrate it. Our discipline is well-versed in systematically examining patterns of illicit activity and drawing conclusions based on objective empirical evidence – a research practice that is much needed in the study of terrorist behavior.

In fact, after scanning several reviews of the terrorism literature, it becomes clear that until the September 11th terrorist attacks in 2001, scholarly work designed to systematically examine the activities of terrorist organizations was surprisingly rare. Thirteen years before the historic September 11th attacks, Schmid and Jongman

(1988: 177) conducted an extensive review of the terrorism literature and characterized it as 'impressionistic, superficial, and at the same time often also pretentious, venturing far-reaching generalizations on the basis of episodal evidence'. They continue to describe it as 'too often narrative, condemnatory, and prescriptive' (ibid: 179). Little has changed since that assessment according to a more recent account of the literature by Kennedy and Lum (2003). Between 1975 and 2002, 96 per cent of all the terrorism-related articles in peer reviewed journals were characterized as 'thought pieces', lacking any systematic case study or empirical analyses. Furthermore, more than half (54 percent) of all articles covering the 27-year period were published in the last two years, 2001 and 2002, demonstrating the increased interest among scholars and funders to better understanding terrorism since the September 11th attacks (Kennedy and Lum, 2003). Despite the demand for high-quality empirical and generalizeable research on terrorism, without data that was recently compiled by two criminologists (including this author) that systematically documents terrorist attacks our understanding of terrorists might have remained centered on case studies that provide in-depth views of only the most active organizations, lacking generalization to other, less notorious, yet menacing groups.

Some of the most studied terrorist organizations include the Irish Republican Army (IRA) who mostly attack British targets in Northern Ireland and other parts of the UK (Bell, 1980; Campbell and Connolly, 2003; Horgan and Taylor, 1997; O'Leary, 2005; O'Leary and McGarry, 1993; LaFree et al., 2009; Peroff and Hewitt, 1980; Soule, 1989), Euskadi ta Askatasuna (ETA) or Basque Homeland and Freedom who fight for Basque independence in Spain (Clark, 1984; Gillespie, 1999; Reinares, 2004; Sanchez-Cuenca, 2007; Shepard, 2002), Sendero Luminoso or the Shining Path, a communist organization in Peru (Gorriti, 1999; McCormick, 2001; Werlich, 1984), and the Palestinian Liberation Organization (PLO) in Israel and the Palestinian Territories (Becker, 1985; Cobban, 1984). Scholars have translated documentation on and communiqués by these and other clandestine groups into insightful discussions on topics such as terrorist organizational structure (Crenshaw 2001), terrorist tactics (Jackson et al., 2005), effectiveness of counter-terrorist strategies (LaFree et al., 2009; Soule, 1989), terrorist mindsets (Cordes, 2001), and how terrorist groups end (Cronin, 2006; Jones and Libicki, 2008; United States Institute for Peace, 1999). While such scholarship is crucial for efforts to end terrorism, their conclusions are based on only the most conspicuous terrorist organizations. Further, these micro-investigations were conducted in the absence of the broader, more global view of all terrorist organizations and their campaigns. In order to capture a more objective characterization of terrorist organizations, scholars must draw upon the entire universe of terrorist groups. Until the advent of a comprehensive database that captures terrorist incidents across the globe over an extended period of time (see Box 12.1), this task would have been deemed impossible. This chapter introduces the Global Terrorism Database (GTD) and shows how it can be used to study the patterns of activity for all terrorist organizations across the globe. The recently compiled GTD chronicles terrorist attacks from 1970 to 2007, making it the most comprehensive database on both international and domestic terrorism. With these data, scholars can finally step back and observe the behavior of *all* terrorist organizations over a 38-year period.

This chapter begins by introducing the Global Terrorism Database (GTD). Here I describe the efforts that went into compiling the GTD, and the implications of using this type of open-source incident-based data to document the activities of all known terrorist organizations. I introduce the

process of transforming the GTD into a database of terrorist organizational activity in order to describe the lifecycles of terrorist organizations. A terrorist organizational lifecycle, in theory, would include information on when the organization formed, how its membership grew, the timing of its first attack, details on all attacks, any splits or transformations experienced by the group, coalition memberships, when its activity ceased, and the date it disbanded. Yet, because the GTD is an open-source incident database, we only have access to information on attacks that are attributed to specific groups (see Box 12.2). Thus, the analysis described at the end of this chapter characterizes organizations by the length of time that the media attributes attacks to them, their attack rates, and their fatalities rates, all characteristics suggesting a high level of threat.

THE GLOBAL TERRORISM DATABASE

In this section, I describe the history of the GTD and the steadfast efforts required to construct the database. In essence, the GTD was compiled through three data collection endeavors, although the data used for this chapter comes from only the first two. Both collection efforts are discussed in detail, with special attention paid toward their merger. This section ends with a description of important problems and limitations that are especially relevant when using the GTD to study the activities of terrorist organizations.

The GTD – history

The GTD began as several stacks of 58 boxes containing nearly 70,000 index-sized cards, each recording the details of a single terrorist attack or co-ordinated attack (often including the perpetrator) for the entire world from 1970 to 1997.[1] This unique database was originally collected by the Pinkerton Corporation's Global Intelligence Service (PGIS), a private security corporation and an offspring of the famous Pinkerton Detective Agency from the late 1800s. The collectors of the PGIS terrorist incident database aimed to record every known terrorist event across nations and over time. They originally collected this information from multi-lingual news sources for the purpose of performing risk analysis for US business interests. For example, individuals interested in the risk associated the moving their business to an international location could hire PGIS to run a risk analysis for the region of interest. In addition, PGIS used the data to produce annual reports of total terrorist attacks by different categories,

Box 12.1 Terrorist incident databases

One of the main reasons the universe of terrorist organizations has never yet been successfully chronicled is simply due to the long-time absence of comprehensive databases on terrorist organizations and their activity. Several organizations now maintain databases on terrorist incidents, including the National Counter Terrorism Center's Worldwide Incidents Tracking System; the Jaffee Center for Strategic Studies in Tel Aviv (see Falkenrath, 2001); the RAND Corporation (see Jongman, 1993); the ITERATE data base (see Mickolus, 1982; Mickolus et al., 1993); the Monterey Institute of International Studies (see Tucker, 1999), and, of course, the GTD (LaFree and Dugan, 2007). All of these databases are populated by scanning unclassified media reports or other open sources that are available to the general public. These typically include wire services, such as Reuters; government reports; and US and foreign newspapers such as the *New York Times*, the British *Financial Times*, and Latin America's *El Diario* (LaFree and Dugan, 2007). Collectors of these data typically employ multilingual staff in order to scan reports from non-English papers. Details of each attack are then recorded in the fields of the databases.

Clearly this strategy is quite unconventional when we consider how crime databases are typically constructed. LaFree and Dugan (2007) discuss the infeasibility of collecting terrorist information through any of the three primary sources of crime data: law enforcement (e.g., Uniform Crime Reports), through self-reporting, or through victimization surveys. They explain that while it would be impractical to collect crime data through media reports, they are an ideal source for collecting terrorism data because terrorists, unequivocally, seek public attention. In fact, Jenkins (1975) points out that terrorists, unlike more common criminals, carefully choreograph their attacks in order to attract attention from the press. This makes open-source media the single most consistent resource for documenting the universe of terrorist attacks.

While several databases have been constructed over the past four decades, only the GTD has attempted to capture the universe of international and domestic attacks over an extended period of time (see LaFree and Dugan, 2007, for a comparison across the databases). Despite knowing that instances of domestic terrorism greatly outnumber instances of international terrorism, until 1998 all existing publicly available databases excluded domestic attacks. While this may seem short-sighted, at first the decisions were appropriate at the time the databases were developed. For example, one reason the RAND Chronology restricted its earlier content to only international terrorist attacks was to accommodate the concerns of the US government at the time it was developed (Dugan et al., 2008). Falkenrath (2001: 164) explains that the exclusive focus on international terrorism is 'an artifact of a simpler, less globally interconnected era'. While today some terrorist groups (e.g., al-Qaeda, Mujahedin-E-Khalq) now have global operations that cut across domestic and international lines, others (e.g., Abu Nidal, Kurdistan Workers' Party, and Popular Front for the Liberation of Palestine) have operations in multiple countries and hence, may simultaneously be engaged in acts of both domestic and international terrorism. By recording only their international activities, we artificially capture only part of the picture. In short, the divide between domestic and international terrorism has become more artificial as cultures become more global. In order to better understand the life spans of all terrorist organizations with relatively little bias, the data source must include attacks by organizations regardless of whether they only attack within one country or whether they cross national borders. The GTD captures both international and domestic terrorist attacks from 1970 to 2007, making it the best data source for this endeavor.

Box 12.2 Measuring the life cycle of a terrorist organization

INFORMATION WE WANT

This includes (1) date the organization formed; (2) how its membership grew; (3) date of its first attack; (4) details on all its attacks, whether recorded by the media or not; (5) whether it split to form new organizations; (6) to which coalitions it belonged; (7) all names under which it operates; (8) the names of all its factions; (9) the date of its last attack; and (10) the date it disbanded.

INFORMATION WE HAVE IN THE GTD

The dates and descriptions of attacks attributed to it by any media source that was captured by GTD staff.

CONSEQUENCE

The life cycles derived from the GTD data only measure the first publicized attack and all publicized attacks afterwards. Any attacks perpetrated by the organization that are unattributed to the group remain uncounted.

such as region or event type, and a narrative description of regional changes in terrorist event counts from the previous year.

PGIS trained their employees to identify and code all terrorist attacks they could identify from a variety of multi-lingual sources, including: wire services such as Reuters and the Foreign Broadcast Information Service, US State Department reports, other US and foreign government reporting, US and foreign newspapers, information provided by PGIS offices throughout the world, occasional inputs from such special interests as organized political opposition groups, and data furnished by PGIS clients and other individuals in both official and private capacities. Although about two-dozen persons were responsible for collecting information over the years, only two individuals were in charge of supervising data collection and the same basic coding structure was used throughout the entire data collection period.

The definition of terrorism employed by the original PGIS data collectors was exceptionally broad, widening the net to capture attacks by even the most obscure terrorist organizations. Definitions of terrorism are a complex issue for researchers in this area. In fact, compared to most areas of research in criminology, researchers studying terrorism spend an exceptional amount of time defining it. Thus, many of the most influential academic books on terrorism (e.g., Schmid and Jongman, 1988; Hoffman, 2006) devote their first chapters to definitions of terrorism. And in fact one of the commonly cited challenges to the empirical study of terrorism (Falkenrath, 2001:165) is that the various publicly available databases have used different definitions of terrorism. We retained the original PGIS definition for the GTD data because it is especially inclusive:

> the threatened or actual use of illegal force and violence to attain a political, economic, religious or social goal through fear, coercion or intimidation (LaFree and Dugan 2007: 184).

Compare this definition with the ones used by the US State Department:

> premeditated, politically motivated violence perpetrated against noncombatants targeted by subnational groups or clandestine agents, usually intended to influence an audience (Hoffman 2006: 31).

The Federal Bureau of Investigation (FBI) gives:

> the unlawful use of force or violence against persons or property to intimidate or coerce Government, the civilian population, or any

segment thereof, in furtherance of political or social objectives (ibid.).

While the Department of Homeland Security (DHS) gives:

> any activity that involved an act that: is dangerous to human life or potentially destructive of critical infrastructure or key resources; and ... must also appear to be intended (i) to intimidate or coerce a civilian population; (ii) to influence the policy of a government by intimidation or coercion; or (iii) to affect the conduct of a government by mass destruction, assassination, or kidnapping (ibid.).

We see that none of the definitions of terrorism used by the three government agencies listed above include threats of force. Yet as Hoffman (2006: 32) points out, '[T]errorism is as much about the threat of violence as the violent act itself.' In fact, most hijackings involve only the threatened use of force (e.g., 'I have a bomb and I will use it unless you follow my demands'). Similarly, kidnappers almost always employ force to seize the victims, but then threaten to kill, maim or otherwise harm the victims unless demands are satisfied. Note also that the State Department definition is limited to 'politically motivated violence'. The FBI definition is somewhat broader, including social along with political objectives as fundamental terrorist aims. However, the GTD definition also includes economic and religious objectives. For example, an economic objective for a terrorist group might be to kidnap a foreign national in order to acquire a ransom to pay for continued terrorist activity.

Based on coding rules originally developed in 1970, the persons responsible for collecting the original PGIS database sought to exclude criminal acts that appeared to be devoid of any political or ideological motivation and also acts arising from open combat between opposing armed forces, both regular and irregular. The data coders also excluded actions taken by governments in the legitimate exercise of their authority, even when such actions were denounced by domestic and/or foreign critics as acts of 'state terrorism'. However, they did include violent acts that were unofficially sanctioned by government, even in cases where many observers believed that the government was openly tolerating the violent actions. For example, many attacks on Israel by Hezbollah are suspected to have been financed by the Iranian government.

In sum, the fact that the GTD data were collected by a private corporation for a business purpose can be regarded as an important advantage over other datasets in order to more accurately link the attacks to specific terrorist organizations. Because the goal of the data collection was to provide risk assessment to corporate customers, the database was designed to err on the side of inclusiveness. The justification was that being overly inclusive best serves the interest of clients – an employee of a corporation about to move to Colombia would be concerned about acts of violence against civilians and foreigners, even if these acts were domestic rather than international, threatened rather than completed, or carried out for religious rather than political purposes. While there is at present no universally accepted definition of terrorism, the definition used to generate the PGIS (and now GTD) data is among the most comprehensive. Thus, the two primary reasons that the GTD is the most comprehensive is because: (1) it includes domestic and international attacks from as far back as 1970s; and (2) its definition is broad enough to capture violent events that other data collectors are likely to exclude.

GTD1 and GTD2: Production of each

From 2002 until 2005, staff at the University of Maryland computerized the nearly 70,000 index-sized cards describing terrorist incidents recorded by PGIS from 1970 through 1997. While the cards all contained similar information (who, what, where, when, and to whom), their design changed three times over the 27-year period. From 1970 through 1985, the PGIS coded each attack literally on index cards with handwritten numbers that represented each item. The coding was unique to each event type, which were assassination,

bombing, facility attack, hijacking, or kidnapping (See Appendix A for a list of PGIS definitions for each event). The card shown in Figure 12.1 is a facility attack that was perpetrated by the Argentine Youths for Sovereignty on January 26, 1978, in Buenos Aries, Argentina against the LAN Chile Airlines. Note that the original source of for this incident was the Foreign Broadcast Information Service-Latin America (FBIS LA), dated January 30, 1978. From the middle of 1985 through 1988, PGIS coded the events on a field-formatted card that was unique to each event type. Figure 12.2 presents an example of this hybrid card that was coded for the April 12, 1988, assassination of police officer Samuel Lopez,by the Manuel Rodriguez Patriotic Front in Chile, Peru. The final version of the PGIS coding card, used from 1989 through 1997, was generic in design so that it could be used to code any type of terrorist event (see Figure 12.3).

In order to transfer the information from the three different versions of coding sheets into an electronic database, we first designed a web-based interface that closely matched all three card types. Dropdown menus were used wherever possible to reduce error. Nearly 100 undergraduate students were trained to enter the data from the cards into the interface. In order to assure quality control, 10 percent random samples were drawn of each coder's work and checked against the original cards. When error was found, the remaining cases by that coder were verified and the coder was either retrained or let go depending on the nature of the error. See LaFree et al. (2006) for further detail of on the data entry process.

After the data were entered, GTD staff scoured other data sources to supplement cases or add

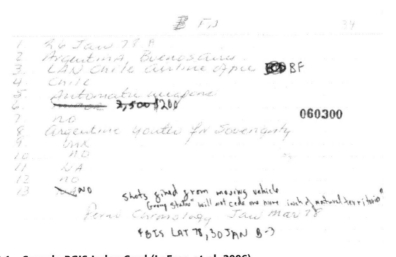

Figure 12.1   Sample PGIS Index Card (LaFree et al. 2006)

Figure 12.2   Sample PGIS Hybrid Card (LaFree et al. 2006)

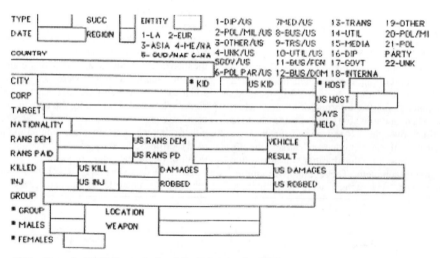

Figure 12.3   Sample PGIS Generic Card (LaFree et al. 2006)

additional events. As scholars and graduate students cleaned the data for their research purposes, additional sources were found to supplement the GTD cases. For example, the version of the GTD used by LaFree et al. (2009) was supplemented by the Conflict Archive on the INternet (CAIN), when it became apparent that the original PGIS data were missing some attacks by republicans in Northern Ireland. CAIN is a project funded by Access Research Knowledge (ARK) beginning in 1996, which is jointly supported by between the University of Ulster and Queens University Belfast. The purpose of CAIN is to

provide a wealth of source material for researchers on the troubles in Northern Ireland from 1968 to the present. Focused data collections like this helped staff at the Department of Homeland Security's (DHS) Center for the Study of Terrorism and Response to Terrorism (START) to supplement the original PGIS data. While it is unclear why PGIS missed some of these cases, their omission incentivized an ongoing effort to compare the GTD data with other data sources on an ongoing basis. The GTD maintains a field that indicates original data source of each specific case (e.g., PGIS, CAIN).

By the time the original GTD was finally coded in 2005, its latest recorded event was nearly eight years old. START obtained funding to extend the GTD data through 2007, with the goal of developing an ongoing data collection strategy through real time into the future. This effort was initiated by Gary Ackerman and Charles Blair of the Center for Terrorism and Intelligence Studies (CETIS) in 2006. Because the new data collection was inherently different from the original collection, we referred to the 1970–1997 data as GTD1 and the 1998–2007 data as GTD2. Once the two datasets were adequately synthesized, we dropped the suffixes retaining the simpler GTD title.

Prior to collecting the GTD2 data, CETIS formed a GTD advisory board composed of an international team of terrorism experts including the principle investigators to the GTD1 to develop the criteria for the GTD2 collection (LaFree and Dugan, 2007).[2] The goal was to improve the flexibility of the new data, while preserving the original collection criteria and data fields. The new GTD2 codebook included a total of 120 variables, whereas the original GTD1 was comprised of fewer than 30 fields. For example, the original GTD1 allowed up to four different weapons that included general categories such as firearms and explosives. The GTD2 matched those weapons classifications and expanded upon them with more weapon sub-types (e.g., automatic weapons, handguns, or rifles for firearms and grenades, landmines, letter bombs, or others for explosives).

The advisory board also developed a set of more specific selection criteria rather than relying on a definition that could be vaguely construed. The goal of the selection criteria was to allow users to create their own definition by including or excluding different criterion according to their own definition. In order to develop a set of criteria that would (1) include the PGIS definition and (2) expand the flexibility of the GTD, the CETIS team organized a GTD Advisory Board, comprised of experts on terrorism and terrorism databases. The resulting criteria are as follows (START, 2009: 4–5).

In order to consider an incident for inclusion in the GTD, *all three* of the following attributes must be present:

1 *The incident must be intentional* – the result of a conscious calculation on the part of a perpetrator.
2 *The incident must entail some level of violence or threat of violence* – including property violence, as well as violence against people.
3 *The perpetrators of the incidents must be subnational actors.* This database does not include acts of state terrorism.

In addition, *at least two* of the following three criteria must be present for an incident to be included in the GTD:

Criterion 1: The act must be aimed at attaining a political, economic, religious, or social goal. In terms of economic goals, the exclusive pursuit of profit does not satisfy this criterion. It must involve the pursuit of more profound, systemic economic change.

Criterion 2: There must be evidence of an intention to coerce, intimidate, or convey some other message to a larger audience (or audiences) than the immediate victims. It is the act taken as a totality that is considered, irrespective if every individual involved in carrying out the act was aware of this intention. As long as any of the planners or decision makers behind the attack intended to coerce, intimidate or publicize, the intentionality criterion is met.

Criterion 3: The action must be outside the context of legitimate warfare activities. That is, the act must be outside the parameters permitted by international humanitarian law (particularly the prohibition against deliberately targeting civilians or non-combatants).

Once the criteria and codebook were finalized, the CETIS team organized a group of more than 75 research assistants from graduate programs across the US. The team included students who were fluent in French, Spanish, Russian, Arabic, and Mandarin. They accessed more than 25,000 different news sources through OpenSource.gov and Lexis-Nexis to search for terrorist incidents throughout the world beginning in 1998 (Blair, 2007). Using the selection criteria, the individual data collectors evaluated each potential terrorist attack to determine whether it met these criteria; and all decisions were reviewed by GTD supervisory staff. However, while these criteria appear to be unambiguous, potential terrorist attacks reported by media are sometimes equivocal making them necessary for additional review. For example, it was unclear whether the following incident met criterion 3 (outside the context of legitimate warfare). On March 16, 2008 a 13-year-old boy was killed and a US soldier was hurt when a suicide bomber attacked a NATO convoy in Afghanistan. Members of the GTD Advisory Board were available to assist in these sorts of decisions. For this specific case, because the NATO convoy is a group of peacekeepers and because a non-combatant was killed, criterion three was considered met. Cases that remained uncertain, but could reasonably be considered terrorist incidents were included in the GTD but marked as 'doubt terrorism proper' (START, 2009). In fact, because the example case mentioned above could also have been classified as an insurgency, doubt terrorism proper was marked with the case noted as a possible insurgency. Just over a quarter of the case in the GTD2 are marked as doubt terrorism proper (25.65 percent).

Merging GTD1 and GTD2 to form the GTD

In May 2007 the GTD was released to the public as two separate datasets, GTD1 and GTD2. The GTD team preserved the divide between the two datasets because the first relied on a definition and the second, a set of criteria. In 2008, CETIS and GTD staffs applied the GTD2 criteria to the GTD1 incidents to form a more comprehensive database. Furthermore, whenever possible, information on the additional GTD2 fields was coded in the GTD1. This process required the review of each of the nearly 70,000 GTD1 incidents. Incidents that failed to meet the criteria were removed from the newly synthesized GTD.

Despite the best efforts of the CETIS and GTD staff to produce a comparable GTD before and after the 1997–1998 divide, little can be done to change the fact that GTD1 and GTD2 were collected using very different methodologies. The PGIS staff collected the GTD1 data in real time. Thus, within days of an attack being reported through the media, it was likely recorded by one of the PGIS staff. CETIS, on the other hand was attempting to reconstruct terrorist attacks years after they occurred. Because some of the original media sources have since become unavailable and others provide no electronic archive, it is impossible to retrospectively capture the universe of terrorist attacks years after the fact. Thus, as the synthesized GTD data transitions from 1997 to 1998, the level of attacks drops. This drop is likely a combination of unrecorded attacks (i.e., measurement error) and an actual drop in the level of terrorism. No other dataset exists to help estimate the actual change in terrorism between these two periods.[3] For this reason, users of the GTD are cautioned against ignoring the differing data collection methods across the entire series. For the analysis presented here, all GTD data are combined but distinctions are preserved when examining the series over time.

Challenges with open-source databases

While the GTD data have important strengths that will enhance the ability to document the activities of all known terrorist organizations, it is important to recognize that its inherent weaknesses will limit this endeavor. In essence, by relying on media sources to record terrorist events, all open-source databases are subject to biases and inaccuracies that are inherent in media reports. I outline a few of them here and discuss their implications on the analysis. First, because all open-source terrorism databases rely on data gleaned from news sources, selection will be biased toward (1) the most newsworthy forms of terrorism, and (2) successful attacks that avoided early detection by authorities (Falkenrath, 2001). Although the GTD database includes events that were prevented by authorities whenever that information was available, it is certain that some thwarted terrorist attacks never came to the attention of the media and are thus excluded. Because of this bias, the 81,799 attacks recorded in the GTD can be thought of as the most newsworthy and successful of the universe of attacks. For example, an undetonated explosive that was discovered by officials but kept away from the media in order to facilitate an investigation will not be recorded in the GTD.

A second weakness is due to conflicting information on terrorist attacks reported by various media sources (e.g., local newspapers, international cable networks and electronic press). With relatively few measures of reliability in news reporting, researchers may be unable to discern the most accurate of conflicting sources. More specific to this analysis, media may inadvertently attribute an attack to the wrong organization. In fact, it is likely that a certain percentage of the GTD incidents will be attributed to the wrong organization, making the descriptions of the life cycles of terrorist organizations only estimates of their true patterns of perpetration. Furthermore, in the more newsworthy events, this type of attribution mistake will likely be corrected and updated in the GTD, making this more of an issue for the less consequential attacks reducing GTD's overall error. As with most estimates, because these mistakes are unlikely to be systematic toward specific terrorist organizations, I expect the overall patterns to remain valid recognizing that the patterns of organizational activity associated with more newsworthy events will more closely approximate the actual patterns in order to get a sense of the magnitude of this problem.

A third and probably the most important limitation for this research is that nearly half of the attacks in the GTD are unattributed to any terrorist organization. This means that none of the original news articles describing the attack mentioned the identity of the perpetrating group. Without further investigation into each incident (and usually even with such investigation), it is impossible to discern whether these attacks were perpetrated by groups found in the GTD or by others. In actuality, the unattributed attacks are likely a mixture of both. Thus, in the GTD, when none of the original sources mention a perpetrator, that field is left blank.

Creating a database of organizational activity

In order to create a longitudinal database on the activity of terrorist organizations from the incident-based GTD, the GTD staff first linked attacks that were perpetrated by the same organizations. However, terrorist organizations often have several variations to their name, each with unique spellings. Furthermore, the original PGIS coders of the GTD sometimes used their own notation to refer to specific terrorist organizations (see Figures 12.1 and 12.2 for examples). Both problems make it difficult to link attacks by the same organization artificially inflating the number of actual terrorist organizations represented in the GTD. Consequently, the 1970 to 1997 GTD originally listed more than 5,000 unique terrorist organizations. After several years of standardizing the list and researching specific incidents, the GTD staff reduced this number to 1,599. After synthesizing the GTD1 with the GTD2, the 1971 to 2007 GTD records attacks by 2,013 unique terrorist organizations. This figure is based on data downloaded in May 2009. Subsequent analyses reflect this state of the database.

It would be misleading to suggest that all terrorist organizations adhere to the simple form that is characterized by this new organizational database (i.e., organizations become active until they become inactive). Among the variations found in the GTD, terrorist groups, like all organizations, experience internal strife and sometimes split into entirely new organizations. Also, factions may form to execute more specialized operations. Finally, multiple groups form coalitions and operate together under new names. Unfortunately, there is no central registry to document these organizational changes making it necessary for us to rely on research by others that chronicles these changes. As with the other limitations mentioned above, the accuracy will be biased toward those organizations that have been active enough to precipitate the interest of scholars.

The GTD documents these organizational changes as best as it can. For terrorist organizations that form factions as the original organization remains intact, the GTD keeps the group name constant for all attacks regardless of whether the splinter or larger group perpetrate the operation. If the splinter group is responsible for the attack, then it is recorded in the GTD as the group's sub-name. One notorious example comes

from one of the most active terrorist organization today, Revolutionary Armed Forces of Colombia (FARC) and its many military units, including, for example, the 1st through 15th Fronts. The organizational database links all activities by FARC's military units to FARC, thus absorbing all faction activity into the organization. However, activity by factions that are unrecognized by the GTD staff will erroneously appear to be perpetrated by a separate organization.

Organizations that splinter into new organizations are documented as distinct groups in the GTD. Because splits often result from ideological or operational disagreements, it would be misleading to impose the original organizational name on the new splinter. For example in 1984, Italy's Red Brigades split and formed the Red Brigades-CCP (Communist Combat Party) and the Red Brigades-UCC (Union of Combatant Communists). All three are recorded as separate organizations in the GTD. Similarly, in the organizational database used in the analysis below, activity by the Red Brigades and its splinter groups are recorded separately. A similar strategy is used when distinct organizations collaborate to form a separate coalition organization. Both the GTD and the organizational database used here record attacks by the coalition as separate attacks than those perpetrated by its member groups. For example, the Nicaraguan Resistance formed from the merger of various Contra rebel groups in 1987 (Merrill, 1993). After that merger, member groups like the Nicaraguan Democratic Force appear inactive in the GTD. While the GTD staff is continuously updating the database to document splinters, factions and coalitions, it is likely that some organizational changes were undetected by media or scholars and will remain as measurement error in the GTD and its derived organizational database. Similarly, the GTD will also likely miscode some of those terrorist organizations that change their name to avoid detection. Scholars at the START center are currently coding attacks in the GTD by the responsible movement in order to absorb some of the variation that is due to splinters, factions, coalitions and unattributed attacks (Miller, 2009). For example, attacks by Fatah, Hamas, and the PLO will all be linked through the Palestinian movement.

Finally, as mentioned above, nearly half (49.7 percent) of the attacks in the GTD are unattributed to any terrorist organization. Included amongst these attacks are those where the perpetrator was only generally described by its ideology (e.g., Sikh extremists), location (e.g., Palestinians), or the situation (e.g., angry farmers). Of the unattributed attacks, 22.3 percent had some form of generic attribution. Figure 12.4 shows the trends of total attacks, partitioned by whether the attacks

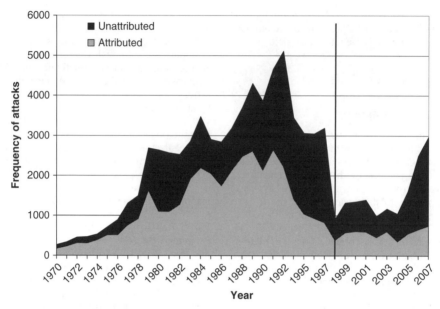

Figure 12.4   Total, Attributed, and Unattributed Attacks, 1970 to 2007

were attributed or unattributed over the entire period from 1970 to 2007. A vertical line separates the different data collection methods described above to distinguish the GTD1 series from the GTD2 series. We see that the overall trend peaks in 1992 with 5,116 attacks. A larger portion of these attacks are unattributed to a specific group (56.4 percent). This year also marks the peak for unattributed attacks (2,887 unattributed attacks), while 1989 is the peak year for attributed attacks (2,614 attributed attacks).

The second part of the series (GTD2) peaks in 2007 with 2,968 attacks. It is obvious from this figure that a majority of these attacks were entirely unattributed to a specific group. In fact, nearly three quarters of all the 2007 attacks were unattributed (74.97 percent) and a large portion of these attacks (43.7 percent) took place in Iraq, which was fraught with anonymous violent outbursts since the US invasion in March 2003. In fact, other analyses of terrorist attacks during this period explicitly exclude attacks in Iraq due to ambivalence as to whether they meet the criteria of terrorism (LaFree et al., 2010a, 2010b). That year also marks the peak percentage of unattributed attacks over the entire series. Other local peaks include 1997 with 74 percent unattributed and 1980 with 58 percent unattributed (both of which are in GTD1).

Figure 12.5 presents the distribution of attributed and unattributed attacks across regions. The countries for each region are listed in Appendix B.

Here we see that terrorist attacks in five predominantly Western regions were attributed to a specific organization more than half of the time (North America, Central America and Caribbean, South America, Southeast Asia and Western Europe). Attacks in the remaining regions were mostly perpetrated by unknown entities. This contrast is especially profound for Central Asia and Russian regions where only 6.6 percent and 4.0 percent of the attacks were attributed to specific perpetrators. Countries in both of these regions were part of the former Soviet Union. Perhaps these unusually low rates were due to the extreme controls imposed on media investigating and reporting by the Soviet Government or, more recently, problems faced by overwhelmed new governments after the Soviet collapse.

When I examined the distribution of attributed and unattributed attacks across countries and territories, I find that *all* of the attacks in 39 countries or territories were unattributed to any specific organization. However, most of these countries were also relatively unaffected by terrorism, experiencing less than five attacks over the 38-year period. Still countries like Albania (71 attacks), Togo (48 attacks), and Ukraine (29 attacks) experienced a sufficient number of attacks to make the 100 percent unattributed rate somewhat surprising. Thus, countries with relatively few attacks are likely to have unusually high percentages of unattributed or attributed attacks. For example, a country with only one attack will

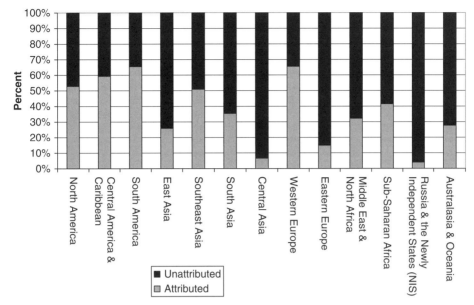

Figure 12.5   Percent Attributed and Unattributed Attacks by Region, 1970–2007

have either 100 percent attributed or 100 percent unattributed attacks, depending on the perpetrator of that single attack. To get beyond the potentially misleading impact of these countries, I examine only those countries in the top quartile (or top 20 countries) with regard to the frequency of terrorist attacks to get a sense of which of the most affected countries have the highest proportions of unattributed and attributed attacks. Table 12.1 lists the 20 countries in this upper quartile that have the largest percentage of unattributed attacks. Given Figure 12.5, it is unsurprising that Russia tops this list with nearly 97 percent of its attacks unattributed. However, Russia is the only country from that region that is listed in the top 20. The countries in this list appear to be distributed more heavily on the Eastern and Latin portions of the globe with a slight majority representing the Middle East (and North Africa). As mentioned above, the Iraq war has led to an unusual number of unattributed attacks leading to Iraq's ranking as fourth among these nations with just over of attacks 90 percent unattributed. South Asia is also well represented in this list with four countries experiencing a large percentage of unattributed attacks.

Table 12.2 lists the top 20 countries that experienced the largest percentage of attacks attributed to a specific terrorist organization. This list has a greater Western representation with half the countries or territories from the Western hemisphere. Angola tops this list with more than 85 percent of its attacks attributed to specific organizations.

In fact, more than 80 percent of all attacks in Angola were attributed to the National Union for the Total Independence of Angola (UNITA), a leftist organization that controlled the southeast portion of the country (TOPS, 2008). It is unsurprising that Peru also tops this list since this country is the birthplace of one of the most active terrorist organizations to date, Sendero Luminoso, or Shining Path. Shining Path was responsible for nearly 4,500 attacks in Peru between 1978 and 2007. Western Europe is better represented in this list with Northern Ireland, Spain, Great Britain, and France. The popular terrorist campaigns of the IRA, the Basque Fatherland and Freedom (ETA) and the Corsican National Liberation Front (FLNC) were spread throughout these areas. Other well-known terrorist campaigns that helped their countries make this list include FARC in Colombia, the Tamil Tigers (LTTE) in Sri Lanka, and the Nicaraguan Democratic Force – the earliest Contra group – in Nicaragua.

LIFE CYCLES OF TERRORIST ORGANIZATIONS, 1970–2007

Because the focus of this chapter is to demonstrate how we can use the incidents of the GTD to inform us about the life cycle of terrorist organizations world wide from 1970 through 2007, we now only examine those attacks that were

Table 12.1   20 Upper Quartile Countries with the Largest Percent of Unattributed Attacks, 1970 to 2007

Country	Region	Attributed Attacks	Unattributed Attacks	Percent Unattributed
Russia	Rus. & NIS	29	896	96.86%
Haiti	CA & Car.	16	184	92.00%
Thailand	SE Asia	79	825	91.26%
Iraq	ME & NA	296	2673	90.03%
Nepal	S Asia	49	319	86.68%
Brazil	S America	35	218	86.17%
Pakistan	S Asia	359	2140	85.63%
Burundi	SS Africa	53	288	84.46%
Somalia	SS Africa	57	303	84.17%
Nigeria	SS Africa	40	171	81.04%
Bolivia	S America	69	241	77.74%
Algeria	ME & NA	412	1233	74.95%
India	S Asia	1088	3185	74.54%
Guatemala	CA & Car.	523	1509	74.26%
Ecuador	S America	53	151	74.02%
West Bank and Gaza Strip	ME & NA	395	977	71.21%
Iran	ME & NA	174	406	70.00%
Israel	ME & NA	404	932	69.76%
Bangladesh	S Asia	222	453	67.11%
Germany	W Europe	274	526	65.75%

Note: The regions are abbreviated as follows: Russia and the Newly Independent States (Rus. & NIS), Central America and the Caribbean (CA & Car.), Southeast Asia (SE Asia), Middle East and North Africa (ME & NA), South Asia (S Asia), South America (S America), Sub-Saharan Africa (SS Africa), and Western Europe (W Europe).

Table 12.2   20 Upper Quartile Countries with the Largest Percent of Attributed Attacks, 1970 to 2007

Country	Region	Attributed Attacks	Unattributed Attacks	Percent Attributed
Angola	SS Africa	414	66	86.25%
Peru	S America	5105	935	84.52%
Mozambique	SS Africa	183	40	82.06%
Northern Ireland	W Europe	3040	734	80.55%
Spain	W Europe	2534	635	79.96%
Nicaragua	CA & Car.	1568	419	78.91%
Great Britain	W Europe	431	161	72.80%
El Salvador	CA & Car.	3732	1598	70.02%
Cambodia	SE Asia	170	74	69.67%
Uganda	SS Africa	217	97	69.11%
Sri Lanka	S Asia	1650	743	68.95%
Philippines	SE Asia	1686	800	67.82%
Colombia	S America	4180	2590	61.74%
France	W Europe	679	448	60.25%
Egypt	ME & NA	289	196	59.59%
Afghanistan	S Asia	651	483	57.41%
United States	N America	767	580	56.94%
Chile	S America	1297	991	56.69%
Turkey	ME & NA	1497	1183	55.86%
Myanmar	SE Asia	119	102	53.85%

Note: The regions are abbreviated as follows: Sub-Saharan Africa (SS Africa), South America (S America), Western Europe (W Europe), Central America and the Caribbean (CA & Car.), Southeast Asia (SE Asia), South Asia (S Asia), Middle East and North Africa (ME & NA), and North America (N America).

attributed to at least one specific terrorist organization. By examining these attacks, we can (1) form a broad picture of the overall patterns of terrorism, and (2) identify those organizations that are the most threatening.

To meet the first goal of presenting the overall picture of terrorist activity for all 2,013 organizations identified in the GTD, I first identify those attacks that were perpetrated by more than one organization. In some cases, the media report listed two groups because it was unsure which was responsible (e.g., al Qaeda or the Taliban). In other instances, organizations actually operated together. For example, on two occasions the Animal Liberation Front appeared to have worked with the Earth Liberation Front in the Pacific Northwest, setting fires to establishments perceived as damaging the environment and harming wildlife. The first was on June 21, 1998, when the US Department of Agriculture's Wildlife Services, Animal Damage Control division was burned using gallons of gasoline. The second attack was on June 1, 2001, when logging trucks were set fire using milk cartons containing gasoline. According to the GTD, 378 attacks record a second perpetrator and 48 record a third. In order to best describe the life cycles of terrorist organizations each attack with multiple perpetrators are recorded under each group, thus inflating the total number of attacks by 426 attacks.

Of the 2,013 organizations recorded in the GTD, the majority of these organizations (52.9 percent or 1,065 groups) have only one attack.

An additional 428 organizations (21.3 percent) only appear in the GTD within a one-year time frame. The three most active of these short-lived organizations were the Dishmish Regiment in India with 43 attacks in 1984, the National Liberation Army in Macedonia with 35 attacks in 2001, and the April 6th Liberation Movement in the Philippines with 31 attacks in 1980. I refer to all 1,493 organizations that were active less than a year as short-lived and the remaining 520 as long-lived (respectively representing 74.2 percent and 25.8 percent of the GTD groups). Figure 12.6 presents the trends of terrorist attacks for both types of terrorist organizations over the years covered in the GTD. Notice that the overall pattern is similar to that of the attributed attacks in Figure 12.4, the only difference coming from the additional 426 attacks mentioned above. More notable, however, is that the vast majority of terrorist attacks were attributed to the long-lived organizations. In other words, 25.8 percent of terrorist organizations were presumably responsible for 93.2 percent of the attributed attacks.

Not surprisingly, when we examine this distribution across regions, the vast majority of attacks in each region were also attributed to long-lived organizations (see Figure 12.7). The only exceptions are for those attacks in the Central Asian and the Russian regions. A quick glance at Figure 12.5 should remind you that most of the attacks in those regions were unattributed, suggesting that these proportions were calculated from relatively few attacks. In fact, Central Asia only had 20

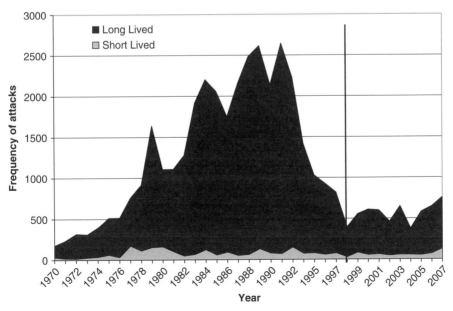

Figure 12.6   Attacks Attributed to Short-Lived and Long-Lived Attackers, 1970 to 2007

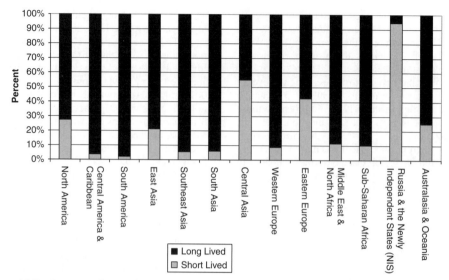

Figure 12.7   Percent of Attacks Perpetrated by Long- and Short-Lived Organizations by Region, 1970–2007

attributed attacks, with only 9 perpetrated by long-lived organizations (Hizb al-Tahrir al-Islami (HT) in Tajikistan and Uzbekistan and Islamic Movement of Uzbekistan (IMU) in Kyrgyzstan and Uzbekistan). Russia and the Newly Independent States region (see Appendix B for countries) experienced only 36 attributed attacks, with two perpetrated by long-lived terrorist organizations (Belarusian Liberation Army in Belarus and Communist Party of Nepal-Maoist (CPN-M) in Russia). In absolute numbers, most of the short-lived organizations attacked in Western Europe (821 attacks) and in the Middle East (including North Africa) with 512 attacks.

In order to have one final look at the activities of the short-lived terrorist organizations, I direct our attention on those countries in the upper quartile of attributed terrorist attacks. Table 12.3 lists the 20 countries from that quartile with the highest proportion of attributed attacks perpetrated by short-lived organizations. Topping this list is Mexico with 42.7 percent of its attributed attacks perpetrated by short-lived organizations. These 76 attacks were perpetrated by 20 different organizations; the most active being Union of the People who attacked 21 times from September 1977 to March 1978. The Popular Revolutionary Army was another active short-lived group that perpetrated 17 attacks from July of 1996 to May of 1997. The 102 attacks by long-lived groups in Mexico were perpetrated by 13 different organizations. The most active of these organizations was the 23rd of September Communist League, which was active from 1970 to 1980.

Table 12.3 shows that short-lived terrorist organizations have been active across the globe in both the Western and Eastern Hemispheres. Greece is probably the nation most notorious for generating short-lived terrorist organizations because of its groups' talent for creating the most descriptive names. Short-lived Greek organizations include such groups as Arsonists for Social Cohesion (three attacks), Erotic Anti-Authority Cells (one attack), Friendly Company (one attack), and Nihilists Faction (one attack). We see that Israel and the Palestinian Territories also make the top 20 list of short-lived terrorist organizations, despite their reputation for attracting attacks by well-known long-lived organizations such as the PLO and Hamas. The most active of the short-lived organizations found in the GTD is called Jewish Terror, which was active in 1983 with 10 attacks. This group has also been called the Gush Emunim Underground, which is part of a nationalistic religious group that spearheaded the Jewish Settlement movement in the West Bank (Kelly, 1984). Other short-lived organizations include both Israeli organizations (Terror Against Terror and David's Sword) and Palestinian organizations (Hizballah Palestine and the fundamentalist Islamic Swords of Justice in the Land of Ribat).

The second goal of this analysis is to demonstrate how we can use the GTD to identify those organizations that are most threatening. We do this by focusing exclusively on the long-lived organizations – or those that have been active for at least a year. Figure 12.8 presents a chart that shows

Table 12.3 20 Upper Quartile Countries with the Largest Percent of Attributed Attacks by Short-Lived Terrorist Organizations, 1970 to 2007

Country	Region	Short-Lived Attacks	Long-Lived Attacks	Percent Short-Lived
Mexico	N America	76	102	42.70%
Italy	W Europe	250	534	31.89%
Greece	W Europe	134	302	30.73%
Iraq	ME & NA	90	208	30.20%
United States	N America	166	546	23.31%
Lebanon	ME & NA	162	538	23.14%
France	W Europe	135	540	20.00%
Iran	ME & NA	31	145	17.61%
Japan	E Asia	25	126	16.56%
Honduras	CA & Car.	19	112	14.50%
West Germany (FRG)	W Europe	19	121	13.57%
India	S Asia	141	1009	12.26%
Germany	W Europe	33	239	12.13%
Bangladesh	S Asia	26	194	11.82%
Argentina	S America	33	253	11.54%
Israel	ME & NA	44	370	10.63%
Great Britain	W Europe	36	392	8.41%
West Bank and Gaza Strip	ME & NA	34	388	8.06%
Indonesia	SE Asia	13	154	7.78%
Algeria	ME & NA	32	382	7.73%

Note: The regions are abbreviated as follows: North America (N America), Western Europe (W Europe), Middle East and North Africa (ME & NA), East Asia (E Asia), Central America and the Caribbean (CA & Car.), South Asia (S Asia), and South America (S America).

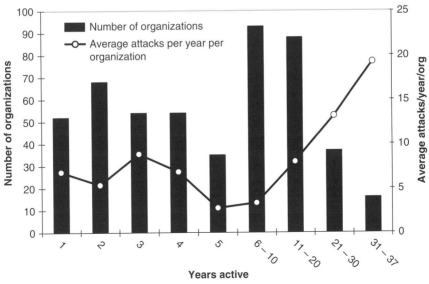

Figure 12.8 Activity Length and Intensity for Long-Lived Terrorist Organizations, 1970–2007

both the distribution of longevity and intensity for the longest-lasting terrorist organizations found in the GTD. Longevity is measured by the total number of years between each group's first recorded attack to its last. Intensity is measured by the average number of attacks per year for each group. Thus, groups that averaged two or three attacks a year are considered less intense than groups that average twenty to thirty attacks a year. While this measure ignores the impact of each attack, fatalities are considered later. For this figure, organizations that began after 2003 and were still active in 2007 are excluded to avoid distortion because these 13 groups may still be active today. The year 2003 was chosen because later calculations compare those groups that ended by year 5 to those that lasted longer. As Figures 12.4 and 12.6 demonstrate, these 509 organizations account for the majority of terrorist attacks over this period.

Yet, we see in Figure 12.8 that more than half of all terrorist organizations (attributed in the GTD) are inactive after five years (53.9 per cent). The average number of attacks per year per group for these organizations is 5.93, which is substantially and statistically lower than the average number of attacks for the groups that remained active after five years (16.2; $p < 0.01$). This difference and the dramatic rise in the average number of attacks after five years shown in Figure 12.8, suggest that the longer-lived terrorist organizations are also the most active.

In order to get a better sense of the lifecycle of these terrorist organizations, three top ten lists are reproduced in Table 12.4, ranking the groups according to their longevity (time between their first and last attack), activity (average number of attacks per year), and lethality (average number of fatalities per attack). The average number of fatalities per attack is used to measure lethality as a way to identify those organizations that may have the desire or potential to produce mass casualties. Because all three characteristics are potentially threatening to national security, only by examining all three lists are we better able to identify those groups that have been problematic, those that still are, and those that might become problematic.

Table 12.4 includes the region where they perpetrated most of their attacks, the range of years that the GTD lists them as active, the average number of attacks per year, and the average number of fatalities per attack. Not surprising, all ten of longest running organizations began in the 1970s and were active after the turn of the century. In fact, for five of the organizations the GTD lists their first attack as in 1970. It is likely that these organizations were well active prior to the start of the GTD data. According to Terrorist Organization

Profile (TOPS) data housed at START, Basque Fatherland and Freedom (ETA) was formed in 1959 in Spain; the New People's Army (NPA) formed in 1969 in the Philippines; the Popular Front for the Liberation of Palestine (PFLP) formed in 1967 in Israel and the Palestinian Territories; the IRA formed in 1922 in Northern Ireland, and the Ulster Volunteer Force (UVF) formed in 1966 in Northern Ireland (TOPS, 2008). Similarly the seven organizations that were still active in 2007 are likely still active today. Thus, because this table only presents the available information during a specific slice of time it is only an estimate of the ten longest running organizations.

The ten most active organizations are measured by the average number of attacks per year. Our first observation is that only two of the longest active organizations are also listed among the most active: the IRA of Northern Ireland and ETA of Spain. This demonstrates the high degree of organization in these groups that they are able to risk exposure while perpetrating a large number of attacks; and yet still survive longer than 20 years. The most active terrorist organization was the highly lethal Nicaraguan Democratic Force (FDN), which was the first rightist Contra rebel organization in Nicaragua. It was active from 1983 though 1987 as it opposed the communist Sandinista government. We see that in 1987, the same year of the infamous US Iran–Contra hearings, the Nicaraguan Resistance formed from the merger various Contra rebel groups (Merrill, 1993), virtually extending the life of FDN through another organization. Table 12.4 indicates that the new Nicaraguan Resistance was only about a third as active (and as lethal) as its predecessor.

The four most active groups averaged far more than 100 attacks a year and, with the exception of the People's Liberation Front (JVP), were based in Latin America. FMLN averaged more than 200 attacks a year in El Salvador and was an umbrella organization for five leftist organizations who were attempting to overthrow the military dictatorship in El Salvador and replace it with a communist regime (TOPS, 2008; Haggarty, 1988). Shining Path became violent that same year in Peru and had the more extreme goal of destroying all Peruvian political institutions and creating a 'new state of workers and peasants' (McCormick, 2001: 113). The final of the top four, JVP, also a leftist organization, formed in 1965 as a Marxist Sinhalese political party in Sri Lanka in reaction to the perceived collaboration between the existing leftist parties and the capitalist government (Gunaratna, 1990). According to the GTD it was only violent for four years from 1987 to 1990, averaging close to 150 attacks a year that resulted in about 2 deaths each. The JVP became violent in

Table 12.4 Top 10 Organizations Measured by Longevity, Activity, and Lethality

Longest Running	Modal Region	Years Active	Attacks per Year	Fatalities per Attack
Basque Fatherland and Freedom (ETA)	W Europe	1970–2007	53.68	0.41
New People's Army (NPA)	SE Asia	1970–2007	29.46	3.01
Popular Front for the Liberation of Palestine (PFLP)	W Europe	1970–2007	3.24	1.46
Irish Republican Army (IRA)	W Europe	1970–2006	74.14	0.69
al-Fatah	ME & NA	1971–2007	1.50	1.80
Ulster Volunteer Force (UVF)	W Europe	1970–2005	7.46	1.39
Ulster Freedom Fighters (UFF)	W Europe	1972–2007	7.20	0.79
National Liberation Army of Colombia (ELN)	S America	1972–2006	36.79	1.34
Corsican National Liberation Front (FLNC)	W Europe	1974–2007	17.12	0.02
Democratic Front for the Liberation of Palestine (DFLP)	ME & NA	1974–2007	1.09	1.83
Most Active				
Nicaraguan Democratic Force (FDN)	CA & Car.	1983–1987	225.00	8.08
Farabundo Marti National Liberation Front (FMLN)	CA & Car.	1978–1994	209.81	2.53
Shining Path (SL)	S America	1978–2007	155.62	2.58
People's Liberation Front (JVP)	S Asia	1987–1990	144.67	2.05
People's Liberation Forces (FPL)	CA & Car.	1977–1979	83.50	0.74
Nicaraguan Resistance	CA & Car.	1987–1990	77.00	2.55
Irish Republican Army (IRA)	W Europe	1970–2006	74.14	0.69
Manuel Rodriguez Patriotic Front (FPMR)	S America	1984–1997	63.85	0.11
Taliban	S Asia	1995–2007	54.42	2.98
Basque Fatherland and Freedom (ETA)	W Europe	1970–2007	53.68	0.41
Most Lethal				
Ethiopian People's Revolutionary Army	SS Africa	1986–1992	0.67	60.00
National Resistance Movement (NRM)	SS Africa	1984–1985	4.00	57.00
al-Qa'ida	S Asia	1998–2007	10.44	46.52
Movement for Democracy and Justice in Chad (MDJT)	SS Africa	1999–2002	0.67	38.50
Martyr Abu Ja'far Group	ME & NA	1980–1982	1.00	38.00
Communist Party of Nepal- Maoist (CPN-M)	S Asia	1997–2006	2.11	35.16
Oromo Liberation Front	SS Africa	1992–2004	0.67	34.13
Tigray Peoples Liberation Front (TPLF)	SS Africa	1976–1990	0.71	31.70
Popular Front for the Liberation of Palestine, Gen Cmd (PFLP-GC)	W Europe	1970–2003	0.15	31.20
Armed Forces for Liberation of East Timor (FALINTIL)	SE Asia	1992–1995	0.67	30.00

Grayed areas indicate that the organization was also among the 10 longest running organizations.

Note: The regions are abbreviated as follows: Western Europe (W Europe), Southeast Asia (SE Asia), Middle East and North Africa (ME & NA), South America (S America), Central America and the Caribbean (CA & Car.), South Asia (S Asia), and Sub-Saharan Africa (SS Africa).

the wake of the Indio-Sri Lankan Accord and as a reaction to the prospect of Tamil autonomy (Gunaratna, 1990).

Finally, Table 12.4 also lists the ten organizations with the highest average fatalities per attack. As noted above, I use this as a measure of lethality because these are the organizations most likely to engage in mass killings. Because relatively few terrorist organizations have killed more than 500 persons in one attack, world governments are especially concerned about those organizations that demonstrate their desire to produce mass casualties. The first observation worth noting is that none of these organizations were listed among the longest running or most active. In fact, the average lifespan of these groups is 10.2 years, with the PFLP-GC as an outlier with its 34-year tenure. Furthermore, many of these organizations had relatively few attacks, averaging 14.8 total attacks. In fact, in the Ethiopian People's Revolutionary Army's six years, it only had four reported attacks in the GTD, killing a total of 240 individuals. The first attack was the December 1986 kidnapping of two Italian workers and thirty other Ethiopians who were working on a development project in northwestern Ethiopia. Forty persons were killed including dozens of guards and some hostages (Associated Press, 1987a, 1987b). Two more kidnappings of Italian workers occurred in November 1987 and June of 1988; both resulting in no fatalities. The fourth attack was the most deadly as the Ethiopian rebel group attacked a peace march of two million Oromos – the Horn of

Africa's largest ethnic group – with automatic weapons, killing 200 civilians and wounding 300 others. The attack was believed to be a consequence of the ongoing rivalry between Ethiopian People's Revolutionary Army and another rebel group, the Oromo Liberation Front (Reuters News, 1992). This is the last reported incident of the deadly Ethiopian People's Revolutionary Army in the GTD.

Third on this list is al-Qa'ida, which was active from 1997 through 2007. Of all groups listed here, al-Qa'ida was attributed to the most attacks, 94. In fact, Figure 12.9 demonstrates that al-Qa'ida is by far the most active of all the deadly terrorist organizations, peaking with 28 attacks in 2003. While it is listed as being most active in South Asia, nearly 40 percent of its attacks where in the Middle East, Northern Africa region. Al-Qa'ida is well known for being an international organization (Cronin, 2006; Hoffman, 2006), perpetrating attacks in at least 13 countries across the globe. Its most lethal attacks were the 9/11 attacks in the US killing 2,950, the bombing at the US Embassy in Kenya killing 224, and the 2004 suicide attack against Shi'ite pilgrims during the holy month of Ashura, killing 110. Al-Qa'ida is believed to still be active today and likely poses the greatest threat to Western countries because of its penchant for mass casualties. Other lethal organizations that were still active in 2007 and could likely still pose a threat today are Harkatul Jihad-e-Islami in India, and Jemaah Islamiyah in the Philippines and Indonesia.

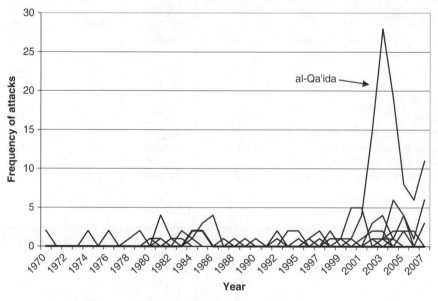

Figure 12.9   Attacks by the Most Lethal Organizations, 1970–2007

CONCLUSION

As criminologists it is important that we continue to further our understanding of violent perpetrators, including terrorists. This chapter was designed to educate scholars about the Global Terrorism Database (GTD), and demonstrate how it can be used to learn more about the lifecycles of terrorist organizations. Only by examining a broad overview of the activity of all terrorist organizations can we identify those groups that pose the most serious threats.

In order to accomplish this task, however, it is critical that scholars understand that the GTD is not a database of organizations. It is an incident database that, more than half the time, specifically attributes the attack to an organization. This means that just under half of the attacks are perpetrated by unknown assailants. Because of this, and a host of other limitations discussed in this chapter, all conclusions are based on only the information available. The life cycles of these terrorist organizations might only represent the 'tip of the iceberg', with other unattributed attacks possibly extending a group's longevity, activity or lethality. For instance, of the 2,013 organizations distinctly listed in the GTD, a subset might represent the same groups differently named. Further, some of the short-lived organizations might have been attacking anonymously to strategically preserve their longevity through secrecy. In fact, the larger terror campaigns with more than 1,000 anonymous attacks in countries such as Iraq, Pakistan, Algeria, India and Guatemala suggest that some organizations are strategically choosing to keep their identities hidden. Despite the missing information on organizations and the potential for error in the GTD, the data list 2,013 unique names that, as far as we know, are different organizations. As the GTD continues to evolve, perpetrator information will be updated and corrected as users provide additional sources to the GTD team.

In the meantime, this chapter sets the global context of the life cycles of terrorist organizations allowing those who conduct micro-studies of specific campaigns to better understand how their research fits within the setting of the larger and broader picture. We see from the above analysis is that the life cycles of terrorist organizations vary markedly across a range of dimensions. The vast majority of these organizations have only one attributed attack; and most of the remaining organizations became inactive within one year of their first attack. Despite the preponderance of these short-lived organizations, most of the world's terrorism damage comes from the remaining quarter of the terrorist organizations – those that managed to persevere beyond the first year and sometimes for more than two decades. In fact, Crenshaw (2001) explains that the primary goal of any terrorist organization is to survive. According to the analysis presented in this chapter, most organizations have failed but hundreds have succeeded.

Only two organizations are highly active among the longest running, the IRA in Northern Ireland and the Basque Fatherland and Freedom in Spain. Another group, Shining Path, also stands out in the GTD by attacking an average of more than 150 times each year over 30 years, demonstrating its ability to persevere. Yet, even this organization is vulnerable. In 1992, its charismatic leader, Guzmán, was captured and recanted his teachings asking his followers to lay down arms (Cronin, 2006). Attacks by Shining Path dropped from more than 200 a year to less to a few dozen, and eventually only 3 attacks were reported in 2007.

When we turn to the most lethal organizations, an almost entirely new list of organizations emerges, revealing those that are most likely to engage in mass killings. All but one of these organizations ceased to be active by 2007, suggesting possible desistance. However, a large number of these groups also averaged less than one attack a year – or one attack every few years, which means that it may be premature to declare some of these groups inactive. In fact, half of the most lethal organizations named in this chapter were active into the twenty-first century, and could easily be planning another mass casualty event. The low number of attacks perpetrated by these deadly groups suggests that they may be dedicating their resources and time into planning less frequent, yet high-impact attacks. The only deadly organization that breaks this pattern is al-Qa'ida, who successfully captured the world's attention with the most deadly terrorist attack to date, killing nearly 3,000 in New York, Washington DC and Pennsylvania on September 11th, 2001. It remains active today, perpetrating as many as 28 attacks in a single year.

By continuing to use datasets like the GTD to monitor al-Qa'ida, other threatening organizations, and new organizations that are potentially threatening, criminologists and others can continue to characterize risk and develop theories to improve our abilities to identify threatening terrorist behavior. Policy makers and law enforcement can be more informed and make more strategic decisions based on the most comprehensive information available to date on terrorist organizations.

NOTES

1 The boxes containing the index cards for incidents from 1993 were missing from this collection. Therefore all analyses exclude data from 1993.

2 The original committee included Gary Ackerman, Victor Asal, Charles Blair, Martha Crenshaw, Susan Cutter, Laura Dugan, Gary LaFree, Clark McCauley, Magnus Ranstorp, Alex Schmid, Kathleen Smarick, and a representative from the Department of Homeland Security.

3 In 1998, the RAND Corporation started collecting both domestic and international cases of terrorism in their chronology. NIJ funded an effort to combine the GTD1 with the RAND data, using RAND's definition of terrorism. The resulting GTD–RAND dataset also produces a drop from 1997 to 1998 (Dugan et al., 2008; see also LaFree and Dugan, 2009).

RECOMMENDED READING

The article by LaFree G. and L. Dugan (2007) 'Introducing the Global Terrorism Data Base.' *Terrorism and Political Violence* 19: 181–204, provides a thorough overview of the Global Terrorism Database from 1970 through 1997.

The GTD data can be accessed at www.start. umd.edu\gtd. This web interface has an advanced search feature making it relatively simple to find specific cases that meet your criteria of interest. The 'I'm a new user' link provides a useful guide to using the data interface (http://www.start.umd. edu/gtd/NewUser.aspx). To obtain a full version of the database, go to contact link (http://www. start.umd.edu/gtd/contact/) and state your action as 'Download full GTD dataset'.

Other terrorists incident databases can be accessed through the following links: National Counter Terrorism Center's Worldwide Incident Tracking System (http://wits.nct.gov/), the RAND Corporation (http://smapp.rand.org/rwtid/terms. php), the ITERATE data (http://www.icpsr.umich. edu/icpsrweb/ICPSR/studies/07947), the Conflict Archive on the INternet (http://cain.ulst.ac.uk/), and others (http://people.haverford.edu/bmendels/ terror_attacks). To learn more about the original collectors of the GTD, go to http://www.pinkertons.com/companyinfo.htm.

REFERENCES

Associated Press. 1987a. 'Guerrilla Group Claims Kidnap of Two Italians in Ethiopia,' January 3, 1987, Saturday AM Cycle.

Associated Press. 1987b. 'Ethiopian Rebels Released Two Kidnapped Italians,' February 6, 1987, Friday AM Cycle.

Becker, J. 1985. *The PLO: The Rise and Fall of the Palestinian Liberation Organization.* New York: St. Martin's Press.

Bell, J.B. 1980. *The Secret Army: A History of the IRA, 1916– 1979.* Cambridge, MA: MIT Press.

Blair, C.P. 2007. 'What is the Global Terrorism Database (GTD) 2 and Why Should You Care?,' presentation for the 2007 Homeland Security Stakeholders Conference, A World in Change, May 23, 2007.

Campbell, C. and I. Connolly. 2003. 'A Model for the "War against Terrorism"? Military Intervention in Northern Ireland and the 1970 Falls Curfew.' *Journal of Law and Society* 30: 341–375.

Clark, R.P. 1984. *The Basque Insurgents: ETA, 1952–1980.* Madison, WI: University of Wisconsin Press.

Cobban, H. 1984. *The Palestinian Liberation Organization: People, Power and Politics.* Cambridge, MA: Cambridge University Press.

Cordes, B. 2001. 'When Terrorist Do the Talking: Reflections on Terrorist Literature,' in D.C. Rapoport (ed.) *Inside Terrorism Organizations* (pp. 150–171). London: Frank Cass.

Crenshaw, M. 2001. 'Theories of Terrorism: Instrumental and Organizational Approaches,' in D.C. Rapoport (ed.) *Inside Terrorism Organizations* (pp. 13–29). London: Frank Cass.

Cronin, A.K. 2006. 'How al-Qaida Ends.' *International Security* 31: 7–48.

Dugan, L., G. LaFree, K. Cragin, and A. Kasupski. 2008. *Building and Analyzing an Open Source Comprehensive Data Base on Global Terrorist Events.* A Final Report to the National Institute of Justice for Grant # 2005-IJ-CX-0002.

Falkenrath, R. 2001. 'Analytic Models and Policy Prescription: Understanding Recent Innovation in U.S. Counterterrorism.' *Journal of Conflict and Terrorism* 24: 159–181.

Gillespie, R. 1999. 'Peace Moves in the Basque Region,' *Journal of Southern Europe and the Balkans* 1: 119–136.

Gorriti, G. 1999. *The Shining Path: A History of the Millenarian War in Peru.* Chapel Hill, NC: University of North Carolina Press.

Gunaratna, R. 1990. *Sri Lanka, A Lost Revolution? The Inside Story of JVP.* Kandy, Sri Lanka: Institute of Fundamental Studies.

Haggarty, R. A. 1988. *El Salvador: A Country Study.* Washington: GPO for the Library of Congress.

Hoffman, B. 2006. *Inside Terrorism.* New York: Columbia University Press.

Horgan, J. and M. Taylor. 1997. 'The Provisional Irish Republican Army: Command and Functional Structure,' *Terrorism and Political Violence* 9: 1–32.

Jackson, B., J.C. Baker, K. Cragin, J. Parachini, H.R. Trujillo, P. Chalk. 2005. *Aptitude for Destruction Volume 2: Case Studies of Organizational Learning in Five Terrorist Groups.* Santa Monica, CA: RAND Corporation.

Jenkins, Brian M. 1975. "International Terrorism: A New Model of Conflict." In *International Terrorism and World Security,* (p. 15) edited by David Carlton and Carla Schaerf. London: Croom Helm.

Jones, S.G. and M.C. Libicki. 2008. *How Terrorist Groups End: Lessons for Countering al Qa'ida.* Santa Monica, CA: RAND Corporation.

Jongman, A.J. 1993. "Trends in International and Domestic Terrorism in Western Europe, 1968–88." *Terrorism and Political Violence* 4:26–76.

Kelly, J. 1984. 'What Next for Israel,' *Time*, Monday July 9, 1984.

Kennedy, L.W. and C. Lum. 2003. *Developing a Foundation for Policy Relevant Terrorism Research in Criminology*. Prepared for the Center for the Study of Public Security, Rutgers University, Newark, NJ.

LaFree, G. and L. Dugan. 2004. 'How Does Studying Terrorism Compare to Studying Crime?' in M. DeFlem (ed.) *Terrorism and Counter-Terrorism: Criminological Perspectives* (pp. 53–74). New York: Elsevier.

LaFree, G. and L. Dugan. 2007. 'Introducing the Global Terrorism Data Base.' *Terrorism and Political Violence* 19: 181–204.

LaFree, G. and L. Dugan. 2009. 'Research on Terrorism and Countering Terrorism,' *Crime and Justice* 38: 413–477.

LaFree, G., L. Dugan, and K. Cragin. 2010a. 'Trends in Terrorism, 1970–2007,' in J.J. Hewitt, J. Wilkenfeld and T.R. Gurr (eds) *Peace and Conflict* (pp. 51–64). Boulder, CO: Paradigm Publishers.

LaFree, G., L. Dugan, H. Fogg, and J. Scott. 2006. *Building a Global Terrorism Database*. A Final Report to the National Institute of Justice for Grant # 2002-DT-CX-0001.

LaFree, G., L. Dugan, and R. Korte. 2009. 'The Impact of British Counterterrorist Strategies on Political Violence in Northern Ireland: Comparing Deterrence and Backlash Models,' *Criminology* 47: 17–45.

LaFree, G., N. Morris, and L. Dugan. 2010b 'Cross-National Patterns of Terrorism: Comparing Trajectories for Total, Attributed and Fatal Attacks, 1970–2006,' *British Journal of Criminology*, 50: 622–649.

McCormick, G.H. 2001. 'The Shining Path and Peruvian Terrorism,' in D.C. Rapoport (ed.) *Inside Terrorist Organizations*. London: Frank Cass Publishers.

Merrill, T. 1993. *Nicaragua: A Country Study*. Washington: GPO for the Library of Congress.

Mickolus, E.F. 1982. *International Terrorism: Attributes of Terrorist Events, 1968–1977. (ITERATE 2)*. Ann Arbor, MI: Inter-University Consortium for Political and Social Research.

Mickolus, E.F., T. Sandler, J.M. Murdock, and P.A. Fleming 1993. *International Terrorism: Attributes of Terrorist Events 1988–91 (ITERATE 4)*. Dunn Loring, VA: Vineyard Software.

Miller, E. 2009. 'Patterns of Decline Among Terrorist Movements,' presentation at the Annual Meeting for the American Society of Criminology, November 6, 2009.

O'Leary, Brendan, and John McGarry. 1993. *The Politics of Antagonism*. London: Athalone Press.

O'Leary, B. 2005. 'Looking Back at the IRA,' *Field Day Review* March–April: 216–246.

Pape, R. 2005. *Dying to Win: The Strategic Logic of Suicide Terrorism*. New York: Random House Publishing Group.

Pedahzru, A. 2005. *Suicide Terrorism*. Cambridge: Polity Press.

Peroff, K. and C. Hewitt. 1980. 'Rioting in Northern Ireland: The Effects of Different Policies,' *Journal of Conflict Resolution* 24: 593–612.

Reinares F. 2004. 'Who are the Terrorists? Analyzing Changes in Sociological Profile Among Members of ETA,' *Studies in Conflict and Terrorism* 27: 465–488

Reuters News. 1992. 'Ethiopian Forces Kill 200, Rival Group Says,' April 8, 1992.

Rapoport, D.C. 2004. 'The Four Waves of Modern Terrorism,' in A.K. Cronin and J. Ludes (eds) *The Campaign Against International Terrorism*. Washington, DC: Georgetown University Press.

Sanchez-Cuenca I. 2007. 'The Dynamics of Nationalist Terrorism: ETA and the IRA,' *Terrorism and Political Violence* 19: 289–306.

Schmid, A P., and A.J. Jongman. 1988. *Political Terrorism: A New Guide to Actors, Authors, Concepts, Databases, Theories and Literature*. Amsterdam: North-Holland.

Shepard, W.S. 2002. 'The ETA: Spain Fights Europe's Last Active Terrorist Group,' *Mediterranean Quarterly* 13: 54–68.

Soule, J.W. 1989. 'Problems in Applying Counter terrorism to Prevent Terrorism: Two Decades of Violence in Northern Ireland Reconsidered,' *Terrorism* 12: 31–46.

START. 2009. *Global Terrorism Database: GTD Variables & Inclusion Criteria*. Available at: http://www.start.umd.edu/gtd/downloads/Codebook.pdf.

TOPS. 2008. *Terrorist Organizational Profiles*. Terrorism Knowledge Base. Available at: http://www.start.umd.edu/start/data/tops/.

Tucker, J.B. 1999. 'Historical Trends Related to Bioterrorism: An Empirical Analysis,' *Emerging Infectious Disease* 5: 498–504.

United States Institute of Peace. 1999. *How Terrorism Ends*. Special Report, No. 48, Washington, DC: United States Institute for Peace.

Werlich, D.P. 1984. 'Peru: The Shadow of the Shining Path,' *Current History* 83: 78–82.

APPENDIX A: GTD1 ATTACK TYPE DEFINITIONS

Assassination

The objective of the act is to kill a specific person or persons. Normally the victim is a personage of note, a policeman, government official, and so on. The key is – what was the objective of the act? For example, an attack on a police jeep usually is a facility attack, but an attack against a single police officer on a post is an assassination; that is, the aim was to kill that specific man. Some incidents of this nature will be judgment calls and may be categorized either as assassinations or facility attacks. Generally, when the attack is against a jeep full of police, a police post, a military outpost, military vehicles, and so on, it is coded as a facility attack. In an assassination, the thrust is concerning an identified person or persons rather than several unknowns, as would be the case in an attack on a police vehicle occupied by several persons or against a police/military post.

Assault

The objective of the act is to inflict pain or injury upon the victim(s), but not cause loss of life or permanent ill effect such as maiming. This normally involves the use of some type of weapon, including such basic devices as stones, bricks, sticks, and so on. This often occurs as the result of political, religious, ethnic and other factional disputes. For the purposes of the PRAS database, it does not include acts of purely personal or criminal nature.

Bombing

The object of the act normally is destruction or damage of a facility through the covert placement of bombs. The action is clandestine in contrast to a facility attack. Normally, the identity of the perpetrator(s) is not known at the time, although claims of responsibility often follow. The devices are usually placed at night or at least covertly and detonate after the bombers have departed. Bombings do not involve taking a facility or installation by attack and then placing bombs. In contrast to a facility attack, which often is aimed at physically taking over the installation, a bombing is designed simply to destroy or damage it. The clandestine nature of bombing separates it from facility attacks, as does the fact there is no intention to take the installation or occupy it, or to take hostages. The target of a bombing often is unoccupied or its occupants asleep.

Facility attack

The objective of the act is to rob, damage or occupy a specific installation. The term 'installation' includes towns, buildings and in some cases, as mentioned previously, vehicles. Thus a bank robbery is a facility attack although all its guards may have been killed. The objective in such an action was robbery of a facility, not killing the guards. The occupation of a town, wherein persons may be killed or wounded, also is a facility

attack since the objective was to take the town (installation), not kill or wound persons. Again, it is the objective of the operation that is the determining factor. The idea or objective of the operation is important if, for example, bombs are left behind by the attackers. In such a case, the bombing of the building was not the aim – the aim was to take it over by assault. Bombs were left to do additional damage and/or cause disruption to facilitate the escape of the attackers. Facility attacks may be carried out using automatic weapons, explosives, incendiaries, and so on. Normally, a multi-member team is involved. The operation is carried out openly, in contrast to the covert placement of bombs at night. Hostages may be taken, but this is not the primary objective of the act.

Hijacking

The objective of the act is to assume control by force or threat of force of a conveyance such as an aircraft, boat, ship, bus, automobile, or other vehicle for the purpose of diverting it to an unprogrammed destination, obtain payment of a ransom, force the release of prisoners, or some other political objective.

Kidnapping

The objective of the act is to obtain payment of a ransom, force the release of political prisoner(s), or achieve some other political objective. If the person is killed in the course of the kidnapping process, this does not make it an assassination. It still remains a kidnapping. Kidnapping is aimed at a specific person(s). A facility attack against a bank, wherein hostages may be taking, is not a kidnapping because the hostage-taking is incidental to the primary objective.

Maiming

The objective of the act is to inflict permanent injury, disfigurement, or incapacitation upon the victim(s) but not cause loss of life. 'Kneecapping' and castration are examples of maimings. For the purposes of the PRAS database, this does not include acts of a purely personal or criminal nature.

APPENDIX B: REGIONAL COMPOSITIONS

North America	Canada, Mexico, United States
Central American and Caribbean	Antigua and Barbuda, Bahamas, Barbados, Beliz, Bermuda, Cayman Islands, Costa Rica, Cuba, Dominica, Dominican Republic, El Salvador, Grenada, Guadeloupe, Guatemala, Haiti, Honduras, Jamaica, Martinique, Nicaragua, Panama, Puerto Rico, St. Kitts and Nevis, Trinidad and Tobago, Virgin Islands (US)
South America	Argentina, Bolivia, Brazil, Chile, Colombia, Ecuador, Falkland Islands, French Guiana, Guyana, Paraguay, Peru, Suriname, Uruguay, Venezuela
East Asia	China, Hong Kong, Japan, Macau, North Korea, South Korea, Taiwan
Southeast Asia	Brunei, Cambodia, Indonesia, Laos, Malaysia, Myanmar, Philippines, Singapore, Thailand, Vietnam, Timor-Leste, South Vietnam
South Asia	Afghanistan, Bangladesh, Bhutan, India, Maldives, Mauritius, Nepal, Pakistan, Seychelles, Sri Lanka
Central Asia	Kazakhstan, Kyrgyzstan, Tajikistan, Uzbekistan
Western Europe	Andorra, Austria, Belgium, Corsica, Denmark, East Germany (GDR), Finland, France, Germany, Gibraltar, Great Britain, Greece, Iceland, Ireland, Isle of Man, Italy, Luxembourg, Malta, Netherlands, Northern Ireland, Norway, Portugal, Spain, Sweden, Switzerland, West Germany (FRG)
Eastern Europe	Albania, Bosnia-Herzegovina, Bulgaria, Croatia, Czechoslovakia, Czech Republic, Hungary, Kosovo, Macedonia, Moldova, Montenegro, Poland, Romania, Serbia, Serbia-Montenegro, Slovak Republic, Slovenia, Yugoslavia
Middle East and North Africa	Algeria, Bahrain, Cyprus, Egypt, Iran, Iraq, Israel, Jordan, Kuwait, Lebanon, Libya, Morocco, North Yemen, Qatar, Saudi Arabia, South Yemen, Syria, Tunisia, Turkey, United Arab Emirates, West Bank and Gaza Strip, Western Sahara, Yemen
Sub-Saharan Africa	Angola, Benin, Botswana, Burkina Faso, Burundi, Cameroon, Central African Republic, Chad, Comoros, Congo (Brazzaville), Congo (Kinshasa), Djibouti, Equatorial Guinea, Eritrea, Ethiopia, Gabon, Gambia, Ghana, Guinea, Guinea-Bissau, Ivory Coast, Kenya, Lesotho, Liberia, Madagascar, Malawi, Mauritania, Mozambique, Namibia, Niger, Nigeria, Rhodesia, Rwanda, Senegal, Sierra Leone, Somalia, South Africa, Sudan, Swaziland, Tanzania, Togo, Uganda, Zambia, Zimbabwe
Russia and the Newly Independent States	Armenia, Azerbaijan, Belarus, Estonia, Georgia, Latvia, Lithuania, Russia, Soviet Union, Ukraine
Australasia and Oceania	Australia, Fiji, French Polynesia, New Caledonia, New Hebrides, New Zealand, Papua New Guinea, Samoa (Western Samoa), Solomon Islands, Vanuatu, Wallis and Futuna

Perceptual Dimensions
of Crime

In this section of the handbook we present seven chapters that are concerned with the perceptual dimensions of crime and victimization: how crime and its control are represented by the media; the disjuncture between these representations and how crime and law enforcement are experienced by those on their receiving ends; the very real practical challenges these issues present with respect to the operationalization of concepts and the implementation of research designs across international borders; the utilization of reflexivity in criminological research; and the pleasure and perils of conducting research on subjects – crime, deviance, victimization and social control – the meanings of which are not only densely political, but are also simultaneously taken for granted by many but highly context dependent in practice.

As the chapters themselves reveal, research into the perceptual dimensions of crime has witnessed considerable methodological innovation from within criminology in recent years. A compelling exemplar of this innovation is articulated in Cécile Van de Voorde's chapter, 'Ethnographic Photography in Criminological Research'. A social activist and documentary photographer as well as a criminologist, Van de Voorde is a pioneer of the use of imagery to engage and enliven academic and popular interest in questions of crime, victimization and social control. Her chapter utilizes her own photographs, some gathered in the course of ethnographic enquiry, to illustrate new ways in which criminologists can reach out to wider audiences of non-specialists, including communities damaged by, or recovering from, crime and transgression. Drawing inspiration

from the works of Howard Becker and Margaret Mead, as well as an instructive legacy of photo-journalism addressed to war, Van de Voorde uses photography as a means of illuminating the inter-sections between crime, political protests, immigration and global inequality. Her work illustrates how the production of new and captivating images can facilitate the interrogation of taken-for-granted representations of crime, whether these be predominant political constructions of crime, people's everyday talk, or the responses of interviewees participating in criminological research.

Continuing in this ethnographic vein, the cultural criminologist Jeff Ferrell uses his chapter to explain how autoethnography – the ultra-reflexive method of ethnographically exploring and accounting for the self – can be used to decipher the social and cultural contexts in which deviance occurs and transgressions are policed. Describing the years he spent, first as an urban graffiti writer, then as an urban trash scrounger and rough sleeper, Ferrell illustrates what a profoundly emotional and physical investment good ethnographic research in criminology requires. Ferrell's vivid reflections on the risky situations he chose to put himself in, and the status inconsistency he endured as a consequence, take him to the conclusion that there can be no ethnography within criminology that is not also autoethnographic. For him, there is no avoiding the need to take account of one's own investment in, and impact upon, the field of enquiry: an important lesson for a discipline indebted to so many participant observation studies of illicit behaviour. In so doing, Ferrell reveals the centrality of interpretive narration, and the many forms this may take, to reflexive autoethnographic practice.

Likewise, as Liz Stanley's chapter, 'Interviewing Victims of State Violence', demonstrates, criminological research that involves interviewing can also demand a heightened level of emotional and cultural reflexivity from researchers. Drawing on her groundbreaking fieldwork in Timor-Leste, Stanley explores the intersections between the issues that arose for her as a relatively privileged academic researcher and the challenges involved in disclosure for a community trying to come to terms with pervasive state violence. Through in-depth interviews, Stanley explores the complexities of researching a subject which is almost impossible to 'tell about'; 'torture', by definition, involving the administration of indescribable physical and psychological pain in order to silent dissent and extract confessions. In her account of this remarkable study, Stanley explores some of the practical difficulties of conducting research in places where barriers of language, multiple power differentials, local custom and gossip, and the logistics of travel collude with a history of oppression and colonialism to compound the challenges of gathering data. Stanley's account of working with translators who did not always convey the full force of the sentiment expressed by her interviewees is particularly revealing, and should be of interest to all criminologists interested in cross-cultural research, whatever their approach.

What counts as a systematic approach to examining issues of representation and meaning is a central theme in Moira Peelo and Keith Soothill's chapter, 'Questioning Homicide and the Media: Analysis of Content or Content Analysis?' Peelo and Soothill explain that while mixed-methods approaches were once regarded by many social scientists as something of a compromise best avoided, the necessity of developing responsive research designs, able to evolve, mutate and merge, has encouraged a resurgence of interest in how different approaches might complement each other. In their own study of the relationship between the actuality of homicide and media reporting of it Peelo and Soothill combined content analysis, with utilization of the Offenders' Index, in-depth case study analysis, and more textual, discursive forms of reading news stories. Their mixed methods approach revealed much about the differences between the reality of homicide and media reporting, why some cases attract more media attention than others, and hence the role of homicide in constructing social order. But perhaps more importantly, their chapter also illustrates how research designs can and should evolve within research agendas that extend beyond the confines any discrete project.

The importance of responsive research design is a theme that also unites the three concluding chapters in this section, all of which are specifically concerned with the development and utilisation of crime surveys. The first of this trilogy is Pat Mayhew and Jan Van Dijk's account of the challenges of assessing crime through international victimization surveys. Mayhew and Van Dijk offer an overview of the development of standardized methods that provide alternative measures to officially recorded crime. The most commonly used example is the national household victimization survey – a particular specialism of criminology. Technically, however, there remain many difficulties both in terms of establishing tools that can be used across different countries and in terms of operationalizing those tools in ways that enable valid comparisons to be made once the data are collected. In their insider account of the development of the International Crime Victimisation Survey (ICVS), Mayhew and van Dijk provide criminologists with a rare opportunity to see the development of a new methodological approach likely to be at the frontier of our discipline for years to come. They also outline the key methodological challenges that will need to be overcome ahead of the ICVS' planned roll out in 2013 if its full potential is to be realized.

Of course, household victimization studies have also been used to assess public attitudes towards crime, the mismatch between official and public diagnoses of the risk of victimization having generated a small industry within criminology addressed specifically to understanding the fear of crime. In their chapter, Emily Gray, Jon Jackson and Stephen Farrall provide an overview of the international research that has been conducted on negative emotional responses to the threat of common crimes like burglary, theft and assault. Thereafter Gray et al. outline the major breakthroughs that have been made in terms of capturing the diversity of reactions to crime in terms of their emotional range, frequency and endurance, many of the innovations developed by this particular team of researchers over a number of years. Drawing on the burgeoning psychological literature about responses to surveys, Gray et al. show what more criminologists have to gain from the better use of longitudinal data, and how such approaches enable the many dimensions to crime fear to be captured over time and on a larger scale, without reducing their complexity.

Mapping this complexity accurately is imperative, as Julian Roberts, Matrina Feilzer and Mike Hough demonstrate in their chapter, 'Measuring Public Attitudes to Criminal Justice'. Too often satiating public anger is cited as grounds enough for 'tough' criminal justice policy making. Roberts et al. review the main ways in which public attitudes to criminal justice are measured, setting out the principal differences between opinion polls, surveys and the kinds of experiments that access people's reactions to particular criminogenic scenarios. Roberts et al. illuminate the value of mixed-methods approaches to public attitudes, showing how interviews or focus groups can supplement for the limitations of survey-based approaches. As Roberts et al. illustrate with examples from their own projects, whatever one's method, getting the question wording correct, coping appropriately with participant indecision, and taking account of social desirability effects are all crucial if one is to make sense of the full range of public attitudes towards criminal justice. Taking full account of these complexities is also, perhaps more importantly, crucial if criminologists are to build trust in the capacity of criminological research to represent public opinion accurately: an objective to which the work of Roberts et al. makes an incisive contribution.

13

Ethnographic Photography in Criminological Research

Cécile Van de Voorde

INTRODUCTION

Visual research methods relying on photography, motion films (documentary, ethnographic, observational and full-length feature films) or even video clips easily engage viewers and work wonders against the inertia of the printed word (Pink, 2001; Sooryamoorthy, 2007). Yet, Howard Becker deplored just a decade ago that '[t]he social sciences have lagged behind the natural sciences in the use of visual materials' (Becker, 2000: 333). In anthropology, sociology, and cultural studies, photographic images have now earned an esteemed place in the toolkit of researchers, especially (but not exclusively) ethnographers (see Collier, 2003). In criminology, on the other hand, we have only just begun to give serious thought to the use and usefulness of photographs (see Ferrell and Van de Voorde, 2010). However, the appropriateness of the inclusion of photography in criminological research, and in particular the use of ethnographic photography, is undeniable. In a late modern world saturated with images, where our senses are constantly assaulted and challenged by visual representations and meanings, photography plays no less than a vital role in the critical analysis of crime and deviance, and related social control mechanisms. While the plea for visual criminology has been made for several years (Greek, 2006; Hinds-Aldrich, 2007; Van de Voorde, 2005, 2006, 2007), it is only very recently that a few criminologists vigorously heeded that call. Most noticeably, they have argued that cultural criminology provides the ideal conceptual framework for rich photoethnographic narratives of crime and deviance (Ferrell and Van de Voorde, 2010; Hayward and Presdee, 2010; Van de Voorde, 2009a, 2009b, 2010).

As Margaret Mead (1995) famously emphasized, using photographs in a discipline of words can be daunting. Most criminologists indeed shy away from using documentary photography for analytical purposes, preferring instead the safer confines of the evidentiary value of photographs. What is troublesome, of course, is that '[i]mporting photographs into a discipline defined by words and numbers may create a certain decorative appeal, but of itself it does nothing to address the taken-for-granted dominance of those very words and numbers' (Ferrell and Van de Voorde, 2010: 36). Photography should instead be used to enhance conventional ethnographic narratives for photographs are not mere illustrations of written text: they can be contextualized in relation to text and can also be presented as self-sufficient photo-essays depicting certain events, behaviours, people, cultures or social forms (Ferrell, 2006; Ferrell and Van de Voorde, 2010; Hamm, 2007; Snyder, 2008; Tunnell, 2006, 2009; Van de Voorde, 2005, 2007, 2009a, 2009b).

DOCUMENTARY PHOTOGRAPHY AND THE ROOTS OF ETHNOGRAPHIC PHOTOGRAPHY

Photography takes an instant out of time, altering life by holding it still (Dorothea Lange).

Ethnographic photography as used in criminological research today springs from the photodocumentary tradition. Photojournalism, social documentary photography and war photography have all contributed to the growth of the photographic medium as a source of truthful, candid visual narratives chronicling social reality.

The roots of photojournalism can be traced to European battlefields in the nineteenth century. During the Crimean War (1853–1856), British photographer Roger Fenton and Rumanian artist Carol Szathmàri pioneered the use of photography to tell news stories. Like Fenton's work, photographs taken by US photographer Mathew Brady during the American Civil War were engraved and published in weekly magazines. After the first halftone news photograph was published in New York in 1880, photojournalism (*reportage*) soon became a staple of newspaper and magazine reporting. The golden age of photojournalism (1930s to 1950s) introduced the public to the works of W. Eugene Smith, Margaret Bourke-White, and Robert Capa. Known for his near-limitless temporal and moral commitment to the subjects of his photographs, Smith described his approach as 'photographic penetration deriving from study and awareness and participation' (as quoted in Miller, 1997: 150). French photographer Henri Cartier-Bresson, who is often regarded as the father of modern photojournalism, also gained great fame during this period. Cartier-Bresson mastered candid, *in situ* photography to capture what he termed the 'decisive moment'. The period was also marked by patterns of sensationalized crime coverage and photographic profiteering. Most infamously, Arthur Fellig (Weegee) used photography to document street crime in New York City, sometimes resorting to questionable tactics in order to find and photograph crime scenes before the police could arrive. 'If I had a picture of two handcuffed criminals being booked,' he once said, 'I would cut the picture in half and get five bucks for each.'

Social documentary photography (or concerned photography) is a form of critical photography that views the camera as an instrument of accusation against social injustice. It originated in England in the nineteenth century thanks to the keen eye of John Brinny, Henry Mayhew, and Thomas Annan. In the US, the forerunners of the genre were Jacob Riis and Lewis Hine. As early as 1890, Riis documented the extreme poverty of the New York City slums by focusing on immigrants, the homeless and the unemployed. In the early twentieth century, Hine, a sociologist, promoted the use of photography as an educational and political tool in thousands of photographs documenting the lives of child labourers and destitute immigrants in New York City. Social documentary photography was then popularized when the US Farm Security Administration (FSA), from 1935 to 1944, chronicled the plight of poor farmers across the US. As part of President Franklin D. Roosevelt's New Deal, the FSA was designed to fight rural poverty and highlight the urgency of rehabilitating rural areas. Its photography project yielded nearly 80,000 images by Dorothea Lange, Walker Evans, Russell Lee, Gordon Parks, Arthur Rothstein, and others. Some of these documentary photographs have persisted in collective memory as emblematic representations of the Great Depression and the suffering it engendered, even though many of them were staged or heavily edited once taken (including Lange's iconic 'Migrant Mother').

War photography has evolved tremendously since our earliest photographic records of combat, a series of 1847 daguerreotypes of the Mexican–American War. Nineteenth-century war photographers were unable to provide genuine battle photography and documented the aftermath of battle instead, staging pictures to convey the atrocities of war while overcoming the technological limitations of the times. World War II changed the face of war photography, starting with Robert Capa's work. Capa covered several conflicts, including the Spanish Civil War during which he produced 'The Falling Soldier', the controversial 1937 photograph of a Spanish soldier getting shot. However, he is best known for his work in the 1940s, most notably the dozen images he captured on Omaha Beach on D-Day. 'If your pictures aren't good enough, you're not close enough,' Capa once said – poignant words indeed from a man who risked his life to document warfare and eventually lost it, camera in hand, on an Indochinese battlefield. Today, war photography, much like armed conflict in general, is omnipresent in the mass media. The power of such images on viewers and readers is undeniable. During the Vietnam War, for instance, a public outcry followed the publication of photographs of scores of coffins draped in American flags during the repatriation of dead soldiers; public opinion about the war markedly shifted and the photographs became a significant factor in the withdrawal of US troops from Vietnam. When similar images surfaced in the news within the context of the ongoing conflict in Iraq, they were promptly censored by the Bush Administration.

Documentary photography in its various forms is now widely recognized as a legitimate tool for the representation of people and events. The ever-evolving tradition has many notable exemplars today. James Nachtwey (1999, 2004, 2006) produces ever-startling war photography in some of the most dangerous conflict zones in the world. The socially committed photography of Sebastião

Salgado (2001, 2005) has yielded an astounding body of black-and-white photographs documenting the plight of migrants and refugees in developing countries. Likewise, Steve McCurry (2003, 2006, 2007, 2009) has relentlessly documented the human toll of armed conflict across the globe in countless evocative photographs he has added to his impressive collection over the past three decades. Many more photographers are devotedly contributing to the preservation of photography not simply as an art form but as a public awareness and education medium.

Figure 13.1   Students for a Free Tibet demonstration, New York City, 2007

ETHNOGRAPHIC PHOTOGRAPHY AND THE ADVENT OF VISUAL CRIMINOLOGY

> Photography is a small voice, at best, but sometimes one photograph, or a group of them, can lure our sense of awareness (W. Eugene Smith).

Today we are witnessing the emergence of visual criminology as a bona fide approach to criminological research, and we owe this tardy methodological breakthrough to a splinter group composed of cultural criminologists and a few other dilettantes who have used photographs for documentary and investigative purposes. Some scholars have analyzed print media constructions of the meaning of criminality through the selection and placement of photographs for publication (see Jones and Wardle, 2008; McLaughlin and Greer, 2008). Others have methodically examined genocidal tourism (Morrison, 2004), the Abu Ghraib torture photographs (Hamm, 2007), or visual representations of the wrongfully convicted (Courtney and Lyng, 2007). Yet other scholars have been either producing their own gripping photographic essays and analyses of crime and deviance or theorizing the photograph within the context of crime and transgression (see, for instance, Alvelos, 2005; Brown, 2006; Rodriguez, 2003; Snyder, 2008; Tunnell, 2006, 2009; Van de Voorde, 2009a, 2009b, 2010; Young, 2004).

This new trend in criminological research is concomitant with the revival of ethnographic field research. In recent years, particularly within cultural criminology, ethnography has resurged as the humanistic counterpoint to the sterile data sets found in orthodox criminology. Much like documentary photography, ethnography is both the product and the process of fieldwork (see Ferrell and Hamm, 1998; Freidenberg, 1998; Van de Voorde, 2009b, 2010). More specifically, *ethnography* is

> an approach to experiencing, interpreting and representing culture and society that informs and

is informed by sets of different disciplinary agendas and theoretical principles. Rather than being a method for the collection of 'data', ethnography is a process of creating and representing knowledge (about society, culture, individuals) that is based on ethnographers' own experiences ... It should account not only for the observable, recordable realities that may be translated into written notes and texts, but also for objects, visual images, the immaterial, and the sensory nature of human experience and knowledge (Pink, 2001: 18).

Photography as a methodological tool for criminological research

Ethnographic photography can be described as documentary photography with a specific investigative and narrative purpose. Still photography, like other visual methods, is very useful 'in the process of validating interpretations with study populations and submitting ethnographic renditions to general publics' (Freidenberg, 1998: 169). Thus, 'knowledge is gained by close and repeated interaction with specific individuals who provide information about different cultures and different ways of being or of conceptualizing one's place in the world' (ibid. 170).

Photographs can provide timely, forthright representations for use in ethnographic investigation and narratives. They can be used as 'empirical data' in a realistic, unbiased, and systematic fashion, which answers the continuous call for more sustained empirical analyses of the visual dimensions of culture and crime. Although field photographs may not be ethnographic per se, they can be defined as such by discourse and content and through interpretation and context. Indeed, the 'ethnographicness' of a photograph depends upon

Figure 13.2   Paris, France, 2009

its situation, interpretation, and usage 'to invoke meanings and knowledge that are of ethnographic interest' (Pink, 2001: 19).

For the purpose of ethnographic research in criminology, documentary photography may be used: (1) by *making visual representations* (i.e., producing images via documentary photography); (2) by *examining pre-existing visual representations* (i.e., studying third-party images and graphic displays to gather information about a topic or issue of interest); and (3) by *collaborating with social actors in the production of visual representations* (i.e., co-producing photographs on site or resorting to photo-elicitation to probe the participants' visual meanings and gain new knowledge from their personal narratives).

Ethnographic photography can play an important role in interviews and focused discussions. *Photo-elicitation* can help to determine how people use photographs to reference aspects of their experience and knowledge. Insofar as 'photographs can be *tools* with which to obtain knowledge' (Collier and Collier, 1986: 99), photographic images (produced in the field or obtained from archival visual records) can be shown to participants in order to elicit responses from them and ensure that they actively work with ethnographers in the interpretation of visual representations of reality. The integration of photo-elicitation in ethnography redefines it as a model of *collaboration in research*. It can also be useful to view photographs with the participants when coming across public displays to further explore and create relationships between visual and verbal knowledge. 'By paying attention to how people interweave such images with verbal narratives, researchers may learn about how these individuals construct their lives and histories' (Pink, 2001: 74).

The photograph in Figure 13.3 was taken during a research trip to India. While I was waiting for my interpreter at the main square in Dharamsala, a small town in the Himalayan foothills where many Tibetan exiles live, including His Holiness

Figure 13.3   Dharamsala, India, 2010

the Dalai Lama, I took pictures of passer-bys. A few days later, when I showed this image of two Indian policemen to my interpreter, he exclaimed: 'Oh, these are not nice people! They always stop us Tibetans when we are on motorcycles, but they never stop Indians even if they are speeding or driving the wrong way on a one-way road! But we get stopped and harassed all the time when we reach the square. Sometimes they catch us at the bottom [of the hillside road], but usually they just call these guys up here and they stop us. They take our papers, give us fines for no reasons, and demand bribes from us, too … Now I wear a helmet, so no one knows I am Tibetan. I can drive home from work in peace. And wearing helmets is mandatory now, so everyone should have one! They would avoid all the trouble!'

Photography as an instrument for presenting criminological research

Ethnographic photography enables researchers and viewers to consider photographic images past aesthetic notions and beyond the meaning contained in the very images. Instead, photographs are vessels from which individual viewers extract meaning (Hayward, 2010; Schwartz, 1989; Van de Voorde, 2005, 2007). Given the dynamic (albeit formulaic) interplay between the photographer, the viewer and the photograph, meanings are actively constructed rather than passively picked up. This becomes even more evident if one considers the dynamics of photographs and text in criminological research, a problem that can be at least partially addressed by considering the purpose of images vis-à-vis text, and vice versa. Photographic images ought to be used in ways that transcend their illustrative purpose. To break the yoke of the written word, we have a responsibility to emancipate photographs from textual content by recognizing their intrinsic value not only as *legitimate research instruments* but also as *educational and social justice tools*, all the while recognizing that images and text may very well complement each other wherever appropriate. According to Barthes (1978), photographs are inherently polysemic. 'The viewer of the image receives at one and the same time the perceptual message and the cultural message' (ibid. 36), thus illustrating the communicative power of mass images and the need, at times, for textual explication of the cultural norms and perceptual qualities of photographs. Barthes (1981) and Sontag (1977) further suggest a visual semiotics attuned to the layering of meaning, with *denotation* focusing on what or who is depicted, and *connotation* emphasizing the various ideas and values that are expressed through the content and structure of representation (see also Ferrell and Van de Voorde, 2010).

For all practical purposes, the final *compositional phase* of a photoethnographic study is significant insofar as it highlights the interconnectedness of education, research, and praxis. The compositional structure of the narrative should reflect the theory development goals of the research. The significance of the findings, whether cast in academic or practical terms, is as important as the rigour with which the research was conducted. They can be disseminated in one or more formats, including but not limited to written reports and scholarly articles, mass media publications, monographs, photographic essays (inserted in text or published as self-standing essays in pertinent outlets), seminars, workshops, and public visual displays or photo exhibitions. They can also be used in the classroom to familiarize students with the relevance, significance and usefulness of innovative, integrative and interpretive research, which can lead to curricular and professional development opportunities for students at all levels.

TEACHING AND LEARNING ETHNOGRAPHIC PHOTOGRAPHY

To take photographs means to recognize – simultaneously and within a fraction of a second – both

Figure 13.4   May Day 2010 demonstration against anti-immigration law reforms, New York City

the fact itself and the rigorous organization of visually perceived forms that give it meaning (Henri Cartier-Bresson).

The priority of research methods instruction in criminology is often to provide students an adequate set of skills to tackle quantitative problems. If a course includes a segment on field research, it is typically limited and more interpretive qualitative methods, including ethnography, are often overlooked. Visual methods are glaringly absent from the extant criminological literature, as noted above, and they are virtually non-existent in criminology lesson plans today. Nonetheless, photographs can be invaluable pedagogical tools. Even though ethnographic photography cannot be quantified or explained with the help of mathematical analysis or advanced computer programs, it can still be easily taught by criminological research methods instructors. Students, who today have near universal access to picture-making technology via small digital cameras and mobile phones, need not be accomplished photographers, nor do they have to have a sophisticated knowledge of art theory or aesthetics, advanced technical skills or a superior understanding of the history of photography. Photoethnographic research can effectively be taught in a similar fashion as ethnography is – by promoting the acquisition and development of three essential research skills: *observation*, *analysis* and *interpretation*.

Experiential learning is a *sine qua non*. Whereas investigation (understood here as the act of collecting information from created or gathered photographs as well as the elicitation of information via the use of photographs in semi-structured or open interviews) may be explained abstractly or didactically, the observation and interpretive analysis phases cannot. Although some basic photoethnographic observational and analytical skills can be acquired within the confines of a lecture hall, students must learn from direct experience with the photographic medium and be active participants at all three levels. Indeed, observation 'requires both intensive training and self-discipline' and students need to learn how to 'be attentive to both significant and seemingly insignificant aspects of social life' (Leblanc, 1998: 62). They should be taught and then scrupulously train themselves to keep regular field notes detailing their observations in addition to what is captured in the photographs. Likewise, students must be keenly involved in the iterative process of interpretive analysis in order to systematically generate theory; this is a rigorous but crucial phase of any photoethnographic project that cannot be limited to a lecture framework. Evolving outside of a classroom in a truly interactive environment in

Figure 13.5   Paris, France, 2004

which they will have opportunities to fully embrace the significance of visual methods, especially the photographic medium, is a must for students at any level.

Documenting social reality, whether on photographic film or an electronic sensor, implies a decision-making process that takes a fraction of a second, a keen eye and much practice. For a good start, students should learn about basic image composition (positioning of the subjects or objects, background, distance between camera and subjects), black and white *versus* colour, flash *versus* ambient light, vertical *versus* horizontal format, candid *versus* posed images (documentary style can include both). Dramatic changes in the resulting photograph will incur based on very simple (and typically rapid) decisions made by the photographer, who is not merely pressing a button to take pictures but rather actively involved in the making of each photograph.

It should be emphasized that an interest in ethnographic photography does not automatically translate into a need to invest in expensive, complex professional equipment. Technology has certainly improved in the past decade alone, but the switch to sophisticated digital cameras is not necessary. One of the many advantages of high-end digital cameras, especially medium-format models, is that they enable professional photographers to output very large prints (40 × 60" or more) for exhibitions. For qualitative research methods instruction and assignments, the use of such technologically advanced and often prohibitively priced equipment is unwarranted. A simple point-and-shoot model is convenient and adequate. Even digital cameras are not compulsory in the toolkit of a field ethnographer or experimenting documentary photographer. Like many professional photographers today, I own several digital single-lens reflex (D-SLR) models, and yet I still shoot with 35 mm and medium-format film cameras and print my own black

Figure 13.6   New York City subway, 2007

and white photographs. The possibilities truly are endless.

Photographs are created to be looked at. It is not the technology used to make them that matters but the act of *seeing* the photographs. The 'decisive moment' (*l'instant décisif*) that defined his 'images on the run' (*images à la sauvette*) set the pace for future generations of documentary photographers and photojournalists. 'To photograph is to hold one's breath,' Cartier-Bresson once said, 'when all faculties converge to capture fleeting reality. It is at that precise moment that mastering an image becomes a great physical and intellectual joy.' While the camera is merely a research tool, close attention must be paid to the cadence of the photograph-making process and the *organic rhythm* of the photograph. Photographic images capture fleeting moments and convey infinitesimal parts of reality. They flow harmoniously at the speed of the events they depict, and yet they also fix moments in time, thus establishing their value as vigorous expressions of the relationship between subject and form.

The instruction of ethnographic photography should build upon *learning activities* designed to keep students interested, challenged and actively involved in the learning experience. Systematically monitoring skill acquisition and development is a requisite aspect of teaching visual research methods. Wherever possible, instructors should use formative assessments; that is, assignments that provide feedback and help prepare for summative/graded activities, assess prior knowledge, or serve as motivational activities. Smaller thematic assignments can be created and mini-portfolios assembled to help students acquire and develop the necessary skills for the completion of a full-blown photoethnographic project. Learning activities should also allow peer review and self-assessment (e.g., short reflection exercises focused on student perceptions of field experience, setting/meeting goals).

KEY METHODOLOGICAL CHALLENGES

The camera is my tool. Through it I give a reason to everything around me (André Kertész).

Research design and conceptual framework

A photoethnographic project should be designed as a first-hand, contextualized, naturalistic, hypothesis-generating, emic (insider) study. Inasmuch as its goal is to generate theory in a rather inductive fashion, it can be viewed as closely related to the grounded theory tradition. Ethnography is a full-blown methodology encompassing multiple methods, requiring the collection and analysis of multiple elements of information, and involving a sustained engagement in contexts of production (the participants' worlds). It offers rich opportunities for contextualized studies of multi-faceted issues and makes it possible to explore and track dynamic situated meanings and practices, which in turn favours the development of holistic understandings of complex social phenomena (Brewer, 2000). A stated goal of academic research is to reach towards context and contextualization, and ethnography has much to offer at both levels. Moreover, ethnography must be understood as *deep theorizing* (Blommaert, 2007). Indeed, it fundamentally challenges the traditional ways in which pressing social issues and their respective contexts are conceptualized as separate phenomena, and thus provides outstanding analytical tools to narrow that gap. Ethnographic photography can only help solidify underlying themes and highlight greater social issues by methodically probing into the meanings – understood, apparent, hidden, constructed, taken for granted, ignored, or otherwise – of the phenomena criminologists strive to explain.

Cultural criminologists have been pressing for a more systematic use of visual methods in criminological research, especially photography (Ferrell and Van de Voorde, 2010; Hayward, 2010). Cultural criminology is a theoretical, methodological, and interventionist approach that highlights the continuous generation of meaning surrounding human interaction (Ferrell et al., 2008). This inter-disciplinary approach is all the more relevant here as ethnography and theory are mutually informative: theory focuses and sharpens ethnography while ethnography grounds theory in the richness of social life (Peirce, 1995). A theoretically engaged photoethnography can facilitate dialogue across fields and methods by providing a trans-situational language. In addition, it will promote visually *and* ethnographically based contributions to policy or intervention, which would be a welcome innovation in both research and practice. By adopting a critical outlook rooted in cultural criminology, photoethnographic projects also align themselves with a post-modern penchant for situating research in its social context and determining how knowledge is shaped by the values of human agents and communities involved in power differences.

Doing ethnographic photography, and 'doing it right'

The use of documentary photographs for ethnographic representation and knowledge generation involves three fundamental activities: observation, analysis and interpretation. Photography is indeed an art and a method of *observation* consisting of making visual representations, examining pre-existing visual representations, and/or collaborating with social actors in the production of visual representations. To decide what to photograph, a thorough inventory is necessary. Furthermore,

> how and where to begin photographing requires some strategic planning, because the act of making photographs may serve as the community's introduction to the photographer, her activities and her aims. Data produced during this stage of an ethnographic study require closer inspection later on – the status of initial pictures is uncertain, their value as data is determined during the course of the research (Schwartz, 1989: 124–5).

One could start with photographing a physical environment, so as to create a descriptive record of basic architectural features. Making oneself visible in the field is also important at this early stage, so people may be aware of the photoethnographer's presence in the community. In addition to recording physical surroundings, researchers ought to observe patterns of daily activity and systematically record their observations, as well as descriptions of their own photographic endeavours, in detailed field notes. It is always helpful to also ponder upon the role of the camera as a tool to gain access, a starting point for conversations, and a catalyst for networking within and sometimes even beyond the community. Its potentially negative impact should also be considered. Special attention should constantly be paid to the role played and, essentially, the space occupied by the researcher. If a telephoto lens is used, for example, does it enable direct, unobtrusive observation or does it facilitate unethical, covert shooting tactics and likely breaches of privacy? What may be the 'contaminating' effects of the camera? Does its presence merely serve the purpose of recording

behaviours or practices, or can it effectively elicit performance?

Photoethnographic research yields a profusion of rich visual data that must be meticulously organized and analyzed, both continuously and iteratively. In order to structure and interpret the meanings derived from the raw visuals, the latter must be methodically transcribed, coded, categorized and analyzed through each phase of the project. Hence, the analytical process is *inductive, recursive* and *interactive*. It enables researchers to build patterns, categories and themes from the bottom up by organizing the data into increasingly more abstract units of information. They need to work back and forth between themes and their database until a comprehensive set of themes is established. Participants should also actively collaborate throughout the analysis so they may provide additional insight and help shape emerging themes or abstractions. Such a thorough approach will move a photoethnographic study beyond 'thick description' (Geertz, 1973) and information-rich analysis; indeed, beyond bridging gaps in the extant literature. It represents a remarkable opportunity to test and generate theory. Perhaps more importantly, it is a unique catalyst for sharing one's fieldwork experience and disseminating insightful findings in and beyond a publication or a classroom via symposia, workshops, and photography exhibits, so that others in academia and the general public may benefit intellectually and practically from recurring exposure to critical fieldwork and visual research.

The meanings of a photograph emerge in the viewing process itself. This is not a limitation since 'the multiple meanings negotiated by viewers can be mined for the rich data they yield' (Schwartz, 1989: 122). Photographs ought be duly coded, organized and compared in order to explore the processual and sequential character of visible social arrangements (Ball and Smith, 1992). Both the analysis and the interpretation of the images will typically draw from three key concepts: (1) the *content* (what is given in the photo); (2) the *referent* (what the photo is of); and (3) the *context* (the physical or social presentation of the photographs made).

There are many ways to analyse ethnographic photographs. A simple yet effective method is *layered analysis*, whereby photographs are examined in continuously greater depth so as to explore 'the connections between each consecutive stratum of explanation' (Dowdall and Golden, 1989: 187). The approach includes three layers:

• *Appraisal:* Compare ethnographic photographs with written (historical or cultural) records. What information do the photographs present? Is it in accordance with written (historical or cultural) records? If there are discrepancies, note possible explanations for them. Are the misrepresentations deliberate or did they result from other physical factors, crime practices, social stigma, cultural issues or crime control mechanisms? Quantitative analysis of the images is acceptable at this stage.

- *Inquiry*. Focus on emerging themes in the entire set of images. The photographic images are considered as a whole, whether they were created for the specific purpose of the ethnographic project or collected from third parties. Themes and patterns will emerge (both subtle and more salient ones). It is important at this stage to bear in mind that 'photographs convey emotion and sentiment, not just neutral information' (ibid. 194). This could effectively lay the foundation for visual grounded theory.

- *Interpretation*: Conduct an in-depth examination of each individual photograph. Adequate descriptions of social events and phenomena require thick description; that is, observing and collecting everything needed to provide a detailed account of places, people and activities within a given social setting. It enables researchers to focus on details that are important to the study participants, so as to explore what is significant for participants within a specific context. Local knowledge is therefore indispensable (Boeije, 2010; Richards, 2009). However, since this third layer of the analytical process relies on prior inquiry, 'the interpretation is necessarily contextual and historical' and the way that 'we "read" the photographic text' is going to be naturally influenced by the 'base of information gleaned from other sources' (Dowdall and Golden, 1989: 188). Analyzing individual photographs is a difficult task, and yet it is most rewarding as it enhances our understanding of textures and nuances.

Threats to the integrity of photoethnographic studies

The purpose of photoethnographic research is to engage in knowledge making as a human activity, not to produce value-free knowledge of the social world as an objective entity. Such a normative and interpretive approach to human inquiry requires a practical and theoretical sensitivity to various issues related to observation, analysis, and interpretation. The trustworthiness of such a qualitatively driven approach depends on its truth-value, consistency, applicability and neutrality (Lincoln and Guba, 1985).

Truth-value: Researchers must focus on the *credibility* of their study and whether the people studied will agree with the produced images and text (if any). To increase the truth-value of a photoethnographic study at the observation phase, researchers can use *multiple methods* and *multiple sources* of evidence (triangulation) so as to encourage convergent lines of inquiry and establish a useful chain of evidence. During the final composition phase, key informants should be asked to *review the draft* case study report (which will also enhance the reliability of the study).

Consistency: The *dependability* of a study hinges upon its consistency. Concern for consistency arises if inferences are made when events cannot be directly observed. *Pattern matching* can be used to compare empirically based patterns in the photographic data with predicted ones. Consistency will be higher where patterns coincide. *Explanation building*, an iterative process linked to pattern-matching logic, should also be used to formulate a general explanation that fits each individual case. *Rival explanations* (from researcher bias to rival practices or theories) may also be considered, defined and tested, wherever applicable. Finally, *logic models* can help stipulate complex chains of events over time by matching empirically observed events/issues to theoretically predicted events/issues at the individual and organizational levels.

Applicability: The applicability of the study depends on whether its findings can be extended or transferred – either as grounded theory or as an analytic synthesis that may be used by other researchers to further research the phenomenon or at least appreciate comparable cases. This addresses whether knowledge can be produced not by replicating the study but, rather, where extensive corroborating information gathered via additional photoethnographic studies (or more positivist analyses) of the chosen issue becomes available. The *transferability* of the findings will be maximized by focusing on: (a) the researcher's role and relationship with the study participants; (b) the site and key informant selection process; (c) the social context of both the phenomenon of interest and the photoethnographic study itself; (d) the observation and analytical strategies; (e) the accuracy of textual and visual data; (f) the typicality of the selected groups or sites; (g) the specificity and flexibility of the analytic framework; and (h) potential alternative interpretations.

Neutrality: The debate surrounding the potential subjectivity of photographs unsurprisingly impacts the claims of neutrality or *confirmability* that photoethnographers can make. If the photographs are viewed as works of art, they likely embody the personal concerns or views of the artist. They may express personal emotions and will certainly have a discernable aesthetic significance. If, on the other hand, the photographs are considered as mechanical reproductions of reality, then they are simply objective records that provide dispassionate and unmediated visual evidence of a specific action or moment in time.

As visual ethnographic documents, photographs are invaluable tools for the portrayal and explanation of deviance, transgression and social injustice by criminologists (as socially and politically engaged documentarists, rather than artists). However, photographs build upon the paradoxical nature of the photographic medium, which is lauded for its realism but typically subject to a multitude of perceptions and interpretations. Some doubts still linger today about the truth-value of documentary images produced by field researchers (see Ferrell and Van de Voorde, 2010; Pink, 2001). As Hayward (2010) points out,

> it is not just a case of image proliferation – contemporary society's keen sense of the visual demands that images also be both mutable and malleable. Here the 'logic of speed' meets liquidity of form, as images bleed from one medium to the next. Uploaded and downloaded, copied and cross-posted, Flickr-ed, Facebook-ed and PhotoShop-ped, the image today is as much about porosity and manipulation as it is about fixity and representation. This, of course, poses a question: what does the term 'image' actually mean under contemporary conditions?

It should thus be noted that the *documentary* nature of photography entails an *objective representation* (a mechanical record of something factual) and a *subjective interpretation* (a representation of the paradigm in which it was constructed) with meanings ascribed to the image by the photographer and the viewer. Photographs always have a context. Indeed, 'an ethnographic photograph cannot be reduced to the mere expression of the meaning that lies within it' since it is 'embedded in links of a general, historical, social, and personal nature' (Heintze, 1990: 131).

Consequently, it is crucial to assess the circumstances of image production. If one is producing one's own photographs, it is important to ensure that they will not be staged, faked, digitally altered or otherwise modified once taken (unless faces need to be blurred to conceal and protect the identity of the people pictured). If third-party images are used, the conditions in which they were produced and later disseminated have to be carefully researched and taken into consideration before they are used in the analysis or for photo-elicitation purposes. Given the profusion of images

readily available today – in musty photographic archives or just a click away on the Internet – the immediate and wider context(s) in which the photographs stand *must* be considered. Today, technological advances allow photographers to store thousands of images as digital files in a single memory card, bystanders can become 'citizen journalists' upon snapping shots on the street with their cell phones, and just a few clicks in a photo-editing software program can rework an image and result in not only a new visual representation but also a different interpretation of social 'reality'. Researchers are therefore well advised to proceed with extreme caution when they are processing their own images or considering using pre-existing ones for their analysis and interpretation of a given phenomenon. The images below illustrate the effects of simply angling, cropping, and captioning photographs.

Figure 13.7 Spontaneous shrine on Broadway (New York City) in honour of an 18-year-old graffiti artist killed by a driver with a suspended licence

A research protocol should be developed and explicitly recorded. Additionally, whether they produce their own images or not, researchers ought to not only systematically and meticulously document the procedures followed at the data collection stage, but also create and maintain a detailed database of the issue(s) or case(s) under study. *Research bias* can be systematically monitored and subjectivity therefore reduced by: (a) keeping a *field log* of dates, times, locations, people, and activities for every set of photographs created or collected; (b) keeping a *field journal* in order to record all decisions made while designing the study (including rationale for such decisions and data consistency/applicability evaluation); (c) documenting pertinent *ethical considerations*; that is, logging ethical issues, decisions, or actions where applicable; (d) ensuring *audibility* by documenting the techniques, codes, and categories used to manage the photographs; and (e) formally *corroborating initial findings* via confirmation interviews.

The neutrality of photoethnographic research can be optimized by prolonging on-site observation in order to ensure the dependability of the findings by providing more concrete information upon which to base the interpretative analysis of the phenomenon of interest. Moreover, triangulating across methods and sources should be a priority, so as not to rely exclusively on one type of observation. Photographs can thus be analyzed in conjunction with direct observations, open-ended or focused interviews, or documents (letters, memoranda, administrative reports, formal site studies, articles in the mass media, community newsletters, etc.). All of these additional sources of information can be used in order to corroborate and supplement photographic evidence. Finally, it is imperative to have participants actively check and corroborate the interpretation of all collected information and to collect referential materials in order to complement or support the photographic evidence collected on site.

Field issues

Access to the sites may be difficult. If the research requires permits from federal, state, or local government authorities, they must be requested *prior to* entering the field and photographing people, objects or places. If the project involves the use of pre-existing, third-party images, proper authorizations to access and use said images have to be secured as well. Accessing sites will generally not be difficult when the research involves locations open to the general public. Indeed, observing public behaviour and taking photographs at public events is typically freely permitted and acceptable.

If regulations change, of course, the research protocol has to be modified before any activities can be undertaken or continued. Overall, if public photography is not explicitly forbidden or discouraged, including street photography, then no formal permission is required to photograph and consent need not be obtained from individuals present in the public setting. However, this is not an absolute rule. Special circumstances might warrant extra caution out of courtesy and respect for special needs, emergency situations, or local customs.

Wherever fieldwork involves direct interaction with participants, it is crucial to develop a relationship based on mutual trust in order for access to be granted and for a *rapport* to be built. The nature of this relationship shapes the knowledge generated by the photoethnography. Instead of a more distanced perspective, as formalized in applicable ethical codes, it is possible to opt for a more contemporary and dynamic approach to fieldwork that values the interpersonal and interactive dimensions of research, especially if photography is used. Indeed, 'there can be formal guidelines for ethics, but ethics in fieldwork are relational and subject to local contingencies' (De Laine, 2000). Therefore, an unorthodox, critical approach can help restructure the research process and promote the views of those who are often silent or marginalized (see Ferrell and Hamm, 1998; Van de Voorde, 2009a, 2009b).

Direct or participant observation may pose additional problems if the researcher has limited experience with fieldwork or as a documentary photographer. Whereas advanced knowledge of ethnographic or photographic techniques is not a must, those interested in photoethnographic research should first acquire some basic skills. In particular, it is essential to have a good command of the mechanics of observing as a non-participant, from photographing to keeping detailed field notes to funnelling a massive amount of observational data into a manageable amalgam of information. This can be taught formally and informally in a classroom environment, to some extent, but experiential learning is the best ally budding photoethnographers will ever have. This requires being actively and regularly involved in the field photographic adventure, being willing and able to reflect upon the experience, developing and using analytical skills to conceptualize the experience, as well as implementing new ideas with the help of one's improved decision-making and problem-solving skills. This is a perfect illustration of the adage 'practice makes perfect' – not every photography novice can intuitively capture a decisive moment, but any and all aspiring documentary photographers can strive to develop their instinct and train their eye to capture that significant

Figure 13.8   New York City, 2010

moment in a single shot. Yet, Zana Briski and Ross Kauffman's Academy-Award-winning documentary *Born Into Brothels* (2004) recorded the oft horrid lives of children of prostitutes in Sonagachi, the red light district of Kolkata, India, showing that even children with disposable cameras and no prior knowledge of photography history or art theory can provide compelling images as any seasoned documentary photographer or photojournalist would. The film also gave us a unique insider's perspective that no participant-observation research protocol could have possibly achieved. Projects that would not pass the test of ethics committees can sometimes provide most insightful, rich visual narratives of crime deviance.

Ethical issues

In the US, the Federal Policy for the Protection of Human Subjects (*Common Rule*) can be found in the *Code of Federal Regulations*. Ethnographic photographic field research, even though it involves photographing people in their natural environment, typically does *not* involve the use of human subjects, and is therefore not subject to the Common Rule. Nonetheless, rules regarding informed consent need to be addressed. Provisions pertaining to informed consent are detailed in Section 46.116 of the Common Rule ('General Requirements for Informed Consent').

Specifically, Section 46.117(c) allows for a *waiver of written consent* where the signed consent form would be the only document linking the subject and the research and if the risk of harm would derive from the breach of confidentiality or if the research is of minimal risk and signing a consent document would be culturally inappropriate in that context. *Oral informed consent* can be authorized pursuant to Section 46.116(d) of the Common Rule if: (1) the research is of no more than minimal risk; (2) the change in consent procedures will not harm the respondents; (3) the research could not practicably be carried out without the waiver or alteration; and (4) whenever appropriate, additional information will be provided to subjects after participation. These regulations can additionally be interpreted as providing alternative means of obtaining consent within the peculiar context of ethnographic fieldwork. Consent can be assumed in instances where the respondent is free to converse or not with the researcher and is free to determine the level and nature of the interaction between participant and researcher.

In a photoethnographic project, documenting informed consent prior to photographing people can preclude the making of candid portraits or the casual observation of social or cultural practices. According to the American Anthropological Association (AAA) *Code of Ethics*, which may serve as a key guideline for photoethnographic research in criminology, informed consent does not necessarily imply or require a particular written or signed form (AAA, 2010). Indeed, it is the *quality* of the consent that is most relevant, not its format. In addition, if the photoethnographic project has to take place in developing countries where the population is not uniformly literate or where a legacy of human rights abuses has created an atmosphere of fear amongst the population, demanding that people read and sign forms may simply be impractical if not completely unfeasible. Consequently, it may be necessary to obtain a *waiver* to written informed consent so that another (more appropriate) mean of obtaining informed consent may be utilized: *oral informed consent*.

Once it has been clearly established that the research population is the optimal target for a photoethnographic study, the research proposal should argue that there may be no actual or potential direct benefits to individual participants, save perhaps the production of visual materials and other documents that are relevant to the phenomenon of interest or their culture in general. If informal interviews and focused discussions are planned, they can further affirm the value of the participants' life experiences and constitute rewarding experiences in and of themselves. In any case, the overall benefits of photoethnographic research can be long-term and far-reaching. For instance, it can help a disenfranchised group record their ways of life as part of their cultural heritage and gain further recognition of their needs and rights. It also contributes to our understanding of the complex challenges that social institutions and individual members of a marginalized community face on a daily basis.

The proposal should also ascertain that, following the ethical principle of beneficence, risks associated with the research project have been minimized and will be managed throughout the course of the study. This includes hazards to the safety of the researcher, too. Even though there may not be substantial direct benefits for the individual participants, the proposal must clearly explain the importance of the knowledge to be gained from the research, the contributions its findings will make to our understanding of the phenomenon of interest, and the policy implications of the study. The proposal should also state that the activities pose no immediate physical, psychological, emotional, social or economic risk to the subjects. Researchers shall then follow standards established by their institution, as well as relevant professional organizations. The paramount obligation of field researchers is to the people they study and with whom they work. Accordingly, photoethnographers should be fully aware of not only their responsibilities to scholarship and science, but also their professional and ethical obligations to the communities and societies in which they are going to live and work. They must do everything in their power to not only respect and honour the rights, dignity, privacy and diversity of the participants, but also protect their physical, psychological and social welfare.

Regardless of the legal status of their photoethnographic project, researchers are obligated to clearly inform all participants about the purpose and procedures of the study, its potential risks and benefits, and plans for the use and protection of photographic and ethnographic materials gathered during the study. Even if the research only involves secondary analysis of pre-existing images, wise decisions must be made with regard to the inclusion of archival visual materials showing, for instance, the faces of people who may still be alive. Researchers must also always make inquiries about and comply with the laws and regulations of the foreign countries in which photoethnographic research is to be conducted (if applicable). Finally, if required by the ethics committee in charge of reviewing and green lighting a photoethnographic project, a *photographic image release form* should be drafted and distributed to participants whose images will be used in the final narrative.

'ONWARD THROUGH THE FOG': ETHNOGRAPHIC PHOTOGRAPHY AND THE FUTURE OF CRIMINOLOGY

The use of visual ethnographic analysis is a novel approach in criminology whereby images, instead of being mere illustrations, actually engage readers/viewers in a genuine analytical investigation of the visual. Because it is highly applicable to both research and social action, the intellectual merit and broader impact of criminological research relying upon ethnographic photography are indisputable. Photoethnographic research essentially expands the traditional framework associated with qualitative methods by enhancing the theoretical and practical impact of both ethnographic fieldwork and documentary photography. This highlights the interconnectedness of education, research and praxis, which can not only promote a more activist form of criminology but also help implement national and international research networks and distinctive educational opportunities. In effect, this also roots ethnographic photography in an important but often forgotten goal of criminological research: to reach out to and communicate with a wider audience of non-specialists, including individuals in communities affected by crime and transgression, in furtherance of our lofty ideal of social justice.

Today ethnographic photography is breathing new life into the conceptual and methodological frameworks of orthodox criminology. It enables us not only to study a wide range of culturally patterned behaviours and representations of crime and deviance, but also to document emerging patterns and developments in this ever liquid, rapidly evolving late modern society. Furthermore, it can provide invaluable access to more remote or isolated communities, or even less noticed manifestations of crime and transgression. Consequently, it would behove culturally attuned criminologists to set forth on a visual exploration of subjects that have been marginalized by mainstream criminology, and to do so both in the spirit of social documentary photography and as keenly as visual anthropologists and sociologists thus far.

We have just begun our analysis of visual depictions of the putative, constructed Other. In order to dispel the 'myths of Otherness' (Scherer, 2003: 207), we need to learn more about how different cultures or sub-cultures see themselves and interpret photographic representations in line with 'culturally specific symbolic meanings and functions' (ibid.). Intrinsically, ethnographic photography is a form of socially and politically engaged field research. Through the lens of cultural criminology in particular, it focuses our gaze upon the meaning of crime and transgression for those involved in undertaking it – or even preventing it (see Ferrell and Van de Voorde, 2010). As a mode of political activism, it can therefore allow criminological research to effectively give the disenfranchised and the marginalized a voice in the ongoing debate on crime and deviance. And so, while visual criminology – especially ethnographic photography – is in its infancy and slowly producing encouragingly rich narratives based on photographs either produced or collected by cultural *outsiders*, we ought to also actively promote the indispensable viewpoint of the *insiders*. Perhaps, then, we can reasonably look forward to the inclusion of the even more privileged insight of photographs and photographers indigenous to the cultures or sub-cultures under study.

RECOMMENDED READING

Becker, H.S. (1981) *Exploring Society Photographically* (Evanston, IL: Northwestern University Press) for words of wisdom or encouragement by a leading advocate of visual research;

Collier, M. (2001) 'Approaches to analysis in visual anthropology' in T. Van Leeuwen and C. Jewitt (eds), *Handbook of Visual Analysis*, pp. 35–60 (London: Sage) for additional information on visual analytic processes applicable to photoethnographic research in criminology;

Sontag, S. (2004) *Regarding the Pain of Others* (New York: Picador), a seminal meditative analysis of the iconography of human suffering replete with historical, literary and photographic references;

Stanczak, G. (ed) (2007) *Visual Research Methods: Image, Society, and Representation* (London: SAGE), an edited volume that skilfully synthesizes images with analytic questions about the world 'out there'.

For more information on cultural criminology, please visit http://www.culturalcriminology.org/, a website maintained by Dr Keith Hayward and his team at the University of Kent.

REFERENCES

Alvelos, H. (2005) 'The glamour of grime', *Crime, Media, Culture* 1(2): 215–217. American Anthropological Association (2010) *Code of Ethics*. Available at: http://www.aaanet.org/committees/ethics/ethicscode.pdf

Ball, M.S., and Smith, G.W.H. (1992). *Analyzing Visual Data*. Newbury Park, CA: Sage.

Barthes, R. (1978) *Image-Music-Text*. New York: Hill & Wang.

Barthes, R. (1981) *Camera Lucida*. New York: Hill & Wang.

Becker, H.S. (2000) 'What should sociology look like in the (near) future?' *Contemporary Sociology* 29(2): 333–336.

Blommaert, J. (2007) 'On scope and depth in linguistic ethnography', *Journal of Sociolinguistics*, 11(5): 682–688.

Boeije, H. (2010) *Analysis in Qualitative Research*. London: Sage.

Brewer, J.D. (2000) *Ethnography*. Buckingham: Open University Press.

Briski, Z., and Kaufman, R. (2004) *Born Into Brothels*. [film]

Brown, M. (2006) 'The aesthetics of crime' in Bruce Arrigo and Christopher Williams (eds), *Philosophy, Crime, and Criminology*, pp. 223–256. Urbana, IL: University of Illinois Press.

Collier, J. (2003) 'Photography and visual anthropology' in P. Hockings (ed), *Principles of Visual Anthropology* (3rd ed.), pp. 235–254. Berlin: Mouton de Gruyter.

Collier, J.J. and Collier, M. (1986) *Visual Anthropology: Photography as a Research Method*. Albuquerque, NM: University of New Mexico Press.

Courtney, D. and Lyng, S. (2007) 'Taryn Simons and the Innocence Project', *Crime, Media, Culture* 3(2): 175–191.

De Laine, M. (2000) *Fieldwork, Participation and Practice: Ethics and Dilemmas in Qualitative Research*. London: Sage.

Dowdall, G.W. and Golden, J. (1989) 'Photographs as data: An analysis of images from a mental hospital', *Qualitative Sociology* 12(2): 183–213.

Ferrell, J. (2006) *Empire of Scrounge*. New York: New York University Press.

Ferrell, J. and Hamm, M. (eds) (1998) *Ethnography at the Edge*. Boston: Northeastern University Press.

Ferrell, J., Hayward, K. and Young, J. (2008). *Cultural Criminology: An Invitation*. London: Sage.

Ferrell, J. and Van de Voorde, C. (2010) 'The decisive moment: Documentary photography and cultural criminology' in K. Hayward and M. Presdee (eds), *Cultural Criminology and the Image: Framing Crime in Late Modernity*, pp. 36–52. London: Routledge.

Freidenberg, J. (1998) 'The social construction and reconstruction of the others: Fieldwork in El Barrio', *Anthropological Quarterly* 71(4): 169–185.

Geertz, C. (1973) *The Interpretation of Cultures*. New York: Basic Books.

Greek, C. (2006) 'Visual criminology: An international case study in police and citizen interaction', presented at the American Society of Criminology Annual Meeting, Los Angeles, California, November 2006.

Hamm, M. (2007) '"High Crimes and Misdemeanors": George W. Bush and the Sins of Abu Ghraib', *Crime, Media, Culture* 3(3): 259–284.

Hayward, K. (2010) 'Opening the lens: Cultural criminology and the image' in K. Hayward and M. Presdee (eds), *Cultural Criminology and the Image: Framing Crime in Late Modernity*, pp. 1–16. London: Routledge.

Hayward, K. and Presdee, M. (eds) (2010) *Cultural Criminology and the Image: Framing Crime in Late Modernity*. London: Routledge.

Heintze, B. (1990). 'In pursuit of a chameleon: Early ethnographic photography from Angola in context', *History in Africa* 17: 131–156.

Hinds-Aldrich, M. (2007) 'Visualizing protest arson: The phenomenological Promise of protest photography', presented at the American Society of Criminology Annual Meeting, Atlanta, Georgia, November 2007.

Jones, P. and Wardle, C. (2008) '"No emotion, no sympathy": The visual construction of Maxine Carr', *Crime, Media, Culture* 4(1): pp. 53–71.

Leblanc, L. (1998) 'Observing reel life: Using feature films to teach ethnographic methods', *Teaching Sociology* 26(1): 62–68.

Lincoln, Y.S. and Guba, E.G. (1985). *Naturalistic Inquiry*. Newbury Park, CA: Sage.

McCurry, S. (2003). *The Path to Buddha: A Tibetan Pilgrimage*. London: Phaidon.

McCurry, S. (2006). *Looking East: Portraits*. London: Phaidon.

McCurry, S. (2007). *In the Shadow of Mountains*. London: Phaidon.

McCurry, S. (2009). *The Unguarded Moment*. London: Phaidon.

McLaughlin, E. and Greer, C. (2008) 'Reporting Murder', paper presented at the Crime, Culture and Conflict Conference, London, England, March 2008.

Mead, M. (1995) 'Visual anthropology in a discipline of words' in P. Hockings (ed), *Principles of Visual Anthropology* (2nd ed.), pp. 4–10. The Hague, Netherlands: Mouton de Gruyter.

Miller, R. (1997) *Magnum*. New York: Grove.

Morrison, W. (2004). '"Reflections with memories": Everyday photography capturing genocide'. *Theoretical Criminology* 8(3): 341–358.

Nachtwey, J. (1999). *Inferno*. London: Phaidon.

Nachtwey, J. (2004). *War:USA.Afghanistan.Iraq*. Milbrook, NY: de.MO.

Nachtwey, J. (2006). *Forgotten war: Democratic Republic of the Congo*. Milbrook, NY: de.MO.

Peirce, B.N. (1995) 'The theory of methodology in qualitative research', *TESOL Quarterly* 29: 569–576.

Pink, S. (2001). *Doing Visual Ethnography*. London: Sage Publications.

Richards, L. (2009) *Handling Qualitative Data: A Practical Guide* (2nd ed.). London: SAGE.

Rodriguez, R.T. (2003) 'On the subject of gang photography' in L. Kontos, D. Brotherton and L. Barrios (eds), *Gangs and Society: Alternative Perspectives*, pp. 255–282. New York: Columbia University Press.

Salgado, S. (2001) *The Impact of War on Children*. Hampshire: Palgrave Macmillan.

Salgado, S. (2005) *Migrations*. New York: Aperture.

Scherer, J.C. (2003) 'Ethnographic photography in anthropological research' in P. Hockings (ed.), *Principles of Visual Anthropology* (3rd ed.), pp. 201–216. Berlin: Mouton de Gruyter.

Schwartz, D. (1989) 'Visual ethnography: Using photography in qualitative research' *Qualitative Sociology* 12(2): 119–154.

Snyder, G. (2008) *Graffiti Lives*. New York: New York University Press.

Sontag, S. (1977) *On Photography*. New York: Picador.

Sooryamoorthy, R. (2007) 'Behind the scenes: Making research films in sociology', *International Sociology* 22: 547–563.

Tunnell, K. (2006) 'Socially disorganized rural communities', *Crime, Media, Culture* 2(3): 332–337.

Tunnell, K. (2009) 'Photos and filed notes from visual research', presented at the American Society of Criminology Annual Meeting, Philadelphia, Pennsylvania, November 2009.

Van de Voorde, C. (2005) 'Rethinking visual ethnography: Towards a criminology of aesthetics', presented at the American Society of Criminology Annual Meeting, Toronto, Canada, November 2005.

Van de Voorde, C. (2006) 'Ethnographic photography: Using images to enrich traditional narratives of crime and deviance', presented at the American Society of Criminology Annual Meeting, Los Angeles, California, November 2006.

Van de Voorde, C. (2007) 'Cultural criminological applications of visual semiotics and iconography to photographic meaning and representation', presented at the American Sociological Association Annual Meeting, New York, August 2007.

Van de Voorde, C. (2009a) 'Invisible soldiers: A photoethnography of child combatants', presented at the Academy of Criminal Justice Sciences Annual Meeting, Boston, Massachusetts, March 2009.

Van de Voorde, C. (2009b) 'Cultural genocide and politicide in the land of snow lions: Exploring the Tibetan tinderbox', presented at the American Society of Criminology Annual Meeting, Philadelphia, Pennsylvania, November 2009.

Van de Voorde, C. (2010) 'Exiled: Photoethnographic insight into the lives of Tibetan refugees in India and Nepal', presented at the John Jay College International Conference on Crime & Justice, Marrakesh, Morocco, May 2010.

Young, A. (2004) *Judging the Image*. London: Routledge.

14

Autoethnography

Jeff Ferrell

INTRODUCTION

I celebrate myself,
    And what I assume you shall assume,
For every atom belonging to me as good belongs
to you (Walt Whitman, 'Song of Myself'[1]).

Like Walt Whitman, I deliver this account of autoethnography – and so this song of myself – to you in the first person. This seems appropriate enough; autoethnography – the ethnographic exploration of the self – is after all the one criminological method that is most obviously and admittedly focused as much on the researcher as on the research. But I warn you, it's also a trick, this first person writing. It's actually a series of tricks. Fall for them at your own risk.

To provide some initial sense of autoethnography as a criminological method, and to begin exploring some of the tricks of identity and presentation that this method can play on the unsuspecting, we can start by dispensing with two mythic positions. That is, we can usefully begin by exploring two possibilities that are in fact not possibilities at all. The first of these is that there could exist any sort of ethnography – that is, any sort of participatory field research – that is not to some degree also autoethnography. If at a minimum autoethnography suggests that ethnographers account for their own participation in field research, and in some way turn the 'ethnographic gaze' (Kane, 1998) on themselves as well as on others, then an autoethnographic sensibility is inherent – must be inherent – in the ethnographic research process. Ethnography is if nothing else a profoundly personal research approach, requiring the ethnographer's own physical, emotional and perceptual presence amidst the subjects under study. Because of this, ethnographers always operate both as researchers and as themselves subjects of their own research; they inevitably intermingle with those they research by way of interactive nuances, shared emotions, and collective experiences. The ethnographer is the medium through which ethnographic research is conducted, and as always, the medium is part of the message (McLuhan, 1964).

Putting it bluntly, ethnographers unable or unwilling to account for their own presence in the research process would strike me as very poor ethnographers indeed. And in this sense, while ethnography can and should be carefully attuned to the dynamics of groups and situations, it cannot be made to be 'objective' – it cannot be honestly divorced from the ethnographer's own reflexive presence in the research process. To pretend otherwise, it seems to me, is to perpetuate a sort of positivist fraud, to overlay assumptions about objectivity and rationality onto what is an inherently subjective and inter-subjective process. Ethnography entails ongoing collaboration between the ethnographer and those others that we call 'research subjects', and to deny the ethnographer's role in this collaboration, and the importance of a reflexive accounting of this role, would be to deny that which gives ethnography its very depth and power. All ethnography is and must be, at least in part, autoethnography.

But if that is true, then to begin to understand autoethnography and its tricks we must also explore and dispense with a second impossibility: that there could exist any autoethnography that is not also ethnography. If sociology teaches us anything, it is surely this – that to explore ourselves is to explore others. Even the most tightly focused autoethnography – a crime victim's exploration of the crime's emotional damage, for example – is also an ethnography of all those past people and experiences, all those past processes of socialization and acculturation, that made those emotions what they now are. It is also inevitably an exploration of those patterns of age, gender, ethnicity and occupation that help shape personal experience, and help craft the emotions that a particular crime may elicit. Beyond this, such an autoethnography might well emerge also as a study of the mass media and popular culture, and of the ways in which even the most intimate of emotions reference and recall cultural scripts that circulate throughout everyday life. The more closely we look at ourselves, it seems, the more broadly we must account for those social and cultural forces by which our selves are constructed.

And there's more to it than that. To the extent that autoethnography is an account of oneself and one's own experiences, it is also an account of the particular and immediate situation in which those experiences occur – and so as much an ethnography of the situation, and of those that occupy it, as it is an autoethnography of self-examination. Autoethnography occurs *in situ* – embedded, that is, in particular places and situations – and the situations that autoethnographers choose to occupy, or in which they find themselves caught, in many ways define their accounts of self and self-experience. As symbolic interactionists would remind us, the self is not only shaped by past experiences and interactions; it is always in the process of *being shaped* by ongoing experience and interaction. Because of this, an account of my experiences in any new or unfamiliar situation is also an account of that particular situation, and of the ways in which it partially reconstructs the very self about which I write (Chawla, 2003). And so the first trick of writing autoethnography, and of writing in the first person, is revealed: when I write 'I', I really mean 'we' – for, as Whitman says, every atom belonging to me as good belongs to you.

In this sense I'm not particularly interested in sharply distinguishing more traditional practices of ethnography from newer practices of autoethnography, in my own work or more generally. Each, it seems to me, contains and incorporates the other – and certainly in contrast to positivist/quantitative methods, they are more similar than they are different. In thinking about this sort of methodological approach, then, the real question for me is not whether a particular piece of field research constitutes ethnography or autoethnography, but rather where it falls along a long continuum that stretches between the two scholarly impossibilities already noted: positivist objectivity on the one end and isolated, individual self-examination on the other. Neither extreme of the continuum promises much in the way of insight – but in between are all sorts of autoethnographic possibilities, and all manner of insights into crime, criminality, and ourselves.

AUTOETHNOGRAPHY AS ETHNOGRAPHIC METHOD

The initial factor that situates autoethnographic method along the continuum of self and social investigation, it seems to me, is the immediate social setting within which the method is employed. In my own ethnographic work and more generally, then, I give priority not to the reflexive, self-examining aspects of autoethnography, but rather to the social and cultural context within which such autoethnography goes forward. My guiding principle is: *first an ethnographer, and only then an autoethnographer*. That is, I start not by exploring self-awareness, but by exploring the dynamics of a particular group or setting, and only then my role within it. Among other things, this approach has the salutary effect of countering the unfortunate tendency among academics (including myself) toward an inflated sense of self-importance and self-evaluation. As odd as it may sound, I would argue that autoethnography – on the face of it, the self-study of the self – must begin not with the self but outside the self. To borrow from the Buddhists, you can best begin an autoethnography by killing your ego – by turning your initial gaze outward rather than inward. And so a second trick of the trade: autoethnography may end up in the first person, but it should be founded in the second.

There is another layer to this as well. I have no doubt that there can exist insightful autoethnographic accounts of crime and transgression within the social and institutional worlds of doctoral students, instructors, and tenure-track professors. Certainly there's much material ready-made for self-examination: plagiarism, the padding of curricula vitae, excessive drinking and drug use, theft of services, sexual impropriety, and the like. Certainly autoethnographic accounts of these issues might go a long way toward showing that the insights of criminology as regards subcultures, labeling and social control apply as much to ourselves as to others. And certainly, when situated in broader contexts of social class and cultural marginality, such reflexive accounts can serve to critically deconstruct the structures of academic life (Muzzatti and Samarco, 2006). Yet it seems to me that in undertaking this sort of work we also risk reproducing at a disciplinary and professional level the very sort of myopic self-importance noted already. After all, excessive self-examination can occur collectively as well as individually.

To put it another way, autoethnography is not simply autobiography; when best used as a tool of criminological research, it transcends autobiography by rupturing in some fashion the usual experiences and understandings that make up the autoethnographer's personal and professional identity. In this light my own autoethnographic work has over the years centered on some mix of two such ruptures: exploring those aspects of my own life already affiliated with marginalized worlds outside the confines of my academic life, and putting myself into new groups and situations defined by cultural marginality and legal vulnerability. Such strategies, I've found, forcefully attune me both to ethnography and to autoethnography; that is, they compel me to make sense of a new or alternative social world, and of myself as an emergent member of it. This approach is not unlike travelling through a foreign country for the first time, or relocating to another society as an expatriate: inevitably, such dislocation compels us not just to learn something of the new country's cultural patterns, but to reconsider our own patterns of self-identity and self-presentation as participants in this new setting. To undertake this sort of research, then, is to account for a learning process – a process of learning a new culture and of learning something new about oneself – and so to intertwine ethnography with autoethnography (e.g., Ferrell, 1996; Snyder, 2009). The 'self' that autoethnography studies is of course never static, but in such situations it seems especially malleable and emergent, and because of this especially useful as a subject of reflexive criminological analysis.

Significantly, autoethnography of this sort resonates with longstanding understandings of knowledge and discovery in other fields. Phenomenologists like Husserl (1999) explored the importance of epoché – that is, the 'bracketing' of everyday assumptions and understandings, and the temporary suspension of usual moral judgments – in the process of philosophical inquiry. Without such bracketing, they argued, explorations of human existence inevitably remain clouded by taken-for-granted assumptions – but with such bracketing, new understandings can be achieved as scholars are able to confront, examine and move beyond some of their own taken-for-granted limitations. Recalling this tradition and integrating it with the sociological analysis of everyday social structure, ethnomethodologists (Garfinkel, 1967) likewise engineered 'breaching procedures' in an attempt to expose the invisible order of everyday social interaction. These procedures were designed to violate the sorts of patterned assumptions that no one generally notices – the spatial rules governing proper behavior in an elevator, for example – and so to bring them into the open for analysis and critique. Like autoethnography undertaken in situations marginal to the professional life of the researcher, such approaches affirm the scholarly value of a self knocked off center. Cultural discomfort is itself a sort of enlightenment; strangers in a strange land see and sense things that others don't.

AUTOETHNOGRAPHY AND STATUS INCONSISTENCY

Thought of in sociological terms, we might likewise say that the most useful autoethnography involves embracing – maybe even engineering – the experience of *status inconsistency*. As used by sociologists, the concept of status inconsistency suggests an often jarring disjunction between the social roles that an individual occupies, especially as regards the standing of those roles in the social order; classic examples would include a powerful female attorney who goes home to the degradations of a dominating husband, or an accomplished African-American actor who, upon leaving the theatre, can't get a cab to stop and pick him up. These experiences of course embody the injustices of inequality and discrimination, and in their glaring inconsistency begin to reveal the ways in which such injustices are structured and enforced. For autoethnographers immersed in new or marginal settings, the disjunction between their status as an academic and their status in this new setting can likewise be jarring – and can likewise force open a space in which to examine critically both sorts of status, and their larger meanings. Such experiences of status inconsistency often push into the open taken-for-granted assumptions about scholarly roles and scholarly research, and as much so unexamined assumptions about the group or setting under study. Given this, these experiences are not an unfortunate by-product of autoethnographic research; they are in fact one of its great strengths, and one of the primary means by which autoethnography is experientially integrated with ethnography.

Christine Mattley (1998: 150–1, 153), for example, took a job as a phone sex worker as part of her ethnographic research into the emotional labour and emotional commodification involved in such work. She was successful in moving inside this world, establishing personal connections with other women there, and forging an understanding of the work – but throughout the research process, it was the disjunction between her status as female professor and phone sex worker that was perhaps most revealing to her. Her application for research funding was denied, in part because a feminist scholar dismissed the research as 'titillating'. Her discovery that many of the workers were forced to deal with the 'salacious curiosity' of others was paralleled by the reactions of male colleagues and other men to her research:

[M]en generally first responded by saying (always smiling), 'Well, you have a great voice for it!' Then, 'So, what do you say? What do you talk about?' I usually answered, 'Just exactly what you would think.' Not being deterred, they continued, 'Like what?' I never told them, never described calls to them, but rather tried to steer them away from such questions by saying, 'This is not the point of my research.' If they persisted, I told them, 'It costs $1.25 a minute to find out' … Within the department I have also noticed that some men who were previously respectful toward me … now sometimes giggle, make double entendres, and allude to things like dirty movies, etc., in my presence. I have become sexualized to them.

Female colleagues, meanwhile, at times made it clear to her that 'while they could never do "that sort of work", there must be something about me that made it easy for me to do that sort of work'. As Mattley says, 'talking to other workers about the stigmas they endured helped me recognize the one applied to me' – and the disjunctive stigma of her ethnographic work helped her to understand broader issues of sexuality, identity and power common to the phone sex line and the academy.

Stephanie Kane (1998: 134, 138, 140) likewise experienced this sort of stigmatized status inconsistency in the course of ongoing field work into sex workers and sexual risk-taking. In fact, she experienced it twice; as she says, 'I found two points at which a white male gaze of a certain negative kind, directed at me, made me feel the sickness that is racism and sexism, and feeling it, I knew it in a way that book learning and participant observation in the usual mode couldn't begin to communicate.' In the first case a white man shot her a glance of 'utter disgust' while she mingled with a sexually charged, mixed race crowd in a Belizean bar; in the second, while in the company of a black man, she was mistaken for a prostitute by the white managers of a Chicago pawnshop, who looked at her 'like I was a piece of slime on the floor'. She emphasizes that the ethnographic insights about race, gender, and sex work that she gleaned from these glances derived in large part from the status inconsistency they forced upon her:

Twice glanced, I was shown that my identity as a middle-class white woman is so loosely bound to

my body that if I am inhabiting a social space in which white middle class-ness is not evident through context, if I do not fulfill the conditions required to represent white middle class-ness, the privileges will be immediately withdrawn … In fieldwork, such a glance thus blurs the lines between personal and professional, causing the ethnographer a certain amount of productive turmoil. The glance, repeated, keyed me to the importance of determining the particular ways in which race structures the organization of sex work.

Christine Mattley's and Stephanie Kane's accounts in turn came about as part of a larger collective effort to bring an autoethnographic sensibility to ethnographic research into crime and deviance. For this project – the book *Ethnography at the Edge* (Ferrell and Hamm, 1998) – Mark Hamm and I enlisted criminological ethnographers to reflect on their own research experiences, and to consider the ways in which these experiences contributed to the research itself. In this way the book by its very nature grounded autoethnography in ethnographic practice – and as it turned out, the book documented both the inevitability and the value of this autoethnographic dimension in ethnographic research. As the book's collected accounts revealed, Mattley and Kane weren't the only ethnographers who had endured inconsistencies of status and self in the process of field research, and who had come to understand the autoethnographic insights offered by such experiences. Engaged in field research with militarized police units, trading macho boasts and firing high-powered weapons, Pete Kraska (1998: 107) reluctantly found himself 'enjoying militarism', and so realizing that part of militarism's dangerous appeal results from the fact that it 'has been and continues to be a seductive, pleasurable, and embedded component of social life'. Researching domestic terrorists, tracking Timothy McVeigh's path to the Oklahoma City bombing, Mark Hamm (1998) checked himself into the same cheap motel room in which McVeigh holed up just before the bombing – and, finding his own sense of self overwhelmed by the dark swirl of place and politics, learned something about the seductions of terror. Having researched and theorized 'edgeworkers' for years, Steve Lyng (1998) finally went over the edge himself – and from the other side, recovering from the high-speed, bone-crushing motorcycle accident that all but killed him, began to reconsider his own theoretical model of edgework.

In light of these accounts, you may appreciate the book's original title, the one that the publisher insisted we change: *True Confessions*. For a female scholar to admit that she's been sexually trivialized by her academic peers or mistaken for a prostitute, for a male scholar to admit to enjoying militarism or to being overwhelmed by fear and regret, is indeed to make the sort of professionally lurid confession that tends to create discomfort among publishers and colleagues alike. But of course this very discomfort affirms the essential place of such autoethnographic confessions in exposing the deep structures of gender, identity and power that run through deviance and criminality, and as much so through policing and crime control. Putting themselves in situations of social and physical risk, stripped of the comfort that their professional roles provided, these researchers were left vulnerable to the sorts of experiences and emotions encountered by those they studied. And if such vulnerability in this sense constitutes a temporary failure of professional identity, to be confessed and carefully considered, it for this very reason also constitutes a significant methodological *achievement*. Through it, researchers are able to contrast one world with the next, to experience this contrast with a special sort of emotional sharpness, and to find in their confessed emotions and experiences another window into the situations they study.

Revealing tensions of status and context likewise surface in the autoethnographic work of those whose own life histories have left them caught between contrasting worlds. Both Devika Chawla (2003: 278) and Deborah Reed-Danahay (1997), for example, document the profound cultural dislocation brought about by 'leaving home', whether as a resident of rural France seeking an education or as a Pakistani refugee seeking political asylum in India. In both cases, this dislocation leads to sociological analysis and methodological insight – in Chawla's case, ultimately, the distinct ability as an ethnographer and autoethnographer to occupy an 'in-between space [that] is conceptual, textual, spatial, emotional, and physical'. Interrogating his own family's fluid shifting between 'Mexican' and 'Spanish' self-identification, Nick Trujillo (2003) likewise is able to explore the cultural construction – and ongoing cultural ambiguity – of ethnicity. Other work echoes, on a different scale, the sorts of physical and emotional trauma suffered by Mark Hamm and Steve Lyng. Living in Romania under the dictatorship of Nicolae Ceausescu, physically disabled and politically disenfranchised, Aurel Balan nonetheless manages to create an extensive ethnography/autoethnography of his life and his village, thereby engaging in what David Kideckel (1997: 47) calls 'autoethnography as political resistance'. Similarly, as Henk Driessen (1997: 108) argues, the political abduction of popular Algerian/Kabyle singer Lounes Matoub leads Matoub to a form of 'ethno-autobiographic writing that speaks to issues larger than the events in his personal life'.

AUTOETHNOGRAPHY OF AN AUTOETHNOGRAPHER

You will perhaps have noticed that I have to this point made few 'true confessions' regarding my own research, accounted for few of my own inconsistencies of status and context. Of course this delay might constitute yet another trick, another way of suggesting that a method that seems to put the individual first may in fact work best when much else comes before. But in any case, I do have much to confess; 20 years of ethnographic research has provided more than a few disturbing and revealing autoethnographic moments. In fact, though I didn't set out with this in mind, it seems in retrospect that my methodological approach has always intertwined autoethnography with ethnography. Immersed since my graduate school days in philosophical critiques of social scientific positivism and artificial 'objectivity', I could simply never find much justification for removing my presence from my own ethnographic research, nor in any case much motivation for doing so. As a result, even in my first book-length ethnography – the result of a five-year participatory study with underground graffiti writers (Ferrell, 1996) – I wove myself into the story now and then, and attempted to account for my presence as researcher and participant. In subsequent ethnographies my presence, and my sense of myself as an appropriate subject of study, only increased, to the point that a recent book-length account of urban trash scrounging (Ferrell, 2006) was, I suppose, as much autoethnography as ethnography. In my own work, anyway, I never could see much difference – and I've seen less and less as I've gone along. While the following confessions and accounts certainly embody aspects of professional rupture and status inconsistency, then, they are not actually anomalies; they are more like episodic embodiments of my general approach to ethnography.

A good enough place to start is in the middle of that five-year graffiti study, in the middle of the night, too, down a dark urban alley, as I'm being arrested for 'destruction of private property' – that is, for painting a graffiti mural on the back wall of a vacant warehouse. As I've detailed elsewhere (Ferrell, 1997; Ferrell, 2001: 1–2, 179–91), that moment captured all sorts of criminal and criminal justice dynamics, and served to situate me ever more firmly in the midst of them all. The moment demonstrated the collective nature of graffiti, and the strengths and weaknesses of graffiti 'crews'; though I had been painting alongside Eye Six, a veteran member of the crew to which I belonged, we were missing other essential crew members that night – and worse yet, were accompanied by beginner or 'toy' writers whose boisterous inexperience likely drew the attention that led to my arrest. The moment of arrest also confirmed the aggressive politics of the city's anti-graffiti campaign then underway. As I knew they would, the arresting officers included in their report a special notation alerting the district attorney and the judge that the case was one of graffiti vandalism (I was subsequently convicted and sentenced to a year's probation). And when the officers compelled me to state my occupation, their 'utter disgust' for me was much like that experienced by Stephanie Kane, but with two differences. It was spoken, repeatedly, as well as glanced, and it came as no surprise – the overall vitriol of the local anti-graffiti campaign all but predicted it. As an active graffiti writer and field researcher, it was the sort of in-your-face status inconsistency I'd long assumed would accompany any encounter with the police.

Though getting caught was certainly not my intention, I did over the next few years quite purposefully put myself in a series of similarly risky situations as part of a long-term ethnographic exploration of urban space, urban social movements and emerging practices of urban control (Ferrell, 2001). Increasingly, my intention was not only to participate with those I studied, and to immerse myself in situations where their political practices intersected with practices of legal control, but in some way to channel those contested practices through my own experience. With this in mind, I spent many days and nights busking with other musicians on the streets, playing music for passers-by, noting how our performances organized urban space, and noting also the legal statutes and policing strategies meant to contain us. I went on the air with illegal underground radio stations, sharing the collective energy of an illicit broadcast; hung out at the clandestine workshops where participants manufactured do-it-yourself broadcast equipment; and learned from activists their (not always successful) strategies for staying on the air and out of jail in the face of Federal Communications Commission enforcement campaigns. I rode with Critical Mass bicycle activists, clogged rush hour traffic with collective bike rides designed to 'take back the streets' from the automobile – and found myself once again the recipient of a revealing arrest, this one for 'obstructing traffic'. Both the arrest and subsequent trial hinged on a contested negotiation of my identity – bicyclist? activist? professor? – and because of this, both spawned narratives and

counter-narratives on law, activism and the urban environment that would have been unavailable to me otherwise.

As already suggested, my recent ethnography of urban trash scrounging (Ferrell, 2006) tipped the balance toward autoethnography further still. In part this was because my research circumstances pushed me closer than usual to 'becoming the phenomenon'; resigned from a tenured professorship, sans other employment or grant money or book contract, I undertook to live as best I could from items I scrounged from trash piles and skips. To account for myself, then, was not only to document my experiences as a researcher, but also to document the lived experience of trash scrounging. In comparison to my immersion in the collective worlds of graffiti writers or Critical Mass riders, much of my trash scrounging also emerged as solitary activity; my accounts of such activity tended, naturally, toward the personal. Yet as always, these personal accounts chronicled scene and setting, too: the yells of homeowners to 'get out of my trash', the expressions of support from others, the roving private security patrols hell-bent on guarding corporate trash, and for a change, a general attitude of kindness from police officers, anti-trash scrounging laws notwithstanding. Most important in terms of autoethnographic insight, though, was the way in which trash scrounging ruptured my professionally honed sense of identity, space and time. Freed from salary and college classes and writing deadlines, learning to make do with what I could find, I found myself slowing, relaxing, riding the peripatetic rhythms of day-to-day survival. This, I discovered, was perhaps the most revealing part of becoming the phenomenon: the process of becoming a different sort of person in time and space, an outsider to bureaucratic schedules and professional panic, scrounging existential reorientation as surely as urban trash (Ferrell, 2009a).

AUTOETHNOGRAPHY AND *VERSTEHEN*

With this experience of emerging as a person remade by the temporal and spatial arrangements of scrounging – as with Mattley and Kane's confronting the stigma of sexually degraded identity, or Kraska and Hamm's succumbing to the seductions of violence and terror – autoethnography circles back into the practice of ethnography by way of a key ethnographic dynamic. This is the dynamic of *verstehen* – the process by which researchers seek, and as best they can achieve, empathic understanding with those they study. As developed by Max Weber (1978), and later applied to criminological scholarship (Ferrell, 1997), *verstehen* is central to any research that undertakes to understand the *meaning* of social life. From this view it is not enough for researchers to observe interactions or to document patterns of behavior; they must in addition seek to understand the meaning of these interactions for those who engage in them, to participate in the emotions that animate them, and so to capture the human feel and texture of the situations they study. This is of course a demanding and in many cases dangerous endeavor for those studying crime, deviance and victimization, and one never fully realizable in any case due to differences between researcher and research subjects in terms of personal history, social status and professional consequence. Yet to the extent that it is accomplished, *verstehen* marks in many ways the epitome of ethnographic research; for a researcher to achieve it, even in part, is to move the researcher's own experiences and emotions inside the subject matter itself.

In this sense, *verstehen* constitutes the essential experiential and epistemic link connecting ethnography to autoethnography. Experiences of risk and vulnerability shared by researcher and research subjects not only forge the sorts of inter-personal bonds necessary for ongoing field research, but imply that a researcher's self-understanding of these experiences becomes an understanding of subjects and setting as well. Moments of shared emotional resonance create insights that are as much visceral as intellectual, taking the research into social and cultural depths otherwise unavailable; as Stephanie Kane (2010) says of her experience of being robbed while among Brazilian beach condominium dwellers, 'the crime radically alters my communicative relationships among the condo dwellers, giving me entrée to the undercurrent of fear and racism papered over by the myth of brasilidade ['Brazilianness'] and the pleasures of beach life'. Shared interpretive understandings of crime or law or victimization, shared codes of honor or conduct, allow the researcher to conduct analysis from within the categories of research subjects and research setting – not to think *for* those under study, but to think *with* them. In moments of *verstehen*, ethnography and autoethnography intertwine; in the best moments, perhaps one simply becomes the other.

If *verstehen* in this way pulls researchers out of their own selves and into the research setting, it also affirms the deeply personal nature of both ethnography and autoethnography. Further, it suggests a somewhat subversive methodological insight: that the methods of ethnography and autoethnography must be learned not only from essays like this one, but from the process of research itself, from those with whom ethnography and autoethnography are conducted. For both these reasons, the summary guidelines in Box 14.1 should be taken as suggestive at best, and should be tempered with large doses of creative autonomy on the part of individual autoethnographers.

AUTOETHNOGRAPHY AS NARRATIVE

Over the past two or three decades scholars have increasingly understood ethnography as both a process of research and a process of communication. Specifically, in light of such works as James Clifford and George Marcus's *Writing Culture* (1986), they have explored ethnography as a form

---

Box 14.1   Autoethnography as method

1   Good autoethnography examines the self as situated in social and cultural context; in this sense autoethnography always requires ethnography as well. Because of this, autoethnography usefully begins with a critical awareness of the researcher's social situation, and only then flows toward the researcher as self-aware subject. Remember: an ethnographer first, an autoethnographer second.
2   Good autoethnography accounts for the self not as a fixed entity, but as a mutable subject. It is in this way an ethnography of the researcher's own learning process during the course of research.
3   In the course of field research, and especially criminological field research, this learning process is unlikely to be a smooth one; instead it will often be fraught with risk and vulnerability, and so will force upon the researcher ruptures in social status and troubling experiences of status inconsistency. Such experiences are particularly appropriate subjects for autoethnography, in that they force into view unexamined assumptions and otherwise hidden dimensions of social life.
4   To the extent that ethnographic research is designed to achieve *verstehen* – a sympathetic appreciation of meaning and emotion between research and subjects of research – ethnography and autoethnography come full circle in the shared experiences of field research.

of research that intertwines a researcher's field experiences with the modes of communication by which such experiences are recorded, categorized and disseminated. A naïve view is that ethnographers 'do' ethnography, next record their ethnographic findings in field notes, and subsequently rewrite these field notes into articles or books. Recent reconsiderations suggest a more sophisticated and realistic understanding: ethnographic research takes shape in an ongoing, dialectical relationship with the media through which it is imagined and encoded. The 'writing up' of research, in a moment's field notes or a later scholarly work, is as much a part of ethnography as are field interviews and careful observations; in many ways this writing defines the possibilities offered by these interviews and observations. Once again, the medium remains at least in part the message – and for a method that relies on the researchers' ability to construct thick (Geertz, 1973), thoroughgoing accounts of the subject under study, this is especially so. Ethnography is, inevitably, story telling – and stories short or long can be told in all sorts of ways, through all sorts of media, and with greater or less passion and persuasion.

If the accounts by Mattley, Kane and me seen previously are reconsidered in this context, yet another dimension of autoethnography emerges. In many ways the ethnographies on which these accounts are based are no different from other ethnographies; in these ethnographies of sex work or graffiti or trash scrounging, as in others, the researchers are by definition present as their research is undertaken. The difference in these accounts, then, is not so much methodological as *narrative*; that is, it is *the decision of the ethnographers to include themselves as characters in their ethnographic stories*. This decision, it is worth noting, is not likely to have been one taken in earlier times. In considering the emerging role of such 'self-narratives' in ethnography, for example, Deborah Reed-Danahay (2007: 407) quotes the anthropologist Ruth Behar's claim that 'in anthropology, which historically exists to "give voice" to others, there is no greater taboo than self-revelation'. For traditional ethnographers in anthropology and other disciplines, then, the ethnographic narrative included the subjects of study, but intentionally omitted its own author as subject. With the advent of 'autoethnography' – Carolyn Ellis and Arthur Bochner (2000: 739; see Anderson, 2006, and Reed-Danahay, 1997: 4–9) date the term to the late 1970s – and with broader recent trends in the social sciences toward reflexive scholarship, ethnographers are increasingly deciding to include themselves as characters in their ethnographic accounts. Autoethnography in this sense constitutes a new form of narrative, or

perhaps an emergent narrative strategy, within ethnographic work, and so raises a question: how does autoethnography operate as a narrative device?

At a minimum, autoethnographic accounts often create a sort of surrogate presence for the reader, moving the reader a narrative step closer to the ethnographic action and deeper into the dynamics of the ethnographic scene. The double role of the ethnographer as narrator of the story and participant in the story tends to close the gaps separating subject matter, author and reader; encountering an author who is also a character in the narrative, I've found, seems to create in readers a particularly strong emotional involvement with the author and the ethnography. Further, judging from readers' responses to my own autoethnographic writing, it serves to confirm the importance of the ethnographic research by way of experiential legitimacy; the ethnographer's willingness to participate in marginal or dangerous worlds, and then to account for this participation, affirms the significance of the research and research subject. When the ethnographer's experiences of status inconsistency and existential disruption are included, this sort of writing in turn animates the narrative with dramatic tension and personal pathos, and creates a form of ongoing character development that can help lead readers through the larger ethnographic account. In all of this, the presence of the ethnographer in the ethnographic story usefully serves to pull readers into the ethnography – to create a type of narrative *verstehen* echoing that which the ethnographer achieves with research subjects in the field – and to aid in the construction of engaging ethnographic accounts.

This form of autoethnographic writing highlights the power of what Carolyn Ellis (2004) and others call 'evocative autoethnography' or 'emotional autoethnography' – that is, autoethnography that overtly avoids 'objective' claims about research or research subjects, and instead strives to create a shared subjective experience between the autoethnographer and the reader of the autoethnographic account. Yet as Leon Anderson (2006) argues, if such an approach is to avoid devolving into a myopic focus on ethnographers and their emotional adventures, it must remain connected to larger ethnographic accounts and larger social issues. I would agree, and add that in my own experience, these necessary connections have been made and explored in a number of ways. One has been to begin with small moments of evocative emotionality – moments that help craft a bond between the autoethnographer and the reader – but then to telescope the narrative out from these moments so as to explore the ways that they embody broader themes. So, for example, I wrote the account of my middle-of-the-night arrest for graffiti writing in part as a narrative 'hook' – a hook to pull the reader into larger issues of crime and law enforcement, and into larger disciplinary concerns regarding criminological ethnography as well (Ferrell, 1997). A second approach has been to utilize emotionally engaging experiences not only anecdotally, but also as 'grounded theory' – that is, as the basis for emergent analytic categories or narrative structures. Writing about my arrest for 'obstructing traffic' while a participant observer with Critical Mass activists, for instance, I recalled a derisive comment that the arresting officer made to me – 'Maybe you should read the statute and consider what's reasonable' – and then reproduced this comment as the heading and organizing scheme for a section of the larger ethnography that explored tensions between law, law enforcement and political action (Ferrell, 2001: 121–9).

Here, then, is yet another trick of first-person autoethnography: as a form of narrative persuasion, an autoethnographic narrative can effectively pull readers into emotional involvement with the ethnographer and the ethnographic project, but also into analytic involvement with larger social or disciplinary issues. Yet it is worth emphasizing that this 'trick' does not denote inauthenticity or duplicity; it is simply one among many narrative strategies to be utilized, when appropriate, in the process of translating (auto)ethnographic experience into inter-subjective communication. After all, *any* after-the-fact account of ethnographic work is an act of translation; as James Agee (Agee and Evans, 1960) and others have taken pains to remind us, words or images on the page are not the thing itself, but always media of translation. In this light the question is not whether we will translate – and therefore change – ethnographic experience into forms of post hoc communication, but rather how we can best go about doing so. In the case of autoethnographic writing, this question suggests that we would do well to learn from traditions that have long explored the power of first-person narrative: biography, autobiography, playwrighting, documentary filmmaking and others (see Brettell, 1997). Plot continuity, foreshadowing, character development, theatrical 'through lines' that keep the character connected to the larger story – all these are techniques, tricks even, that can be utilized to communicate the authenticity of ethnographic and autoethnographic experience, as Box 14.2 suggests.

Box 14.2   Autoethnography as narrative

The first of these two passages – taken from *Empire of Scrounge* (Ferrell, 2006: 43–5), my ethnography of street scavenging and trash picking – is written as an autoethnographic narrative. The second passage reproduces this account, but in a more traditional ethnographic/non-autoethnographic manner. While the emotional register changes between the two accounts, the subject matter remains the same. Or does it?

I see ahead on the right one of those big clean-out-the-house thrash piles, and two people already digging in it, their half-full grocery cart sitting in the middle of the street. Cycling up, I offer greetings … The woman – older, white, gray hair parted in the middle – strikes up a conversation … Meanwhile, she's already pulling clothes and coats out of the pile and handing them to me … She assures me I should have them, and continues to pull clothes out of the pile for me … [Later] I'm thinking about the old lady who helped me scrounge the big trash pile, taking the trouble to find clothes for me when she had few enough for herself. I'm thinking about doting grandmothers, sorting through the sale racks at Macy's or the strip mall, pulling out clothes for the grandkids – grandmothers that might or might not be sympathetic to the plight of an old homeless woman, digging in the trash. I'm thinking about my own grandmother, a central Texas farm woman known on occasion to haul home cast-off clothes or stray animals herself, an old woman that's a long time gone and sometimes still around.

While a variety of groups are engaged in street scavenging and trash picking, the group perhaps most typically associated with this activity – homeless individuals, pushing rickety shopping carts piled with scrounged items – are certainly present as well. Among this population of street scavengers are individuals not only marginalized by homelessness, but left especially vulnerable by age and gender; elderly women forced to survive by scrounging embody this problem especially. Yet it would be a mistake to understand these elderly women only as passive victims of social inequality; they are also active agents in engineering their own survival. Moreover, they often scrounge not just to survive, but in order to share with others as part of a larger if scattered community of those living on the streets.

AUTOETHNOGRAPHY: TRAJECTORIES WITHIN AND BEYOND CRIMINOLOGY

The growing popularity and practice of autoethnography within criminology cannot be understood apart from broader scholarly trends within and beyond the discipline. Because of this, deciding whether or not to employ autoethnography in the research process, or deciding how it might be best used in a particular research situation, is not simply a matter of method. It is also a matter of considering these broader trajectories, and one's place within or against them.

Central among these is the resurgence of qualitative inquiry within a criminological discipline whose mainstream in the US, and to a somewhat lesser degree elsewhere, has remained largely defined by survey research, governmental datasets, statistical analysis and other quantitative approaches. While certainly not confined to the work of cultural criminologists, the creation of this qualitative revival has in many ways accompanied the recent development of cultural criminology as a theoretical alternative to the mainstream criminological paradigm. Significantly, this alternative methodological space has emerged not only from the various ethnographic studies for which cultural criminology has become known, but also from cultural criminology's critique of quantitative methods and their positivist underpinnings (Ferrell et al., 2008). I and other cultural criminologists (e.g., Morrison, 2004) have aimed this critique at a variety of criminological targets: the early positivism on which 'scientific' criminology was historically founded, the epistemic presumptions underlying current quantitative methodologies, and the limits of positivist methods for making sense of an increasingly fluid and mediated world. For cultural criminologists and others, then, ethnography exists as both a method and a disciplinary alternative – an alternative to the sort of positivism that privileges 'objective' data and statistical calculation within criminological research and analysis.

If ethnography in this way challenges the positivist assumptions that criminologists can remain emotionally detached from their criminological research, and that methods can stand apart from those who employ them, then autoethnography pushes this challenge further still. To put it in other terms: if engaging in ethnography locates a criminologists within certain epistemic and methodological frameworks, then choosing autoethnography surely moves the researcher deeper still into these frameworks. With autoethnography, the lines separating researchers from their methods and from their subjects of study cross and blur – and with this blurring, critical

subjectivity replaces scientific objectivity as the standard of research. Taken to its extreme, autoethnography even begins to suggest a sort of post-methodological criminology, a criminology that has moved beyond method as a formal procedure and toward more fluid, holistic, and personal forms of inquiry (Ferrell, 2009b). I would argue that this trajectory is a healthy one, and one long overdue in a discipline sometimes made moribund by its adherence to methodological positivism. Still, it's worth remembering that many conventional criminologists would passionately disagree – and worth remembering that, because of this, autoethnographic work can invite critique, even rejection, within more conventional criminological worlds. In fact, initial autoethnographic work might in some cases even spawn its own reproduction – that is, later autoethnographic accounts of journal rejection, tenure denial, or an alternative career (Holt, 2003).

There are other ways as well in which autoethnography challenges conventional understandings of criminology as a discipline. In my own case, I have at times used accounts of my own ethnographic adventures in law-breaking and status inconsistency to push for a reconsideration of criminology's past – that is, to argue that many of the founding works in modern criminology were based not on positivist methods, but on similarly 'unprofessional' and legally ambiguous adventures in field research (Ferrell, 1997). Autoethnography can in this sense become part of the contest for criminology's past as well as its present – as, for example, in Eric Goode's (2008) recent re-evaluation of C. Wright Mills and his often unsuccessful fight to intertwine biography, and his own autobiographical narrative, with the practice of modern sociology. Likewise, contemporary autoethnography resurrects a question that has haunted criminology both historically and in its more recent affiliations with criminal justice: should we takes sides, and if so, whose side are we on (Becker, 1967)? Autoethnography answers this question at the level of method itself, and in a way that challenges once again models of positivist objectivity. It is after all one thing to conduct an ethnography of graffiti writers or drug users; it is quite another to *become* a graffiti writer or drug user, and to account for this experiential affiliation, this experiential taking of sides, through autoethnographic reflection. And yet this answer raises still other questions: what, for example, would be the moral and professional limits of similar autoethnographic work with armed robbers or violent offenders – or their victims?

Another contemporary trajectory within criminology suggests that autoethnographic accounts may well increase in the future – and may well work to alter criminology's disciplinary self-image. Many students from marginalized or alternative backgrounds who are now finding their way into criminology seem less willing than some previous cohorts to disavow these backgrounds in the interest of professional socialization; in fact, in my experience, they seem increasingly ready to embrace their past life experiences for the critical perspectives these experiences can bring to crime, criminal justice, and criminology. In these cases, the autoethnographic insights offered by status inconsistency are reversed and reimagined; it is not the disjunction between existing academic status and subsequent ethnographic experience that creates space for critical analysis, but the disjunction between previous lived experience and current academic involvement. Mike Presdee (2000, 2004: 41), for example, has intertwined an autobiographic account of his own upbringing as a trouble-prone working class youth with his broader analysis of inequality, crime and transgression, and has in turn used his own autoethnographic insights to challenge what he calls the 'fact factories' of administrative criminology and criminal justice. A new generation of 'convict criminologists' – criminologists with prior experiences of incarceration – are likewise today drawing on these past experiences to create sharp-edged, inside-out critiques of contemporary criminal justice policy and mass incarceration (Richards and Ross, 2001). Similarly, young scholars emerging from the worlds of gang life or graffiti writing are now creating theoretically informed accounts of their past experiences, and utilizing these to confront conventional criminological understandings of these worlds (e.g., Ferrell and Weide, 2010). Much like anthropology – where the 'natives' who were once the subject of anthropological study are now themselves becoming anthropologists, and so claiming the right to write about themselves – some who were once the focus of criminology's examination now turn their own critical examination and self-examination back on criminology itself (Motzafi-Haller, 1997; Reed-Danahay, 2007).

Finally, innovations within the practice of ethnographic research also portend new possibilities for autoethnography. Drawing on their analysis of criminal events as moments of seductive emotion and dramatic performance, for example, cultural criminologists have begun to explore *instant ethnography* and the *ethnography of performance* – forms of ethnography that emphasize the close investigation of ephemeral events over more traditional ethnographic orientations towards long-term engagement. Likewise, cultural criminologists have begun to imagine forms of *liquid ethnography* – ethnography attuned to shifting

identities and cultural movement, in place of ethnography situated within stable social groups – in response to the increasingly uncertain circumstances of late modern globalization (Ferrell et al., 2008). These innovations suggest all sorts of autoethnographic possibilities: autoethnographies that deconstruct researchers' most transgressive moments, that explore researchers' various performances in the field, or that examine mutable selves made vulnerable to endless construction and reconstruction (e.g., Muzzatti, 2008). Along with this, new media for ethnography and autoethnography are increasingly available, and with them fresh possibilities for creating photographic, filmic or virtual autoethnographic accounts. In the same way that autoethnography pushes the boundaries of criminological research, these new developments push ahead the potential for autoethnographic research itself – the potential, that is, for singing Whitman's song of ourselves, but in the key of contemporary culture, crime and transgression.

NOTE

1 Scrounged September 2009, during the writing of this chapter, and as part of my ongoing ethnographic research into urban trash scrounging (Whitman, 1986).

RECOMMENDED READING

Chang, H. 2008. *Autoethnography as Method*. Walnut Creek, CA: Left Coast Press. A guidebook for autoethnographic research that situates autoethnography within cultural and multi-cultural dynamics.

Ellis, C. and A. P. Bochner. 2000. 'Autoethnography, Personal Narrative, Reflexivity: Researcher As Subject', in N. Denzin and Y. Lincoln, eds., The Handbook of Qualitative Research, 2nd ed. Thousand Oaks, CA: Sage, pp. 733–768. A wide-ranging autoethnographic narrative that includes considerations of autoethnography's historical, theoretical, and methodological foundations.

Ferrell, J. and M.S. Hamm (eds). 1998. *Ethnography at the Edge: Crime, Deviance and Field Research*. Boston: Northeastern University Press. A collection of 'true confessions' and autoethnographic reflections from researchers who have conducted ethnography with deviant and criminal sub-cultures.

Reed-Danahay, D. (ed.). 1997, *Auto/Ethnography*. Oxford: Berg. An interdisciplinary and cross-culture collection of essays that critically explore the practice and politics of autoethnography; especially useful for the international breadth of its collected studies.

REFERENCES

Agee, J. and W. Evans. 1960. *Let Us Know Praise Famous Men*. New York: Ballantine.

Anderson, L. 2006. 'Analytic Autoethnography' *Journal of Contemporary Ethnography* 35(4), 373–395.

Becker, H.S. 1967. 'Whose Side Are We On?' *Social Problems* 14, 239–247.

Brettell, C. 1997. 'Blurred Genres and Blended Voices: Life History, Biography, Autobiography, and the Auto/Ethnography of Women's Lives' in D. Reed-Danahay, ed., *Auto/Ethnography*. Oxford: Berg, pp. 223–246.

Chawla, D. 2003. 'Rhythms of Dis-Location: Family History, Ethnographic Spaces, and Reflexivity' in R. Clair, ed., *Expressions of Ethnography*. Albany: State University of New York Press, pp. 271–279.

Clifford, J. and Marcus, G. 1986. *Writing Culture*. Berkeley: University of California Press.

Driessen, H. 1997. 'Lives Writ Large: Kabyle Self-Portraits and the Question of Identity' in D. Reed-Danahay, ed., *Auto/Ethnography*. Oxford: Berg, pp. 107–121.

Ellis, C. 2004. *The Ethnographic I: A Methodological Novel about Autoethnography*. Walnut Creek, CA: AltaMira Press.

Ellis, C. and A.P. Bochner. 2000. 'Autoethnography, Personal Narrative, Reflexivity: Researcher As Subject' in N. Denzin and Y. Lincoln, eds., *The Handbook of Qualitative Research*, 2nd ed. Thousand Oaks, CA: Sage, pp. 733–768.

Ferrell, J. 1996. *Crimes of Style*. Boston: Northeastern University Press.

Ferrell, J. 1997. 'Criminological Verstehen: Inside the Immediacy of Crime' *Justice Quarterly* 14(1): 3–23.

Ferrell, J. 2001. *Tearing Down the Streets*. New York: Palgrave/McMillan.

Ferrell, J. 2006. *Empire of Scrounge*. New York: New York University Press.

Ferrell, J. 2009a. 'Scrounging: Time, Space, and Being' in R. Lippens and D. Crewe, eds., *Existentialist Criminology*. Abingdon: Routledge-Cavendish, pp. 127–144.

Ferrell, J. 2009b. 'Kill Method: A Provocation' *Journal of Theoretical and Philosophical Criminology* 1(1): 1–22.

Ferrell, J. and Hamm, M.S., eds. 1998. *Ethnography at the Edge: Crime, Deviance and Field Research*. Boston: Northeastern University Press.

Ferrell, J., Hayward, K., and Young, J. 2008. *Cultural Criminology: An Invitation*. London: Sage.

Ferrell, J. and Weide, R. 2010. 'Spot Theory' *City* 14(1–2): 48–62.

Garfinkel, H. 1967. *Studies in Ethnomethodology*. Englewood Cliffs, NJ: Prentice-Hall.

Geertz, C. 1973. *The Interpretation of Cultures*. New York: Basic Books.

Goode, E. 2008. 'From the Western to the Murder Mystery: The Sociological Imagination of C. Wright Mills' *Sociological Spectrum* 28(3): 237–253.

Hamm, M.S. 1998. 'The Ethnography of Terror' in J. Ferrell and M.S. Hamm, eds., *Ethnography at the Edge*. Boston: Northeastern University Press, pp. 111–130.

Holt, N. 2003. 'Representation, Legitimation, and Autoethnography: An Autoethnographic Writing Story' *International Journal of Qualitative Methods* 2(1). Available at: http://www.ualberta.ca/ijqm.

Husserl, E. 1999. *The Essential Husserl*. Bloomington, IN: Indiana University Press.

Kane, S. 1998. 'Reversing the Ethnographic Gaze' in J. Ferrell and M.S. Hamm, eds., *Ethnography at the Edge*. Boston: Northeastern University Press, pp. 132–145.

Kane, S. 2010. 'Beach Crime in Popular Culture: Confining the Carnivalesque in Salvador da Bahia, Brazil' in M. Deflem, ed., *Popular Culture, Crime and Social Control* (*Sociology of Crime, Law and Deviance*, Volume 14). Bingley: Emerald Group.

Kideckel, D. 1997. 'Autoethnography as Political Resistance: A Case from Socialist Romania' in D. Reed-Danahay, ed., *Auto/Ethnography*. Oxford: Berg, pp. 47–70.

Kraska, P. 1998. 'Enjoying Militarism' in J. Ferrell and M.S. Hamm, eds., *Ethnography at the Edge*. Boston: Northeastern University Press, pp. 88–110.

Lyng, S. 1998. 'Dangerous Methods: Risk Taking and the Research Process' in J. Ferrell and M.M Hamm, eds., *Ethnography at the Edge*. Boston: Northeastern University Press, pp. 221–251.

Mattley, C. 1998. '(Dis)courtesy Stigma: Field Work among Phone Fantasy Workers' in J. Ferrell and M.S. Hamm, eds., *Ethnography at the Edge*. Boston: Northeastern University Press, pp. 146–158.

McLuhan, M. 1964. *Understanding Media*. New York: McGraw Hill.

Morrison, W. 2004. 'Lombroso and the Birth of Criminological Positivism' in J. Ferrell, et al., eds, *Cultural Criminology Unleashed*. London: Routledge-Cavendish, pp. 67–80.

Motzafi-Haller, P. 1997. 'Writing Birthright: On Native Anthropologists and the Politics of Representation' in D. Reed-Danahay, ed., *Auto/Ethnography*. Oxford: Berg, pp. 195–222.

Muzzatti, S. 2008. 'Reduction in the Seduction of Speed?' Paper presented at the American Society of Criminology's 2008 Annual Meeting, St. Louis, Missouri.

Muzzatti, S. and C.V. Samarco, eds. 2006. *Reflections from the Wrong Side of the Tracks: Class, Identity, and the Working Class Experience in Academe*. Lanham, MD: Rowman and Littlefield.

Presdee, M. 2000. *Cultural Criminology and the Carnival of Crime*. London: Routledge.

Presdee, M. 2004. 'The Story of Crime: Biography and the Excavation of Transgression' in J. Ferrell et al., eds., *Cultural Criminology Unleashed*. London: Routledge-Cavendish, pp. 41–48.

Reed-Danahay, D. 1997. 'Leaving Home: Schooling Stories and the Ethnography of Autoethnography in Rural France' in D. Reed-Danahay, ed., *Auto/Ethnography*. Oxford: Berg, pp. 123–143.

Reed-Danahay, D. 2007. 'Autobiography, Intimacy, and Ethnography' in P. Atikinson et al., eds., *Handbook of Ethnography*. London: Sage, pp. 407–425.

Richards, S. and Ross, J. 2001. 'Introducing the New School of Convict Criminology' *Social Justice* 28(1): 177–190.

Snyder, G. 2009. *Graffiti Lives*. New York: New York University Press.

Trujillo, N. 2003. 'In Search of Naunny's Ethnicity: An (Auto) Ethnographic Study of a Family's Ethnic Identity' in R. Clair, ed., *Expressions of Ethnography*. Albany: State University of New York Press, pp. 257–269.

Weber. M. 1978. *Economy and Society*. Berkeley: University of California Press.

Whitman, W. 1986 [1855]. *Leaves of Grass*. New York: Penguin.

15

Interviewing Victims of State Violence

Elizabeth Stanley

INTRODUCTION

Criminologists have increasingly turned their attention to state-led violence against civilian and military populations. Authors such as Green and Ward (2004), Parmentier and Weitekamp (2007) and Rothe (2009), among others, have enhanced criminological thinking with writings that question the fundamental nature of states, violence, human rights and justice. These authors have identified the criminological reticence to engage with crimes conducted by state officials; they have also exposed the massive suffering and harm that often results from state violence.

Fortunately, given criminology's stance to 'explain crimes and the behaviour of offenders and victims' (Parmentier and Weitekamp, 2007: 110), and given the diverse methodological skills held by criminologists, the discipline is well positioned to advance thinking on a whole range of violent acts, including those directed by state agencies. To give just one example, criminologists Hagan, Rymond-Richmond and Parker (2005) have recently used victimization survey data from third-party sources to show how the Sudanese Government directly supported the killings and rapes of Darfurians. Through statistical and regression analyses, they illustrated the racial targeting of African Darfurians by state actors and, in doing so, bolstered the case for naming these events as state-sponsored genocide. Their study presented a unique analyses of crime (genocide) that has strong theoretical and policy implications; it exemplified the usefulness of criminologists to the area of state violence.

This chapter focuses on the author's own qualitative contributions to debates on state violence. In particular, it examines my research on/with victims of torture. This work has emerged over the last decade with projects that have focused on the implementation of 'transitional justice' bodies within South Africa, Chile and Timor-Leste. Transitional justice bodies refers, in my studies, to the court processes and truth commissions that are established to provide truth and justice in states that are 'transitioning' from extensive (often state-led) violence to more democractic situations. My focus has attended to how these truth and justice mechanisms have been experienced by the individuals who have suffered the most serious of state violence, torture, and who are still alive to 'tell the tale'.

The following section evaluates the ways in which torture has been researched by criminologists, as well as by colleagues in related disciplines such as law, psychology and history. This broad-brush overview is followed by a reflexive exploration of doing research 'on' those who have survived torture. Given that the focus here is a population made vulnerable by state actions and structural forces, the repercussions regarding the practical approaches of doing research are detailed. Attention is paid to some of the challenges and questions raised in my most recent interviews, with victims of torture in Timor-Leste. Finally, the chapter establishes some future methodological challenges of pursuing this kind of work, especially in terms of questioning the transformative potential of producing knowledge about state-led violence and oppression.

RESEARCHING TORTURE

Torture is a specific form of state violence. According to the UN Convention against Torture and Other Cruel, Inhuman or Degrading Treatment or Punishment (Art 1.1), to be defined as torture, an act must encompass a number of factors: (i) it must cause severe pain or suffering, whether physical or mental; (ii) it must be inflicted by a public official or person of official standing, or undertaken with their consent/acquiescence or at their instigation; (iii) it must be intentionally inflicted, for a purpose such as to obtain a confession or information, or to punish, intimidate or coerce a person or another party; and, (iv) the pain or suffering should not arise from, or be an incidental or inherent feature of, any lawful sanction. In practice, the boundaries of torture are subject to vigorous debate – for instance, does a tortured person have to be detained? Can rape be a form of torture? Where does psychological pressure, or degrading treatment, end and torture begin? These questions cannot be answered here but they illustrate the ongoing contentious nature of how torture is defined, legitimized or challenged.

Many academics will 'know' about torture through reading social literature – media reports, ground-breaking exposés (such as Danner, 2004), documents from human rights bodies (like Amnesty or Human Rights Watch) or books (such as Ortiz, 2002) that highlight personal experiences of torturing regimes. Fewer academics have actually studied this violation in more detail. One reason for this is that doing research on torture is, as Rejali (1994: 2) noted, something of 'a methodologist's nightmare'. If torture is ongoing, countries can be 'black boxes to the outside world' (1994: 2). States tend to deny their involvement in torture. The vast majority of perpetrators do not wish to be identified, and those who attempt to expose them can find themselves subject to threats, attacks and even death. For different reasons, victims of torture are also often hidden, they can be in positions of extreme vulnerability and many victims prefer to remain silent about what has happened to them. Doing primary research on this topic is not easy. Nonetheless, academic attention to torture has continued to grow and develop. Box 15.1 highlights some of the perspectives that can be found in the criminological, and related, literature.

My work has built upon many of the approaches identified in Box 15.1. It has focused upon the social, political, legal and cultural impact of experiencing torture, and it has assessed the specific needs of victims in relation to the concerns of truth and justice. With regards to the latter, I have sought to understand the official 'justice' responses

---

Box 15.1 Academic research on torture

Academic writings on torture are largely positioned around a number of approaches, including analyses on:

- *The historical use of torture.* Rejali (1994) undertook documentary analysis to illustrate the historical use of torture (and subsequent reforms) within Iranian punishment systems while, in an analysis of the documentary archives from 'S-21' (a torture and death prison in Cambodia), Chandler (1999) establishes how torture can be institutionally legitimized.
- *Torture and the law.* Evans and Morgan (1998) chart the development of European law and administrative services to counter torture while Sands (2008) shows how law can be circumnavigated in the support of torture.
- *The institutional, societal or structural basis of modern torture.* Huggins (2010) provides a 'torture essentials' model that illustrates the conditions in which torture operates, across all kinds of political states; Rejali (2007) establishes how stealth techniques of torture have become entrenched within modern democratic states; the edited collection by Crelinsten and Schmid (1995) highlights the institutional, social, political and psychological frameworks in which torture is practiced.
- *The socio-psychological underpinnings of torture.* The experiments of Milgram (1974), who highlighted the propensity of individuals to follow orders from those presumed to be in authority, as well as Zimbardo (Haney et al., 1973) who exposed how individuals could enact authoritarian/sadist or rebellious/passive (prison officer or prisoner) personalities, are well known in this regard. While these studies would struggle to advance beyond current University Ethics Committees, researchers continue to focus on how individuals can be drawn into torture. For instance, from interviews with ex-military policemen and their victims in Greece, psychologist Haritos-Fatouros (2002) develops an analysis of the psychological origins of torturers and their supporters while Huggins et al. (2002), in work on Brazil, show how torturers make sense of, or justify, their violence.
- *Studies on victims' health and social needs.* The journal *Torture* advances research on the range of social, medical and psychological repercussions faced by torture victims, their families and communities.

to torture. Truth commissions and international courts are now relatively commonplace bodies; indeed, they are now almost a knee-jerk response to deal with state violence. Yet, while academic analyses on transitional justice has developed, it tends to focus on debates of international law, the institutional difficulties of gathering 'truth', the problems that transitional justice professionals will face, and so on. Strangely, victims' experiences – or community-wide experiences – of these mechanisms are regularly absent. Thus, my research has examined how victims of torture have experienced these commissions and courts.

Overall, my research has aimed to address a number of research questions:

1   How has torture been experienced by victims? (How was torture used? What was the impact of torture on victims, their families and communities? How was torture resisted?)
2   How, if at all, have transitional justice institutions provided 'truth' and 'justice' for victims? (What do victims know about these institutions? How have they experienced them? Have these institutions fulfilled victims' needs?)
3   How do torture victims experience life in the wake of violation? (On a longer-term level, how does torture link with other forms of violence?)

Given these aims, my research centralizes victims' experiences and needs. Subsequently, my work operates at a personal, interpretive and contexual level – a position that is relatively rare within the torture literature.

RESEARCH AS A CHALLENGE TO TORTURE

At a personal-political level, my research has been based on a belief that human suffering in all its forms should be acknowledged and, preferably, responded to in ways that will alleviate its causes and conditions. It reflects a consideration that research may assist towards breaking down the 'cultures of denial' that surround acts of violence (Cohen, 2001). Over recent periods, when the methods and calibration of torture have been discussed with seemingly little concern for victims, as if there is no terror or pain, such research on torture may have value. I have consequently aspired to write '*against* rather than simply *about*' human rights violations (Sim, 2003: 247).

Critical criminologists (such as Scraton, 2007; Sim, 2003; Tombs and Whyte, 2003) have exposed the need for research that emphasizes 'the view from below', to highlight the experiences of those who are silenced or misinterpreted through popular and official channels. The reason for this approach is that 'mainstream' ideologies frequently work to conceal 'the processes which oppress and control people' (Harvey, 1990: 6). In relation to torture, for instance, victims can be denied their victimhood through common depictions that they are deserving of their treatment because they are 'terrorists', 'subversives', 'dangerous prisoners', and so on (Huggins et al., 2002; Stanley, 2004). My research position has been that these ideological boundaries are unhelpful, at the very least, and that there is a need to 'dig beneath the surface of historically specific, oppressive, social structures' (Harvey, 1990: 1) to illustrate violations and victims for what they are.

A critical analysis also requires an understanding that events, identities and the formation of knowledge are 'derived and reproduced, historically and contemporaneously, in the structural relations of inequality and oppression that characterise established social orders' (Chadwick and Scraton, 2001: 72). Subsequently, within this critical approach, it is apparent that torture, as a form of state violence, cannot be examined in isolation from other forms of 'structural violence' or 'pathologies of power' that underline and obscure violations (Farmer, 2003). State violence is often 'embedded in entrenched structural violence' (ibid. 219). It tends to be directed to those who hold the most vulnerable positions – for instance, towards those who may be poor, or marginalized on 'racial', gendered or other grounds. Torture can also be directed to those who are made vulnerable by political or social exclusion; for instance, many Chilean torture victims were middle-class professionals – academics, health professionals, legal or media workers – who were depicted as political 'subversives' by the Pinochet regime (Stanley, 2004).

It also soon becomes apparent that these forms of violence are sustained across global power dynamics. For example, the lived realities of Indonesian-led torture in Timor-Leste could not be understood without analytical tracking of the Indonesian Government, political organizations in Timor-Leste, other states, the UN, the World Bank, corporations, militia members, among others, as well as of the structural priorities that give rise to gross inequalities across the world.

As shown in Box 15.2, a critical approach presents an opportunity to unpack the ways in which torture is undertaken, experienced, talked about and resisted. It is an opportunity to counter the taken-for-granted attitudes about torture, truth and justice. However, acknowledging such 'views from below' is difficult when faced with a hidden and often silent group of respondents.

Box 15.2   A critical approach to researching torture

Taking a critical framework, researchers can:
- ground their work in historical, political, social, economic and cultural analyses;
- reflect on the structural determining contexts (for instance, linked to class, 'race', gender, age, ability or political status) that underpin the use of torture;
- examine how political and ideological factors obscure the reality of torture, and lead to its legitimization;
- expose the 'voices' of those who are commonly silenced, ignored or obscured within discourses on torture;
- be self-conscious about their own values and status, and the political purposes of their research;
- engage in strategies of resistance, such as to direct their research to struggles of prevention, acknowledgement or accountability.

THE SILENCING CONTEXT OF TORTURE

I have previously detailed how and why torture victims often remain silent about their experiences (Stanley, 2004). There are a host of reasons for this silence, including that many victims want to protect themselves and others, or they may not want to be recognized as a victim. In addition, victims face problems in communicating their experiences to others. This, of course, raises a fundamental methodological challenge.

To understand this silencing requires some reflection on torture's use. Torture is often used to spread fear, humiliate, control or punish particular groups or individuals. However, it also focuses on communication – one common understanding is that torture is used to retrieve information from individuals. Through the application of physical or psychological pain, torturers seek to control who says what, when and how. In these respects, the 'voice' of the victim is simultaneously directed and destroyed by the torturer (Scarry, 1985). Through pain, torturers can make victims 'talk'. For the victim, talking (or not talking) can become an issue of survival – and silence can be a chosen form of resistance (Ross, 2003). In this context, talking about torture – even in the safest of spaces – is difficult. The experience of this violence, that can destroy the body, mind and voice, is such that speech becomes useless to provide an insight into pain. The experience can become impossible to re-tell (Stanley, 2004).

This 'impossibility of telling' about torture represents a personal position in which victims can find no way to explain their experience. Yet, the language to explain torture only really exists 'within a collectivity' (de Saussure, 1974: 14). Communicating about torture is not just about the victim's ability to articulate pain and stress, it is also about the ability of others to listen. Stories of torture can be silenced as victims sense that listeners cannot take in their account of what happened. There can be a social and institutional retience to hear painful or chaotic stories that challenge common-sense notions of state protection. The 'public' also want testimonies to be easily digestible, chronological and sensical yet how victims talk about state violence can be scattered, ad hoc and disjointed; some things do not 'make sense'. Silence can be attributed to the way in which audiences shut out or do not hear difficult stories. It might also derive 'much more from the others' need to forget and to not have to deal with the pain involved in encountering survivors of violence' (Rosenthal, 2003: 926).

This silencing may also result from continued fears about renewed victimization from the state. For example, in work on a recent Chilean Commission on Torture, Bacic and Stanley (2005) showed that many Chilean torture victims continued to maintain their silence, decades after their violation. Despite changes in government, and the seemingly benign attempt by the state to expose testimonies of torture and to make amends, victims continued to remain fearful and suspicious of government initiatives. Many victims felt that government officials could not be trusted to represent their needs and that, to talk, would compromise their future safety. Such an example illustrates the very different implications of being a victim of state violence compared, for instance, to being a victim of 'ordinary' violence. After all, when individual state officials engage in violence, they represent the whole state system. Trust is broken on individual, social and institutional levels.

In these circumstances, there is a concern that public attention on torture might just augment state power. Following evidence of torture at Abu Ghraib, for instance, the exposure on torture did not readily equate to increased support for, or understanding of, victims. Instead, the discourse (dominated by politicians, military officials, legal personnel, academics, corporate workers and the few highlighted perpetrators) revolved around the questions of the deviance or limited training of officers and the legitimacy of torture or 'torture lite' in the face of threats to the state. Little was reported from the victims' perspectives and connections were more clearly drawn with the perpetrators – seen, for example, in the websites that allow individuals to post photographs of themselves in poses similar to those taken by particular torturers (Stanley, 2009).

A related issue is whether research and subsequent writing on torture actually serves to insulate bystanders from the horror of state violence. Any publications on torture might have 'the effect of softening and cleaning what went on' (Chandler, 1999: 144). Certainly, in describing agony and emotions, writers struggle to depict torture in a way that correlates with how it is experienced. In this context, the role of critical research may be just that of 'bearing witness', of 'breaking the silence and calling … atrocities … by the name they deserve' (Becker, 2004: 9).

THE 'STORYTELLING' REMIT

Storytelling is a foundation for human interaction. The stories people tell about themselves and their lives both constitute and interpret those lives (Ewick and Silbey, 1995). Indeed, the act of attempting to tell a story is part of the process of making sense of situations, it is 'at the core of constructing interpretation and memory' (Hackett and Rolston, 2009: 360). Stories do not occur naturally; rather, they are shaped and told and re-told. In their re-telling, they provide an opportunity for less powerful actors to build or regain control over definitions, experiences and discourses. Further, a storytelling approach can counteract the tendency to fracture peoples' experiences – in avoiding a reduction of individual experiences to a 'question and answer' format, storytelling can demonstrate the complexity of peoples' lives in ways that relate individuals, and their experiences, to their social and structural contexts.

In this sense, stories are 'saturated with meaning' (Lawler, 2002: 252). They have the potential to reveal truths that have previously been silenced or denied. For instance, stories of life in places such as Timor-Leste, Chile or South Africa, have exposed the 'breadth of degradation' (Ross, 2003: 48) during periods of repression. State violence – from direct acts of physical violence through to the everyday intrusions of the state and the continuing, normalized fear of state officials and their powers – can be uncovered.

Nonetheless, storytelling is not without its 'troubles'. As a researcher, I have been faced with stories that contradict each other, that expose misunderstandings of events or are just factually wrong. Further, all stories are mediated and victims will always be engaged in some form of self-presentation (Hackett and Rolston, 2009). Like any teller, victims will speculate on what a researcher wants and tailor their stories to meet a receptive audience. They sometimes downplay events or mask the wider political, social and ideological realities in which their lives are contextualized (Huggins et al., 2002). Stories, like all forms of collated data, are imperfect. Yet, taken together, 'multiple stories … have the capacity to undermine the illusion of an objective, naturalised world which so often sustains inequality and powerlessness' (Ewick and Silbey, 1995: 198–9).

Storytelling can, then, be problematic for researchers. However, this is equally so for the teller. If done carelessly, the experience of storytelling might contribute to the victim's sense of inequality or alienation. Victims of state violence can face numerous repercussions in exposing their story. For instance, in drawing attention to themselves as 'victims', they simultaneously highlight that they, or their friends or family, were implicitly regarded by the state as being threatening or suspicious. In turn, they may face future mis-recognition as being potentially polluted or dangerous figures (Ross, 2003).

Moreover, stories made public can contribute to fixing the teller's identity – the torture victim becomes forever known as 'the torture victim'. Specific acts of violence, that in real time might account for a fraction of a life, begin to dominate a whole life story. Stories can freeze identities and victims may lose the nuance of their range of identities as survivors, family members, lovers, workers, and so on. Victims also sense that they may be subsequently regarded as being weak, damaged, emotional, biased or non-analytical (Hackett and Rolston, 2009). Similarly, the recorded story can also become 'freeze dried text' (Plummer, 2001: 234). That is, the experience of torture can be fixed so that the victim's interpretation, at a particular time and in a specific context, becomes *the* defining story of violence. In the face of these problems, many victims choose not to be identified as having suffered (Stanley, 2009).

Nonetheless, many victims do want to tell their stories. Part of the reason for this is that storytelling also looks to the future – what people say, how they say it, and who to, is often dependent on emotive, political, legal or moral expectations. The process of storytelling becomes a social practice itself, demonstrating cultural values, power relations and aspirations (Ewick and Sibley, 1995) and victims can have clear motivations with regard to their participation.

During my research, individuals frequently connected the wider acknowledgement of their stories with social change. Numerous victims told their story to me in a bid to tell 'Western states' of their collusion in violence. Timorese victims, for instance, continually highlighted the role of the British Government in the ideological and military support of the Indonesian Government; similarly, Chilean victims were quick to point out the British bolstering of the Pinochet regime. Victims also used the opportunity to argue for prosecutions, reparations and social change.

So, while storytelling has an emotional and personal resonance, it is also intensely political. In some instances, stories can even be used to send messages to a wider 'community'. For example, in Timor-Leste, Antonio agreed to be interviewed on the proviso that it was to take place in the yard outside his office. The actual story was then related not just to myself and the interpreter, but to approximately 20 other individuals. As Antonio told his story, the audience would listen, sometimes nod, and occasionally add further comment. Politically attuned, Antonio turned his storytelling into a public narrative; a means to express opinion, persuade others and progress social debate (Stanley, 2009).

At the same time, a story marks the boundaries of what individuals are prepared to tell (Graham, 1984). In seeking out victims of state violence, I have met numerous victims who have refused to engage with my project, sometimes because they had already told their story (to aid agencies or lawyers or truth commissions) and they felt disillusioned about the lack of subsequent action. Other victims saw that stories can just be re-appropriated by others for their own ends, stories can be used for the advancement of others, and there is no personal benefit to be gained from relating a painful past once more.

INTERVIEWING VICTIMS OF TORTURE IN TIMOR-LESTE

My primary research on Timor-Leste was conducted, over three fieldwork visits to the country, from February 2004 to December 2005. During this period, I undertook interviews with 74 individuals (21 victims of torture, 18 legal workers, 16 truth commission workers and 19 workers from human rights groups and other non-governmental organizations (NGOs)). In addition, I directed a project for a local NGO, the Judicial System Monitoring Programme, in which outreach staff conducted interviews with 15 torture victims. Alongside interviews, I observed criminal justice and truth commission proceedings, and undertook informal meetings with victims, transitional justice workers and other individuals. Of course,

such data belies the messy reality of actually *doing* the research.

In many ways, this research was often a case of 'making it up as I went along'; however, there were some particular concerns that I faced. In particular, these revolved around how I might access respondents, respond to power differentials, deal with difference and distance, communicate with speakers of different languages and cope with emotions.

Accessing respondents

The journey from Wellington to Dili is reasonably long, and it would generally take me over 24 hours from leaving home to standing on the Dili tarmac. In retrospect, this journey was relatively easy compared to some of the interview travel within Timor-Leste. Within Dili itself, the standard US$1 cab fare for short trips around town – while unattainable for many locals – was relatively cheap for me. These taxis were not, however, always reliable as drivers did not have the money or skills to repair broken cars (which were often damaged from very poor road conditions or the heat). On one occasion, when I was late for an interview about a kilometre away, I travelled in five taxis to get to my destination; the first four all broke down en route. Over 90 minutes late, after consolingly inspecting each broken car with its driver, I jubilantly arrived to discover that my interviewee had gone for a long lunch. I walked back. Outside Dili, the roads are much worse and often inaccessible, particularly when it rains. All journeys were hot and slow, and regularly accompanied by 'logic problems' of building makeshift bridges to cross certain sections. Yet, besides the company of fellow travellers, the beautiful scenery more than compensated for protracted, winding drives.

Of course, the issue of 'access' is not just about travel, it also involves convincing others to spend their time with you and 'open up'. In this regard, access to professional workers was relatively easy. The main issue, here, was that they were all incredibly busy so timing and flexibility on my part was crucial. However, negotiating access to victims was, as one might expect, considerably more difficult. I primarily negotiated access through two local NGOs (the Judicial System Monitoring Programme and the International Catholic Migration Commission) that operated outreach programmes with survivors of serious violations. After a range of informal vetting procedures, through which organizational workers basically 'sussed me out', I was provided with a list of potential interviewees and their general location.

Following this, I would attempt to find the individuals and explain the research. This was, by no means, simple: most Timorese have no access to phones, there is no effective postal service, most roads do not have names, directions were often vague, given names would sometimes be unrecognizable to local people (as it is not unusual for Timorese people to have a variety of names) and potential interviewees would be at work or had moved. And, of course, when I did find some individuals, they did not always want to talk to me. This latter response resulted from a variety of factors – it reflected the personal stance of individuals (why, after all, would anyone really want to talk about their torture to a complete stranger?), however it could also emerge because people were sceptical about my credentials. Occasionally, my work could also be downgraded by association – for instance, one respondent would not speak to me because he did not like the person who had put me in touch with them.

Connections also came through other unlikely sources including from the cleaners of the small hostel in which I twice stayed. While I generally enjoyed a good relationship with them, these three women 'warmed' to me on the thirteenth anniversary of the massacre at Santa Cruz; principally, I suspect, because I was an 'international' who knew about it and had tried to talk to them about it, through poor Tetum and mime. When they subsequently discovered my research topic (and found out that I had also had a Catholic upbringing), they escorted me to their friends and family who had been victimized. In these instances of direct connection, interviewees were always open to the research. Trust, in these circumstances, is a crucial factor.

The range of interviewees, and their own personal circumstances, meant that interviews were conducted in various settings: offices, homes, restaurants, my hotel room, school rooms, courtyards, gardens, under trees and even on a beach. Essentially, if the interviewee was comfortable with the situation, I would speak with them anywhere. With the exception of six interviewees (principally legal workers) all interviews were recorded. Unanimously, victims were happy to be taped and often stressed the importance of the recording.

Responding to power differentials

The economic, social and environmental conditions in which this research progressed has inevitably advanced reflexive questions about my own position within the research. After all, '*What* we do and *how* we do it is informed by who we are, how we think, our morals, our politics, our sexuality, our faith, our lifestyle, our childhood, our "race", our values' (Clough and Nutbrown, 2002: 70).

The ability of Western researchers, to 'give voice' to people's suffering and to re-write stories for their own ends, illustrates privilege. The reproduction of victims' stories reflects the researcher's own status and power. Indeed, that most researchers can 'study, rather than endure' torture is a reminder of the benefits that follow for some from the 'nature and distribution of assaults on dignity' (Farmer, 2003: 224). Research has to be undertaken with an acknowledgement of the positioning and status of those involved. Even in the best of circumstances, this can be an unequal exchange (Skeggs, 2002).

Historical experience indicates that Western researchers can readily position themselves as 'those who know'. 'Data' can be readily re-appropriated into a commodity and interviewees can lose ownership over their stories. There are significant questions on who 'owns the story' as the dissemination of painful experiences can become 'wholly cut off from the life of the teller' (Plummer, 2001: 216). This issue is intensified by unequal resources and access to global information flows in which stories (that are repeatedly circulated in the media, on the Internet and reproduced by scholars around the world) are not accessible to interviewees (Ross, 2003).

These realities led to a situation in which, unsurprisingly, many victims were outspoken with regards to their concerns and scepticism about the cultural capital that western academics, with ready access to publishing sources, possess. They understood the nature of the work – that I would return to a prosperous country and then produce publications that, while having next-to-no direct impact on their lives, would probably deepen my cultural resources further. In addition, a number of victims also challenged me on how my status had been achieved thus far. For example, Fransisco remarked that my education had probably been paid from monies derived from British Ministry of Defence sales. For him, my status, as an academic born and educated in the UK, was clearly linked to the suffering of the Timorese people. This argument, that I could not contest given extensive weapon sales from the UK to Indonesia, illustrated the everyday expressions and enactment of power relations. There were times in this research when power relations changed and the interviewee held more power than I, the researcher (Huggins and Glebbeek, 2003). In this instance, Fransisco claimed power in response to the values and meanings he attributed to me, as a white, British, academic female.

In the midst of such challenges, I took on the mantle of an 'involved outsider', 'one who is personally connected' to victims through a stance that violations are wrong, and that victims' demands for truth and justice are paramount

(Hermann, 2001: 79). I approached with 'a sort of political certificate of honesty' (ibid. 84) in which I emphasized that my research did have an academic 'agenda', that it would admittedly 'not change the world' but I would communicate findings in diverse ways and push for change for Timor-Leste. I, like Bell (2001), maintained criteria of ensuring that the work had practical value and that respect for interviewees would override any of my own research objectives. In terms of the latter, I prioritized victims' needs during, and in the wake of, interviews. In many respects, Timorese people thought this too and individuals regularly asked for some financial or social assistance. At its bluntest, I had indicated that I wanted to expose and change 'the view from below', so how committed was I? In response, aside from my academic contributions, I gave money to individuals and organizations, put victims in touch with rare support groups and also helped out with domestic chores. These actions never, however, felt adequate.

My status raised tensions with some victims; however, it permitted far clearer access to professional workers. While this was not a homogenous group, my background was generally viewed as a mark of approval and, indeed, some Timorese individuals later claimed that they had failed to access some of these workers because, as they saw it, they did not share my international, professional status. As Green (2003: 173) notes, 'Being foreign, always to some extent on the outside looking in, is probably more of a help than a hindrance'. Further, I am also certain that being a relatively young woman combined with other features 'to help secure some interviewees and to produce among them some greater openness' (Huggins and Glebbeek, 2003: 372). It was evident, particularly with some male professional interviewees, that I was viewed as an unthreatening character, one that would not merit suspicion or a guarded approach.

Dealing with difference and distance

Throughout the research, I faced the generic research issues of building rapport, being nonjudgmental, assuring confidentiality and establishing trust. Part of my strategy, here, was to establish active listening principles. Thus, I took an approach to 'decipher what the interviewee has said', signal my 'interest in understanding more' and show a 'willingness to be open to the other's feelings' (Rosenthal, 2003: 919). Nonetheless, given the cultural, social and economic differences between our 'worlds', interviews were inevitably fractured. Similar to the human rights research undertaken by Lambert et al. (2003: 42),

I sometimes found myself in a situation in which 'Words slipped and fell about … [because] we did not have shared meanings built from shared histories.' Our very identities, understandings and experiences meant that the research was limited as it lost the nuance and complexity of life. Active listening strategies could not always break through our differences so that I might fully understand the meanings of what was being said.

Agger and Jensen's (1996) landmark text, on interviewing torture survivors and Chilean therapists (many of whom had been traumatized by political repression), provided a guide for my thinking on responding to difference. They establish the distinction between 'empathetic listening' (that any individual might do) and the listening required in research practice. The latter requires empathy with the listener, however it also needs the researcher to continually reflect on their place within the research, and to acknowledge the difference and distance between research parties.

The difference between our lives meant that I was not always sure how far I might 'push' or 'probe' into victims' experiences. Moreover, sometimes, questions that I would anticipate to be 'difficult' for victims – such as on sexual torture – would be directly and fully answered while other questions, that I would consider to be 'lighter' – say, on political connections – would endure strained responses. These events highlighted the limits of my understanding about the long-term harmful, or discomfiting, outcomes of repression. Acknowledging my ignorance, the best I could do was to take care not to 'work against the interviewee's defenses' (Rosenthal, 2003: 919).

Communicating across languages

The storytelling approach allows individuals to speak in their own language and in their own words (Graham, 1984). Many of the professionals working in the truth commission and serious crimes process were English-speakers, making communication comparatively straightforward. While I learnt Tetum (a principal indigenous language in Timor), clear communication with Timorese people was not so easy. There are different reasons for this. First, my Tetum was very basic and I regularly mistook words with Te Reo Māori, which I had also been learning after arriving in New Zealand. Second, despite the relatively wide use of Tetum, there are over 20 indigenous languages in Timor-Leste and many are quite localized. Third, at the time of my research, there was some conflict over official languages – Portuguese, Bahasa Indonesia and English were each used by administrators (the former two languages now have ascendancy). Given all this, my much-needed interpreters regularly struggled to circumnavigate the discussions, and they had to hold a strong knowledge of numerous languages.

The interpretation of discussions brought its own issues which skewed the research process. Even the best translations can be problematic, as they 'unavoidably impair the authenticity of the data, and hence the validity of [the] analyses' (Hermann, 2001: 83). Translations can regularly fail to expose the cultural nuances and complexity of language or meaning that may be more apparent in direct communication (ibid.). This is an issue that researchers using interpreters always face.

Concerns about the use of interpreters were intensified in the context of this research on torture in a still-decimated country (in which over 90 per cent of all infrastructure had been destroyed when Indonesia left the region). In Timor-Leste, there are few professional interpreters and these individuals were already occupied under more lucrative UN contracts. Added to this, given recent circumstances, Timorese people were suspicious of those they 'do not know' – there were continual questions about what people had done or not done, who they were related to, could they be trusted, and so on. As Brounéus (2008: 64) comments, 'Two risks arise if there is a relationship of distrust ... first, the interviewee may choose to not speak freely; second, the interpreter may hide facts or distort information according to their own opinion. In both cases the interview material will lose its value.'

The withholding of facts is, undoubtedly, one of the most serious of risks in the use of interpreters. This occurred during this research, although it emerged from the sensitivity of an interpreter who managed his translation so as not to offend. During one interview, a torture victim spent a few minutes in an animated flow of speech. During this time, Casimiro, the interpreter, nervously glanced at my expression and smiled at me. He then started to look agitated as the speech continued. Finally, I intervened and asked him to translate. He shrugged his shoulders, smiled again, and quietly said, 'She says that your country has caused much destruction in Timor. She says that the UK is responsible too.' Casimiro later admitted that he had not wanted to translate the parts that he saw as an affront to my nationality as he thought it would make me upset. This occurred despite the fact that I had previously spoken to him about my critical approach and my understanding of the role of the UK Government. His personal and cultural commitment to ease tensions, and look after me, overtook his focus on a neutral translation.

Coping with emotions

Within the storytelling approach, it is hoped that while interviewees might relate painful or problematic pasts, they will finish their story by talking about good, secure areas of life (Rosenthal, 2003). Yet, Timorese people have little personal security; during interviews, Timorese victims talked about their constant economic worries, health problems, housing troubles, and many were anxious about the possibilities of renewed violence. Insecurities included threats of direct physical violence and structural violence (linked to the lack of food, water, shelter, health services, and so on). Most interviewees continued to have an uncertain future. This was clearly illustrated in the surge in violence during 2006 – after the completion of my data collection – which left many Timorese in refugee camps and without homes once more. These insecurities frequently led to a questioning of research ethics – for instance, should I actually undertake research in situations of continuing insecurity? In response, I clearly answered 'yes' as I saw that my work might assist Timorese people, or other populations who have faced torture. However, this led to a second question: how can I do research that does not cause further harm?

While interviews were always conducted to create the least pain possible (for example, by encouraging interviewees to bring along support people, or by connecting interviewees to social or religious support organizations), the exposure of torturous events undoubtedly brought feelings of anguish and trauma to the fore. After all, it is impossible to conduct research that details exactly what state violence means and 'feels like' to victims, without emotion and to some extent harm. This is intensified when victims, having opened the trauma, have to return to a difficult environment in which violence continues albeit in different forms.

Emotional involvement means that researchers need to acknowledge the 'unpleasant emotions and self-doubts' that are generated by requesting such accounts of harm and violence (Huggins and Glebbeek, 2003: 378). These feelings affect everyone involved – the teller, the interpreter and the researcher. This research was, then, attentive to the forces of emotionality as a central methodological issue. Like Pickering's (2001: 498) experiences in Northern Ireland, I have experienced a wide range of emotions through these interviews– including joy, pain, horror, sadness, shame, disgust, fear, guilt, amusement, anger, disbelief and outrage. I have also been confronted with strong emotional expressions by interviewees and interpreters that could not go unacknowledged.

Furthermore, I have been forced to re-invigorate my conscious engagement and to continually question my ideas about what interviewees 'are like'. Certainly, I have been confronted by the vast differences between victims. Despite what I have read and thought I understood about violence and victimhood (for instance, that victims of political violence may also be perpetrators of violence within the private sphere), I have been challenged by the ambiguous status of some interviewees, who could be both oppressed and oppressing. During one interview, I had to rein in my despair and disgust to one male victim of torture who would occasionally 'bark out' instructions to his bruised and sullen wife. Alternatively, in other instances, I have had to question the 'seduction' of certain interviewees' stories (Robben, 1995). That is, some interviewees have been thoroughly engrossing, persuasive and moving in their stories, so much so that I am certain that my critical engagement was diminished.

While my experiences have made me somewhat hardened to hearing about state brutality, confronting reactions can emerge at the most unexpected times. Like Agger and Jensen (1996), I also faced days during the research process when I had an urgent and overwhelming need to sleep, my body essentially shut down. Now, years after my primary research, I often wonder about whether I said or did the right things in relation to particular victims; I regularly struggle to watch television news about state violence elsewhere without wondering about the human experiences of those on the ground or how particular interviewees are faring today; and I often feel (poor me!) status-based guilt about my pleasant life while Timorese populations continue to face survival struggles on a daily basis.

This emotionality has had a number of outcomes. On a personal level, it has pulled apart my own 'expert' status (Pickering, 2001). It gave me concerns about my own inadequacies as a researcher, as my experiences certainly did not fit with mainstream social research texts that often cast researchers as being efficient, objective and non-emotional. Yet, at the same time, my basic 'human' responses have meant that I have retained my attention on victims, and their human experiences. In many ways, our emotions have ensured that I have little trouble in formulating and sustaining my analytical framework and focus.

FUTURE METHODOLOGICAL CHALLENGES

Human rights research, and studies that traverse geographical, political, social and cultural boundaries, are becoming more common within

criminological literature. Increasingly, criminologists are doing research with marginalized communities within their own state or are packing their bags to travel abroad for research outside their nation-state borders. In this way, criminologists are undertaking interviews with groups representing diverse cultures, languages, histories and experiences; and, research on state violence is developing. With this in mind, there are some methodological issues that are worthy of further consideration.

First, criminologists might be mindful of maintaining a critical agenda. Research about state violence has expanded exponentially over the last decade or so. However, doing research on human rights, or torture, or transitional justice does not necessarily equate with critical analysis. For instance, the advance of governments, transnational agencies and corporations to fund such research adds a layer of concern that researchers can be used to build non-reflective and 'state-approving' knowledge that enhances power inequalities. Further analysis of state power is required here. Moreover, the 'cheerleading' that often exists about the benign nature of human rights or international justice measures can 'blind' researchers into thinking that these advances are unproblematic. A closer inspection can reveal that institutions like truth commissions or international courts may actually make matters worse for victims and their communities – they can entrench global discrimination, and inequalities of power or access to justice in new ways (Stanley, 2009). Thus, critical reflection is imperative – particularly on the things that, as a researcher, you might support most.

Second, criminologists might continue to hone an honesty, or awareness, about the political nature of their work. After all, 'Research that focuses on serious civil disorder ... and the use of state-legitimated force, and negligence by those in authority, is conceived, formulated and realised in volatile circumstances. Its agenda, *a priori*, is political' (Scraton, 2007: 11). State violence is politicized – and this will impact on any kind of research regardless of whether it is undertaken with a critical agenda or not.

Third, criminologists might re-invigorate their thinking on how research really impacts on the people and communities that they research. Through this research, I have faced many questions on this, such as: How might research be 'improved' to ensure that people (interviewees, researchers) feel supported and safe, and that they are not unduly stressed or harmed by research? How may interviewees be engaged in more hybridized research ventures, in which respondents truly guide and participate in the project? How can projects be structured so that they do not result in colonizing or ethnocentric research? How can research be undertaken in a way that has clear boundaries about the 'ownership' of stories? Further, in a world in which academics are increasingly forced down a route to disseminate their work in specific spaces, how might research on state violence be used to propel positive change at individual, community, national or global levels? That is, how can research be undertaken in a way that moves beyond good analysis? All of these questions need to be asked before, during and after the research.

CONCLUSION

In many respects, the critical methodology that has underpinned this author's work brought an 'additional burden of high expectations' for continual direct action during the research process (Sim, 2003: 248). How far I might 'stand on side' with those facing troubles came down, ultimately, to daily personal decisions. The issue of actually doing this research revolved around a consolidating awareness of global politics; the process was certainly not a 'hygienic affair' but one that evolved from my 'own personal values', understandings and aspirations (Clough and Nutbrown, 2002: 68).

At an individual level, the research has encompassed change. However, the question remains whether such work can lead to ameliorative actions for respondents. As Farmer (2003: 226) details, the role of academic researchers can be called into question,

> No more adequate, for all their virtues, are denunciation and exhortation, whether in the form of press conferences or reports or harangues directed at students. To confront, as an observer, ongoing abuses of human rights is to be faced with a moral dilemma: does one's action help the sufferers or does it not?

My research has attempted to bolster the idea that we are implicated in each others' lives and to progress the stance that the first act to take against torture is an acknowledgement that it is not acceptable … even for those who might challenge us with their own violence. This recognition of commonalities, as well as differences, is what enables individuals to take steps to progress social, political and economic change, and to take actions that demonstrate care for others (Cohen, 2001). Conversely, 'Not to look, not to touch, not to record, can be the hostile act, the act of indifference and of turning away' (Scheper-Hughes, 1992: 28).

In summary, this work has been based on a transformative recognition, not just for the struggles that continue in Timor-Leste but also to those that will duly 'flourish' in future 'brutal regimes' (Huggins et al., 2002: 18). In this regard, criminologists have positive skills to offer, and extensive opportunities for further analysis and action.

RECOMMENDED READING

The article by Huggins, M. and Glebbeek, M. (2003) 'Women Studying Violent Male Institutions: Cross-Gendered Dynamics in Police Research on Secrecy and Danger', *Theoretical Criminology*, Vol 7, No 3, 363–387, is both analytically and practically useful. It highlights issues that emerge when females research powerful male officials and male-dominated state agencies.

Pickering, S. (2001) 'Undermining the Sanitized Account: Violence and Emotionality in the Field in Northern Ireland', *British Journal of Criminology*, Vol 41, No 3, 485–501, provides a reflexive account of the emotional impact of researching conflict zones, and explores the theoretical and epistemological consequences of ignoring emotion in research.

Readers might also wish to consult Scraton, P. (2007) 'Challenging Academic Orthodoxy: Recognising and Proclaiming 'Values' in Critical Social Research' in *Power, Conflict and Criminalisation* (London: Routledge). This work details the emergence of a critical research agenda to the social sciences, and encourages academics to break the silence on repressive or discriminatory practices.

Finally, the edited collection by Tombs, S. and Whyte, D. (eds) (2003) *Unmasking the Crimes of the Powerful: Scrutinizing States and Corporations* (New York: Peter Lang) provides a range of invaluable case studies, from around the world, on researching the powerful.

REFERENCES

Agger, I. and Jensen, S.B. (1996) *Trauma and Healing under State Terrorism.* London: Zed Books.

Bacic, R. and Stanley, E. (2005) *Dealing with Torture in Chile*, Nuremburg Human Rights Centre, available at: www.menschenrechte.org/beitraege/lateinamerika/Dealingwithtorture.htm.

Becker, D. (2004) 'Dealing with the Consequences of Organised Violence in Trauma Work', in *Berghof Handbook for Conflict Transformation*, available at: www.berghof-handbook.net.

Bell, P. (2001) 'The Ethics of Conducting Psychiatric Research in War-Torn Contexts' in Smyth, M. and Robinson, G. (eds) *Researching Violently Divided Societies.* London: Pluto.

Brounéus, K. (2008) 'Truth-Telling as Talking Cure? Insecurity and Retraumatization in the Rwandan Gacaca Courts', *Security Dialogue*, Vol 39, No 1, 55–76.

Chadwick, K. and Scraton, P. (2001) 'Critical Research' in McLaughlin, E. and Muncie, J. (eds) *The Sage Dictionary of Criminology.* London: Sage.

Chandler, D. (1999) *Voices from S-21: Terror and History in Pol Pot's Secret Prison.* Berkeley: University of California Press.

Clough, P. and Nutbrown, C. (2002) *A Student's Guide to Methodology.* London: Sage.

Cohen, S. (2001) *States of Denial: Knowing about Atrocities and Suffering.* Cambridge: Polity.

Crelinsten, R. and Schmid, A. (1995) *The Politics of Pain: Torturers and their Masters.* Boulder: Westview Press.

Danner, M. (2004) *Torture and Truth: America, Abu Ghraib, and the War on Terror.* New York: New York Review Books.

De Saussure, F. (1974[1959]) *Course in General Linguistics*, trans: Baskin, W. London: Fontana.

Evans, M. and Morgan, R. (1998) *Preventing Torture: A Study of the European Convention for the Prevention of Torture and Inhuman or Degrading Treatment or Punishment.* Oxford: Clarendon Press.

Ewick, P. and Silbey, S.S. (1995) 'Subversive Stories and Hegemonic Tales: Towards a Sociology of Narrative', *Law and Society Review*, Vol 29, No 2, 197–226.

Farmer, P. (2003) *Pathologies of Power: Health, Human Rights, and the New War on the Poor.* Berkeley: University of California Press.

Graham, H. (1984) 'Surveying through Stories' in Bell, C. and Roberts, H. (eds) *Social_Researching: Politics, Problems, Practice.* London: Routledge and Kegan Paul.

Green, P. (2003) 'Researching the Turkish State' in Tombs, S. and Whyte, D. (eds) *Unmasking the Crimes of the Powerful: Scrutinizing States and Corporations.* New York: Peter Lang.

Green, P. and Ward, T. (2004) *State Crime: Governments, Violence and Corruption.* London: Pluto Press.

Hackett, C. and Rolston, B. (2009) 'The Burden of Memory: Victims, Storytelling and Resistance in Northern Ireland', *Memory Studies*, Vol 2, No 3, 355–376.

Hagan, J., Rymond-Richmond, W. and Parker, P. (2005) 'The Criminology of Genocide: The Death and Rape of Darfur', *Criminology*, Vol 43, No 3, 525–561.

Haney, C., Banks, W. and Zimbardo, P. (1973) 'Interpersonal Dynamics in a Simulated Prison', *International Journal of Criminology and Penology*, Vol 1, 69–97.

Haritos-Fatouros, M. (2002) *The Psychological Origins of Institutionalized Torture.* London: Routledge.

Harvey, L. (1990) *Critical Social Research.* London: Unwin Hyman.

Hermann, R. (2001) 'The Impermeable Identity Wall: The Study of Violent Conflicts by "Insiders" and "Outsiders"' in

Smyth, M. and Robinson, G. (eds) *Researching Violently Divided Societies.* London: Pluto.

Huggins, M.K. (2010) 'Modern Institutionalized Torture as State-Organized Crime' in Chambliss, W., Michalowski, R. and Kramer, R. (eds) *State Crime in the Global Age.* Cullompton: Willan.

Huggins, M.K. and Glebbeek, M. (2003) 'Women Studying Violent Male Institutions: Cross-Gendered Dynamics in Police Research on Secrecy and Danger', *Theoretical Criminology*, Vol 7, No 3, 363–387.

Huggins, M.K., Haritos-Fatouros, M. and Zimbardo, P.G. (2002) *Violence Workers: Police Torturers and Murderers Reconstruct Brazilian Atrocities.* Berkeley: University of California Press.

Lambert, C., Pickering, S. and Alder, C. (2003) *Critical Chatter: Women and Human Rights in South East Asia.* Carolina: Carolina Academic Press.

Lawler, S. (2002) 'Narrative in Social Research' in May, T. (ed.) *Qualitative Research in Action.* London: Sage.

Milgram, S. (1974) *Obedience to Authority: An Experimental View.* New York: Harper Collins.

Ortiz, D. (2002) *The Blindfold's Eyes: My Journey from Torture to Truth.* New York: Orbis Books.

Parmentier, S. and Weitekamp, E. (2007) 'Political Crimes and Serious Violations of Human Rights: Towards a Criminology of International Crimes' in Parmentier, S. and Weitekamp, E. (eds) *Crime and Human Rights.* Oxford/Amsterdam: JAI Press.

Pickering, S. (2001) 'Undermining the Sanitized Account: Violence and Emotionality in the Field in Northern Ireland', *British Journal of Criminology*, Vol 41, 485–501.

Plummer, K. (2001) *Documents of Life 2: An Invitation to a Critical Humanism.* London: Sage.

Rejali, D. (1994) *Torture and Modernity: Self, Society and State in Modern Iran.* Boulder: Westview.

Rejali, D. (2007) *Torture and Democracy.* Princeton: Princeton University Press.

Robben, A. (1995) 'The Politics of Truth and Emotion among Victims and Perpetrators of Violence' in Nordstrom, C. and Robben, A. (eds) *Fieldwork under Fire: Contemporary Studies of Violence and Survival.* Berkeley: University of California Press.

Rosenthal, G. (2003) 'The Healing Effects of Storytelling: On the Conditions of Curative Storytelling in the Context of Research and Counseling', *Qualitative Inquiry*, Vol 9, No 6, 915–933.

Ross, F.C. (2003) *Bearing Witness: Women and the Truth and Reconciliation Commission in South Africa.* London: Pluto.

Rothe, D. (2009) *State Criminality: The Crime of All Crimes.* Plymouth: Lexington Books.

Sands, P. (2008) *Torture Team: Rumsfeld's Memo and the Betrayal of American Values.* London: Palgrave.

Scarry, E. (1985) *The Body in Pain: The Making and Unmaking of the World.* Oxford: Oxford University Press.

Scheper-Hughes, N. (1992) *Death Without Weeping: The Violence of Everyday Life in Brazil.* Berkeley: University of California Press.

Scraton, P. (2007) 'Challenging Academic Orthodoxy: Recognising and Proclaiming 'Values' in Critical Social

Research' in *Power, Conflict and Criminalisation*. London: Routledge.

Sim, J. (2003) 'Whose Side are We Not On? Researching Medical Power in Prisons' in Tombs, S. and Whyte, D. (eds) *Unmasking the Crimes of the Powerful: Scrutinizing States and Corporations*. New York: Peter Lang.

Skeggs, B. (2002) 'Techniques for Telling the Reflexive Self' in May, T. (ed.) *Qualitative Research in Action*. London: Sage.

Stanley, E. (2004) 'Torture, Silence and Recognition', *Current Issues in Criminal Justice*, Vol 16, No 1, 5–25.

Stanley, E. (2009) *Torture, Truth and Justice: The Case of Timor-Leste*. London: Routledge.

Tombs, S. and Whyte, D. (2003) 'Scrutinizing the Powerful: Crime, Contemporary Political Economy, and Critical Social Research' in Tombs, S. and Whyte, D. (eds) *Unmasking the Crimes of the Powerful: Scrutinizing States and Corporations*. New York: Peter Lang.

16

Questioning Homicide and the Media: Analysis of Content or Content Analysis?

Moira Peelo and Keith Soothill

INTRODUCTION

As researchers who explore the reporting of crime, analysis of newspaper content for us has always been a varied activity, calling on a range of research methods to further our understanding of criminology and requiring careful sifting and analysis. It is, we contend, the focus for research which should define research, not data sources or methods alone. Interest in homicide betrays our concern for criminological problems – that is, as a social issue which focuses on crime. In this sense, we occupy a similar space to that of Beckett and Sasson in that we are interested 'in the rhetorical practices through which crime-related problems are constructed' (2000: 7), and situate these in a political and social context. It is, we argue, only on a basis of detailed, systematic evidence about the *actuality* of homicide that one can move on to analyse how society defines illegal killing as a criminological problem.

While homicide is a fascinating topic of itself, to us it has represented one of the places where social commentaries on crime meet individual crime events to the most telling effect concerning how society both expresses disapproval and withholds disapproval for its worst of crimes. While all concerned perceive events differently (e.g., as victim or as perpetrator), homicide remains resolutely a 'reality', even allowing that there are deaths which cannot be defined as either naturally caused or illegally caused. As one of the most shocking and violent of events that society recognizes as unacceptable, it attracts much media attention in both fiction and non-fiction. In examining newspaper reporting of homicide we are systematically looking at two key aspects in criminological problems: the social context and the individual event.

Hence, in our studies, newspaper text provides data that represent a barometer about public narratives surrounding homicide. What makes this different to content analysis in linguistic, management or social studies are the types of questions we wish to explore: close analysis of text may be satisfying, but not necessarily helpful in exploring criminal problems fully. Yet release from the computation and computerized textual detail of traditional content analysis does not mean that we do not use text systematically. As we will go on to illustrate by drawing on five published papers (under 'Principles into Practice'), we sift and compare data systematically but derive detail from many sources in order to achieve an informed understanding of the representation of homicide. However, before entering the realm of homicide and the media in detail, further explanation is needed as to why we adopt what we have called a 'social questioning' approach which, on a larger research stage, currently aligns most closely with the 'mixed methods' label.

PRINCIPLES UNDERPINNING THE RESEARCH

Dominant paradigms and the place of social questioning

Research biographies can often sound a little too neat and tidy, too purposive and planned to be entirely credible. The narrative leaves out important elements of happenchance: the unplanned conversation by the photocopier and the shared misunderstandings that get ironed out along the way and are then forgotten. What emerged for us as authors was a shared agnosticism, albeit approached from quite different directions. 'Mixed methods', as this agnosticism is usually called, has sometimes been assumed to represent muddled thinking, and its resurgence has led to what Bergman has described as unhelpful calls for 'pragmatism' (2008: 12) due to the continued underlying schism between users of qualitative and quantitative methods. This pragmatic drawing of lines between two camps perhaps explains why, while researchers are no longer likely to be actively shunned when using mixed methods, they may well be faced with unspoken (a) pity (*surely* they cannot be so ignorant or unaware of the need to choose?) or (b) distrust (are these people opportunists, playing both ends of the research game against the middle?).

Bergman rightly questions the boundaries between the dominant paradigms, arguing that they need to be redrawn to enable social researchers to move beyond the pragmatic impasse of accepting perceived difference. Rather, he argues the lines drawn in the current détente 'are drawn mostly for political and strategic, and less for substantive reasons' (ibid. 2). We would go further and argue that, in part, the pressure to commit to one side of the divide or the other arises out of the social construction of research as labour and not always out of the logic of the research questions or problems themselves. Choice of research methods, as experienced in the last 30 years or so, can function as a social filter in academe, and the act of commitment works as a membership ticket for distinct and different communities of practice (using Lave and Wenger's [1998] term fairly loosely). Inherent in choice is a definition of 'other' as alien and inherently bad (essential for strengthening bonds within a group). Slowly, methods of research become elided with the paradigm they were once meant only to be illustrative of or to represent and, instead, *become* the paradigm.

A shared agnosticism, then, in this case includes discomfort with the subtle shift over time from researchers accounting for the lenses through which they view society and data to the more simplistic assumption that accompanying research methods must reflect positioning vis-à-vis a schismatic divide. We have long since accepted that commitment to a paradigm can be genuinely felt and is not in all cases driven by a desire for group membership; however, membership of international communities of practice is an essential part of conducting academic careers and the two can easily become entwined. For students, this may be merely a linguistic confusion arising from the unnecessary elongation of words: 'method' inappropriately becomes 'methodology' and choice of methods is accepted as shorthand for any given paradigm, rather than as representative of the epistemology underpinning the research frame (which, quite rightly, does indicate paradigms of knowledge and value systems, but these need to be unpacked rather than assumed in unthinking, prejudiced ways).

There have always been researchers who never fully accepted the absolutist schism that is sometimes presented as being an inevitable part of latter-day social science (see, e.g., Bryman, 1988; Tashakkori and Teddlie, 1998). While many have focused on the differences, Bryman in his useful text, *Quantity and Quality in Social Research* (1988), was an early exponent of stressing that 'it is important not to minimize the importance of similarities between the two traditions [of quantitative and qualitative research]' (ibid. 172). Certainly in the last two decades since Bryman wrote those words, researchers have been more ready to carry out research incorporating techniques which stem from the two traditions. The general aim is usually stated as building on the identified strengths of each technique (what Bergman objects to as a 'pragmatic' approach). Yet, rather than being presented as a clear divide between qualitative and quantitative research methods, in practice the ways in which methods are used suggest that there has been a continuum along which methods sit. In this more accurate representation, methods resume their position as artefacts being shaped by thinking rather than, themselves, shaping research thinking and decisions.

Before illustrating what we mean by 'mixed methods' by giving examples from our studies of newspaper representation of homicide, we need first to ask some basic questions about the purposes of social research (particularly using media sources) and to present something of our research values; and to question what makes research different to other types of knowledge.

Mixed methods and critical questioning

For us, fundamental to social research is a critically questioning mindset about why to engage in social research at all. This basic mindset is often left unexplored in research that engages with popular culture or media sources; and when this omission occurs, leaves media research outcomes in danger of appearing to be no different to the more general, cultural consumption of infotainment for personal satisfaction. Analysis of data can appear to be an isolated act of researcher preference; hence, before engaging with advanced analysis or social commentary, we believe that clearer accounts of why researchers are analyzing popular culture are needed at this fundamental level. So, newspapers are a public and easily accessible source of information that are a part of the means by which some murders become infamous, while others go unnoticed in the wider world. Hence, the choice of homicide reporting for research relates to its position as the focus for much media attention, social disapproval and yet, nonetheless, this worst of crimes shows variations in levels of disapproval – indicating a rich focus for exploring the complex social construction of criminality surrounding what, as a crime event, is rightly one of society's most feared transgressions.

In this, we echo elements of Ericson et al. (1991) and Schlesinger et al. (1991), arguing for a need to recognize the complex, interactive – indeed, even iterative – processes that surround newspaper reporting of major crimes. There is a long tradition, leading back to Rowntree, of analysing the relationship between individuals (or individual criminal events) and their social context, and the conversation between the two; and recent decades have seen a need to integrate the role of media and mediated experience into this frame. Altheide and Johnson (1980) have argued that 'impression management' leads to bureaucratic propaganda that actively shapes culture, rather than being only a cultural outcome (see especially chapter 1). Beckett and Sasson (2000), also situating their analysis within the American political system, chart the development of specific political discourses, particularly in the 1980s and 1990s, that eschew social and welfare policy for tough stances on crime (see especially chapter 4, 'The Politics of Crime', pp. 47–74). Garland (2001) has theorized the nature of change in policy and thinking about social order and control that, he argues, has occurred since the 1970s. A key part of these changes has been the emergence of a highly politicized, populist policy-making process which has overturned accepted ways of thinking and previously acknowledged expertise. Hence, a 'highly charged political discourse now surrounds all crime control issues, so that every decision is taken in the glare of publicity and political contention and every mistake becomes a scandal' (ibid. 13).

Representation of crime issues and surrounding social commentaries are conceptualized here, then, as a matter of political advantage within an era that emphasizes the drama of crime, criminality and fearfulness. Within our version of this framework, choosing a mixed methods approach arises out of a set of views about the role of research as a form of social action and the need to produce critical, evidenced commentaries that question key social issues. This is predicated on notions of criminological research as potentially having a role in a quest for social justice through a process of raising awareness of social issues, providing recognizable accounts of the social phenomena surrounding criminality, and a sceptical questioning of known accounts.

There is an another basic question to be answered: what is it that makes research different to other types of knowledge, including, for example, practitioner experience, journalism, scholarship, learned values or instinct? The social importance of a topic means that a desire to find convincing explanations of crime phenomena (contextualized historically and socially) is what leads the choices in methods and types of data sought rather than prior conformity to specific research groups' approaches. However, the expectation that research knowledge is different to other types of knowledge leads us to see two elements as distinguishing research-led commentaries from other types of analysis: (1) systematic collection and analysis; and (2) evidenced interpretations. So, our resulting research is a systematic use of methods that we believe illuminate the specific problem being considered and that research-led social commentaries emerge from carefully, systematically collected, organized and analyzed data and are evidenced. Evidence, in this arena, allows for varieties of data, variety in questions whose answers are further varied in nature (e.g., their depth, acting as an overview, the accuracy of data, or its illustrative function).

In the rest of this chapter, then, we will describe this process by focusing on five articles we have published on the topic of homicide and the media. These five articles essentially probe four main questions (reflected in the aims of each paper) and we had to identify the appropriate choice of methods in order to pursue each aim.

1 *How do the media contribute to reproducing social order?* In a complex and fragmented society, legal systems work not only to protect individuals and prosecute others in order to maintain 'law and order', but they also define the boundaries of what are the agreed social values and symbols which we decide to protect. Against this backcloth, we wanted to try to understand the complex role of newspaper reporting in these

debates and we chose to focus on the press coverage of one case (Peelo and Soothill, 2000).

2 *Does the media reporting of homicide accurately record the actuality of homicide?* There has been much discussion about the distorted nature of the media reporting of homicide, even though it might be expected that official statistics reasonably reflect the number of homicides. Hence, we investigated the press reporting of 2,685 homicides in England and Wales in three national newspapers and compared them with an index of homicides. By systematically charting the nature of reporting distortions, we explored the contribution of newspapers to the social construction of homicide (Peelo et al., 2004).

3 *Is there a media hierarchy among homicide cases?* This question distinguishes media-homicides in terms of the extent of coverage, forming groups headed 'mega-cases', 'mezzo-cases' and 'routine cases' (Soothill et al., 2002). A further probe considers how some mega-cases can escalate to become 'moral panics' (Soothill et al., 2004).

4 *How do newspapers invite readers to identify with victims and victimhood?* The focus here is on the newspaper techniques which help to contribute to the construction of public narratives about homicide. It is argued that researchers, as well as working at a macro level, need to research at the micro level of textual analysis when researching media (including visual media) in order to understand how media framing contributes to the construction of public narratives (Peelo, 2006).

PRINCIPLES INTO PRACTICE

In this section we focus on how we have used different approaches and methods in practice. Our studies offer examples that range from using just one reported homicide to a series of over 2,500 homicides, as well as examples of using both qualitative and quantitative approaches and highly detailed analyses of text.

How do the media contribute to reproducing social order?

The first paper focused on one case study (Peelo and Soothill, 2000), that of the trial of the Taylor sisters, Michelle and Lisa, for the murder of Alison Shaughnessy, for which they were convicted and then, later, released on appeal. A case study approach was chosen because of the apparently exceptional nature of the crime and its coverage. The offence itself took place in June 1991

and, for a while, the case can aptly be described as having the characteristics of a 'national soap opera' in Britain. While the coverage substantially died down after the appeal and the acquittal of the Taylor sisters, the case – because the benchmark appeal held that the press coverage of the trial created a real risk of prejudice against the defendants – will always remain important in the annals of crime reporting (Taylor and Taylor, 1994).

Our central question asked how the media contribute to reproducing social order. The study looked in detail at aspects of the coverage of the trial in two broadsheet newspapers, *The Times* and the *Guardian*, and two tabloid newspapers, the *Daily Mirror* and *The Sun*. Our aim was not to assess the fairness or otherwise of press coverage, but to examine in what ways, if at all, the coverage can be said to be a 'public narrative' which contributes to definitional debates concerning the boundaries of acceptable morality. Detailed analysis of the photographs, headlines and language showed the ways in which the Taylor sisters' trial had become essentially a public narrative in the form of a fairy story about solving crime masquerading as justice. Fairy stories are underpinned by traditions of good and evil and so what emerges is that the narrative subtly (and sometimes not so subtly) transmutes from being about a brutal murder into a tale about sexual morality. In short, it is lifestyle which is found guilty in a public arena. Detailed analysis explained the process by which it becomes a trial about an affair between the victim's husband, John Shaughnessy, and the accused, Michelle Taylor; and with that an inherent judgment of appropriate womanhood.

In their authoritative study, Ericson et al. (1991: chapter 1) have argued that what newspapers pick out as exceptional or newsworthy is predicated on an assessment of what is morally acceptable at the time. Ericson et al. go further than simply seeing newspapers and broadcast media as interesting indicators of an underlying agreement about social morality. Rather, they see the news values represented as being a part of the agencies which actively reproduce social order, particularly in the case of murder: '[T]he news media are as much an agency of *policing* as the law-enforcement agencies whose activities and classifications are reported on' (Ericson et al., 1991: 74). However, social morality and values are not static and there is a tension in newspapers between conformity and moving with social change among their readerships. Hence, we argued, that we need to recognize that mass-circulation newspapers are the new 'public scaffold'. Kai Erikson reminded us that 'morality and immorality meet at the public scaffold and it is in this meeting that the line between them is drawn' (1966: 12).

By studying one case study in detail, and by choosing an exceptional case of homicide, we illustrated how the desire for safety in the face of disorder (after such an extreme crime as murder) dominates the narrative. The confirmation of morality following a display of immorality, the desire for punishment, revenge or the re-establishment of a sense of control may be all-important desires within a society that lead to the reproduction of social order. However, in achieving them, society may be supporting an injustice which, ironically, allows the criminal to remain a threat to us all. Certainly in the Taylor sisters' case it seemed that once the 'bad' elements had been established, then there was no need of clear evidence of homicide. By its nature, it remains an exceptional case study that cannot inform us about the 'routine' nature of homicide and the relationship between the spectacular and the routine may, in fact, be a complex one. Hence, our next task was to focus much more on the routine.

Does the media reporting of homicide accurately record the actuality of homicide?

If the question had simply been 'is newspaper reporting of homicide ever distorted?' then the answer from existing literature is certainly clear. Previous evidence (e.g., Johnstone et al., 1994; Sorenson et al., 1998) has shown that it can. However, we were interested in the nature or form of that distortion and its degree rather than reinforcing existing findings. Nor did our paper examine editors' decision-making processes or the production and ownership of newspapers; rather, we explore the *outcomes* of selection decisions made. Within our framework, method is a cornerstone of social criticism, in that the systematic examination of a known phenomenon – in this case illegal killing – is the basis on which perceptions, inter-relationships and personal accounts can, at a later

stage, be explored. The notion that there is a 'reality' in the occurrence of crime which is, in any way, distinct from the experience, understanding or social response to crime is one that needs to be systematically explored and demonstrated. So, exploring how reported cases construct a public narrative of homicide at odds with its reality requires systematically relating the newspaper coverage to data about actual homicides.

The data from this study, then, compares an account of the national statistics of illegal killing in England and Wales with their representations in the print press. First, definitions are crucial. We took as our sample all cases initially recorded as homicide, rather than those finally determined to be homicide. In other words, we were concerned with newspaper reporting of what is perceived at the time to be homicide, whatever the later outcome. We used the Homicide Index, a computerized Home Office database of all initially recorded homicides in England and Wales, as our basic source. This contains details of all cases dealt with by police forces in England and Wales from 1977 onwards. 2,685 initially recorded homicide cases were identified in England and Wales in the period 1993–1996. These were initially classified into 2,396 murders, 282 manslaughter cases and 7 infanticide cases. Three homicide cases[1] with a terrorist motive were excluded from the analysis. Fewer than 4 per cent of the cases (95) had a multiple victim, but 18.3 per cent of the cases where suspects had been identified had more than one suspect. One hundred and seventy cases (6.3 per cent) had not yet identified a suspect by the end of 1999.

The basis for our newspaper study is shown in Box 16.1. We adopted as our measure of homicide reporting whether a particular homicide case had been reported in a particular newspaper or not. This allowed us to assess newsworthiness – whether a case was judged interesting enough to report or not. The study analyzed a wide range of variables to explain homicide story salience. The circumstance of the killing was found to play a

---

Box 16.1   How we did it

The *reporting* of these homicide cases was examined in three national newspaper titles: *Times*, representing a broadsheet newspaper title (and consisting of *Times*, *Sunday Times* and supplements[4]), the *Mail*, middle-brow right-of-centre newspaper titles (*Daily Mail* and *Mail on Sunday*) and the *Mirror*, tabloid left-of-centre newspaper titles (*Daily Mirror* and *Sunday Mirror*). All stories from the start of 1993 to the end of 1997 relating to homicide were traced and examined (excluding stories on terrorist killings). As we were comparing with a database on homicides in England and Wales between 1993 and 1996 (inclusive), homicides first recorded outside this period or taking place outside England and Wales were excluded from the analysis.

crucial role in whether a homicide is reported, with sexual homicides and motiveless acts being more likely to be reported. Homicides involving young children are highly likely to be reported, but infant homicides are not. Our analysis is that these public narratives construct homicide differently to the reality of illegal killing, highlighting particular versions of 'otherness' and danger. These distorted contributions may, we argue, foster particular political and social responses to homicide that are not based on statistical reality but on media representations of reality.

Is there a media hierarchy among homicide cases?

The next question takes us from consideration of the routine back to the unusual (i.e., such cases which attract exceptional coverage such as that of the Taylor sisters). In earlier work, Soothill and Walby (1991: 25) noted in their study of newspaper coverage of sex crime in 1985 that just 3 cases (out of 114) accounted for one-third (32 per cent) of the total newspaper coverage of rape cases in England and Wales. Certain homicide cases, as we have already noted, have a similarly extraordinary impact on a national consciousness. Hence, rather than focusing on just one major homicide case this time, we aimed to systematically examine the intensity of coverage by exploring the hierarchy within 'media-homicides' that we subsequently distinguished in terms of 'mega-cases', 'mezzo-cases' and 'routine cases'. Hence, understanding the impact of newspaper reporting is a much more complex social and cultural phenomenon than is usually understood through counting the traditional binary 'reported/non-reported' approach.

In this part of our homicide study we focused on the coverage of homicide by a leading British newspaper (*The Times*) over a period of 23 years (1977–1999 inclusive) considering which were the top cases (i) each year and (ii) over the whole period. Our focus on the 'mega-cases'

demonstrated the importance of unusualness and cultural context in fully understanding how, in particular, homicides become mega-cases (Soothill et al., 2002). In broad terms, the top cases in *The Times* tend to be killings by strangers, principally with multiple victims and/or involving children and females. In our study there were over 4,000 different homicide cases from the UK reported in *The Times* in the 23-year period and so the 13 cases which we defined as 'mega-cases' were only a very small percentage. However, these 13 cases contributed 2,860 stories – of a total of over 15,000 stories – and thus a sizeable amount of news space was devoted to these top cases. The bulk of the mega-cases resonate because they are in some way straightforwardly shocking, disturbing and hardest for society to reconcile itself with. They stand out from other cases, perhaps in the quantity of victims or betrayal of duty and trust.

While mega-cases may vary, they share the capacity to touch a public nerve. A particular killing may link to wider concerns; for example, if an individual case becomes representative of a particular 'social problem', such as gun culture, errant youth or stranger danger. In so doing, they may help to spawn the development of specific 'moral panics', a concept taken from Cohen's pioneering fieldwork in the 1960s (Cohen, 1972). In short, mega-cases contribute disproportionately to what we call the 'general knowledge of homicide' (see Box 16.2 for how we use the idea of a 'general knowledge' of homicide).

We argue that the continuance of the reporting of high profile cases over a sustained period may combine both chance happenings and a cultural context that provides sustenance to this kind of reporting. The mid-1980s after the Yorkshire Ripper case[2] had reached its zenith and the mid-1990s immediately after the Bulger case[3] may have provided such a context in Britain. Further, examining reporting over time shows that their unusualness is not the complete story, for one also needs to appreciate the wider, contemporary discourses within Britain that contributed to them becoming mega-cases. So, for example, Stephen

---

Box 16.2 General knowledge of homicide

Examining coverage of a case over time allowed us to explore a process that is often missed: the way that mega-cases become, cumulatively and over time, a part of the cultural context within which we understand homicide and within which journalistic choices about reporting are made. Paradoxically, repeated reporting of the unusual feeds into the context by which we make sense of 'routine', 'mezzo' and 'mega' cases as they emerge through reporting as part of our 'general knowledge' of killing. We argue that the variables normally identified for multiple regression analysis fail to capture the importance of the wider contextual debates and the possible importance of time in that contextual framework.

Lawrence, a black youth who was killed on 22 April 1993, was in many respects like several other homicide victims. However, while the murder of Stephen Lawrence was reported in most newspapers from the outset, it was a developing concern that institutional racism within the police was hindering progress on the case which led to the later, more widespread media coverage.

How do newspapers invite readers to identify with victims and victimhood?

Peelo (2006) has explored some of the techniques whereby newspapers engage readers in a stylized dialogue that further contributes to the construction of public narratives about homicide; and the framing of homicide for readers as 'mediated witness'. In the context of the present chapter, Peelo (2006) is essentially arguing that researchers, as well as working at a macro level of quantification, social analysis and comparison of datasets (which was necessary to understand how the Stephen Lawrence case, for example, became of such importance), need also to research qualitatively at the micro level of textual analysis when researching media (including visual media) in order to understand the precise framing of homicide that contributes to public narratives. This form of textual analysis was not about quantification but about a careful sifting of discourse and meaning.

Her argument continues by illustrating how newspapers develop the 'victim' role in major crimes by inviting us to witness and take part on the side of those closely affected by a killing (Peelo, 2006). In focusing on the side of the offended-against and being encouraged to feel the hurt, there are techniques of the crime-reporting genre, such as the defamiliarization and objectification of homicide victims, which help to mediate certain paradoxes. In our earlier study (Peelo et al., 2004) we showed how the profile of *actual*

homicides is quite different to those usually reported: what makes a mega-killing especially newsworthy is the exceptional quality of its horror, its oddness. However, a part of what makes a murder into entertainment is the shock of ordinariness invaded by the brutal or the corrupt. The offence to society of a killing is greater according to its invasion into homely cosiness, and the greater the shock the harder it becomes to regroup our sense of social order. 'Mediated witness' brings homicide closer to personal experience through reporting moments and objects of familiarity that, thereby, become grotesque by a process of defamiliarization, bringing us closer to the chaos and disorder that we fear. One particularly well-known moment of virtual witness shaped by defamiliarization is the touching trust shown in the video clip of two-year-old James Bulger, raising his hand in the child's universal – and commonplace – expectation of care. Shocking events distort the ordinariness of lives and its meaning to people but what shocks may vary over time (see Box 16.3 for Orwell's view of what once were the ingredients of the 'English murder').

However, the cruelty is that, while survivors of homicide understandably experience their lives as changed forever, the rest of society will move on and probably quite swiftly. The objectification of homicide victims is part of a social process of neutralizing anguish. Peelo (2006) uses the reports of the killing of the headmaster, Philip Lawrence, who was stabbed to death by a 15-year-old boy to illustrate the point. The killing – while tragic of itself – raised the spectre of an ordinary event made sinister: that of children coming out of school. Peelo notes how reports moved rapidly through (a) reflecting parents' fears to (b) accounts of social disintegration, and then to (c) defining 'otherness' and 'bad' in the world at large. Hence, the tragedy of one person's brutal killing becomes strangely depersonalized and held to represent a mass of social discontent.

Box 16.3   Change over time

In a celebrated essay, 'Decline of the English murder', George Orwell (1946: 345) argued that 'one finds a fairly strong family resemblance running through the greater number' of murders which have become best known to the British public. He pointed to the period between roughly 1850 and 1925 as 'our great period in murder' and pointed to various murderers, such as Jack the Ripper, Dr Crippen and Joseph Smith, whose reputation has stood the test of time. In fact, he regards the Jack the Ripper case as 'in a class by itself' (ibid. 346), but from various others he constructs 'from a *News of the World* reader's point of view', the 'perfect' murder as one in which readers identify with the murderer. But our findings tell a very different story from Orwell, as our top cases from *The Times* echo Garland's analysis in that they do not invite the reader to identify with the murderer, but more usually to identify with vulnerability. In other words, newspapers invite readers to identify with victims and victimhood as a route to engaging readers in 'human interest' stories.

CONCLUSION

From this analysis it can be seen that we expect media researchers in the area of crime to be able to engage in a variety of research activities in order to fully explore research questions. Newspapers provide researchers with easy access to source material, but quantification of content needs to go beyond the simplicity of what is reported/what is not reported to encompass the complexities of mediated crime narratives. So, for example, the concept of the 'general knowledge of crime' was made possible because analysis of reporting homicides over time made clear how some crimes are revisited over many years, thereby acting as benchmarks for exceptional wrongdoing. Probing the nature and style of coverage and how reporting fits into more long-term cultural and social consciousness requires a variety of approaches. Our quantitative work provided a systematic framework, establishing what a 'unit' is (a newspaper article, a TV programme, etc.), establishing a target population and its boundaries. The qualitative work contributed predominantly to the analytical style – not measuring or counting per se but probing in depth what happens within the framework. Hence, the examples which Peelo (2006) chooses to discuss are not selected at random but emerge from the earlier quantitative analysis whereby top/mega cases were identified.

All crimes are framed by the perspectives of those involved (such as the victim, their friends and families, neighbours and colleagues, as well as perpetrators, their kith and kin, etc.); however, the death of a homicide victim has an actuality independent of perspective or opinion. Yet in our example of homicide and the media we are focusing on different types of reality: that is, the world that is 'captured' by official statistics and the world that is 'captured' by the media. In using the quantitative approach to consider homicide as portrayed in official statistics, this provides a baseline from which we can explore the cases reported in the media in some depth. Qualitative approaches consider more processual questions of what actually happens within the framework; for example, the focus on language, photographs and the court interaction.

Reiner (2002) has discussed the way in which quantification in traditional content analysis has tended to present itself as value-free, as if its categories for analysis arise without underpinning assumptions – not least, that 'the categories used necessarily presuppose some theory of meaning, usually about likely consequences' (ibid. 378). The same, of course, can be argued for qualitative methods that are unexplained or chosen unthinkingly rather than for their appositeness to the research focus. In our studies of homicide, we

have clear concerns about possible meanings and consequences: we believe that, if one accepts Garland's thesis concerning the politicization surrounding crime and the social policy arena, then the gulf between rhetoric and reality – between public narratives and people's life experiences and interactions with the public sphere – becomes a matter of importance. In terms of social justice, the gulf between rhetoric and lived experience has the potential to contribute to injustice.

If criminology is to contribute to social action via its critical commentaries on complex crime phenomena, then these need to be systematically evidenced and match the complexity of the research focus with its research methods and analysis. One challenge, then, for future researchers is to develop methods that are both systematic and flexible to understand the effects of an increasing range of media available, as well in charting how different media representations of serious crime (e.g. on television, film or Internet) interact with each other.

ACKNOWLEDGMENTS

Work on this chapter was partially supported by the UK Economic and Social Research Council under the National Centre for Research Methods initiative (grant number RES-576-25-0019).

NOTES

1 The Warrington shopping centre bomb, the Bishopsgate bomb in the City of London in 1993, and the Canary Wharf bomb in East London in 1996 had five victims in total.

2 Peter Sutcliffe (the 'Yorkshire Ripper') was convicted of the murder of 13 women aged from 16 to 47. Despite a massive police operation to find him, his murder rampage lasted over five years before he was eventually arrested. He was sentenced to life imprisonment in 1981.

3 In February 1993, two-year-old James Bulger was abducted from Bootle Shopping Centre by two ten-year-old boys, Jon Venables and Robert Thompson. The subsequent search for him was covered extensively by the media as was the search for his abductors/killers. The trial was held in November 1993 and both boys were ordered to be detained at Her Majesty's Pleasure. They have since been released.

4 The supplements are the *Times Literary Supplement*, *Times Educational Supplement* and *Times Higher Educational Supplement*. All are separate products from the main newspaper.

RECOMMENDED READING

Interested readers may wish to look further at:

Bergman, M. (ed.) (2008) *Advances in Mixed Methods Research: Theories and Applications* (London: Sage) for discussions of the philosophical and practical implications of mixed methods in a variety of social science settings.

Jewkes, Y. (2004) *Media and Crime: a Critical Introduction* (London: Sage) which combines understanding of both media analysis and criminology, providing some basic building blocks alongside theoretical depth for researchers working in this cross-disciplinary space.

Reiner, R. (2002) 'Media made criminality: the representations of crime in the mass media' in Maguire, M., Morgan. R. and Reiner, R. (eds) *The Oxford Handbook of Criminology*, 3rd Edition (Oxford: Oxford University Press) pp. 376–416, provides an authoritative discussion of the extensive literature on media portrayals of crime; moving on from traditional concerns with the impact of media representation as either subversive or socially controlling, instead he provides three useful categories for analysis – content, consequences and causes of mass media representations.

REFERENCES

Altheide, D.L. and Johnson, J.M. (1980) *Bureaucratic Propaganda*. Boston: Allyn and Bacon.

Beckett, K. and Sasson, T. (2000) *The Politics of Injustice: Crime and Punishment in America*. Thousand Oaks, CA: Pine Forge Press.

Bergman, M. (ed.) (2008) *Advances in Mixed Methods Research: Theories and Applications*. London: Sage.

Bryman, A. (1988) *Quantity and Quality in Social Research*. London: Unwin Hyman.

Cohen, S. (1972) *Folk Devils and Moral Panics*. Oxford: Martin Robertson.

Ericson, R.V., Baranek, P.M., and Chan, J.B.L. (1991) *Representing Order: Crime, Law and Justice in the News Media*. Buckingham: Open University Press.

Erikson, K.T. (1966) *Wayward Puritans: A Study of the Sociology of Deviance*. New York: John Wiley.

Garland, D. (2001) *The Culture of Control: Crime and Social Order in Contemporary Society*. Oxford University Press: Oxford.

Johnstone, J., Hawkins, D. and Michener, A. (1994) 'Homicide reporting in Chicago dailies', *Journalism Quarterly*, 71(4): 860–872.

Lave, J. and Wenger, E. (1998) *Communities of Practice: Learning, Meaning and Identity*. Cambridge University Press: Cambridge.

Orwell, G. (1946) 'The Decline of the English Murder' in: *Essays* (1984) Penguin: London.

Peelo, M. (2006) 'Framing homicide narratives in newspapers: Mediated witness and the construction of virtual victimhood', *Crime, Media and Culture*, 2(2): 159–175.

Peelo, M., Francis, B., Soothill, K., Pearson, J. and Ackerley, E. (2004) 'Newspaper reporting and the public construction of homicide', *British Journal of Criminology*, 44(2): 256–275

Peelo, M. and Soothill, K. (2000) 'The place of public narratives in reproducing social order', *Theoretical Criminology*, 4(2): 131–148.

Reiner, R. (2002) 'Media made criminality: the representations of crime in the mass media', in: Maguire, M., Morgan. R. and Reiner, R. (eds) *The Oxford Handbook of Criminology*, 3rd Edition (pp. 376–416). Oxford: Oxford University Press.

Schlesinger, P., Tumber, H., and Murdock, G. (1991) 'The media politics of crime and criminal justice', *British Journal of Sociology*, 42(3): 397–420.

Soothill, K., Peelo, M., Francis, B., Pearson, J., and Ackerley, E. (2002) 'Homicide and the media: identifying the top cases in *The Times*', *Howard Journal of Criminal Justice*, 41(5): 401–421.

Soothill, K., Peelo, M., Pearson, J. and Francis, B. (2004) 'The reporting trajectories of top homicide cases in the media: a case study of *The Times*', *Howard Journal of Criminal Justice*, 43(1): 1–14.

Soothill, K. and Walby, S. (1991) *Sex Crime in the News*. London: Routledge.

Sorenson, S., Peterson Manz, J. and Berk, R. (1998) 'News media coverage and the epidemiology of homicide', *American Journal of Public Health*, 88(10): 1510–1514.

Tashakkori, A and Teddlie, C. (1998) *Mixed Methodology: Combining Qualitative and Quantitative Approaches*. Thousand Oaks: Sage.

Taylor and Taylor (1994) *Criminal Appeal Reports* 98: 361–369.

17

Assessing Crime Through International Victimization Surveys

Pat Mayhew and Jan Van Dijk

INTRODUCTION

Victimisation surveys (or 'victim' or 'crime' surveys as they are sometimes called) are in the scale of things a relatively new way of studying crime. Essentially they take a sample of the population (usually householders) to ask them if in the recent past they have been a victim of crime and whether or not they reported what happened to the police. Since to a very large extent, figures of crimes recorded by the police depend on the number of crimes reported by victims, victimisation surveys provide an alternative count of crime to the police count. Several studies have shown that survey-based estimates can give a more reliable picture of the volume of, and trends in, crime than police figures. Victimisation surveys also collect social and demographic information to show which social groups are most vulnerable to victimisation. This is important as police data usually provide very little information on this front. Victimisation surveys have developed substantially over the past two or three decades, as costs in data collection and data analysis software have been cut.

This chapter deals mainly with 'general purpose' household victimisation surveys. It also deals in particular with household surveys that have used standardised methods to address crime in an international context. The emphasis throughout is more on methodological issues than on substantive results.

The next section considers the development of victimisation surveys generally, and the place they hold alongside police figures to assess the volume and nature of crime, and how it changes over time. The section describes some of the main technical features of victimisation surveys, the ground they usually try to cover, and the way in which the surveys have been administered. The material here is relevant to comparative surveys, which were informed by the foci and methods of other household victimisation surveys. There is also a discussion of the limitations of such surveys. We then move on to describe the development of standardised comparative victimisation surveys. A major focus is the International Crime Victimisation Survey (ICVS). This was set up to overcome the substantial difficulties of comparing police statistics, or the results of freestanding victimisation surveys – dependent as they are on the approach taken to counting victimisation. Both of us have been very closely involved in the ICVS, so we can speak from the heart about the challenges it posed. Finally, we raise some issues about future prospects and make some concluding points.

THE DEVELOPMENT OF VICTIMISATION SURVEYS

The most important early victimisation survey was carried out in the US for the President's

Crime Commission in the 1960s. This was followed in 1972 by the first round of what is now called the National Crime Victimisation Survey (NCVS). It has been conducted continuously ever since (see Rand, 2009, for latest results). Although it now has to rein in costs, it is still by far the largest of any of the national surveys, with 135,300 people aged 12 or more currently interviewed in 76,000 households a year.

Elsewhere, early household victimisation surveys were carried out in Finland, the Netherlands, Switzerland, Canada, Australia and the UK. These countries still conduct stand-alone 'bespoke' national victimisation surveys. So too now do many other countries: for instance, New Zealand, Belgium, Denmark, Italy, Sweden and South Africa. The surveys are done on a regular basis, though not necessarily annually. In some countries, victimisation questions have been added to other generic household surveys (France, Ireland Italy and Romania are examples). In other countries, the ICVS has been adopted as the national survey, using augmented samples (Argentina, Estonia, Poland and Japan are examples).[1]

National surveys of householders have been the most common genre, although they are often analysed by type of area, to see where victims most often live. There have also been household surveys with a focus on cities or 'high-crime' areas. In the Netherlands, household surveys are now conducted in the majority of local administrative areas, to track local levels of victimisation and local police performance. The British Crime Survey (BCS) also offers some measures of victimisation and confidence in policing for each police force area in England and Wales. In the US, local community surveys have gone forward apace, especially since the Bureau of Justice Statistics and the Office of Community Oriented Policing Services (COPS) developed software for localities to conduct their own telephone surveys of residents. Some local surveys have also been conducted to evaluate crime prevention programmes, looking at 'before and after' risks and changes in perceptions of risk. In the UK, for instance, they were used in an evaluation of 'reassurance poling' initiatives (see Singer, 2004), and in testing the effectiveness of improved street lighting (see Farrington and Welsh, 2002). They often intended to complement the picture from police figures which might change simply because crime prevention programmes often encourage reporting to the police (and better recording by the police). Victimisation questions also sometimes appear in polls conducted by major polling agencies. The form of the questions varies widely, and the victimisation measures tend to be somewhat crude.

In many countries, household victimisation surveys have been complemented by surveys focussing on special groups, or particular forms of victimisation. Violence against women (VAW) surveys have featured particularly large, since 'general purpose' household surveys are not considered to provide especially good measures of sexual or assaultive victimisation, which often involves those well known to the victim. Some VAW surveys have been national ones, such as in the US (see Tjaden and Thoennes, 1998), but some take selected populations of women. (There are a plethora of studies amongst students – a convenient group for university researchers.) VAW surveys sometimes take men as a comparator group, but often they do not. The surveys are notable for their wide differences in approach, particularly as regards the sorts of questions asked. This has meant that they have produced widely different estimates of harm to women (see, e.g., Percy and Mayhew, 1997). Some estimates are high ones, albeit with a relatively low threshold of harm.

Business (or commercial) victimisation surveys are growing in popularity too (see Hopkins, 2002), although they fall far short of the number of household surveys. Sampling methods and the types of business sectors taken have varied. Retailers and manufacturers have been a common focus, but one of us made a refreshing excursion into the victimisation of house builders in Australia (Sakurai et al., 2004). Recently, there has been much activity in terms of measuring cybercrime (or 'e-crime) amongst businesses. In the US, the Bureau of Justice Statistics and the Department of Homeland Security estimated the number of cyber attacks, frauds, thefts of information, and resulting losses during 2005 (Rantala, 2008). There has also been a global, comparative survey of economic crimes against businesses, including cybercrime (Bussmann and Werle, 2006; PricewaterhouseCoopers, 2005).

Victimisation surveys have also focused on other special groups (for instance, tourists, the disabled, and the mentally ill), usually showing them to be more at risk of victimisation than the public at large. Of increasing interest are ethnic minorities as victims of crime, and the degree to which their different experiences are due to racial prejudice, or to broader structural factors which negatively influence victimisation risk.

Methodology

The methods used in household victimisation surveys vary to quite an extent. The main features are summarised below, overlooking several deviations from the norm. (The design of the NCVS, for instance, is singular.) The features of most household victimisation surveys are pertinent to the

ICVS and the few other standardised household comparative surveys, which have not deviated greatly from the procedures described below.

- *Samples.* The surveys generally adopt a stratified random sampling approach to achieve a representative sample in terms of age, gender and geographical area. (Post-survey weighting is often done to improve representativeness.) Virtually all national surveys are cross-sectional (taking a different sample in each round). Sometimes, 'booster' samples are added: for instance, of ethnic minorities or those in inner cities. For national estimates, the booster samples are down-weighted, but are available for separate analysis.
- *Respondents.* Usually one person in each household is interviewed. This is generally someone aged 16 or 18 years or older, since it is felt that incidents of 'household' victimisation may not be well reported by youthful respondents.
- *Mode of interview.* The mode of interviewing has changed somewhat over time. Box 17.1 shows the main current modes, with their main advantages and disadvantages. Face-to-face interviewing was the 'gold standard' in the earlier days. This was partly because of high response rates,

and the belief that interviewers could build more rapport with respondents. Also, though, telephone penetration was not considered high enough to be an acceptable alternative. Where face-to-face interviews are still done, the interviewer now generally uses a laptop (Computer Assisted Personal Interviewing, CAPI).

Telephone interviewing has now increased, bringing cost savings. Also, the premise that respondents would be unwilling to answer questions of a sensitive nature over the telephone interviews has not been borne out. For instance, extensive testing in relation to the first Canadian VAW survey showed higher levels of admissions than in face-to-face interviews – perhaps because simply because of a lack of a 'face' provides some degree a degree of anonymity (Smith, 1989). Telephone interviews are now virtually always done through Computer Assisted Telephone Interviewing (CATI), where samples are typically drawn using some form of random digit dialling. Experience shows that long questionnaires do not work well in telephone interviews.

In both CATI and CAPI, the questionnaire is programmed into the computer which the interviewer uses to enter responses. A by-product of

---

Box 17.1 Different modes of interviewing in victimisation surveys

		Advantages	Disadvantages
Face-to-face interviewing		Higher response Better rapport?	Expensive
Paper and pencil interviewing	PAPI		Data entry mistakes
Computer Assisted Personal Interviewing	CAPI	Cleaner data entry Allows possibility of CASI	
Computer Assisted Self Interviewing	CASI	More anonymity	Has to take account of literacy levels
Telephone interviewing		Cheaper than face-to-face	Does not allow show cards Long interviews difficult
Computer Assisted Telephone Interviewing	CATI	Cleaner data entry Allows possibility of CASI	
Computer Assisted Personal Interviewing	CASI	More anonymity	Has to take account of literacy levels
Mail questionnaires		Cheap	Generally poor response Have to take account of literacy levels Do not suit complicated routing

CAPI is the potential to allow respondents to use the computer themselves to answer questions of a sensitive nature – a technique known as Computer Assisted Self Interviewing (CASI). CASI imposes limits on the complexity of questions that can be asked, but has nonetheless proved valuable. Levels of sexual and domestic violence revealed in CASI modules in the BCS, for instance, are substantially higher than from the survey's main face-to-face screening methods (see, e.g., Hoare and Jansson, 2008). In Japan, CASI has also been found to increase reports of domestic violence.

Mail surveys are not unknown, and Germany has recently used them in pilot testing for a European Union-wide victimisation survey that is discussed later. Mail surveys are relatively cheap, but the questions have to accommodate the 'lowest common denominator' in literacy terms. Respondents may also have to cope with a complicated set of routings, depending on their victimisation status. Mail surveys also rarely achieve high response rates. Low response would not necessarily be a problem if those who do respond are representative, but there is reason to doubt this.

- *The screening process.* Respondents are screened for experiences of victimisation over a given 'recall period' (see below). The screener questions typically describe 'volume' crimes using definitions and concepts taken from colloquial language rather than from law. The screener questions usually aim simply to elicit a 'yes' or 'no' answer, with further questions about the nature of what happened coming later. (A respondent faced with a long list of questions immediately after saying 'yes' may well be inclined to say 'no' to a following screener.) The count of victimisation sometimes comes from affirmative answers to screener questions (the ICVS procedure). Sometimes surveyors post hoc count and define the crimes using more detailed information about what happened in the victimisation incident. In many surveys (the ICVS included), it is common for the selected respondent to answer questions about possible victimisations that can be seen as affecting the household as a whole: for instance, burglary and vehicle crime. For personal crimes (such as sexual offences, assault and robbery), respondents answer only about their own experience, since it not felt that personal victimisations are necessarily always shared with other household members.
- *The recall period.* Victimisation surveys aim to estimate victimisation over a limited time period. There is a balance to be made about the period over which experiences are likely to be reliably remembered, and generating enough victimisation incidents to report upon. Methodological

work shows that many less serious victimisation incidents are soon forgotten, although they fall within the legitimate victimisation survey count. At the same time, serious incidents tend to be pulled forward in time (so-called 'forward telescoping'). The NCVS measures victimisation over the last six months, although many surveys (without the vast samples of the NCVS) have a 'recall period' of one year.[2] To avoid forward telescoping, some surveys (the ICVS included) ask people about possible victimisation over a longer time-period (the ICVS takes five years) and then ask specifically whether this happened last year or longer ago.

- *Contextual information.* All household victimisation surveys collect socio-demographic information to assess how risks for different groups vary. This always includes 'harder' measures (such as household income and personal education level). Some surveys have also tried to measure 'lifestyle' or 'routine activities', which the victimological literature has shown to be important in explaining why some people are more often than others in the wrong place at the wrong time, or behave in ways that 'attract' victimisation (e.g., Felson, 1998; Garofalo, 1978; Hindelang et al., 1978).
- *Other crime-related information.* Since making successful contact with a respondent is the biggest survey cost, surveyors typically take the opportunity to address other crime-related issues, as well as victimisation. The questions asked have varied considerably in scope, and even when similar topic areas have been covered, it has been with different questions. Popular topics have been the use of crime prevention measures, and attitudes to criminal justice agencies (in particular the police). Fear of crime has also featured regularly, although with many different approaches, reflecting lack of academic consensus about how 'fear' is best measured (see, e.g., Gray et al.. 2008, and also Chapter 18, this volume)

It is worth saying that while the focus of household victimisation surveys remains on 'volume' crimes (such as burglary, car crime, assault and robbery), some surveys have been expanded to take up issues of emerging interest. Examples include stalking, identity theft, 'plastic card' fraud, Internet fraud, computer viruses, hacking, and receiving harassing or offensive email or mobile phone messages. Counts of these are usually not added to the conventional crime count. Drawing on information about the victimisation incident, some surveys now also try to assess the extent of 'hate crime' – that is, crimes committed because of a victim's race, ethnicity, religion, disability, gender or sexual orientation.

The limitations of household victimisation surveys

Household victimisation surveys have limitations that have been extensively discussed (see, e.g., Lynch and Addington, 2007; Mayhew, 2007). Briefly, the main ones are:

- Sample surveys do not represent the entire population completely. The most common household sampling frames exclude those in communal establishments, for instance, and the homeless. Their omission makes little difference to national victimisation estimates in fact, although it obviously precludes building up a full picture of victimisation patterns.
- As only a sample of the population is questioned, findings are subject to sampling error. Margins of error are obviously greater for surveys with smaller samples – an issue that is pertinent to the ICVS. Estimates are most imprecise for types or sub-types of crimes that happen relatively infrequently, and for answers to follow-up questions such as whether reporting victims were satisfied with their treatment by the police. The experience of the ICVS has shown that sample sizes of a few thousand per country suffice to obtain rough estimates of national crime problems that can be used for comparative purposes. For more accurate estimates, and for estimates of sub-populations, considerably larger sample sizes are needed. Household victimisation surveys provide incomplete coverage of crime. For instance, they omit 'victimless' crimes (such as drug possession), and crimes against businesses and society at large (e.g., racketeering, grand corruption, and environmental pollution). There are omissions even for crimes against private individuals. The victimisation of children is largely ignored. There is no victim to be interviewed in the case of homicide. And it is difficult to cover fraud well, since people will not always be aware they have been victimised.
- By no means all potential respondents can be contacted, and some who are approached do not wish to take part, either through lack of time or interest. Possible bias from non-response needs to be acknowledged, although its extent is somewhat contested. One view is that those who cannot be contacted, or who refuse to take part may have 'more to say' in victimisation terms. The other view is that people who are available and willing to be interviewed are those who have 'something to say'. This point is returned to in the context of the ICVS.
- Other types of response bias are a problem in victimisation surveys. Serious victimisation incidents may, as said, be over-counted because of 'forward telescoping'. Counter to this, many incidents may well be undercounted. Some relatively minor incidents are simply forgotten (memory loss). These include incidents which could be on the borderline of what people actually regard as criminal (e.g., street brawls). Incidents of a sexual nature and/or those perpetrated by someone well known to the victim are also likely to be undercounted. This is because incidents between intimates may not be perceived as 'criminal', or because respondents are reluctant to talk to unknown interviewers about issues deemed private or sensitive. (As said, dedicated surveys are often seen as more suitable here, although the use of more anonymous modes of questioning within a conventional household survey may also help.)
- There is a further challenge as regards what is known as 'series' victimisation – that which is repetitive in nature (such as domestic violence). It can be hard for respondents to remember incidents as discrete and definitionally tidy events and locate them accurately in time. Series incidents pose a problem in terms of counting the number of victimisations spread across a given number of respondents ('incidence rates'). Respondents often cannot give a reliable numeric value, and very high values, taken at face values, can distort risk estimates for some groups. (Surveyors have taken different approaches to dealing with series incidents. They often set an arbitrary ceiling as to the number counted.) Reporting simple 'prevalence rates' (the number of respondents victimised once or more) is another option, and one which the ICVS has taken.

In sum, then, household victimisation surveys leave out populations that may be more at risk; there is inevitable imprecision in their risk estimates; they cannot claim to cover all offences that directly or indirectly affect private citizens; and they are susceptible to a number of response biases. The count of crime from household victimisation surveys, then, is both incomplete and possibly biased. With the exception of forward time-telescoping and statistical sampling error, the way victimisation is counted will tend to underestimate rather than overestimate the extent of victimisation actually experienced, principally because of memory loss.

COMPARATIVE VICTIMISATION SURVEYS

Prior to the ICVS, there were a few early attempts to compare crime across countries using victimisation surveys. Some studies took results from stand-alone national surveys but they largely ran into the sand because the victimisation count was so heavily influenced by survey design and counting protocols (cf. Lynch, 2006). A few studies mounted standardised surveys in a limited number of countries, for instance in Scandinavia. These exercises have largely sunk into obscurity.

The ICVS, which is dealt with below, is by far the most serious attempt to obtain survey-based measures of victimisation in different countries using a standardised measure. However, a few other exercises are worth mentioning.

- In 1996, the Eurostat Division of the European Commission piloted a small 'Eurobarometer of Crime' (covering the populations of the EU member states). It included questions about victimisation experience, albeit with rather small samples of 1,000 in most countries (Van Dijk and Toornvliet, 1996).
- As part of the ICVS programme, a comparative International Commercial Crime Survey (ICCS) was mounted in eight countries in 1994, although problems of different sector coverage and small sample sizes meant that little became of it (though see Van Dijk and Terlouw, 1996). A very similar questionnaire was later used in six other countries. It focused on experiences of business victimisation, safety around the business area, pollution issues, and the extent and cost of security. The ICCS questionnaire was modified by the United National Interregional Criminal Justice Research Institute (UNICRI) in the late 1990s to include more items on fraud, corruption, extortion and intimidation. Surveys took place in 2000 with small samples of 500 managers in eight capital cities in Central and Eastern European countries (Alvazzi del Frate, 2004).[3] As mentioned, there has also been a global, comparative survey of economic crimes against businesses.
- In terms of violence against women, a multi-country World Health Organisation survey collected data between 2000 and 2003 from women in 12 countries, although there appears to be some differences in samples and survey administration (Garcia-Moreno et al., 2005). A tighter comparative exercise was the International Violence Against Women Survey, which used a fully standardised questionnaire and analysis methods. Between 2004 and the end of 2005, surveys were conducted with women in 11 countries. Five of the surveys used CATI; the remainder used face-to face interviewing (see Johnson et al., 2007).
- There has been a recent move to mount an EU-wide survey of selected immigrant and ethnic minorities' experiences of discrimination and criminal victimisation. At the end of 2006

and beginning of 2007, the European Union's Fundamental Rights Agency (FRA) conducted pilots in six EU member states to test different probability sampling approaches to identify selected ethnic minority and immigrant groups in countries where population data on minorities is often limited. The pilots were the forerunner to the European Union Minorities and Discrimination Survey (EU-MIDIS) conducted in 2008 across the EU member states. The victimisation questions were taken mainly from the ICVS questionnaire. Risks for ethnic minority residents were considerably higher than for others (EU-MIDIS, 2009).

The International Crime Victimisation Survey (ICVS)

The ICVS was initially set up at the end of the 1980s by a small group of criminologists (the two authors among them) who were knowledgeable about national victimisation surveys techniques and had something of a passion for international comparisons of crime. It was clear then (and still is) that using police statistics for these was fraught. This is because of variations in the way the police define, record, and count crime, and differences in the extent to which victims in different countries might choose to involve the police. Police figures are also strongly affected by the scale and effectiveness of policing activities. This influences the amount of crime recorded, and contaminates trend data insofar as policing efforts or priorities change.

The first ICVS took place in 1989 in 13 industrialised countries (see Van Dijk et al., 1990). It has since been repeated four times – in 1992, 1996, 2000, and 2004/2005. Some of the initial 1989 survey countries took part again (though not in all subsequent rounds). Other new countries joined. From 2000 onwards, efforts were made by UNICRI in Italy to execute surveys (usually at city level) in a selection of countries in transition and developing countries (see Gruszczyńska, 2004, and Alvazzi del Frate, 1998 for results).[4]

The most recent fifth round of the ICVS in 2004/2005 was organised rather differently from previous rounds. Whilst mainly co-ordinated through the UN offices in Turin and Vienna and the Dutch Ministry of Justice (as previous rounds were), there were two survey exercises. The first was the European Survey on Crime and Safety (EU ICS) in which all the 15 older member states of the EU took part. This was organised by a consortium lead by Gallup Europe, and financed by the European Commission's Directorate General for Research and Technology Development. Results are in Van Dijk et al. (2007). The second set of surveys was done in countries outside the EU, co-ordinated by the UN. Van Dijk et al. (2008) report on the results for all countries, in and outside the EU. All told, 30 countries were covered at national level, with another 33 surveys in main or capital cities.

Across all rounds of the ICVS over a period of nearly 20 years, more than 140 surveys have been done in over 78 different countries (with national level surveys in 37). Over 320,000 respondents have been interviewed with a questionnaire that has been translated into thirty or more languages (see Box 17.2). The full dataset can be consulted at http://rechten.uvt.nl/icvs/ICVS2005_3full.zip.

The ICVS methodology

The thrust of the ICVS has been to use the same questionnaire and analysis methods to produce equivalent across-country results. To ensure further consistency, much of the data collection in each round of the ICVS was supervised by one polling company. In the first four rounds, survey co-ordinators were appointed in each country liaising with the central team to minimise deviations from the central ICVS model (or 'template'). Country co-ordinators were invited to preparatory meetings, made responsible for correct translation of the questionnaire, and for briefing of interviewers.

Many features of the methodology of the ICVS are similar (and deliberately so) to those adopted in bespoke national surveys. The surveys target a nationally representative sample of householders in which one randomly chosen respondent (aged 16 or more) is selected. The model for the ICVS surveys was that national samples should be at least 2,000 respondents, although some countries increased sample size to aid better local measurement. The rather modest sample size requirement was to curb costs, whilst allowing 'top level' comparisons across different countries for broad categories of prevalent crimes, rather than precise estimates of a larger number of specifically defined types of crime. Criticism of the ICVS sample sizes is justified for analysis tasks based on small numbers. However, comparative analyses of national (or city) risks are sound enough. (The main measures used are the proportion of those victimised once or more in the previous year (prevalence rates), published with their margins of error at the 90 per cent confidence level.)

The ICVS template is to interview respondents using the CATI technique. In countries where there is insufficient national telephone penetration, face-to-face interviews are conducted in the main cities, generally with samples of 1,000–1,500 respondents. Since its inception, the ICVS screener questions have covered ten types of 'conventional' crime that affect private citizens. The selected respondent answers on behalf of the household about household crimes (theft of a car, theft from a car, theft of a motorcycle or moped, theft of a bicycle, burglary and attempted burglary). The respondent answers about his /her experience in relation to personal crimes (theft of personal property, robbery, sexual offences and assault and threats). In later rounds of the ICVS,

---

Box 17.2 Issues in translating the ICVS questionnaire

The ICVS questionnaire has been translated into more than 30 languages	
• Country co-ordinators are responsible for translating the questionnaire (written in UK English) into the host language.	
In the first (1989) round of the ICVS, foreign language questionnaires were 'back translated' to English, which is ideal.*	
• Back translation has not always occurred for other foreign-language questionnaires. This made it difficult to know whether the correct terminology was always used.	
Some concepts and terms did not cross linguistic boundaries very well. Some examples are:	
• 'Seriousness' of a crime	• 'Stranger' (in some countries it is nearer to 'immigrant'
• 'Vans' (as a target of theft) – 'trucks' and 'pick-ups are terms more often used in some countries	• 'Robbery' (often synonymous with 'burglary')
• 'Bribery' – too serious a term in some countries for the type of low level bribery the ICVS was meant to capture. More appropriate terms to use could be 'backhander', *un petit cadeau*, *pot-de-vin*, *smeergeld* (Dutch), 'illegal commission' (Southern Europe)	

Notes: * The foreign language questionnaires were those administered in: Belgium, Finland, France, Germany, Japan, the Netherlands, Norway, Spain, and Switzerland.

additional questions have been added on experiences with street level corruption, consumer fraud (including Internet-based fraud), credit card theft, drug-related problems, and hate crime.

The initial ICVS 'recall period' is five years, although the main measure of victimisation is for the calendar year prior to the survey. To minimise memory loss about what happened in the previous calendar year, the ICVS template is for surveys to be conducted as early as possible in the following year. (Respondents are asked whether what happened occurred in the interviewing year, the previous calendar year, or in the period before this.) Details of victimisation incidents are collected about the 'last' incident of a particular type (the most recent incident of assault for instance). This approach reduces interviewing time, although it may risk bias insofar as respondents choose a 'last' incident which is most salient to them, or about which they have more to say.

Because, as said, the ICVS has tried to provide a measure crime which is independent of police records, it has been important to assess levels of reporting to the police, differences in which can help explain variations in police figures at country level. The proportions of crimes reported, can also serve as a measure of confidence in the police. Reporting rates show considerable variation across countries, even among developed countries. (Asking about reasons for *not* reporting has provided additional contextual information, as has the assessment of those who have reported crimes to the police about how well the police dealt with their report). One consistent question has been about all respondents' views of local police performance. (Internationally, this has shown marked differences. In countries where victims are less likely to report, police performance tends to be rated as poorly.

Questions about fear of crime have been modest in scope in the ICVS. One regular question asks about the perceived likelihood of becoming a victim of burglary in the coming year. (Again, it shows substantial across-country variation.) Another question is the ubiquitous one which asks, 'How safe do you feel walking alone in your area after dark?' This has achieved currency through repetition, although it does not mention fear of crime, and may be tapping other concerns about general 'pavement safety', particularly amongst the elderly (e.g., Allen, 2006). There have also been questions to victims in the ICVS on their need for victim support. Finally, all respondents are asked about attitudes towards sentencing, and the use of common household security measures (for instance, burglar alarms and secure window locks). This last question has been surprisingly problematic, seemingly raising respondents' suspicions about the credentials of the survey.

How far does the ICVS provide a good comparative measure?

The limitations of household victimisation surveys in providing a reliable measure of victimisation experience were discussed above. The limitations also apply of course to the ICVS. A central question, though, is whether the ICVS has achieved its purpose both in terms of standardisation and culturally relevant measures of crime.

To enable reliable and comparative measures of the impact of crime in different jurisdictions, the ICVS should ideally have been done in all countries using the same questionnaire, the same fieldwork periods, and the same interviewing mode. It should also have tapped into crime concerns which have common resonance. Much has been achieved on these fronts, but it is fair to say that the ICVS has fallen short of full standardisation. This was especially so perhaps in the surveys in developing countries. Here, face-to-face interviews were mainly used, and sometimes less experienced interviewers. Marginalised groups living in informal housing were also hard to reach, as were the more affluent living in gated communities living in South America for instance (Kury et al., 2002). While there is no reason to assume that comparability has been seriously compromised, divergent design features and the way respondents in different countries react to the survey may have affected results in unknown ways. Some of the main issues are set out below.

- *Translating the questionnaire.* The ICVS questionnaire was written in English and obviously needed to be translated for use in the large majority of countries. The translation process was not without problems (see Box 17.2). Country coordinators were responsible for ensuring that the English language ICVS questionnaire was translated into host languages to reflect as precisely as possible what the questions were meant to address. In the first round, all translations were checked by the co-ordinating group. Particularly demanding here was translating the concepts and terms of the screener questions. There was also a problem with some other questions. For instance, one question asked victims how 'serious' they felt the crime to be. This seemed to be a term that was difficult to translate, since in some countries proportionately more crimes were considered 'serious', even though the relative rankings of different types of crime in seriousness terms were nonetheless very similar to rankings elsewhere. Thus, it is hard to know how precisely key concepts could be captured in translation. On other fronts, too, it was inevitable that some countries were resistant to strictures of a standardised questionnaire, feeling that 'they could do better' or that some questions were inappropriate. (Poland, for instance, did not acknowledge the relevance of questions about 'victim support', a concept unknown in the country at the time.) Also problematic was the option of 'labour camps' as a special form of imprisonment in the question about sentencing preferences. Some countries were also keen to add additional questions, or restructure the ordering of questions, thereby introducing possible 'context effects'. Some countries took it upon themselves to make minor change to the ordering of response categories, causing huge complications in analysis.

- *Response rates.* These have been variable across country and sometimes rather low. This was so especially in the first 1989 round, when privacy protection prohibiting sufficient re-contacting of non-respondents applied in some countries. While response rates generally improved subsequently, they fell again in the 2004/2005 ICVS round, reflecting a general trend in survey research. While it cannot be ruled out that variable and low response affects ICVS results, the extent of non-response bias is contested, as has been said. In the context of the ICVS, analysis of results from the fifth round of the survey showed no statistical relationship in developed countries between the number of attempts needed to reach a respondent and overall victimisation rates (Van Dijk et al., 2007). This suggests – at least insofar as initial refusal may be taken as a proxy for eventual refusal – that reluctance to take part in telephone interviews may not have a serious impact on cross-national comparability. Whether the situation is the same in developing countries is more arguable. Non-contact may be a particular problem where marginalised groups (especially those residing in informal housing) or privileged groups (living in highly secured areas) are difficult to contact for face-to-face interviews. If anything, this may contribute to an underestimation of victimisation rates in developing countries.
- *Mode of interview.* An obvious challenge is whether ICVS surveys done in face-to-face and CATI mode produce similar results. Analysis of ICVS results so far have not pointed to any systematic bias such that one mode produced higher victimisation rates than the other (e.g., Scherpenzeel, 2001). This is also in accord with tests in the US in relation to the NCVS (Catalono, 2007). Available evidence from a number of methodological tests suggests that the single most important factor determining survey productivity is quality control (e.g., the selection, training and supervision of interviewers).
- *Cultural sensitivity.* It is very difficult to say whether people in different countries will answer questions about victimisation with the same

degree of readiness. There may also be different cultural thresholds for defining certain behaviours as crime. Cultural sensitivity may be most pertinent in relation to violence between intimates and sexual victimisation – the Achilles heel of comparative surveys. For instance, rates of minor sexual victimisation have typically been higher in those Western countries where the social position of women is most advanced (including North America and the Scandinavian countries). This may be because subjective thresholds are lower (Kangaspunta, 2000). In pilot tests for the proposed European Security Survey (to be discussed later) there were high refusal rates in relation to sexual and intimate partner offences in some Eastern European countries specifically. The jury is still out on how well a standardised survey can cope with cultural sensitivity in this domain.

A rather different question is whether any one survey can adequately address experience of and reactions to 'crime across the globe'. On the one hand, one might suppose that the globalisation of markets and mass media information has brought some attitudinal consistency as regards most conventional crime, especially in urban environments. (Japan, for instance, may be thought of as singular in many criminological respects, but the ICVS has been well received there.) Moreover, the ICVS has shown that victims – at least in Western countries – hold strikingly similar views about the relative seriousness of different offence types about which they are asked (see Mayhew and Van Dijk, 1997). On the other hand, there are inevitable limitations to the ICVS as a fine-tuned measure of the impact of crime. For one, despite much common ground in terms of people's usual experience of victimisation, some countries may have particular concerns which bespoke surveys could cover better. For instance, in many developing countries where cattle are a vital resource, theft of livestock is perceived by victims as one of the most serious victimisation experiences. Questions on bribery and corruption, too, are very susceptible to different interpretations as to what constitutes such events, and how seriously they are assessed. In former Soviet countries, such as Georgia, for instance, street-level extortion in the form of neighbours asking to borrow money is a key concern.

What has the ICVS methodology achieved?

This is not the place to go into detail about what the ICVS approach has achieved in the way of adding to criminological knowledge about the risks and responses of victims of crime in different cultural settings, or the attitudes and perceptions of different populations towards crime and its control. Suffice it to say that the ICVS has over the years been used as a data source for hundreds of academic publications and student papers across the world.

However, it is worth singling out two main contributions of the ICVS. The first is what it has shown as to the level crime in different countries compared to the picture from police figures (leaving aside differences in their coverage). The second contribution concerns what ICVS measures of *trends* in crime show relative to trends according to police figures.[5]

Levels of crime

On levels of crime, analysis by Van Dijk (2009) looked at 39 countries across the world in relation to 'total ICVS crime' and 'total recorded crime'. (The latter measure comes mainly from the 2000 UN Crime Survey, which collects a wide range of criminal justice statistics). Figure 17.1 shows the results. 'Total ICVS crime' is generally more restricted in scope than 'total recorded crime', with the result that in some countries (Sweden, the UK and Finland, for instance), total recorded crime per capita is higher.

The results in Figure 17.1 shows that there is no correlation between the actual level of victimisation and the rates of crime recorded by the police ($r = 0.212$; $n = 39$; not significant). Some countries with exceptionally high numbers of recorded crimes also show comparatively high victimisation rates (for instance, South Africa), but many others such as Finland, Canada and Switzerland do not. Comparisons between country rankings according to the ICVS and police recorded crimes were repeated for different types of crime. The results showed positive correlations for robbery ($r = 0.663$; $n = 37$), and car theft ($r = 0.353$; $n = 34$), but much weaker (and statistically insignificant) correlations for other types of crime. The results echo previous analyses of a global nature (e.g., Mayhew, 2003), as well as those that have been restricted to Europe and North America (e.g., Aebi et al., 2002; Gruszczynska and Gruszczynski, 2005; Howard and Smith, 2003). In relation to the data on which Figure 17.1 is based, the concordance between recorded crimes and ICVS crimes *reported to the police* was rather closer, testimony to the fact that victim reporting habits are one of the factors determining the officially recorded output of police forces.

Trends in crime

Of the countries which have taken part in the ICVS since 1989, there are 15 developed countries about which information is available from at least four different rounds, enabling an analysis of trends in crime over the last 10–15 years. (The average victimisation rates for these countries showed them to have peaked halfway the 1990s but declined since. The pattern for individual countries was nearly always the same. The drops are most pronounced in vehicle-related crime and burglary.)

Van Dijk's (2009) analysis looked at what the ICVS had shown in terms of trends in overall crime, compared to the police picture. The analysis reiterated, first, earlier results for the five countries that have had entered the ICVS four times between 1989 and 1999 (Van Kesteren et al., 2000). (The countries were England and Wales, Finland, the Netherlands, Canada, and the US.) The ICVS picture was compared to that from overall police figures (with some adjustments made to bring the two measures closer in line as regards coverage).[6] The overall picture was that the two measures largely converged. Very broadly, crime increased on both measures between 1988 and 1991, stabilised or decreased between 1991 and 1995, then further decreased between 1995 and 1999. The magnitudes (and timing) of the rises and fall in crime in the five counties according to the two measures, however, was far from exact. This is not surprising, however, given that the ICVS and police measures of crime are not the same in scope, for instance.

The analysis also looked at trends in five specific types of crime between 1999 and 2003/2004 in 15 countries according to police statistics and more recent ICVS results.[7] The results were rather different from the picture for the period between 1989 and 1999. Only for motor vehicle theft and robbery were weak positive correlations found between movements in police figures and the ICVS; for theft and assault, there was no correlation between the two measures; for sexual offences there was a negative one. These results are broadly in line with those of Cook and Khmilevska (2005). They also echo results of trends in overall crime (or some subsets) as indicated by the bespoke national surveys of England and Wales, the Netherlands, France and Switzerland and the police figures for the four countries (Van Dijk, 2009). The picture is complex, but the broad conclusion was that trends in many types of crimes according to the survey and police indicators have diverged. Improvements in police recording and, to a lesser extent, increased reporting by victims to the police is the most likely explanations for the generally higher increases in police figures (cf. Shepherd and Sivarajasingam, 2005). The bottom line drawn is that there is little room for optimism about how well police figures reliably monitored changes in volume crime over time in the four countries, and

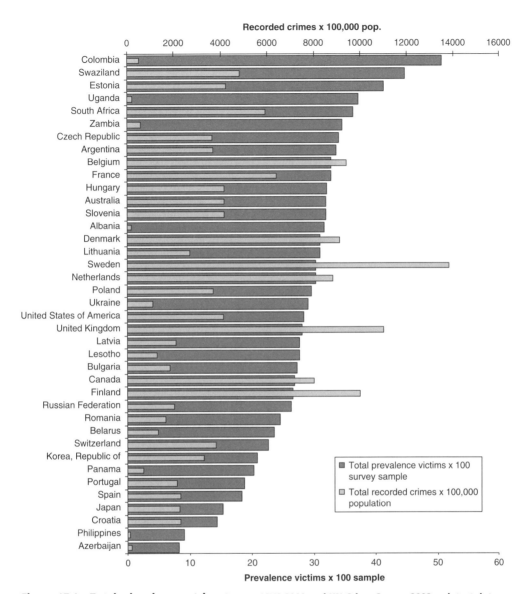

Figure 17.1   Total crime by countries. Source: ICVS 2000 and UN Crime Survey 2002 or latest data available (Van Dijk, 2009)

probably in others including the US (cf. Lynch and Addington, 2007).

FUTURE DEVELOPMENTS

The UN office in Vienna has produced a *Manual on Victimisation Surveys* which provides an overview of organisational and methodological issues (see 'Recommended Reading'). The existence of this manual should help those who have made no

in-roads into victimisation surveys, although it is no guarantee that comparable surveys will be carried out. The experience of comparing independent surveys in the 1980s, and the subsequent experience of the ICVS, has shown that the reasonably high level of methodological standardisation that is critical for producing reliable comparative results requires organisational coordination and, preferably, collective core funding.

At the time of writing, there are definite plans for standardised surveys in 2013 in all 27 member states of the European Union (EU), to be called the EU Security Survey. This is being co-ordinated by Eurostat, with part funding from Eurostat and part funding from the Directorate General for Justice, Liberties and Security. There have been pilot tests in 17 countries, looking at different modes of interviewing for one. The questionnaire content is not as yet decided although comparability with a set of core questions from the ICVS seems assured. Sample sizes and sample design are also undecided. So too is the degree of stringency that can be imposed as regards interview mode. Dictating a common mode is unrealistic given different survey capabilities in different countries, but some degree of 'pressure' towards standardisation seems advisable.

In tandem, the International Government Research Directors (IGRD) group is piloting surveys using a reduced version of the questionnaire used in the fifth ICVS, carried out in 2004/2005.[8] The pilots are centred largely on testing different modes of survey administration, including CAWI (Computer Assisted Web Interviewing) – essentially a form of CASI using the Internet.

Policy interest in international comparisons of crime using victimisation survey techniques has been considerably enhanced by the results to date. This means that countries are likely to be keen to enter into future comparative survey exercises. This is especially so if they do not have to fund their own fieldwork costs. But even where self-funding is necessary, countries that have not so far taken part in any standardised survey may wish to sign up, particularly when they do not have the resources for a bespoke national survey. This makes it attractive for them to ride on the back of another survey vehicle, especially when there are comparisons with other countries on offer. This said, the conduct of victimisation surveys in developing countries seems to have stalled. This is regrettable since statistics of recorded crimes are of poor quality, or even lacking altogether in many developing countries. Here, victimisation surveys are the most viable option for collecting information about national or local crime problems, and about the performance of the police.

The logistical challenges of carrying out international comparisons through victimisation surveys remain. So too do the methodological challenges of improving the measurement of crime internationally through survey techniques that are hard to standardise in diverse environments. 'Survey saturation' in westernised countries may also become an obstacle, whatever mode of interviewing is adopted. Over the lifetime of the ICVS, the development of CATI has been a major bonus, reducing fieldwork costs and facilitating consistent questionnaire administration. A problem to be faced, however, is that many people (particularly younger ones who are more heavily victimised) are forsaking landlines for mobile phones. Internet-based voice services like Skype are also growing. How far viable representative samples can be obtained from the growing diversity of telephone provision remains to be seen – although it is a problem that survey companies will be keen to solve across a wide range of business. The inclusion of mobile phone users in sampling designs is an obvious priority.

With increasing Internet use, CAWI clearly provides a window of opportunity for surveys in the future, particularly in terms of cost. In the Netherlands and Finland, pilot testing for the 'bespoke' national victimisation surveys has begun with CAWI, with fairly encouraging results.[9] However, the methodological challenges of CAWI cannot be denied (cf. Rand, 2007). There is possible bias due to differential access to the Internet, and a degree of respondent self-selection (with or without incentives). Response rates may also be low. In the medium to long term, however, ways round these problems may be found, particularly by using incentives and representative panels that polling companies are increasingly likely to offer.

CONCLUSION

Victimisation surveys are now part of the tool kit of criminological researchers, although they are relatively new compared to other methods of investigating crime. Stand-alone national surveys have earned their place in showing more about the dimensions of 'ordinary' victimisation, who is most affected by it, and what the public feels about a number of crime-related issues. They have also paid their way in offering an alternative picture of trends in crime to that from local police figures. These surveys now inform the public and the political debate on crime in many developed countries, both nationally and locally.

Using surveys for the purposes of international comparisons of crime has been a rather newer enterprise. It has taken off against a background of increasing recognition of how much police figures are influenced by national legal definitions, recording practices of the police, and the readiness of victims to report their experiences to the police. This recognition was something of a kiss of death for comparative criminology, although it is fair to say that there has been increasing rigour of late in at least documenting the problems of non-comparability. For instance, the *European Sourcebook of Crime and Criminal Justice Statistics* now itemises the difference in legal definitions and counting protocols, and so on, that affect police statistics (Aebi et al., 2006).

The ICVS has shown that it is feasible to conduct standardised surveys in a large number of countries, albeit that it takes huge logistical effort. While the ICVS has not provided data that are impeccable by any means, or entirely comprehensive, it has arguably improved on what can be derived from police records as regards comparative levels and patterns of victimisation in different parts of the world. The information from standardised surveys on trends in crime has also been an important addition to the picture from police records. Our judgement about the achievements of the ICVS, of course, may be tainted by familiarity and many night candles burnt.

Some of the main lessons of the ICVS are practical ones. Conducting surveys in a standardised way, more or less on time, and with sound adherence to the ICVS design template, was logistically tortuous. To ensure consistency, tight oversight from the central team was needed to make certain that country co-ordinators engaged with tedious technical detail. Financial matters were also time-consuming and a continuing challenge, especially with regard to developing countries. The ICVS had other special problems too. Although all results were, with some delays, made available for secondary analysis, there were nevertheless occasional issues as regards the ownership of results, and the way in which participating countries could share or could use their own results[10] When and how the results were released was also something of a minefield – clearly so, as crime 'league tables' can be politically sensitive. For countries taking part that had their own national surveys (and there were several), country co-ordinators also sometimes needed to be able to explain why the ICVS could give different results as to victimisation risks.

NOTES

1 In 2005, the United Nations Office on Drugs and Crime (UNODC) and the United Nations Economic Commission for Europe (UNECE) attempted an inventory of surveys conducted or planned in the 56 Economic Commission for Europe (ECE) member countries (including Europe, North America and Central Asia). The inventory located 32 dedicated national victimisation surveys (carried out in 23 countries), and 26 other surveys with a module on victimisation (carried out in 16 countries). The ICVS questionnaire was used in full or in part in 18 surveys.

2 Many VAW women surveys ask about experience over the lifetime or since the age of age 16. One problem here is that it is hard to know whether the lower levels of victimisation reported by older people are due to lower levels of violence in the past,

a greater a reluctance to disclose events, or simply not being able to remember pertinent incidents over a greater period of elapsed time.

3 They were co-ordinated by Gallup, with funding from the Netherlands and Hungary.

4 These had financial support from the Dutch Ministry of Development Aid. (Until the 2004/2005 ICVS round, Western industrialised countries have largely paid their own way in the ICVS.)

5 Both these questions were most recently addressed at a conference in 2008 – one of a number funded by the European Commission devoted to Assessing Deviance, Crime and Prevention in Europe (CRIMPREV) (see Van Dijk, 2009).

6 The main adjustment was to exclude from the ICVS count incidents of threats and offensive sexual behaviour; since these were unlikely to be recorded by the police.

7 These were: theft of motor vehicles, other theft, robbery, assault, sexual offences, and 'total contact crime'.

8 There were pilot surveys in 2008 in four countries (Canada, Germany, Sweden and the UK). Further ones are planned for early 2010 in the same four countries, as well as Denmark and the Netherlands. The work is being organised in the Netherlands through the NICIS Institute. It is being done at the request of the Research and Documentation Centre (WODC) of the Dutch Ministry of Justice, whose director is a member of the IGRD. NICIS has subcontracted the survey work through an EU tendering process. NICIS is responsible for overall co-ordination of the pilots, data management and reporting of the pilot results.

9 The Netherlands, for instance, is using sequential mixed mode approach. Respondents contacted by mail are invited to fill in the questionnaire by CAWI or by mail. Those who do not answer are subsequently approached with a request to participate in CATI mode. Possible non-responders can also be visited at home for a CAPI interview.

10 The full dataset is currently available at http://easy.dans.knaw.nl/dms?query=icvs, or http://rechten.uvt.nl/icvs20053full.zip

RECOMMENDED READING

Lynch and Addington's (2007) book *Understanding Crime Statistics* (Cambridge: Cambridge University Press) usefully reviews the differences between (and scope of) police statistics and victimisation surveys in the US. The European research group, CRIMPREV, has issued a collection of essays comparing police statistics with survey results from several European countries (see Van Dijk, 2009). Jan Van Dijk's (2008) book *The World of Crime* (Thousand Oaks, CA: Sage) covers global results of household surveys and surveys of violence against women, as well as a critical review of available international statistics on police-recorded crimes The UN *Manual on Victimisation Surveys* gives a useful introductory overview of design and implementation issues. This can be found at http://www.unodc.org/documents/data-and-analysis/Crime-statistics/Manual_on_Victimization_surveys_2009_web.pdf.

REFERENCES

Aebi, M., Aromaa, K., Aubusson de Cavarlay, B., Barclay, G., Gruszczynska, B., von Hofer, H. et al. (2006) *European Sourcebook of Crime and Criminal Justice Statistics 2006*. Available at: http://www.europeansourcebook.org.

Aebi, M.F., Killias, M. and Tavares, C. (2002) 'Comparing crime rates: the International Crime (Victim) Survey, the European Sourcebook of Crime and Criminal Justice Statistics, and Interpol statistics'. *International Journal of Comparative Criminology* 2(1): 22–37.

Allen, J. (2006) *Worry about crime in England and Wales: findings from the 2003/04 and 2004/05 British Crime Survey*. Online Report No. 15/06. London: Home Office.

Alvazzi del Frate, A. (1998), *Victims of Crime in the Developing World*. Publication 57. Rome: UNICRI.

Alvazzi del Frate, A. (2004) 'The International Business Survey: findings from nine Central-Eastern European cities'. *European Journal on Criminal Policy and Research* 10: 137–161.

Bussman, K-D. and Werle, M. (2006) 'First findings from a global survey of economic crime'. *British Journal of Criminology* 46: 1128–1144.

Catalona, S.M. (2007) 'Methodological change in the NCVS and the effect of convergence'. In, J. Lynch and L. Addington (eds) *Understanding Crime Statistics*. Cambridge: Cambridge University Press.

Cook, P.J. and Khmilevska, N. (2005) 'Cross-national patterns in crime rates'. In M. Tonry and D. Farrington (eds) *Crime and Justice: An Annual Review of Research*, Volume 33. Chicago: University of Chicago Press.

EU-MIDIS (2009) *European Union Minorities and Discrimination Survey: main results report*. European Union Agency for Fundamental Rights (fra.europa.eu/eu-midis)

Farrington, D.P. and Welsh, B.C. (2002) *Effects of improved street lighting on crime: a systematic review*. Home Office Research Study No. 251 London: Home Office.

Felson, M. (1998) *Crime and Everyday Life*, 2nd edition. Thousand Oaks, CA: Pine Forge.

Garcia-Moreno, C., Jansen, H., Ellsberg, M., Heise, L. and Watts, C. (2005) *World Health Organisation multi-country study on women's health and domestic violence against women: initial results on prevalence, health outcomes and women's responses*. Geneva: World Health Organisation.

Garofalo, J. (1987) 'Reassessing the lifestyle model of criminal victimization'. In M.R. Gottfredson and T. Hirschi (eds) *Positive Criminology*. Newbury Park, CA: Sage.

Gray, E., Jackson, J. and Farrall, S. (2008) 'Reassessing the Fear of Crime'. *European Journal of Criminology* 5(3): 363–380.

Gruszczy ska, B. (2004) 'Crime in Central and Eastern European countries in the enlarged Europe'. *European Journal on Criminal Policy and Research* 10: 123–136.

Gruszczynska, B., and Gruszczynski, M. (2005) 'Crime in enlarged Europe: comparison of crime rates and victimization risks'. *Transition Studies Review* 12: 1337–1345.

Hindelang, M.J., Gottfreson, M.R. and Garofalo, J. (1978) *Victims of Personal Crime: An Empirical Foundation for a Theory of Personal Victimization*. Cambridge, MA: Ballinger.

Hoare, J. and Jansson, K. (2008) 'Extent of intimate violence, nature of partner abuse and serious sexual assault, 2004/05, 2005/06 and 2006/07 BCS'. In D. Povey (ed.) *Homicide, Firearms Offences and Intimate Violence 2006/07*. Home Office Statistical Bulletin 03/08. London: Home Office. Available at: http://www.homeoffice.gov.uk/rds/pdfs08/hosb0308.pdf.

Hopkins, M. (2002) 'Crimes against business: the way for future research'. *British Journal of Criminology* 42: 782–797.

Howard, G.J. and Smith, T.R. (2003) 'Understanding cross-national variations of crime rates in Europe and North America'. In K. Aromaa, S. Leppa, S. Nevala and N. Ollus (eds) *Crime and Criminal Justice Systems in Europe and North America, 1995–1997*. Helsinki: HEUNI.

Kangaspunta, K. (2000) 'Secondary analysis of integrated sources of data'. In A. Alvazzi del Frate, O. Hatalak and U. Zvekic (eds) *Surveying Crime: A Global Perspective*. Rome: ISTAT/UNICRI.

Johnson, H., Ollus, N. and Nevala, S. (2007) *Violence Against Women*. New York: Springer-Verlag.

Kury, H., Obergfell-Fuchs, J. and M. Würger, M. (2002) 'Methodological problems in victim surveys: the example of the ICVS'. *International Journal of Comparative Criminology* 2(1): 38–56.

Lynch, J. (2006) 'Problems and promise of victimization surveys for cross-national research'. In M. Tonry and D. Farrington (eds.) *Crime and Justice: An Annual Review*, Volume 34 (pp. 229–287). Chicago: University of Chicago Press

Lynch. J.P. and Addington, L.A. (eds) (2007) *Understanding Crime Statistics: Revisiting the Divergence of the NCVS and UCR*. Cambridge: Cambridge University Press

Mayhew, P. (2003) 'Operations of the criminal justice system'. In K. Aromaa, S. Leppä, S. Nevala, and N. Ollus (eds) *Crime and Criminal Justice Systems in Europe and North America 1995–1997*. Helsinki: HEUNI.

Mayhew, P. (2007) 'Researching the state of crime: national and international and local surveys'. In R. King and Wincup, E. (eds) *Doing Research on Crime and Justice*, 2nd edition. Oxford: Oxford University Press.

Mayhew, P. and van Dijk, J.J.M. (1997) *Criminal Victimisation in Eleven Industrialised Countries*. The Hague: Ministry of Justice, Research and Documentation Centre.

Percy, A. and Mayhew, P. (1997) 'Estimating sexual victimisation in a national crime survey: a new approach'. *Studies in Crime and Crime Prevention* 6, (2): 125-150.

PricewaterhouseCoopers (2005) *Global Economic Crime Survey 2005*. In collaboration with Martin Luther University.

Rand, M. (2007) 'The National Crime Victimisation Survey at 34: looking back and looking ahead'. In M. Hough and M. Maxfield (eds) *Surveying Crime in the 21st Century*. Crime Prevention Studies, Volume 22. Cullomptom, Devon: Willan Publishing.

Rand, M. (2009) *Criminal Victimisation 2008*. NCJ 227777. Washington DC, US Department of Justice. Available at: http://bjs.ojp.usdoj.gov/content/pub/ascii/cv08.txt.

Rantala, R. (2008) *Cybercrime Against Businesses*. NCJ 221943. Washington: US Dept of Justice.

Sakurai, Y., Mayhew, P. and White, M. (2004) *Theft and Vandalism at Residential Building Sites in Australia*. Technical and Background Paper Series No. 29. Canberra: Australian Institute of Criminology.

Scherpenzeel, A. (2001) *Mode effects in panel surveys: a comparison of CAPI and CATI*. Neuenberg: Bundesamt für Statistik.

Shepherd J. and V. Sivarajasingam (2005) 'Injury research explains conflicting violence trends'. *Injury Prevention* 1: 324–325.

Smith, M.D. (1989) 'Women abuse: the case for surveys by telephone'. *Journal of Interpersonal Violence* 4: 308–324.

Singer, L. (2004) *Reassurance Policing: An Evaluation of the Local Management of Community Safety*. Home Office Research Study No. 288. London: Home Office.

Tjaden, P. and Thoennes, N. (1998) *Extent, Nature and Consequences of Violence Against Women: Findings from the National Violence Against Women Survey*. Washington DC: National Institute of Justice and Centers for Disease Control and Prevention.

Van Dijk, J.J.M. (2008) *The World of Crime; Breaking the Silence on Problems of Crime, Justice and Development Across the World*. Thousand Oaks, CA: Sage.

Van Dijk, J.J.M. (2009) *Approximating the Truth About Crime*. Available at: www.crimprev.eu

Van Dijk, J.J.M., Manchin, R. Van Kesteren, J, and Hideg, G. (2007) *The Burden of Crime in the EU: A Comparative Analysis of the European Crime and Safety Survey (EU ICS) 2005*. Brussels: Gallup Europe. Available at: http://www.europeansafetyobservatory.eu/downloads/EUICS_The%20Burden%20of%20Crime%20in%20the%20EU.pdf.

Van Dijk, J.J.M, Mayhew, P. and Killias, M. (1990) *Experiences of Crime Across the World: Key Findings of the 1989 International Crime Survey*. Daventer, Netherlands: Kluwer.

VAN DIJK, J.J.M. and TERLOUW, G.J. (1996) 'An international perspective of the business community as victims of fraud and crime', Security Journal 7(3): 157–167.

Van Dijk, J.J.M. and Toornvliet, L.G. (2006) 'Towards a Eurobarometer of Public Safety'. Paper presented at the Seminar on the Prevention of Urban Delinquency linked to Drug Dependence, European Commission, Brussels, November.

Van Dijk, J.J.M., Van Kesteren, J.N. and Smit, P. (2008) *Criminal Victimisation in International Perspective: Key Findings from the 2004–2005 ICVS and EU ICS*. The Hague: Boom Legal Publishers. Available at: http://rechten.uvt.nl/icvs/pdffiles/ICVS2004_05.pdf.

Van Kesteren, J.N., Mayhew, P. and Nieuwbeerta, P. (2000) *Criminal Victimisation in Seventeen Industrialised Countries. Key Findings from the 2000 International Crime Victims Survey*. The Hague: Ministry of Justice.

18

In Search of the Fear of Crime: Using Interdisciplinary Insights to Improve the Conceptualisation and Measurement of Everyday Insecurities

Emily Gray, Jonathan Jackson,
Stephen Farrall

INTRODUCTION

The body of work on the 'fear of crime' is vast, spans several decades and continents, and attracts continuing interest from politicians and academics alike. Most of this work focuses on negative emotional responses (fear, worry or anxiety) to the threat of common crime categories (burglary, theft, assault, etc.). Surveys suggest that the fear of crime is widespread amongst members of many contemporary westernised societies. Since 2000 the British Crime Survey has found that around one-sixth of the population have reported high levels of worry about burglary, car theft and violent crime (Nicholas et al., 2007). Studies undertaken in the US (Skogan and Maxfield, 1981), Australia (Enders and Jennett, 2009), Europe (Holland [van der Wurff et al., 1989]; Switzerland [Killias and Clerici, 2000]; Germany [Kury and Obergfell-Fuchs, 2008]; Sweden [Heber, 2007]; and Spain [Serrano-Maillo and Kury, 2008]), and

newly industrialised economies like China (Zhang et al., 2009) and Brazil (Dammert and Malone, 2006) also testify to heightened public insecurities about falling victim to crime.

Fear of crime is often seen to constitute a social problem in and of itself (Hale, 1996), reducing quality of life and public health (Jackson and Stafford, 2009; Stafford et al., 2007), restricting movements (Ferraro, 1995), eroding social and neighbourhood bonds (Lavrakas, 1981), and shaping the very organisation and zoning of a city. Yet while reducing fear and providing reassurance to the community has, at times, become *as* important as the reduction of actual crime among policy makers, understanding the nature of fear has been fraught with challenges and pitfalls. On the one hand there seems a mismatch between officially modelled 'likelihood' statistics (self-reported victimisation) and lay perceptions of risk; on the other hand standard survey designs may inadvertently exaggerate the extent of the fear of crime

(Farrall and Gadd, 2004; Lee, 1999), distort the nature of fear as it is experienced in everyday life (Gabriel and Greve, 2003), fail to recognise the functional aspects of worry (Jackson and Gray, 2010), and struggle to capture the 'expressive' properties of crime fears (Farrall et al., 2009; Girling et al., 2000; Jackson, 2006;).

This chapter reviews the history of fear of crime research methodology and addresses some common questions on the topic. *How much* fear of crime is there? (i.e. is the fear of crime a common experience for citizens living in the industrialised world?). *Why* it is that people feel fearful? *And what avenues remain* profitable for future research? We touch on several sets of debates not just in criminology, but also in survey research and question design. We explore not just what the fear of crime 'is', but also unpack the history of the fear of crime as a concept and object of enquiry. And we consider the latest thinking on the psychology of answering survey questions and methodological innovations from psychology and sociology.

THE HISTORY OF FEAR OF CRIME RESEARCH

We first chart the emergence of the fear of crime from the policy-relevant victimisations surveys of the 1960s in America, to its increasing influence through the 1970s and 1980s, to its transformation into a staple feature of government statistics and performance indicators. It is worth noting in advance that anxieties about crime are not a recent phenomenon; historians have charted public anxiety about an increasingly 'out of control' youth offender population for over two centuries (Shore, 1999), and how the mass media stoked anxieties about the 'Jack the Ripper' murders in late nineteenth-century London (Curtis, 2001), to name just two examples.

The President's Commission on Law Enforcement

But the emergence of public concerns about crime as a topic of research can be dated back to a Commission initiated by the American President, Lyndon Johnson, in 1965. Concerned with a perceived growth in public anxiety about crime and eager to attend to voters insecurities, the President's Crime Commission on 'Law Enforcement and the Administration of Justice' (1967)[1] was tasked to 'find out precisely what aspects of crime Americans are anxious about, whether their anxiety is a realistic response to actual danger, and how

anxiety affects the daily life of Americans' (President's Commission, 1967: 49). The Commission funded three crime surveys (Biderman et al., 1967; Ennis, 1967; Reiss, 1967) to count victimisation and measure public attitudes towards crime.

Of chief importance in the beginnings of fear of crime research was the report of the first survey, in which an 'index of anxiety' was developed that incorporated five subjective reports on (1) the chances of being beaten up, (2) whether neighbours created disturbances, (3) if respondents would move if they could for reasons of 'trouble', (4) whether safety or moral characteristics were the most important feature in their neighbourhood, and (5) if crime was getting better or worse in their local area. On inspection of the data the researchers were surprised by the discrepancy between actual victimisation (using police recorded crime statistics and self-reported victimisation) and perceived risk (using the 'index of anxiety'), whereby an individual's anxiety often seemed out of proportion with their objective risk. This paradox set the scene for future debates about the 'rationality' of public anxieties about crime.

What attracted less attention, by contrast, was the argument of Biderman and colleagues about the symbolic nature of crime, in which public anxieties gather their meaning in relation to the deeper significance that crime and disorder represent in the public consciousness. 'The intensity of public reaction to [crime] is understandable in that it reveals weaknesses of the moral order on which not only everyone's safety depends but also almost everything else that is important and precious in life' (Biderman et al., 1967: 164). Such a comment rightly draws our attention to the political and social context of America in the mid 1960s. Not only was recorded crime on the rise, but disorder and unrest had become national anxieties. Civil rights issues erupted into riots, and the movement's leader, Martin Luther King Jr, was assassinated in 1968. It was against this background of urban conflict that a number of Republican politicians started to focus their political campaigns on 'law and order', exploiting the issue of 'insecurity' and 'crime in the streets' (Lee, 2007).

Fear of crime reaches a wider audience

The trend to identify public anxieties about crime for political leverage was not limited to the political arena in America however. During the 1970s and 1980s, right-wing politicians in the UK also began to organise their political campaigns around issues of law and order, claiming the populace did not feel 'safe on the streets'. The Home Office, hoping to quell the mounting media 'panics' about rising crime and disorder (see Hall et al., 1978), set about establishing the British Crime Survey not only to measure unrecorded crime but also to assess respondent's perception of risk and safety. The results captured the zeitgeist. Interest in the fear of crime was buoyed up an ever-growing news media, hungry for salacious stories about crime and criminals, and fear of crime emerged as fodder for high-profile election campaigns, premised on the idea that the public were increasingly concerned about their safety. As Garland (2001) observed, after the 1970s people in the US and UK began to feel that life was becoming more risky in general. Not only was the rehabilitative ideal of treatment seemingly failing, leaving crime on the increase. There also emerged a sense of social malaise, related to the idea that common values were deteriorating, and that modern life was increasingly unfamiliar, unpredictable and hazardous.

More recently, President Clinton's pursuit of symbolic law and order policies, such as 'zero tolerance' in the 1990s led to a re-focusing on issues of disorder, fear and crime, and inspired similar policies in the UK, and to a lesser extent parts of Europe – specifically in the Netherlands (Burney, 2005). In the UK,'anti-social behaviour' assumed priority status and became attached to a huge range of nuisance or petty crimes in the UK. The perceived need to 'get tough' with anti-social 'yobs', who disproportionately damaged the harmony and appearance of communities provided an opportunity for a range of new civil and criminal control mechanisms, most notoriously in the shape of the Anti-Social Behaviour Order (ASBO).

As fear of crime remained at the front of the electorate's mind, so it stuck as an object of political substance, and moving forward to the present day, fear of crime still has weight in election campaigns. In particular it is now a performance indicator for numerous police forces in North America and Europe, with its reduction often forming a key aspect of 'reassurance' interventions and day-to-day operations.

TRIAL AND ERROR: OPERATIONALISING 'FEAR OF CRIME'

Fear of crime remains a slippery subject – a concept that lacks clarity, with real methodological complexities at its core. We next examine some of the problems with common survey questions.

We outline some important breakthroughs from feminist and 'left realist' scholars, and we highlight advances using experience-based questions and the 'expressive' dimensions of public insecurities about crime.

'Walking around in the dark': early methodological difficulties

The questions used in the three early surveys commissioned by President's Commission provided a patchy collection of indicators that, with hindsight, lack theoretical specification (Farrall et al., 2009; Ferraro and LaGrange, 1987; Garofalo and Laub, 1978; Hale, 1996). But among the items was a set of questions that soon found its way into subsequent large-scale victimisation surveys: 'How safe do you feel walking alone in your neighborhood after dark?', 'Have you wanted to go somewhere recently but stayed home because it was unsafe?' and, 'How likely is it a person walking around here at night be held up or attacked?' (Ennis, 1967). Criticism of the measures soon followed however. Garofalo and Laub (1978) pointed out that these safety questions (1) did not mention crime, (2) failed to provide a specific geographical reference, and (3) provided a hypothetical situation. Instead of measuring fear of crime, they argued, these questions tapped into to a broader sense of urban insecurity. The Figgie Report (Figgie, 1980) continued this critique, distinguishing between 'formless' fear (measured by perceptions of safety and abstract threats to one's security) and 'concrete' fear (self-reported concern about becoming a victim of various personal crimes).

After reviewing the fear of crime indicators, Ferraro and LaGrange (1987: 715) concluded that survey questions designed to measure fear should include the following characteristics: (1) use 'how afraid' – a 'helpful way to examine an emotional state of fear'; (2) make reference to specific crimes; (3) avoid using hypothetical formats; and (4) state 'in your everyday life' to bring 'a touch of reality to the questions'. This advice proved influential, with standard items now asking respondents to summarise their levels of 'worry' (UK) or 'fear' (US) about specific crimes or their perceived likelihood of victimisation. But technical difficulties still remained. Criminologists have highlighted the leading nature of the question wording of 'how worried are you about...?' that includes an assumption that the respondent already does or should have an opinion on this topic, which can prompt biased or invalid responses (Tourangeau et al., 2000). There is also the limited emotional pallet of the questions, failing to acknowledge other socially significant emotions

---

Box 18.1   Key problems with early survey questions on the fear of crime

The earliest types of questions employed to measure the fear of crime (which asked about how safe an individual felt (or *would* feel) walking alone in their neighbourhood after dark) have been criticised for:

- starting with the word 'how' (believed to be leading; Moser and Kalton, 1971: 325);
- failing to mention crime at all (Ferraro and LaGrange, 1987: 76);
- referring to a vague geographical area ('neighbourhoods'; Ferraro and LaGrange, 1987: 76);
- asking about something which many people may only do rarely, or not at all ('walking alone after dark'; Ferraro and LaGrange, 1987: 76–7);
- mixing fears and risk assessments (Ferraro and LaGrange, 1987: 77);
- failing to refer to a specific time period (Farrall and Ditton, 1999); and
- conflating the intensity and frequency of feelings (Farrall, 2004a).

---

like anger, frustration or even indifference (Ditton et al., 1999). And the validity of asking respondents for details about past emotional experiences has also come under the spotlight. Robinson and Clore (2002a, 2002b) have argued that beyond a two week time-span memories of emotional experience draw on 'semantic' knowledge which is not grounded in the specifics of time and place but is imbued with people's general beliefs related with this particular event. Indeed, until recently surveys have rarely asked about the frequency or intensity of the emotions reported, not enquiring whether the fear experienced took place on a constant basis throughout the day, or whether it was concentrated at certain times or in particular places. See box 18.1 for a summary of the key methodological weaknesses associated with early fear of crime research.

Feminist research – enter stage, left.

As the methodological difficulties became more widely recognised, some scholars concluded that large-scale surveys were simply too crude a method to capture the intricacies and nuances of emotional reactions to crime risk. Smaller-scale qualitative studies subsequently proved successful in teasing out some of the more intimate and personal features of crime fears (Bannister 1993; Girling et al., 2000). Feminist researchers (e.g., Stanko, 1988, 1990) challenged the notion that certain groups, in this case women, were apparently 'irrational' in their response to crime (given their objective 'risk' as measured by recorded crime and national crime surveys). By employing ethnographic and life-history research and female interviewers, feminist studies were able to draw attention to the 'hidden' nature of crimes (such as domestic and sexual violence) that were not only concealed from police statistics, but to large-scale

victimisation surveys. Such discoveries effectively put to rest the idea that women (or other 'vulnerable' groups) often reported fears in wild excess of their objective risk.

Meanwhile, a number of commentators began to conduct spatial analysis and were able to make links between deprivation and public disorder. Specifically, 'left realists' argued for more locally based victim surveys to show the geographic and social distribution of criminal victimisation and fear of crime (Jones et al., 1986; Young, 1986). Local surveys, they argued, were able to challenge the idea that crime was a rare occurrence and began to highlight the problems of 'relative deprivation', repeat victimisation and racially and sexually motivated crime. New and secondary analysis of the British Crime Survey also confirmed the link between crime and deprivation (Hope and Hough, 1988; Nicholas et al., 2007); however, the relationship emerged as a complicated one. Both national and local victimisation surveys have reported extensive geographic variations in risks and perceptions, even within small boundaries.

'Fear' of crime; an event or frame of mind? Perhaps both?

If researchers found they were opening a can of worms in studying the fear of crime, one thing became clear: it is difficult to measure the everyday experience of *fear* of *crime*. A number of thorny questions emerged. Might respondents be trying to recall the number of occasions on which they have worried and calculating some sort of average? How were they weighing up feelings of intensity with the frequency of emotional episodes? Were worrying thoughts future- or past-orientated? Were they worried for themselves or their family? Perhaps answers included an overall fusion of these elements? In short, it is likely that people would struggle to identify and articulate precisely how they felt for the purposes of a questionnaire.

Comparing survey data with in-depth interviews in which participants frequently modified or qualified their answers, Farrall et al. (1997) analysed 'mismatches' between quantitative and qualitative data. The authors concluded that incidences of fear were rare, and that standard questionnaires consistently overestimated levels of worry about crime. Exaggeration occurred as respondents tried to summarise their experiences, with their most vivid or recent events at the forefront of their minds – inferred to be representative of their overall experiences. Crucially, when asked to think carefully about their specific instances of worry, many revised their reports and concluded they worried less frequently than reported in the questionnaires. The paper concluded: 'The results of fear of crime surveys appear to be a function of the way the topic is *researched,* rather than the way it *is*. The traditional methods used are methods which seem consistently to over-emphasize the levels and extent of the fear of crime' (Farrall et al., 1997: 676)

It is at this stage worth referring to a short debate which took place between Farrall and Hough in 2004 (See Farrall, 2004a, 2004b; Hough, 2004). Farrall (2004a) argued that because of the poor state of fear of crime methodology, researchers ought to refine their conceptual tools to better pinpoint particular aspects of fear of crime, and that questions on frequency and intensity (of the last event) may be more accurate indicators (compared to standard measures) because they directed respondents to specific moments in their lives rather than ask for one overall summary of fear. Fearful experiences could be recalled as distinct incidents with relatively accurate information, he claimed. On the other hand Hough (2004) suggested that the fear of crime should be conceived of as mental *state* which was not reducible to episodic measurement: 'When we talk about

mental states such as anxiety or worry, we are concerned with *intensity,* not *frequency*. Leaving aside acute anxiety attacks, anxiety is not comprised of a series of events that can be located in space and time' (Hough, 2004: 174). In this respect, worry about crime might be more of an 'underlying uneasiness' that peaks and flows. Similarly, Warr (2000: 453) concluded that fear is 'an emotion, a feeling of alarm or dread caused by an awareness or expectation of danger', and since respondents of crime surveys were unlikely to be in the process of experiencing fear at the time of interview, they were probably drawing upon a more generalised anxiety, rather than fear when answering questions.

Evidence soon emerged in the UK that actual incidences of fear or worry about crime were perhaps less frequent than previously thought. These studies (Farrall 2004a; Farrall and Gadd, 2004; Gray et al., 2008) developed and tested new sets of measures with two unique aspects: (a) the use of a filter question, followed by (b) an assessment of the frequency in the past year and the intensity of the most recent event (see Box 18.2). Farrall and Gadd (2004) found that frequency questions yielded smaller estimates of the fear of crime than 'old' standard questions (i.e., 'worry about ...' or the 'safety walking' items). An alternative strategy is to ask individuals how often they have worried over the past month (Jackson, 2004, 2005).

A sub-sample of the British Crime Survey (2003/2004) fielded both the standard fear of crime questions (How worried are you about...?) and the new measurement strategy. Answers to the two question sets could thus be compared, and since the new questions were likely to achieve lower estimates of fear, it was expected that some people would say they worried about a crime to the standard question, when they reported no (or very few) incidences of worry on the new questions. Top line findings, reported in Gray et al. (2008), confirmed this hypothesis. Not only did responses to these two measurement strategies not

---

Box 18.2 Measures to test the 'frequency' of episodes of worry about crime

The strategy employs a narrow time frame of 12 months to allow respondents a specific reference period which is believed to be more accurate for recall purposes (Farrall and Gadd, 2004; Gray et al., 2008).

Q1: 'In the past year, have you ever felt worried about...' (car theft/ burglary/robbery);
Q2: [if YES at Q1] 'How frequently have you felt like this in the last year' [number of times recorded];
Q3: [if YES at Q1] 'On the last occasion how fearful did you feel?' [not very worried, a little bit worried, quite worried, very worried or cannot remember].

neatly reflect one another; responses to the standard questions demonstrated that 35 per cent of respondents were worried (summing 'fairly' and 'very') about being robbed, 47 per cent reported being worried about being burgled, and 45 per cent reported being worried about having their car stolen. Crucially, the picture was markedly different when drawing on the new question strategy, based on frequency; 85 per cent said they had *not* worried about robbery in the last 12 months. Similarly, 68 per cent stated they had not actually worried about being burgled or having their car stolen in the preceding year. Moreover, where participants had worried, the frequency of these events was surprisingly low – very few people had worried more than once a month during the previous year.

What these data demonstrated was that significant proportions of the sample reported that they were worried about crime, even if they could not recall an episode of worry in the previous 12 months. In fact, worrisome experiences were an infrequent occurrence among the sample. This begs the question; how many manifestations of 'worry' are there? For some people there were tangible moments of worry about crime that they could recall – for example, perhaps clear memories of worry about their car being stolen, or being followed home. For others, there was a form of worry about crime that did not involve memorable stand-alone episodes of worry. Perhaps, as Biderman et al., (1967: 164) commented all those years before, fear of crime questions also tapped into deeper assessments of moral order and community health?

Given the above, rather than opt for an 'either/or' account, fear of crime research might benefit from attending to various 'streams' of fear. The distinction between concrete moments of fear (which can be measured in terms of frequency) and a more diffuse but emotionally tinged anxiety about crime (which is invoked by standard questions; e.g., How worried are you...?) can deepen our understanding of the phenomenon at an empirical and theoretical level. Indeed, such hypotheses were explored by Jackson (2004) and Farrall et al., (2009), who found that while many respondents can be classified as 'unworried', it was also possible to identify people who reported high levels of worrying episodes – typically found among people who reside in places where crime, disorder and social problems are concentrated. Meanwhile another group – the anxious – did not report moments of worry about crime, but expressed concerns about crime and society more generally. Anxiety about crime consisted of beliefs, perceptions or attitudes concerning the cultural meaning of crime, social relations and environmental cues.

The interpretative approach; fear of crime as a proxy for broader social anxiety

If fear of crime research sometimes captures more than just those frightening, albeit rare moments in which one is worried about victimisation, what else, *exactly*, is it capturing? What are these broad anxieties that are invoked by fear of crime questions? Qualitative and quantitative research has extended the analysis to demonstrate that people's perceptions about crime in everyday life ultimately registers with, and is entangled in, questions of social order, politics, culture and justice. Studies have shown how social and political contexts can shape individuals perceptions of risk. For example, Ferraro's (1995) work suggests that an individuals' perception of their community shapes their subjective estimates of victimisation. Key here are symbols of neighbourhood deprivation and disorder, where urban environmental 'cues' are linked by observers with the threat of crime (Bannister, 1993; Jones et al., 1986; Lewis and Maxfield, 1980; Pain, 1993).

Relational concerns about group values, normative concerns, and moral authority may also shape how individuals make sense of neighbourhood disorder (Jackson, 2004). This accords with the findings of Sampson and Raudenbush (2004), who found that the same 'cue' can be interpreted in two different areas as being indicative of two different potential crime risks. Therefore, it is not simply the presence of crime or disorder that is crucial, but how people interpret and perceive crime and all the various ingredients which are associated with the threat of crime. At the root of fear of crime may be public unease about the health of local order, as well as broader anxieties about the pace and direction of social change (cf. Girling et al., 2000). Moreover, the very ways in which people talk about and share stories about crime might be bound up with perceptions of and anxieties about social relations and changing values and morals in society (Sparks, 1992).

In sum, public concerns about crime have a 'long reach,' articulating worries about social, psychological and ontological safety. As Elias notes, 'The strength, kind and structures of the fears and anxieties that smoulder or flare in the individual never depend solely on his own "nature".' Rather they are 'always determined, finally by the history and the actual structure of his relations to other people' (1982: 327). Fear of crime research has thus emerged as an 'absorbent' topic bound up in an individual's response to 'place' *and* 'community' (Banks, 2005; Girling et al., 2000). As Girling et al. conclude:

> Whatever 'it' might be 'fear' turns out to involve multiple dimensions, vicarious as well as direct

experiences and be open to varying conceptualisations as 'an expression of uneasiness', a judgement of government competence to deliver collective security and an 'expression of powerlessness and uncertainty'. In other words it involves abstractions from experience – and hence by definition their meanings and attributions as well as the immediate impact of victimisation as such (2000: 15).

SHARPENING THE METHODOLOGICAL TOOLBOX; LESSONS FROM INTERDISCIPLINARY RESEARCH

We next review what criminologists studying the fear of crime might learn from interdisciplinary research. In particular, we consider the psychology of survey response, studies in 'everyday emotions' (as well as relevant niche areas within psychology and sociology), and we encourage the better use of quantitative techniques and longitudinal data in order to capture the multidimensional and dynamic nature of fear over time.

Lessons from the psychology of survey response

Developing out of work started in the late 1970s and early 1980s, a considerable body of research and theorising has emerged on the ways in which respondents answer survey questions. Taking a psychological perspective, the approach argues that the processes by which people understand, interpret and answer survey questions are part and parcel of the ways in which people ordinarily process information cognitively (e.g., Tourangeau et al. 2000; Zaller and Feldman, 1992). Below we summarise some of the most relevant and insightful aspects of this work with respect to asking people about their emotional responses to crime.

'Leading' questions

All survey questions, to some extent, assume that the respondent has an opinion about a topic or has experienced a certain social situation and can recall it in sufficient detail to provide reliable answers about it. Questions which are poorly worded or imply the respondent ought to have an opinion are referred to as leading questions. Such questions can cause respondents to 'recall' events as if the presupposition were true, even if it is not (Tourangeau et al., 2000: 42). The presupposition is not rejected unless the respondent believes it to be false (so those with no firm opinion on the topic, may tend to agree with it). In sum, leading

questions are *directional* in that, whilst they do not indicate an answer, they guide the person in a desired direction. Question design must be carefully worded to avoid influencing a participant's response. Unfortunately, as described above, fear of crime surveys have frequently involved questions of a leading nature.

Socially desirable responding

Some questions have a tendency to illicit socially desirable responses. These are answers which do not necessarily reflect the respondent's true feelings, but rather the answer which they feel best fits the image of themselves which they wish to portray to the interviewer. For example, work by Sutton and Farrall (2005, 2009) has suggested that gender differences may have less to do with actual differences in fear estimates, and more to do with men being less willing to report fear than women.

Attitudes and non-attitudes

Attitudinal items do not often refer to objective facts and almost always present the respondent with a pre-coded set of responses ('strongly agree' to 'strongly disagree', for example). Research now suggests that, after reading and comprehending the question, respondents often report what might be called 'non-attitudes.' Although respondents may be poorly informed, surveys appear to be for the 'common good', and respondents may attempt to give answers which they hope will be both helpful and constructive. If the topic is salient enough in the minds of politicians and social commentators and resonates at some level with popular beliefs, then, over time, the topic may become one which is 'produced' via repeated surveys on that topic (Osborne and Rose, 1999). Surveys in this situation may not merely measure fear they may actually 'create' and 'recreate' it (Lee, 2007).

Lessons from interdisciplinary research on emotions

Research into emotions has become increasingly prominent (see Davidson et al. 2003; Turner and Stets, 2005). As Karstedt (2002) insists, there has been a 'return of emotions' in criminal justice via the increasingly prominent voice of the victim, the use of restorative justice, and the emotionalised cultures of late-modern societies. Meanwhile, there has been an increasingly rich and diverse understanding of emotions outside the criminological field. One of the largest studies of emotions focused on emotional experiences in everyday life and their socio-demographic and situational antecedents (Scherer et al., 2004). This body of work has also encompassed a number of ethnographic studies concerned with 'how emotions work' (Katz, 1999), how emotions are 'managed' across the settings of everyday life (Hochschild, 1983) and the development of a diverse 'sociology of emotions' (Kemper, 1990; Williams and Bendelow, 1998). These contributions are noteworthy, not only because they offer a conceptual vocabulary that may well have much to offer criminological research, but also because they address pertinent methodological questions.

Frequency of everyday emotions

Scherer and colleagues asked over 1,000 participants to record and describe emotional events of the previous day. Over half the sample reported at least one strong emotion. Notably, while fear was often thought to be a culturally significant and common emotion, it was one of the least frequent emotions in this study, experienced by only 1.2 per cent (although anxiety was more common, 6.5 per cent). They concluded that 'serious fear situations are few and far between in the normal course of events' (2004: 520).

The rich palette of emotions

The emotional complexity of everyday life was underlined by Scherer's study. Respondents used 775 different words and phrases to describe their emotions from the previous day. The authors concluded that there were as many emotions as there were 'appraisal combinations' or interpretations. The richness of Scherer's data reminds us of the plentiful ways in which people interpret and understand their emotional responses

The ways we experience emotions

Reviewing the literature from the 'sociology of emotions', Turner and Stets (2005) highlighted the distinct ways in which emotions are experienced. These can include biological, cultural, linguistic, physical and perceptual reactions to given stimuli. The authors also suggest that not all of these elements need to be present for emotions to exist. In this regard emotions should be a considered to be a multi-dimensional process and be researched as such.

Emotional evaluation

Thinking about facts and events is subject to considerable subjective interpretation. Goldie (2004) has noted how one event may be considered highly significant by one individual and irrelevant by another, depending on their personal, cultural and biological characteristics. In fact, as Warr notes, simply *imagining* a situation of potential danger may elicit fear or worry in one person but not in another (Warr, 1984).

Other studies have documented substantial discrepancies between peoples' concurrent and retrospective reports of emotional experiences (Robinson and Clore, 2002a, 2002b). This has been attributed to the fluctuating nature of emotions over time and place-to-place (Brandstatter, 1983), to the nature of memory (Scherer et al., 2004), and to the way respondents integrate and reconstruct their experiences when they are accessing historical events (Kahneman, 1994).

Examples of alternative methodologies

Methodologists have long been concerned with the results from surveys, since simple measurement errors can easily affect the validity and reliability of the data. Here are just some of the methods employed by researchers from psychology, sociology and socio-psychologists who have conducted emotion research.

Qualitative methods

Katz (2004: 611) argues that formalised survey research 'functions as a surgical courier service for distant intellectual audiences, hastily cutting out and neatly packaging experiences that have taken subjects a messy lifetime to form.' Social phenomena, he stresses, are better approached through alternative ways: ethnographically, interactionally, diachronically, and with attention to corporeal practices. Life-histories and narrative research are other popular methods for psychosocial (and other) researchers as a means of gathering information on the subjective essence of one person's life (see Gadd and Jefferson, 2007; Holloway and Jefferson, 2000).

Diary methods

Numerous studies have employed diaries to study fluctuations in emotions. Some use the 'day reconstruction method' which asks respondents to reconstruct the *previous* day by completing a structured self-administered questionnaire (Scherer et al., 2004). Event History Calendars (Belli, 1998) can take a longer-term approach, and ask participants to record particular events in a chronological order. These methods facilitate retrieval from autobiographical memory and help avoid biases commonly observed in retrospective reports.

Recall time-scales

Research has revealed that respondents are simply not very good at recalling emotional responses for survey purposes beyond two weeks (Robinson and Clore, 2002a, 2002b), and quite often draw upon their most vivid memory (Scherer et al., 2004). Narrowing the time frame is one method for minimising response error.

Cognitive interviewing

These techniques were designed by an interdisciplinary team in the 1980s to estimate the impact of measurement errors. The aim is to use cognitive theory to get feed-back from participants on how they interpreted the interview questions to identify potential problems that may arise in prospective questionnaires (see Beatty and Willis, 2007; Campanelli, 1997).

Audio-visual

What people sometimes say, do and feel are sometimes at odds with one another. However, audio-visual equipment can observe body language and voice-reflections in a way not possible with cognitions. Using a researchers 'eye's and ears' could extend the range of research on fear of crime. Along these lines Sampson and Raudenbush (2004) videotaped social and environmental observations to explore the basis on which individuals formed perceptions of disorder.

Better utilisation of quantitative techniques and longitudinal designs

It is often said that fear of crime is best defined as not just emotional responses to the threat of crime, but also thoughts (cognitive appraisals of risk) and behavioural responses (precautions against crime and reactions to the sense of the threat). Yet quantitative work rarely captures the interplay between the constituent dimensions (for exceptions, see Farrall et al., 2009; Jackson, 2009; Ferraro, 1995). Latent variable modelling[2] is best placed for this task (Everitt, 1984). Such techniques allow researchers to assess the structural paths between feelings, thoughts and behaviours, treating the various concepts as collective properties of multiple manifest indicators. By first empirically assessing the number of underlying dimensions, secondly by treating the joint distribution of the multiple indicators as the measurement of individual constructs (Jackson, 2005), and by third locating fear of crime as the interplay between feelings, thoughts and behaviours, we can begin to capture this social phenomena in a more sophisticated and rigorous manner (Gray et al., 2011).

Fear of crime can also be treated as a dynamic set of processes over time. We might, for example, treat fear as a reciprocal process where crime-related anxieties damage public health and in turn poor health elevates levels of anxiety (Jackson and Stafford, 2009; Stafford et al., 2007). An explanation such as this incorporates its psychological significance. Equally, fear may generate sensitivity to disorderly cues, and where perceptions of neighbourhood disorder feed back into individual's assessments of their environment and maintain or elevate fear. In this sense public evaluations incorporate topics of community cohesion and moral consensus as well as specific experiences of 'fear' of 'crime' – treating fear as a way of seeing as well as a way of feeling.

CONCLUSION

There is an extensive and expanding body of psychological and socio-psychological research on emotion and survey design. Such work has opened up new ways of looking at emotional responses and provided a multi-dimensional view of our emotional life. It has also employed a range of creative research methods and illuminated how we, studying fear of crime, might improve internal as well as construct validity in our research. Emotions are indeed complex thought processes that individuals experience in personal and diverse ways. So is the business of exploring the incidence and experience of the fear of crime. Being alert to the issues we have argued in this chapter will not only increase the general validity of any study, but also will better inform our understanding of how people comprehend, process and 'manage' the fear of crime.

We have pinpointed key stages in the development of this corpus of work. Despite the many conceptual and methodological issues that have required careful thought and attention by criminologists (as well as psychologists, geographers, sociologists and others) studying fear of crime, the topic has made considerable progress over four decades. It was in the late 1960s that fear of crime made its debut as an object of academic and political significance. Since then, it has emerged as an enigmatic, rich and elaborate field of inquiry, and its intimate relationships with culture, politics, emotions and justice have been rightfully identified. Just how these subjects inter-relate has yet to be fully realised, but these questions provide fruitful opportunities for future research and the accumulation of new data. Employing more sensitive methodologies has already allowed researchers to fashion a more unified account of the fear of crime; as a phenomenon with economic, cultural, political and psychological dimensions, that is rooted in time and place, but also varies between people and is subject to a host of global, national and local influences.

Perhaps members of the research community have, at times, been guilty of expecting too much of fear of crime survey questions to deliver 'on all fronts'. No one methodology is capable of being 'all things to all people'. There has, however, been a distinct lack of ambition and imagination to fully exploit alternative methodological tools required to explore the public's emotional reactions to crime. In our view, promoting high-quality research means embracing a range of methodologies, designed to meet the specific goals of the respective project. For example, studying women's or men's 'worry' about crime, studying 'anxiety' in rural communities, or the economic costs of 'public insecurity', will require dedicated thought at each point of the design, collection and analysis stages. By summarising some of the most interesting developments in the field, we hope to have demonstrated the broad range of methodologies and research knowledge available. Certainly, the field will benefit from more theoretical integration, more efforts to link macro, micro and meso theories together, and greater attention to what is meant by the emotional arousal and beyond. Exactly how do worries about crime affect people in their daily lives? What impact does it have on behaviour? How are political opinions influenced by crime concerns? How should politicians respond to an anxious public?

Shortcomings aside, fear of crime research continues to proffer rich pickings. The theoretical and methodological difficulties are now well established and amply documented, the topic remains politically and culturally relevant and new technologies, and methods are available to allow researchers to measure the full range of emotional processes. In closing the chapter we wish to highlight some of the most interesting new directions fear of crime research is exploring.

The functional and dysfunctional aspects of fear

As Gladstone and Parker (2003) note, worry is not a typically pathological process: worry can have functional properties. One relevant study (Jackson and Gray, 2010) has been able to differentiate between a *dysfunctional* worry about crime that erodes quality of life and a *functional* worry that motivates vigilance and routine precaution. Around one-quarter of those research participants who said they were worried about crime in this study also viewed their worry as something akin

to problem solving. In sum, they took precautions that made them feel safer and did not experience a reduction in quality of life as a result of their worry or cautionary activity.

Psychosocial methods

Psychosocial research methods explore topics through an analysis of individual biographies and psychodynamic perspectives. Gadd and Jefferson (2007) highlight the potential for these methods to move beyond the individualistic approach that have thus far been the norm in relation to fear of crime (see Hollway and Jefferson, 2000), exploring broader issues such as how some people are influenced and affected by discourses of populist punitiveness and fear of crime while others remain indifferent to them. A notable example of this method can be found in Evans (2003) who used a psychoanalytic approach to explore the motivations of an anti-paedophile action in the context of 'responsibilising' criminal justice policy.

Special populations

While it is appropriate to situate research in particular contexts and environments, it is also necessary to integrate developing understanding of social and political identities. However, research knowledge about certain social groups remains sparse and there is little on the experiences of the mentally ill, homeless people, sex workers and young men, who are perhaps most at risk from crime, but are rarely the focus of dedicated research. Notably, there is also little information about young people's emotional reactions to crime and victimisation. This is particularly surprising given young people's frequent occupation of public and leisure space; that they are at increased risk of victimisation (Pain, 2001), in addition to being the focus upon which considerable fears and anxieties about crime are projected (Burney, 2005). Nayak (2003) has highlighted a dichotomy in the literature which constitutes children and young people as either 'angels' who need adult protection from predatory adult criminals (particularly paedophiles) (Delemont, 2001) or 'devils', whose very presence in public space makes others feel threatened (Pain, 2001).

NOTES

1 Also known as the Katzenbach Commission after its Chair, Nicholas de B. Katzenbach.

2 'Latent' or 'hidden' constructs, such as 'quality of life' or 'attitudes towards punishment,' are not

easily subject to direct measurement. Construction of a suitable measurement strategy for latent variables is an important part of basic social research, and a necessary step in the exploration of relationships between concepts. This kind of research has a long history in psychology and education but is less developed in criminology. Specifically, latent variable modelling is a statistical technique for exploring relationships between multiple variables, where some or many of the variables are 'unobserved' or 'latent'. 'Confirmatory factor analysis', 'path analysis' and 'structural equation modelling' are the most commonly used procedures.

RECOMMENDED READING

Farrall, S., Jackson, J. and Gray, E. (2009) *Social Order and the Fear of Crime in Contemporary Times* (Oxford: Oxford University Press, Clarendon Studies in Criminology). This book provides an up-to-date synthesis of empirical and theoretical research on 'fear of crime', as well as presenting novel avenues of thought regarding the measurement of emotional responses to victimisation insecurity.

Ferraro, K.F. (1995) *Fear of Crime: Interpreting Victimization Risk* (New York: SUNY Press). Ferraro's seminal work was the first to use national data to examine fear of crime across various types of offence. Central here is the concept of 'perceived risk' to the interpretative process and the study employs a range of perceptual, environmental and personal variables.

Katz, J. (1999) *How Emotions Work* (Chicago, IL: University of Chicago Press). Using a vast range of oral, observational and ethnographic sources, Katz demonstrates the complex nature of human emotionality – highlighting the challenges social researcher's face in accurately understanding how emotions lead us to behave.

Tourangeau, R., Rips, L.J. and Rasinski, K. (2000) *The Psychology of Survey Response* (Cambridge. Cambridge University Press). This final suggestion provides a comprehensive and critical review of the complex psychosocial processes at play when individuals complete surveys. The authors stress the implications for best practice in question and survey development.

Online resources

Social Science Research Network (SSRN) allows members to publish or download a wide range of social science research – often free of charge – as well as hosting a number of specialised research networks. Available at: http://ssrn.com/

The Economic and Social Data Service (ESDS) is a UK-based data service providing access to key economic and social data, both quantitative and qualitative, spanning many disciplines and themes, including the British Crime Survey, as well as other British, European and international data. Available at: http://www.esds.ac.uk

UK-based statistics and government research relating to crime and justice from the public, police forces and other justice agencies are published at: http://www.statistics.gov.uk/hub/crime-justice

American-based government statistics and government research on crime, criminal offenders, victims of crime, and the operation of justice systems at all levels of federal and national government. Available at: http://www.ojp.usdoj.gov/bjs

GERN is a research network from the fields of sociology, history, and law, who work on issues of norms and deviance in ten European countries (Belgium, France, Germany, Italy, the Netherlands, Poland, Portugal, Spain, Switzerland and the UK). The website includes publications and information of local seminars. Available at: http://www.gern-cnrs.com/gern/

REFERENCES

Banks, M. (2005) 'Spaces of insecurity: media and fear of crime in a local context', *Crime, Media, Culture*, 1(2), 169–187.

Bannister, J. (1993) 'Locating fear: Environmental and ontological security' in Jones, H. (Ed.), *Crime and the Urban Environment*. Aldershot: Avebury.

Beatty, P. and Willis. G. (2007) 'Research synthesis: The practice of cognitive interviewing', *Public Opinion Quarterly*, 71(2), 287–311.

Belli, R. (1998) 'The structure of autobiographical memory and the event history calendar: Potential improvements in the quality of retrospective reports in surveys', *Memory*, 6, 383–406.

Biderman, A.D., Johnson, L.A., McIntyre, J. and Weir, A.W. (1967) 'Report on a pilot study in the District of Columbia on victimization and attitudes toward law enforcement'. *President's Commission on Law Enforcement and Administration of Justice, Field Surveys I*. Washington DC: US Government Printing Office.

Brandstatter, H. (1983) 'Emotional responses to other persons in everyday life situations', *Journal of Personality and Social Psychology*, 45, 871–883.

Burney, E. (2005), *Making People Behave: Anti-Social Behaviour, Politics and Policy*. Devon: Willan.

Campanelli, P. (1997) 'Testing survey questions: New directions in cognitive interviewing', *Bulletin de Methodologie Sociologique*, 55, 5–17.

Curtis, L.P. (2001) *Jack the Ripper and the London Press*. New Haven: Yale University Press.

Dammert, L. and Malone, M.F. (2006) 'Does it take a village? Policing strategies and fear of crime in Latin America', *Latin American Politics and Society*, 48(4), 27–51.

Davidson, R.J., Scherer, K.R. and Goldsmith, H.H. (Eds) (2003) *Handbook of Affective Sciences*. New York: Oxford University Press.

Delamont, S. (2001) *Changing Women, Unchanged Men? Sociological Perspectives on Gender in a Post-industrial Society*. Buckingham: Open University Press.

Ditton, J., Bannister, J., Gilchrist, E. and Farrall, S. (1999), 'Afraid or angry? Recalibrating the 'fear' of crime', *International Review of Victimology*, 6(2), 83–99.

Elias, N. (1982) *The Civilizing Process*, vol. 2, State Formation and Civilization. Oxford: Basil Blackwell.

Enders, M. and Jennett, C. (2009) 'Revisiting the fear of crime in Bondi and Marrickville' in Lee, M. and Farrall, S. (Eds), *Fear of Crime: Critical Voices in an Age of Anxiety*. London: Routledge.

Ennis, P.H. (1967), 'Criminal victimization in the United States: A report of a national survey'. *J President's Commission on Law Enforcement and Administration of Justice, Field Surveys II*. Washington DC: US Government Printing Office.

Evans, J. (2003) 'Vigilance and vigilantes: a psychoanalytic view on anti-paedophile protesters', *Theoretical Criminology*, 7(2), 163–189.

Everitt, B.S. (1984) *An Introduction to Latent Variable Models*. London: Chapman-Hall.

Farrall, S. (2004a) 'Revisiting crime surveys: emotional responses without emotions', *International Journal of Social Research Methodology*, 7(2), 157–171.

Farrall, S. (2004b) 'Can we believe our eyes: a response to Mike Hough', *International Journal of Social Research Methodology*, 7(2), 177–179.

Farrall, S., Bannister, J., Ditton, J. and Gilchrist, E. (1997), 'Questioning the measurement of the fear of crime: findings from a major methodological study', *British Journal of Criminology*, 37(4), 657–678.

Farrall, S. and Ditton, J. (1999) 'Improving the measurement of attitudinal responses: an example from a crime survey', *International Journal of Social Research Methodology*, 2(1), 55–68.

Farrall, S. and Gadd, D. (2004) 'The frequency of the fear of crime', *British Journal of Criminology*, 44(1), 127–132.

Farrall, S., Jackson, J. and Gray, E. (2009), *Social Order and the Fear of Crime in Contemporary Times*. Oxford: Oxford University Press, Clarendon Studies in Criminology.

Ferraro, K.F. (1995) *Fear of Crime: Interpreting Victimization Risk*. New York: SUNY Press.

Ferraro, K.F. and LaGrange, R.L. (1987) 'The measurement of fear of crime', *Sociological Inquiry*, 57, 70–101.

Figgie, H.E. (1980) *The Figgie Report on Fear of Crime: America Afraid. Part 1: The General Public*. Ohio. Willoughby.

Gabriel, U. and Greve, W. (2003) 'The psychology of fear of crime: Conceptual and methodological perspectives', *British Journal of Criminology*, 43, 600–614.

Gadd, D. and Jefferson, T. (2007) *Psychosocial Criminology: an introduction*, London. Sage.

Garland, D. (2001), *The Culture of Control*. Oxford: Oxford University Press.

Garofalo, J. and Laub, J. (1978) 'The fear of crime: broadening our perspective', *Victimology*, 3, 242–253.

Girling, E., Loader, I. and Sparks, R. (2000) *Crime and Social Change in Middle England*. London: Routledge.

Gladstone, G. and Parker, G. (2003), 'What's the use of worrying? Its function and its dysfunction'. *Australian and New Zealand Journal of Psychiatry*, 37(3), 347–354.

Goldie, P. (2004) 'The life of the mind: commentary on Emotions in everyday life', *Social Science Information*, 43(4): 591–598.

Gray, E., Jackson, J. and Farrall, S. (2008) 'Reassessing fear of crime in England and Wales', *European Journal of Criminology*, 5(3), 309–336.

Gray, E., Jackson, J. and Farrall, S. (2011) 'Feelings and Functions in the Fear of Crime: Applying a New Approach to Victimisation Insecurity' *British Journal of Criminology*, 51(1), 75–94.

Hale, C. (1996), 'Fear of crime: a review of the literature', *International Review of Victimology*, 4, 79–150.

Hall, S., Critcher, C., Jefferson, T., Clarke, J. and Roberts, B. (1978) *Policing the Crisis*. London: Macmillan.

Heber, A. (2007) *Var Rädd om Dig!* Stockholm: Stockholm University Press.

Hochschild, A. (1983) T*he Managed Heart: The Commercialization of Human Feeling*. Berkeley, CA: University of California Press.

Hollway, W. and Jefferson, T. (2000) *Doing Qualitative Research Differently: Free Association, Narrative And The Interview Method*. London: Sage.

Hope, T. and Hough, M. (1988) 'Area, crime and incivilities: Findings from the British Crime Survey', in Hope, T. and Shaw, M. (Eds), *Communities and Crime Reduction*. London: HMSO.

Hough, M. (2004), 'Worry about crime: Mental events or mental states?' *International Journal of Social Research Methodology*, 7, 173–176.

Jackson, J. (2004) 'Experience and expression: Social and cultural significance in the fear of crime', *British Journal of Criminology*, 44(6), 946–966.

Jackson, J. (2005) 'Validating new measures of the fear of crime', *International Journal of Social Research Methodology*, 8(4), 297–315.

Jackson, J. (2006) 'Introducing fear of crime to risk research', *Risk Analysis*, 26(1), 253–264.

Jackson, J. (2009) 'A psychological perspective on vulnerability in the fear of crime', *Psychology, Crime and Law,* 15(4), 365–390.

Jackson, J. and Gray, E. (2010) 'Functional fear and public insecurities about crime', *British Journal of Criminology* 50(1): 1–22.

Jackson, J. and Stafford, M. (2009) 'Public health and fear of crime: A prospective cohort study', *British Journal of Criminology,* 49(6), 832–847.

Jones, T., Maclean, B. and Young, J. (1986) *The Islington Crime Survey*. Aldershot: Gower.

Kahneman, D. (1994) 'New challenges to the rationality assumption', *Journal of Institutional and Theoretical Economics*, 150, 18–36.

Karstedt, S. (2002) 'Emotions and criminal justice', *Theoretical Criminology*, 6(3), 299–317 .

Katz, J. (1999) *How Emotions Work*. Chicago, IL: University of Chicago Press.

Katz, J. (2004) 'Everyday lives and extraordinary research methods', *Social Science Information*, 43(4), 609–619.

Kemper, T. (Ed.) (1990) *Research Agendas in the Sociology of Emotions*. New York: SUNY Press.

Killias, M. and Clerici, C. (2000) 'Different measures of vulnerability in their relation to   different dimensions of fear of crime', *The British Journal of Criminology*, 40(3), 437–450.

Kury, H. and Obergfell-Fuchs, J. (2008) 'Measuring the fear of crime' in Kury, H. (Ed.), *Fear of Crime – Punitivity; New Developments in Research and Theory*. Bochum: Universitatsverlag Brockmeyer.

Lavrakas, P.J., Herz, L. and Salem, G. (1981) 'Community organization, citizen participation, and neighbourhood crime prevention.' Paper presented at the Annual Meeting of the American Psychological Association.

Lee, M. (1999) 'The fear of crime and self-governance: Towards a genealogy', *The Australian and New Zealand Journal of Criminology*, 32(3), 227–246.

Lee, M. (2007) *Inventing Fear of Crime: Criminology and the Politics of Anxiety*. Cullompton: Willan.

Lewis, D.A. and Maxfield, M.G. (1980) 'Fear in the neighborhoods: an investigation of the impact of crime', *Journal of Research in Crime and Delinquency*, 17 (2) 160–189.

Moser, C. and Kalton, G. (1971) *Survey Methods in Social Investigation*, 2nd edition. London: Heinemann.

Nayak, A. (2003) 'Through children's eyes: Childhood, place and the fear of crime', *Geoforum*, *34*, 303–315.

Nicholas, S., Kershaw, C. and Walker, A. (2007) *Crime in England and Wales 2006/7*, 4th edition. London. Home Office.

Osborne, T. and Rose, N. (1999) 'Do the social sciences create phenomena?', *British Journal of Sociology*, 50(3), 367–396.

Pain, R. (1993) 'Women's fear of sexual violence: Explaining the spatial paradox' in Jones, H. (Ed.), *Crime and The Urban Environment*. Aldershot: Avebury.

Pain, R. (2001) 'Gender, race, age and fear in the city', *Urban Studies*, 38(5–6), 899–913.

Reiss, Jr., A.S. (1967), 'Studies in crime and law enforcement in major metropolitan areas, volume I'. *President's Commission on Law Enforcement and Administration of Justice, Field Surveys III*. Washington DC: US Government Printing Office.

Robinson, M.D. and Clore, G.L. (2002a) 'Belief and feeling: Evidence for an accessibility model of emotional self report', *Psychological Bulletin*, 128, 934–960.

Robinson, M.D. and Clore, G.L. (2002b) 'Episodic and semantic knowledge in emotional self-report: Evidence for two judgment processes', *Journal of Personality and Social Psychology*, 83, 198–215.

Sampson, R.J. and Raudenbush, S. (2004) 'Seeing disorder: Neighborhood stigma and the social construction of broken windows', *Social Psychology Quarterly*, 67(4), 319–342.

Scherer, K.R., Wranik, T., Sangsue, J., Tran, V. and Scherer, U. (2004) 'Emotions in everyday life: probability of occurrence, risk factors, appraisal and reaction patterns', *Social Science Information*, 43(4), 499–570.

Serrano-Maillo, A. and Kury, H. (2008) 'Insecure feelings and punitivity' in Kury, H. (Ed.), *Fear of Crime – Punitivity; New Developments in Research and Theory*. Bochum: Universitatsverlag Brockmeyer.

Shore, H. (1999) 'Cross coves, buzzers and general sorts of prigs: Juvenile crime and the criminal "underworld" in the early nineteenth century', *British Journal of Criminology*, 39(1), 10–24.

Skogan, W. and Maxfield, M. (1981) *Coping with Crime*. Beverly Hills, CA: Sage.

Sparks, R. (1992) *Television and the Drama of Crime*. London: Open University Press.

Stafford, M., Chandola, T. and Marmot, M. (2007) 'Association between fear of crime and mental health and physical functioning', *American Journal of Public Health*, 97, 2076–2081.

Stanko, E. (1988) 'Hidden violence against women', in Maguire, M. and Pointing, J. (Eds), *Victims of Crime. A New Deal?* Milton Keynes: Open University Press

Stanko, E. (1990) 'When precaution is normal: A feminist critique of crime prevention', in Gelsthorpe, L., and Morris, A. (Eds), *Feminist Perspectives in Criminology*. Milton Keynes: Open University Press.

Sutton, R. and Farrall, S. (2005) 'Gender, socially desirable responding, and the fear of crime: are women really more anxious about crime?', *British Journal of Criminology*, 45(2), 212–224.

Sutton, R. and Farrall, S. (2009) 'Untangling the web: Deceptive responding in fear of crime research' in Lee, M. and Farrall, S. (Eds), *Fear of Crime: Critical Voices in an Age of Anxiety*. London: Routledge.

Tourangeau, R., Rips, L.J. and Rasinski, K. (2000) *The Psychology of Survey Response*. Cambridge: Cambridge University Press.

Turner, J.H. and Stets, J.E., (2005) *The Sociology of Emotions*. Cambridge: Cambridge University Press.

Warr, M. (1984) 'Fear of victimization: Why are women and the elderly more afraid?', *Social Science Quarterly*, 65, 681–702.

Warr, M. (2000), 'Public perceptions of and reactions to crime' in J. Sheley (Ed.), *Criminology: A Contemporary Handbook*, 3rd edition. Belmont, CA: Wadsworth.

Williams, S. and Bendelow, G. (Eds) (1998) *Emotions in Social Life: Critical Themes and Contemporary Issues*. London: Routledge.

van der Wurff, A. and Stringer, P. (1988) 'Measuring Fear of Crime in residential Surroundings' in Stephenson, L.G., Sozzka, L., Jesuino, C. and Cantor, D. (Eds), *Environmental Social Psychology*. The Hague: Nijof.

Young, J. (1986) 'The failure of criminology: the need for a radical realism', in Matthews, R. and Young, J. (Eds), *Confronting Crime*. London: Sage

Zaller, J. and Feldman. (1992) 'A simple theory of the survey response: answering questions versus revealing preferences', *American Journal of Political Science*, 36(3), 579–616.

Zhang, L., Messner, S.F., Liu, J. and Zhuo Y.A. (2009) 'Guanxi and fear of crime in contemporary urban China' *British Journal of Criminology*, 49(4), 472–490.

19

Measuring Public Attitudes to Criminal Justice

Julian Roberts, Martina Feilzer, Mike Hough

INTRODUCTION

In recent years, academics as well as policy makers have shown increased interest in the nature of public attitudes to criminal justice. One consequence of this has been a steady growth in empirical research and commercial public opinion polls. Much of this research has explored public punitiveness which has been associated with more repressive penal policies (most prominently, but not exclusively, in the UK, the US and New Zealand) (Pratt et al., 2005: xi–xxv; Roberts et al., 2003). If we are to understand public opinion on crime and criminal justice it is essential to have valid and accurate ways of measuring it. Using surveys to measure peoples' *experience* of crime creates a wide range of technical challenges, but the conceptual issues are fairly straightforward. Measuring public attitudes to criminal justice is far more challenging, and these challenges are the subject of this chapter.

Defining terms

The terms 'public opinion' and 'public attitudes' are often used interchangeably, although differences can be identified. Political philosophers such as Bentham pioneered thinking about the role of *public opinion* and by the middle of the last century the term was well embedded both in the political realm and in academic social psychology (cf. Noelle-Neumann, 1977: 143; Speier, 1950: 376). The term was used in both realms with connotations of communication: public opinion was something that by definition was communicated – or ought to be communicated – to political institutions, or to individuals within a group.

Public *attitudes*, on the other hand, relate to the aggregation of individual attitudes, defined as evaluations based on emotions, beliefs, past experience or behaviour (Petty and Wegener, 1998: 324). The term is free of the connotations of communication: the fact that an attitude is held does not imply that it is, or ought to be, communicated to others. People may or may not hold attitudes regardless of their willingness or ability to communicate them. In the political sphere, public opinion can be regarded as a cornerstone of democracy, as 'primarily a communication from the citizens to their government' (Speier, 1950: 376). Public opinion defined through the notion of communication to the government would include questions about the suitability and appropriateness of particular sentences which in turn may well be linked to the attitudes that individuals hold on the purpose of punishment and other normative questions.

Whether (and how) criminal justice should respond to public opinion is a matter of considerable controversy (see discussion in Roberts, 2008). However, there is general agreement in mature democracies about two propositions. First, decisions taken about individuals – by prosecutors, judges, magistrates or parole boards – should not be influenced by public opinion. Regardless of the level of public animosity towards a particular offender, a sentencing court should not make public antipathy a reason for imposing a tougher sentence. Similarly parole boards' decisions about release should not be shaped by public opinion.

Second, that although individual decisions should not be affected by public opinion, there must be some degree of public support for, or at least acceptance of, criminal justice policies. If judges imposed sentences using mitigating factors which the public thought were unrelated to sentencing, community confidence in the courts would surely suffer. Similarly, if courts imposed lenient sentences for very serious crimes (in violation of the well-known principle of proportionality in sentencing) the public would be outraged and confidence would decline. On a general level then, policy makers and politicians often seek to know what the public think about criminal justice policy. For this reason, polls have been conducted on almost every stage of the criminal justice process from policing through to sentencing and parole. In addition, within each of these domains polls have explored public reaction to a wide range of specific criminal justice policies, including the death penalty, alternatives to custody, and victim impact statements – to name but a few (see Cullen et al., 2000; Roberts and Hough, 2005a; Roberts and Stalans, 2000; Wood and Gannon, 2009, for reviews).

Chapter overview

This chapter reviews the methods used by researchers to measure public attitudes to issues in criminal justice. It is important to consider issues relating to methodology because different methodologies generate differing portraits of public opinion. Throughout the chapter, we provide illustrations of studies that have used different methodologies drawing on examples from a range of countries and a range of criminal justice issues.

MEASURING PUBLIC ATTITUDES: WHAT ARE THE OPTIONS?

Public opinion researchers in the field of criminal justice use a variety of approaches to measuring public opinion. Each approach has its own advantages and disadvantages, which we shall discuss in due course. First, however, it is worth addressing the central decision confronting a researcher, namely whether to use a *quantitative* method – such as a survey using a representative sample of respondents, or a *qualitative* method – such as a focus group. Traditionally, the choice between

quantitative and qualitative research methods was determined by accepting and following one of the main paradigms or world-views presented as being fundamentally opposed: positivism/post-positivism and constructivism/interpretivism (Creswell and Plano Clark, 2007). Put simply, positivists believe that there is a single reality which can be discovered by objective and value-free inquiry using mainly quantitative research methods. In contrast, constructivists contend that there is no such thing as a single objective reality and that 'subjective inquiry is the only kind possible to do' (Erlandson et al., 1993: xi; see also Palys and Atchison, 2008: chapter 1). There have been significant developments and advances on these rather rigid positions and many more nuanced positions have been developed by feminists, postmodernists, poststructuralists and critical rationalists. Nevertheless, they still inform much of our understanding of an appropriate research method (Teddlie and Tashakkori, 2009).

Quantitative or qualitative?

Both approaches have their advantages and disadvantages, although quantitative research accounts for the vast majority of public opinion studies conducted in Western nations. Quantitative surveys have a number of limitations, but with respect to assessing public opinion for the purpose of guiding policy decisions they are generally to be preferred over qualitative designs. If policy makers want to know where the population stands with respect to a particular policy question – for example whether young offenders should be punished less severely than adult offenders – there is no substitute for a representative survey, from which inferences about the population response can be reasonably drawn from the responses of a small sample. When a polling company reports a finding based upon a representative sample, we know, within the limits of probability, how the overall population would respond to the same question.

A specific example illustrates what we mean. In a survey of public attitudes to youth justice in Britain (Roberts and Hough, 2005b), we included a question that was asked of a sub-sample of 558 people: 'A 16-year-old has been convicted of assault. He has two previous convictions for assault and selling stolen property. Choosing your answer from this card, what sentence do you think he should receive?' In response, 62 per cent of our sub-sample opted for 'detention followed by community supervision'. This percentage represents simply an *estimate* of how the overall population in the country would answer this question.

Sampling error

The degree of precision of the estimate – or its 'sampling error' can be calculated, however. In the study discussed above, the small (*n* = 558) sample size means that the estimate is actually quite imprecise: allowing for the way in which the sample was constructed, one can say with 95 per cent certainty that if the entire adult population were asked this question, between 57 per cent and 67 per cent would have opted for detention and community supervision. Had the sample been larger – say, 2,000 – the margin of error would have been much smaller, with the estimate falling within 2.5 percentage points of the 'true' figure.

The clear advantage of representative polls is their demonstrable *replicability*. If two properly executed sample surveys are carried out on the same population at the same time, they will generate very similar findings allowing for some variation dependent on the confidence interval, provided they are using valid questions (for a discussion of variability of survey responses to 'poor' questions over time, see Ditton and Farrall, 2007: 225–227). The implication of this is that well-conducted polls repeated over time can yield reliable trends. For many issues in the field of criminal justice, particularly confidence in justice, policy makers are interested in trends over time. Although polls have their limitations, these are generally constant. If the wording is the same, repeating a question year after year permits pollsters to track changes in public confidence in the police, for example, or support for capital punishment. In addition, politicians and policy makers are sometimes interested in making international comparisons: how do levels of confidence in criminal justice compare across jurisdictions? A number of polls have now been conducted using the same question across different countries (see Hough and Roberts, 2004a, for a review).

Limitations of public opinion surveys

Despite their popularity as a tool for public opinion researchers in the field of criminal justice, surveys are subject to a number of weaknesses. Methodological criticisms are levelled against public opinion surveys generally and they are not new. Survey limitations are discussed at length in the relevant methodological literature and have been rehearsed for well over 50 years (for comprehensive critiques, see Blumer, 1948, and Bourdieu, 1993). Nevertheless, these limitations are of particular relevance in the field of criminal justice as survey results are often used as indicative of public opinion and, recently, of public confidence in the criminal justice system and such readings of

public opinion can influence penal policy (Roberts and Hough, 2002: 4; Rock, 1995: 2). Surveys are used, of course, for a range of different purposes. Often they are used to chart people's experience or status – what levels of health they enjoy, for example, or whether they have been the victims of crime. The methodological issues raise by the surveying of *experience* will not be covered here (though readers are referred to Chapter 18 by Gray et al.) for a discussion of the measurement of fear of crime). We are concerned specifically with issues that affect the measurement of attitudes.

We have already mentioned that sample surveys produce estimates, and these have a level of imprecision as a result of sampling error. But factors apart from sampling procedures can also impose limitations on the value of surveys. Respondents are often incentivised to participate in surveys and will respond to cues indicating what is expected and desired of their survey responses. The most important of these limitations relates to the quantification of attitudes, which may fail to capture the subtlety of people's viewpoints. Surveys typically offer respondents a limited number of responses to simple questions. Thus they might have only five options from which to choose when asked if sentences are tough enough: 'much too tough; a little too tough; about right; a little too lenient; or much too lenient'. A thoughtful person might well be reluctant to generalise in the way required by the question. People may feel that some sentencers were far too tough on some crimes, and others were too soft on others, or that sentencing is too lenient for some crimes, appropriate for others. But the interviewer will push the respondent to make a single choice from a limited range of options. In this way, an attitude towards the courts is shaped, or, some might say, created by the measuring instrument.

The importance of providing adequate response options

A sound sampling technique is essential to the integrity of any public opinion survey. However, the most carefully constructed and conducted survey will provide a false reading of public attitudes if the response options are inappropriate or insufficient. Most polls employ a fixed-choice format in which respondents are asked to choose from among a limited number of alternatives. When this method is used, researchers have to ensure that the options represent a full and realistic range of possibilities. Otherwise public support may simply reflect the alternatives that the researchers have identified.

Consider a poll conducted in Britain in 2000. Respondents were asked to identify the strategies that would do the most to reduce the volume of crime in Britain (MORI, 2000). Most of the response options provided were punitive in nature – including tougher prisons for young offenders, capital punishment for offenders convicted of murder, longer prison sentences, and so forth. Given this restrictive list of options respondents have no way of expressing their support for other, non-punitive crime prevention strategies such as social prevention or situational crime prevention. Since respondents are encouraged to make a choice, and are discouraged from refusing to answer, responses to this list will convey a false sense of the degree of public support for the limited range of strategies that are on offer. When measuring public attitudes to an issue such as crime prevention, it is essential to develop appropriate lists of options that actually include all the main categories that most people are likely to want to select. Developing such a list usually requires piloting, and often benefits from prior qualitative work using focus groups or in-depth interviews.

Kubiak and Allen (2008) provide a similar illustration of the importance of providing an adequate range of response options. The purpose of their research was to determine the level of public support for life without parole (LWOP) – an alternative to capital punishment which appears to appeal to many people. Usually, respondents are asked to simply agree or disagree with a sentencing policy which mandates imprisonment for the offender's natural life. Kubiak and Allen found that support for LWOP was significantly lower when survey respondents were given a comprehensive array of sentencing options, rather than just being asked to agree or disagree with LWOP. Box 19.1 summarises this study.

Inappropriate or leading question wording

Polls are often used by politicians to bolster a particular position or penal policy. The tool to measure public opinion therefore becomes a means of manipulating public attitudes. Many examples of misleading or manipulative polls exist. An extreme example comes from New Zealand. Respondents to a poll conducted in 1999 were asked the following question: 'Should there be a reform of our justice system placing greater emphasis on the needs of victims, providing restitution and compensation for them and imposing minimum sentences and hard labour for all serious offenders?' Given the wording of this question it is impossible to be in favour of better treatment for victims without also endorsing minimum sentences (see Roberts et al., 2003, for other examples of manipulative questions).

Social desirability effects

Researchers in the field of social psychology have long been aware of social desirability effects in research. There is a natural human inclination to respond in a way that places the respondent in a good light. Polls that explore stereotypes, for example, may well underestimate the extent to which members of the public subscribe to negative ethnic or national stereotypes for the simple reason that is people do not want to be seen to be prejudiced. Similarly, in the field of criminal justice, participants may feel that it is inappropriate to express some views in response to poll questions. For example, residents of countries which long ago abolished the death penalty may be less inclined to express support for capital punishment – surveys measuring support for restoration of this penalty will have overcome this tendency in respondents.

Box 19.1 Measuring public attitudes to life without parole (LWOP) for juveniles

At the time this study was conducted, 42 US states had the option of imposing life without parole or capital punishment on juveniles convicted of murder. The study focused on public support for a policy permitting LWOP in the state of Michigan which has one of the highest rates of committing youth to life imprisonment with no possibility of ever being released. The researchers were interested in measuring the level of public support for this controversial policy. A representative sample of the public was first asked whether they agreed or disagreed with Michigan's policy. In response to this simple agree/disagree question, almost half the sample expressed agreement. They were then given a series of options including alternatives such as, 'Life in an adult prison with the possibility of parole after 20 years.' When given a list of less severe alternatives such as this one, only 8 per cent of the sample who had originally agreed with the current Michigan policy chose the sanction associated with that policy. The implication is clear: the level of support for a punitive policy that permits life without parole for teenagers is much lower than one might believe on the basis of a simple question (see Kubiak and Allen, 2008).

The social desirability effect could also affect respondents' answers to attitudinal questions. Wilkins contended that 'if one asks the average citizen for his opinion on a topic, the most honest response may well be, "Frankly, until you asked me, I had not given it a moment's thought"' (1984: 83). However, rather than admitting to not having an opinion many people will attempt to construct one either on the basis of general values and pre-dispositions or specific beliefs about the issue in question (Tourangeau et al., 2000: 172). Alternatively, they may select a non-committal 'middle ground' response option to mask the fact that they have no real views on the topic.

Requiring respondents to make categorical judgements

We describe another weakness with polls in criminal justice as the 'categorical error'. By this we refer to the tendency to ask the public to arrive at a decision about issues such as capital punishment, sentencing or parole in terms of a category, rather than with respect to individual cases. For example, polls examining attitudes to parole often ask respondents whether they support or oppose parole for prisoners serving terms for crimes of violence. The error is frequently compounded by asking people whether they support parole for 'violent offenders', which summons to the respondent's mind images of dangerous individuals with lengthy criminal records. Parole boards do not make decisions about categories of offending, and it is accordingly inappropriate to ask the public to judge offenders in this way. The best way of understanding the level of public support for an issue such as parole or capital punishment is to ask respondents to make choices that relate to individual cases.

When this approach is adopted, a far more refined and accurate portrait of public opinion emerges. This has been demonstrated in a number of research projects. For example, in Canada, Cumberland and Zamble (1992) found high levels of support for restricting parole to non-violent offenders when respondents were asked a general question. However, confronted with specific parole applications to review, public attitudes look quite different. For example, approximately four-fifths of the sample supported granting parole to a burglar, and over half the sample favoured parole for an offender convicted of aggravated assault and robbery (see Cumberland and Zamble, 1992: table 1).

Legitimate indecision?

Another illustration of the importance of wording comes from the US. As the only major Western democracy that retains the death penalty, public opinion polls routinely address the issue of capital punishment. The standard question posed by the Gallup organisation is the following: 'Are you in favour of the death penalty for a person convicted of murder?' (Gallup Organisation, 2010). People are allowed to respond negatively or affirmatively. If they respond, 'don't know', or refuse to answer, their responses are ignored, or they are classified as respondents with, 'no opinion' (Gallup Organisation, 2010). In all probability, few people have no opinion about this issue; but many are undecided or conflicted about their view (see Unnever et al., 2005). Attitudes to the death penalty are far more nuanced and complex than this simple question would suggest.

Simple 'yes/no' wording prevents the respondent from expressing the degree to which he or she supports or opposes capital punishment. Nor does the question permit people to give contingent answers such as, 'I support the death penalty, but only for certain categories of murder.' And, finally, the question fails to allow people to express an *agnostic* view, to state that they are 'undecided'. In reality, few proponents of capital punishment favour the death penalty for all cases, in all contexts. Even the wording used by Gallup – which does not permit people to be 'undecided' – generates a significant number of respondents who appear undecided. Thus in 1995, fully 10 per cent of the population responded 'don't know'; this corresponds to approximately 30 million Americans. Question wording is therefore important. Consider the issue of the 'undecided' or ambivalent respondent with respect to capital punishment. Jones (1994) examined different ways of posing the question about death penalty attitudes. He found that if you simply ask the respondent whether he or she is in favour of the death penalty, 20 per cent spontaneously responded 'depends' or 'don't know'. If people are first asked whether they have an opinion, and then asked to express that opinion, this percentage rises to 38 per cent, a very significant shift. Box 19.2 provides an example of a study which demonstrates that support for custody as a sanction is largely created by researchers failing to provide respondents with all possible alternatives.

Limited time for respondents to consider the issues

Another limiting factor is that surveys often allocate respondents limited time for the consideration of the complex issues in the field of criminal justice. Attitudes to issues such as capital punishment, mandatory sentencing or sex offender registers must be measured within the space of a few

---

Box 19.2   Public support for alternative sanctions

When most people think about sentencing, imprisonment is the disposal that usually comes to mind (Indermaur, 1987; Roberts and Hough, 2005a). Indeed, one of the barriers to the greater use of community penalties has been the lack of public knowledge of alternatives. A British survey tested the hypothesis that the public will accept community penalties *if they are made aware of them* (see Rethinking Crime and Punishment, 2002).

Respondents were randomly assigned to impose sentence in one of two cases: a theft by a repeat offender with a number of related prior convictions and an assault with serious consequences for the victim. Respondents were asked to choose between custody, a community penalty or a fine. Those who chose custody for the case of theft were then asked: 'Supposing the courts decided to impose the following sentence: an order to pay compensation of £500 to the victim, and a community order involving probation supervision and 300 hours unpaid work. Would you accept this as an acceptable alternative to sending the offender to prison?' Around three quarters (73 per cent) of the sample favoured custody, 18 per cent a community sentence and 9 per cent a fine. Once respondents had been provided with the alternative however, almost half (47 per cent) of these 'custody' respondents indicated that they found the alternative acceptable. For the assault case, respondents choosing imprisonment were asked a similar question involving a community order requiring probation supervision and 300 hours unpaid work. Thirty-nine percent of respondents choosing custody now reported finding the community penalty to constitute an acceptable alternative to imprisoning the offender. Thus there was a relatively high degree of public acceptance of an alternative to imprisonment in both cases. This finding is consistent with earlier research in other jurisdictions (see Roberts and Hough, 2005a).

---

minutes using a few simple questions. The consequence is that polls oversimplify both the issue under examination, and the nature of public opinion towards the issue. To say that two-thirds of the public believes that sentences should be harsher, or that capital punishment should be reinstated fails to reflect the complexities of public attitudes to these issues. One solution is to ask follow-up questions – for example, to first ask people whether they are in favour of, or opposed to, the death penalty, and then follow this up by asking them to consider a list of offences. When this method is adopted, it reveals that most advocates of capital punishment favour the death penalty only for the most serious forms of murder (see Cullen et al., 2000; Oberwittler and Qi, 2009).

Limited information on which to base a decision

The process of rapid quantification of opinion is by no means the only limitation upon opinion polls. Arguably, a more insidious limitation concerns the limited information available to the respondent. Again, attitudes to punishment represent a good illustration of the problem. Asking people whether sentences are severe enough yields large majorities verdict in favour of tougher punishment whenever and wherever the question is posed (see Roberts and Hough, 2005a, for a review). The problem with this approach is that pollsters cannot control the images of offences and offenders in respondents' minds when they

answer the question. And we know that most people think about serious crime committed by repeat offenders when answering these general questions (Doob and Roberts, 1988). These images 'drive' the response offered. This is why it is important, wherever possible, to specify a particular case before asking members of the public about the appropriateness of sentencing patterns.

Simple questions, posed at a high level of generality, tend to elicit a punitive response from respondents. When people are provided with more time, more questions, or more information about the topic explored in the survey their reactions become less punitive, and more in line with the practice of the criminal justice system. This is perhaps the best-documented – and most important – lesson from public opinion research in the field of criminal justice. Many demonstrations of this effect exist, going back at least 40 years and in many different countries (e.g., Doob and Roberts, 1983; Hough and Roberts, 2004b; Knight, 1965).

A related weakness of large-scale surveys of attitudes towards specific criminal justice policies is that they fail to take into account the limited levels of public knowledge about the subject. For example, many polls over the past 30 years have asked members of the public whether they support the abolition of parole. These surveys often find support for eliminating early release provisions. However, pollsters fail to take into account the reality that public knowledge of the way that parole functions, and important parole statistics (such as grant rates, failure rates of parolees and so forth) is poor.

Representative and 'convenience' samples

All research designs, including true experiments and quasi-experimental designs, face a number of threats to their 'external validity'. External validity or generalisability is present when conclusions drawn from the research can confidently be applied to populations other than the one examined (Bachman and Schutt, 2003: 22). External validity is concerned with examining whether the researchers were justified in drawing the conclusion which generalises the findings of cause and effect from the 'experimental group'; that is, their sample, to 'the public'. When measuring 'public opinion' using survey research it is vital that sample survey participants are representative of the 'public'. This will result in externally valid and generalisable results.

This is not the place for a thorough discussion of sampling issues, and the reader is referred to the list of further reading for this. However, we should make one point here, which is that researchers often have to make pragmatic decisions between the desirable and the practical. Large-scale representative surveys are not always an option for research, partly due to resource constraints, partly due to questions of appropriateness. Good research designs employ methods with the best potential fit to answer the research question. Is it really necessary to have a representative sample if the research aim is to establish whether the provision of information has an effect? Convenience samples thus make no claims about statistical representativeness; rather, they further explore the processes of

why people express particular opinions; that is, determining whether it is because of a lack of knowledge or misinformation.

The most commonly used group for convenience samples is the student population, despite the fact that students are obviously very different from the general population. Thus, any findings on student responses to particular stimuli are of limited value. As a consequence, some researchers have aimed to make their convenience samples more 'ecologically valid' (Roberts and Doob, 1990: 455); that is, more *like* a representative sample. Two examples of the use of convenience samples in public opinion research are included in Box 19.3.

The importance of qualitative research

Acknowledging the inherent limitations of survey research, social scientists have turned to other methods of measuring public opinion. Focus groups, deliberative polls, and small-scale studies using 'convenience' samples of the public are often promoted as a more appropriate way to find out what people feel and think about crime and criminal justice (see discussion in Green, 2006: 132–135; Roberts and Stalans, 2000, 14–20).

Focus groups account for most qualitative studies in the field. They can play an important role in developing understanding of the nuances of public opinion, of how people feel and talk about crime and criminal justice and in producing an appreciation of the dynamics of attitude formation. For example, prior to conducting a poll on public attitudes to the police, it would be prudent to carry out some focus groups to better understand the issues that people are 'talking about' and 'how they are talking about them' (see Hough, 1996).

Box 19.3 Use of 'convenience' samples

Three studies were carried out which progressively tested how media representation of sentencing shapes public perception of judicial leniency. The researchers chose to ask visitors to a Canadian science museum to volunteer to participate in the study. Sample sizes varied between 99 and 157. The population sampled from was not representative of the general Canadian population thus forming a convenience sample. However, the purpose of the studies was not to generalise about public opinion but 'rather to compare reactions of randomly created groups of subjects' (Doob and Roberts, 1983; Roberts and Doob, 1990: 455). Participants were exposed to media coverage of sentencing stories and where asked to assess their appropriateness. The three studies varied in the type of stimulus provided to assess the effect of media coverage of sentencing on its audience. Rather than 'simply' measuring public views of sentencing, the research was interested in the processes that may influence the finding that 'the public' regard sentencing as too lenient. Thus, it concluded that simplistic assertions about public opinion made on the basis of 'superficially expressed responses to a single poll's question' are either 'naïve, dishonest, or cynical'. For another example of this approach, see Horst et al. (2007) who employed a convenience sample of people approached on trains, in local government offices, and at post offices across the Netherlands.

A good example of using qualitative research to inform the design of surveys is the use of cognitive interviewing techniques. Cognitive interviews represent a combination of qualitative and quantitative research which can take a number of different forms. It usually entails 'administering draft survey questions while collecting additional verbal information *about* the survey response' (Beatty and Willis, 2007: 288; emphasis in original). The verbal elaboration can relate to the construction of the survey answer, interpretation of survey questions, or difficulties in answering the question. The commentary can be prompted through explicit 'probing by an interviewer or through the encouragement of "thinking aloud"' (Beatty and Willis, 2007: 289). Cognitive interviewing is primarily 'concerned with how respondents interpret and comprehend questions and the process behind making a response' (Adamson et al., 2004: 144).

In-depth interviews or ethnographic work are rarely used in isolation in public opinion research. Interviews represent a qualitative approach to data collection, designed to go beyond the simplistic answers provided through a tick-box questionnaire and to seek open-ended, qualified answers. Rather than offering research participants a limited number of pre-selected answers, the in-depth interview aims to elicit responses which 'provide access to the meanings people attribute to their experiences and social worlds' (Miller and Glassner, 1997: 100). However, the limitations of interviews in ascertaining the opinion of a sample large enough to be externally valid; that is, representative, are obvious. Nevertheless, considering the limitations of public opinion polls as outlined above, support is growing to move towards assessing public opinion on issues of policy relevance such as appropriate and acceptable sentencing guidelines through more deliberative and qualitative methods such as focus groups and deliberative polls in particular (see below). The Sentencing Advisory Panel in England has used qualitative methods to assess whether their proposals for sentencing guidelines would be acceptable to the public (see Hough et al., 2008, 2009). Such an approach resonates strongly with growing calls for a more deliberative democracy and notions of considering the views of an informed public in the process of making decisions on criminal justice policy (see, for example, Green, 2006).

Multi-method approaches to research

Mixed- or multi-method research has, by some, been hailed as a panacea for the respective problems inherent in quantitative and qualitative research. Multi-method approaches offer the possibility of a truce in these paradigm 'wars' (for a discussion of the main paradigms, see Creswell and Clark, 2007; Feilzer, 2010; Morgan, 2007). The rationale behind mixing methods is that mono-method designs are regarded as limited as they only measure one aspect of social phenomena, and that multi-method designs are better able to answer research questions relating to complex social phenomena, such as public opinion.

Let's consider an actual research example to illustrate the strengths of using more than one methodology. The research question here is straightforward: what kinds of factors do the public take into account when they sentence offenders? The Sentencing Advisory Panel in England and Wales was interested in soliciting public views about the sentencing of offenders convicted of driving offences resulting in death – for example, dangerous driving causing death. In particular, the panel wanted to know where the public stood with respect to mitigating or aggravating factors in such cases.

There are two ways of determining the nature and relative importance of sentencing factors for members of the public. One method involves asking respondents directly whether specific factors should mitigate or aggravate the severity of the sentence imposed. The proportion of respondents choosing a particular factor is then taken as an estimate of the importance of the factor to the population. This approach has been used in a number of previous explorations of public opinion and sentencing factors (e.g., Roberts, 1988; Russell and Morgan, 2001).

A more sophisticated approach involves providing respondents with a series of scenarios, and manipulating the presence or absence of various factors. Respondents are asked to sentence the offender and the degree to which the severity of sentence changes as the factors are introduced provides a measure of the power of the factor to mitigate or aggravate sentence. This method of gauging public reaction to sentencing factors can provide a direct measure of the importance of the factors and does not rely on respondents' self-reports. (The approach, known as 'conjoint analysis', is described more fully by Hough et al., 2008).

Respondents were asked to consider a specific case of an offence in which the offender was a 28-year-old male and the victim a 35-year-old female: 'The offender was driving along a quiet road in daylight. Another car pulled out from a side road, well in front of the offender. The offender failed to notice this other car, crashed into it and killed the other driver.' This description was then changed on the screen as various mitigating and aggravating factors were introduced for the respondent to consider. For the purposes of illustration, Table 19.1 provides a hierarchy of the

Table 19.1   Impact of aggravating and mitigating factors on sentence length

Sentencing factor	Change in number of months imposed
Second person killed in other car	+11 months
Offender clearly expresses no remorse	+8 months
Offender using a mobile phone at time of accident	+7 months
Offender fled the scene	+7 months
Parents of victim said to be devastated and ask court to impose severe penalty	+7 months
Offender was driving 20 mph over speed limit	+4 months
Offender was on medication which he knew would impair his driving ability	+5 months
Victim was a close friend of the offender	+3 months
Offender had only recently learned to drive	−2 months
Offender helped the victim and called emergency services	−4 months
Offender clearly expressed remorse for the crime	−3 months
Offender was driving 10 mph over speed limit	+1 month
Offender had been driving for several hours and was feeling very tired	+1 month
Offender was an experienced driver	−1 month
Offender was himself badly injured	−1 month
Parents of the deceased have forgiven the offender and now ask the court to be lenient	No change

Source: Hough et al. (2008)

sentencing factors. The number of months changed in the sentence may be taken as an index of the relative importance of the factors. In this way the importance of different factors is measured directly, without having to rely on the respondents' self-report of how important each factor is at sentencing (see also Applegate et al., 1996).

Attitude measurement and hypothesis testing

Most public opinion polls conducted for governments or special interest groups in the field of criminal justice simply measure opinions. For example, the government may be interested in knowing how much public support there is for mandatory sentencing or abolishing parole. Academic researchers in recent years have become increasingly interested in testing specific hypotheses about the processes and factors that influence how attitudes to crime and justice develop and evolve. Sometimes this kind of research is performed in university laboratories, sometimes using a representative sample of the public. The advantage of a university laboratory is that subjects, typically university students, are available for around an hour of research time. The downside is that university students are not representative of the general population. On the other hand, when researchers test hypotheses using a representative

sample of the general population, the respondents are available for only a few minutes, therefore severely restricting the kinds of hypotheses that may be tested.

Experimental approaches

Laboratory experiments
Public attitudes to criminal justice have been explored experimentally in a number of studies. This line of research generally involves manipulating some variable such as the amount of information provided to participants, and then measuring the effect of this variable on some dependent variable. In Box 19.4 we provide a good example of this approach to research.

Experiments involving surveys
In the early days of polling, all respondents were given the same questions and the same response options. Today, many surveys use a split-sample approach in which sub-groups of the total sample are given different variations on the question, or different amounts of information. Whether any given respondent receives version A or B of a question is randomly determined; such surveys are therefore true experiments. The essence of an experiment is that any differences between conditions on the *dependent* variable (that which is

---

Box 19.4   Experimental research

One of the important questions relating to the death penalty is whether there is a relationship between the level of information people have about capital punishment and the degree to which they endorse this punishment. A US Supreme Court judge once hypothesised that if the public knew the facts about the administration of the death penalty, people would conclude that it was immoral. Bohm et al. (1991) put this hypothesis to the empirical test. Students taking a course in the death penalty at a university in Alabama were asked about their level of support for the death penalty before and after the course had ended – with the hypothesis being that students would be more informed on the second administration and that support for the death penalty would decrease. These researchers found support for the hypothesis.

Box 19.5   Researching the effect of previous convictions on public sentencing preferences

Some scholars argue that sentencing a repeat offender more harshly because he has prior convictions is unfair – after all he has already paid the price for those previous offences. Others argue that offenders with prior convictions are more blameworthy and should be punished more severely than first offenders for this reason. Where do the public stand on this question? In a recent study (Hough et al., 2009) several approaches were used to determine where the public stands on this important issue. First, a representative sample of the public was asked whether having previous convictions increased the seriousness of the case. In response, the majority (65 per cent) said it always increased crime seriousness. But we also wanted to test the hypothesis indirectly. We wanted to see whether people would *actually sentence* more harshly when the offender had prior convictions. One way of doing this would be to use a 'within subjects' design. This would involve giving respondents three offenders to sentence, one with no record, one with a short record and one with a long record. The problem with this approach is that people might guess that we were testing to see whether they took previous convictions into account, and respond accordingly. So instead we used a 'between subjects' design in which respondents were asked to sentence only one offender.

   The sample was divided randomly into thirds. Respondents in each third were asked to sentence the same offender (convicted of assault) but under a different criminal history description: no previous convictions; two previous convictions; or five previous convictions. So this was a true experiment: all extraneous factors have been held constant (the crime description is exactly the same, the only thing that has changed is the number of prior convictions). People were asked to choose between imposing custody, a community order, or a fine. Even a relatively short criminal record (i.e., two prior convictions) had an impact on public sentencing preferences. The percentage of respondents imposing custody across the three experimental conditions rose from 11 per cent for the first offender to 65 per cent for the offender with two prior convictions, and then to 83 per cent for the offender with four priors. This pattern of findings suggests that the public appear to support a policy of imposing harsher sentences on repeat offenders.

---

measured) must be a consequence of the *independent* variable (which is manipulated by the researcher). Box 19.5 reports an experimental manipulation in which different groups of respondents are given a different version of the same criminal case to read. All respondents are then asked the same question, namely to state the sentence that they would impose.

Field experiments

Most research into public opinion and criminal justice is conducted by means of opinion surveys or focus groups where people discuss the issues in a rather artificial setting. A more naturalistic approach involves collecting information in the field. Field experiments have become more popular in recent years. One of the authors conducted a long-running field study (Feilzer, 2007) which is summarised in Box 19.6. The arena of public opinion research has evolved considerable over the years and moved away from its over-reliance on survey research. As reservations about the quality of some survey research and validity of survey research generally increased, creative research designs making use of the full range of quantitative and qualitative research methods have greatly enhanced our understanding of the nature

---

Box 19.6   The Oxford Crime Scene study

This study aimed to measure the impact of the provision of information on crime and criminal justice to members of the public through a local newspaper, thus going beyond the traditional laboratory experiment (see Feilzer, 2007). The novelty of the project lay in testing whether facts about crime and criminal justice transmitted through the media could transcend the daily deluge of information in contemporary society. The intervention consisted of the author writing 26 columns on crime and criminal justice for a weekly local newspaper which were published every week for six months.

The impact of the columns was measured using a mixed methods quasi-experimental research design. Research methods consisted of a large-scale repeat survey (total of 1,311 surveys returned), 38 in-depth interviews with survey participants, and contextual data which included six exploratory interviews with media 'insiders' (the editor, a sub-editor, a columnist, and the crime reporter at the local newspaper) and 'opinion leaders' (a restorative justice manager at the local Youth Offending Team and the Acting Chief Constable of Thames Valley Police), the shadowing of the crime reporter, and a fieldwork diary. The Crime Scene study was a local study and the contextual data were vital to locate the study in space and time. The experimental intervention, that is, the columns, was fairly modest and the research found that readership of the column was low and had no measurable impact on its readers. Thus, the combination of different research methods and the nature of the research as a field experiment gave rise to a number of findings questioning views that public confidence in criminal justice can be improved simply by the provision of facts about crime and the criminal justice system. It further highlighted the need to be cautious when interpreting survey results as accurate and valid representations of public opinion. Similarly, a field experiment carried out in the Netherlands found that their experimental intervention had no measurable impact (Elffers et al., 2007).

---

of public opinion and the complexities and controversies surrounding the use of the concept. Field experiments exchange the controlled environment of the laboratory which enables random allocation of subjects to control or experimental group for the messiness of the 'real' world. Thus, rather than laboratory studies which measure, for example, whether the 'media can produce certain effects' (MacBeth, 1996; emphasis in original), natural or field experiments intend to measure the effects that occur in 'reality'.

Deliberative polls

The survey method can sometimes prove crude and reductionist in the sense that it reduces complex questions to simple 'yes/no' or 'agree/disagree' responses. There is an alternative, although costs prevent it from being widely used. The 'deliberative poll' is designed to give people the time, space and information to develop *considered* views on a topic. This technique marries the advantages of qualitative research with those of quantitative approaches. As with focus groups, deliberative polls provide respondents with time to absorb information and to think about and develop their viewpoints. However, deliberative polls also aim to quantify opinion in ways that are properly generalisable. Researchers conduct a representative survey to measure public attitudes regarding a wide range of issues. Respondents are also asked if they are prepared to take part in a seminar,

typically run over a weekend. Such an event is subsequently held, and attitudes are measured at the beginning of the event (to ensure that the sample has not been biased or skewed by the 'volunteer' effect) and at the end. In between, participants hear presentations on the issues, and have extensive opportunities to discuss and debate them. The participants constitute a representative sample – so inferences may be drawn about the attitudes of the population. At the same time, the experience lasts more than just a few minutes; this gives researchers the opportunity to provide information to the participants, who can then deliberate (hence the title) before responding. To our knowledge only two such polls have been conducted in criminal justice (e.g., Hough and Park, 2002), because they are so expensive. However, there is no reason why a deliberative poll may not be mounted for a single evening, rather than a weekend. This would dramatically reduce the costs, and also increase the proportion of the original sample attending.

Current controversies and future directions

To summarise, public attitudes towards issues as complex as criminal justice can be understood only by utilising a variety of methodologies. Over the past century, research assessing public opinion of crime and justice has evolved not only in the type of methods used but also in the types of questions asked of research. Although the representative survey remains the principal tool, findings from this approach must be regarded with caution. Qualitative methods of exploring public opinion are also important, and mixed methods research has emerged as an approach better able to deal with the complexities of public opinion of crime and justice. A good example of this can be found in the research reported by Hutton (2005). This project contained three components: a large, representative survey, a series of focus groups, and a form of 'deliberative poll' in which participants were asked to complete sentencing exercises after having been exposed to presentations by experts in the field.

Internationalisation of public attitudes research

To date, a considerable amount of research on public attitudes has accumulated in most Western nations. However, this research has been jurisdiction-specific. With a few exceptions, researchers have been concerned with measuring public attitudes towards criminal justice programs and policies in their own country, without regard to trends elsewhere. This is now changing. There is growing interest in cross-jurisdictional surveys. One such instrument is the International Crime Victimisation Survey (ICVS). This instrument is now administered in over 30 countries (Van Kesteren, 2009; and Chapter 17, by Mayhew and van Dijk). Primarily a survey of crime victims, it also contains a measure of public attitudes: respondents are asked to impose sentence in the case of a repeat burglar. The ICVS therefore provides a fairly simple measure of public punitiveness using a question common to respondents in all countries in which the survey is administered.

At the time of writing, one of the authors is involved in a further comparative project that forms part of the European Social Survey (see www.eurojustis.eu and www.europeansocialsurvey.org). Unlike the ICVS, this will focus specifically on public attitudes to justice, and will document trends in public trust in justice across European countries. Work of this sort should help to develop a more sophisticated understanding of the factors that shape public views about justice, and should be able to offer pointers about the best ways of building public trust and confidence.

FURTHER READING

There is by now a vast literature on measuring public opinion, going back to the 1930s as well as a more specific literature which explores measurement issues in the field of criminal justice.

General methodology texts

Asher, H. (2004) *Polling and the Public. What Every Citizen Should Know.* Washington, DC: Congressional Quarterly.

Ferguson, S. (2000) *Researching the Public Opinion Environment. Theories and Methods.* Thousand Oaks: Sage.

Manza, J., Cook, F. and Page, B. (2002) *Navigating Public Opinion.* Oxford: Oxford University Press.

Moser, K. and Kalton, G. (1971) *Survey Methods in Social Investigation*, 2nd Edition. Glasgow: Heinemann. (A classic text, republished 1985 by Ashgate)

Specialist works on attitudes to crime and justice

Stalans, L.S. (2002) Measuring attitudes to sentencing. In: J.V. Roberts and M. Hough (eds) *Changing Attitudes to Punishment. Public Opinion, Crime and Justice* (Cullompton: Willan Publishing). This chapter provides a concise summary of attitude measurement in the field of criminal justice. It is a useful primer for the non-specialist.

Roberts, J.V. and Hough, M. (2005) *Public Attitudes to Criminal Justice.* Maidenhead: Open University Press.

Tendayi Viki, G. and Bohner, G. (2009) Achieving accurate assessment of attitudes toward the criminal justice system: methodological issues. In: J. Wood and T. Gannon (eds) *Public Opinion and Criminal Justice* (Cullompton: Willan Publishing). This chapter is the most recent description of methodological approaches to measuring public opinion.

REFERENCES

Adamson, J., Gooberman-Hill, R., Woolhead, G. and Dononvan, J. (2004) 'Questerviews': using questionnaires in qualitative interviews as a method of integrating qualitative and quantitative health services research. *Journal of Health Services Research Policy*, 9: 139–145.

Applegate, B., Cullen, F., Link, B., Richards, P. and Lanza-Kaduce, L. (1996) Determinants of public punitiveness toward drunk driving: A factorial survey approach. *Justice Quarterly*, 13: 57–79.

Bachman, R. and Schutt, R. (2003) *The Practice of Research in Criminology and Criminal Justice*, 2nd Edition. Thousand Oaks: Sage.

Beatty, P.C. and Willis, G.B. (2007) Research synthesis: The practice of cognitive interviewing. *Public Opinion Quarterly*, 71(2): 287–311.

Blumer, H. (1948) Public opinion and public opinion polling. *American Sociological Review*, 13: 542–549.

Bohm, R., Clark, L. and Aveni, A. (1991) Knowledge and death penalty opinion: A test of the Marshall hypothesis.

Journal of Research in Crime and Delinquency, 28: 360–387.

Bourdieu, P. (1993) Public opinion does not exist. (R. Nice, trans.). In: P. Bourdieu (ed.) *Sociology in Question*. London: Sage.

Creswell, J.W. and Clark, V.L.P. (2007) *Designing and Conducting Mixed Methods Research*. Thousand Oaks: Sage.

Cullen, F., Fisher, B. and Applegate, B. (2000) Public opinion about punishment and corrections. In: M. Tonry (ed.) *Crime and Justice. A Review of Research*. Chicago: University of Chicago Press.

Cumberland, J. and Zamble, E. (1992) General and specific measures of attitudes toward early release of criminal offenders. *Canadian Journal of Behavioural Science*, 24: 442–455.

Ditton, J. and Farrall, S. (2007) The British Crime Survey and fear of crime. In: M. Houg and M. Maxfield (eds) *Surveying Crime in the 21st Century*. Cullompton: Willan.

Doob, A. and Roberts, J.V. (1983) *Sentencing: An Analysis of the Public's View*. Ottawa: Department of Justice Canada.

Doob, A.N. and Roberts, J.V. (1988) Public punitiveness and public knowledge of the facts: Some Canadian surveys. In: N. Walker and M. Hough (eds) *Public Attitudes to Sentencing*. Aldershot: Gower.

Elffers, H., Keijser, J.W.d., Koppen, P.J.v. and Haeringen, L.v. (2007) Newspaper juries: A field experiment concerning the effect of information on attitudes towards the criminal justice system. *Journal of Experimental Criminology*, 3: 163–182.

Erlandson, D.A., Harris, E.L., Skipper, B.L. and Allen, S.D. (1993) *Doing Naturalistic Inquiry: A Guide to Methods*. Newbury Park, CA: Sage.

Feilzer, M.Y. (2007) Criminologists making news? Providing factual information on crime and criminal justice through a weekly newspaper column. *Crime, Media, Culture*, 3: 285–304.

Feilzer, M.Y. (2010) Doing mixed methods research pragmatically – implications for the rediscovery of pragmatism as a research paradigm. *Journal of Mixed Methods Research*, 4(1): 6–16.

Gallup Organization (2010) *Gallup Poll Social Series: Crime*. Retrieved at: http://www.gallup.com/poll/144284/Support-Death-Penalty-Cases-Murder.aspx

Green, D.A. (2006) Public opinion versus public judgment about crime. *British Journal of Criminology*, 46: 131–154.

Horst, M., Kuttschreuter, M. and Gutteling, J.M. (2007) Perceived usefulness, personal experiences, risk perception and trust as determinantsof adoption of e-government services in the Netherlands. *Computers in Human Behavior*, 23: 1838–1852.

Hough, M. (1996) People talking about punishment. *Howard Journal of Criminal Justice*, 35: 191–214.

Hough, M. and Park, A. (2002) How malleable are attitudes to crime and punishment? In: J.V. Roberts and M. Hough (eds) *Changing Attitudes to Punishment*. Cullompton: Willan.

Hough, M. and Roberts, J.V. (2004a) *Confidence in Criminal Justice. An International Review*. ICPR Research Paper No. 3. London: King's College.

Hough, M. and Roberts, J. (2004b) *Youth Crime and Youth Justice: Public Opinion in England and Wales*. Researching Criminal Policy Paper. Bristol: Policy Press.

Hough, M., Roberts, J.V., Jacobson, J., Bredee, A. and Moon, N. (2008) *Attitudes to the Sentencing of Offenders Convicted of Offences Involving Death by Driving*. London: Sentencing Advisory Panel.

Hough, M., Roberts, J.V., Jacobson, J., Moon, N. and Steel, N. (2009) *Public Attitudes to the Principles of Sentencing. Sentencing Advisory Panel Report No. 6*. London: Sentencing Advisory Panel.

Hutton, N. (2005) Beyond populist punitiveness? *Punishment and Society*, 7: 243–248.

Indermaur, D. (1987) Public perception of sentencing in Perth, Western Australia. *Australia and New Zealand Journal of Criminology*, 20: 163–183.

Jones, P. (1994) It's not what you ask, it's the way that you ask it: question form and public opinion on the death penalty. *The Prison Journal*, 73: 32–50.

Knight, D. (1965) Punishment selection as a function of biographical information. *Journal of Criminal Law, Criminology and Police Science*, 56: 325–327.

Kubiak, S. and Allen, T. (2008) Public opinion regarding juvenile life without parole in consecutive statewide surveys. *Crime and Delinquency*, online first, 10 June 2008.

MacBeth, T.M. (1996) Indirect effects of television. In: T.M. MacBeth (ed.) *Tuning in to Young Viewers: Social Science Perspectives on Television*. Thousand Oaks: Sage

Miller, J. and Glassner, B. (1997) The 'inside' and the 'outside'. In: D. Silvermann (ed.) *Qualitative Research - Theory, Method and Practice*. London: Sage.

Morgan, D.L. (2007). Paradigms lost and pragmatism regained. *Journal of Mixed Methods Research*, 1: 48–76.

MORI (2000) *Crime and Punishment Poll*. MORI poll, 16 July 2000. Available at: www.mori.com/polls/2000/ms000714.shtml

Noelle-Neumann, E. (1977) Turbulences in the climate of opinion: methodological applications of the spiral of silence theory. *The Public Opinion Quarterly*, 41: 143–158.

Oberwittler, D. and Qi, S. (2009) *Public Opinion and the Death Penalty in China*. Freiberg: Max Planck Institute for Foreign and International Criminal Law.

Palys, T. and Atchison, C. (2008) *Research Decisions. Quantitative and Qualitative Perspectives*. Toronto: Pearson.

Pratt, J., Brown, D., Brown, M., Hallsworth, S. and Morrison, W. (2005) *The New Punitiveness*. Cullompton: Willan.

Petty, R.E. and Wegener, D.T. (1998) Attitude change: multiple roles for persuasion variables. In: D.T. Gilbert, S.T. Fiske and G. Lindzey (eds) *The Handbook of Social Psychology (Vol. 1)*. New York: Oxford University Press.

Rethinking Crime and Punishment (2002) *What do the public really feel about non-custodial penalties?* London: Esmee Fairburn Foundation.

Roberts, J.V. (1988) *Public Opinion and Sentencing: the Surveys of the Canadian Sentencing Commission*. Ottawa: Department of Justice Canada.

Roberts, J.V. (2008) The role of public opinion in the development of sentencing policy and practice. In: A. Freiberg and K. Gelb (eds) *Penal Populism, Sentencing Councils and Sentencing Policy*. Cullompton: Willan Publishing.

Roberts, J.V. and Doob, A.N. (1990). News media influences on public views of sentencing. *Law and Human Behaviour*, 14: 451–468.

Roberts, J.V. and Hough, M. (2002). Public attitudes to punishment: the context. In J.V. Roberts and M. Hough (eds) *Changing Attitudes to Punishment*. Cullompton: Willan.

Roberts, J.V. and Hough, M. (2005a) *Understanding Public Attitudes to Criminal Justice*. Maidenhead: Open University Press.

Roberts, J.V. and Hough, M. (2005b) Sentencing young offenders: public opinion in England and Wales. *Criminal Justice*, 5: 211–232.

Roberts, J.V. and Hough, M. (2010) Custody or community? Exploring the boundaries of public punitiveness in England and Wales. *Criminology and Criminal Justice*.11: 185–202.

Roberts, J.V., Hough, M., Jacobson, J. and Moon, N. (2009) Public attitudes to sentencing purposes and sentencing factors: an empirical analysis. *Criminal Law Review*, November: 771–782.

Roberts, J.V., Hough, M., Jacobson, J., Bredee, A. and Moon, N. (2008) Public attitudes to sentencing offenders convicted of offences involving death by driving. *Criminal Law Review*, July: 525–540.

Roberts, J.V. and Stalans, L.J. (2000) *Public Opinion, Crime, and Criminal Justice*. Colorado: Westview Press.

Roberts, J.V., Stalans, L.S., Indermaur, D. and Hough, M. (2003) *Penal Populism and Public Opinion. Lessons from Five Countries*. Oxford: Oxford University Press.

Rock, P. (1995). The opening stages of criminal justice policy making. *British Journal of Criminology*, 35: 1–16.

Russell, N. and Morgan, R. (2001) *Sentencing of Domestic Burglary*. Research Report. Sentencing Advisory Panel. Available at: www.sentencing-advisory-anel.gov.uk/saprr1.htm.

Speier, H. (1950) Historical development of public opinion. *American Journal of Sociology*, 55: 376–388.

Teddlie, C. and Tashakkori, A. (2009) *Foundations of Mixed Methods Research*. Thousand Oaks: Sage.

Tourangeau, R., Rips, L. and Rasinski, K. (2000) *The Psychology of Survey Response*. Cambridge: Cambridge University Press.

Unnever, J., Cullen, F. and Roberts, J.V. (2005) Not everyone strongly supports the death penalty: assessing weakly-held attitudes about capital punishment. *American Journal of Criminal Justice*, 20: 187–216.

Van Kesteren, J. (2009) Public attitudes and sentencing policies across the world. *European Journal of Criminal Policy and Research*, 15: 25–46.

Wilkins, L.T. (1984) *Consumerist Criminology*. London: Heinemann.

Wood, J. and Gannon, T. (eds) (2009) *Public Opinion and Criminal Justice*. Cullompton: Willan Publishing.

Criminal Justice Systems: Organizations and Institutions

In this section we present six chapters all addressed to the challenges of researching criminal justice systems. Each explores methodologies that address the processes, people, cultures, organizations and institutions through which these systems function. As all of the contributions in this section reveal, the question of how criminal justice organizations, institutions and systems function has inspired much methodological innovation. On the one hand, it has caused criminologists to develop methodologies designed to assess 'what works': whether or not particular sanctions or interventions achieve the effects their advocates claim of them. Whether, for example, particular styles of policing deter or reduce crime more than others? Whether offenders are less likely to offend if subjected to community sentences as opposed to imprisonment? On the other hand, it has also motivated criminologists to explore the many other ways in which criminal justice systems and processes operate, often resulting in outcomes that appear quite antithetical to officially stated aims. Why, for example, minority groups often feel they have been treated unjustly by criminal justice organizations committed to equality principles, or why greater law enforcement often fails to increase feelings of security. Hence, most of the chapters in this section pay attention to the different ways in which criminal justice objectives are translated into practice, providing methodological guidance on how to explore the impact of occupational cultures, under-resourcing, or conflict within and between different professionals upon this translation process. Some chapters also provide advice on how to explore the competing meanings

victims, offenders and professionals attribute to criminal justice outcomes and processes. Others address cultural, structural and comparative issues, including the methodological challenges presented by comparative studies across large regions and/or discrete countries.

As readers who take on all six chapters in this section will discover, while it was once the case that researchers pursuing the question of 'what works' concerned themselves principally with how best to approximate experimental designs, there are few criminologists who would argue that this method alone is capable of assessing whether or not any particular criminal justice intervention or organization is successfully delivering or not. This is certainly the argument to be found in Wesley Skogan's chapter on the use of quasi-experimental research methods. By describing the implementation of successive evaluation efforts in Chicago – one of the largest cities in the world to test the effectiveness of community policing – Skogan illustrates the importance of engaging with stakeholders in order to establish what counts as success. A mixture of survey techniques, officer reports, police call data, and community beat consultation meetings were used in the various studies undertaken by Skogan and his colleagues over a 12-year period. Through methodologically rich examples, Skogan reveals how certain ethnic and socio-economic groups differed with respect to the criteria against which they wanted successful policing to be benchmarked. Ultimately, some of those neighbourhoods with the greatest social and economic capital were able to exert more political influence with respect to which problems were deemed the proper focus of community policing, influence which in turn shaped the research methodology deployed. As well as detailing the technicalities involved in identifying relevant comparison sites, establishing baseline data and controlling for displacement effects, this chapter reveals exactly the kind of difference responsive and democratically responsible research design can make.

What connects Skogan's chapter to this section's second chapter is the insight that what actually happens where criminal justice interventions are implemented and what programme designers intend are often quite different things. In her chapter, Janet Chan explores the ways in which longitudinal mixed methods approaches involving both ethnography and self-report accounts can add to an understanding of police culture. Using her own study of the socialization of new recruits to the Australian police as illustrative, Chan examines the challenges of developing methodological strategies able to illuminate the structures and processes that inform, maintain and change organizational cultures, especially the more racially discriminatory elements regarded by many as endemic within police services. Chan's own research involved field observation over two years, in-depth qualitative interviews, a questionnaire-based survey, and a ten-year follow-up study. What her research illustrates is how effective mixed methods are in terms of making sense of criminological processes that are in some way coveted. Chan and her team discovered that in policing, multiple layers of authority and access, paranoia about the true intentions of the research, and the desire to fit in with more established officers tended to collude to present a picture of 'cop culture' that was more monolithic, hostile and homogenous than it really was. Chan explains that if criminologists are to avoid presenting overly pessimistic analyses of organizational cultures within criminal justice then they need the skills to make sense of organizational defensiveness and move beyond it in the immediate term, as well as research strategies for reconnecting with individual participants over the longer term.

It is because of its capacity to capture the contingencies through which subtle nuances of meaning are negotiated that Aaron Kupchik, Joseph De Angelis and Nicole Bracy advocate the use of ethnomethodology to explore the various settings in which juvenile justice is performed. Having distinguished ethnomethodology from ethnography through a review of the classic ethnomethodological works of Harold Garfinkel, Robert Emerson and Aaron Cicourel, Kupchik et al.'s chapter highlights the advantages of this under-utilized approach to studying the nature of the justice experienced by children and young people. They explore the power of ethnomethodology, sometimes assisted by conversation analysis, to unearth the effects of processes that are so mundane and routine as to be taken for granted. Within criminal courtrooms, for example, ethnomethodology has been used to explore why some sentencers give light sentences to those they sternly admonish. Likewise, the experiences of researchers in schools where law enforcement now operate can be understood as akin to Garfinkel's 'breaching experiments': children are disorientated by the presence of adults who are neither teachers nor law enforcers. If one knows how to read them, children's disorientated reactions to researchers can reveal much about the counterproductive effects of social control on those who are ordinarily powerless to alter the thinking of the professionals who deem them unruly.

None of this negates the importance of knowing whether work with those who do breach the law is effective, as Karen Tusinski Miofsky and James Byrne argue in their chapter. As they explain, probation is the sanction of choice for most categories of convicted offenders the world over, but its effects have rarely been researched as thoroughly as those of imprisonment. More therefore needs to be done to understand the effectiveness of probation in terms of traditional outcomes, such as cost, community protection and individual offender change. Tusinski Miofsky and Byrne thus provide an overview of the available evaluation research in order to identify the key elements of sound methodological approaches to the measurement of probation program implementation and impact. As their review reveals there are very few methodologically sound studies nuanced enough to capture the multi-dimensional nature of probation, the quality and scale of its dosage, and the conditions of its applications. Consequently, policy has been made on the basis of a handful of studies which present unjustifiably pessimistic analyses of what might work. Tusinski Miofsky and Byrne's chapter concludes by exploring what a methodologically sophisticated approach to evaluating the effectiveness of probation supervision applied to high-risk offenders might look like.

Overcoming both political and methodological challenges is a theme explored further by Alison Liebling, Susie Hulley and Ben Crewe in their account of a succession of studies designed to improve the measurement of quality of life in prisons. A not uncontentious project in and of itself, Liebling et al.'s work has been motivated by a desire to develop techniques able to hold prison service providers to account in terms of the effects of poor service provision on prisoners' perceptions of fairness and quality of life, pose questions of comparability and value for money across the prison estate, and transcend the predominant 'what works' focus on treatment effectiveness. While the product of Liebling et al.'s efforts has been the creation of a pioneering survey tool that measures the moral quality of prison life in ways that policy audiences have found persuasive, the development of the tool required the use of methods of appreciative inquiry. These appreciative methods sought to capture what could be positive in otherwise painful prison experiences. Consequently, the survey measures that were developed from this appreciative work retained meaning and depth in terms of their conceptualization of prisoners' experiences. They ensured the critical relational dimensions of prisoners' experiences were captured by the survey instrument that had, ultimately, to speak to a managerialist agenda; and hence delivered findings that have been used to make prisons fairer and more humane.

Comparative studies of criminal justice across nations and cultures are no less challenging. They confront criminologists with numerous methodological problems. These range from the pitfalls of data collection to epistemological questions of cultural relativism, the general possibility of taking comparative studies beyond the in-depth analysis of a single case, the limitations of understanding a culture that is not our own, and the risk of overgeneralization. Susanne Karstedt's chapter provides insights into the methods used by comparative criminologists when navigating these problems. The chapter starts with a brief overview of the expanding field of comparative criminology, and its links with processes of globalization. Throughout Karstedt reveals the wealth of opportunities open to criminologists willing to engage in cross-cultural research, in particular the ever-increasing range and accessibility of data sources for comparative studies of crime and criminal justice. The chapter moves on to identify the two major methodological challenges for cross-cultural research: the problem of autonomy of the sphere of culture; the problem of coherence and homogeneity of culture in contrast to its internal differences and variation; and finally the question of understanding, interpreting and analyzing a culture that is not the researcher's own. General comparative strategies that address these problems are presented, and questions of practical research design are discussed: selecting units, cases and samples; and identifying, reconstructing and measuring culture. The chapter concludes with an outline of new methodological challenges that arise from migration and the study of minority cultures in multicultural societies, and from more rapid cultural change.

20

Researching Police Culture: A Longitudinal Mixed Method Approach

Janet Chan

INTRODUCTION

The study of the organization, practice and culture of public police has had a long and distinguished history in criminology. Participant observation has emerged as an important research technique for uncovering routine, taken-for-granted features of policing. Researchers such as Westley (1970), Skolnick (1966), Reiss (1971), Black (1971), Bittner (1967) and Cicourel (1967) have pioneered observational studies of specific aspects of police practice. Van Maanen (1973) has applied this approach to the study of police socialization. This tradition continued over the next decades from Manning's research on police work (1977/1997), Ericson's studies of police detectives and patrol officers in Canada (1981/1993; 1982), Holdaway's (1983) and Young's (1991) participant observation of British police, Dixon's comparative study of law in policing in the UK and in Australia in the mid 1990s (Dixon, 2011), Herbert's (1997, 1998) and Parks et al.'s (1999) research on policing in America, to more recent studies such as Marks' (2004, 2005) study of post-apartheid public order policing in South Africa and Huey's (2007) comparative study of skid row policing in Edinburgh, San Francisco and Vancouver.

Although field observation is often the most appropriate and fruitful way of gaining an in-depth understanding police culture and practice, researchers have also made use of other research techniques, such as formal interviews or questionnaire surveys to supplement, or replace, field observation (e.g., Ericson and Haggerty, 1997; Fielding, 1988; Huey, 2007; Marks, 2005). This chapter describes a research project that used a longitudinal design to study the occupational culture and socialization of recruits in an Australian police organization (Chan et al., 2003). The research consisted of multiple rounds of questionnaire surveys, interviews and field observation over two years, together with a ten-year follow-up study. The chapter is organized as follows. In the next sections, I will describe the research problem that drove the research, the research design adopted, and how the design was implemented. I will then discuss the strengths of the approach, some of the methodological challenges, as well as legal and ethical issues, before summarizing the lessons learnt and commenting on the future of policing research in the concluding section.

UNDERSTANDING POLICE CULTURE

My interest in police culture originated from my field experience in the pilot phase of Richard Ericson's (1982) project on police patrols and a study of youth bureau police with Tony Doob. The youth bureau project (Doob and Chan, 1982) was my first serious encounter with police culture. Having spent three months as a participant observer in the bureau, I was both appalled and intrigued by the 'widely accepted practice of denigrating minorities and telling racist jokes within the station' (Chan, 1997: 10). I assumed then, as others did, that racism was very much part of police culture and this would always be the case. It was not until a decade later, when I was researching community policing in Australia, that I started to question the conventional wisdom about police culture. I was wary of the pessimistic implications of the way police culture was conceptualized – a uniform, all-powerful and unchanging set of practices and values that would make police reform all but doomed to failure. Police culture, with a few notable exceptions (e.g. Goldsmith, 1990; Shearing and Ericson, 1991), was often cast as negative and recalcitrant. In the area of police–minorities relations, there was a sense that police racism was institutionalized and minority groups were helpless victims of police oppression. Even though I felt strongly about racism as a social issue, I wanted to move beyond the political rhetoric and examine these relations more closely and more carefully.

I was critical of some of the underlying assumptions behind the way police culture had been understood: its universality, homogeneity, omnipotence and recalcitrance (Chan, 1996, 1997). To me, the challenge for researchers was how to conceptualize police culture in such a way that cultural change was possible. I began searching for an alternative theoretical framework that would accommodate the existence of multiple cultures, recognise the agency of police officers in shaping their culture, situate cultural practice in the political context of policing and provide a theory of cultural change. The framework I came up with was first laid out in Chan (1996) and Chan (1997) and subsequently refined in Chan et al. (2003). I made use of the French sociologist Pierre Bourdieu's theory of practice—in particular the notions of field, habitus and capital—which provides excellent tools for thinking about the relationship between police cultural knowledge and the structural conditions of policing (see Bourdieu and Wacquant, 1992).

THE RESEARCH PROJECT

The original 'Police Culture and Professionalism' project was jointly funded by the Australian Research Council and the New South Wales Police Service as an 'industry partner'. The Police Service executive team at the time was remarkably progressive and open to innovative ideas. Apart from contributing a substantial amount of cash for the three-year project, the Service also granted the research team unprecedented access to the police academy and the organization. Not only were we given permission to interview recruits, academy staff and field training officers, we were able to observe the activities of recruits during their field training and after they had graduated as police constables.

The project set out to examine the experience of a cohort of recruits during their first two years of joining the police. Although it also investigated how recruits learnt the craft of policing and developed their concept of 'good' and 'bad' policing, the main focus was to try to understand how 'police culture' was transmitted from one generation to another through the socialization process. Consistent with the theoretical framework, the project was open about whether there was a single police culture or a diversity of cultures; it was designed to capture the agency of recruits and other officers in shaping the culture, and to reveal any fluidity in the culture and socialization process amidst the changing field of policing.

The project was designed to follow the progress of a cohort of approximately 150 police recruits at regular intervals for two years. A mix of research techniques was employed, including face-to-face interviews, questionnaires and observation. In addition, documentary material such as course outlines, police internal documents and official reports were used as supplementary data. The original project was carried out in 1995–1997. A follow-up study of the 118 remaining members of the same cohort was conducted in 2004–2005; it involved a mail-out questionnaire survey as well as face-to-face interviews.

Table 20.1 summarizes the research design, schedule of activities and the participation outcomes (see Chan et al., 2003: chapter 2, for full details of the sampling methods, response rates and the types of information sought in the original study; see Chan and Doran, 2009, for details of the follow-up study). The research instruments were designed to capture the experience of recruits at different stages of their careers. The questionnaire surveys recorded demographic data, training experiences, as well as a number of attitudinal measures, some of which were repeated in subsequent surveys to detect changes over time. For example, perception of the community appeared in Survey 1 and was repeated in Surveys 2 and 3. Other such attitudinal measures include: perception of the criminal justice system (Surveys 1 and 3), ethical values (Surveys 1, 2 and 3), attitudes towards and responses to specific conduct scenarios (Surveys 1 and 3), and satisfaction with chosen career as police officer (Surveys 2, 3, 4 and 5). Interview questions provided a relatively unrestricted space for interviewees to recount their experiences and express their views. While questions for each

Table 20.1   Research design, schedule and outcomes

Month	Stage of training	Survey	Interview	Observation
1–2	1. Academy	#1 (n = 147)	#1 (n = 73)	–
3	2. Field observation	–	–	#1 (19 shifts)
4–6	3. Academy	#2 (n = 127)	#2 (n = 59)	#2 (Debrief)
7–12	4a. Field training (Demo patrols)	–	–	#3a (30 shifts)
13–17	4b. Field training (Training patrols)	–	–	#3b (28 shifts)
18	5. Academy	#3 (n = 134)	#3 (n = 54)	–
19–24	Work as constable	#4 (n = 87)	#4 (n = 53)	#4 (38 shifts)
Follow-up project				
9–10 yrs	Mid-career officers	#5 (n = 42)	#5 (n = 44)	–

round of interviews were designed to relate to each stage of the participant's training or career, some questions were repeated to detect changes over time. For example, the questions: 'Did you see any examples of good [bad] police work?' were asked at interview rounds 2, 3, 4 and 5 so that changes in conception of good practice can be tracked. Similarly, recruits who were female, from a non-Anglo background, or older (over 25 years of age at entry) were asked at rounds 2 to 5 to reflect on whether their gender, ethnicity or age had made a difference to their training/working experience.

Research assistants who conducted field observation were given a half-day training, written instructions (See Box 20.1 for a summary of the instructions), and opportunities for debriefing. During the training, fieldworkers were provided with a set of 'sensitizing concepts' to guide their observation. For example, in accordance with the framework in Chan (1996), fieldworkers were asked to focus on the socialization of the recruits with particular reference to the dimensions of cultural knowledge (the *habitus*); for example, how members of the public were categorized, how things were normally done in the local area, how things were supposed to be done in specific situations, and how recruits and other officers regarded their work and its rationale. Fieldworkers were also asked to observe the distribution of various types of capital in the *field* in which learning takes place, including the rank and power structure of the local area command, the amount of resources available, the degree of supervision, the amount of paperwork required, the rules and regulations, the socio-economic mix of the local community, the political climate, legal constraints, policy directives, and so on. They were asked to note any variations within the patrol in terms of attitudes and values and any references to differences between patrol and 'headquarters' values. Given the generally negative use of the term 'police culture' in

public discourse—partly as a result of the way police culture was denigrated in a famous inquiry into police corruption in Queensland (Fitzgerald Report 1989)—the title of the project was presented as 'A Study of Police Recruits' in the questionnaires; the term 'police culture' was not used explicitly anywhere until round 4 of the interviews to minimize potential resistance to the research.

THE RESEARCH PROCESS

It is obvious from the design of the original project that there were strict constraints on the schedule of fieldwork activities. The first survey was administered in a classroom at the police academy during the first week of training. This was relatively straightforward as recruits saw the project as part of what they were asked to do; they dutifully turned up and completed the very lengthy questionnaire without any complaints. The response rate was 98.7 per cent. It was more difficult to organize 75 interviews during the same week, as recruits' schedules were packed with training activities during the day. Interviews had to be conducted in the evenings. This necessitated the use of a team of research assistants who were trained to conduct semi-structured interviews. Similarly, observation of recruits in the field had to be carried out by a team of research assistants, some more experienced than others in the intricacies of field observation. Because recruits were sent to different stations across the State at different stages of their training, we decided to sample a variety of shifts and stations in order to get a reasonably representative overview of field experience. Sampling was partly determined by geographical, socio-economic and workload characteristics of the patrol areas. This differs from traditional fieldwork where researchers spend a considerable amount of time at one location.

Box 20.1   Field observation instructions

POLICE CULTURE AND PROFESSIONALISM: GUIDE FOR OBSERVERS

Purpose

- To get a first-hand understanding of the settings, people and activities that take place
- To gain an insider's view of police practices and how police interpret these practices

What to observe

- Physical setting
- Social environment
- Activities and behaviours
- Informal interactions and unplanned activities
- Language used
- Non-verbal communication
- Documents
- What does not happen

Field notes

- Descriptive, detailed and concrete
- Include date, time, place, who, etc., quotes, your own feelings, reactions, reflections, insights, interpretations, preliminary analysis, working hypotheses, etc.
- To be completed in prose form as soon as possible after each day.

Useful techniques

- Cover sheet for field notes – date and time, summary of activities, information on members being observed.
- Take note of actual time and activities throughout the period of observation.
- Assure people of anonymity and confidentiality. All data are to be used for research only.
- Note names and organizational role/title of members encountered but do not write actual names in field notes (Manager X).
- Note sex, age or estimated age, appearance, status, etc. of people encountered.
- Note what people do, without using any judgment, and record as faithfully as possible all types of activities, including coffee breaks, joking, shopping, slacking off, sleeping, etc. Do not put these in your notebook in a way that is recognizable if someone got hold of your notes.
- Note significant actions/omissions in relation to what members are supposed to do.
- Observe and note any differences between what people say and what they do (also between what they did and what they said they did).
- Be open and non-judgmental, you may discover what other researchers have failed to discover. You should be like a sponge, taking in whatever is around you.
- Make use of any opportunity to interview people informally. It's important to observe as well as obtain participants' accounts of what happened.

In total, we observed 80 different members of the cohort working over 58 day shifts, 42 evening shifts and 14 night shifts, in 40 different local areas. Female recruits were observed in 45 shifts (39 per cent) while male recruits were observed in 70 shifts (61 per cent).

Given the magnitude and complexity of the original project, there were a host of implementation issues which were detailed in Chan et al. (2003: chapter 2) and will only be highlighted

here. First of all, communication within an organization of 13,000 police officers was not always ideal. Even though the project was strongly supported by the police executives, fieldwork arrangements had to be negotiated locally with nominated contact persons. This was a frustrating process that often involved multiple phone calls and repeated delays, and at times was exacerbated by changes in police personnel, last-minute changes in shift or duty, no-shows and various forms of miscommunication. The timing of the project coincided with a major Royal Commission inquiry into police corruption. This added an extra hurdle for researchers to get through, as some shift supervisors and officers became suspicious of outsiders observing their work (Chan et al., 2003: 53). Apart from concerns about the Royal Commission, officers were also anxious that researchers might have been 'spies' working for Internal Affairs, the Independent Commission Against Corruption, or some performance evaluation projects sponsored by management. Researchers' practice of note-taking only added to the paranoia of officers who were concerned about what was being recorded. One researcher was told not to take notes during a police interview of a suspect 'as it might get [the police] in trouble'. The fieldwork experience was varied: officers' reactions to researchers ranged from 'indifference, simple curiosity, genuine interest and support, through to suspicion, abrasiveness or rudeness' (Chan et al., 2003: 55–6).

STRENGTHS OF THE APPROACH

Findings of the original research and the follow-up study have been reported in a number of publications (Chan, 2001, 2007a, 2007b; Chan and Doran, 2009; Chan et al., 2003) and will not be repeated here. I will discuss the strengths of the approach taken in this section and describe some of the methodological challenges in the next section.

One obvious strength of a longitudinal design is the ability to observe and measure change or stability. The use of the same questionnaire item over two or three surveys or the same questions over two or three interviews provided some empirical support for the changes in attitudes and values (habitus) among recruits over the years. However, it is the use of mixed methods that gave the research its most important edge: we were able to compare and reconcile survey results with interview and observation data. For example, the survey data revealed that

> [r]ecruits' attitudes towards the community became progressively and significantly more negative over the eighteen months of their training … Over the course of their training, recruits developed a more negative attitude towards the criminal justice system. Although there was no significant change in their general attitudes towards the rule of law, corruption and work practice during the first six months of training, there was a significant and negative change over their period of field training (Chan et al., 2003: 306).

These changes were consistent with what the majority of recruits told us in interviews: that they had lost some of their idealism and become more cynical, suspicious, less tolerant and more likely to stereotype people. By the end of their field training, many had become disillusioned with the job, and 'picked up some typical elements of the occupational habitus of street-level policing: cynicism, dislike of paperwork, and distrust of management and outsiders, including the general public' (2003: 305).

Where there was convergence between the quantitative and qualitative data, we had a lot more confidence in the validity of our findings, but often they told very different stories, or different aspects of the same stories. This points to the strength of the multiple-method approach: if we had relied solely on the survey data, we would have arrived at a very pessimistic conclusion about police reform. This is because the increasingly negative attitudes towards the public, the criminal justice system, management, and even the job itself, could be interpreted as the failure of the new recruit-training program to produce the 'reflective practitioner' and professional officer that it was designed to do. The survey data could be interpreted as evidence that once recruits left the police academy, they quickly became integrated with the cynical 'street-cop culture'. The surveys, however, only told one side of the story. Our interviews with recruits and our observation in the field painted a much more nuanced and dynamic picture of how recruits interacted with operational police officers. First of all, consistent with the theoretical framework adopted, operational police culture was not homogeneous: recruits' training experience varied according to the work styles of their partners, supervisors, and managers. Second, recruits were generally much more discerning about role models than the traditional conception of socialization would suggest. In fact, they were much more reflective and strategic in their action than we had expected:

> Recruits' lack of confidence and practical experience when they first entered the operational field made [the FTO's] criticisms [of academy training] particularly poignant. Their desire to 'fit in' and be accepted by operational police also meant that they would never openly contradict these criticisms. But when we interviewed probationers away from the field, some of them admitted that the negative view of the Academy was partly perpetrated by officers in the field—a fact confirmed by our observation during Phase 4 … A few recruits told us that they did not agree with these criticisms of the Academy. They thought that the Academy provided the basic knowledge which could then be drawn upon in the field. They felt

that there was a place for theoretical knowledge and Academy training was not meant to replace field training, which was where practical training was supposed to take place ...

Probationers also commented on how workers adapted to the inconsistent styles and expectations of different shift supervisors and shift partners. Probationers' adaptations to their work environment did not consist of blanket acceptance of everything they were told in the field. When given the opportunity to express their views, some probationers were quite willing to criticise and distance themselves from certain practices. Individual probationers formed judgments about police work and the police organization based on their own experiences and were able to distinguish between 'good' and 'bad' models. Some interviewees felt that having been exposed to different policing styles, they could make up their own mind about the type of police they want to become. This was true especially of older probationers (Chan et al., 2003: 307–8).

Third, we were able to mobilize other documentary evidence to describe changes in the field of policing – in particular, the impact of the Royal Commission – and relate them to the interview and survey data which indicated changes in the way the cohort members viewed corruption, professional integrity and solidarity issues. As a result of these major political and regulatory changes in the field of policing, both police culture and the socialization process were shifting: while police were more willing to formally report misconduct because they could lose their job if they were found to have been involved in a cover-up, they were also unsure about the nature of 'the game' because rules were constantly changing.

Another major advantage of the longitudinal approach is that we got to know the recruits and, in many cases, gained their trust to the extent that they would tell us about their experience in a much more honest and open way than if they were interviewed only once. This was especially salient when we launched the follow-up study: we had no idea what the response rate would be, and was in fact quite pleasantly surprised that over 40 of the 118 officers who remained in the police organization were willing to talk to us after almost a decade. This trust also allowed us to ask the cohort to talk openly about police culture at the fourth interview:

These accounts are unusual in that researchers have traditionally derived notions of police culture from their observation of police officers in action (e.g. Skolnick 1966; Ericson 1981, 1982). Some of these were insiders' accounts as the researchers were themselves former police officers

(e.g. Holdaway 1983; Young 1991). It has been rare, however, for researchers to actually ask serving police to define and describe police culture. Since recruits had been quite willing to share their experience with us over the two years, it seemed natural to tackle the topic directly with them. Given the frequent mention of 'police culture' in the Fitzgerald and Wood inquiries, the term would have been familiar to every Australian police officer. We were confident that recruits would want to have a say about this topic. As it turned out, our questions generated some extremely thoughtful responses and important insights (Chan et al., 2003: 248–9).

METHODOLOGICAL CHALLENGES

The project faced many methodological challenges. These include the validity of findings given the problem of access, issues of reliability and causality, and the challenges of analyzing the large volume of qualitative data.

Access and validity

First, it was always going to be difficult for academic outsiders to penetrate a close-knit organization to examine its culture and work practices. So the study of police culture was very likely to be inhibited by the culture itself. For example, we wondered whether the logistical difficulties we experienced in fieldwork were part of the paranoia, secrecy, siege mentality and cynicism often associated with police culture. The financial and moral support of police executives did make the research possible and get researchers a foot in the door, but it could not guarantee an easy passage at the operational level. In a sense this, too, was consistent with a street-cop culture that was suspicious of management whose endorsement of our research only made it more worthy of resistance. As it turned out, focusing on recruits was a very good way to both gain access to the organization and understand the complexity of the socialization process. By listening to the accounts of new recruits and observing their experiences, we were guided through the labyrinth of this large and somewhat closed organization to places and moments of interest in recruits' socialization journey. But as our recruits became more integrated into their new workplace, the rapport we had built up at the beginning of the study appeared to fade: response rates of surveys and interviews showed a gradual decline[1], and an invisible wall eventually came between us. We will never find out whether the failure of the vast majority of recruits to hold on to the unique identification number they were assigned for the surveys was a symptom of their paranoia about us or simply an unrealistic expectation on our part. Similarly, we will never know whether the experiences and opinions of the non-respondents were the same or very different from those of the respondents. Nevertheless, the response rates for the original study were very good for research of this kind; even those for the follow-up study were quite acceptable given the amount of time that had elapsed since the last contact.

Reliability

Another methodological challenge related to inter-observer reliability. Fieldworkers' ability to establish rapport with the police could vary by age, sex, ethnicity, skills and experience, and as a result, the type and quality of information they obtained could also vary substantially (Chan et al., 2003: chapter 2). There were, however, trade-offs in advantages between young graduates and highly experienced researchers. For example, I consider myself an experienced field researcher, but it was obvious that the presence of an older female academic of Chinese descent in the back seat of a police car was not necessarily the most effective way to put officers at ease. Most officers were polite and tried to be on their best behaviour; others were determined to show me some 'action' as in a gratuitous high-speed chase on one shift. In contrast, a young male social science graduate established such excellent rapport with male officers that they regularly talked about sex and swore in his presence. In general:

> Experienced researchers may have an advantage in their ability to 'see' what inexperienced researchers do not; at the same time, their age and maturity can act as barriers in dealing with younger subjects. Similarly, familiarity with the concepts, jargon, and procedures of the group being studied can be an asset in field observation … Yet familiarity can also be a handicap when researchers fail to notice, let alone explore the meanings and complexities of taken-for-granted assumptions and concepts (Chan et al., 2003: 57).

There is no doubt that fieldworkers' presence had an impact on officers' speech and action, and there is always going to be a question as to the authenticity of what we observed. Ethnographic researchers who spend a long period of time with one group of subjects are more likely to capture typical behaviour because it is difficult for people to put up false appearances over time. This is an advantage not available for our study as we

decided to sample shifts and subjects to ensure a representative coverage. The use of multiple sources of data was one way to improve the validity of our findings.

Internal validity

The issue of internal validity or causality can be a vexed issue with longitudinal studies (Chan et al., 2003: chapter 2). In other words, we could not conclude that the changes in attitudes among recruits over time were caused by their socialization into the prevailing police culture because of the usual factors such as history, maturation, mortality and testing (Campbell and Stanley, 1963). For example, these changes could equally have been caused by the changes in political conditions due to the Royal Commission, the appointment of a new police commissioner, or the major reforms to the accountability structures and processes which all happened during the research project. Similarly, the maturation of the recruits, the attrition of the cohort, and the repeated use of questionnaire items could all have resulted in changes not caused by the socialization process. Attrition was particularly salient for the follow-up study where about 20 per cent of the original cohort were no longer working in the police force. In the original study we tried to contact those who left to find out more about their reasons for leaving, but we were not able to secure any interviews after repeated requests. It was impossible to include this group in the follow-up study because we did not have their current contact information. Once again, these issues did not affect the validity of our findings because our analysis was based on multiple sources of data as well as a theoretical framework that conceptualized police attitudes and practices in a dynamic and relational way, taking into account the changing field of policing.

Qualitative analysis

A final methodological challenge not often discussed by researchers is the volume of qualitative data generated by research of this kind. With nearly 240 interviews and 900 hours of observation in the original study, we were faced with over 5,000 pages of transcripts and field notes to analyze. It is obvious that any systematic analysis of this volume of data would require a great deal of work, which, as it often happens, has to be done after the project funding has run out. My experience over many projects has also shown that it is very difficult to share the task of qualitative analysis among team members as the same text could be interpreted in different ways by different researchers. The selection of excerpts from interview transcripts and field notes to be included in subsequent publications requires the art of compromise: researchers are constrained by word limits in journals and books and have to make a choice between breadth and depth. To represent the full breadth of the study, there will never be sufficient space for more than a sampling of the research findings in an inevitably decontextualized way. On the other hand, a fully contextualized and in-depth examination of a small segment of the research may not do justice to the variations that exist across the whole study. We struck a compromise by using quantitative data to provide an overview of the distribution of responses which were then filled out by the presentation of qualitative data. Even so, we were asked by the editor to cut about one-third of the qualitative material from the manuscript because the book became too long and repetitive. Although researchers may be justifiably reluctant to relinquish 'choice quotes' from their precious data, the editor's advice turned out to be a sensible one, as the book actually benefited from a more parsimonious use of qualitative data: less can be more when communicating results to readers.

LEGAL AND ETHICAL ISSUES

A number of legal and ethical issues arose in the study. In Chan et al. we discussed the ambiguity of informed consent in a command-and-control organizational setting; we also discussed how we ensured that confidential information and the identity of the subjects were protected (2003: chapter 2). One issue not raised directly but of central concern at the time was the extent to which we were able to honour our undertaking to protect the identity of our subjects should they engage in misconduct while we were observing. Under the law, police officers have an obligation to report misconduct that they come across. I was well aware of the legal issues that police researchers such as Richard Ericson (1993/1981) and Richard Leo (1995) had encountered. Because the original project was conducted at the height of the Royal Commission, there was a distinct possibility that the data could have been subpoenaed by the Royal Commission. To protect the identity of the subjects, research assistants were given instructions to write field notes in such a way that names of police station, suburb, and officers encountered during fieldwork were replaced by codes such as officer X or [suburb], although a confidential master list existed that documented the date, location, and name of the recruit being observed.

Another important legal issue was the safety of fieldworkers. At the time of the research, the university did not have any written guidelines on fieldwork safety, but this was something we clearly needed to consider. As pointed out in Chan et al. (2003), the following precautions were taken:

> The NSW Police Service (NSWPS) was protected from legal liability in relation to the fieldworkers by an indemnity signed by the University of New South Wales. Observers were instructed to follow the advice of the police they were attached to in terms of safety issues and exclusion from particular situations. Many patrol commanders, shift supervisors and contact personnel instructed the officers to treat observers as student police officers in terms of safety and procedure: they were to be dropped off if there was a high speed chase, or if room had to be made for an offender to be transported in the car. Observers were advised to always have sufficient taxi money for such situations (Chan et al., 2003: 50).

High speed driving was one of the hazards fieldworkers encountered. In about 10 per cent of the 115 shifts we observed, fieldworkers commented on the 'very high speed' or dangerousness of the driving, with the speed of the patrol car at 170 km per hour in one instant (Chan et al., 2003: 321, note 8). Box 20.2 illustrates an instance of such dangerous driving behaviour on the part of the senior partner in the patrol team. In this case, the observer, a social science graduate and a former police officer, was so traumatized by the experience that she decided to quit the project, citing safety as the primary reason. This was a disappointing outcome as the project lost an excellent fieldworker, who could have gone on to become a fine police researcher, as was her ambition. Apart from highlighting the danger of fieldwork, the incident revealed a serious deficiency in the field training of police recruits at the time: there was obviously no mechanism to control the quality of officers who were, in effect, role models for new recruits.

A final ethical issue arose after the completion of the follow-up study. It would have been logical and interesting to document the 'life stories' of the police officers over the ten-year period since their recruitment. Such real-life case studies are rare in police research and would have made a valuable contribution to the literature. However, once I started compiling these life stories, it became clear that the details would have identified the officers involved and in some cases caused damage to their reputation. Given that both the name of the police organization and the starting year of the original study were published facts, it would

---

Box 20.2   Excerpts from fieldnotes (Chan et al., 2003: 182–4)

[The probationer and her partner constable C were called to attend a robbery]. C was driving and he reversed the vehicle at high speed down the driveway that ran beside the police station. He reversed the vehicle straight across the pedestrian footpath without even slowing or checking for anybody who may have been walking along the footpath. He then proceeded to drive (with lights and sirens activated) at high speed up a main road towards the small shopping centre where the alleged robbery had taken place. During this time he frequently went onto the wrong side of the road and directly into the path of oncoming vehicles. The traffic was quite heavy and it was obvious that other road users were confused or unaware of where the police car was coming from. He was driving in a frenzied state and seemed to be oblivious to the danger he was posing to other road users. C drove through two red lights with only a cursory attempt to slow down. If at any stage another vehicle had been approaching or moving through these intersections C would have certainly caused a major accident.

   When we reached the small shopping centre C started yelling out to [the probationer] PC that he didn't know where the take-away shop was located. It appeared that in his frenzied departure from the police station he had neglected to get the address of the shop. We drove past all the shops but we couldn't see a sign of any disturbance. By this stage C was hunched over the wheel, with no seat belt on, and was obviously completely obsessed with capturing the armed robbers. It was obvious to me that anybody who had robbed the shop would have been long gone as such an offence is usually committed within a matter of minutes. This fact seemed to have completely escaped C who was in a state of extreme agitation.

   At this point C must have decided that he was looking for the shop in the wrong shopping centre. As it happened there was another small shopping centre about one km down the road from where we were currently looking. C did a U-turn and then proceeded to head in the direction of this other shopping centre. The road that led to these shops was a main two-lane roadway. There was about a 1/2 km steep downhill run before the road went up and over a crest (with traffic lights on top of this crest). The shops we were heading towards were on the other side of the crest. C drove down this road at extremely high speed and as we were heading down a steep hill the vehicle gathered an excessive amount of speed.

   As C was hunched directly over the steering wheel I could not see the speedometer but I could see that he was pushing the vehicle to its maximum speed. I estimate from the shuddering of the vehicle that we were going 120-140 km per hour. As the vehicle was a caged Hi Lux truck it was therefore not a stable vehicle at extremely high speeds. At this point in time C had exceeded the point of acting in a rational manner in the execution of his duties. He was driving in a highly dangerous manner which put at risk the lives of those in the police vehicle and the lives of other road users. He was driving at such an excessive speed that he was not in proper control of the vehicle. At such a speed loss of control of the vehicle would most certainly have resulted in fatalities. At the crest of the hill the traffic lights were red. C was going so fast that his cursory touch on the brakes would have been insufficient to stop the vehicle in time had any other vehicle been at those lights. Upon reaching the shops at the end of the road all was quiet. C again turned the vehicle around and drove in exactly the same dangerous manner back to the original shops from where we had come. As we reached these shops we saw [another police car] parked outside a take away shop and the police manning that vehicle were inside the shop taking details from the victim of the robbery … In summary, C had driven in such a manner as to exceed all his powers as a police officer. Urgent duty runs are undertaken only by the consent and courtesy of other road users and the police have no legal dispensation to exceed the speed limit or disobey traffic lights. C acted irrationally and illegally. He had no right to endanger other people's lives for his own personal gratification in seeking to come face to face with alleged armed robbers. It appeared that he was unable to rationalise his actions and weigh up risk versus outcome. Apart from this, his actions clearly indicated his total unsuitability for a role in training new police.

---

be difficult to conceal the identity of the officers from others in the organization if full facts of their sex, age, current rank and duty, as well as details of their career trajectory were described. It may be possible to alter some of the characteristics in order to protect officers' identity, but the authenticity of the life stories would be compromised. Besides, some characteristics, such as ethnicity or Aboriginality, are extremely central to the life stories, but at the same time highly identifying.

The frankness of some of our subjects had meant that sensitive personal issues were discussed in interviews, and even though these issues had bearing on their attitudes, motivations, practices and career trajectories, it would be unethical to reveal them if there was a possibility that their identities could be disclosed. I have not been able to resolve these ethical dilemmas, and as a result, the life stories of recruits have remained an unfinished project.

NEW HORIZONS

This chapter has described our experience of designing and implementing a major empirical study of police culture and socialization in Australia. The uniqueness of the project is its ability to study police socialization and police cultures over an extended period of time and in considerable depth. The successful use of mixed methods in a longitudinal design suggests that researching police culture could benefit from combining ethnographic and quantitative data, comparing direct observation with self-report accounts, and taking into consideration both structures and processes that inform the constitution, maintenance or change of organizational culture.

The challenges we encountered, while substantial, are not uncommon in any large-scale project involving longitudinal tracking and the coordination of a team of researchers. There are, of course, issues peculiar to the study of police organizations: the challenge of penetrating a close-knit occupation generally suspicious of outsiders, and the difficulty of eliciting frank views among members whose principal reflex is to protect themselves. Reflecting on the experience of this project years later, I recognize that we were extremely lucky to have been given permission as well as resources to conduct such a unique and groundbreaking study of the socialization of a class of recruits. We were also fortunate that the organizational and political upheaval brought about by the Royal Commission had made it possible for us to observe the diversity, fluidity and shifting nature of police culture in a changing field.

Whether police organizations will continue to be open to the scrutiny of researchers is a very important question for the future of police research. Police research has had a long and illustrious history of scholarly writing and methodological innovation. In part this remarkable history is due to the hard work and brilliance of policing scholars, who have gone to great lengths to immerse themselves in and make sense of a culture quite unlike their own and distil from their fieldwork useful insights and elegant theorizing of what they saw. On the other hand, these achievements would not have been possible without the willingness of police organizations to open their doors, to take the risk of having the behaviours and attitudes of their members scrutinized by outsiders. This takes courage on the part of police leaders and cooperation (or, at the very least, tolerance) on the part of rank-and-file officers. Police researchers must not forget that they are themselves operating within the field of policing. Their symbolic capital as researchers is dependent on the perceived integrity, rigour and usefulness of their work. Being allowed to enter the field is a great privilege, but such a privilege cannot be taken for granted. When the field of policing becomes politicized, when police legitimacy is challenged, or when researchers are critical of police practice, police organizations can become defensive and uncooperative. Ironically, this is precisely the time when police organizations are in need of high quality independent advice based on solid research. For the sake of both the future of policing and the future of police research, researchers and police should keep their doors ajar, if not widely open.

NOTE

1 Response rates for the five questionnaire surveys were: 99, 89 and 96, 60 and 34 per cent, the last two being mail-out surveys. Response rates for the five rounds of interviews were: 99, 89, 89, 87 and 36 per cent.

RECOMMENDED READING

Interested readers may wish to consult:

Marks, M. (2004) 'Researching Police Transformation: The Ethnographic Imperative' *British Journal of Criminology* 44: 866–888, for a lively and sobering analysis of the challenges of field research in policing.

Mastrofski, S.D., Parks, R.B., Reiss, A.J. Jr, Worden, R.E., DeJong, C., Snipes, J.B. and Terrill, W. (1998) *Systematic Observation of Public Police: Applying Field Research Methods to Policy Issues* (Washington: National Institute of Justice) for a useful guide for conducting systematic observation in a team.

Van Maanen, J. (ed.) (1983) *Qualitative Methodology* (Beverly Hills: Sage) for a theoretically informed discussion of the variety of qualitative methodologies useful for organizational research.

Van Maanen, J. (1988) *Tales of the Field: On Writing Ethnography* (Chicago: University of Chicago Press) for the art of writing about cultures.

REFERENCES

Bittner, E. (1967) 'The Police on Skid Row', *American Sociological Review* 32: 699–715.

Black, D. (1971) 'The Social Organization of Arrest', *Stanford Law Review* 23: 1087–1111.

Bourdieu, P. and Wacquant, L.J.D. (1992) *An Invitation to Reflexive Sociology.* Cambridge: Polity Press.

Campbell, D.T. and Stanley, J.C. (1963) *Experimental and Quasi-Experimental Designs for Research.* Boston: Houghton Mifflin Company.

Chan J. (1996) 'Changing Police Culture', *British Journal of Criminology* 36(1): 109–134.

Chan, J. (1997) *Changing Police Culture: Policing in a Multicultural Society.* Melbourne: Cambridge University Press.

Chan, J. (2001) 'Negotiating the Field: New Observations on the Making of Police Officers', *Australia and New Zealand Journal of Criminology* 34(2): 114–133.

Chan, J. (2007a) 'Making Sense of Police Reforms', *Theoretical Criminology* 11(3): 323–345.

Chan, J. (2007b) 'Police stress and occupational culture', in M. O'Neill, M. Marks and A.-M. Singh (eds) *Police Occupational Culture: New Debates and Directions.* Oxford: Elsevier, pp. 129–151.

Chan, J., with Devery, C. and Doran, S. (2003) *Fair Cop: Learning the Art of Policing.* Toronto: University of Toronto Press.

Chan, J. and Doran, S. (2009) 'Staying in the Job: Job Satisfaction among Mid-Career Police Officers', *Policing: A Journal of Policy and Practice* 3(1): 66–77.

Cicourel, A.V. (1967) *The Social Organization of Juvenile Justice.* New York: John Wiley and Sons.

Doob, A.N. and Chan, J. (1982) 'Factors Affecting Police Decisions to Take Juveniles to Court', *Canadian Journal of Criminology* 24(1): 25–37.

Dixon, D. (2011) 'Reflecting on Fieldwork in Comparative Policing', in L. Bartels and K. Richards (eds) *Qualitative Criminology: Stories from the Field.* Sydney: Federation Press, pp. 230-241.

Ericson, R.V. (1982) *Reproducing Order: A Study of Police Patrol Work.* Toronto: University of Toronto Press.

Ericson, R.V. (1993) *Making Crime: A Study of Detective Work*, 2nd Edition. Toronto: University of Toronto Press. (First published in 1981 by Butterworth).

Ericson, R.V. and Haggerty, K. (1997) *Policing the Risk Society.* Toronto: University of Toronto Press; Oxford: Oxford University Press.

Fielding, N. (1988) *Joining Forces: Police Training, Socialization, and Occupational Competence.* London: Routledge.

Fitzgerald Report (1989) *Report of the Commission of Inquiry Pursuant to Orders in Council dated (1) 26 May 1987; (2) 24 June 1987; (3) 25 August 1988; (4) 29 June 1989.* Brisbane: Queensland Government Printer.

Goldsmith, A. (1990) 'Taking Police Culture Seriously: Police Discretion and the Limits of Law', *Policing and Society* 1: 91–114.

Herbert, S. (1997) *Policing Space: Territoriality and the Los Angeles Police Department.* Minneapolis: University of Minneapolis Press.

Herbert, S. (1998) 'Police Subculture Reconsidered', *Criminology* 36: 343–369.

Holdaway, S. (1983) *Inside British Police.* Oxford: Basil Blackwell.

Huey, L. (2007) *Negotiating Demands: The Politics of Skid Row Policing in Edinburgh, San Francisco, and Vancouver.* Toronto: University of Toronto Press.

Leo, R. (1995) 'Trial and Tribulations: Courts, Ethnography, and the Need for an Evidentiary Privilege for Academic Researchers' *The American Sociologist,* 26(1): 113–134.

Manning, P. (1997) *Police Work: The Social Organization of Policing*, 2nd Edition. Prospect Heights: Waveland Press. (First edition 1977).

Marks, M. (2004) 'Researching Police Transformation: The Ethnographic Imperative', *British Journal of Criminology* 44: 866–888.

Marks, M. (2005) *Transforming Robocops: Changing Police in South Africa.* Scottsville: University of KwaZulu-Natal Press.

Parks, R.B., Mastrofski, S.D., DeJong, C. and Gray, M.K. (1999) 'How Officers Spend Their Time with the Community', *Justice Quarterly* 16: 483–518.

Reiss, A. (1971) *The Police and the Public.* New Haven: Yale University Press.

Shearing, C.D. and Ericson, R.V. (1991) 'Culture as Figurative Action', *British Journal of Sociology* 42: 481–506.

Skolnick, J.H. (1966) *Justice Without Trial: Law Enforcement in a Democratic Society.* New York: John Wiley and Sons.

Van Maanen, J. (1973) 'Observations on the Making of Policemen', *Human Organization* 32(4): 407–418.

Westley, W.A. (1970) *Violence and the Police: A Sociological Study of Law, Custom and Morality.* Cambridge, MA: MIT Press.

Young, M. (1991) *An Inside Job: Policing and Police Culture in Britain.* Oxford: Oxford University Press.

21

Quasi-experimental Research on Community Policing

Wesley G. Skogan

INTRODUCTION

This chapter describes an evaluation of community policing in Chicago. Although Chicago was
not the first city in the US to adopt community
policing, it is among the largest. The city developed a program that reorganized the work of
patrol officers to tie them more closely to the community, incorporated the public in identifying
priority neighborhood problems, and coordinated
the work of an array of city agencies in order to
address those problems. It was dubbed 'CAPS',
for Chicago's Alternative Policing Strategy. After
a brief planning period the program began in 5 (of
25) test police districts in April 1993. By March
1995, important elements of the initiative were in
place throughout the city. A team of academic
researchers headquartered at Northwestern
University, which is close to Chicago, became
involved in evaluating this effort during its planning phase. Over the years more than 75 faculty
students and researchers worked on the evaluation. Regular reports and three books resulted
from the project. The first (Skogan and Hartnett,
1997) analyzes the political origins of the program, its planning and implementation, how the
city staffed and paid for it, and the impact of community policing in the five test districts where it
was first set in motion. The second (Skogan et al.,
1999) assesses the program's problem-solving
component. It presents a detailed, on-the-ground
description of police and community problem
solving efforts in 15 selected areas of the city. The
final book (Skogan, 2006) describes the development of community policing in Chicago over a

12-year span, and examines trends in crime, fear
and satisfaction with policing in the city's diverse
neighborhoods.[1]

This was not the first evaluation of neighborhood-
oriented policing, or something resembling it. In
the early 1980s I was involved in studying a precursor to many of the community policing programs that came later. In that project, police in
Houston, Texas, and Newark, New Jersey, tried to
engage with the public by opening storefront
offices, distributing newsletters, and going door to
door to inquire about local problems. In Houston,
a team of officers was trained in community
organizing, and another provided new support for
crime victims. Newark experimented with foot
patrols, a neighborhood clean up, opening schools
at night to provide recreational opportunities for
youths, and aggressive order maintenance efforts
on busses and busy street corners (Pate et al.,
1986).

The research design and many of the survey
questionnaires our team used in Chicago drew
from that experience. So too did our interest in the
impact of community-oriented policing on a broad
range of outcomes, including fear of crime, disorder reduction, physical decay and community
self-help. It was apparent in both Houston and
Newark that engaging the public brought new
issues to the fore, and that a narrow focus on traditional measures of crime victimization would
miss many important aspects of 'public safety'
more broadly conceived. The evaluation strategies
employed in Houston and Newark influenced
ensuing studies of community-oriented policing
in a long list of cities. The findings of many of

these investigations, which took place between 1986 and 1990, are summarized in Skogan (1994).

Many more studies of community policing appeared in the 1990s, but they were released only after we had launched our work in Chicago. As we began, the Vera Foundation published an evaluation of the assignment of dedicated neighborhood officers in New York City (McElroy et al., 1993), and Sadd and Grinc (1993) issued a comparison of community policing projects in eight US cities. Studies then appeared describing projects in Australia, Britain and Canada. In the UK, Trevor Bennett (1991) evaluated a pioneering fear-reduction project that was conducted in both Birmingham and London. Fifteen years later, the Home Office was busily replicating many aspects of the program and the evaluation in communities all over England and Wales (Quinton and Tuffin, 2007). Meanwhile, an edited collection by Dennis Rosenbaum (1994) provided an outlet for a large number of studies that had been completed but were as yet unpublished.

As all of this research activity suggests, community policing was being widely adopted. The concept was proving immensely popular with the public, and thus with politicians, and as a result few police chiefs wanted to be caught without adopting something they could point to and call community policing. Chicago was no exception.

This chapter describes the evaluation and some of what we found. Early sections introduce the evaluation and the program, and review the kinds of data we gathered to assess its major components. There is a discussion of general issues that drove the design and execution of the project. A final section places the findings for Chicago in larger context, comparing them with the results of evaluations of other community policing initiatives.

THE EVALUATION

Because of its magnitude, the developmental nature of the project, and its decentralized character, it was important to understand what the program actually looked like in the field, as well as to systematically assess how effectively it addressed the city's problems. These twin interests called for two kinds of evaluations, and we did both.

Process evaluations examine program design and implementation. They document a program's 'theory', or how its developers thought it was supposed to have an impact. Process evaluations also document the actual implementation of the program, for there is often a gap between plans and reality. Uncovering what really happened on the

ground is particularly important in the case of community policing. In Chicago, as in many cities, the program involved decentralizing authority and responsibility, moving it out of police headquarters and down the organizational hierarchy. Especially in the early years, this inevitably led the program in different directions, depending upon neighborhood conditions. It turned out that sometimes we knew more than the senior management about how key elements of the program were evolving. At the same time, community policing challenged many deeply rooted 'business as usual' aspects of the organization. The program was not initiated by the department; rather, it was imposed on it by the city's political leaders, who were responding to public concern about crime and dissatisfaction with policing in the city. Thus there was ample reason to fear that officers and commanders would fall back upon their familiar routines when no one was watching, and our early reports frequently concluded that the organization was not properly structured to ensure that the city's plan was actually being carried out. It almost collapsed in 1999, and our report that year warned that 'CAPS is dead in the water'. The ensuing crisis lead to a successful re-engineering of supervision and accountability processes in the organization, and the program weathered the storm.

Impact evaluations analyze the effects that programs have on the problems that they target, and look to see if they have unexpected or unintended consequences as well. As I describe below, one thing we feared was that there would be unequal outcomes by race. The strength of an impact evaluation is dependent upon its design and how well it measures what the program might accomplish. This chapter describes how we took advantage of the trial run of the program in a few districts, plus a (rare) opportunity to gather benchmark data before the program actually began, to assess the impact of community policing in a diverse set of neighborhoods. Later, after the program expanded to encompass the entire city, the evaluation focused in detail on how specific components of the program were working, while it continued to monitor trends on a broad set of outcome measures.

THE PROGRAM

Police departments embracing community policing typically adopt three inter-related organizational strategies: they (a) decentralize and adopt a local neighborhood orientation, (b) facilitate community input in defining and prioritizing their activities, and (c) adopt a broadly focused, problem solving orientation toward their work. CAPS encompassed all three of these program elements.

Decentralization

Chicago's first move was to reorganize the work of its patrol officers to support community policing. Small teams of officers (usually nine, plus part of the time of a supervising sergeant) were given round-the-clock responsibility for each of the city's 279 small police beats. The emergency 911 system was reconfigured, effectively restructuring the daily routines of thousands of patrol officers. The system prioritizes dispatching in a way that keeps team officers concentrated on their beat, often with some 'unassigned' time available for getting out of their cars to attend meetings and talk with residents, merchants and building managers. Officers assigned to beat teams are expected to engage in identifying and dealing with a broad range of neighborhood problems in partnership with neighborhood residents, community organizations and other city agencies. Beat team officers regularly attend public meetings that are held monthly with local residents. There they review their progress on problems and discuss emergent issues. Other police units were decentralized, so that local commanders had somewhat more control over investigators and gang-crime specialists and could integrate their efforts with plans being developed at the grassroots level.

One tool for evaluating how this new turf orientation was working was surveys of police officers. During the course of the evaluation we surveyed about 13,600 police officers, some undoubtedly more than once. To control our costs, questionnaires were distributed in group settings, either at the roll-call meetings held when officer's shifts began or when they gathered for training sessions. We found that officers surveyed before the program began were quite dubious about the community policing enterprise, as were their immediate supervisors, but that both groups grew more positive over time. At almost every point their reactions to community policing were tied to race; African-American officers were the most optimistic about CAPS, while white officers were more skeptical by a very large margin. White officers felt welcome at public meetings where most of the residents attending were white, but otherwise were uneasy. Latino officers felt less welcome at meetings hosting a large proportion of Spanish-speaking Latinos; apparently, Spanish-speakers in attendance were making heavy demands on them. On the other hand, the views of African-American officers were unaffected by the racial composition of the meetings they attended, and a large majority

felt welcome everywhere. Initially, most officers suspected that other city agencies would not help out with their problem-solving projects, but later reported that they did. Over time, the surveys revealed a host of program glitches; for example, that sergeants were not intervening to make the new dispatching system work, and the brief meetings that were to be held between team officers beginning and ending their work shifts were a waste of time.

We used data on individual police officers to monitor the department's ability to manage the process of linking beat officers with community residents. An anticipated feature of CAPS was that residents would come to know the officers who regularly attend beat meetings, and the officers would also be the ones that answered calls and could be seen around the neighborhood. On their part, beat team officers needed to stay in one place long enough for residents to meet and learn to trust them. Time would also help officers develop a personal sense of 'ownership' of their turf and develop an ethos of teamwork.

However, police in Chicago regularly bid for their district and shift assignment by seniority. In addition, personnel transfers, vacations, relief duties, court appearances, and compensatory time off made it hard to maintain staffing stability. The resulting turnover of officers from public meeting to public meeting did not go unnoticed, and both regular attendees and community organizations periodically complained about it. To assess the department's ability to make stable assignments happen, we examined the brief reports that are filed about each beat meeting and recorded the unique employee identification number of each officer listed as present. For example, during 1998, an average of five to seven police attended each beat meeting, and during the course of the year 4,650 different officers showed up for at least one meeting. Beats meet an average of ten times per year, so officers were classified as 'regular participants' if they attended at least five meetings in a beat during that period, a generous standard. By this standard, 14 percent of beats did not have any regular officers at all. We judged that only one-third of the beats had adequate personnel stability, with at least five officers attending meetings regularly. Continuity of officer participation in beat meetings was far from random. In particular, poor African-American areas least often had a full compliment of regular participants; only 26 percent of those beats had five regularly attending officers. Beats in predominately Latino areas did not do much better (28 percent). Better-off African-American beats did better still; 42 percent of those beats saw a large complement of officers on a regular basis. On the other hand, more than 60 percent of predominately white, middle-income beats had five or more police officers attending meetings on a regular basis.

We tried to use data on emergency calls from the dispatching center to assess stability of assignment, but it was in terrible shape. Until the late 1990s, information on each call and dispatch was handwritten and passed around the dispatching center on paper slips, then later punched on cards for bulk processing on a computer with vacuum tubes. Neither we nor the police could get a clear handle on the effectiveness of CAPS' reorganization of the dispatching of beat teams until they acquired new information-processing capacity. The goal was to keep beat teams on their beat 70 percent of the time, and the actual figure turned out to be 68 percent.

Engaging with the public

In Chicago, the primary mechanism that police have for engaging with the public is beat meetings. These are regular – usually monthly – gatherings of small groups of residents and a number of the officers who actually work in the beat. The meetings are held at night in church basements, park buildings and hospital cafeterias all over the city. During the evaluation an average of 6,700 residents attended about 250 meetings each month. They met with an average of five to seven police officers, most of whom regularly patrol in the area. Police serving in specialized units, such as gang teams or detectives, are often present as well, along with a representative of the district's neighborhood relations unit. Meetings are sometimes attended by representatives of the city's service departments and area community organizations, and the local aldermen's staff. Most meetings are co-led by a civilian recruited from the neighborhood. The meetings provide a forum for exchanging information and identifying, analyzing and prioritizing problems in an area. Local crime maps, lists of the most frequent crimes on the beat, and other informational materials are distributed at the meetings, following a printed agenda. There is always a discussion of what has happened with regard to issues raised at the last meeting, and this provides a bit of community oversight of police activity. The new business segment of the meetings focuses on identifying new issues and debating whether they are general problems or just the concern of one resident. Beat meetings are also a very convenient place to distribute announcements about upcoming community events, circulate petitions, and call for volunteers to participate in action projects. Importantly, they also provide occasions for residents and the officers who work in the area and will likely answer their calls to get acquainted.

One very important evaluation question was, 'What actually goes on at beat meetings?' This was a difficult and expensive question to answer. Because they are held night after night in hundreds of locations all over the city, it is hard even for the police department to know what is going on. An officer who attends fills out a brief form reporting the number of people who came and summarizes what was talked about, but not much information is recorded, and other observers might have a different view of what transpired. Our city-wide surveys asked respondents if they had attended a beat meeting in the past year, and in a typical year about 22 percent of adult Chicagoans indicated they had. The surveys found that a very large majority of them thought the meetings were useful and led to improvements in their neighborhood, but they could tell us few details about how the meetings actually functioned.

In order to examine the dynamics of beat meetings more closely, observers working on the evaluation attended hundreds of them between 1995 and 2002. They completed forms recording specific details about the sessions, including where it was located and how long it lasted. They counted the number of police and residents who attended, by race and sex. They reported on the languages that were spoken and the kinds of printed materials that were distributed. Using a checklist, they noted the issues that were raised by residents during the course of the meeting. They noted which participants identified problems and solutions to problems that were discussed. The observers were trained to make judgments about such matters as how effectively police and civilian leaders conducted the meetings, and they classified the roles played by police and other city employees. The previous description of what happens at beat meetings was drawn from the resulting data.

In addition, we surveyed participants at the meetings on several occasions. At a prearranged moment the observers rose, explained who they were, and distributed questionnaires to both the police and residents who were in attendance. In 1998, observers attended one meeting each in 253 beats and surveyed 5,293 residents and 1,050 officers. In 2002 they observed two or three (if we could) meetings in each of a random sample of 130 beats, and surveyed 3,495 residents and 643 officers. A 1995 study involved 161 beats clustered in selected districts. The surveys asked about conditions in the beat, the quality of local police service, resident involvement in CAPS-related activities, how frequently they attended the meetings, and assessments of the meetings they had attended. The questionnaires for residents were available in both English and Spanish.

In the field, we found that, at the average meeting, about one-third of those in attendance were there for the first time, another third reported attending two to three meetings in the past year, and the remainder were loyal participants. But because they came frequently, the latter group accounted for a very large percentage of those who showed up in the course of a year. Compared to census reports on the composition of the beats, frequent attenders were older, did not have as many children at home, were more often retired, and were more likely to be long-term residents and homeowners. In short, there was an 'establishment bias' of major proportions in beat meeting involvement. However, a comparison of participants' ratings of neighborhood problems with the findings of surveys of residents of the same beat found that the meetings actually represented the interests of their 'constituencies' fairly well. We concluded that this was because 'small is beautiful'. Chicago's beats are small in population and geographically compact. Some of the residents attending meetings may be college graduates and others high school dropouts, but they still walk to the same bus or train stop and shop at the same supermarket. They pass by the same graffiti-clad schools and abandoned automobiles. Living together, their fates are linked to those of their neighbors despite differences among them.

Broadly focused problem solving

One of the most interesting aspects of community policing is that police departments find that they must take on a much broader range of issues than they did before, a consequence of opening themselves up to public input. At community meetings residents complain about bad buildings, noise and people draining their car radiators at the curb, not just about burglary. If police reply, 'But that's not our responsibility', and try to move on, no one will come to the next meeting. As a result, they need to find partners that can help them. These frequently include city departments responsible for health, housing, garbage collection, and even street lighting. From the beginning, the delivery of services in Chicago was linked to community policing. Procedures were developed to link agencies to requests for assistance from the beat teams and in response to complaints lodged at beat meetings. Officers were able quickly to mobilize building inspectors, street cleaners and repair trucks, and other city resources. They could easily get abandoned cars towed away, empty buildings boarded up, and vacant lots cleared of trash. Department employees orchestrate neighborhood cleanups and graffiti paint-outs by volunteers and city workers, and take note of burned-out street lights and trees that needed trimming. Police districts have 'problem-buildings officers' who inventory dilapidated and abandoned structures and track down property owners for civil prosecution over building, health, fire, sanitation, and business-license violations. This broad focus led us to include measures of physical deterioration on our checklist of program outcomes.

One of our tools for identifying changes in neighborhood conditions was a large-scale survey that involved interviewing, and later re-interviewing, randomly selected samples of residents. We were able to do this early on, before the program began, and then again while it was in operation in only a few police districts. The re-interviews thus enabled us to measure changes that took place following the introduction of the program, and in addition to compare those to over-time changes in areas where the program had yet to be introduced (there is more on this later). The surveys were conducted by telephone. This was principally a budgetary matter, but telephone surveys have advantages. We were able to re-contact sample numbers many times (as many as 22 times), enabling us to reach mobile and frequently-not-at-home individuals. We could also afford to re-contact households that initially refused to be involved in the study. Very importantly, it could be dangerous for interviewers to walk the streets of many of the neighborhoods we were studying, and evaluation staff safety considerations were always at the top of our checklists.

There are many advantages to two-wave surveys, in particular that they directly measure individual-level changes in attitudes and self-reported behavior. However, they typically suffer from significant attrition. Americans move frequently, especially so in high crime areas and immigrant communities, so the capacity of telephone surveys to successfully re-contact survey respondents after an extensive period of time is always limited. Across all areas we successfully contacted and re-interviewed 59 percent of the original survey respondents, which was about normal for paired interviews over an 18-month interval. We were least likely to find and re-interview Latinos, who are the youngest and most mobile component of the city's population. We adjusted the survey data to account for this attrition in several ways: by weighting the data we did collect using census estimates of the total population, and by controlling for the under-representation of groups in the statistical analysis.

A key role for the surveys was to gauge possible changes in the extent of crime, disorder and decay problems in each area. A survey is a good instrument for doing so, for many of the problems that concern residents are not captured by official record-keeping systems or are very poorly recorded when they are. For example, street drug dealing appears in official statistics only when arrests are made, and arrest numbers simply did not reflect the wide-open street drug markets that plagued several of our study neighborhoods. Graffiti is only rarely reported to police (most people do not connect it with making an emergency 911 call), and before CAPS began it was not dealt with even when they did call. No one in Chicago kept official statistics on problems like junk-strewn vacant lots and loose garbage in the alleys, but these concerned residents of some of the study neighborhoods a great deal. Using surveys enabled us to gather uniform and comparable measures of a broad mix of problems. Respondents were quizzed about a long list of specific issues that we anticipated would be problems in various parts of the city. Neighborhood residents were asked to rate each of them as 'a big problem', 'some problem' or 'no problem'. In addition, the surveys also measured the victimization experiences of those we questioned. This enabled us to assess changes in crimes like burglary, vandalism, street robbery, and auto theft. Because personal crime and car theft could take place virtually anywhere, the surveys had asked victims if the incident took place in their neighborhood or not, so this could be accounted for.

We also examined time-series trends in officially reported crime. Surveys in the five prototype districts found that auto thefts, burglary, and assault were among the public's top concerns, and we could track both official crime figures and survey reports of victimization by these crimes. This was not easy. In the early 1990s police databases were a mess. Department records were maintained on an aging mainframe computer and stored on reels of computer tape that kept breaking. Information on such vital points as the address of the offence was keyed in haphazardly, with many variations in spelling and abbreviations. We had to individually clean up many thousands of computer records for the early 1990s, before the department made our life simpler by acquiring a modern computer and database system.

The surveys documented the disparate character of community priorities across the five prototype areas. Only two problems were of virtually universal concern: street drug dealing was nominated among the top four problems in every area, and 'shooting and violence by gangs' was a leading problem in four of the five prototypes. Gangs and drugs are challenging issues that lay near the core of the city's crime problems in the 1990s. They present a difficult target for community policing and, indeed, policing strategies of any style. Otherwise, a wide range of problems were identified as particularly troubling, and many issues that loomed large in some areas were scarcely problems at all in other districts. In two areas car vandalism was near the top of the list, and in two others household vandalism ranked high. Auto theft, burglary, disruptions around schools, abandoned buildings and 'vacant lots filled with trash and junk' each stood near the top of the list in at least one district.

ISSUES DRIVING THE EVALUATION DESIGN

Chicago is large yet divided

The central city itself if home to almost three million residents, but most look to their immediate neighborhoods and identity groups when they decide how they are faring. The city is particularly segregated by race, and the racial composition of the city's neighborhoods provides a template that describes the distribution of almost every social ill. In 2009, African-Americans constituted about 35 percent of the population. A majority of them are poor, for beginning in the 1970s many better-off blacks migrated to close-in suburbs on the fringe of the city, searching for nicer, safer housing and schools. About 30 percent of the population is white. They are divided roughly evenly by lifestyle, with younger, more affluent and college-educated whites clustering by the lakeshore, while blue-collar and lower-middle class whites cling to the far reaches of the city proper, far from Lake Michigan. During the mid-2000s, Latinos passed whites to become the second largest group in the city. Along with a far-smaller number of Asians they are the only group that is growing, and it is quite possible that by 2012 or so Latinos will surpass African-Americans and become the largest group in the city. They are divided by immigration status. The numbers of newcomers and second-generation or more Latinos are both growing rapidly, but the flood of immigrants that came to Chicago from Mexico in the 1990s and 2000s has had the greatest impact on the growth of dense, Spanish language barrios (neighborhoods) around the city's core.

The contested nature of the city shaped the evaluation in fundamental ways. First, it was clear that we had to be able to be able to speak separately to the concerns of major population groups. They faced different problems, and the community activists and politicians who represented them would only be interested in findings that related to their constituencies. Instead of watching the program unfold in a few selected places, the evaluation needed to be based on large samples of residents, activists, patrol officers and police beats, so that the findings could describe general trends in Chicago *and* have enough detail to break out what was happening to its largest groups. While in-depth studies of individual neighborhoods, police teams or specific problem solving efforts might have been informative, it would have been difficult for us to conduct them in a sufficient number and variety of locations. What people wanted to know was what happened in their neighborhoods, or at least in their kind of community.

The contested character of the city also made it imperative that the evaluation consider the *distributive* consequences of community policing, and not just its overall impact. I knew from experience that community policing threatens to become polarized. Policing by consent can be difficult in places where the community is fragmented by race, class and lifestyle. If, instead of trying to find common interests in this diversity, the police deal mainly with elements of their own choosing, they will appear to be taking sides. It is very easy for them to focus on supporting those with whom they get along best and whose outlook they share. But as a result, the 'local priorities' that they represent will be those of some in the community, but not all. My evaluation of community policing projects in Houston found that the way in which programs in various areas were run favored whites, homeowners and established interests in the community. Police worked well with members of those groups, but less affluent residents did not hear about the programs and did not participate in them. The positive effects of community policing turned out to be confined to whites and homeowners; African-Americans and Latinos saw no visible change in their lives. As a result of this experience, at every turn we considered the possibility of differential outcomes by race and class.

Concern about distributional issues proved to be well founded. The main findings of the evaluation were reflected in the subtitle of my 2006 book, *A Tale of Three Cities*. In a nutshell, blacks, whites and Latinos began the program facing different problems, and their communities went in different directions over the course of the next decade. Conditions were initially worst in the city's African-American neighborhoods, but things improved there a great deal and they saw the most benefits from the program. Beat meeting participation was highest in black neighborhoods, and crime there dropped most. Satisfaction with police performance rose by 14 percentage points among generally skeptical blacks. Whites, on the other hand, were already well off, and there was not much room for them to show many gains. They could already get things done when they needed, through strong neighborhood organizations and political channels, and they were already

friendly with the police. But over the course of the 1990s things grew worse in the city's predominately Latino neighborhoods, and by the 2000s they were by some measures worse off than the blacks. The influx of immigrants from Mexico drove down wages and levels of education and home ownership. The Latino community cleaved in two during the 1990s. The poorer, more disorganized and immigrant segment grew faster and became more concentrated in new city barrios. Awareness of CAPS actually declined among Latinos, and few got involved in the program. In the end, the inability of the city to engage with its large and fast-growing immigrant Latino population was the biggest shortfall of community policing in Chicago. Police faced challenges thrown up by demographic turmoil and globalization of the economy in their own back yard, and they did not make much headway.

The evaluation was not an 'experiment'

Experiments, strictly speaking, demand a great deal of control on the part of the researcher. Experimenters must be able to control where or who gets the program, and they use this power to assign their subjects at random to program and control groups. They also control the intervention itself, determining who gets what 'treatment' and how much of it (the 'dosage') they receive. It is the ability of researchers to control who receives how much of what treatment, and thus to make unambiguous claims about their causal effects, that grants 'gold standard' status to randomized experiments in the social sciences. We had none of these powers.

What we had instead was a fairly brief time period – about 18 months – during which the police would be trying out their program plan in a few selected areas of the city, while in other places policing would continue as usual. They had developed a fairly elaborate plan for reorganizing the work of patrol officers and involving the public in identifying priority problems in their neighborhood, but they did not know if it would work. So, in a wise move, they decided to try out the plan first in five of the city's 25 police districts, a number that was selected because they thought they, and we, had the resources to monitor how well it would go there. These were officially dubbed 'prototype' districts, to connote that the program there was still a work in progress. The prototypes kept their existing personnel and leadership; in the words of one department executive, they did not 'stack the deck in favor of success', for they knew that once the program encompassed the entire city it had to work with the people and talent that the department already had.

However, the sheer size of the city ensured that this stage of the evaluation would still be large in scope. If just the five police districts in which the program was first tested had been independent, they would have been one of the larger cities in the US. Together, more people lived in the prototypes than in the city of Seattle, and they were only slightly outnumbered by the population of Boston. If the police officers in the five districts were to form their own department, it would have been far larger than the agencies serving the cities of Atlanta, Miami, Kansas City or New Orleans. The size and diversity of the prototype districts led us to anticipate that each district would evolve a somewhat different program over the course of the experimental period, because at the outset no one in Chicago had a clear idea about what community policing should look like. This was another reason why the evaluation needed to speak separately about each area, and about each area's problems.

While the evaluation was not an experiment, the decision to work first in the prototypes at least gave us both program districts and (for a while) 'business-as-usual' areas to work with. However, we had no power to determine which parts of the city would be involved at the outset. By a few months before the process was to begin, word about it had spread among community activists and political leaders, and everyone wanted to be first. The final call as to which districts would be among the prototypes was determined by City Hall. One district that was not on the candidate list submitted by the police department was inserted by the mayor after behind-the-scenes maneuvering by powerful politicians and by well-connected community activists who besieged him, demanding that their districts be selected. In this district, our first survey found that burglary was the top-ranked neighborhood problem, but that only 10 percent of residents gave it a high rating. There was not much room for improvement on many of our outcome measures in this fairly well-off community. However, between them the five districts did represent a range of communities that also included some of the city's worst-off African-Americans and dense concentrations of recent immigrants, giving us enough variation to work with.

A next step was to select sections of the city which closely matched the newly announced program areas. The matching factors for selecting these were race, home ownership, and features of the housing stock such as the percentage of residents living in single family or high-rise buildings. Crime rates were not used for matching purposes – it is bad practice to 'match on the dependent variable' – but each pair of evaluation areas turned out to have similar levels of officially

recorded crime. Because they were far from randomly selected, we dubbed these 'comparison' areas. In a true experiment the comparison areas would have been the 'control groups' against which changes in the program areas could be compared, and the areas would be almost exactly similar. However, none of these areas were randomly selected and they each had a distinctive character, population, and history. Because the match of each experimental and comparison area was imperfect, if the program was received differently among various social groups (say, by race or social class) the population mixes of the areas might account for some of the changes that we interpreted as effects of the program. So too could unique local events and other neighborhood factors that might influence either the experimental or comparison areas, but not both. We patched up these design flaws as well as we could, by monitoring events in the program and comparison areas and statistically controlling for some of the remaining race and class differences between residents of the paired communities. The comparison areas were selected so each included parts of at least three police districts, so that we could adjust at least some of our data for any independent community policing efforts that district commanders might decide to put in place during the course of the first year of the program. We could not control our 'control groups' either.

In the evaluation, the comparison areas were the 'counterfactual'. Changes over time in conditions in the comparison areas were used to represent what would have happened in the experimental districts if there had been no program. This is a far stronger research design than a simple 'before-and-after' description of trends over time in program areas. With before-and-after designs one has no idea what other factors may have contributed to changes that occurred; these might include the weather, general economic conditions, the coverage of crime and the police in the media, or even other programs or the efforts of other agencies. Changes over time in the matched comparison areas provided a benchmark against which changes in the program areas could be contrasted.

A significant feature of this evaluation is that we were afforded the luxury of being able to organize the evaluation and gather baseline data before the program began. This is often not the case. More typically, evaluations are almost an afterthought, and they are funded and begun after the agony and excitement of getting the program into the field has worn off. We had to hurry, but planning for the evaluation began almost four months before the program was launched, and we were able to gather enough money from private foundations and the federal government to staff the study, select the comparison areas, and conduct large surveys in the program and comparison neighborhoods before it began. The result is that we could field something approximating a 'quasi-experimental' evaluation: there were before-and-after measures of the presumed outcomes of the program in both program and comparison areas (see Shadish et al., 2002).

We found modest but consistently positive effects of community policing. In the surveys, the extent of neighborhood physical decay was measured by ratings of the extent of vacant lots filled with trash and junk, abandoned cars, abandoned buildings and graffiti. Decay went down significantly in the three most troubled experimental areas. For two of these there was no parallel decline in matched comparison areas, and for the third district there was a smaller although still significant decline in the comparison area as well as the experimental area. In the worst-off area we studied, residents themselves prioritized two physical decay problems among their top four concerns. Both were the targets of concerted efforts by the police there, and both declined by a very substantial margin. The other two experimental areas were better off, and they were visibly cleaner and in better repair even before CAPS began. Respondents in one of those districts identified graffiti as a top-four problem, but it did not decline significantly there during the months after the program began. There were two measures of social disorder in the evaluation. Disorder in and around schools was identified by respondents in one district as a top-four problem, and over the course of the evaluation it declined noticeably but not significantly; there were no changes in the matched comparison area. Likewise, vandalism to parked cars declined but not significantly in another experimental area, but did not decline at all in its comparison area. The program led to a reduction in other forms of crime in three of the five areas. As measured by surveys, crime dropped in all five police districts, but did not all outpace trends in some of the matched comparison areas. Gang and drug problems declined significantly more in three districts. For example, in the worst-off district, reports of serious street drug markets dropped from 62 to 49 percent, and from 66 to 53 percent in the next-worst areas. Officially recorded auto theft, burglary, robbery and assault generally declined (or remained stable) in parallel with the survey findings.

We also had to deal with the issue of displacement. This was the possibility that the introduction of new policing strategies to some extent pushed problems elsewhere, out of the program areas. While there was evidence of significant declines in a wide range of problems in Chicago's experimental police districts, there lingered the possibility that some were simply displaced elsewhere rather than truly being resolved. The possibility of displacement questions the results of virtually every crime prevention program, but rarely are researchers in a good position to monitor this possible outcome. The possibilities for displacement are numerous. Depending on the problem, displacement might be geographical: the program may push it into another neighborhood, or somewhere down the highway. However, an effective program might instead displace a problem in time, to a period when residents or police are not patrolling; or, offenders might switch to another type of crime, with no guarantee that the neighborhood will be better off due to their taking up a new line of work.

Of all these possibilities, we were able to consider only the possibility of geographical displacement, and then only tentatively. To monitor displacement we identified the program areas in which problems that we judged to be the most displaceable – gang violence, street drug sales, and street crime – declined significantly. We then identified potential displacement zones around these program districts that were areas where we had also conducted evaluation surveys (they were parts of the comparison areas for this study). Those potential displacement areas were defined as the first two tiers of census tracts along the borders of the prototype areas. The survey responses of those who lived in potential displacement areas were contrasted with those of respondents living deeper in the comparison areas and were presumably less vulnerable to geographical displacement.

We then examined Wave 1–Wave 2 changes in gang violence, street drug sales, and street crime, accounting separately for changes in the prototypes, the potential displacement zones, and the (now shrunken) comparison areas. We examined change scores for the three areas and statistically combined all of the data. In no case was there evidence of a significant increase in drug, gang or street crime problems in a potential displacement zone. If anything, there was a hint of a diffusion of benefit rather than displacement of crime (see Clarke and Weisburd, 1998). In the aggregate, gang problems went up in the relevant comparison areas, but remained steady in the displacement zones near the prototypes. Street crime remained steady in the comparison areas, but went down in the displacement zones. There were no apparent shifts in drug problems, other than their significant decline in the prototype districts. While none of the gang or street crime changes in the displacement zones were statistically significant, the number of survey respondents living in the potential displacement areas was not large, so we were not tempted to claim that the *benefits* of community policing spilled over from the prototypes into surrounding areas, but that hypothesis was at least as credible as fears about displacement.

CAPS had few formal goals

One goal of community policing is to open departments up to local input so that they can effectively discern differences in problems and priorities among neighborhoods, and to tailor their operations to respond appropriately. Chicago's policing plan did not specify particular targets for the program, or anticipate how much impact it might have. Our life as evaluators would have been much simpler if the department's leadership had announced goals and target figures – say, a 20 percent reduction in household burglary – but they did not. This reflected the bottom-up approach to policing they were developing. The planners' vision was that teams of officers meeting and working with the public would identify different kinds of problems, and differing priorities for them, in the city's many communities. The goal was to be 'responsive' to what they turned up, and to find effective ways to deal with it. Our evaluation in turn needed to be responsive to this agenda.

To establish whether CAPS successfully addressed priority neighborhood issues, the evaluation focused on the issues identified by neighborhood residents themselves as the most serious problems facing their communities. Our first analysis of the impact of the program examined the four biggest problems that residents of each area nominated in their first interview. We then compared them to ratings given the same issues more than a year later. This analysis let residents set the agenda for the evaluation through their expressions of concern about neighborhood conditions. Focusing on a fixed number of problems in each area helped protect us against random fluctuations in the measures. In the Chicago study there were five program areas, but several dozen outcome measures. If we looked at changes in every measure in every area, some differences almost inevitably would be due to chance fluctuations in the measures. This would be true whether the outcomes were measured by surveys or by official statistics, so disciplining ourselves by looking only at a clearly defined set of 'priority' problems was important.

A largely unstated goal of CAPS was to improve the image of the police in the city's poor neighborhoods. As in many cities, Chicago police faced a 'legitimacy deficit' of major proportions, and their more sophisticated executives knew that this was undermining their effectiveness. Shootings by police and charges of brutality were commonplace in African-American neighborhoods, and our first survey found very large gaps between whites, blacks and Latinos in their evaluations of the quality of police service. Memories of the 1991 Rodney King episode – visions of a black man being pummeled by a large number of officers in Los Angeles while a video camera rolled – were still vivid in 1992 and 1993 when discussions took place in City Hall about what to do about policing in Chicago.

The surveys enabled us to track changes in the perceived quality of police service delivered to the experimental and comparison areas. We asked respondents to rate the performance of the police on several dimensions: on their effectiveness (at keeping order, reducing crime and helping victims), responsiveness (to community concerns and the problems that bother people, plus working together with residents) and demeanor (are they fair, polite, concerned and helpful?). We also questioned them about their recent contacts with the police, and asked those who had called or been stopped by the police to rate their effectiveness and the fairness with which they had been treated. Because views of the police are deeply divided by race and class, our analysis paid close attention to differences among social groups in this regard.

Before community policing began, almost two-thirds of the respondents already averaged a positive score on the police demeanor index. In general, whites perceived that police treated people well even in the early 1990s, and there was not much room for improvement. However, positive perceptions of police demeanor rose by about 10 percentage points among both Latino and African-American respondents and ended on a high note. Perceptions of police responsiveness to community concerns improved steadily. Perceived responsiveness went up the most among African-Americans and Latinos, rising by almost 20 percentage points between 1993 and 1999. The views of whites, which were more positive even before CAPS began, improved by about 10 percentage points. Finally, at the outset Chicagoans were mostly negative in their views of how well police performed their traditional tasks. Over time, the index measuring this aspect of police service improved significantly, rising from a low of 36 percent in 1994 to a high of 51 percent in 2003. Note, however, that for all of these changes, opinion *gaps* between the races closed not at all. While positive trends were apparent, racial polarization around policing issues changed hardly at all. A decade after the program began, the contrast between the general optimism of whites and the still-widespread pessimism of African-Americans was almost as large in 2003 as it had been in the beginning.

Our role as evaluators in *creating* goals for the program is best illustrated by our effort to evaluate beat meetings. Following a series of reports indicating that program implementation was faltering, new meeting requirements were announced that matched line-by-line the evaluation criteria that we had developed to assess them. Meetings were required to have printed agendas, and crime maps and city service reports were to be distributed each time. Distinct segments of the meetings were to be devoted to reviewing progress on problems identified at past meetings and on new crime and disorder problems. Participants were to identify tasks to be performed and a timetable, and officers sought volunteers from the group and assigned them jobs. Both the beat team sergeant and the managing lieutenant had to sign off on the official report that these things had taken place. If all the new requirements actually were met, a beat would have gotten a perfect score in our 1998 study, which concluded instead that they were meeting only half of their goals. This was no accident; beat meeting procedures were redesigned *in order* to get a perfect score from us, and also because our scoring criteria reflected the department's unrealized plan for them.

CONCLUSION

The structure of the CAPS evaluation was at all points driven by the nature of the program and the character of the city. Because we got involved before the program plan was even finalized, our evaluation team could gather pre-program baseline information, a luxury that many studies of real-world, politically driven projects do not enjoy. The police department choose to phase in the implementation of the program so that they could fix any problems that emerged early, while they were still small in scale. This enabled us to contrast changes in the prototype districts with parallel trends in matched areas of the city, drawing on data collected after the program had been in operation in a few communities. The large and diverse character of Chicago compelled us to design an evaluation that could encompass the entire city. Instead of watching the program unfold in a few selected places, the evaluation would be based on samples of residents, activists, patrol officers, and police beats representing the entire city, so that the findings could describe general trends in Chicago and what was happening in its three major communities.

The evaluation continued, and over the years we learned a great deal about the operation of key elements of community policing. This included how to gain the attention of the community through effective marketing and what it took to run a productive beat meeting; the organizational and leadership factors associated with effective neighborhood problem solving; and what did not work (for mostly it did not) when it came to involving the city's new immigrants in community policing. However, the strongest conclusions about whether the program itself caused changes in quality of life, fear of crime, and confidence in the police in the city's neighborhoods come from the first two years of the study.

Was Chicago's effort a success? In Skogan and Hartnett (1997) we put Chicago's accomplishments in context by comparing the results of our impact analyses with evaluation findings from other cities. By this accounting, Chicago's success rate was about that of other cities that have conducted carefully evaluated community policing programs.

The baseline for this comparison was a review of a large stack of largely unpublished community policing evaluations, which concluded that these interventions had a success rate of just over 50 percent (Skogan, 1994). The reviewed projects targeted victimization, fear of crime, drug markets, and the perceived quality of police service. They were carried out in experimental neighborhoods in Houston, Newark, Oakland, Birmingham, Madison and Baltimore. Each was evaluated using roughly the same approach that we employed in Chicago: matched comparison areas, two waves of resident surveys, and the analysis of census, crime, and other archival data. To give an example of the findings, fear of crime was a target in all of the projects, and it went down – probably as a result of the program – in half of them. Overall, compared to what happened in the comparison areas, positive changes were recorded in 27 of the 51 outcomes that were monitored. That constituted a 'success rate' of 53 percent.

In Chicago there was evidence of program impact on nine of the 20 top priority problems, for a success rate of 45 percent. As described earlier, we also assessed the impact of CAPS on four clusters of outcome measures for each district: drug and gangs problems, serious crime problems, physical decay problems, and perceived police responsiveness to community concerns. There was evidence of significant program effects for 10 of the 20 clusters, for a success rate of 50 percent.

Thus Chicago hit about the national mark. It fielded somewhat different community policing efforts of varying quality in five experimental districts; the programs in other cities also varied considerably in type and quality. Like in Chicago, some projects were well conceived and well executed, while others did not get very far. In the aggregate they succeeded about half the time.

Whether a success rate for community policing of 50 percent will be pronounced 'a success' or 'a disappointment' is a political rather than a research question. In Chicago it was viewed to be a considerable success, and by early 1995 the program had expanded to encompass the entire city. Running on its popularity, the mayor who insisted on reforming policing has since been re-elected several times, by widening margins and with increasing support among African-American and Latino voters. The democratic processes by which people who initiate programs are held accountable is another way to assess their effectiveness, and by that measure CAPS was successful indeed.

NOTE

1 All of the reports and other published material from the evaluation can be found at: http://skogan.org/ChicagoCAPS.htmlhttp://skogan.org/ChicagoCAPS.html

RECOMMENDED READING

In addition to the material cited above, interested readers may wish to consult:

Foster, A. and Jones, C. (2010) 'Nice to do' and Essential: Improving Neighbourhood Policing in an English Police Force' *Policing: A Journal of Policy and Practice,* 4, 395–402; for a study of the implementation of community policing in the UK.

Skogan, W. and Frydl, K, (eds) (2004) *Fairness and Effectiveness in Policing: The Evidence.* (Washington D.C., National Academies Press) for a comprehensive review of the field of police research in the United States.

Weisburd, D. and Braga, A. (eds) (2006) *Police Innovation: Contrasting Perspectives* (Cambridge: Cambridge University Press) for a set of eight 'debates' between leading police scholars over the implementation and effectiveness of recent innovations in policing.

REFERENCES

Bennett, Trevor. 1991. 'The Effectiveness of a Police Initiated Fear Reducing Strategy.' *British Journal of Criminology,* 31: 1–14.

Clarke, Ronald V. and David Weisburd. 1994. 'Diffusion of Crime Control Benefits: Observations on the Reverse of Displacement.' In Ronald V. Clarke (ed.) *Crime Prevention Studies Vol. 2,* Monsey NY: Criminal Justice Press, pp. 165–183.

McElroy, Jerome E., Colleen Cosgrove and Susan Sadd. 1993. *Community Policing: The CPOP in New York.* Newbury Park, CA: Sage Publications.

Pate, Antony, Mary Ann Wycoff, Wesley G. Skogan and Lawrence W. Sherman. 1986. *Reducing Fear of Crime in Houston and Newark.* Washington DC: National Institute of Justice and the Police Foundation.

Quinton, Paul and Rachel Tuffin. 2007. 'Neighbourhood Change: The Impact of the National Reassurance Policing Programme'. *Policing,* 1: 149–160.

Rosenbaum, Dennis P. (ed.) 1994. *The Challenge of Community Policing: Testing the Hypotheses.* Newbury Park, CA: Sage Publications.

Sadd, Susan and Randolph Grinc. 1993. *Issues in Community Policing: An Evaluation of Eight Innovative Neighborhood-Oriented Policing Projects.* New York City: Vera Institute of Justice.

Shadish, William R., Thomas D. Cook and Donald T. Campbell. 2002. *Experimental and Quasi-Experimental Designs for Generalized Causal Inference.* Boston: Houghton-Mifflin.

Skogan, Wesley G. 1994. 'The Impact of Community Policing on Neighborhood Residents: A Cross-Site Analysis.' In Dennis P. Rosenbaum (ed.) *The Challenge of Community Policing: Testing the Hypotheses.* Newbury Park, CA: Sage Publications, pp. 167–181.

Skogan Wesley G. 2006. *Police and Community in Chicago: A Tale of Three Cities.* New York: Oxford University Press,.

Skogan, Wesley G. and Susan M. Hartnett. 1997. *Community Policing, Chicago Style.* New York: Oxford University Press.

Skogan, Wesley G., Susan M. Hartnett, Jill DuBois, Jennifer T. Comey, Marianne, Kaiser and Justine H. Lovig. 1999. *On the Beat: Police and Community Problem Solving.* Boulder, CO: Westview Publishing Co.

22

Order in the Court: Using Ethnomethodology to Explore Juvenile Justice Settings

Aaron Kupchik, Joseph De Angelis,
Nicole L. Bracy

INTRODUCTION

The term 'ethnomethodology' is a broad designation that covers a diverse body of work involving different analytical approaches (Coulon, 1995; Francis and Hester, 2004; Maynard and Clayman, 1991). Yet ethnomethodologists tend to share at least one thing in common – a devotion to studying the mundane, obvious, and 'natural' grounds of routine action that characterize social life in concrete everyday settings (Pollner, 1987). Whether exploring turn-taking in conversations (Sacks et al., 1974), studying how statistical categories are constructed (Cicourel and Kitsuse, 1963; Meehan, 1989), or describing the structure of emergency telephone calls (Whalen and Zimmerman, 1990), ethnomethodologists are concerned with the subtle methods that people use to intuit the social world and create orderly sets of social relations. In this chapter, we explore the logic of using ethnomethodology to study social relations in justice institutions, with a particular focus on juvenile justice settings. In particular, we describe ethnomethodology's basic theoretical tenets, its most common methodological approaches, and some of the obstacles that researchers face when using this approach to study issues in juvenile justice.

This chapter is divided into five sections. In the first section we outline ethnomethodology's theoretical and methodological orientation by briefly reviewing the foundational work of Harold Garfinkel, as well as some 'classic' applications in criminal justice settings. The second section of the chapter focuses on how this approach has been applied to the study of juvenile justice. We briefly examine the major works in this area and discuss how ethnomethodological methods have been refined over the last 30 years. We then review Aaron Kupchik's recent study of how judges speak to youth in criminal courts as a way of demonstrating how ethnomethodology can be used to examine symbolic rituals and identity construction in juvenile justice. In the third section, we explore some of the challenges that researchers may face when adopting an ethnomethodological approach in institutional settings. To do this, we discuss the recent work of Nicole Bracy to illustrate some of the challenges associated with adopting an ethnomethodological approach to the study of juvenile justice. In the final sections, we first consider the importance of ethnomethodology in juvenile justice, and then discuss opportunities for ethnomethodological work to make additional contributions in the field of juvenile justice.

ETHNOMETHODOLOGY: THE CLASSICS

It is difficult to describe ethnomethodology as a specific method. Rather, it has been alternatively characterized as a theory, a methodology (Maynard and Clayman, 1991), a research perspective (Coulon, 1995), and a form of life (Mehan and Wood, 1975). While commonly affiliated with sociology, ethnomethodological work can be found in a wide range of academic disciplines including criminal justice, anthropology, communication studies, English and linguistics. Even given this diversity, when people talk about ethnomethodology, they are generally referring to the study of the methods that individuals use to construct the meaningful, patterned and orderly social situations that characterize their everyday lives (Rawls, 2002). As Coulon (1995: 2) describes it, ethnomethodologists study the 'ordinary methods that ordinary people use to realize their ordinary actions'. This approach assumes that social action is guided by sets of rules and structures, which can be discovered through close, empirical examinations of social behavior in everyday, naturally occurring settings (Psathas, 1994).

Ethnomethodology's core ideas were initially developed by Harold Garfinkel in the 1940s and entered mainstream sociology in the late 1960s (Rawls, 2005). In his book, *Studies in Ethnomethodology,* Garfinkel (1967) demonstrated that social behavior is not chaotic or random, as it sometimes may appear, but instead has a relatively patterned and orderly character. Unlike previous sociologists, however, Garfinkel argued that forms of social action do not emerge simply because actors have internalized pre-existing sets of norms, values, ideas and beliefs that constrain and govern their action in social situations (Garfinkel 1967; see also Maynard and Clayman 1991). In fact, as Pfohl (1985: 292–3) notes, ethnomethodologists do not adhere to the assumption that people share the same symbolic meanings. Instead, they argue that people engage in interpretive work during social interaction that allows them to cooperatively define 'what's happening' in any given social situation. From this perspective, social order emerges through the concerted action of individuals who are acting for practical reasons in concrete social situations (Maynard and Clayman, 1991). In simpler terms, 'people do what they do, right there and then, to be reasonable and effective and they do so for pervasively practical reasons and under unavoidably local conditions of knowledge, action and material resources' (Boden, 1990: 189; cited in Edles, 2002: 166).

In attempting to describe ethnomethodology, it is important to distinguish it from more traditional forms of ethnographic fieldwork. Ethnomethodology shares certain features in common with ethnography. For example, both generally focus on describing grounded social situations and they both pay close attention to the details of mundane, everyday types of interaction (Sacks, 1992). Ethnography and ethnomethodology diverge strongly, however, when it comes to exploring motivations for action. Unlike ethnography, ethnomethodologists are not primarily concerned with how individuals 'see' the social worlds they inhabit or with exploring how individuals explain their internal motivations (Maynard and Clayman, 1991). Rather, ethnomethodologists generally focus on the *observable* acts and methods that individuals actually use to collaboratively enact stable social routines. For example, Harvey Sacks argues that one of the shortcomings of ethnography, as conducted in the tradition of the Chicago School, is that these early sociologists tended to rely on informants to tell them what is going on, rather than having the sociologist observe in detail what is actually happening in specific social activities (Sacks, 1992).

This orientation can be seen most clearly in Garfinkel's (1967) use of 'breaching experiments' to explore how 'common sense' social rules are created and sustained in everyday interaction. Rather than asking people about how they understand the social rules in any given situation, Garfinkel sought to empirically demonstrate the existence of social rules by having his students violate them in social settings. For example, he had his students act as if they were boarders in their own home and behave toward family members in a polite but formal manner (ibid. 47). By violating the background expectations in this type of social situation (i.e., replacing casual interaction between family members with a more formal style of interaction that would be appropriate for a guest), the breaches tended to generate anxiety, confusion and outbursts of anger among both the research subjects and onlookers. For Garfinkel, these types of reactions served to demonstrate the existence of tacit social rules and highlighted the steps that people will take to 'normalize' breaches of interactive expectations (Garfinkel, 1967).

Ethnomethodology in criminal justice

The most common ethnomethodological approaches to the study of justice institutions fall into two distinct areas: conversation analysis and institutional ethnomethodology (Atkinson and Drew, 1979; Maynard and Clayman, 1991). Conversation analysis focuses on the 'order/organization/orderliness of social action, particularly those social actions that are located in everyday interactions, in discursive practices, and in the sayings/telling/doings of members of society'

(Psathas, 1994: 2). Often relying on the analysis of texts or detailed transcriptions of audio and video material, conversation analysts are concerned with examining the basic methods people use to achieve interaction through talk. Like many ethnomethodologists, conversation analysts focus on the methods of conversation, not necessarily because they are interested in understanding the sets of meaning that conversation holds for the participants, but because they hope to discover the basic organizational patterns and rules of talk that emerge in everyday social situations (Edles, 2002: 170). Within sociology, there have been a large number of studies in a wide range of settings, including the examination of the sequential ordering of mundane conversations (Schegloff, 1986), news interviews (Greatbatch, 1988), booing (Clayman, 1993), and political speeches (Atkinson, 1984).

While the use of conversation analysis has been less common in criminology than in sociology in general, there have been a number of important studies that relate to issues in crime and justice. Whalen and Zimmerman's (1987, 1990) research on the structure of emergency calls to police has been particularly influential. In their early research, Whalen and Zimmerman (1987) describe the differences between mundane telephone calls (e.g., calls between friends) and calls that are designed to elicit an institutional response (e.g., calls to police). They find that while mundane calls may have an elaborate series of turn taking as part of the opening of the conversation, emergency calls tend to have a much more truncated and focused opening. In later research, Whalen and Zimmerman (1990: 469–80) outline what they see as the five interactional segments of calls to the police: (1) an opening/identification/acknowledgement ('Mid-City police and fire'); (2) a request ('[can you] get somebody over here right away'); (3) an interrogative series 'You don't know what's wrong with her though'); (4) a response ('Okay we'll get somebody over there'); and (5) a closing sequence ('Thank you'). They conclude that this pattern emerges not because both parties have a pre-existing cognitive template for how these types of calls should work, but rather results from *in situ* negotiation as the callers orient their descriptions of the troublesome event in a way that is meant to assuage the suspicions and doubts of dispatchers.

A second type of ethnomethodological research is best described as institutional ethnomethodology (Maynard and Clayman, 1991). Like conversation analysts, institutional ethnomethodologists often focus on spoken interaction. Unlike conversation analysts, however, who commonly rely on transcriptions of audio or video data, institutional ethnomethodologists often use observational

fieldwork to produce highly detailed examinations of micro-level interactions in 'natural' institutional environments (Cicourel, 1987; Maynard and Clayman, 1991). Institutional ethnomethodologists may also conduct interviews with research subjects to develop a better understanding of patterns of commonsense reasoning (Mehan, 1991). This form of ethnomethodology has been conducted in a wide range of settings and on a variety of topics, including traffic court (Pollner, 1987), plea bargaining (Sudnow, 1965), jury decision-making (Garfinkel, 1967), the use of codes in correctional settings (Wieder, 1974), police interrogations (Watson, 1983), crime statistics (Meehan, 1989), juvenile court (Cicourel, 1968), and police work (Bittner, 1967).

A good illustration of this approach is Maynard's (1989) study of the plea bargaining process, which was radically different than most ethnographic attempts to study courtroom negotiation. Ethnographers have explained patterns of courtroom interaction and outcomes by reference to the development of courtroom communities, where prosecutors, defense attorneys, and judges coordinate their actions based on a shared worldview (see Eisenstein et al., 1988; see also Ulmer, 1997, for a more recent example). In contrast, Maynard sought to study negotiations by strictly focusing on the basic sequences in plea-bargaining talk. Unlike previous ethnographic accounts of courtroom activities, he was not necessarily interested in excavating the sets of meaning that prosecutors or defense attorneys bring to negotiations. Rather, he focused on the actual observable methods that the courtroom actors use to negotiate pleas. He explored how pleas could be introduced or solicited. Rather than assuming that plea bargains naturally flow from pre-existing values, ideas, or norms, Maynard's ethnomethodology illustrated how pleas are created and recreated through the collaborative discursive labor of the courtroom actors themselves in the everyday conduct of their work.

ETHNOMETHODOLOGY IN JUVENILE JUSTICE

Soon after Garfinkel's treatise on ethnomethodology, sociologists Aaron Cicourel and Robert Emerson each performed important ethnomethodological work in juvenile justice. Their books, *The Social Organization of Juvenile Justice* and *Judging Delinquents*, respectively, are still perhaps the best-known and most influential texts about the juvenile court.

In *The Social Organization of Juvenile Justice*, Cicourel (1968) illustrated an important advantage of ethnomethodology: that one can analyze how situations are created without being held captive by existing data or perspectives. By studying how police, juvenile court judges and probation officers decide which youth should receive the label 'delinquent', Cicourel uncovered the process by which youth are assigned the identity of being a juvenile delinquent. He used an ethnomethodological process to understand how juvenile justice decision makers conceive of delinquents, and how they then turn this conception into reality. Youth who get arrested and 'adjudicated delinquent' (convicted) in juvenile courts are not necessarily more violent or disruptive than other youth; instead they fit the image of a delinquent, and this image is shaped by race and social class. In contrast, if one were instead to study the problem of delinquency by using official statistics, then one would only see the youth who fit the preformed definition of what a delinquent is supposed to look and act like. His work makes clear how an ethnomethodological approach offers a unique contribution to studying juvenile justice, since it allows us to understand how delinquent identities are achieved through social interaction.

In *Judging Delinquents*, Robert Emerson (1969) studied juvenile courts as organizations whose actions are shaped by both external politics (how they interact with other organizations such as child welfare and correctional institutions) and internal politics (shared understandings among court workers). He illustrated how court workers collaborate within these political spheres to achieve common goals – namely, reaching consensus on what to do with juvenile cases. In order to make these decisions, courts judge the moral character of each youth and sort youth into three different categories: normal, hardcore and disturbed. Court workers' assessments of moral character are based on subjectively interpreted cues of a youth's personality, and these assessments are contingent on relations within the court and with other organizations. Emerson's work, too, shows the importance of ethnomethodology, since he produces these insights into how courts work only by exploring the subjective and dynamic process of identity construction as it is shaped by the negotiation among individuals involved in collective action.

Despite their somewhat different approaches and goals, these two classic texts have a lot in common. Each questions traditional understandings of what delinquency is and who delinquents are. Each seeks to explore the constructed social order of the juvenile justice system by looking at the process through which common understandings about youth and their behaviors are reached. Each seeks to understand the process by which juvenile justice workers come to shared understandings that sort and label juveniles into categories.

There have been relatively few efforts to do ethnomethodology in juvenile justice since these two texts. The few that we have seen in the past 40 years have taken a somewhat different tack than those of Cicourel and Emerson. Whereas Cicourel and Emerson established how juvenile justice workers subjectively define youth, much of the recent work in this area has taken for granted that this is true and turned attention instead to how this process works in different settings. For example, Cavender and Knepper (1992) studied juvenile parole board hearings, focusing on how the board members meet behind the scenes to agree on a script for the formal hearing to follow, which they then perform in a ceremony intended to send the youth a message. Bortner and Williams (1997) studied a juvenile correctional institution that had recently shifted from a custody-oriented approach to a treatment-oriented one. By observing youth residents and staff members alike, they illustrated how the reality of the new correctional program is very different than what it was intended to be. Because of individuals' perceptions and the institutional demands of the facilities, the new treatment-oriented initiatives wind up taking a backseat to coercive control instead of replacing it. Bortner and Williams illustrated how correctional staff and administrators respond to contradicting missions and constraints as they construct an operating paradigm.

Recent ethnomethodologies also consider how policy shifts have reshaped (or not) juvenile justice practices in varying contexts and across national borders. In Box 22.1, we discuss the work of Stewart Asquith (1983), who used an ethnomethodological perspective to compare how juveniles are processed in England's and Scotland's juvenile justice systems. More recently, Kupchik (2004) used an ethnomethodological approach to analyze what happens when juveniles are transferred to criminal (adult) court to be prosecuted as if they were adults. He writes about the problems judges face when trying to deal with juveniles in an adult court – that they need to communicate defendants' criminal responsibility, while also taking into account their reduced blameworthiness due to their age. Judges have to balance these concerns while working within a system not designed to deal with youth and with few options that are geared towards helping youth. Thus, judges' actions are constrained by their subjective perceptions of how blameworthy youth are, and also by the organizational constraints they face by being in a criminal rather than a juvenile court.

Admonishing adolescents in court is one response to this set of circumstances. Judges use harsh talk to admonish juveniles in an attempt to

---

Box 22.1   Steward Asquith's *Children and Justice*

In *Children and Justice*, Stewart Asquith (1983) uses an ethnomethodological perspective to consider how juvenile justice decision-making is shaped by laws, institutional practices, and ideologies of delinquency. He compares juvenile justice in England, which uses juvenile courts, and Scotland, which disbanded its juvenile courts in favor of 'children's hearings'. The systems in both countries have similar formal goals: a commitment to age-appropriate treatment, help for youth and prevention rather than punishment, and diversion from formal court processing when possible. England's system is more formal than Scotland's, and as Asquith's research shows produces more punitive justice. For example, by relying on magistrates and police officers (in England), rather than laypeople with no legal training (in Scotland), the English courts pay more attention to youths' offenses and to personal responsibility, and less to the juveniles' welfare considerations. Members of these forums pursue different hearing goals and seek out different pieces of information about juveniles (guided by what he calls their 'frames of relevance'), which leads to distinct treatment for youth. Though it is unsurprising that hearings and courts proceed in different ways and result in different outcomes, Asquith makes a substantial contribution to the literature by using an ethnomethodological perspective to uncover the rules by which social order is shaped. These patterns of interaction are complex: they are shaped by participants' training and predispositions, the organizational characteristics of the forums in which they work, and the interactions and negotiations among participants.

---

communicate the seriousness of their offenses but also let them off the hook somewhat by sparing them from serious punishment. Essentially, the judges yell at the defendants, tell them how horrible their actions were, and personalize the offense, such as by asking a defendant, 'How would you feel if someone did this to your mother?' Yet judges then tell the juvenile that s/he will not have to go to prison as long as s/he stays out of trouble, and the judges prescribe counseling and supervision services. This tactic lets judges feel that they are adding a punitive bite to a lenient sentence while still holding the youth accountable for his/her actions. In the end, judges define youthful defendants' identities: as youth who are salvageable but deserve some blame.

Like prior work by Cicourel, Emerson, and others, Kupchik's analysis is substantially shaped by his use of ethnomethodology rather than a different perspective. His analysis includes the attempt to understand how social actions and identities are created through interaction using ceremonial and symbolic language, and how these actions are shaped by the particular contexts in which they are situated. Had he instead recorded only the outcome of these hearings rather than the ceremonial process of reaching these outcomes, his analyses would have been very different.

PRACTICAL ISSUES IN INSTITUTIONAL ETHNOMETHODOLOGICAL RESEARCH

Applying an ethnomethodological perspective to research in juvenile justice settings requires that the researcher navigate through a number of potentially problematic steps. While a great deal of academic work has been done on conversation analysis (see Hutchby and Wooffitt, 1998; Psathas, 1994; Schegloff, 2007; Ten Have, 2007), less attention has been paid to the practical problems that researchers face when trying to conduct ethnomethodological research in institutional settings. The following section discusses some of these steps and the difficulties that one might encounter when doing institutional ethnomethodological research in juvenile justice settings, using examples from a recent study by Nicole Bracy (2011), which draws on both ethnomethodological and ethnographic strategies to examine the social order of high-school disciplinary systems.

Schools in the US have invested a considerable amount of resources in discipline and security agendas, which can be seen through the broadening of school rules and punishments and the now regular presence of non-teaching personnel (like police officers and security guards) on school campuses. Bracy spent one school year in two public high schools observing and documenting interactions between students, school police officers (called School Resource Officers, or SROs), and school principals and disciplinary staff, with a focus on the how the social environment of each school shapes the way these groups interact, particularly in disciplinary situations. She examines how certain students in the schools come to be labeled as troublemakers and how this label persists and spreads across teachers and school disciplinarians, making it less likely that these students get a fair 'hearing' when they are suspected of having done something wrong. Her results suggest that while, in theory, school discipline and security strategies promote safer, more orderly schools, in reality they can have the opposite effect as they alienate and disempower students.

Obtaining access

One of the first and most critical steps when embarking on a research project with an institutional ethnomethodological approach is gaining access to the population one intends to study. While most research projects involve this step of gaining access, in an ethnomethodological study this process can be especially difficult; the researcher is sometimes asking for a longer-term, more time-intensive commitment from research subjects, and one's presence as an ethnomethodological researcher may be more intrusive (as compared to administering a survey, for example), especially since ethnomethodology requires the research to scrutinize subtle interactions among study subjects.

When a research project involves youth or other vulnerable populations, these access challenges can be compounded. For researchers, schools are logical (though not problem-free) settings for ethnomethodological studies of youth, as they are hubs of routine actions through which almost all youth pass during their lives. Schools are also an increasingly logical setting for a criminologist, given that schools in the US are becoming more and more intertwined with the juvenile justice system (see Kupchik and Monahan, 2006). However, to members of a school community, a researcher's presence may feel unnatural and gaining access to schools for ethnomethodological research can be time-consuming, complicated, and likely involves getting permission from multiple institutional gatekeepers. Before beginning ethnomethodological research in schools, researchers may need to convince school officials at various levels, including school administrators, school district officials and even school boards, that the proposed research does not threaten student or staff privacy.

In Bracy's project, two researchers were involved in data collection. The lead researcher first met with school district officials to explain the proposed project and discuss potential school sites that would be appropriate to study and meet the research goals. Involving the district in site selection can be beneficial to the project in two ways: presumably, the district knows its schools very well and can suggest schools based on study-specific characteristics and familiarity with school leadership (not all school administrators may be equally welcoming to the idea of participating in research, for example); second, by asking for the district's input the researcher creates a cooperative spirit, and in doing so may help dispel any feeling the district may have of being invaded by who they might perceive as a 'know-it-all' academic. The second important step in gaining access to research sites for Bracy's school study was meeting directly with the selected schools' administrators and SROs. Arranging a meeting like this gives school officials an opportunity to ask questions and express concerns, which may help to assuage their apprehensions and can also clue ethnomethodological researchers in on potentially sensitive issues for the site (or specific site members) of which to be cautious when in the field.

Developing rapport with research subjects

Even if the research proposal is deemed sound and access is granted, an ethnomethodological researcher in a school setting may find it challenging to establish rapport within the school. School administrators might feel apprehensive or self-conscious about having an unfamiliar researcher in the school; they might question the researcher's motive, feel like someone is looking over their shoulder, checking up on them, or questioning their actions and decision-making. It is important for an ethnomethodological researcher to be conscious of these types of reactions to her presence in a research setting as they can be barriers to establishing rapport and can alter the dynamics of the social behavior being studied.

Through the course of Bracy's research, there were a few staff members at each school with whom it was difficult to establish rapport. She quickly noticed that these staff members tended to stay away and did not engage with (or even acknowledge) her when encountering her around the schools' buildings. The reactions of these staff members suggest that they interpreted Bracy's outsider presence as a violation of the social rules of the school community. While sometimes efforts can be made to overcome these rapport-building challenges, other times it may be best to follow the lead of these reluctant research subjects and give them space, lest one risk completely alienating them. Regardless of whether one is able to eventually gain their trust, individuals like these are informative in ethnomethodology, since they can cue the researcher to a set of rules that may be violated by the researcher's presence. In this case, for example, opposition to her presence led Bracy to realize that some staff members distrusted the school administration and were concerned about surveillance by the school principal or school district officials. Though this insight was not directly related to her subject of study (school discipline and security) these individuals helped Bracy to refine her ethnomethodological perspective by alerting her to the fact that the social rules guiding staff members' actions can be shaped by distrust of school administrators. Certainly, difficulties like reluctant research subjects encountered during fieldwork should be noted and explored when analyzing the data and writing up the results.

In addition to challenges with institutional gatekeepers, researchers employing an ethnomethodological approach in juvenile justice settings may also encounter difficulty establishing rapport with youth in the research setting. Unlike conversation analysts, ethnomethodologists that study verbal and non-verbal action in institutional contexts will often conduct interviews with research subjects to develop a better understanding of the social context that is guiding their action (Maynard and Clayman, 1991). As a result, they have to take steps to ensure that the research subjects are comfortable talking to them about the social activities that are taking place. One should not underestimate the impact that age and gender differences between the researcher and the research subjects can have on the data collection process and, consequently, the overall results of the research project. Youth may not be trusting of adult researchers, particularly those that they do not know well, but yet who are suddenly interested in talking to them, knowing their perspective, and asking them for their opinions. This may be especially true in the broader spectrum of juvenile justice settings, such as in cases where researchers are working with youth that have been arrested, incarcerated or involved in the child welfare system. These youth may be particularly guarded and view the researcher as a threatening or intimidating adult figure, not dissimilar to a police or probation officer, an attorney or a judge.

In Bracy's research, she found that students in the schools she was studying were sometimes confused about her role in the school. They did not know if she was a teacher, principal, disciplinarian or someone visiting from the school district to evaluate school staff. While visiting the schools, she often spent time in the in-school suspension rooms, in principals' offices or walking through halls of the school building while shadowing the school's police officer. Students may have seen her as closely associated with these other adults, and/or collaborating with them. As a result students may have been reluctant to honestly express concerns about police and school employees. To deal with this issue, when interacting with students, Bracy made an effort to explain who she was (i.e., not someone working for or associated with the school) and was mindful, when around students, not to bring up information she learned through conversations with school administrators. In Box 22.2 we describe one instance of how she attempted to build rapport with students.

Developing a data analysis strategy

In their analyses, ethnomethodologists seek to dig beneath the obvious and look closely at how 'normal' becomes normal in a given social context. The realization of this goal requires a careful, strategic data analysis plan. Because ethnomethodologists seek to understand norm construction, a single source cannot provide all of the necessary information; ethnomethodological data analysis frequently involves the identification of themes and patterns across multiple types of data in order to draw meaningful conclusions about how social meanings and actions are constructed. In Bracy's

---

Box 22.2 Explaining the researcher's presence

In the following field notes, Bracy (2011) describes an interaction with a student during which the student inquired about who she was. In addition to explaining who she was and why she was there, Bracy attempted to build rapport with the student by helping with a school task, and in the process learned about one student's view of discipline at her school:

Steve was helping a White female student named Samantha with her Spanish assignment. There was an African-American male student sitting at another table also working on an assignment. 'Hey that's a pretty good accent' I told Steve when I heard him pronouncing a few of the Spanish words. He said that he had studied abroad in Spain but had also stayed awhile in Argentina. I helped Samantha translate a few words she and Steve were unsure about. I then introduced myself to her and she asked if I worked here. I told her that I was visiting from [the nearby university], doing research about school discipline. I asked her what she thought about it. She said 'Discipline? They don't discipline nobody here.'

research, for example, she compares discipline practices across two schools with an eye towards how rules are created and sustained in two different social environments, but also compares discipline practices across administrators *within* both schools.

Because ethnomethodological research can produce a large amount of data, proper organization of these data is necessary in preparation for effective analysis. Researchers may find qualitative software programs like Atlas.ti, MAXqda V2, or NVivo (formerly NUD*IST) useful for organizing qualitative data and ultimately helpful as a data analysis tool (see Hwang, 2008; Lewis, 2004; Silver and Fielding, 2008). These software programs allow a researcher to load multiple word-processing files (that may contain field notes or interview transcripts, for example) into one central location and link them together to create one or more datasets. Once linked, a researcher can easily search within and between data files to identify and create codes based on emerging themes in the data and mark each occurrence of the code/theme for quick retrieval at a later date.

Writing about youth

One of the great values in conducting ethnomethodological research in schools (like other juvenile justice settings) is that it allows juveniles to be represented as agents within the social order of the school. Ethnomethodological research presents an opportunity to discuss, in depth, how students act within a unique situation and setting. Social science research too often represents students as the passive recipients of school disciplinary processes. Instead, ethnomethodology allows the researcher to highlight how students, alongside teachers, administrators and police officers, together produce the social organization of the disciplinary system. Using this approach, criminologists can elucidate how students talk about having a police officer in school, how they represent the role of the officer in their school and how they use both verbal and non-verbal social action to resist, accept or re-shape their school's disciplinary processes.

Bracy's article (2011) offers examples of writing strategies that can be used when disseminating the results from an ethnomethodological study involving youth. She writes about how school administrators in the two public high schools she studied 'do discipline' in a way that leaves students feeling frustrated and powerless, as shown in Box 22.3. She uses the data from field notes to share students' descriptions of how the discipline process transpires – how their experiences are shaped by school administrators' actions and comments.

These students discuss how they lack opportunities to tell their side of the story when in trouble, and that adults in their school are not interested in what they have to say and would not believe them if they tried to defend themselves or dispute a charge levied against them. This was true of students in both high schools studied, but was particularly acute in the school that was more disorderly and where school staff expressed a much lower opinion of the student body overall. To highlight differences found between schools, Bracy juxtaposes quotes from students at each school, coupled with data about the social environment of each school.

Unlike writing that emerges from other research methods, ethnomethodological writing provides rich descriptions of social environments that give context to youths' behaviors. This kind of discourse can be uniquely empowering for youth in that it does not participate in the hegemonic repetition of the 'taken-for-granted', but instead challenges it by questioning how and why it came to be. In ethnomethodological research, youth are not treated merely as subjects being studied for some greater purpose, but are recognized as participants that play varied roles in shaping their own environments. Similarly, ethnomethodological writing avoids imposing 'truths' upon youth, but instead recognizes that all truths are socially constructed and seeks to understand how truth is created and reinforced.

TAKING STOCK: UNIQUE CONTRIBUTIONS OF ETHNOMETHODOLOGY

The goal of this chapter is to describe what ethnomethodology is and how criminologists have and can use ethnomethodological methods to study juvenile justice institutions. We paid particular attention to recent work by Kupchik in juvenile courts and by Bracy in schools. Our discussion demonstrates ethnomethodology's unique contributions to the study of juvenile justice institutions. Most importantly, ethnomethodology allows the researcher to examine, in detail, the micro-sociological context within which juvenile justice works. This is particularly useful when studying juveniles, since less detailed analyses or approaches that fail to consider how participants actively construct justice settings may not understand the nuanced and complicated world of adolescents. Simply stated, the world looks different through the eyes of a juvenile than it does through the eyes of an adult, and juveniles interact socially in different ways than adults do. This makes it important to focus on the active process through

---

Box 22.3   Constructing discipline. In the following field notes, Bracy (2011) uses both students' comments and her own observations to illustrate how school administrators actively construct school discipline situations in a way that leaves students powerless.

Students at Cole and Vista high schools are frustrated with the way punishments are handed down in their schools. An African-American female Vista High School student explained:

> This school is more 'take action' than 'ask questions'. So you may do something, it may not even be your fault, but you'll get suspended ... or they'll already have it written up and then you explain it, but they already got their minds made up so [they'll say], 'Okay well you have a detention next week,' or something. You know what I'm saying? It's nothing like both sides of the story at all.

At Cole High School, students express similar aggravation:

> Interviewer: How fair do you think teachers are in general in the way they deal with students?
> Student (white male): Like detention, like all that other stuff, like write ups?
> Interviewer: Yeah, just in general.
> Student: Not fair at all. They write up people like there's no tomorrow. There's no detentions, I mean there are detentions, but they'll skip detention [and] go straight to [formally 'writing up' a student]. They want them out of the class and they want suspension.

While visiting Vista and Cole High Schools I observed many instances where students were disciplined without having the opportunity to explain what happened, lending credibility to the claims students made in interviews. At Vista High School, for example, the school principal responded to staff concerns that students become upset when told that they are suspended by making the following suggestion at a staff meeting:

> The principal said that one tactic that works is to calm the student down, and don't tell him/her that he/she is suspended. Let the student go home, then call the parents, tell them their child has been suspended, and let them tell the student. This way, the parents will understand, and the student will get upset at home rather than at school.

This excerpt of text, taken from fieldnotes of a school disciplinary staff meeting, reveals what is usually unseen about the educational system in the US. The objective of order in schools is so highly valued that the Vista High School principal suggests shifting any potential disorder to a student's home.

---

which social situations involving juveniles are constructed, rather than assuming that social order can be described without attention to how it comes to be or relying on the researcher's own presumptions to interpret a situation, which may not accurately acknowledge the peculiarities of interactions involving juveniles.

Though other criminological research methods – especially ethnography – pay careful attention to the social world of juveniles, ethnomethodology does so in a manner that emphasizes the processes that juveniles and those in authority use to actively create juvenile justice. This approach avoids assumptions about pre-existing social structures or cultural forces, and instead explores how order emerges in juvenile justice institutions (like schools) by closely examining *in situ* social behavior. By exploring how juveniles and adults create and recreate routine social encounters, the ethnomethodologist can highlight the agency juveniles have and the ways they are manipulated in social situations, rather than assuming they are passive actors who always bend to the will of adults.

FUTURE DIRECTIONS FOR ETHNOMETHODOLOGY

While ethnomethodology is an important approach for the study of juvenile justice, and criminal justice issues generally, there are a number of controversies that involve this approach. Ethnomethodology has certainly been the target of criticism for such things as the complicated nature of its language (Gidlow, 1972; Peyrot, 1982; Swanson, 1968) and for having what some see as an unduly behaviorist and empiricist orientation (for a review of this criticism see Atkinson, 1988). Critics argue that ethnomethodological approaches to criminology would be improved by incorporating tenets from other approaches, particularly ethnography. This is an interesting development since 'traditional' ethnomethodologists have long sought to distinguish ethnomethodology from other methodological approaches. For example, Wieder (1974), in his classic text, *Language and Social Reality*, sought to demonstrate the fundamental differences between ethnomethodology and ethnography. In this book, Wieder used both ethnography and ethnomethodology to examine the place of a 'convict code' in a halfway house for narcotics offenders. In order to highlight the differences between these two approaches, Wieder provides an ethnographic account in the first half of the book and describes how deviance emerges among the residents as a result of their adherence to the sub-cultural 'convict code' (i.e., the pre-existing code 'causes' residents to resist agency rules and staff directives). In the second half of the book, Wieder provides a more traditional ethnomethodological account of the same code. In this section, Wieder focuses on the residents' language and especially how they 'tell the code' – that is, how the residents (and staff) use the code as a sense-making interpretive device, which they use in a self-serving manner to frame their motives and to rationalize their conduct. In this account, it is social action through talk that brings the code into existence. Thus, in Wieder's research, ethnography and ethnomethodology are distinct frameworks that can be used to explore different aspects of the same social phenomena.

More recently, some researchers have gone a step further than Wieder and have attempted to explicitly blend ethnography and ethnomethodology together to form a hybrid perspective. In this approach, which can be described as ethnomethodological ethnography (Jimerson and Oware, 2006), researchers attempt to preserve ethnomethodology's empirical focus on the methods that people use to create social order *in situ*, while simultaneously using ethnography (and especially informant interviews) to understand the intentions and sets of cultural meaning that influence people's actions in those grounded social settings. In one of the best examples of this approach, Moerman (1988) argues that conversation analysts cannot adequately understand interaction-through-talk without having some information about the historical, cultural, and personal contexts out of which that talk emerges. Thus he argues that analysis of transcripts needs to be supplemented with ethnographic work that explores the cultural knowledge that provides the context for the speaker's social action. Jimerson and Oware (2006)

combine ethnographic and ethnomethodological approaches to explore how the 'code of the street' influences the conduct of African-American basketball players (ethnographic approach), but also how those same players recursively recreate the code by rationalizing their conduct through 'telling the code' (ethnomethodological approach). Finally, the orientation toward using ethnographic tools to inform ethnomethodological work has had a strong influence on Bracy's (2011) aforementioned research on school discipline. In this article, she argues that one cannot understand interaction between students and school authorities without having some appreciation for the motives, intentions and personal contexts that inform their behavior. Thus, she uses ethnographic and ethnomethodological approaches in a complementary way, where interviews are used along with field observations in order to understand the sets of meanings that guide the actions of students, teachers, administrators and SROs within the school disciplinary system.

Beyond the controversies that have marked ethnomethodology, there are a range of new directions in which it can be applied to the field of juvenile justice. While there has been some work on how language is used to construct the social order of juvenile justice, much of this research has tended to emphasize the action of authority figures (e.g., judges and attorneys), rather than the juveniles themselves. So there is an important space in the current literature that can be filled by using ethnomethodology to more actively explore how juveniles contribute to the social order of different types of juvenile justice settings. For example, more ethnomethodological research could focus on the interactional order of police interrogations of juveniles, or on how juveniles use language to either support or resist symbolic rituals in juvenile justice settings such as teen courts or juvenile drug courts.

Another interesting direction for ethnomethodology is to consider how juvenile justice settings are reshaped by the growing use of technology, especially technological surveillance. It seems likely that improved surveillance and data sharing systems such as electronic monitoring, drug testing, and online databases will alter juvenile justice settings, since juvenile justice workers will have more information available to them about youths' deviant acts. Whether these technologies reshape the social organization of juvenile justice is a question that ethnomethodologists are well suited to address. What's more, technological advances might alter the range of offenses that lead to juvenile justice involvement. As the current generation of youth grows up using mobile phones, email, and the Internet, their experiences with juvenile justice institutions might be different from those of a generation ago. For example, we know little about the ways that norms are created and enforced regarding juveniles who commit cyber-bullying (bullying that occurs online), or who send sext-messages (sexually explicit text and video messages through mobile phones) and are caught. Given the priority that ethnomethodology places on the subtleties of interaction, ethnomethodology is well suited to study how changes in interaction that arise due to technological advances shape and reshape juvenile justice.

Certainly, these are just a few examples of how ethnomethodology can continue to contribute to the field of criminology, and particularly the study of juvenile justice. Whether ethnomethodology is used on its own or in conjunction with other methodological approaches, it offers a unique perspective that is especially helpful when studying juveniles and the social worlds they inhabit.

RECOMMENDED READING

Coulon, A. 1995. *Ethnomethodology* (London: Sage Publications) is a very concise introduction to ethnomethodology, and is particularly appropriate for advanced undergraduates and graduate students.

Francis, D. and Hester, S. 2004. *An Invitation to Ethnomethodology: Language, Society, and Interaction* (Thousand Oaks, CA: Sage) provides an accessible introduction to ethnomethodology and observational methods. It does a particularly good job of using empirical examples to demonstrate ethnomethodological ideas.

Garfinkel, H. 1967. *Studies in Ethnomethodology* (Cambridge: Polity Press) is the pioneering work that propelled the use of ethnomethodology in sociology and criminology.

Maynard, D. and Clayman, S. 1991. 'The diversity of ethnomethodology' *Annual Review of Sociology* 17: 385–418, provides an outstanding review of the basic theoretical issues in ethnomethodology.

Ten Have, P. 2007. *Doing Conversation Analysis* (Thousand Oaks, CA: *Sage Publications*) is a well-written book that provides an excellent introduction to conversation analysis.

REFERENCES

Asquith, S. 1983. *Children and Justice: Decision-making in Children's Hearings and Juvenile Courts.* Edinburgh: University of Edinburgh Press.
Atkinson, J. 1984. *Our Master's Voices: The Language and Body Language of Politics.* London: Methuen.
Atkinson, J. and Drew, P. 1979. *Order in Court: The Organisation of Verbal Interaction in Judicial Settings.* London: Macmillan.
Atkinson, P. 1988. 'Ethnomethodology: A critical review' *Annual Review of Sociology* 14: 441–465.
Bittner, E. 1967. 'The police on skid row: A study of peace-keeping' *American Sociological Review* 32(5): 699–715.
Boden, D. 1990. 'The world as it happens: ethnomethodology and conversation analysis.' In G. Ritzer (ed.), *Frontiers in Social Theory*, pp. 185–213. New York: Columbia University Press.
Bortner, M.A. and Williams, L.M. 1997. *Youth in Prison: We the People of Unit Four.* New York: Routledge Press.
Bracy, N.L. 2011. 'Student perceptions of high security school environments.' *Youth and Society* 43(1): 365–395.
Cavender, G. and Knepper, P. 1992. 'Strange interlude: An analysis of juvenile parole revocation decision making' *Social Problems* 39(4): 387–399.
Cicourel, A.V. 1968. *The Social Organization of Juvenile Justice.* New York: John Wiley.
Cicourel, A.V. 1987, '*Interpenetration of communicative contexts:* examples from medical encounters' *Social Psychology Quarterly* 50(2): 217–226.
Cicourel, A. and Kitsuse, J. 1963. *The Educational Decision Makers.* Indianapolis: Bobbs-Merrill.
Clayman, S. 1993. 'Booing: the anatomy of a disaffiliative response' *American Sociological Review* 58(1): 110–130.
Coulon, A. 1995. *Ethnomethodology.* London: Sage Publications.
Edles, L. 2002. *Cultural Sociology in Practice.* Malden, MA: Blackwell.
Eisenstein, J., Flemming, F. and Nardulli, P. *1988. The Contours of Justice: Communities and Their Courts.* Boston, MA: Little, Brown.
Emerson, R.M. 1969. *Judging Delinquents: Context and Process in Juvenile Court.* Chicago: Aldine Publishing.
Francis, D. and Hester, S. 2004. *An Invitation To Ethnomethodology: Language, Society And Interaction.* Thousand Oaks, CA: Sage Publications.
Garfinkel, H. 1967. *Studies in Ethnomethodology.* Cambridge MA: Polity Press.
Gidlow, B. 1972. '*Ethnomethodology-a new name for old practices*' *British Journal of Sociology* 23(4): 395–405.
Greatbatch, D. 1988. 'A *turn-taking system for* British news interviews' *Language in Society* 17(3): 401–430.
Hutchby, I. and Wooffitt, R. 1998. *Conversation Analysis: Principles, Practices, and Applications.* Cambridge: Polity Press.
Hwang, S. 2008. 'Utilizing qualitative data analysis software: A review of Atlas.ti' *Social Science Computer Review* 26(4): 519–527.
Jimerson, J. and Oware, M. 2006. 'Telling the code of the street: An ethnomethodological ethnography' *Journal of Contemporary Ethnography* 35(1): 24–50.
Kupchik, A. 2004. 'Youthfulness, responsibility and punishment: Admonishing adolescents in criminal court' *Punishment & Society* 6(2): 149–173.

Kupchik, A. and Monahan, T. 2006. 'The New American School: Preparation for postindustrial discipline' *British Journal of Sociology of Education* 27(5): 617–631.

Lewis, R. 2004. 'NVivo 2.0 and ATLAS.ti 5.0: A Comparative Review of Two Popular Qualitative Data-Analysis Programs' *Field Methods* 16: 439.

Maynard, D. 1989. 'On ethnography and analysis of discourse in institutional settings.' In J.A. Holstein and G. Miller (eds), *Perspectives on Social Problems, Vol. 1* (pp. 127–146). Greenwich: JAI Press.

Maynard, D. and Clayman, S. 1991. 'The diversity of ethnomethodology' *Annual Review of Sociology* 17: 385–418.

Meehan, A.J. 1989. 'Assessing the 'Police-worthiness' of Citizens' Complaints to the Police: Accountability and the Negotiation of "Facts"', in D.T. Helm, W.T. Anderson, A.J. Meehan and A.W. Rawls (eds), *The Interactional Order: New Directions in the Study of Social Order* (pp. 116–140). New York: Irvington.

Mehan, H. 1991. 'The school's work of sorting students', in D. Bodre and D. Zimmerman (eds), *Talk and Social Structure: Studies in Ethnomethodology and Conversation Analysis* (pp. 71–90). Berkeley: University of California Press.

Mehan, H. and Wood, H. 1975. *The Reality of Ethnomethodology*. New York: John Wiley and Sons.

Moehrman, M. 1988. *Talking Culture*. Philadelphia: University of Pennsylvania Press.

Peyrot, M. 1982. 'Understanding ethnomethodology: A remedy for some common misconceptions' *Human Studies* 5(4): 261–283.

Pfohl, S. 1985. *Images of Deviance and Social Control: A Sociological History*. New York: McGraw-Hill.

Pollner, M. 1987. *Mundane Reason*. Cambridge: Cambridge University Press.

Psathas, G. 1994. *Conversation Analysis: The Study of Talk-In-Interaction*. Thousand Oaks, CA: Sage Publications.

Rawls, A. 2005. *'Respecifying the Study of Social Order'* In H. Garfinkel (ed.) *Seeing Sociologically: The Routine Grounds for Social Action* (pp. 1–99). Boulder, CO: Paradigm Publishing.

Sacks, H. 1992. *Lectures on Conversation*. Oxford: Basil Blackwell.

Sacks, H., Schlegoff, E., and Jefferson, G. 1974. 'A simplest systematics for the organization of turn-taking for conversation' *Language* 50(4): 696–735.

Schegloff, E. 1986. 'The routine as an achievement' *Human Studies* 9(2): 111–151.

Schegloff, E. 2007. *Sequence Organization in Conversation Analysis: Vol. 1: A Primer in Conversation Analysis*. Cambridge: Cambridge University Press.

Silver, C. and Fielding, N. 2008. 'Using computer packages in qualitative research' In C. Willig and W. Stainton-Rogers (Eds.) *The Sage Handbook of Qualitative Research in Psychology* (pp. 334–351). London: Sage.

Sudnow, D. 1965. 'Normal crimes: sociological features of a penal code in a public defender's office' *Social Problems* 12(3): 255–276.

Swanson, G. 1968. 'Review of Harold Garfinkel, *Studies in Ethnomethodology*' *American Sociological Review* 33(1): 122–124.

Ten Have, P. 2007. *Doing Conversation Analysis*. Thousand Oaks, CA: *Sage Publications*.

Ulmer, J.T. 1997. *Social Worlds of Sentencing: Court Communities Under Sentencing Guidelines*. Albany, NY: State University of New York Press.

Watson, D.R. 1983. 'The presentation of victim and motive in discourse: the case of police interrogations and interviews' *Victimology* 8(1): 31–52.

Whalen, M. and Zimmerman, D. 1987. 'Sequential and institutional contexts in calls for help' *Social Psychology Quarterly* 50(2): 172–185.

Whalen, M. and Zimmerman, D. 1990. 'Describing trouble: Practical epistemology in citizen calls to the police' *Language in Society*, 19(4): 465–492.

Wieder, D.L. 1974. *Language and Social Reality: The Case of Telling the Convict Code*. The Hague: Mouton.

23

Evaluation Research and Probation: How to Distinguish High Performance from Low Performance Programmes

Karin Tusinski Miofsky,
James M. Byrne

INTRODUCTION

Over the past two decades, the total population of adults under some form of community supervision in the US nearly doubled from 2.6 million in 1990 to 5.2 million offenders today, the equivalent of about 1 in every 45 adults (Bonczar and Glaze, 2009). Probationers represent the majority (84 percent) of the country's community corrections population, totaling 4,270,917 offenders in 2008 (Byrne, 2009; Glaze and Bonczar, 2009). Examination of longer-term trends in corrections populations reveals that the growth of the US probation population has outpaced the pace of growth in prison, jail and parole populations. In 1980, there were a little over a million offenders under probation supervision; by year end 2008, the population was four times larger, with over 4.2 million offenders under probation supervision.

For these offenders, a probation sanction included three unique elements: *punishment* (loss of rights and privileges), *control* (limits on behavior, associations, and movements) and *reformation* (i.e., efforts to induce offender change in risk-related areas, such as drug and alcohol use, lack of education and job skills, etc., utilizing various treatment interventions). While a number of observers have documented the increased control orientation of probation sanctions in the US and in other countries over the past few decades (longer terms of probation, more conditions of supervision, stricter enforcement, and higher revocation rates), there is a paucity of empirical research linking these changes directly to probation outcomes (Byrne, 2009). We know that using standard, accepted outcome measures – such as re-arrest, reconviction, technical violations and/or return to prison – today's probationers 'fail' much more often than probationers in the 1970s; but we do not know why.

In the following chapter we examine the available empirical research on probation, highlighting what we currently know – and do not know – about the effectiveness of current probation strategies. Based on this review, we identify the key steps that are needed to conduct a quality evaluation of a probation program, focusing on four key implementation measures: (1) quantity of supervision, (2) style of supervision, (3) enforcement of conditions, and (4) response to positive and negative offender change. We also discuss the importance of model specification, research design choice, sample size, and choice of criterion measures. We conclude our review by identifying new directions in probation and then considering the methodological challenges associated with rigorous evaluation of these new initiatives.

WHAT IS PROBATION?

Probation has its origins in the simple notion that prison and jail terms may be too harsh a sanction for certain categories of offenders, and the belief that prisons and jails may actually make some offenders worse, undermining the deterrence component of the sanction. Probation systems have been designed to manage offenders in their communities while imposing the sanctions ordered by a criminal court. These penalties involve the control of offenders in the community through direct supervision, monitoring compliance with the conditions of probation, and promotion of treatment resources from the immediate community to support law-abiding behaviors (McCarthy et al., 2001). As with other forms of corrections, probation has grown enormously in the last decade and

its clientele have changed from predominately misdemeanor offenders to both misdemeanants and low-level felons.

Today, as in the past, almost two-thirds of all convicted offenders serve their sentences on probation (DOJ, 2009). While there is no escaping the fact that we have been on a recent incarceration binge in the US (the number of convicted offenders sent to prison increased 700 percent between 1970 and 2005, from 190,000 offenders in federal and state prison to 1.5 million), it is important to recognize that, for most categories of crime, probation is the sanction of choice in this country. Although there has been considerable discussion and debate about how we incarcerate, it should be noted that our community corrections population has actually increased at a much faster rate in the past 25 years than our prison/jail population (see Figures 23.1 and 23.2). We rely on community corrections to sanction offenders for a variety of reasons, but certainly one rationale for community-based corrections is the belief that we can punish most offenders in the community *without compromising public safety*. In fact, there is some evidence that community corrections sanctions contribute much more to public safety than either a prison or jail sentence (Byrne and Roberts, 2007; Stemen, 2007).

According to the most recent data from the Bureau of Justice Statistics (Bonczar and Glaze, 2009) there are now over 4 million offenders on probation, representing approximately 60 percent of the total correctional population in this country (7,000,000). About half of all offenders sentenced to a term of probation have been convicted of a felony; three quarters of all probationers are males, and blacks (29 percent) and

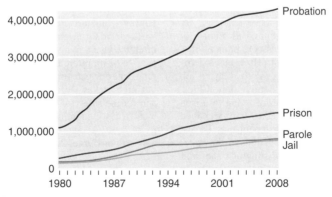

Figure 23.1   Probation population trends in the US. *Source*: **Bureau of Justice Statistics Correctional Surveys (The Annual Probation Survey, National Prisoner Statistics Program, Annual Survey of Jails, and Annual Parole Survey) as presented in Correctional Populations in the United States, Annual Prisoners in 2008, and Probation and Parole in the United States, 2008**

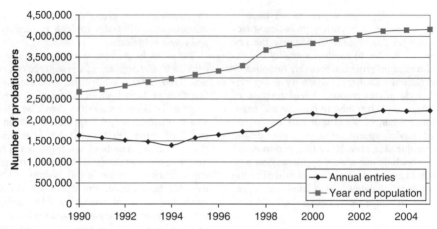

Figure 23.2   Annual probation population and entries to probation, 1990–2005.
Source: **Annual Probation Survey and Annual Parole Survey**

Hispanic/Latinos (13 percent) are overrepresented in the probation population. For offenders on probation, the most common criminal offenses were *drug law* violations (about one in three probationers) followed by DUI (driving while intoxicated) offenders, who comprise about one in six probationers, and offenders convicted of *larceny theft* (about one in ten probationers). In addition, about one in five probationers were convicted of some form of *assault* (sexual assault, 3 percent; domestic violence 6 percent; other assault, 10 percent).

It should be noted that not all probationers are directly sentenced to probation alone. When sentencing offenders to a term of probation, judges may use a *split sentence* (a short term of incarceration in prison or jail, followed by a longer period of community supervision). Today, almost 20 percent of all offenders under probation supervision fall into the split sentence category. By comparison, in 1995, 13 percent of all probationers were split sentence cases. Of course, if a period of time in either jail or prison has a detrimental effect on offenders – due to reduced job prospects, disrupted personal/family relationships, and the negative consequences of living in prison with a group of criminals – then what we gained in the area of retribution/punishment may be lost in the area of deterrence. Evaluations of the effectiveness of probation must distinguish the split sentence from the direct-to-probation offender in order to examine these potential effects.

Finally, it is important to keep in mind that only a portion of all offenders sentenced to a term of probation are *actively* supervised by probation officers. In 2008, 71 percent of probationers nationwide were actively supervised at the time of the Bureau of Justice Statistics (BJS) status review;

by comparison, 76 percent of all probationers were actively supervised in 2000 (Glaze and Bonczar, 2009: 24, appendix table 5). However, active supervision means different things in different jurisdictions and there is wide variation in supervision contact levels, and supervision styles both within and across state probation systems in the US (Byrne, 2009). In some US jurisdictions, the majority of probationers are placed on administrative supervision, with no direct contact with – or supervision by – probation officers. In these jurisdictions, a decision has been made to focus limited probation resources on those offenders who pose the greatest risk to the community. Nationwide, 8 percent of all offenders were identified as inactive in 2008, with another 30 percent classified as active, but in need of minimal supervision (Byrne, 2009; Glaze and Bonczar, 2009). However, all jurisdictions weigh more than *risk* when deciding who should be supervised, how often they need to be seen, and the conditions that need to be monitored. Sex offenders, for example, represent one category of low risk (for re-offense) but high stakes (for the legitimacy of probation and for the safety of residents) offenders that will receive close attention not based on the *probability* of a new crime, but rather the *possibility* of a new crime (Byrne, 2009).

HOW DO WE IDENTIFY A SUCCESSFUL PROBATION SYSTEM?

There is no simple metric than has been devised to rank the most effective – and least effective – probation systems in the US. This is certainly one

Table 23.1 Distribution of types of felony sentences imposed in State courts, by gender of felons and offense, 2002

Most serious conviction offense	Total	Percent of felons sentenced to – Incarceration			Nonincarceration		
		Total	Prison	Jail	Total	Probation	Other
Male							
All offenses	100	71	41	30	29	26	3
Violent offenses	100	80	54	27	20	18	2
Murder /a	100	96	92	4	4	4	0
Sexual assault /b	100	84	59	25	16	14	2
Robbery	100	88	70	18	12	11	1
Aggravated assault	100	75	43	32	25	23	2
Other violent /c	100	76	40	36	24	22	2
Property offenses	100	70	40	30	30	27	3
Burglary	100	75	48	27	25	22	3
Larceny /d	100	69	36	33	31	29	2
Fraud /e	100	61	31	30	39	36	3
Drug offenses	100	65	38	27	35	31	4
Possession	100	60	32	28	40	34	6
Trafficking	100	67	41	26	33	30	3
Weapon offenses	100	74	39	34	26	24	2
Other offenses /f	100	71	33	38	29	27	2
Female							
All offenses	100	56	25	31	44	40	3
Violent offenses	100	64	32	31	36	34	3
Murder /a	100	88	81	7	12	11	1
Sexual assault /b	100	71	44	27	29	25	4
Robbery	100	74	50	24	26	24	1
Aggravated assault	100	58	23	35	42	39	3
Other violent /c	100	68	37	31	32	29	3
Property offenses	100	53	22	31	47	44	3
Burglary	100	73	30	43	27	25	3
Larceny /d	100	52	19	33	48	45	3
Fraud /e	100	49	22	27	51	48	3
Drug offenses	100	54	26	28	46	41	5
Possession	100	51	21	30	49	43	6
Trafficking	100	56	29	27	44	40	4
Weapon offenses	100	60	27	33	40	35	5
Other offenses /f	100	64	25	39	36	33	3

Note: See note on tables 1.2 and 2.1. Detail may not sum to total because of rounding.

– Less than 0.5%.

a/ Includes nonnegligent manslaughter.

b/ Includes rape.

c/ Includes offenses such as negligent manslaughter and kidnaping.

d/ Includes motor vehicle theft.

e/ Includes forgery and embezzlement.

f/ Composed of nonviolent offenses such as receiving stolen property and vandalism.

source : 2002 National Judicial Reporting Program.

area where corrections research lags far behind medical research. In medical research it is possible to both the most effective treatment interventions and the most successful treatment providers for a wide range of serious medical problems and life-threatening diseases, from cancer to cystic fibrosis (Gawande, 2007). Because probation systems vary widely in offender population characteristics, and various organizational dynamics (including structure, personnel, technology, classification procedures, supervision levels, length, styles, revocation practices, and resource and capacity levels) probation in one jurisdiction may not be directly comparable to probation in another jurisdiction. Despite this caveat, it is our view that performance measures for probation can be established and used to identify both high performance and low performance probation systems. We recommend a multiple indicators approach to measuring probation success. In the following section, we identify the most promising measurement techniques available to distinguish high performance from low performance probation systems.

The most commonly cited measure of probation 'success' is the percentage of probationers in a given jurisdiction who successfully complete their probation terms in a given year. In the US, state level data on the number/percent of offenders who exit probation are available from the BJS (see Glaze and Bonczar, 2009: 22, appendix table 4). Using these data, we can determine the percentage of *successful* probation exits; in 2008, 2,165,083 offenders exited probation, and of this total, less than half were classified as successful terminations (1,041,695). However, these data do not include offenders supervised at the county level. In addition, several state probation systems – including Massachusetts, New Hampshire, New Jersey, Rhode Island, and New Mexico – refused to provide these state-level data to the Bureau of Justice Statistics. Without these data, we cannot accurately rank order the states using successful probation exits as the criterion measure. The BJS has attempted to address this problem by estimating the likely exit rates for those states with reporting problems. Using these estimation procedures, the overall (national) success of probation increases to 63 percent (See Glaze and Bonczar, 2009: 4, table 3).

Using the national BJS estimates, it is possible to track long-term changes in the effectiveness of probation, using the successful exit measure. In 2008, the percentage of adults who successfully completed their probation terms was 63 percent, using the BJS national estimate (but less than 50 percent using the available state level data). There was a long-term downward trend in the success rate of probation, between 1970 and the early 1990s (1970s – 80 percent successful completions;

1980s – 70 percent successful completions; 1990s – 60 percent successful completions). However, the success of probation – as measured by successful exits each year, nationally – has remained relatively stable over the past two decades. Perhaps recognizing the negative consequences of split sentences, direct sentences to probation have increased during this period, while the percentage of split sentences (10 percent) was much lower than it had been a decade earlier (15 percent).

While successful exits from probation is one possible measure of probation success, it probably tells us more about how the probation system monitors, controls and sanctions offenders than it does about the behavior of probationers. This suggests that we need to create additional measures of probation success. The most common measure you will find in the probation evaluation research literature is *re-arrest* during a specified follow-up period (one-year, two-year, three-year, etc.). When calculating re-arrest, a decision will need to be made regarding whether any re-arrest will be counted (e.g., driving related offenses, minor public order). Some researchers focus only on a specified subgroup, such as felony or misdemeanor arrests, while others use a broad brush approach (any re-arrests). Remarkably, it is currently impossible to examine the percentage of offenders who are re-arrested while on probation supervision, because no national database exists. While it would be helpful to identify those state probation systems with the lowest – and highest – re-arrest rates, these data are not available for review.

In addition to re-arrest, the success of probation could be measured by examining *technical revocation rates*; that is, the percentage of probationers who had their probation revoked because they failed to adhere to the conditions of probation imposed. Using this outcome measure in conjunction with re-arrest, researchers can provide answers to a basic question about what works in probation: will high technical revocation rates result in lower re-arrest rates for a probation system? This is a critical question to answer, but we currently do not collect the necessary data to answer it. When an offender has his/her probation revoked, there are a number of possible judicial sanctions, including continuation on probation with new conditions, placement in a secure correctional treatment facility, or incarceration. As Petersilia et al. (2009) has observed, offenders on probation often have their probation revoked for a *combination* of technical violations and new arrests. Rather than prosecute these offenders for their alleged new crimes, formal revocation proceedings are used to fast track many of these offenders to prison. Unfortunately, we do not collect detailed revocation data on probationers.

This limits our ability to measure probation performance using this indicator.

Incarceration is another outcome of interest to probation researchers. If probation is an effective alternative to prison then it should reduce the need for incarceration among certain categories of convicted offenders. Researchers have examined subsequent incarceration patterns of probationers during various follow-up periods as a measure of probation's effectiveness as an alternative sanction. In 2008, 17 percent of all offenders exiting probation were incarcerated; three-quarters of these offenders had their probation revoked, while one-quarter were convicted of a new crime and sentenced to a prison term. Unless we begin to collect outcome data that allows us to distinguish between technical violators and individuals arrested and convicted of new crimes, we will not be able to answer important questions about the impact of various monitoring and control strategies.

Up to this point, we have discussed outcome measures based on the dual notions of offender control and offender change. However, there is another element of the probation sanction that should be measured: *punishment*. The limits placed on offenders sentenced to probation represent the multidimensional, punishment/control component of probation. Punishment – as it is applied via probation – is a multi-dimensional concept; it represents more than 'loss of liberty' because it may also be viewed in terms of *loss of rights* (e.g. right to vote, occupational disqualification), *loss of privileges* (e.g. driving, drinking, socializing) and *loss of freedom* (e.g. residential location restrictions, movement restrictions, curfews, mandated reporting, mandated treatment, mandated employment, drug testing, computer monitoring). First, an offender with a criminal record will find that his/her conviction will have consequences for where he/she lives, what jobs he/she can apply for and/or successfully get hired, and even his/her ability to vote in a federal, state or local election. Being labeled a convicted offender is a punishment in itself, even without the need to abide by the rules of probation.

The multiple conditions of probation represent the second punishment dimension of probation. When an offender receives a direct sentence to probation, he/she must abide by a series of conditions designed essentially to change and/or control the lifestyle of offenders, including mandatory treatment conditions for a variety of offender problems (alcoholism, drug abuse, mental illness, etc.), mandatory meetings with a probation officer, and a series of restrictions on *where* an offender can live, work, socialize and travel, *when* an offender can leave his/her residence (curfews), *with whom* an offender can associate, *what* jobs the offender may apply for, *whether* the offender can have a computer and/or whether access to certain areas of the Internet is prohibited, *how* much money he/she must pay in fines and restitution to the victim, and even *which* (if any) substances (drugs, alcohol) he/she may consume while on probation. Failure to abide by these conditions may result in subsequent incarceration in all but one state (namely, Washington).

For a significant number of offenders, restrictions on lifestyle decisions (or forced *lifestyle change*) may actually constitute a more severe form of punishment than incarceration, which can be described as short-term *lifestyle interruption* (as contrasted with long-term offender change). Rather than face the prospects of curfews, drug and alcohol testing, attendance at treatment programs, job training and full time employment, at least some offenders would rather simply do their time in prison or jail without the restrictions and hassles (and controls) associated with community supervision (Petersilia, 2003; Travis and Visher, 2005).

Our point is straightforward: community sentences carry with them elements of freedom and control. And while to some people a probation sentence may seem lenient, it actually captures the multi-dimensional nature of punishment more fully than a prison sentence. With a few exceptions, researchers have largely ignored punishment as an outcome of interest, but it appears to be an important consideration in the sanctioning process. This raises an interesting empirical question: can the success of probation as punishment be measured; and if so, how? We argue here that it can, using such basic measures as number of hours of community service, number of licenses revoked, number of curfew hours, number of occupational disqualifications, number and type of other restrictions imposed (voting, residence, locations). To date, assessments of the punishment component of the probation sanction have been based on surveys of legislators, offenders, community residents, and/or probation personnel on what the exchange rate should look like when a prison or jail sentence is replaced by a period of time on probation (e.g. a six-month jail sentence could be exchanged for a six-year probation sentence based on the calculation that a year on probation is roughly equivalent to a month in jail). Aside from the work of Andrew von Hirsch (1992) on exchange rates in the early 1990s, very little research has focused on this outcome measure.

In defining and measuring probation success, it should be highlighted that success is positive in its nature (Mead, 2005/1937; Rossi et al., 2004). Many researchers consider success as something far more fundamental than mere absence of failure.

No acceptable evaluation of probation success can be achieved simply by counting up violations – those individuals who are routinely referred to as probation failures – or by measuring the proportion of such violators to the entire group supervised on probation (Mead, 2005/1937). Do researchers truly recognize whether success achieves genuine improvement in the behavior of those on probation? Researchers need to continually devise ways to determine not only the simple fact of improvement in behavior, but also the degree of improvement.

It is in this context that we consider the final element of probation performance that needs to be systematically measured: *service provision*. It can be argued that a probation system is a success if it: (1) classifies offenders correctly in terms of individual-level risk-related problems (such as mental health, substance abuse, lack of job skills, lack of education, and other individual problems related to criminal behavior); (2) links these offenders to appropriate services; (3) monitors offender progress in treatment; and (4) adjusts the treatment protocol and services based on offender progress. Unfortunately, we do not routinely collect these types of service provision data on a national, state, or local level in the US (Taxman et al., 2007).

While there are certainly a number of other outcome measures that could be employed by researchers studying offenders on probation – including changes in either the rate of offending or the seriousness of offending among offenders during a pre/post comparison period (Byrne and Kelly, 1989), or self-report measures of criminal activity, we believe that the measures of success identified here – re-arrest, reconviction, incarceration, technical violations resulting in revocation, punishment and service provision – highlight the need for a multiple indicators approach to the measurement of probation performance.

METHODOLOGICAL APPROACHES TO PROBATION

The credibility of probation as a stand-alone sanction depends, to a certain degree, on whether it can exhibit its effectiveness through rigorous evaluation. Well-conducted evaluations are efficient at recognizing the degree at which probation is accomplishing its intentions, and also which components are most effective, for whom and under what conditions (Healy and O'Donnell, 2005; Rossi et al., 2004). This provides beneficial information to policy makers in reference to which elements of probation should be

widespread, abandoned or revised. Yet, what should a 'rigorous' evaluation look like?

Methodology refers to the approach that researchers employ to conduct a study. These techniques can be surprisingly simple or quite elaborate, employing highly refined measures and sophisticated statistical models (MacKenzie and Hickman, 1998). The quality of the methodology used in evaluations of probation is generally regarded as low, based on systematic review criteria (note: for more details on systemic reviews and the criteria used to rank evaluation quality, see the Campbell review link in the 'Recommended Reading' section at the end of the chapter).

The vast majority of research studies conducted in the probation field have employed *non-experimental* research designs. These studies provide a necessary first look at probation, but more rigorous research designs must be employed before we can draw any conclusions about probation performance. Typically, these studies provide information about the implementation and impact of probation strategies at a single site, with no pre/post comparisons and/or no attempt to identify a comparison group that did not receive the intervention.

A smaller number of studies employ *quasi-experimental* research designs; these studies identify the target group included in a particular program to be evaluated, and then attempt to identify an appropriate comparison group using a variety of matching techniques. This approach consists of identifying a suitable comparison group for the experimental group of probationers and matching relevant characteristics such as age, sex and criminal record (Raynor, 2008). If the matching is done well, the findings will certainly be useful to policy makers and practitioners; but if the matching rules are poorly constructed, you can end up with a comparison between apples and oranges.

The most rigorous evaluations of probation have employed *experimental* designs, with random assignment to treatment and control groups. Unfortunately, only a few random assignment experiments have been conducted in the field of probation (Barnes et al., 2010; Gill, 2010; Petersilia and Turner, 1990). Until recently, true experiments have been viewed as an unreasonable methodology because of the need for random assignment to treatment (intervention) and control groups. As Colledge and colleagues observed: 'In rare circumstances, it may be possible to set up control groups by random allocation of offenders to the programme of interest and to a control group which does not receive the programme. However, usually such randomised control groups are not possible for practical reasons' (Colledge et al., 1996: 16). Overcoming resistance to experimental research is now a major topic of interest to researchers worldwide (Weisburd, 2010). Random assignment is the scientific ideal for identifying the effects of an intervention program because it reduces the likelihood that one group differs from the other. With an experimental design, the researcher can demonstrate that the only difference between the two groups of probationers is the intervention. However, we should emphasize that even with random assignment to treatment and control groups, the researcher will need to measure the 'dosage' (or intervention) differences between treatment and control groups.

It appears that probation administrators have been frightened away from true experiments based in part on the notion that if you have a strategy that you think will work, you should use it on *all* eligible offenders; because if an offender in the control group commits a serious crime during the evaluation then it could be argued that the evaluation put the community unnecessarily at risk. However, there is a logical counter-argument that can be raised. Since we do not know which strategies are effective, we need to conduct the necessary research to demonstrate the need for a particular program or intervention strategy. With limited resources, it is important to correctly determine what works, with whom, and why. This is the underlying message of the evidence-based corrections movement, both in the US and internationally (Note: see the link to the Credos web page in the 'Recommended Reading' section; CREDOS, 2010).

EARLY SYSTEMATIC REVIEWS OF PROBATION: MARTINSON REVISITED

In order to progress with rigorous evaluations of probation, it is essential to examine prior studies on the effectiveness of probation. Thirty years ago, Michael Gottfredson observed that the review of the treatment literature most often cited by advocates of the 'nothing works' position was the examination of 231 institutional and community treatment program evaluations by Lipton et al. (1975). However, as Gottfredson (1979) pointed out, this early 'systematic review' actually provides support for the advocates of rehabilitation, while at the same time underscoring the need for standard research review criteria. All too often in systematic, evidence-based reviews, these review criteria are defined in ways that raise doubt about the conclusions offered by reviewers. After reviewing the Lipton et al. (1975) assessment of rehabilitation, Gottfredson (1979) offered the following assessment: it all depends on how you assess the

quality of the research studies, summarize key findings, and aggregate the results. Consider the following:

> These authors reviewed 231 treatment studies in the field of corrections, published between 1945 and 1967 ... of these 231 studies only 138 used some measure of recidivism as a criterion. Of these, only 65 used a design that met the minimum standards for scientific confidence ... [O]f these 65, the treatment advocates are likely to stress that 32 (49%) reported positive results. If the field of studies is further restricted according to the quality ratings given by Upton et at 1975 to only 'A' studies acceptable for the survey with no more than minimal shortcomings, then the number falls to 40. Of these, 19 (48%) reported positive results (Gottfredson, 1979: 11).

The Lipton et al. review included a wide array of institutional and community based treatment programs. Only a very small number of the 40 'A' studies cited above were evaluations of probation or parole programs. In fact, Gottfredson and Gottfredson (1988) pointed out that you can count the number of adult probation studies included in this review on one hand. Actually, there were seven and only one randomly assigned offenders to different types of probation (see Lipton et al., 1975: 26). If one considers for a moment that this was a review of the evaluation literature during a 25-year period, then US researchers were producing one good study on probation every five years! While it would be difficult to conclude anything about the effectiveness of various forms of probation from just five studies, many subsequent probation reform efforts – in particular, the movement toward surveillance and control-based probation and parole strategies – begin by citing the Lipton et al. review as definitive evidence that nothing works.

What did Lipton et al. actually conclude about community supervision's rehabilitative effects? In his now classic article, 'What works? Questions and answers about prison reform,' Martinson (1974) summarized the group's findings related to the intensive supervision of adults. The best evidence he could find came from an experimental study, not of probationers but of parolees. He focused his review on the intensive supervision of adult parolees in California's experimental Special Intensive Parole Unit (SIPU). According to Martinson, positive findings were only found in one of four phases of the SIPU experiment Phase III. His comments on these positive results bear careful consideration:

> Here, it was indeed found that a smaller caseload improved one's chances of parole success.

There is, however, an important caveat that attaches to this finding: when my colleagues and I divided the whole population of subjects into two groups – those receiving supervision in the North of the state and those in the South – we found that the 'improvement' of the experimentals success rates was taking place primarily in the North. The North differed from the South in one important aspect: its agents practiced a policy of returning both 'experimental' and 'control' violators to prison at relatively high rates. And it was the North that produced the higher success rates among its experimentals. So this improvement in experimental's performance was taking place only when accompanied [by] a 'realistic threat' of severe sanctions. What this suggests is that when intensive supervision does produce an improvement in offenders' behavior, it does so not through the mechanism of 'treatment' or 'rehabilitation' but instead through a mechanism that our studies have almost totally ignored – the mechanism of deterrence (Martinson, 1974, reprinted in Martinson et al., 1976: 32).

Martinson's summary of findings is essentially correct, but the conclusions he draws about the relative power of deterrence *versus* rehabilitation are not, for one basic reason: if it really was simply a deterrent effect at work in this phase of the project, then there should have been no significant difference between experimental and control offenders in the North, since the return to prison rate was high in the North for both groups. However, examination of Table 23.2 reveals that there were significant overall differences between experimental and control court offenders in the North. In addition, the success rates of offenders was higher for experimentals than for controls within all risk classification levels in the North and in three of four risk levels in the South.

One other difference worth noting is that offenders on intensive supervision in the North did somewhat better than offenders on intensive supervision in the Southern region. Is this evidence of a specific deterrent effect? A more likely scenario is that the threat of prison resulted in a higher level of compliance with the rehabilitative aspects of intensive supervision, which in turn led to lower recidivism. In other words, the deterrent component of intensive supervision may have had an indirect effect on recidivism through increased compliance with the treatment component of the program. Thus, the results of the early round of intensive supervision programs – although very preliminary and based on parolees – suggest that probation and parole policy makers need to develop supervision programs which attempt both to rehabilitate and to deter. They certainly do not reveal any glaring flaw in the rehabilitative strategy which would justify the abandonment of this approach to community corrections. Program developers involved in the current wave of intensive supervision programs seem to recognize this point, since specific forms of treatment and strict revocation policies are standard elements of intensive supervision (Byrne and Pattavina, 2007; Paparazi, 2006; Taxman, 2008).

These findings are interesting to consider, but they do not tell us anything about probation effectiveness, beyond the usual caveat: the necessary research has not been done. In 1979, the National Institute of Law Enforcement and Criminal Justice disclosed the findings from a review on probation evaluation literature (Fitz Harris, 1979). The review was dispersed into three categories: (1) studies that compared the effectiveness of probation with that of alternative sentencing options, (2) studies that measured probation outcome without any form of comparison, and (3) studies that attempted to isolate the factors that enhance the

Table 23.2   Success and failure rates for experimentals and controls in percentages by region and risk category (California Special Intensive Parole Unit Studies [SIPU])

	Northern region				Southern region			
	Experiment		Control		Experiment		Control	
Risk level	Success*	Failure***	Success*	Failure***	Success*	Failure**	Success*	Failure***
Poor Risk	28	37.6	26.3	39.9	21.7	30.8	22.7	32.5
Medium-Poor	35.6	29.9	27.9	36.7	35.9	21.1	32.6	27.5
Medium Good	47.3	28.4	36.5	33.7	44.2	22.5	35.5	26.4
Good Risk	64.3	17.9	59.6	20.2	62	11.6	61.2	14.5
Overall†	44.6	28	37.2	32.7	40.2	21.7	37.2	25.6

* Success rate defined as the no-arrest rate: one-year follow-up period; ** failure rate defined as the return-to-prison rate; † differences between the success rates of exp. and control groups are significant (p <.05) only in the *Northern* region.

Source: Adapted from Lipton et al., 1975: 122, table 8.

likelihood of probation success (McCarthy et al., 2001). Notably, only five studies methodologically compared the effectiveness of probation with another sanction. Three evaluations compared probation with incarceration through the examination of their experiences (McCarthy et al., 2001). Another two evaluations compared a mixed group of offenders to those of a burglary offense (McCarthy et al., 2001). The results concluded that probation did produce lower recidivism rate, but only for the burglars. A third evaluation focused only on female offenders, and found no difference between female probationers and female prisoners (McCarthy et al., 2001).

A fourth study compared probationers, persons sentenced to probation following a jail term, and persons sentenced only to jail. Each group was followed for 12 months within their community. The probation group produced the lowest rate of recidivism, with roughly two-thirds of the probationers having no subsequent arrests (Fitz Harris, 1979).

The fifth evaluation examined misdemeanor probationers through a comparison of probation supervision to an alternative sanction. The participants were randomly assigned to either the experimental or the control group. The experimental group received supervision, while the control group received non-supervision probation. Measuring probation success as a probationer only having a conviction for a new offense, 22 percent of the supervised probationers and 24 percent of the non-supervised probationers recidivated (Fitz Harris, 1979).

PROBATION RESEARCH: 1980–2010

A number of research studies were conducted in the 1980s and early 1990s on the effectiveness of the wave of intermediate sanctions – including residential community corrections, boot camps, intensive probation supervision, day reporting centers, and electronic monitoring – that were being touted as a new surveillance and control-oriented approach to the community supervision of offenders. However, it should be emphasized that despite their media popularity, only a small proportion of all offenders (no more than 10 percent in any given year over the last three decades) were actually placed in these programs. As before, traditional probation was still – and continues to be – the sanction of choice for most categories of non-violent offenders, along with a significant number of violent offenders. The fact that traditional probation was largely ignored by evaluators is a problem, because much of the research evidence that is cited in support of evidence-based

probation practice is *not* research on probation; it is research on intermediate sanctions. We still know remarkably little about the effectiveness of federal, state and local probation systems in the United States. Gottfredson and Gottfredson (1988: 198–9) examined over 130 probation studies conducted over the previous two decades (1960–1980) and found that only 10 studies met their minimum review criteria. The key findings identified in their review of these 10 studies are important to consider:

1. The necessary research has not been done to permit a determination of whether probation is more effective than imprisonment as a rehabilitative treatment.
2. Evidence tends to support the conjecture that the personal characteristics of offenders are more important than the form of treatment in determining future recidivism.
3. From limited evidence, it appears that intensive supervision may result in more technical violations known and acted upon and also to fewer new offense convictions; thus, the size of the caseload may have some effect on recidivism.
4. There is limited evidence to indicate what forms of treatment and supervision provide more effective results when applied to probationers generally or to any particular classification of offenders, and even that evidence is mixed (As quoted in Byrne et al., 1989: 23).

The most often cited US studies on probation effectiveness were conducted by RAND researchers in the late 1980s. (For an overview, see Petersilia, 1989; or Byrne et al., 1992). In 1985, the RAND Corporation reported results of a study on felony probation. The study utilized data from more than 16,000 offenders convicted of felonies in 17 California counties, as well as recidivism data on 1,672 probation felons in Los Angeles and Alameda counties, who were tracked for a 40-month period (Petersilia et al., 1985). The purpose of the research was to answer two questions:

1 What criteria are used by the courts to determine which offenders will be imprisoned and which will be granted probation?
2 How many of these probationers are ultimately re-arrested, re-convicted, and re-imprisoned?

The researchers reviewed court data on each offender, including offenses, prior record, and victim. The researchers found that many probationers were indistinguishable from prisoners, in terms of their crimes and prior record. One key finding reported in this study was that probationers with histories and offenses comparable to prisoners were roughly 50 percent more likely to be re-arrested than were other probationers (RAND, 1985). Overall, two-thirds of the probationers in the RAND study were re-arrested during the three-year follow-up. More than half of the total number of probationers was re-convicted, and 34 percent were re-incarcerated. About two-thirds of those recommended for probation and two-thirds recommended for prison were subsequently re-arrested. Using factors associated with probation success, the researchers concluded that only about 3 percent of prisoners could have been safely placed on probation. The researchers presumed that felony probation within these jurisdictions posed a considerable threat to public safety.

Although it is unclear whether felony probation in California accurately reflects felony probation elsewhere, the RAND study provided further impetus to efforts already under way to improve offender classification and to emphasize the need for the close monitoring and supervision of felony probationers. When considering these findings, it is important to keep in mind that this study utilized a non-experimental design, and secondary analyses of available data. No attempt was made in this study to analyze data on probation supervision strategies (e.g. contact levels, number of conditions, supervision styles, monitoring and enforcement of conditions of probation), and/or to link the use of different supervision strategies to outcomes of interest (such as cost, recidivism, technical violations, and improvements in risk-related problem areas, such as mental health, substance abuse and employment).

Researchers at RAND also conducted a large multi-site evaluation of intensive probation supervision in 14 separate jurisdictions using random assignment to treatment and control groups (Petersilia and Turner, 1993). However, in several of the sites, there were problems with small sample size, due to restrictive target population criteria, rendering the identification of statistically significant effects difficult in several sites. To address the small sample size issue, researchers pooled results across sites, which is an acceptable method only if the sites were operating similar programs with similar target populations. Unfortunately, this was not the case, a point subsequent reviewers have largely ignored. It is this multi-site evaluation that is most often cited as evidence that surveillance-oriented intensive probation supervision programs did not reduce recidivism (MacKenzie, 2006). The fact that the researchers conducted a randomized experiment across 9 states and 14 sites is impressive, but the research conducted at each of these sites must be reviewed carefully. In our assessment, we actually learned relatively little about intensive supervision

from these evaluations, for two simple reasons; (1) sample size was too small in most sites to identify effects; and (2) researchers focused only on the surveillance component of intensive supervision in their experiment, making it impossible to assess the individual and combined effects of changes in either – or both – the surveillance and treatment components of intensive supervision. To their credit, the researchers acknowledged this limitation in their final report of study findings (Petersilia and Turner, 1993)

One interesting side note: in two of the intensive supervision experimental sites, offenders were randomly assigned to a short term of incarceration or intensive probation supervision. Since inclusion in the RAND study at these two sites was voluntary, offenders could opt out of the pool of eligible participants. In one jurisdiction, one in four offenders refused to participate; these offenders were incarceration-bound, which meant they simply went to prison as sentenced. One interpretation of this decision is that for some offenders, lifestyle interruption (a short stay in prison/jail) may be preferable to lifestyle change (via intensive supervision). This is an avenue for further research that needs to be investigated further.

Another investigation into probation supervision comes from a self-reported study completed by MacKenzie and colleagues (1998). The researchers asked offenders to report their criminal activities during the year before arrest and during probation. The results demonstrated that the criminal activities of the offenders declined dramatically when the pre-arrest period was compared to the probation period. This suggests probation was effective in reducing the criminal activities of these offenders. Similarly, behaviors that constituted a violation of conditions of probation, such as heavy drinking or illegal drug use, were associated with increased criminal activity. The researchers found no evidence that increases in the intrusiveness of conditions, the agent's knowledge of misbehavior, or how the agent responded to misbehavior were associated with changes in criminal activity. According to this study, while probation appears to be effective in reducing criminal activities and the violations of conditions signaled criminal activities, little else done during probation had a crime reduction effect.

Recently, Villetez et al. (2006) conducted a systematic review comparing prison against a variety of community-based sanctions, including probation, community service, and electronic monitoring. Only studies comparing custodial *versus* non-custodial sanctions were included in this review. Three hundred research studies were originally examined, but only 23 studies met the minimum criteria for inclusion. In total, 18 quasi-experiments and 5 experimental studies were identified and analyzed. Focusing on the 5 experimental and 18 quasi-experimental studies investigating custodial versus non-custodial sanctions, the authors reported that

[a]lthough a vast majority of the selected studies show non-custodial sanctions to be more beneficial in terms of reoffending than custodial sanctions, no significant difference is found in the meta-analysis based on four controlled and one natural experiments (Villetez et al., 2006: 3).

One study comparing prison to probation (Bergman, 1976) showed probationers fared significantly better; however, a second study comparing prison to community service had mixed results (Killias et al., 2000), while a third natural experiment comparing the effects of a 14-day prison term to a suspended sentence reported mixed results as well (Van der Werff, 1979). Turning to the quasi-experiments, the authors reported that 11 of the 18 studies they reviewed showed positive effects for a range of non-custodial sanctions, including probation, home confinement, community service and mandatory alcohol treatment in drunk driving cases (Villetez et al., 2006).

What have we learned about probation performance generally and the effectiveness of specific probation practices in particular? While some progress has been made through the past 30 years, there is a tremendous amount of work which remains to be done before researchers can hope to make any scientific assessment of probation effectiveness. There are four dimensions of probation practice that need to be systematically evaluated: (1) supervision quantity (Gill, 2010), (2) supervision quality (Taxman, 2009), (3) enforcement of conditions (Byrne and Kelly, 1989), and (4) response to violations (Byrne, 2009). These four measure of probation implementation need to be linked to specific outcomes of interest, including cost, recidivism, punishment and service provision. In the following section, we describe the methodological challenges associated with the evaluation of probation, and then provide a framework for future research and evaluation on probation.

METHODOLOGICAL CHALLENGES

As is now well documented, the response from probation's leaders to the negative research findings related to most surveillance-oriented community supervision programs was the rediscovery of rehabilitation (Cullen, 2007; Cullen et al., 2009). Unfortunately for the field, the research basis for this community corrections paradigm shift owed more to *negative* evaluation findings from a small number of boutique programs (Taxman, 2009), than to the *positive* evidence supporting the move toward rehabilitation (Farabee, 2005). Despite the claims of the 'What Works' movement, which identified the key programmatic elements of effective, evidence-based probation supervision, we do not have sufficient research evidence to support these policy and practice recommendations.

It is important that probation evaluations cover all aspects of the probation process, including offender targeting, classification, supervision strategies (quantity, style, enforcement, response), probation completion and multiple probation outcomes. Because of the economy, the costs associated with most correctional control strategies are viewed by many as unreasonably high; consequently, several states have developed strategies designed to reduce the size of the prison population, and allocate additional resources for the supervision and treatment of offenders in the community (Byrne, 2009). In many jurisdictions, probation administrators are now embracing the notion of evidence-based practice, which should bode well for researchers looking to evaluate the effectiveness of various probation interventions. The potential downside with this new evidence-based approach to resource allocation decisions is that policy makers may not rely on high quality, gold standard evidence-based reviews to make these decisions (Byrne and Miofsky, 2009). The field needs to recognize that we still need to conduct the necessary research before we can offer evidence-based policy recommendations about probation. There are no shortcuts.

The majority of evaluation researchers encounter obstacles when conducting sound research. Evaluations have been affected by problems of project design and implementation (Raynor, 2004), including, for example, low completion rates or selection effects. Moreover, there are a number of methodological challenges in implementing rigorous evaluations of probation. First, the offender's conduct is problematic because measuring behavioral change is methodologically complex (Jones, 1995). Behavioral changes in such areas as criminal thinking, problem solving, anger management and decision making can be difficult to uncover and assess (Taxman et al., 2010). The aim of supervision is to minimize harm to the community and the offender by reducing the frequency and/or the seriousness of offending. An added possibility might be the evaluation in terms of risk reduction. Actuarial risk assessment devices have been accessible for some time and are now viewed as fairly to moderately reliable. An offender's behavioral change may be correlated to a reduction in the level of risk or recidivism over time (Byrne and Pattavina, 2006). One way to measure this risk reduction effect involves examination of changes in an offender's risk score over time (e.g., a researcher could compare an offender's initial risk score on a particular variable – substance abuse, employment – to his/her risk score at reassessment and/or termination). Researchers need to attempt to document the impact of probation on offender change in specified risk-related problem areas. Without this information, we will not be able to link changes in these intermediate outcomes to changes in criminal behavior.

An additional challenge for probation researchers involves obtaining a sample size that is large enough to draw generalizable conclusions. With small samples, it is difficult to detect a statistically significant difference between conditions unless the effect is very large (Cunningham, 2002; Lipsey, 1995; Rossi et al., 2004) and previous research suggests the impacts (or effect sizes) of treatment are fairly modest (Lipsey, 1995). Petersilia (1989) stated one of the bigger difficulties in attempting to employ evaluation research develops from the use of targeting within an experimental design, specifically on the impact of target population decisions on the size of the sample identified in the initial screening and referral process. Probation officials would often identify and refer ineligible offenders – and not refer eligible ones – for these interventions, which made assessments of likely sample size difficult. In order to address this potential problem, we recommend that probation researchers conduct a preliminary pipeline study before determining likely study sample size. Pipeline studies examine the flow of offenders through the probation system during a specified review period. Once the flow of offenders meeting study inclusion criteria is examined, a more accurate assessment of likely sample size will emerge. Perhaps more importantly, researchers will have a baseline for monitoring case flow once the study begins. This represents an important tool for addressing case flow issues related to inappropriate referrals.

A third methodological challenge focuses on the criterion used to measure probation success. It would be helpful to acquire information about subsequent consequences through an advanced model rather than the use of a dichotomous variable which measures merely the presence or absence of re-offending. Fourth, it is important for researchers to consider the impact of geographic location on probation impact. A richer representation of probation supervision – disaggregated by location – might expose factors (social service availability) that would otherwise remain unknown (Bachman and Schutt, 2007 ; Hipp et al., 2010).

In addition to acquiring a large enough sample size, obtaining a representative comparison sample is also a barrier of evaluation research. Complications develop in research designs which consist of comparison groups. Are the comparison groups truly comparable? Many evaluation studies control for differences in the risk of re-offending, but control only for static factors and not dynamic ones (Merrington and Stanley, 2004). There may be factors relating to why probationers who complete supervision have a lower recidivism rate, including personal motivation or willingness to conform, both of which do not have a probation effect.

Another finding surfacing from recent research concerns probation completion. Several probation systems report relatively low probation completion rates. This may be a result of an *offender* characteristic such as risk, personal motivation or *supervision* characteristics such as length of supervision, and/or the number and type of conditions being monitored (Andrews et al., 1990; Van Voorhis and Brown, 1996). Completion rates must be increased if an offender is going to benefit from what probation has to offer. Probation supervision is meant to provide a service provision objective. In our view, this objective may be undermined if an offender fails to complete his/her term successfully. While researchers have conducted basic, descriptive assessments of probation success and failures, we know very little about how probation supervision and probation service referrals – particularly voluntary referrals – affect these outcomes. We also know very little about what the optimal length of probation supervision should be, given what we know about time to failure (Byrne, 2009; Petersilia, 2009). Research demonstrates that probation completers tend to have a relatively lower re-offending rate than those not completing the supervision (due to technical violations). Within probation, the importance of raising completion rates has been recognized, but there is little empirical research available on this important topic.

Because assessment of probation has become a major issue in modern corrections, probation success must be monitored to determine if the goals are achieved, and if probation is as cost-effective in comparison to other forms of correctional disposition. A typical problem with probation evaluation involves the definition of success. Well-defined evaluation measures provide an accurate appraisal of probation effectiveness, and offer probation officials with practical information with which they can improve the competence of the initiatives.

The primary measure of probation effectiveness has been the outcome measure of recidivism. However, this outcome measure does not provide much support to probation officials in determining the day-to-day impact of supervision. Traditionally, recidivism considers the long-term effect of probation supervision. Numerous problems are related with using recidivism as the sole measure for probation effectiveness. These include a wide range of definitions for recidivism, and the vagueness surrounding the proper measure of success (Maltz, 1984; Mears and Travis, 2004; Snyder and Sickman, 2006; Travis, 2005).

Outcomes for success rates of probation supervision will fluctuate depending upon the definition of recidivism applied, from a high of 65 percent re-arrest rate of probationers in California (Petersilia, 1985) to a lower estimate such as that reported by Vito (1987) of an 18 percent reconviction rate among probationers in Kentucky. Notably, these studies differ in many regards, mostly from inconsistent operational definitions of recidivism, and the amount of time probationers are followed up for the research. Some studies on probation define recidivism as re-incarceration; however, previous research has operationalized recidivism as *simple recidivism*, specific recidivism, re-arrest, re-conviction and re-incarceration (Klein, 1974; Rempel, 2005; Webb, 1976). Each of these are a valid measure of recidivism, but each measures something different and will lead to widely varied conclusions. *Simple recidivism* is built on the notion that any contact with the criminal justice system constitutes a failure of the correctional program. As an outcome measure, success only occurs if the offender stays out of trouble for a selected length of time. *Specific recidivism* deems probation a failure if the offender commits a crime similar to the original offense. This definition permits the offender who was arrested for a specific crime, such as battery, to be arrested for drug possession without regarding the program to be a failure. Re-arrest regards the probation a failure if the offender is re-arrested, while re-conviction entails the action of the criminal justice system. Using arrests as the decisive criteria for recidivism will result in a higher recidivism rate. Re-conviction is a more limiting criterion which results in a lower recidivism rate. Re-incarceration is measured as the date of return to prison after a newly convicted felony or repeated probation violations. In an ideal world, correctional agencies would employ a universal operational definition of recidivism. But it is clear that the choice of criterion can be used to make probation appear more or less successful.

Petersilia (1985) commented that 'the success of community corrections should not be based solely on some post-program assessment of behavior'. She suggested a substitute to recidivism – applying performance-based outcome measures for probation effectiveness. In 1993, the National Institute of Justice recommended the implementation of alternative outcomes measures used by community corrections agencies to evaluate overall agency performance, including what they do and how well they do it (Boone and Fulton, 1996). Specifically, performance-based measures examine agency values and goals, activities for accomplishment, and measures for evaluating effectiveness. Such measurements can facilitate the professional and organizational growth that needs to continue in community corrections.

As it is clearly possible to overcome many of the methodological problems associated with conducting quality evaluations of supervision communities, why has the practice of better-quality evaluation not taken hold in the US? It is imperative to match evaluation methods with the needs and characteristics of the community supervision agency. Evaluation researchers should recognize that there is a hierarchy of design quality; with certain methodological designs rated as superior to others (Healy and O'Donnell, 2005, 2008). At minimum, we need to design probation evaluations to capture both the level of implementation of a particular program or strategy, and the impact of the intervention strategy and/or program under review. It seems logical to assume that most probation strategies are not always implemented as designed. Unless we measure level of implementation and then examine the link between level of implementation and impact (e.g., reduction in recidivism during a specific follow-up period), we may miss important findings about the effectiveness of a particular program or strategy. Byrne and Kelly (1989), for example, demonstrated that while there were no overall differences in outcomes across experimental and control groups in their evaluation of the Massachusetts Intensive Probation Supervision (IPS) program, this was due to the fact that the IPS program was not fully implemented at several sites. However, those offenders (about one in three) who did receive the full intensive supervision 'dosage' had significantly lower recidivism levels than (1) other experimentals who received a lower level of the program, and controls, who – by design – received standard probation supervision services and controls. In this case, the evaluators found that the Massachusetts IPS program worked quite well *when it was implemented as designed.*

This leads us to an important point: evaluation researchers need to measure level of implementation regardless of research design choice (non-experimental, quasi-experimental, or experimental design). Byrne and Kelly (1989) offer one possible approach to this measurement issue by developing an index of implementation with four key components found in all probation systems: (1) quantity of supervision, (2) quality of supervision, (3) enforcement of conditions and (4) response to violations. Let us briefly consider how each of these probation components can be measured.

Measuring supervision quantity

There is currently considerable debate about the importance of probation contacts. A recent review of experimental and quasi-experimental research by Gill (2010) identified 14 separate research studies that examined the impact of reduced caseload size on adult probation outcomes (e.g., re-arrest, during a specified follow-up period). Of these 14 studies, 8 linked smaller caseload size and increased contacts to higher re-arrest rates, while 6 linked smaller caseload size and increased contacts to lower re-arrest rates (see Gill, 2010, appendix D). Clearly, the field needs a more definitive answer to the question: does supervision quantity matter? To get such an answer, we need to offer a standard definition of supervision quantity.

One reason for the mixed findings reported by Gill (2010) is that the operational definition of the quantity of supervision for the experimental group varied from study to study. In addition, the level of supervision in the comparison groups used in these studies varied as well. In one study, for example, the comparison was between 15:1 caseload size in the experimentals *versus* 90:1 caseload size in the control group. In another study, the comparison was much closer: 20:1 experimental *versus* 45:1 control. Given these differences, it is not surprising that the overall findings were mixed.

There are a number of techniques that can be used to measure the quantity of probation supervision provided in a given program, including calculation of a probation officer's caseload size (15:1; 30:1, etc), the total number of contacts between probation officers and probationers on a weekly or monthly basis, and the specific types of contacts made by probation officers (face-to-face; and collateral, such as address and employment verifications and criminal record checks). To accurately measure supervision contact levels, it is necessary to review individual case files and collect/code detailed data on the number and types of contacts between probation officers and probationers throughout the supervision period, because in many jurisdictions, both the number and types of contacts are likely to vary over time. Byrne and Kelly (1989) collected detailed contact data on each of the following types of contacts: face-to-face, office visits, home visits, work visits, telephone contacts, employment verifications, address verifications and record checks. They used these data to construct a quantity of supervision scale

(scores ranged from 0 to 10) with the following components: average total monthly contacts, average face-to-face contacts, average record checks per month; and average employment verifications. This is one possible approach to the measurement of supervision quantity.

Measuring supervision style and quality

A second component of probation involves the style (and quality) of supervision used by the probation officer to manage his/her caseload. There are a number of different strategies that probation officers can employ to supervise offenders, but we know very little about the impact of different supervision styles on probation outcomes (Taxman, 2009). To measure supervision style it will be necessary to survey probation officers on their preferred supervision styles, and then to follow up this survey research with a qualitative review, combining case file examination with direct observations of probation officers in action.

Perhaps equally important, we also need to measure the impact of supervision *quality* on outcomes. One approach to the measurement of supervision quality involves a close examination of what probation officers are expected to do in the course of supervision. To conduct such a review, researchers would need to assess the accuracy of the probation officer's initial classification, whether mandatory referrals were made as required, and how the probation officer responded to the problems and needs of offenders under their direct supervision. In their examination of the Massachusetts IPS program's implementation, Byrne and Kelly (1989) addressed this measurement challenge by creating a Quality of Supervision Scale, which was designed to measure whether probation officers were supervising offenders in a manner consistent with the program model. Their index included the following items:

1 *Risk/need consistency for both alcohol and drug problems.* One simple measure of the diagnostic skills of probation officers is the consistency of their substance abuse assessments between risk and need classification. If a probation officer indicates on the risk assessment form that an offender has a drug and/or alcohol problem, then he/she should also identify this item (or items) on the need form.

2 *Mandatory referrals for special conditions.* A second measure of probation quality is whether the probation officer made a referral to fulfill the requirements of a special condition established by a judge at disposition (e.g., counseling, drug testing, restitution).

3 *Mandatory referrals in risk-related high need areas (such as substance abuse, employment, and individual/family counseling.* A third measure identified by Byrne and Kelly (1989) focused on whether the probation officers made referrals based on their own assessments of offender problems, regardless of whether a special condition was set. Interestingly, they reported that probation officers in Massachusetts were much more likely to make referrals (referrals made 70 percent of the time) when ordered by a judge, than based on their own assessment (referrals made 50 percent of the time).

4 *Evidence of supervisory review.* A fourth measure of supervision quality is evidence of supervisory review of the case file. In the Byrne and Kelly study, there were two review points identified (four-month review and termination review.)

5 *Probation officer non-response rate.* A final measure of supervision quality is based on an examination of the probation chronology (in the case file), where the probation officer indicates what progress is being made during supervision, identifies specific offender problems, and describes his/her actions and recommendations. Using this information, it is possible to calculate the percentage of times a probation officer identifies a problem; and when identified, how often the probation officer responds appropriately. Byrne and Kelly focused on the first ten face-to-face contacts between probation officers and probationers, and found something that underscores the need for detailed case file reviews of this kind: by the third face-to face contact, over half of the case files indicated no problem noted; by the tenth face-to-face contact, two-thirds of all probation chronologies indicated no problem noted. Given the extent of the drug, alcohol, employment, and personal problems identified in this population, this suggests that it is the first two face-to-face contacts where problems are addressed; after this point, the visits appear to be more routine. In addition to determining the nature of the face-to-face visits, it is possible to calculate the number of times a particular problem was noted, but the probation officer did not respond. In the Massachusetts evaluation, the researchers found that during the first ten face-to-face contacts, probation officers identified a problem but made no specific response in 17.6 percent of the cases reviewed.

Once a quality of supervision scale is created, researchers will be able to examine the link between supervision quality and probation outcomes. A similar measurement strategy can be employed to examine the link between supervision style and probation outcomes (Taxman, 2009).

Measuring probation enforcement

Most probation systems have specific policies and procedures in place to address non-compliance by probationers to the conditions of probation supervision. Probation officer enforcement practices represent another component of probation that needs to be measured accurately. To create a measure of enforcement, researchers need to examine both the overall level of compliance with probation conditions by probationers, and to examine how probation officers respond to evidence of non-compliance with the conditions of probation that they identify in their case files. One approach advocated by Byrne and Kelly (1989) focuses on the use of surrenders for various types of technical violations, such as failure to report, failure to notify probation officer of change of address, failure to attend drug/alcohol counseling, failure to pay fine/restitution, or some combination of these violations. Using these data from probation case files, it will be possible to measure the level of enforcement attained in a particular jurisdiction. In the Massachusetts study, 16.7 percent of the offenders in the IPS program were found to be in non-compliance, but were not surrendered, compared to 19.4 percent of control group offenders supervised following standard practices. This finding of no significant differences led researchers to conclude that enforcement practices did not change as expected in the original program model.

Measuring administrative and judicial response to violations

The final component of probation supervision process that needs to be accurately measured is what actually happens after surrender is issued for a technical violation. When a probation officer requests a formal revocation hearing, and the result of that hearing is a lenient administrative/judicial response, it could be argued that the probation officers' authority has been undermined. When the response is stricter, it could be viewed as reinforcing the authority of the probation officer. Unfortunately, we know very little empirically about the impact of administrative/judicial decisions on the subsequent behavior of offenders. One possible measure to consider is the return to prison rate for a technical resulting in a revocation. In the Massachusetts IPS evaluation, researchers found that

over 60 percent of all cases where noncompliance was identified with technical conditions by probation officers, nothing happened to the offender, due to one of three factors: (1) no surrender was issued, (2) no revocation hearing was held, or (3) the judge either discontinued probation in the case or continued the offender on probation with no changes in his/her conditions of supervision (Byrne and Kelly, 1989: 190).

Importantly, no significant differences between experimental and control groups in administrative/ judicial response to non-compliance were identified in the Massachusetts evaluation. There are only a handful of studies that have addressed the non-compliance issue. Similarly, there are no studies that have addressed the equally important question: how should probation departments respond to the compliant offender? Petersilia (2009) has recommended shortening probation sentences considerably, based on the behavior of offenders during their first year of probation, a strategy based on the notion of behavioral contracting. We need to conduct empirical research on policy recommendation before it is adopted.

There are a number of possible techniques that can be applied to the measurement of probation's key components; the key is to systematically evaluate the link between level of implementation and level of impact. By measuring the level of implementation of each component of the program, the Massachusetts' intensive probation supervision researchers were able to determine that only two of the four components of the program – supervision quantity and supervision quality – varied significantly across experimental and control courts. Apparently, some components of probation practice are more difficult to change than others. If we fail to measure the implementation of probation programs, we run the risk of falsely identifying probation programs and strategies as ineffective.

CURRENT CONTROVERSIES AND NEW HORIZONS

To this point, we have focused on what researchers need to consider as they attempt to evaluate the implementation and impact of probation initiatives. In this section, we will highlight current controversies that probation researchers may be able to resolve, while suggesting several emerging strategies that probation researchers will likely be evaluating in the near future. First, it is apparent that probation research needs to become more sophisticated. Generally speaking, evaluation research should attempt to conduct randomized, controlled experiments, but there is still an important place for both quasi-experimental and non-experimental research, particularly in the early

stages of program development (Byrne and Miofsky, 2009; Weisburd, 2010). In addition, some of our most enduring research comes from the use of qualitative research methods, particularly interviews with line staff and probationers on the nature of the officer–client relationship, and observational studies of probation. While much of the debate over corrections strategies focuses on the application of formal social control mechanisms, researchers are now beginning to examine the impact of informal social control mechanisms in the desistance process (Byrne and Taxman, 2005; National Research Council, 2007). It is certainly plausible to view the probation officer–probationer relationship as one such informal social control mechanism. Further research – both quantitative and qualitative – on the nature of this relationship and the possible link to desistance is needed.

Second, we need to separate the science from the nonsense (or non-science) in the discussion of evidence-based practice (Byrne, 2008; Byrne and Miofsky, 2009). Probation policy makers and program administrators cannot incorporate evidence-based practice into community corrections, because the necessary research has not been completed. Several scholars have noted that probation research has made premature assumptions regarding the success or failure of particular programs (Byrne and Miofsky, 2009; Cullen, 2007; Gottfredson, 1979; Palmer, 1975, 1978; Van Voorhis and Brown, 1996). This has not stopped the proliferation of evidence-based guides for practitioners, both in the US and abroad. While our own review of the available evaluation research underscores this point, we can offer some preliminary broad statements about what works in the area of probation: it appears that probation programs that attempt to balance the control and treatment components of probation are the most effective, across a wide range of outcome measures (Byrne, 2009). The challenge ahead for probation researchers will be to identify that tipping point between control and treatment in various probation programs. This effort will require the type of detailed implementation assessment described earlier in this chapter, followed by well-designed experimental and/or quasi-experimental research linking implementation 'tipping points' to positive outcomes.

Third, there are always new probation initiatives and new probation programs to be evaluated. Byrne (2009) recently suggested a new wave of community corrections programming targeting three maximum impact points: high-risk offenders, high-risk times and high-risk locations. Research has demonstrated that a sub-group of high-risk offenders can be identified; the challenge before us is to develop effective risk reduction strategies for these high-risk offenders. There is emerging evidence that concentrating both services and supervision on these higher risk, higher rate offenders will result in significant reductions in crime and victimization (Byrne, 2008; MacKenzie, 2006; Petersilia, 2007). According to Byrne (2009), we need to evaluate the impact of supervising higher-risk offenders using: (1) smaller caseloads; (2) new supervision strategies that emphasize the importance of the relationship between probation officers and probationers in terms of informal social control; and (3) employ new technological innovations for monitoring offenders' movements, drug and alcohol consumption, and progress in treatment.

Research has also revealed that offenders on community supervision are at the highest risk of re-arrest during the first months of community supervision (National Research Council, 2007). In 2007, the National Research Council produced results from over 240,000 offenders released from prisons in 13 states, and reported the probability of arrest is roughly twice as high in the first month of community supervision as it is in the fifteenth month. We need better research on the time to failure patterns of probationers; we also need to examine the impact of concentrating probation resources – essentially frontloading both supervision and services – during the beginning months of probation supervision.

The third dimension of a Byrne's maximum impact strategy is the concentration of probationers by geographic location, which has implications for probation, both in terms of offender supervision (e.g., the allocation of geographically determined caseloads) and offender programming (e.g., location of services and programs in higher risk neighborhoods). A disproportionate segment of probationers reside in neighborhoods that may increase an individual's risk of re-offending (Byrne and Pattavina, 2006; Hipp et al., 2010; Kubrin et al., 2007). Kubrin and Stewart describe the effects of neighborhood context on recidivism:

> Neighborhood context is fundamental to our understanding of why individuals offend, and potentially even more important for understanding why former offenders offend again, yet we know very little about how the ecological characteristics of communities influence the recidivism rates of this population (Kubrin and Stewart 2006: 167).

New initiatives based on Byrne's maximum impact, concentrated supervision strategy need to be implemented and empirically evaluated. Targeting offender, time, and location may pave the way for progressively more accurate measurements on the degree of success for probation agencies. However, we need to learn an important lesson from history: do not forget to evaluate mainstream probation practice. In our rush to evaluate new technology and new boutique probation programs, we often ignore the need to measure the performance of traditional probation programs and practices. Without this empirical foundation, we will not be able to identify evidence-based probation strategies. Ensuring probationers lead crime-free lives and follow the rules of community supervision are difficult tasks; a considerable amount of work remains to be accomplished on the scientific evaluation of outcomes for probation.

CONCLUSION

In sum, this chapter has demonstrated the need to conduct high-quality scientific research on the implementation and impact of federal, state and local probation systems, not only in the US but internationally. In-depth critiques of the last 50 years of probation research expose clear flaws in the methodology of many probation studies, including research design flaws, inappropriate comparison groups, small sample sizes, and imprecise measurement of key predictor and criterion variables. We have provided a framework for improved research and evaluation, which is based on what we have learned from reviewing this body of research.

The new generation of probation programs – aimed to target high-risk offenders, high-risk times, and high-risk locations – have yet to be fully implemented, and as a consequence, the needed evaluative research has yet to be conducted on the effectiveness of this approach. Pressure for evaluating effectiveness is on the increase. The present situation, in which states are aggressively investigating techniques to reduce crime and corrections costs, offers policy makers a valuable opportunity to test and benefit from sound, independent evaluation research. As Cheetham et al. (1992: 5) noted, there is a 'general ethical and professional obligation upon social workers not simply to do their best for people who need their help but to offer the help most likely to be effective'. To do this in the field of probation, we need to know what works, with whom and why. As we highlight in this chapter, the next generation of probation researchers need to undertake the task of defining the meaning of probation success and then using these performance indicators to distinguish high-performing from low-performing probation systems.

RECOMMENDED READING

MacKenzie, D. 2006. *What Works in Corrections: Reducing the Criminal Activities of Offenders and Delinquents* (New York: Cambridge University Press). This book highlights the results of systematic research reviews on the effectiveness of both institutional and community –based programs, including rehabilitation programs, intensive supervision and electronic monitoring programs, boot camps, and drug courts/ drug treatment programs.

Byrne, J. 2009. *Maximum Impact: Targeting Supervision on Higher-Risk People, Places and Times.* Public Safety Policy Brief, no. 9: July, 2009 (Washington, DC: The PEW Charitable Trusts), available at: www.pewtrusts.org. This brief monograph highlights what we currently know – and don't know – about community corrections initiatives designed to target high-risk offenders, times and places.

Taxman, F., Shepardson, E. and Byrne, J. 2004. *Tools of the Trade: A Guide for Incorporating Science into Practice.* Washington, DC National Institute of Corrections. This monograph describes how probation departments can implement a proactive community supervision strategy, utilizing such techniques as motivational interviewing, and non-coercive offender change strategies.

Kleiman, M. 2009. *When Brute Force Fails: How to Have Less Crime and Less Punishment.* Princeton, NJ: Princeton University Press. The author presents a review of research on the effectiveness of a wide range of sanctions, including probation. He proposes a new model of probation and parole supervision, based on his research on the effectiveness of Hawaii's Project Hope, based on the principles of earlier zero tolerance policing strategies.

Web resources

CREDOS (Collaboration of Researchers for the Effective Development of Offender Supervision)

Available at: http://www.sccjr.ac.uk/projects/Collaboration-of-Researchers-for-the-Effective-Development-of-Offender-Supervision-CREDOS/29, CREDOS is an international network of researchers, and policy and practice partners in research, who share a common interest in the effective development of offender supervision. It was established following a seminar in Prato, Italy, in September 2007. CREDOS aims to support, encourage and engage in high-quality, collaborative and comparative research and scholarship exploring:

- How best to measure effectiveness in offender supervision
- The nature and features of effective offender supervision
- The characteristics, styles and practices of effective offender supervisors

- The qualities and features of effective relationships between offenders and those that work with them
- The social, political, cultural, organizational and professional contexts of effective offender supervision and how these contexts impact upon it.

Campbell Collaborative: Crime and Justice Coordinating Group

Available at: http://www.campbellcollaboration.org/crime_and_justice/index.php, the Crime and Justice Coordinating Group (CCJG) is an international network of researchers that prepares and disseminates systematic reviews of high-quality research on methods to reduce crime and delinquency and improve the quality of justice. It welcomes the participation of researchers, practitioners, policy makers, teachers, students, media, and concerned citizens from anywhere in the world.

Center for Advancing Correctional Excellence (ACE!):

Available at: http://cls.gmu.edu/ace, the Center for Advancing Correctional Excellence (ACE!) seeks a revisiting of contemporary policies that focus on using the criminal justice and correctional umbrella as a response to a variety of social problems. With an expanding correctional landscape of over 8 million adults and adolescents under correctional control, these incarceration-focused punitive policies have contributed to unhealthy people and communities by increasing the very same risk factors that advocates of punishment believed would deter criminal behavior. ACE seeks to conduct research and assist policy makers and correctional practitioners with using evidence-based practices and treatments in crafting new policies that are focused on preventing criminal behavior, instead of responding to it.

REFERENCES

Andrews, D., Bonta., J., and R. Hoge. 1990. Classification for effective rehabilitation: rediscovering psychology. *Criminal Justice and Behavior,* 17: 19–52.

Bachman, R. and Schutt, R. 2007. *The Practice of Research in Criminology and Criminal Justice,* 3rd Edition. Thousand Oaks: Sage Publications.

Barnes, G., Ahlman, L., Gill, C., Sherman, L.W., Kurtz, E., and Malvestuto, R. 2010. Low-intensity community supervision for low-risk offenders: A randomized, controlled trial. *Journal of Experimental Criminology,* 6(2): 159–189.

Bergman, G.R. 1976. The evaluation of an experimental program designed to reduce recidivism among second felony criminal offenders. Unpublished doctoral dissertation, Wayne State University, Detroit, Michigan.

Bonczar, T., and Glaze, L. 2009. *Probation and Parole in the United States 2008.* Washington, DC: Bureau of Justice Statistics. NCJ 228230.

Boone, H., and Fulton, B. 1996. *Implementing Performance-Based Measures in Community Corrections.* National Institute of Justice: Research in Brief.

Byrne, J.M. 2008. The social ecology of community corrections: Understanding the link between individual and community change. *Criminology and Public Policy,* 7(2): 263–274.

Byrne, J.M. 2009. *Maximum Impact: Targeting Supervision on Higher Risk People, Places, and Times.* Washington, DC: Pew Charitable Trusts.

Byrne, J.M., and Kelly, L. 1989. *Restructuring Probation as An Intermediate Sanction: An Evaluation of the Massachusetts Intensive Probation Supervision Program.* Final report to the Research Program on the Punishment and Control of Offenders, National Institute of Justice, February, 1989.

Byrne, J.M., Lurigio, A., and Baird, C. 1989 *The Effectiveness of the 'New' Intensive Supervision Program.* Monograph prepared for the 'Research in Corrections' series, Volume 2, Issue 2, National Institute of Corrections, Washington, DC.

Byrne, J., Lurigio, A., and Petersilia, J. 1992. *Smart Sentencing: The Emergence of Intermediate Sanctions.* Newbury Park, CA: Sage.

Byrne, J. and Miofsky, K. 2009. From preentry to reentry: An examination of the effectiveness of institutional and community-based sanctions. *Victims and Offenders,* 4(4): 348–356.

Byrne, J.M., and Pattavina, A. 2006. Assessing the role of clinical and actuarial risk assessment in an evidence-based community corrections system: issues to consider. *Federal Probation,* 70(3): 64–66.

Byrne, J.M., and Roberts, A. 2007. New directions in offender typology design, development, and implementation: Can we balance risk, treatment, and control? *Aggression and Violent Behavior,* 12: 483–492.

Byrne, J. and Taxman, F. 2005. Crime control is a choice: Divergent perspectives on the role of treatment in the adult corrections system. *Criminology and Public Policy,* 4(2): 291–310.

Chapman, T. and Hough, M. 1998. *Evidence Based Practice: A guide to effective practice.* HM Inspectorate of Probation/ Home Office.

Cheetham, J., Fuller, R., McIvor, G., and Petch A. 1992. *Evaluating Social Work Effectiveness.* Buckingham: Open University Press.

Collaboration of Researchers for the Effective Development of Offender Supervision (CREDOS). 2010. American Society of Criminology, Division of Corrections and Sentencing Newsletter, Fall 2010, p. 2.

Colledge, M., Collier, P., and S. Brand. 1996. *Crime Reduction Programme and Constructive Regimes in Prison. Programmes for Offenders: Guidance for Evaluators.* London: Research, Development and Statistics Directorate, Home Office.

Cullen, F.T. 2007. Make rehabilitation corrections' guiding paradigm. *Criminology and Public Policy,* 6: 717–728.

Cullen, F.T., Smith, P., Lowenkamp, C., and Latessa, E. 2009. Nothing works revisited: Deconstructing Farabee's Rethinking Rehabilitation. *Victims and Offenders* 4(4): 101–124.

Cunningham, A. 2002. *One Step Forward: Lessons Learned from a Randomised Study of Multi-Systemic Therapy in Canada.* Ontario: Centre for Children and Families in the Justice System.

Farabee, D. 2005. *Rethinking Rehabilitation: Why Can't We Reform Our Criminals?* Washington, DC: AEI Press.

Fitz Harris, T.L. 1979. *Proposition 13 – Its Impact on Probation in California.* US Department of Justice, National Institute of Law Enforcement and Criminal Justice, National Institute of Justice Publishing.

Gawande, A. 2007. *Better: A Surgeon's Notes on Performance.* New York: Picador.

Gill, C. 2010. The effects of sanction severity on criminal conduct: A randomized low intensity probation experiment. Publicly accessible Penn Dissertations. Paper 121. Available at: http://repository.upenn.edu/edissertations/121.

Glaze, L.E., and Bonczar, T.P. (2009). Probation and parole in the United States, 2008. Fact Sheet US Department of Justice No. NCJ 228230. Retrieved from Bureau of Justice Statistics website: www.ojp.usdoj.gov/bjs/.

Gottfredson, M. 1979. Treatment destruction techniques. *Journal of Research in Crime and Delinquency,* 16: 39–54.

Gottfredson, M., and Gottfredson D., 1988. *Decision-making in Criminal Justice: Toward the Rational Exercise of Discretion.* New York: Plenum.

Healy, D., and O'Donnell, I. 2005. Probation in the Republic of Ireland: Context and Challenges. *The Journal of Community and Criminal Justice,* 52(2): 56–68.

Healy, D., and O'Donnell, I. 2008. Calling time on crime: Motivation, generativity and agency in Irish probationers. *Probation Journal,* 55(1): 25–38.

Hipp, J., Petersilia, J. and Turner, S. (2010) Parolee recidivism in California: The effect of neighborhood context and social service agency characteristics. *Criminology,* 48(4): 947–979.

Holsinger, A., Lurigio, A., and Latessa, E. 2001. Practitioners' guide to understanding the basis of assessing offender risk. *Federal Probation,* 65(1): 46–50.

Jones, M., 1995. Predictors of success and failure on intensive probation supervision. *American Journal of Criminal Justice,* 19(2).

Killias, M., Aebi, M., and Ribeaud, D. 2000. Does community service rehabilitate better than shorter-term imprisonment? Results of a controlled experiment. *Howard Journal of Criminal Justice,* 39(1): 40–57.

Klein. M. 1974. Labeling, deterrence, and recidivism: a study of police dispositions of juvenile offenders. *Social Problems,* 22(2): 292–303.

Kubrin, C.E., and Stewart, E. 2006. Predicting who offends: The neglected role of neighborhood context in recidivism studies. *Criminology,* 44: 165–197.

Kubrin, C.E., Squires, G., and Stewart, E. 2007. Neighborhoods, race, and recidivism: The community-reoffending nexus and its implications for African Americans. *Race Relations Abstracts,* 32(1): 7–37.

Lipsey, M. 1995. What do we learn from 400 research studies on the effectiveness of treatment with juvenile delinquents? In J. McGuire (ed.) *What Works: Reducing Re-offending. Guidelines from Research and Practice.* Chichester: John Wiley and Sons.

Lipton, D., Martinson, R., and Wilks, J. 1975. *The Effectiveness of Correctional Treatment: A Survey of Treatment Evaluation Studies.* New York: Praeger.

MacKenzie, D. 2006. *What Works in Corrections: Reducing the Criminal Activities of Offenders and Delinquents.* Cambridge: Cambridge University Press.

MacKenzie, D., and Hickman, L. 1998. *What Works in Corrections? An Examination of the Effectiveness of the Type of Rehabilitation Programs Offered by Washington State Department of Corrections.* Available at: www.webarchive.org.

Maltz, M.D. 1984. *Recidivism.* US Department of Justice: National Institute of Justice. Academic Press.

Martinson, R. (1974). What works? Questions and answers about prison reform. *The Public Interest,* 34: 22–54.

Martinson, R., Palmer, T., and Adams, S. 1976. *Rehabilitation, Recidivism, and Research.* Hackensack, NJ: National Council on Crime and Delinquency.

McCarthy, B., McCarthy, B., and Leone, M. 2001. *Community-Based Corrections.* Belmont, CA: Wadsworth/Thomson Learning.

McGuire, J. 1995. (ed.) *What Works: Reducing Reoffending.* Chichester: Wiley.

Mead, B. 2005. Is there a measure of probation success? *Federal Probation: A Journal of Correctional Philosophy and Practice.* 69(2). Originally published in the May/June 1937 issue of Federal Probation.

Mears, D.P. and Travis, J. 2004. Youth Development and Reentry. *Youth Violence and Juvenile Justice,* 2(1): 3–20.

Merrington, S., and Stanley, S. 2004. 'What works?': Revisiting the evidence in England and Wales. *The Journal of Community and Criminal Justice,* 51(1): 7–20.

National Research Council. 2007. *Parole, Desistance from Crime and Community Reintegration.* Washington DC: National Academy Press.

Nay, J., and Kay, P. 1982. *Government Oversight and Evaluability Assessment.* Toronto: Lexington Books.

Palmer, T. 1975. Martinson revisited. *Journal of Research in Crime and Delinquency,* 12(2): 230.

Palmer. T. 1978. *Correctional Intervention and Research: Current Issues and Future Prospects.* Lexington, MA: Lexington Books.

Paparozzi, M. 2006. Responding to 'nothing works' in correctional treatment. *Journal of Community Corrections.*

Petersilia, J. 1985. Probation and felony offenders. *Federal Probation,* 49(4).

Petersilia, J. 1989. Implementing randomized experiments: Lessons from BJA's intensive supervision project. *Evaluation Review,* 13: 435–458.

Petersilia, J. 1992. Probation and felony offenders. In L.F. Travis, III. M.D. Schwartz and T.R. Clear (ed.) *Corrections: An Issues Approach.* Cincinnati: Anderson.

Petersilia, J. 2003. *When Prisoners Come Home: Parole and Offender Reentry.* New York: Oxford University Press.

Petersilia, J. 2007. Employing behavioral contracting for earned discharged parole. *Criminology and Public Policy,* 6(4): 807–814.

Petersilia, J, Lin, G., and Beckman, M. 2009. Parole violations and revocations in california: analysis and suggestions for action. *Federal Probation,* July: 2–13.

Petersilia, J., and Turner, S. 1990. *Intensive supervision for high-Risk probationers: Findings from three California experiments.* Santa Monica, CA: RAND

Petersilia, J. and Turner, S. 1993. Intensive probation and parole. *Crime and Justice: A Review of Research,* 17: 281–335.

Petersilia, J., Turner, S., Kahan, J., and Peterson, J. 1985. *Granting Felons Probation: Public Risks and Alternatives.* R-3186-NIJ, The RAND Corporation. Available at: www.rand.org.

Raynor, P. 2004. The Probation Service 'Pathfinders': Finding the path and losing the way? *Criminal Justice,* 4(3): 309–325.

Raynor, P. 2008. Community penalties and Home Office research: One the way back to 'nothing works'? *Criminology and Criminal Justice,* 8(1): 73–87.

Rempel, M. 2005. *Action Research: Using Information to Improve Your Drug Court.* Bureau of Justice Assistance, Office of Justice Programs, US Department of Justice.

Rosenfeld, R. 2008. Recidivism and its discontents. *Criminology and Public Policy,* 7(2): 311–318.

Rossi, P., Lipsey, M., and Freeman H. 2004. *Evaluation: A Systematic Approach.* Thousand Oaks, CA: Sage Publications.

Shadish, W., Cook, T., and Campbell, D. 2002. *Experimental and Quasi-experimental Designs for Generalized Causal Inferences.* Boston: Houghton-Mifflin.

Snyder, H.N., and Sickman, M. 2006. *Juvenile Offenders and Victims: 2006 National Report.* Washington, DC: US Department of Justice, Office of Justice Programs, Office of Juvenile Justice and Delinquency Prevention.

Stemen, D. 2007. *Reconsidering Incarceration: New Directions for Reducing Crime.* New York: Vera Institute of Justice.

Taxman, F. 2008. No illusions: Offender and organizational change in Maryland's proactive community supervision efforts. *Criminology and Public Policy,* 7(2): 275–302.

Taxman, F. 2009. Effective community punishments in the United States: probation. *Criminal Justice Matters,* 75: 42–44.

Taxman, F., Byrne, J., Pattavina, A., and Ainsworth, S. 2010. *Risk, Need, Responsivity (RNR) Simulation Tool.* Working paper prepared for the Bureau of Justice assistance and presented for review at the Annual Meeting of the American Society of Criminology, San Francisco, CA, November 17, 2010.

Taxman, F.S., Perdoni, M., and Harrison, L. 2007. Treatment for adult offenders: A Review of the state of the state. *Journal of Substance Abuse Treatment,* 32(3): 239–254.

Travis, J. 2005. *But They All Come Back: Facing the Challenges of Prisoner Reentry.* Urban Institute Press.

Travis, J., and Visher, C. (eds) 2005. *Prisoner Reentry and Crime in America.* New York: Cambridge University Press.

Van der Werff, C. 1979. *Speciale Preventie.* Den Haag, NL: WODC.

Van Voorhis, P., and Brown, K. 1995. *Evaluability Assessment: A Tool for Program Development in Corrections.* Monograph Prepared for National Institute of Corrections. Available at: *www.citeseerx.ist.psu.edu/viewdoc/summary?doi= 10.1.1.131.362.*

Villetez, P., Killias, M., and Zoder, I. (2006). The effects of custodial vs. non-custodial sentences on re-offending: A systematic review of the state of the evidence. Available at: http://www.campbellcollaboration.org/doc-pdf/Campbell-report-30.09.06.pdf.

Vito, G.F. 1987. Felony probation and recidivism: Replication and response. *Federal Probation*, 50: 17–25.

von Hirsch, A., (1992) Proportionality in the philosophy of punishment. *Crime and Justice,* 16: 55–98.

Webb, V.J., Hoffman, D.E., Wakefield, W.O., and Snell, J. 1976. Recidivism: In search of a more comprehensive definition. *International Journal of Offender Therapy and Comparative Criminology*, 20: 144–147.

Weisburd, D. 2010. Justifying the use of non-experimental methods and disqualifying the use of randomized controlled trials: challenging folklore in evaluation research in crime and justice. *Journal of Experimental Criminology*, 6: 209–227.

24

Conceptualising and Measuring the Quality of Prison Life

Alison Liebling, Susie Hulley, Ben Crewe

Science is a continuous enterprise in which advance is made by successive approximations to 'the truth' and by a never-ending series of small excursions into the unknown (Foreword to Lewin, 1997/1951).

In empirical science everything depends on how fruitfully and faithfully thinking intertwines with the empirical world of study ... and since concepts are the gateway to that world, the effective functioning of concepts is a matter of decisive importance (Blumer, 1969: 143–4).

INTRODUCTION

How can the social environment of a prison be accurately assessed? What is it important to measure? How should the prison experience be represented in empirical research? How do we capture distinctions between prisons, which can be good or bad in so many different ways? What kind of conceptual framework is relevant to the measurement of prison quality? This chapter will outline one attempt to address these questions in England and Wales, outlining the development of a recently revised 'quality of life' measure for prisons. There is considerable consensus about the inadequacy of narrow and selective performance measures, such as hours spent in purposeful activity or number of serious assaults, in representing prison quality. The difficulties are both methodological and conceptual; for example, prison operational managers can be very imaginative in defining all kinds of routine prison activities as apparently

'purposeful'. Official measures often reflect what is measurable rather than what matters most. We argue that, whilst all empirical measurement attempts can be revised and improved, and some important aspects of prison life change over time, the prisoner survey we outline here represents a useful measure of the quality of prison life. It provides a basis for understanding and improvement, and for the exploration of causal relationships, as well as for critical analysis.

MEASURING PRISON ENVIRONMENTS

Most early attempts to assess prison quality were conducted in a quest for 'therapeutic effectiveness': what kinds of penal regimes led to positive outcomes on release? The framework within which such studies were conceived consisted of a set of beliefs about the 'people-changing' nature of institutions and their potentially rehabilitative effects and the growing recognition of the role of the social environment or 'field' in shaping behaviour (Murray, 1938; Lewin, 1997/1951). Moos, for example, applied the methods he had developed in his evaluations of treatment environments in psychiatric settings to correctional environments during the 1960s and 1970s. His scale was developed to provide a measure of the 'social climate' of psychiatric wards and was based on a number of items, which were used to form subscales. These sub-scales were empirically derived from respondents in these environments (Moos, 1975: 20).

Moos's 90-item scale – the Correctional Institutions Environment Scale (CIES) – assessed nine dimensions of the social climate of correctional programmes. It was adapted from the Ward Atmosphere Scale, used in hospitals. New items were devised, informed by the relevant literature, discussions with staff and residents on various correctional programmes, and certain statistical criteria (e.g., items should discriminate significantly among units; and each scale should have ten items each, half scored true and half scored false). Items with low item-to-sub-scale correlations were eliminated; and other sub-scales were collapsed into one. Three broad categories of dimensions were developed, clearly linked to therapeutic concepts so that, for example, relationship dimensions included involvement, support and expressiveness; personal development included autonomy, practical orientation and personal problem orientation and was a proxy for 'treatment'; system maintenance included order and organisation, clarity and officer control (see the CIES scale and the sub-scale dimensions in Moos, 1975: 41).

These sub-scales were not conceived as wholly independent from each other but as recognisable and inter-related aspects of prison life. A moderate degree of sub-scale intercorrelation existed. The items included 'the residents are proud of this unit' (in Involvement) and 'staff go out of their way to help residents' and were scored 'true' or 'false'. The scale was consistent with findings on other perceived environment scales in that assessments were relatively independent of background variables such as age, sex and length of stay (Moos 1975: 47). The scale was administered to random samples of prisoners using paper and pencil questionnaires, under conditions of anonymity.

The CIES was developed in order to evaluate specific treatment programmes and to link their characteristics to outcomes. It was used to describe and compare institutional climates, longitudinally and cross-sectionally, in evaluations of the effects of training, new treatment programmes and other interventions. Moos recognised that this kind of research was developmental. However, his model is limited because his measures were conceptually and ideologically linked to 'treatment' or behaviour modification, whereas the prison experience is about much more than this. The interest in staff was limited to their perceptions of prisoner behaviours and attitudes. Staff perceptions of the 'treatment climate' are always found to be more positive than prisoners' perceptions. There was no separate attempt to evaluate how staff saw and experienced their working climate. Whilst this chapter focuses on the prisoner survey, staff perceptions also form an important aspect of any

measurement of a prison's climate. We describe that part of our work elsewhere. Applications and developments of this early work in a range of custodial environments include studies by Clarke and Martin (1971), Gunn et al. (1978), Heal et al. (1973), Jones and Cornes (1977), Sinclair (1971), Thornton (1987) in the UK and Hans Toch (1982) in the US.

A shift from a rehabilitative or correctionalist to a pragmatic and managerialist approach occurred in the 1980s so that later work by Saylor (1984) and Logan (1992) in the US, and King and McDermott (1995) in the UK, included a greater emphasis on less aspirational 'custodial' goals such as security and order. The 'confinement model', as Logan (1992) described it, brought with it a move away from the focus on social and individual change, in favour of 'relatively precise concepts' that were 'susceptible to operationalisation and empirical measurement', like levels of staff sickness, or cost per place. With this development, however, the relevance of measurement to the prisoner *experience* was lost.

Despite significant efforts made to develop and improve measurement of prison quality throughout the 1980s and 1990s, many limitations to these measurement or evaluation techniques have been identified. These limitations reflect an underlying major theoretical gap in approaches to the task (see further Liebling, assisted by Arnold, 2004). They are shown in Box 24.1.

THE 'MEASURING THE QUALITY OF PRISON LIFE' STUDY

[T]he essential nature of the work of the scientist consists of making a proper translation from phenomena to concepts (Lewin, 1997/1951: 160).

Our attempt to conceptualise and measure prison quality returns to the spirit of Murray and Lewin in emphasising the importance of perceptions and experiences, but seeks to avoid the narrow constraints of either a correctionalist or managerialist framework in identifying what should be measured. Instead, our methods began with prisoner and staff experiences and worked 'upwards', towards measurement, from a thoroughly grounded analysis of prison life.

The original study in which a measuring the quality of prison life survey was developed consisted of organised observation and deep conversation in five prisons over a one year period.[1] Our task was to identify what mattered, to whom and why. This was achieved in two ways. The first part of our research was based on appreciative inquiry (AI); briefly, a search for what is life-giving out of

---

Box 24.1   Limitations of techniques used to measure and evaluate prison quality

- A failure to address key dimensions in statements of aims (such as the term 'humanity' in the Prison Service Statement of Purpose)
- A lack of clarity about the meaning of key terms, such as 'respect' and 'safety'.
- A managerialist concern with performance-as-service-delivery, and poor operationalisation of this narrowly conceived agenda.
- Limitations in the use of specific measures: such as recorded assaults as a measure of 'safety'.
- A 'process compliance' and 'componential' framework for standards, where one practice is apparently unrelated to another.
- Insufficient information from prisoners and staff about a sufficiently broad and relevant range of areas of prison life.
- A failure to compare information from diverse sources (e.g., audits, performance data and inspectorate reports).
- A failure to analyse or interpret data in detail.
- Low 'face validity'; that is, the rejection by staff (and prisoners) of the accuracy of the world painted by these data.

---

what is experienced as painful, in order to move beyond 'existing reified patterns of discourse' (Ludema et al., 2001: 189; see also Elliott, 1999; and Liebling, assisted by Arnold, 2004) and was largely inductive. AI begins with exercises aimed at imaginative conversation and continues into loosely structured interviews. The method has certain similarities with symbolic interactionism and grounded theory: it is creative and mainly qualitative; it is concerned with theory generation and with the development of sensitising concepts; and it is concerned with 'lived experience', narrative, and meaning (Liebling et al., 1999). We worked closely with groups of staff and prisoners in workgroup exercises over a number of days in each prison. The facilitated workshops were intended to explore as fully as possible best and worst experiences of life in each prison, with participants trying to 'imagine' each prison at its best, drawing on experiences of 'appropriate treatment' in order to talk to each other and to us in depth about what mattered most to them. Throughout this process, we departed with all our notes and flip charts in the evenings, then returned each morning with a digested account of the previous day's work, for discussion (and rejection of anything we had 'got wrong'). It was clear from these exercises that the prison environment was multi-dimensional and primarily *relational*. This process led to the identification of themes which became the basis for agreeing a set of dimensions each group would wish to see reflected in any attempt to measure it. Via this circuitous route, we arrived in each prison at a list of important but difficult to measure conceptual dimensions such

as 'respect', 'humanity', 'safety' and 'trust', and devoted the remainder of our time to exploring the meaning of these often used terms, in conversation, in the relevant literature, and in concrete examples from experience, until we arrived at conceptual definitions and were satisfied that they could be operationalised. We were surprised by the level of consensus achieved about the identification of relevant dimensions, but this enabled us to move to the second 'measurement' stage sooner than we had originally anticipated. The key dimensions identified were: respect, humanity, staff-prisoner relationships, support, trust, fairness, order, safety, well-being, personal development, family contact, power, meaning, and decency, as shown in Table 24.1. 'Respect' and 'humanity' almost always emerged first and were given the strongest emphasis.

The second main approach was deductive and involved the development and administration of a detailed quality of life survey, which was informed and supplemented by the method of AI and structured around the dimensions identified in the first part of the study. Over 100 items (or statements) thought to reflect the various dimensions were crafted, from interview data and with the help of staff and prisoners, and these were tested in early versions of the survey. Prisoners responded to each statement on a five-point Likert Scale, from 'strongly agree' to 'strongly disagree'. Some of the items were worded positively and others negatively. Later refinements were made via statistical analysis (particularly factor analysis and reliability checks), but our decisions were informed by our growing understanding of the prison

Table 24.1 Original quality of life dimensions, with reliabilities

Respect	0.80
Humanity	0.82
Staff-prisoner relationships	0.71
Trust	0.78
Support	0.77
Fairness	0.90
Order	0.71
Safety	0.73
Well-being	0.84
Personal development	0.92
Family contact	0.62
Decency	0.74
Power/authority	0.70
Prisoner social life	0.75
Individual items	
Meaning	
Quality of life	

environment and the meaning of terms as used in this environment.

Our aim was to draw together the sociologically imaginative and rich with the empirically precise, and to end up with a quantitative measure that had strong qualitative foundations. The dimensions were both empirical and theoretical constructs. We needed data that were amenable to quantification. But we also wanted to retain

meaning, depth and individual contact in qualitative interviews. We continued to regard the exercise as exploratory even when a first workable version of the survey was devised. Once the design of the survey was complete, questionnaires were administered in five comparable prisons, to 100 randomly sampled prisoners in each, as one part of long one-to-one interviews. We continued to use appreciative questions in the interviews, before or after administering the more structured questionnaire, in order to allow for continual clarification of meaning. Examples of three of the dimensions are given in Box 24.2.

The dimensions shown in Table 24.1 reflect some subtle normative thinking about the sort of institution a prison ought to be, as well as identifying areas on which establishments are known to vary. Our method of discovery was organised conversation, with the aim of establishing principles of general applicability in the prison setting. We referred to the outcome as a measure of the 'moral performance' of prisons (Liebling, assisted by Arnold, 2004). In the language used by others, the survey provides an assessment (by prisoners) of the 'interior legitimacy' of an individual prison (Sparks, 1994; Sparks and Bottoms, 2008).

Several revised and improved versions of the survey were developed in later studies for particular reasons, including an evaluation of a suicide prevention initiative in 12 prisons during which stronger emphasis was placed on measuring distress and well-being, and on identifying aspects of the quality of prison life that explained variations in levels of well-being and distress (Liebling et al., 2005). Such was the level of practitioner interest

Box 24.2 Statement items for the original dimensions: humanity, relationships and well-being

Humanity	Staff–prisoner relationships	Well-being
I am being looked after with humanity in here. I am treated as a person of value in this prison. Some of the treatment I receive in this prison is degrading. Staff here treat me with kindness. I am not being treated as a human being in here.	Relationships between staff and prisoners in this prison are good. Personally, I get on well with the officers on my wing. Staff are confrontational towards prisoners in this prison. There is a strong sense, or culture, of 'them and us' in this prison. The level of staff interaction with prisoners is low.	The atmosphere in this prison is relaxed and friendly. My experience of imprisonment in this particular prison has been stressful. I can be myself in this prison. I feel tense in this prison. My experience in this prison is painful. Morale amongst prisoners here is high. Generally I fear for my psychological safety.

in the questionnaire, several versions of the survey were adopted by the Prison Service (and continue to be used) as a supplement to their usual Standards Audit procedure. It added 'colour and meaning' to these process-oriented measures of quality and performance (McConnell, pers. comm., 2001).

The most recent and thoroughly revised version of the survey took place during an ESRC-funded study of 'values, practices and outcomes in public and private sector corrections' (award ref RES-062-23-0212). In this seven-prison study, described below, efforts were made to strengthen our grasp of aspects of prison life relating to security, order and policing (the use of authority) to balance and complement the more explicitly relational aspects of prison life emphasised in the first study. Prisoners appreciate fair and respectful treatment, but also order and organisation, as we explain further later. There is an element of authority – used appropriately – in legitimacy.

MEASURING PRISON QUALITY IN PUBLIC AND PRIVATE SECTOR PRISONS

One of the developments to stimulate interest in accurate measurement of prison quality has been the onset of prison privatisation. Perrone and Pratt have argued, amongst others, that we do not know enough about the relative quality of public versus private prisons (2003; see also Gaes et al., 1999), and that there is no consensus on 'the best way to conceptualise and measure prison quality' (ibid. 317; Logan, 1992). As the Public Administration Select Committee has stated, 'the need for proper assessment, in a way that is transparent and open to scrutiny and challenge, is fundamental' (House of Commons, 2002: 13). The development of a satisfactory measure would be an important step forward in this field.

In March 2007, the authors embarked on an ESRC-funded study of 'values, practices and outcomes in public and private sector corrections'. The study included an observation, interview and questionnaire-based study of senior managers in public and private sector corrections; and an ethnographic and survey-based study of two public and five private sector prisons. We felt that the first version of our quality-of-life survey had captured relational or 'harmony' dimensions of prison life more satisfactorily than 'safety and security' dimensions, not least because these aspects of prison life are extremely difficult to measure in ways that distinguish between the aggravations of security procedures and their benefits to prisoners. Despite their emphasis on the relational aspects of prison quality, we found, using Valerie Braithwaite's terminology, that prisoners were 'moral dualists'; that is, they wanted respectful and decent treatment, but they did not appreciate chaos or inappropriate distributions of power (see Braithwaite, 1998; and Liebling, assisted by Arnold, 2004). The under-use of authority could pose as many problems in prison as the over-use of power (although these problems are distinctive). The mainly relational focus of the first version of the MQPL survey may have been advantageous to the private sector, given that 'the private sector was effectively invited to provide more 'humane' and reasonable treatment than the public sector had been achieving throughout the 1980s and 1990s' (Liebling, assisted by Arnold, 2004: 98). In our research up to that date, private sector prisons had scored well on dimensions related to these aspects of prison life.

The MQPL (Measuring the Quality of Prison Life) survey was revised and extended in this project during its early qualitative phase, to represent 'missing' aspects of the prison experience and new issues prisoners were raising in the context of the changing contours of prison life (e.g., how the introduction of Imprisonment for Public Protection [IPP] sentences, recall and other features of the new indeterminacy impacted on the 'weight', 'depth' and 'tightness' of prison life (see Crewe, 2009; Downes, 1988; King and McDermott, 1995)). Specifically, 38 new items were added to the survey.

The establishments were selected for fieldwork following a lengthy consultation process with senior managers in NOMS. We attempted to find two 'pairs' of public and private sector establishments that were similar in age, size and function. For this reason, we excluded establishments for women, young prisoners, high security prisons, and establishments that were over 20 years old. We also excluded Altcourse from the original private sector sample, because we were informed that it operated under the most expensive contract and was therefore unrepresentative of private sector prisons. We selected establishments that were used for other matching purposes (e.g., cost comparisons), so that they were already regarded as a 'fair match' by those working in the field. Inevitably, the matches were imperfect, but they constitute a 'best case fit'. The three additional private prisons were included in the study during its later stages for different reasons: Rye Hill, because we were invited to use our survey there as part of a formal performance review process; and Lowdham Grange and Altcourse, because prisoners in our main research sites talked about them relatively positively and we were curious about what they were like.

In each of the seven prisons involved in the study, the revised MQPL survey was delivered alongside a staff survey, SQL (Staff Quality of

Life survey) during an extended period of fieldwork. The research team spent between six to nine weeks in the four main prisons and one week each in the three additional prisons. Table 24.2 shows the main characteristics of the prisons included in the research at the time of our fieldwork.

In each of the four main prisons, extensive periods of observation were undertaken of daily life. Informal discussions were held in various areas of each prison and staff and prisoners were formally interviewed. Detailed research diaries were kept and notes were circulated among the team members for discussion.[2] New 'sensitising concepts' and related additional items were developed out of these conversations and tested in new versions of the survey. The formation of new dimensions and final decisions as to their titles came later, as we shall describe below.

THE NEW QUALITY OF LIFE SURVEY

At each of the seven prisons in the study, the MQPL survey was administered during pre-arranged focus groups. Each group lasted about an hour, which normally left some time after completion of the survey for discussion. A random sample of prisoners was drawn up from a list of the current population, organised by prison wing. Around 10 per cent of the population on each wing were selected. Prisoners were asked by staff and/or the research team whether they were willing to attend the group, and were reassured about confidentiality, anonymity and the independence of the research team. Notices were circulated alerting staff and prisoners to the exercise. Outlying areas, such as Healthcare and the Care and Separation Unit, were sampled separately due to their specific functions and the complexity of managing the research in these locations: here, surveys were supplied to a small number of prisoners who volunteered to undertake them.

In each prison, a liaison officer assisted with the organisation of the survey, usually suggesting days and times that suited particular wings. Liaison officers often gathered prisoners together and escorted them to the focus group venue. In all prisons, response rates were high, a fact assisted by the 'semi-official' nature of the research and by a lack of alternative activities for prisoners. The pace of action was often fast, and sometimes staff would include prisoners not on the original lists in their efforts to try to be helpful. Some of these departures from strict random sampling went unrecorded, so the final figures included a minority of prisoners obtained by 'opportunity sampling'. Exceptionally, in some prisons, prisoners

on one wing were under-represented. This was due to difficulties in communication with staff on that wing, or regime conflicts; for example, when the time allotted to survey a wing conflicted with gym sessions. The group sessions were normally held in an association room on the wings, or in other areas of the prison such as the visits room, education block or faith centre. No staff were present in these sessions. Often, two members of the research team were present so that the questionnaire could be completed under supervision and questions could be answered. Mars bars or chocolate biscuits were provided as an incentive and a way of thanking prisoners for their participation.

A total of 1145 prisoners completed the survey in the seven prisons. Table 24.3 details the sample size at each establishment. We aimed to achieve a minimum of 100 prisoners in each sample.

Prisoners personally completed the survey during the focus groups, following a brief introduction, the distribution of pens, and the answering of any questions. Each survey contained 147 statements or items, which the respondents were asked to agree or disagree with on a five-point Likert Scale (from 'strongly agree' to 'strongly disagree') (see Box 24.3 for details of how responses to these statements were coded).

Once all of the fieldwork, including the survey, had been completed in the first prison (Forest Bank), a factor analysis was carried out on the MQPL survey results, to explore the placement of the new items and their impact on the existing set of dimensions. Factor analysis allows a large number of items in a survey to be organised into smaller or more compact dimensions, which cluster together. The dimensions constitute empirical and conceptual constructs or small clusters of survey items (measurable variables), which represent concepts that are considered to characterise key elements of a prisoner's 'quality of life' – a latent or underlying construct (also see Gray et al., this volume; and Field, 2005: 736). Each dimension consisted of between three and nine items. The overall dimension score for each prison was then calculated as the mean of these values and represented as a score ranging from one to five. The relative quality of aspects of prisoners' lives is represented by the mean score for each dimension. Table 24.4 shows the working dimensions developed at this stage, which were used during the research in the six remaining prisons. Whilst the analysis was based on a relatively small sample size ($n = 188$) it reflected the practice of continuous reflection and conceptual revision adopted since the earliest versions of the MQPL were developed and helped to make sense of the data for feedback to the prisons involved in the project.

Table 24.2 Details of the seven prisons involved in the ESRC values and practies research

	Main (matched) prisons				Additional prisons		
	Forest Bank	Bullingdon	Dovegate	Garth	Rye Hill	Lowdham Grange	Altcourse
Sector (company)	Private (Kalyx)	Public	Private (Serco)	Public	Private (G4S)	Private (Serco)	Private (G4S)
Year of opening	2000	1992	2001	1988	2001	1998	1997
Region	North West	South East	West Midlands	North West	East Midlands	East Midlands	North West
Function	Cat B Local	Cat B Local and Cat C Training	Cat B Training	Cat B Training	Cat B Training	Cat B Training	Cat B Local
Operational capacity	1124	963	860	847	664	680	1324
Fieldwork dates	Sept–Oct 2007	April–May 2008	Nov 2007–Jan 2008	Sept–Nov 2008	Sept 2008	Jan 2009	April 2009

Table 24.3   Sample size at each establishment

Prison	Sample
Forest Bank	188
Bullingdon	187
Dovegate	159
Garth	186
Rye Hill	167
Lowdham Grange	158
Altcourse	100

Box 24.3   Coding the survey statement responses

The structured questionnaire data were entered and analysed using the computer software package SPSS.

- Every response to each of the 147 statements in the questionnaire was coded on a '1' (strongly agree) to '5' (strongly disagree) scale, corresponding to the Likert Scale structure of the questionnaire.
- Eighty-four of the 147 items were worded 'positively' (where agreement with the statement constituted a positive response) and 63 were worded 'negatively' (where agreement with the statement indicated a negative perception). This format was employed in order to minimise acquiescence bias.
- To ensure that the higher the score or value, the better the quality of prison life, the scoring method had to be reversed for the 84 'positively' worded items. For example, if a prisoner replied 'strongly agree' to the statement 'staff address and talk to me in a respectful manner', this response would originally be scored as '1', but would then be re-coded in order that a score of '1' would become a '5'.
- Any missing answers (of which there were few) were coded as '99' and treated as missing values. A small number of 'not applicable' responses were coded as '77' and excluded from the analysis.

Table 24.4   MQPL working dimensions during the study

Working dimensions
Entry support
Distress on entry into custody (later 'Entry into custody')
Assistance for the vulnerable
Individual care
Dignity and material needs
Relationships
Respect
Fairness
Order and security
Physical safety
Care and safety (later 'Psychological safety')
Policing and sub-culture
Meeting needs
Personal development
Family contact
Personal autonomy
Well-being
Frustration
Compliance/resistance
Relationships with peers

The dimensions in Table 24.4 were useful as a working guide during the remainder of the fieldwork, but as the study progressed, and extended periods were spent in the remaining prisons, our understanding of prisoners' experiences grew. For example, greater emphasis on the 'responsibilisation' of prisoners and the experience of new, indeterminate sentences (such as the IPP sentence) meant that prisoners were under enormous pressure to personally manage their progression through the sentence. This led to a new sense of urgency in prisoners' need for staff assistance and expertise: to signpost them to the relevant form or department, to explain their sentence conditions, and to support them in their attempts to access the necessary information or personnel to progress through the system. As a result of prisoners' descriptions of their experience in each establishment, we observed that the term 'respect' was being used not only in terms of the way staff spoke to and treated them in general, as we had found in the original study, but also in relation to their ability to 'get things done' (see Hulley et al, in preparation). It was clear too that issues such as staff professionalism would be particularly salient to the research. What mattered to prisoners, and the precise meaning of concepts applied in practice in prisons, had changed (see below).

Informed by the qualitative fieldwork and by the quantitative survey results that emerged from the seven prisons, we began to reconsider the dimensions, leading to a new and more conceptually-informed factor analysis of the final data set.

THE NEW DIMENSIONS: THE MORAL QUALITY OF PRISON LIFE

Based on the overall sample of 1,147 prisoners from the seven establishments, the 148 items were entered into a principal components analysis (see Field, 2005, for details). In the first analysis, 32 factors emerged (factors were only retained where their substantive importance was confirmed using Kaiser's 1960 criterion). Principal components analysis was repeated on those initial factors upon which a large number of items loaded (i.e., eight items or more).

The final dimensions were developed using a combination of conceptual and statistical methods. Theoretical reflection on the factors generated by the quantitative analysis led to revisions, which were then re-tested statistically. The process was deliberative and iterative, drawing on our fieldwork experiences and interviews. Conceptually plausible changes to the placement of items that did not significantly lower the statistical reliability

of a factor remained. Where reliability was compromised, further options were considered until reliability and qualitative interpretation were in accord (i.e., factors were split, or items were removed or added from other factors). Where reliabilities were somewhat low (although they all emerged at 0.561 or higher) dimensions only remained in use where they were deemed conceptually important and no alternative was found. Factors were retained only if they contained at least three unique loadings. The set of dimensions arrived at are shown in Table 24.5.

Once the final set of dimensions had been agreed, they were clustered thematically into five overarching categories: Harmony dimensions; Professionalism dimensions; Security dimensions; Conditions and Family Contact dimensions; and Well-being and Development dimensions. These categories reflected our broader thinking and theorising about the content and meaning of the survey overall. We retained the term 'moral' as the survey dimensions reflected, as originally, the way

Table 24.5   Dimensions measuring the moral quality of prison life

Dimension	Reliability
Harmony dimensions	
Entry into custody	0.618
Respect/courtesy	0.886
Staff–prisoner relationships	0.867
Humanity	0.889
Decency	0.636
Care for the vulnerable	0.803
Help and assistance	0.772
Professionalism dimensions	
Staff professionalism	0.885
Bureaucratic legitimacy	0.801
Fairness	0.820
Organisation and consistency	0.836
Security dimensions	
Policing and security	0.751
Prisoner safety	0.734
Prisoner adaptation	0.623
Drugs and exploitation	0.780
Conditions and Family Contact dimensions	
Regime decency	0.705
Family contact	0.635
Well-being and Development dimensions	
Personal development	0.875
Personal autonomy	0.664
Well-being	0.786
Distress	0.561

prisoners feel morally treated by the institution (i.e., largely by staff).

Some of the dimensions in each of the theoretical categories are outlined below as an illustration of this final stage of the analysis, during which the themes were identified, the dimensions were defined and descriptions of the items and concepts were developed. The following dimensions have been selected to demonstrate the range of concepts included in the survey and as examples of our attempts to capture important aspects of prison life and quality (as described previously).[3]

Harmony dimensions

This group of dimensions represent the mainly interpersonal and relational aspects of the prison experience.

Respect/courtesy: Positive, respectful and courteous attitudes towards prisoners by staff

The term 'respect' has broad and subtle meaning in the prisons context, including overall treatment by staff, the expression of courteous attitudes and also the question of whether staff respond effectively to prisoners' needs. 'Courtesy' was an important but not exclusive or defining aspect of respect.

Respect/courtesy items	Correlation
I feel I am treated with respect by staff in this prison.	0.782
This prison is poor at treating prisoners with respect.	0.709
Most staff address and talk to me in a respectful manner.	0.691
Relationships between staff and prisoners in this prison are good.	0.669
Staff speak to you on a level in this prison.	0.651
Staff are argumentative towards prisoners in this prison.	0.646
Personally I get on well with the officers on my wing.	0.561
This prison encourages me to respect other people.	0.533

Staff–prisoner relationships: Trusting, fair and supportive interactions between staff and prisoners

It is widely agreed that 'staff–prisoner relationships lie at the heart of the prison system', for reasons that have been well documented (Home Office,

1984; Liebling and Price, 2001). It was the topic most often raised by prisoners and the term was readily acknowledged and understood. Whilst arguably all the dimensions under this general heading reflect aspects of the staff-prisoner relationship, this dimension was its most direct measure.

Staff–prisoner relationships items	Correlation
I receive support from staff in this prison when I need it.	0.723
Overall, I am treated fairly by staff in this prison.	0.704
I trust the officers in this prison.	0.687
Staff in this prison often display honesty and integrity.	0.683
This prison is good at placing trust in prisoners.	0.602
I feel safe from being injured, bullied, or threatened by staff in this prison.	0.550
When I need to get something done in this prison I can normally get it done by talking to someone face-to-face.	0.550

Humanity: An environment characterised by kind regard and concern for the person, which recognises the value of the individual

The term 'humanity' is at the centre of the English Prison Service's Statement of Purpose, but critics have argued for a long time that none of the service's key performance indicators measure or reflect it. The dimension below retained all of the original items in the first version of our MQPL survey but, in addition, we found that items incorporating notions of care and concern belonged in the concept of humanity.

Humanity items	Correlation
Staff here treat me with kindness.	0.736
I am treated as a person of value in this prison.	0.734
I feel cared about most of the time in this prison.	0.716
Staff in this prison show concern and understanding towards me.	0.709
I am being looked after with humanity in here.	0.698
Staff help prisoners to maintain contact with their families.	0.609
I am not being treated as a human being in here.	0.593
Some of the treatment I receive in this prison is degrading.	0.534

Professionalism dimensions

The Professionalism dimensions represent key aspects of the 'craft' of prison work, shaping the way it is carried out, involving communication and other skills, general expertise, knowledge, reliability and experience, and internalised as well as organisational values. This set of dimensions emerged out of our observations of and conversations with staff and prisoners, as we came to understand the significance of 'delivery', authority (used carefully, rather than avoided) and confidence in the experience of prisoners. They bring together 'harmony' and 'security' values, in the sense that whilst they are essentially *relational*, they forge (or prevent) a link between attitudes and behaviour: between staff orientation towards prisoners and the way in which they approach their daily tasks. The largest differences between prisons were found in these dimensions. Under-uses of authority were regarded as 'illegitimate' as well as over-uses of authority.

Staff professionalism: Staff confidence and competence in the use of authority

The daily application of prison rules and procedures involves considerable skill and discretion and is a low visibility activity. How staff approach, interpret and apply 'the rules', or avoid them, constitutes one of the most significant variations between prisons. Staff action in this domain can be related to confidence and experience as well as expertise. This dimension contains items related to the way in which staff use their authority and discretion.

Staff professionalism items	Correlation
Staff here treat prisoners fairly when applying the rules.	0.747
Staff here treat prisoners fairly when distributing privileges.	0.734
Privileges are given and taken fairly in this prison.	0.718
Staff in this prison have enough experience and expertise to deal with the issues that matter to me.	0.659
Staff in this prison tell it like it is.	0.587
The rules and regulations are made clear to me.	0.587
Staff carry out their security tasks well in this prison.	0.586
The best way to get things done in this prison is to be polite and go through official channels.	0.556
If you do something wrong in this prison, staff only use punishments if they have tried other options first.	0.538

Bureaucratic legitimacy: The transparency and responsiveness of the prison/prison system and its moral recognition of the individual

The term 'bureaucratic legitimacy' arose in our discussions about some of the new aspects of prison life being described by prisoners. It reflects a 'new penological' (see Feeley and Simon, 1992) treatment of the individual prisoner as part of an aggregate, risk-averse management strategy that deepens and 'tightens' the experience of imprisonment and makes the sentence more difficult to navigate (Crewe, 2009). These issues were of major concern to prisoners, particularly in the category B training prisons, and were among the major focus of their complaints about the prison experience.

Bureaucratic legitimacy items	Correlation
I have to be careful about everything I do in this prison, or it can be used against me.	0.617
I feel stuck in this system.	0.570
All they care about in this prison is my 'risk factors' rather than the person I really am.	0.548
Decisions are made about me in this prison that I cannot understand.	0.531
Decisions are made about me in this prison that I cannot influence.	0.526
When important decisions are made about me in this prison I am treated as an individual, not a number.	0.495
To progress in this prison, I have to meet impossible expectations.	0.452

Fairness: The perceived impartiality, proportionality and legality of punishments and procedures

Fairness is one of the most important aspects of prison life. Lack of fairness has been linked to a number of serious disorders in English prisons (Home Office, 1991; Sparks et al., 1996; Liebling, assisted by Arnold, 2004) as well as to levels of distress among prisoners (Liebling et al., 2005). The concept of fairness measured here is primarily *procedural justice*: the application of prison rules and procedures in a flexible, accountable and unbiased manner.

Fairness items	Correlation
My legal rights as a prisoner are respected in this prison.	0.653
The regime in this prison is fair.	0.632
In this prison things only happen for you if your face fits.	0.612
This prison is poor at giving prisoners reasons for decisions.	0.590
In general I think the disciplinary system here is unfair.	0.553
Control and restraint procedures are used fairly in this prison.	0.476

Security dimensions

The security dimensions reflect those aspects of a prison's environment concerned with the rule of law and the proper use of authority, the regulation of behaviour, and the provision of safety.

Policing and security: Staff supervision and control of the prison environment

The policing of the prison environment requires a careful balance between imposing and under-enforcing the rules to facilitate the 'smooth flow' of prison life (Sykes, 1958; Liebling, 2000). The role of staff is to monitor, regulate and challenge prisoners' behaviour, and to maintain the appropriate balance of power for the purpose of ensuring the safety of staff and prisoners. Failure to supervise and control the prison environment leads to an 'authority vacuum' (Bottoms, 1999: 239) and is regarded as illegitimate by prisoners.

Policing and security items	Correlation
Staff in this prison turn a blind eye when prisoners break the rules.	0.562
Supervision of prisoners is poor in this prison.	0.540
This prison is run by prisoners rather than staff.	0.505
This prison does very little to prevent drugs being smuggled in.	0.444
Staff in this prison are reluctant to challenge prisoners.	0.398
There is a lot of trouble between different groups of prisoners in here.	0.384
In this prison, there is a real 'pecking order' between prisoners.	0.374
This prison has too few staff.	0.357
Staff respond promptly to incidents and alarms in this prison.	0.287

Well-being and Development dimensions

The dimensions under this general heading reflect prisoners' perceptions of their own well-being, capacity to act autonomously, levels of support for their personal development, and help with progression. They refer to a prisoner's present and future prospects.

Personal development: An environment that helps prisoners to address their offending behaviour, prepare for release and develop their potential

Since the advent of 'what works' and a renewed commitment to 'public protection' or risk reduction, much greater emphasis has been placed in prisons on responsible engagement with offending behaviour programmes and other activities or courses thought to challenge thinking and behaviours relevant to offending. The availability of opportunities to undertake such programmes or engage with relevant services differs between establishments. The provision of and focus of psychologists, the number of accredited courses on offer, and the size and scope of the education department, for example, can influence a prisoner's chances of 'making progress'. Progression (or a sense of progression) is influenced by prison staff, as well as by availability, as officers are often the gatekeepers to much of the information and personnel necessary to apply for, find out about and be accepted onto such courses.

Personal development items	Correlation
My needs are being addressed in this prison.	0.690
I am encouraged to work towards goals/targets in this prison.	0.689
I am being helped to lead a law-abiding life on release in the community.	0.683
Every effort is made by this prison to stop offenders committing offences on release from custody.	0.660
The regime in this prison is constructive.	0.650
My time here seems like a chance to change.	0.655
This regime encourages me to think about and plan for my release.	0.592
On the whole I am doing time rather than using time.	0.477

Together, these and the remaining dimensions (in Table 24.5), represent a carefully balanced conceptual framework for thinking about the moral quality of a prison, as experienced by prisoners. The survey constitutes a tool for reflection and analysis, and for the 'identification of symptoms' indicating moral failings as well as strivings for legitimacy. Exploring relationships between the dimensions, between these and various 'outcomes' (such as rates of suicide, or reconviction) and looking closely at lowest and highest scoring dimensions overall, tells us much about the contemporary prison experience.

THE ROLE OF SOCIAL SCIENCE AND NEW HORIZONS

Blumer argued in *Symbolic Interactionism* (1969) that we should always be self-critical and cautious about how well social-scientific variables (or dimensions) indicate the complex abstract categories they are designed to measure. Part of the long-term project giving rise to the new survey was explicitly concerned with the identification of and relationships between complex and important aspects of prison life that mattered to prisoners. The survey only has value to the extent that these complex aspects of the prison experience have been identified, and translated into items reflecting the social, relational and moral atmosphere of a prison. If this has been achieved, even if to a modest extent, then we can begin to move from description to explanation (e.g., which aspects of the moral quality of prison life give rise to suicides in prison?) and to interpretation. We would always advocate deep and messy qualitative work, alongside use of the survey, so that interpretation and meaning (a picture of 'human beings in their particular world'; ibid: 131) can be appropriately anchored in 'empirical instances of their occurrence' (ibid. 148). The concepts we are seeking to measure are intricate, so that any attempt to fix their content or meaning is premature. There are dangers in using this type of survey naively or instrumentally, or out of context. What we have attempted to do is make a meaningful contribution to the sociological analysis of the prison, and to make it possible to find relatively stable patterns otherwise impossible to observe in the experience (and provision) of imprisonment. Neither the concepts nor their definitions are intended to be definitive.

We are satisfied that in this extended exercise we have found considerable confirmation of the original 'core' dimensions. 'Quality of life' is a 'latent construct' (Gray et al., this volume) amenable to operationalisation in the prison setting.

That we have grown its 'security and policing' components in this study is a considerable advance on where we had got to in previous studies, and a reflection of areas where we think we have found important differences between the public and private sectors (see Crewe et al., under review). This is, we propose, a patient, slow and careful enterprise, worthy of effort and self-conscious critique. As Blumer argued, the role of the concept in social science is to 'sensitise perception' (1969: 152) – to change the perceptual world, so that consciousness of fairness and unfairness, differential uses and abuses of power, and the intended and unintended effects of changing punishment provisions are brought into existence. That is the underlying purpose of the survey.

There are many limitations to this survey (as with all surveys) including its failure to take into account age, location, architecture and other characteristics of the prison, or differences between population groups in their capacity and tendency to be critical (long-term prisoners are far more aware of their rights and entitlements that young prisoners, for example). Surveys are inherently time bound and restrictive, as they force respondents into fixed choice categories that leave no room for elaboration. Prisoners prefer open conversation, and they sometimes have such powerful individual stories to tell that a survey item looks inadequate as a reflection of their experience. We hope that the overall methodological strategies we use offset, to some degree, some of these inevitable limitations. We have focused here on the basic measurement task, rather than on our results, or on explanations for those results: what shapes prison life? Why is one prison so much better or worse than another? What is the role played by governors, management teams, staff culture, in the experience of prison life for prisoners? These and other questions like them will be the focus of other work. The survey we have developed here provides an ongoing methodological and conceptual foundation, upon which we and others might continue to work.

Formal statistical analysis has (we suggest, analytic guidance) value only in so far as the 'groundwork' has been carefully completed – that the concepts, their operationalisation and any methods of data collection have meaning and validity. The material subjected to mathematical exploration should be 'mature' (Lewin 1997/1951: 169). The point of all empirical research is to help us take (often small) steps towards solving analytic puzzles about the nature of the social world. Once the data are available in their most carefully statistically analysed form, we have arrived at the beginning of a process of meaning-making. At this stage, it is our exposure to 'the field' we need to draw upon, to formulate understanding. We should strive for rigour and precision, whilst knowing that the best social science is always approximate, intuitive and developmental.

In relation to the prison, the important questions raised by this methodological journey remain: is it possible to construct a form of imprisonment whose basic structure and daily practices are more or less acceptable to those who endure it, despite their domination and commonly low social position (Liebling, assisted by Arnold, 2004)? Are prisoners slaves or citizens? If they retain their citizenship, then certain things follow. If it were possible to construct a form of imprisonment whose basic structure and daily practices were more rather than less acceptable to those who undergo it, then the effects of this form of imprisonment might be less damaging and more socially constructive. There are further questions to be asked about the extent to which the prison setting – a context of punishment – shapes the meaning of concepts like 'trust', 'frustration', and 'relationship'. To feel 'safe' in a prison may be a very different experience from feeling 'safe' (or conversely, unsafe) in one's home or work environment. The meaning of terms like 'well-being' may be peculiarly narrow in the context of a 25-year prison sentence. Our work attempts to provide valid tools for meaning-making, appropriate means for 'dissecting the social' in the strange and complex environment of prison. We are confident that there is relevance beyond the prison in much of what we have learned and that the use of authority, the way power works, and the links between legitimate treatment and psychological well-being work in similar ways 'outside'. Our focus is on understanding the contemporary experience of imprisonment, and on finding methodologically legitimate ways of doing so. In pursuing this work developmentally over a number of years, we have learned much about the craft of social science, its methods and its difficulties. We have learned above all that empirical research is critical to the development and clarification of conceptual understanding, and vice versa.

NOTES

1 This research project was carried out under the Home Office's *Innovative Research Grant* scheme, under the title, *'Measuring the Quality of Prison Life and Locating the Energy for Change'*. See Liebling and Arnold (2002). In the original MQPL research, HMP Doncaster (a privately run prison) had outperformed four public sector prisons on the relational qualities of prison life. There were, however, some weaknesses in security (see Liebling, assisted by Arnold, 2004).

2 In one of the three additional prisons (Altcourse), the MQPL was delivered by the Prison Service Audit and Assurance Unit as part of their auditing programme, with a researcher from the project present to ensure consistency of research methods and to gain insights from the discussions.

3 With the exception of Conditions and Family Contact dimensions, which are the most straightforward and easily measurable category.

RECOMMENDED READING

The origins and methodological and conceptual underpinnings for the survey can be found in Liebling, A., assisted by Arnold, H. (2004) *Prisons and their Moral Performance: A Study of Values, Quality and Prison Life* (Oxford: Clarendon Press). An application of the methods to suicides in prison, as well as a more general overview of the literature on the effects of imprisonment can be found in Liebling, A. and Maruna, S. (eds) (2005) *The Effects of Imprisonment* (Cullompton: Willan); and Liebling, A. (1999) 'Prison Suicide and Prisoner Coping' in M. Tonry and J. Petersilia (eds) *'Prisons', Crime and Justice: A Review of Research*, vol. xxvi (Chicago: University of Chicago Press), pp. 283–360. The main findings from the most recent version of the survey, applied to public–private sector imprisonment, can be found in Crewe, B., Liebling, A., Hulley, S. and McLean, C. (under review) 'Prisoner Quality of Life in Public and Private Sector Prisons'.

REFERENCES

Blumer, H. (1969) *Symbolic Interactionism: Perspective and Method.* New Jersey: Prentice-Hall.

Bottoms, A.E. (1999) 'Interpersonal Violence and Social Order in Prisons' in M. Tonry and J. Petersilia (eds) *'Prisons, Crime and Justice: A Review of Research*, vol. xxvi. Chicago: University of Chicago Press, pp. 205–282.

Braithwaite, V. (1998) 'The Value Balance of Political Evaluations', *British Journal of Psychology*, 89: 223–247.

Clarke, R.V., and Martin, D.N. (1971) *Absconding from Approved Schools.* Home Office Research Studies. London: HMSO.

Crewe, B. (2005) 'Prisoner Society in the Era of Hard Drugs', *Punishment and Society*, 7(4): 457–481.

Crewe, B. (2009) *The Prisoner Society: Power, Adaptation and Social Life in an English Prison.* Oxford: Oxford University Press.

Crewe, B., Liebling, A., Hulley, S., and McLean, C. (under review) 'Prisoner Quality of Life in Public and Private Sector Prisons'.

Downes, D. (1988) *Contrasts in Tolerance: Post-War Penal Policy in the Netherlands and England and Wales.* Oxford: Oxford University Press.

Elliott, C. (1999) *Locating the Energy for Change: An Introduction to Appreciative Inquiry.* Winnipeg: International Institute for Sustainable Development.

Feeley, M., and Simon, J. (1992) 'The New Penology: Notes on the Emerging Strategy of Corrections and its Implications', *Criminology,* 30: 449–474.

Field, A. (2005). *Discovering Statistics Using SPSS,* 2nd Edition. London: Sage.

Gaes, G.G., Flanagan, T.J., Motiuk, L.L., and Stewart, L. (1999) 'Adult Correctional Treatment' in M. Tonry and J. Petersilia (eds) *'Prisons', Crime and Justice: A Review of Research,* vol. xxvi. Chicago: University of Chicago Press, pp. 361–427.

Goffman, E. (1967) 'Where the Action is' in E. Goffman (ed.) *Interaction Ritual: Essays on Face-to-Face Behaviour.* New York: Doubleday Anchor, pp. 149–270.

Gunn, J., Robertson, G., Dell, S., and Way, C. (1978) *Psychiatric Aspects of Imprisonment,* London: Academic Press.

Haney, C. (1997) 'Psychology and the Limits to Prison Pain: Confronting the Coming Crisis in the Eighth Amendment Law', *Psychology, Public Policy and Law,* 3/4: 499–588.

Heal, K., Sinclair, I., and Troop, J. (1973) 'Development of a Social Climate Questionnaire for use on Approved Schools and Community Homes', *British Journal of Sociology,* 24/2: 222–235.

Home Office (1984) *Managing the Long-Term Prison System.* The Report of the Control Review Committee, Cmd. 3175. London: HMSO.

Home Office (1991) *Prison Disturbances April 1990: Report of an Inquiry by the Rt. Hon. Lord Justice Woolf (Parts I and II) and his Honour Judge Stephen Tumim (Part II),* London: HMSO.

House of Commons (2002) Home Affairs Public Administration Select Committee, *The Public Service Ethos,* Seventh Report of Session 2001–2 263-II, London: Stationery Office.

Hulley, S., Liebling, A. and Crewe, B. (under review) 'Respect in Prisons: Prisoners' Experiences of Respect in Public and Private Sector Prisons'.

Jones, H., and Cornes, P. (assisted by Stockford, R.) (1977) *Open Prisons,* London: Routledge and Kegan Paul.

Kaiser, H.F. (1960) 'The application of electronic computers to factor analysis', *Educational and Psychological Measurement,* 20: 141–151.

King, R.D., and McDermott, K. (1995) *The State of Our Prisons.* Oxford: Oxford University Press.

Lewin, K. (1997) *Field Theory in Social Science.* London: Harper and Row. (1st edition 1951).

Liebling, A., Price, D. and Elliot, C. (1999) 'Appreciative Inquiry and Relationships in Prison', *Punishment and Society: The International Journal of Penology,* 1(1), pp. 71–98.

Liebling, A. (2000) 'Prison Officers, Policing and the Use of Discretion', *Theoretical Criminology,* 4/3: 333–357.

Liebling, A., and Arnold, H. (2002) *Measuring the Quality of Prison Life: Research Findings 174.* London: Home Office.

Liebling, A.; assisted by Arnold, H. (2004) *Prisons and their Moral Performance: A Study of Values, Quality, and Prison Life.* Oxford: Oxford University Press.

Liebling, A., Durie, L., Stiles, A., and Tait, S. (2005) 'Revisiting Prison Suicide: The Role of Fairness and Distress' in A. Liebling and S. Maruna (eds) *The Effects of Imprisonment.* Cullompton: Willan Publishing, pp. 209–231.

Liebling, A., and Price, D. (2001) *The Prison Officer.* Leyhill: Prison Service and Waterside Press.

Logan, C.H. (1992) 'Well-Kept: Comparing Quality of Confinement in Private and Public Prisons', *Journal of Criminal Law and Criminology,* 83/3: 577–613.

Ludema, J., Cooperrider, D., and Barrett, F. (2001) 'Appreciative Inquiry: The Power of the Unconditional Positive Question' in P. Reason and H. Bradbury (eds) *Handbook of Action Research.* London: Sage, pp. 189–199.

Moos, R.H. (1975) *Evaluating Correctional and Community Settings.* New York: Wiley Press.

Murray, H.A. (1938) *Explorations in Personality.* New York: Oxford University Press.

Perrone, D. and Pratt, T.C. (2003) 'Comparing the Quality of Confinement and Cost-Effectiveness of Public Versus Private Prisons: What We Know, Why We Do Not Know More, and Where to Go from Here', *The Prison Journal,* 83(3): 301–322.

Saylor, W.G. (1984) *Surveying Prison Environments.* Washington: Federal Bureau of Prisons.

Sinclair, I. (1971) *Hostels for Probationers.* Home Office Research Studies. London: HMSO.

Sparks, R. (1994) 'Can Prisons be Legitimate?' in R. King and M. McGuire (eds) *Prisons in Context.* Oxford: Clarendon Press.

Sparks, R. and Bottoms, A.E. (2008) 'Legitimacy and Imprisonment Revisited: Notes on the Problem of Order Ten Years After' in J. Byrne, F. Taxman and D. Hummer (eds) *The Culture of Prison Violence.* Boston: Pearson/Allyn and Bacon.

Sparks, R., Bottoms, A.E. and Hay, W. (1996) *Prisons and the Problem of Order.* Oxford: Clarendon Press.

Sykes, G. (1958) *The Society of Captives.* Princeton: Princeton University Press.

Thornton, D. (1987) 'Assessing Custodial Adjustment' in B.J. McGirk, D.M. Thornton, and M. Williams (eds) *Applying Psychology to Imprisonment.* London: HMSO, pp. 445–462.

Toch, H. (1982) 'Studying and Reducing Stress' in R. Johnson and H. Toch (eds) *The Pains of Imprisonment.* London: Sage.

25

Comparing Justice and Crime Across Cultures

Susanne Karstedt

THE IMPORTANCE OF COMPARING

During the past decade comparative perspectives flourished in criminology to a hitherto unseen extent. Handbooks and textbooks on *Transnational Crime and Justice* (Reichel, 2005), on *Crime: Local and Global* (Muncie et al., 2010), *Global Criminology and Criminal Justice* (Larsen and Smandych, 2008) or on white collar and corporate crime (Pontell and Geis, 2007) testify to the increasing interest in cross-national and cross-cultural comparisons in our field. As early as 1997, Neapolitan and Schmalleger (1997) gave an overview of cross-national research on crime. Van Dijk's *The World of Crime* (2008) provides an encompassing view of developments in crime and justice across the world and a rich source of data that offer a vivid picture of differences as well as similarities across nations, cities and what we might preliminary conceptualise as 'cultures'. David Nelken (2010) presents an insightful treatise on the advantages of *Comparative Criminal Justice* alongside the problems and pitfalls of the comparativist's endeavour in this field. When a leading criminologist (Zimring, 2006) confesses to having become a 'recent convert' to the cause of comparative studies we have reason to assume that comparative and trans-national perspectives are presently more important than ever. The field has evolved from a niche and 'peripheral and none-too-important suburb of empirical study of crime and social control' (Zimring, 2006: 615) into a major field of research and teaching in criminology.

This chapter focuses on cross-cultural research and thus addresses only part of the body of comparative research in criminology. However, the problems explored here equally apply to other comparative research, in particular cross-national research that does not explicitly address questions concerning 'culture'. 'Culture' is an umbrella concept that can be comprised of political culture, of economic as well as religious practices, values and beliefs. As such, even if a number of exemplary studies are not explicitly defined as studies of culture, they often use and touch upon conceptual dimensions otherwise defined as such. Like other types of comparative research in criminology, cross-cultural research covers a broad area and a multitude of actors. According to Sutherland's definition of criminology, it uses the tools of comparison for the analysis of law making, law breaking and reactions to law breaking. This implies covering types of cultures from sub-cultures to regional and national cultures, and to legal cultures. It includes all types of actors, from offenders and victims to police, actors within the legal system to politicians and the general public. It does not only comprise those actors whose decisions affect crime and justice, or who are affected by these decisions, but in addition families, networks, corporations, markets and societal institutions other than criminal justice institutions. Nelken (2010) in particular draws attention to the fact that any comparison of criminal justice (and its outcomes) has to acknowledge the multitude of actors and stages that are involved in criminal justice decision making, and each of which can hugely affect any global measure of 'punitiveness' of the system.

The expansion of cross-cultural research across the past decade had a clear focus on comparative perspectives on criminal justice and crime prevention, partially driven by the increase of imprisonment rates across Western democracies and what has been termed the 'punitive turn' in public opinion and political decision-making. David Garland's study, *The Culture of Control* (2001), set the scene for a number of studies to follow over the first decade of the twenty-first century. Given the extensiveness of this body of writing, this chapter will concentrate on cross-cultural studies of criminal justice and its outcomes that present methodologically exemplary work. In the next section, I will give a brief overview of the major developments that have driven the cross-cultural enterprise in criminology. Thereafter, I will give an outline of the concept of culture, as well as of major problems that cross-cultural research encounters in general and in criminology particularly. I will then address different general strategies of comparison, and of cross-cultural comparison in particular. The two following sections will look at how these general strategies are translated into different methodologies: usage of large and small samples, and case studies; units of analysis; and finally, the challenges entailed in identifying, reconstructing and measuring culture. The chapter concludes by exploring new directions in cross-cultural research on crime and justice.

TRANSCENDING LOCAL KNOWLEDGE: GLOBALISATION AND COMPARATIVE PERSPECTIVES IN CRIMINOLOGY

The reasons for the increasing relevance of comparisons are manifold and obvious. Globalisation has certainly played a major role in this development. International bodies and agencies increasingly pressurise for comparative measurements of both crime and justice (see Van Dijk, 2008). International human rights regimes require comparative perspectives on victims' and prisoners' rights alike, on prison conditions as well as on criminal procedures. Crime prevention policies like 'zero tolerance' travel from their country of origin to foreign shores, and not always with beneficial or entirely predictable effects (Karstedt, 2002a; Nelken, 2010; Newburn and Sparks, 2004). Pressures towards harmonisation in crime prevention and criminal justice have made comparisons an 'intrinsic part' of the search for 'best practice' (Nelken, 2010: 2). But it is not only crime policies that travel in the era of globalisation; other policies that impact on crime and justice, and as such represent the drivers of global changes in crime and justice travel, too. In their analysis of 12 penal

systems Cavadino and Dignan (2006) identify the global spread of neo-liberalism and respective market-driven economic policies as the major causes of rising imprisonment in these countries (cf. Nelken, 2009).

Notwithstanding these pressures towards convergence, globalisation has also fostered differences and contrasts. Increasing mobility across the globe and streams of migrants have spawned more diversity into countries and cultures where people had hitherto regarded themselves as ethnically homogenous or even indigenous. This has made the endeavour of comparing crime and justice cross-nationally not only more rewarding but also more challenging. How do 'migrating' or 'hybrid' cultures help us to gain a new understanding of cross-cultural differences in crime and justice? Will it still be possible to compare 'cultures' between nation states? Even if we concede that 'the effects of rapid globalisation have changed social, political and legal realities' in ways that have eradicated clear national differences (Larsen and Smandych, 2008: XI), important differences between countries persist. Crime rates, the prevalence of corruption and organised crime and imprisonment rates differ widely, as do the fear of crime, public reactions toward crime and justice as well as the public's confidence in the justice system. Further to this, legal systems as well as legal cultures and the 'law in practice' shape criminal justice as well as its outcomes. Far from rendering comparative and international approaches obsolete and inadequate to deal with new challenges in criminology, globalisation begs the question of exactly how different societies are affected by globalisation and with what particular consequences (Van Dijk, 2008).

Criminology as a discipline has profited immensely from internationalisation and globalisation over the past few decades. Even if criminal justice and criminology are still 'parochial' in their perspectives (Karstedt, 2002a), the ways in which we perceive and position ourselves are increasingly informed by how we compare ourselves to others. Zimring (2006: 615) aptly illustrates this point with the cherished concept of 'American exceptionalism'. The notion of exceptionalism is a fundamentally comparative concept and 'based on assumptions that only comparisons can test'. Criminology has particularly profited from the exponential growth and accessibility of international and comparative data sets on crime and justice (see Mayhew and Van Dijk, this volume; Van Dijk, 2008). Criminologists have embarked on putting together sourcebooks on crime and justice like the *European Sourcebook of Crime and Criminal Justice Statistics* (2010). National and international government bodies make data and reports available, like the Country

Reports produced by the US State Department. The International Crime Victims Survey (ICVS) provides the best source of crime data beyond official statistics (Mayhew and Van Dijk, this volume). The Global Terrorism Database covers terrorist incidents across several decades and a large number of countries (Dugan, this volume). Non-governmental organisations, like Transparency International, collect and make available annual data on corruption extracted from a variety of survey sources. International surveys like the World Values Survey offer an array of public perceptions of crime and justice spanning the period from the 1980s until 2005.

While these data sources provide measures of crime, security and justice across the world, others give easy access to structural, social and cultural factors that criminologists conceptualise as causes and drivers of difference across the world. International surveys are a rich source of public attitudes and thus of cultural factors that we think shape crime policies in various ways. The huge body of statistics and indicators provided by the United Nations makes it possible for criminologists to analyse economic, demographic and structural factors that account for differences in violent crime rates, corruption, as well as in criminal justice throughputs (see, e.g., Sung, 2006). Data on political systems and cultures, including indicators of the justice system and legal cultures, are provided by the Polity Index or the Freedom House Index and numerous other data sets, collected by academics or non-governmental institutions. Databases which comprise indicators of culture based on anthropological studies, like the Human Relations Area File and the Standards Cross-Cultural Sample, lend themselves to being used by criminologists interested in cross-cultural research (see later for further information on databases).

Far from being 'inadequate to capture the full complexity ... on a global scale' as Larsen and Smandych (2008: XI) contend, comparative cross-national and cross-cultural perspectives in criminology have the potential to enhance the complexity of questions that can be asked in a global environment. They provide more profound and sophisticated knowledge on similarities and differences between countries and the particular shape and nature of crime and punishment beyond the overarching concept of globalisation. The analysis of globalisation needs to be informed by comparative perspectives as much as the latter need to be informed by the former. Paradoxically, the process of globalisation and trans-nationalisation has sharpened notions of our own criminal justice system. Large datasets as well as small case studies might position us side by side with others to whom we do not like to be compared.

They may also make us ask uncomfortable questions about our own, often taken for granted, environments of crime, public opinion and criminal justice reactions (see, e.g., Karstedt, 2002b).

GOING CROSS-CULTURAL: CONCEPTS AND PROBLEMS

Crime, justice and culture are intricately linked. As Alexander and Smith (1993, 157–8) write, '[T]he conflict between good and bad functions inside of culture as an internal dynamic ... It is for this reason that transgression and purification are key rituals in social life.' Values set off 'the good from the bad ... the sainted from the demonic'. Crime, social control and criminal justice thus become expressions of these internal dynamics, and as Nelken (1994) has aptly concluded, they can be seen as illuminating culture. The ways in which societies punish, how they react to particular exceptional cases of crime (Green, 2008), and how they respond to victims, can all be analysed as signifiers of a particular culture.

What is culture? Presumably some new definitions have been added to the 200 plus that were counted at the end of the last century (Karstedt, 2001: 288). Most of these definitions converged on a common core: culture is defined as a historically shaped set of meanings, values, interpretations and practices or habits that are shared between members of a community, nation or even a number of nations; it forms a specific social force independently of and partially autonomous of social structure and institutional contexts (Alexander and Smith, 1993). Values, and interpretations provide a stock of cultural symbols and knowledge that are used to give meaning to experience and to generate action, and as such define identity, express commitment and give rise to the 'rules of the game' embodied in institutions. Culture is embedded in the social system as much as in the minds of people (Hofstede, 1984). Culture is thus ' about who we are, not just what we do' (Nelken, 2004: 1).

From these definitions two problems arise for the cross-cultural study of crime and justice. The first of these concerns the *coherence and homogeneity of cultures*, and conversely the difference between cultures that cross-cultural research seeks to explore. Are consensus, homogeneity and integration necessary requirements of a concept of culture (Karstedt, 2001) that is useful in cross-cultural comparisons, and how much coherence and homogeneity do we need? Whether we seek to explain differences or whether we seek to explain a particular culture itself, in each case we have to assume a certain level of coherence within the set of values, beliefs, meanings and practices of the unit we are analysing, and that difference and variance between cultures is higher than within a culture. However, cultures vary as to the extent of homogeneity and consensus (Smith et al., 2006: 38). This corresponds to a lack of similarity and congruence between the patterns and configurations of values on individual and country level indicating that these represent different types of structures (Fischer et al., 2010). While the patterns of values at the individual level reflect the requirements for individuals to function within their social relationships, at the country/societal level value patterns reflect their function as guidance and justification for societal institutions, and their salience for the social systems as a whole.

Perceiving of cultures as *monolithic entities* which are defined by a single or a small number of particular characteristics ('culture complex'; Fiske et al., 1998) will certainly overrate their coherence as well as their distinctness compared to others. This is the risk when describing cultures as 'macho', ' honour-based' or as 'shame-' or 'guilt-culture'; it equally applies when overarching cultural concepts like 'Confucianism' or 'Asian values' are used in comparative research and as explanatory concepts (see Karstedt, 2001). In contrast, conceptualising culture as *multidimensional* will result in a more contingent notion of culture, more able to accommodate difference, diversity and subtle changes over time. It further allows particular combinations of dimensions of culture to be recognised. Different cultures are defined by different structural relationships, weights and combinations of values and practices shared at the collective level. They occupy a specific position on these dimensions, or are part of a typical cluster where a specific type of values, practices and institutions coalesce. A (multi-)dimensional perspective on culture will rest on the assumption that cultures vary along a small number of dimensions which they all have in common, and according to which they differ from each other. This assumption equally applies to single-trait conceptualisations of culture, which mainly are based on contrasting cultures where a specific trait is absent or present. Whichever route is taken, embarking on cross-cultural research implies the basic assumption that cultures can be compared according to a conceptual framework, even if a case study of a single culture is used (e.g. in Garland's 2010 study of the death penalty in the US).

The second problem concerns the question of understanding, interpreting and analysing cultures that are not our own. This problem is cast as the 'two opposing dangers' (Nelken 2009: 291) of *ethnocentrism* and *relativism* in comparative cultural research. *Ethnocentric* is the term used to criticise those whose analyses are informed by the biases of their own culture; it implies that the researcher assesses the values and practices in other cultures in the light of these, or starts comparative research with the assumption of finding similar patterns as well as significant 'deficits' in others. Community crime prevention schemes or community policing according to the UK model are hard to find in continental Europe and in particular in Germany where a very different notion of 'community' prevails and is historically rooted (e.g. Lacey and Zedner, 1998). The presumption that other countries, like Germany, can simply import community policing UK style could, therefore, be said to be ethnocentric. Likewise Nelken (2009) alerts us to the dangers of using 'neo-liberalism' as a conceptual frame for understanding international imprisonment rates and overall punitiveness of criminal justice, as such an approach is based on an ethnocentric perspective informed principally by policies that might only be present in the US and UK (see Cavadino and Dignan, 2006). *Relativism,* by contrast, is the argument that each culture has to be understood, interpreted and analysed in its very own terms. Taken to its logical conclusion this could make any comparison between cultures obsolete. Is it possible for an outsider to 'understand' a culture that is not their own? Does the researcher always need to be part of the culture in order to understand it fully?

There are no easy answers to these questions. However, cross-cultural research is based on the presumption that the capacity to learn a culture is innate to human beings. We are all capable of learning our own cultures. We must therefore be also capable of learning and understanding those of others, even if inevitably accomplished with varying degrees of competency. It is not ethnocentric to have value preferences and to endorse human rights, even if these are occidental in origin and part of our own culture (Nelken, 2010: 20). A relativistic approach does not necessarily imply the exclusive use of more qualitatively orientated methods of interpreting culture (Pakes, 2004: 13). Likewise, quantitative, multi-dimensional approaches need not necessitate the taking of an ethnocentric position. There is hardly a better exercise in alerting researchers to the relative position of their own culture than inspecting a figure that positions countries alongside two dimensions, like prison conditions and egalitarian values for example (Karstedt, 2011 a; see, for many examples, Van Dijk, 2008). Such a figure shows diversity, common cores, values shared by close 'culture neighbours' and all their nuanced variations. However, in order to explain and understand cultures and their impact on crime and justice it is necessary to do this in the context of their own values, structures and expectations (Nelken, 2010: 21), independent of whether these are measured in terms of multiple dimensions or just single and exceptional traits. We need carefully designed strategies to navigate these pitfalls of cross-cultural research.

'WAYS OF SEEING': STRATEGIES OF CROSS-CULTURAL COMPARISON

Strategies of cross-cultural comparison can be conceptualised in terms of the general solutions that they provide for the two problems outlined above. As such they define basic approaches and the type and numbers of units chosen for the research, the details of the method of comparison and the way in which culture is conceptualised and 'measured'. There are two main strategic approaches to cross-cultural research on crime and criminal justice.

The first of these is variously termed 'explanatory' (Nelken, 1994, 2010), 'distributional' (Zimring, 2006) or 'multi-dimensional and extensive' (Karstedt, 2001). This approach has as its central focus 'a variety of different places' or different cultures (Zimring, 2006: 617). It aims to discover a range of variations in crime and justice, distributions across cultures, and links between these distributions and one or more of the social dimensions by which these cultures differ. Its objective is to explain differences (and similarities) in crime and justice through one or more defining dimensions of culture. Van Dijk (2008) provides numerous examples of such correlates of punishment, crime and justice across the globe. An exemplary study is Greenberg and West's (2009) analysis of the impact of religion and other cultural factors on the abolishment of the death penalty for 193 countries. My own research explores the impact of democratic values like individualism and collectivism on violent crime (2006) as well as on state violence (Karstedt, 2011b, in press); I also analysed these value dimensions and their impact on punishment for a sample of more than 60 countries, using both imprisonment rates and prison conditions as indicators (Karstedt, 2011a).

The opposite strategy has been defined as 'interpretative' (Nelken, 1994, 2010) 'contextual' (Zimring, 2006: 617) or 'single trait and intensive' (Karstedt, 2001: 290). This strategy aims at identifying and isolating the 'distinguishing features' (Zimring, 2006: 617) of a single place or culture by a case study or a selection of cases used for dyadic and triadic comparisons. Typically, the country of the researcher provides a starting point from which to venture into cross-cultural comparisons. Green's study of reactions toward exceptional cases *When Children Kill Children* (2008) in the UK and Norway, or Zimring and Hawkins' (1997) comparative study of crime rates in the US and other countries are examples of this approach. Research on 'American exceptionalism' can be counted in this group too (Garland, 2010). Alternatively, a study of one or a small number of cases can be used to contextualise these within a particular region, set of cultures or time frame.

The following gives a brief overview of exemplary studies using this strategic approach: Johnson and Zimring's (2009) study of the death penalty in Asia addresses a regional set of countries/cultures; Whitman's (2003) study of the origins of 'harsh punishment' in France, Germany and the US provides an exemplar of strategic dyadic and triadic comparisons; single case / country studies include a study of Russian prisons (Piacentini 2004), and a study of policing housemaids in Bahrain (Strobl 2009). Downes' (1988, 2007) analysed the development of penal culture in the Netherlands covering two decades. All of these studies represent in-depth explorations of cases which give space to cultural narratives and particular institutional design; they situate these within the context of the meaning of crime and justice that is particular to a culture. Rarely, they start with a pre-conception of defining characteristics of this culture, and these characteristics rather emerge as a result of the research.

While such a framework that clearly juxtaposes these two strategies defines paradigmatic routes for research, there is agreement that the two strategies represent ideal types in the Weberian sense . In short, they do not mirror the realities of comparative research. Most authors argue that these two strategies are interdependent, and 'distributional work provides contextual perspective' and vice versa (Zimring, 2006). They suggest that a mix of explanatory and interpretative strategies (Nelken, 1994) are required in order to get beyond such alternatives, which tend to over-emphasise the contrast between quantitative and qualitative, and between theory-driven and grounded-theory-focused cross-cultural research (Karstedt, 2001).

The sociologist Charles Tilly (1984: 80) provides a more differentiated scheme of comparative strategies as 'ways of seeing'. Comparative strategies can be classified according to two dimensions which signify 'reasonable aims' of comparative analysis: Tilly defines these as 'share of all instances' and 'multiplicity of forms'. The first dimension ranges from a single instance to all instances of a phenomenon; this implies that we can proceed from a correct identification of the cultural characteristics of one case to isolating the characteristics of all cases. A smaller number of strategically selected cases can then be used to refine the analysis. 'Multiplicity' implies that comparisons can range from a single form, where all instances of the phenomenon have common properties, to multiple forms, where instances vary considerably. Thus we could assume either that the neo-liberal state represents a single form and comes in a single shape, or in contrast that neo-liberalism is actually a very multi-faceted phenomenon. Figure 25.1 shows the four different strategies that result from cross-classifying these two dimensions: a continuum between individualising and universalising constitutes one dimension; a continuum between encompassing and variation-finding comparative strategies constitutes the other.

A purely *individualising strategy* takes each case as unique at a certain period of time, and aims at 'minimizing its common properties with other instances'. Identifying the features of American or Scandinavian exceptionalism (Pratt 2008a, 2008b) is a fitting example here; another exemplar of this strategy is Whitman's (2003) study, which analysed the impact of revolution on status politics with a view to understanding the different ways prisoners were treated in the US, Germany and France. At the *universalising* end

we find those comparisons that aim to establish a common cause, mechanism or stages through which countries and cultures will necessarily pass. Universalising strategies are best exemplified by cross-cultural and cross-national research on violent crime that are based on the notion of a process of modernisation (see Karstedt, 2001, for an overview) or what Elias' referred to as the 'civilising process' (Eisner, 2001). Purely universalising strategies are less frequently used in comparative research on penal systems. But the assumption that the adoption of neo-liberal policies and the establishment of the neo-liberal state necessarily increase the use of imprisonment has certainly informed recent comparative studies, like Cavadino and Dignan's (2006) analysis of the growth of imprisonment in 12 countries.

On the opposite side of Figure 25.1, variation-finding and encompassing comparisons are located. Variation-finding comparisons aim to establish a 'principle of variation in the character or intensity of a phenomenon by examining systematic differences among instances' (Tilly, 1984: 82). Variation-finding comparisons are often based on multi-dimensional concepts of culture and large samples. Research on the impact of democratic cultures and institutions as well as on the process of democratisation provides a number of

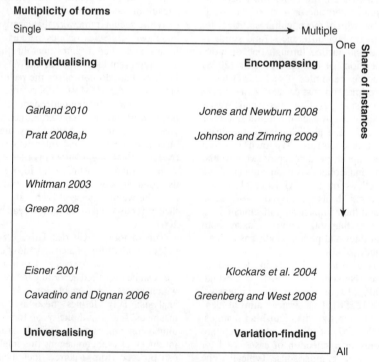

Figure 25.1 'Ways of seeing': Comparative strategies. Source: Tilly, 1984: 81

exemplary studies comprising both variations in violent crime and criminal justice across a large sample of countries (Karstedt and LaFree, 2006). A seminal variation-finding study is Greenberg and West's (2008) research on the death penalty in 193 nations. Klockars et al. (2004) used a standardised survey instrument for their study of police integrity respective misconduct and corruption in 14 countries, which measured general and specific characteristics of police culture. All variation-finding comparisons need to use 'parallel methods' of comparison; this implies either using a set of indicators across all countries, or research instruments that are tasked to elicit exactly similar and comparable types of information across the sample (Karstedt, 2001).

Encompassing strategies of comparison place 'different instances at various locations within the same system' with the aim of 'explaining their (individual) characteristics as a function of their varying relationships to the system as a whole' (Tilly, 1984: 83). They neither isolate the specific characteristics of a case nor do they search for variations in crime and criminal justice 'across the globe' among isolated and totally unconnected instances of a phenomenon. What they do instead is seek to contextualise cultural characteristics and their variations within networks and regions. Encompassing strategies thus open up routes toward integrating globalisation with comparative perspectives, and the global with the local. They are therefore best situated for answering questions about why regions differ in terms of crime and criminal justice, in what ways regional traditions shape criminal justice, and particularly how crime policies travel around the globe (Newburn and Sparks, 2004). Birkbeck's study (in press) aims at teasing out fundamental differences in the meaning and concept of imprisonment in North and South America in terms of cultural similarities and linkages within each of these two regions. Jones and Newburn (2008) analyse the convergence and exchange of penal policies between two countries with traditional and close links, the US and UK. They include three major and globally important policies: zero-tolerance policing, prison privatisation and mandatory sentencing. Johnson and Zimring's study (2009) on the death penalty in Asia similarly explores links and transfers between the countries of that region.

SAMPLES, UNITS AND THE PROBLEM OF SIMILARITY AND DIFFERENCE

How can we know that the characteristics that we isolated for a single or a few cases are actually decisive or even causal in shaping penal policies?

Are the systematic variations and regularities that we found between countries actually meaningful, or do they gloss over particularities and subtle differences between countries? What makes a case 'exceptional', and when can we use the term 'exceptionalism'? It is a common experience among comparativists that they will always be confronted with the 'exception' of a country or case that does not fit, and where their analyses do not apply. Does this render the comparative effort futile? These questions refer to strategies of sampling, to sample size and to the definition of units in cross-cultural research, and the ways in which we establish similarities and difference.

There is 'no safety in numbers' as Tilly (1984: 76) reminds us; not in the single case, and neither in small nor in large samples. Cross-cultural research is often based on small numbers, and the sample can be termed a 'convenience sample' of countries where the research team had access like in Klockars et al.'s (2004) study of police integrity, or in Cavadino and Dignan's (2006) research on the penal systems of 12 countries. These studies comprise a number of case studies, with each analysed as a single case, and differences and similarities distilled from their specific characteristics. There is nothing to object in principle to such convenience samples, as they are often the only route towards collecting in-depth information on cases. They also have the advantage of involving 'cultural insiders' who can offer particular insights into the system of criminal justice.

Cross-cultural research lends itself to the study of extremes and opposites (Mills, 1970), in particular as cultural characteristics and dimensions are often constructed as 'polar types'. Japan and the US were contrasted as two highly developed and modernised countries, of which Japan had not developed the particular mix of violent and property crime, and high crime rates that were supposed to be concomitants of the process of modernisation (see Karstedt, 2001, for an overview). Green (2008) analysed penal populism and political culture in the UK and Norway, and chose these countries because they represented 'polar types' in their public and political reactions to cases of children killing children. Such binary conceptions of cross-cultural research and dyadic comparisons have some in-built problems. They can lead to privileging one case over another, either as being the 'standard' or 'normal' case in contrast to the deviation, or seen as the one that 'does better' as it has all the characteristics that the researcher contends will improve criminal justice, like more and better welfare, inclusion and solidarity (Nelken, 2009: 292; see, e.g., Pratt 2008a, 2008b on Scandinavian countries). Similarities and common ground are pressured to dissolve in such juxtapositions of two cases.

Differences are exaggerated and constructed as causal factors or signifying characteristics. A triadic method of selection of cases and analyses can avoid these problems by choosing cases which vary in their distance towards each other in terms of their characteristics. Whitman's (2003) study of the 'widening divide' of criminal punishment between Europe and the US is exemplary in using a triadic selection and comparison. He constructs three different pathways that ultimately lead to contemporary differences in the harshness of punishment between these countries. While the US represents a 'polar type' in contrast to the two European countries, his analysis avoids simply contrasting the US and Europe as he identifies differences in the political culture and their historical trajectories between the two European countries.

Comparative studies based on a small number of cases present some general problems when researchers aim at causal explanations of differences and similarities, and try to arrive at 'big conclusions' (Lieberson, 1991). These are not problems of generalisation but rather of causal inference, and they indicate methodological pitfalls. Implicitly they are based on John Stuart Mill's (1872) method of agreement and difference, and thus the search for 'significant absences' (Lacey and Zedner, 1998) or respectively 'presences' of a particular characteristic in comparisons can count as an application of Mill's method. This method proceeds by eliminating any common features between the cases, until finally the one characteristic is found that differs between them, be it by absence, presence or typical variation, and causal significance is assigned to it. This can be achieved by strategically sampling cases, which are similar in important characteristics, or by selecting polar types and eliminating what they have in common. However, causal inference from small numbers is based on several assumptions, which contradict a realistic appraisal of most social and cultural processes that shape criminal justice. First, such research needs to assume a deterministic approach, which would contradict the often contingent and incremental nature of penal policy making (see, e.g., Jones and Newburn, 2008), and certainly is not appropriate for the comparison of crime rates between countries. Second, it is necessary to assume the existence of only one cause, and the presence of more than one common causal variable makes it impossible to sort out the actual cause (Tilly, 1984). Finally, the absence of interactions between these variables is a necessary assumption. In particular, the latter two assumptions are unreasonable when comparing cultures, crime and criminal justice, and contradict what we know about each of them.

Large samples allow for a clearer picture of variation and co-variation of cultural contexts and their impact on criminal justice. They are less restricted in terms of assumptions concerning determinism, multiple causation and interaction between causal factors. They are, however, not necessarily superior to small numbers in cross-cultural research mainly for two reasons. First, unbiased samples of cultures are not available, as data collection on crime and criminal justice depends very much on conditions that are linked to both, like GDP, welfare, education or the strength of governments and the polity. African countries are suspiciously absent in most of these samples (see, e.g., Van Dijk, 2008: chapters 1 and 2). Official crime and justice data have well-known problems which restrict the type of crimes and indicators of penal systems that can be used, leading to the use of homicide and imprisonment rates as 'gold standards' for comparative research in our field. International surveys that provide both crime victimisation rates and cultural variables are mostly conducted in countries that have the infrastructure for such surveys in place and can afford them.

Second, cross-cultural research with large samples is based on a limited number of cultural indicators and measurement of values, practices and institutions that provide comparable and quantifiable dimensions of culture. This deprives these measurements of the rich contextual data about culture that small samples can provide, and reduces concrete differences between cultures to rather abstract commonalities (Geertz, 1973). International surveys allow for exploring people's beliefs about crime and justice; however, the resulting country-level measures of sharing and consensus easily gloss over dissent and variation within a culture, especially regional differences (Hofstede et al., 2010). Indicators of the justice system can be rather rough, and biased by those who collect them: what does an indicator like 'independence of justice' (e.g., Freedom House) actually measure (Nelken, 2010)?

Using large samples therefore implies diligent choices with respect to the type of indicators used for measuring both criminal justice and culture. Greenberg and West's (2008) study of the death penalty is exemplary in these respects. Data on the abolishment, retention and use of the death penalty are available for most countries; their indicator of culture was religion, again available for most countries, and they meticulously relate concepts and ideologies of punishment to each of the major religions. Their control variables covered a large number of countries. They achieved a total and unbiased sample of 193 countries.

It might be useful to follow Tilly's advice (1984: 77): 'Stick with careful comparisons of small numbers until you have a very clear idea what you need from large numbers and how to make the comparisons valid.' Even if this might not be asked from the individual researcher, the collective of cross-cultural criminologists provides opportunities to follow this route. My study of democratic culture and institutions and penal punishment was based on Whitman's analysis of three cases of revolutionary and persisting patterns of status politics, and used a sample of 60 countries, including mature democracies as well as autocratic states. Both imprisonment rates and prison conditions were used as indicators of penal punishment, and these were complemented by a scale of 'Physical Integrity' (Cingranelli and Richards, 2007) measuring state violence exerted through the criminal justice system, as Whitman had focused on the treatment of offenders and prisoners. The measurement of cultural indicators closely followed the distinct characteristics of status politics that he had identified: respect for the individual and individual autonomy; egalitarian values; and patterns of status difference, either based on explicitly meritocratic or more inclusionary orientations. I used Hofstede's (2005/2010) cultural dimensions of Individualism/Collectivism and Egalitarianism/Power Distance for the former and data from the World Values Survey for the latter (Karstedt, 2011a, b, in press).

What 'units of culture' can be used in cross-cultural research on crime and justice? As most indicators of crime and justice are only available at the level of nations and countries, cross-cultural research necessarily has to be done with cultural indicators at this level of aggregation, or revert to primarily quantitative signifiers of diversity, like ethnic, religious and linguistic differentiation within a country (see Alesina et al., 2003; Greenberg and West, 2008). Even if researchers choose to start from specific cases like Green (2008), or use scandals as their focal lens through which they observe and analyse cultural difference (West, 2009), they finally have to use countries as units of cultural analysis. Given the nature of cultural patterns and of the institutional arrangements that embody and foster these, the more or less forced choice of country-level data is nonetheless justified. Theoretical models and simulations of cultural diversity indicate that within the boundaries of a state, culture tends towards homogenisation, even with initially high levels of diversity (Axelrod, 1997). As such, social, political and economic institutions create an environment which pressures toward a certain extent of homogenisation of individual mentalities and behavioural patterns (Smith et al., 2006: 58). More important is the fact that institutional arrangements are bounded by the nation state, and reflect the will of its polity and the values and

demand of communities. In particular, legal institutions are established at the level of countries, and hence are the legal cultures to which these institutions give rise. Federal states might encompass different justice systems and criminal policies, but even these are bound by overarching constitutional principles and subject to decisions by higher courts and federal government. However, the assumption of a unified and shared set of values, beliefs and practices that is confined within the boundaries of the nation state will become more contested with increasing migration and ethnic difference within nation states, and might be wrong from the outset for specific global regions, where countries are comprised of a number of groups and regions that differ substantially in terms of ethnicity, language and/or religion.

Cross-cultural research can, however, use and combine units at different levels of aggregation, individuals within countries, countries within regions, or federal states within a nation state. As cultures are embedded in the social system and in the minds of people, they are equally embedded within regions. Contact, networks, modelling and travelling all contribute to sharing at least some core features of culture. In this context, 'nested designs' provide a methodological way forward: individual belief and value patterns are analysed within the context of difference and consensus at the level of countries, or country-specific patterns are contextualised within regional patterns, as Johnson and Zimring (2009) do for Asia and selected case studies. International surveys like the ICVS, the World Values Survey or the European Social Survey allow for the analysis of relationships between cultural patterns, crime and perceptions of justice at the individual and aggregate country level. The US represents a special case, as criminal justice and outcomes of penal policies differ hugely between federal states, equalling variations between European countries. Notwithstanding such differences, they are embedded in an overarching cultural and institutional pattern. Barker's (2009) study of democratic process and culture in three states (California, Washington and New York) and their impact on penal policies takes advantage of the 'natural' contextual and nested design that the US offers.

MEASURING CULTURE, CRIME AND JUSTICE

Measuring crime and justice is at the core of the criminological enterprise, and criminologists are well aware of the pitfalls of measurement, whether they use official crime and justice data, survey data from self-reports of victimisation and offending, or the respective data sources from police, courts and other criminal justice agencies. Measuring culture necessitates venturing into the foreign terrain of other disciplines and methods of data collection. The very notion that 'culture' can be 'measured' begs a number of questions, and it might be advisable to use a different term. 'Identifying' core patterns and configurations of culture seems to be more inclusive, as it encompasses both the use of qualitative data as well as quantification of dimensions of culture. This section will first give a brief overview of the state of the art and problems of measurement of crime and justice and then proceed to a discussion of identifying culture.

As outlined previously, the problems of national official data are exacerbated at the international level. Van Dijk (2008: chapters 1 and 2) gives a succinct overview over the state of international crime and justice statistics, which he describes as 'the sorry state of art' (ibid. 4). Notwithstanding numerous efforts at improvement, their quality and range remains deplorable, and even seem to have deteriorated during the past decades. The United Nations Survey on Crime Trends and the Operations of the Criminal Justice System offers a wealth of indicators, ranging from broadly defined types of crime to a number of indicators of policing and different segments of the criminal justice system. However, as these data are collected through an administrative questionnaire and based on official statistics, they are susceptible to a number of biases, not the least political manipulation (Van Dijk, 2008: chapter 1). This can occur when they are seen as affecting the image of a country with severe ramifications for internal security and the economy.

Criminologists therefore have reverted to other sources of data for good reasons: international surveys of victimisation and offending; data collected and compiled by other international agencies like the World Bank or the World Health Organisation; data collected by insurers and other private companies for the purpose of risk assessment; and data collected by non-governmental organisations. The ICVS is the most important and encompassing amongst these surveys, covering households in 78 countries (37 nationwide) across the period from 1989 to 2005. In addition to the sources described above (see previous section), specialised surveys provide data on particular crimes and groups, like the International Violence against Women Survey, the International Crime Business Survey or the Global Crime Survey from international auditing companies (PricewaterhouseCoopers). Data combining victimisation and offending, including fraud, bribe paying, tax evasion and other 'middle class crimes'

are available from the European Social Survey for 2002 (see Karstedt and Farrell, 2006). Self-report data on offending are rare in comparison to victimisation data. Two waves of the International Self-Report Delinquency Study provide information about young offenders.

While indicators of crime and victimisation have their own problems in terms of different legal definitions, scope of categories, range of types of crimes and issues of perceptions, the data sources named above mostly offer viable solutions to these problems. In contrast, indicators of criminal justice, performance and outcomes are burdened with problems of definition or measurement due to their conceptual breadth. Is it possible to use imprisonment rates as indicator of 'punitiveness', or do we need to take into account other data like the rate of life sentences, sentence length and actually served sentences, or prison conditions? What can count and be counted as 'police performance'? In the field of legal culture, in what ways can concepts like 'rule of law' or 'penal populism' be assessed and measured? The UN Survey provides data on the different segments of the criminal justice system, their respective strength and operational outcomes (e.g. prosecution and conviction rates; see Sung, 2006). The most comprehensive and reliable data file on the death penalty is provided by Amnesty International. With regard to imprisonment rates, most comparativists in criminology use Walmsley's World Prison Population List (1999–2009). More detailed assessments of average length of prison sentence and actual time served for equivalent cases are only available for a small number of countries (Farrington et al., 2004). Indicators of police performance are mostly constructed from data on reporting and victim satisfaction with the police from the ICVS. Surveys of businesses provide data on the reliability of police and protection against crime (World Economic Forum). The International/World Values Survey and the European Social Survey include data on public trust and confidence in police and the justice system across nearly three decades. As an indicator independent of public perceptions, Van Dijk (2008: 219) suggests the conviction rate for homicide as a more 'objective' measurement of police performance.

For most evaluative indicators of the criminal justice system, criminologists will have to look beyond the UN Survey data. General assessment of the state of the rule of law and measurements are compiled by political scientists and often by institutions outside of academia. Widely used are data from Freedom House, a US-based organisation, and its annual survey of global political rights and civil liberties. The Freedom House Index includes general indicators of the rule of law and independence of the judiciary. The World Economic Forum provides data from surveys of business leaders on political independence and corruption of the judiciary (Van Dijk 2008: 249). The Country Reports of the US Department of State are a valuable source for the assessment of prison conditions. Observance of and compliance with human rights standards by governments – in particular in the treatment of offenders and prisoners – are increasingly important measures of performance and 'justice gaps' in the criminal justice system. The Political Terror Scale compiled by Amnesty International and the Index of Physical Integrity constructed by Cingranelli and Richards (2007) include 'unlawful and arbitrary deprivation of life', 'disappearances', 'torture' and 'political imprisonment'. It is important to note that most of these indices are composed from a number of sources and expert ratings, and therefore often rank countries and assign scores.

Van Dijk (2008) advocates composite indices of crime and justice, which should be used as 'diagnostic tools' and for 'bench marking' rather than exact measurements. His 'index of punitiveness' (ibid. 270) is aimed at relating severe violent crime to imprisonment; countries were ranked on both rates, and ranks for imprisonment rates were subtracted from the ranks for homicide rates, resulting in positive and negative scores. High positive net scores indicate low imprisonment rates given levels of lethal violence, while high negative scores indicate an excess of imprisonment and more severe punishment. A Composite Index of Police Performance is based on two objective measures (victim reporting rate from the ICVS, and homicide conviction rate from the UN Survey) and three subjective measures (victim satisfaction and citizen satisfaction, both from the ICVS, and business leader satisfaction from the World Economic Forum Survey). For cross-cultural research, his composite index 'Culture of Lawfulness' is of particular interest, and he demonstrates its value as a diagnostic tool. This index combines overall victimisation rates (ICVS), the Composite Index of Organised Crime (Van Dijk, 2008), the Corruption Perception Index of Transparency International, as well as the Composite Index of Police Performance and measures of political independence and integrity of the judiciary (World Economic Forum), covering 158 countries.

With rare exceptions, cross-cultural research makes wide use of these quantitative data, even if mostly in a descriptive way. The identification of culture and its measurement however mostly relies on different types of data sources and different types of measurement. Data on crime and justice aim to be strictly comparable, and therefore use what is termed *parallel methods* in cross-cultural

research (Karstedt, 2001). Parallel research design and measurement uses the same variables, operationalisations, samples and data sources across all units. In contrast, *equivalent methods* are used when culture per se is the subject; these are adapted to the cultural context, and consequently dimensions, sources and samples will differ and produce equivalent data rather than strictly comparable data. Equivalent methods are required where cultural research is aimed at achieving rich contextual data that define core patterns, fine-grained mechanisms and behavioural patterns, and as contexts vary so might the need for context-specific information. Equivalent methods are more flexible, as they are linked to the research process and outcomes at each of its stages. Structural differences require different points of data collection, different subjects and different spaces. This applies in particular to research on legal cultures: according to mechanisms and structures of decision making in criminal justice agencies, and their relative importance, the researcher will need to focus on different agencies, levels in the hierarchy and different experts and interview partners to collect relevant and contextual information.

Cross-cultural research has its roots in anthropological research and its ethnographic methods; Geertz (1994) famously termed its richly nuanced and contextualised accounts of cultural patterns as 'thick descriptions'. Ethnography is explicitly or implicitly wedded to the notion of the case study, and when reconstructing cultural values, practices and institutional mechanisms ethnographic research uses 'cases' ranging from particular events and spaces situated within a culture to cultural units as a whole. Case studies use multiple sources of data: observations, narratives, interviews, media, historical accounts, and all types of 'products' of institutional decision making embedded in files and records. For the cross-cultural criminologist, two developments of ethnographic/case study methods are particularly important. The 'extended case method' (Burawoy, 2000, 2009) situates the case within its spatial and temporal context, adding historical trajectories and spatial networks to the reconstruction of contemporary patterns that are analysed. 'Discourse analysis' is useful in analysing and reconstructing the 'interpretive repertoires' present in a cultural setting; that is, the specific and coherent ways in which people talk about events, objects and practices (Green, 2008: 105). Discourse analysis probes into the stock of knowledge present in a cultural setting and relates it back to seminal values and institutional practices. It is a way to explore the beliefs of people about good and bad, crime and justice, political and judicial decision-making, as well as the public spaces where such discourses merge in contemporary societies, such as the media. Discourse analysis lends itself to explorations of political culture and how it shapes criminal justice across countries.

Johnson and Zimring's (2009) study of the death penalty in Asia excellently demonstrates how the extended case study method can be set to work in comparative research, though they do not explicitly use an ethnographic approach. For each country they provide a historical account of relevant developments in their political and criminal justice systems, as well as of the political and legal culture. They look into Western and international as well as regional influences, the models that Japan, for example, strived for, and where and when it became 'exceptional'. They analyse change and persistence in public opinion on the death penalty as well as specific cases that were focal for public and political debate using multiple sources of data. The five in-depth country studies are complemented by short accounts of six other countries that add to the regional context.

With its focus on media and policy discourse in order to illuminate differences in penal populism and political culture between Norway and the UK, Green's (2008) study is an exemplar of cross-cultural discourse analysis. He identifies four ways in which discursive–analytic approaches contribute to comparative research in criminology: first, 'they render observable culturally distinct penal sensibilities'; second, 'they expose political motives … (of) criminal justice policy makers by unpacking the rhetoric used to justify dominant approaches'; third, they 'can offer possible explanations for the dominance of one or more discourses over others'; and fourth, they 'allow us to untangle the dominant discourses, trace their origin and understand, why they are so well transmitted and accepted.' (ibid. 113). He analyses the discourse in the media through all stages of the two cases of children killing children for a year and for all coverage. He then links the themes of this discourse to characteristics of the political culture in each country, including the media–political complex, institutional characteristics, political parties and crime policies. Green adds to these 'arenas' of public discourse the one of 'experts and criminal justice practitioners', and thus relates arenas and discourses through the focal lens of the case in each country.

Cross-cultural psychology and social psychology offer an alternative approach that is aimed at literally measuring culture in quantifiable terms, with comparable efforts in political science and sociology. These are based on multi-dimensional concepts of cultures and on parallel methods, and mostly used with large samples. The most common data sources are cross-national surveys of cultural values and practices, either of samples of the whole population or selected and seminal groups matched for all cultural settings. These are probably the most suitable data sources for exploring people's beliefs about crime and justice, either directly or contextualised within wider belief systems and cultural practices. At the aggregate level these sources provide indicators of the shared beliefs and social practices common to a culture, both as 'citizen means', 'most common' characteristics within a nation state, or as typical 'profiles' of the salience of values, and their specific links to each other. Such measurement of cultural dimensions can be complemented by other indicators of culture such as majority religious affiliation and practices. Indicators of culturally important institutional settings like the political system, welfare, the economy and education can be added from other data sources (e.g. Greenberg and West, 2008). As long as these data sources cover multiple waves like the World Values Survey, they provide the opportunity to probe into cultural change across several decades.

Three major cross-cultural /cross-national surveys have been most influential in the field of cross-cultural research: the Hofstede project, the World Values Survey (initiated and conducted by political scientist Inglehart and his collaborators), and the Schwartz Values Surveys (see, for details, Smith et al., 2006). The European Social Survey mirrors the World Values Survey and includes the set of Schwartz Values for some of its waves. They all construct cultural dimensions and value patterns by using factor analysis both on the individual and the aggregate or 'ecological' (Hofstede) level, and as outlined above, with different patterns emerging at the individual and aggregate level. As such they are based on a conceptualisation of culture that stresses universal and core dimensions, common to all cultures and humanity, along which cultures differ in their unique and characteristic patterns. Thus cultural patterns can be ranked according to the distance and similarity between them, or clusters of countries with similar cultural patterns can be identified. A cautious note needs to be added: the sample of countries is biased towards the global north, Western industrialised and wealthier countries, and the global south is under-represented. However, there is considerable overlap in the samples of all three cultural surveys, which allows for combining country-level cultural dimensions from the different sources. A brief description of each of them is given below, exploring their potential for cross-cultural research on criminal justice and crime.

Hofstede's study can be deemed the most influential in shaping the field of cross-cultural social psychology for decades to come (Hofstede, 1984; 2005/2010). In particular the dimensions of

Individualism/Collectivism and Power Distance/ Egalitarianism have since become a widely used measure of cross-cultural differences (Triandis, 1995; Smith et al., 2006). Presently, data for at about 70 countries are available (Hofstede, 2005/ 2010). Hofstede's value dimensions can be regarded as fundamental, long-term and stable dimensions for cross-cultural research, as the relative positions of countries across time indicates a high stability of *relative* cultural differences despite the changes caused by the process of modernisation during the two decades between 1970 and 1990 (Inglehart, 1997, Triandis and Trafimov, 2001). Both Individualism/Collectivism and Power Distance/Egalitarianism emerge as cultural patterns that shape criminal justice as well as levels of criminal behaviour. They are related to interpersonal lethal violence (Karstedt, 2006) and state violence (Karstedt, 2011b), as well as to levels of corruption and organised crime (Karstedt, in press). They determine the ways in which offenders are punished and how they are treated in prisons (prison conditions, Karstedt, 2011a).

The World Values Survey comprises five waves between 1982 and 2005, and combined these now include nearly 70 countries (Inglehart, 1997; Inglehart and Welzel, 2005). Originally designed to delineate cultural change cross-nationally and globally, it has achieved a much broader relevance in identifying two distinct cultural dimensions. Rational–Legal Authority versus Traditional Authority define the ways in which authority is exerted, legitimised and accepted within a culture. Self-Expression versus Survival define the extent of tolerance of ambiguity and deviant behaviour, the acceptance and expression of individual identity, and the prioritisation of security over individual difference. Besides these two dimensions the World Values Survey offers a wealth of data for the criminological comparativist: moral judgments; attitudes towards inequality and welfare; and trust and confidence in others and institutions, including the justice system and the police (see Karstedt, in press).

The Schwartz Value Survey explicitly aims at understanding the links between individual-level and culture-level value patterns. Separate samples of students and school teachers are used for each nation, and presently samples from 67 countries are available. In addition, the European Social Survey provides population samples for 25 countries from its 2002 wave. Schwartz and his colleagues found distinct patterns on the individual and country level. At the nation level, values are patterned according to seven dimensions: Harmony with the Environment *versus* Mastery; Intellectual and Affective Autonomy *versus* Embeddedness Within Social Networks; Egalitarianism *versus* Hierarchical Order. As the European Social Survey

includes a number of items on crime victimisation and offending as well as perceptions of criminal justice it offers a rich source for cross-cultural analyses (Karstedt and Farrell, in press).

Cross-cultural criminologists, whether as ethnographers or survey researchers, are confronted with a major though often under-rated problem in identifying and measuring culture: language and translation. Even if English-speaking criminologists can take advantage of the fact that they can communicate with professionals at higher echelons of criminal justice institutions in their own language, this will hardly be possible when conducting research at the lower levels. Those who aim at using media and political discourse in their cross-cultural research will need more than rudimentary mastery of the foreign language when they are looking for richly nuanced narratives and subtext. Those who embark on extended case studies of one or more foreign countries (and more than one language) will need considerable language support when sifting through and using documents. Even as cross-national surveys are available in the *lingua franca* of our times, constructing and designing questionnaires in different languages is a major undertaking. In which ways do cross-cultural criminologists address these problems?

Stanley (this volume) gives a vivid account of the problems of language and translation when researching torture victims in Timor Leste, with more than one official language and numerous indigenous languages. Her several translators often needed the mastery of more than one of each. Green (2008) collaborated with native speakers at different stages of his analysis of Norwegian newspapers, who translated all articles for him. Additional translation support was needed when coding the translated files. The team of Johnson and Zimring (2009) included one researcher with in-depth knowledge of Japan, and they relied on numerous collaborators in each country who collected and translated documents; they also discussed draft chapters with local experts. Cavadino and Dignan (2006) relied on criminology colleagues in each of the 12 countries, who were experts in the field of their local penal systems.

Translation of cross-national surveys involves a set of sophisticated procedures in order to ensure the requirements of parallel measurement and cross-national validity of the data. The European Social Survey used state-of-the-art procedures of translation. First, a source questionnaire in English was produced, which was translated by teams in each country. Draft translations were discussed in team meetings with bilingual experts and final versions were produced through back-and-forth translation (Harkness et al., 2004). In their study of middle-class crime Karstedt and Farrall (2006) took advantage of the fact that they were both native speakers of each of the languages of the questionnaire. They designed each question and item together in what can be termed a 'simultaneous translation method', and the final German questionnaire was edited by the German author.

NEW HORIZONS FOR CROSS-CULTURAL RESEARCH

The prospects for comparative perspectives and cross-cultural research in criminology have never been better. Far from being inimical to comparative perspectives, globalisation has sparked fresh and intriguing visions. Students and researchers from other countries and cultures help us better to understand our own criminal justice systems as we help them to contextualise their own experiences and research within a global framework. A wealth of data resources is easily available. The gap between quantity and quality in particular of international data sources on crime and criminal justice will be – if only slowly – closed by efforts from international agencies, NGOs and the international scientific community. All these developments will increase the knowledge and understanding of crime patterns and trends, and of the performance of criminal justice systems, and will help to develop mutually beneficial ways of preventing crime and improving criminal justice. I will briefly outline three topics and opportunities that the future holds for cross-cultural research: relating the global and the local, and 'cultures within cultures'; crossing different levels of analysis; and cultural change.

Flows of migrants across the globe have increased the diversity of cultures inhabiting the space of nation states, and hybrid cultures are evolving. Cross-cultural research therefore can start at home, and reach out to the countries of origin of these migrants. How do their cultural inheritance and their adaptations impact on common and joint understandings of crime and criminal justice? In what ways do criminal justice systems adapt to such diversity? The well-worn concepts of culture conflict acquire a new meaning in more diverse societies, and offer new opportunities for cross-cultural research within countries.

Cross-cultural research is mostly used to analyse values, beliefs and social practices at the aggregate level and as consensual and shared between individuals. It has thrived on contrasting cases or comparing cultures as unrelated and 'stand-alone' units, particularly when using larger samples. New and sophisticated methods of multilevel and hierarchical data analyses are available that help to embed individuals within their cultural context, and to contextualise countries within larger regions. These methods will also be useful when comparing cultures and ethnicities within a society. Such nested designs are more receptive to the contextual nature of culture, including the networks of encounters in and through which culture emerges. They tease out bottom-up rather than top-down conceptualisations of culture, and view culture as produced by rather than imposed on, individuals. Nested designs give a more nuanced understanding of similarities and differences, of variation between and within cultures, and of regional links and exchange.

The flows of migrants, knowledge and goods (in illegal as well as in legal trade) that connect cultures across the globe will result in cultural change at both ends – in originating as well as in receiving countries. In our field, the travel of crime, crime prevention policies and criminal justice institutions is exemplary of this facet of globalisation. Cross-cultural research needs to engage more with trajectories of cultural change and its impact on criminal justice. The World Values Survey covers nearly three decades and was designed to measure change; it offers numerous indicators that can be related to changes in criminal justice, punitiveness and penal populism across cultures. Political change and transitions that affected numerous countries over the past decades can be used to analyse trajectories of such abrupt changes across different cultures.

Finally, cross-cultural research has to engage with the 'justice deficit' in many countries (Van Dijk, 2008: 310). These are regions and countries that suffer from the highest rates of violence and property crime and where criminal justice systems are particularly weak, and often violate basic human rights of offenders and victims. Corruption and other state crimes are endemic. Cross-cultural research can help to identify where such deficits are entrenched, and where they are imposed and imported from outside. It can provide a better understanding of how and where criminal justice reforms that are rooted in local culture can improve justice and security and thus reduce the justice deficit.

RECOMMENDED READING

In addition to the material above, interested readers might wish to consult the following.

On comparative perspectives on crime and punishment

Lacey, N (2008) *The Prisoners' Dilemma. Political Economy and Punishment in Contemporary Democracies* (Cambridge: Cambridge University Press).

Tonry, M. (ed.) (2007) *Crime, Punishment and Politics in Comparative Perspective. Crime and Justice, Vol. 36.* (Chicago: University of Chicago Press).

Tonry, M. & Farrington. D.P. (eds) (2005) *Crime and Punishment in Western Countries 1980 – 1999, Crime and Justice, Vol. 33.* (Chicago: University of Chicago Press).

On ethnography

Atkinson, P., Coffey, A., Delamont, S. et al. (eds) (2007) *Handbook of Ethnography* (Los Angeles: Sage).

Evens, T.M. and Handelman, D. (eds) (2006) *The Manchester School. Practice and Ethnographic Praxis in Anthropology* (New York: Berghahn Books).

Hammersley, M. and Atkinson, P. (2007) *Ethnography. Principles in Practice* (London: Routledge).

Website information

Getting started

Crime and Society – a comparative criminology tour of the world. Available at: http://www-rohan. sdsu.edu/faculty/rwinslow/

Links to Internet resources for comparative criminology are available at: http://www-rohan. sdsu.edu/faculty/rwinslow/links/newlinks.html

The International Centre for Comparative Criminological Research (ICCCR) website is available at: http://www.open.ac.uk/icccr/

Data sources: Surveys and sourcebooks

Information on the International Crime Victim Survey, Law School, University of Tilburg is available at: http://rechten.uvt.nl/icvs/

European Values Study Group and World Values Survey Association. ASEP/JDS, Madrid, Spain and Tilburg University, Tilburg, the Netherlands. File Distributors: ASEP/JDS and GESIS, Cologne, Germany. Information is available at: www.worldvaluessurvey.org

The European Sourcebook of Crime and Criminal Justice Statistics is available at: http:// www.europeansourcebook.org/

Information on the Polity IndexPolity IV Data Set is available at: http://www.systemicpeace.org/ inscr/inscr.htm

Information on The Transparency International Corruption Perception Index is available at: http:// www.tranparency.org

Information on the World Prison Population List (1st–8th editions) is available at: http://www. prisonstudies.org

Information on the European Social Survey is available at: www.europeansocialsurvey.org

Ethnography

A standard cross-cultural sample is available at: http://eclectic.ss.uci.edu/~drwhite/courses/ SCCCodes.htm

The Human Relations Area File eHRAF Collection of Ethnography is available at: http:// www.yale.edu/hraf/

Journal

The *World Cultures eJournal* welcomes articles, data, and comparative research material dealing with any aspect of human behavior. Publication of any comparative database, regional or worldwide are considered. Available at: http://escholarship. org/uc/wc_worldcultures

REFERENCES

Alesina, A., Devleeschauwer, A., Easterly, W., Kurlat, S. and Wacziarg, R. (2003) 'Ethnic Fractionalization'. *Journal of Economic Growth* 8: 155–194.

Alexander, J.C. and Smith, P. (1993) 'The Discourse of American Civil Society: A New Proposal for Cultural Studies'. *Theory and Society* 22: 151–207.

Axelrod, R. (1997) 'The Dissemination of Culture. A Model with Local Convergence and Global Polarization'. *Journal of Conflict Resolution* 41(2): 203–226.

Barker, V. (2009) *The Politics of Imprisonment. How the Democratic Process Shapes the Way America Punishes Offenders.* Oxford: Oxford University Press.

Birkbeck, C. (in press) 'Imprisonment and Internment: Comparing Penal Institutions North and South' in C. Wood (ed) *Crime, Law and Governance in the Americas.* Santiago: Editorial Catalonia.

Burawoy, M. (2000) *Global Ethnography: Forces, Connections, and Imaginations in a Postmodern World.* Berkeley: University of California Press.

Burawoy, M. (2009) *The Extended Case Method: Four Countries, Four Decades, Four Great Transformations, and One Theoretical Tradition.* Berkeley: University of California Press.

Cavadino, M. and Dignan, J. (2006) Penal Systems. *A Comparative Approach.* London: Sage.

Cingranelli, D.L. and Richards, D.L. (2007) The Cingranelli-Richards (CIRI) Human Rights Dataset. Available at: http:// humanrightsdata.org.

Downes, D. (1988) *Contrast in Tolerance.* Oxford: Oxford University Press.

Downes, D. (2007) 'Visions of Penal Control in the Netherlands' in M. Tonry (ed) *Crime, Punishment and Politics in Comparative Perspective*. Crime and Justice, Vol. 36, pp. 93–127. Chicago: Chicago University Press.

Eisner, M. (2001) 'Modernization, Self-control and Lethal Violence. The Long-term Dynamics of European Homicide Rates in Theoretical Perspective'. *British Journal of Criminology* 41: 618–638.

European Sourcebook of Crime and Criminal Justice Statistics, 4th edition. (2010) Available at: http://www.europeansourcebook.org/

Farrington, D.P., Langan, P.A. and Tonry, M. (2004) *Cross-National Studies in Crime and Justice*. Washington DC: US Department of Justice, Office of Justice Programs, Bureau of Justice Statistics.

Fischer, R., Vauclair, C.-M., Fontaine, J.R.J. and Schwartz, S.H. (2010) 'Are Individual-Level and Country-Level Value Structures Different? Testing Hofstede's Legacy With the Schwartz Value Survey'. *Journal of Cross-Cultural Psychology* 41 (2): 135–151

Fiske, A.O., Kitayama, S., Markus, H.R. and Nisbett, R.E. (1998) 'The Cultural Matrix of Social Psychology' in D.T. Gilbert, S.T. Fiske and G. Lindzey (eds) *The Handbook of Social Psychology*, Vol. II, 4th edition, pp. 915–981. Boston: McGraw-Hill.

Garland, D. (2001) *The Culture of Control*. Oxford: Oxford University Press.

Garland, D. (2010) *Peculiar Institution. America's Death Penalty in an Age of Abolition*. Oxford: Oxford University Press.

Geertz, C. (1973) *Local Knowledge: Further Essays in Interpretive Anthropology*. New York: Basic Books.

Geertz, C. (1994) 'Thick Description: Toward an Interpretive Theory of Culture' in M. Martin and L.C. McIntyre (eds) *Readings in the Philosophy of Social Science*, pp. 213–232. Cambridge MA: MIT Press.

Green, D.A. (2008) *When Children Kill Children*. Oxford: Oxford University Press.

Greenberg, D.F. and West, V. (2008) 'Siting the Death Penalty Internationally'. *Law and Social Inquiry* 33(2): 295–343.

Harkness, J.A., Pennell, B.E. and Schoua-Glusberg, A. (2004) 'Survey Questionnaire Translation and Assessment' in Presser, S., Rothgeb, J.M., Couper, M.P., Lessler, J.T., Martin, E., Martin, J., and Singer, E. (eds) *Methods for Testing and Evaluating Survey Questionnaires*. pp. 453–473. New Jersey: John Wiley and Sons.

Hofstede, G. (1984) *Culture's Consequences: International Differences in Work-Related Values*, 2nd edition. Beverly Hills: Sage.

Hofstede, G. (ed.) (2005/2010) *Cultures and Organizations. Software of the Mind*, 2nd edition. New York: McGraw-Hill Professional.

Hofstede, G., Garibaldi de Hilal, A.V., Malvezzi, S., Tanure, B. and Vinken, H. (2010) 'Comparing Regional Cultures within a Country: Lessons from Brazil.' *Journal of Cross-Cultural Psychology* 41: 336–352.

Inglehart, R. (1997) *Modernization and Postmodernization: Cultural, Economic, and Political Change in 43 Societies*. Princeton: Princeton University Press.

Inglehart, R. and Welzel, C. (2005) *Modernization, Cultural Change and Democracy*. Cambridge: Cambridge University Press.

Johnson, D.T. and Zimring, F.E. (2009) *The Next Frontier. National Development, Political Change, and the Death Penalty in Asia*. Oxford: Oxford University Press.

Jones, T. and Newburn, T. (2008) *Policy Transfer and Criminal Justice*. Milton Keynes: Open University Press.

Karstedt, S. (2001) 'Comparing Cultures, Comparing Crime: Challenges, Prospects and Problems for a Global Criminology.' *Crime, Law and Social Change* 36: 285–308.

Karstedt, S. (2002a) 'Durkheim, Tarde and Beyond: The Global Travel of Crime Policies'. *Criminal Justice* 2: 111–123.

Karstedt, S. (2002b) 'Emotions and Criminal Justice'. *Theoretical Criminology* 6: 299–317.

Karstedt, S. (2006) 'Democracy, Values and Violence: Paradoxes, Tensions, and Comparative Advantages of Liberal Inclusion'. *Annals of the American Academy of Political and Social Science* 605: 50–81.

Karstedt, S. (2011a) 'Liberty, Equality and Justice: Democratic Culture and Punishment' in A. Crawford (ed.) *International and Comparative Criminal Justice and Urban Governance: Convergence and Divergence in Global, National and Local Settings*, pp. 356–385 Cambridge: Cambridge University Press.

Karstedt, S. (2011b) 'Our Sense of Justice: Values, Justice and Punishment' in S. Parmentier, L. Walgrave, I. Aertsen, J. Maesschalck and L. Paoli (eds) *A Sparking Discipline: The Contribution of Criminology to Social Justice and Sustainable Development*, pp. 33–58. Leuven: Leuven University.

Karstedt, S. (in press) *Democracy, Crime and Justice*. London: Sage.

Karstedt, S. and Farrall, S. (2006) 'The Moral Economy of Everyday Crime: Markets, Consumers and Citizens'. *British Journal of Criminology* 46: 1011–1036.

Karstedt, S. and Farrall, S. (in press) 'Respectable' Citizens – 'Shady Practices': The Moral Economy of Modern Life. Oxford: Oxford University Press.

Karstedt, S. and LaFree, G. (eds) (2006) Special issue on 'Democracy, Crime and Justice'. *Annals of the American Academy of Political and Social Science* 605.

Klockars, C.B., Ivkovic, K. and Haberfeld, M.R. (2004) *The Contours of Police Integrity*. Thousand Oaks: Sage.

Lacey, N. and Zedner, L. (1998) 'Community in German Criminal Justice: A Significant Absence?' *Social and Legal Studies* 7(1):7–25

Larsen, N. and Smandych, R. (eds) (2008) *Global Criminology and Criminal Justice. Current Issues and Perspectives*. Peterborough, CA: Broadview Press.

Lieberson, S. (1991) 'Small N's and Big Conclusions: An Examination of the Reasoning in Comparative Studies Based on a Small Number of Cases'. *Social Forces* 70(2): 307–320.

Mill, J.S. (1872) *A System of Logic, Vol 2*, 8th edition. London: Longmans, Green and Company. (Reprinted in 1949.)

Mills, C.W. (1970) *The Sociological Imagination*. New York: Pelican Books.

Muncie, J., Talbot, D. and Walters, R. (eds) (2010) *Crime: Local and Global*. Cullompton: Willan.

Neapolitan, J.L. and Schmalleger, F. (1997) *Cross-National Crime: A Research Review and Sourcebook*. New York: Greenwood Press.

Nelken, D. (1994) 'Whom Can You Trust?' The Future of Comparative Criminology' in D. Nelken (ed.) *The Futures of Criminology*, pp. 220–244. London: Sage.

Nelken, D. (2004) 'Using the Concept of Legal Culture'. *Australian Journal of Legal Philosophy* 29: 1–28.

Nelken, D. (2009) 'Comparative Criminal Justice: Beyond Ethnocentrism and Relativism'. *European Journal of Criminology*, 6(4): 291–312.

Nelken, D. (2010) *Comparative Criminal Justice*. Los Angeles: Sage.

Newburn, T. and Sparks, R. (eds) (2004) *Criminal Justice and Political Cultures. National and International Dimensions of Crime Control*. Cullompton: Willan.

Pakes, F. (2004) *Comparative Criminal Justice*. Cullompton: Willan.

Piacentini, L. (2004) *Surviving Russian Prisons. Punishment, Economy and Politics in Transition*. Cullompton: Willan.

Pontell, H.N. and Geis, G. (eds) (2007) *International Handbook of White Collar Crime and Corporate Crime*. New York: Springer.

Pratt, J. (2008a) 'Scandinavian Exceptionalism in an Era of Penal Excess. Part I: The Nature and Roots of Scandinavian Exceptionalism'. *British Journal of Criminology* 48(2): 119–137.

Pratt, J. (2008b) 'Scandinavian Exceptionalism in an Era of Penal Excess. Part II: Does Scandinavian Exceptionalism have a Future?' *British Journal of Criminology* 48(3): 275–292.

Reichel, P. (ed.) (2005) *Handbook of Transnational Crime and Justice*. London: Sage.

Smith, P., Bond, H. and Kagitcibasi, C. (2006) *Understanding Social Psychology Across Cultures*. Los Angeles, London: Sage.

Strobl, S. (2009) 'Policing Housemaids: The Criminalization of Domestic Workers in Bahrain'. *British Journal of Criminology* 49: 165–183.

Sung, H. (2006) 'Democracy and Criminal Justice in Cross-National Perspective: From Crime Control to Due Process'. *Annals of the American Academy of Political and Social Science* 605: 311–337.

Tilly, C. (1984) *Big Structures, Large Processes, Huge Comparisons*. New York: Russell Sage Foundation.

Triandis, H.C. (1995) *Individualism and Collectivism*. Boulder: Westview.

Triandis, H.C. and Trafimov, D. (2001) 'Cross-national Prevalence of Collectivism' in C. Sedikides and M.B. Brewer (eds) *Individual Self, Relational Self, Collective Self*. pp. 259–276. Ann Arbor: Taylor and Francis.

Van Dijk, J. (2008) *The World of Crime*. Los Angeles: Sage.

Walmsley, R. (1999–2009) World Prison Population List, 1-8th edition. Available at: http://www.prisonstudies.org.

West, M.D. (2009) *Secrets, Sex and Spectacle*. Chicago: University of Chicago.

Whitman, J. (2003) *Harsh Justice. Criminal Punishment and the Widening Divide between America and Europe*. Oxford: Oxford University Press.

Zimring, F.E. (2006) 'The Necessity and Value of Transnational Comparative Study: Some Preaching from a Recent Convert'. *Criminology and Public Policy* 5(4): 615–622.

Zimring, F.E. and Hawkins, G. (1997) *Crime is not the Problem: Lethal Violence in America*. New York: Oxford University Press.

Preventing Crime and Improving Justice

In 1974, Robert Martinson published the results of a systematic review of studies on offender rehabilitation under the heading 'What works? Questions and answers about prison reform.' Martinson had made use of the then nascent method of 'meta-analysis'. Somewhat prematurely, the question he posed as to whether 'nothing works' became a mantra among criminologists. By way of contrast, Martinson argued, that before this question could be answered, criminologists would need to: (1) conduct many more 'truly rigorous' studies (1974: 48); (2) engage more theoretically with the relationships between crime, its causes, and interventions in work that attends to treatment or other criminal justice effects; and (3) conduct research which also attends to the 'moral dimension of crime and punishment' (ibid. 50).

In this section we present eight chapters that demonstrate the advances that criminologists have made on these three fronts. The first three chapters, in particular, attend to the question of what methodologically rigorous evaluations should look like. As Heather Strang and Lawrence Sherman explain in this section's opening chapter, large-scale field-trials are particularly demanding. They require long-term planning, considerable cooperation between practice and science-based communities, large groups of research staff, and budgets generous enough to cover the costs of implementing interventions and measuring success over the long-term. Illustrating with reference to a 15-year programme of research in the field of restorative justice, Strang and Sherman explain the strength that the randomized control trials provide with respect to claims about fairness,

crime prevention and alternatives to custody. Strang and Sherman demonstrate what might just be achieved in criminal justice when research projects are sufficiently rigorous, and why it is important to take advantage of the relatively rare opportunities for developing randomized control designs when they arise. While the suitability of this kind of science to criminological research problems remains fiercely debated, what is clearly demonstrated by Strang and Sherman's chapter is how similar the skill set needed to conduct good randomized control trials is to that needed to conduct action research, surveys and observational studies. The effectiveness of randomized control trials at deciphering intervention effects depends heavily on the commitment of practitioners, programme managers, policy makers and whole organizations and systems to the scientific endeavour. The allocation of subjects to different conditions has to be genuinely and consistently randomized. Protocols have to be consistently applied. Interventions have to carefully observed and monitored with particular attention paid to detail. All in all, this methodology depends, perhaps more than any other, on the willingness of the researched to be researched and of practitioners to live with the uncertainty of not knowing whether what they have been doing is best or better practice until the experiment concludes.

In another exemplar of methodological rigor, Manuel Eisner, Tina Malti and Denis Ribeaud address the problems of dissemination trials; or otherwise, experimental methods 'writ-large'. Dissemination trials examine the effects of an intervention under conditions close to those under which a programme is to be distributed. Because they operate under real-world conditions, dissemination trials are critical for translating research findings into policy recommendations. Dissemination trials are based on fully developed and manualized programmes that are supported by adequate infrastructure, training mechanisms and technical support structures, often with considerable costs attached. Even if they do not differ conceptually from the experimental methodology that Strang and Sherman propose, dissemination trials come with additional challenges for researchers. An important requirement is assurance of the independence of the research team. Dissemination trials have to be conducted by independent researchers in order to understand whether effects can be maintained without the active involvement of the programme developers. Questions addressed by Eisner et al. include: What kind of preparation is necessary for a large-scale field trial? What is required to achieve valid and reliable measurement of the intervention process and its outcomes? What can be done to address ethnic and cultural diversity in the target population? And, what should be put in place to ensure consistent implementation quality with respect to the intervention? Throughout, the chapter draws on Eisner et al.'s experience with a large-scale field trial for the early prevention of aggression and delinquency, known as the Zurich Project on the Social Development of Children (z-proso). This included two programmes that targeted risk factors at the family and school levels among primary school children.

This section's third chapter, by Martin Schmucker and Friedrich Lösel, revisits the case for more systematic reviews of empirical studies in criminology, using examples from the authors' own meta-analytic research on the effectiveness of sex offender treatment programmes. Schmucker and Lösel commence with two outstanding and well-known studies of developmental crime prevention – one effective, the other not – and scrutinize the factors that can explain the different outcomes of both studies. From here, Schmucker and Lösel take the reader through the steps involved in conducting systematic literature reviews (meta-analyses): the development of the research question and the definition of relevant concepts; the searching for relevant studies that fit the definition; coding these studies with respect to their characteristics and outcomes; quantitative analysis of the data, both to integrate study results as well as differentiate between them and the interpretation and reporting of the meta-analyses to different audiences. As Schmucker and Lösel show, meta-analytic approaches not only provide decisive knowledge about the effectiveness of specific types of interventions for stakeholders,

they also draw attention to deficiencies in the primary studies of treatment effectiveness and the impact of various corrupting factors. The authors conclude by explaining how improving the quality of primary studies would enhance the capacity of meta-analyses to answer policy-relevant questions.

Ken Pease's chapter is based on the experience of a criminologist who has been more deeply involved than most in day-to-day operational police work. Based on this experience, Pease makes a case for research that is palpably helpful to both frontline police officers and their managers. Researchers, Pease argues, need to make the case for the collation of specific types of crime data that can be easily interpreted and thus made useful in everyday policing operations. Making such knowledge and data available within the organization and implementing proper collection, interpretation and transfer into police practices entail research challenges over and above those ordinarily incurred in the course of navigating organizational police culture and the external pressures to produce results. First, the researcher has to focus on the concentration of crime across time and space. Second, the researcher needs to develop theoretical concepts responsive to the key characteristics of police work. Pease suggests that Signal Detection Theory provides one powerful means of assisting police managers to make decisions on the basis of imperfect data. This theory reflects the type of information that police officers have to use, and the uncertain and risky contexts in which they have to make decisions. Exemplary signals, Pease explains, include repeated calls to the police from one household or a single area. These need to be interpreted and assessed as signals of a wider range of problems that might require police intervention, including rapid policing responses. In the chapter, Pease expands upon his method for the 'chunking' of crime events into 'problems' which can then be addressed by managers and officers. He illustrates this point through the utilization of data pertaining to both chronic victimization and the concentration of crime in localities. He adds to these data unobtrusive measurements of crimes, or 'crime proxies', such as alcohol consumption, evidence of broken glass from car windows, and the repair costs of vandalized bus shelters.

Whether real or imagined, the costs of crime have become a major driver of investment in crime prevention and law enforcement initiatives in recent years. Yet, as much as they are common coinage in policy discourses, it is incredibly hard to estimate costs in ways that are reasonable, robust and reliable. The problems involved in estimating costs of burglary or violent crime pale against those that confront the criminologist who takes up the challenge to estimate the costs of the hardly visible and most secretive, but nonetheless very common crime of fraud. As Michael Levi explains in his chapter, these challenges include the task of identifying a broad range of fraudulent activities, from minor and everyday incidents to major and large-scale fraud committed across borders by numerous and highly sophisticated parties. Victims of fraud vary no less and include citizens, companies, NGOs and the public sector. How should criminologists assess these costs? As Levi explains the costs of fraud do not end with the experience of victimization. This is because the proceeds of fraud can be used to undertake further criminal activities like organized crime and terrorism. Regulating against fraud and undertaking detective work and prosecutions also require high levels of investment and impose considerable costs on the public and private sector. Drawing on his research for the Association of Chief Police Officers, Levi reviews the strengths and weaknesses of the different kinds of fraud data collection strategies; explains the criminologist's reliance on information from business and wealthy individuals, together with the reluctance of the private sector to share and publicise fraud data; and outlines the lacunae of self-report studies on fraud. Levi draws two major methodological conclusions from his research. He suggests that criminologists need to develop better access to non-reporting sectors using random or strategic sampling techniques. He also explains why it is important to not only generate an overall estimate of the costs of 'fraud', but also to be able to explain which sectors of the population are most victimized by particular kinds of frauds.

Cyndi Banks' chapter, 'The Other Cultural Criminology', is the first of three chapters that take the ethics and practice of research into new dimensions. Banks takes up the topic of researching cultures that are not our own, and of which 'cultural outsiders' often have only scant knowledge. She does this by using neither the kind of comparative perspective (advanced by Karstedt, this volume), nor ethnography (see Ferrell, this volume). Instead, Banks uses a kind of participatory approach that has drawn inspiration from social anthropology. Banks' particular version of cultural criminology suggests a major role for action research, which in itself is well suited to cope with the many practical constraints on research in poorer parts of the world. In her research, Banks explores how continuous improvements in a programme for juvenile offenders in Bangladesh were achieved through action research styles of engagement with a range of competing stakeholders. What is particularly distinctive about the approach that Banks' advocates is its close attention to issues of cultural specificity in the

design and implementation of research, right through to the dissemination and utilization of findings. Banks explains that in parts of the developing world, donor interventions comprising programs for law reform and rule of law projects often present the only means and opportunity to conduct sufficiently culturally specific research. Because donors often do not allow for adequate time and resources for large-scale evaluations, modes of action research are the most suitable method cultural criminologists have at their disposal for trying to understand crime and justice problems and assist local populations in solving them.

In their chapter, Gail Mason and Julie Stubbs explore the role of feminist theory in research on crime and justice. They refute the notion of an orthodox methodology prescribed by feminist criminology. Rather, Mason and Stubbs explain that feminists in the field of criminology have tended to adopt a series of methodological preferences. They are inspired by the insights of gender theory; they take the need for social change seriously; they seek to advance post-positivist epistemologies; they recognize the importance of experience (including that of the researcher's) in understanding crime and justice; and they are committed to breaking down the power relations inherent in research through processes of reflexivity. Fleshing out how these preferences have shaped their own research on violence against Filipino migrants and on homophobic violence against women, Mason and Stubbs illustrate the importance of feminist research conducted at the crossroads between different theories, epistemological orientations and methodological preferences. Four themes are featured in Mason and Stubb's account of their own methodological praxis: the difficulties of operationalizing intersectionality; the problem of surmounting the dichotomy of victim/agent without denying the deeply patterned nature of victimization and criminalization; the need to acknowledge and redress the uneven power dynamics intrinsic to the research process epistemologically and methodologically; and the question of how to design research projects that do justice to experiential accounts of crime and criminalization as simultaneously 'real' and constructed.

Criminologists like to believe that they behave in ways that are morally virtuous, but like many offenders, when it comes to dealing with ethical review, they tend toward techniques of neutralization, casting themselves as victims of an ever-increasing bureaucratic apparatus that obstructs good research practice. In their chapter, Mark Israel and Iain Hay confront the reluctance of criminologists to deal with ethical challenges head-on. Drawing on examples from many contemporary studies, including some of those described within the chapters of this volume, Israel and Hay argue that criminologists need to extend their capacity to think seriously and systematically about what constitutes ethical conduct and to develop better understandings of the political and social contexts within which ethics are regulated. Israel and Hay start with setting out the new terrain of ethical review and research governance that now confronts criminologists, and ask questions about the vexed relationships between ethical conduct and ethical regulation in criminological research. Informed consent, confidentiality, harms and benefits, research integrity, and investigators' relationships are all focal concerns of the chapter, as are the challenges of ethical criminological research in international contexts and/or via the Internet. In the second part of the chapter, Israel and Hay suggest how criminologists might engage constructively with the regulatory challenges that ethical conduct now necessitates. They provide guidance for researchers on how to recognize ethical challenges when they appear and how to explore the implications of particular approaches to research methodology and relationships with research funders and participants. It is a particular asset of this chapter and an achievement of the authors that they engaged many criminological colleagues in this discussion. In so doing, they provide evidence that the criminologists who represent the many methodological traditions set out in this volume are taking the challenge of conducting ethical research more seriously than ever.

REFERENCES

Martinson, R. (1974) What works? Questions and answers about prison' reform. *Public Interest*, 35(Spring): 22–54.

26

Experimental Criminology and Restorative Justice: Principles of Developing and Testing Innovations in Crime Policy

Heather Strang, Lawrence W. Sherman

INTRODUCTION

Experimental criminology is a means for generating scientific knowledge about crime and justice discovered from random assignment of different conditions in field tests, and is the preferred way to estimate the average effects of one variable on another, holding all other variables constant (Sherman, 2010). While the experimental method is not suitable to answer all criminological questions, opportunities exist to work in partnership with operational agencies to develop and test many theoretically coherent ideas about reducing crime and the harm that it causes, as well as to evaluate interventions, pure and simple. Randomized field experiments can provide the ideal test of theories concerning both the prevention and causation of crime: Farrington and Welsh (2005) report 83 such experiments carried out between 1982 and 2004 in policing, crime prevention, corrections, courts and community interventions. The authors' programme of research in restorative justice (RJ) over a 15-year period provides a strong example of this application.

Notwithstanding their advantages as rigorous and reliable tests of theory and policy, randomized experiments depend on the capacity of those who set them up to succeed in achieving the many necessary elements of an unbiased comparison between the experimental and control conditions. The attention over a sustained period that successful experiments require is exceptionally demanding. Without it, the quality of studies is often reduced. This attention involves, among other things, establishing the experiments' intellectual and social foundations, agreeing the research protocol, setting up the management arrangements, setting in train the supply of cases, screening for eligibility, monitoring random assignment and treatment delivery, measuring treatments delivered and measuring outcomes. All of these components require specific skills of a kind not usually employed in observational criminology.

The objective of this chapter, therefore, is to discuss each of these components and thus to provide guidance in the design and conduct of experiments. In the course of this discussion we draw on the authors' experiences in RJ research as a 'case study' in the development and testing of crime policy. First, however, we place the chapter in a broader context of alternative research designs in criminology,

OVERVIEW: RANDOMIZED EXPERIMENTS IN CRIMINOLOGY

The experimental method

An experiment is a method of research in which the person doing research 'manipulates' or changes something in order to observe what results from that manipulation. In exact sciences like physics, this manipulation will always produce the same result – for example, Galileo dropping a large and small object from the Tower of Pisa. But many sciences are 'inexact', meaning that identical manipulations in experiments do not always get the same result. These sciences include the 'basic' science of biology, and almost all applied sciences, such as medicine, agriculture and clinical psychology. These sciences deal with highly variable entities (usually people) and often with varying environments that affect the results of experiments: criminology shares this character. A widely accepted solution to this variability is the *randomized* experiment (Fisher, 1935).

Randomized experiments

A randomized experiment is one in which a relatively large number of independent units of analysis are treated in different ways, with the treatment for each unit determined by pure chance: a 'lottery' of experimental conditions. This means that each unit, no matter what its characteristics may be, has an equal chance of being assigned to each condition. There is no purer equality that mathematics can achieve in the allocation of policies or programmes than by random assignment. With a large enough number of units, most of the characteristics by which the units differ will be distributed in even proportions in each group of experimental conditions. Thus, not only will readily apparent features such as age, hair colour or employment status be distributed evenly between the groups through random assignment, but also factors one may not even have thought of or be able to measure, such as genetic factors or underlying health or psychological issues.

Experimental control

This means, for example, that if 900 people are randomly assigned to be prosecuted for drinking and driving (50 per cent) or diverted to a RJ conference without gaining criminal record (50 per cent), then each group of 450 people should have roughly equal proportions of men and women, blacks and whites, young and old, employed and unemployed, university graduates and school

leaver drop-outs, people with and without prior criminal records, and so on. The experiment can then be said to have 'controlled' for all of those characteristics by holding them 'constant' between the prosecution and RJ groups.

Observational criminology

Why is random assignment important? Because it solves the major problem of inferring causation in the inexact sciences, namely selection bias. If we simply *observed* the differences between people police selected for each treatment based on their subjective judgment of 'appropriateness,' or observed the differences between people who volunteer for RJ and those who do not, our results would be subject to a statistical form of *bias*. In this context, bias simply means that the groups may differ in key characteristics that could not be controlled for in an observational study. Thus if 80 per cent of the people selected for prosecution had a criminal record but only 20 per cent of those selected for RJ, we could not be certain whether to ascribe any difference in subsequent offending to the treatment received or to factors associated with prior offending. That is the main reason that randomized experiments are preferable for highly specific questions about policy innovations. While some observational criminologists have objected that randomized controlled trials (RCTs) have no inherent superiority over observational methods even for policy research (Sampson, 2010), we find such arguments unpersuasive, since they lack specific examples of how an observational study could ever answer *without bias* such precise questions as what impact RJ can have on the life course of a criminal offender.

Quasi-experimental criminology

To be sure, most criminology has been and will continue to be 'observational'. By that we mean that there is no manipulation of any condition, but rather pure data collection on crime and punishment without attempting to intervene in the object of study. It is rare, however, that purely observational methods are used to evaluate such innovations in criminal policy as RJ. It is much more common that a 'quasi-experimental' research design is used to evaluate such programmes. These designs feature some kind of manipulation, but they lack the 'control' provided by random assignment. They may include, for example, placing every drink-driving offender in an entire police district into an RJ diversion, while comparing their outcomes to all the offenders in the adjacent police district, all of whom were prosecuted.

This method may shed some insights on RJ, but it retains a large threat of bias. The kinds of people arrested in the two districts, for example, could be very different, in ways that might not even be measurable. Thus the difference in the sample characteristics could still account for the differences in results, rather than the difference between RJ and prosecution. In general, quasi-experiments in criminology tend to produce more favourable estimates of how well a programme is working than RCT designs do (Weisburd et al., 2001) because the evaluation method is less rigorous.

What is restorative justice?

This chapter illustrates the RCT approach with 12 tests of a single theory and policy: voluntary face-to-face meetings between admitted offenders, their victims and their respective families and friends, led by a trained facilitator whose job is to lead a discussion of three questions:

1   What did the offender(s) do and what do they think about it?
2   What harm did it cause, to the victims and those who care about them?
3   What should the offenders do to repair the harm they have caused?

While there are many other justice procedures that have been called 'restorative,' this is the consistent approach taken in all 12 of the experiments discussed in this chapter.

What are the control groups?

The control groups in these experiments varied by research site. In Canberra, Australia, four experiments used the usual prosecution process as the control group and RJ was randomly assigned to be conducted *instead of* prosecution. In England, in seven RCTs, RJ was randomly *added to* the usual criminal justice process, while the control group experienced the criminal process usual for their offence without the addition of RJ. In Indianapolis, Indiana, the control group experienced various forms of diversion from prosecution in juvenile court, while the experimental group was diverted to RJ. Table 26.1 describes the offences, offenders and point in the criminal justice process for each experiment.

'Batch' versus 'trickle-flow' experiments

In all 12 RJ experiments discussed here, the cases were randomly assigned to RJ or control conditions on a 'trickle-flow' basis. This means that random

assignment was done almost every day the experiments were in operation, as the eligible cases 'trickled in' to the research team is small numbers. In Canberra, the research team took phone calls 24 hours a day, one case at a time, to take the case details and then open a sealed envelope containing the randomly assigned treatment for that case number. Whether sealed envelopes are used or the more modern approach of secure computer programmes with an instant algorithm to generate the treatment once the identifiers are typed in, the case-by-case assignment of experimental conditions is what we mean by trickle-flow.

In contrast, much experimental criminology consists of 'batch' random assignment. Sherman and Weisburd's (1995) hot spots patrol experiment, for example, randomly assigned 110 hot spots all on the same day to either the control condition (no change in patrol patterns) or the experimental condition (much more frequent patrol). Ariel's (2009) experiment in tax compliance in Israel randomly assigned a batch of over 15,000 taxpayers to different conditions all on one day. In general, however, trickle-flow experiments are more common in any experiment testing the treatment of individual offenders or victims in the criminal justice process, since their cases are constantly trickling in to the criminal justice system itself.

Testing theory versus policy

This chapter draws particular attention to the important distinctions between testing a theory and testing a policy. In general, this contrast addresses the pragmatic nature of applied sciences. In medicine, the identical concepts are called 'efficacy' of a medical treatment under 'ideal' conditions, such as nurses giving patients all the right pills at the right time – versus 'real-world' conditions, such as patients going home and becoming responsible for taking their own pills (which they may often forget). So while the *theory* that a pill like aspirin has great efficacy in preventing heart attacks, a *policy* of prescribing aspirin may have less effectiveness than the theory suggests because so many people may forget to take their pills. Similarly, not everyone assigned to have RJ, or even to be prosecuted, will actually get that treatment. Under such conditions, it is fairer (and pragmatic) to say that the RCT is testing the policy of RJ rather than the theory of how effective it could be if every case administered it fully and correctly.

Treatment integrity

The issue of theory *versus* policy is only one aspect of the larger problem of 'treatment integrity'.

Table 26.1

Name	Location	Offences	Offenders/point in criminal process	Years of sample intake
Juvenile violent crime	Canberra	Violent Crimes	Offenders up to age 29, at point of prosecution	1995–2000
Juvenile property crime	Canberra	Property Crimes	Offenders up to 18, at point of prosecution	1995–2000
Juvenile shoplifting in large stores	Canberra	Shop theft without personal victims	Offenders up to 18, at point of prosecution	1995–2000
Drinking- driving	Canberra	Driving while blood alcohol level in excess of legal limit (no victims)	Adult offenders, at point of prosecution	1995–2000
Crown Court robbery	London	Robbery and street crime	Adult offenders, in court, post guilty plea, pre-sentence	2002–2004
Crown Court burglary	London	Burglary and aggravated burglary	Adult offenders, in court post guilty plea pre-sentence	2002–2004
Probation for violent crime	Thames Valley, UK	All violent crime	Adult offenders, post-conviction in the community	2002–2004
Prison for violent crime	Thames Valley, UK	All violent crime	Adult offenders, post-conviction, in prison	2002–2004
Magistrates' Court for violent crime	Northumbria, UK	Middle-level seriousness assault	Adult offenders, in court post guilty plea, pre-sentence	2002–2004
Magistrates' court for property crime	Northumbria, UK	Middle-level seriousness property crime	Adult offenders, in court post guilty plea, pre-sentence	2002–2004
Juvenile reprimands and warnings	Northumbria, UK	Property and assault	Offenders up to age 18, police warnings	2002–2004
Juvenile diversion	Indianapolis, Indiana	Low level property and assault	Offenders 7–14 years	1998

By 'integrity' we mean that all the rules of the experimental protocol are followed, including screening cases for eligibility before they are randomized, delivering the treatments that are randomly assigned, not prosecuting a case assigned to RJ, if at all possible (where RJ is a diversion), not giving RJ to a control case, running the RJ conference in the same way that facilitators were trained to run them, and many other rules that must be followed. In general, experimental criminology stands or falls on how good the treatment integrity is in each experiment.

Summary: Why do randomized experiments?

In an age of austerity in public funding, governments increasingly demand precise estimates of the cost-effectiveness of criminal justice. Even prison (at long last) and police patrol are subjected to this demand in countries like the UK, and many states across the US. Regardless of their relative strength and weakness, RCTs hold the greatest potential for yielding the cost-effectiveness estimates that may increasingly drive policy choices that affect the lives of millions of crime victims and offenders worldwide.

ELEMENTS OF SUCCESSFUL EXPERIMENTS

Intellectual foundation – the research question

In deciding what questions to test, we propose that experimentalists have first to develop an appreciation about which ones are the most theoretically important; they also need a technical appreciation of which hypotheses are practically testable and a grasp of how useful or practical an answer to the question will be, particularly with respect to costs and benefits.

It is often assumed that the evaluation of new programmes is the primary application of experimental criminology but it is our contention that experiments can be most useful when the focus is on their theoretical implications. Whereas the independence of the evaluator relative to the programme being evaluated is often reified by those commissioning the evaluation, we suggest that the active engagement of experimental criminologists in shaping the programme prior to testing is often a more sensible use of scarce research resources. The authors' own experience, for example, in designing a series of tests of the theory of re-integrative shaming (Braithwaite, 1989) via a series of 12 completed RCTs in RJ, provided the opportunity for better measurement of elements of the theory and consequent revision of it (Braithwaite, 2002). In theory, as in policy, the fewer ambiguities the more useful the results. It is because experiments are better than most other methods at eliminating or at least limiting competing explanations that they can make a unique contribution to criminological theory (Sherman, 2010). This occurs through the process of random assignment that we described earlier. With large enough samples, similar distributions will naturally occur of the independent variables that serve as potential rival explanations of any difference between the experimental and control groups. When the only difference between the groups is the presence or absence of the intervention being tested, then any difference between the groups can be confidently attributed to the intervention.

The capacity of experiments to provide clear answers to utilitarian questions, such as the relative cost-effectiveness of different interventions, is one of their greatest strengths. Experiments need to be planned to measure costs both in 'start-up' mode and in 'roll-out' mode because they will vary substantially in these two conditions. Inevitably additional costs are involved in getting new programmes established whereas there may be reduced costs from 'mass production' and experiments must take both into consideration when they are designed. In addition, measures of personnel time, travel costs, equipment and so on in both experimental and control conditions need to be captured during the course of the experiment rather than pieced together retrospectively.

Finally, in framing the research question, besides testing important theories, testing expensive strategies makes more sense than expending the time and energy required by the research design on small and inexpensive ones. Testing a programme with the rigour of an experiment for reducing murder makes more sense than one reducing car theft, and likewise focusing on people or places involved in the most crime has the greatest potential for demonstrating large differences in the cost-effectiveness of available policy choices.

RJ provided the ideal subject matter for experimental research according to these criteria. Its rise in the early 1990s as a radical and theoretically powerful innovation in criminal justice, underpinned by Braithwaite's (1989) theory of re-integrative shaming, provided precisely the kind of research question most suited to successful experiments: is it superior in its effects on re-offending and victim satisfaction with their treatment compared to 'normal' criminal justice processing?

Braithwaite's theory was joined soon after by the equally compelling theory of procedural justice being developed at that time by Tyler (1990), together with Sherman's defiance theory (1993); all of these lent themselves to rigorous testing by means of an experiment in RJ. When the opportunity for an experiment arose in Canberra in 1995, with an enthusiastic police chief willing to cooperate with a research team for this purpose, a perfect opportunity presented itself for an experiment.

Our Canberra research consisted of four experiments, all involving offences that would normally be dealt with in court. Although all these experiments showed moderate to high levels of victim satisfaction with RJ relative to court (Strang, 2002), results on re-offending were mixed. In brief, RJ backfired in the juvenile property experiment, with offenders randomly assigned to court re-offending at a lower level than their RJ counterparts, while only small differences between the groups were found in the drink-driving and shoplifting experiments. We found, however, that RJ was significantly more effective than the courts in reducing re-offending by violent offenders. The British Home Office was impressed by these findings and as a result decided to fund a comprehensive test of RJ in a range of social settings, with more serious adult offenders at different points in the justice system, with an emphasis on violent crime. Table 26.1 sets out for all of these experiments the kind of offences, the age of the offenders (all of whom had admitted responsibility for the crime), the point in the criminal process at which they were randomly assigned, and the years during which the experiments were conducted.

Replication of experiments is always desirable (Sherman, 1992) and the authors enthusiastically accepted the challenge of conducting a further series of experiments in RJ in the UK to deepen our knowledge of the following central research question: under what conditions is RJ superior to normal criminal justice processing in reducing re-offending and increasing victim satisfaction?

Social foundation – partnering with an operational agency

The essential prerequisite in experimental criminology is the establishment of a set of human relationships and social networks between the research team trained in experimental design and the operational partners who control the cases to be randomly assigned. The latter are usually inside a criminal justice agency, school or other entity delivering the intervention to be tested. They may be heavily invested personally in the intervention and can easily feel threatened by outsiders whom they believe are there specifically to test their 'baby' to extinction. Alternatively, they may be completely indifferent to the intervention and indifferently helpful in providing the kind of cooperation essential to the research team in getting the experiment up and running. Both possibilities and a myriad of intermediate positions need to be taken into account in a coherent and systematic way by the research team.

An understanding of the constituent social elements of experiments is fundamental to a successful partnership. These elements include the funders, the leadership of the operational agency, the operational staff delivering the treatment to be tested who will most likely be the day-to-day contact for the researchers and, if separate, the staff who provide the cases.

Funders may have been convinced by logic of the superiority of randomized controlled trials in testing an intervention but they may not be familiar with the pace at which experiments can be set up or the feasibility issues around establishing eligibility criteria or outcome measures. Frequent communication is essential at this level, with timely warnings of delay or the need for additional resources so that surprises are minimized. The pace of our Canberra experiments was a painful case in point when data collection that we had hoped would be completed in two years stretched out to five years, with the need for additional funding along the way.

The agency leadership, whose expressed support for the experiment is essential, need not be involved at all in day-to-day issues but must be available to the principal investigator in the event of trouble. The absence of strong support from the top can be an almost fatal blow to the enterprise. The research team must then rely on formal contractual arrangements negotiated at the outset, but even these rarely serve as a substitute for personal backing of the project. Our experience in Canberra brought home to us this truth when the police chief with whom we originally negotiated the RJ experiments was replaced by an RJ sceptic. The new chief was bound by our Memorandum of Understanding negotiated with the Australian Federal Police at the outset to continue the experiments but his lack of support soon became known throughout the organization of 600 sworn officers. As a consequence, our case flow was badly affected. Over the course of the five years our experiments ran in Canberra the police had two more changes of leadership, making a total of four police chiefs in this period. The resulting uncertainty was reflected in our fluctuating case flow.

In our UK work, by contrast, we had much greater stability in the leadership of the numerous agencies we worked with, though we did encounter a wide range of attitudes to our experiments at the day-to-day level. Where we worked with magistrates' courts, for example, real problems arose because the experiments entailed inserting an RJ stage into court processing at a time when, in the face of criticism about the snail's pace of justice, the government wanted to speed up cases through the courts as much as possible. The unfortunate timing of this policy decision, when RJ inevitably meant a short delay in finalizing the case, proved a serious difficulty throughout the three years the experiments ran. Magistrates' Courts clerks were unfailingly pleasant but even the Lord Chancellor, Lord Falconer, asking in person that they cooperate fully with us failed to solve the case flow problem. This issue did not affect our work in the Crown Courts in the same way, however.

Here, relentless effort by our imaginative and determined research staff in getting to know judges, endlessly explaining the purpose of the research, bringing cakes for their staff and being visibly in court day after day all paid dividends in case flow.

The operational staff delivering the treatment are critical partners for the experimentalists on a day-to-day basis. Ideally, they should be volunteers with a lively interest in the experiment. Additionally, it is extremely useful to have a primary link on the operational site to act as permanent liaison for the duration of the study. The authors were blessed in our UK RJ experiments with extremely competent contacts; indeed the absence of such a person in our Canberra experiments proved very problematic and almost fatal to the integrity of the project. When no one person on the operational side is charged with responsibility for the success of the enterprise, difficulties soon arise in relation to eligibility questions, the pace of case referral, treatment integrity and all the other issues at the operations/research interface.

Enthusiasm for the project may, however, sometimes be confused with a strong commitment to the value of the treatment to be tested and it is often necessary to explain the difference between a clear experimental result and a result that shows that a programme 'works'. Operational staff are usually not exposed to a research mindset which values the former more than the latter and it is the daily job of the research team to make this distinction clear.

Often the staff with whom the research team has the most contact are not in fact the staff on whom the flow of cases depends. These are usually 'frontline' people dealing directly with incidents, offenders and victims as the central role of their working lives. It is these people who, often amidst drama and confusion, are being asked to make assessments of the eligibility of these cases for an experiment they may feel rather distant from, at a time when they have much on their minds. But their cooperation is vital and they must be won over to the value of the research. Failing to reach sample size goals is the fear that haunts every experiment and failing to persuade frontline staff to provide the cases is the most common reason.

Even when initial enthusiasm abounds, it is never enough as it will flicker and diminish over the course of the experiment, but the social foundation established at the outset between all the partners must be strong enough to build on and withstand the *longeurs* of experimental research. As for maintaining momentum and morale on a day-to-day basis, whether in finding cases or delivering treatment, all social life is grist to the mill: dinners, lunches, pep-talk sessions, as well as straightforward meetings in which operational people discuss openly with the research team their experiences and anxieties about the experiment and the intervention being tested. Time and resources spent engendering strong social relations with the senior staff, the treatment deliverers and with the case suppliers is simply essential and will repay the investment many times over.

Experimental protocol

This is simply the written design for performing the experiment, setting out the way in which it will be conducted and the elements that are needed. Developing the experimental protocol can be both a frustrating time-waster and an essential safety net for the research team. Where the research takes place under the aegis of a university, the protocol becomes a legal requirement for Institutional Review Boards or Ethics Boards of any stripe, so it has to be negotiated. It is not always necessary; conducting research on behalf of police authorities in the UK did not require any contractual agreement or specified protocol (though it did in Australia). Instead, the research team entered into a series of less formal procedural rules with the various criminal justice agencies involved, a much more efficient process when it is impossible to delineate with great certainty at the outset what the final protocol will look like.

But the discipline of a carefully constructed protocol can help avoid pitfalls as the experiment unfolds. Weisburd (1993) observes that many experiments in criminology have violated good design standards or failed to report fundamental information that would allow for much greater transparency in interpreting results and analysis. The CONSORT statement (Consolidated Standards on Reporting of Trials), (see 'Web Resources' section at end of the chapter) published in 1996 and designed specifically for medical trials, provides a model that could be usefully adopted in experimental criminology. It consists of a set of recommendations for reporting experiments in medicine, offering a blueprint for consistent reporting about how the trial was designed, analyzed and interpreted. This is achieved via a 25-item checklist, aided by a flow diagram that displays how all participants progress through the trial and showing rates of attrition at every stage. The items include statements about the participants, interventions and objectives of the study, as well as the sample size, recruitment, participant flow, numbers analyzed and interpretation.

Box 26.1   Crim-PORT 1.0

Crim-PORT 1.0 consists of the following elements:

1 Name and hypotheses
2 Organizational framework
3 Unit of analysis
4 Eligibility criteria
5 Pipeline: recruitment or extraction of cases
6 Timing
7 Random assignment
8 Treatment and comparison elements
9 Measuring and managing treatments
10 Measuring outcomes
11 Analysis plan
12 Due date and dissemination plan

The CONSORT statement, however, is only a reporting system that alerts the research team to what needs to be known at the end of the experiment. An experimental protocol, on the other hand, will lay out what is needed to make the experiment succeed. The particular requirements of criminological research, experiments for which differ in important ways from those in medicine, education, agriculture and other research fields, call for the development of a format for a standard protocol in this field. The authors have laid out a first version of such a protocol, known as Crim-PORT 1.0 (Criminological Protocol for Operating Randomised Trials) Box 26.1.

This protocol consists of both formal elements and also the managerial elements involved in making the experiment happen. The formal elements include two particularly important features, informed consent and statistical power. Informed consent in a randomized trial is usually an ethical necessity and must be obtained prior to randomization so that only consenting participants are assigned to the treatment conditions. Statistical power is a means for establishing in probability terms the capacity of any test to detect a significant effect; that is, one not achieved merely by chance. Power analysis is used to calculate the sample size needed to detect a significant difference between the two groups.

The Cambridge Institute of Criminology website (listed in the 'Website Resources' section at the end of this chapter) will soon provide the opportunity for experimental criminologists to register their RCT protocols before their trials actually start. Some of the most prestigious medical journals now require studies to have been registered before their results can be published. Registering experiments in this way avoids the 'file-drawer problem'; that is, the systematic bias that results from failure to report the results of experiments with equivocal or undesired outcomes. This problem is especially troubling in meta-analyses and other systematic reviews of findings across a range of studies on a particular topic which tend to rely on published research, which in turn has tended to favour studies with unequivocal (positive) findings.

The authors were as guilty as any other researcher in their RJ experiments in failing to report many of these basic data elements initially, though with some careful work we have been able to reconstruct most of what the CONSORT statement requires for all the experiments. Reconstruction was not impossible because much of it was essential to record for everyday case management. We believe adherence to CONSORT in fact makes much easier the business of recording what is needed to make sure the experiment is on track; for example, it is vital to be able to see where cases are being lost between the point at which they are identified as ostensibly eligible and the point at which the experimental and control treatments are delivered (or not delivered, as the case may be).

Recruiting and training key people

Most criminological research is funded by government agencies and carried out in universities in collaboration with operational partners. Unlike medicine with its close links between teaching hospitals and academic institutions, in criminal justice practitioner-investigators are rare. Senior police officers, for example, will probably not be in a position to design the protocol nor to benefit in the way medical researchers do from publishing their results. This may be changing though: several police agencies in the UK have sought their own funding and established their own research units to collaborate with the Cambridge Institute of Criminology on particular experiments and may ultimately have the expertise to run their experiments entirely independently. At the present time, however, the usual model is for the academic principal investigator (PI), having successfully applied for funding and having engendered a collaborative relationship with an appropriate criminal justice agency to carry out an experiment on a defined topic, to be seen and held accountable as the leader of the experiment. Experience has shown that when no one is clearly seen in the role of PI, the experiment is likely to fail.

The PI, however, usually operates at arm's length both physically and intellectually from the operational aspects of the experiment and cannot know about day-to-day problems in the field, or how to interpret accumulating data, without an independent source of intelligence at close quarters to the experiment. This is the role occupied by the project manager, who must be totally enmeshed in the everyday issues of the experiment. When the study depends on the trickle-flow of cases, the issues of eligibility, consent, correct assignment and, above all, the volume of cases are such that rarely a day goes by without the need to adjust, consult, discuss and above all problem-solve issues between the operational staff on the one hand and the research team on the other. Funds must always be made available for this lynchpin individual who has day-to-day responsibility for holding the experiment together. Intellectual attainment is necessary but not sufficient for this role; the essential qualities are emotional intelligence and pragmatic problem-solving ability.

In a large experiment, the project manager may supervise other research staff who interact at a direct personal level with the operational staff on a daily basis and may be co-located with them. They remain, however, unequivocally on the research team. Their main point of liaison is usually an operational field manager who is employed by the partner agency and who is responsible for the staff supplying the cases, administering the treatment or any other operational task. This is where 'the rubber hits the road' experimentally: close and collegial relations between all these people is vital for the success of the venture. The only member of the team best kept at a little distance from the research site is the data manager, whose expertise with the numbers provides a second source of checking on the progress of the experiment.

Our RJ experiments in Canberra provided some useful experience here that we were able to benefit from in our later experiments in the UK. Because the Canberra police chief who enthusiastically embraced the experiments at the outset believed that RJ was a skill that all his officers could use (based on no empirical evidence), all 600 Canberra police officers were trained in RJ techniques on the basis that all would both identify eligible cases for the experiment and then, as required, administer the RJ programme. Not surprisingly we found that not all officers shared their chief's enthusiasm – many of them in fact felt RJ was a complete waste of time. After several months of trial and error we changed the model so that while all operational staff were aware of the kinds of cases we needed, only a small and more highly trained cadre of officers actually facilitated the RJ meetings. We were able to apply this experience in our UK experiments, relying on a small team of extremely effective individuals to talk to eligible offenders and their victims about taking part in the study and then actually facilitating the meetings.

Starting the experiment and keeping it going

There are essentially two ways in which eligible cases can be captured – 'batch' and 'trickle-flow'. As we described at the outset, in a 'batch' design the experimenter may spend months or even years in negotiation with many people around issues of eligibility and procedure but finally, 'at the press of a button', all cases can be randomly assigned at once. In a 'trickle-flow' design, on the other hand, the aim is to capture the cases as they arise, typically in criminology at the point of arrest, prosecution, sentence and so on. The machinery for delivering these eligible cases to the random assignment moment may require the cooperation of dozens, perhaps hundreds, of people. How to reach all these people is a major preoccupation at the start of an experiment. All forms of publicity can be used, and especially one-on-one lobbying with key individuals.

In our Canberra RJ experiments, the cases were referred by police officers on the street to the research team who randomly assigned them and then referred the experimental cases to the unit of highly trained police officers who administered the RJ. In our UK experiments, however, the referral process was much more complicated. Here, the cases were more serious and RJ was being tested as an addition to standard criminal justice treatment rather than as a diversion. Cases therefore had to be captured as they entered different points of the justice system: after a guilty plea in court but before sentence; at sentence where RJ could form part of a probation order; or after a custodial sentence had been imposed. A very high order of social skill and emotional intelligence was demanded of our research team in negotiating with, in one site alone, over 700 individuals and agencies.

Getting the cases

The same skills needed to get the experiment underway have to be employed repeatedly to keep the momentum going until the requisite number of cases are finally secured. Maintaining case flow is actually an even greater challenge than launching the experiment. Information technology can be used to identify where cases are 'leaking' from the experiment, but it is up to the skill and ingenuity of the research team to address the problem. Unless the operational people with access to the cases feel in some way invested in or emotionally connected to the study, case flow dwindles as time goes by. They will become bored with the study, which will always take longer than most people expect, they will be distracted by their own priorities, they will forget their promises, they will be replaced by new people who have never heard of the study or who have no interest in cooperating, and above all they will doubt the value of such a massive research effort, especially if they are privately convinced that they already know the answer to the research question.

Challenging these problems is the stuff of everyday life for the research team and all of these problems were encountered in our RJ work at one time or another. When the flow of cases begins to dry up, ingenuity is needed to rekindle awareness and enthusiasm among those supplying the cases – afternoon tea parties, late-night ride-alongs with beat officers, endless explaining about the nature of the programme being tested and the purpose of the research. One of the unintended consequences, however, of engendering high levels of support among operational staff is sometimes a commitment to the programme being tested that is not based on empirical evidence, but on the same 'gut-reaction' that can also result in a programme being dismissed on non-empirical grounds. The research team would sometimes be told that an individual wanted to help in getting cases because they 'really believed' that RJ works to reduce re-offending. Of course, the primary purpose of the research was to find out the answer to this very question but this was a hard message to deliver to operational staff who were used to dealing with certainties and may have been unclear about the ethical basis for doing the experiments at all, namely that we really did not know whether RJ was more or less effective than business as usual. Some of our supporters in our Canberra experiment for people charged with driving with a blood alcohol reading over the legal limit were mocked by their colleagues for their loyalty to an intervention that they thought was a waste of time: it was a difficult day when we had to tell our supporters that indeed RJ worked no better than court in reducing future offending and in some cases made re-offending worse (see the website of the Australian Institute of Criminology, listed in the 'Web Resources' section, for reports on all aspects of results from the Re-integrative Shaming Experiments in Canberra).

Eligibility screening

Preventing ineligible cases from entering the study is even more important in randomized trials than in other research designs. This is because once a case has been randomly assigned within a sequence of random numbers, it cannot be deleted without causing the very selection bias random assignment is designed to control by upsetting the equivalence of the groups. Even professional researchers sometimes believe that it is possible to delete ineligible cases post-random assignment: it certainly is one of the most troubling aspects of experimental design to explain to a lay person why doing so can fatally undermine the entire study.

The research team therefore needs to be very vigilant about eligibility and rigorous procedures at the point of case acceptance is vital. This can be achieved through good planning and protocols and ensuring that clear eligibility criteria are articulated and complied with as the cases are referred to the 'random assigner'. It is always more difficult to get it right when trickle-flow means that staff need to be rostered on duty to receive calls at any time; officers phoning in the cases on night shift may be wide awake but researchers sometimes are not. We safeguarded our integrity of the experiments as far as possible by listing ten or so questions for the researcher to ask the officer presenting the case to ensure that the case was eligible.

'Phase 1' testing

A crucial stage in establishing experiments which is ignored by the inexperienced and which can result in disaster concerns the need for a 'Phase 1' (as it is termed in medical clinical trials) or piloting of the experimental treatment. Without this stage we do not know whether the treatment itself may yield unintended consequences or whether the proposed procedures are workable. For example, in McCold and Wachtel's (1998) experiment in RJ, offenders who would normally have been dealt with in court were randomly assigned to RJ or court without their prior consent. The researchers had assumed that offenders would perceive RJ as a preferable option to court as it meant they would not get a criminal record. As it happened, many of the offenders randomly assigned to RJ strongly resisted participating in this treatment, resulting in about half of this group going to court anyway. The researchers felt this problem made the results of the experiment almost impossible to interpret, given the strong selection bias.

Problems in case flow or eligibility may also be uncovered by several weeks or even months of Phase 1 testing which will save an enormous amount of unnecessary effort when the experiment 'proper' gets underway. Weisburd (1993) found that case flow problems often led researchers to widen their eligibility criteria, introducing more heterogeneity in the kinds of cases accepted, but that doing so led to more variance and greater difficulty in interpreting findings. A well-conducted Phase 1 study will reveal such potential difficulties and allow them to be solved before the experiment becomes 'a ship at sea', when fixing them becomes much more complicated.

Random assignment

Responsibility for actual random assignment must always remain with the research team; furthermore, they must retain custody of the random number sequence of assignments to experimental and control conditions at all times and under strict security – for example in a locked filing cabinet in a locked office, as a minimum – though generating the random assignment only as the need arises is a more reliable means for maintaining security.

The integrity of the entire experiment is only as good as the integrity of the randomization procedures. Every case treated other than as assigned reduces the likelihood that the groups will be equivalent so that causal inference becomes increasingly compromised. These consequences were famously clear to see in the Lanarkshire school milk experiment of 1930, designed by two medical practitioners, Leighton and McKinlay, to test the value of providing free milk to school children (an experiment that might not have been granted ethics approval these days). The experiment was elegantly critiqued by WS Gosset (known as 'Student') (1931). He pointed out that because the randomization had been left in the hands of the school teachers there was no equivalence between the experimental and control groups. The teachers had naturally felt that the experimental group which would receive the milk should consist disproportionately of malnourished children. As a result, the evidence in favour of milk for school children was actually diminished because the weight gain achieved in the experimental group was less than it would have been if the malnourished children had been equally distributed between the two groups.

It is necessary to be vigilant about the possibility in any experiment that randomization will be undermined by those who genuinely believe that the alternative treatment is more suitable for a particular case. But much more likely is a degree of carelessness that can intrude when the 'random assigner' is not highly invested in ensuring correct procedures. Complete separation between the people providing the cases or treatment and the people assigning randomization places the process above suspicion.

Even though mechanisms such as coin tosses, odd/even birth dates and many others have been used to create equal probability of assignment, it is generally accepted that the fairest mechanism for random assignment is through computer generation of random number sequences. Once the assignments have been made then various methods can be used to apply them to actual cases, provided complete security is retained over the sequence. In our low-tech Canberra RJ experiments one of the authors spent several hours cutting up pieces of paper bearing the case number and the random assignment and placing each, carefully folded so that it was impossible to read the assignment, in a small envelope with the case number recorded on the outside, and then sealing it with red sealing wax so that any improper opening of the envelope would be apparent. To assure security these envelopes were always in the custody of the research staff member rostered on to take calls. In our higher-tech UK experiments, no one, including members of the research team, ever knew what assignment would come up next because it became known only when the police officer with the case called a member of our staff in Philadelphia to have the random assignment generated by a computer.

Consistency of treatment delivery

For both cases and for treatments, anything causing a difference can produce a misleading result. The greater the heterogeneity within the experimental and control groups, the less power in the test (Weisburd, 1993). Strong adherence to eligibility rules can minimize differences in the kinds of cases accepted.

It is more difficult however to ensure that standardized treatment is delivered, though how difficult depends on the composition and complexity of the treatment. Some experimental treatments may be starkly difference from the control; for example, custody *versus* no custody, which is easy to observe and audit. Other treatments may require repeated contacts, lengthy interactions with offenders and an emotional dimension to the encounter the content of which may be theoretically very relevant.

It is sometimes difficult for researchers to ensure the consistent delivery of all these elements, though the need for them to monitor the training and development is clear. In our experiments the research team ensured that the same training, by the same trainers, was delivered in the same way to all facilitators in all sites. This enabled us to aggregate the experimental results, confident that the same intervention had been tested everywhere.

Measuring delivered treatments

Monitoring of treatment delivery by the research team can help though, through solid investment in observations and interviews so that at least consistency can be measured even if it is not guaranteed. Failing to measure treatment delivery is a common problem in experiments because of the assumption by inexperienced researchers that once a treatment is assigned it will be delivered as agreed. Some treatments lend themselves to automated monitoring; for example, recording through GPS technology the location of police officers. More often though this task falls again to the research team and the expenditure of the social capital it has built up with operational partners to persuade them to comply. In addition, careful data management recording will reveal where treatments are not conforming to what is expected. Certainly investment in the training of staff is needed for this to be done consistently, and attention to their morale and engagement in the project will pay dividends handsomely in terms of the integrity and value of the experiment.

The research team had a critical role in recording what happened in the RJ and court cases that came into our Canberra experiments. A member of the team attended each RJ and court event for all cases and completed a semi-structured questionnaire for each of them, noting the attendees, their attitudes and demeanour as well as the content of the event. This observation instrument was extensively tested at the outset for inter-rater reliability, given the inherently subjective nature of the content, and proved to be a rich source of data. We were unable to monitor the content of most of our UK cases in the same way, though research staff were present at most of the RJ meetings. At the request of the Crown Court judges who were hearing most of our burglary cases we prepared lengthy summaries of the content of the RJ events experienced by the experimental group so that the judges could make up their own minds about the likely sincerity of any remorse expressed by the offender and the degree of satisfaction expressed by the victim. We were very aware, however, that we lost much valuable data by not being able to observe or interview our UK cases as painstakingly as our Canberra cases.

MEASURING OUTCOMES

Agreeing primary outcome measures based on theoretically sustainable concepts at the very outset of the experiment is essential to avoid arguments about 'fishing' for significant results in a set of results with many null findings. Registering experiments following the CrimPORT model discussed earlier would solve this problem. There are, however, some practical principles that can be employed in identifying the most useful outcome measures.

It is usually preferable to select universal measures over low response rate measures when the choice is presented. For example, arrest and conviction records apply to the whole population whereas interview data are subject to bias resulting from response problems. Of course interview data can provide information not available from any other source, but when it is possible to use a universal source, it should be used in preference to another measure with a lower response rate.

Likewise, it is preferable when testing crime prevention strategies to choose crime frequency over prevalence as the outcome measure. Frequency in this setting refers in this case to the number of *offences* that have been committed (or prevented) while prevalence refers to the number of *offenders* who have re-offended, on a yes–no basis. From the community perspective we suggest that it is preferable for fewer offences to be committed post-intervention, rather than to have fewer offenders (many of whom may have reduced their repeat offending as a result of the intervention, as was the case with our UK experiments, without necessarily desisting entirely). Whereas prevalence of repeat offending has been more commonly used in assessing outcomes, simply because it is easier to measure, frequency is actually a far more useful measure when the objective of the strategy is to reduce overall crime incidence, because it is so much more sensitive and reliable.

Finally, it is relevant to weigh seriousness of repeat offending rather than simple counts when the impact of crime on the community is at issue: clearly a reduction in armed robbery would be viewed as more significant than a reduction in a less serious offence such as shoplifting. Seriousness can also be converted into a useful cost measurement using established metrics, providing useful information about the cost-effectiveness of the intervention (see, e.g., Shapland et al., 2008, which documents the striking cost savings associated with the use of RJ across a range of offence types, using Ministry of Justice estimates for the costs of different kinds of crime).

Analysis of results

While data analysis is a technical matter addressed by many statisticians, there are some basic principles that underpin any analysis in randomized experiments. First, RCTs lend themselves to simplicity. Their elegance derives from the fact that the research design has already taken care of many of the problems for which sophisticated statistical techniques have been developed. People with little or no statistical training can understand the meaning of a difference between 'before treatment' and 'after treatment' measures of the variable of interest in the experimental and control groups. The clarity of the technique makes the results all the more powerful when one considers the issues involved in communicating to lay people results derived from complex statistical modelling.

A second principle concerns the testing of policies rather than treatments per se. A treatment may be perfectly useful but if fewer than 100 percent of people selected are prepared to participate, or to finish it, we cannot know its effect without taking into account the likely take up rate if the treatment became a policy. What we do know, however, is that there will never be 100 per cent take up and the experiment will likely suffer the same kind of failure of participants to take up the treatment that would occur if the programme were rolled out as policy. Thus measuring non-compliance and comparing experimental and control results on the basis of the intended treatment rather than the delivered treatment is in effect a test of the *policy* rather than the *treatment*. This is actually far more useful to policy makers than testing a treatment that may never be taken up in sufficient volume to be useful, no matter how effective it is. Indeed, without near-perfect delivery of the experimental treatment to all and only the experimental group participants and without content consistency in all cases, it is actually impossible to answer the question of the effect of the treatment per se.

Communicating results

The purpose of most experiments is to test the effectiveness of adopting a particular intervention to solve a real-world problem faced by policy makers. It is essential therefore to be able to communicate the experiment's findings in a clear and concise manner readily comprehended by people who simply want to see whether an intervention 'works' or not. Needless to say, all findings must be supported by rigorous analysis but whether or not the findings will be implemented may well depend upon whether or not key people can understand them.

Synthesizing results

All knowledge is provisional and one experiment's findings in one location or under one set of conditions may be at odds with another experiment tested under different conditions. Not only can we learn about variations in effectiveness under different conditions of any intervention, we can also use techniques of meta-analysis and systematic reviews of the evidence to estimate average effects across all these conditions. These methods allow us to combine results from any number of rigorous studies on any subject (such as RJ) to show the range of results across them all and then to show whether or not on average the results favour the treatment group or the control group. Thus experiments can have value far beyond the immediate time and place in which they are reported, as findings from replications and other research become available.

CONCLUSION

Much has been said by government in both the US and the UK in recent times about the desirability, indeed the imperative, for policy to be evidence-led. Experiments need to be seen in that context as they are the obvious mechanism for determining what is the best way to proceed, free of ideology. Experiments are often attractive to governments to commission, but many obstacles may lie in the path of the implementation of their conclusions.

As David Howarth, former MP for Cambridge, deftly described the process of policy formation in his speech to the Cambridge University Institute of Criminology 3rd International Evidence-Based Policing Conference (http://www.crim.cam.ac.uk/news/ebp; 'How should ministers and parliament be educated on evidence?'), arriving at a decision in government about what to do about any issue often involves very little attention to evidence. Ministers worry about a problem, usually highlighted in the media, decide what to do based on a mixture of ideological predisposition and attention to media reaction (the surrogate for public reaction) and act expediently. The high-water mark of policy formation in this manner may have been the 'sofa government' style of the UK Blair government (between 1997 and 2007) whose informal decision-making practices have been comprehensively criticized (see, e.g., Hastings, 2006). Such a style ostensibly freed government ministers from the dead hand of bureaucratic procedures but at the same time created an atmosphere often characterized by indiscipline and lack of accountable practices that did not require evidence as a basis for action. Evidence-based government will ask rather: what do we know and how do we craft a response to a problem based on evidence? Ironically, it may be in tighter economic times, when less money is available for research, that research evidence is more likely to be sought – when governments cannot afford to act on the basis only of what they think they know but instead need a more rigorous and less ideological approach. Experimental criminology provides the means to achieve this evidence.

RECOMMENDED READING

Shapland, J., Atkinson, A., Atkinson, H., Dignan, J., Edwards, L., Hibbert, J. et al. (2008). *Does Restorative Justice Affect Reconviction? The Fourth Report From the Evaluation of Three Schemes* (London: Ministry of Justice) reports findings on re-offending from the RJ studies conducted in the UK.

Sherman, L. (2010). 'An introduction to experimental criminology' in A. Piquero and D. Weisburd (eds) *Handbook of Quantitative Criminology* (New York: Springer) provides a comprehensive and thorough explanation of the use of experiments in criminology.

Strang, H. (2002). *Repair or Revenge: Victims and Restorative Justice* (Oxford, Oxford University Press) provides a more detailed account of the RJ experiments in Canberra as well as a comprehensive evaluation of the victim's perspective in the criminal justice process.

Weisburd, D. (1993). 'Design sensitivity in criminal justice experiments' in M. Tonry (ed.) *Crime and Justice: A Review of Research* (Chicago, University of Chicago Press) provides a definitive analysis of methodological issues in experiments, and the critical issue of sample size versus sample homogeneity in maintaining treatment integrity.

Web resources

The statement of the Consolidated Standards on Reporting of Trials (CONSORT) is available at: http://www.consort-statement.org/consort-statement/

The Criminological Protocol for Operating Randomized Trials, known as Crim-PORT 1.0 for short, is available at: http://www.crim.cam.ac.uk/experiments

Reports on all aspects of results from the Reintegrative Shaming Experiments in Canberra are available at: http://www.aic.gov.au/en/criminal_justice_system/rjustice/rise/

The four reports by Joanna Shapland and her team at the University of Sheffield (Anne Atkinson, Helen Atkinson, Becca Chapman, James Dignan, Marie Howes, Jennifer Johnstone, Gwen Robinson and Angela Sorsby) on various aspects of the three schemes funded by the Ministry of Justice, including the UK experiments discussed in this chapter, are available at: http://www.justice.gov.uk/publications/

Sherman, Lawrence and Heather Strang. *Restorative Justice: The Evidence* (London: Smith Institute) provides a summary of RJ research findings up until 2007. Available at: www.smith-institute.org.uk/publications.htm.

REFERENCES

Ariel, B. (2009) *Taxation and Compliance: an Experimental Study*. PhD dissertation, Hebrew University of Jerusalem, Israel.

Braithwaite, J. (1989) *Crime, Shame and Reintegration*. Cambridge: Cambridge University Press.

Braithwaite, J. (2002) *Restorative Justice and Responsive Regulation*. New York: Oxford University Press.

Farrington, D. and Welsh, B. (2005) 'Randomized experiments in criminology: What have we learned in the last two decades?' *Journal of Experimental Criminology* 1(1): 9–38.

Fisher, R. A. (1935) *The Design of Experiments*, Edinburgh and London, Oliver and Boyd.

Hastings, M. (2006) 'The sofa government of Blairism has been an unmitigated disaster.' Available at: http://www.guardian.co.uk/commentisfree/2006/may/16/comment.labour

McCold, P. and Wachtel, B. (1998) *Restorative Policing Experiment: The Bethlehem Pennsylvania Police Family Group Conferencing Project*. Bethlehem, PA: Community Service Foundation.

Sampson, R. J. (2010) 'Gold Standard Myths: Observations on the Experimental Turn in Quantitative Criminology', *Journal of Quantitative Criminology*, Published online 18 September.

Shapland, J., Atkinson, A., Atkinson, H., Dignan, J., Edwards, L., Hibbert, J. et al. (2008) *Does Restorative Justice Affect Reconviction? The Fourth Report from the Evaluation of Three Schemes*. Ministry of Justice Research Series 10/08. London: Ministry of Justice.

Sherman, L. (1992) *Policing Domestic Violence*. New York: Free Press.

Sherman, L. (1993) 'Defiance, deterrence and irrelevance' *Journal of Research in Crime and Delinquency* 30(4): 445–473.

Sherman, L. W. and Weisburd, D. (1995) 'General Deterrent Effects of Police Patrol in Crime Hot Spots: A Randomized, Controlled Trial.' *Justice Quarterly* 12(4): 635–648.

Sherman, L. (2010) 'An introduction to experimental criminology' in A. Piquero and D. Weisburd (eds) *Handbook of Quantitative Criminology*. New York: Springer.

Strang, H. (2002) *Repair or Revenge: Victims and Restorative Justice*. Oxford: Clarendon Series Oxford University Press.

'Student' (WS Gosset) (1931) 'The Lanarkshire Milk Experiment' *Biometrika* 23(3/4): 398–406.

Tyler, T. (1990) *Why Do People Obey the Law?* New Haven: Yale University Press.

Weisburd, D. (1993) 'Design sensitivity in criminal justice experiments' in M. Tonry (ed.) *Crime and Justice: A Review of Research.* Chicago: University of Chicago Press.

Weisburd, D. Lum, C. and Petrosino A. (2001) 'Does Research Design Affect Study Outcomes in Criminal Justice?', *Annals of the American Association of Political and Social Science* 578: 50–70.

27

Large-Scale Criminological Field Experiments

Manuel Eisner, Tina Malti,
Denis Ribeaud

INTRODUCTION

Large-scale experiments on the effectiveness of crime prevention and reduction in real world settings are as close as criminology gets to big science. They need long-term planning, involve the cooperation between practice and science, require large groups of research staff, and entail considerable costs for implementing an intervention and measuring its success. If conducted well, they can provide policy makers and practitioners with the best knowledge that criminology can offer on how to effectively reduce crime. However, large-scale field experiments are complex projects that require a broad set of methodological skills if they are to be successful.

This chapter first explains how criminological field experiments differ from other experimental studies, and why these characteristics lead to specific methodological problems. It then provides an introduction to the conceptual, organisational and practical challenges that arise during the various stages of large-scale field experiments. Throughout, we use experiences made in the Zurich Project on the Social Development of Children (z-proso) to illustrate how researchers can address critical challenges (for an overview of the study see Eisner and Ribeaud, 2005). This large-scale field trial combines a longitudinal study with the evaluation of two universal prevention programmes, both implemented at the start of primary school with the aim of reducing aggressive behaviour problems amongst children.

WHY EFFECTIVENESS AND DISSEMINATION TRIALS?

In prevention and intervention research a distinction is made between efficacy, effectiveness, and dissemination trials (Elliott and Mihalic, 2004; Flay, 1986; Glasgow et al., 2003; Schoenwald and Hoagwood, 2001). *Efficacy trials* attempt to answer whether an intervention has effects under optimal conditions of delivery. In such studies the researchers have tight control over the implementation of the intervention, the treatment is delivered by trained and motivated research staff, the participants are screened to meet inclusion criteria, and potential confounding factors are carefully controlled. In efficacy trials the number of participants is typically small and outcomes are often assessed shortly after the treatment was received. *Effectiveness trials* try to establish whether an intervention has a desirable effect under real-world conditions. Such studies are typically of a larger scale, require the collaboration between researchers and a variety of agencies, entail the delivery of the programme by practitioners, usually deliver the intervention to a heterogeneous target group, and often try to establish the kinds of longer-term effects that are of interest to policy makers and politicians. *Dissemination trials* examine the effects of an intervention under conditions close to those under which a programme is to be distributed. They examine the effects of fully developed and manualised programmes that are supported by adequate infrastructure, training mechanisms and technical support structures. Ideally, dissemination trials are conducted by independent researchers in order to understand whether effects can be maintained without the active involvement of the programme developers. Effectiveness and dissemination trials share many methodological characteristics and will subsequently discussed as 'large-scale field trials'.

Efficacy trials are an important first step in the evaluation of interventions to reduce crime and delinquency. However, broad adoption of a programme should be based on solid knowledge on whether it works when delivered by trained practitioners to a more varied target group, and whether the effects can be maintained over a period that is practically and politically relevant. The importance of this distinction has been highlighted in meta-analyses that have examined factors which affect the size of treatment effects in criminology, the health sciences and prevention science (Beelmann and Lösel, 2006; Petrosino and Soydan, 2005; Piquero et al., 2009; Wilson et al., 2003a). In many of these studies a similar pattern emerges: significant positive intervention effects tend to be found when the number of study participants is small (Farrington and Welsh, 2003), the intervention is delivered to very high standards, the programme developer is directly involved in the evaluation (Petrosino and Soydan, 2005), and the effects are measured shortly after the intervention (Beelmann and Lösel, 2006). In contrast, much smaller effects tend to be found in studies with a large number of participants, intervention delivery by trained practitioners, limited implementation quality, no direct involvement of the programme developer, and an assessment of effects over months or years.

This suggests that the generalisability of efficacy trials is limited and that larger effectiveness and dissemination trials are critical for translating research findings into policy recommendations. Such studies are complex, time-consuming, and often expensive. Also, the concept of 'research methods' acquires a much broader meaning than is usually the case in criminological research. Of course, the usual business of getting research questions and hypotheses right, of developing an adequate sampling and measurement strategy, and of performing the right kind of statistical analyses plays an important role. However, effectiveness and dissemination trials require an understanding of partnerships between researchers and stake holders, knowledge about communication with the various parties involved, programme implementation, and so on (see box 27.1).

EFFECTIVENESS AND DISSEMINATION TRIALS IN CRIMINOLOGY

Possibly because of its traditional link to policy making, possibly also due to the enthusiastic support by world-leading scholars like Sherman (2002), Farrington (1983), Weisburd (2000), and Lipsey (1995), criminology is an area of social science research that is comparatively supportive of randomised controlled trials. This is expressed, amongst others, in the foundation of the Academy of Experimental Criminology in 1999 and the initiation of the *Journal of Experimental Criminology* in 2004. Large-scale field trials can be found in many areas related to criminology including, for example, hot spots policing (e.g., Braga, 2005; Weisburd, 2005), the early developmental prevention of anti-social behaviours (e.g., Olds, 2002), the school-based prevention of bullying, substance abuse and delinquency (Gottfredson et al., 2006; Patton et al., 2003), restorative justice programmes (Sherman et al., 2005) or offender treatment programmes (e.g., Timmons-Mitchell et al., 2006). For an overview of randomised trials in criminology see Farrington and Welsh (2005, 2006).

Our own experience with a large-scale dissemination trial comes from the z-proso project (for an overview of the study see Eisner and

---

Box 27.1   Characteristics and goals of large-scale effectiveness and dissemination trials

- Test the effects of interventions in real-life settings, often with large Ns
- Give realistic estimates of intervention effects in routine applications
- Interventions delivered by trained practitioners rather than research staff
- Examine both short and long-term effects, often continue for many years
- Try to understand effects of interventions embedded in the life-course of people
- Try to add to knowledge about the conditions for successful dissemination
- Usually entail intensive cooperation between practitioners and researchers

Ribeaud, 2005). It combines a longitudinal study with the evaluation of two universal prevention programmes. As an evaluation study, the project aims at providing policy makers with research-based knowledge about whether prevention programmes implemented at the beginning of primary school can reduce externalising problems during childhood, and delinquency during adolescence. The study also aims at contributing to the question of whether programmes found to be effective in other countries could be successfully transferred to an ethnically diverse urban context in continental Western Europe.

The implemented interventions are well known and had been previously tested both in efficacy and effectiveness trials. At the family level, the parenting skills programme Triple P (Positive Parenting Programme; see, e.g., Sanders, 1992, 1999) was implemented, while at the school level the social skills programme PATHS (Promoting Alternative Thinking Strategies; see, e.g., Greenberg et al., 1998; Kusche and Greenberg, 1994) was administered. From the onset, the study was designed as a close collaboration between a research team at the Universities of Zurich and Cambridge, and an intervention team of the municipality of Zurich.

To assess the effectiveness of these programmes 56 schools in the city of Zurich were randomly allocated to four treatment conditions, namely Triple P only, PATHS only, Triple P and PATHS, and no intervention. Participants of the study were all 1,650 children who entered year 1 of primary school in one of the participating schools in the fall of 2004. The interventions were delivered during years 1 and 2 of primary school. Data collection currently includes four waves of child interviews, primary caregiver interviews, and teacher assessments during years 1, 2, 3, and 5 of primary school.

HOW ARE EFFECTIVENESS AND DISSEMINATION TRIALS DIFFERENT?

All experiments have the same general logic: the experimenter manipulates a particular component of a system and sets up monitoring devices to measure a signal of the outcome which is theoretically expected to react to the manipulation of the presumed cause. Researchers therefore need to solve two problems: the manipulation of the input needs to be well-defined, controlled and systematic; and the instruments for capturing the signal need to measure what they are meant to measure, to be precise, and sensitive to change within the range of variation likely to be produced by the

manipulation. Almost all specific challenges of large-scale field trials relate to the difficulty of maintaining this basic set-up of an experimental design and drawing the correct conclusions from the results (also see Welsh et al., 2010). They can be described by the following four questions:

- How can the intervention (i.e., treatment, programme, policy) be delivered at a larger scale so that the actual manipulation of the system corresponds to what was intended? This is known as the problem of maintaining *treatment fidelity* in field trials.

- How can a field study be designed and set up so that the variation in the signal (e.g., conduct problems, bullying, repeat offending) due to the experiment can be unambiguously distinguished from all the other sources of variation found in natural settings? This is the core challenge of preserving *internal validity* (Shadish et al., 2002).

- How can we assure that the measurement instruments are of sufficiently high quality to capture the signal even if a large number of people are involved in the data collection? Answers to this question relate to the challenge of achieving high *construct validity* in large-scale studies.

- How can a field experiment be conducted so that its findings provide unbiased estimates of the effects that can be expected when the intervention is delivered in other places, by other people? This is a core element of the problem of achieving *external validity* or generalisability.

In the subsequent sections we introduce general strategies that can help to solve these challenges, using the z-proso study to illustrate possible solutions.

THE PREPARATION STAGE

Large-scale field trials require detailed long-term planning. Often it is advisable to conduct a *feasibility study* before the main project begins. Issues addressed in a feasibility study may include the following: a resource and needs assessment in the target site; an evaluation of possible interventions suitable for the target site; an examination of site readiness including an evaluation of the financial and organisational resources available for implementing the intervention; a review of social and demographic characteristics of the target site with a view to understanding barriers, risk factors, and resources in the respective communities; and an overview of the various stake-holders with whom partnerships need to be built up and maintained during a field experiment.

UNDERSTANDING AND RESPONDING TO COMMUNITY NEEDS

A careful choice of the most appropriate intervention is important. Elliott and Mihalic (2004) distinguish three factors that influence the selection of an appropriate intervention for effectiveness and dissemination trials: (1) the organisational capacity of the intervention, (2) the fit of the intervention with existing organisational structures and resources, and (3) the readiness of the planned intervention field.

Organisational capacity refers to all the components that influence the ability to effectively deliver a programme with fidelity. Components include the existence of high-quality published manuals and, where required, teaching materials; the ability to train, certify and supervise the trainers; the infrastructure to provide technical assistance; and a tested process of recruitment and delivery of the programme. Generally, effectiveness or dissemination trials should only be conducted for interventions that have been demonstrated to work in efficacy trials, that are based on strong theoretical models, and that are fully documented.

Fit with existing structures and resources refers to whether the planned intervention fills gaps in the existing provision, whether it can be delivered within existing structures, and whether there exists sufficient organisational and financial support to deliver the intervention. The choice of an intervention should be based on a thorough needs and resources assessment in the target area (Hawkins et al., 2002). In particular, such assessments should include an overview of particularly salient risk factors in the target area, an assessment of potential barriers to implementing programmes, and an overview of existing activities, measures and mechanisms for preventing or reducing crime and delinquency.

Site readiness, finally, relates to how prepared a community, a school, or a criminal justice institution is to endorse and support an intervention and a field trial. Factors that influence site readiness include, for example, a well-connected and respected local champion, strong administrative support, formal organisational commitments and organisational/staffing stability, up-front commitment of necessary resources, and programme credibility within the community (Elliott and Mihalic, 2004).

Site readiness and organisational capacity are variables that researchers should try to influence. Thus, any large-scale field trial requires a coherent approach to *building partnerships* with agencies and engaging with stake holders (Spoth et al., 2004). This process entails different organisational levels and changing activities during the stages of a trial (Goodman, 2000). For example, it is useful to distinguish the macro or policy level (e.g., national or local policy makers), the meso-level of actors with managerial roles (e.g., heads of schools, senior police officers), and the micro-level of staff directly involved in the delivery of the interventions (e.g., teachers, social workers, prison officers). For each level, different communication styles and channels may be most appropriate to maintain and promote enthusiasm for the project.

A major goal of the z-proso study was to provide the local authorities with research evidence on programmes that could later be implemented on a broader basis. It was therefore important to carefully assess which programmes should be included in the field trial. The Effective Violence Prevention and Intervention among Children and Adolescents in Zurich project – a feasibility study carried out in 2002 – served this purpose. It aimed at achieving four goals: (1) to thoroughly examine and describe the problem situation in the target site; (2) to review existing knowledge about the causes and risk factors associated with youth violence in a way accessible to political decision makers; (3) to assess existing resources in the target site, including a comprehensive overview of prevention and intervention activities already in place in Zurich; and (4) to present an overview of current knowledge about effective universal prevention programmes amenable to implementation.

We then combined this needs and resources assessment with a review of universal, selective and indicated programmes that had a good evidence base internationally. In addition to summarising existing reviews of US-American research (e.g., 'Blueprints of Violence Prevention' website run by the CSVP (Center for the Study and Prevention of Violence) at the University of Colorado), we also tried to include findings from evaluations carried out in Europe. On this basis, the final report recommended nine model programmes to be considered for implementation in the city of Zurich. These programmes share four qualities: (1) they had been shown to be effective in high-quality evaluation research elsewhere; (2) they target risk factors that can be shown to be relevant in the context of the city of Zurich; (3) they fill gaps not yet covered by ongoing prevention and intervention programmes; (4) they can be evaluated by means of a randomised experiment within a longitudinal study.

In meetings with representatives of the city authorities it was subsequently determined that Triple P and PATHS would be implemented as universal prevention programmes, aimed at primary school children, and targeting risk factors at the family (poor parenting skills), the school (school climate), and the individual (emotional skills and self control) levels. The programmes were chosen because they filled significant gaps in the current local provision, available evidence from previous evaluations was sufficiently positive to warrant a large-scale randomised trial, and the local government was prepared to provide the financial and organisational support needed for implementing the interventions with high quality.

Advisory boards can be very helpful when developing an effectiveness or dissemination trial. In the z-proso study we established two boards that served different functions. The first was a scientific advisory board of leading scholars in the field who had previous experience in conducting similar studies and who brought in a range of methodological competencies. It proved to be extremely useful for the final design of the study. The second board was set up by the municipality of Zurich and served as a communication and discussion forum between the research project and the various agencies interested in and affected by the study. It comprised representatives, amongst others, of the school authorities, social services, the police, the urban planning department, the health and prevention department, and the organisation of school psychologists.

DEVELOPING THE RESEARCH DESIGN

A research design is a plan of how the experimental manipulation (i.e., the intervention) is to be delivered, how units are to be allocated to experimental and control conditions, and when and how the baseline, post, and follow-up measurements are to be taken. Several issues need to be addressed when a large-scale field experiment is being developed. First, the study needs to be large enough to allow an assessment of whether the expected effects were achieved. To assess this question, researchers need to familiarise themselves with a technique called *power analysis* (Cohen, 1988). In non-technical terms, the purpose of power analysis is to determine how big the study sample must be so that the researcher has a good chance of discovering an intervention effect, if such an effect does exist. As we saw above, interventions are likely to have lower effects in effectiveness and dissemination trials than in efficacy trials. It is therefore advisable to design field trials so that they can detect even relatively small, but practically relevant, intervention effects.

Second, you will need to develop a plan of how to allocate units to control and treatment conditions. Details about various experimental designs can be found in Shadish et al. (2002) and Rossi and Freedman (2004). An important topic in criminological field trials relates to randomisation

not by individuals but by larger units. Thus, many criminologically relevant real-world interventions are delivered at the level of schools, courts, probation officers with several clients, concentrations of crime (i.e., crime 'hot spots') or prison wings (Weisburd and Taxman, 2000). To the extent that field trials strive for external validity the research design should reflect the treatment delivery in bundles. Such designs are called *cluster-randomised experiments* and require knowledge of the specialist literature.

Finally, consideration needs to be given to the timing and organisation of the data collection. Usually this will entail at least a baseline measurement (before the intervention) and a post assessment (after the intervention). Also, field trials often distinguish between short-term and long-term effects of an intervention.

In the z-proso study, several considerations influenced the final research design. First, decisions needed to be made regarding the most appropriate units of randomisation. As the classroom-based skills programme PATHS required classes as the smallest treatment delivery units, we first considered randomisation by class. However, this entailed the risk of contamination (i.e., the transfer of treatment effects to classes in the control condition) between adjoining classrooms. It was therefore decided to use schools as the randomisation units.

Also, we decided to use a *factorial design* for allocating schools to the treatment conditions. Factorial designs can be used when two or more interventions are tested simultaneously. In a factorial design units are allocated, with an equal probability, to any combination of treatments (Shadish et al., 2002: 263). In our case the combination of the parent training and the social skills training led to a 2×2 factorial design with the four treatment conditions: 'control', 'Triple P only', 'PATHS only' and 'Triple P and PATHS combined'. Major advantages of such designs are that they are more cost-effective because they require smaller samples than if each intervention was tested separately and that they allow testing interactions; that is, whether the combination of both interventions is more effective than each intervention separately.

Third, the precise randomisation procedure had to be determined. An important factor here was that the targeted sample size of 1,200 participating children corresponded to about 50–60 schools. With such a small number of units the direct randomisation would have entailed a large risk of imbalance between the randomised groups. The reason is that random allocation can only be expected to result in equivalence of the treatment groups if the number of allocated units is relatively large. Imbalance means that the individuals allocated to the treatment conditions would differ in various respects. We therefore decided to use a *randomised block design*. In such a design the units chosen for randomisation (i.e. schools) are first subdivided into groups that are relatively similar, and allocation to treatment conditions is then done within each group (Boruch, 1997: 111). In our case we created 14 blocks of 4 schools whereby the schools within each block came from the same school district (meaning that social background of the catchment area was comparable) and were similar in the size of the school. Within each block schools were then randomly allocated to the treatment condition.

Finally, we had to work out how to interlock the data collections and the interventions (see Figure 27.1 for a schematic overview). The succession of the interventions was partly determined by practical considerations. Triple P had already been available commercially for several years before the start of the study. We could therefore rely on existing programme material and a pool of providers who had been licensed by the distributors. For PATHS, in contrast, a fully operational German version needed to be developed as part of the study. This included translating and adapting the PATHS curriculum, developing a teacher training programme, testing preliminary versions of the curriculum, and training the coaches who were to provide teacher training and supervision. Because of the time required to develop an operational version of PATHS, it was decided to offer Triple P during year 1 of primary school and to implement PATHS in year 2. The waves of data collection were timed so that wave 1 could be fully completed before the start of the parent training and wave 3 was conducted after the

completion of the social skills programme. For wave 2 of the data collection some temporal overlap between the start of the skills programme in the classrooms and the completion of all child and parent interviews could not be avoided. For this reason, the data from wave 2 were not used in subsequent analyses of the effects of the social skills programme.

MEASUREMENT INSTRUMENTS

Every experiment examines whether the manipulation of a hypothesised mechanism results in the predicted change of the outcome. The minimal required data, therefore, consist of two components, namely correct measures of the manipulation and valid, change-sensitive and reliable measures of the outcome. In efficacy and dissemination trials the design of measurement instruments for both components requires careful attention. One reason is that researchers and practitioners expect that large-scale criminological field trials yield more than an answer to the simple question, 'Was the intervention effective?'. Rather, the large organisational and financial investment into field-trials usually warrants answers to questions such as: 'why did it work?', 'for whom?', and 'under what circumstances?'.

As regards measurement of the treatment it is therefore pivotal to develop a comprehensive bundle of instruments that help to observe systematically how the intervention was delivered to the target population. Without such data, it is impossible to determine whether treatment was received

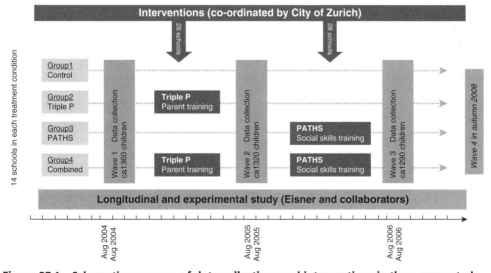

Figure 27.1   Schematic sequence of data collections and interventions in the z-proso study

as planned, which components of the intervention contributed most to the overall effect, whether possible non-significant results are due to an ineffective programme or poor implementation, or how the effectiveness of a programme can be improved (Dane and Schneider, 1998). Every large-scale field experiment therefore needs comprehensive measures of *fidelity* (sometimes also referred to as *integrity*); that is, the extent to which the intervention was delivered as intended by the programme developers (Dusenbury et al., 2003). Dane and Schneider (1998) distinguish five dimensions of fidelity: (1) the extent to which all the components of an intervention were delivered (adherence); (2) the amount of programme content received by the participants (dose); (3) the level of engagement and competence with which the programme was delivered (quality of delivery); (4) the extent to which participants actively engaged in the intervention (participant responsiveness); and (5) which specific elements of a programme were present in an intervention (programme differentiation).

Data on treatment delivery are often collected from multiple informants. In the z-proso study, for example, four monitoring devices were put in place to measure the implementation of the parent training programme: enrolment and attendance sheets recorded every stage of programme exposure from the initial intent to participate to the full completion of all four training sessions; programme providers completed standardised questionnaires to assess the course climate and the delivered programme components; parent questionnaires were administered to measure various components of customer satisfaction; participant observation by a member of the research team provided qualitative data on a subset of courses; and finally, questions in the parent interview at wave 2 (i.e., a few months after the intervention) provided information about the extent to which parents effectively used the techniques they had learned in daily life (see Eisner et al., in press).

The design of outcome measures should be based on the *programme theory* of the intervention. Programme theory means the theoretical model of the mechanisms assumed to be activated by the intervention and believed to be responsible for its direct and indirect effects (Bickman, 1987; Rogers et al., 2000). Thus, researchers embarking a large-scale field study should not be satisfied with a 'black box' model of their intervention. Rather, measurement instruments should be designed so that they represent all proximal mechanisms and more distal outcomes implied in the underlying theory of the intervention. A parent training programme, for example, uses parents as therapeutic change agents whereby the change in

the parenting behaviour is believed to be causally relevant for the change in children's antisocial behaviour. An evaluation of parent trainings should therefore examine whether the training did affect the parenting behaviour as the proximal mechanism, whether the training resulted in a change in child problem behaviour as the distal outcome, and whether the change in problem behaviour was mediated through the change in parenting.

Outcome measures must be change sensitive; that is, able to capture information on the change triggered by the stimulus associated with the intervention. In order to be change-sensitive, measures must be both reliable and valid. For example, instruments that measure the outcome with a low precision tend to underestimate the true effects of an intervention. When conducting large-scale field experiments researchers are well advised to use measurement instruments that have been previously tested and shown to react to the kinds of interventions similar to that implemented in the study.

Furthermore, researchers need to consider multiple sources to elicit information about change in the target outcome. For example, simply relying of official measures of crime (e.g., arrests) may be insufficient because the intervention may have triggered processes that also affect the likelihood of arrest. Similarly, exclusive reliance on teacher assessments in a school based intervention is insufficient as teacher ratings of children may be biased by their own involvement in programme delivery. As a general rule, it is therefore advisable to adopt a *multi-trait multi-method approach* to measuring intervention effects (Campbell, 1959). This means that outcomes should be assessed by different sources of information and that the instruments should comprise all target domains believed to be affected by the intervention. In the z-proso study, for example, identical measures of child problem behaviour were administered to the teachers, the parents and the children themselves.

ORGANISING DATA COLLECTION AND MANAGEMENT

Data-collection for a large-scale field experiment is a major organisational challenge. It entails resolving issues such as how to develop a realistic time plan, how to hire qualified staff, how to train and monitor interviewers, how to achieve high participation and retention rates, and how to organise the collection and storage of data (Stouthamer-Loeber and Kammen, 1995). This is particularly the case if data are to be collected from multiple informants and if follow-up measures are planned over longer periods of time.

In the z-proso study, up to 30 interviewers had to be recruited and trained for each wave of data collection. Interviewer training comprised two days and included one afternoon of practical exercises with the questionnaire. Also, 60-page interviewer handbooks were developed for the child and the parent interviews. They comprised detailed guidance about, for example, how to contact the parents, how to explain the study, how to react to concerns about the study, how to conduct the interviews, how to cope with difficult situations, and how to communicate with the project administrators. In order to facilitate standardised data collection and efficient transfer of the data, the child and the parent interviews were set up as computer-aided personal interviews, whereby the interviewers could transfer the encrypted data electronically to our server. Furthermore, interviewers were required to attend weekly meetings with project administrators and discuss progress, problematic cases or issues regarding the questionnaire. For the child interviews, which were conducted in separate rooms during regular school hours, organisational details needed to be discussed in advance with the heads of schools and the teachers. Also, recruitment of interviewers included a vetting procedure, and prior experience in working with children of a similar age was required.

ETHNIC AND CULTURAL DIVERSITY

In contemporary societies, target sites for criminological field experiments are often characterised by considerable ethnic and cultural diversity. Researchers who consider a large-scale efficacy trial may therefore have to acquire specialist knowledge about how diversity affects the planned study. Depending on the specific study this may entail knowledge about how to best *translate survey instruments* (Harkness et al., 2003), whether the planned interventions need *cultural adaptation* (Castro et al., 2004), and how ethnic minority participants are best recruited and retained in the study (Yancey et al., 2006). Box 27.2 lists some of the questions that may need to be addressed.

For the intervention component the main questions to be resolved is whether the recruitment approach, the delivery format and language, or the programme content should be adapted. Adaptation may be meaningful for various reasons. Minorities may differ in the salience of risk factors, requiring adaptation in the emphasis of different components of a programme. Also, ethnic groups may differ in the responsiveness to various delivery formats such as face-to-face meetings or Internet-based distance learning. Finally, similar messages of a programme may require culturally adapted packaging.

The extent to which cultural adaptation is desirable or necessary has been hotly debated amongst prevention and intervention researchers during the past 20 years. A review by Miranda et al. (2005) provides an overview of findings related to psychosocial interventions for ethnic minorities. In an informative paper, Castro et al. (2004) outline various types of mismatch between a prevention programme and its consumers, and how they may be resolved. Also, Lau (2006) discusses when and to what extent cultural adaptations of evidence-based interventions may be meaningful. Generally, however, decisions to culturally adapt programme *content* should not be taken lightly. Reviews suggest that many standardised prevention and treatment programmes are equally effective amongst minority and majority groups (Elliott and Mihalic, 2004; Wilson et al., 2003b). Also, substantive adaptations of a programme should be considered a different intervention, which requires an alteration of the basic design of your study.

Box 27.2 Questions arising from conducting an efficacy trial in an ethnically diverse context

- What is the ethnic and cultural composition of the target group?
- What specific measures are required to contact and recruit minority members for study participation?
- Does data collection (interviews, questionnaires) have to be multilingual?
- How can measurement instruments be translated to high standards?
- Are specific instruments needed to measure culture-specific patterns of response behaviour (e.g. social desirability)?
- How can cross-culturally competent interviewers be recruited and trained?
- Should interventions be modified to suit ethnic minority needs?

A second set of questions relates to the consequences of ethnic diversity for study participation, interviewer recruitment and data collection. Conclusions about different treatment effects amongst minorities and the majority are only valid if the collected data are of equally high quality for all participating groups. In ethnically and culturally diverse contexts a number of measures may be needed to achieve this goal: to the extent that minority members are less likely to participate, adapted recruitment strategies may be required; also cross-culturally competent interviewers may need to be recruited and trained; finally, one may consider translating contact material and questionnaires into different languages. Good entry points to the respective specialist resources include the *Cross-Cultural Survey Guidelines* developed by the Comparative Survey Design and Implementation (CSDI) Guidelines as well as the edited volume, *Cross-Cultural Survey Methods*, by Harkness et al. (2003).

In the z-proso study, diversity was a major issue. Data collected during the feasibility study suggested that about 56 per cent of parents in the city of Zurich had an immigrant background and that most immigrant groups were concentrated in disadvantaged neighbourhoods and had low economic and educational resources. Furthermore, a significant proportion of these parents could not be expected to read or speak German well enough to understand written information or to conduct an interview. The most important mother-languages of immigrant minorities were Albanian (9 per cent), Portuguese (7 per cent), Serbian (5 per cent), Tamil (5 per cent), Spanish (5 per cent), Turkish (5 per cent), Italian (4 per cent), and Croatian (4 per cent).

We tried to address the resulting challenges with a comprehensive package of measures. In respect of study participation and data collection it mainly comprised four components (for details, see Eisner and Parmar, 2007; Eisner and Ribeaud, 2007): (1) all contact material (i.e., letters, project information, informed consent forms) was translated into the ten languages of the most important immigrant minorities and sent out in conjunction with the respective German versions; (2) the parent questionnaire was translated into all languages using an expert team approach (Harkness, 2003: 37), and was then loaded onto the laptops so that interviewers could choose the appropriate language at the beginning of the interview; (3) bilingual and cross-culturally competent interviewers were recruited and trained for each language minority; and (4) adapted and more extensive recruitment strategies were developed to contact minority parents. As regards the delivery of the interventions the main measure consisted in

offering Turkish, Albanian, and English versions of the Triple P parent training programme. While additional efforts were made to recruit minority parents into these courses, the delivery format and the substance of the training remained unchanged.

PLANNING AND COORDINATING THE INTERVENTION

A large body of research suggests that poorly implemented interventions do not work and there is no need for more research on that issue (Dane and Schneider, 1998; Dusenbury et al., 2003b; Greenberg et al., 2005). Achieving high intervention fidelity in large-scale field trials is a demanding task: the target population is more diverse than in small-scale interventions; the programme is delivered by practitioners who have to balance various competing demands; and the intervention is received in everyday environments where many contextual factors cannot be controlled.

Researchers who want to take their own programme from the stage of an efficacy trial to an effectiveness trial need to consider that this step requires considerable additional investments. This includes a fully manualised version of an intervention, a training schedule for intervention providers, quality control and supervision mechanisms, and the production of teaching material. If researchers consider evaluating programmes developed by others it is essential to get a full picture of what is required for implementing the programme as intended by the developers. Mihalic (2004) provides a general overview of criteria for assessing implementation quality. Also, the 'Blueprints of Violence Prevention' website run by the CSVP (Center for the Study and Prevention of Violence) at the University of Colorado provides insight into the critical issues. For each of the eleven Model Programmes recommended by the CSVP a booklet details the requirements for high-quality implementation.

In the z-proso study, the challenge of achieving high implementation quality differed between the two programmes. For the parent training intervention, Triple P, we could rely on an established distributor who had experience in licensing providers. The primary task was therefore limited to selecting the ablest providers, in collaboration with Triple P Switzerland, amongst a pool of applicants. Additionally, a local supervision mechanism was set up and a researcher monitored a selection of courses.

In respect of the PATHS programme the guidance provided as part of the Blueprints of Violence Prevention initiative (Greenberg et al., 1998) was an important resource when the implementation planned. It explains, in great detail, how the teacher training should be organised, how often the programme should be delivered, and what supervision arrangements are expected. Additionally, an expert from the Netherlands, where PATHS had been introduced in the 1990s, was invited to advise the implementation team on the modalities of setting up a teacher training programme. Furthermore, the implementation team from Zurich visited PATHS schools in the Netherlands to get a real-life understanding of how the programme is run.

DATA ANALYSIS

Any properly conducted large-scale criminological field experiment will produce a large amount of data. Analysing these data adequately will require solid statistical skills. It is beyond this introduction to describe the various statistical methods that can be used to examine whether an intervention had the desired effect (but see the contributions in Piquero and Weisburd, 2010). But it is useful to summarise some of the principles that should guide outcome evaluations.

First, it is important to fully document which measurements were taken during the study and how the data were used to derive psychometric scales on, for example, parenting, impulsivity or aggressive behaviour. In the z-proso study, we produced *technical reports* that are accessible online and that describe in detail each instrument, its administration during the study, and its psychometric properties.

Second, how participants were allocated to treatment conditions, what proportion of the target group initially participated in the study (study participation rate), and what proportion of initial participants dropped out of the study at various stages (attrition rate) will need to be documented carefully. In the z-proso study we used the suggestions included in the CONSORT statements (Altman, 2001; Campbell, 2004) about how this information can be presented transparently in flow diagrams that document the participation and attrition rates at the various stages of an experimental study. As part of these analyses you will usually also assess whether the randomisation was successful; that is, whether treatment groups were equivalent.

Third, any empirical analysis of an effectiveness or dissemination trial should comprise a detailed report on how the treatments were delivered, how treatment fidelity varied, and what factors may have influenced the dose and quality of programme delivery. Such analyses are particularly important in large-scale field trials. For example, in the z-proso study only about 25 per cent of the parents who were offered the free parent training programme effectively attended the course. While this is better than the participation rates reported in many other similar studies, it required an analysis of who participated in the intervention and how recruitment into similar programmes could be improved in the future. Respective analyses suggested that participating parents were more likely to live in breadwinner families, to be of Swiss rather than immigrant background, and to be highly integrated in neighbourhood networks. Such findings can subsequently help to learn about shortcomings in the recruitment process and to develop policy recommendations about how specific target groups could be reached.

Analyses of the treatment effects themselves can often be sub-divided into two stages. The core stage relates to analyses of whether the intervention had the expected effects on proximal or distal outcomes for all participants who were originally allocated to the treatment conditions; that is, without excluding non-compliant cases or subgroups who received only parts of the planned intervention (Boruch, 1997: 201). These so-called *intention-to-treat (ITT) analyses* are critically important in efficacy and dissemination trials because they provide policy makers and practitioners with the realistic estimates of what effects can be expected in the wider population, if the treatment was disseminated as delivered in the trial. In order to be unbiased, ITT analyses need to be conducted and published on all outcomes where effects were initially expected. In a subsequent stage researchers may wish to examine the extent to which the intervention effects were contingent on factors such as treatment fidelity, background characteristics of groups of participants, or the presence of certain components of an intervention.

RESEARCH ETHICS

Randomised criminological field trials touch on almost every domain of research ethics. Ethical questions need to be addressed on at least four levels: (1) the selection of the intervention; (2) the randomised allocation to treatment conditions; (3) the collection and storage of data; and (4) the analysis and publication of the findings. Thus, large-scale trials are only appropriate in situations where there is sufficient prior research suggesting consistent positive effects and there is no evidence suggesting negative effects. Random allocation to treatment conditions is an ethical issue that is often raised by policy makers and occasionally by study participants. Weisburd (2003) makes an ethical case for randomised trials in criminological and criminal justice research. Further, researchers need to develop comprehensive plans on how to comply with confidentiality and data protection requirements, and how informed consent is sought and obtained. Also, one needs to carefully consider the health and safety of hired interviewers involved in the data collection. In the z-proso study, for example, interviewers had detailed written instructions about situations when they were *not* allowed to conduct interviews, and contingency plans were put in place in the case of any safety threats to the interviewing staff.

Finally, researchers need to develop a plan about how to present and report research findings in such a way that other researchers, policy makers and practitioners get a full picture of study outcomes. Unbiased information is a thorny issue in efficacy and dissemination trials. Interests from policy makers, programme developers, stakeholders and practitioners will often stack up in favour of positive findings. Researchers should therefore protect themselves against the potential impact of wishful thinking on their analyses and findings. For example, they may write a plan for the data analysis before the experiment begins, and have the analytic plan reviewed by an expert in the field. Also, researchers should prepare themselves for the possibility of finding adverse effects and think about how they would be communicated. McCord's (2003) overview of the Cambridge-Somerville Youth Study is a telling reminder that even well-designed and theory-based interventions sometimes do have negative effects, and that communicating such findings requires a lot of personal and academic integrity.

The most salient ethical issue we encountered in the z-proso study related to the publication and interpretation of research findings. To our disappointment we found no evidence in support of positive effects of the parent training intervention Triple P on children's problem behaviour (Malti et al. in print). This is in contrast to much previous research on Triple P, part of which was conducted with similar target populations and comparable study designs (for an overview, see Nowak and Heinrichs, 2008). After the results of the z-proso study had been verified using different approaches, it was therefore important to find out why.

We adopted two approaches to this problem. First, when publishing the findings related to the parent training component of the trial we took care to present all relevant details regarding the study design, the implementation of the intervention, the outcome measurement, and the approach to statistical analysis. This allowed readers to assess whether there are any major flaws in the z-proso study that may explain the lack of effects. Also, both in discussion with policy makers and in academic publications we tried to highlight any limitation of the z-proso study that may have been responsible for the lack of positive effects.

However, our interpretation of findings is that the study design of z-proso is sound. The lack of positive effects is a true statement about the study population rather than an artefact of the study. Eisner (2009) therefore suggested that it might be possible that evaluations conducted by the programme developers are subject to a number of subtle biases which result from the conflict between the role of neutral scientific observer and the material or immaterial interests as programme developer. The hypothesis has led to a lively academic debate (Olds, 2009; Sherman and Strang, 2009), which highlights the ethical requirements and potential conflicts that researchers who conduct an experimental study may experience.

CONCLUSION

For various reasons, large-scale field trials that empirically examine the effectiveness of criminal justice or psychosocial interventions in real-life settings are likely to become even more important than they are to date. While meta-analyses and systematic reviews in several research fields demonstrate that some types of interventions can be effective, there is also widespread recognition that we do not yet understand how such effects can be transported into real-life settings, and how effects can be maintained over time (Welsh et al., 2010). In addition to evidence-based programmes there is therefore a need for evidence-based dissemination. The past 20 years have seen the introduction, in many Western countries, of recommendation lists or accreditation procedures for preventative or therapeutic programmes. Demonstration of effectiveness in at least one independent large-scale dissemination trial is increasingly becoming a critical requirement for inclusion in such lists. Many programmes and strategies still fail this test, meaning that there remains considerable work to be done. There is still a considerable lack of large-scale effectiveness and diffusion trials in places other than the US and the extent to which findings of effective interventions can be generalised across countries is still largely unknown and requires further efforts (see box 27.3).

Box 27.3   In the beginning – a starter kit

Researchers who contemplate conducting a criminological field trial for the first time should be aware that they will have to find solutions to many issues as they go along. However, many mistakes can be avoided if researchers acquire good knowledge, before the start of study, in the following four areas.

First, you will need to understand the logic of experimental and non-experimental designs as a way to draw correct conclusions about the causal effects of an intervention. There exist excellent introductions to evaluation research in the social sciences. We recommend the great book *Experimental and Quasi-Experimental Designs for Generalized Causal Inference* by Shadish et al. (2002). In conjunction novices should also have the newest edition of Rossi et al. (2004) *Evaluation: A Systematic Approach.* It guides students through all the methodological steps of an evaluation study including the selection of programmes, their implementation, and the measurement of effects.

Second, researchers need to become familiar with all substantive research in their targeted intervention domain; for example, on the developmental risk factors implied in the causation of conduct problems, the mechanisms of policing, or the processes associated with persistence and desistance amongst serious offenders. Also, you should acquire a solid understanding of what is already known as regards effective prevention and intervention programmes. The volume by Sherman et al. (2002) on *Evidence-Based Crime Prevention* still provides valuable overviews for most types of criminological interventions, but researchers should also familiarise themselves with specialist systematic reviews such as the reports conducted for the Crime and Justice Group of the Campbell Collaboration.

Third, practical things such as collecting data, conducting interviews, coordinating a team of researchers, and implementing interventions need to be understood. The monograph by Boruch (1997) (*Randomized Experiments for Planning and Evaluation: A Practical Guide*) is a useful resource to understand how to see through an experimental field study. In studies with a significant number of interviews, *Data Collection and Management: A Practical Guide* by Stouthamer-Loeber and van Kammen (1995) is invaluable. Finally, researchers should develop a good understanding of the practical challenges associated with delivering an intervention with fidelity at a larger scale. Good overviews of the issues that require consideration can be found in Rohrbach et al. (2006), Elliot and Mihalic (2004), Domitrovich and Greenberg (2000) and Durlak and DuPre (2008).

Over the past ten years professional bodies have developed valuable guidelines and checklists. We mention two that are particularly useful. First, the Committee on Law and Justice of the US National Research Council published a report in 2005 entitled *Improving Evaluation of Anti-crime Programs (National Research Council, 2005).* It provides methodological and practical guidance about how to design and implement evaluation research 'in a manner that provides valid and useful results of sufficient quality to be relied upon by policy makers' (Lipsey et al., 2006: 272). Also, the Society of Prevention Research has developed standards for identifying effective prevention programmes (Flay et al., 2005). These 'Standards of Evidence' specify methodological criteria to establish whether an intervention had desirable effects at the level of efficacy trials, effectiveness trials and dissemination trials.

Additional useful web-links

Campbell Collaboration: http://www.campbellcollaboration.org/
Consort Statement: http://www.consort-statement.org
Cross-Cultural Survey Guidelines: http://ccsg.isr.umich.edu/index.cfm

---

REFERENCES

Altman, D.G. (2001). The revised CONSORT statement for reporting randomized trials: explanation and elaboration. *Annals of Internal Medicine, 134*(8), 663.

Beelmann, A., and Lösel, F. (2006). Child social skills training in developmental crime prevention: Effects on antisocial behavior and social competence. *Psycothema, 18*(3), 603–610.

Bickman, L. (1987). The functions of program theory. *New Directions for Program Evaluation, 1987*(33), 5–18.

Boruch, R. (1997). *Randomized Experiments for Planning and Evaluation: A Practical Guide.* Applied Social Research Method Series, No 44. Thousand Oaks: Sage.

Braga, A. (2005). Hot spots policing and crime prevention: A systematic review of randomized controlled trials. *Journal of Experimental Criminology, 1*(3), 317–342.

Campbell, D.T. (1959). Convergent and discriminant validation by the multitrait-multimethod matrix. *Psychological Bulletin, 56*(2), 81.

Campbell, M.K. (2004). CONSORT statement: extension to cluster randomised trials. *British Medical Journal (Clinical Research Edition), 328*(7441), 702.

Castro, F.G., Barrera, M., and Martinez, C.R. (2004). The cultural adaptation of prevention interventions: Resolving tensions between fidelity and fit. *Prevention Science, 5*(1), 41–45.

Cohen, J. (1988). *Statistical Power Analysis for the Behavioral Sciences.* New York: Academic Press.

Dane, A.V., and Schneider, B.H. (1998). Program integrity in primary and early secondary prevention: are implementation effects out of control. *Clinical Psychology Review*, *18*(1), 23–45.

Domitrovich, C.E., and Greenberg, M.T. (2000). The study of implementation: Current findings from effective programs that prevent mental disorders in school-aged children. *Journal of Educational and Psychological Consultation*, *11*(2), 193–221.

Durlak, J., and DuPre, E. (2008). Implementation matters: A review of research on the influence of implementation on program outcomes and the factors affecting implementation. *American Journal of Community Psychology*, *41*(3), 327–350.

Dusenbury, L., Brannigan, R., Falco, M., and Hansen, W.B. (2003). A review of research on fidelity of implementation: implications for drug abuse prevention in school settings. *Health Education Research*, *18*(2), 237–256.

Eisner, M. (2009). No effects in independent prevention trials: can we reject the cynical view? *Journal of Experimental Criminology*, *5*(2), 163–183.

Eisner, M., Meidert, U., Ribeaud, D., and Malti, T. (2011). From enrollment to utilization – stages of parental engagement in a universal parent training program. *Journal of Primary Prevention*, *32*, 83–93.

Eisner, M., Nagin, D.S., Ribeaud, D., and Malti, T. (submitted). Effects of a universal parenting program for highly adherent parents: A Propensity Score Matching Approach.

Eisner, M., and Parmar, A. (2007). Doing criminological research in ethnically and culturally diverse contexts. In R.D. King and E. Wincup (eds) *Doing Research on Crime and Justice* (pp. 171–199). Oxford: Oxford University Press.

Eisner, M., and Ribeaud, D. (2005). A randomised field experiment to prevent violence: The Zurich Intervention and Prevention Project at Schools, ZIPPS. *European Journal of Crime, Criminal Law and Criminal Justice*, *13*(1), 27–43.

Eisner, M., and Ribeaud, D. (2007). Conducting a criminological survey in a culturally diverse context. *European Journal of Criminology*, *4*(3), 271–298.

Elliott, D.S., and Mihalic, S.F. (2004). Issues in disseminating and replicating effective prevention programs. *Prevention Science*, *5*(1), 47–53.

Farrington, D.P. (1983). Randomized experiments on crime and justice. In M. Tonry and N. Morris (eds) *Crime and Justice*, Vol. 4 (pp. 257–308). Chicago: Chicago University Press.

Farrington, D.P., and Welsh, B.C. (2003). Family-based prevention of offending: A meta-analysis. *Australian and New Zealand Journal of Criminology*, *36*(2), 127–151.

Farrington, D.P., and Welsh, B.C. (2005). Randomized experiments in criminology: What have we learned in the last two decades? *Journal of Experimental Criminology*, *1*(1), 9–38.

Farrington, D.P., and Welsh, B.C. (2006). A half century of randomized experiments on crime and justice. *Crime and Justice*, *34*(1), 55–132.

Flay, B.R. (1986). Efficacy and effectiveness trials (and other phases of research) in the development of health promotion programs. *Preventive Medicine*, *15*(5), 451–474.

Flay, B.R., Biglan, A., Boruch, R., Castro, F., Gottfredson, D., Kellam, S. et al. (2005). Standards of evidence: Criteria for efficacy, effectiveness and dissemination. *Prevention Science*, *6*(3), 151–175.

Glasgow, R.E., Lichtenstein, E., and Marcus, A.C. (2003). Why don't we see more translation of health promotion research to practice? Rethinking the efficacy-to-effectiveness transition. *American Journal of Public Health*, 93(8), 1261–1267.

Goodman, R.M. (2000). Bridging the gap in effective program implementation: From concept to application. *Journal of Community Psychology*, *28*(3), 309–321.

Gottfredson, D., Kumpfer, K., Polizzi-Fox, D., Wilson, D., Puryear, V., Beatty, P. et al. (2006). The Strengthening Washington D.C. Families project: A randomized effectiveness trial of family-based prevention. *Prevention Science*, *7*(1), 57–74.

Greenberg, M.T., Domitrovich, C.E., Graczyk, P.A., and Zins, J.E. (2005). *The Study of Implementation in School-Based Preventive Interventions: Theory, Research, and Practice*, Vol. 3. Rockville: Center for Mental Health Services, Substance Abuse and Mental Health Services Administration.

Greenberg, M.T., Kusché, C.A., and Mihalic, S.F. (1998). *Blueprints for Violence Prevention, Book Ten: Promoting Alternative Thinking Strategies (PATHS).* Boulder, CO: Center for the Study and Prevention of Violence.

Harkness, J.A. (2003). Questionnaire translation. In J.A. Harkness, F.J.R. van de Vijver and P.P. Mohler (eds) *Cross-Cultural Survey Methods* (pp. 35–57). New York: John Wiley.

Harkness, J.A., Van de Vijver, F.J.R., and Mohler, P.P. (eds) (2003). *Cross-Cultural Survey Methods.* New York: John Wiley.

Hawkins, D.J., Catalano, R.F., and Arthur, M. (2002). Promoting science-based prevention in communities. *Addictive Behaviors*, *27*(6), 951–976.

Kusche, C.A., and Greenberg, M.T. (1994). *The PATHS Curriculum.* Seattle: Developmental Research and Programs.

Lau, A.S. (2006). Making the case for selective and directed cultural adaptations of evidence-based treatments: Examples from parent training. *Clinical Psychology: Science and Practice*, *13*(4), 295–310.

Lipsey, M.W. (1995). What do we learn from 400 research studies on the effectiveness of treatment with juvenile delinquents? In J. McGuire (ed.) *What works? Reducing Reoffending* (pp. 63–78). New York: John Wiley.

Lipsey, M.W., Petrie, C., Weisburd, D., and Gottfredson, D. (2006). Improving evaluation of anti-crime programs: Summary of a National Research Council report. *Journal of Experimental Criminology*, *2*(3), 271–307.

Malti, T., Ribeaud, D. and M. Eisner (in print). The effectiveness of two universal preventive interventions in reducing children's externalizing behavior: A cluster randomized controlled trial. *Journal of Clinical Child and Adolescent Psychology.*

McCord, J. (2003). Cures that harm: Unanticipated outcomes of crime prevention programs. *The ANNALS of the American Academy of Political and Social Science*, *587*(1), 16–30.

Mihalic, S.F. (2004). The importance of implementation fidelity. *Emotional and Behavioral Disorders In Youth*, *4*, 83–105.

Miranda, J., Bernal, G., Lau, A., Kohn, L., Hwang, W.-C., and LaFromboise, T. (2005). State of the science on psychosocial interventions for ethnic minorities. *Annual Review of Clinical Psychology*, *1*, 113–142.

National Research Council (2005). Improving Evaluation of Anticrime Programs, Committee on Improving Anticrime Programs, Committee on Law and Justice, Division of Behavioral and Social Sciences and Education. Washington, D.C.: National Academy Press, 2005.

Nowak, C., and Heinrichs, N. (2008). A comprehensive meta-analysis of Triple p-positive parenting program using hierarchical linear modeling: effectiveness and moderating variables. *Clinical Child and Family Psychology Review*, *11*(3), 114–144.

Olds, D.L. (2002). Prenatal and infancy home visiting by nurses: From randomized trials to community replication. *Prevention Science*, *3*(3), 153–172.

Olds, D.L. (2009). In support of disciplined passion. *Journal of Experimental Criminology*, *5*(2), 201–214.

Patton, G., Bond, L., Butler, H., and Glover, S. (2003). Changing schools, changing health? design and implementation of the Gatehouse Project. *Journal of Adolescent Health*, *33*(4), 231–239.

Petrosino, A., and Soydan, H. (2005). The impact of program developers as evaluators on criminal recidivism: Results from meta-analyses of experimental and quasi-experimental research. *Journal of Experimental Criminology*, *1*(4), 435–450.

Piquero, A.R, Farrington, D.P., Welsh, B.C., Tremblay, R., and Jennings, W. (2009). Effects of early family/parent training programs on antisocial behavior and delinquency. *Journal of Experimental Criminology*, *5*(2), 83–120.

Piquero, A.R., and Weisburd, D. (eds) (2010). *Handbook of Quantitative Criminology*. New York: Springer.

Rogers, P.J., Petrosino, A., Huebner, T.A., and Hacsi, T.A. (2000). Program theory evaluation: Practice, promise, and problems. *New Directions for Evaluation*, *2000*(87), 5–13.

Rohrbach, L.A., Grana, R., Sussman, S., and Valente, T.W. (2006). Type II translation: transporting prevention interventions from research to real-world settings. *Evaluation and Health Professions*, *29*(3), 302–333.

Rossi, P.H., Lipsey, M., and Freeman, H.E. (2004). *Evaluation: A Systematic Approach*, 7th edition. Beverly Hills: Sage.

Sanders, M.R. (1992). *Every Parent: A Positive Guide to Children's Behavior*. Sydney: Addison-Wesley.

Sanders, M.R. (1999). Triple P-Positive Parenting Program: Towards an empirically validated multilevel parenting and family support strategy for the prevention of behaviour and emotional problems in children. *Clinical Child and Family Psychology Review*, *2*(2), 71–89.

Schoenwald, S.K., and Hoagwood, K. (2001). Effectiveness, transportability, and dissemination of interventions: What matters when? *Psychiatric Services*, *52*(9), 1190–1197.

Shadish, W.R., Cook, T.D., and Campbell, D.T. (2002). *Experimental and Quasi-Experimental Designs for Generalized Causal Inference*. Boston: Houghton-Mifflin.

Sherman, L.W., Farrington, D.P., Welsh, B.C., and MacKenzie, D.L. (eds) (2002). *Evidence-Based Crime Prevention*. London: Routledge.

Sherman, L.W., and Strang, H. (2009). Testing for analysts' bias in crime prevention experiments: Can we accept Eisner's one-tailed test? *Journal of Experimental Criminology*, *5*(2), 185–200.

Sherman, L.W., Strang, H., Angel, C., Woods, D., Barnes, G.C., Bennett, S. et al. (2005). Effects of face-to-face restorative justice on victims of crime in four randomized, controlled trials. *Journal of Experimental Criminology*, *1*(3), 367–395.

Spoth, R., Greenberg, M., Bierman, K., and Redmond, C. (2004). PROSPER community–university partnership model for public education systems: Capacity-building for evidence-based, competence-building prevention. *Prevention Science*, *5*(1), 31–39.

Stouthamer-Loeber, M., and van Kammen, W.B. (1995). *Data Collection and Management: A Practical Guide*. Thousand Oaks: Sage.

Timmons-Mitchell, J., Bender, M.B., Kishna, M.A., and Mitchell, C.C. (2006). An independent effectiveness trial of multisystemic therapy with juvenile justice youth. *Journal of Clinical Child and Adolescent Psychology*, *35*(2), 227–236.

Weisburd, D. (2000). Randomized experiments in criminal justice policy: Prospects and problems. *Crime and Delinquency*, *46*(2), 181–193.

Weisburd, D. (2003). Ethical practice and evaluation of interventions in crime and justice: The moral imperative for randomized trials. *Evaluation Review*, *27*(3), 336–354.

Weisburd, D. (2005). Hot spots policing experiments and criminal justice research: Lessons from the field. *The ANNALS of the American Academy of Political and Social Science*, *599*(1), 220–245.

Weisburd, D., and Taxman, F.S. (2000). Developing a multicenter randomized trial in criminology: The case of HIDTA. *Journal of Quantitative Criminology*, *16*(3), 315–340.

Welsh, B.C., Sullivan, C.J., and Olds, D.L. (2010). When early crime prevention goes to scale: A new look at the evidence. *Prevention Science*, *11*(2), 115–125.

Wilson, S.J., Lipsey, M.W., and Derzon, J.H. (2003a). The effects of school-based intervention programs on aggressive behavior: A meta-analysis. *Journal of Consulting and Clinical Psychology, 71*(1), 136–149.

Wilson, S.J., Lipsey, M.W., and Soydan, H. (2003b). Are mainstream programs for juvenile delinquency less effective with minority youth than majority youth? A meta-analysis

of outcomes research. *Research on Social Work Practice, 13*(1), 2–26.

Yancey, A.K., Ortega, A.N., and Kumanyika, S.K. (2006). Effective recruitment and retention of minority research participants. *Annual Review of Public Health, 27*(1), 1–28.

28

Meta-Analysis as a Method of Systematic Reviews

Martin Schmucker, Friedrich Lösel

NARRATIVE LITERATURE REVIEWS AND THE ADVENT OF META-ANALYSIS

Although developmental crime prevention is becoming an increasingly important topic within criminology, two classic studies stick out as landmarks: one is the High/Scope Perry Preschool Project (Schweinhart et al., 1993, 2005); the other is the Cambridge-Somerville Youth Study (McCord, 1978, 2003). These projects evaluated the efficacy of prevention programmes from childhood onwards into middle adulthood. Both studies are not only outstanding with regard to the length of follow-up, but also for their methodological quality. Both used randomized control trials (RCTs).

The High/Scope Perry Preschool Project targeted three- to five-year-olds from high-risk areas at Ypsilanti (Michigan). It combined daily education and cognitive stimulation of the children in a preschool with a parent training and weekly home visits over approximately two years. Evaluations that tracked participants through to age 40 showed desirable effects, not only on crime indicators such as lower arrest rates, but also on intellectual competencies, income, home ownership and other markers of positive development.

The Harvard-based Cambridge-Somerville Youth Study addressed boys between five and thirteen years and their families in deprived urban areas of Massachusetts. The programme lasted five years and contained regular home visits and family counselling, academic tutoring, medical assistance, sports groups, summer camps and other community measures to prevent anti-social development. The findings in middle adulthood, however, were disappointing. With respect to criminality, alcohol abuse, family problems, mental illnesses and early deaths it revealed either no significant differences or even slightly more problems among the treatment group relative to the randomized control group.

It is not clear why these two outstanding studies had such conflicting results. Research suggests that numerous variables may lead to different outcomes of similar interventions, for example the content of the programmes; integrity/quality of implementation; risk level and age of participants; proportion of dropouts; sample size; evaluation design; features of the control condition; type of outcome measures; characteristics, training and supervision of staff; relations between staff and clients; and the involvement of the researchers in programme development and delivery (Lipsey and Wilson, 1998; Lösel, 2007a). Whether one or the other factor is relevant for outcome variation cannot be clarified by only comparing two studies. It requires a broader knowledge about the research findings in the respective field and, in particular, a systematic review and comparison of as many relevant studies as available.

Traditionally, such research syntheses have been carried out as narrative literature reviews. Although this approach is still most widely used and appropriate in areas with only a few relevant studies, it typically contains at least four key shortcomings. First, and most importantly, narrative literature reviews are subject to bias. A reviewer who is biased towards specific theoretical concepts, interventions, authors, research designs, and so on, may rigorously criticise studies that reach unwanted conclusions and not criticise other studies that reach more palatable conclusions in line with his/her biases. Second, narrative reviews rarely detail the methods used to search the literature, often fail to explain why studies were included or excluded, concentrate primarily on easily available journals and books in English, and are frequently one-off exercises that soon become out of date. In the case of biased study selection, such reviews often fail to adequately represent the breadth of the research on the respective topic. This is sometimes referred to as the 'file-drawer problem', an issue we return to later in this chapter. Third, narrative reviews tend also to describe studies and outcomes one by one. To the extent that there is an attempt to synthesize results, this is often done using a 'vote-counting' or 'box-counting' method that counts the number of statistically significant or non-significant results out of the number of tests. Counting only statistically significant results ignores issues of effect size and practical significance. Because statistical power is inversely related to sample size, there could be a number of small-scale studies that all point in a desirable direction but do not reach an agreed level of significance. However, were these samples to be merged, one might discover an important and highly significant effect. Finally, narrative reviews often fail to address interaction effects between programme features, offender characteristics, variables of the social context, and so forth.

Of course, traditional narrative research reviews vary in quality and some of the above-mentioned problems reflect insufficient practice rather than the review method per se (e.g. Cook and Leviton, 1980). However, only recently have criminologists started to show greater awareness of the basic prerequisites of sound literature reviews. This is due to the increasing dissemination of systematic review methods and, in particular, meta-analyses. A meta-analysis is a scientific approach for integrating the empirical evidence on a specific topic in a systematic, representative and transparent manner by using quantitative techniques. It is not a single method but a perspective with various techniques of measurement and statistical analysis (Cooper et al., 2009). Typically, meta-analyses contain a precise definition of the respective topic, a systematic and comprehensive search for primary studies, a reliable coding of the methodological and content characteristics of the single studies, a computation and integration of effect sizes, an analysis of relations between study characteristics and effect size, and a transparent presentation of findings. These procedures will be described in detail later in the chapter.

Meta-analyses were introduced in the late 1970s (Glass, 1976; Smith and Glass, 1977) and since then have been widely applied on both intervention and correlation studies. Psychology, medicine, economics, education and other disciplines quickly adopted meta-analytic methods. There were also early applications on criminological topics, particularly with respect to the effects of offender treatment (e.g. Andrews et al., 1990; Garrett, 1985; Gottschalk et al., 1987; Lipsey, 1988; Lösel et al., 1987). However, it took more than a decade until meta-analytic reviews became widespread in other areas of criminology. The Campbell Collaboration has played an important role in this development.

The Campbell Collaboration is an international bottom-up initiative of researchers that was established in 2000 (Farrington and Petrosino, 2001; Petrosino et al., 2001). It is named after the founder of modern evaluation research who urged the research community and policy makers to conceive 'reforms as experiments' (Campbell, 1969). In this spirit, the Campbell Collaboration aims to promote evidence-based policy and practice by systematic reviews in three areas: crime and justice, education and social welfare. The Campbell Collaboration (C2) follows the model of the Cochrane Collaboration (C1) in medicine. Named after the British epidemiologist Archibald Cochrane, C1 aims 'to help people make well-informed decisions about healthcare by preparing, maintaining and promoting the accessibility of systematic reviews of the effects of healthcare interventions' (Chalmers, 1993). Within a little more than a decade the Cochrane Library and Register became the best international evidence on effective healthcare. The famous *Lancet* journal even sees the Cochrane Collaboration as an enterprise 'that rivals the Humane Genome Project in its potential implications for modern medicine'.

The Campbell Collaboration has not yet reached such a status. However, it has successfully developed an infrastructure that initiates, coordinates, supervises and disseminates systematic reviews on many topics. For example, the Campbell Crime and Justice Coordinating Group edited systematic reviews on the effects of cognitive–behavioural programmes for criminal offenders (Lipsey et al., 2007), closed-circuit television surveillance on crime (Welsh and Farrington, 2008), custodial *versus* non-custodial sentences (Killias et al., 2006), anti-bullying programmes (Farrington and Ttofi, 2009), hot spots policing (Braga, 2007), mentoring programmes for the prevention of juvenile delinquency (Tolan et al., 2008), correctional boot camps (Wilson et al., 2005), and other topics (see www.campbellcollaboration.org). Reviews also showed a lack of methodologically sound studies in areas such as counter-terrorism strategies (Lum et al., 2006) and non-custodial employment programmes (Visher et al., 2006).

This function of detecting a shortage of sound research in specific areas is also an important aim of systematic reviews that should lead to more and more appropriate primary studies.

Campbell reviews quickly became a model for systematic reviews in criminology. As far as possible they concentrate on high-quality studies, include published as well as unpublished studies, have an international scope, undergo rigorous peer review, are transparent and objective, and aim for regular updates. However, there is also an increase in the use of criminological meta-analyses outside the Campbell Collaboration. Similar to Campbell reviews, many of these address measures of prevention and intervention. For example, Wilson et al. (2003) analyzed the effectiveness of school-based interventions against anti-social behaviour and Mitchell et al. (2007) reviewed custodial drug programmes. Another area of meta-analyses is prediction. Leistico et al. (2008), for example, reviewed the relationship between psychopathy and recidivism/institutional refractions, whereas Hubbard and Pratt (2002) studied predictors of delinquency among girls. Meta-analyses are also used for criminological theory testing. For example, Pratt and Cullen (2000) addressed Gottfredson and Hirschi's self-control theory and Ortiz and Raine (2004) reviewed studies on the relationship between heart rate level and anti-social behaviour that is relevant for neurobiological theories.

These and many other examples demonstrate that meta-analysis became an important method in criminology and related areas (Lösel, 2008; Pratt, 2010). Therefore, this chapter will present the method in some detail. We will now describe the steps needed to undertake sound systematic reviews in criminology and address both technical issues of methodology, as well as the many decisions that are required in a meta-analysis.

CARRYING OUT A META-ANALYSIS

Typically, meta-analyses contain the following steps:

1 development of the research question and the definition of the relevant concepts;
2 searching for relevant studies that fit the definition;
3 coding of studies with respect to both their characteristics and outcomes;
4 quantitative analysis of the data, both to integrate study results (mean effects) as well as differentiate study results (moderating effects); and
5 interpretation and reporting with regard to different audiences (e.g., researchers, practitioners, policy makers).

In this section we illustrate each of these steps in detail. We also discuss the pros and cons of different strategies and the pitfalls that have to be taken into account when conducting a meta-analysis. We draw mainly on our meta-analysis of the effectiveness of sexual offender treatment (Lösel and Schmucker, 2005) to exemplify the decisions that have to be taken at the different stages of the meta-analysis process.

Development of the research question

As with any research, before conducting a meta-analysis the researcher has to define what he/she aims to investigate. This includes the formulation of the principle research question (e.g., 'How effective is the treatment of sexual offenders?'), setting the inclusion criteria for selecting relevant studies and possible intervening variables. Each of the concepts included in the research question – in this instance, 'effectiveness', 'treatment' and 'sexual offenders' – has to be carefully defined by the meta-analyst in order to avoid confusion of terms in all subsequent procedures and decisions.

However, a meta-analysis has to take some limitations into account. By drawing on already available research, those conducting meta-analyses are not as free as those conducting primary research to define their variables. A meta-analysis must deploy constructs consistent with the ways in which they have been used in primary research studies. Accordingly, a meta-analyst has to be sufficiently familiar with the primary research in the respective domain before he/she writes a protocol for the analysis. Even then it might still be necessary to refine definitions at later stages in order to fully capture the relevant pre-existing primary research.

Setting the inclusion criteria

The inclusion criteria have to make clear which studies are eligible for the meta-analysis and which are not. Apart from defining the content of the studies this also refers to methodological aspects such as study design or measures used and general features such as time frame. As an example, in our meta-analysis on the effectiveness of treatment for sexual offenders we used the following eligibility criteria. The study must

1 deal with sexual offenders;
2 evaluate treatment;
3 apply recidivism as an outcome measure;
4 include a control group;
5 have a sample size of 10 or greater; and
6 provide sufficient data for effect size computation.

There were no explicit restrictions regarding time and location of the study, although there may have been implicit restrictions due to the availability of some studies in literature databases and the like.

The first two criteria refer to the basic research question. The other criteria set methodological standards. Each of these inclusion criteria needed to be defined in order to be applicable. We cannot detail all of those criteria here, but highlight some thoughts about the importance of a thorough definition of the concepts. For example, there are many interventions for sexual offenders that would not strictly fall under the category treatment, like measures of diversion or pure deterrence. These have to be clearly distinguished. At the same time, the focus of our meta-analysis was on the effects on re-offending. So we included evaluation studies on therapeutic interventions as long as they aimed at reducing re-offending. Other treatments are not specific for sexual offenders but include sexual offenders among others. We decided that such evaluation studies should be included if they reported results for sexual offenders separately. Regarding outcome measures we restricted these to re-offending. Offender treatment may not directly influence re-offending but rather intervening variables like anti-social attitudes, coping strategies or empathy. We did not include measures of such intervening variables. A treatment may effectively increase empathy, for example, but if this does not translate into less re-offending, the aim of the treatment would not have been achieved. However, we included different measures of recidivism such as official convictions and arrests as well as self reported data.

A difficulty that can occur in research integrations has been metaphorically labeled as the 'apples and oranges' problem or, in a more scientific manner, the 'incommensurability problem' (Glass and Kliegl, 1983, Sharpe, 1997). This is the problem of integrating studies that deal with rather different issues. When defining the constructs in a meta-analysis one has to deal with the question of whether the primary studies provide answers to a meaningful research question. The pioneering meta-analysis on the effectiveness of psychotherapy by Smith and Glass (1977) has been criticized as being too broad because it included all sorts of psychotherapy for all sorts of clients and data on all sorts of outcome. Indeed, different psychotherapeutic approaches work differently and vary in their results, especially with respect to different mental disorders. The apples and oranges metaphor, however, lends itself to a more detailed look at the problem. Of course, apples and oranges are not the same, but they are both fruits. On the other hand, even apples are different from each other. So the basic question is: how broadly or narrowly defined should the constructs be in order to render meaningful results? There is no simple answer to this question. The very general question of whether psychotherapy works may be useful, for example, when considering its funding in the healthcare system. However, in the case of broadly defined constructs a meta-analyst should be aware that a closer look may reveal systematic differences in the results of the integrated studies. Meta-analysts should always check whether the studies provide a homogenous result pattern and, furthermore, what characteristics have led to differences in results. In fact, such analyses often give valuable clues as to the relevant distinguishing features. Or to stay in the metaphor, they help answer the question: In what ways do apples and oranges differ?

In our meta-analysis on the effectiveness of sexual offender treatment we defined sexual offending broadly to include offenses as diverse as rape, child molestation and exhibitionism. This broad definition conformed well with the definitions used in most primary studies. It also conformed with the reality of treatment; that is, that most treatment programmes for sexual offenders treat different types of sexual offenders together. However, to avoid inappropriate merging of different categories we examined offense types as a moderating variable. The same holds for our definition of the treatment procedures. These were quite diverse and ranged from psychotherapy to organic surgery and medication. For the general question of whether therapy for sexual offenders works, the integration of such diverse treatment modalities is defensible. Yet again, the meta-analysis would be incomprehensive if it did not investigate potential differences in the effectiveness of different measures.

Study quality

Apart from defining the content of the integrated studies the inclusion criteria have to address the validity of the studies. The results of a meta-analysis can only be as valid as the body of integrated studies. Or as Eysenck (1978) put it: 'Garbage in – garbage out.' A meta-analysis has to define appropriate standards in study quality.

In their classic work on quasi-experimentation, Cook and Campbell (1979) provided an invaluable collection of threats to validity. The more such threats are present the less one can assume a causal relationship between the independent and dependent variables. Although the scheme of Cook and Campbell may be too differentiated to be regularly used in meta-analyses (Wortmann, 1994) it has successfully been employed in some studies (e.g. Lösel and Köferl, 1989) and has guided the development of rating schemes.

Although some discussions of research designs suggest the contrary, there is no clear-cut line between 'good' *versus* 'bad' design quality. In fact, the 'perfect study' may not even exist. Rather the validity of studies lies on a continuum from 'not interpretable at all' to 'perfectly interpretable'. There are a number of schemes that address this continuum (see Farrington, 2003; Moher et al., 1995; Moyer and Finney, 2005; Wortmann, 1994). Defining minimum quality standards as inclusion criteria for a meta-analysis requires a cut-off point that separates studies that are reasonably good from those that are not. In fields that are extensively researched one may be able to define a conservative threshold and restrict integration to studies of the highest quality, namely RCTs (e.g., Lösel and Beelmann, 2003, on the effects of child skills training on anti-social behavior). However, even then there remains the problem that the quality of studies cannot always be reduced to one dimension (Valentine, 2009). For example, if two experiments on a correctional treatment programme use very different outcome indicators (e.g., official recidivism *versus* personality scales) and points of assessment (e.g. at the end of imprisonment *versus* long-term follow up) issues of measurement validity may become as important as randomization. In addition, drawing only on very strictly defined high-quality studies may result in a study pool that does not allow for any reasonable analysis. For example, a meta-analysis by White et al. (2005) on sexual offender treatment ended up with only three studies because they restricted their integration to RCTs. Although this is a relevant finding (too few randomized trials on sexual offender treatment), it does not provide much information of use for either treatment practice or theory.

In our meta-analysis on sexual offender treatment we used an adapted version of the Maryland Scale of Scientific Rigor (Sherman et al., 1997) to define study quality. Our adaptation emphasized the presence and adequacy of a control group and identified five categories:

1 no control or comparison group;
2 non-equivalent control or comparison group: There are differences on important variables between the treated and comparison groups which are not controlled for (e.g., subjects who refuse any treatment as comparison group);
3 control or comparison group with no reason for assuming differences related to recidivism between groups or sound statistical control of such differences;
4 systematic strategy to attain equivalence of control or comparison group (e.g., individual matching procedure basing on relevant variables) or comprised random assignment;

5 random assignment of treated and untreated subjects without obvious differences between groups.

We chose a rather low cut-off point and included all studies that had a controlled design (i.e., Maryland Scale rating of 2 and above). We did this because we wanted to keep a reasonably big pool of studies to realize more complex moderator analyses. This permitted us to test whether weak studies would show systematically different results relative to better-designed studies. Apart from this we also coded in what ways treatment and comparison groups differed. In fact, results showed that design quality – as determined using the Maryland Scale of Scientific Rigor – was not significantly related to better or worse outcomes. However, we were aware of the problems of Level 2 studies and updated our review when a sufficient number of Level 3 studies were available (Schmucker and Lösel, 2009).

Searching for relevant studies

While searching the literature is a key feature of any work that integrates research, the 'meta-analytic philosophy' puts special emphasis on a comprehensive and fully transparent search procedure (White, 2009). In principle the literature search can be compared to subject sampling in primary studies. However, meta-analyses usually do not sample from the population of studies referring to the research question. Instead, they try to tap the full population of studies in the respective field. Therefore, methods used in the literature search aim at revealing the population of relevant studies.

The file-drawer problem

One of the most hideous problems in meta-analyses is the file-drawer problem (Rothstein et al., 2005). Many studies never see the light of day and remain unpublished. Although they belong to the population of studies that should be integrated, they are not easily fetched, if at all. Whether a study is published or not may not be a random process but related to the research results; that is, studies that yield negative results may have a higher chance of not being published (e.g., because of author and journal editor decisions). There is no easy way to solve this problem of a publication bias. Of course one should reduce the impact of this bias by searching for unpublished studies (e.g. 'grey literature', student theses, conference reports, etc.). However, even this will not fully rule out the possibility of a bias because some studies with disappointing results may never have left the desk of the researcher. Rosenthal (1979) proposed the 'fail safe N' measure. This gives the number of nil findings that would be necessary to render the determined mean effect insignificant. Obviously the fail-safe N measure itself does not reduce the bias as such. But it gives an idea of whether the results of any particular meta-analysis are relatively stable or fragile.

Sources for the search and strategies

There are different sources to identify studies that meet the inclusion criteria and no single one that is best. Therefore, a variety of sources should be used. We recommend strategies that increase the inclusion of unpublished studies whenever possible to reduce the impact of a publication bias and to enlarge the available study pool. In areas that are of high interest for practice many studies are funded or conducted by institutions that evaluate programmes to improve their policy and quality management. They may not be interested in publishing the results from the very start; probably even more so if the results are unfavorable. In an unbiased meta-analysis the following sources and strategies to identify relevant research should be tried out.

Previous research integrations

A convenient place to start a search is with previous research integrations in the respective field. This is a relatively easy way to get a stock of relevant studies because earlier reviewers already have conducted a more or less extensive literature search. However, there are a number of drawbacks. First, existing research integration cannot cover the most recent work. Second, there is no control over how the search was performed. And third, the search strategies and inclusion criteria in the previous reviews may introduce a more or less severe bias. Therefore, this method is helpful in beginning to build up a study pool, but needs to be supplemented by a number of other sources.

Scientific databases

Scientific databases give easy access to references and usually sound content information which helps to decide whether a study could be considered for inclusion (Reed and Baxter, 2009). Depending on the research question different databases have to be considered. Most databases include only published work, but there are some databases that also include unpublished material such as the National Criminal Justice Reference Service of the US Department of Justice. Many research funders also provide searchable databases with information on the respective research projects.

Any database has more or less detailed search options. Using the search tools is not as easy as it may seem at first glance. This is because the aim of searching when undertaking a meta-analysis is to retrieve all relevant references contained in the database. Most others searching such databases, by contrast, are satisfied merely to discover the most pertinent references on their topic. Therefore, for meta-analytic purposes the recall of the search has to be maximized. Because it is unrealistic to individually scan all references in a database, one needs to make the search as precise as possible. These two aims – high recall and high precision – are inversely related and need to be balanced. It helps when databases allow for more complex search phrases. A strategy we found helpful in optimizing the recall–precision balance is to first search for reference pools that each fit single inclusion criterion and then look at the overlap of these pools. This represents the pool of references which fit all criteria. For example, in our meta-analysis on sexual offender treatment we first searched for studies that dealt with deviant sexuality in the broadest sense, then we restricted these 'hits' to those about offending behavior. Then we further restricted the search within these 'deviant sexuality' AND 'offending behavior' hits to studies that dealt with treatment in the broadest sense. Finally we excluded studies that had not evaluated the treatment. As an example the following search phrase was used for the PsycInfo database:

[article refers to sexually related behavior including abnormal sexuality]

(sex* OR paraphil* OR rape OR rapist OR molest* OR exhibitionis* OR voyeur* OR pedophil* OR incest* OR fetish* OR necrophil* OR frotteur*) AND

[article refers to criminal behavior/delinquency]

((offen* OR crim* OR delinquen* OR perpetrator* OR prison*) in DE,SU) AND

[article refers to treatment/intervention]

((treat* OR therapy OR psychotherapy OR intervention OR training OR correction* OR rehabilitation OR prevention OR management) in DE,SU) AND

[article includes evaluation/measure of effectiveness]

((evaluation OR evaluate OR evaluated OR outcome OR outcomes OR effect OR effects OR effectiveness OR impact OR recidivism OR re-offen* OR reoffen* OR follow-up OR followup OR relapse) in DE,SU)

In defining a search phrase so exactly one has to take into account the structure of a database and tailor it specifically. To optimize the search it is helpful to look up whether articles located via other sources are included in the database and then check whether they are tracked using the search phrase. If this is not the case one should figure out why the articles did not show up and eventually adapt the search phrase accordingly. Unfortunately, in most databases some articles, especially older ones, are very poorly indicated. It is also a common experience of meta-analysts that scientific databases turn out to be less informative than one would expect.

Snowball method

Located studies can be further scanned for other relevant primary studies. Usually articles that report a study put their results in relation to other work in the field or even have a more or less general review of the research relating to the study.

Manual search of important journals

Often, some journals are of special significance for a certain topic. Such journals should be manually searched to make sure that important articles are not missed. This can even be appropriate for journals that are indexed in databases because at times articles are not properly indexed in such databases. A manual strategy is also particularly useful for journals that are not indexed in the respective databases. Whether this strategy can be applied in an economic manner depends on the relevance of non-major journals for the specific research topic. Nowadays, most journals have at least some online tables of contents and abstracts. So it takes only little effort. On the other hand, most journals of high quality are included in literature databases and therefore this strategy may not yield many otherwise unfound references.

Internet searches

Searching the Internet sounds simpler than it really is when it comes to systematic searches. First, it is difficult, if not impossible, to properly document Internet searches. This is a clear drawback with regard to objectivity. Second, the Internet contains a huge amount of – mainly irrelevant – information. Typical search engines cannot be used because it is impossible to appropriately balance the search with regard to recall and precision. For example, if one searches Google for the term 'sex offender treatment' one gets roughly 130,000 links. Even a further restriction using the term 'effectiveness' does not yet give a manageable amount of results. It is not only impossible to follow all those links but they represent a rather small subset of the relevant pages (e.g. they do not

even contain pages dealing with 'sexual offender treatment', etc.). The Internet can nevertheless be a valuable tool in searching for relevant studies, especially unpublished ones. For the purpose of our meta-analysis we mainly inspected the sites of important institutions (e.g. Sites of the Departments of Corrections) dealing with the treatment of sex offenders to find relevant studies or links to such studies.

Congress proceedings

Congress proceedings and the programmes of congresses can help in identifying the most recent research. Often, congress information, including titles of the papers and sometimes abstracts, may be available online. Therefore, this is an easy source that can be combined with the Internet search.

Contacting leading researchers in the field

A personal inquiry with experts in the respective field is a particularly valuable tool to retrieve new or unpublished studies. On the one hand, these experts can be asked about research they conducted themselves. On the other hand, they often have a good overview and may informally receive information from colleagues about ongoing projects.

As stated above the different search sources overlap but may each reveal articles that are not traceable via other sources. Table 28.1 gives an overview of the 'success' of different sources in establishing the pool for our sexual offender meta-analysis ($n = 66$). Obviously each source had 'hits' for articles that did not make it to the study pool due to ineligibility. These are not counted here. In total more than 2,000 articles had received a closer look, but were stepwise excluded according to inclusion criteria. As can be seen each source revealed at least one article that would not have been detected otherwise.

Study coding

Once the study pool has been completed the retrieved studies need to be coded. Coding includes two main areas: (1) effect size coding which is central for the later integration of research results; and (2) coding of study descriptors. The coding scheme has to include the variables that describe the different features of each study, as well as the outcomes (effect size coding). The aim of this coding is to describe the study pool as a whole and set the basis for differentiated moderator analyses; that is, to check whether specific features of studies correlate with the outcomes.

Table 28.1   'Successes' for different sources used to build the pool for Lösel and Schmucker (2005)

Source	Located via this source	Exclusively located via this source
Earlier reviews and snowball method	39	14
Scientific databases	33	6
Manual searches of journals	7	1
Internet search (incl. congress proceedings)	—[a]	8
Experts	—[b]	2

Notes. [a] Studies found via Internet searches that had already been identified using other sources were not specifically documented; [b] experts were sent a list of already identified studies and asked to add not yet included studies

Effect size coding

A basic aim of a meta-analysis is the quantitative integration of the results of individual studies. As a prerequisite, the results of each study have to be transformed into a common metric. This is done by effect size coding. Each outcome that is presented and fits the defined outcome criteria is transformed into an effect size measure of choice. There are numerous effect size measures that can be used. Although the common effect size measures can usually be transformed to other effect size measures, the need for this should be reduced to a minimum, mainly because the transformations can introduce bias. It is desirable that the effect size can be directly calculated from the results presented in the study. Therefore, the decision for the effect size measure to be used in a meta-analysis depends on the typical outcome measures used in the primary studies and the typical research design and question. Table 28.2 lists the most commonly used effect size measures. For a more thorough overview, readers are referred to textbooks on meta-analysis (e.g. Borenstein et al., 2009; Cooper et al., 2009; Lipsey and Wilson, 2001).

In our meta-analysis on sexual offender treatment the common outcome measure was the recidivism rate and by definition studies included a group comparison. Therefore, we chose to use odds ratios (OR) as an effect size measure. The odds ratio is easily calculated and has some advantages over other measures for dichotomous measures (Farrington and Loeber, 2000; Fleiss and Berlin, 2009). It is based on the odds of the (non-)occurrence of an event; for example, re-offending:

$$\text{Odds} = \frac{\text{No. of cases who did not re-offend}}{\text{No. of cases who did re-offend}}$$

The odds of the treated group and the odds for the control group are then set in relation:

$$OR = \frac{\text{Odds}_{TG}}{\text{Odds}_{CG}}$$

If the odds are the same for both groups, then $OR = 1$, what signifies a 'zero effect'. If the treated group did better, $OR > 1$. If the treated group did worse than the control group, then $OR < 1$.

Most of the outcome research on sexual offender treatment reports recidivism rates or

Table 28.2   Typical research situations and common effect size measures

Outcome measure	Research design/question	Typical effect size measure
Metric (e.g., test scales)	Group comparison	Cohen's *d*
	Correlation	Pearson correlation (*r*)
Dichotomous (e.g., recidivism rates)	Group comparison	Odds ratio (*OR*)
	Correlation	Phi (Φ)

frequency tables enabling odds ratios to be easily computed. At times, however, results are presented in a more sophisticated manner. For example, authors may use Cox Regression which not only takes into account whether a re-offense occurred but also the time until a re-offense occurred. In addition, a Cox Regression can include variables to control for differences between treated and untreated offenders. Therefore, the results of a Cox Regression give a better account of the treatment effect than simple recidivism rates. As an outcome the Cox Regression reports hazard ratios, which is a measure of the relative risk of re-offense of treated compared to untreated offenders. In our own meta-analysis, we preferred such hazard ratios over the simple recidivism rates. We used the hazard ratio to estimate corrected recidivism rates for the control groups and then used these to calculate the odds ratio. Sometimes other metrics are reported; for example, the mean number of re-offenses in the treated *versus* the comparison group. In such cases Cohen's *d* could be estimated and then transformed into odds ratios using a reversed logit transformation (see Lipsey and Wilson, 2001).

The precision of the effect size estimate varies from study to study. For example, results that are based on small samples are relatively prone to sampling errors; that is, the effect size computed from a small sample is a rather imprecise estimate of the population effect it represents. For studies using larger samples the effect size estimate is more reliable. This has to be taken into account when integrating the study results. There are different approaches regarding the measure being used to individually weight the effect sizes according to their precision. For example, Hunter and Schmidt (2004) use the sample size in their model for the integration of correlation effect size data. Meta-analytic integration following the Hedges and Olkin (1985) model uses the standard error of the effect size during integration. For each effect size that is calculated, a standard error must be coded as well. Therefore, it is essential that the chosen effect size measure allows the computation of standard errors.

It is also desirable that the sampling distribution of the effect size measure has good statistical properties (e.g. normal distribution). The odds ratio, for example, has not – it is strongly skewed. Therefore, statistical analyses are conducted on the natural log of the odds ratio which has a nearly normal distribution. Besides, the calculation of the standard error is straightforward for the log odds ratio.

It is beyond the scope of this chapter to present details of effect size coding. As a rule, however, all efforts should be taken to compute valid effect sizes. If in a research domain it is common not to report detailed results for insignificant findings, the exclusion of those outcomes in effect size coding would lead to a clear bias. If no other information is given it might be appropriate to estimate a zero effect for non-significant findings in this situation. Whenever studies have to be excluded due to insufficient outcome reporting this means a threat to the validity of the integration.

Adjusting effect sizes

The standard error indicates the (im)precision of the results due to sampling error. It thus reflects a random error. There are, however, other influences on study results that represent systematic biases. For example, effect sizes are systematically lower when outcomes are based on unreliable measures. In such cases the error variance of the outcome variable is higher and thus obscures 'true' variance. In principle, effect size calculation is a standardization procedure and is thus influenced by error variance. The lower the reliability of the outcome measure, the higher the variance and accordingly the lower the effect size estimates. This can be corrected in the following way (standard errors will have to be adjusted the same way; see Hedges and Olkin, 1985):

$$ES_{corr} = \frac{ES}{\sqrt{r_{tt}}}$$

Hunter and Schmidt (2004) have developed adjustments to correct for a number of biases. The purpose of such corrections is to estimate a true, unbiased effect; that is, an effect size that would result from 'flawless research'.

Using these sorts of corrections requires reasonable estimates of the bias. To correct for an unreliability bias one needs to know the reliability of the outcome measure. For standardized tests reliability indices are usually reported. But for other measures it is often difficult or even impossible to gather a reasonable estimate of the reliability. The latter surely is the case for recidivism data. While it is obvious that re-offense measures are not fully reliable (offenses committed may not be detected or there may be false accusations), it is very difficult to establish precisely how reliable such measures actually are. For this reason we refrained from using corrections in effect size coding in our own study. As a consequence our effect sizes were probably conservative estimates of the true effects of the treatment programmes. For our research question this conservative strategy seemed more adequate than running the risk of over-correcting the effect size estimates.

Coding of study descriptors

While the outcome of a study is a main feature for the integration, it is important to realize that every study has individual characteristics and that the study pool is a collection of more or less similar studies. The coding of study descriptors thus gives an overview of the characteristics of the collected studies and serves two functions. First, it allows for more detailed analyses (i.e., whether certain characteristics go along with higher or lower effects); second, it simply helps describe the study pool. This is important for generalizing the findings of a meta-analysis. This descriptive function also helps to identify weaknesses in the research area. In sexual offender treatment, for example, different interventions are not equally well evaluated. While there are a number of studies evaluating cognitive behavioral interventions, other psychotherapeutic approaches are hardly evaluated at all. Furthermore, evaluations of organic treatment methods are mainly based on rather weak study designs.

Which study descriptors should be coded depends on the topic of research. But as a general rule the following domains should be taken care of in any meta-analysis:

1 characteristics of the independent variable(s) (e.g., treatment characteristics);
2 features of the study sample/population (e.g., offender classifications);
3 methodological issues (e.g., study design);
4 general study features (source descriptors; e.g., publication year).

In our analyses of sexual offender treatment we coded 61 items that included treatment characteristics (e.g., treatment mode, setting of the treatment), offender characteristics (e.g., offense types, age of treated offenders), general study characteristics (e.g., time and setting of the study, publication status) as well as methodological features (e.g., method of control group formation, time of follow-up, measure of re-offending).

Coding scheme and coding manual

On the one hand, a coding scheme should be comprehensive enough to account for relevant features. On the other hand, one has to cut back on less central variables in order to keep the coding manageable and concentrate on information that is sufficiently reported in the primary studies. In fact, insufficient information in study reports is the most severe problem of coding. Often, variables cannot be coded because they are missing for a large portion of the integrated studies. In the latter case, these variables will be of limited value for moderator analyses. It can still be wise to incorporate such variables in the coding scheme if they are of special relevance for the research question. Although they may not be usable for the moderator analyses, the descriptive analysis of such variables will be able to demonstrate weaknesses in reporting habits. For example, we decided to code whether the treatment under evaluation was implemented successfully although we were aware that such information is rarely reported. We checked the articles for measures of implementation, staff supervision or training and reported implementation problems. Not surprisingly, 57 out of 80 comparisons did not report anything about treatment implementation. Therefore, we could not analyze these data in a differentiated manner. Nevertheless, documenting this lack of information serves as a feedback for improving future evaluation studies in the field of sexual offender treatment.

In order to make the coding process as objective as possible, a detailed coding manual should be compiled. The coding manual includes the description of the different variables that are coded, what values the variables represent and how to assign values to them. A detailed coding manual enables other researchers to reconstruct the coding. It also serves as the blueprint for double coding. Double coding should be done with at least a sub-set of the studies to check the reliability of the coding scheme. Variables that show poor inter-rater agreement should be defined more precisely. We tested our coding scheme in a subset of studies and found an average inter-rater agreement of 91 per cent. For core variables such as study design or treatment type there was full agreement.

Even a detailed coding manual will leave insecurities in the coding of items because of unclear information in the reports of primary studies. Therefore, it can be helpful to include confidence ratings for some important variables. Instead of item-based confidence ratings, we decided to include the coding of threats to descriptive validity as conceived by Lösel and Köferl (1989) as a more general measure. This approach refers to the quality of documentation in the study reports.

Defining independent units of analysis

When it comes to the integration of outcomes the statistical procedures assume that the data points are independent (i.e., that the effect sizes are derived from independent samples). Often studies present several outcome measures. Those have to be either combined, or one of them has to be chosen above the others. In combining different outcome measures one has to deal with the apples and oranges problem mentioned above. Combining effect sizes can have pros and cons. An advantage is that the composite effect size may be more reliable than a single measure. A disadvantage is that crucial differentiating information can get lost. If the outcome measures refer to different constructs one should not mix them but conduct separate analyses for the different constructs.

In our meta-analysis of sexual offender treatment evaluations we coded outcomes referring to sexual re-offending. Some studies also reported other re-offending (e.g., non-sexual violent or general re-offending). We were interested in such outcomes but coded and analyzed them separately. Things look different when it comes to re-offense definitions. This could be convictions, arrests, charges and so forth. Different studies used different definitions and sometimes multiple definitions are used within a single study. In principle, the different definitions refer to the same type of outcome, albeit on different levels. Therefore, after we had checked that the different definitions did not yield systematically different effects, we aggregated them to a mean effect for each study.

Usually, the unit of analysis is defined at the study level; that is, each study delivers one effect size per analysis. In most cases, this is reasonable because primary authors design the study and report on it on this level as well. Sometimes, however, it can be useful to choose another level. If, for example, the study reports on sub-groups this may increase differentiation. In our example, we chose to treat sub-group comparisons as independent units if, on this level, treated and comparison groups were better matches regarding the risk for re-offending as demonstrated by relevant variables. This gave us 80 independent comparisons from 69 studies. Of course, this bears some dependencies. For example, the sub-groups have had the same treatment in the same setting, and so on. In deciding whether to choose such sub-groups as units instead of the study level one has to carefully balance such dependencies *versus* an increase in differentiation. In other instances a part of the sample may be identical across different articles or studies. Often, these dependencies cannot be clearly resolved. The most straightforward solution in such cases is to select one of them according to validity criteria, or to combine them to one unit, if this is feasible.

Quantitative integration and moderator analyses

So far, the steps had to do with gathering the data for the meta-analysis. The core of a meta-analysis is the quantitative integration of the individual study results. In its simplest form this means averaging the individual effect sizes to a mean effect. The individual study effects constitute a sampling distribution. The differences between these effects are regarded as sampling errors. By averaging the individual study effects these errors should level out and provide an estimate for the population mean.

However, there are a number of pitfalls when integrating study results. First, different studies differ with regard to the probability of larger or smaller sampling errors. Studies with small samples are more susceptible to sampling error than large studies. Second, the assumption of sampling errors leveling out across studies is only true if the individual studies belong to the same population; that is, they have to represent a common population effect. If the individual studies do not only differ in outcomes but in characteristics that systematically influence outcomes (e.g., different treatment modes differ in effectiveness), simple averaging would obscure the true differences between studies and their outcomes. These problems have to be taken into account when integrating studies.

Different methods for the integration of effect sizes have been proposed (e.g. Hedges and Olkin, 1985; Hunter and Schmidt, 2004; Rosenthal, 1991; for comparisons see Field, 2001, Hall and Brannick, 2002). In our integration of the effectiveness of sexual offender treatment we drew on the methods developed by Hedges and Olkin (1985; Hedges and Vevea, 1998) because these enable rather differentiated analyses.

Estimating the mean effect

To overcome the problem of results varying in precision across different studies, the study effects should be weighted accordingly. The standard error (SE) of an effect size is a measure of its imprecision. Therefore, Hedges and Olkin (1985) proposed to assign weights (w) as the inverse of the error variance:

$$w_i = \frac{1}{SE_i^2}$$

On this basis, one can calculate a weighted average across studies that will represent individual studies according to their precision in estimating the true effect:

$$\overline{ES} = \frac{\sum w_i \times ES_i}{\sum w_i}$$

The standard error for the mean effect size corresponds to the square root of the inversed sum of the weights and can be used for significance testing via a z-test or for calculating confidence intervals:

$$SE_{\overline{ES}} = \sqrt{\frac{1}{\sum w_i}}$$

This basic and rather simple way of weighted integration is labeled as 'fixed effects model'. 'Fixed effects' means that all study outcomes refer to the same – that is, fixed – population effect. If this is not the case, the fixed effects model will misrepresent the true mean effect. Whether the assumption holds or not should first be judged theoretically: can one assume that the integrated studies constitute mere variations of the same constructs or do they differ more substantially? Wilson (2001) notes that for meta-analyses in criminology the first case may be the exception rather than the rule. Whether or not the fixed effects model is appropriate has far-reaching consequences with regard to the results of the meta-analysis. The fixed effects model has higher statistical power compared to models that assume heterogeneous effect sizes. On the other hand, it is overly liberal when applied in situations where the homogeneity assumption is violated (Overton, 1998).

In addition to theoretical reasoning the assumption of homogeneous effect sizes should be tested statistically. If the effect size differences were indeed only due to sampling error they should be distributed regularly. The effect size of large studies should be close to the overall mean. For small studies a somewhat broader range can be expected. The Q statistic is a χ^2-distributed score for the homogeneity of the effect size distribution:

$$Q = \sum w_i \times (ES_i - \overline{ES})^2$$

with $df = k - 1$ (k being the number of comparisons).

In our analyses on the effectiveness of sexual offender treatment we had expected heterogeneity from the start and this was confirmed in homogeneity analyses for all outcome areas under study (sexual, violent and any recidivism).

A significant Q score indicates that the effect sizes are not distributed randomly, which in turn means that the fixed effects model is not suitable. There are a number of reasons for heterogeneous effect size distributions and a number of ways to deal with such situations. In any case, if the effect size distribution is heterogeneous one should take efforts to figure out the reasons. This can be done via moderator analyses that check whether certain study characteristics are related to smaller and larger effect sizes.

However, heterogeneity can also be induced by some single values that are very far off the mark. It is wise to scrutinize the effect size distribution for such outliers because they can severely distort the overall results. In identifying outliers one can draw on different markers but one should keep in mind that labelling a value as an outlier or not is a more or less arbitrary decision. In our meta-analysis on sexual offender treatment we used two markers to check for outlier values. First, we checked how far off a value was from the overall mean and regarded values differing by more than ± 2 standard deviations as extreme. Second, we checked whether these extreme values could be expected under the assumption of sampling errors. Here we drew on the 'sample-adjusted meta-analytic deviancy statistic' (SAMD) developed by Huffcutt and Arthur (1995). The SAMD takes into account that even extreme values can be the result of sampling error in small sample studies while such extreme values are very improbable in studies with larger samples. We only defined values as outliers if they were extreme values and if the SAMD indicated that they were not in the expectancy range. In fact, none of the effect sizes regarding sexual or general re-offending met these criteria. When an outlier is detected via statistical criteria one should also have a closer look at the respective study to check whether the study has specific characteristics that might explain the extreme value. If outliers are detected, discarding the value from further analyses is only one option. In such instances, it can be helpful to do the analyses both with and without the outlier values to check what changes occur when outlier values are discarded. Another option is to cut the effect sizes back to less extreme values, a process that is referred to as 'windsorizing'.

Outlier values need not only refer to the effect sizes. For example if the study pool contains studies with extremely large samples and extremely small standard errors, their extremely large weights can distort overall results considerably. This may be particularly the case when it comes to moderator analyses. In our meta-analysis we had three studies that exceeded a sample size of 1,000 and a few more studies with samples larger than 500. We therefore controlled our results by conducting sensitivity analyses (for the whole study pool the median sample size was 118). First, we checked the results excluding the very large sample studies. Second, we truncated studies with sample sizes above 500 to a value of 500. For both checks the results changed only marginally. This indicated that the results were pretty robust against such outliers.

If the effect size remains heterogeneous even after controlling for outliers one should refer to a random effects model to integrate effect sizes. The random effects model assumes that the individual effect sizes do not refer to a single population mean but represent different population effects. Therefore, the random effects model does not only take into account the variance that is due to sampling error (SE_i^2) but also adds a variance component that arises from the heterogeneity between the population effects (SE_{random}^2). The value of the random variance takes into account the heterogeneity of the effect size distribution (via the Q value; for details, see Hedges and Olkin, 1985). The individual effect size weights are thus reduced:

$$w_{random(i)} = \frac{1}{SE_i^2 + SE_{random}^2}$$

The higher the heterogeneity the larger the reduction. The formulas for determining the mean effect size and its standard error are the same as stated above for the fixed effects model, the only difference being that of the corrected weights. Compared to the fixed effects model the random effects model thus has less power and the respective confidence intervals are broader. This is of course intended because the estimate of a mean effect is less reliable under these circumstances.

In the random effects model the individual weights are not as different between the studies because for any study the random variance component is the same. As a consequence, the account of sample size gets less important for the relative weights of the individual studies. This in turn can lead to substantial changes in the overall mean when sample size is correlated with effect size. Unfortunately, this is often the case in treatment evaluation. In our meta-analysis, for example, the (not appropriate) fixed effects analysis revealed an overall mean odds ratio of 1.24 with a confidence interval (95 per cent) from 1.12 to 1.38 whereas the (appropriate) random effects analysis resulted in a mean odds ratio of 1.70 ($CI_{96\%}$: 1.35–2.13). In both cases this was a highly significant effect ($p < 0.001$) that justified the conclusion that treatment with sexual offenders on average has a positive influence on re-offending. However, the fixed effect model would have led to a smaller overall effect estimation.

This points to a very basic problem of a mean effect estimated via the random effects model. When the integrated studies do not refer to the same population mean, a mean estimate can only serve to give a rather rough idea regarding the principle research question, in our case the general effect of sexual offender treatment. If different studies yield systematically different outcomes, the more important question is what characteristics are responsible for those differences in effect size. This can be done via moderator analyses.

Analyzing moderating effects

Whenever the studies pooled in a meta-analysis constitute a heterogeneous set one should take a closer look at what accounts for these differences. A researcher should always be prepared for this situation and should have developed a system of potentially relevant variables that might moderate outcomes during the definition and coding stages. In fact, this is one basic reason for coding study characteristics as mentioned earlier. In the moderator analyses these variables are checked for their influence on the effect size distribution. With regard to content specific variables such as the type of an intervention or the characteristics of the participants, the benefit of moderator analyses is obvious. The results can guide decisions in treatment planning and programme development or can provide expectations of the effects of programmes that have not (yet) been evaluated.

Hedges and Olkin (1985) have described modified versions of the one-way analysis of variance and regression analysis that allow one to analyze categorical variables (analog to the ANOVA) as well as metric variables (weighted multiple regression) as moderators. It is beyond the scope of this chapter to go into the statistical details of these procedures. We want rather to exemplify how such moderator analyses can help to clear up heterogeneous effect-size distributions and then explain what difficulties remain.

Both methodological variables (e.g., study design) as well as content variables (e.g., mode of treatment) need to be considered. In our analysis we considered a broad scope of treatments. Specifically, we also included studies on surgical castration. These studies (eight comparisons altogether) clearly stood out as a group. Not only did they show very high effect sizes but also the effect size distribution of these eight comparisons was rather homogenous. Apart from this, the studies on surgical castration had very weak designs (castrated offenders were highly selected and probably particularly motivated). Surgical castration is also very controversial ethically and currently rarely practised even if an offender actively wishes to have it. We thus decided to exclude this group of studies for further analyses. The heterogeneity of the remaining studies was clearly reduced although it remained inhomogeneous and analyses revealed a number of further relevant moderators regarding the treatment concept, setting or types of treated offenders.

Methodological variables are of interest in order to test whether researcher decisions regarding the design of the study, outcome measurement and the like have a systematic influence on the results. Knowing such effects can be helpful in interpreting the results of single outcome studies. Other variables such as insufficient reporting of study characteristics can be subsumed here. In fact, even 'missing information' can exert influence. In our analyses the threats to descriptive validity (Lösel and Köferl, 1989) correlated significantly with effect size. The better documented a study was, the larger the treatment effects. At first glance, this result – knowing that not knowing things about a study makes a difference – may not seem helpful. However, such a result should alert study authors, publishers and reviewers to closely scrutinize whether relevant information has been omitted. 'Non-information' may well be 'hidden information' that would be better out in the open.

Methodological variables can also be used as control variables when it comes to the analysis of treatment variables. When treatment variables show up with moderating effects these may in fact be artifacts derived by being confounded with certain methodological features. Quite often, different study characteristics are interrelated (Lipsey, 2003). In our example, evaluations of hormonal medication more often drew on self-report measures which were themselves related to better outcomes. Moderator analyses on single variables cannot resolve such multiple relationships. Just as in primary research this requires multivariate modeling.

Multiple regression can be applied for meta-analysis (Hedges, 1982). In our meta-analysis on sexual offender treatment we fitted a hierarchical regression model in order to sequentially control for less treatment-specific variables and to finally test whether different treatment orientations would make a difference at all. The model included four steps:

1 methodological (including unspecific) variables;
2 offender variables;
3 general treatment characteristics; and
4 treatment contents.

The full model explained 60 per cent of outcome variance. However, the biggest part of this was already covered in the first step (45 per cent). Nevertheless, each consecutive step explained a significant portion of effect size variability and thus demonstrated that content specific variables do indeed moderate outcomes over and above non-content related variables.

While hierarchical regression can help to disentangle 'real' moderators, there are a number of caveats. First, in theory, all relevant variables must be considered. Possible confounders that don't enter the analysis remain uncontrolled. This requires a comprehensive coding scheme. It also demands that relevant information is reported in primary studies, which is often not the case. Second, with a hierarchic procedure non-content related facets may be overly pronounced. Common variance is automatically counted for the preceding step and discounted from later variables. Third, complex multivariate analyses necessitate a large number of available comparisons to enter the meta-analysis. In particular, when strict inclusion criteria are applied (with good reasons) or rather narrow research areas are under investigation such analyses may not be possible. We had 72 comparisons available for our analyses. This is not a very large number in the context of the number of variables we had to take care of. And we even had to 'buy' this number of comparisons by including methodologically weaker studies. Otherwise a more detailed multivariate analysis would not have been feasible at all.

Sensitivity analyses

As shown in the preceding paragraphs a researcher has to take a multitude of decisions when conducting a meta-analysis. Each of these decisions can impact upon the results. To get an idea how single decisions influence results, sensitivity analyses can be conducted. Sensitivity analyses reiterate the original analyses with the decision under question being taken differently. For example, a certain inclusion criterion can be put differently and one can check whether this would change the results. In part, such sensitivity analyses are implicitly conducted during moderator analyses. In our meta-analysis we checked whether general design quality as measured via the Maryland Scale of Scientific Rigor did systematically influence effect sizes. Sometimes the sensitivity analyses are more explicit (like our above-mentioned analyses on outliers in sample size). It would be foolish, though, to conduct sensitivity analyses on every single decision because there are just too many. Such analyses need to be restricted to decisions of special importance (like the decision on the minimum study design quality required). Sensitivity analyses can greatly improve the interpretation of meta-analytic results when they show that the decisions taken do not substantially change the outcomes. Or they can lead to a note of caution when they demonstrate substantial outcome differences.

Reporting the results

On the whole, reporting a meta-analysis is not much different from reports of primary research. In fact, the reporting of a meta-analysis resembles more an empirical primary study than it resembles a traditional narrative review. This is not only due to the quantitative nature of meta-analytic results. Traditional reviews often almost exclusively focus on the results while not much information is given on the processes that led to them. In contrast, meta-analyses, in the effort to create an objective and reproducible integration of primary studies, should put greater emphasis on delineating the methods used and decisions taken. Providing a list of the included studies is mandatory. A list of the excluded studies, ideally together with the reason for exclusion, should be prepared as well.

Still, the final results are usually the main interest for most readers. For meta-analyses, the recipients can be quite diverse regarding their knowledge of methods as well as on the constructs being studied. Often, meta-analyses are used as a start to get an overview of a topic. Meta-analyses are also highly relevant for people who are not well grounded in research at all. As mentioned in the introduction, Campbell reviews explicitly target practitioners and policy makers, as well as researchers. For such target groups the report must be understandable and not overloaded with technical issues (which could go into an appendix). Effect sizes, for example, are rather abstract measures. And at times one may wonder whether the classification of effect sizes provided by Cohen (1962) is a help or a hindrance. In criminology, so called 'small' effects can be of high practical relevance and even cost-effective (e.g. Welsh et al., 2001). Odds ratios, which we used in our study of sexual offender treatment, have both strengths and weaknesses. The odds ratio has very convenient mathematical properties which explains its popularity as an effect size measure in meta-analyses. But it is easily misinterpreted as changes in probability although it really represents changes in odds. This misinterpretation is especially problematic with higher base rates. If, for example, the recidivism rate is 30 per cent for treated offenders and 60 per cent for untreated offenders, the odds ratio is 3.5. This means that the odds, not the probability, to re-offend are 3.5 times higher in the untreated group. The probability to re-offend is only doubled. Confusion can be avoided if the odds ratios are translated back to concrete rates of re-offending in treatment and control groups. For other effect size measures there are other ways to transform abstract effect size measures into more understandable formats, such as the *binomial effect-size display* for correlations (Rosenthal and Rubin, 1982). Such translations usually enhance the understanding of the practical significance of the results.

Graphics can help illustrate the findings and there are numerous formats that can be used (Borman and Grigg, 2009). Histograms or stem-and-leaf plots can give a general picture of the effect size distribution. They do not, however, inform about the standard errors differing across the studies. Forest plots contain a graphical listing of the integrated effect per study with an error bar. They are rather common in meta-analyses and give an idea of a general trend across the studies as well as their heterogeneity. Funnel plots, plotting the effects of the studies against the sample size, can help illustrate a publication bias. However they need cautious interpretation because a skewed funnel plot need not necessarily be a consequence of publication bias. Error bar charts are useful in contrasting the categories of moderator variables.

Overall mean effects are catchy because they promise to be the essence of what is in the data, and they are useful, of course, especially when the effect size distribution is homogeneous. But with heterogeneous effects they may be misleading and obscure differences. Often, the variance in the results is more important than the average. Then, the partitioning of this variance, that is, the results of the moderator analyses, should be given particular emphasis.

Presenting descriptive analyses of the study characteristics is crucial with respect to the generalization of the results. It also helps highlight gaps in primary research. Such descriptive results thoroughly and well presented can instigate future research. Methodological shortcomings afford special consideration here. These are particularly important with regard to the validity of the results of the meta-analysis and how much confidence can be put in them.

CURRENT CONTROVERSIES AND NEW HORIZONS

It was the aim of this chapter to demonstrate the importance of systematic reviews of criminological research and to show how these should be carried out. We hope that we convinced the reader that methodologically sound meta-analyses provide the best (i.e., most objective, comprehensive, transparent and systematic) evidence on a specific research question. If such analyses become more widespread in criminology they will form a powerful tool for evidence-based policy making. Of course, scientific evidence is not the only guide for political decision making (Lösel, 2007b). However without consensus on basic empirical facts the role of criminology in policy making and practice would be weak. Therefore, the Campbell Collaboration's mission to promote systematic reviews is very important. And beyond a direct policy orientation there is also little doubt that the methodological standards of meta-analyses will shape the future of literature reviews in research projects or in doctoral students' theses. As a consequence, methods of systematic reviews should become an integral part of university courses in criminology. It should also become more common knowledge that meta-analyses are not a quick and easy type of 'desk research' but are as demanding as complex fieldwork. In practice, those undertaking systematic reviews have to solve many problems similar to those undertaking primary research. Accordingly, meta-analytic publications should be adequately recognized in research assessment exercises and career promotion.

This chapter also demonstrated that meta-analyses require many decisions within the research process. To make these decisions as clear and explicit as possible is a specific value of sound meta-analyses. Following such a strategy, our example showed relatively consistent evidence in a highly controversial field such as sexual offender treatment. Although single evaluations of sexual offender treatment programmes varied in outcomes, there was an overall positive effect (i.e. a statistically and practically significant reduction of re-offending). However, there are other meta-analyses on sexual offender treatment whose mean effects are substantially larger or smaller (Schmucker and Lösel, 2007). Reviews that used similar inclusion criteria and methods of effect size integration revealed comparable results (e.g., Aos et al., 2006; Hanson et al., 2002; Lösel and Schmucker, 2005; Schmucker and Lösel, 2009). This example shows that the many explicit or implicit decisions in meta-analyses can lead to rather heterogenous findings. Therefore one should not take every meta-analysis as definitive evidence in a specific field. As in primary research, evidence comes by replication. This underlines the importance of the above-mentioned discussion of methodological inclusion criteria and suggests the necessity of systematic comparisons of meta-analyses (Lipsey and Cullen, 2007; Lösel, 1995).

Another controversial issue is whether meta-analyses should address relatively narrow or broad research questions. Again, there is no general answer to this question because it depends on the number of available studies. If there are only very few studies on a specific type of programme a broader definition may be advantageous because it allows for more comparisons and moderator analyses. Our study revealed various factors that accounted for differences in outcome. These should be addressed in further programme development and implementation. However, our example also confirmed a frequent experience in meta-analyses, namely the lack of sound and

sufficiently detailed studies to answer more specific questions. In our case, for example, there was not enough research that addressed the question of which treatments best fit particular types of sexual offenders. To answer such questions, it is necessary to get more detailed information on the factual implementation of a programme, its integrity, impact on different clients, dependence on context factors, and so forth (Lösel and Köferl, 1989; Shaffer and Pratt, 2009). Such deeper digging and fine-tuning of reviews is often more important for practice than information on mean overall effects.

More information would also be necessary with regard to the cultural context of findings. In contrast to the natural sciences, research on crime and criminal justice cannot simply be generalized across cultures, countries and legal systems. The majority of meta-analyses concentrate on English-language reports and indeed North American studies are most frequent in many criminological fields. However, it is rarely asked how far such findings can simply be transferred to other cultures and contexts. Only a few meta-analyses investigated the impact of national framing conditions on the outcome (e.g. Welsh and Farrington, 2008).

Meta-analysts love to conclude that more and, in particular, more differentiated and high quality research is needed. Sometimes this is annoying for recipients in practice and policy because they want definitive answers. However, meta-analysis cannot be more definitive than the pool of integrated studies. And shortcomings in primary studies are probably the single most important restricting feature for any meta-analysis.

RECOMMENDED READING

There are a number of books and resources on meta-analysis and systematic research integration more generally. The following is merely an annotated bibliography to help the interested reader in criminology.

Lipsey and Wilson's (2001) *Practical Meta-Analysis* (Thousand Oaks: Sage) gives an excellent introduction on how to conduct a meta-analysis. Two features of the book are especially helpful for criminologists who plan to conduct a meta-analysis for the first time: First, it often draws on research examples from criminology. Second, it provides good assistance for beginners because it pays special attention to the practical implementation of meta-analytic strategies. David Wilson also provides some tools like macros for standard statistical programme packages that are very convenient when conducting a meta-analysis following the book's guidelines on his website (http://mason.gmu.edu/~dwilsonb/ma.html).

The second edition of Cooper et al.'s (2009) *The Handbook of Research Synthesis* (New York: Russell Sage) is the revised version of a real classic, originally published in 1994. It is a valuable resource that includes chapters on all steps of a meta-analysis, each authored by specialists on the topic at hand.

Borenstein et al.'s (2009) *Introduction to Meta-analysis* (Chichester: Wiley) is focused on the quantitative integration issues of a meta-analysis. It gives a rather complete account of effect size estimation and integration. Although this basically means statistical procedures, the book takes special care to provide an understanding of the procedures, as opposed to a purely mathematical account. It does not include much of the surroundings of quantitative integration (like formulating the research question or searching the literature).

Cooper's (2009) *Research Synthesis and Meta-analysis: A Step-by-step Approach* (Los Angeles: Sage) by contrast, takes a broader perspective and pays special attention to the steps preceding the quantitative aspect of a meta-analysis while the statistical integration of the studies is – albeit not spared – less central.

Web resources

A resource especially interesting for criminologists is the Campbell Collaboration website (http://www.campbellcollaboration.org/). Apart from issuing systematic research integrations on many criminological issues (see the Coordinating Group on Crime and Justice), it also offers information on methodological issues surrounding systematic research integrations.

The Cochrane Collaboration (www.cochrane.org) is dealing with systematic research integrations on medical health issues and it served as a template for the above mentioned Campbell Collaboration. Among other things it features the comprehensive *Cochrane Handbook for Systematic Reviews of Interventions* edited by Julian P.T. Higgins and Sally Green in 2008 (www.cochrane-handbook.org).

REFERENCES

Andrews, D.A., Zinger, I., Hoge, R.D., Bonta, J., Gendreau, P. and Cullen, F.T. (1990) Does correctional treatment work? A clinically relevant and psychologically informed meta-analysis. *Criminology*, 28(3), 369–404.

Aos, S., Miller, M. and Drake, E. (2006) *Evidence-based Adult Corrections Programs: What Works and What Does Not*. Olympia, WA: Washington State Institute for Public Policy.

Borenstein, M., Hedges, L.V., Higgins, J.P.T. and Rothstein, H.R. (2009) *Introduction to Meta-analysis*. Chichester: Wiley.

Borman, G.D. and Grigg, J.A. (2009) Visual and narrative interpretation. In H. Cooper, L.V. Hedges and J.C. Valentine (eds) *The Handbook of Research Synthesis*, 2nd edition. New York: Russell Sage.

Braga, A. (2007) The effects of hot spots policing on crime. Available at: www.campbellcollaboration.org/reviews_crime_justice/index.php

Campbell, D.T. (1969) Reforms as experiments. *American Psychologist*, 24(4), 409–429.

Chalmers, I. (1993) The Cochrane Collaboration: Preparing, maintaining, and disseminating systematic reviews of the effects of health care. *Annals of the New York Academy of Sciences*, 703(1), 156–165.

Cohen, J. (1962) The statistical power of abnormal-social psychological research: A review. *Journal of Abnormal and Social Psychology*, 65(3), 145–153.

Cook, T.D. and Campbell, D.T. (1979) *Quasi-experimentation. Design & Analysis Issues for Field Settings*. Boston: Houghton Mifflin.

Cook, T.D. and Leviton, L.C. (1980) Reviewing the literature: A comparison of traditional methods with meta-analysis. *Journal of Personality*, 48(4), 449–472.

Cooper, H.M. (2009) *Research Synthesis and Meta-analysis: A Step-by-step Approach*. Los Angeles: Sage.

Cooper, H., Hedges, L.V. and Valentine, J. (eds) (2009) *The Handbook of Research Synthesis*. New York: Russell Sage.

Eysenck, H.-J. (1978) An exercise in mega-silliness. *American Psychologist*, 33(5), 517.

Farrington, D.P. (2003) Methodological quality standards for evaluation research. *Annals of the American Academy of Political and Social Science*, 587(1), 49–68.

Farrington, D.P. and Loeber, R. (2000) Some benefits of dichotomization in psychiatric and criminological research. *Criminal Behaviour and Mental Health*, 10(2), 100–122.

Farrington, D.P. and Petrosino, A. (2001) The Campbell Collaboration Crime and Justice Group. *The Annals of the Academy of Political and Social Science*, 578(1), 35–49.

Farrington, D.P. and Ttofi, M. (2009) School-based programs to reduce bullying and victimization. Available at: www.campbellcollaboration.org/reviews_crime_justice/index.php

Field, A.P. (2001) Meta-analysis of correlation coefficients: A Monte Carlo comparison of fixed- and random-effects methods. *Psychological Methods*, 6(2), 161–180.

Fleiss, J.L. and Berlin, J.A. (2009) Effect sizes for dichotomous data. In H. Cooper, L.V. Hedges and J.C. Valentine (eds) *The Handbook of Research Synthesis*, 2nd edition. New York: Russell Sage.

Garrett, C.J. (1985) Effects of residential treatment on adjudicated delinquents: a meta-analysis. *Journal of Research on Crime and Delinquency*, 22(4), 287–308.

Glass, G.V. (1976) Primary, secondary and meta-analysis of research. *Educational Researcher*, 5(10), 3–8.

Glass, G.V. and Kliegl, R.M. (1983) An apology for research integration in the study of psychotherapy. *Journal of Consulting and Clinical Psychology*, 51(1), 28–41.

Gottschalk, R., Davidson, W.S. II., Mayer, J. and Gensheimer, G.K. (1987) Behavioral approaches with juvenile offenders: a meta-analysis of long-term treatment efficacy. In E.K. Morris and C.J. Braukmann (eds) *Behavioral Approaches to Crime and Delinquency: A Handbook of Application, Research, and Concepts* (pp. 389–422). New York: Plenum.

Hall, S.M. and Brannick, M.T. (2002) Comparison of two random-effects methods of meta-analysis. *Journal of Applied Psychology*, 87(2), 377–389.

Hanson, R.K., Gordon, A., Harris, A.J.R., Marques, J.K., Murphy, W.D., Quinsey, V.L. and Seto, M.C. (2002) First report of the collaborative outcome data project on the effectiveness of psychological treatment for sex offenders. *Sexual Abuse: A Journal of Research and Treatment*, 14(2), 169–194.

Hedges, L.V. (1982) Fitting continuous models to effect size data. *Journal of Educational Statistics*, 7(2), 245–270.

Hedges, L.V. and Olkin, I. (1985) *Statistical Methods for Meta-analysis*. Orlando: Academic Press.

Hedges, L.V. and Vevea, J.L. (1998) Fixed- and random-effects models in meta-analysis. *Psychological Methods*, 3(4), 486–504.

Huffcutt, A.I. and Arthur, W.J. (1995) Development of a new outlier statistic for meta-analytic data. *Journal of Applied Psychology*, 80(2), 327–334.

Hunter, J.E. and Schmidt, F.L. (2004) *Methods of Meta-analysis. Correcting Error and Bias in Research Findings.* Thousand Oaks, CA: Sage.

Hubbard, D.J. and Pratt, T.C. (2002) A meta-analysis of the predictors of delinquency among girls. *Journal of Offender Rehabilitation*, 34(3), 1–13.

Killias, M., Villettaz, P. and Zoder, I. (2006) The effects of custodial vs. non-custodial sentences on reoffending: A systematic review of the state of knowledge. Available at: www.campbellcollaboration.org/reviews_crime_justice/index.php

Leistico, A.-M., Salekin, R.T., De Costa, J. and Rogers, R. (2008) A large scale meta-analysis relating the Hare measures of psychopathy to antisocial conduct. *Law and Human Behavior*, 32(1), 28–45.

Lipsey, M.W. (1988) Juvenile delinquency intervention. In H.S. Bloom, D.S. Cordray and R.J. Light (eds) *Lessons from Selected Program and Policy Areas* (pp. 63–83). San Francisco: Jossey-Bass.

Lipsey, M.W. (2003) Those confounded moderators in meta-analysis: Good, bad, and ugly. *Annals of the American Academy of Political and Social Science*, 587(1), 69–81.

Lipsey, M.W. and Cullen, F.T. (2007) The effectiveness of correctional rehabilitation: A review of systematic reviews. *Annual Review of Law and Social Science*, 3(1), 297–320.

Lipsey, M.W., Landenberger, N.A. and Wilson, S. (2007). Effects of cognitive-behavioral programs for criminal offenders. Available at: www.campbellcollaboration.org/reviews_crime_justice/index.php

Lipsey, M.W. and Wilson, D.B. (1998) Effective intervention for serious juvenile offenders. In R. Loeber and D.P. Farrington (eds) *Serious and Violent Juvenile Offenders* (pp. 313–345). Thousand Oaks, CA: Sage.

Lipsey, M.W. and Wilson, D.B. (2001) *Practical Meta-analysis*, Thousand Oaks, CA: Sage.

Lösel, F. (1995) The efficacy of correctional treatment: A review and synthesis of recent meta-evaluations. In J. McGuire (ed.) *What Works: Effective Methods to Reduce Re-offending* (pp. 79–111). Chichester: Wiley

Lösel, F. (2007a). It's never too early and never too late: Towards an integrated science of developmental intervention in criminology. *Criminologist*, 35(2), 1–8.

Lösel, F. (2007b) Doing evaluation in criminology: Balancing scientific and practical demands. In King, R.D. and Wincup, E. (eds) *Doing Research on Crime and Justice*, 2nd edition, (pp. 141–170). Oxford, Oxford University Press.

Lösel, F. (2008) Meta-analysis. In G. Towl and D.P. Farrington (eds) *Dictionary of Forensic Psychology* (pp. 107–109). Cullompton: Willan.

Lösel, F. and Beelmann, A. (2003) Effects of child skills training in preventing antisocial behavior: A systematic review of randomized evaluations. *Annals of the American Academy of Political and Social Science*, 587(1), 84–109.

Lösel, F., Köferl, P. and Weber, F. (1987). *Meta-Evaluation der Sozialtherapie* [Meta-evaluation of social-therapeutic prisons]. Stuttgart: Enke Verlag.

Lösel, F. and Köferl, P. (1989) Evaluation research on correctional treatment in West Germany: A meta-analysis. In H. Wegener, F. Lösel and J. Haisch (eds) *Criminal Behavior and the Justice System* (pp. 334–355). New York: Springer.

Lösel, F. and Schmucker, M. (2005) The effectiveness of treatment for sexual offenders: A comprehensive meta-analysis. *Journal of Experimental Criminology*, 1(1), 117–146.

Lum, C., Kennedy, L.W. and Sherley, A.J. (2006). The effectiveness of counter-terrorism strategies. Available at: www.campbellcollaboration.org/reviews_crime_justice/index.php

McCord, J. (1978). A thirty-year follow up of treatment effects. *American Psychologist*, 33(3), 284–289.

McCord, J. (2003). Cures that harm: Unanticipated outcomes of crime prevention programs. *Annals of the American Academy of Political and Social Science*, 587(1), 16–30.

Mitchell, O., Mackenzie, D.L. and Wilson, D.B. (2007) The effectiveness of incarceration-based drug treatment: An empirical synthesis of the research. In D.P. Farrington and B.C. Welsh (eds) *Preventing Crime: What Works for Children, Offenders, Victims, and Places* (pp. 103–116). Dordrecht, NL: Springer.

Moher, D., Jadad, A.R., Nichol, G., Penman, M., Tugwell, P. and Walsh, S. (1995) Assessing the quality of randomized controlled trials. *Controlled Clinical Trials*, 16(1), 62–73.

Moyer, A. and Finney, J. (2005) Rating methodological quality: Toward improved assessment and investigation. *Accountability in Research: Policies and Quality Assurance*, 12(4), 299–313.

Ortiz, J. and Raine, A. (2004) Heart rate level and antisocial behavior in children and adolescents: A meta-analysis.

Journal of the American Academy of Child and Adolescent Psychiatry, 43, 154–162.

Overton, R.C. (1998) A comparison of fixed-effects and mixed (random-effects) models for meta-analysis tests of moderator variable effects. *Psychological Methods*, 3(3), 354–379.

Petrosino, A., Boruch, R.F., Soydan, H., Duggan, L. and Sanchez-Meca, J. (2001) Meeting the challenges of evidence-based policy: The Campbell Collaboration. *The Annals of the American Academy of Political and Social Science*, 578(1), 14–34.

Pratt, T.C. (2010) Meta-analysis in criminal justice and criminology: What it is, when it's useful, and what to watch out for. *Journal of Criminal Justice Education*, 21(2), 152–168.

Pratt, T.C. and Cullen, F.T. (2000) The empirical status of Gottfredson and Hirschi's general theory of crime: A meta-analysis. *Criminology*, 38(3), 931–964.

Reed, J.G. and Baxter, P.M. (2009) Using reference databases. In H. Cooper, L.V. Hedges and J.C. Valentine (eds) *The Handbook of Research Synthesis,* 2nd edition. New York: Russell Sage. pp. 73–102.

Rosenthal, R. (1979) The 'File Drawer Problem' and tolerance of null results. *Psychological Bulletin*, 86(3), 638–641.

Rosenthal, R. (1991) *Meta-analytic Procedures for Social Research.* Newbury Park, CA: Sage.

Rosenthal, R. and Rubin, D.B. (1982) A simple, general purpose display of magnitude of experimental effects. *Journal of Educational Psychology*, 74(2), 166–169.

Rothstein, H.R., Sutton, A.J. and Borenstein, M. (eds) (2005) *Publication Bias in Meta-analysis.* Chichester: Wiley.

Schmucker, M. and Lösel, F. (2007) Meta-analyzing sexual offender treatment efficacy: An integration of research syntheses. Paper presented at the 59th Annual Meeting of the American Society of Criminology, 14–17 November 2007, Atlanta, US.

Schmucker, M. and Lösel, F. (2009) A systematic review of high-quality evaluations of sexual offender treatment. Paper presented at the Annual Conference of the European Society of Criminology, 9–12 September 2009, Ljubljana, Slovenia.

Schweinhart, L.J., Barnes, H.V., and Weikart, D.P. (1993) *Significant Benefits: The High/Scope Perry Preschool Study Through Age 27.* Ypsilanti, MI, High/Scope Press.

Schweinhart, L.J., Montie, J., Xiang, Z., Barnett, W.S., Belfield, C.R. and Nores, M. (2005) *Lifetime Effects: The High/Scope Perry Preschool Study Through Age 40.* Ypsilanti, MI, High/Scope Press.

Shaffer, D.K. and Pratt, T.C. (2009) Meta-analysis, moerators, and treatment effectiveness: The importance of digging deeper for evidence and program integrity. *Journal of Offender Rehabilitation and comparative Criminology*, 50(2), 672–690.

Sharpe, D. (1997) Of apples and oranges, file drawers and garbage: Why validity issues in meta-analysis will not go away. *Clinical Psychology Review*, 17(8), 881–901.

Sherman, L., Gottfredson, D., Mackenzie, D., Eck, J., Reuter, P. and Bushway, S. (1997) Preventing crime: What works, what doesn't, what's promising. Report to the US Congress, Washington, DC.

Smith, M.L. and Glass, G.V. (1977) Meta-analysis of psychotherapy outcome studies. *American Psychologist*, 32(9), 752–760.

Tolan, P., Henry, D., Schoeny, M. and Bass, A. (2008) Mentoring interventions to affect juvenile delinquency and associated problems. Available at: www.campbellcollaboration.org/reviews_crime_justice/index.php

Valentine, J.C. (2009) Judging the quality of primary research. In H. Cooper, L.V. Hedges and J.C. Valentine (eds) *The Handbook of Research Synthesis,* 2nd edition. New York: Russell Sage. pp. 129–146.

Visher, C.A., Coggeshall, M.B. and Winterfield, L. (2006) Systematic review of non-custodial employment programs: Impact on recidivism rates of ex-offenders. Campbell Systematic Review, available at: www.campbellcollaboration.org/reviews_crime_justice/index.php

Welsh, B.C. and Farrington, D.P. (2008) Effects of closed circuit television surveillance on crime. Available at: www.campbellcollaboration.org/reviews_crime_justice/index.php

Welsh, B.C., Farrington, D.P. and Sherman, L.W. (eds) (2001) *Cost and Benefits of Preventiong Crime.* Boulder, CO: Westview Press.

White, H.D. (2009) Scientific communication and literature retrieval. In H. Cooper, L.V. Hedges and J.C. Valentine (eds) *The Handbook of Research Synthesis,* 2nd edition. New York: Russell Sage. pp. 51–71.

White, P., Bradley, C., Ferriter, M. and Hatzipetrou, L. (2005) Managements for people with disorders of sexual preference and for convicted sexual offenders. Cochrane Review, *The Cochrane Library*, Issue 4.

Wilson, D.B. (2001) Meta-analytic methods for criminology. *Annals of the American Academy of Political and Social Science*, 578(1), 71–89.

Wilson, D.B., Mackenzie, D.L., Mitchell, F.N. and Hammerstrom, K.T. (2005) Effects of correctional bootcamps on offending. Campbell Systematic Review, available at: www.campbellcollaboration.org/reviews_crime_justice/index.php

Wilson, S.J., Lipsey, M.W. and Derzon, J.H. (2003) The effects of school-based intervention programs on aggressive behavior: A meta-analysis. *Journal of Consulting and Clinical Psychology*, 71(1), 136–149.

Wortmann, P. M. (1994) Judging research quality. In H. Cooper, L.V. Hedges and J.C. Valentine (eds) *The Handbook of Research Synthesis,* 2nd edition. New York: Russell Sage. pp. 97–109.

29

Crime Concentration and Police Work

Ken Pease

INFORMATION, COMMUNICATION AND POLICING

The present chapter seeks to link information inputs to police work with policing resource allocation and day-to-day decision making. Its intellectual heritage is indebted to signal detection theory (SDT). It discusses the distribution of crime victimization across places and people, and suggests how these might be measured and understood. It concludes with the suggestion that methods informed by SDT could provide a new and applicable focus to police decision making.

Police officers' current awareness of the extent, type and concentration of crime events is necessarily imperfect. The distinctions they are required to make are moulded by legal categorization and by organizational pressures and exigencies. A multi-faceted call for service must initially be classified mentally as crime/no crime. Once a crime is inferred, it must be provisionally classified as to offence type. Are three boot marks on a door criminal damage or attempted burglary? How does one assess recklessness as to a sexual partner's consent? The choice determines whether a rape charge will stand up. Next, in some forces a judgment of crime solubility is required which determines how much follow-up effort is expended. Characteristics of a suspect pool must be delineated. If a putative perpetrator is identified, a prosecutor's decision about evidential sufficiency has to be anticipated. Other decisions have routinely to be made requiring Solomonic wisdom. For example, in the aftermath of a sudden infant

death, how does one square sensitivity with the need to exclude the possibility of murder? What experience and organizational imperatives can one bring to bear on such decisions, given that police organizational memory is estimated at two years (see Wright and Pease, 1997). Into this heady mix is added a police culture emphasizing immediacy of action and solidarity with colleagues which persists over time. Loftus concludes from her recent ethnographic research that 'the underlying world view of officers displays remarkable continuity with older patterns' enduring because 'the basic pressures associated with the police role have not been removed' (Loftus, 2010: 1). Loyalties and allegiances persist beyond retirement, with the National Association of Retired Police Officers 'representing retired police officers of all ranks and police widows from police forces throughout England and Wales'.[1]

In short, policing is extraordinarily difficult, and a stream of ambiguous data gives rise to daily dilemmas which are played out against a backcloth of organizational culture and testing external pressures. Majoring on crime concentration is, in the writer's view, the most realistic emphasis for applicable policing research, at least in the short term. Put crudely, a researcher cannot hope to encompass the complexity of police work. A focus on the data with which the police officer has to work is feasible and may be seen as readily communicable to police officers, and has a fighting chance of being regarded as helpful by them. The writer spent the last 15 years of his working life in operational police stations. This taught him many things, not the least important of which was the miniscule extent to which research currently informs both front-line policing and police management. In the words of one officer 'we just crack on with the job'. If bridges are to be built, research must initially focus on what is palpably helpful.

How does one helpfully think about the information on which policing practice is built? Despite its neglect, a reasonable place to start is with the eponymous mathematical theory classically set out by Shannon (1948) and its offshoot developed by ergonomists and psychologists, signal detection theory (SDT). For both information theory and SDT, the danger lies in the use of facile and superficial applications (Pierce, 1980). Information theory can, nonetheless, defensibly be brought to bear on the measurement of crime concentration. If all crime occurs at one spot, the location of the next crime conveys no location information. Uncertainty is not reduced. If crime is distributed randomly, the location of the next crime is maximally informative. The ideal state of affairs for policing (but not for the community) is the former, and police sting and honeypot operations are attempts to move to a state of complete predictability of crime. The same applies to the distribution of crime across offenders. If all crime is committed by one person, knowing the perpetrator of the next crime conveys no information. Space precludes developing the perspective as it applies to offenders, but readers should see Roach (2010) for analyses which can be interpreted in information theory terms. Another concept within information theory which will be referred to later involves the 'chunking' of information. For example, skilled Morse operators work by envisaging sequences of dots and dashes equivalent to words, rather than individual letters. This is aided by the redundancy of language, whereby (for example) 'th' is usually followed by 'e' and never by 'q'. It will be speculated that skilled police problem-solvers 'chunk' events into precipitating problems which are then addressed as a single entity.

The basics of SDT will be outlined here, in the belief that it can be faithfully applied to police work. An excellent detailed account of SDT and its associated methodology is provided by Wickens (2002). At its root, SDT is about individuals making decisions under uncertainty, something equally applicable to medical diagnostics, police work and earthquake prediction. An individual must decide whether a condition (signal) is present. In the original classic demonstration, the person must respond according to whether an auditory signal is present against a background of white noise. The action alternatives are distinct, but the evidence on which a decision must be based is ambiguous. For example a police officer must decide to patrol in area A in the belief that more crime is more likely to be committed there.

If she chooses to patrol in area A, the outcomes may be that a crime is committed (hit) or no crime is committed (false alarm). If she chooses not to patrol in area A, there are two outcomes; a crime was committed in area A (miss) or no crime was committed in area A (correct rejection). The parallel with the original signal–noise situation will be clear. Plotting the hit rate against the false alarm rate yields a curve known as the receiver operating characteristic (ROC) which defines the quality of individual performance, in terms of how well the actor can distinguish between signal (crime) and noise (no crime).

In the simple case, the optimal observer will be equally concerned with avoiding the two types of error. Real life, however, usually means that the consequences of the two types of error (false alarm and miss) are different. ROC curves will be influenced by the consequences of false alarms and misses. For example, a crime victim in a prosperous area may complain about police absence (miss) more than a victim in a poorer area. If such complaints were more vociferous than complaints in poorer areas about police presence (false alarm) patrols would congregate in better-off areas than would be optimal. The police decision to put a case forward for prosecution is a false alarm if the Crown Prosecution Service decides not to proceed. 'Misses' (i.e., cases where the Crown Prosecution Service would have proceeded had the case been referred to them) are effectively invisible to the officer. In such circumstances the observer will be subject to bias and make many decisions not to refer to prosecutors cases which they would have proceeded with. In the writer's view, *all* criminal justice decisions could profitably be addressed by thinking them through in SDT terms. Tentative steps were taken by the writer and colleagues three decades ago to apply SDT to criminal justice decisions (Pease *et al.*, 1977). Further developments in the application of SDT to policing are imminent (Bouhana *et al.*, in prep.). The approach's benefits include identification of officers who are the most discriminating decision makers, and those who need training; the degree of bias introduced by unequal consequences of misses and false alarms (in all policing activities); and the provision of a reasoned basis for resource allocation. To make explicit the application to methodology, measurement of hits, misses, false alarms and correct rejections are the necessary data for applicable analyses.

THE FLUX OF CRIME

Are counts and rates of crime and disorder to be considered information for the police? In 1829 at the inception of London's Metropolitan Police Service Sir Richard Mayne wrote:

> The primary object of an efficient police is the prevention of crime: the next that of detection and punishment of offenders if crime is committed. To these ends all the efforts of police must be directed. The protection of life and property, the preservation of public tranquillity, and the absence of crime, will alone prove whether those efforts have been successful and whether the objects for which the police were appointed have been attained (Metropolitan Police Service, 2010).

Mayne set the hurdle high by writing that the presence of tranquillity and the absence of crime 'will alone prove' police efficacy. He was wrong. The absence of crime may be ascribed to a number of reasons of which police efficacy is only one candidate for a causal role. The drop in crime common across Western countries in the late 1990s is (arguably) most plausibly ascribed to changes in levels of security (Farrell *et al.*, 2008, 2010, in press) rather than police action, but the fact that the issue remains contested illustrates the difficulty of making cause–effect inferences about policing and crime.

Policing impacts influence, and are influenced by, decisions largely outside frontline police control. These decisions are of two kinds. The first concerns the processing of offenders. These decisions include the decision to charge, the choice of charge, the decision to prosecute, the decision to bail or imprison on remand, the decision as to guilt and the sentence imposed. The consequences of these decisions feed back into policing burdens, with, for example, offenders freed on bail remaining at liberty to commit crime, and police officers in consequence being abstracted from normal duties to appear in court. The second set of decisions impacting on, and impacted by, police work, involves attempts to change the precipitating circumstances of crime. These sets of decisions include publicity and advice campaigns to the public, and attempts to persuade designers to incorporate security in their products and services. Taken together, these contextual decisions muddy the evaluation waters considerably. In SDT terms, the signal–noise ratio is low.

Notwithstanding the attendant difficulties, Mayne's criterion must be relevant insofar as the absence of tranquillity and the presence of crime are not compatible with assertions of policing success, however defined. The last two decades have seen a change of emphasis in policing, from police officers as direct enforcers, to the police as enablers of crime-reductive action by the community and by other agencies (see, e.g., Byrne and Pease, 2008). For instance, Green Bay Wisconsin

police cleared a problem area by a range of methods which included publicizing which bars were sites of crime and disorder, and briefing and supporting citizens wishing to take action against proprietors of trouble spots.[2] In Portsmouth, UK, vehicle crime was reduced by the extraordinarily simple expedient of finding the streets most prone to such crime, asking the residents what was happening, and taking appropriate action.[3] Some 40 years ago, the writer was teaching a group of frontline officers, and it emerged in discussion that the burglary problem in a nearby town was caused by the fitment of poor-quality front doors in its social housing, which gave way under modest pressure. I asked the officer who supplied the information why he did not tell the relevant local authority. He replied, 'That's more than my job is worth,' suggesting he would be disciplined for exceeding his role, which was simply to respond to a call for service. Now, he would be encouraged to report this, and channels have been established to provide means of doing this. The expansion of the police role can be illustrated (but is not confined to) the development of problem-oriented policing. What does the new emphasis on the police as enablers of community crime prevention mean for understanding data?

The problem-oriented policing (POP) movement advocates the clustering of events into problems, which are then addressed by wide-ranging remedial action. This is exemplified by the projects in Green Bay and Portsmouth cited earlier. This has interesting and unexplored parallels with SDT, where the 'chunking' of information refers to a strategy for making more efficient use of cognitive resources by recoding information (see Gobet *et al.*, 2001). In Green Bay the project leader, Bill Bolger, describes in his presentations the mindset which it seeks to dislodge. In morning briefings before his project began, a daily award was given, in a spirit of irony, to the officer who had taken longest dealing with a call during the previous day. Taking a long time over calls was seen as heaping additional burdens on colleagues who had to deal with other incoming calls. Bolger's attempt to 'chunk'–that is, to identify remediable problems which underlay repeated events which led him to spend more time on individual calls–caused him to receive the award frequently. When his project succeeded, there were (of course) fewer calls to deal with, so his colleagues did not need to work so hard to minimize the time they spent at the location to which they were called. All the (currently 61) practice guides issued by the Center for Problem-Oriented Policing take essentially the same approach (see, e.g., Kooi, 2010).

If chunking events into problems and dealing with the problems, as reflected in POP, is the way ahead, the rate, distribution *and patterns* of crime and disorder, collectively rendered here in terms of concentration, should represent a key measure of police performance. Of course, these things are knowable only imperfectly. Some crime victims are unaware that they have been offended against (e.g., very young victims of paedophile attack and the elderly suffering from Alzheimer's disease or other forms of dementia who are targeted by fraudsters or burglars by deception). Some people are reluctant to report their victimization (e.g., those suffering domestic violence and whose own legal status is questionable; Sparks, 1981). Many victims, usually of less serious crime, forget or decide not to have official notice taken of their experience because of their perceptions of police impotence to help. These limitations are well recognized and described in the literature on victimization surveys (Hough and Maxfield, 2007; Lynch and Addington, 2007). Taken together, these factors mean that crime levels and variation as reflected in calls for police service provide a poor basis for deciding whether Mayne's sole criterion of police effectiveness has been met. Better criteria are available to the able methodologist, as the rest of this chapter explains.

GRAPPLING WITH CRIME'S DISTRIBUTION

For many criminologists, one of the most shocking facts about crime is the inequality of its distribution. This is true across nations (Farrell and Bouloukos, 2001) but also across areas intranationally, and across individuals and households within areas (Tseloni and Pease, 2005). The conventional measurement of inequality by geographers and economists is the Lorenz Curve and its associated Gini coefficient (Marsh, 1988; Smith, 1979). The calculation and use of Lorenz curves (and to a lesser extent in academic contexts Gini coefficients) provides an excellent means, rarely used in the crime context, of depicting the equity of distribution of social ills (or goods).

In its crime usage, the Gini coefficient can be explained as follows. Think of a situation of perfect equality of victimization across people (or households or businesses, or whatever is the relevant unit of count). In this case, 25 per cent of units suffer 25 per cent of crimes, and so on. Think of the opposite, a situation where a single unit accounts for all victimization; that is, a position of maximum possible inequality of victimization. The Gini coefficient expresses the position of an actual distribution relative to these two extremes. The Gini's companion measure, the Lorenz curve, plots the cumulative proportion of the total crimes (y) suffered by the bottom x per

cent of the population. This is illustrated by Figure 29.1, which uses British Crime Survey (BCS) data on crimes against the person. The figure is somewhat simplified for ease of calculation by dividing BCS sampling points into deciles, with the x axis having at point 1 the 10 per cent of sampling points which suffered least personal crime, at point 2 the 20 per cent (because the data are cumulative) of sampling points which suffered the least personal crime, and so on. The straight line represents the position under complete equality. The actual BCS line is, by contrast, bowed, indicating much areal inequality. If Figure 29.1 were printed on graph paper, you could roughly calculate the Gini coefficient by counting the squares on the graph paper below the diagonal (perfect equality), then counting the squares between the straight line and the bowed curve, and expressing the second as a proportion of the first. In the spirit of this chapter we need to express the inequality revealed in terms recognizable to police officers. For that, Gini is unnecessary. We can look at Figure 29.1 and see that 10 per cent of areas (decile 10) accounts for over half of all personal crime. The massive implications for allocation of resources will be clear from that alone.

The precise formula for the Gini coefficient depends upon the data studied, but in the present case can be taken as

$$G_1 = 1 - \sum_{k=1}^{n} \left(X_k - X_{k-1} \right) \left(Y_k + Y_{k-1} \right)$$

being roughly 0.45 in this case. X refers to cumulative units of count (in this case area deciles), Y is the cumulative proportion of crime in those areas, and n is the number of units of count (in this case 10). So one sums from $k = 1$ to 10, and subtracts the total from 1.

The Gini and Lorenz should be used with care, with different units of count (here grouped areas) appropriate for different purposes, but they have

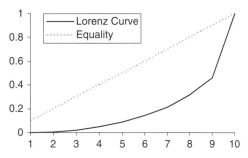

Figure 29.1   Personal crime inequality in BCS

huge advantages insofar as policing is concerned with fairness in the sharing of the burden of crime. They can be used to compare crime distributions across countries, police forces and beats. They can show trends in inequality of crime victimization over time. They are scale invariant, so it does not matter whether one is comparing large or small sectors. There are numerous calculated Lorenz curves and Gini coefficients to be found in Tseloni and Pease (2005) together with a discussion of the advantages and difficulties of the approach.

For the local police station, the level of inequality of victimization will be masked by the fact that they are aware only of crimes reported to them (or which they target). Figure 29.2 shows the proportion of unreported crime falling in area deciles ranked by amount of reported crime. Looking at Figure 29.2, decile 1 (the 10 per cent of areas with the least *reported* crime) hosts only some 2 per cent of all *unreported* crime. By contrast, the 10 per cent of areas with most reported crime suffers some 19 per cent of all unreported crime. Put another way, the areas that are worst when one looks from the police commander's office; that is, in terms of reported crime, are much, much worse when one factors in unreported crime. In the worst decile, some 60 per cent of crimes remain unreported, so the inequality there is of high significance and should feature in police resourcing decisions.

The above discussion was concerned with how to think about measuring fairness in the distribution of victimization. At the area level, this could provide a radical new basis for monitoring police performance. Traditionally, this has been conceived in terms of rates of crime, measures of public confidence, or sanction detections. I have suggested (often to the general bemusement of policy-making audiences) that the level of reported crime in the most crime-ridden area (ward or beat) should be no more than twice the rate in the least crime-ridden area. In that way, police attention would be directed towards increasing the equity, as well as decreasing the level of victimization in the high-crime areas. Residents of the least crime-challenged areas can be relied upon to command police attention. This is not true of the most crime-ridden areas. The effect was described by Townsley and Pease (2002) as the 'winter in Florida, summer in Alaska' phenomenon. That is to say, when a low crime area has a period when it suffers crime (winter in Florida) it sees itself as having a problem. When a high crime area has a period when it suffers less crime (summer in Alaska) it feels relative relief. This is true despite the fact that winter in Florida is still warmer than summer in Alaska. In other words, if an area becomes habituated to a particular level of crime, deviations from that level will evoke feelings of relief or distress. Only a policing approach which adopts a general standard of crime victimization independent of such highly relativized local feelings can serve to resource an area equitably. How in fact resourcing equates to the presenting problem will be discussed later. Before leaving the discussion of inequality, however, we should think about variations in victimization at the individual level.

SEPARATING PREVALENCE AND CONCENTRATION

Drawing a parallel with medicine, let us consider cancer as analogous to victimization. We have two

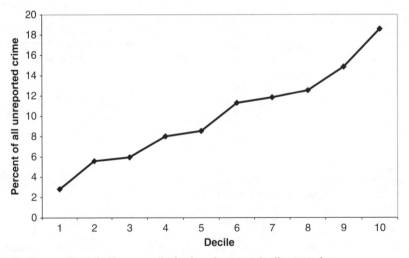

Figure 29.2   Proportion of all unreported crime by area decile: BCS data

relevant populations, the second a subset of the first. First there is the number of people capable of developing cancer (i.e., everyone, to varying extents). Second is the population of those diagnosed with cancer. Treatment success is traditionally measured as n year survival rates of those diagnosed; that is, the second population distinguished above. In survival rates, the number of people who have already contracted cancer (population 2) is the denominator, with the number of people still alive after n years is the numerator. The process does not start with the population at risk of contracting cancer (population 1), since a variety of factors such as exposure to carcinogens and lifestyle (which medical science cannot reasonably be expected to change) determines the number of people who fall ill. If policing success were assessed like cancer treatment success, one should measure the absence of further victimization *of those who have previously called for police service*. The more recent emphasis on policing as agency of social change should be reflected in a decrease in the number of people seeking help. In this it has similarities with the specialism of public health within medicine, and indeed violence was declared a public health issue by the World Health Assembly in 1996 (see Krug *et al.*, 2009, for later developments).

Distinguishing the two modes of evaluation requires conventionally reported crime rates to be refined in order to provide an indication of how police action may be working. Incidence (i) is a product (both literally and arithmetically) of prevalence (p), being the proportion of people/places available to be victimized which are victimized. Concentration (c), is the number of victimizations per victimized person or place, with

$$i = p \times c$$

Concentration *among victims* reflects the extent to which victims are aided (or otherwise) to avoid further victimization. Prevalence is the extent to which the community generally is aided to prevent an experience of crime.

The crucial importance of separating prevalence and concentration in understanding crime trends and policing impacts can be illustrated by the study of domestic violence carried out by Farrell and Buckley (1999). Domestic violence is notoriously poorly reported. Thus an increase in the prevalence of reports of domestic violence is to be welcomed because it means that more of those suffering the problem bring it to police attention. In their Merseyside study, Farrell and Buckley showed that the introduction of an improved service for victims of domestic violence was associated with an *increase* in the number of

women reporting to the police (p). Because a decent service was now being offered, there was also a desirable *decrease* in the average number of calls made per complainant (c). The increase in prevalence and decrease in concentration, however, cancelled each other out when incidence was considered. The total volume of calls (i) remained the same giving the impression that the initiative had no effect. In fact that conclusion had been reached in Merseyside before the Farrell and Buckley study showed otherwise.

The concentration of crime across victims is virtually always underestimated. There are many reasons for this. They include the following:

1   Some places are described differently or misspelled. In an early study we found that crime at the local hospital, Anytown Royal Infirmary, was spelled (or mis-spelled) in 17 different ways. Unless there were multiple or open-ended searches, the huge degree of repeat victimization of the hospital would be missed. Geocoded police data, where accurate, will reduce the importance of this reason, but checks should *always* be made.
2   Some people have their names mis-spelled, or forename and surname placed in wrong fields. This latter issue is a particular problem for ethnic minority victims of crimes away from their home. For example the Western name Judith Anne Parker would, as a Chinese name, be rendered as Parker Judith Anne.
3   People repeatedly victimized have a diminishing probability of reporting to the police the crime they have suffered (Pease, 1998).
4   Repeats are calculated within a time window (three months, six months, etc.). While a substantial proportion of repeats happen quickly, the length of the time window determines the volume of repeats captured. Figure 29.3 is re-analyzed from Farrell *et al.* (2002) to illustrate the point. The data, from three US cities (Baltimore, Dallas and San Diego) is indexed to 100 with a time window of one year. Thus a time window of six months will miss over half of the repeats that happen within three years, and a time window of one year will miss some 40 per cent. Put another way (more important for practical policing) repeats tend to occur quite quickly. A third of all repeats within three years will in fact happen within three months. This points towards speed of reaction being necessary after a burglary event in order to maximize prevention and detection possibilities.

The possible detection advantage of temporary measures taken after a burglary is suggested by Anderson *et al.* (1995). In a study in Huddersfield, West Yorkshire, silent intruder alarms were

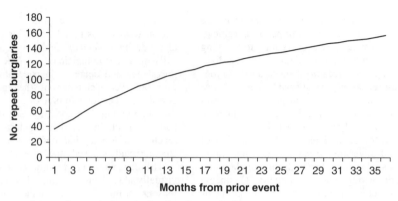

Figure 29.3   Volume of repeat burglaries by time window

allocated to those who had suffered two or more burglaries during the previous 12 months. These alarms, when activated, sounded in the local police station, allowing (hopefully) arrest of burglars at the crime scene. Elsewhere in West Yorkshire, allocation of such alarms was made on the basis of individual officer assessment of risk, as had hitherto been the case in Huddersfield. Table 29.1 sets out the 'pre-project' and 'during project' experience. It will be seen that the proportion of installations based on prior victimization which led to an arrest was much higher than for allocation based on officer assessment of risk. The rate of arrests in Huddersfield rose during the project, in contrast with a decline elsewhere in West Yorkshire. Combined with true misses (where an offence occurred, but the police did not arrive in time to make an arrest) some 21 per cent of alarms installed *for a period of just six weeks* were activated by a real crime in progress. This was substantially higher than elsewhere in the force before or during the project, and higher than had traditionally been the case in Huddersfield before the alarms were installed. The suggestion is that basing risk on awareness of the probability of revictimization can yield more efficient deployment of police detection resources.

Separation of incidence into concentration and prevalence is difficult in police recorded crime data, as noted above. One would expect the problem to be absent from victimization surveys. It is not.

The problem lies in the arbitrary maximum number of offences deemed plausible for an individual to have suffered over the course of a year at the hands of the same person or people. Thus the concentration measure in the BCS is arbitrarily capped at five events (Farrell and Pease, 2007). The effect of this exclusion of the most chronically victimized is to reduce the level of crime captured by some 29 per cent, the effect being most marked for crimes against the person. A similar picture emerges in the US (Planty and Strom, 2007). Table 29.2 shows the degree of under-counting found by Farrell and Pease consequent upon the capping process. Planty and Strom comment powerfully as follows:

[A]nnual estimates [excluding series victimizations] published by the government are severely underestimated. For example in 1993 the … counting rules did not include 58% of all violent victimizations … Second, the magnitude of the undercount varies by crime type and victim demographics. Subsequently, certain groups disproportionately affected by the counting rule may be severely underrecognised as groups prone to victimization. Integrating series incidents into annual victimization rates challenges the basic foundation of our knowledge and understanding of the characterization and risk of victimization (Planty and Strom 2007: 198).

Table 29.1   Temporary silent alarm deployment effects

	Huddersfield pre-project	*Rest of force pre-project*	*Huddersfield during project*	*Rest of force during project*
Installations	104	616	171	713
Arrests	4 (4%)	50 (8%)	24 (14%)	31 (4%)
True misses	2 (2%)	21 (3%)	12 (7%)	19 (3%)

Table 29.2   Crime in England and Wales in thousands (BCS 2005–6)

Crime category	Official count	Actual count	% difference
Property Crime			
Vandalism	*2731*	*3376*	*24*
Vehicle vandalism	1697	1846	9
Other vandalism	1034	1528	48
Burglary	*733*	*877*	*20*
With entry	440	515	17
Attempts	293	362	24
With loss	315	342	9
No loss	418	535	28
Vehicle thefts	*1731*	*1779*	*3*
Theft from	1121	1159	3
Theft of	185	185	0
Attempts	425	436	3
Bicycle theft	*439*	*446*	*2*
Other h/hold theft	*1158*	*1361*	*18*
Theft from person	*576*	*584*	*1*
Snatch theft	71	71	0
Stealth theft	504	512	2
Other theft	*1196*	*1213*	*1*
Violence			
Common assault	*1490*	*2956*	*98*
Wounding	*547*	*1060*	*94*
Robbery	*311*	*333*	*7*
All BCS violence	**2420**	**4421**	**83**
Domestic violence	357	857	140
Acquaintance	817	2093	156
Stranger	863	1067	24
Mugging	382	404	6
All h/hold crime	**6792**	**7838**	**15**
All personal crime	**4120**	**6250**	**52**

The reason for government agencies excluding series victimization is primarily to ensure stability of annual estimates of crime. Including them would mean that estimates would depend upon the number of very frequently victimized people captured in the victimization survey sample. Consequently, statistical convenience is privileged over the reality of suffering. Indeed, the problem may be more pervasive than the above figures suggest. While repeat victimization has been most studied in relation to burglary and personal violence, there is much evidence that the disproportionate victimization of some individuals and businesses also characterizes crimes in cyberspace (see, e.g.,Titus and Gover, 2001; Moitra and Konda, 2004).

To reiterate, emphasis here is on the front end of police work, the data available and how to organize and interpret it, how to chunk it and convert it into uncertainty-reducing information by linking it to practice choices. The separation of concentration and prevalence is as important in principle as it is rare in practice. Yet it seems crucial in interpreting crime trends, as well as police performance. The crime drop in England and Wales between 1995 and 2006 was much larger for repeat crime (51 per cent) than for single incidents of crime (16 per cent). In particular, the decline in the number of repeat incidents has been the main contributor to the overall decline in BCS violence (Thorpe, in Jansson *et al.*, 2007: 93). Thus, whatever caused the crime drop, it had more to do with those already victimized than those not yet victimized. Grove (2010: 139) in a systematic review of projects seeking specifically to prevent repeat victimization concluded, 'The weighted mean effect size, calculated using the random effects model, is 1.212 (low = 1.093, high = 1.345) indicating that overall, programmes which focus crime prevention resources on existing victims of crime are successful.'

AREA INEQUALITY AND THE ECOLOGICAL FALLACY

There is a general tendency to equate deprivation and crime, and to advocate general area improvement as a crime control measure. In information theory terms, knowing the level of area deprivation is taken to be substantially uncertainty-reducing, with consequences for the preferred balance between false alarms and misses (see previous SDT discussion). A recent significant study of area effects and crime (Kershaw and Tseloni, 2005; Tseloni, 2006) found that area attributes based on census and regional variables, including deprivation measures, are linked with local crime rates, but the relationships are surprisingly weak. *Crime rates are generally not satisfactorily explained by area characteristics and region*. This goes against received wisdom. *Individual* characteristics are known to significantly explain crime risks (see Hindelang et al., 1978; Kershaw et al., 2000) and rates (Osborn and Tseloni, 1998). Between-household variability is 9.5 and 19 times greater than the between-area variability of total household crime and thefts and burglaries, respectively (Tseloni, 2006). Socio-demographic measures are better at measuring fear and perceived disorder than they are at measuring crime itself. There is thus no obvious substitute for crime itself as a predictor of crime. There are many excellent reasons for providing a decent environment for people to live and grow up in. That can be regarded as a moral imperative. Moreover, there *is* an association between various measures of crime and area deprivation; and unusually high offender activity and crime rates have been found in deprived areas in various locations in Britain (Herbert, 1977, in Cardiff; Hirschfield et al., 1995, in Merseyside; Baldwin and Bottoms, 1976, in Sheffield). But we must not get carried away. Kershaw and Tseloni's (2005) work shows the association is loose. Whatever the underlying dynamics, the direct relationship between deprivation and crime is not powerful enough for deprivation to substitute for crime itself as an index of area crime. This needs to be said plainly and unequivocally: the use of area classification schemes appeals to a simplistic notion that area characteristics, such as deprivation, powerfully drive crime rates. This notion is misguided, even though they tend to appeal to government. For example, an Audit Commission paper opined, 'As well as directing effort, the adoption of this core policy has been used to convince local communities and businesses that policing should concentrate on crime hot spots and/or deprived communities' (Smith, 2002: 2). The 'and/or' suggests that deprivation is a sufficient criterion for crime-reductive resource concentration even in the absence of high crime. The same approach is common at a local level. For example, Calderdale Council argues, 'Several socio-economic factors affect the likelihood of being a victim as well as committing an offence. In Calderdale the postcodes with the highest levels of crime tend to rank highest in terms of deprivation.'[4] Sometimes the link between crime and poverty is taken as given: 'ConDem plans to slash police budgets will create a North–South divide. Eight of the 10 forces due to be hit hardest by Home Office cuts are in the North … They cover some of the poorest areas in England and Wales where crime and social deprivation is high.'[5]

The relationship between wealth and burglary also provides a beautiful example of the ecological fallacy. Readers will recall that the fallacy contends, in essence, that a relationship at the aggregate level does not necessarily hold at the individual level; in the most familiar instance, Durkheim's (1897) classic observation that predominantly Catholic countries suffered lower rates of suicide than predominantly Protestant countries. He proceeded with an interpretation in terms of varying theologies which assumed that more Protestants killed themselves than did Catholics. This (we can say with hindsight and a reasonable social science education) does not follow. For example, if majority Catholic communities were nicer to their minorities than majority Protestant communities, the area differences would be as Durkheim found, even though most of those in Catholic countries who killed themselves were Protestants. Numerous examples of ecological fallacies are to be found in the literature, many in the context of medical research (Greenland and Robins, 1994). If the relationship between wealth and burglary is the same at the individual and area level, there is some justification for deploying crime-reductive resources *throughout* poorer areas. If, however, the relationship differs at household and area levels, that is inappropriate.

Tseloni et al. (2002) showed that the association was indeed different at area and household levels, with the two levels interacting. Insofar as deprivation was relevant to burglary, it worked in different directions at the area and household

Table 29.3 Prevalence rates (per 1000 homes, six year period) for detached and terraced housing by deprivation quintile

Prevalence rate	Detached	Terraced
Quintile 1	1793 10.32	498 18.87
Quintile 2	1038 17.85	2485 18.44
Quintile 3	579 27.46	6150 21.31
Quintile 4	336 57.83	7751 21.95
Quintile 5	391 71.29	6924 25.91

levels. Specifically, the houses most liable to burglary were the homes of affluent people in poorer areas. This was confirmed by Bowers *et al.* (2005) and is illustrated in Table 29.2. Considering the risk of burglary *per se*, Table 29.3 shows the risk, expressed as a rate per 1,000 households, of being burgled for four different housing types in each of five different areas. These areas were defined by including the most affluent 20 per cent of areas in quintile 1, the next most affluent 20 per cent into quintile 2, and so on, with the most deprived 20 per cent of areas being categorized as quintile 5. The quintiles were produced by using the ward level Index of Multiple Deprivation 2000. Using this approach, each of Merseyside's 118 local authority wards were assigned to one of the five quintiles. Rates were produced using counts of each property type falling into each quintile for the whole of Merseyside.

It will be seen that the prevalence rate of burglary against terraced houses is 19 in the least deprived quintile and 26 in the most deprived. By contrast, the prevalence of burglary against detached homes is 10 in the least deprived quintile, but 71 in the most deprived, four times as much, and three times the prevalence of burglary against terraced homes in the most deprived quintile. The householders at greatest need of burglary prevention help, it turns out, are those in detached homes in deprived areas. The moral is this: if you insist, against the evidence, to allocate crime reduction resources according to area deprivation indices rather than historical rates of crime, you should give greatest priority to people in the biggest houses in the most deprived areas.

FUNDING BY AREA

Police resources deployed in an area have to be funded. In England and Wales, the Police Funding Formula (PFF) is used to determine the distribution of money from central government amongst police forces in England and Wales. The formula was introduced following the Police and Magistrates' Courts Act 1994. Its underpinning assumptions are that the policing need of an area can be inferred from the characteristics of the area and its population, that these characteristics are capable of measurement, and that the relationships are sufficiently precise to form an equitable basis for the allocation of funding. The process whereby the PFF was constructed was very sophisticated, and like many sophisticated measuring devices, it easily diverts attention from the essence of its function. The Catch 22 of the formula is that while it seeks to resource forces in proportion to the problems which they face, received wisdom suggests that it must not do this in any way which makes use of measures of crime and disorder, lest the police become exposed to perverse incentives. If recorded crime and disorder were the indices on the basis of which funds were disbursed, organizational self-interest would dictate that a force would seek to maximize the amount of crime and disorder it recorded. The forces that showed greatest ingenuity in boosting their crime figures would then get most money. The easiest way to boost figures is to target so-called victimless crimes, and one could anticipate crackdowns, *inter alia*, on drug use and prostitution, whose identification flows directly from police presence. Put colloquially, detecting such crimes is like shooting fish in a barrel. The officer does not have to detect anyone, merely be at a place where criminal transactions often take place. The grant offers a basic sum per resident of the area to be policed plus a basic sum per person projected to be in an area during a 24-hour period (such as commuters and clubbers). This is supplemented by 11 top-up factors. The indicators used to derive the top-up factors include:

- the number of claimants of unemployment-related benefits with a duration of unemployment more than one year;
- the proportion of terraced households;
- the proportion of student households;
- the proportion of lone-parent households;
- the number of overcrowded households[6]; and
- the number of bars per 100 hectares.

The relationship between the factors incorporated in the top-up measures and the presenting crime problem turn out to be so approximate as to allow only the crudest allocation. In short, the assumption that the various kinds of policing needed in an area can be related to the characteristics of the area and its population is unjustified. The key statistic reported is R^2, the coefficient of determination.

This shows how much of the variation in the item of interest is accounted for by the factors in the equation. For example, the amount of auto-crime was predictable from the demographic factors used in the equation with $R^2 = 0.49$, so that half of the variability in auto-crime is not captured by the formula. Property crime had $R^2 = 0.60$, and other coefficients were likewise less than impressive. The PFF captures 60 per cent of the variation in policing need. The rest is either random or reflects force efficiency. The interpretation of the variance in crime and disorder not accounted for in the PFF is a crucial issue for understanding the evaluation of police performance generally.

The discussion of the PFF above indicates a need for an alternative basis for allocation of funds from central government to police forces. Allocation of resources within forces is the responsibility of senior officers. In a recent analysis (Ross and Pease, 2008), the association between crime and number of police officers allocated to an area was calculated. At the crudest level, number of crimes stands as a proxy for policing need. First, it was shown that at the force level, doubling the number of crimes to be dealt with is associated with approximately a 62 per cent increase in the number of police officers available to deal with them. So, at the force level, doubling the problem does not double the resource to deal with it. Next, 'basic command units' within one large force were examined in the same way. It shows that a doubling of crime is associated with a mere 23 per cent increase in police strength. Finally, analysis by beats within one basic command unit of a different force showed, on the face of it, that a doubling of crime corresponds with roughly a 36 per cent increase in the number of dedicated officers. These analyses are crude but suggest that, even more than is the case at force level, policing resource does not keep pace with the problem as reflected in presenting crime data. There is a case for saying that doubling the crime problem should mean more than doubling the policing response, since processing an alleged offender takes a police officer away from the streets for several hours, so the more arrests, the more 'down-time' from active policing.

Taken together, if the critique of the PFF as a basis for resourcing is correct, and if the Ross and Pease analyses of the relationship between crime and resourcing are generalizable, the areas which are the least adequately policed are the most crime-prone beats in the most crime-prone command areas in the most crime-prone forces. If socio-demographic measures will not do as a proxy input measure for crime, what are the alternatives? One is to fund on the basis of crimes almost universally reported for insurance reasons, such as theft-taking of motor vehicles. A more contentious alternative is to fund on the basis of total crime and disorder figures from three years ago, three years being the rough average tenure of area police commanders. The rationale is that no police commander will spuriously inflate crime numbers so that his or her successor will be funded more generously. Rather the commander will seek to reduce crime during their own tenure.

EVERYDAY PROXIES FOR CRIME NUMBERS

The writer spent the last 15 years of his working life in operational police stations. This experience gave him abundant sympathy for those engaged in frontline policing. It would thus be remiss, after discussing to this point data types and patterns which will inform frontline policing indirectly because of their appeal to senior officers and crime analysts, to neglect data sources which are uniquely available to police officers on the street. Some officers have already developed a sensitivity to the patterns illustrated below. They represent a police 'nose'. For the researcher, this section is intended to serve two purposes. First, it serves to remind her of a branch of the literature too often ignored. Second, it helps to take forward a research tradition which seeks to uncover elements of the craft of policing.

The use of unobtrusive or non-reactive research measures was advocated by Webb et al. in 1966, and developed by Webb and others in 1981. Unobtrusive measurement concentrates on the traces of human action, on the signature scrawled on the environment by human agency. For example, market researchers will find it very useful to know the stations to which potential customers tune their car radios. Street surveys are a possibility, asking car drivers which station they usually listen to. There are problems with social desirability in such an approach, where the over 35s might insist that they listen to Classic FM, whilst the under 25s claim that they listen to local popular music stations. The unobtrusive measurement alternative would be to pay mechanics servicing and repairing cars to have their staff check the station to which each car radio was tuned on arrival. The content of waste bins can be used to monitor the consumption of takeaway foods amongst young women in catered university accommodation (cited in Rathje, 1984), and the wear of floor tiles marking favoured exhibits in museums (Duncan, 1963, cited in Webb et al., 1966). Graffiti is useful to explore the demarcation of gang territories (see Robson, 1993, for a precursor of this use).

Unobtrusive measurement has several crucial advantages over the alternatives. It is normally cheap (often utilizing data already collected by authorities), it is not liable to response bias, and is seldom attached to any single individual, reducing ethical problems associated with invasion of privacy. For example, injectable drug use can be monitored by counting or weighing the contents of street bin collection points and monitoring change across time, comparing reports of needles and other drug-taking paraphernalia via street cleaners, or public complaints. Sales of cigarette paper provides a reasonable proxy for local drug smoking. The signal crimes perspective of Martin Innes is a variant on the unobtrusive measures technique, with the added benefit of identifying the signs of crime and disorder which the public finds most troubling (Innes, 2004).

Problems likely to be susceptible to quick analysis using non-reactive measures include the following (modified from Garwood et al., 2000):

- Traces of public alcohol consumption can be found in litter bins in parks and public gardens, with the kind of drink (alcopops, cheap wine, sherry, cider or lager) suggesting who may be doing the drinking, and sales tags or carrier bags suggesting who may be doing the selling.
- Seat repair costs in soccer grounds are a good proxy for disturbance. It is likely that such damage will be higher in the away section of grounds, since travelling supporters are typically more committed and volatile. It is predicted that damage will be highest in the seats at the territorial divide between home and away fans, since fans who choose such seats are those most interested in taunts and confrontation.
- Abnormal local cost of repairs to buses (see Sturman, 1976), bus shelters and telephone boxes are a good proxy for vandalism.
- Non-standard maintenance costs in school and between tenancies in council-owned housing will give an indication either of damage inflicted by tenants or to void properties between tenancies. That is to say, a certain expected maintenance cost is to be expected by dint of normal wear and tear. A signature of abnormally high costs provide a proxy for vandalism.
- The paraphernalia of smoking heroin is distinctive, with matches and burned foil. The utility rooms of multi-storey blocks and the toilets of pubs in which drug use is extensive are characterized by debris of this kind. Clubs that host much amphetamine use may be characterized by a high rate of sale of water and soft drinks.
- Markers of incivility include visible abuse of the Orange Badge scheme. This can be seen from different viewpoints. First, the number of non-Orange Badge holders parking in disabled bays can be counted (some authorities already book cars for this); second, illegal use of orange badges by trade vehicles (such as builders) act as a further indicator of incivilities. In a sense, this reflects the thinking of the massively influential 'broken windows' hypothesis (Kelling and Coles, 1997), whereby the existence of a broken window which remains unreplaced is a marker for indifference to the locale.
- Positive markers for improvement of feelings of safety in an area are also possible. Increased sales of bus passes and takeup of free or reduced price bus passes amongst the elderly could, along with records of the concessionary fares, be very useful for this purpose. A further indicator is increased takings from streetside pay and display units. Meter takings were used in the US to measure the success of a newspaper strike as long ago as 1963 (Mindack et al., 1963).

One step further, the former chief constable of Thames Valley sees it as extremely important to determine the level of 'social glue' (Sir Charles Pollard, pers. comm.). There are many ways of checking this – for example, levels of redirection of deliberately misdirected mail, levels of pension collection on behalf of a pensioner, levels of use of schools for communal purposes, the extent to which people return the wheelie-bins of their neighbours after refuse collection has taken place. Changes in the level of reports of broken or failed street lamps, and uneven paving, or complaints to highways that pavements have not been repaired properly or are dangerous, may give a clue to the levels of feelings of perceived control and social cohesiveness. Such indicators of 'social glue' may be particularly useful in establishing the presumptive mechanism of change. Some scattered work of a similar kind has already been undertaken, as is indicated by the occasional references given above. Other examples include Coleman's (1985) measures of dog faeces and the like to indicate area breakdown (although the way in which she combined and interpreted these is open to question). Rates of infective hepatitis have been used as proxies for the amount of drug use by injection (Joint Committee on the New York Drug Law Evaluation, 1978).

Some of these traces of crime, disorder and incivilities will already be on record, but not have been collated (e.g., parking in disabled bays without an Orange Badge); others will need collecting and codifying, such as infective hepatitis figures; others, such as debris from heroin smoking will need to follow on from the development of methodologies for data collection, such as those of the North American 'Le Project du Garbage (Hughes, 1984; Rathje and Hughes, 1984).

One example may be given of actual use of such a technique, albeit very modest in scale. An undergraduate student at Huddersfield University, Colette Felvus, sought to count heaps of toughened glass in the car park of the Meadowhall Shopping Centre, Sheffield. Such heaps, found by the roadside or in car parks, are almost certainly indicators of theft from cars. She found the vast majority of such heaps in one small section of the car park, characterized by the absence of passing people on foot, and with easy egress to wasteland. The number of such piles of glass, when annualized, exceeded the total number of reported thefts from cars in the entire police division in which the car park is sited. It is well known from all sweeps of the British Crime Survey that theft from vehicles is greatly under-reported, but to find that one technique (window breaking) in one car park exceeds the recorded total for a division gives dramatic evidence of the extent of under-reporting. Also, it is well known that police records are poor at locating offences within large public areas. In this case, it is difficult to imagine an adequate substitute for glass-counting. Interviews with window replacement personnel might serve a different purpose, measuring incidence rather than location of offences.

BACK TO THE FUTURE

The past may be a good guide to the future, but it is not a perfect one. Multiple victimization of the same target is a special case of a general tendency of risk to be communicated across time and space (Bowers et al., 2004; Johnson and Bowers, 2004; Townsley et al., 2000, 2003). For example, households close to a burglary have an increased likelihood of suffering the same offence. The increased risk declines with distance from the initial target and with time, typically over 400 metres and one month. Townsley et al. used statistical techniques from epidemiology to demonstrate how burglaries are 'infectious'. They found this to be particularly the case in areas with uniform housing type and layout, with higher repeat rates in areas of more diverse housing type. Johnson and Bowers looked at ecological theory to characterize the burglar as an 'optimal forager'. A grazing animal would like to consume the most nutritious grass in a field. The effort expended in getting to the juiciest stuff must also be taken into account. Starting at the best clump of grass in the field, our forager must decide whether the next most promising clump, some way across the field, is a sufficient improvement over the nearby grass to make the amble worthwhile. This provides a plausible analogue of burglar behaviour, at least as can be inferred from

patterns of repeats and near repeats. It squares with the following facts:

- Detached houses are disproportionately burgled in areas where terraced housing predominates (the juiciest grass is chosen first: Bowers et al. (2005).
- Detached houses are *repeatedly* burgled most in areas where terraced housing predominates (the forager goes back to the juiciest grass when the next juiciest grass isn't very juicy: Bowers et al. (2005))
- Near repeats are greatest in areas of uniform housing (when the grass is pretty much the same all over the field, you don't bother going very far: Townsley et al. 2000, 2003).

The work of Johnson, Bowers and Townsley has been translated into predictive mapping software which takes the phenomena of repeats and near repeats and puts them to work in prediction. The software is called ProMap (for **Pro**spective **Map**ping) and is revolutionary (see Johnson, 2010). So far it has been applied to domestic burglary in several countries and police force areas, to bicycle theft (Johnson et al., 2008; Thorpe et al., 2011) and to motor vehicle crime (Johnson et al., 2006; Summers et al., 2007), with essentially the same results. It has even been successfully applied to the prediction of explosive devices detonated in Baghdad (Townsley et al., 2008). Since the burglary research is furthest advanced, it will be used in illustration here. The ProMap work shows that every burglary event confers an elevated level of risk on nearby homes. The closer the home to the one burgled, the greater the risk conferred. This risk is transient, returning to its prior level after a month or so. In ProMap, every burglary event leads to the revision of risk for every nearby home, and every elapsed day leads to a diminution of that risk. Any new burglary event confers transient extra risk on homes nearby. It has already been established that ProMap substantially outperforms the most sophisticated alternatives in predictive accuracy and importantly the predictions of police officers serving the area (McLaughlin et al., 2007).[7] It has been trialled operationally with encouraging results (Johnson et al., 2007). A particularly interesting and welcome development is how the Johnson and Bowers work has been taken up by mathematicians and even seismologists (e.g., Mohler et al., 2010).

FUTURE CHALLENGES AND NEW DIRECTIONS

Virtually none of the measures advocated above are routinely incorporated in inputs to operational policing. Separating prevalence from victim concentration in crime statistics is difficult and time-consuming. The Lorenz curve is a stranger to most police analysts. The police funding formula still delivers funding to places in a very approximate way, and chief constables distribute money in a way which leaves the most crime-challenged areas under-resourced. In the UK, ProMap attracts some interest but no funding.

In the UK the landscape of police evaluation may change in the light of policies of the coalition government elected in 2010. The first policy statement from the Home Secretary May in July 2010 (Home Office, 2010) stressed the substitution of democratic for bureaucratic accountability of the police. The means by which this is envisaged to arise are

1 the direct election of local police and crime commissioners;
2 the abolition of centrally imposed performance targets;
3 the creation of a National Crime Agency to fight organized crime, alongside the abolition of the Serious and Organised Crime Agency (SOCA) and the National Policing Improvement Agency (NPIA).

This will have implications for research into policing. The most probable one will be the increase of defensive research undertaken locally, whereby police officers demonstrate that they are doing what they have been tasked to do, in the places where they have been tasked to do it. For example, Leicestershire Constabulary have pioneered their IR3 software, which allows monitoring of the location of all their vehicles and officers at all times (when on duty – Big Brother has not yet invaded police homes).[8] This will surely be irresistible to police commanders dogged by local commissioners. They will at least be able to prove where their officers were! Whether where they are is where they will have greatest effect is a different question, and it is instructive that answering this question is not part of the Leicestershire initiative. To an academic, the obvious research task is to demonstrate how crime and disorder patterns are shaped by officer presence revealed by IR3. Whether there will be any future police interest in this is questionable. Even given such interest, whether there remains enough loose change in police budgets to fund such work after paying the developers of IR3 is still more questionable.

As a final remark to the aspirant researcher of policing, my final word should be – let none of the problems put you off. Policing is important. Policing is only slightly evidence led. Research across a range of topics is urgently needed. Go to it. If one message has to be stressed, it is bringing

to bear the insights of information theory and SDT, which has been applied to many decisions of less import than those daily made by frontline police officers. As claimed earlier, the writer can think of no aspect of police decision making which could not be advanced by this route, and no discussion of the equity of police deployment and funding that could not be facilitated by it.

NOTES

1 http://www.narpo.org.uk/
2 http://www.popcenter.org/library/awards/goldstein/1999/99–22(W).pdf
3 http://www.popcenter.org/library/awards/goldstein.cfm?browse=abstracts&year=2004
4 http://www.calderdale.gov.uk/community/safety/audit/victim.html
5 *Daily Mirror*, 4 November 2010, p. 23
6 Actually, the natural logarithm of that number. Logarithmic transformations are sometimes used, as they are here, to make data sets more consistent with the assumptions underpinning the statistics used.
7 An interesting incidental finding was that police officer confidence in their predictions bore no relationship to their accuracy.
8 http://www.landaconsultants.com/Products/Ir3Police.aspx

RECOMMENDED READING

Averdijk, H. (2010) *Individuals' Victimisation Patterns Over Time* (Amsterdam: NSCR) is an up-to-date and thorough account of victim 'careers', with their attendant crime reduction implications.

Grieve, J., McVean, A. and Harfield, C. (eds) (2008) *The Handbook of Intelligent Policing* (Oxford: Oxford University Press). The notion of 'intelligent' or 'evidence-led' policing is in vogue. Though an odd notion (is normal policing stupid or ignorance-led?) the handbook contains a variety of scholarly and practitioner-led perspectives on the topic.

Newburn, T. (2008) *Handbook of Policing* (Cullompton: Willan) is essential background reading for those undertaking police research. It is encyclopaedic in academic content, albeit somewhat short on practitioner input.

Ratcliffe, J. (2008) *Intelligence-Led Policing* (Cullompton: Willan). Jerry Ratcliffe is perhaps the leading student of crime mapping, and this book is an accessible introduction to the geography of crime and disorder, and policing responses to it. Jerry's website is also a good source. http://jratcliffe.net/

Tilley, N. (ed.) (2005) *Handbook of Crime Prevention and Community Safety* (Cullompton: Willan) is valuable as a reflection of the context within which crime-reductive policing must take place, with chapters on the 'hot topics' in the area.

Webb, E.J., Campbell, D.T., Schwarts, R.D., Sechrest, L. and Grove, J.B. (1981) *Nonreactive Measures in the Social Sciences* (Boston: Houghton Mifflin) is a classic study of 'traces', and describes an approach which is unduly neglected in policing research and practice.

Williamson, T. (ed.) (2008) *The Handbook of Knowledge-Based Policing* (London: Wiley). Tom Williamson was deputy chief constable of Nottinghamshire and held a doctorate in criminology. This posthumously published collection is distinctive in its emphasis on application of criminology to police work.

Online resources

The Social Science Research Network (SSRN) allows members to publish or download a wide range of social science research – often free of charge – as well as hosting a number of specialized research networks. Available at: http://ssrn.com/

The Economic and Social Data Service (ESDS) is a UK-based data service providing access to key economic and social data, both quantitative and qualitative, spanning many disciplines and themes, including the British Crime Survey, as well as other British, European and international data. Available at: http://www.esds.ac.uk

UK-based statistics and government research relating to crime and justice from the public, police forces and other justice agencies are available at: http://www.statistics.gov.uk/hub/crime-justice

American-based government statistics and government research on crime, criminal offenders, victims of crime, and the operation of justice systems at all levels of federal and national government are available at: http://www.ojp.usdoj.gov/bjs

The Centre for Problem-Oriented Policing website provides completed projects in the problem-oriented policing tradition, over 50 practice guides, detailed descriptions of winning projects in annual competitions, and copious background literature. Available at: http://www.popcenter.org/

A range of research and statistics relating to crime, policing, immigration, drugs, and other areas of Home Office responsibility are available at: http://rds.homeoffice.gov.uk/rds/

The Research and Documentation Centre (WODC) of the Dutch Ministry of Justice deposits cutting edge research and knowledge in the broad field of Justice. Available at: http://www.wodc.nl/

The Institute for Canadian Urban Research Studies website contains useful research reports and factsheets around the mapping of crime concentration and people movements. Available at: http://www.sfu.ca/icurs/

A massive collection of crime and justice data and statistics is available at: http://bjs.ojp.usdoj.gov/

Jerry Ratcliffe's homepage provides details, including downloadable presentations, of the work of this leading scholar on intelligence-led policing. Available at: http://jratcliffe.net/

The homepage of the Jill Dando institute describes itself as the first university department in the world devoted specifically to reducing crime. It does this through teaching, research, public policy analysis and by the dissemination of evidence-based information on crime reduction: http://www.jdi.ucl.ac.uk/

REFERENCES

Anderson, D., Chenery, S. and Pease, K. (1995) *Preventing Repeat Victimisation: A Report on Progress in Huddersfield*. Police Research Group Briefing Note 4/95. London: Home Office.

Baldwin, J. and Bottoms, A.E. (1976) *The Urban Criminal*. London: Tavistock Publications.

Bouhana, N., Sally, H. and Johnson, S.D. (in prep.) *An Examination of Burglar Modus Operandi Consistency*.

Bowers, K.J., Johnson, S.D. and Pease, K. (2004) 'Prospective hot-spotting: the future of crime mapping?' *British Journal of Criminology*, 44, 641–658.

Bowers, K.J., Johnson S.D. and Pease, K. (2005) 'Victimisation and revictimisation risk, housing type and area: a study of interactions.' *Crime Prevention and Community Safety: An International Journal*, 7, 7–17.

Byrne, S. and Pease, K. (2008) 'Crime reduction and community safety.' In Newburn, T. (ed.) *Handbook of Policing*, 2nd edition. Cullompton: Willan.

Coleman, A. (1985) *Utopia on Trial*. London: Hilary Shipman.

Durkheim, E. (1897) *Le suicide*. Paris: F. Alcan.

Farrell, G. and Buckley, A. (1999) 'Evaluation of a police Domestic Violence Unit using repeat victimization as a performance indicator.' *Howard Journal of Criminal Justice and Crime Prevention*, 38, 42–53.

Farrell, G. and Bouloukos, A. (2001) 'International overview: a cross-national comparison of rates of repeat victimisation.' In Farrell, G. and Pease, K. (eds) *Repeat Victimization*. Monsey, NY: Criminal Justice Press.

Farrell, G., Sousa, W.H. and Weisel, D.L. (2002) 'The time window effect in the measurement of victimisation.' In Tilley, N. (ed.) *Analysis for Crime Prevention*. Monsey, NY: Criminal Justice Press.

Farrell, G. and Pease, K. (2007) 'Crime in England and Wales: More violence and more chronic victims.' *Civitas Review*, 4, 1–8.

Farrell, G., Tilley, N., Tseloni, A. and Mailley, J. (2008) 'The crime drop and the security hypothesis.' *British Society of Criminology Newsletter*, 62, 17–21.

Farrell, G., Tilley, N., Tseloni, A. and Mailley, J. (2010) 'Explaining and sustaining the crime drop: Clarifying the role of opportunity-related theories.' *Crime Prevention and Community Safety*, 12, 24–44.

Farrell, G. Tilley, N., Tseloni, A. and Mailley, J. (2011) 'The crime drop and the security hypothesis.' *Journal of Research in Crime and Delinquency*. Online version now available at http://jrc.sagepub.com/content/early/2011/02/10/002242 7810391539

Garwood, J., Rogerson, M. and Pease, K. (2000) 'Sneaky measurement of crime and disorder.' In Jupp, V., Davies, P. and Francis, P. (eds) *Doing Criminological Research*. London: Sage.

Gobet, F., Lane, P.C.R., Croker, S., Cheng, P.C.H., Jones, G., Oliver, I. and Pine, J.M. (2001). 'Chunking mechanisms in human learning.' *Trends in Cognitive Sciences*, 5, 236–243.

Greenland, S. and Robins, J. (1994) 'Ecologic studies: biases, misconceptions and counterexamples.' *American Journal of Epistemology*, 139, 747–760.

Grove, L.E. (2010) Synergies of Synthesis: A Comparison of Systematic Review and Scientific Realist Evaluation Methods for Crime Prevention. PhD thesis, Loughborough University.

Herbert, D.T. (1977) 'An areal and ecological analysis of delinquency residence: Cardiff 1966 and 1971.' *Tijdschrift voor Economische en Sociale Geographie*, 68, 83–89.

Hindelang, M.L., Gottfredson, M.R. and Garofalo, J. (1978) *Victims of Personal Crime: An Empirical Foundation for a Theory of Personal Victimisation*. Cambridge: Ballinger.

Hirschfield, A.F.G., Bowers, K.J. and Brown, P.J.B (1995) 'Exploring relations between crime and disadvantage on Merseyside.' *European Journal on Criminal Policy and Research*, 3, 93–112.

Home Office (2010) *Policing in the 21st Century: Reconnecting Police and the People*. CM 7925. London: HMSO.

Hough, J.M. and Maxfield, M. (ed.) (2007) *Surveying Crime in the 21st Century*. Cullompton: Willan.

Hughes, W.W. (1984) 'The method to our madness: the garbage project methodology, special issue on household refuse analysis, theory, method and applications in social science'. *American Social Scientist*, 28, 41–50.

Innes, M. (2004) 'Signal crimes and signal disorders: notes on deviance as communicative action.' *British Journal of Sociology*, 55, 335–355.

Jansson, K., Budd, S., Lovbakke, J., Moley, S. and Thorpe, K. (2007) *Attitudes, Perceptions and Risks of Crime: Supplementary Volume 1 to Crime in England and Wales 2006/7*. London: Home Office Statistical Bulletin 19/07.

Johnson, S.D. and Bowers, K.J. (2004) 'The burglary as clue to the future: the beginnings of prospective hot-spotting.' *European Journal of Criminology*, 1, 237–255.

Johnson, S.D., Birks, D.J., McLaughlin, L., Bowers, K.J. and Pease, K. (2007) *Prospective Crime Mapping in Operational Context: Final Report*. Home Office online report 19/07. webarchive.nationalarchives.gov.uk/20110220105210/http://rds.homeoffice.gov.uk/rds/burglary1.html

Johnson, S.D., Sidebottom, A. and Thorpe, A. (2008) *Bicycle Theft*. Problem-Oriented Guides for Police Problem-Specific Guide 52. Washington DC: US Department of Justice.

Johnson, S.D. (2010). 'Prospective Mapping.' In Fisher B. and Lab S. (eds) *Encyclopedia on Victimology and Crime Prevention*. London: Sage.

Joint Committee on the New York Drug Law Evaluation (1978) *The Nation's Toughest Drug Law: Evaluating the New York Experience: Final Report*. Washington, DC: National Institute of Law Enforcement and Criminal Justice, LEAA.

Kelling, G. and Coles, C. (1997) *Fixing Broken Windows*. New York: Free Press.

Kershaw, C., Budd, T., Kinshott, G., Mattison, J., Mayhew, P. and Myhill, A. (2000) *The 2000 British Crime Survey, England and Wales*, Home Office Statistical Bulletin 18/2000. London: Home Office.

Kershaw, C. and Tseloni, A. (2005) 'Predicting crime rates, fear and disorder based on area information: Evidence from the 2000 British Crime Survey.' *International Review of Victimology*, 12, 295–313.

Kooi, B.R. (2010) *Theft of Scrap Metal*. Problem Guide 58. Washington DC: Center for Problem-Oriented Policing.

Krug, E., Mercy, J., Dahlberg, L. and Zwi, A. (2009) 'The World Report on Violence and Health.' *The Lancet*, 360, 1083–1088.

Loftus, B. (2010) 'Police occupational culture: classic themes, altered times.' *Policing and Society*, 20, 1–20.

Lynch, J.P. and Addington, L.A. (2007). *Understanding Crime Statistics*. Cambridge: Cambridge University Press.

Marsh, C. (1988). *Exploring Data: An Introduction to Data Analysis for Social Scientists*. Cambridge: Polity Press.

McLaughlin, L.M., Johnson, S.D., Bowers, K.J., Birks, D.J. and Pease, K. (2007) 'Police perceptions of the long and short-term spatial distribution of residential burglary.' *International Journal of Police Science and Management*, 9, 99–111.

Metropolitan Police Service (2010) *History of the Metropolitan Police*. Available at: http://www.met.police.uk/history/definition.htm accessed October 1st 2010.

Mindack, W.A., Neibergs, A. and Anderson, A. (1963) 'Economic effects of the Minneapolis newspaper strike'. *Journalism Quarterly*, 40, 213–218.

Mohler, G.O., Short, M.B., Brantingham, P.J., Schoenberg, F.P. and Toita, G.E. (2010) *Self-exciting point processes in the modeling of crime*. Available at: www.math.ucla.edu/~gmohler/crime_point_process.pdf

Moitra, S.D. and Konda, S.L. (2004) 'An empirical investigation of network attacks on computer systems.' *Computers and Security*, 23, 43–51.

Osborn, D.R. and Tseloni, A. (1998) 'The distribution of household property crimes.' *Journal of Quantitative Criminology*, 14, 307–330.

Pease, K. (1998) *Repeat Victimisation: Taking Stock*. London: Home Office.

Pease, K., Tarling, R. and Meudell, P. (1977) 'Decisions in the criminal justice process and signal detection theory: a note.' *Quality and Quantity*, 11, 83–89.

Pierce, J.R. (1980) *An Introduction to Information Theory*, 2nd edition. New York: Dover.

Planty, M. and Strom, K.J. (2007) 'Understanding the role of repeat victims in the production of annual US victimisation rates.' *Journal of Quantitative Criminology*, 23, 179–200.

Rathje, W.L. (1984) 'The garbage decade special issue on household refuse analysis, theory, method and applications in social science.' *American Social Scientist*, 28, 9–30.

Rathje, W.L. and Hughes, W.W. (1984) 'Introductory comments, special issue on household refuse analysis, theory, method and applications in social science.' *American Social Scientist*, 28, 5–8.

Roach, J. (2010) *Finding the Usual Suspects*. PhD thesis, University College London.

Robson, C. (1993) *Real World Research*. Oxford: Blackwell.

Ross, N. and Pease, K. (2008) 'Community policing and prediction.' In Williamson T. (ed.) *The Handbook of Knowledge-Based Policing*. London: Wiley.

Shannon, C.E. (1948) 'A mathematical theory of communication.' *Bell System Technical Journal*, 27, 379–423, 623–656.

Smith, D.M. (1979) *Where the Grass is Greener*. Harmondsworth: Pelican.

Smith, K. (2002) 'Policing deprived areas.' *Policy Review*, 8th November.

Sparks, R.F. (1981) 'Multiple victimisation: evidence, theory and future research'. *Journal of Criminal Law and Criminology*, 72, 762–778.

Sturman, A. (1976) 'Damage on buses: the effects of supervision.' In Mayhew, P. *et al*. (eds) *Crime As Opportunity*. Home Office Research Study 34. London: HMSO.

Summers, L., Johnson, S.D. and Pease, K. (2007). 'El Robo de (Objetos en) Vehículos y su Contagio a través del Espacio y el Tiempo: Aplicaciones de técnicas epidemiológicas.' *Revista Electronica de Investigacion Criminologica*, 5(1), 1–22.

Thorpe, A., Gamman, L., Ekblom, P., Johnson, S., Sidebottom, A. and Willcocks, M. (2011) 'Bike Off 2 - Catalysing anti theft bike, bike parking and information design for the 21st century: An Open Innovation research approach.' In Inns, T. (ed.) *Designing for the 21st Century – Interdisciplinary Methods and Understanding*. Aldershot: Gower.

Titus, R.M. and Gover, A.R. (2001) 'Personal fraud: the victims and the scams.' In Farrell, G. and Pease, K. (eds) *Repeat Victimization*. Monsey, NY: Criminal Justice Press.

Townsley, M., Homel, R. and Chaseling, J. (2000) 'Repeat burglary victimisation: spatial and temporal patterns.' *Australian and New Zealand Journal of Criminology*, 33, 37–63.

Townsley, M., Homel, R. and Chaseling, J. (2003) 'Infectious burglaries: a test of the near repeat hypothesis.' *British Journal of Criminology*, 43, 615–633.

Townsley, M.T., Johnson, S.D. and Ratcliffe, J.R. (2008). 'Space-time dynamics of insurgent activity in Iraq.' *Security Journal*, 21, 139–146.

Townsley, M. and Pease, K. (2002) 'Hotspots and cold comfort: The importance of having a working thermometer.' In Tilley, N. (ed) *Analysis for Crime Prevention*. Monsey, NY: Criminal Justice Press.

Tseloni, A. (2006) 'Multilevel modelling of the number of property crimes: Household and area effects.' *Journal of the Royal Statistical Society Series A: Statistics in Society* 169, 2, 206–233.

Tseloni, A., Osborn, D.R., Trickett, A. and Pease, K. (2002) Modelling property crime using the British Crime Survey: What have we learned? *British Journal of Criminology*, 42, 89–108.

Tseloni, A. and Pease, K. (2005) 'Population inequality: The case of repeat crime victimisation.' *International Review of Victimology*, 12, 75–90.

Webb, E.J., Campbell, D.T., Schwartz, R.L. and Sechrest, L. (1966) *Unobtrusive Measures: Nonreactive Research in the Social Sciences*. Chicago: Rand McNally.

Webb E.J., Campbell, D.T., Schwartz, R.L., Sechrest, L. and Grove, J.B. (1981) *Nonreactive Measures in the Social Sciences*. Boston: Houghton Mifflin.

Wickens, T.D. (2002) *Elementary Signal Detection Theory*. Oxford: Oxford University Press.

Wright, A. and Pease, K. (1997) 'Cracking down on crime.' *Policing Today*, 3, 34–50.

30

Assessing the Cost of Fraud

Michael Levi

INTRODUCTION

The principal focus of the criminal law is upon the discrete actions of individuals: stealing from and/or physically injuring other people, or damaging property. Fraud is mainly about getting goods, money or services by 'dishonestly' deceiving other people or institutions who would not supply them (at least on those terms) if they knew the truth; but it can also involve causing losses to others without any obvious benefit to self (other than keeping one's job or getting a performance bonus that otherwise one would not get). Counting the *number* of frauds can be interesting, especially if what is counted is telling us about a coherent class of events (like credit card frauds); but when a single fraud with the same legal label can relate to £50 or £50 million, the limitations of this are plain. My aim in this chapter is to examine how we might assess how harmful different forms of fraud are, touching very briefly also upon related crimes such as 'market abuse' (e.g., insider dealing in which market professionals unlawfully exploit inside non-public information) and money laundering (concealing and disposing of the proceeds of crime).

What is fraud? The legal definition varies over time and in different countries. At least prior to the Fraud Act 2006, both legal and analytical/survey definitions and classifications were varied in England and Wales. To avoid confusion, for the purposes of this chapter, fraud is defined as follows:

> Fraud is the obtaining of financial advantage or causing of loss by implicit or explicit deception; it is the mechanism through which the fraudster gains an unlawful advantage or causes unlawful loss.

The focus of this chapter is on one aspect of criminal harms: the costs of fraud. It was stimulated by my ESRC Professorial Fellowship on economic and organised crime and specifically commissioned by the UK Association of Chief Police Officers' Economic Crime Portfolio to meet the following objectives:

- to determine as accurately as possible – from existing *published* sources of information – the nature, extent, and cost of fraud to the public and private sectors;
- to assess critically the availability and quality of existing evidence on fraud; and
- to recommend appropriate strategies to facilitate the comprehensive and consistent recording of data on fraud (i.e., strategies for future data capture).

The sort of data one focuses on may have an impact on what the visible 'fraud problem' consists of. This is reflected in the literature on white-collar crime, and in the tension between it and those who would concentrate on crimes of deception, whatever the collar of the perpetrator. In fact, the literature on white-collar crime – and other crimes too – has largely neglected the question of cost, contenting itself with vague generalities about it being more harmful than other types of crime because of its impact on trust (Sutherland, 1985/1949). Yet this sort of impact is taken for granted rather than demonstrated, and there are so many different types of fraud (and corporate crimes such as corruption, environmental and health and safety violations) that neither the dependent nor independent variables are specified with any reasonable precision.

WEAKNESSES IN DATA ABOUT FRAUD

Most studies of the costs and prevalence of fraud have avoided rigorous research methods; they paid insufficient attention to the problematic interpretation of the term 'fraud' and – to the extent that fraud is a crime targeted on organisations as much as individuals – the survey exercises carried out share many of the problems associated with corporate surveys rather than with the better-tested surveys of individuals and/or households (e.g. the British Crime Survey and equivalents carried out in Australia, the Netherlands, and the US). Weaknesses in current fraud data can be grouped together around several key issues:

1   *Defining 'fraud'.* Questions about fraud often lack specificity. This does not matter greatly in the simpler forms of fraud, whether against individuals, businesses or public sector. If individuals pay direct for goods from someone they have encountered on eBay, bypassing normal controls, and the goods never arrive and the seller cannot be found, then this clearly is fraud; likewise, the data collected by the UK Cards Association on payment card and cheque frauds are relatively unambiguous reflections of crime. (Although UK Cards data unreliably count the more ambiguous 'first party' fraud (and 'phantom withdrawals' at ATMs by genuine card-holders) and do not include frauds committed in the UK upon the holders of non-UK cards, they do include frauds committed abroad on UK-issued cards). Where data have been collected by means of a survey, however, assumptions are often made that all recipients will share a common understanding of what specific forms of fraud entail. The issue of separating 'bad debt' from 'fraud' also remains a major difficulty. In interviews I conducted recently with company workers supplying consumer credit, I was told that by re-analysis of its bad debt book, one firm was able to enhance its ratio of fraud to write-offs more than threefold. Whether this ratio is generalisable across the credit industry (in the UK and elsewhere) remains unknown.
2   *Readiness to participate in fraud surveys.* Corporate victimisation surveys have become commonplace but it is hard to believe that participation rates are complete, yet refusal rates are almost never reported by survey firms.
3   *Ensuring full survey participation by victims.* The question of what sort of victims one focuses on, and how one contacts poorer consumer/investor victims is largely neglected (although see Office of Fair Trading, 2006). Accounting firms understandably focus on their corporate and public sector clients, but this can lead to a distorted picture of the social distribution of fraud victimisation.
4   *Determining the unit of analysis.* The unit of analysis is often not clarified in data collection exercises and equally often appears to be taken for granted by data providers, not least in questionnaire surveys (written or telephone). For example, with surveys of businesses, it is very seldom clear whether the questionnaire response speaks for the company as a whole (e.g., it has been circulated around different divisions before completion) or simply for the person/section asked. Some surveys take care to give advance notice but in many telephone questionnaires, particularly, it seems to be taken for granted that the person answering the questions has full, immediate knowledge of the issues at hand. There are reasons to be sceptical about whether this is always so. The summary of fraud studies outside the financial services sector suggests that different responses will be obtained depending on whether it is head office or local branches answering questions (and there are positive and negative aspects of both). In financial services, especially but not exclusively, different consequences may arise for bonuses and for staff accountability if a loss is classified as bad debt or as fraud. This may distort the data by the time it reaches the person filling in the questionnaire and/or considering whether to file administrative reports on bad debt or fraud.
5   *Determining where the fraud was committed.* It is inherently difficult in the case of transnational frauds to determine where the fraud has occurred, since the answer might be in more than one country. Thus, in the case of international companies, where there is a group audit for the business as a whole (or a region of the world such as 'Asia-Pacific'), it is far from clear in which country the fraud occurred. This may not matter to the company – which may want to know only what its risks are – but it is relevant to assessing 'the impact on the UK' (or on any other specific country).
6   *Accounting for the time lapse between the commission and reporting of fraud.* The duration of the process by which frauds come to light creates difficulties for the placement of fraud within an annualised time frame, let alone real-time 'hot-spotting' of fraud events. There are of course modest lagged effects in relation to some frauds – such as payment card frauds, where the cardholder may become aware of the fraud only weeks after the event, generally when his/her statement arrives (although proactive card scheme and issuer detection systems may spot these much sooner). However, the events themselves are tightly time-bound. Procurement frauds, cartels and real estate frauds involve particular timed events which may require 'retrospective allocation' when learned about

some time later. On the other hand, if there are suspicions/beliefs that fraud occurred, but no criminal convictions or even prosecutions, can one properly label this 'crime'?

7 *Aggregating data and deriving UK-wide estimates.* The task of extrapolating – from limited data – the extent of fraud affecting a particular business sector, or even country, requires much more sophistication than is commonly recognised. Some extrapolations clearly test the bounds of credibility: though there was a caveat in its original report, the much-publicised Association for Certified Fraud Examiners (ACFE, 2002, 2006, 2008) study was a membership survey in the US that had only a 10 per cent response rate, so to extrapolate from that even to the US let alone the UK would defy the normal canons of research. Likewise, the frequent absence of ranges in fraud estimates may make clear newspaper headlines, but cannot possibly be defended when it comes from a research study other than one which, like the KPMG Fraud Barometer and the BDO Fraud Track in the UK, reports cases that are coming or have come to court. The question of whether different surveys could 'double count' the same fraud events has been discussed earlier, and represents a major risk when attempting to pool the results of different data collection exercises.

8 *The irregularity in data collection exercises.* Since the original research by Levi et al. (2007), discussed later in this chapter, the National Fraud Authority was created, and this has updated some of the data, concluding that on the basis of fuller data available on some aspects of fraud, in 2009, fraud cost the UK over £30 billion (National Fraud Authority, 2010a, 2010b), rising to £38.4 billion in 2010 (National Fraud Authority, 2011). However, less detail is available on how some of these data were generated. Whether funds will continue to be available for this sort of exercise is uncertain. No parallel broad-ranging exercises have been undertaken in any other countries to date.

JUDGING COST AND HARM: A FRAMEWORK FOR THE RESEARCH QUESTIONS

The impact of any fraud or series of frauds depends not just on the amount of money involved but also on how well we can afford the loss, and what the implications of fraud are for our institutional and personal reputation, which itself has a commercial and a social value. At a governmental level, Jeremy Bentham viewed the collection of crime statistics as a way of measuring social health.

We might look at what information on crime is collected *and what is not collected* as an indication of concern about social 'problems' as felt by those managing the state.

The collection of information is not the end of the issue. Bentham assumed that we would publish what we have collected. An open society (and a modern transparent company) will face up to its fraud and other crime problems rather than suppress them, but this is easier if other countries and other companies are doing likewise. Indeed, the first British fraud victimisation study of major UK-based companies by this author found that companies favoured being required to publish their fraud data, but only if others had to do likewise – they were mostly confident that their companies were no more vulnerable than the norm, but were afraid that they might suffer a comparative disadvantage if they were incorrectly *seen* to be more vulnerable (Levi, 1987). That study was conducted by semi-structured interviews in collaboration with accountancy firm Ernst & Young to enhance credibility and reduce concern about respectability in the eyes of senior directors, at a time before corruption and fraud surveys became routinised. In the particular case of fraud, it is also expensive to construct credible evidence sources (e.g., via individual and business crime victimisation surveys which cover a representative sample of the population), and recorded crime statistics are poor guides to harm or to financial crime victimisation rates, since so many decision-stages lie between the fraudulent act, its discovery, the decision to report (or not) and its recording by the authorities. Reporting is itself a costly business. Very few victimisation or crime surveys include the cost of any type of fraud. Since governments are the primary funders of such studies, this omission reflects populist and political constructs of which crimes are important as well as technical problems of defining fraud and getting sufficient responses to be worth reporting. (Though low fraud rates are interesting in themselves, those who organise the surveys understandably look for statistically significant data that they can report, generating an unintended bias in data collected.)

Despite all the victimisation surveys that have been carried out in Australia, Europe and the US, and to a far lesser extent elsewhere, the collection of information on impacts (beyond reporting and 'confidence in the police') has been quite crude and simplistic. Moreover, harm (and threat) is not just about how much things cost us. 'Organised fraud', for example, intermingles actual impacts with the social construction of malevolence and 'dangerous groups'. But what if we do not know whether or not particular fraudsters are connected with 'organised crime groups' or are financing terrorism? Should we take the agnostic position that they are not connected and therefore are less harmful than they would have been? And why should having such connections be worse than the frauds of schemers like Bernie Madoff who stole roughly $15 billion from a variety of charities and relatively wealthy individuals and firms over a 15-year period, despite numerous attempts to alert the authorities (Markopoulos, 2010)? For illustrations of major frauds, for which there is no space here, see Doig (2006), Rosoff et al. (2009), Punch (1996), Wells (2007) and Zagaris (2010).

Zemiology – the study of social harms – has been treated as a useful tool with which to batter the obsessions of conventional criminology with household and street crime (Hillyard et al., 2008). The aim of some of its advocates is to transform our priorities so that we might do more about road and industrial accidents than about terrorism; and perhaps more about corporate food poisoning than about what is normally thought of as criminal poisoning. However, Sparrow (2008) emphasises that it is absurd to neglect the relevance of perceptions of future dangerous intentions (as in 'Islamic violence' post-9/11) when assessing harm, for this is part of their cultural impact and also ought to trigger our strategic interventions. I would argue that we should not ignore planned (and foreseeable unplanned) harm-doing in constructing risk assessments and crime control methodologies, however problematic politically it may be to incorporate such crime risk elements into general social planning (Dorn and Levi, 2006; Edwards and Levi, 2008). But irrespective of the current operational use of harm data, the latter (and crime seriousness studies) remain sociologically interesting and socially important.

One of the reasons that economists have flourished and have permeated the administrative culture so effectively is that they offer a common metric – money – through which social impacts (costs and benefits) of social interventions can be filtered and value-for-money assessed across the board. However assessing the costs of different forms of crime is not straightforward. For those crimes that have identifiable individual or collective victims, which sorts of crime victims do we collect 'data' on, in what terms do we view financial costs (e.g., in raw numbers or as a proportion of individuals' wealth/income or corporate profits), and 'collateral damage' such as emotional trauma, changed saving and investing behaviour of those defrauded and others who hear about the frauds? Fraud has both collective and individual dimensions. The former include loss of confidence by people in one's country or company because of a perceived lack of integrity, with serious consequences in the willingness to lend (think of Nigeria), and the costs of policing and prosecution; and unlike most other crimes, many fraud

victims may not realise that they are victims but think that they have merely been unlucky.

Maguire (2007) has reviewed the evidence on general crime measurement in the UK, and there is no need here to replicate these critiques of crime data that are familiar to criminologists, even if they are ignored by news media in their crime reportage in the UK and internationally. The UN's periodic International Crime Victimisation Surveys (van Dijk et al., 2008), and the European one funded by the European Commission (van Dijk et al., 2007) yield important comparative insights, though their small samples mean that they have greater error margins, and the only questions they ask relevant to this review are about perceived frauds on consumers and about everyday local corruption. There have been some modest and intermittent attempts to estimate the prevalence and incidence of *some* white-collar offences (Bussman and Werle, 2006; Kane and Wall, 2006; Karstedt and Farrall, 2006; Pricewaterhouse-Coopers, 2007; Rebovich and Kane, 2000 – see also successive surveys by Ernst & Young and PricewaterhouseCoopers). However, the *financial* costs and other impacts of deception offences have tended to be more the subject of rhetoric than of serious empirical investigation. Unlike offences of interpersonal violence, whether as conventionally defined or as part of corporate health and safety crimes (Tombs and Whyte, 2007), the victim of fraud may not know about the social or other background of the offender. The latter would in any event require us to look at fraud against business and government, as well as fraud against individuals. The social scientific question of how many people in different sectors of society are harmed by deceptions emanating from which sectors is part of the broader question of who is harmed by whom via which mechanisms. This might be used to generate a more sophisticated construction of 'cost' in terms of its impact rather than using a standardised monetisation.

A further dimension of cost is how much we spend on dealing with crimes. Paradoxically, if we include the costs of responses to crime as part of 'the costs of crime' – as is conventional in the US and in Home Office practice (Cohen, 2005) – the less that is done about them, the lower are the 'costs of crime'. In white-collar crimes – even after the enhanced profile after the global economic crisis in 2008–2009 – relatively modest resources overall are expended in investigation, prosecution and imprisonment, despite the fact that high-profile cases individually may be extremely expensive to investigate and to prosecute. This would mean that the serious fraud component of 'the costs of crime' is much lower than in public order or street and household crimes. Thus, out of police expenditure of £14.55 billion in 2008–2009 nationally, only the City of London police spend more than an insignificant part of their budget on pursuing fraudsters (who are seldom linked to domestic terrorism or local disorder risks). However there is substantial non-police public expenditure on combating fraud; there are significantly more Department of Work and Pensions social-security fraud investigators than there are police, tax and trading standards fraud investigators combined (see Doig, 2006, for some data). Because of the dangers that existing expenditure on policing distorts our judgments of the harmfulness of the activity and reinforces a cycle of repetitive attention and control approaches (as in illegal drugs), it is preferable to separate out the costs of controlling crimes from 'the costs of crime' (Levi et al., 2007; Levi and Burrows, 2008).

However difficult it is to maintain that *anything* the public and media care about is *not* serious, harm reduction has clearly moved from the policy margins to the mainstream in the UK, though to a lesser extent elsewhere. In addition to the more general Home Office *crime* reduction objectives, the UK's Serious and Organised Crime Agency (SOCA), set up in 2006 and planned to be merged with other bodies into a National Crime Agency in 2012, is explicitly justified as a 'harm reduction' rather than merely a 'law enforcement' body. But how can the harm caused by 'fraud' (or, as I prefer to conceptualise it, by frauds of various types) be analysed and agreed upon (and by whom?), and to what extent does it reach into the popular consciousness? The origins of our sentiments about the harmfulness of crimes are themselves an important research issue, but they will not be addressed here beyond a superficial level. Levi (2006) argues that white-collar and other financial crimes of deception are treated by the mass media as extensions of 'infotainment'. They typically focus on issues such as: individual and corporate celebrities in trouble; a drugs, gambling or sex craze altering the 'normal' life course of otherwise successful, honest people, whether in the UK or internationally; readily visualisable and often quite short fraud events like the copying of data from payment cards used in UK fuel stations and sent electronically (often to Malaysia or Sri Lanka) to be copied onto false cards; or the loss or insecure storage/transportation of personal financial data that *may* be used for 'identity fraud' (or may not). The impact of the data loss upon those who learn that their electronic identity has been compromised may be unrelated to whether or not a financial loss has occurred – this is empirically an open question.

An examination of media reports following the publication of surveys by large accountancy, consulting and law firms reveals that there is almost no seriously critical examination of these survey results and their extrapolations of costs from often low or unreported response rates (Levi, 2006). The media commonly repeat the press handouts from firms and treat trends in cases coming to court as trends in 'current fraud', thereby distorting the fact that it may have taken years to find out about the frauds or to investigate them. The effects of such publicity upon enforcement resources or public perceptions are unknown, but since these exercises involve at least modest costs, the consultancy firms clearly believe them to be worthwhile. Likewise money laundering 'estimates' of trillions of dollars worldwide annually are uncritically re-quoted endlessly, becoming 'facts by repetition' despite the dismal state of our underlying knowledge regarding what criminals do with their money (van Duyne and Levi, 2005; Levi and Reuter, 2006, 2008). These figures are treated as evidence of the harm done by 'organised crime' to the legitimate economy, without questioning the extent to which laundering increases the harm done by the original offences that generated the illicit income. Explaining why such extravagant estimates of cost and harm are so commonly and readily accepted is itself a research question of some importance.

Crime victims vary in the 'collateral damage' caused and how well placed they are to recuperate from their losses, economically and psychologically. Apart from psychological damage, there are other dimensions of harm and risk such as:

- the growing attractiveness of fraud to conventional major criminals and to previously noncriminal technophiles alike; and
- the possibilities of crimes which – unlike other forms of property crime – can be committed from remote places beyond the easy reach not just of victims but also of law enforcement or civil recovery.

However these harm measurement issues were outside the brief of the study.

THE STUDY

This section primarily reports on a Rapid Evidence Assessment of the costs of fraud in the UK (Levi et al., 2007). The study was not resourced – financially or in time available – to conduct original research to get a closer approximation to the 'true cost of fraud'. Such a goal is anyway impossible, since despite the broadening of the construct of fraud under the Fraud Act 2006, there will always be room for legitimate dispute about, for example, what proportion of a failed company's losses was due respectively to fraud or to lawful misfortune, or indeed whether there was sufficient intent or recklessness to constitute fraud. But it is important to appreciate that it benefits from a greater amount of attention by public and private sectors to fraud costs in the UK than is the case in other European or other countries, and the willingness of the audit bodies to reveal their findings.

Our task was to review the evidential value of existing studies of fraud in the private and public sectors in the UK, and to build up a composite picture of the cost of fraud from those datasets that had an 'adequate' level of validity. This involved a judgment call to leave out the more speculative studies and those where there was insufficient evidence of method to cast doubt (after first contacting the reports' authors). Some estimates such as 'Corporate fraud loses UK business £72bn each year' (Wachman, 2005) turned out to be done in a more sophisticated way than we had initially thought: the non-representative sample's results were compared with the US 'data' from the Association of Certified Fraud Examiners and then adjusted for the relative size of the UK and US economies (disregarding or being ignorant of the fact that the ACFE data themselves had only a 10 per cent response rate). However, this showed that clever arithmetic manipulation is valueless if the underlying data are invalid. What the effects were of such publicity on fear of fraud, fraud reduction and consultancy income were not measured.

Given the difficulties of getting responses, we had to be more tolerant of studies than would be ideal or accepted; for example, in government victimisation surveys. This generated some controversy amongst some commercial studies who considered that they should be included.

The studies of the costs of fraud reviewed broadly fell into four categories:

1 those that reproduce, in a digest form, data derived from criminal justice processed cases (prosecuted frauds above a certain figure – the KPMG Fraud Barometer and the BDO Fraud Track, for example);
2 reports derived from networks of organisations (often sharing a common membership of an umbrella body) aggregating key administrative data to monitor trends and patterns; for example, HM Treasury's annual review of external fraud against government departments; CIFAS' annual reviews of the costs of credit and identity fraud; Financial Fraud Action UK (formerly APACS) reports on the costs of payment card, cheque and online retail banking frauds;
3 surveys that aimed to generate a more general portrait of fraud or particular forms of fraudulent conduct (e.g. CIFAS, 2011a, 2011b); and

4 those that scientifically sample frauds within agencies or departments and then extrapolate from them.

The level of scientific sampling in fraud is commonly below that normally accepted in social scientific surveys, and it is rare for commercial organisations to give any hint of refusal or non-response rates. At the quality end, there are proper – if only episodically administered – statistical surveys such as (for corporations) the Home Office's Commercial Victimisation Survey (Mirrlees-Black et al., 1995) and the annual British Retail Crime Survey, that meet conventional criteria for social scientific research. Then there are corporate victimisation surveys in which some care has been taken to develop questions, pilot them and administer them properly, though response rates and the questionnaires are not available for reasons of intellectual copyright and commercial competitiveness (Bussman and Werle, 2006; Levi, 1987). Reluctantly, a decision was taken to include such studies, because otherwise it would have been impossible to generate any contemporary figure at all. As stated earlier, there are also studies where not only are response rates and information on firms sampled unknown, but dubious extrapolations are made; these were excluded, despite occasional protests from the firms involved (who are not named here).

The studies reviewed encompass worldwide surveys (from which national data can often be derived), national-level surveys, through to national data collection exercises using administrative data compiled by 'trade associations', often focusing on particular types of fraud (as reflects their funding and member interests). Indeed, in the absence of a more systematic overview such as this, something of a 'free market' in information about the cost of fraud has developed in which organisations (including the government, for example on 'identity fraud' – Cabinet Office, 2002; Home Office, 2006) feel pressurised to generate ever-higher 'estimates' of fraud, publicity about which bears little relationship to the scientific rigour (or cost) of the studies themselves. With so little pressure to produce rigorous data, there are many opportunities for people who seek to profit from business and social alarm to take advantage.

In analysing the cost of fraud, the study adopted a conservative position based on the lower end of estimation ranges, avoiding the normal practice of taking the mean or median estimate (e.g. NERA, 2000; estimated UK fraud between just over £10 billion and over £18 billion). One consequence of that is that the aggregate cost figures in some sectors are lower than might be expected if better research were available. (In most countries, where less fraud data are available, the equivalent exercise would generate lower figures still.) The data in this study are mainly from 2005 or shortly before, but the lag in awareness of longer-term frauds mean that some will date back years. Moreover, following situational opportunity models of crime causation, the extent and nature of fraud are shaped by organisations' business and service activities as well as by their culture, transparency and prevention efforts (plus offender skills/energy). It is helpful to distinguish between (1) frauds against manufacturing, retail and wholesale businesses – the 'real economy' as it might be traditionally viewed; and (2) the financial services sector – the 'new' economy which deals not just in retail financial services but also the sophisticated and less tangible financial instruments that (especially prior to 2009) enriched many professionals in the City of London, Wall Street and other financial centres around the world, and helped to generate the large and growing social inequalities that had collateral impacts upon rates of 'ordinary' crime via relative deprivation.

WHO ARE 'THE VICTIMS' OF FRAUD?

Some frauds are confined to one class of victim: thus central government (or, in the longer run, the taxpayers) suffer from most tax or social security fraud, and the costs of insurance fraud are typically borne by the insurance industry (or by others who take out insurance and do not defraud). At the other end of the spectrum, every public body and private sector business is susceptible to embezzlement and procurement fraud. Up to a variable limit (in 2011) of £58,000 for deposits, investments and home finance, losses from frauds and defaults committed by regulated persons/firms are covered by the Financial Services Compensation Scheme (FSCS) or, in some cases, by professional bodies like the Law Society (or by the firms themselves): this figure was raised in 2008 after the Northern Rock and other banking 'runs'. However other investment frauds are compensated only if the offender can be found and made to repay (following conviction or civil recovery action). The same applies to frauds on company pension holders and to cheque frauds. In the case of payment card frauds, there are four potential losers – the card issuer, the merchant acquirer (who for a fee reimburses the merchant for his card transactions), the merchant and the cardholder. Unless the cardholder can be shown to have committed – or been complicit in – the fraud, or to have handled the PIN negligently, he/she will not have to bear the loss (though the introduction of 'chip and pin' technology transfers the cost of fraud from the card issuers to those merchants who do not comply with agreed standards). Such transfers of costs vary between countries, and this illustrates the importance of understanding the institutional context in which fraud occurs.

Of course, individuals (the public-at-large) are ultimately the victims of most fraud, as they generally bear the costs of fraud through higher insurance premiums, reduced dividends or pensions, higher credit card fees or interest rates, higher fees for banking services, higher taxes, and so on (including psychiatric services and redundancies). In special cases such as betting frauds, individuals may lose bets that they should have won – or occasionally, by accident, *vice versa* – and in electoral frauds, their right to the democratically chosen candidate.

APPLYING A TYPOLOGY TO FRAUD

Information on fraud losses is typically identified and reported by immediate and/or ultimate victims, and this recognition led the review to employ a *victim-centric approach* to thinking about types of fraud and their measurement (Levi and Burrows, 2008). Victims may be separated into two general categories: victims from the private sector (one way of categorising this is in terms of financial services and non-financial services firms) and individual members of the public); and victims from the public sector (central bodies and local bodies).

Table 30.1 sets out a typology of frauds within each, and further sub-divides those sectors. The typology is influenced by the sources of information available, which are mostly reports of fraud levels/losses made by or about organisations and individuals as victims. The use of this kind of matrix makes it easier to determine where gaps exist in fraud data, and enables clearer thinking on how the costs of fraud can be allocated. The third column in Table 30.1 includes examples of types of fraud; although by no means comprehensive in its coverage of all frauds, this column seeks to separate frauds that are mutually exclusive and collectively exhaustive for each sub-sector (although the same types of fraud and sorts of fraud technique may be used against different victim sectors).

However, quite apart from the frauds that are poorly documented and analysed, some costs of fraud are difficult to attribute to any particular sub-group of victims, and some frauds may impact simultaneously on several sub-groups, for example. Moreover, organisations themselves may not find it convenient or useful for risk-management or other purposes to sub-divide fraud

Table 30.1   A Typology of Fraud Victimisation

Victim sector	Victim sub-sector	Examples of fraud
Private	Financial services	Cheque fraud
		Counterfeit intellectual property and products sold as genuine
		Counterfeit money
		Data-compromise fraud
		Embezzlement
		Insider dealing/market abuse
		Insurance fraud
		Lending fraud
		Payment card fraud
		Procurement fraud
	Non-financial services	Cheque fraud
		Counterfeit intellectual property and products sold as genuine
		Counterfeit money
		Data-compromise fraud
		Embezzlement
		Gaming fraud
		Lending fraud
		Payment card fraud
		Procurement fraud
	Individuals	Charity fraud
		Consumer fraud
		Counterfeit intellectual property and products sold as genuine
		Counterfeit money
		Investment fraud
		Pension-type fraud
Public	National bodies	Social Security benefit fraud
		Embezzlement
		Procurement fraud
		Tax fraud
	Local bodies	Embezzlement
		Frauds on municipal taxes
		Procurement fraud
	International (but affecting local public)	Procurement fraud [by national against foreign companies and government to obtain foreign contracts]
		EU/UN/World Bank funds fraud

in this way, and since little can be done to compel them, this framework may be 'academic'.

The victim-centric approach also assists the distinction between primary victims, the natural or legal persons (individual or business or public body) who initially suffer the harm of fraud; and secondary victims, those who ultimately pay for the economic component of fraud losses. These sometimes will be the primary victims; in other cases, they may be financial institutions, insurers or industry/professional compensation schemes who, by contract or following interventions by regulators, agree to reimburse some or all economic costs to primary fraud victims; plus taxpayers and/or those who are deprived of services which they would otherwise have received.

The label 'fraud' is not always a natural category however. In many failed businesses, it may be difficult to decide whether or not the company or person has traded whilst insolvent; if it did, this could be classified as 'fraudulent trading' (Levi, 2008). Part of the aim of the fraudster is to make targets believe that they and their transactions are genuine, so whether conduct is labelled as fraud may be a matter of some delicacy (e.g., with bad debt *versus* fraud, or with pyramid/high yield investment schemes). And it may be a matter of some considerable confusion for victims, who may well *believe* that they were victims of fraud, but may be *treated* by the authorities only as victims of unfortunate trading conditions and are not legally 'fraud victims'. Reactions to the global economic crisis may lead many to consider that they have been cheated, rather than merely unfortunate; conversely, fraudsters have an interest in portraying themselves as being merely unlucky rather than as swindlers (Levi, 2008). Surveys of victims, for example, will often ask, 'Have you been a victim of this or that fraud?' – yet many of these types of frauds are complex, and even seasoned anti-fraud professionals are unclear on the exact meaning of certain terms. The implication is that victim-centric measures of fraud are not always precise even when they are drawn from victim 'knowledge'.

'Identity fraud' is often used as a category of crime, but (like terrorism), it is a method of crime rather than a clear victim category, since it spans commercial businesses, financial institutions, governments and individuals. This is why it was not included in the table. In other contexts there may be good reasons for aggregating the creation, circulation and use of fictitious or copied/misattributed personal data for economic gain – in short, all conduct that involves an individual pretending to be someone he/she is not – under this broad label. But conventionally, financial institutions have broken the various forms of identity theft and fraud down, in order to define for risk management or preventative action purposes more specialised acts such as 'application fraud' and/or 'corporate website fraud', or 'account takeover fraud' (using 'stolen' personal details to open accounts in the name of living or dead people without their knowledge). In addition, confusion is sometimes caused by the use of the term 'identity theft', which is usually applied whenever an unauthorised outsider gets hold of someone's personal details from a database, yet the 'identity theft victims' often will still be able to use their own identity or credit facilities, and it is possible that no-one may actually seek to use their identities for a criminal purpose.

ASSESSING THE EXTENT AND COSTS OF FRAUD

Costs of crime may be estimated by 'bottom-up' and/or 'top-down' methods. A 'bottom up' approach seeks to evaluate the costs of fraud from the perspective of the producer or defrauded organisation. An example of the bottom-up method might be the use of administrative data on payment card fraud reported to the UK Cards Association (in which the annual volume/value terms simply represent the sum of all reported frauds). A 'top down' approach seeks to estimate the economic implications of fraud from a national perspective. (See my suggestion above regarding the collective and individual dimension of costs.) An example of a top-down method might be as follows: X percent of cheques appear to be fraudulent (perhaps determined through some sort of audit), the mean loss per fraudulent cheque is Y GBP, and Z cheques are used in the UK annually, so $X \times Y \times Z$ would yield the cost of fraudulent cheques. If the costs of the fraudulent cheques are initially met by banks, they would want to recoup them by charging more for cheque services or levying a wider interest rate spread. In both cases, customers end up paying more.

Additionally, the issue of 'who bears the cost' is often a complex one. It is also one reason why the likelihood of double counting is a major concern in the fraud field. An individual who has been victim of an investment or pension fraud may report this fact in the course of a survey on fraud, but so too will any organisation that provided all, or part of, compensation to that individual for associated losses. This presents a significant challenge to aggregating the costs of fraud to the economy.

Further, determining the true costs of goods and services obtained by fraud can present difficulties. Certain types of fraud – for example, those that facilitate terrorism or distort election results – may produce immense collateral damage, but their estimation will be exceedingly difficult without rafts of assumptions.

Other types of fraud may be perpetrated not specifically to defraud the system (i.e., not to generate income or cause a loss directly) but rather to gain access to services. For example, a fraudulent driver's licence may be used not to obtain money or goods in some sort of identity-related fraud but rather to gain access to the road network and associated services, like motor insurance, or to reduce traceability to surveillance by the police or to avoid municipal congestion charges (e.g., in London).

FINDINGS BY ECONOMIC SECTOR

Substantial and varied data about many types of fraud in the UK (though not elsewhere) are available. As explained above, for each sector, this research seeks to summarise:

- data availability and deficiencies;
- the reasons underpinning data collection
- data collection methods; and
- the known costs of fraud – divided into the direct (transfer) costs of the fraud, the costs of preventing fraud and the costs of responding to fraud after the event.

Data on the costs of responding to fraud and of fraud prevention are particularly sparse, and for clarity, they have been kept disaggregated from fraud losses to victims (see Levi et al., 2007, for a more detailed review of sources.)

Losses affecting the private sector

The *minimum* extent of the losses borne (excluding responses to fraud) by victims in the private sector was judged to be as follows:

1 For businesses in the financial service sector (i.e., banks, building societies, finance houses, insurance companies and their agents), some data are quite robust and some result from the administrative record-keeping of members, which means that the data could be used tactically to prevent and/or respond to fraud. From the best evidence available (see further, Levi et al., 2007), financial services' fraud losses were estimated at £1.005 billion in 2005.
2 For businesses in the non-financial services sector (the majority of businesses by volume) data are largely derived from surveys, and their value has thus to be restricted to policy development and more strategic crime reduction approaches. The coverage – both in terms of business sectors and different types of frauds – is patchy.[1] Here, fraud losses to businesses other than financial services were estimated at £0.934 billion in 2005.
3 The losses in the sectors above are complicated by the fact that a number of surveys of frauds against businesses do not separate out financial services from other sector losses in their reports. There may be some modest double-counting with

the datasets above, but survey findings (Bussman and Werle, 2006; PricewaterhouseCoopers, 2005) suggest that at least another £1.821 billion should be added to the total costs of fraud against businesses, mainly in 2005, though one cannot tell whether these losses are to financial services or to other businesses since the surveys themselves are insufficiently rigorous in separating the categories. This is a particular problem with multinational corporations which have diversified businesses.

4 Fraud against *private individuals* paradoxically has received very little attention in any of the studies, being covered neither in the corporate fraud surveys nor in the public sector reviews. Although it is not certain that all 'scams' against private individuals (in the national victimisation survey by the Office of Fair Trading, 2006) meet the criteria of 'a crime', and these data do not include the costs of consumer fraud by corporations against individuals via price-fixing and product adulteration, fraud losses against private individuals were estimated at £2.75 billion in 2005. It is important to appreciate that without this Office of Fair Trading study, fraud against private individuals would have been a much smaller proportion of the whole, simply because there would have been no such dataset to use.

Losses affecting the public sector

The losses borne by victims in the public sector were judged to be as follows:

1 For *public bodies at the national level* there is much the same variation in the availability and quality of fraud data noted in the private sector. Considerable progress has been made in specific fields, notably by the NHS Counter-Fraud and Security Management Services and by the Audit Commission's National Fraud Initiative, which has steadily broadened in scope, reinforced by the Serious Crime Act 2007. Tax fraud is (and probably always will be) a far more significant source of economic loss than any other single area of public or, for that matter, private sector fraud; and VAT/Missing Trader Intra-Community (MTIC) frauds and large income tax frauds may comprise the largest single categories. National public sector fraud losses can be conservatively estimated at £6.434 billion, mostly in 2005–2006 but due to data time lags, sometimes in earlier years. But this sum *excludes* two major items which might be expected to make a substantial difference to the public sector fraud total. One is income tax fraud, where no valid figures are currently available and which this study has set at zero. The other gap in evidence on public sector

fraud is the UK's share of fraud (a) against the EU, where annualised estimation of fraud (as opposed to irregularities and inefficiencies) is deeply problematic, and (b) against other international bodies such as the UN and World Bank.

2   For public bodies at the local level, losses are conservatively estimated at £0.04 billion in 2005–2006. Some deceptions against council tax may also cause losses to central government departments (like the Department of Work and Pensions), so it is difficult to allocate losses to one rather than the other.

Overall fraud losses

The above fraud loss figures are merely indicative. The existing sources of data on fraud are neither mutually exclusive nor collectively exhaustive. Many high value cases that appear to meet the criteria of criminal fraud are investigated by forensic accounting and law firms, and are treated as civil matters for litigation and negotiation with 'suspects' and third parties. Before an 'actual' fraud comes to be counted as such, it has to go through a process of being suspected, investigated and identified as such, whether through accident or a more formal audit process aimed at uncovering fraud. A decision then has to be made as to whether to make the fraud public in some way, in aggregate form (as in UK Cards data on plastic frauds) or as an identified individual case (e.g., via formal reporting to a policing body). The study by Levi et al. (2007) essentially evaluated and summarised data that reach the final stage.

Overall, available sources suggest that excluding the cost of doing something about them, the direct losses from frauds of all types were at least £12.98 billion (mostly) in 2005; and it would be surprising if the true total was not much larger than this.

In addition, the known and separately identified private and public costs of acting against fraud – both before the event and in response to it – total £0.937 billion, and this is certainly a significant underestimate.[2] Together, the known costs of fraud and of dealing with fraud were at least £13.9 billion in 2005.

CONCLUSION

The process of compiling, plausibility testing[3] and then aggregating data made a significant contribution to clarifying what is currently known about fraud in the UK. With modification, it is hoped that this can also serve as a model for other countries. The patchiness of the data is self-evident,

and some results were left out altogether because aggregation even within victim categories was impossible. An unintended effect may be to present patterns of fraud that reflect the level of effort and ease of compilation, rather than the portrait that might appear if careful and rigorous assessment were attempted across the board. (See also ONS, 2011, for a review that highlights deficiencies in fraud and e-crime victimisation statistics.) A 'true picture of fraud' is a chimera, but a better and truer picture of fraud is possible and will have to await improved fraud awareness and collection strategies within business as well as by consumer and trade bodies, regulators and the public police, in the UK and in other countries that are stimulated to get a better grasp on their fraud problems.

In the UK, the Fraud Review (2006) running in tandem with this study, recommended the establishment of a National Fraud Reporting Centre (later funded by government and on-stream from 2009 as 'Action Fraud'). The practical aspect of this follows a similar model of online reporting adopted in Canada and the US, in collaboration with the National White-Collar Crime Center there. A centralised body to 'champion' the improved reporting and recording of fraud is plainly a good thing, but in the context of very high current levels of fraud, and the potential enormity of what might follow if victims were encouraged to report all instances, there is a real danger of raising expectations that the police or other central bodies cannot meet, and some effort has to be paid to managing expectations. This impact is an area worthy of study in its own right, from both a victim perspective and a policing perspective. Some initial scoping work by Portsmouth University based on interviews with victims illustrates some aspects of victim expectations (National Fraud Authority, 2009), but the expectations and after-the-fact reactions of victims to reporting to Action Fraud require elaboration, as do the ways in which the police actually deal with this intelligence, analytically and operationally.

Furthermore, whether the more complex frauds – where criminality is more ambiguous – will be reported in an online environment remains doubtful. Such cases may take days to explain, let alone to investigate, hence the rise of private policing and investigation for those who can afford it and are willing to 'throw good money after bad'. In the absence of an insurance rationale, the incentives for reporting frauds may be weak for most actors. Methodologically, this means that reliance on those businesses and wealthy individuals who report fraud to the police is inadequate. We have to develop access to non-reporting sectors; for example, by random or strategic sampling beyond police data. Up to a point, this has been done by corporate fraud surveys of firms such as Ernst & Young, KPMG and PricewaterhouseCoopers. Many frauds are reported not as crime complaints but via the 'suspicious activity reports' anti-money laundering regime of the national Financial Intelligence Unit – the Serious and Organised Crime Agency (SOCA) – submitted by 'regulated' financial intermediaries. However, their costs and other impacts are not drawn out of those reports, which in any case are under-utilised because of cost constraints on SOCA and police forces. This under-utilisation is a universal problem. Even in countries where data collection is poor, fraud is currently a very significant socio-economic crime problem, and represents a rational modern form for illicit profits, whether against citizens, companies and governments of one's own country or against those of other countries. Consequently, unless we develop a better awareness and manage fraud risks better, there is no reason whatever to suppose that its costs, level or significance will diminish *naturally* over time. What is important is not merely to generate an overall figure for 'fraud', but also to generate data about which sectors of the population – individuals and businesses – get victimised by which sorts of frauds, preferably also identifying the sources of those threats. In this way we can set about demystifying the nature of financial crimes and showing what types of fraud, market abuse (e.g., insider dealing) and laundering we lack analytically robust information about. Gradually, this should improve the quality of public policy-making and move us away from a situation in which bodies feel that the only way they can get more attention and resources is to estimate/invent huge figures that are usually conveyed uncritically by a sensation-hungry media.

NOTES

1 For example, although some intellectual property (IP) offences plainly cause physical as well as economic harm, the published data do not validly distinguish between cases in which purchasers were deceived as to the legitimacy of the products and those – probably the great majority - in which they knew perfectly well that they were buying counterfeits: therefore IP fraud costs have not been included.

2 There are severe difficulties in separating ongoing costs of computer systems and of compliance with anti-money laundering regulations from the costs of anti-fraud measures. Some private and public organisations also wish to keep their fraud control costs private.

3 For example, intellectual property costs were rejected because the assumption in intellectual property fraud that people would pay full price for all counterfeit products bought cheaply is plainly incorrect. Identity fraud and payment card fraud partly double-counted the same phenomena of using cards that had been stolen or their data copied onto magnetic strips of blank cards.

RECOMMENDED READING

Bussman, K. and Werle, M. (2006) 'Addressing crime in companies: first findings from a global survey of economic crime', *British Journal of Criminology*, 46, 1128–1144.

Cohen, M. (2005) *The Costs of Crime and Justice*. London: Routledge.

Dorn, N., Levi, M., Artingstall, D. and Howell, J. (2009) *Impacts of Financial Crimes and Amenability to Control by the FSA: Proposed framework for generating data in a comparative manner*, London: Financial Services Authority. Available at: http://www.fsa.gov.uk/pubs/other/scale_and_impact_paper.pdf

Levi, M. and Burrows, J. (2008) 'Measuring the impact of fraud: a conceptual and empirical journey', *British Journal of Criminology*, 48(3), 293–318.

Levi, M., Burrows, J., Fleming, M. and Hopkins, M., with the assistance of Matthews, K. (2007) *The Extent, Nature and Economic Impact of Fraud in the UK*. Report for the Association of Chief Police Officers' Economic Crime Portfolio. Available at: http://www.acpo.police.uk/asp/policies/Data/Fraud%20in%20the%20UK.pdf

Web-based resources:

http://www.attorneygeneral.gov.uk/nfa/Pages/default.aspx
http://www.nfib.police.uk/
www.financialfraudaction.org.ukwww.financialfraudaction.org.uk
http://www.cifas.org.uk/

REFERENCES

ACFE (2002) *2002 Report to the Nation: on Occupational Fraud and Abuse*. Available at: http://www.acfe.com/documents/2002RttN.pdf

ACFE (2006) *2006 ACFE Report to the Nation: on Occupational Fraud and Abuse*. Available at: http://www.acfe.com/documents/2006-rttn.pdf

ACFE (2006) *2008 ACFE Report to the Nation: on Occupational Fraud and Abuse*. Available at: http://www.acfe.com/documents/2008-rttn.pdf

BDO Stoy Hayward (2006) *'Inside Job': Fraud Track 3: Rising Fraud in the Spotlight: Annual Survey 2006*. BDO Stoy Hayward UK.

Brand, S. and Price, R. (2000) *The Economic and Social Costs of Crime*. Home Office Research Study no.217. London: Home Office.

British Retail Consortium (2006) *Retail Crime Survey 2004–2005*. London: British Retail Consortium.

Bussman, K. and Werle, M. (2006) 'Addressing crime in companies: first findings from a global survey of economic crime', *British Journal of Criminology*, 46, 1128–1144.

Cabinet Office (2002) *Identity Fraud*. London: Cabinet Office.

CIFAS (2011a) *Fraudscape*, London: CIFAS. Available at https://www.cifas.org.uk/secure/contentPORT/uploads/documents/CIFAS%20Reports/CIFAS_Fraudscape_2011.pdf

CIFAS (2011) *Staff Fraudscape*, London: CIFAS. Available at https://www.cifas.org.uk/secure/contentPORT/uploads/documents/reports/2._CIFAS_Staff_Fraudscape_2011.pdf

Cohen, M. (2005) *The Costs of Crime and Justice*. London: Routledge.

Committee of Public Accounts (2004) *32nd Report: HM Customs and Excise Standard Report*. HC 284. London: HMSO.

Doig, A. (2006). *Fraud*. Cullompton: Willan.

Dorn, N. and Levi, M. (2006) 'From Delphi to Brussels, the Policy Context: Prophecy, Crime Proofing, Impact Assessment', *European Journal on Criminal Policy and Research*, 12, 213–220.

Dubourg, R., Hamed, J. and Thorns, J. (2005) *The economic and social costs of crime against individuals and households 2003/04*. Home Office On-Line Report 30/05.

Edwards, A. and Levi, M. (2008) 'Researching the organisation of serious crimes', *Criminology and Criminal Justice*, 8(4), 363–388.

Fraud Review (2006) *Final Report*. London: Attorney's Office.

GetSafeOnline (2006) *The GetSafeOnline Report*. Available at: http://www.getsafeonline.org

HM Treasury (2005) *2004–05 Fraud Report: An analysis of reported fraud in Government Departments*. London: HMSO.

Hillyard, P., Pantazis, C., Tombs, S., Gordon, D. and Dorling, D. (2008) *Criminal Obsessions*, 2nd edition. *Why Harm Matters More Than Crime*. London: Crime and Society Foundation. Available at: http://www.crimeandjustice.org.uk/criminalobsessions2.html

Home Office (2006) *Updated Estimate of the Cost of Identity Fraud to the UK Economy*, 2 February 2006. London: Home Office. Available at: www.identity-theft.org.uk

House of Commons Committee of Public Accounts (2003) *Tackling Fraud against the Inland Revenue: First Report of Session 2003–04*. London: HMSO.

Kane, J. and Wall, A. (2006) *The National Public Household Survey 2005*. Virginia: National Center for White-Collar Crime NWC3.

Karstedt, S. and Farrall, S. (2006) 'The Moral Economy of Everyday Crime: Markets, Consumers and Citizens', *British Journal of Criminology*, 46, 1011–1036.

KPMG (2004) *Fraud Survey 2004 Report*. Available at: http://www.kpmg.com.my/kpmg/publications/fas/fsurvey_2004.pdf

KPMG (2006) *KPMG Fraud Barometer*. Press release appendix.

Levi, M. (1987) *Regulating Fraud*. London: Routledge.

Levi, M. (1992) 'White-collar crime victimization', in K. Schlegel and D. Weisburd (eds) *White-Collar Crime Reconsidered*. Boston: Northeastern University Press.

Levi, M. (2006) 'The media construction of financial white-collar crimes', *British Journal of Criminology*, 46, 1037–1057.

Levi, M. (2007) 'Pecunia non olet? The control of money-laundering revisited', in F. Bovenkerk and M. Levi (eds) *The Organised Crime Community*, New York: Springer, pp. 161–182.

Levi, M. (2008) *The Phantom Capitalists*, 2nd edition. Andover: Ashgate.

Levi, M. and Burrows, J. (2008) 'Measuring the impact of fraud: a conceptual and empirical journey', *British Journal of Criminology*, 48(3), 293–318.

Levi, M., Burrows, J., Fleming, M. and Hopkins, M., with the assistance of Matthews, K. (2007) *The extent, nature and economic impact of fraud in the UK*. Report for the Association of Chief Police Officers' Economic Crime Portfolio. Available at: http://www.acpo.police.uk/asp/policies/Data/Fraud%20in%20the%20UK.pdf

Levi, M. and Reuter, P. (2006) 'Money Laundering' in M. Tonry (ed), *Crime and Justice: A Review of Research*, Vol.34: 289–375, Chicago: Chicago University Press.

Levi, M. and Reuter, P. (2009) 'Money Laundering'. *Handbook on Crime and Public Policy* [Editor M. Tonry] New York: Oxford University Press. Pp. 356–380.

Maguire, M. (2007) 'Criminal statistics', in *The Oxford Handbook of Criminology*, 4th edition. Oxford: Oxford University Press.

Markopoulos, H. (2010) *No One Would Listen: A True Financial Thriller*. New York: John Wiley.

Mirrlees-Black, C. and Ross, A. (1995) *Crime against Retail and Manufacturing Premises: Findings from the 1994 Commercial Victimisation Survey*. Home Office Research Study no. 146. London: HMSO.

National Audit Office (2003) *Tackling Fraud against the Inland Revenue*. London: National Audit Office.

National Fraud Authority (2009) 'Fraud victims voice concerns over lack of support'. Available at: http://www.attorney-general.gov.uk/nfa/WhatAreWeSaying/NewsRelease/news-releases-2009/Pages/fraud-news-dec09-fraud-victims-voice-concerns-over-lack-of-support.aspx

National Fraud Authority (2010a) *Annual Fraud Indicator*. London: National Fraud Authority.

National Fraud Authority (2010b) 'Identity fraud costs UK £2.7billion every year'. Available at: http://www.attorneygeneral.gov.uk/nfa/whatarewesaying/newsrelease/pages/identity-fraud-costs-27billion.aspx

National Fraud Authority (2011) *Annual fraud indicator*, London: National Fraud Authority.

NERA (2000) *The Economic Cost of Fraud*. London: HMSO.

Office of Fair Trading (2006) *Research on impact of mass marketed scams*. London: Office of Fair Trading. Available at: http://www.oft.gov.uk/shared_oft/reports/consumer_protection/oft883.pdf

ONS (2011) *National Statistician's Review of Crime Statistics: England and Wales. Newport*: Office of National Statistics

PricewaterhouseCoopers (2005) *Global Economic Crime Survey – United Kingdom*. London: Pricewaterhouse-Coopers.

PricewaterhouseCoopers (2007) *The 4th Biennial Global Economic Crime Survey – Singapore*. Available at: http://www.pwc.com/extweb/pwcpublications.nsf/docid/A10C86 8A6D3F7852CA257370002FFE33/$file/gecssg2007.pdf

Punch, M. (1996) *Dirty Business: Exploring Corporate Misconduct: Analysis and Cases*, London: Routledge.

Rebovich, D. and Layne, J. (2000) *The 1999 National Public Survey on White-Collar Crime Completed*. Morgantown: National White-Collar Crime Center.

Rosoff, S. Pontell, H., and Tillman, R. (2009) *Profit without Honor*. New York: Prentice-Hall.

Sparrow, M. (2008) *The Character of Harms*, Cambridge: Harvard University Press.

Sutherland, Edwin (1985) *White-Collar Crime: the Uncut Version*, Princeton: Yale University Press.

Tombs, S. and Whyte, D. (2007) *Safety Crimes*. Cullompton: Willan.

van Dijk, J.J.M., Manchin, R., Van Kesteren, J., Nevala, S., and Hideg, G. (2007) *The Burden of Crime in the EU. Research Report: A Comparative Analysis of the European Crime and Safety Survey (EU ICS) 2005*. Available at: www.europeansafetyobservatory.eu/.../EUICS%20-%20The%20 Burden%20of%20Crime%20in%20the%20EU.pdf

van Dijk, J., van Kesteren, J. and Smit, P. (2008) *Criminal Victimisation in International Perspective, Key findings from the 2004–2005 ICVS and EU ICS*. The Hague: Boom Legal Publishers.

Van Duyne, P. and Levi, M. (2005). *Drugs and Money: Managing the Drug Trade and Crime-Money in Europe*, London: Routledge.

Wachman, R. (2005) 'Corporate fraud loses UK business £72bn each year' *Guardian Online*, 20 November 2005. Available at: http://www.guardian.co.uk/business/2005/nov/20/corporatefraud.observerbusiness

Wells, J. (2007) *Fraud Casebook: Lessons from the Bad Side of Business*. New York: John Wiley.

Zagaris, B. (2010) *International White Collar Crime: Cases and Materials*. Cambridge: Cambridge University Press.

31

The Other Cultural Criminology: The Role of Action Research in Justice Work and Development

Cyndi Banks

INTRODUCTION

It ought to be possible to accept that societies are also incontrovertibly different but still to include them within our intellectual universe. In stressing the differences rather than the similarities in people's arrangements, one would challenge that monstrous ethnocentrism that extends understanding only so far as the observer is prepared to recognize in the devices of others similarities and parallels to devices of his or her own (Strathern, 1988: 32–3).

Few criminologists, whether indigenous or outsiders, conduct research into crime in developing countries. The reasons for this absence of research studies range from lack of personal interest by outsider criminologists, the reluctance of grant awarding bodies to fund such research, difficulties in gaining country access and, in the case of indigenous researchers, the relatively small number of such researchers due to the absence of schools of criminology in state universities in developing countries. The traditional parochialism and ethnocentrism of criminology is a further major factor (Hardie-Bick et al., 2005: 1). I have been fortunate enough however, to undertake what I term 'cultural criminology' research since 1988 in the developing countries of Papua New Guinea, Bangladesh, Iraq, Sudan and Timor Leste. In most cases I have lived in the country concerned for at least six months and, in the case of Papua New Guinea, for more than 12 years. The *other* cultural criminology I advocate differs from that of Ferrell and Sanders (1995) and Ferrell et al. (2008) in that while they are concerned primarily with issues of representation and style, I am concerned with cultural specificity.

I will argue here that because of the significant constraints affecting cultural criminological research in the developing world, donor interventions comprising programs for law reform and rule of law projects in such countries often provide the only means and opportunity to conduct culturally specific research. Also, given donor reluctance to allow sufficient time and resources for sustained periods of research, modes of action research are often the best method in the overall goal of understanding the cultural criminology of the society in question.

This chapter is divided into four sections. The first section outlines the meaning, scope and content of cultural criminology (the other cultural criminology germane to the title to this chapter); the second builds upon the concept of cultural criminology by exploring methodological issues associated with that concept; the third discusses action research as a mode of cultural criminological research in the context of justice reform or rule of law projects in developing countries, and the fourth sets out action research I conducted in Bangladesh on juvenile justice, identifies constraints and challenges, and offers a view of the way forward in developing the cultural criminologies of the developing world.

TOWARDS A CULTURAL CRIMINOLOGY

In my book *Developing Cultural Criminology: Theory and Practice in Papua New Guinea* (2000), I reviewed theoretical approaches to third world criminology and suggested key constituents that I believe ought to be taken into account in formulating a cultural criminology for a third world state. In particular I explained the need to transcend the limits of both modernization theory and underdevelopment theory.

The theoretical framework of modernization theory views crime in the third world as the logical outcome of an evolutionary process, or as Cohen (1988: 178) quips, 'not just the price for progress but an index of progress'. It presumes that 'traditional societies' will, through the process of social change comprising rapid economic growth, urban migration, and the retooling of political, economic and social institutions necessary for economic development, become images of the 'modern societies' found in Western nations (Clinard and Abbott 1973: 7). From this view, educated elite nationals in third world nations working in government structures are expected to shape modernization through advancing policy initiatives in education, employment, and communications (Clinard and Abbott 1973: 6–11). Rapid growth and modernization are assumed to create dramatic increases in officially reported crime rates, engendering a breakdown of norms and alienation, otherwise known as *anomie* (Durkheim, 1951). Constructing modernization in these terms the difference between the developed and developing countries to be construed primarily in crime rates as opposed to general causes of crime Birkbeck (1985: 218).

Underdevelopment theory, by contrast, presumes that crime and justice in the 'third world' should be linked to the 'processes and effects of underdevelopment' (Sumner, 1982: 1). Sumner, in his outline of this approach emphasizes, 'the difference in patterns and forms of social control between nineteenth-century Europe and Third World societies' in a way that rather unfortunately reproduces the colonial experience of 'third world' nations (Clegg and Whetton, 1995: 31; Cohen, 1988). In so doing he

assumes that the experience of colonialism and 'underdevelopment' is largely similar everywhere, failing to explain marked differences in rates and

patterns of growth between contemporary Third World countries (Clegg and Whetton, 1995: 32).

Like the modernization approach, underdevelopment theory has thus also been insensitive to issues of cultural specificity. And yet, 'culture' is a crucial component in any criminological project (Ferrell and Sanders, 1995; Ferrell et al., 2008; Garland, 1990; Nelken, 1994), particularly so in comparative research (Karstedt, 2008, and this volume). In trying to extend this argument I have suggested that constructing an adequate cultural criminology for a developing nation requires the incorporation of four key principles: (Banks, 2000).

1   Descriptions, analyses and discussions of culture (or aspects of it) must be grounded in the context of the particular culture under study (Geertz, 1993: chapter 1). Ideas about crime are culturally embedded and must be understood as such (Henry and Milovanovic, 1994: 118; Nelken, 1994: 14), in relation to both general and local definitions of crime.

2   The syncretic processes followed by many, if not all cultures, which have endured colonial contact must be fully appreciated. Hence, cultures constantly appropriate parts of new cultural formations, and reject, subvert and refashion others. They, as Clifford expresses it, 'live by pollination, by (historical) transplanting' (1988: 15).

3   The notion of cultural specificity as applied to a culture must include an understanding of the pre-colonial history, colonial and post-colonial changes within a specific culture (Loomba, 1993; Mohanty, 1993). It also entails sensitivity to commonalties and differences where there are diverse societies within a culture. The aim is to emphasize the importance of the whole and the interdependence of its parts so that specific acts and events of interest to criminology can be viewed within the particular cultural context.

4   To be culturally specific, then, is to present a 'bottom up' approach which complements the customary analyses based on the political, economic and structural aspects of a society undertaken by those advocating the standpoints of modernization, underdevelopment or otherwise, and to explore how it resonates with more 'top-down' formulations.

THE ROLE OF ACTION RESEARCH WITHIN CULTURAL CRIMINOLOGY

For this reason, cultural criminologists cannot afford to invest in methodological chasms. They must make use of all knowledge in all relevant disciplines, qualitative or quantitative studies, including historical records of contact, any pre-colonial knowledge, the records compiled by colonial administrations, especially those that explore the notion of justice in the society under study and the introduced changes, and studies that examine the post-colonial society's meanings and interpretations of relevant concepts and notions of justice. However, they have also to make a special place for action research which provides special tools for responding to cultural change instigated through contemporary development assistance processes.

The contemporary development assistance process through which wealthy Western nations provide forms of aid and assistance to developing nations opens up limited opportunities for Westerners to conduct criminological research in these states. Commonly such assistance projects incorporate technical assistance, which is normally provided by qualified consultants who are often outsiders and who may be engaged for very short terms of a month or less or, at best, no more than a few years. The assistance is often directed at 'capacity building', which involves developing the skills of indigenous bureaucrats and civil society members. Sometimes, although infrequently, a specific research component is built into a project or occasionally a project may exclusively comprise research. An example within the justice sector is recent donor interest in conducting research into traditional dispute settlement processes in Afghanistan. In many cases, executing rule of law and law reform programs within developing nations provides the only means of generating a partial cultural criminology for those nations.

As I will explain in what follows, action research is uniquely able to deliver the cultural sensitivity research in these kinds of contexts, where inequalities of power are acute and the legacy of a colonial past has left an unmistakable imprint. Action research has a broad theoretical base drawing on pragmatic philosophy (Dewey, James, Pierce), critical thinking, democratic practice, and liberationist thinking. Paulo Freire (1972), the Brazilian educator and author of *Pedagogy of the Oppressed*, is perhaps the most significant figure in education action research, but action research has also become well established in some forms of psychology, constructionist theory and systems theory too (Reason and Bradbury 2002: 2). The notion of action research originated from the assumption that theory can be expressed in action and 'ways of doing' (Gustavsen, 2002: 17). Unlike much academic research, action research does not seek to undertake a review of the knowledge in a subject area, rather, it aims to be 'flexible and creative as it improvises the relevance of different types of theory at different

stages' (Winter, 2002: 27). This suggests to me that action research has the capacity to produce the kind of grounded theory that is developed from qualitative research studies by merging practice with appropriate theoretical frameworks. Winter (2002) also advises that of necessity, action research be a reflexive process because such is the centrality of the process of conducting action research that every stage in the process contributes to the knowledge produced. Importantly, he also notes that one of the aims of this research is to challenge existing interpretations.

Action research (also known as participatory action research) has been most strongly developed within the fields of education, heath and social welfare (McTaggart, 1997). This method of research focuses on change (in the case of development assistance, usually social change is the broad rubric under which such studies are subsumed) and the aim is to find a local solution to a local problem. As noted by Robin McTaggart (1997: 34), social change as an outcome of action research requires that participatory groups collectively bring about change through an analysis of problem areas and through iterative study. Individuals cannot themselves accomplish this change but instead operate as change agents in the overall research process of planning, research, action, observation and reflection. This process involves 'a systematic learning process in which people act deliberately, although remain open to surprises and responsive to opportunities' (McTaggart, 1997: 36). Rather than promote and support an expert-oriented form of knowledge production, action research attempts to democratize the acquisition and use of knowledge (Stinger, 1999).

The essence of action research is that those who implement change must be direct participants in the issues associated with change. According to McTaggart (1997: 6), legitimate participation requires that all participants contribute, not only to the actual research itself, but also to its conceptualization. The action research process introduces new practices and an iterative process of testing proposals for change until they are refined into the final implementation plan. The test of the efficacy of the research is not the publication of a paper in a peer-reviewed journal; rather, it is the actual implementation of the outcome of the research process. Where an interpretive approach is taken, the production of data is not an end in itself because the knowledge produced must be incorporated into an approach that develops action strategies to improve a situation in some meaningful manner (ibid: 38). Research outcomes are validated through diverse methods especially

by establishing credibility among participants and informants, by participant confirmation, by the deliberate establishment of an 'audit-trail' of data and interpretations and by testing the coherence of arguments being presented in a 'critical community' (McTaggart, 1997: 13).

As noted in many texts concerned with action research (McTaggart, 1997; Kemmis and McTaggart, 2000), this mode of study encompasses diverse practices. While there is no single definition of action research, Reason and Bradbury capture its essence when they describe it as

a participatory, democratic process concerned with developing practical knowing in the pursuit of worthwhile human purposes, grounded in a participatory worldview ... It seeks to bring together action and reflection, theory and practice, in participation with others, in the pursuit of practical solutions to issues of pressing concern to people, and more generally the flourishing of individual persons and their communities (Reason and Bradbury, 2002: 1).

In other words, action research entails 'the study of a social situation with a view to improving the quality of action within ... [the] total process – review, diagnosis, planning, implementation, monitoring effects' (Elliott, 1982 in Winter 1989: p. ii, p. 1). Consequently, it often entails a 'cyclical process' involving 'critical reflection on ... practice to identify a problem which is then researched and the findings are translated into a plan for change. The plan is then implemented and evaluated' (Noakes and Wincup, 2004: 16).

All of this renders the action researchers' professional capacity central to the success of the process, for the researcher must seek to merge their own professional perspective with local knowledge in order to develop the kind of understanding that validly resolves the practical problem under examination. Essentially, action research follows a trajectory of active experimentation through which new knowledges are created. In action research the power of the expert researcher to control the research process must be confronted (McTaggart, 1997: 33) because the process must be fully participatory. In development assistance work where international declarations recognize the necessity for the host country to take 'ownership' of a project it is even more crucial that researchers from outside relinquish control. As McTaggart (ibid. 39) points out, action research is not research undertaken 'on' other people; rather, it is research carried out 'by' those people themselves, sometimes on their own work, with the aim of improving their life conditions. In other words, they are not 'objects of research' but 'knowing agents' in the research process.

ACTION RESEARCH AND JUVENILE JUSTICE IN BANGLADESH

Having offered a broad overview of action research here I want to describe the action research I conducted in Bangladesh employing the principles and methodologies of cultural criminology discussed earlier. As indicated previously, I believe the cultural specificity of any culture must be taken into account in designing any project or program of development assistance for that country. However, development assistance projects in law reform and rule of law fields commonly fail to allow space for research and investigation to establish cultural specificity. In fact, even though the very concept of the rule of law is quite problematic, such projects scarcely ever provide for sustained, in- depth research (Carothers, 2006).

In the discourse and practice of rule of law and justice reform in the West globalization has contributed to a convergence of justice policies and practices based on Euro-centric models. Policies and practices have migrated to the developing world as elements of development assistance projects in which compilations of planned interventions are to be implemented with the aim of building country capacity to administer justice and enforce the rule of law. Project designs and plans follow Western models, adopt 'top down' approaches and are implemented by Western justice practitioners who sometimes have little or no experience of any justice system but their own (and sometimes not much of their own either). Stromseth et al. (2006: 188) point out that in rule of law work, 'transplanting lessons and approaches from one context to another, without sufficient cultural and historical knowledge can be ineffective at best or deeply counterproductive'. An indigenous criminologist from West Africa, Biko Agozino, writes that third world criminologists must cease to rely on imported Western crime control models with their 'imperialist logic' in the form of police training, security and prison administration and must focus on the links between criminology and colonialism to begin the 'decolonization ' of criminology (2004: 355).

It is however, simplistic to contend that planned interventions from outside are accepted uncritically and unproblematically in developing nations. Despite hegemonic and globalizing tendencies, these countries find ways of resisting, and even subverting Western models. For example, in an exploration of the articulation between the global and the local in the field of juvenile justice in Bangladesh, I have argued that globalization has not produced, and will not deliver, a universalistic juvenile justice system and that 'local contingencies and especially assertions about cultural differences will figure in debates about implementing these universalist discourses' (Banks, 2007: 393). Development sociologist, Norman Long, has called for a planned intervention to be deconstructed 'so that it is seen as it is – an ongoing, socially constructed, negotiated, experiential and meaning-created process, not simply the execution of an already–specified plan of action with expected behavioral outcomes' (Long, 2001: 25). In this context, he notes that government officials confronted with a planned intervention must necessarily grasp the organizational and cognitive elements of the social change they are facing by devising appropriate strategies (ibid. 27). As Long explains, development interventions lack 'sharp boundaries in time and space' and 'are always part of a chain or flow of events located within the broader framework of the activities of the state ... and the actions of different interest groups operative in civil society' (ibid. 32). Local actors can overcome or adapt the global to meet local needs and circumstances and defeat interventions that are founded on the notion that 'one size fits all'. Consequently, action research techniques have the capacity to create a space within which the flows of knowledge possessed by experts and local groups can fuse and bring about socially beneficial outcomes.

From 2002 until 2005 I worked in Bangladesh as the juvenile justice specialist on a Canadian government funded justice reform project. The project comprised three elements, one of which was concerned with capacity building and law reform in juvenile justice. The project was principally directed at developing the capacity of government officials who were responsible for running the juvenile justice system and I interacted constantly with this group of local actors. I initially collaborated with juvenile justice officials in a range of research activities with the aim of producing an assessment of the current state of juvenile justice. This work enabled a determination of intervention points for future collaboration. The collaborative process produced a research report for the overall project and involved:

- reviewing numerous texts produced by non-government organizations (NGOs) and donor projects;
- interviewing all relevant stakeholders in government including police, judges and magistrates, civil society actors (national and international) other donor project personnel, and juveniles themselves, as well as the UN agencies involved in child protection;
- collecting statistical data relevant to juvenile justice and compiling the research report.

This part of the process established a broad baseline from which to implement a range of reform and capacity-building activities devised in conjunction with local officials. Activities included: formal training courses, mentoring, supporting infrastructure development, addressing the need for juveniles in contact with the law to receive legal aid from public or private sources, and promoting alternatives to juvenile detention.

Bangladesh is a poor and largely agricultural country, with an estimated population of 156,050,883 (World Fact Book, July 2009). The country has had a traumatic history having been part of India up to partition in 1947 when it was assigned to the newly created Pakistan as East Pakistan because of its largely Muslim population. According to Khair (2001: 55) the country's juvenile justice system has its foundations in the colonial Bengal Code and Prisons Act 1894 which stipulated separate trials for adults and children. Subsequent laws provided for the trial of children in juvenile courts and institutionalization in reformatory schools. Ved Kumari notes that the alternative of a reformatory for delinquent children rather than prison originated in concern about bad prison conditions in India generally and from the recognition that children needed to be incarcerated separately from adults (2004: 63). At present, the Children Act 1974 and the Children Rules represent the law on juveniles being modeled on Indian legislation of the same name passed in the 1940s. Siddiqui (2001: 26) comments that the Act 'not only remains unimplemented but is often disregarded by law enforcers. In fact, the police in Bangladesh are notorious for exhibiting extreme cruelty with young "offenders" such as child prostitutes, "vagrant" children and other young violators of the law.' As well as suffering outdated colonial laws, the juvenile justice system is massively under-resourced.

In Bangladesh there are approximately 54 million children and adolescents up 14 years of age with 27 million boys and 26.9 million girls. According to the Department of Social Welfare, Government of Bangladesh (GOB) children in the 0–14 age group make up about 43 percent of the total population and those in the age group 0–16 years, 55 percent. The country maintains three institutions for juveniles (two for males and the other for females) housing both delinquents and those detained for status offenses. No donor or government diversionary project for juveniles had ever been established in Bangladesh at the time I conducted my research. It was agreed that an action research project would be designed and executed to establish such a scheme, as a pilot project, in a city of about one million, approximately five hours drive from the capital, Dhaka. In this city, Jessore, the project was pursuing numerous juvenile justice reform activities following a 'bottom up' approach in collaboration with a community group comprising government officials, NGOs and representatives of the community. The group I worked with was known as the Association for Correction and Rehabilitation of Offenders (ACRO).

Extensive research was already ongoing in relation to juvenile justice issues. The diversion project, however, required further attention. Research there was conducted in collaboration with a discrete working group specifically organized to plan, implement, supervise, and monitor and evaluate it. The working group, a kind of micro policy network, was drawn from ACRO and comprised a district judge, juvenile court magistrate, a magistrate nominated by the deputy commissioner, the probation officer of the magistrates court and probation officer of the juvenile court, the district coordinator of the CIDA, Canada, Legal Reform Project (employed by the project and located in Jessore), the director of the Diversion Program, the superintendent of police and the NGO participating in the project known as Banchte Shekha. The composition of the working group was aimed at directly meeting the needs of the diversion project and was the outcome of extensive consultation with all members.

Members of the working group and I conducted baseline research for the diversion project. The research process included visits to the juvenile correction centers in the country, interviews with staff as well as the boys and girls detained in the centers, a lengthy review of juvenile records, lengthy discussions with the juvenile magistrate and district judge concerning the legalities associated with the proposed diversion project, and extended discussions with the staff of Banchte Shekha planning the scope and nature of the involvement of Banchte Shekha in the project. Also, we organized and conducted a workshop in Jessore on the practice of juvenile diversion to raise awareness of its operation and effect. Participants included members of ACRO, local NGOs, and actors from the court system in the district including the local bar association, totaling more than one hundred. International experts on restorative justice and diversion practice also attended. The workshop provided a venue within which to share the research data and gain the perspective of the community on the proposed project.

Research for the diversion project aimed to capture the cultural specificity of juvenile delinquency and of sanctioning juveniles so that this knowledge could be incorporated into the design and operation of the diversion project. Without this specific knowledge the diversion project would lack legitimacy within the local community and probably not be sustainable. Also, the juvenile court might well refuse to divert juveniles into the project. Action research associated with the diversion project revealed elements of the specificity of punishing juveniles in the form of: attitudes of stakeholders, including parents and guardians and juvenile corrections staff toward punishment of juveniles generally; notions of 'seriousness' in explicating delinquency; and the nature of juvenile offending (relevant to the issue of seriousness of delinquent acts). Box 31.1 gives a summary of the major issues.

The research revealed that local cultural norms concerning children's development include proscriptions against 'spoiling' children. In fact, once a child is regarded within the local community as spoiled, his or her parents may be ostracized if they do not sever relationships with the child. This cultural pressure may explain the willingness of parents to commit their children to confinement in the juvenile institute as an 'uncontrollable child' at least for a period of time. There was some suspicion amongst my informants that parents pay a bribe for the privilege of having their child committed under this provision. According to Blanchet (1996), all classes of Bangladeshi society believe that children will be spoiled if parental control and authority is weak. This sometimes leads parents to impose severe physical punishment in the hopes of bringing their children back to the right path. When parents volunteer information concerning the punishments they inflict on their children they are conveying that they have not neglected their parental responsibilities. It is also believed that children can become spoiled through a bad environment or neighborhood. Children are thought to lack autonomy and spoiling is always seen as an outcome of the actions or inactions of others or of environmental conditions.

'UNCONTROLLABLE' CASES

Whenever the parents or guardians petitioned the court to detain a child as being 'uncontrollable' the court social caseworker would meet with the child and parents/guardians to collect information for an investigation report from which the court would base its decision about whether to confine or release the child. Parents and guardians described the condition of their child's uncontrollability in terms of conduct that included using drugs, staying out all night, vagrancy, theft, pickpocketing and complaints from the community about the child's behavior. Sometimes the juvenile court magistrate was unsatisfied with the parents' or guardians' explanations about the 'uncontrollability' of the child and the juvenile would remain only a few days at the institution. However, 90 percent of the parents were poverty stricken and

---

Box 31.1: Jessore Correctional Institute

In Bangladesh, two of the three juvenile correctional centers are located in, or in close proximity to, the capital Dhaka, with one being situated at Jessore where the project maintained an office and where it was intended to launch the diversion project. Courts having jurisdiction over juveniles, defined in Bangladesh as a child under the age of 16 years, including the juvenile court, are empowered to send children to a juvenile correctional centre during the pre-trial stage as a remand in custody to await the trial of his/her case and post-trial may commit him/her to detention in a center following the determination of his/her case. Largely for purposes of convenience, all three correctional centers include a juvenile court, a remand home for the children awaiting trial, as well as a correctional institute for those ordered to be detained. This close proximity was supposed to simplify logistics, especially when taking children to and from court hearings.

On inspection, the Jessore Correctional Institute exhibited the starkness and lack of amenities commonly found in Western barrack-type accommodation. Nevertheless, according to living standards in a country where poverty is endemic, the facilities were adequate. The Correctional Institute building had been constructed in 1992 but was not occupied until 1996 when funding from the government for operational needs commenced. The institute housed a trade building where specialist staff taught electrical work, welding, and woodworking. The superintendent of the institute expressed support for further developing the vocational and trade skill training that would provide the children with certificate level skills and help them find jobs after their release. Given the poverty of the children and their families, this was regarded by the local actors as a solution to the children's involvement in crime or indiscipline.

There were 46 staff at the Jessore institute and one vehicle provided by the project. The institute facilities comprised a number of separate buildings including dormitory blocks accommodated according to category of juvenile ('under trial' and 'undergoing correction' post trial) with rooms housing three to four juveniles, toilet and shower block, a dining area, and recreation room while the school rooms were located in another building. The daily routine involved schooling and vocational training in the morning and afternoon, periods of exercise, religious instruction, rising at 5 am and lights out at 10 pm.

At the time of inspection the juvenile population comprised five specific categories: parent referred correction cases where parents had requested a juvenile be detained as an 'uncontrollable' child and the court had made the order accordingly; detainees undergoing correction after having been prosecuted and convicted of an offense were called police referred cases; under trial cases referred by parents; under trial cases referred by police; and juveniles who had been permitted leave of absence from the institution due to some family emergency.

---

felt unable to control their children because both parents had to work to survive. There were no community programs available for uncontrollable children and therefore the magistrate frequently detained uncontrollable children who were parent-referred for a minimum period of six months after which time she would review the case and decide whether to extend the period or release the child. Rarely were lawyers available to represent the children, although the magistrate said lawyers attended her juvenile court for bail applications, after which she never saw them again.

NGO reports on delinquency and my own research after interviewing children, corrections staff and police was supplemented by a published qualitative research study conducted by an indigenous researcher, Abdul Sarker (2001) who interviewed 40 juveniles detained in the correctional institute mostly as 'uncontrollable children' as defined by section 33 Children Act, 1974. Sarker used a self-report method to discover the kinds of 'delinquencies' the boys most frequently engaged in. Sarker's study enumerated the

following 'offenses' as described by the boys and he ranked them from the most to the least prevalent:

- stealing small amounts of money and property from the child's own home;
- truancy from school;
- wandering in the street, rowdyism, and vandalism – including playing football, 'making mischievous fun', 'making hue and cry through obscene language', climbing over roofs, gathering at street corners and annoying people, gambling, breaking windows with stones, boxing and fighting, splashing walls with ink or ugly drawings, stealing flowers and fruit and gossiping;
- returning home late and 'passing the night outside of their homes'. The reasons given for this conduct included associating with friends or carrying out business activities, but many said they were afraid of their parents or guardians because of previous misbehavior;
- smoking cigarettes/tobacco;
- excessive witnessing of movies and VCR shows;

- stealing money/property from outside the home – including asking for loans from relatives or close neighbors and not repaying them, pilfering in stores in the absence of the storekeeper and stealing goods from loaded trucks or other vehicles;
- pilfering of fruits and flowers from street sellers;
- sexual offenses/misbehavior – this conduct includes 'visiting red light areas', homosexuality, 'engaging in sexual acts with elderly women', and 'other perversions';
- running away from home;
- gambling and fraud;
- loitering and 'girl teasing'; that is, shouting obscene language at girls in public places.
- pick pocketing;
- addiction to drugs and alcohol; and
- hijacking – the act of snatching valuable things from the possession of a person by force or through creating a distraction.

Sarker's (2001: 240) study discloses parental sanctions for perceived acts of juvenile delinquency to be both physical and psychological with the former most often taking the form of assaults, using hands or sticks. Other sanctions included refusing to provide food or delaying meals, restrictions on movement, chaining the youth's legs together, and locking the child away in a room for a period. Eighty-two percent of the guardians and parents interviewed admitted having beaten their boys with their hands and over 64 percent had used wooden, iron or bamboo sticks. As an alternative to physical punishment, some parents and guardians had sent their children to hostels, placed children under the care of relatives, or changed the child's schooling from academic to religious education.

In relation to punishment generally, researchers from the international NGO Save the Children reported widespread belief by police, juvenile corrections staff and parents and guardians that a coercive and rigorous system was better for the children than any other measures. Specific punishment practices imposed by juvenile corrections staff for violations of rules and regulations were listed by the children as: requiring them to carry heavy loads, severe beatings and sometimes being hung up by rope tied around the wrists. Also, some boys were required to wear handcuffs at night.

DIALOGUE AND THE ACTION RESEARCH PROCESS

As I explained earlier, action research necessitates constructing a strategy that continually evolves through engagement with local actors. Thus, the diversion project was the outcome of an iterative process of research, planning and participation as proposals were made, discussed, discarded, varied and endorsed in the working group meetings. The working group dialogue was sustained and intense and revealed a collection of discrete interests, agendas, and resources which were continually re-negotiated, within a context of shifting power relations. For example, the probation officer at one point took the position that Bangladesh law did not permit the operation of a diversion scheme of the kind envisaged at all but was overruled by the district court judge who, as a member of the district judicial elite, could not be challenged extra-judicially on such an issue. The director of the NGO was the only non-government member of the group, and as a Christian woman in a largely Islamic society sometimes struggled to have her voice heard in the male-dominated group despite being well known and respected among government circles in the city. To an extent, she was the victim of anti-NGO discourse promoted at all levels of government in the country. Ultimately, agreement was reached that the following would be the foundational principles of the diversion project:

- Institutionalization of juveniles would be a last resort as stipulated by the United Nations Convention on the Rights of the Child.
- The diversion project would provide a stable environment for juveniles who had come into contact with the law and who would benefit by being 'corrected' through participating in the project.
- Stakeholders would aim to instill an attitude that valued work and self-reliance in juveniles participating in the diversion project.
- The project would promote and provide access to formal and non-formal education.
- The project would promote and provide access to vocational skills.
- The project would promote a healthy and productive lifestyle.
- Diversion should have the capacity to assist in reducing the incidence of minor crime committed by juveniles in Jessore.
- The project would create awareness among juveniles in contact with the law concerning their legal and human rights.

These principles reflected the cultural specificity of the issue of juveniles in contact with the law. In particular, the legitimacy of the diversion project in the eyes of the working group and therefore of the community in Jessore depended on it being regarded as a form of 'correction' of juveniles. It was deemed necessary then that the project would equip those committed to it with training and skills that would enable them to find employment. 'Correcting' juveniles in local terms meant not spoiling juveniles and giving them the means to lift themselves out of poverty at a young age.

POWER RELATIONS

Bangladesh is a donor-rich environment in which the numerous donor interventions are often seen by the local elites as policy drivers and instruments for imposing Western models based on liberal conceptions of the public good. The configuration and structure of the diversion project, including the working group itself, constituted a 'structure of domination' (Scott, 2001) because almost all resources for the diversion project would be provided out of donor funds and because project professionals had initiated the notion of this juvenile diversion project in Jessore. Nevertheless, participants in the action research resisted, debated and shaped the nature of the project. They identified as Bangladeshi citizens negotiating with non-citizens over a project providing for the punishment of their juvenile citizens; through their status as senior and elite government officials residing and working in the city of Jessore and exercising significant local administrative and legal powers; and through their extant knowledge of bargaining with aid donors in various fields gained over a long period of time resulting from their senior positions in district government.

Using an action research methodology entails always trying to remain conscious of the positionality of the academic researcher as 'expert' and controller of knowledge production. As noted by numerous commentators, the extent of stakeholder participation in action research can be assessed by the location of power and control; that is, who actually controls the research process (Hampshire et al., 2005: 340). In this project and in the juvenile diversion micro-project, my international and academic status was enhanced by my possession of the professional title, 'juvenile justice specialist.' My interactions with project stakeholders always occurred within a context of donor assistance to the country and within the relations of domination engendered by that context. As Mark Hobart notes, 'The relationship of developers and those-to-be developed is constituted by the developers' knowledge and categories' (1993: 2). Therefore, power relations were, from the outset, asymmetrical.

In trying to assess the extent of participation and control by local stakeholders it can be helpful to draw on typologies because they provide a starting point and initial framework for assessing the extent of participation and control in a particular project. Biggs (1989), for example, identifies four modes of participation and control:

contractual: researchers contract local people as research subjects;

consultative: local people are consulted for their opinions prior to the start of the research project;

collaborative: researchers and local people work together on projects that are designed, implemented and supervised by the researchers; and

collegiate: researchers and local people work in concert as colleagues offering varying skills in a mutual learning process but the local people have control (Biggs, 1989).

In most instances, however, such typologies are better thought of merely as characterizations, not least because during the course of project work power relations tend to ebb and flow according to the issue under discussion, whether explicit or implicit, or led by the researchers or local citizens. From my position, the process of action research in Bangladesh resonated with a collegiate standard, but the dominance of 'knowledge' possessed by the outsiders and the paramount position of the project as the funder of this diversion scheme tended to mitigate the notion of complete local control. Mediating the tension between an acceptable participatory standard of action research and local project control was a major challenge in the process.

Nevertheless, the tensions were mediated well enough to enable the diversion project to come into being with the consent of all stakeholders. During its initial pilot period of operation ten boys were placed on probation and as a condition of probation agreed to participate in the diversion project for six months. They were housed in facilities provided by the Jessore NGO, supervised by NGO staff, and received training and instruction from specialists in mechanical and electrical skills and computer usage. The project was continually monitored by the working group and evaluated after two months and again after six months in an iterative process designed to identify and resolve operational issues.

CONCLUSION

I have argued for an approach to third world criminology that is culturally specific and that seeks to gain access to the cultural criminology of a nation. I have suggested that the action research method should be given prominence in this undertaking and that it should inform political, economic and institutional analyses. There are significant constraints affecting cultural criminological research in the developing world. Nevertheless, within these constraints donor interventions for law reform and rule of law projects can provide an opportunity to conduct culturally specific action research of a participatory kind. Given donor reluctance to allow sufficient time and resources for sustained periods of research, action research in its various forms and with all its imperfections offers an 'as good as it gets' methodology. In the context of development assistance work, the merits of good action research lie in its recognition of the importance of local participation from the outset and during the research process, and in the imperative that action research must produce socially useful outcomes.

In the field of law reform and rule of law, the dominating Euro-centric models of practice and policy are permeated with Western cultural assumptions, beliefs and expectations. In confronting this knowledge, developing countries are able to deploy their own situated practices constituted by a past and changing history of practices. Where local citizens are empowered and have a foundational stake in reforms, they can ensure that globalization unfolds in locally specific ways and critically assess how local social processes are shaped by global forces. Action research is one of the best methods criminologists have at their disposal for helping developing countries to achieve this.

Committed cultural criminologists engaging with action research can help shape social practice and formulate transformative plans in important justice policy fields. In developing countries, exciting fields of inquiry such as 'traditional' justice processes for dispute settlement, transitional justice and gaining access to legal and human rights often exemplify the challenges to legal, social and political development. Cultural criminologists will test their skills in ensuring that research processes pursue an iterative path toward the intersection of theory and practice, according to the needs of participants. Also, in conducting research, they must constantly monitor the dynamics of local participation and, where necessary, undertake radical changes to ensure legitimate collaboration and genuine local ownership.

RECOMMENDED READING

Readers interested in my study where I began to develop the tenets of cultural criminology might wish to consult: Banks, C. (2000) 'Developing cultural specificity for a cultural criminology.' in C. Banks (ed.) *Developing Cultural Criminology: Theory and Practice in Papua New Guinea*

(Sydney: University of Sydney, Institute of Criminology), pp. 15– 50.

For an early (1983) view of methodological and epistemological issues in comparative criminology, see Beirne, P. (1983) 'Cultural relativism and comparative criminology.' *Contemporary Crisis* 7: 371–91.

A seminal essay on the export of Western models of crime control to the third world as well as insights concerning indigenous social controls is Cohen, S. (1988). 'Western crime control models in the third world: benign or malignant?' In S. Cohen (ed.) *Against Criminology* (New Brunswick: Tansaction Books), pp. 172–202.

McTaggart, R. (1997) *Participatory Action Research: International Contexts and Consequences*. (New York: State University of New York Press) contains chapters on modes of action research in Germany, Columbia, Australia, Spain, Thailand and the US as well as a useful explanation of the guiding principles for participatory action research.

Winter, R. (1989) *Learning from Experience: Principles and Practice of Action Research* (Lewes: The Falmer Press) was written primarily for teachers but remains one of the best and most comprehensive explanations of action research.

REFERENCES

Agozino, B. (2005) 'Crime, criminology and post colonial theory.' In J. Sheptycki and A. Wardak (eds) *Transnational and Comparative Criminology*, Australia: The GlassHouse Press, pp. 117–134.

Banks, C. (2000) (ed.) *Developing Cultural Criminology: Theory and Practice in Papua New Guinea*. Sydney: University of Sydney: Institute of Criminology Monograph Series.

Banks, C. (2007) 'The discourse of children's rights in Bangladesh: International norms and local definitions.' *International Journal of Children's Rights* 15(3–4): 391–414.

Biggs, S. (1989) 'Resource – poor farmer participation in research: a synthesis of experiences from nine national agricultural research systems.' OFCOR (On-Farm Client-Oriented Research) Comparative Study Paper 3. The Hague: International Service for National Agricultural Rewards.

Birkbeck, C. (1985) 'Understanding crime and social control elsewhere: a geographical perspective on theory in criminology.' *Research in Law, Deviance and Social Control* 7: 215–246.

Blanchet, T. (1996) *Lost Innocence, Stolen Childhoods*. Dhaka: The University Press Limited.

Carothers, T. (2006) 'The Problem of Knowledge.' In T. Carothers (ed.) *Promoting the Rule of Law Abroad: In Search of Knowledge*. Washington, DC: Carnegie Endowment for International Peace, pp. 15–30.

Clegg, I. and Whetton, J. (1995) 'In search of a Third World Criminology.' In L Noaks, M. Levi and M. Maguire (eds) *Contemporary Issues in Criminology*. Cardiff: University of Wales Press, pp. 26–51.

Clifford, J. (1988) *The Predicament of Culture: Twentieth Century Ethnography, Literature, and Art*. Boston: Harvard University Press.

Clinard, M. and Abbott, D. (1973) *Crime in Developing Countries: A Comparative Perspective*. New York: John Wiley & Sons.

Cohen, S. (1988) 'Western crime control models in the third world: benign or malignant?' In S. Cohen (ed.) *Against Criminology*. New Brunswick: Transaction Books, pp. 172–202.

Durkheim, E. (1951) *Suicide*. J.A. Spaulding and G. Simpson, trans. New York: The Free Press.

Ferrell, J. and Sanders, C. (1995) *Cultural Criminology*. Boston: Northeastern University Press.

Ferrell, J., Hayward, K. and Young, J. (2008) *Cultural Criminology: An Invitation*. Thousand Oaks: Sage Publications.

Freire. P. (1972) *Pedagogy of the Oppressed*. New York: Penguin.

Garland, D. (1990) *Punishment and Modern Society*. Oxford: Oxford University Press.

Geertz, C. (1993) *The Interpretation of Cultures*. London: Fontana Press.

Gustavsen, B. (2002) 'Theory and practice: the mediating discourse.' In P. Reason and H. Bradbury (eds) *Handbook of Action Research: Participative Inquiry and Practice*. London: Sage Publications, pp. 17–26.

Hampshire, K., Hills, E. and Iqbal, N. (2005) 'Power relations in participatory research and community development: a case study from Northern England.' *Human Organization* 64(4): 340–349.

Hardie-Bick, J, Sheptycki, J. and Wardak, A. (2005) 'Introduction: Transnational and comparative criminology in a global perspective.' in J. Sheptycki and A. Wardak (eds) *Transnational and Comparative Criminology*. London: Glasshouse Press, pp. 1–16.

Henry, S. and Milovanovic, D. (1994) 'The constitution of constitutive criminology: a postmodern approach to criminological theory.' In D. Nelken (ed.) *The Futures of Criminology*. London: Sage Publications, pp. 110–133.

Hobart, M. (1993) 'Introduction: the growth of ignorance?' In M. Hobart (ed.) *An Anthropological Critique of Development: The Growth of Ignorance*. London: Routledge, pp. 1–30.

Karstedt, S. (2008) "Comparing Cultures, comparing crime: challenges, prospects and problems for a global criminology" in N. Larsen and R. Smandych (eds). *Global Criminology and Criminal Justice: Current Issues and Perspectives*. Buffalo, NY: Broadview Press, pp. 23–46.

Kemmis, S. and McTaggart, R. (2000) 'Participatory action research.' In N. Denzin and Y. Lincoln (eds) *Handbook of Qualitative Research*. London: Sage Publications, pp. 567–605.

Khair S. (2001) 'Street children in conflict with the law: The Bangladesh experience.' *Asia-Pacific Journal on Human Rights and the Law* 2(1): 55–76.

Kumari, V. (2004) *The Juvenile Justice System in India From Welfare to Rights*. New Delhi: Oxford University Press.

Long, N. (2001) *Development Sociology*. London: Routledge.

Loomba, A. (1993) 'Overworlding the "Third World".' In P. Williams and L. Chrisman (eds) *Colonial Discourse and Post-Colonial Theory: A Reader*. Hertfordshire: Harvester Wheatsheaf, pp. 305–323.

McTaggart, R. (1997) *Participatory Action Research: International Contexts and Consequences*. New York: State University of New York Press.

Mohanty, C. (1993) 'Under western eyes: feminist scholarship and colonial discourses.' in P. Williams and L. Chrisman (eds) *Colonial Discourse and Post-Colonial Theory: A Reader*. Hertfordshire: Harvester Wheatsheaf, pp. 196–220.

Nelken, D. (1994) 'Reflexive criminology?' In D. Nelken (ed.) *The Futures of Criminology*. London: Sage Publications, pp. 7–42.

Noaks, L. and Wincup, E. (2004) *Criminological Research: Understanding Qualitative Methods*. London: Sage Publications.

Reason, P. and Bradbury, H. (eds) (2002) 'Inquiry and participation in search of a world worthy of human aspiration.' In P. Reason and H. Bradbury (eds) *Handbook of Action Research: Participative Inquiry and Practice*. London: Sage Publications, pp. 1–14.

Sarker, A. (2001) *Juvenile Delinquency: Dhaka City Experience*. Dhaka: Human Nursery for Development.

Scott, J. (2001) *Power*. Cambridge: Polity Press.

Siddiqui K. (2001) *Better Days, Better Lives: Towards a Strategy for Implementing the Convention on the Rights of the Child in Bangladesh*. Dhaka, Bangladesh: The University Press Limited.

Stinger, E.T. (1999) *Action Research*, 2nd edition. Thousand Oaks: Sage.

Strathern, M. (1988) *The Gender of the Gift: Problems with Women and Problems with Society in Melanesia*. Berkeley: University of California Press.

Stromseth, J., Wippman, D. and Brooks; R. (2006) *Can Might Make Rights?: Building the Rule of Law after Military Interventions*. Cambridge: Cambridge University Press.

Sumner, C. (1982) 'Crime, justice and underdevelopment: beyond modernisation theory.' In C. Sumner (ed.) *Crime, Justice and Underdevelopment*. London: Heinemann, pp. 1–39.

Winter, R. (1989) (ed.) *Learning from Experience: Principles and Practice of Action Research*. Lewes: The Falmer Press.

Winter, R. (2002) 'Managers, spectators and citizens: Where does 'theory' come from in action research.' In C. Day, J. Elliott, B. Somekh and R. Winter (eds) *Theory and Practice in Action Research*. Oxford: Symposium Books. pp. 27–44.

World Fact Book, (2009) Available at: https://www.cia.gov/library/publications/the-world-factbook/geos/bg.html

32

Feminist Approaches to Criminological Research

Gail Mason, Julie Stubbs

INTRODUCTION

There is no orthodoxy to feminist research methods in criminology. Rather than adherence to particular methods, feminist research is better characterized as arising from methodological and ethical concerns related to theory, ontology (beliefs about the nature of the world) and epistemology (theories of knowledge), and to political engagement. Feminist work from the outset has been deeply concerned with methodological issues. It has been open to innovative approaches to research and to deploying established methods in new ways. Feminist criminological approaches commonly have a concern with the production and authorizing of knowledge, and with questions such as: who can know, what counts as knowledge and whose knowledge counts? While some of these concerns may be shared by other critical approaches to criminology, feminist research is typically marked by a concern with social relations as organized by reference to sex/gender. These issues have implications for the choice of methods but there is no necessary link between a feminist approach and a particular method.

Theoretical developments in feminist criminology have begun to permeate mainstream criminology (the concept of intersectionality is a good example), and the benefits of research methodologies favoured by feminist criminologists are gradually being recognized by other streams of criminology; for instance, feminist approaches have reshaped developments in victimology (Walklate, 2007). Carol Smart (2009) argues with respect to sociology that feminist methodologies have come to provide a foundation for innovative research and for highlighting the importance of theoretically informed research. However, feminist research continues to be given scant attention in many methodological texts within criminology. Feminist criminology is committed to an interdisciplinary approach that employs blended research methods. Like all feminist research, feminist criminology is 'in a state of constant challenge and continual reformulation' that makes it 'its own most trenchant critic' (Smart, 2009: 296).

We begin with an overview of feminist criminology, identifying selected methodological features that are characteristic of a feminist approach to research. We flag key debates and emerging themes related to feminist research on violent victimization. We have selected four themes for more detailed examination: the challenge of intersectional work; moving beyond the victim/agent dichotomy; the integrity of the research process in the interpretation and analysis of research data; and the implications of the so called 'textual turn'. We demonstrate the challenges of engaging with these issues through case studies based on our own research.

OVERVIEW

Mainstream criminology has focused on producing an etiological, explanatory approach to crime, charting the patterns of crime and monitoring the practices of police, courts and corrections towards improving the efficiency and effectiveness of criminal justice (Gelsthorpe, 2002). Criminology has largely sought to do this through empirical inquiry and the development of theoretical frameworks grounded in this inquiry. Feminist criminology of the 1970s and 1980s sought to address two main problems with this criminological enterprise: neglect of women in the study of crime; and distorted, stereotyped and one-dimensional accounts of women's offending and consequent problems in the management of female crime within the criminal justice system (Gelsthorpe, 2002; Heidensohn, 1985; Morris, 1987; Smart, 1976).

Under-representation of women and girls in official crime statistics made it easy to exclude them from mainstream criminological theories, grounded in empirical research largely conducted on male subjects and crime patterns. As Daly (2010) notes, feminist criminology identified a 'generalizability problem': so called general explanations of crime were in fact theories about male offenders that were inappropriate and inadequate for explaining criminal behaviour (or its absence) amongst women and girls. Distorted accounts of women's experiences of crime were the product of stereotypes about female psychology and behaviour, and traditional gender-role expectations that led to assumptions about 'normal' and 'deviant' behaviour for women (Gelsthorpe, 2002). Early feminist criminology worked to expose the influence of these stereotypes on criminal justice policy and practice, and within attempts to explain crime committed by, and towards women. It has also been associated with calls to work beyond the limitations of criminology (Cain, 1990).

Building on this critique, feminist criminology began to investigate the absence of gender theory in the study of crime as a whole. Male offending was too often analyzed without an adequate investigation of the relationship between crime and masculinity. This evolved into a focus on crime as a way of 'doing masculinity' (Messerschmidt, 1993). As critiques emerged (Collier, 1998), 'doing gender' developed into more nuanced accounts of 'situated/structured action' (Miller, 2002) and the idea of 'gendered lives' shaping offending and non-offending behaviour (see Daly, 2010).

From the 1980s, more analyses emerged of the differences not just between women and men but also between women of different circumstances and cultures. An appreciation, led by Black feminist thought, of the intersectionality of gender, class and race allowed for more varied and divergent understandings of female experiences of crime, as victims and offenders. In the 1990s, some feminist criminologists started to draw upon the post-modern trend in wider feminist theory of 'deconstructing' the traditional sex/gender distinction with a view to highlighting the discursively constructed and performative nature of gender identity. Together with a post-modern scepticism about 'grand theories' and definitive, linear and causal explanations for human behaviour, with crime no exception, this led some feminist theorists to suggest that the notion of a *single* feminist criminology is neither theoretically possible nor politically desirable.

In summary, feminist criminological approaches have sought to: bring the specific experiences and representations of women into focus as victims, offenders and agents in the criminal justice system, whilst remaining attuned to multiple and sometimes contradictory ways in which gender interacts with other aspects of identity; critique and reform the processing of women within the criminal justice system; and draw upon the insights of gender theory to challenge and reconstruct theories of crime and the model of social science through which criminological knowledge is produced.

This scholarship would not have been possible without the leadership of early feminists who challenged both dominant and emerging radical criminological perspectives for failing to attend to gender, and participated in debates that contributed to feminist developments in criminology and beyond (Carlen, 1983; Chesney-Lind, 1986; Heidensohn, 1985; Klein, 1973; Smart, 1976). Nor would it have been possible if some criminologists had not taken up the feminist challenge to develop new research methodologies. The theories used, the questions asked, the subjects studied and the data gathered required feminist criminologists to look beyond the disciplinary boundaries of criminology for inspiration and practical advice. Initially, they found guidance in the burgeoning field of feminist methodology and epistemology that was influencing many disciplines across the sciences and humanities (Harding, 1987; Stanley and Wise, 1983). As fracture lines started to appear in methodological praxis, feminist criminologists began to draw from a larger pool of methodological resources, including reinventing approaches favoured by various forms of traditional criminology such as ethnography, qualitative interviews or crime victimization surveys and using quantitative methods in a more considered way (Gelsthorpe, 1990; Kelly, 1990).

Given the dynamic and multi-faceted nature of feminism, it should come as no surprise that there is little agreement on epistemological questions of how, and what kind of, feminist knowledge should be produced. Over the last 40 years, debates about ways of creating knowledge and doing research have produced multiple methodological loyalties and options. With an eye to these methodological issues, Sandra Harding (1987) grouped feminist thinking in the social sciences according to three broad epistemological orientations: feminist empiricism, standpoint feminism and post-modern feminism.

Within criminology, feminist empiricism describes research that focuses on the production of data about women in order to analyze women's victimization, criminality and engagement with the criminal justice system. The assumption is that such knowledge will bring greater objectivity to criminological theory and research that prioritizes men. Empirical research of this nature attempts to improve criminology as a science by adding women but without questioning the underlying assumptions of positivism and the hypothetico-deductive model of science which it favours (Naffine, 1997). Such empirical research contin-ues to make an important contribution to knowl-edge within feminist criminology and recent work has often been responsive to criticisms of earlier empiricism.

One of the most significant challenges to this understanding of knowledge has been the devel-opment of feminist standpoint epistemology (Harding, 1987). Borrowing from Marx and Hegel, this approach prioritizes women's views of the world and was quickly expanded to the idea of a woman's standpoint (Harding, 1987) or a Black feminist standpoint (Collins, 1990). Standpoint epistemology treats women's experiences as the foundation for feminist knowledge. In some ver-sions of standpoint epistemology, research that commences from this marginalized social position is 'scientifically preferable' because it originates in, and is tested against, a 'more complete and less distorting kind of social experience' (Harding, 1987: 184). Critics argue that this epistemological position reduces women's experience to a univer-sal and essential benchmark that is incapable of deconstructing the power relations embedded in criminology's truth claims, or, of adequately accounting for differences of race, ethnicity, sexu-ality and the like (Cain, 1990; Naffine, 1997).

Feminist post-modernism is a broad term that includes feminist approaches that are influenced by post-modern or post-structural theory (such as by Derrida or Foucault). It rejects the positivist claim that research can produce a universal, objec-tive and certain account of the social world and the standpoint assertion that experience is a pre-ferred origin for the production of knowledge. Instead, it argues that 'reality', subjectivity and 'truth' are constructed and produced through dis-course, power and knowledge (such as legal, criminological, scientific or artistic discourses). This sometimes focuses on deconstructing the binary oppositions that profoundly shape human knowledge (mind/body, male/female,

masculinity/femininity, black/white, heterosexual/ homosexual, agent/victim, etc.). An influential body of feminist thinkers have applied this strong version of constructionism to reinvent the sex/ gender distinction as a matter of corporeality and performativity (Butler, 1990). This has been picked up by a number of feminist researchers on crime (Howe, 1994; Mason, 2002; Naffine, 1997; Young, 1996). For example, Carol Smart proposed the idea of the 'woman of legal discourse', arguing that '[w]oman is a gendered subject position which legal discourse brings into being' (1992: 34).

It is helpful to identify the differences between these epistemological positions but we should not see them as either chronological stages or as mutually exclusive. Feminist criminological research has become so diverse and flexible – with individual researchers often employing a combi-nation of different methodological approaches within and between studies – that it is difficult for such classifications to do justice to the richness of this scholarship. It is more helpful to think of feminist research in criminology as involving a series of key methodological preferences, or imperatives, that shape how we design, implement and analyze research. Feminist research has few essential ingredients but, rather, engages with the epistemological issues discussed previously while not being determined by them. These preferences, in turn, influence how we anticipate the results of our research could, or should, be applied in prac-tice. While some of these preferences are unique to feminist research (such as the commitment to a gendered analysis), others are shared by related criminological approaches (such as critical crimi-nology) or adapted from fields outside criminol-ogy. Feminist research is thus a question of process rather than simply one of definition: it is not just *what* we do but *how* we do it that makes a project feminist. Below we describe and explain these preferences.

Feminist/gender theory

One defining characteristic of feminist crimino-logical research is an engagement with feminist theory. Although there is no single approach to feminist theorizing, and studies vary in how much emphasis they give to feminist theory, it is diffi-cult to see how research can be feminist without some commitment to feminist thinking. However, the fact that a project has an analysis of sex/gender differences is not sufficient to make it feminist. The subject matter and research questions of a feminist approach are informed by, and sympa-thetic to, feminist theory as an account of sex/ gender as an organizing principle and power relation in social life (Gelsthorpe, 2002: 135).

This doesn't mean that feminist research only uses feminist theory; it brings a feminist sensibility to bear upon a variety of theories from within and outside criminology. Developments in feminist theorizing have had important implications for research methodology, and research findings and political activism have also shaped feminist theorizing.

Over time feminist theory has developed a deeper and more complex engagement with gender relations, moving from a focus on patriarchy to a more differentiated understanding of power and beyond a dichotomous conception of gender, and also undertaking a critical examination of masculinity (Gelsthorpe, 2002). Contemporary feminist projects commonly analyze and interpret sex/gender as a relation of power that operates across multiple levels and sites including individual, structural and discursive levels, and intersects with other axes of power (see 'Intersectionality' later). Kathy Daly makes the point that '[f]ew feminist scholars are interested to devise a grand theory of crime' (2010: 232) because they recognize that offending behaviour is a social construct that is shaped by multiple, shifting and context-dependent variables.

More complex conceptions of sex/gender have offered challenges for researchers, and perhaps more so for researchers who rely exclusively on quantitative methods; sex/gender cannot be adequately captured as a trait, or variable, and researchers need to engage with the meanings of social processes and interactions (Daly, 2010). Mixed-method approaches, drawing from both qualitative and quantitative methods, may address these concerns although care must be taken in attempting to integrate approaches that have inconsistent epistemological foundations (Tashakkori and Tedlie, 2008).

Experience

For theoretical, epistemological and political reasons, feminist research has emphasized women's experiences as a subject of research, and a source of knowledge. It typically links individual or micro-level experience with gendered power relations at the macro level. Giving voice to women has been associated with democratizing research, validating women and acknowledging women's agency, redressing their absence from criminology and criminological analysis, recognizing the private sphere, challenging universal criminological accounts and offering a more complete account of social relations. Experience is given greatest emphasis within standpoint feminism which usually privileges qualitative methods. Attention to women's experience does not preclude an examination of men or masculinity, nor does it preclude men conducting research within a feminist framework (Collier, 1998).

In the 1970s and 1980s documenting women's experiences of offences like domestic violence and sexual assault was a focus of feminist research, commonly using methods such as interviews based on convenience or purposive samples, and localized victimization surveys. Much of this research and associated political activism emphasized the common experiences of women. Critical reflection on the inadequacies of conventional research methodologies and methods for such purposes shaped future developments in feminist research and in criminology more generally such as the refinement of crime victimization surveys (Walklate, 2007), approaches to evaluation (Griffiths and Hanmer, 2005), and arguably the move towards mixed methods. Such research also opened up new areas of enquiry and had a profound influence on criminal justice policy.

However, the role of experience, and especially the valorization of subjectivity, became a vexed issue for feminist researchers and has been debated from several perspectives. Strong versions of standpoint feminism attracted criticism for seeming to endorse a singular standpoint, imposing a false unity and failing to attend to differences between women including but not limited to those of race, class and sexuality; for some the category 'woman' became untenable. For instance, research about the experiences of lesbian (and gay male) victims of intimate partner violence (Renzetti and Miles, 1996) challenged simple dichotomous conceptions of sex/gender, and research concerning Black women's experiences exposed constructs such as Battered Women Syndrome as largely based on white, middle-class experience (Allard, 1991). From a different perspective Joan Scott has critically examined the claim that experience might provide an 'unassailable' basis for knowledge. In a more complex argument than can be summarized here, she observes that when 'meaning is taken as transparent', experience 'reproduces rather than contests given ideological systems' (1991: 778). For Scott '[i]t is not individuals who have experience, but subjects who are constituted through experience' (1991: 779); '[w]hat counts as experience is neither self-evident nor straightforward; it is always contested, and always therefore political' and thus 'the discursive nature of experience' needs critical analysis (1991: 797).

Such criticisms have encouraged ongoing reflection on how experience is used and represented. Feminist research has responded by seeking to give richer accounts of women's experiences and differences, for instance, by using ethnographies (Maher, 1997), life histories

(Richie, 1996) and feminist pathways analysis (Daly, 1994), attending to the gendered, situational contexts of violence (Miller, 2008), deploying constructs such as intersectionality (Maher, 1997), and by analyzing how discourses constitute women (Young, 1996). We return to these issues below. Documenting women's and girls' experiences of violence continues to be a significant concern, especially to highlight issues specific to particular groups and to demonstrate failures in laws, policies and practices.

Social change

A defining feature of feminism is a commitment to social change in the interests of women (Gelsthorpe, 2002). Thus, feminist research is commonly seen as having political utility, informing social change and social justice. However, together the focus on women's experiences and a preference for political engagement offers a profound challenge to conventional ideas about value neutral research and objectivity (Harding, 1987). These characteristics are consistent with aspects of other post-positivist research traditions (Mertens, 2008; Tashakkori and Tedlie, 2008) and critical criminological approaches. A feminist preference for consciously partial and purposive research projects does not signal a departure from rigorous and sound methodology but may be entirely consistent with effectively integrating theoretical, ethical, epistemological and methodological concerns.

This commitment to change tends to encourage certain research questions and topics: the application of feminist theory to feminism's preferred subject matter, women's and girl's experiences, produces research questions that characterize feminist methodology. Asking questions about women's experiences of violence has been one of feminism's major contributions to criminal justice reform. A commitment to social change may also be associated with allowing the perspectives of women, children or other marginalized groups to be heard through research, and through linking research with practice and practitioners. The feminist commitment to social change is sometimes incorporated directly into the project in an 'action research' design. Haviland et al.'s study (2008) on the effects of mandatory arrest was specifically designed to advocate change and affect policy on domestic violence. The advocacy-researcher partnership technique they adopted sought to move away from dispassionate observational methods typical in this area. Their project approaches the task of data collection and research as an aspect of social action rather than social study.

Post-positivism

Scepticism amongst feminists about the capacity of criminology to deliver neutral or universal accounts of crime has prompted a disavowal of positivist epistemology which includes a belief in the existence of a single reality, a conviction that value-free and independent research is possible, a search for cause-and-effect relationships, and a belief in the ability of research to generalize to the wider population (Lincoln and Guba, 1985). Like other post-positivists, feminists acknowledge that research is influenced by the values of the researcher and the theory that he/she uses and can ever only hope to represent a constructed version of reality (Tashakkori and Tedlie, 2008). This has methodological implications for research practice. Instead of undertaking quantitative analysis on large datasets in order to test hypotheses derived from grand theories of crime, feminists have favoured small-scale qualitative studies and inductive modes of analysis. This preference is apparent from an examination of the pages of the journal *Feminist Criminology*. The majority of articles published since its inception employ comparable designs of qualitative research including: (1) a selection of samples drawn from volunteers; (2) use of semi-structured interviews; and (3) coding of themes in interview transcripts by hand or by using qualitative software.

In seeking to capture the dynamic, contradictory nature of experience, feminist criminologists have also borrowed a range of qualitative methods from other disciplines (such as oral history and ethnography) and engaged with objects of analysis (fiction, media or photographic images) and/or modes of analysis (literary analysis or psychoanalysis) that provide alternate cultural or experiential views of crime (Hollway and Jefferson, 2001; Young, 1996). For example, adopting a psychoanalytic orientation, Robinson (2007) uses a single-subject clinical case study to explore the subjective experiences of a 'delinquent' adolescent mother within a theoretical model that sees gender, race, trauma and power as fluid and interwoven constructs. Treatment (including the exchange of emotion between client and therapist) and treatment outcomes of this single case study are given policy implications through extrapolation to 'a larger population exhibiting similar constellations of thoughts, feelings and behaviors' (2007: 32).

It would be a mistake, however, to assume that feminist criminology is wedded to qualitative research alone. Admittedly, in the beginning, the need to build a firm epistemological foundation for feminist inquiry meant that quantitative research was often viewed with suspicion or accompanied by an apology. Yet, the problem has never been with quantitative research itself but rather with 'insensitive quantification' (Gelsthorpe, 1990: 91). While qualitative data gathering still dominates feminist criminology, increasingly we see the use of innovative and careful statistical analysis to answer feminist-inspired questions about crime (Griffiths and Hanmer, 2005). Recent examples include research on attrition rates in sexual assault cases (Kelly et al., 2005) and measuring the costs of domestic violence (Stanko, 2001).

Reflexivity and power

Feminism's sensitivity to questions of power and experience extends beyond the research subject to the researcher herself. One hallmark of feminist methodology is a commitment to acknowledging and breaking down the power relations that operate between the researcher and her participants. Reflexivity describes research that attempts to: (1) de-objectify research participants by enabling them to have greater input into a research project; and (2) consciously insert the researcher into the research process with the view to producing a more honest, ethical and balanced form of knowledge. Reflexivity is one of the means used by feminist criminologists to avoid the myth of objective and value-free research. Although there are limits on the extent to which the power imbalance between researcher and research participant can be neutralized, particular methods (usually qualitative) are thought to be better at moderating and minimizing this imbalance. For example, the social change objectives of action research mean that it is geared towards involving research subjects in project design and implementation (Gelsthorpe, 1990). Something as simple as describing one's research project in the first person can also remind the writer and the reader that the research results are shaped by subjective decisions made by the researcher at every step of the way (e.g., 'I chose to ask my research participants questions about their perceptions of domestic violence education programs because I had good reason to believe …').

One of the complexities of breaking down the power relations in research has been the question of 'who speaks for whom?' raised particularly by women of colour. For instance, how can a privileged white, middle-class feminist academic hope to speak on behalf of a disenfranchised, working-class, indigenous woman whose life has been deeply affected by criminalization and/or victimization? Whilst distinctions between speaking 'for', speaking 'about' and speaking 'with' have consumed considerable feminist attention, the issue is more helpfully approached, as noted by post-colonial critic Gayatri Spivak (1988), as less about who does the speaking and more about what we say, how we say it and who listens.

In summary, it is the preferences described above that make a project distinctly feminist or give it a feminist 'edge'. Criminological research that takes feminism seriously will most likely address, or adopt, one or more of these features. We have chosen Lisa Maher's study (1997) of women's lives in a Brooklyn drug market as an exemplar of feminist criminological research (see Box 32.1).

EMERGENT THEMES AND ONGOING DEBATES: VIOLENCE AND VICTIMIZATION

In this section we draw out some themes that reflect recent trends, ongoing debates or conundrums for criminologists engaged in feminist research, with reference to feminist research on violence. In the 1970s, the violent victimization of women became a focal point of feminist politics,

---

Box 32.1 Sexed work: gender, race and resistance in a Brooklyn drug market by Lisa Maher

This study draws on criminology, anthropology and other disciplines. Maher locates the women's offending, and victimization, within the context of their lives and work in the informal and formal economies, in sex work and drug markets. She pays careful attention to women's agency, while acknowledging the significant constraints on that agency. This is a theoretically sophisticated study, using an intersectional approach that engages race, gender and class, and works across levels connecting individual experience, with the situational context and structural conditions. Maher demonstrates how structural conditions and cultural narratives shape identities and reproduce inequalities. She uses triangulated methods, giving a rich ethnographic account based on detailed observations, interviews with a wide sample, and repeated interviews with a deep sample. She is respectful of the research subjects and deeply reflexive, recognizing the limits on claims of allowing women to tell their stories since she is the author of the text.

spawning a massive movement seeking to expose, challenge and prevent men's violence towards women and children, particularly domestic violence, rape and child sexual assault. Much of this work was conducted at the 'coal face' of service provision to women survivors of violence (e.g., women's refuges and rape crisis centres) but quickly developed close and enduring ties with feminists in academia and government agencies. The policy reforms and shifts in social attitudes that were sought called for new theoretical and empirical knowledge on women's and girl's experiences of violence. Although this concern was at odds with the 'new criminology' that was developing amongst left-leaning critical criminologists (Carrington, 2008), feminist criminologists were insistent on the need to develop a comprehensive and critical body of scholarship in this area of victimology. This research has been highly influential in bringing visibility, and giving voice, to women's and girl's experiences as the victims of violence, their treatment in the criminal justice system and our understanding of these processes. It has changed the face of criminology and the practices of the criminal justice system. Feminist scholarship on the violent victimization of women and girls has also been at the forefront of methodological innovation. Ongoing debates about how best to research and represent women as the victims of violence have tapped into deeper theoretical and epistemological questions. The following selected themes give some sense of the complexity of issues that are currently leading methodological discussion in this area.

Intersectionality

Useful reviews of the call for an intersectional approach within criminology are provided by Burgess-Proctor (2006) and Sokoloff and Dupont (2005) who apply intersectionality to domestic violence. Intersectionality is a shorthand term that reflects the complexity of experience and relations of power, especially but not limited to the intersection of gender, race (and or ethnicity) and class. It recognizes that these relations are 'dynamic, historically grounded, socially constructed power relationships that simultaneously operate at both micro-structural and macro-structural levels' (Burgess-Proctor, 2006: 37), although 'particular social identities may be more salient in one context than another' (Daly, 2010: 237). In part it has grown out of recognition of the limitations of a unitary account of women's experiences, that the category 'Woman/en' is essentialist, and in response to criticisms especially from women from minorities. Feminist legal scholar Kimberle Crenshaw (1991) has been

very influential; she examined violence against women of colour with reference to intersecting social categories at structural, political and representational levels. However, intersectionality has been used in various ways and has no singular meaning.

In examining the methodological implications of intersectionality, Burgess-Proctor (2006) sees qualitative approaches as offering the capacity to examine experience, and mixed-methods approaches as having the potential to engage both macro and micro levels as commonly required from an intersectional frame. Some feminist criminological studies of victimization (directly or indirectly) have used an intersectional approach, in conjunction with methods such as the integration of interview data and a post-structural analysis (Mason, 2002), ethnography (Maher, 1997) and case studies (Cunneen and Stubbs, 1997; Stubbs and Tolmie, 1995). However, as Daly suggests, few researchers are actually doing intersectional analyses of crime and giving effect to intersectionality remains complex, and subject to debate (2010: 1994). For instance, which differences count, and for whom, and what are the limits, if any, of taking intersecting social identities into account? Does intersectionality imply the use of a highly specific account of individual experience? As Snyder notes the latter can be a useful means of 'unsettling essentialist narratives about dominant men and passive women' (2008: 185), but does not resolve the challenges of moving beyond narrative to analysis and interpretation. Sokoloff and Dupont's (2005) concern that recognizing differences among women who experience violence should not obscure the need to examine structural oppression captures one part of the debate, but ways of thinking about intersectionality are not limited to those that emphasize either structure or the multiplicity of factors that shape identity.

Victim/agent

How to research women's experiences of victimization without erasing their agency or casting women as inevitable victims is an ongoing challenge. Feminist political campaigns concerning the victimization of women have been very important, but may have had unintended consequences such as reinforcing an association of the category 'victim' with that of 'women', and underplaying the agency of victims. Recent research and advocacy has sought to redress this concern; for instance, by challenging the victim/agent dichotomy, recognizing the blurred boundaries between victim and offender and re-examining the category of victim (and offender), how it is deployed and with what political and other effects (Walklate, 2007). The term survivor is often used to signal that victimization does not define the individual and to respect their agency and subjectivity.

Popular discourses and criminal justice practices often assume an idealized victim, and in consequence some victims of crime are constructed as deserving of concern and support and others as undeserving and complicit in their own victimization. Critical engagement with these issues is well developed in research on sexual violence (Estrich, 1987) and has been undertaken with respect to the responsibilization of victims within crime prevention literature (Stanko, 1997). Jan Jordan's (2008) study of women's narratives of surviving attacks by a serial rapist, demonstrates flaws in conventional understandings of active resistance *versus* passive victims. The women used psychological and other strategies to resist the rapist's dominance and control; they were 'victims in survivor mode' (Jordan, 2008: 28).

The blurred boundary between victimization and offending is commonly recognized with respect to incarcerated women (Richie, 1996) and in research concerning battered women who offend against abusers (Ferraro, 2006; Stubbs and Tolmie, 1995). This recognition has also helped disrupt essentialist depictions of women as victims and men as offenders (Carrington, 2008: 87). However, this approach carries the risk of too neatly accounting for women's offending by reference to their victimization (Daly, 1994) which may erase their agency. Lisa Maher recognized that women were '[constrained by] sexism, racism and poverty' but also the 'active, creative and often contradictory choices, adaptations and resistances that constitute these women's criminal agencies' (1997: 201). A 'gendered lives approach' that starts with women's lives, rather than with their offending or victimization, may offer one way beyond the methodological limitations of victim/agent and victim/offender dichotomies.

Integrity and analysis

Early leaders in feminist methodology, Liz Stanley and Sue Wise, described the relationship between researcher and research subject as 'obscene' and 'morally unjustifiable', aligning it with sexual objectification (Stanley and Wise, 1983: 170). Although few feminists would describe the dilemma in the same terms today, that is partly because there are now well-established techniques for minimizing the hierarchical relationship between researcher and research participant. These include: allowing participant input into various stages of the research process; sharing one's own experience with participants; reproducing

unabridged participant narratives; minimizing the application of analytical categories upon participant experiences; and, maintaining an open and honest reflexivity over the research process by describing the assumptions, hiccups and mistakes we make.

It is not easy putting these strategies into practice. Analysis is a case in point. Analysis is the process by which experiential knowledge is transformed into scholarship: the application of a conceptual framework to personal narratives of violence renders them meaningful within wider social and legal paradigms. Feminist research on violence treads a fine line here because it is often working with 'data' on deeply personal and traumatic experiences of violation. Ethically, the researcher is bound to maintain the 'voice' of these experiences by avoiding a 'slice and dice' analysis that transforms them into easily digestible categories. It is the responsibility of the feminist scholar – a politics which may not be shared by her research participants – to reveal how these experiences function with other experiences, discourses, structures and power relations even if this does require their dissection and classification. In other words, feminist researchers must do more than let these experiences speak for themselves. A good example of how to balance these competing interests is the recent work by Segrave et al. (2009) on sex trafficking which successfully brings together the voices of women who have been trafficked with trafficking 'experts' and policy makers across three continents to unearth the way in which discourses of race, gender and criminal justice frame international trafficking policies and practices.

As feminist theory becomes more comfortable with multivocality (Snyder, 2008), feminist research methods become more adept at drawing out the multiple readings that can be made of the experience of victimization. For example, in her analysis of semi-structured interviews on mother-daughter sexual abuse, Peter (2006) encouraged her research participants to revisit, reconsider and rationalize their attitudes towards their abusive mothers, thereby developing more nuanced positions. Whilst this reflexivity offers a genuine opportunity for participants to contribute to analysis and to receive something in return for their efforts, it raises the question of where to draw the line between research and therapy. Feminist criminology aims to minimize the power discrepancies between researcher and research participant but, ultimately, the final analytical responsibility rests with the researcher. While researchers often seek to convey the multiple, contradictory and 'messy' nature of everyday life, it is no longer *de rigueur* to under-analyze data on the grounds that it diminishes the integrity of participants' experiences.

The textual turn

Daly and Maher (1998) have identified a tension in feminist criminology between the 'woman of discourse' and the 'real' woman. Picking up on Smart's articulation of gender identity as a product of discourse – an idea born of feminism's engagement with post-structural theory – the former focuses on the construction of women/femininity and men/masculinity (gender) through legal, economic and social discourses (Smart, 1992). It prioritizes texts (such as film, fiction, media, legal documents) and deconstructive approaches to discourse analysis (Howe, 1994; Naffine, 1997; Young, 1996). The latter emphasizes experiential accounts of women's lives, victimization and criminalization, using methods such as surveys, interviews and ethnographies to understand these lives (Dobash and Dobash, 1998; Stanko, 1990). In the field of gendered violence, it is the latter approach, particularly from a standpoint perspective, that has had the most influence, promoting qualitative, reflexive methods that take women's experiences of victimization as the starting point for understanding violence.

In the context of gendered violence, two issues lie at the heart of this tension between 'women of discourse' and 'real' women: power and experience. Faced with the realities of men's violence against women, many researchers working directly with experiential accounts of violence have been comfortable analyzing violence as a tool of oppression within a structural model of gendered power relations (albeit an increasingly intersectional model). Liz Kelly's (1988) work on the continuum of sexual assault is an excellent example of insightful and influential research in this style. Drawing upon alternative articulations of power – such as Foucault's model of disciplinary power as a shifting force that creates subjectivities – other feminist researchers have been increasingly interested in the way in which representations of violence feed into the maintenance of fixed and essential gendered identities. Sharon Marcus' (1992) work on the 'rape script' is a good example of scholarship in this vein from outside criminology. In terms of experience, feminist criminologists drawn to post-modern theory tend to be wary about privileging personal narrative as evidence of the material 'facts' of violence, much less a superior form of evidence. As noted previously, this concern has much to do with the belief that individuals do not simply *have* experience but, rather, are constructed *through* experience (Scott, 1991), and thus experience cannot provide a self-evident beginning for knowledge because it is itself a cultural construct that demands explanation. Some feminist criminologists have rejected research methods that use empirical accounts of experience as a foundation for understanding violence, focusing instead on textual representations of such violence. A small number of projects have sought to integrate empirical research on women's experiences of violence with a theoretical framework attuned to post-structural thinking about experience and power (Bell, 1993; Mason, 2002).

CASE STUDIES

In the following case studies from our own research we seek to illustrate the methodological themes discussed previously. We consider some of the difficulties of feminist methodological praxis in researching different types of violence against women and how we sought to deal with some of the issues faced.

Violence against Filipino women in Australia (Chris Cunneen and Julie Stubbs)

When Chris Cunneen and I began to examine the high number of homicides of Filipino women in Australia, it was clear that most women were killed by a partner or former partner (Cunneen and Stubbs, 1997, 2004). Using a national homicide database, and epidemiological advice, we established that Filipino women were almost six times over-represented as victims of homicide compared with other women in Australia. Unlike other immigrant groups, Filipino women had a higher homicide rate than Filipino men. Most offenders were not Filipino; this too was distinctive as homicide tends to be intra-racial. The well-developed literature on intimate partner homicide was helpful but insufficient as a framework for understanding these deaths. Neither did mainstream criminological theory seem to be adequate; for instance, theories such as those related to culture conflict offered few insights into the complex factors that shaped the women's immigration to Australia, and rendered them vulnerable once there.

An intersectional approach offered a framework that explicitly recognized that gender, race/ethnicity and class were key factors related to how these women were situated. Class related to both the women's economic circumstances, and to international political economy which underlies migration patterns. Unlike other immigrant communities, the Filipino community in Australia is predominantly female. In the Philippines emigration is common, but many Filipino women can only qualify to migrate to Australia as spouses or fiancées of Australian men. In part, this highly gendered and racialized pattern of migration reflects immigration policy which has devalued occupational skills categories common to women, and does not provide visas for domestic labour. Decisions to immigrate are not just individual or family decisions; immigration is supported by the Filipino government and, at the time of our research, the remittances sent to the Philippines by overseas nationals constituted the country's largest foreign exchange earner.

Our research was instigated by women from the Filipino community who lobbied the Human Rights and Equal Opportunities Commission for the study; the commission sought submissions related to this issue, which together with some case files and media accounts collated by the community provided resources for our work. We undertook further research of media sources and transcripts of cases where prosecutions had occurred; using a case study approach, we examined 27 homicides. We also undertook internet-based research of sites promoting international marriages with Filipino or other Asian women after this emerged as a concern from the submissions. Later in the project we travelled to the Philippines for consultations with government and non-government agencies, and visited a community that was the source of many immigrants to Australia.

Intersectionality offered a way to frame our research, but did not determine how best to analyze and interpret the case studies. We benefited from community activists who helped us reflect on our analysis and the emerging themes. Some of these analytical challenges are illustrated in Box 32.2.

Economic disadvantage and lack of technological access limited the capacity of Filipino women to contest how they are represented in international marriage marketing through internet sites. These sites commonly deployed essentialized images of Filipino women, or other Asian women, as passive, exotic, and highly desirable for Western men, and thus also incorporated a particular understanding of masculine desire. Some sites also promoted sex tourism. Myths about naturally submissive, sexually accommodating Filipino women can function to authorize male power and control, although we recognized that culturally dominant discourses are not necessarily determinative of gendered behaviour and practices. However, our analysis suggested that in at least some of the cases, men used violence against their (ex) partners to impose conceptions of sex/gender consistent with such discursive constructions. Like intimate partner homicides generally, these cases commonly occurred in the context of previous domestic violence, at separation, or when the victim tried to end the relationship. This was consistent with Polk's 'masculine scenario of violence' (1994), or the use of violence as a form of 'doing gender' (Messerschmidt, 1993), but more was happening here. The meaning of the violence could not be grasped by reference to masculinity alone; violence both reflected and sought to reimpose a racialized order that authorized the entitlement of 'first world' men to 'third world' women discursively constructed as available to meet their desires. That media reports, and court decisions often deployed similar gendered and racialized stereotypes suggests that such discourses are deeply embedded across a range of institutional settings.

Box 32.2 Absent voices

A key concern in studies of homicide is that it is typically the defendant, other legal actors and the media whose accounts construct what we know about victims; it is rare to have access to any account by the victim. In this study we were also aware that discourses concerning 'mail order brides' were widely circulating and typically demeaning of the women, often stripping them of agency by characterizing them as 'naturally submissive' or else over-endowing them with agency by representing them as calculating and manipulative of their sponsors. We were conscious, too, that we risked being seen as problematizing intimate partnerships across race or ethnicity, when that was not our intention. However, as new immigrants, the women were dependant in many ways on their sponsoring partners, who were established residents in the country, and they were legally dependant since their immigration status rested on their relationship. We examined how the women were constructed discursively through media accounts, Internet sources and legal texts and juxtaposed this with the material reality of the women's lives. In some cases this revealed conflicting accounts; for instance, demonstrating previous attempts by the woman to seek protection from domestic violence when the defendant denied prior violence. One case involved a young woman who married the offender in the Philippines at age 15 and was only 17 when he killed her. The judge apparently accepted the evidence of a psychiatric expert that the young woman was demanding and uncompromising; this account was based on the expert's interview with the *offender*. Evidence of the escalating violence that had been used against the young woman, available in police reports and from her friends, was muted in the sentencing decision.

Researching homophobic violence against women (Gail Mason)

Feminist research in criminology is often conducted at a crossroads between different theories, bodies of literature, epistemological orientations and methodological preferences. Some years ago, I conducted an in-depth study of women's experiences of homophobic hostility and violence using individual and group interviews as well as focus groups (Mason, 2002). My research participants were all women who identified as gay, lesbian or bisexual. Although most were Anglo-Celtic, others came from diverse cultural and linguistic backgrounds including Chinese-Australian, Indian, Greek-Australian and Jewish. My aim was to understand both the contexts for and the implications of homophobic violence against women (and to extrapolate to gay men as far as possible). At the time, the literature was largely divided into two distinct fields which barely acknowledged the other: research on homophobic violence grounded in gay men's experiences; and research on violence against women grounded in the experiences of heterosexual women. The normative effect was that violence towards lesbians tended to be reduced to a problem of *either* gendered violence *or* homophobic violence. I hoped to move between these polarities by capturing the interaction between embodied subjectivities of sexuality *and* gender and by layering this with questions of ethnic and racial difference. It is challenging to put this kind of multi-faceted conceptual framework into practice. I learnt that it was impossible to always do justice to a sexuality–gender–race configuration at every stage of the research (not to mention other cultural formations such as class).

I found the 'solution' – for my project at least – in the process of reflexivity. My approach to interviewing was not just to gather experiences of violence but also to actively garner participants' interpretations of their own experiences. Some participants remarked that although their everyday lives were shaped by the interaction of sexual, gendered and racial hierarchies of difference, particular constructions of difference dominated at certain times and places. For example, an act of violence may be primarily motivated by racist sentiment even though the way that racism is acted out is refracted through the gender relations between perpetrator and victim: a white male perpetrator may be 'differently racist' towards a male Asian victim than towards a female Asian victim. See Box 32.3 for further illustration of these issues.

Although the victim's experience of such hostility is lived through specificities of gender and sexuality, it may well be their racial identity that feels primarily under attack. In practice, it was appropriate and necessary to prioritize particular formations of power/difference over others at given points (whether through the kinds of questions I asked or the analysis). Ultimately, it was my responsibility to decide how I incorporated this experiential insight into my analysis but I would not have arrived at it so readily without the analytical input of my participants.

Violence is very real for those who are on the receiving end. Feminist methodology provides us with the tools for making this reality visible so as to better understand and respond to it. However, in this I was also drawn to a post-structural and Foucauldian framework that suggests that we cannot treat the 'realities' of violence that women recount during research as either objective facts in the positivist sense or the foundation for a superior knowledge as standpoint epistemology suggests. One of the insights of post-structural theory is that experience is always constituted within discourse and is itself part of the process by which seemingly natural identity categories (such as lesbian, homosexual, woman, Black and so on) are constructed. This created a conundrum for my research. How could I position qualitative accounts of violence as the starting point for my analysis of homophobic violence when I accepted that lesbian women do not simply *have* these experiences but,

---

Box 32.3   Reflexive voices

One of the women I interviewed, So Fong, emigrated from Hong Kong as a child and had lived in Australia for approximately 20 years. In talking of the privileges attached to being white, she suggested that race can interact with gender to produce a specific and more acute experience:

> If I were a white woman, if I were you, I'd still have to be worried about all the violence that is handed out to women. But I wouldn't also have to worry that every time I step off my own bit of turf I might be entering racist territory, or that men might be more sexist to me because they're also racists. The difference of race is as simple as that (Mason, 2002: 71).

rather, become who they are *through* those experiences? Concerns of this kind have led some post-structural feminists to reject experiential accounts as a suitable object of analysis. In contrast, other feminists have rejected post-structural thinking as appropriate for feminist research on violence (Hester et al., 1996) (as mentioned above, feminist antagonism towards post-structural theory also relates to the ways in which it conceptualizes power).

I was frustrated by the chasm that seemed to have developed between these different feminist epistemologies and determined not to have to choose between the notion of 'real' women and 'women of discourse'. There were two layers to the methodological strategy I developed. First, despite post-structural criticism, I accepted the political and intellectual enterprise of making women's experiences of homophobic violence visible as an indispensable first step in understanding the cultural contexts that encourage such violence and the ways it functions in the reproduction of larger power relations of heteronormativity. Second, I equally accepted that empirical narratives of violence neither speak for themselves nor represent a foundational form of knowledge. My purpose was not to make experiences of homophobic violence visible for their own sake but, instead, to make them visible so as to render them available for critique and analysis. Rather than thinking of identity as the authoritative and 'real' origin of these experiences, I approached the lesbian/gay/bisexual identities of my research participants as a medium through which they voiced and interpreted their encounters with violence. Ultimately, I conceptualized homophobic violence as an embodied experience that feeds into the constitution of identity categories in ways that are deeply problematic yet constantly resisted. This is explored in box 32.4.

Feminist methodology does not ask us to accord a superior or 'untouchable' epistemological status to the experience of violence. It asks us to find the best way possible to investigate and analyze the multiple avenues via which violence and power reinforce each other.

CONCLUSION

It would be heartening to be able to conclude a chapter on feminist research in criminology with the observation that Carol Smart has recently made about the discipline of sociology, which is that feminist approaches have influenced sociological research practice to the point that they have 'become taken for granted or normal practice' (Smart, 2009: 297). Despite the now respectful relationship between feminist and mainstream criminology, it would be going too far to say the same about feminism's influence on criminology. However, just as feminism as a political movement and a theory have shaped the way that we think about and analyze crime and the criminal justice system, so too have research approaches favoured by feminists influenced the methodologies that many criminologists use.

As feminist methodologies are increasingly applied to a wider range of criminological subject matter (such as terrorism, hate crime and state crime), the debates that we have identified in the context of research on gendered violence will continue to challenge criminologists who wish to benefit from the methodological innovations and insights of feminism, irrespective of their field of study. These include: the difficulties of operationalizing intersectionality in research praxis; the problem of how to break down the dichotomy between victim/agent without denying the deeply patterned nature of victimization and criminalization; the need to acknowledge and redress the uneven power dynamics intrinsic to the research process; and the question of how to design research projects that do justice to experiential accounts of crime and criminalization as simultaneously 'real' and constructed. Feminist methodology has no quick answers to these dilemmas

---

Box 32.4 Constitutive voices

Samantha, a young white woman who identified as gay, described how an experience of homophobic abuse engendered a belittled sense of sexual identity yet was ultimately resisted:

> It's kind of like being told, 'We don't think you're as good as us, or we don't think you belong here with us.' But you know that really most of the time you don't feel that way ... You only feel it when you come up against it ... later on, this huge part of who I am takes control again and says, 'Fuck off, I know who I am!' (Mason 2002: 111).

about knowledge production but it recognizes the importance of continuing to ask the questions.

RECOMMENDED READING

Interested readers might consult Stanko, E. and Curry, P. (1997) 'Homophobic violence and the self "at risk": Interrogating the boundaries', *Social and Legal Studies*, 6(4): 513–532, for a useful example of analyzing empirical material within a theoretical framework attuned to feminist and post-structural concerns.

The edited collection Dobash, R.E. and Dobash, R.P. (eds) (1998) *Rethinking Violence Against Women* (Thousand Oaks: Sage) provides several chapters that reflect on methodological debates in researching violence against women and offers examples of multi-disciplinary research that reflects theoretical and methodological developments in feminist research.

See also the following journals for examples of the breadth and diversity of current feminist research in criminology and on violence:

Violence Against Women, available at: http://vaw. sagepub.com/
Feminist Criminology, available at: http://fcx. sagepub.com/

REFERENCES

Allard, S. (1991) 'Rethinking battered women's syndrome: A Black feminist perspective', *UCLA Women's Law Journal*, 1: 191–207.

Bell, V. (1993) *Interrogating Incest: Feminism, Foucault and the Law*. London: Routledge.

Burgess-Proctor, A. (2006) 'Intersections of race, class, gender and crime: Future directions for feminist criminology', *Feminist Criminology*, 1(1): 27–47.

Butler, J. (1990) *Gender Trouble: Feminism and the Subversion of Identity*. New York: Routledge.

Cain, M. (1990) 'Feminists transgress criminology' in M. Cain (ed.) *Growing Up Good: Policing the Behaviour of Girls in Europe*. London: Sage, pp. 1–18.

Carlen, P. (1983) *Women's Imprisonment*. London: Routledge & Kegan Paul.

Carrington, K. (2008) 'Critical reflections on feminist criminologies' in T. Anthony and C. Cunneen (eds) *The Critical Criminology Companion*. Sydney: Hawkins Press, pp. 82–93.

Chesney-Lind, M. (1986) 'Women and crime: The female offender', *Signs*, 12(1): 78–96.

Collier, R. (1998) *Masculinities, Crime and Criminology: Men, Heterosexuality and the Criminal(ised) Other*. London: Sage.

Collins, P.H. (1990) *Black Feminist Thought: Knowledge, Consciousness, and the Politics of Empowerment*. Boston: Unwin Hyman.

Crenshaw, K. (1991) 'Mapping the margins: Identity politics, intersectionality, and violence against women', *Stanford Law Review*, 43(6): 1241–1299.

Cunneen, C. and Stubbs, J. (1997) *Gender, Race and International Relations: Violence Against Filipino Women in Australia*. Sydney: Institute of Criminology.

Cunneen, C. and Stubbs, J. (2004) 'Cultural criminology: Engaging with race, gender and post-colonial identities' in J. Ferrell, K. Hayward, W. Morrison and M. Presdee (eds), *Cultural Criminology Unleashed*. London: Glasshouse Press, pp. 97–108.

Daly, K. (2010) 'Feminist perspectives in criminology; A review with gen y in mind' in E. McLaughlin and T. Newburn (eds), *The Handbook of Criminological Theory*. London: Sage, pp. 225–246.

Daly, K. (1994) *Gender, Crime, and Punishment*. New Haven: Yale University Press.

Daly, K. and Maher, L. (1998) 'Crossroads and intersections: Building from feminist critique' in K. Daly and L. Maher (eds) *Criminology at the Crossroads: Feminist Readings in Crime and Justice*. New York: Oxford University Press, pp. 1–17.

Dobash, R. and Dobash, R.E. (1998) *Rethinking Violence Against Women*. Thousand Oaks: Sage.

Estrich, S. (1987) *Real Rape*. Cambridge, MA: Harvard University Press.

Ferraro, K. (2006) *Neither Angels nor Demons: Women Crime and Victimization*. Boston: Northeastern University Press.

Gelsthorpe, L. (1990) 'Feminist methodologies in criminology: A new approach or old wine in new bottles?' in L. Gelsthorpe and A. Morris (eds) *Feminist Perspectives in Criminology*. Buckingham: Open University Press, pp. 89–106.

Gelsthorpe, L. (2002) 'Feminism and criminology' in M. Maguire, R. Morgan and R. Reiner (eds) *The Oxford Handbook of Criminology*. Oxford: Oxford University Press, pp. 112–143.

Griffiths, S. and Hanmer, J. (2005) 'Feminist quantitative methodology: evaluating policing of domestic violence' in T. Skinner, M. Hester and E. Malos (eds) *Researching Gender Violence: Feminist Methodology in Action*. Cullompton UK: Willan, pp. 23–43.

Harding, S. (1987) 'Conclusion: Feminism and epistemology' in S. Harding (ed.) *Feminism & Methodology*. Bloomington: Indiana University Press, pp. 181–190.

Haviland, M., Frye, V. and Rajah, V. (2008) 'Harnessing the power of advocacy-research collaborations: Lessons from the field', *Feminist Criminology*, 3(4): 247–275.

Heidensohn, F. (1985) *Women and Crime*. Houndmills, UK: Macmillan.

Hester, M., Kelly, L. and Radford, J. (eds) (1996) *Women, Violence and Male Power*. Buckingham: Open University Press.

Hollway, W. and Jefferson, T. (2001) *Doing Qualitative Research Differently: Free Association, Narrative and the Interview Method*. London: Sage.

Howe, A. (1994) *Punish and Critique: Towards a Feminist Analysis of Penality*. New York: Routledge.

Jordan, J. (2008) *Serial Survivors: Women's Narratives of Surviving Rape*. Annandale: Federation Press.

Kelly, L. (1988) *Surviving Sexual Violence*. Cambridge: Polity Press.

Kelly, L. (1990) 'Journeying in reverse: possibilities and problems in feminist research on sexual violence' in L. Gelsthorpe and A. Morris (eds) *Feminist Perspectives in Criminology*. Milton Keynes: Open University Press, pp. 107–114.

Kelly, L., Lovett, J. and Regan, L. (2005) 'Study of attrition in rape cases: "A gap or a chasm?"', *Home Office Research Study No: 293*. London: Home Office Research, Development and Statistics Directorate. Available at: http://www.homeoffice.gov.uk/rds/pdfs05/hors293.pdf

Klein, D. (1973) 'The aetiology of female crime: a review of the literature', *Issues in Criminology*, 8(2): 3–30.

Lincoln, Y. and Guba, E. (1985) *Naturalistic Inquiry*. Thousand Oaks: Sage.

Maher, L. (1997) *Sexed Work: Gender, Race and Resistance in a Brooklyn Drug Market*. Oxford: Clarendon Press.

Marcus, S. (1992) 'Fighting bodies, fighting words: A theory and politics of rape prevention' in J. Butler and J. Scott (eds) *Feminists Theorise the Political*. New York: Routledge, pp. 385–403.

Mason, G. (2002) *The Spectacle of Violence: Homophobia, Gender and Knowledge*. London: Routledge.

Mertens, D. (2008) 'Mixed methods and the politics of human research' in V. Plano Clarke, and J. Cresswell (eds) *The Mixed Methods Reader*. Los Angeles: Sage, pp. 68–104.

Messerschmidt, J. (1993) *Masculinities and Crime: Critique and Reconceptualization of Theory*. Lanham: Rowman & Littlefield.

Miller, J. (2008) *Getting Played: African American Girls, Urban Inequality and Gendered Violence*. New York: New York University Press.

Miller, J. (2002) 'On gang girls, gender and a structured action theory', *Theoretical Criminology*, 6(4): 461–476.

Morris, A. (1987) *Women, Crime and Criminal Justice*. Oxford: Basil Blackwell.

Naffine, N. (1997) *Feminism and Criminology*. St. Leonards: Allen & Unwin.

Peter, T. (2006) 'Mad, bad or victim? Making sense of mother-daughter sexual abuse', *Feminist Criminology*, 1(4): 283–302.

Polk, K. (1994) 'Masculinity, honour and confrontational homicide' in T. Newburn and E. Stanko (eds) *Just Boys doing Business? Men, Masculinities and Crime*. London: Routledge, pp. 189–213.

Renzetti, C. and Miles, C. (eds) (1996) *Violence in Gay and Lesbian Domestic Partnerships*. New York: Harrington Park Press.

Richie, B. (1996) *Compelled to Crime: The Gender Entrapment of Battered Black Women*. New York: Routledge.

Robinson, R. (2007) '"It's not easy to know who I am": Gender salience and cultural place in the treatment of a "delinquent" adolescent mother', *Feminist Criminology*, 2(1): 31–56.

Scott, J. (1991) 'The evidence of experience', *Critical Inquiry*, 17(4): 773–797.

Segrave, M., Milivojevic, S. and Pickering, S. (2009) *Sex Trafficking*. Cullompton: Willan Publishing.

Smart, C. (1976) *Women, Crime and Criminology: A Feminist Critique*. London: Routledge & Kegan Paul.

Smart, C. (1992) 'The woman of legal discourse', *Social and Legal Studies*, 1(1): 29–44.

Smart, C. (2009) 'Shifting horizons: Reflections on qualitative methods', *Feminist Theory*, 10(3): 295–308.

Snyder, R.C. (2008) 'What is third-wave feminism? A new directions essay', *Signs: Journal of Women in Culture and Society*, 34(1): 175–196.

Sokoloff, N. and Dupont, I. (2005) 'Domestic violence at the intersections of race, class, and gender: challenges and contributions to understanding violence against marginalized women in diverse communities' *Violence Against Women*, 11(1): 38–64.

Spivak, G. C. (1988) 'Can the subaltern speak?' in C. Nelson and L. Grossberg (eds) *Marxism and the Interpretation of Culture*. London: Macmillan, pp. 271–313.

Stanko, E. (1990) *Everyday Violence: How Women and Men Experience Physical and Sexual Danger*. London: Pandora.

Stanko, E. (1997) 'Safety talk: Conceptualizing women's risk assessment as a "technology of the soul"', *Theoretical Criminology*, 1(4): 479–799.

Stanko, E. (2001) 'The day to count: reflections on a methodology to raise awareness about the impact of domestic violence in the UK', *Criminology and Criminal Justice*, 1(2): 215–226.

Stanley, L. and Wise, S. (1983) *Breaking Out: Feminist Consciousness and Feminist Research*. London: Routledge & Kegan Paul.

Stubbs, J. and Tolmie, J. (1995) 'Race, gender and the Battered Woman Syndrome: an Australian case study'. *Canadian Journal of Women and Law*, 8(1): 122–158.

Tashakkori, A. and Tedlie, C. (2008) 'Introduction to mixed method and mixed mode; studies in the social and behavioural sciences' in V. Plano Clarke and J. Cresswell (eds) *The Mixed Methods Reader*. Los Angeles: Sage, pp. 7–28.

Walklate, S. (2007) *Imagining the Victim of Crime*. Maidenhead UK: Open University Press.

Young, A. (1996) *Imagining Crime: Textual Outlaws and Criminal Conversations*. London: Sage.

33

Research Ethics in Criminology

Mark Israel, Iain Hay

INTRODUCTION

While few criminologists have written about or even taught research ethics (Rhineberger, 2006), there is an oral tradition as criminologists – like many other researchers – swap stories about their dealings with various research ethics and research committees. These accounts tend to be dominated by horror stories or suggestions for ways of mollifying committees. As a result, little time has been spent describing positive interactions and not much systemic effort has been invested in exchanging models of good practice.

In this chapter we move to repair this situation by taking up two major challenges. First we lay some basic groundwork, setting out the ethical terrain that now confronts criminologists, asking questions about the meaning of ethics, the relationships between ethical conduct and ethical regulation, and the key ethical issues encountered by criminologists in our work. These include, for example, informed consent, confidentiality, and harms and benefits, as well as the questions we face when conducting research in new contexts, including international or Internet-based activities.

We follow this in the second major component of the chapter with suggestions for constructive ways of responding to the day-to-day and regulatory challenges that ethical conduct brings. Unfortunately, many researchers find that it is more difficult to act ethically than it should be. Often, researchers in our field do not have the philosophical training to negotiate sometimes difficult ethical terrain. As researchers, we do not always recognize ethical challenges when they

appear, nor do we necessarily have the time to make the best decisions. Moreover, the regulatory mechanisms that now surround ethical research offer the potential for perverse outcomes. David Dixon – a criminologist with extensive ethics review experience – provides a fair summary of the objections that many other criminologists have raised:

> [T]he current ethics process diverts attention from the key question of whether conduct of a research project is ethical. It does so by the bureaucratic apparatus of committee procedures, consent forms and information sheets which so consume and alienate many researchers that they see the ethics process as an unnecessary obstacle to doing research. Even turning from poacher to gamekeeper, I underestimated the antagonism felt by many researchers to the process. (David Dixon, University of New South Wales, e-mail to Mark Israel, 6 October 2004)

We hope to go some way to reducing the antagonism to which Dixon refers. We take up criminologists' deep concern with ethical conduct, arguing that not only do we need to extend our capacity to think seriously and systematically about what constitutes ethical conduct but that we also need to develop better understandings of the politics and contexts within which ethics are regulated, wherever we find ourselves working (Israel and Hay, 2006).

This chapter updates, synthesizes and extends work that we have published elsewhere (see 'Acknowledgements'). Where possible, we have based our discussion on examples outlined elsewhere in this handbook. In other cases, we have contacted colleagues and worked with them to develop illustrative material drawn from their research experiences.

ETHICS OR REGULATION?

As empirical researchers, criminologists face two distinct difficulties. First, we must develop ways of working that can be regarded as ethical. Second, we have to meet the demands of regulators of research ethics. These are not always the same thing. At best, research ethics committees and frameworks help researchers respond to ethical issues. Sadly, however, there is a considerable international literature (Bosk and De Vries, 2004; Israel, 2004b; Lewis et al., 2003; Social Sciences and Humanities Research Ethics Special Working Committee, 2004) that reveals how ethical research can be compromised by bureaucratic procedural demands, particularly when 'researchers see ethics as a combination of research hurdle, standard exercise, bureaucratic game and meaningless artefact' (Holbrook, 1997: 59).

The two requirements act simultaneously; our need to behave ethically and to satisfy regulatory requirements operates through the entire research process. Scholars might be tempted to see research ethics approval as a one-off 'sheep dip' or a gate to be passed through, but most committees intend their decisions to have an impact on what follows and would imagine that their work shapes what occurs before the formal review process.

In Israel and Hay (2006), we suggested that some researchers might be inclined to focus their approach to research by identifying both the key intellectual debates they wish to consider and the means by which they expect to investigate them. Such an approach might involve, at best, some broad and tentative explorations of the ethical implications of choosing particular methodologies but little in the way of rigorous contemplation. This should not come as much of a surprise, given the training that criminologists have provided and received.

Typically then, it is not until such researchers are compelled to respond to research ethics committee requirements that they give detailed consideration to ethical issues. It is at this point that investigators with little experience may confront serious difficulties. For instance, the biomedically derived hard architecture of some ethics forms can lead criminologists to offer particular responses to committee demands because they cannot conceive or justify any alternative.

In short, for some researchers, the formal process of ethics review offers both disadvantages and advantages: it can unreasonably restrict ethical responses but it can also offer a significant mechanism for stimulating ethical reflection. Sadly, having received the formal stamp of regulatory approval, some researchers appear to believe that the time for ethical reflection is over. However, no matter how well prepared they are, no matter how thoroughly they have constructed their research project, and no matter how properly they behave, researchers are likely to have to deal with a variety of unanticipated ethical dilemmas and problems once their study commences. Ethical consideration is never a 'done deal'.

More experienced researchers can draw on their knowledge of how they and their colleagues have developed research plans, interpreted ethical guidelines, engaged with research ethics committees, and managed the practicalities of negotiating ethics in the field. From the outset of their research, they may anticipate many of the problems they are likely to encounter in their research as well as the issues they may face having their proposed work accepted by a research ethics committee. By comparison with more junior colleagues, they may have broader scholarly networks to draw on for advice and greater negotiating power with regulators, though some very senior social scientists have expressed on record their frustration with review processes (Israel, 2004b; Social Sciences and Humanities Research Ethics Special Working Committee, 2004). More thoughtful – though not always more experienced – researchers know that ethics needs to be designed into a project from the outset; is 'what happens in every interaction' (Komesaroff, in Guillemin and Gillam, 2004: 266); and continues well after the research is concluded.

WHAT IS ETHICS?

Ethical behaviour helps protect individuals, communities, and environments and offers the potential to increase the sum of good in the world. Ethical research conduct assures trust and helps protect the rights of individuals and communities involved in our investigations. It ensures research integrity and, in the face of growing evidence of academic, scientific and professional corruption, misconduct and impropriety, there are now emerging public and institutional demands for individual and collective professional accountability.

Ethics, in the words of Beauchamp and Childress (1994: 4) is 'a generic term for various ways of understanding and examining the moral life'. It is concerned with perspectives on right and proper conduct. One branch of ethical philosophy, normative ethics, offers the moral norms which guide, or indicate what one should do or not do, in particular situations. While this ethics literature can be quite daunting to most non-philosophers – and that includes us as writers on research ethics – in summary, there are two major ways of assessing whether people's actions and decisions are 'right' or 'wrong', 'bad' or 'good'.

- *Consequential or teleological* approaches see the judgement of acts as ethical or not on the basis of the consequences of those acts.
- *Non-consequential or deontological* approaches suggest that our evaluation of moral behaviour requires consideration of matters other than the ends produced by people's actions and behaviours.

We do not want to oversimplify ethics. There are other alternative and derivative approaches, including casuistry and virtue ethics which we will not discuss here. And, in the past two decades in particular (as feminist criminologists will be well aware), advocates of feminist ethics have challenged traditional constructions of the purposes of research, the role of the researcher and the way in which researchers interact with research participants, arguing for greater concern with relationship, particularity and inclusion (Halse and Honey, 2005; Preissle, 2007). In some cases, this has been expressed in terms of an 'ethics of care' as an alternative or, as is more commonly argued, complement to traditional 'ethics of justice'. We shall return to the 'ethics of care' later in this chapter, when we consider the responsibilities that researchers might have to individuals, groups and organizations who are not actually participants in the research.

WHAT MAJOR ETHICAL ISSUES AFFECT CRIMINOLOGY?

Informed consent

Most professional and institutional, national and international guidelines and ethical codes for research demand that, other than in exceptional circumstances, participants agree to research before it commences. That consent should be both *informed* and *voluntary*. In most circumstances, researchers must provide potential participants with information about the purpose, methods, demands, risks, inconveniences, discomforts and possible outcomes of the research, including whether and how the research results might be disseminated. What is going to happen to them and why? How long will it take? What are

the risks? What are the potential benefits? Who is funding the work?

In some cases, providing information to ensure informed consent may take considerable time and effort for both researchers and research participants. In other cases, it may be sufficient to provide potential participants with a list of their entitlements and a range of information they can request. Researchers are usually expected to record participants' agreement to take part.

Generally, researchers have to negotiate consent from all relevant people (and organizations, groups or community elders), for all relevant matters and, possibly, at all relevant times. Several researchers have argued that consent should be dynamic and continuous and not limited to the beginning of the research project. There are plenty of examples, of course, where this has not happened, including the extensive non-therapeutic experimentation on prisoners in the US (Advisory Committee on Human Radiation Experiments, 1996; Hornblum, 1998) and Philip Zimbardo's creation of a mock prison at Stanford University in 1971 (Zimbardo et al., 1999).

In their work on bioethics, Faden and Beauchamp (1986) depicted informed consent as an autonomous action, committed intentionally, with understanding, and without controlling influences resulting either from coercion or manipulation by others or from psychiatric disorders. However, researchers may find it difficult to assess whether potential participants' circumstances allow them such freedom. In consequence, special procedures are often adopted when attempting to obtain consent or assent from vulnerable and dependent groups. For example, in some cases, it may be appropriate to obtain parental consent or assent when interviewing their children. On the other hand, telling parents that you are interviewing their children because of their active membership of a gang or requiring young offenders to sign consent forms in the presence of adult witnesses may be wildly inappropriate. While undertaking work on juvenile gangs in St Louis, Decker and van Winkle (1996) appointed a university employee to act as an advocate for each juvenile participant. As advocate, the colleague made sure that interviewees understood both their rights in the research process and the nature of the confidential assurances. By comparison, the Human Research Ethics Committee at University of New South Wales insisted that Janet Chan and Jenny Bargen collect signatures documenting consent for their research between 2000 and 2002 on the New South Wales Young Offenders Act 1997:

> When dealing with people in conflict with the law, especially young people, the insistence on written

consent, which in turn had to be witnessed and signed by an independent person, is quite unreasonable – it discourages participation and appears (at least to the subjects) to contradict the assurance of anonymity. (Janet Chan, University of New South Wales, e-mail to Mark Israel, 8 October 2004)

The American Sociological Association (1999) requires its members to obtain consent from both children and their guardians except where: the research imposes minimal risk on participants; the research could not be conducted if consent were to be required; and the consent of a parent 'is not a reasonable requirement to protect the child' (s.12.04b) as in, for example, cases where the child has been abused or neglected. A similar exception is outlined in the Economic and Social Research Council's (ESRC's) Framework for Research Ethics (2010: 30).

Several criminologists undertaking research in prisons or with the police or private security agencies have pointed out how difficult it may be to ensure that they have obtained informed consent from all relevant parties (Liebling, 1992; Norris, 1993; Rowe, 2007; Waddington, 1994). First, it can be difficult for researchers to assess whether many potential participants have freedom of action – people held in detention may believe that they will be punished if they refuse to take part in research, for example. Second, the nature of information given to participants may be incomplete. This might be because the nature of the interview would make it difficult to predict what might be uncovered (see Gadd, this volume, on the Free Association Narrative Interview Method) but it might also be by design. One has to wonder whether researchers have always explained to offenders that the purpose of their research on, for example, burglars might be to make it more difficult for burglary to take place. In some cases, nevertheless, it may be possible and appropriate to develop methodologies that help promote autonomy and rebuild capacity.

The complexities of informed consent have proved particularly problematic for researchers engaged in covert research or deception. Deception could compromise both the informed and voluntary nature of consent but some researchers have argued that consent need not be obtained where any harm caused by lack of consent might be outweighed by the public benefit obtained. In addition, it might be impossible to gain access to some participants if other people are not deceived. For example, Paweł Moczydłowski (1992/1982), later to become director-general of prisons in postcommunist Poland, entered Polish prisons to undertake his research by joining study groups of questionnaire-wielding students. Researchers have

also had difficulty with the ethics review process when institutionally standardized consent processes have been imposed that mandate excessively formal information sheets, signed consent forms, or extend such processes to secondary use of interview data (see Godfrey, this volume). This might jeopardize the safety and autonomy of research participants, the quality of the research, as well as the integrity of the consent process itself.

Confidentiality

When people allow researchers to investigate them, they often negotiate terms for the agreement. Participants in research may, for example, consent on the basis that the information obtained about them will be used only by the named researchers and only in particular ways. The information is private and is offered voluntarily and in confidence to the researcher in exchange for possibly not very much direct benefit. While social science research participants might be hurt by insensitive data collection, it is important to be aware that more significant risks are typically posed by what happens to data *after* it has been collected.

In some research projects, negotiations around confidentiality may be fairly straightforward. Some criminologists operate in relatively predictable contexts where standardized assurances about anonymity may be included in a covering letter with a questionnaire. However, other work takes place in informal and unpredictable environments, where agreements need to be negotiated with individuals and groups and renegotiated during the course of lengthy fieldwork as new issues emerge, ranging from the use of interpreters to the discovery of past or impending criminal activity.

Lizzy Stanley has investigated the activities of transitional justice bodies within South Africa, Chile and Timor-Leste. Working in Timor posed considerable problems when it came to safeguarding confidentiality:

Timor is a small place and it also has a 'gossipy' culture. Maintaining confidentiality is difficult – you can ultimately control your own behaviour but not that of interpreters, translators, transcribers. However, some victims were also attuned to this. For instance, one victim took me to one side and gave me a story, in stilted English, that he didn't want the interpreter to hear. He'd never met the interpreter and didn't know him... but he was a Timorese and he didn't know who he might know. (Lizzy Stanley, Victoria University of Wellington, e-mail to Mark Israel, 10 November, 2009)

A further complication may arise if the participant has commercial interests to protect and the resources and expertise to ensure that these protections are stipulated in any agreement. However, obligations of confidentiality cannot be considered absolute and in some situations – such as when gross injustice is uncovered – researchers have contemplated disclosing to a particular person or group information received under an implied or explicit assurance of confidentiality. Lowman and Palys (2000) argued that in such cases of 'heinous discovery', researchers should distinguish between the kinds of serious harm that they could anticipate discovering during a particular piece of research and those that they could not. In the first instance, Lowman and Palys argued that researchers had two options: either be prepared to hear about such activities and keep quiet, or do not undertake the research. Having witnessed police violence during his doctoral research in the UK, Clive Norris (1993) reached a similar conclusion:

> Given that I had expected to encounter police deviance but had, none the less, still made promises of anonymity and been sensitive to the issue of informed consent, then I had no right to change my mind when confronted with such behaviour. (Norris, 1993: 140)

While not every research participant may want to be offered or even warrant receiving assurances of confidentiality, most do. Social researchers have developed a range of methodological precautions in relation to collecting, analyzing and storing data as well as strategies to respond to challenges to the confidentiality of their data. (Israel, 2004a) These include:

- not recording names and other data at all, or removing names of people and places and identifying details of sources from confidential data at the earliest possible stage;
- disguising the name of the community where the research took place;
- masking or altering data;
- covertly sending files out of the jurisdiction;
- avoiding using mail or telephone systems so that data can not be intercepted or seized by police or intelligence agencies.

Yet there are examples where British researchers have failed to hold data securely (Aldridge et al., 2010; BBC, 2001) and, given the apparent vulnerability of government laptops and computer disks to loss and theft (Dowling, 2008; Summers, 2007), it seems unlikely that hardware owned by social scientists should not also have gone astray.

Some Canadian, Australian and American researchers may receive statutory protection for their data. But recognizing that full confidentiality may not be assured, some British, Canadian and Australian regulators have required researchers to offer only limited assurances of confidentiality indicating to participants that they could be forced to hand data over to courts (Economic and Social Research Council, 2000; Fitzgerald and Hamilton, 1996). This practice has been criticized as undermining the relationship of trust between researcher and participant (Adler and Adler, 2002; Palys and Lowman, 2001). Nevertheless, several researchers have indicated that they would breach confidentiality to protect vulnerable groups such as children (Barter and Renold, 2003; Cowburn, 2005; Harne, 2005; Tisdall, 2003), or to protect the security of correctional institutions (Zinger et al., 2001).

Over ten years of research exploring the lives of ex-offenders in the UK, Stephen Farrall has limited his offers of confidentiality by telling interviewees that anything they said was confidential, unless they 'confessed to planning to commit murder or offences which could hurt someone'. Such wording was designed to cover harm to others or to the interviewee him/herself. This meant he felt justified in warning the Probation Service when one ex-probationer had been violent in a restaurant, and another had threatened to kill employees of the Department of Social Security. On the other hand, he chose not to report a prisoner who confessed to planning post office hold-ups while in prison as the individual concerned was unlikely to be able to commit such offences for the foreseeable future (Stephen Farrall, University of Sheffield, e-mail to Mark Israel, 2 October, 2009).

Harms and benefits

Contemporary researchers are normally expected to minimize risks of harm or discomfort to participants in research projects (the principle of non-maleficence). Although harm is most often thought of in physical terms, it also includes psychological, social, environmental and economic damage.

Researchers should try to avoid imposing even the *risk* of harm on others. Of course, most research involves some risk, generally at a level greater in magnitude than the minimal risk we tend to encounter in our everyday lives (Freedman et al., 1993). The extent to which researchers must avoid risks may depend on the degree of the risk (prevalence) as well as the weight of the consequences that may flow from it (magnitude). Researchers may adopt risk minimization strategies which might involve monitoring participants, maintaining a safety net of professionals who can provide support in emergencies, excluding vulnerable individuals or groups from participation where justifiable, considering whether lower risk alternatives might be available, and anticipating and counteracting any distortion of research results that might act to the detriment of research participants. In some cases, specific risk minimization strategies may compromise a more general concern to maintain informed consent. Drawing on his experience of conducting research with victims and perpetrators of violence, David Gadd, for example, pointed out that researchers might be justified in deciding not to return to participants to negotiate the use of quotes gathered earlier for fear of opening up old wounds:

> Young people who have lived in institutional care homes or in prisons are typically quite distraught young people and often very angry. When they participate in research they are often willing to disclose distressing experiences, knowing they won't have to see the researcher again. Returning to participants at a later date in order to reaffirm informed consent, may remind them of how hurt and angry they used to be. It could be very damaging indeed. (David Gadd, Keele University, e-mail to Mark Israel, 2 October, 2009)

One way of minimizing the possibility of harming participants is by incorporating in the planning and running of the research members of those communities who are the focus of the work.

In some circumstances, researchers may also be expected to promote the well-being of participants or maximize the benefits to society as a whole (the principle of beneficence). For example, over and above conducting the study, researchers on domestic violence could provide emotional and practical support for victims, offering information about, and organizing access to, formal and informal services, providing feedback to the study community and relevant agencies, and supporting or engaging in advocacy on behalf of abused (Ellsberg et al., 1997; Usdin et al., 2000). Work on victims of state violence may also advocate broader political change (see Stanley, this volume, on her work in Timor-Leste). On the other hand, interventions by researchers are not always well judged and may be regarded as betrayal by those the researcher intended to help, as Montgomery (2007) acknowledged after she sought medical treatment for a young boy during her anthropological fieldwork with children engaging in prostitution in Thailand.

Even research that yields obvious benefits may have costs. It is likely to consume resources such as the time and salary of the researcher, or the time of participants. It may also have more obvious negative consequences, causing various harms.

In general, obligations to do no harm override obligations to do good. However, there may be circumstances where this may not be the case such as occasions where we might produce a major benefit while inflicting a less substantial harm. As Lizzy Stanley observes in this volume, '[I]t is impossible to conduct research, that details exactly what state violence means and "feels like" to victims, without emotion and to some extent harm.'

It may be tempting to over-generalize obligations of beneficence and non-maleficence on the basis of principles developed to meet the needs of medical research. Indeed, several ethical codes do. However, some research undertaken in the social sciences may quite legitimately and deliberately work to the detriment of research subjects by revealing and critiquing their role in causing 'fundamental economic, political or cultural disadvantage or exploitation' (Economic and Social Research Council, 2010: 27). Researchers working to uncover corruption, violence or pollution need not aim to minimize harm to the corporate or institutional entities responsible for the damage though, as far as the Framework for Research Ethics is concerned, they might be expected to minimize any personal harm. As the Canadian Tri-Council Policy Statement (2003) acknowledges: 'Such research should not be blocked through the use of harms/benefits analysis' (2003: 7).

Research integrity

Researchers owe a professional obligation to their colleagues to handle themselves honestly and with integrity. This covers matters relating to a researcher's own work and his or her colleagues' scholarship: intellectual honesty in proposing, performing, and reporting research; accuracy in representing contributions to research proposals and reports; fairness in peer review; and collegiality in scientific interactions, including communications and sharing of resources.

In 2000, the United States Office of Science and Technology Policy published the Federal Policy on Research Misconduct. The policy defines research misconduct in terms of fabrication, falsification and plagiarism (or 'FFP').

- *Fabrication* is 'making up data or results and recording or reporting them'.
- *Falsification* is 'manipulating research materials, equipment, or processes, or changing or omitting data or results such that the research is not accurately represented in the research record'.
- *Plagiarism* is the 'appropriation of another person's ideas, processes, results, or words without giving appropriate credit'.

In 2006, the British government, research and higher education funding councils and the pharmaceutical industry established the UK Research Integrity Office. The Office is to provide support and advice to whistleblowers, and develop institutional codes of good practice. Currently, its work only extends to health and biomedical sciences and it has decided not to examine specific cases of misconduct. In 2009, however, the Research Councils UK released a Policy and Code of Conduct on the Governance of Good Research Conduct, which is mandatory for those projects funded by grants from the various UK Research Councils. The code describes unacceptable research conduct and includes the issues of fabrication, falsification and plagiarism identified in the United States Federal Policy, but also pointed to matters of misrepresentation of data, interests, qualifications or involvement, undisclosed duplication of publication, and breach of a researcher's duty of care.

Researchers face enormous pressures to publish or, at least, look like they are publishing as they struggle to obtain grants or jobs. One consequence has been that problems have arisen over the attribution of authorship either because someone who has insignificant involvement has been added – gift authorship; or because junior staff who made significant contributions have been omitted – ghost authorship. Occasionally, these omissions are part of a larger disinformation strategy. In biomedical research, evidence was uncovered in 2008 that suggested a pharmaceutical company was supplying North American, British and Australian academics with ghost-written articles that contained conclusions supporting use of the company's products (Singer, 2009). The articles were subsequently published by the academics under their own name.

The International Committee of Medical Journal Editors (2010), under the Vancouver Protocol, requires the following three conditions to be met if someone is to be included as an author:

1 substantial contribution to conception and design, or acquisition of data, or analysis and interpretation of data;
2 drafting the article or revising it critically for important intellectual content;
3 final approval of the version to be published.

A slightly weaker version of this forms the basis of the authorship provisions in the National Health and Medical Research Council's Australian Code for the Responsible Conduct of Research (2007). Many criminology journals are yet to catch up with such practices in publication ethics.

Conflicts of interests occur in social science when: researchers have co-existing personal, financial, political and academic interests; and, the *potential* exists for one interest to be favoured over another that has equal or even greater legitimacy, in a way that might make other reasonable people feel misled or deceived. Researchers risk appearing negligent, incompetent or deceptive (Davis, 2001).

Such conflicts have been best explored in the biomedical literature where academics obtaining financial benefit from industry through research funding, consultancies, royalties or by holding shares in companies are more likely to reach conclusions that favour their corporate sponsor. On some occasions, they have conducted research of lower quality and less open to peer review than colleagues with fewer commercial ties.

Although criminologists may be less likely to have a financial stake in their research area than biomedical scientists, they may still have to negotiate financial or contractual relationships with corporations or government agencies. So, should they accept contracts where clients hold a veto over publication, disclose corporate or government affiliations when advising the public or publishing research, assess grant applications from commercial competitors? Many research institutions are developing enterprise cultures which make such conflicts of interest more likely (Geis et al., 1999; Israel, 2000).

Criminologists often use 'conflict of interest' to describe role conflicts – where their relationships with research participants involve multiple roles as researchers as well as perhaps as teachers, clinicians, activists, colleagues or friends. This can occur wherever researchers are embedded as insiders in the research site, notably in action research. In such circumstances, it may be particularly difficult to negotiate informed consent, guard confidentiality, avoid harm and convince research ethics committees that the research relationship has not been exploitative.

In 2008, Mark Halsey and a colleague were asked by an Attorney-General's Department in Australia to undertake research on a group of young repeat offenders that had been identified as trouble-makers by the media and government. Halsey was already in the middle of research that involved some members of this group:

[T]his offered a significant opportunity to be involved in crime and public policy 'in the real world' and for drawing on various criminological theories of youth offending, policing, social exclusion and the effects of incarceration. However, I knew from the outset that such work was likely to involve – for me, at least – a conflict of interest. This conflict centred on the fact that a proportion of the young persons named and discussed in the context of the pending consultancy work would, as a matter of high probability, be those who I had interviewed – and intended to further interview – in my own Australian Research Council funded research examining the repeat incarceration of young males in South Australia. (Mark Halsey, Flinders University, e-mail to Mark Israel, 26 October 2009)

Halsey obtained permission from his university's relevant ethics committee for the following approach. He spoke face-to-face with all those 'identified as persons of interest to the South Australian Government' who were already part of his project and told them about the government consultancy.

They were given the opportunity to clarify any issues of concern and subsequently to continue participation or to decline to be interviewed. The declaration of these dual roles and of participants' knowledge and understanding of such was digitally recorded at the outset of each interview. All participants consented to ongoing participation. (Mark Halsey, e-mail to Mark Israel, 26 October, 2009)

Institutional conflicts of interest may influence the governance and conduct of research. Some ethically acceptable research proposals might be blocked in the ethics review process because of, for example, a desire by the reviewing institution to avoid legal action. Commercial relationships maintained by research institutions can also place individual researchers in invidious positions – even if individual researchers are not directly compromised by their home institution's corporate relationships, they could be influenced by the knowledge that their own institution's financial health may be affected by the results of their research or, at least, be seen to be influenced.

Other relationships

While most work on research ethics is based on universal notions of justice, since the late 1970s, feminist writers such as Gilligan (1977, 1982), Baier (1985) and Noddings (2003) have elaborated an ethics of care. For such writers, people develop and act as moral agents through social relationships. These relationships derive strength and meaning from each party's willingness to listen, include, care for and support the other. An ethics of care has obvious implications for ethics in research. Among other things, it forces us to think about a broad range of relationships that fall well outside those with research participants and

the academy that are the traditional focus for most codes of research ethics. However, far from resolving traditional ethical problems, 'trading a detached, distant and hierarchical stance for an intimate, close, and equitable position' (Preissle, 2007) may, of course, generate its own problems.

Criminologists sometimes work in teams and senior researchers may have supervisory responsibility for junior colleagues. Team leaders have responsibility for the ethical behaviour of members of their staff and for ensuring that team members are appropriately briefed 'about the purpose, methods and intended possible uses of the research, what their participation in the research entails and what risks, if any, are involved' (Economic and Social Research Council, 2010: 3). Team leaders must also ensure the physical safety and emotional wellbeing of their staff. Some projects require research team members to deal repeatedly with subject matter that might have a traumatic effect on them (see, e.g., Campbell, 2002; Liebling, 1999).

As pressures increase on academics to find external funding for their research, and as the centre of academic enterprise has moved from a humanities and social science core to 'an entrepreneurial periphery' (Slaughter and Leslie, 1997: 208), university-based social scientists may find themselves working for clients. As an employee or consultant, researchers and their institutions may be bound to secrecy or commercial-in-confidence agreements. They may be questioned about the propriety of accepting money from a particular source such as the British Foreign and Commonwealth Office (Houtman, 2006), an American counter-insurgency program (THES Editorial, 2000), or being embedded within military units (American Anthropological Association, 2009) and find themselves increasingly vulnerable to charges of conflicts of interest, or having their own interpretation of the need to minimize harm and maximize benefits to participants challenged by colleagues and sponsors.

Emerging issues

As the environment within which research occurs evolves, so we can expect changes in the ethical challenges faced by researchers. Social scientists are increasingly interested in international- and internet-based research. Both were identified as significant issues by the ESRC in its 2010 framework though the document falls short of providing detailed guidance.

The conduct and governance of research raises significant issues for those conducting investigations outside their home jurisdictions or who secure funding from external sources that require ethical review in accordance with the regime applying in the jurisdiction where the research will occur, and for those with external students who must conduct research within courses taught by flexible delivery or at offshore sites. In the case of international research, the framework requires British researchers to 'be alert to potential difficulties while staying true to the principles of the FRE' (s.1.15.5). While there are obvious complications that might arise from, for example, the possibilities of increased risks to both researchers and participants, differing conceptions of rights and harm (Montgomery, 2007), and the role and demands of gatekeepers, there are also additional governance issues. Australian criminologists have identified problems: when no comparable ethical review structure exists in the overseas country; when their own research ethics committee has no understanding of cultural values and norms impinging on the ethical conduct of research; if the researcher has, prior to entering the field, limited knowledge of circumstances in which research will be conducted; where the potential for conflict exists between local and Australian law, local laws and Australian ethical guidelines, and between ethics committees operating within different jurisdictions; and where data needs to be transferred between jurisdictions (Israel, 2004b).

Criminologists have become increasingly interested in the internet either as a tool for research or a site of study in its own right. While many of the ethical issues we have already discussed are equally relevant online, researchers may need to find new ways of responding to them. For example, internet-mediated research poses particular problems in verifying the identities and status of participants, providing debriefing or in redacting data (British Psychological Society, 2007). Of course, we need to remain aware that cyberspace is a differentiated and heterogeneous space (Madge, 2007) and should be wary of overgeneralization.

The ESRC Framework accepts that the use of information held in the public domain is not considered to be data collection and it therefore not subject to scrutiny by a research ethics committee (s.1.3.2.5). So, data obtained from public bulletin boards and open websites are likely to fall within this category. However, personal emails and exchanges within closed chat rooms are more likely to be interpreted as private and use of data from these sites would therefore generally require the informed consent of participants. Nevertheless, there are defenders of covert research on the internet when the harm caused by failing to observe privacy of, for example, a particular violent group may be outweighed by the benefits of publicizing and opposing their activities (Glaser et al., 2002).

HOW CAN WE RESPOND TO ETHICAL PROBLEMS?

How can criminologists decide what to do when presented with an ethical dilemma? Most ethical difficulties might be resolved by reference to one of the three principles initially formulated in the US in the Belmont Report – justice, beneficence and respect for others – and that form the basis for most codes of research ethics (National Commission for the Protection of Human Subjects of Biomedical and Behavioral Research, 1978). However, more challenging dilemmas may arise if it becomes necessary to violate one basic principle in order to meet the needs of another.

In such situations, decision-making can be grounded in an appreciation of both normative approaches to ethical conduct. As we noted earlier, the teleological or consequentalist approach focuses on the practical consequences of actions whereas the deontological approach rejects the emphasis on consequences, and suggests instead that certain acts are good in themselves. These two positions underpin a strategy for coping with ethical dilemmas that we develop in the following section.

Identify the issues, identify the parties

Ethical dilemmas rarely categorize themselves, so the first step is to identify the nature of the problem. It is also important to recognize the different stakeholders involved: who will be affected and how? We might think of stakeholders in progressively larger groupings starting first with those immediately affected by a situation or decision; moving through the relevant institutions (e.g., university, employer, sponsor); to the communities of social science researchers; and finally to society more broadly.

Identify options

Researchers may be able to respond to ethical problems in a range of ways and it is important that possibilities are not discarded prematurely.

Consider consequences

Researchers should consider the range of positive and negative consequences associated with each option: who or what will be helped; who or what will be hurt; what kinds of benefits and harms are involved and what are their relative values; what are the short- and long-term implications of any decision; which option produces the best combination of benefit-maximization and harm-minimization?

Analyze options in terms of moral principles

Then, setting aside consideration of consequences, investigators need to adopt a deontological approach, examining options against moral principles like honesty, trust, individual autonomy, fairness, equality, and recognition of social and environmental vulnerability. In some instances, some principles may be regarded as more important than others.

Make your own decision and act with commitment

Consequences and principles to reach an independent, informed, should be thoroughly considered, and each justifiable decision should be evaluated. However, it is possible that every option will yield adverse consequences or violated principles. Ultimately, we may find ourselves choosing the lesser of several 'evils'. It may be helpful to use casuistry to clarify the nature of the value conflict through analogies: are there any precedents – how have other similar cases been handled and what were the outcomes; is the issue similar to or different from the analogy; what if certain elements or individuals in the scenario were changed or if the 'stakes' were higher or lower?

Several prompts can be used to promote thoughtful reflection on the proposed action: will I feel comfortable telling a close family member such as my mother or father what I have done; how would I feel if my actions were to attract media attention; how would I feel if my children followed my example; and is mine the behaviour of a wise and virtuous person?

Consider future responses

We owe it to our discipline, our colleagues and all those who are affected by research in our field to reflect on how the dilemma we faced arose and, where appropriate, to take steps to minimize the prospects of a similar situation arising again. In some situations, we might need to draw attention to systemic difficulties or to work collectively as a discipline to develop new responses to such a situation (see Israel, 2004b).

DEALING WITH ETHICS COMMITTEES

The vast majority of ethics committee members do not seek to obstruct research. For little reward, they invest considerable time to provide ethical oversight and, in many cases, are able to offer constructive and practical suggestions to improve the quality of research proposals. Nevertheless, in many institutions, and in a great number of countries, academics have felt that the processes adopted by research ethics committees have been excessively bureaucratic and arbitrary. Social scientists have complained that committees have been found to be slow to respond or, even, entirely unresponsive to problems raised by researchers. In addition, researchers have discovered that some committees lack the expertise necessary to judge their work (Dingwall, 2007; Haggerty, 2004; Lewis et al., 2003).

Problematic ethical encounters can be minimized by good procedural regimes and for many researchers committee review presents a useful opportunity to reflect critically on research practices. Unfortunately, some have found that in the review process ethical questions may be swamped by the need to meet bureaucratic demands or assuage the fears of those responsible for risk management.

How criminologists prepare applications can depend – among other things – on: the nature of the research; the composition, policies and practices of the relevant ethics review committee; and the local, national and professional regulations and codes that govern the research. Often, the nature of the review process will differ between institutions, countries and disciplines.

Some writers give straightforward advice to researchers preparing ethics applications (see, e.g., Oakes, 2002; Israel with Hersh, 2006). Generally aimed at postgraduate students or early career researchers, they recommend that applicants think strategically in completing the application form, drawing on skills in research, networking and negotiation.

Consider the ethical aspects of your study from the very beginning

Ethics needs to be designed into a project from the outset. It is present in every interaction and continues well after the research is concluded.

Identify the regulations that govern your work

Researchers need to be sensitive to the review requirements for their particular project in all relevant jurisdictions – both where they are employed and where they will be conducting research – and should be careful not to carry inappropriately one community or jurisdiction's formal and informal approaches to ethics into another.

Find out how your local research ethics committee works

A research project may also be subject to a wide range of review bodies that need to be dealt with in a particular order. For instance, some institutions require researchers to apply to a university research ethics committee, some to a departmental one, others to both. It may also be necessary to apply to the ethics committee of the institution where researchers are collecting their data.

Some committees have different levels of review – perhaps allowing a 'light touch' or expedited review for research with minimal risks. While the ESRC Framework does not define minimal risk, it does list various projects that would not be considered in this category (s. 1.2.3). It might be argued that research where the only foreseeable risk is of discomfort might fall within this category.

Where this is the case, researchers should ensure they apply for the right level of review: too high and time is wasted preparing unnecessary documentation; too low and applicants may be asked to approach the right committee, answer more questions and supply further documentation, by which time they may have missed a meeting of the appropriate committee. Completing the documentary requirements for research ethics committee consideration can be a significant burden. Not only are applications typically lengthy and detailed, but some researchers also bristle at questions that reflect a singular and inappropriate approach to their inquiry.

Answer the committee's questions in a simple and straightforward manner

Members of research ethics committees have reported that some applications by social scientists are under-prepared. In particular, criminologists need to improve their ability to justify their methodologies and articulate the benefits of their research in terms that fit forms that may not be designed for the purpose, and research ethics committees that have little experience in such methodologies. Qualitative criminologists may groan each time they are asked questions about their 'human subjects', 'interview schedule' or 'experimental hypotheses' but it is still generally worthwhile for us to answer such questions fully and courteously. It is often useful to seek advice from colleagues and read examples of successful applications. Criminology departments could usefully maintain files of successful research ethics applications.

Be prepared to educate your committee

Find out what kinds of expertise your committee has – are you writing for social scientists or for medical researchers, or both? Are there criminologists on the committee? In your application, explain why the research is necessary, justify your choice of methodology and explain how other researchers have used it without causing harm. The committee may know very little about the methodology that you propose to use, the topic or the population that you are studying, or the location for your research. Locate your research within past practice – who has used this methodology before – and explain to the committee why your proposal makes sense given the context within which you will operate.

Talk to your local committee

If you have questions, telephone and talk to your research ethics committee administrator or chair. Find out how often the committee meets and when applications are due. In some cases, you may be allowed or asked to appear before the committee and answer questions. If you disagree with a research ethics committee's decision, read their regulations and then ask for a meeting.

Be prepared for delays

Some committees take a very long time to reach decisions. Although rare, Australian social scientists and British health researchers have reported waiting almost two years for approval (Israel, 2004b; Nicholl, 2000). In some cases, this can be because committees meet infrequently or proposal submission dates do not coincide with committee meeting dates, because committees raise objections to unaltered parts of submissions that had already been modified to meet an earlier set of objections, or because researchers have to shuttle between different committees. If you need approval from outside agencies, be prepared to wait. Some government agencies use delays in the processing of applications as a way of maintaining control over work in their institutions by external researchers. All this can be particularly distressing for students who are trying to complete their degrees.

Be prepared to adapt your work

Our experience in Australia, where researchers have greater familiarity dealing with university research ethics committees than in the UK, suggests that few research proposals are rejected outright by committees. However, some projects would have been abandoned in the face of conditions that researchers felt could not be accommodated. The more usual outcome is a process of negotiation between committee and researcher – sometimes protracted, and at times fraught – after which approval is given, conditional upon modifications to the scope and/or methodology of the research. Clearly, it is to researchers' advantage to be well prepared for any such negotiations. Researchers may be able to obtain some help from their professional societies, particularly those like the British Society of Criminology with sub-committees that focus on ethical issues (see 'Resources' at the end of this chapter).

Contribute to reform

Individual criminologists would do well to follow the advice of Bosk and De Vries (2004) to expand their knowledge of, and participation in, the review process, undertake empirical investigations of the ethics review boards, and educate board members. Collectively, social scientists could play an important role in advocating changes to the policies, procedures and systems adopted by particular committees. This might happen at the national level in countries such as the UK through the ESRC, or at a local level where, for example, researchers could encourage institutions to adopt helpful, consistent, transparent and appropriate practices.

Professional associations also have a responsibility to encourage theoretically informed, self-critical and perceptive approaches to moral matters. Our associations share responsibility with higher education institutions to ensure that material on ethics and ethical governance is integrated into undergraduate and postgraduate courses as well as into professional development programmes. The British Society of Criminology's Professional Affairs and Ethics Sub-Committee has the potential to act as a forum where ethical matters may be aired, best practice disseminated (among academics, postgraduates, government and non-government organisations) and grievances with regulatory systems may be collected. It might also:

- monitor problems members have with research ethics committees;
- lobby funding, host and regulatory agencies to support more appropriate governance;
- engage with the processes of law reform so that legislators consider the impact of their activities on social research;
- broker the development of ethics training materials, some of which could be used to help educate ethics committee members about discipline-specific matters;
- exchange information and resources with other professional associations across disciplinary and national boundaries (see Israel, 2004b, for a review of the activities of ethics committees within other societies of criminology).

CONCLUSION

As we noted at the outset of this chapter, criminologists have had a difficult history working with research ethics bureaucracies. In some cases, long-standing practices have been questioned and banned. Indeed, a number of researchers who generously contributed case studies to this chapter indicated that they were relieved that someone else might actually benefit from their struggle to satisfy the needs of regulators. No doubt, there is some value in identifying the points at which criminologists have struggled to gain approval for their work and we would encourage researchers to document these difficulties and share their experiences with colleagues. But we also need to be careful to move on constructively from recitations of frustrated and sometimes angry 'war stories'. And we need to avoid any related temptation to dismiss ethics review processes as overzealous and unwarranted obstacles to research conduct.

Instead, as implied by several of those colleagues to whom we have spoken, we advocate engaging more comprehensively with ethics, from theory to regulation. As researchers concerned with ethical conduct, each one of us needs to develop our understanding of the conceptual underpinnings to ethical decision-making, an enhanced capacity to recognize actual and prospective ethical challenges, and the tools to negotiate those challenges as they arise – anticipated or otherwise. Together these should offer us the wherewithal as individuals and as a scholarly community to shape and reshape the mechanisms by which ethical research in criminology is regulated.

Taking up these ethics challenges successfully offers not only the prospect of continued criminological research at the highest of ethical standards but also the capacity to offer more informed and expert input to the shape of the regulatory mechanisms that currently surround – and sometimes thwart – our work.

ACKNOWLEDGEMENTS

Earlier versions of parts of this resource were first published as Israel (2004b), Israel and Hay

(2006, 2007), and Hay and Israel (2008). Material is reproduced here by permission of Sage Publications, and the United Kingdom Centre for Legal Education, both of whom retain their existing copyright.

RECOMMENDED READING

Israel, M. and Hay, I. (2006) *Research Ethics for Social Scientists: Between Ethical Conduct and Regulatory Compliance.* London: Sage.

Israel, M. and Hay, I. (2007) *Good Ethical Practice in Empirical Research in Law.* Web Resource for the United Kingdom Centre for Legal Education. Available at: http://www.ukcle. ac.uk/research/ethics/index.html

Mertens, D.M and Ginsberg, P.E. (2009) *The Handbook of Social Research Ethics.* Thousand Hills: Sage.

Research ethics blogs and RSS feeds

The Research Ethics Blog (Canada). Available at: http://www. researchethics.ca/blog/

The Institutional Review Blog (United States). Available at: http://www.institutionalreviewblog.com/

Journals with a focus on research ethics

Journal of Academic Ethics (Canada). Available at: http:// www.springerlink.com/content/111139/

Journal of Empirical Research on Human Research Ethics (United States). Available at: http://www.csueastbay.edu/ JERHRE/

Research Ethics (United Kingdom). Available at: http://www. research-ethics-review.com/

Selected national and international codes and guidelines

British Psychological Society (2006) Code of ethics and conduct. Available at: http://www.bps.org.uk/sites/default/ files/documents/code_of_ethics_and_conduct.pdf

British Psychological Society (2007) Conducting Research on the Internet: Guidelines for Ethical Practice in Psychological Research Online. Available at: http://www. bps.org.uk/sites/default/files/documents/conducting_ research_on_the_internet-guidelines_for_ethical_practice_ in_psychological_research_online.pdf

British Society of Criminology (2006) Code of Ethics for researchers in the field of criminology. Available at: http:// www.britsoccrim.org/codeofethics.htm

British Sociological Association (2002) Statement of Ethical Practice for the British Sociological Association. Available at: http://www.britsoc.co.uk/equality/Statement+Ethical+ Practice.htm

Economic and Social Research Council (ESRC) (2010) Framework for Research Ethics. Swindon Economic and Social Research Council (online). Available at: http://www. esrc.ac.uk/_images/Framework_for_Research_Ethics_ tcm8-4586.pdf

Office for Human Research Protections (2010) International Compilation of Human Research Protections. Available at: http://www.hhs.gov/ohrp/international/intlcompilation/ intlcompilation.html

The RESPECT Code of Practice (2004) The RESPECT Code of Practice for Socio-Economic Research. Brighton: Institute of Employment Studies. Available at: http://www.respect- project.org/code/index.php

Social Research Association (2003) Ethical guidelines. Available at: http://www.the-sra.org.uk/guidelines.htm

Socio-Legal Studies Association (2009) Statement of principles of ethical research practice. Available at http://www.slsa. ac.uk/content/view/247/270/

REFERENCES

Adler, P.A. and Adler, P. (2002) 'The reluctant respondent', in J.F. Gubrium and J.A. Holstein (eds), *Handbook of Interview Research: Context and Method.* Thousand Oaks: Sage, pp. 515–535.

Advisory Committee on Human Radiation Experiments (1996) *The Human Radiation Experiments: Final Report of the President's Advisory Committee.* New York: Oxford University Press.

Aldridge, J., Medina, J. and Ralphs, R. (2010) 'The problem of proliferation: guidelines for improving the security of qualitative data in a digital age', *Research Ethics Review* 6: 3–9.

American Anthropological Association (2009) *Commission on the Engagement of Anthropology with the US Security and Intelligence Communities (CEAUSSIC) Final Report on The Army's Human Terrain System Proof of Concept Program.* Submitted to the Executive Board of the American Anthropological Association, October 14, 2009.

American Sociological Association (1999) *Code of Ethics,* Available at: http://www2.asanet.org/members/coe.pdf

Baier, A. (1985) 'What do women want in a moral theory', in A. Baier (ed.), *Moral Prejudices: Essays on Ethics.* Cambridge: Cambridge University Press, pp. 1–18.

Barter, C. and Renold, E. (2003) 'Dilemmas of control: methodological implications and reflections of foregrounding children's perspectives on violence', in R.M. Lee and E.A. Stanko (eds), *Researching Violence: Essays on Methodology and Measurement.* London: Routledge, pp. 88–106.

BBC (2001) Inquiry into sex abuse files blunder, 1 September. Available at: http://news.bbc.co.uk/2/hi/uk_news/ 1519889.stm

Beauchamp, T.L. and Childress, J.F. (1994) *Principles of Biomedical Ethics,* 4th edition. New York: Oxford University Press.

Bosk, C.L. and De Vries, R.G. (2004) 'Bureaucracies of mass deception: Institutional Review Boards and the ethics of ethnographic research', *Annals of the American Academy of Political and Social Science,* 595, September: 249–263.

British Psychological Society (2007) Conducting Research on the Internet: Guidelines for ethical practice in psychological research online. Available at: http://www.bps.org.uk/document-download-area/document-download$.cfm?file_uuid=2B3429B3-1143-DFD0-7E5A-4BE3FDD763CC&ext=pdf

Campbell, R. (2002) *Emotionally Involved: the Impact of Researching Rape.* London: Routledge.

Cowburn, M. (2005) 'Confidentiality and public protection: Ethical dilemmas in qualitative research with adult male sex offenders', *Journal of Sexual Aggression,* 11: 49–63.

Davis, M. (2001) 'Introduction', in M. Davis, and A. Stark (eds), *Conflict of Interest in the Professions.* New York: Oxford University Press, pp. 3–19.

Decker, S.H. and van Winkle, B. (1996) *Life in the Gang: Family, Friends and Violence.* Cambridge: Cambridge University Press.

Dingwall, R. (2007) 'Comment on the Presidential Address: 'Turn off the oxygen…', *Law and Society Review,* 41(4): 787–795.

Dowling, R. (2008) 'Ministry of Justice loses 45,000 personal records', *Times Online,* 16 August.

Economic and Social Research Council (2000) *Guidelines on Copyright and Confidentiality: Legal issues for social science researchers.* Swindon: Economic and Social Research Council.

Economic and Social Research Council (2010) *Framework for Research Ethics.* Swindon: Economic and Social Research Council (online).

Ellsberg, M., Liljestrand, J. and Winvist, A. (1997) 'The Nicaraguan network of women against violence: using research and action for change', *Reproductive Health Matters,* 10: 82–92.

Faden, R.R. and Beauchamp, T.L. (1986) *A History and Theory of Informed Consent.* New York: Oxford University Press.

Fitzgerald, J. and Hamilton, M. (1996) 'The consequences of knowing: ethical and legal liabilities in illicit drug research', *Social Science and Medicine,* 43(11): 1591–1600.

Freedman, B., Fuks, A. and Weijer, C. (1993) '*In loco parentis*: mimimal risk as an ethical threshold for research upon children', *Hastings Center Report,* 23: 13–19.

Geis, G., Mobley, A. and Schichor, D. (1999) 'Private prisons, criminological research, and conflict of interest: a case study', *Crime and Delinquency,* 45: 372–388.

Gilligan, C. (1977) 'In a different voice: women's conceptions of self and of morality', *Harvard Educational Review,* 47: 481–503.

Gilligan, C. (1982) *In a Different Voice: Psychological Theory and Women's Development.* Cambridge, MA: Harvard University Press.

Glaser, J., Dixit, J. and Green, D. (2002) 'Studying hate crime with the internet: what makes racists advocate racist violence?', *Journal of Social Issues* 58: 177–93.

Guillemin, M. and Gillam, L. (2004) 'Ethics, reflexivity and "ethically important moments"', in research', *Qualitative Inquiry,* 10: 261–280.

Haggerty, K. (2004) 'Ethics creep: Governing social science research in the name of ethics', *Qualitative Sociology,* 27: 391–414.

Halse, C. and Honey, A. (2005) 'Unravelling ethics: Illuminating the moral dilemmas of research ethics', *Signs: Journal of Women in Culture and Society,* 30(4), 2142–2161.

Harne, L. (2005) 'Researching violent fathers' in T. Skinner, M. Hester and E. Malos (eds), *Researching Gender Violence: Feminist Methodology in Action.* Devon: Willan, pp. 167–189.

Hay, I. and Israel, M. (2008) 'Private people, secret places: ethical research in practice', in M. Solem, and K. Foote (eds), *Aspiring Academics.* New York: Prentice-Hall, pp. 165–176.

Holbrook, A. (1997) 'Ethics by numbers? An historian's reflection of ethics in the field', in M. Bibby (ed.), *Ethics and Education Research, Review of Australian Research in Education, no. 4.* Coldstream: Australian Association for Research in Education, pp. 49–66.

Hornblum, A. (1998) *Acres of Skin: Human Experimentation at Holmesburg Prison.* New York: Routledge.

Houtman, G. (2006) 'Double or quits', *Anthropology Today,* 22: 1–3.

International Committee of Medical Journal Editors (2010) *Uniform Requirements for Manuscripts Submitted to Biomedical Journals.* ICMJE (online).

Israel, M. (2000) 'The commercialisation of university-based criminological research in Australia', *Australian and New Zealand Journal of Criminology,* 33(1): 1–20.

Israel, M. (2004a) 'Strictly confidential? Integrity and the disclosure of criminological and socio-legal research', *British Journal of Criminology,* 44: 1–26.

Israel, M. (2004b) *Ethics and the Governance of Criminological Research in Australia: A Report for the New South Wales Bureau of Crime Statistics and Research.* Sydney: New South Wales Bureau of Crime Statistics and Research.

Israel, M. and Hay, I. (2006) *Research Ethics for Social Scientists: Between Ethical Conduct and Regulatory Compliance.* London: Sage.

Israel, M. and Hay, I. (2007) Good Ethical Practice in Empirical Research in Law. Web Resource for the United Kingdom Centre for Legal Education. Available at: http://www.ukcle.ac.uk/resources/israel_and_hay.html

Israel, M. with Hersh, D. (2006) 'Ethics', in N. Gilbert (ed.), *From Postgraduate to Social Scientist: A Guide to Key Skills.* London: Sage, pp. 43–58.

Lewis, G., Brown, N., Holland, S. and Webster, A. (2003) *A review of ethics and social science research for the Strategic Forum for the Social Sciences. Summary of the Review.* York: Science and Technology Studies Unit.

Liebling, A. (1992) *Suicides in Prison.* London: Routledge.

Liebling, A. (1999) 'Doing research in prison: breaking the silence', *Theoretical Criminology,* 3: 147–73.

Lowman, J. and Palys, T. (2000) *The Research Confidentiality Controversy at Simon Fraser University.* Available at: http://www.sfu.ca/~palys/Controversy.htm

Madge, C. (2007) 'Developing a geographers' agenda for online research ethics', *Progress in Human Geography*, 31: 654–674.

Moczydłowski, P. (1992) *The Hidden Life of Polish Prisons*. Bloomington and Indianapolis: Indiana University Press. [Originally published in Polish in 1982.]

Montgomery, H. (2007) 'Working with Child Prostitutes in Thailand: problems of practice and interpretation', *Childhood*, 14: 415–430.

National Commission for the Protection of Human Subjects of Biomedical and Behavioral Research (1978) *The Belmont Report: Ethical Principles for the Protection of Human Subjects of Biomedical and Behavioral Research*. Washington DC: US Government Printing Office.

National Health and Medical Research Council (2007) *Australian Code for the Responsible Conduct of Research*. Canberra: Commonwealth of Australia.

Nicholl, J. (2000) 'The ethics of research ethics committees', *British Medical Journal*, 320: 1217.

Noddings, N. (2003) *Caring. A Feminine Approach to Ethics and Moral Education*, 2nd edition. Berkeley, CA: University of California Press.

Norris, C. (1993) 'Some ethical considerations on field-work with the police', in D. Hobbs and T. May (eds), *Interpreting the Field: Accounts of Ethnography*. Oxford: Clarendon Press, pp. 123–143.

Oakes, J.M. (2002) 'Risks and wrongs in social science research. An evaluator's guide to IRB', *Evaluation Review*, 26: 443–479.

Office of Science and Technology Policy, United States (2000) 'Federal policy on research misconduct', *Federal Register*, 65: 76262–76264.

Palys, T. and Lowman, J. (2001) 'Social research with eyes wide shut: the limited confidentiality dilemma', *Canadian Journal of Criminology*, 43: 255–267.

Preissle, J. (2007) 'Feminist research ethics', in S.N. Hesse-Biber (ed.), *The Handbook of Feminist Research: Theory and Praxis*. Thousand Oaks: Sage.

Research Councils UK (2009) *Policy and Code of Conduct on the Governance of Good Research Conduct*. Swindon: Research Councils UK.

Rhineberger, G.M. (2006) 'Research methods and research ethics coverage in criminal justice and criminology textbooks', *Journal of Criminal Justice Education*, 17(2): 279–296.

Rowe, M. (2007) 'Tripping over molehills: ethics and the ethnography of police work', *International Journal of Social Research Methodology*, 10(1): 37–48.

Singer, N. (2009) 'Medical papers by ghostwriters pushed therapy', *New York Times*, 5 August, pp. A1.

Slaughter, S. and Leslie, L.L. (1997) *Academic Capitalism: Politics, Policies, and the Entrepreneurial University*. London: Johns Hopkins Press.

Social Sciences and Humanities Research Ethics Special Working Committee (2004) *Giving Voice to the Spectrum*. Ottawa: Interagency Advisory Panel on Research Ethics.

Summers, D. (2007) Personal details of every child in UK lost by Revenue & Customs. *The Guardian*, 20 November.

THES Editorial (2000) 'The fundraising deal: we get cash, you get kudos', *The Times Higher Education Supplement*, 8 December.

Tisdall, E.K.M. (2003) 'The rising tide of female violence? Researching girls' own understandings and experiences of violent behaviour', in R.M. Lee and E.A. Stanko (eds), *Researching Violence: Essays on Methodology and Measurement*. London: Routledge, pp.137–152.

Tri-Council (Medical Research Council of Canada, National Science and Engineering Research Council of Canada, Social Sciences and Humanities Research Council of Canada) (2003) *Policy Statement: Ethical Conduct for Research Involving Humans*. Ottawa: Public Works and Government Services (online).

Usdin, S., Christfides, N., Malepe, L. and Aadielah, M. (2000) 'The value of advocacy in promoting social change: implementing the new domestic violence act in South Africa', *Reproductive Health Matters*, 8: 55–65.

Waddington, P.A.J. (1994) *Liberty and Order: Public Order Policing in a Capital City*. London: UCL Press.

Zimbardo, P. G., Maslach C. and Haney, C. (1999) 'Reflections on the Stanford Prison Experiment: genesis, transformations, consequences', in T. Blass (ed.), *Obedience to Authority: Current Perspectives on the Milgram Paradigm*. Mahwah, NJ: Erlbaum, pp. 193–237.

Zinger, I., Wichmann, C. and Gendreau, P. (2001) 'Legal and ethical obligations in social research: the limited confidentiality requirement', *Canadian Journal of Criminology*, 43(2): 269–274.

Name Index

Index